PRINCIPLES
AND PRACTICE
OF MARKETING

PRINCIPLES AND PRACTICE OF MARKETING

Jim Blythe

SOUTH-WESTERN
CENGAGE Learning

Australia • Brazil • Japan • Korea • Mexico • Singapore • Spain • United Kingdom • United States

SOUTH-WESTERN
CENGAGE Learning

Principles and Practice of Marketing, Second Edition
Jim Blythe

Commissioning Editor: Charlotte Loveridge

Content Project Editor: Leonora Dawson-Bowling

Manufacturing Manager: Helen Mason

Senior Production Controller: Maeve Healy

Marketing Manager: Vicky Fielding

Typesetter: Macmillan Publishing Solutions

Cover design: Adam Renvoize

Text design: Design Deluxe, Bath, UK

For product information and technology assistance,
contact emea.info@cengage.com.

For permission to use material from this text or product,
and for permission queries,
email clsuk.permissions@cengage.com.

The Author has asserted the right under the Copyright, Designs and Patents Act 1988 to be identified as Author of this Work.

This work is adapted from *Principles and Practice of Marketing*, 1st Edition, 2006 © Cengage Learning.

British Library Cataloguing-in-Publication Data
A catalogue record for this book is available from the British Library.

ISBN: 978-1-4080-114-78

Cengage Learning EMEA
Cheriton House, North Way, Andover, Hampshire. SP10 5BE.
United Kingdom

Cengage Learning products are represented in Canada by Nelson Education, Ltd.

For your lifelong learning solutions, visit
www.cengage.co.uk

Purchase e-books or e-chapters at:
http://estore.bized.co.uk

Printed by C&C Offset, China
1 2 3 4 5 6 7 8 9 10 – 11 10 09

Brief contents

WK 1: Intro to marketing → What is mktg. Selling. Cust Service (Questionnaire)

Contents

Part one
Concepts and Contexts 2

Lect 2

Part two
Markets and People 100

Part three
Strategy 324

Part four
Marketing in Practice 390

22 People, process and physical evidence 705

List of case studies

Preface

Introduction

O ver the past 20 years or so, marketing has become one of the most popular and exciting disciplines in most business schools and universities. The reasons for this are obscure, but may well lie in the fact that we are all consumers. Understanding how the exchanges between sellers and buyers operate, and understanding what motivates people to buy, are subjects which all of us can relate to.

Perhaps less creditably, marketing has been seen as a kind of magic wand for making businesses succeed: many company directors seem to think that bringing in a top-class marketer will make customers flock in. In fact, marketers are not magicians, and merely drafting in someone with marketing expertise will not make any difference to a firm's success unless it is backed up with a real concern for, and understanding of, customer needs.

Since the publication of the first edition, the world economy has seen some turbulent times: during this period, marketing has become even more important to companies, since only those firms which look after their customers have been able to survive and prosper.

Aim and structure of the text

The intention of this book is to explain the received wisdom about marketing, and at the same time provide the counter-arguments which moderate the debate. The book examines what marketing will and will not do, and seeks to strike a balance between academic thinking and practical experience. The book begins with some of the key theoretical underpinnings of marketing thought, the concepts and contexts within which academic marketers consider marketing issues.

The second section of the book deals with markets and people. People are at the heart of all businesses, but marketers are especially concerned with customers and consumers: markets are themselves made up of buyers and sellers, so a concern for people and their needs is central to marketing thought. The third section of the book looks at the strategic issues in marketing – positioning the firm and its products advantageously against competitors, and building relationships with customers.

The final, and largest, section of the book deals with the tactics of marketing. For most non-marketers, the tactical aspects (promotion, personal selling, pricing, new product development) are the most prominent part of marketing. It is common to say that these elements are like the tip of an iceberg, with the most important marketing activities happening out of the sight of onlookers. This may be true, but in fact it is the tactical aspects of marketing that occupy most of the attention of practitioners – the salespeople, media buyers, brand managers, advertising executives, and so forth who are engaged in marketing on a day-to-day basis.

Text book features

To help you get the most from the book, there are various features in the text. First, each chapter contains three or four Marketing in Practice boxes. These are intended to give live, up-to-date examples of current marketing issues and practice: they are additional to examples in the text, and go into more detail. Second, there are two cases studies in each chapter: one opens the chapter in order to flag up the issues, and is revisited at the end to show how the company involved solved its difficulties. The second case offers an opportunity for you to test your understanding of the issues contained in the chapter. The case studies have all been updated for the second edition.

Third, each chapter contains a set of Talking Points: these are boxed statements which challenge the accepted views in the text. Talking Points are intended to stimulate argument and deeper thought about the issues: they are deliberately provocative! You should try to use these to understand the debate, and to develop critical thinking: you should not simply accept the view that, because something is printed in a textbook, it must be true.

Fourth, each chapter has a set of chapter review questions at the end. These link to the key points in the chapter, and are for you to use to check your understanding of the chapter.

'Signposting' the chapter is achieved by outlining the key learning objectives at the beginning: these are reprised at the end in the Summary, and at various points in the chapter there are markers to show where the key objectives are covered. These pointers should be used for revision purposes, however – it would be difficult or impossible to understand the chapter just by looking for the key points!

Supplementary material

There is a website to accompany the text, the details of which are printed on page xxi. This book and its accompanying materials are not a substitute for your lectures, but they should give you a solid basis on which to build an understanding of current marketing thought and practice.

ExamView®

This testbank and tBst generator provides a huge amount of different types of questions, allowing lecturers to create online, paper and local area network (LAN) tests. This CD-based product is only available from your Cengage Learning sales representative.

Thanks

I would like to acknowledge the people who have helped me in writing this book. First, my friends and colleagues at Cengage Learning, Anna Carter and Jennifer Pegg, who worked with me on the first edition, and who showed great patience and support. In particular they remained positive about me and the book during the difficult times. For this edition, Charlotte Loveridge has guided the revision process with equal patience and forbearance, and Leonora Dawson-Bowling has kept the production timetable moving despite my having absented myself on numerous occasions.

Second, I would like to thank my colleagues at the University of Glamorgan for help, advice, friendship and practical guidance, and more recently my colleagues at Plymouth Business School. Third, I should thank my wife Sue for bringing me tea and calming me down.

Finally, I would like to thank my many students. Some were excellent scholars who asked me difficult questions and made me think, some were terrible scholars who made me work harder as a teacher, some were 'class comedians' who made me laugh: wherever you are and whatever you are doing, thanks for being such fun to work with!

Acknowledgements

T he publisher would like to thank the following lecturers for their invaluable feedback in shaping the second edition:

Andrea Beetles, Cardiff Business School
Fiona Ellis-Chadwick, Loughborough University
Andrea Prothero, University College Dublin
Alexander Muresan, London Metropolitan University
Gary Warnaby, University of Salford
Heather Farley, University of Ulster
Efthymios Constantinides, University of Twente
Drew Li, Liverpool John Moores University
Carol Deane, University of Ulster
Richard Helsdown, Cardiff Business School
Paul Moore, University of Hertfordshire

We are also indebted to the following lecturers for their review feedback on the first edition:

Mary Brennan, University of Newcastle
Manto Gotsi, University of Aberdeen
Chris Hackley, The University of Birmingham
Matthew Higgins, University of Leicester
Maria Hopwood, University of Teesside
Alice Maltby, University of the West of England
Piet Pauwels, University of Maastricht
Jenny Reid, Napier University
Nina Reynolds, University of Wales Swansea
Eva Ronström, University of Jonkoping
Mark Seager, Trinity and All Saints College, Leeds

Walk through tour

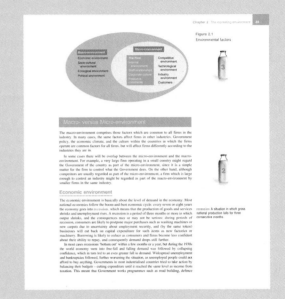

Learning objectives appear at the start of every chapter to help you monitor your understanding and progress through the chapter. Each chapter also ends with a summary section that recaps the key content for revision purposes.

Learning logo When the Learning Objectives are covered within the text they are identified clearly in the margin, acting as a useful revision tool.

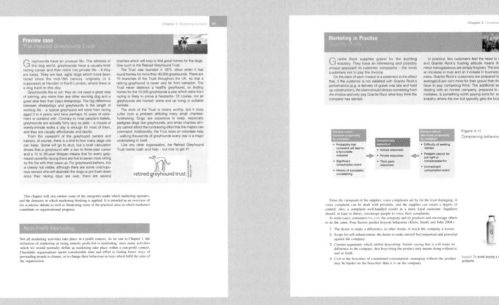

Preview case Each chapter begins with an in-depth case study which sets the scene for the chapter. The case study is then revisited at the end of the chapter and shows the reader how the knowledge learned within the chapter is integrated within the real world example.

Marketing in practice boxes are provided throughout which illustrate how marketing is applied in the real world.

Talking points are provided throughout the text: these challenge the theory within the text, and provoke critical thinking and discussions in class.

Glossary terms are highlighted in colour throughout and explained in full in a Glossary at the end of the book, enabling you to find explanations of key terms quickly.

E-Marketing in practice boxes show the role that electronic communications technology plays in marketing and provide up-to-date examples.

Summary Each chapter ends with a comprehensive summary that provides a thorough recap of the key issues in each chapter, helping you to assess your understanding and revise key content.

Review questions are provided at the end of each chapter to help reinforce and test your knowledge and understanding, and provide a basis for group discussions and activities.

Case studies close each chapter and show how each chapter's main issues are applied in real-life marketing situations. Each case is accompanied by questions to help you test your understanding of the issues.

Further reading and references Comprehensive references and annotated further reading at the end of each chapter allow you to explore the subject further, and act as a starting point for projects and assignments.

About the website

Media rich learning resources are available on our new interactive companion website. Visit www.bized.co.uk/share/blythe to view the added-value content.

For over ten years, *Biz/ed* has delivered unsurpassed online resources for business studies education. Supporting this new edition of *Principles and Practice of Marketing*, we have teamed up with *Biz/ed* to bring you an innovative educational space which launches the companion website into the digital age.

Blythe on Biz/ed Share helps educators and students save time by accessing added-value resources, and compelling new content on an innovative new platform. In addition to the resources you would usually find accompanying our books, this brand new platform supports Web 2.0 tools such as blogs and RSS.

Lecturers are able to use and comment on content provided by Jim Blythe, *Biz/ed* and other users. Using the website, lecturers can download new content and exchange materials they wish to share with others.

Students also have their own dedicated space with study tools such as interactive multiple choice questions, glossary terms and a guide to writing marketing plans.

Among the resources hosted on this site are:

- everything you would expect to find on a typical book companion website, including PowerPoint slides, electronic copies of the book's figures and an instructor's manual
- author-generated additional material, including lecture plans, useful web links and teaching notes
- extra case studies with supporting notes and discussion questions
- multi-media learning including video cases and a selection of the best publicly available marketing video content
- *Biz/ed*'s own unique materials linked to textbook chapters
- up-to-date sources of industry news including RSS feeds and blogs

Blythe on Biz/ed Share gives educators the tools they need and students the learning they want, all in one easily accessed space.

Part one
Concepts and Contexts

This section is intended to lay the theoretical and conceptual groundwork for the rest of the book. Like any other business activity, marketing functions within a set of concepts and has a set of antecedents: this section seeks to outline the boundaries and constraints on both marketing practice and marketing thought.

Chapter 1 explains how theory from other disciplines has contributed to the development of marketing thought. Marketing is a hybrid discipline, and a relatively young one which is still building its body of theoretical research: marketing has grown from practice, and academics have sought to explain the workings of marketing by using theories already developed elsewhere.

Chapter 2 looks at marketing within the wider business world: the environment within which marketing operates, and the influences of the environment on marketing activities.

Chapter 3 is about the areas in which marketing has a role. It covers the different types of marketing, and the role marketing has in different business contexts. The chapter seeks to show where the boundaries lie: what is and is not marketing.

Chapter 1
Managing the exchange process

Learning objectives

After working through this chapter, you should be able to:

1 Compare the different definitions of marketing in common use.

2 Explain marketing's role in managing the exchange process.

3 Explain the importance of customers to marketing.

4 Describe the relationship between marketing and other business specialisms.

5 Explain the role of needs and wants in marketing.

6 Describe the contribution other disciplines have made to marketing thought.

7 Describe the different subdivisions of marketing.

Introduction

Marketing has been variously defined. It is a relatively new discipline, so academic debate is varied and lively: it is a business function which is continually growing and developing, with practitioners introducing new techniques and approaches at a rate which would be unthinkable for lawyers and accountants, and difficult even for engineers and designers. It is a philosophy for orientating business strategy, and it is a co-ordinating mechanism for uniting corporate activities.

Marketers act at the interface between the company and its customers. They need to coordinate the company's activities with the needs of customers, and to communicate the company's offerings to its target groups. This chapter outlines the development of marketing, and the contributions which have been made by other disciplines.

Perhaps strangely (considering the powerful role of communication in marketing) the profession has generally received a bad press. Marketing has commonly been associated with tricks or gimmicks, and there is a commonly-held perception that marketing is about persuading people to buy things they do not need or want. In fact, these criticisms are unfair: marketing is about creating value, not creating needs, and is concerned with creating and retaining customers. The ideal situation for any marketer is that customers return

Courtesy of Mitchells & Butlers plc

Preview case
Mitchells and Butlers

Mitchells and Butlers is one of the largest pub operators in the UK, running some 2000 public houses and restaurants throughout the country. The company had its beginnings in the 19th century, when two family brewers from the English Midlands merged: a series of mergers over the next hundred years or so resulted in the formation of the Bass Charrington conglomerate, but in 1989 the Monopolies and Mergers Commission decided that concentration in the pub industry had reached the level where competition was becoming severely restricted, and the break-up of Bass Charrington into smaller independent units was ordered.

Mitchells and Butlers was eventually spun out from its parent company in 2002, and became established in the form in which it exists today. The company runs several themed chains of pubs, including O'Neill's Irish theme pubs.

Mitchells and Butlers believe that there are specific growth areas in the pub market, despite an overall decline in pub drinking in the UK in recent years: they believe that young professionals, women, families, and the over 50s represent growth areas in the market, and they aim to service those segments effectively. They see the national ban on smoking in pubs (brought in during 2007) to be an opportunity rather than a threat, since they

believe that many of their target markets are deterred by the smoky atmosphere of the traditional British pub. This is especially true for pubs which serve food – and Mitchells and Butlers do serve a lot of food. With only 3 per cent of the nation's pubs under its control, Mitchells and Butlers still manage to capture 10 per cent of the market, but much of this comes from food sales rather than the higher-margin alcohol trade. The company serves 107 million meals a year, almost two meals for every person living in the UK: Mitchells and Butler is the largest on-trade caterer in the country.

The company have done well out of the UK property boom, and have sold some pubs to generate cash – typically, these have been pubs where the company see little or no scope for generating food sales. Some commentators have questioned whether Mitchells and Butlers' business is actually about pubs at all, or whether they are in fact running a restaurant chain – food sales outstrip beer sales for this company.

Providing customers with what they want is a challenging affair in the twenty-first century – especially in an industry which is ever more regulated, and which has seen an overall decline in popularity in recent years. The challenge for pub chains like Mitchells and Butlers is to maintain a competitive edge in a beleaguered market.

regularly and buy again and again – a situation which is unlikely to occur if the customers did not feel that they had been fairly treated in the first place. It is well-known that it is cheaper to keep an existing customer than it is to recruit a new one, and research shows that it is up to six times more expensive to recruit than to retain (Rosenberg and Czepeil 1983). Long-term customer satisfaction can only happen if the organisation offers value for money – not necessarily cheapness, but good value.

Marketing is therefore concerned with providing people with products and services which work effectively, continue to work effectively in the longer term, and are offered at a fair price.

Definitions of Marketing

Unlike accountancy or the legal profession, marketing still needs to define its remit to non-marketers. There are several definitions of marketing in current use, and each suffers from some weaknesses: a universally-agreed definition of what marketing is has not yet been achieved.

American marketing guru Philip Kotler defines marketing as follows (Kotler *et al.* 2003):

Marketing is a social and managerial process by which individuals and groups obtain what they need and want through creating and exchanging products and value with others.

This definition includes the concept of **value**, which is an important aspect of marketing. Value is the relationship between what is paid and what is received, and can be increased or reduced by marketing activities. For example, marketers can include an extra quantity of the product (10 per cent extra free) as a way of increasing value for the customer, or (more profitably) might add an extra feature which costs the firm very little but which greatly increases the value for the customer. The problem with Kotler's definition is that it tries to include all human exchange processes, and does not differentiate between the buyer and the seller. This makes the definition very broad, and some might argue that the definition is too broad to be of much use in deciding what is marketing and what is not. For example, Kotler is apparently arguing that a parent who offers a child a trip to the zoo in exchange for tidying up his room is engaged in marketing, and (more importantly) that the child himself is also engaged in marketing. This would strike many people as being somewhat odd.

> **value** The benefit a customer obtains from a product.

Another interesting aspect of the Kotler definition is the use of the terms '**need**' and '**want**'. To most non-marketers, a need is something which is essential to survival, whereas a want is something which is no more than a passing fancy. For marketers, these definitions are inadequate because there are so many products which are essential to some people, luxuries to others, and actually dangerous for others. For example, diabetics need insulin in order to survive, but for non-diabetics an injection of insulin could easily prove fatal. Even for the same individual, a product might be essential for survival at one time, but a luxury at another. At the extreme, if one were starving, then a plate of caviar might be essential to life, but in a restaurant it would be a luxury. This is not inherently a problem with the Kotler definition, but such definitions of terms need to be addressed if the Kotler definition is to be understood and applied.

> **need** A perceived lack of something.
> **want** A specific satisfier for a need.

The Chartered Institute of Marketing (CIM) uses the following definition:

> *Marketing is the management process which identifies, anticipates, and supplies customer requirements efficiently and profitably.*

This definition tries to capture a somewhat complex set of ideas concisely. The concept of putting the **customer** at the centre of the business strategy is key to marketing, and the definition also includes the idea that we are not interested in any and every customer, but only those whose needs can be satisfied profitably. Identifying customer needs and supplying products and services which satisfy those needs covers a wide range of activities from **market research** through to new product development. The definition also says that marketing is a management process; in other words, it requires planning and analysis, resources, investment of money and time, and monitoring and evaluation.

> **customer** One who decides on payment for a product.

> **market research** Investigations intended to improve knowledge about customers and competitors.

On the other hand, the definition has several weaknesses. First, there is a branch of marketing which deals with non-profit organisations such as charities or Government departments. Few people would argue that a campaign carried out by the NSPCC against child abuse or an anti-smoking advertising campaign carried out by the Department of Health are not marketing activities, yet they are outside the scope of the CIM definition because they are not profit-orientated. Second, the definition excludes other stakeholders such as employees and shareholders. In each case, marketers have an input in communicating with, and meeting the needs of, these groups. Third, the people whose needs are being met are not always customers – for example, a mother who buys football boots for her ten-year-old son is a customer, but it is not her needs which are being met (except in the limited sense that she needs to be regarded as a kind and generous mother).

Another commonly-quoted definition is that provided by the American Marketing Association (AMA 2004), as follows:

> *Marketing is the process of planning and executing the conception, pricing, promotion, and distribution of ideas, goods and services to create exchange and satisfy individual and organisational objectives.*

This definition agrees that marketing is a management process, and that it is about satisfying individual objectives: it also introduces the idea that marketing is about

What goes into crisps goes into you.

Some crisps contain 33% cooking oil.

creating exchange, and that it is about meeting organisational objectives whether this means profit or not.

The definition still suffers from a narrow focus, however. For example, marketers are often concerned about competitors, but neither of the foregoing definitions addresses this. Companies and other organisations might do an excellent job of meeting customer needs at a fair price, but still fail simply because other companies offer even better products or even better prices – or, more confusing still, might offer a product which is actually worse and more expensive, but is offered at a more convenient location or time. For example, a traveller arriving late at night in a strange town is not in a position to shop around for hotels and will probably stay at the first one with an available room.

Another definition, which includes this idea, is offered by Jobber (2003):

Marketing is the process of achieving corporate goals through meeting and exceeding customer needs better than the competition.

stakeholders People who are impacted by corporate activities.

The implication of this is that all the activities of the company should be geared towards meeting customer needs rather than those of other stakeholders. This is not necessarily unreasonable: after all, without customers there is no business. Peter Drucker stated:

Because the purpose of business is to create and keep customers, it has only two central functions: marketing and innovation. The basic function of marketing is to attract and retain customers at a profit. (Drucker 1999).

From the viewpoint of the student, studying marketing is complicated somewhat by the lack of a clear definition of what marketing is. It is obviously difficult to know what to study if one does not know what the boundaries of the subject are. To clarify things a little, it may be useful to consider the development of marketing as an academic subject, and also to consider the contributions made to it by other, older disciplines.

The Marketing Concept

The philosophical idea underlying all marketing thought is that corporate success comes from satisfying customer needs. The idea of placing customers at the centre of everything the company does is basic to marketing thought: this idea of customer centrality is the key concept in marketing. Recent research has shown that there is a positive association between customer satisfaction and shareholder value: this is a clear vindication of the marketing concept (Anderson, Fornell and Mazvancheryl 2004).

The marketing concept did not arrive fully-formed. It is popularly supposed to have developed through series of business orientations, as shown in Table 1.1.

Some marketers have moved the concept a step further by referring to societal marketing. Societal marketing includes the concept that companies have a responsibility for the needs of society as a whole, so should include environmental impact and the impact of

Table 1.1 Business orientations

Production orientation	A focus on manufacturing, on improving the process so as to reduce costs and increase efficiency, and on making a profit through selling large volumes of goods.
Product orientation	The focus here is on quality, and on product features. Product orientation aims to produce the best possible product with the maximum number of features.
Selling orientation	The company seeks to use aggressive and sometimes devious selling techniques to move the product. Profit comes from quick turnover and high volume.
Marketing	Defining what customers want and ensuring that the company's activities are arranged in a way which will achieve customer satisfaction.

Marketing in Practice
Fairtrade

In a globalised world, major companies hold most of the cards, especially dealing in agricultural products from poor countries. For example, the major American fruit importers virtually own countries such as Honduras and Costa Rica – the so-called banana republics – because they represent the only customers for these countries' products. Bananas which cost fractions of a penny from the producers sell for hundreds of times the price in retail outlets in the wealthy nations of Europe and the Americas. If business is bad, the major companies simply cut the price they pay to the growers – thus transferring wealth from the poor to the rich. The same is true of coffee growers, tea pickers, and many other Third World producers.

Fairtrade is an attempt to redress this imbalance. The Fairtrade aim is first to ensure that growers always receive enough for their crops to maintain a good standard of living. Whatever price increase this means for the growers is passed on to consumers, but because the growers' price is so low to start with, even a doubling of the price does not lead to a proportionate doubling of price when the product reaches the consumers.

Of course, prices do go up at the retail stores, so the Fairtrade companies make a point of explaining that the product has been bought from independent growers who have been paid a fair price. For many consumers, especially those with a strong social conscience, this actually represents an advantage: knowing that the products have come from growers who are not being exploited is a comforting thought, and in fact one which is worth paying for.

their products on non-users (Kotler *et al.* 2003). For societal marketers, sustainability is a key issue, as well as impact assessment of the long-term results of use of the product. For example, there is an argument that car manufacturers should reduce noise pollution by making cars quieter to run, but many manufacturers simply make the car more sound-proof for its occupants and do not worry overmuch about the neighbours.

This issue has been debated by marketing academics on the grounds that marketing needs to have some boundaries. The idea that marketing is everything, because so much human activity revolves around exchanges or the results of exchanges, is an idea which has been brought into disrepute by many academics. There are, of course, many adherents to the societal marketing concept, although it is difficult to implement in practice and few companies are in a position to adopt such an altruistic approach.

Production orientation had its beginnings at the start of the Industrial Revolution. Until the nineteenth century, almost everything was hand-made and made to measure. Clothing was tailored to fit almost exactly, houses and vehicles were produced to customer specification, and relatively few items were standardised. This meant that items were relatively expensive. When machines were introduced to speed up the manufacturing process, costs dropped dramatically, so much so that prices could also be cut provided the goods could be sold rapidly. The longer the production run, the lower the costs and consequently the greater the profit: at the same time, customers were prepared to accept items which were not exactly meeting their needs, on the basis that the prices were a fraction of what they would have had to pay for the perfect, tailor-made article. For manufacturers, the key to success was therefore ever more efficient production, but at the cost of meeting individual customers' needs.

Product orientation was a result of oversupply of basic goods. Once everyone already owned the basic products, manufacturers needed to provide something different in order to find new customers. Better-quality products, often with more features, began to be introduced. By the late nineteenth century, extravagant claims were being made for products on the basis of their quality and features. Manufacturers recognised that different customers have different needs, but sought to resolve this by adding in every possible feature. The drawback is that the price of the product increases dramatically under product orientation, and customers are not always prepared to pay for features they will

Courtesy of The Fairtrade Foundation

Fairtrade is about ensuring that Third World producers get a reasonable return.

production orientation The belief that corporate success comes from efficient production.

product orientation The belief that corporate success comes from having the best product.

never use. Modern examples of product orientation include the Kirby vacuum cleaner, which has a multitude of features and can clean virtually anything, and Microsoft Windows software. In the case of the Kirby cleaner, the end price of the product is perhaps ten times that of a basic vacuum cleaner, a price which most people are unable or unwilling to pay. In the case of Windows software, the marginal cost of adding extra features to the CD set is tiny compared with the cost of producing separate CDs for each customer group, so it is vastly more efficient to send out everything to everybody and allow each customer to install and use the features they need.

The basic difficulty with both production orientation and product orientation is that they ignore the diversity of customers and consumers. Customers differ from each other in terms of their needs – there is no such thing as 'the customer'.

sales orientation The belief that corporate success comes from having proactive salespeople.

Sales orientation assumes that people will not buy anything unless they are persuaded to do so. Sales orientation should not be confused with personal selling: sales people do not operate on the basis of persuasion, but rather on the basis of identifying and meeting individual customers' needs.

Sales orientation, on the other hand, concentrates on the needs of the seller rather than the needs of the buyer. The assumption is that customers do not really want to spend their money, that they must be persuaded, that they will not mind being persuaded and will be happy for the salesperson to call again and persuade them some more, and that success comes through using aggressive promotional techniques.

Sales orientation is still fairly common, and often results in short-term gains. In the longer term, customers will judge the company on the quality of its products and after-sales service, and (ultimately) on value for money.

marketing orientation The belief that corporate success comes from understanding the relationships in the market.

Marketing orientation means being driven by customer needs. One of the key elements of marketing orientation is that customers can be grouped according to their different needs, so that a slightly different product can be offered to each group. Differentiation allows the company to provide for the needs of a larger group in total, because each target segment of the market is able to satisfy its needs through purchase of the company product. The assumption is that customers actually want to satisfy their needs, and are prepared to pay money for products which do so. Marketing orientation also includes the idea that customers need information about the products, advice about using the products, advice about availability of products, and so forth. In other words, marketers believe that customer needs go beyond the basic core benefits of the product itself. For example, recent research has shown that American consumers no longer know how to choose fresh produce: this means that, increasingly, people seek the reassurance of a brand (even if it is the local supermarket's guarantee of quality). This has opened up opportunities for farmers and others in the food supply chain to provide the type of quality assurance modern consumers need (Stanton and Herbst 2005).

Marketing orientation also implies that customer needs are the driving force throughout the organisation. This means that everyone in the organisation, from the salespeople through to the factory workers, need to consider customer needs at every stage. Quality control in the factory, accurate information given by telephonists and receptionists, and courteous deliveries by drivers all play a part in delivering customer value. Narver and Slater (1990) identified three components which determine the degree to which a company is marketing-orientated: competitor orientation, customer orientation, and inter-functional coordination.

customer orientation The belief that corporate success comes from understanding and meeting customer needs.

Customer orientation is the degree to which the organisation understands its customers. The better the understanding, the better able the firm is to create value for the customers. Since value is defined by the customers not by the firm, customer orientation means that the firm can make better offers to customers and thus receive better payments in return. Research shows that at least some consumers regard consumption as being like voting – they show approval of companies by buying their products, and avoid companies of which they disapprove (Shaw, Newholme and Dickson 2006).

competitor orientation The belief that corporate success comes from understanding competitors.

Competitor orientation is the degree to which the company understands what other firms are offering to customers. These firms may be offering radically different products:

Customer orientation

Market research.

Opening hours geared to customers' purchasing needs, not staff social needs.

Prime car park spaces reserved for customers, not senior managers.

Advertising based on what customers need to hear, not on what managers want to say.

Competitor orientation

Competitors and their products are monitored carefully.

Potential competitive response is considered when new initiatives are discussed.

Channels of distribution bypass competitors.

Company is aware of how customers perceive them relative to competitors.

PROFITABILITY

Employees have the power to correct customer complaints as they occur.

Goods are distributed through channels which are most convenient for customers.

Staff are trained to put the customer first.

Inter-functional coordination

Figure 1.1

Elements in marketing orientation

the issue is whether the customer perceives the products as offering the same (or better) value. For example, a couple looking for a night out may compare the relative merits of cinemas, night clubs, restaurants, bowling alleys, or theatres. Each of those companies is competing with the others, but the nightclub may only consider other nightclubs as competition, or the bowling alley may not recognise competition from the restaurant. Interestingly, people find the wide range of choice empowering in the long run – although initially a wider choice is actually frightening (Davies and Elliott 2006).

Interfunctional coordination is the degree to which the internal structure of the organisation and the attitudes of its members combine to deliver marketing orientation. There is no point in marketing managers developing good ideas for improving the company's offering to its customers if the employees of the firm are prevented from delivering the promises, or are unwilling to do so.

Of course these three components can be broken down into smaller elements. Figure 1.1 shows the main elements in marketing orientation.

In order to achieve a marketing orientation, firms need to be close to their customers and consumers. For some companies this is not a problem, because they have direct contact with the ultimate consumers. Service industries such as airlines, restaurants and hairdressers have direct contact with the end users of their products, and can fine-tune the delivery to meet customer needs. Other industries such as the food canning industry have contact with their customers (the wholesalers and retailers who handle their products) but do not have contact with the end consumers. These companies may use market research to find out what consumers actually need, or may rely on the retailers to understand the customers and pass on their requirements.

Table 1.2 Internal conflicts with non-marketers

Situation	Problem	Resolution
Credit control	The customers may want longer credit terms. This will cause cash-flow problems, which creates problems for the finance director.	Allow customers to pay extra for the credit. Marketing is not about giving customers everything they want: it is about selling customers everything they want.
New product development	Each customer wants slightly different features, but production economics rely on long production runs.	Identify groups of customers with similar needs. If the group is big enough to support a large production run, there is no problem: if the group is small, but is prepared to pay more for a custom product, again there is no problem.
Delivery service levels	Customers may want regular small deliveries (for example, car parts for small garages). This means that delivery vehicles are sometimes running with small loads, or even empty.	Arrange for a 'return load' pick-up system, or subcontract the deliveries to a parcel delivery company which can deliver to many small firms. In the motor industry there are specialist firms called motor factors which do this.
Handling complaints	Customers may not always be satisfied with the firm and its services, which creates a problem for everyone. Some firms only respond when sued, relying on the contract to cover themselves against dissatisfied customers.	Complaints can be repeated elsewhere: word-of-mouth is a powerful medium for destroying a firm's reputation. On the other hand, research shows that complaints which are handled entirely to the customer's satisfaction actually increase customer loyalty and encourage positive word of mouth (*Coca-Cola Company 1981*).
Purchasing of supplies	Purchasing departments can become overly concerned with price to the exclusion of other considerations. Standardisation of components makes inputs cheaper, but reduces flexibility.	The growth of relationship marketing (see Chapter 11) and just-in-time purchasing have helped to bring marketers and purchasers closer together. An understanding of the reasons for retaining flexibility will, of course, help in this context.

One of the main problems in becoming marketing orientated is that other departments within the firm find that it creates conflicts. For example, the firm's marketers may identify a group of consumers who have a need for a particular set of product features. This may cause the firm's engineers a problem in developing a product with those features. Table 1.2 illustrates some of the conflicts which occur when a firm needs to consider the needs of consumers.

These conflicts can be helped by explaining the reasons for adopting a customer focus. The problem is that some people will interpret customer focus as meaning that the company should give the customers everything they want – low prices, high quality, perfect after-sales service and so forth. This is not actually what the marketing concept says: to give everything away would mean losing money, which of course is not the way to run a business. The marketing concept implies that companies should offer a selected group of customers everything necessary to meet their needs (within the specific product category) because this is the most effective way of justifying the higher prices necessary to provide the product and make a profit. There is evidence to show that satisfied customers are prepared to pay more for the products they buy – and why should this not be so? Better to pay a little more for something that meets a need than buy a cheap product which does not work (Homburg, Koschate and Hoyer 2005). Perhaps surprisingly, there is evidence to show that engineers are generally positive towards marketing and marketers (Shaw and Shaw 2003).

Talking Point

Some writers have taken the view that all employees are marketers now, because everybody in the organisation has a responsibility for customer satisfaction. The problem with this view is a conceptual one: if everybody in the organisation is a marketer, what role remains for the marketing managers? Presumably marketing must have some boundaries!

Customer Needs

Customers in general have a set of generic needs which marketers seek to fulfil. These are shown in Table 1.3.

Customer needs therefore go beyond the product itself, and (since customers are human beings) go beyond the simple physical needs of food, clothing and shelter.

Table 1.3 Customer needs

Type of need	Example
Current product needs	All customers for a given product have needs based on the features and benefits of the product. This also relates to the quantities they are likely to buy, and any problems they might experience with the products.
Future needs	Predicting future demand is a key function of market research. Typically, this is carried out by talking to potential and actual customers and making an assessment of likely purchase quantities. Like any other predictions of the future, the results are unlikely to be perfect, but sales forecasting is essential if resources are to be put in place to ensure that supplies are available to meet demand. Equally, over-optimistic forecasts can result in over-supply and consequent problems in getting rid of excess product. Selling off excess product at cut prices generates problems beyond the immediate loss of profit: damage to the reputation of the brand may continue for years afterwards.
Desired pricing levels	Customers will naturally want to buy products at the lowest possible prices. Pricing is not straightforward for marketers: it is not simply a matter of adding up what it costs to supply the product, adding a profit margin and then selling the product. Customers will only pay what they feel is reasonable for the product, basing this on what they perceive to be the benefits they will get from buying the product. Customers will therefore not pay more than the 'fair' price, and charging them less is simply giving away profit. There is more on this in Chapter 14.
Information needs	Customers need to know about a product and understand what benefits will accrue from buying it. They also need to know what the drawbacks are of owning the product, but this information is unlikely to be provided by the organisation. For major purchases, customers will seek this information elsewhere. Information needs to be presented in an appropriate place and format, and should be accurate.
Product availability	Products need to be in the right place at the right time. This means that suppliers need to recruit the appropriate intermediaries (wholesalers and retailers) and ensure efficient transport systems to move the products to the point of sale in a way that ensures that they arrive in good condition, but at the same time in as economical a manner as possible.

Figure 1.2

Maslow's Hierarchy of Need

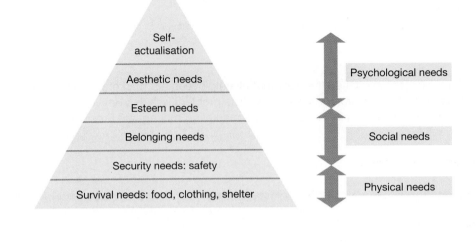

Talking Point

How do we define need? Is it something without which life would be impossible? Is water a need? Maybe – but what about people who drink orange juice, beer, tea, or even Coca-Cola, but rarely drink a plain glass of water? And if water is so essential, does that mean that Evian or Perrier are essential to life?

Perhaps beer is a luxury. But beer is often the basis of a person's social life, and people who have no social life go mad, or at least a little odd. Defining whether a product is a need or a want or a luxury is really not very easy – what is a luxury to one person is a necessity to another, because people are not driven simply by their animal needs. In fact, in modern, wealthy, Western nations very few people have to be concerned about their physical needs. Most of us are concerned about our social and psychological needs – which is why teenagers 'need' the latest trainers!

People need many things apart from survival, and in the Western world people are wealthy enough that they can afford to meet higher-level needs. Needs can be categorised: perhaps the most famous model for this is Maslow's Hierarchy of Needs (Maslow 1954). Maslow postulated that everyone has the same basic needs, and that these needs are met in order. The model assumes that people need to meet their survival needs first, then security needs, then the need to belong, then esteem needs, then aesthetic needs, and finally the need for self-actualisation (see Figure 1.2). If we imagine someone stranded on a desert island, it is easy to see that the first priority is to find food, drinking water, and shelter. Once these have been found, our castaway will seek to secure them, but once these physical needs have been met, the castaway is likely to consider trying to find some other people to relate to. Having found a group to belong to, the castaway might seek to become respected by the group. Having sufficient supplies to meet survival needs, and being a respected member of a group, our castaway is able to turn to the finer things in life: art, music, and so forth. Finally our castaway is able to consider the future, and what he or she would like to achieve in life.

This hierarchy of need is a useful concept because it clearly illustrates how human beings' needs differ from those of most animals. Because we have social needs and psychological needs as well as physical needs, our behaviour is more complex than most animals and we become engaged in exchange processes. Purchasing behaviour is thus directly affected by these higher-order needs.

The main problem with Maslow's hierarchy is that it is not actually a hierarchy. People are far more complex than this, and also are far more individual than this. The clichÅ of an artist starving in a garret is a prime example: people will often go without the basic physical necessities of life in order to self-actualise or meet aesthetic needs. A graphic instance of this occurred in Nazi concentration camps during the Second World War, when prisoners would sometimes exchange food for clothing in order to maintain appearances (Klein 2003). Likewise, a homeless person might well seek out the company of others (thus meeting a social need) without knowing where the next meal is coming from, or having a bed for the night. Having said that, it seems likely that the main preoccupation of a homeless person is likely to be finding food and shelter, even if other needs are met along the way, and that a wealthy person is unlikely to spend much time thinking about whether their survival is threatened.

What Marketers Do

Marketing management is responsible for handling specific aspects of the marketing function. In practice, these functions may appear in departments other than the marketing department as such, but they are nonetheless marketing functions, since they directly address customer needs. These aspects are known collectively as the marketing mix.

Several models exist for defining the marketing mix, and each model has drawbacks. One of the earliest attempts to define the mix came from McCarthy (1987), and defined the marketing mix in terms of product, price, place and promotion. This conveniently pigeonholed everything into four categories (all starting with P) but was an incomplete picture. The four P model has been widely criticised, not least because it has an internal orientation (it refers exclusively to the company, not the external marketplace) and it lacks personalisation (Constantinides 2006). In 1981, Booms and Bitner added three more Ps (people, process and physical evidence) to encompass the extra elements present in service industries, which after all represent the bulk of products in a modern society. This 7P model has been widely adopted, not so much for its accuracy (because like most models it omits a great deal) but because it is easy to remember and understand.

Product is the bundle of benefits which the supplier offers to the purchaser. The particular set of benefits on offer will appeal to a specific group of consumers: it is extremely unlikely that any product will appeal to everyone. Even Coca-Cola, which is sold worldwide and is the world's most recognised brand name, has only a minority share of the soft drinks market. Many people simply do not like it, or think it is too expensive, or prefer other drinks which meet their needs better. Attempts to create a 'perfect' product which suits everybody are likely to result in over-complex, over-expensive products, which is why product orientation has fallen into disrepute.

Price is the total cost to the customer of buying the product. It therefore goes beyond the simple monetary costs: customers also consider the difficulty of purchase, the cost of ownership of the product, and even the 'embarrassment' factor of owning the wrong brand. Some products have psychological associations which customers find costly. However, even the financial cost of purchase is by no means simple, because there is a complex relationship between money, price and value. Price has a strategic dimension for marketers, in that there is (for most products) a relationship between price and sales volume. The lower the price, the greater the volume (in general). On the other hand, there is also a reverse relationship between price and perceived quality (the higher the price, the greater the quality). Balancing these different elements of price is a function of marketing management, not a function of financial management. Price is a fairly flexible element of the mix, since it is relatively easy to change prices in response to demand fluctuations, but continually changing prices can lead to confusion (and even suspicion) on the part of customers.

Place is the location where the exchange takes place. This may be a retail store, it may be a catalogue, it may be a restaurant, or it may be a website. Deciding on the appropriate place for the exchange is not merely a matter of moving goods around (although physical distribution is one aspect of the process) but is rather a strategic issue. The decisions revolve around making it as easy as possible for customers to find the goods and make the purchase, and also using channels which give the appropriate image for the product. For example, retailing a product through discount stores gives a completely different impression from retailing the same product through exclusive department stores. A final issue in place decisions is the problem of power relationships in the distribution channels. In the food industry, the major supermarkets essentially control the market, with farmers

product A bundle of benefits.

price The exchange that the customer makes in order to obtain a product.

place The location where the exchange takes place.

Agricultural markets are good places for buyers and sellers to meet.

and food processing firms having to accept whatever conditions are applied by the retailers. In other industries (notably the hamburger industry), the producers have the upper hand, with retailers being compelled to accept the terms laid down.

promotion Marketing communications.

Promotion is such a large part of marketing that it is often mistaken for the whole of marketing. Promotion encompasses all the communications activities of marketing: advertising, public relations, sales promotions, personal selling and so forth. Promotion is not simply a hard sell, however: it is a way of meeting customers' information needs, at least in part. It is also, to an extent, persuasive, in that most marketing communications emphasise the good aspects of owning products and downplay the bad aspects. In recent years promotion strategies have been thrown into turmoil by the Internet: the changes have been far-reaching and the full implications have still to be assessed.

people The individuals involved in providing customer satisfaction.

People are crucial to success in marketing, particularly in service industries. Customers in a restaurant are not simply buying a meal: they are buying the skill of the chef in preparing and presenting the food, the service of the waiters in delivering the food, and even the quality of the washer-up in ensuring clean cutlery and crockery. The same is true in other industries, because companies do not buy or sell products – a company is a legal fiction. People buy and sell products, sometimes on behalf of organisations, and by so doing go some way towards meeting their own needs.

process The set of activities which together produce customer satisfaction.

Process is the set of activities which lead to delivery of the product benefits. In service industries, the process of delivery makes a difference to the benefits obtained. For example, consider the process of going out for a hamburger. In a corner take-away the hamburger will be cooked to order (which means waiting a few minutes) and will be eaten either standing up in the shop or on the street while walking somewhere else. The process is quick, but basic, and is useful to someone who likes freshly-cooked food but does not at present have much time for a meal. Further up the scale of service would be a hamburger chain such as McDonald's or Burger King, where the food is not as fresh but is delivered quickly and can be eaten either on the street or sitting down at clean but basic tables. This process meets the needs of someone who is in a hurry, and likes reliable food, but is not too worried that the burger might have been sitting under a warming grill for several minutes. Next up the scale might be Hard Rock CafÅ, where the burgers are freshly-cooked and served by a waiter or waitress, where the ambience is exciting and interesting, where music is played and where the process becomes an experience. This would meet the needs of someone who has an interest in music, or who is perhaps on a date or out with friends. Finally, an expensive restaurant might have waiters in jackets, soft lights and soft music, a wine list and silver cutlery. The hamburger is now called a Vienna steak, and would suit the needs of someone who likes to know what he is eating, but is on a special date. Note that the same person could fit into each of these categories at different times, depending on circumstances.

physical evidence The tangible proof that a service has taken place.

Physical evidence is the tangible proof that the service has been delivered. In the case of a restaurant, the food and the surroundings provide good physical evidence of the quality of the service (and probably the price, too). For an insurance company, physical evidence might be the policy documents. Physical evidence is important in services marketing because often (as in insurance) the customer is buying a promise. The policy document is therefore a reassurance that the insurance actually exists. The reverse can also be the case: the lack of physical evidence of a booking on a ticketless airline reassures the customer that every possible cost has been cut, while the physical evidence of a modern aircraft assures the customer that essential costs have been met.

Mixing the 7Ps in the correct way should help the organisation to achieve a competitive advantage, which is of course essential to any business. However, the concept of the marketing mix has been criticised. First, the mix has been criticised on the grounds that it implies a set of sharp boundaries between its elements. In fact, each element impinges on every other element to some extent – as mentioned above, the retailer in which the product is sold gives an impression of the product, which is presumably part of promotion. Likewise, the process of delivery of a hamburger provides different benefits in each case, so is presumably part of the product. Examples of other crossovers abound.

Marketing in Practice
Drink Up!

Process is often subject to local customs and habits. In the UK, patrons of bars pay for their drinks as they get them: they go to the bar to buy the drinks and then move away from the bar to tables or to standing areas away from the bar itself in order to allow other drinkers to order. Apart from an occasional foray to collect glasses, the bar staff remain firmly separated from the customers. No-one ever gives a tip in a pub, although one might occasionally offer to buy a drink for the bar staff if one is a regular customer.

In Spain, on the other hand, drinks are paid for at the end of the session, before leaving the bar. Drinkers may stand at the bar, or sit at tables, or of course sit outside: bar staff will bring drinks over for patrons who are away from the bar, and in many Spanish bars free snacks are also provided. Spaniards do not usually drink without eating: food and alcohol are seen as natural accompaniments to one another. The free snacks (tapas) do not appear with every drink – beer, wine and some cocktails are regarded as before-meals drinks, and tapas will be served. Bailey's, Cognac and some liqueurs are regarded as after-dinner drinks, and no tapas will appear. Tipping happens, but it's usually only a few small coins left for the person who clears the table. It is usual to drop any shellfish shells, nut shells, cigarette ends and used serviettes onto the bar floor, because a dirty floor is a sign of a good bar – the staff are too busy to clean up.

In Brazil, it is usual in many bars to pay for the drinks in advance and present the till receipt to the bar staff in order to be served. Food is not commonly available in Brazilian bars, but high-powered alcohol is. There are no licensing laws in Brazil, so in some major cities (notably Rio de Janeiro) street bars spring up in the evenings, with people selling beer out of cold boxes and cooking food over open-air barbecues, with dancing to impromptu bands or portable disco equipment.

In the United States people pay for their drinks as they get them, and commonly sit at the bar to be served.

Waiter service is available at tables, but tipping is almost mandatory and runs from 15 per cent of the bill upwards. Bars are kept spotlessly clean, and in many states, as in the UK, smoking in bars is illegal – in California it is even illegal to smoke on the street immediately outside the bar.

In Australia, bars frequently double as betting offices, with gambling machines and horse racing bets being taken either through machines or over the bar. Australian bars are sometimes ankle-deep in discarded betting slips. Australians pay for their drinks as they get them, and do not usually tip – the bars are often called hotels, although they do not all have rooms for guests. Table service is unlikely.

In India, several states do not allow alcohol at all. In the others, bars are often hidden away as drinking is regarded as shameful and for men only – most bars do not allow women in at all, except those in tourist areas. The range of alcoholic drinks on offer is extremely limited – usually only beer is available, but occasionally gin or whisky will also be on the menu. Indian tonic water is unknown, somewhat surprisingly.

In Thailand, drinkers get together in bars or restaurants and order a full bottle of spirits each. Typical Thai drinkers drink in order to get drunk, and do so as quickly as possible. Violence as a result of this is extremely rare – but a lot of singing and laughter does result. Bar staff frequently join in the party, which can make getting served somewhat problematic.

In Saudi Arabia, alcohol is illegal, so expatriates working there get together at private parties to drink alcohol. If they are caught they can be severely punished – flogging has been known to happen – but this does not prevent them from enjoying an occasional party.

Throughout the world, people get together to drink alcohol and talk. Yet each country has different processes for doing this, and each country's marketers need to address these different purchasing customs. Cultural differences such as these pervade all aspects of marketing.

Second, the mix has been criticised because it does not cover everything that marketers do. There is nothing about internal marketing (the establishment of relationships and exchanges within the organisation). There is nothing about competition. There is nothing about managing long-term relationships with customers.

Third, the marketing mix concept implies that marketing is something which is done to customers, rather than something which seeks cooperation and interaction between customers and the organisation.

Fourth, the mix is almost entirely focused on consumers, whereas in fact the bulk of marketing activity is carried out between businesses (Raffia and Ahmed 1992). This business-to-business marketing is perhaps less well-researched and generally attracts less attention because it operates at a lower profile. In business-to-business marketing, success does not come from manipulation of the marketing mix components, but from establishing long-term relationships between the firms concerned. If these relationships are strong enough, they act as a barrier to entry for other suppliers (Ford, Hakansson and Johanson 1986).

These criticisms do not mean that the model is of no use. All models are an abstract of reality, so do not give the whole picture. The model does help in considering issues or planning ways of managing the business, but it should not be treated as if it provides all the answers.

Talking Point

Models often seem to be flawed. Any model can be criticised – and often is! So why do we use them at all? Is it possible to create the perfect model?

A model is an abstraction of reality, a simplification intended to make reality easier to understand. Therefore some things have to be left out, which means there will be gaps in our understanding, and the model may not always be easily applied in practice. We all know that a model railway is a good way of seeing how railways operate – the tracks, the carriages, the signal boxes, the points and so forth can all be made up as miniature replicas of the real thing. But if we need to go from London to Glasgow, we need a real train!

Antecedents of Marketing

Marketing has developed as a result of inputs from many other disciplines. Essentially, marketing is an applied social science, and therefore it owes a great deal to other social sciences.

Economics

An early examination of the mechanics of exchange processes came from Adam Smith. Smith was the first writer to state that the customer is king, and he outlined the law of supply and demand, which he thought explained how prices are fixed (see Figure 1.3). Essentially, as the supply of a given product increases, the suppliers need to reduce prices in order to sell their goods: as the supply shrinks, customers must offer more in order to obtain the product. Higher prices will attract more suppliers into the marketplace, until the price stabilises at a point where supply equals demand, and likewise lower prices will force some suppliers out of the market.

Although this is a useful concept, it makes several assumptions which are unlikely to be true in the real world. First, it assumes that all the suppliers are providing identical products, whereas in the real world suppliers go to considerable trouble to differentiate their products from competing products. Second, the model assumes that consumers will

Figure 1.3

Supply and demand

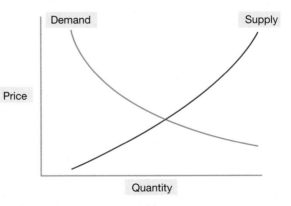

be prepared to shop around, and will know where the cheaper products are available. Third, it assumes that no supplier (or customer) has sufficient 'clout' to affect the price, which is of course unlikely. Some examples do exist of this type of market, however: international money markets and stock exchanges are two such examples.

Smith also contributed the concept that different countries have what he called natural advantages in producing some goods, and that therefore international trade could only be advantageous, since each country could produce what it could most easily and cheaply produce, and therefore maximum efficiency would result. The general principle that fair exchange leaves both parties better off is fundamental to marketing thinking: if it were not the case, trade would be impossible, since one or other party would not go ahead. This concept eventually led to the development of the Edgeworth Box (see Figure 1.5), which explains how trade operates.

The Edgeworth Box has its starting-point in the concept of **indifference curves**. An indifference curve assumes that an individual has a trade-off between different items in his or her portfolio of wealth. For example, most people have a store of food in their houses and a store of money in the bank. Up to a point, it does not matter much if one spends some of the money (reducing the store of cash) in order to increase the store of food, but as the imbalance grows the level of food which needs to be bought to compensate for the reduction in savings will have to increase. In other words, if the freezer is already full the consumer would have to see a really irresistible bargain in frozen turkeys in order to make the purchase. The same is true in the other direction – if food stocks go too low, the individual will certainly spend a portion of his or her savings to restock the larder, and the bank would have to offer an extremely high interest rate to prevent this happening. An indifference curve which illustrates this is shown in Figure 1.4. Note that the curve ends before it reaches the limit – this is because the individual will have a cut-off point, not wishing to have no money at all but plenty of food, or no stocks of food but plenty of money.

If we consider a simple case of two individuals, each of whom has a supply of food and a supply of money, we can map the total supply of food and money as shown in Figure 1.5. Here, Individual A and Individual B are each indifferent to how much food or money they have, provided the totals fall somewhere along the indifference curve. However, it is possible to consider point C, which is a point at which the total amount of food and money could be divided between the two people, but which lies above each of their indifference curves. This means that both are actually better off in terms of both food and money. Point C is on the contract line, which is a line along which either party would be better off. Note that the nearer point C is to an individual's indifference curve, the better off the other individual will be, so the actual point at which the exchange is made will depend on the negotiating skills or power relationships of the parties. In the figure, Individual B is obviously not as skilled a bargainer as Individual A.

indifference curve A diagrammatic representation of the trade-offs people have between products.

Figure 1.4
Indifference curve

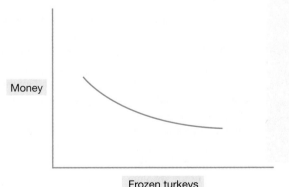

Figure 1.5

Edgeworth Box

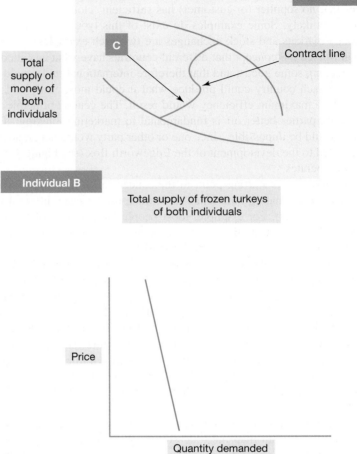

Individual A

Total supply of money of both individuals

C

Contract line

Individual B

Total supply of frozen turkeys of both individuals

Figure 1.6

Inelastic demand curve

Price

Quantity demanded

elasticity of demand The degree to which people's propensity to buy a product is affected by price changes.

In desert countries, people have to buy drinking water – a luxury? Or a necessity?

At first, it appears counter-intuitive that an exchange results in both parties being better off in terms of both money and food. This apparent anomaly comes about because each individual has a different view of the relative values of food and money. This is clearly the case if the individuals are, respectively, a grocer and a consumer. The grocer would rather have the money than have the food, since he or she has more than enough food for personal use, whereas the consumer would clearly prefer to have the food rather than the money. This concept is important because it negates the idea that market value is fixed. All values are subjective, and depend on the perceptions and situation of the individual.

Another useful contribution by economists is the concept of **elasticity of demand**. This model says that the demand for different products is affected by price to differing extents. For example, the overall demand for wedding rings or artificial limbs is unaffected by price (even though individual manufacturers' wedding rings or wooden legs might be). Such products are said to be price inelastic. On the other hand, other products are affected seriously by very small changes in price: these are said to be price elastic, as shown in Figure 1.6 and Figure 1.7. Price elasticity of demand affects the degree to which marketers can set prices relative to their competitors, and also in an absolute sense relative to other products.

An interesting point which arises from the price elasticity concept is that there is no product which is totally price inelastic.

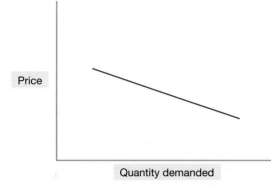

Figure 1.7
Elastic demand curve

Table 1.4 Competition

Type of competition	Explanation
Perfect competition	This is a condition in which there are many suppliers, none of whom is large enough to control the market, many customers who also cannot individually influence the market, and a product which is homogeneous, i.e. does not differ from one supplier to another. Perfect competition also assumes that all parties have complete knowledge of the market. In practice, this type of competition does not exist, apart from a few special cases such as the international money markets.
Oligopoly	An oligopoly exists when a few companies control the supply of goods. Oligopolies almost always fix prices, either by agreeing prices between themselves (a practice which is illegal in most countries) or by being very careful not to start a price war by undercutting each other.
Monopoly	This is a circumstance in which one company supplies the entire market. Very few monopolies exist, since they almost invariably lead to companies setting excessively high prices and earning excessively high profits. In most countries monopolies are carefully regulated, and even prevented, by Government intervention. However, there are cases where a monopoly is almost inevitable – the railway systems in most countries are monopolies, for example.
Monopolistic competition	This occurs when one large company has a controlling share of the market and other small companies follow its lead in setting prices and producing goods. This is the commonest type of competition.

In other words, there is no known product which people would buy no matter what the price charged. This is important because it means that there is no single product which can truly be classed as a necessity of life – if such a product existed, it would be totally price inelastic. The corollary to this is that no product (presumably) exists which can be defined entirely as a luxury, since such a product would be totally price elastic – even a tiny rise in price would prevent any sales, since no-one actually needs the product. The idea that people will not buy things that do not meet their needs is central to the marketing concept.

oligopoly A situation in which a group of companies control the market between them.

Economists also contributed to competition theory. The main types of competition are shown in Table 1.4.

Finally, economists have contributed the concept of the economic choice. This means that money which is spent on one thing cannot be spent on another – so an individual is forced to make choices. The decision to buy one thing can be translated as a decision not to buy something else. This means that competition is by no means clear-cut: marketers

economic choice The inability to spend the same money twice.

are not only competing with other firms in the same industry, they are (in effect) competing with all other ways in which consumers can spend their money. If mortgages rise, spending on consumer durables will fall, for example.

In recent years many former Government-owned enterprises have been privatised and competing organisations have been set up. In the UK, the telephone system, electricity and gas production and delivery, and even the railways were all former Government monopolies, but are now privately owned and operate in competitive markets.

Yet surely all this means is that there is duplication of effort, and a degree of confusion for consumers? Train tickets are only valid on some routes, there are several competing companies providing directory enquiries, people are unable to take their telephone numbers with them if they move house, and so forth.

On the other hand, advocates of privatisation say that duplication of effort is better than no effort at all, which is too often what happens in nationalised industries. Price competition between energy companies has kept prices lower than they might otherwise have been, most public telephone boxes work now, and some rail companies have been investing in some very impressive rolling stock.

The problem with most economic models is that unrealistic assumptions are made for the purpose of simplifying the model. For example, economists often assume that buyers are rational, that consumers have perfect knowledge of the market, that people act in ways which maximise their welfare, and that all brands are essentially interchangeable. In fact none of these assumptions stands up to close scrutiny.

Sociology

Sociology is the study of human beings in groups. Group behaviour is extremely important to human beings: how our friends and family see us, what we have to do to be effective employees, and what we feel about our place in society colours all our behaviour, including our purchasing behaviour.

Human beings are all members of several groups, and in general wish to be part of one or more groups. In order to join or remain in a given group, individuals need to act in particular ways, and this often means buying the right items or the right services. Some examples of groups are the family, friends, work colleagues, clubs or societies, and even those groups to which we belong by reason of gender or race. There are also groups to which we do not belong, and would not want to belong to: for example, most of us would not want to be thought of as stupid, naïve or uneducated, so we may go out of our way to learn about specific subjects in order to appear knowledgeable.

An understanding of how these groups operate is essential to understanding consumer behaviour: there is more on this in Chapter 4.

Psychology

Psychology is the study of thought patterns of individuals. Like sociology, the contribution to marketing lies in the area of consumer behaviour. Such areas as perception, learning, motivation, attitude formation and attitude change, and our involvement with brands and products, are basic to our understanding of purchasing behaviour.

Because psychology is concerned with the internal workings of the mind, it has much to tell us about communications and about how people develop relationships with the products they buy. Making those relationships more relevant and important is the role of marketing. Again, there is more on this topic in Chapter 4.

Anthropology

This is the study of human cultures. A culture is a set of shared beliefs which includes religion, language, customs, child-rearing practices, gender roles and so forth. Anthropologists

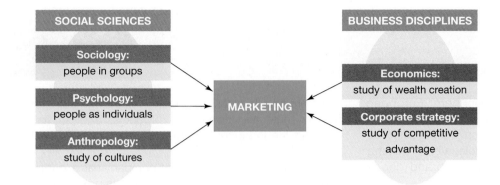

Figure 1.8
Antecedents of marketing

study the way these shared values and beliefs colour behaviour, and marketers can use this information to predict ways in which people will respond to product offerings.

Culture is particularly important in international marketing, where products are crossing cultural barriers. For example, McDonald's hamburgers are made from lamb in India, where the cow is sacred to Hindus.

All three behavioural sciences (psychology, sociology and anthropology) have considerable overlaps with each other (see Figure 1.8). They mainly contribute to marketing in the areas of buyer behaviour (understanding how people make purchasing decisions and act on them) and marketing communications (understanding how people interpret and remember messages).

Corporate strategy

Strategy is about positioning the organisation correctly for its survival and growth. Strategic thinking comes originally from military management, and much of the terminology used is the same as that of warfare. Marketers talk about campaigns, targets, capturing market share and so forth, but in fact much corporate strategy involves placing the organisation in a niche in the market where it will not upset potential competitors and attract retaliation.

The marketing strategy clearly needs to find a place within the corporate strategy, but for marketing-orientated firms the marketing strategy actually is the corporate strategy.

The Scope of Marketing

Marketing divides into a number of different applications, each of which will be examined in more detail in later chapters of this book. Because marketing embraces such a broad spectrum of human activity (indeed, as we saw earlier, some say that marketing covers virtually everything that humans do) it is inevitable that different branches of applied marketing will emerge.

Consumer marketing

Consumer marketing is concerned with the exchange processes which take place at the end of the supply chain, at the point at which the goods and services are used up and disposed of. Because we are all consumers, this is the area that impinges on our daily lives most, and (for many people) appears to be the whole of marketing. This view is bolstered by the way marketing is taught: examples taken from consumer marketing are most often used because they are easy to relate to.

Consumer marketing has also been the starting point for the development of marketing theory. Because consumer markets are large, with many potential customers and competitors, the markets are complex and interesting. Companies in consumer markets see marketing as providing a suitable competitive edge, and have therefore embraced the marketing concept wholeheartedly.

Within the UK and other Northern European countries, Spar is a well-known brand: however, most people associate it with convenience stores (corner shops). In fact, Spar is a wholesaler, providing full services to retailers, including own-brand goods and promotional materials.

The retailers in the Spar network are actually independent businesses. Each business owner contracts with Spar to buy a major proportion of their stock from the wholesaler in exchange for the use of the Spar brand.

Spar provide business advice, promotional activities, display materials, own-brand products, and so forth enabling the independents to compete more effectively with major supermarket chains.

For Spar, the benefit is that the company has a 'captive audience' of retailers who regularly buy its products. The relationship between wholesaler and retailers is therefore mutually beneficial – Spar has achieved their dominance of the convenience store market simply by understanding the needs of the retailers.

Marketing theory owes much to the development of theories of consumer behaviour, which in turn derive from sociological and psychological theory. These theories have also been applied in areas other than consumer marketing.

Industrial marketing

Industrial marketing examines earlier stages in the supply chain. Although the goods ultimately end up in the hands of consumers, products pass through many stages before arriving on the retailers' shelves. Industrial marketing is concerned with exchanges between organisations and is about supplies of raw materials, components and finished products.

Organisations with a marketing orientation are more successful than those without one (Avlonitis and Gounaris 1997). Business-to-business deals are, ultimately, driven by consumer demand, but ensuring that the needs of the customer business are met is an important stage in the process, because it smooths out inefficiencies in the system and makes the process more effective. At the level of the individual organisation, the company which is best able to meet the overall needs of the customer company will get the business.

In fact, industrial marketing does not receive the attention it deserves. In terms of turnover, industrial markets overall are much bigger than consumer markets, yet have fewer customers, which means that order values are much larger. The success of industrial markets depends on the success of consumer markets, but the reverse is also the case: without an efficient and effective industrial supply chain, consumer needs cannot be met.

Service marketing

A service product is one which is essentially intangible: examples include hairdressing, medical services, accountancy, and insurance.

Some observers do not accept that there is a real difference between physical products and service products, and in some respects there are strong arguments in favour of this viewpoint. Any service product contains some tangible elements, and any physical product contains some service aspects. Since there are numerous examples of situations in which a service product can substitute for a physical one and vice-versa, the distinction can seem to be an artificial one.

Having said that, there are differences in the way that intangible aspects of a product need to be marketed, and there are different information needs on the part of consumers. The service sector is, in most Western countries, the largest proportion of the gross national product and far and away the largest employer, so services marketing is of great importance to national prosperity. In addition, marketers of physical products have found that enhancing the services element of their products is a good way to add value for the consumer. For example, companies selling computers offer online support services as a way of generating extra revenue and at the same time increasing the value of the product to the consumers.

Not-for-profit marketing

Not-for-profit marketing is concerned with those organisations whose goals are something other than a profit. These include charities, hospitals, Government organisations, schools, and some arts organisations. In many cases, the exchange these organisations seek is not monetary at all – the Government might run a campaign to discourage smoking, or to reduce drunken driving, and measure its success in terms of the number of people who quit smoking or the reduction in arrests and accidents caused by drunk drivers.

In other cases, money might change hands. Charities are becoming increasingly sophisticated at fund-raising, using TV advertising campaigns, mailings and even telephone selling to encourage donations. Success is measured by the amount of money raised, but can also be measured in terms of raising the profile of the issues the charity was formed to address. For example, the UK children's charity the NSPCC (National Society for the Prevention of Cruelty to Children) runs advertising campaigns aimed at encouraging people to report cases of child abuse. This advertising also helps with fund-raising. In either case, profit is not the motive: as a charity, the NSPCC is non-profit-making.

Even though the NSPCC is a charity, it still uses marketing techniques.

Small business marketing

Much marketing theory (and practice) focuses on large organisations. Small businesses have specific problems of their own, largely related to their limited resources and non-specialist management. Someone running a small business has to be the marketer, the financial director, the personnel manager, the chief production manager and the head of research and development. Because many small businesses come into existence because the owner has a particular expertise in producing something (whether this is haircuts, hamburgers or electronic components) small businesses tend to have production or product orientation.

International marketing

The conceptual basis for international marketing has recently gone through a transformation in which a distinction has been drawn between the international and the global.

International marketing implies an emphasis on producing goods in one country and selling them in another, perhaps with some local assembly in the destination country. Global marketing implies a wider vision in which the company sources raw materials and components in a variety of countries, manufactures in a variety of countries and markets its goods in the same or different countries.

Globalisation of business has been a major issue in world politics, since fully-globalised companies are difficult to control and can often act as if they are above Government intervention. Also, there are issues about the homogenisation of cultures and the erosion of national diversity, as globalised companies force local businesses to close down. There is perhaps a responsibility on marketers to seek ways of minimising the damage from globalisation while maximising the economies of scale and other advantages which come from addressing global markets.

globalisation The view of the world as a single market and single source of supply.

One of the key drivers for globalisation is the identification of **market segments** which cross national boundaries. This allows for the development of products that have very specific features which appeal to only a tiny proportion of the population, since even a segment representing 0.01 per cent of the world's population is numbered in the hundreds of thousands. Thus a producer will obtain economies of scale in manufacturing for this segment, whereas the same segment (on a national basis) would not support development of the product.

market segment A group of people having similar needs.

In order to operate in global markets (or international markets) firms need to adapt the marketing mix to meet local conditions. For most global firms, this means making compromises. On the one hand, a single marketing message means that the firm benefits from economies of scale in its marketing activities; on the other hand a single message will not appeal to the diversity of cultures which exist worldwide.

Summary

Marketing is a young discipline, yet it has captured the imagination of managers and academics alike. As a result, there is a lively debate about the nature and scope of marketing – which means in turn that definitions of what marketing is and what it should be are still emerging.

For some people, marketing is about managing exchange. For others, it is about meeting customer needs at a profit (or in ways which lead to other organisational objectives). For others, marketing is everything that businesses do, and for yet others marketing is what marketers do. All these definitions have some degree of truth in them.

The key issue in practice is that marketers should not try to please everybody. A marketer should be content to meet some of the needs of some of the customers most of the time – trying to do more is unlikely to be practical. The key points from this chapter are as follows:

- There is no single definition of marketing in common use.
- Marketing is about exchange.
- Marketers put the satisfaction of customer needs at the centre of everything they do.

- Marketing often conflicts with other business specialisms.
- People's needs go far beyond mere survival.
- Marketing draws from many other disciplines, including economics, sociology, anthropology, psychology and corporate strategy.
- Marketing sub divides into specialist areas such as services marketing, non-profit marketing and so forth, each of which has its own set of parameters and techniques.

However marketing is viewed, whether as a quick fix, a function of the business, or as the guiding philosophy of the business, there is no disagreement that companies need to take care of their customers. As Sam Walton, charismatic founder of Wal-Mart (the world's biggest retailer) once said:

There is only one boss – the customer. And he can fire everybody in the company from the chairman on down, simply by spending his money somewhere else.

Chapter review questions

1 Describe how the Edgeworth Box makes trade possible.

2 Which behavioural sciences have contributed to marketing theory?

3 What are some of the practical difficulties in becoming truly customer-centred?

4 What is the difference between needs and wants?

5 What are the problems of defining marketing as being simply the management of exchange?

6 What is the difference between product orientation and production orientation?

7 What are the major drawbacks of the 7P model?

8 What problems might arise in defining who the customer is in a non-profit market?

9 Why might some people feel that globalisation is a bad thing?

10 Explain price elasticity of demand.

Preview case revisited
Mitchells and Butlers

The company see the trade as crystallising along two dimensions – drinks vs food-led pubs, and city-centre vs residential area pubs. This gives a total of four quadrants, as follows:

1 Locals. These are drinks-led pubs in residential areas. The company sees potential for these in terms of improving the amenity levels in the pubs so as to gain market share. In other words, the company seeks to attract local residents to the pub by providing cleaner surroundings and better facilities. They account for 38 per cent of the pubs, and 30 per cent of the company's sales, and operate under the Ember Inns, Scream and Sizzling brand names.

2 Pub restaurants. These are food-led pubs in residential areas. Mitchells and Butlers believe that the advantage in the market lies with existing providers, so they seek to maintain their strong presence in this market. These account for 37 per cent of pubs and 45 per cent of sales. The brand names include Toby, Harvester, Premium Country Dining and Vintage Inns. These are mainly aimed at families eating out in their local area: the demand is for eating places within easy reach of home, so that customers can either walk home or have a short taxi ride, in order to avoid the UK's tough drinking and driving laws.

3 High Street. These are drinks-led pubs in city centres. The company believes that the supply of these establishments is outpacing the (albeit strong) demand, in other words, although the market is growing fast, the number of new pubs being opened is growing faster. The company therefore wants to approach this market with a strong differentiation strategy, and do this through O'Neills (Irish theme), Reflex (an '80s theme) and Flares (a '70s theme). These pubs are deliberately geared around the over-50s: customers at Reflex and Flares easily remember the '70s and '80s the first time round.

4 Restaurants. These are city-centre, food-led establishments. Mitchells and Butlers see this market as

Courtesy of Mitchells & Butlers plc

strongly growing, so they seek to maintain strong brand values in order to keep and grow their share of the market. All Bar One and Brown's are the key brands here, and they are intended to be female-friendly places where one can as easily order a coffee as a beer. They often fill up with office workers enjoying after-work drinks, which has led Mitchells and Butlers to develop Metropolitan Professionals, a new chain aimed at inner-city office workers.

In a tough market, Mitchells and Butlers seem to be managing to grow. Despite changes in the marketing environment (the smoking ban, the Government crackdown on excessive drinking, higher taxation on alcohol, the growth in drinking at home rather then going to the pub, tough drink-driving laws and increased competition resulting from longer licensing hours) the company continues to expand and make respectable profits.

http://www.beerintheevening.com/

Case study
The Lynx Effect

Lynx is a body deodorant manufactured by the Anglo-Dutch giant, Unilever. It is aimed at a male market, and is the brand name used in the UK and Ireland: in the rest of Europe the product is marketed as Axe, but Unilever could not use this name in the UK because another company already owned the brand name.

Axe was launched in 1983 by Fabergé, a Unilever subsidiary, as a 'male version' of their highly successful women's deodorant, Impulse. The Impulse brand was marketed with the implication that wearing it would attract men: in the UK, the strapline 'Men can't help acting on impulse' was used in advertisements showing attractive men pursuing complete strangers in order to give them flowers or otherwise act in a romantic way.

From its inception, Lynx has sought to emulate the Impulse style of promotion, but from a male perspective. The commercials are usually somewhat tongue-in-cheek and humorous (unlike the Impulse advertisements which were decidedly romantic), but they show how a geeky-looking man can spray himself with Lynx and immediately become attractive to women. This is straplined as 'the Lynx effect' and has been used in a great many different commercial formats.

Different versions of Lynx have built on this theme: Lynx Africa showed the 'Lynx effect' in an African setting. Lynx Shower showed a fictitious 'Manwash' based on a carwash: men entered at one end and were washed down by attractive women, before being allowed out at the other end to go out on the town. The latest variant of the product, launched in 2008, is a chocolate flavoured version: since women are widely supposed to prefer chocolate to men (which may say something about men). The chocolate version of Lynx is expected to have even greater 'pulling power' than the standard version.

AS IRRESISTIBLE AS CHOCOLATE. NEW LYNX DARK TEMPTATION.

Courtesy of The Advertising Archives

Clearly no man in his right mind would believe that spraying Lynx all over will result in women chasing him down the street, or will make 'nice' girls start acting 'naughty', but the advertising certainly has an impact. Research shows that women do regard smell as an important factor in male attractiveness, and men are usually very conscious of the way they smell, avoiding bad breath or sweaty body odours when going to meet women. According to Unilever, 53 per cent of British men claim to use at least two shower products (presumably one of these is soap) so there is clearly a perception that smelling good is probably a big help when dealing with women.

Lynx (and Axe) have been incredibly successful in all the markets in which they have been launched. Worldwide, Lynx/Axe sold $873 billion of product in 2006, giving it 11 per cent of global sales of deodorants. Putting this in perspective, Lynx sales were greater than the gross domestic product (GDP) of Australia that year. This made it far and away the most successful brand worldwide.

On the downside, feminists have sometimes complained that Lynx advertising is sexist and degrading, and one children's advocacy group in the United States accused Unilever of hypocrisy in running the Lynx campaigns in parallel with the Dove 'Real Beauty' campaign in which the models are typical woman-next-door types rather than 'beauty queens'. Such criticisms are few, however – most people understand that the Lynx campaigns are intended to be humorous spoofs on traditional advertising, and of course the male actors used in the advertising are hardly traditional 'beefcake' types. Like the Dove advertisements, the actors are guy-next-door types.

Further developments are of course in the pipeline. New variants on the basic brand, and new twists on the basic theme of the advertising, are bound to happen as the brand develops and is refreshed. As a brand, Lynx has been incredibly successful: as an advertising and branding platform, the Lynx Effect has worked on the brand as well as it does for the geeky guys in the advertisements.

Questions

1 What needs does Lynx address?
2 Who is the customer, and who is the consumer?
3 How has globalisation helped Lynx?
4 What problems might arise from the criticisms of the Lynx advertising campaigns?
5 Why does Lynx have variants on the basic product?

References

Anderson, E.W., Fornell, C. and Mazvancheryl, S.K. (2004): Customer satisfaction and shareholder value. *Journal of Marketing* **68**(4), 172–85.

Avlonitis, G. and Gounaris, S. (1997): Marketing orientation and company performance: industrial vs consumer goods companies. *Industrial Marketing Management* **26**(5), 385–402.

Booms, B.H. and Bitner, M.J. (1982): Marketing strategies and organisation structures for service firms. In Donnelly, J.H. and George, W.R. (eds) *Marketing of Services* (Chicago: American Marketing Association, pp. 47–52).

Coca-Cola Company (1981): Measuring the grapevine: consumer response and word of mouth (Coca-Cola Company: Atlanta GA).

Constantinides, E. (2006): The marketing mix revisited: towards the 21st century marketing. *Journal of Marketing Management* **22**(3/4), 407–38.

Davies, A. and Elliott, R. (2006): The evolution of the empowered consumer. *European Journal of Marketing* **40**(9/10), 1106–21.

Drucker, P.F. (1999): *The Practice of Management* (London: Heinemann).

Ford, D.H., Hakansson, H. and Johanson, J. (1986): How do companies interact? *Industrial Marketing and Purchasing* **1**(1), 26–41.

Homburg, C., Koschate, N. and Hoyer, W.D. (2005): Do satisfied customers really pay more? A study of the relationship between customer satisfaction and willingness to pay. *Journal of Marketing* **69**(2), 84–96.

Jobber, D. (2003): *Principles and Practice of Marketing* (Maidenhead: McGraw-Hill).

Klein, J.G. (2003): Calories for dignity: fashion in the concentration camp. *Advances in Consumer Research* **30**(1), 34–7.

Kotler, P., Armstrong, J., Saunders, G. and Wong, V. (2003): *Principles of Marketing* (Harlow: FT Prentice Hall).

Maslow, A. (1954): *Motivation and Personality* (New York: Harper and Row).

McCarthy, E.J. (1987): *Basic Marketing: A Managerial Approach,* 9th edn. (Homewood, IL: Irwin).

Narver, J.C. and Slater, S.F. (1990): The effects of a market orientation on business profitability. *Journal of Marketing* **54** (October), 20–55.

Raffia, M. and Ahmed, P.K. (1992): 'The marketing mix reconsidered'. Proceedings of the Marketing Education Group Conference, Salford, pp. 439–51.

Rosenberg, I.J. and Czepeil, J.A. (1983): A marketing approach to customer retention. *Journal of Consumer Marketing* **2**, 45–51.

Shaw, D., Newholme, T. and Dickson, R. (2006): Consumption as voting: an exploration of consumer empowerment. *European Journal of Marketing* **40**(9/10), 1049–67.

Shaw, V. and Shaw, C.T. (2003): Marketing: the engineer's perspective. *Journal of Marketing Management* **19**, 345–78.

Stanton, J.L. and Herbst, K.C. (2005): Commodities must begin to act like branded companies: some perspectives from the United States. *Journal of Marketing Management* **21**(1/2), 7–18.

Further reading

The material in this chapter is covered in introductory marketing texts rather than in dedicated textbooks. For the arguments in favour of 'marketing is everything' see Kotler, Armstrong, Saunders and Wong: *Principles of Marketing* (Harlow: FT Prentice Hall).

For contributions from economics, John Sloman and Mark Sutcliffe have written *Economics for Business* (Harlow: FT Prentice Hall), which ties economic theory to the real world of business in a way which is interesting and relevant.

For contributions from the behavioural sciences, there are many books on psychology, sociology and anthropology, but you may want to read Chapter 4 first, as there is much more on these topics in that chapter.

Chapter 2
The marketing environment

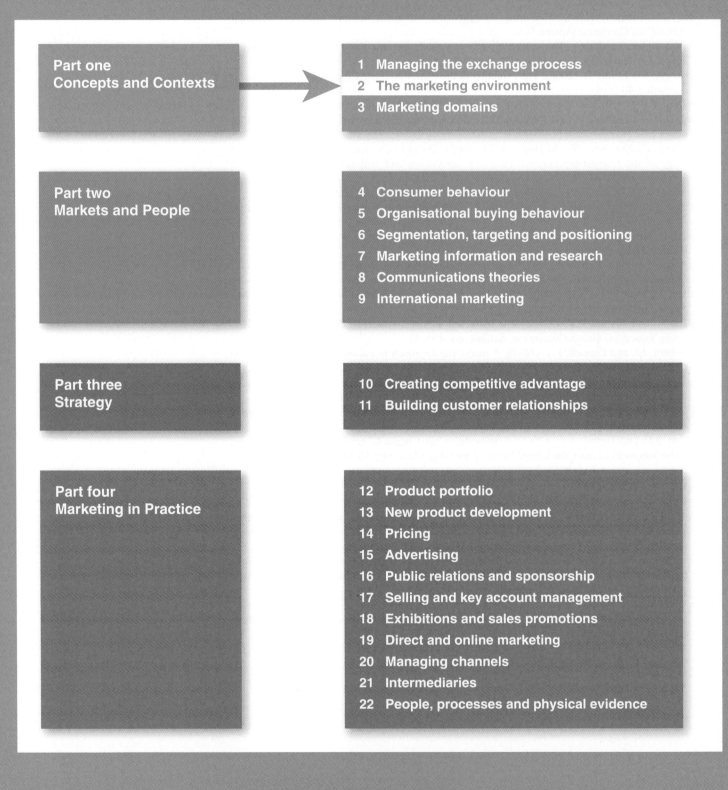

Learning objectives After reading this chapter, you should be able to:

1. Explain the nature of the business environment, and the relationship between the firm and its environment.

2. Understand the problems of dealing with the micro- and macro-environments.

3. Describe the relationship between the elements of the business environment.

4. Explain the methods Governments use for controlling the economy.

5. Explain the effects of demographic change on marketing.

6. Understand the different routes by which business law is created.

7. Discuss the nature and sources of competition.

8. Explain how technological change can transfer between industries.

Introduction

No business operates in a vacuum. Decisions are made within a context of competition, customer characteristics, behaviour of suppliers and distributors, and of course within a legislative and social framework. People working within organisations are contributing to the welfare of society and of each other, and obtaining satisfaction of their own needs in return: this complex network of exchanges results in a better standard of living for everybody.

From a marketing viewpoint, managing the exchange process between the firm and its customers comes highest on the list of priorities, but it would be impossible to carry out this function without considering the effects of customer-based decisions on the other stakeholders involved. More importantly, marketers need to recruit the other stakeholders to the cause of meeting customer needs.

The degree to which the environment can be controlled, and the degree to which the environment controls the business, depends in part on the nature of the environment and in part on the nature of the business. Some environmental factors are easily controlled by managers within the firm, whereas others cannot be changed and must therefore be accommodated in decision-making. In general, the larger the firm, the greater the control over its environment: on the other hand, large firms often find it difficult to adapt to sudden environmental changes in the way that a small firm might.

In order to assess the impact of different environmental factors, managers first need to classify them.

Preview case
Leopard Rock

In the early 1930s a prospector and gold miner, Leslie Seymour-Smith, decided to buy some land in the Eastern Highlands of Zimbabwe. He and his wife decided on the Vumba area, and began to build themselves a house. Local tribesmen warned them that they were building in a forbidden place, but they went ahead with the foundations: suddenly, out of a clear sky, a lightning bolt struck the brickwork near where Leslie was standing. 'OK, Lord' he is reported to have said, 'Fair warning'. They built their house elsewhere, but the original foundations can still be seen today.

When Seymour-Smith joined the Southern Rhodesia Recce Regiment at the beginning of the Second World War, his wife and young daughter were left alone in the house, so they decided to offer accommodation as a way of helping the farm finances. This developed into the idea of opening a hotel, and when Seymour-Smith returned from the war (having been invalided out of his regiment) the family decided to build a hotel as a way of earning money. Despite post-war shortages and difficulties obtaining the necessary permissions, the Leopard Rock hotel was built. In 1953, the hotel hosted a visit by Queen Elizabeth the Queen Mother and the young Princess

Margaret, who were on a holiday tour of what was, at the time, Britain's African dominions. This helped to put the hotel on the map: in the ensuing years the business grew, expanding to include a golf course, a casino and a game reserve.

In the 1970s the hotel was damaged during the liberation struggle, and due to severe shortages and general unrest in the country it was forced to close. A decade later, a tobacco merchant named Tony Taberer bought the hotel and refurbished it to a very high standard indeed.

Unfortunately, after the land reform problems in 1999 and 2000, tourism steadily declined, affecting Leopard Rock severely. By 2008, tourism was in free fall – British Airways stopped flying into Harare in October 2007, stating that the route had become uneconomic. Ethiopian Airlines soon followed suit, and although Air Zimbabwe announced extra flights into London's Gatwick Airport, these were threatened by air regulators, who doubt the company's ability to maintain international standards of safety. Hard information about the Zimbabwe economy is hard to obtain, but the economy is widely reported to be devastated.

macro-environment Factors which affect all the firms in an industry.

micro-environment Factors which only affect one firm.

internal environment Those factors which operate within the firm.

external environment Those factors which operate on all firms.

Classifying Environmental Factors

Factors within the environment can be classified in a number of ways. Firstly, the environment can be considered in terms of those elements which affect all firms within the industry (the macro-environment), as opposed to those elements which only affect the individual firm (the micro-environment). In general, the macro-environment is difficult to influence or control, whereas the micro-environment is much more within the firm's control.

The environment can also be classified as internal or external. The internal environment comprises those factors which operate within the firm (the corporate culture and history, staff behaviour and attitudes, the firm's capabilities) and the external environment comprises those elements which operate outside the firm (competition, government, customers). A problem for firms lies in deciding where the boundaries lie: for a truly customer-orientated company, customers might be considered as part of the internal environment, for example.

Figure 2.1 shows how these factors relate.

In effect, the firm operates within a series of layers of environmental factors, each of which has a greater or lesser impact on the firm's marketing policies. As a general rule, the further out the layer is, the more difficult it is for the firm to control what is happening: only the very largest firms have control, or even influence, on the macro-environment.

Figure 2.1
Environmental factors

Macro-environment

Economic environment
Socio-cultural environment
Ecological environment
Political environment

Micro-environment

The Firm
Internal environment:
Staff relationships
Corporate culture
Resource constraints

Competitive environment
Technological environment
Industry environment
Customers

Macro- versus Micro-environment

The macro-environment comprises those factors which are common to all firms in the industry. In many cases, the same factors affect firms in other industries. Government policy, the economic climate, and the culture within the countries in which the firms operate are common factors for all firms, but will affect firms differently according to the industries they are in.

In some cases there will be overlap between the micro-environment and the macro-environment. For example, a very large firm operating in a small country might regard the Government of the country as part of the micro-environment, since it is a simple matter for the firm to control what the Government does. On the other hand, although competitors are usually regarded as part of the micro-environment, a firm which is large enough to control an industry might be regarded as part of the macro-environment by smaller firms in the same industry.

Economic environment

The economic environment is basically about the level of demand in the economy. Most national economies follow the boom-and-bust economic cycle: every seven or eight years the economy goes into recession, which means that the production of goods and services shrinks and unemployment rises. A recession is a period of three months or more in which output shrinks, and the consequences may or may not be serious: during periods of recession, consumers are likely to postpone major purchases such as washing machines or new carpets due to uncertainty about employment security, and (by the same token) businesses will cut back on capital expenditure for such items as new factories or machinery. Borrowing is likely to reduce as consumers and firms become less confident about their ability to repay, and consequently demand drops still further.

In most cases recessions 'bottom out' within a few months or a year, but during the 1930s the world economy went into free-fall and falling demand was followed by collapsing confidence, which in turn led to an even greater fall in demand. Widespread unemployment and bankruptcies followed, further worsening the situation, as unemployed people could not afford to buy anything. Governments in most industrialised countries tried to take action by balancing their budgets – cutting expenditure until it reached the same level as income from taxation. This meant that Government works programmes such as road building, defence

recession A situation in which gross national production falls for three consecutive months.

Talking Point

contracts, and education were all cut back, with salary cuts for civil servants. This only made matters worse: people lost their jobs in shipyards and on construction projects; even when they still had jobs, they had less money to spend. Eventually the situation was only resolved by the start of the Second World War, when employment in munitions factories and in the Armed Forces kick-started the world economy.

If Governments are so poor at controlling the economy, wouldn't it be better to leave things well alone and let Nature take its course? After all, there are so many factors to take into account in the way the economy works – people's confidence, the availability of manufacturing capacity, the activities of other countries and companies and many more. Governments in the 19th century only concerned themselves with the defence of the realm and the internal security of their citizens – running the Army and the police is a big enough task, surely!

On the other hand, the 19th century was marked by revolutions and rioting throughout Europe, as starving people revolted against their Governments. Maybe having a job and putting food on the table is a security issue, after all.

The management of demand in the economy has been very much a Government responsibility ever since. No country wants to repeat a situation in which only mass destruction and slaughter can create employment and wealth, so Governments worldwide have made attempts to escape from the boom-and-bust cycle. So far these measures have been of limited efficacy, because Government action is often applied too little and too late, but in the 75 years since the beginning of the Great Depression there has not been a repeat of the level of recession experienced then.

In the period immediately following the Second World War, most Governments stimulated their economies by increasing Government expenditure. This approach had been pioneered by Franklin Roosevelt in the United States and by Adolph Hitler in Germany. In both cases the economies had recovered substantially, but eventually the result was inflation (loss of value of the currency). As the post-War period developed, and corporations became larger and more international, Governments were relatively weak in terms of their spending power and could not invest enough to make an appreciable difference to the much larger and wealthier economies that had developed. During the 1970s the situation reached crisis point, with most industrial countries experiencing high levels of unemployment coupled with high levels of inflation. A new paradigm for economic control was needed, and it came in the form of monetarism.

Monetarism seeks to control the money supply by controlling the money markets. The main instrument of economic control used by the Governments of developed countries is therefore interest rates (see Figure 2.2). Interest rates control the economy in two ways: first, a rise in interest rates encourages foreign money dealers to buy the currency, because this enables them to receive a higher rate of interest than they would get on their own currency. As the currency is in greater demand on the world markets, it rises in

Figure 2.2

Effects of interest rate changes

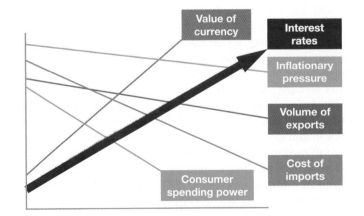

value, which in turn reduces the cost of imports and increases the cost of exports. This causes the national economy to slow down and reduces inflationary pressure. If the Government reduces interest rates, the economy will speed up as the currency falls and it becomes easier to export. The problem here is that imports become more expensive, so that prices rise, which is of course inflationary and reduces the ability of consumers to buy more goods.

The second effect of raising interest rates is more direct. A rise in interest rates reduces demand in the economy, partly because higher rates discourage consumers and firms from borrowing money to finance new purchases, and partly because the cost of existing borrowing (for example mortgages) rises, which reduces consumers' disposable incomes. The same effect is true for commercial organisations. Removing spending power from the economy also reduces inflationary pressures, because marketers are reluctant to raise prices when demand is low, firms are more likely to engage in price wars or similar promotions in order to retain market share.

Governments therefore have a fine balancing act to perform in ensuring that the economy remains stable, and thus provides citizens with a good standard of living and a degree of confidence about the future.

Economic changes can be monitored in several ways. The business press typically provides informed analysis of economic changes, and Treasury officials in most countries also produce impact assessments. These are of variable quality according to the countries concerned. In some countries, the assessments are as objective as it is possible to make them, since this allows companies and individuals to make informed judgements. In other countries, the Treasury produces distorted reports for reasons of political expediency, in order to support the party in power. Some universities and business schools also publish information and forecasts based on their own econometric models, and these may offer a different perspective from those forecasts produced by the Government.

Two problems arise from the forecasting process. First, predicting the future is by no means a simple matter, because there are too many factors to take into account. Second, the impact of economic change will differ according to the business a firm is in, and even according to the structure and positioning of the business within the market. For example, an exporting business will be badly hurt by a rise in interest rates, since this will increase the value of the currency (making exports more expensive) and will also mean that the firm has higher overheads due to servicing debt. Even in the case of two firms within the same industry, one firm might have less reliance on debt than the other and therefore be less affected by a rise in interest rates.

Another source of economic control by Governments is intervention in the markets. Governments can intervene in international money markets, buying or selling their own currencies in order to affect the value of the currency relative to other currencies. They might also intervene in commercial markets, buying up surplus stocks in order to maintain price levels. This type of intervention is a great deal less common than it once was, first because few Governments have the necessary financial reserves or purchasing power to affect global markets, and second because such intervention is often outlawed by international trading agreements, since it amounts to an unfair subsidy of the Government's national industries.

In Figure 2.3 money circulates in a clockwise direction. Companies pay salaries to employees, who in turn use the money to buy goods and services from companies. The Government takes money out of the system in the form of taxes, and puts money back into the system in the form of Government contracts for goods and services and in the form of salaries for its own employees. Money leaves the system to buy imports, and enters the system from exports.

This model is based on the work of Maynard Keynes, a leading economist of the 1930s and 1940s. According to Keynes, Government intervention in the money supply (either by cutting taxes or by increasing expenditure) would increase employment and consequently the amount of money circulating. The more money is in the system, the greater the purchasing power of people, and the greater the demand for goods and

Marketing in Practice
The European Union

After the Second World War, European Governments were faced with the task of rebuilding their national economies and putting them onto a peaceful footing. A large proportion of European manufacturing capacity had been destroyed by bombing or by invading forces: during the late 1940s the few remaining parts of the German industrial capacity were seized by the Allied powers as a form of war reparation, and of course Germany was partitioned. Former occupied countries such as France, Belgium, Holland and Luxembourg had suffered as well, and despite generous American aid to Europe it would clearly be a long time before industry recovered.

The decision was made to 'pool' national resources (initially coal and steel, but eventually virtually everything, including skilled labour) to help trade in the reconstruction period. Trade barriers between the nations of Europe were gradually removed: initially, customs-free movement of goods, capital, labour and enterprise was allowed between just six member states (France, Germany, Holland, Luxembourg, Belgium and Italy). During the 1960s and 1970s more states joined and more barriers were removed, until by 2007 there were 25 member states with virtually no border controls between them.

The effects on trade have been colossal. The European Union now represents a market of 400 million people, and the standard of living of the wealthiest states (including Britain) has now surpassed that of the United States for the first time in over 100 years. Marketers have not been slow to capitalise on the changed situation – brand names have been harmonised (UK brand Marathon became Snickers, Jif cleaner became Cif and so forth) so that the names would resonate better in the different languages of the EU, and technical standards have been harmonised so that an electrical appliance sold in Germany works equally well in France. There is still some work to be done on technical standards – Spanish TV sets do not work in the UK, and there is still no universal European light fitting – but progress has been rapid, largely driven by marketing needs. Likewise, labelling of products in 20 or more languages has caused problems, but these are minor prices to pay for accessing such a large market.

Economies of scale, reduced wastage, less time wasted on pointless border controls, and an effectively greater home market have allowed European companies to build sufficiently to compete on equal terms with American and Japanese conglomerates. Perhaps more importantly, members of the European Union have not had another war with each other – no small consideration on such a small continent.

Figure 2.3

Keynesian economics

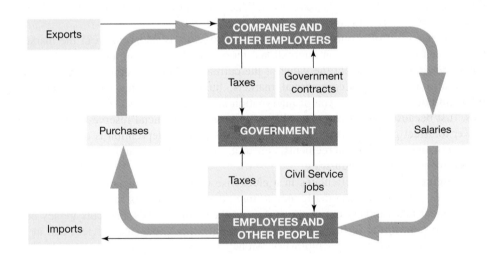

services. In the Keynes model, imports are harmful because money leaves the system, and exports are good because they bring in money. This model turned out to be too simplistic and is now regarded as obsolete: the Government does not have enough spending power to make a big enough difference, and world trade has expanded to the extent that it would be unthinkable to consider controlling imports and exports in any direct manner.

Within the European Union, the common agricultural policy is an example of Government intervention. The European Union intervenes in agricultural markets, buying up and stockpiling food in order to maintain prices and smooth out supplies. However, this policy has resulted in the so-called 'wine lakes' and 'butter mountains' when continuing surplus production is bought and stockpiled, until eventually it has to be dumped on world markets or destroyed. On the other hand, the EU specifically prohibits Governments from favouring their own national suppliers when ordering such items as computers or office equipment – all such tenders must be thrown open to suppliers in all member states (see the E-Marketing in Practice box).

© European Commission, DG ECHO

Surplus food can be donated to poorer countries but this distorts markets.

Socio-cultural environment

Socio-cultural forces fall into four categories, as follows:

1 *Demographic forces.* **Demography** refers to the structure of the population, in terms of factors such as age, income distribution and ethnicity.

2 **Culture**. This refers to differences in beliefs, behaviours and customs between people from different countries.

3 *Social responsibility and ethics.* Derived in part from culture, ethical beliefs (about how marketers should operate) affect the ways in which people respond to marketing initiatives.

4 **Consumerism**. The shift of power away from companies and towards consumers.

The relationship between these elements is shown in Figure 2.4. These relationships will be explained in more detail throughout this section.

Demographic forces are affected by variations in the birth rate and death rate, by immigration and emigration, and by shifts in wealth distribution, which may be caused by Government policies. The demography of Western Europe has shifted dramatically over the last 50 years as the birth-rate has fallen and improvements in medical care have shifted the average age of the population sharply upwards. The birth-rate in Western Europe as a whole is now lower than the death rate, so that the population would be shrinking were it not for immigration from Eastern Europe and the Third World. In some countries the situation is approaching crisis point: for example, Spain has introduced a policy of contacting expatriate Spaniards in Latin America and encouraging them to return home. The Spanish Government estimates that it needs 10 000 immigrants per annum to maintain the population.

The problem of depopulation and the ageing population is that many of the older people are retired, and therefore need to be supported by the productive members of society. Given that more people are staying in education for longer, the average working life has dropped from around 40 years to around 30 years, and certainly the once-common

demographics The study of the structure of the population.

culture The set of shared beliefs and behaviours common to an identifiable group of people.

consumerism The set of organised activities intended to promote the needs of the consumer against those of the firm.

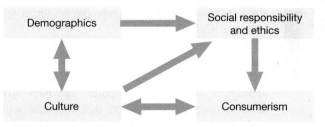

Figure 2.4

Socio-cultural environment

50-year working life has disappeared forever. In the UK and France, this has resulted in the respective Governments examining the possibilities of raising the retirement age: currently, many people in the UK will not be able to accumulate the necessary 40 years of National Insurance contributions to be able to qualify for a State pension.

An influential report prepared for the European Union in 2002 showed that the 15 member states at that time (there are now 25 members) had experienced considerable immigration, virtually no outmigration, and dramatically reduced birth-rates. Coupled with the increased life expectancy (now around 75 for men, 81 for women), the net result has been a reduction in the under-25 age group and increases in both the working population and the elderly population. These changes have happened over a 30-year period from the mid-1970s (Cruijsen, Eding and Gjatelma 2002). The report goes on to say that entry by the new Eastern European member states will change this pattern in the short term, since these countries have lower life expectancies. During the 1990s (following the collapse of Communism in Europe) Eastern European countries have themselves experienced demographic shifts, notably a dramatically reduced birth-rate. These demographic shifts are thought to be the result of worsening health care, fear over job security and less healthy lifestyles. The authors expect the following demographic shifts as a result of expansion:

1 Population decline will occur several years sooner.
2 Population ageing will be slightly suppressed.
3 Population dejuvenation (reduction in under-25s) will become stronger in future decades.
4 Expected decline of the working population will hardly change.

So far, experience has borne out these findings. There have been dramatic shifts in populations (several million Poles have emigrated to other EU states, for example), so there has been no decline in the working population of the original 15 member states.

From a marketing viewpoint, these changes offer both opportunities and threats. Clearly products aimed at a youth market are likely to decline, whereas products aimed at older people will be in greater demand. In practice this may lead to surprises, however: for example, an assumption that almost all 70-year-olds have mobility problems may have been true 30 years ago, but improved health care and healthier lifestyles probably mean that most 70-year-olds in the 21st century are as fit as 50-year-olds were in the 1960s. The increase in the elderly population is not expected to peak until the 2040s, and even this assumption depends on limited improvements in health care and life expectancy of the very old – in other words, it assumes that people will not live much beyond 100 years old (Cruijsen *et al.* 2002).

A further demographic change (general to Europe) is the increase in single-person households. This has come about through an increase in the divorce rate and through increasing affluence: young people no longer live with their parents until they marry, as was the case in the 1950s. At the other end of the age scale, large numbers of widowed elderly people continue to live in the former marital home. In several EU countries single-person households now represent the largest category of household: the UK's 2001 census revealed a 47 per cent increase over a 10-year period in single-person households where the occupant was under pensionable age (Census 2001).

The implications for marketing are widespread. For house builders, smaller homes and starter homes (e.g. flats) will show increased demand. This may mean that smaller models of domestic appliances will be more popular, that pack sizes of cereals and other foods will be smaller, that furniture will be smaller and perhaps more adaptable (for example futons, which convert from

Polish businesses have opened up throughout the UK – in this case, in Wales (the sign is in Welsh, Polish and English).

sofas to beds) and that security devices will be more popular as more people leave their homes unattended when they go to work. Such a rapid increase in single-person households represents a major challenge for many marketers, since it implies a considerable shift in market demand for almost every consumer product.

Income distribution and wealth concentration are also part of the demographic structure. Income is a somewhat fluid concept: pre-tax income does not mean a great deal, since an individual's salary may be heavily or lightly taxed according to the country concerned and the level of income of the individual. Disposable income is the income remaining after income tax and other deductions, but of course this is not the end of the story – basic household expenses need to be met, such as mortgages, local authority property taxes, household bills and so forth. This leaves an amount which the individual can spend in any way he or she chooses: this is called discretionary income. There is, of course, a conceptual problem here in distinguishing between necessities and discretionary purchases. Housing is an example – a relatively wealthy person might choose to live in a small house, and thus have an extremely small mortgage and a correspondingly high discretionary income. Someone else might decide to live in a large house, and have very little discretionary income as a result. In either case, the choice of house was freely made, so the house purchase might be considered in the same way as the purchase of a particular brand of bread or make of car. Clothing is even more problematical – wearing some kind of clothing is obviously essential, but the fashion industry is founded on the basis of attracting discretionary income, so the line between necessity and discretionary purchase is somewhat blurred.

Cultural environment

The cultural environment refers to the shared set of beliefs and behaviours prevalent within the society in which the company operates. These include language, religious beliefs, customary ways of working, gender roles, purchasing behaviour, gift-giving behaviour, and so forth. Social behaviour and cultural attitudes play an enormous role in determining consumer behaviour, but they also play a role in commercial purchasing behaviour and in the way staff behave and expect to be treated by employers.

Socio-cultural issues manifest themselves in several ways, affecting both the external and the internal environments of the organisation. For example, a company operating in Thailand will need to consider the role of Buddhism in Thai life, including the fact that

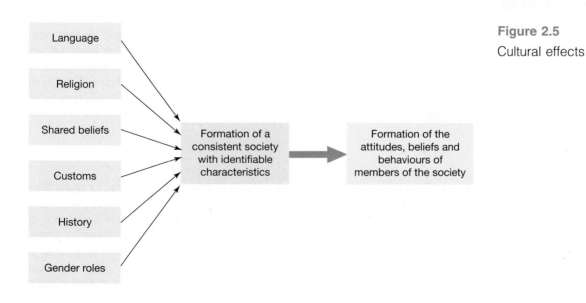

Figure 2.5

Cultural effects

Table 2.1 Cultural problems in the marketing environment

Example	Explanation
Time sense	In many agrarian countries (and warmer countries in general) each day is regarded as being essentially the same as the one before and the one after. Therefore it does not matter if tasks are not completed today: tomorrow is another day. In northern, industrialised countries each day is regarded as unique, so that lost time is regarded as being lost forever.
Gift-giving behaviour	While gift-giving behaviour is common throughout human societies, the occasions on which it happens are not. The Onam festival in Kerala, Christmas in the UK and USA, Twelfth Night in Spain and Portugal, and O-Chugen in Japan are all examples of general gift-giving seasons, but they happen at different times of year and have different traditions behind them.
Meanings of symbols	In advertising, a busy person denotes success to someone from the UK or USA. To an African, the same symbol denotes someone who has no time for others and is selfish.

© iStockphoto.com/Serdar Yagci

Most Thai men become monks for part of their lives.

Talking Point

most Thai men spend several years as monks at some point in their lives. This would be a surprising entry on the CV of a Western employee, but would be normal in Thailand, and indeed regarded as commendable. Also, Thais have the concept of 'sanuk', meaning 'fun', which is applied equally in the workplace as in private life. This means that Thais might expect to spend part of their working day cracking jokes or even singing songs. This can be a difficult aspect of Thai life for Western managers.

Further examples of cultural issues are shown in Table 2.1

Culture can also dictate the ways in which people spend their discretionary income. For example, Irish people spend a high proportion of their incomes on alcoholic beverages (around double the UK figure). This does not necessarily mean that Irish people drink more alcohol than their UK counterparts – in part the figures reflect lower incomes in Ireland and higher taxes on alcohol (Euromonitor 2004). It does, however, reflect the importance that drinking has in the Irish culture: Irish social life centres around the pub, whereas in the UK social life tends to centre on the home.

Changes in taste and fashion are also a component of the cultural environment. Fashions in food, clothing and even ideas can affect marketing effort.

Another aspect of culture which evolves over time is the change in lifestyle expectations. In the 21st century, few people would consider living without a telephone, television, refrigerator, car, bank account and credit cards. Yet in 1960 each of these product categories were owned by a minority of the UK population. At that time it was common for a whole street to have only one or two homes with TV sets, and perhaps one telephone. In 2009 the vast majority of UK homes have more than one television set, and the advent of cellular phones means that many households will have several telephones as well. More recently, the mobile telephone has moved from being a luxury owned only by urban professionals to being widespread among all levels of society: this transformation has happened within a period of less than 10 years.

Earlier it was mentioned that the Spanish Government needs to attract 10 000 immigrants a year to maintain its population balance. All very well, but what about the effect on Spanish culture? In the Middle Ages, Spain was invaded from Morocco, and many of the current icons of Spanish culture (flamenco, olive oil, architectural style) were actually Moorish in origin. The great monuments of Spain (the Alhambra, the walled city of Toledo) date from Moorish times.

Can we expect the same level of cultural change from new waves of immigrants? Should we worry about this? Is this type of change something to be feared – or is it a natural part of human development? After all, if the native Spaniards found that cooking with olive oil rather than pig grease made the food taste better, isn't that a positive cultural change?

Marketing in Practice
The Atkins Diet

During 2003 the revolutionary Atkins Diet suddenly became the 'diet of choice' of over four million British people. Despite warnings from some quarters that the diet was actually dangerous, its proven ability to help weight loss ensured its popularity among the large numbers of obese Britons raised on fish and chips and Mum's treacle pudding.

The Atkins Diet advocates eating large amounts of protein foods and very little carbohydrate. Originally published in 1972, the diet received a tremendous publicity boost after actress Jennifer Aniston and former Spice Girl Victoria Beckham both claimed to have used it successfully. Meat sales grew by 11 per cent, and sales of some fruits (the ones allowed by Atkins, such as watermelons and raspberries) also soared by as much as 64 per cent. The Waitrose supermarket, mainly based in wealthy southern England, saw a 16 per cent increase in meat sales, which a spokeswoman for the firm attributed to Atkins.

On the other hand, sales of bread and potatoes showed corresponding declines. The decline has been steady – of the order of one to two percent per annum, but it's enough to have the bakers worrying. John White, the director of the Federation of Master Bakers, said, 'One can speculate as to the reasons, but personally I have no doubt that Atkins has had an impact. We can only hope that it's a fad that will pass.'

The Flour Advisory Bureau signed up model Denise van Outen to star in commercials promoting flour products. The British Potato Council spent £1m on a makeover for the humble spud, and plans were laid for the potato, rice and flour industries to band together to meet the threat of Atkins.

Other diet products also felt the pinch. Roche's anti-obesity drug, Xenical, suffered a 16 per cent drop in sales, and Slim-Fast (a Unilever product) also showed a sharp decline. As 2004 started, however, some relief was on the horizon in the form of the South Beach Diet. Perhaps a new diet fad would replace Atkins in the public consciousness and save the carbohydrate industry.

Since 2004 many other diets have come and gone. Atkins still has its adherents, as do the others, but people's general confusion over what constitutes a healthy diet has not gone away.

Referring back to Figure 2.4, culture and demographic change are interrelated. Culture dictates the aspirations of the population, which in turn dictates some of the changes in income, education and lifestyle. Movement of population also influences culture, as new influences are brought in by immigrant groups – one has only to consider the influence of Indian immigration into the UK on British eating habits, or the equivalent effect in the Netherlands of Indonesian immigration.

There is more on cultural issues in Chapter 4.

Political and legal environment

Political influences affect businesses in two main ways: firstly, political parties have policies which are often put into legislation, which clearly must be obeyed. Secondly, the ruling party sets the general tone of behaviour in the country as a whole, and in the Government departments in particular. This subtle change in the national culture will also affect business.

The political environment is usually regarded as including the regulatory environment, whether such regulation emanates from the Government or from industry-based bodies. Some examples of Government controls in business are as follows:

1 *Patent legislation.* Governments set the rules about what may and may not be patented and for how long. In high-tech industries such as bioengineering or software design, intellectual property may represent the bulk of the firm's assets. Changes in patent (and copyright) law can have profound effects. This is particularly an issue in the international arena, since there is no such thing as a world

patent: products must be patented in each country separately, and in some countries (notably Taiwan) few products are patentable, so that companies are left open to having their products copied at a fraction of the cost of the 'genuine' product.

2 *Taxation.* Apart from the general taxation regime on corporations, Governments often impose selective taxation on specific products in order to manage demand and raise revenue. This is particularly a problem in the alcoholic drinks industry and the tobacco industry, but in recent years changes in the classification of different products in respect of VAT has had a marked effect on some firms. As with patent legislation, taxation varies from one country to another, and therefore firms need to be particularly careful when entering foreign markets.

3 *Safety regulations.* Products need to conform to national safety regulations. Within the European Union many attempts have been made to coordinate the wildly differing safety laws in the member states, but to no avail: finally, the EU has adopted the stance that any product which is legal in one member state will be legal in all member states unless the Governments concerned can demonstrate that there is a very real danger to human or animal life.

4 *Contract law.* Governments can and do amend contract law, although much contract law is developed through the decisions of law courts. In the UK, contract law is looser than it is in the USA: in the USA, the written agreement is the basis of the law, whereas in the UK verbal contracts are as binding as written contracts. There is, of course, the problem of proof in the case of verbal contracts. The main area of Government intervention in contract law has been in the field of consumer protection, where the contract between the consumer and the retailer is often regulated to compensate for the perceived imbalance of power between individual consumers and large companies.

5 *Consumer protection legislation.* Apart from contract law, mentioned above, Governments often enact legislation designed to protect consumers. In the UK there are several hundred laws relating to consumer protection, covering everything from credit agreements to the quality of goods sold. In general, the old principle of 'caveat emptor' (let the buyer beware) is no longer necessary, since retailers are required to ensure that goods are of suitable quality for the purpose for which they are intended, are being sold at prices that are transparent and reasonable, and can be returned if they are faulty or (often) when the customer changes his or her mind.

6 *Control of opening hours.* In the UK, the opening hours of retail shops are only limited on Sundays, when they may only open for six hours (with exemptions for small businesses). In other countries tougher restrictions apply: in particular, retail hours in Germany are still heavily limited by law. In the past the opening hours of German retailers were even more restricted, the net result of which was the development of one of the largest mail-order markets in the world.

A change in the political nature of the Government can make considerable changes in the general tenor of the law. Left-wing Governments traditionally increase the number of laws and restrictions on businesses (taking the hand of Government approach to ethics mentioned earlier) whereas right-wing Governments tend to reduce restrictions on business (taking the invisible hand approach).

The enforcement of legislation is usually left to specialist bodies such as the Office of Fair Trading and the Trading Standards Institute. Trading standards are enforced at local authority level, with each council in the UK having its own trading standards department. In the United States the same function is carried out by the Better Business Bureau, which is a non-profit body funded by businesses themselves. Businesses fund the BBB in order to keep the rogue operators out – honest businesses are able to compete on a level playing field.

The legal environment is created in two ways: firstly, by Government legislation, and secondly by case decisions made by judges (see Figure 2.6). Case law is created when

Figure 2.6

Sources of law

legislation is put into action: the law is often unclear, and individual circumstances mean that judges (and magistrates) need to clarify matters, usually by referring to other cases which have been decided already. This system of referring to other examples ensures a degree of consistency in decision-making, but of course each case is different in some ways, which is why they need to be argued out in court.

Local government

Local government does not pass law as such (although there may be some local bye-laws affecting businesses) but often has the role of enforcing national law. Local authorities also deal with such issues as planning permission and zoning of business activities (retail parks, residential areas and manufacturing areas). In most cases planning permission presents few problems, but areas which have caused difficulties for marketers include planning permission for signs and displays, location of billboards and zoning of out-of-town retail parks. On the one hand, small businesses tend to oppose the creation of large retail parks, since they represent serious (sometimes fatal) competition, but on the other hand such retail parks offer an opportunity for large firms to grow. The extent to which such regulations affect firms varies from one country to another: in France it is relatively easy to obtain permission for large out-of-town stores or hypermarkets, and a reasonable compromise has been worked out between the hypermarkets and local businesses whereby small businesses are given space within the hypermarket complex. In Italy, on the other hand, restrictions are extremely strict and hypermarkets have great difficulty in obtaining permission to build.

The European Union

The European Union has the role of trying to coordinate business law throughout the member states in order to ensure a fair competitive environment for businesses operating within the EU. Ultimately, the intention is that businesses will be able to compete on an equal basis throughout the EU, but the problems are all but insuperable and it will be some time before there is a single body of regulation covering all member states. Some of the issues are as follows:

1 *Technical standards.* Although most EU countries use the metric system, Britain and Ireland used the Imperial system, which is almost entirely incompatible with the metric system. Simply changing the sizes of such items as plumbing fittings and electrical wiring is not enough – most of the buildings in both countries were built using Imperial measures, which means that any repair work or alterations need to be carried out either using Imperial size components or using conversion fittings where one system joins another. At a more subtle level, the specifications for wiring, plumbing, strength of bricks and so forth vary among member states. Even the television broadcasting systems differ – video recordings made in the UK

Freedom of movement in the European Union has created a large market for holiday and retirement homes.

will not play on Spanish televisions, although they will on French and German systems. Building regulations differ between member states, and even such things as the threads on screws and bolts differ, so that British fixings manufacturers need to retool their factories to be able to do business on the Continent.

2 *Frontier controls.* These have largely been abandoned since 1993, when the European Single Market came into existence. However, Customs officers still have the right to stop vehicles and check for illicit goods, some of which might seem surprising. For example, there is no problem shipping computers, gemstones and alcoholic drinks across European borders, but there is a problem shipping bananas between the UK and Germany. Immigration controls are in place for non-EU citizens, but the difficulty of policing all the former frontiers means that in most cases immigration officers rely on spot checks and occasional tip-offs to catch illegal immigrants.

3 *Safety standards.* Common criteria for safety and health have been agreed, but only at a somewhat minimal level. Provided that a product conforms to basic EU safety regulations, it is given the CE mark and is legal for sale anywhere in the EU. However, such products may not meet the safety standards of products manufactured in the target country.

4 *Currency fluctuations.* The introduction of the Euro for most member states has meant that companies operating between member states no longer have to consider the risks of currency fluctuations. A company doing business between the UK and France has to take account of the possibility that the pound might strengthen or weaken against the Euro, and must therefore fix the price of the goods to allow for the possibility of a fluctuation, or must buy or sell currency in advance in order to minimise the risk of losing money on the contract. Companies dealing between (say) France and Spain do not have this problem, because all prices and costs are calculated in Euros. Sweden, Britain and Denmark were not in the Eurozone at the time of writing: in September 2003 Sweden overwhelmingly rejected membership as a result of a national referendum. In fact, Eurozone countries have found that it has brought problems as well as benefits: soaring prices in Germany, an unwelcome influx of holiday-home buyers in southern Spain, price rises in France and increased smuggling of cigarettes throughout the EU have all followed on from the single currency. In the long run, the benefits are likely to outweigh the drawbacks, but in the meantime the period of readjustment is proving painful for some people.

5 *Advertising.* The EU has made some progress towards harmonising advertising regulations, but apart from introducing a Europe-wide ban on tobacco advertising in broadcast media (TV and radio) there are no regulations which apply throughout the EU.

database marketing Using a list of customers or potential customers stored on a computer to drive the marketing effort.

telephone selling The practice of using telephone communications as a personal selling medium rather than face-to-face meetings.

Meanwhile, the European Union continues to seek ways of unifying marketing law. It would seem likely that the main successes will happen in the new media such as the Internet, database marketing, telephone selling and so forth, simply because national laws in member states are only in their infancy.

Regulatory bodies

Some regulatory bodies are Government-sponsored and run. Most of them are established as independent bodies; in other words, they operate without direct involvement from politicians. These are sometimes called QUANGOS, meaning quasi-autonomous non-governmental organisations. They have a specific task to perform within a limited set of guidelines, and are therefore able to act much more quickly than a Government department could. Here are some examples of UK QUANGOS:

1 *Oftel*. This is the organisation responsible for regulating the telecommunications industry. Since the privatisation and deregulation of the telephone system in the 1980s, several hundred companies have established themselves in the telecommunications market at some level or another, from major landline and satellite providers like British Telecom through to small companies providing answering services.

2 *Ofgas*. The organisation responsible for controlling gas suppliers. Ofgas is concerned with selling practices in the industry, billing problems, difficulties encountered when switching suppliers and disputes between suppliers. Part of the problem for Ofgas has been the practice of doorstep selling of energy services, using salespeople who are unsalaried and who rely on the commissions they get for converting customers. In some cases these salespeople have been less than ethical in their approach to selling, sometimes telling outright lies or even forging signatures. The difficulty for Ofgas is that part of its remit is to encourage vigorous competition between suppliers (Benady 1997).

3 *Independent Television Commission*. In conjunction with its sister organisation, the Radio Authority, the ITC controls commercial broadcasting. Both organisations have the responsibility for issuing licences to broadcast, and have several responsibilities. One is to ensure that programme content meets generally agreed standards of good taste. Second, both are charged with the responsibility of ensuring that the broadcast media do not fall under the control of too small a group of people, so mergers and acquisitions between broadcasters are carefully scrutinised. Third, and perhaps most importantly for marketers, both organisations have responsibility for monitoring and approving broadcast advertising. This includes ensuring that advertising appears at appropriate times (considering that children might be watching or listening), that advertising content is within the bounds of good taste, and that advertising is clearly differentiated from programming. The ITC is also responsible for monitoring product placement (the use of branded products in TV programming). At one time, any reference to a brand name was not allowed, but the impossibility of removing brands from feature films made this ruling unworkable. The current position is that brands can be shown, but the programme makers are not allowed to accept money for including a specific brand (unlike the film industry, where movies are frequently funded by brand owners).

4 *Office of Fair Trading*. This Government organisation has two remits: first, to protect consumers and explain their rights, which it does through advertising campaigns and occasional leaflets, and second to ensure that businesses compete and operate fairly. The OFT tends not to become involved in individual consumer problems, but lays down guidelines and occasionally becomes involved in test cases. In other words, the OFT might become involved in a general problem of unsafe imports from a foreign country, but would not become involved in a case of a customer who has bought faulty double glazing.

5 *Monopolies and Mergers Commission*. The MMC has the responsibility for preventing companies from exercising undue power in the marketplace due to having an excessive share of the market. This does not mean that a monopoly or near-monopoly is not allowed: it merely means that the MMC will monitor such situations carefully to ensure that the company or companies involved do not abuse their power, for example by fixing prices at too high a level or by preventing other companies entering the market. For example, the washing-powder market is entirely controlled in the UK by Unilever and Procter and Gamble. Because of the high cost of the plant and equipment needed to make washing powder,

Figure 2.7

Regulatory bodies

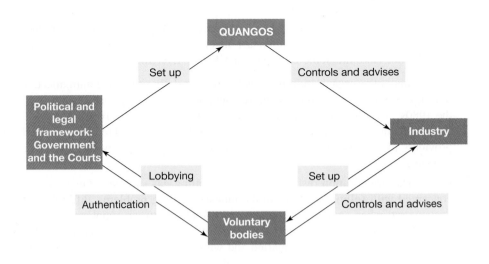

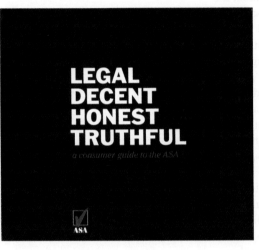

Courtesy of The Advertising Archives

LEGAL DECENT HONEST TRUTHFUL

a consumer guide to the ASA

ASA

Talking Point

other firms cannot economically enter the market, so the MMC monitors the situation to ensure that the two giant firms do not exploit their position.

In the voluntary sector, there are many regulatory bodies which have been set up by industries themselves. In many cases, this has been seen as a way of forestalling Government intervention: if the industry does not have its own regulatory body, the Government might well step in to establish one. This is the case with the Advertising Standards Authority (ASA), about which there is more later in the chapter, and the British Board of Film Censors.

The ASA is probably the voluntary organisation which most impinges on marketers. However, it has no statutory powers to compel advertisers or media such as newspapers and television to comply with its rulings. In practice, the ASA operates on the basis of complaints received, and will act even if only a few complaints come in. The ASA will examine the advertisement concerned, interview the advertisers and their creative people if necessary, and will decide whether the complaint is justified. If the complaint is upheld, the ASA will request the advertiser to withdraw the advertisement. If the advertiser refuses, the ASA will ask the media not to run the advertisement. These requests are rarely refused – in the event that they are, the Office of Fair Trading does have the power (under the Control of Misleading Advertisements Regulations 1988) to apply for a legal injunction to prevent the advertisement being shown, but this is rarely invoked, since no-one in the industry wants the expense of litigation or, indeed, to encourage Government intervention.

If an organisation is set up by an industry, presumably it is funded by that industry and its management is appointed by the industry. So how can such a body have any credibility at all? How can it possibly bite the hand that feeds it by seeking to regulate the activities of its founders?

Maybe the founders of these organisations feel that they are pure in heart themselves, but that the rogues needed to be regulated. All well and good – but everyone's a rogue sometimes. Might there not be a danger of the leading firms being treated more leniently than the small guys struggling to get established by whatever means present themselves?

One of the problems the ASA faces is that it has no authority to vet advertisements before they go out. Thus by the time the ASA has acted, the advertisement has already been seen, and the publicity surrounding its withdrawal often means that the advertisement achieves a much greater impact than it otherwise might have done. Benetton in

Marketing in Practice
Intervention by Regulators

In February 2004 the Office of Fair Trading became involved in a case of misleading advertising. Cyber Travel (UK) Ltd, a Norfolk-based holiday club, agreed to withdraw its misleading advertising. The company has agreed not to give (among other things) the misleading impression that:

- Consumers have been awarded a prize when there is no competitive process.

- Consumers attending a presentation get a free gift, when the gift is available only if an administration fee is paid.

- Membership of the club entitles members to discounted holidays when this is not in fact the case.

- On becoming a member consumers get a 'free weekend break' when in fact they are obliged to buy meals on the premises.

- The holiday club could provide particular holidays or accommodation in specific locations or of the type in specific brochures, when in fact the company has no corresponding inventory of products and services.

- Accommodation is predominantly 'luxury' or 'five-star' when this is not the case.

In the same month, the OFT banned the practice of fly-boarding, whereby estate agents put 'For Sale' signs up outside properties they are not selling to give the impression that they have more properties on their books than is in fact the case. The specific company concerned, Mankind Property Services Ltd, trading as Bairstow Eves, and its manager, Farooq Majeed, were required to give written undertakings not to market properties unless they were acting on instructions from the owner.

Meanwhile, in the voluntary sector, the ASA was also busy. Boots PLC, the UK's biggest pharmaceutical retailer, was requested to withdraw advertisements for Vari-Lash Day and Night mascara when a consumer complained that the model in the 'after' shot of a before-and-after advertisement was obviously wearing false eyelashes. Although Boots claimed that the advertisement was intended to indicate that the product could be used for party wear, and the model was obviously made up for an evening out, the ASA ruled that the advertisement was plainly misleading, since it gave the impression that the mascara would be much more effective than it actually is.

In another case, Agent Provocateur was asked to withdraw an advertisement showing a woman wearing only black stockings and lingerie sitting astride another woman and apparently strangling her with a stocking. The advertisement was held to be obscene, pornographic and degrading to women, and Agent Provocateur (after initially claiming that the ad was intended to be playful) agreed to withdraw it.

Other marketers were feeling less cooperative in February. Bulldog Telecom were upbraided for issuing an advertisement in which they promised each caller a 'free' air machine-gun. The advertisement went on to say, 'There are no charges whatsoever! Call and order as many times as you want! Semi-automatic assault rifle, automatic assault rifle, Colt Uzi rapid fire . . .' and so forth, offering a lengthy list of products. Unfortunately, the order line number was a premium-rate line, and the necessary call to order the goods would cost at least £20. The complainants objected that the advertisements were irresponsible because they encouraged violent and antisocial behaviour, and were also untrue because the products were not free. Bulldog Telecom did not respond to the ASA's requests for information, and therefore the ASA had to ask the media not to carry the advertisements again, and also reported the case to the Committee of Advertising Practice to ensure that other media would not carry the advertisement.

These were only two of the 19 cases decided on a single day (11 February 2004). Most, but by no means all, claims that day were upheld.

particular has been accused of exploiting this situation by deliberately producing highly provocative advertisements in the certain knowledge that the ASA will issue a request for their withdrawal.

Many industries have **trade associations** which police the activities of members. If a firm is a member of a trade association, this provides some reassurance for potential customers, because the trade association will have a code of conduct which its members are expected to adhere to, and which usually provides some redress for disappointed

trade association A group of companies in the same industry, set up to look after the collective interests of the group.

consumers or sanctions against rogue members. Attempts have been made by some trade organisations to coordinate their codes of practice across Europe, but given the widely-differing consumer protection laws and systems in different countries, this is proving somewhat problematical.

Influencing the macro-environment

For smaller firms, the macro-environment usually has to be accepted as it is. Large firms are able to influence some aspects of the macro-environment, however. Advertising campaigns can affect the country's culture in at least a small way, although in most cases this happens more by accident than by design. For example, some advertising slogans have found their way into everyday conversation ('Have a break, have a Kit-Kat' is one well-known example). This can be seen as an example both of the power of advertising to enter the national consciousness, and also the fulfilment of an advertising copywriter's dream.

However, in most cases advertising has only a superficial influence on culture. The main influence that large firms have on the macro-environment lies in the area of lobbying Government for changes in the law, and in playing leading roles in the regulatory bodies. This type of influence is not restricted to businesses, however: pressure groups and even individuals can also lobby Government, even at the simple level of speaking to the local member of Parliament.

For smaller firms, the chances of making any material change to the macro-environment are minimal. The best way of having some effect is to join a trade organisation or other pressure group. In some countries, politicians can be sponsored by pressure groups, and in others pressure groups sponsor political parties in order to receive favourable treatment at a later stage when the party is in power. In the UK, sponsorship of political parties is subject to careful monitoring to ensure that sponsorship does not unduly influence legislation, but in practice the Labour Party is largely financed by trades unions and the Conservative party is largely financed by big business. This sponsorship will inevitably affect the thinking of politicians.

The Micro-environment

The micro-environment comprises those elements of the environment which impinge on the firm and usually its industry, but which do not affect all firms in all industries. The micro-environment is composed of the following elements:

- *The competition*. In a sense, all firms compete with all other firms for the consumer's limited spending power. For most practical purposes, though, consideration of the competition is limited to firms providing similar solutions to the same customer problem.

- *Technology*. Major technological changes such as the advent of satellite communications or cellular telephones clearly affect most industries. Such technological advances are relatively rare, though. In most cases technological change only affects a relatively small sector of the economy: for example, a new manufacturing process for aluminium will have some effect on any firm or customer using aluminium products, but the firms most affected will be aluminium refiners.

- *Industry structure and power relationships*. This may be related to competition, but equally encompasses supply chains and strategic alliances between firms. Some industries operate in a highly competitive manner, while others are more cooperative: for example, funeral directors tend to be fairly cooperative with each other, whereas estate agents are highly competitive.

● *Customers*. The pool of customers, the nature of them, the different segments of the market made up of people with slightly different needs, all affect the firm. For example, a law firm specialising in corporate law will have a very different customer base from that of a firm specialising in house conveyancing. The difference in customer type will affect almost everything about the firm, from the design and location of its offices through to its recruitment policy.

The competition

Competition is a fact of life in any business. There is no such thing as a product that has no competition, because each product (from the consumer's viewpoint) represents a way of solving a problem. Before the product existed, people almost always had some other way of solving the problem: it may not have been as effective, but it existed. For example, television was certainly a radical technological breakthrough, and from the engineering viewpoint it had no competitors. There was, at the time, no other way of transmitting pictures electrically and instantaneously over a long distance. From the consumer's viewpoint, though, television was simply another entertainment device, which was perhaps more convenient than the cinema which it replaced (or the theatre before that), but did not represent a very major change.

Competition can vary greatly between industries, however. As we saw in Chapter 1, competition can be categorised as monopolies (in which one firm controls the market), oligopoly (in which a few large firms control the market between them), perfect competition (in which no single buyer or seller can significantly influence the market) and monopolistic competition, in which one major firm has most of the power in the market, but smaller companies also have significant shares.

Much business strategy is concerned with establishing the firm in a suitable competitive position (there is more on this in Chapter 10). Too rapid growth may lead to unwelcome attention from major firms, whereas too slow growth may lead to being left behind by other small firms. Equally, a large firm cannot afford to be complacent: new challengers arise all the time.

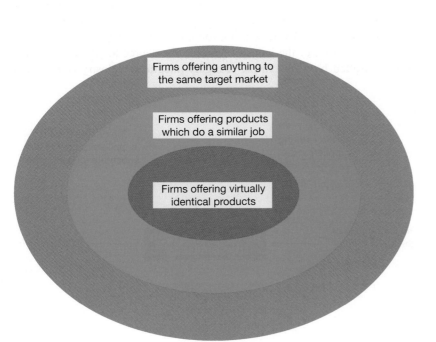

Figure 2.8
Levels of competition

- Firms offering anything to the same target market
- Firms offering products which do a similar job
- Firms offering virtually identical products

Competitor analysis can be carried out using Porter's Five Forces Model (Porter 1990). This model offers a way of assessing the likely strength of competition in any given market. The five forces are as follows:

1 *The bargaining power of suppliers.* If suppliers have strong bargaining power, competitive pressure will be greater.

2 *The bargaining power of customers.* Customers with strong bargaining power will be more demanding and can set one supplier against another. This will make competition fiercer.

3 *The threat of new entrants.* If it easy for new companies to set up in the same business, competition will be strong: if it is difficult for new firms to enter the market, the existing firms can become complacent.

4 *The threat of substitute products and services.* If close substitutes are readily available, competition will be stronger. For example, pizza delivery companies recognise each other as competition, but the business is extremely competitive because of the existence of many other types of takeaway food.

5 *Rivalry among current competitors.* In some industries, firms have a 'live and let live' approach which reduces competition. This is particularly the case in oligopolistic markets, and in markets which are well-established. In new or rapidly-growing markets rivalry will tend to be stronger and therefore competition will be stronger.

Bargaining power of suppliers, if high, can seriously reduce industry profits and thus make competition stronger. Bargaining power of suppliers is determined by the factors shown in Figure 2.9.

If there are few suppliers, the buyer has very little room for bargaining. Suppliers in such circumstances can operate oligopolistically, setting the terms for business between them. For example, hairdressing businesses in the UK have a choice of only six or seven suppliers of hairdressing products. Most hairdressing businesses are small, owner-managed concerns with very little buying power, so they are unable to bargain effectively with their suppliers.

Suppliers' products cannot always substitute for each other. A typical example is the motor industry: spare parts for Ford cars will not fit Toyotas and vice-versa, so the garage business is forced to buy from a small group of suppliers. Likewise, in the computer software industry some software will not run on all operating systems.

vertical integration A situation in which one company controls or owns suppliers and customers throughout the supply chain.

Vertical integration of the industry refers to the degree to which the supply chain is owned or controlled by a few firms. A highly-integrated industry (for example the oil

Figure 2.9

Factors in the bargaining power of suppliers

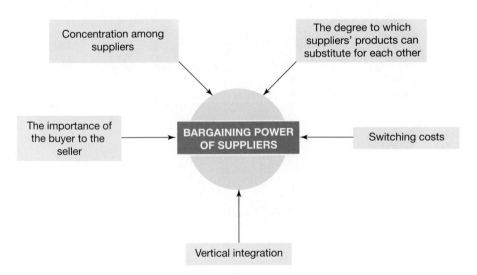

industry, where a few companies control everything from extraction through refining and distribution to the petrol forecourt) does not allow many opportunities for competitors to enter.

The importance of buyers to the supplier is about the extent to which the buyer represents a strategic opportunity for the supplier. Large buyers such as major retailers may control the market – for example, the toy industry is largely controlled by Toys R Us. In general, though, the evidence is that few companies bother (or are able) to develop their suppliers effectively (Wagner 2006).

Finally, if it would be expensive to switch from one supplier to another, the suppliers occupy a strong position. This is the case for firms such as Microsoft, since switching from Microsoft operating systems might well mean making changes to hardware, retraining staff, redesigning administrative systems and so forth.

The bargaining power of customers is determined in much the same way as the bargaining power of suppliers, except that the deciding factors work the other way round.

New entrants to a market can pose a threat for the established companies, but the danger of new firms being able to enter the market is limited by the following factors (see also Figure 2.10):

1 **Economies of scale**. If the industry is such that production can only be carried out efficiently on a very large scale, entry will be less likely. For example, modern steel production only operates efficiently when steel is produced in very large quantities.

2 *Product* **differentiation**. If the products are very similar, new entrants can easily produce copies. If, however, the existing companies have managed to create highly-differentiated products (either by strong branding or by using patented technology) it becomes difficult for new companies to establish a foothold in the market.

3 *Capital requirements*. If the capital outlay needed to enter the market is large, few companies will be able to raise the necessary money, especially without a track record in the industry. For example, for many years the major airlines had little or no serious competition. The cost of buying a fleet of aircraft was prohibitive. However, in recent years the wide availability of good second-hand aircraft has allowed niche operators such as Ryanair and EasyJet to enter the market.

4 **Switching costs**. If it would be prohibitively expensive for the customers and consumers within the industry to change suppliers, new entrants will be unable to gain a toehold in the market. This is a strong barrier to entry.

5 *Access to distribution channels*. If the industry has already integrated the distribution network (the supply chain), new entrants will be unable to obtain distribution. This is a critical determinant of success in markets which are geographically large, such as the United States: the key issue for any new firm is obtaining distribution for its products.

6 *Cost advantages independent of scale*. Sometimes firms within an industry will have access to supplies of raw materials, or will own patents, which mean that newcomers are unable to produce competing products at an economical price.

economies of scale Cost savings resulting from large production runs.

differentiation Factors which distinguish one product from another.

switching cost The expenditure of money and effort resulting from changing from one product to another.

Figure 2.10

The market entry mountain

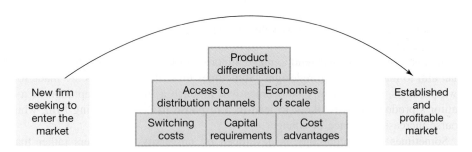

Of course, sometimes it is the newcomer that has the new patent or access to sources of supply, in which case the established firms may have a problem.

Technology

Technological change goes beyond the more obvious changes seen in recent years as a result of communications and electronic technology. For example, Toyota developed new technology for car manufacturing which enabled them to retool a factory to produce a new model in only a few days, instead of the six months or so it took their American and European rivals. This meant that the firm was able to make better use of capital equipment and was also able to be much more flexible in meeting changes in the market.

A technological change can transform an industry. Most of the products in common use today did not exist 100 years ago: refrigerators, televisions, dishwashers, telecommunications satellites, microwave ovens, jet aircraft, computers, frozen foods and many others. The pace of technological change appears to be increasing, as more firms invest in research and development and ideas are more rapidly disseminated due to improved communications. For example, Sony now estimates that a new electronic device has a life of around three months before its replacement will be produced: whether the replacement is produced by Sony or by a competitor is irrelevant to the consumer, so the firm is forced to develop new products that will hurt the sales of its existing products.

The effects of this technological explosion are widespread for the firms concerned. As a threat, the possibility of competitors developing products which will wipe out existing products on the market is very real. All new products replace something else, since people almost always have an existing solution for a real problem. Transistors replaced the electronic valve industry over a period of only a few years, computers have virtually eliminated the carbon-paper industry, and CDs have virtually replaced vinyl records (as vinyl records replaced shellac 78 rpm records, which replaced wax cylinders).

A further problem is that the new technology might arise in an apparently unrelated industry. It would have been impossible for postal services to have recognised the threat from new computer technology in the 1970s, but the advent of cheap personal computers has led in turn to the Internet revolution, and the explosion in emailing. This has undoubtedly had a marked effect on postal services worldwide, as people send emails rather than writing letters. Equally, the development of electronic watches virtually destroyed the Swiss watchmaking industry, which relied on mechanical technology and did not have the necessary expertise or technological infrastructure to make the necessary changes.

Maintaining a technological lead requires firms to make heavy investments in research and development. This in turn means that the investment must be repaid from sales of the product – and given the shorter product life cycles involved, the payback must be very high. This means either that the profit margins per unit of product must be high, or the market must be very large. This is why most companies in rapidly-changing markets such as electronics have adopted a global marketing approach. This is the only way these firms can access a large enough market to be able to obtain the necessary returns on their capital.

Because of the domination of large, globalised firms in high-technology areas, smaller firms find themselves unable to compete effectively. This has resulted in a number of cross-border collaborations. In some cases these have worked well, especially in relatively low-tech industries such as vehicle design and building, but in others the results have been less than exciting.

In most cases companies tend to make minor improvements to existing products rather than aim to make complete redesigns. Sometimes these improvements are made to their own products, but frequently companies will produce a 'me-too' adaptation of a competitor's product. This is likely to lead to a response by the competing firm, which of course increases the pace of change.

Sometimes new technology is developed by university researchers rather than by research departments of companies. For example, the basic technology of the laser was

Marketing in Practice
Airbus Industrie

Airbus Industrie was founded in 1970 as a consortium between Aerospatiale of France and Deutsche Aerospace in Germany. The intention was to compete against the giant American corporations Boeing and McDonnell Douglas in the passenger aircraft business. In the next few years, other firms joined the consortium: British Aerospace, Fokker and CASA of Spain all joined.

Airbus Industrie is headquartered in Toulouse, but manufacture is carried out throughout Europe. The company now has a substantial share of the short-haul passenger aircraft market. In 2007 Airbus launched the A380, a 550-seat double-decker aircraft which is 20 per cent cheaper to run than its closest rival (in fact, its fuel consumption, when full, is equal to that of 550 small cars – so that it uses the same fuel per mile as the passengers would use if they each drove the same distance). The A380 is also quieter than other airliners by a considerable margin. In Spring 2002 Airbus opened its new design and engineering facility – in Wichita, Kansas. This final assault on the homeland of Airbus' greatest competitors is perhaps the company's greatest triumph to date.

The company's success is due to several factors. First, it produces aircraft which meet the needs of airlines, and it works closely with airlines in order to do so. Second, it has a range of products which suit specifically European airlines, which naturally prefer to buy from a company which is conveniently located for spares, repairs and replacement aircraft. Third, Airbus is large enough to create economies of scale which match its largest competitors, and can thus remain price competitive. Finally, the company recognises the wider needs of passengers and society as a whole by producing more environmentally-friendly aircraft.

© Airbus S.A.S. 2005

developed at universities in the United States and Russia, even though the final working model was developed at Hughes Laboratories in California. Even then this revolutionary device had no discernible purpose – it was four or five years before anyone was able to make practical use of lasers. This is an example of the value of pure research (research which has no immediate practical value).

In some cases, technological development is delayed by legislation. New drugs need to go through extremely rigorous testing and in some countries (notably the United States) product liability legislation places a strict liability on manufacturers to ensure that their products are safe. This is another reason for producing 'me-too' products: the competitor has already dealt with the safety issues.

Industry issues

Any competitive act must be considered in the light of possible retaliation. The structure and nature of the industry is crucial in understanding the possible results of any actions. The intensity of competitive response will depend on the following factors:

1. *The degree of concentration in the industry.* The fewer the competitors, the greater the likelihood of oligopoly.

2. *The rate of growth of the industry.* Rapidly-growing industries are usually less stable than established industries, with greater fall-out of companies which are unable to adapt quickly enough.

3 *The degree of differentiation.* If the products are essentially the same (for example, petrol) the nature of competition shifts to other factors. In some cases the other factor is price, but this is a dangerous way to compete because it squeezes profit margins.

4 *Cost structures.* If fixed costs are high (for example because the industry is capital-intensive) profits are dependent on maintaining a high level of sales. The airline industry is a prime example: airlines cannot afford to have planes flying half-empty, so they are prepared to discount seats in order to maintain efficiency.

5 *Investment structures.* If the industry is one in which new investment is made in sizeable chunks, new entrants will make a substantial impact on existing firms until demand catches up. For example, if there are three hotels in a town and a fourth one opens up, the impact will be substantial, at least in the short term.

6 *Competitive information.* If firms in the industry can inform themselves easily about what their competitors are doing, oligopolistic behaviour is the likeliest outcome. On the other hand, some industries (such as farming) operate in almost total ignorance of what other farmers are planting this year, which leads to occasional surpluses or shortages.

7 *Strategic objectives of competitors.* In some industries, the firms have strategic objectives which do not conflict with other firms in the industry. For example, Ford does not compete strongly with Rolls Royce because they are aiming at different sections of the car market.

8 *Cost of leaving the industry.* In some industries, capital assets which have a theoretical book value in the millions may have little or no second-hand value, and thus any firm which leaves the industry will have to leave behind its assets, and thus go bankrupt. Mining and steel production are examples.

Airliners represent a large capital investment.

The industry environment may be controlled by sources of supply, or by lack of customers: for example, the oil industry is controlled in large part by the OPEC countries, who are the producers of petroleum. In the past, the oil companies ran the industry, but during the 1970s the oil-producing countries realised that they held the real power if they were prepared to act together, and they have controlled the world price of oil ever since. At the other end of the supply chain, aircraft manufacturers have relatively few potential customers. Most of the world's airlines are too small to be able to afford new aircraft, so manufacturers can only approach a relatively small number of major national airlines. Equally, there are relatively few aircraft manufacturers in the world.

Internal Environment

The firm's internal environment is the internal culture, staff relationships and resource constraints which colour all of the activities and decisions made by the organisation (see Figure 2.11).

All firms operate with limited resources. Firms create competency in what they do by making appropriate combinations of the resources at their disposal: the more effectively the resources are deployed, the better the firm will do in the competitive environment. Ensuring that the internal environment is working well is an important aspect of management: it is not always part of the marketing manager's remit, but it is, at the conceptual level, marketing.

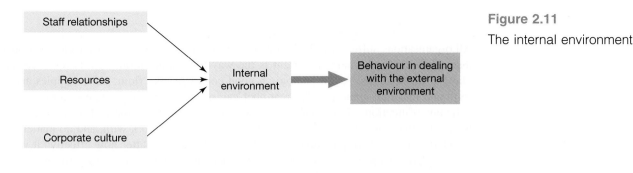

Figure 2.11

The internal environment

Staff relationships

The relationships between staff within the organisation are key in ensuring an effective working environment. While there are many areas of staff relationships that are outside the control of managers, management should be able to create an environment in which staff relationships can flourish.

Organisations have, in general, two structures which work in parallel. The **formal structure** is shown on the company's organisation chart, and shows where each person fits into the overall hierarchy. This structure shows who is answerable to whom, and which department is responsible for which set of activities. People in the formal structure have specific job titles and, usually, fairly clearly-defined responsibilities to the organisation.

The **informal structure**, on the other hand, is not shown on any organisational chart. It comprises the friendships and alliances which are struck up by people who share a lift home, or who have lunch together every day, or who meet at the photocopier or coffee machine. The informal structure cuts right across the organisation chart, and is often more powerful in running the organisation than is the formal structure. Where the formal structure lays down exactly what people should be doing, the informal structure allows people to be flexible in what they do. Problems which have been unaccounted-for in the organisational chart can be solved by people who can call in a favour from a friend in another department. For this reason, managers should encourage the informal structure to develop – it provides flexibility of response in a changing world. Research shows that joint reward systems and social networking are the two most important factors in reducing conflict between marketers and others within the company (Chimhanzi 2004)

formal structure The official relationships between members of an organisation.

informal structure The unofficial relationships between members of an organisation.

Corporate culture

Culture is a set of shared rules and beliefs. Within organisations, beliefs will develop, and a corporate culture will eventually emerge. Corporate culture has been called 'the way we do things round here' and it can be a powerful influence on staff behaviour. Research shows that people are able to have one set of beliefs outside work and an entirely different set of beliefs in the workplace. However, corporate culture and personal ethics should not be too widely separated: staff need to feel that they are working for an ethical organisation (see Chapter 3 for more on this).

Developing the appropriate corporate culture is a lengthy process, since people change slowly. Often the beginning of a corporate culture is the firm's mission statement, in which the company lays down its long-term aims and overall beliefs. In some cases, a charismatic leader will be able to impose a corporate personality on the organisation, but this type of corporate culture sometimes dies with the founder.

Resource constraints

All organisations suffer from lack of resources, but of course some suffer more seriously than others. What is more important is the way the organisation uses its resources and plays to its strengths. As an analogy, a good cook can take flour, butter, apples and so forth and make an apple pie. A great chef can take the same ingredients and produce a delicious confection – but a bad cook can produce an inedible mess. The resources plus the management input constitute what the marketer has to work with, and no matter how wonderful the marketing campaign being planned, and no matter how effective it would be, the plan cannot work if the organisation does not have the necessary resources.

Marketers are frequently faced with the frustrating situation in which senior managers cut the marketing budget because business is bad. Marketers naturally respond by saying that cutting the marketing budget is the worst possible solution, since it will inevitably lead to a further loss of business, but if this argument does not work the marketers are forced into a situation of having to achieve the same results with less resources. This often calls for considerable creativity.

Summary

The environment within which the business operates clearly affects marketing plans. Marketers are always looking outwards, mainly towards the customers and competitors who make up the market, but they also need to consider the internal environment because this is where the resources come from to maintain a marketing plan.

The key points from this chapter are as follows:

- No business operates in a vacuum.
- The macro-environment is largely uncontrollable: the micro-environment is much more susceptible to influence or control.
- The elements of the environment overlap, and also impinge on each other.

- Interest rates are the main tool of Government control of the economy, since globalised business means that most Governments are too small to influence the world economy.
- The ageing population of most industrial countries is often well-off: they represent an opportunity, not a threat.
- Judges create law by making decisions on specific cases.
- Competition may be indirect: it may not even come from the same industry.
- Technological change can also come from unrelated industries.

Chapter review questions

1 What would you expect the Government to do if inflation began to rise?

2 How might a toy manufacturer respond to the changing demography of Europe?

3 Which industries might be affected by the discovery of an anti-ageing drug?

4 How might a large company and a small company differ in their view of a Government regulatory body?

5 How might Governments respond to a cross-border merger between two major steel companies?

Preview case revisited
Leopard Rock

The situation in Zimbabwe is desperate for any company in the tourism business. Unrest in the country, political instability, an economy based on printing money and little else, and international sanctions all serve to create a business environment which is virtually impossible to deal with. Even the wildlife is leaving – Zambians report hundreds of elephants crossing the Zambezi to escape the sound of gunfire, and poachers desperate to feed their families.

Despite these difficulties, Leopard Rock Hotel continues to survive. Visitors to the hotel expressed amazement that, even though the country was suffering so much, 90 per cent of the items on the restaurant menu were still available. The golf course has been highly praised, and is of international standard: in 2008, Leopard Rock joined the Inns of Zimbabwe group, an association of hotels within Zimbabwe, in order to take advantage of the collective marketing possibilities such a group offers. With the Zimbabwe dollar undergoing a period of hyperinflation, all payments are either in South African Rands or in US dollars: the hotel also offers discounts for cash payments.

In June 2008 the UK's Foreign Office advised against any travel to Zimbabwe unless absolutely necessary, hammering another nail in the coffin of Zimbabwean tourism. Following on from the disputed 27 June Presidential elections, when Robert Mugabe was re-elected, a degree of calm was eventually restored – from the viewpoint of Leopard Rock Hotel, this could only be a good thing. In common with many other tourism-oriented businesses in Zimbabwe, the hotel can only hold on and hope for better times to come.

Case study
Nordbrand

For over 500 years the town of Nordhausen, in Thuringia (East Germany) has been famous for producing schnapps. The town was at the centre of a corn growing region, and Nordhauser Doppelkorn is famous throughout Germany and beyond.

In April 1945 the town suffered a disastrous air raid from British and American bombers, trying to destroy the nearby V2 rocket factory. Seventy-five per cent of buildings in the town were destroyed, and a quarter of the population killed: the medieval buildings of Nordhausen's historic centre were destroyed by incendiary bombs and most of the distilleries were destroyed completely.

After the war, Nordhausen became part of Communist East Germany, and it was at this time that distilling was concentrated almost entirely in the huge Nordbrand building in Bahnhofstrasse, Nordhausen. Employing hundreds of workers, the new distillery became the biggest in Germany: the one surviving distillery from medieval times became part of the Nordbrand organisation, and continued using traditional methods of production right into the 21st century, although it is now retained as a working museum and shop for tourists. So popular was Nordhausen Doppelkorn that for a period immediately after the war there was a lucrative smuggling operation across the border between East and West Germany, using special containers made from rocket casings to conceal the Doppelkorn under the smugglers' clothing. When the border between East and West was closed in the early 1960s this practice ceased – crossing the border became virtually impossible.

After reunification, the Nordbrand distillery found itself in the position (like many other East German organisations) of having to compete directly with West German companies. Moving to a market economy from a command economy was far from easy for any company – but for Nordbrand the difficulties were immense. They were now competing in a consumer market against companies throughout the EU – not only did they have to compete against other German schnapps distillers, they were competing against Scottish whisky distillers, Dutch jenever producers, Danish akvavit distillers and so forth. Additionally, in the intervening 40 years or more, the company had lost its original customer base.

Worse was to come. Schnapps drinking was falling out of fashion with younger consumers. It was regarded as an old man's tipple, and young people were drinking more wine, alcopops and pre-mixed drinks such as Bacardi Breezers.

If Nordbrand didn't act fast, their market would start shrinking fast – old soldiers never die, but old drinkers do!

The company began by sending one of its experienced distillers on a tour of Europe to find out about distilling methods in other countries. He visited Scottish whisky manufacturers, Dutch distillers and French brandy stills, among many others, and came back full of ideas. Based in the traditional distillery, he and a small group of workers began producing new variations on Doppelkorn: fruit-flavoured versions, darker-coloured versions, oak-matured versions and so forth. But new products alone were not enough – even the oak-matured Doppelkorn could not compete head-on with whisky unless some aggressive marketing took place.

In 2003 Nordbrand launched an entirely new version of Doppelkorn aimed at a young market. Branded Eiskorn, the new schnapps had a lower alcohol level than Echter Doppelkorn (the flagship product) at only 32 per cent alcohol, since research had shown that younger people preferred a lower-strength spirit to use as a mixer or as a shooter. This lower strength also reduced the taxation level on the spirit. Eiskorn uses glacial water for its manufacture, and the company promote this as water from the Ice Age.

Nordbrand had always used the symbol of a chicken (since chickens eat corn), but for Eiskorn they used a mammoth, to continue the 'ice age' theme. The schnapps was heavily promoted to nightclubs and young people's bars, with special glasses supplied. These glasses were to be kept in the freezer, and the Eiskorn was supposed to be served ice-cold: unlike full-strength spirits, the schnapps will freeze, since its alcohol level is relatively low. The glasses themselves were frosted so that they retained the impression of being frozen.

The brand was an immediate success, and the mammoth symbol soon became known throughout Germany. The company mounted a life-size model of a mammoth outside company headquarters in Nordhausen, and carried out sales promotions in which free stuffed mammoths were given away with bottles of Eiskorn. The brand has caught on so well that the company is now able to sell the glasses through its online store and traditional distillery for £8.95 for six.

Nordbrand still has to make the transition from being a German company to being a European company, but in the 20 years since reunification it has certainly proved that it can survive in a market economy.

Questions

1 How might Nordbrand seek to compete more effectively in a wider market?
2 How has Nordbrand coped with macro-environment problems?
3 What competition does Nordbrand face?
4 How might Nordbrand build on the success of Eiskorn?
5 What are the main positive factors Nordbrand has going for it?

References

Benady, D. (1997): Ofgas must dispel advertising hot air. *Marketing Week*, December, 19–20.

Census (2001): UK Government Statistics Office.

Chimhanzi, J. (2004): The impact of integration mechanisms on marketing/HR dynamics. *Journal of Marketing Management* **20**(7/8), pp 713–40.

Cruijsen, H., Eding, H. and Gjatelma, T. (2002): *Demographic Consequences of Enlargement of the European Union with the 12 Candidate Countries*. Statistics Netherlands, Division of Social and Spatial Statistics, Project Group European Demography.

Euromonitor (2004): *Alcoholic Drinks in Ireland* (London: Euromonitor).

Porter, M.E. (1990): How competitive forces shape strategy. *Harvard Business Review* **57**(2), 137–45.

Wagner, S.M. (2006): Supplier development practices: an exploratory study. *European Journal of Marketing* **40**(5/6), 554–71.

Further reading

This is a somewhat specialised area, with relatively few books dedicated solely to the marketing environment. However, here are some possibilities:

A. Palmer and B. Hartley (1999): *The Business and Marketing Environment* (Maidenhead: McGraw-Hill). This gives a comprehensive coverage of the marketing environment and the management issues surrounding it.

The UK's Chartered Institute of Marketing also publish several study guides on the marketing environment, geared towards the CIM Diploma examinations.

Chapter 3
Marketing domains

Learning objectives After reading this chapter, you should be able to:

1. Explain the main motivations for charitable donations.

2. Describe the main factors in change management.

3. Explain the internal marketing aspects of human resource management.

4. Describe the role staff have in public relations.

5. Describe the types of resistance marketers might face.

6. Understand the basics of negotiation.

7. Understand how to undermine rumours.

8. Explain the relationship between corporate ethics and personal ethics.

9. Understand the role and function of the brand.

Introduction

There has been considerable debate in marketing circles regarding the domains in which marketing operates, or should operate. At the conceptual level, some marketers believe that marketing theory is applicable to all exchanges between people, whether money changes hands or not. This leads to some difficulties when applied in practice, however. For example, a series of advertisements aimed at encouraging people to eat less and exercise more certainly looks like marketing – it uses the tools of marketing to encourage a change of behaviour and manage people's attitudes. On the other hand, it is difficult to see where the exchange is happening. Meanwhile, a mother offering a child sweets in return for good behaviour is clearly engaged in an exchange, but few people would regard this as marketing.

A further problem arises in defining who is a marketer and who is not. If we define marketers as the people who manage the exchange, this implies that interactive websites (for example) in which the customer manages the process without direct intervention from the company making the sale are actually making marketers out of the customers.

For practical purposes, many marketers simply use the definition that marketing is what marketing people do. Although this definition may be intellectually unsatisfying, it does at least have the merit that we can work with it on a day-to-day practical basis. This chapter looks at some of the areas in which marketing professionals work, and outlines the problems which arise from defining the boundaries of marketing.

This chapter will also outline some of the categories under which marketing operates, and the domains in which marketing thinking is applied. It is intended as an overview of the academic debate as well as illustrating some of the practical areas in which marketers contribute to organisational progress.

Preview case
The Retired Greyhound Trust

Greyhounds have an unusual life. The athletes of the dog world, greyhounds have a usually-brief racing career and then retire into private life – if they are lucky. They are fast, agile dogs which have been raced since the mid-19th century, originally (it is supposed) at Hendon in North London, where there is a dog track to this day.

Greyhounds like to run: they do not need a great deal of training, any more than any other working dog and a great deal less than (say) sheepdogs. The big difference between sheepdogs and greyhounds is the length of working life – a typical greyhound will retire from racing aged 3 to 4 years, and have perhaps 15 years of retirement to contend with. Contrary to most people's beliefs, greyhounds are actually fairly lazy as pets – a couple of twenty-minute walks a day is enough for most of them, and they are usually affectionate and docile.

From the viewpoint of the greyhound owners and trainers, of course, there is a limit to how many dogs one can keep. Some will go to stud, but a brief calculation shows that a greyhound with a two to three-year career and a 15 to 20-year lifespan means that for every greyhound currently racing there are five to seven more sitting by the fire with their paws up. For greyhound trainers, this is clearly not viable: although there are some unscrupulous owners who will abandon the dogs or put them down once their racing days are over, there are several

charities which will help to find good homes for the dogs. One such is the Retired Greyhound Trust.

The Trust was founded in 1975, since when it has found homes for more than 40 000 greyhounds. There are 70 branches of the Trust throughout the UK, so that a retiring greyhound is never very far from salvation. The Trust never destroys a healthy greyhound, so finding homes for the 10 000 greyhounds a year which retire from racing is likely to prove a headache. Of course, not all greyhounds are homed: some end up living in suitable kennels.

The work of the Trust is clearly worthy, but it does suffer from a problem afflicting many small charities: fundraising. Dogs are expensive to keep, especially pedigree dogs like greyhounds, and small charities simply cannot afford the fundraising effort that the majors can command. Additionally, the Trust relies on volunteer help – walking thousands of greyhounds every day is a major undertaking in itself.

Like any other organisation, the Retired Greyhound Trust needs cash and help – but how to get it?

Courtesy of the Retired Greyhound Trust

Non-Profit Marketing

Not all marketing activities take place in a profit context. As we saw in Chapter 1, the definition of marketing as being entirely profit-led is misleading, since many activities which we would normally define as marketing take place within a non-profit context. Charitable organisations spend considerable time and effort in finding better ways of persuading people to donate, or to change their behaviour in ways which fulfil the aims of the organisation.

Non-profit marketing falls into two main categories: charitable donations and cause-related marketing. Charities may simply be seeking donations to fund their work, or may be seeking to change public attitudes concerning an issue. For example, Oxfam frequently runs TV advertising asking for donations so that they can build wells or provide food aid, both of which are expensive things to do. On the other hand, the National Society for the Prevention of Cruelty to Children runs campaigns encouraging people to report cases of child abuse, and the Samaritans run advertising encouraging depressed or suicidal people to call the Samaritans for help. The NSPCC campaign raised over £100 million in the biggest-ever campaign by a charity, breaking new

ground in its sector (Pegram, Booth and McBurney 2003). Non-profit organisations are often more brand-oriented than are commercial, profit-making organisations (Napoli 2006).

In non-profit marketing, the question for many marketers is, what is the exchange? What do the contributors to charities gain from their donation? In the case of Government advertising, what do people gain from responding? In most cases, the donors obtain a sense of having done the right thing by giving to charities. The warm glow of generosity that results from a donation recompenses the donor. In the case of business contributions, socially-responsible behaviour on the part of corporations actually boosts sales: also, charities supported by a corporation with a previous poor record of social responsibility often receive higher donations from the public at large (Lichtenstein, Drumright and Braig 2004).

In one study of high-earning young professionals in the City of London, researchers found that these people tended to support charities with well-established reputations, and also liked to be rewarded with 'social' events such as invitations to gala benefit dinners. 'Planned giving' where the donors receive tax breaks were not highly regarded by this group, who evidently enjoy the high profile aspects of being seen to support the charity (Kottasz 2004).

Charities are not always good at marketing, however. Relatively few charities have people on the streets with collecting tins any more, since the amount of money raised is usually so small it would pay better for the person wielding the tin to get a job for the same number of hours and pay their wages to the charity. Charities tend to ask people to commit to regular sums by direct debit, to respond to TV advertising and make a credit card donation over the telephone, or to make donations via websites. Recent research shows that charitable websites are often not very effective (Wenham, Stephens and Hardy 2003) because they ignore the customer's needs and concentrate on the needs of the organisation. Wenham *et al*'s research was conducted with environmental organisations, whose websites were mainly promoting their causes: the researchers found that, although the websites scored well on information provision and even on design, they evidently had not made any attempt to identify customers' needs.

In recent years, not-for-profit marketers have been prepared to take bigger risks with advertising, making it more hard-hitting than in previous years: their remit does not fit the same paradigms as profit-based organisations, so they can afford to take greater risks (West and Sargeant 2004).

The exchange is not always made in financial terms. Charities frequently use volunteers, whose needs must also be met. Volunteers give up their time in order to help the

Figure 3.1

Contributors to charities

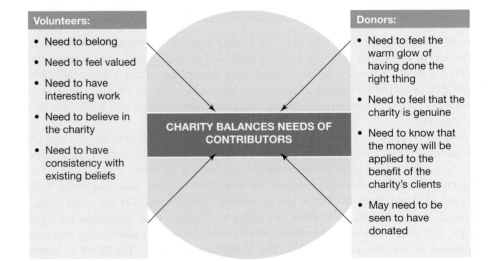

charity, and will need to feel compensated in some way. Sometimes the compensation comes in the form of social contact, because many volunteers are either retired or unemployed and welcome the opportunity to return to a work environment where they can enjoy the company of other people, while at the same time remaining in control of the hours they work and the degree of commitment they give. Women tend to volunteer much more often than do men (Rohrs 1986), although this trend may be reducing as more women have careers outside the home. Although some researchers have found that volunteers are motivated by the desire to help others, such self-reports may not be reliable: other authors suggest that all volunteers are actually motivated by self-interest. In fact, the truth is likely to lie somewhere in between – as might be expected, different volunteers act for different reasons (Wymer 2003).

Talking Point

If people only volunteer to help a charity because there is something in it for themselves, is this really volunteering at all? Shouldn't we be helping out simply because it's the right thing to do – not expecting a ticket of admission to the Kingdom of Heaven for our efforts?

Or perhaps we should give people credit for being the kind of person who derives pleasure from helping others – in contrast to some people who apparently derive pleasure from harming others!

This means that volunteers can be grouped according to the type of motivation that will attract them, and treated accordingly (Kotler 1982). Since many charities assume that their volunteers come forward because they support the aims of the charity, their recruitment campaigns tend to operate in the same way as their fundraising campaigns, which may well not be the correct focus (Kotler 1982). Presumably it would be more realistic to consider how volunteers differ from each other, and try to meet the needs of a group of volunteers who have similar needs (Yavas and Reicken 1985). In a survey of volunteers for a literacy programme, volunteers obtained one or more of the following benefits from volunteering (Wymer 2003):

- Personal satisfaction from making a difference to someone's life.
- Older retired people, especially teachers and librarians, derived a sense of feeling useful and needed.
- Social benefits from interacting with the students and with each other.
- A few volunteers reported that volunteering was consistent with their Christian or other religious beliefs.

In terms of demography, this study found that volunteers tended to come from wealthier households with small families. Gender, age and income were all significant, but personality traits such as self-esteem and empathy do not appear to affect whether someone volunteers or not. Clearly, there is scope for much more research on this topic.

The other aspect of non-profit marketing is that of changing people's attitudes and behaviour. There is a considerable interest in the marketing of political parties, and a view is emerging that political parties have concentrated too much on 'spin' (the manipulation of the news media to create a favourable impression) and not enough on marketing (meeting the needs of their constituents). In particular, information needs of voters are not being met (Mortimore 2003).

As far as changing public opinion on issues of concern goes, various options are available. For example, campaigns encouraging 'safe sex' as a way of combating AIDS have been attempted using three general approaches, as follows:

Marketing in Practice
Canadian Identity

Canada is now the largest country in the world, stretching over 3000 miles from the Atlantic coast to the Pacific, and from the Arctic Circle to the United States. It contains a wide diversity of terrain, people and cultures – everything from the sophisticated French city of Montreal to the Inuit igloos of the North-West. In the West, Vancouver has become a new Hong Kong, with thousands of immigrants (many extremely wealthy) coming in from the former British colony. In the East, Toronto is a busy, modern city with a European feel.

Developing a sense of unity among all this diversity is a major task for the Canadian government. For almost 100 years, campaigns have been run to develop a sense of 'Canadian-ness' among the population, and to foster a view of Canada that goes beyond its former status as part of the British Empire, or its occasional status as a kind of poor relation of the United States. This has led to the creation of certain myths (beliefs unfounded in experience) about what it is to be Canadian (Rose 2003).

Starting from early campaigns to orientate new immigrants in the early 20th century, the Canadian government has run campaigns to answer the complaints of minority groups (notably the French-speaking Quebecois community, who at one time were vocal in seeking independence for Quebec) and the Inuit, and more recently the Olympic Games campaign in 1998. There is therefore a long history of Government advertising in Canada, and even (recently) Government sponsorship of events.

These advertisements have not always been uniformly successful. In 1989 the Canadian Government ran a series of advertisements promoting a change in the sales tax system. This change was extremely unpopular with voters, but the Government saw a need to reform the system in order to ensure that Canadian goods remained competitive. The Government used the Maple Leaf symbol to appeal to Canadians' patriotism, and this was widely seen to be manipulative: one respondent in a research programme described it as a 'snow job', meaning that it was a way of fooling the public.

Eventually, consumer research showed that, although Canadian opinion had moved somewhat towards the view that the tax reform was necessary, a much higher proportion of the public had moved towards the view that the Government should pay more attention to wasteful spending in its own departments. In some respects, therefore, the Canadian Government's campaign had backfired. Of course, taxation is always a difficult thing to 'sell' to the taxpayer – campaigns designed to encourage Canadians to see themselves as a distinct nation, separate from either the UK or the United States, have been a resounding success.

1 *The rational approach.* The advertisement explains what causes AIDS, what the risks are, and what steps might be taken to minimise risk.

2 *Emotional strategy based on a negative message.* Here the advertisements use frightening or shocking imagery to make the audience afraid of the possibility of catching AIDS.

3 *Emotional strategy based on a positive message.* These advertisements used imagery showing how good behaviour is rewarded.

Research shows that the rational strategy created more concern about AIDS, but the emotional strategy based on negative outcomes had the greatest impact on the behaviour intentions of the audience (Marchand and Filiatrault 2002). An experiment in changing adolescents' views about smoking showed that 'cosmetic' appeals (statements that smoking makes you smell bad, etc.) had more effect on adolescent males than long-term health fears: the reverse was the case in adolescent females (Smith and Stutts 2003). One of the problems of dealing with adolescents is that they often think they know all the answers, which makes them less likely to accept the marketing communications they are faced with – sadly, even those who think they are streetwise are often lacking in accurate knowledge, even when they are exposed to social problems such as AIDS and drug abuse within their local area (Parker, Fischoff and de Bruine 2006).

Cause-related marketing also manifests itself in the use of some credit cards. Banks issue the cards as normal cards, but make a contribution to a specific charity whenever the card is used. For the cardholder, this is a painless way of contributing to a charity: for the bank, it offers an added value to the cardholder at very little cost to the bank – not to mention that the cardholders are, by definition, socially-responsible people who are unlikely to default on the credit given. However, it transpires that cardholders are most strongly swayed by the cognitive benefits of the card, and secondly by the feelings they have towards the organisation which benefits from the card. The bank itself ranks third in the equation (Fock, Woo and Hui 2005).

Some people adopt ethical positions regarding advertising itself, and can find themselves in a difficult dilemma when faced with advertising aimed at promoting a specific issue. Beliefs about the ethicality of issue advertising depend on their beliefs about the economic effects of advertising and on the degree to which they already support the issue being advertised (Sego 2002).

Sponsoring a charitable aim, as Playboy sponsors the Design Industries Foundation for AIDS (DIFFA), enhances a firm's ethical position.

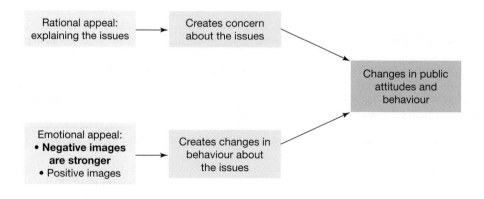

Figure 3.2

Creating changes through cause-related advertising

Internal Marketing

Internal marketing is the group of activities which occur within firms, aimed at moulding the corporate culture. The organisation's internal environment is a microcosm of the external environment. Organisations are composed of people, and as such will develop a corporate culture with its own language, customs, hierarchy and traditions. Sub-groups and individuals within the organisation will have their own agendas and aspirations, alliances will form within groups and pressure groups will form. The organisation will have its own rules and regulations, some of which will be enshrined in the company's official rules, others will be the unwritten rules by which organisation members live and work.

Office parties are good for staff morale.

From the viewpoint of marketing, the members of the organisation are participating in an exchange process. At the very least, individuals are exchanging their time for the organisation's money, but in fact the commitment goes much further than this. In addition, employees contribute a varying amount of commitment to the firm and their colleagues: this is called emotional labour. In other words, people think about their work, talk about it at home, sometimes work extra hours without pay and otherwise go beyond the strict letter of the contract. Such behaviour may or may not be rewarded financially, but in general people do it because they feel a degree of responsibility towards their colleagues and also feel the need to do a good job. Praise or approval from management is part of the reward that staff can reasonably expect from an employer in exchange for emotional labour.

Using the categories outlined in Maslow's famous Hierarchy of Needs (see Chapter 1), Table 3.1 shows examples of work-related need fulfilment.

Since marketing focuses on meeting needs in exchange for value, it seems reasonable to suppose that any request for extra effort from staff should be accompanied by some statement showing how such efforts will result in staff's personal needs being met more closely. Sales managers tend to be adept at this (perhaps because of being marketing-orientated) and can often obtain remarkable effort from the salespeople simply by being attuned to the individual needs of the people they manage.

Table 3.1 Work-related need fulfilment

Need	Example
Physiological needs	Fair salary, comfortable working environment, suitable working facilities and equipment.
Safety needs	Secure employment prospects, safe working environment, medical insurance, pension plan.
Love needs	Respect of management, deserved praise, group membership and feelings of belonging.
Esteem needs	Achievement and recognition of achievement, opportunity to acquire a good reputation, feeling of working for a well-respected organisation.
Aesthetic needs	Pleasant working environment, well-designed working spaces, opportunities to participate in creative activities.
Self-actualisation needs	Opportunity to go on training courses, opportunities for promotion, opportunities to participate in the running of the organisation through participative decision-making.

Marketing in Practice
Southwest Airlines

Southwest Airlines has an unusual approach to its customers. For one thing, the company encourages staff to have fun while working – a playful approach to the job is encouraged, and staff will joke with passengers and even play practical jokes on occasion. Also, Southwest takes the attitude that staff morale is essential to good customer relations – unlike most organisations, the airline takes pride in saying that staff morale comes ahead of customer service. As a result, the company claims that customer service is actually improved, because staff are better-motivated and happier, so that they present a more positive face to the customers.

Embedded within the corporate culture is the notion that business effectiveness depends upon the ability to build strong and caring relationships between staff members. Regardless of position or title, employees are expected to be available to one another, and the firm operates a culture committee to ensure that this happens. One culture committee member shared some interesting comments he had from a senior manager:

While I was out in the field visiting one of our stations, one of the managers mentioned to me that he wanted to put up a suggestion box. And I responded to him by saying 'Sure, why don't you put up a suggestion box right here on the wall and admit you are a failure as a manager?' Our theory at Southwest is, if you have to put up a box so people can write down their ideas and toss them in, then it means you are not doing what you are supposed to do. You are supposed to be setting your people up to be winners. To do that you should be listening to them and available to them in person, not via a suggestion box. And, for the most part, I think that most people employed here know that they can call any one of our vice-presidents on the telephone and get heard, almost immediately. We need to spend at least a third of our time out of the office, walking around. When I do go out in the field, I am much more likely to find that some of the decisions I've made are stupid decisions, and I've seen how my decisions have terribly affected and inconvenienced some of our people. And they definitely pay you with some kind of currency, and if you are incapable of changing things or fixing things or simply doing a self-audit, if you consistently try to sell your employees something they don't want, then what your employees are going to do is fire you! And the problem is, some managers have been fired and don't even know it! But their people won't do business with them any more. They go around them, they're not as committed, they don't have as much energy. When that happens our culture is in trouble.

This approach to communications within the firm sounds as if it should be a recipe for disaster. The managers are apparently going to be spending a great deal of their time listening to complaints from employees, and even more time in trying to elicit comment from the staff. In practice, this does not happen – staff feel empowered, and (for the most part) respect the managers' time and do not waste it. Equally, managers try not to waste employees' time, and go to some trouble to ensure that staff are given sufficient leeway to be able to operate effectively.

From an employee's viewpoint, the firm needs to supply answers to the following questions (D'Apris 1987):

1 What's my job?
2 How am I doing?
3 Does anybody give a damn?

Once the organisation has answered these basic questions, the employee will want answers to others:

1 How are we doing?
2 How do we fit into the whole?
3 How can I help?

Talking Point

The final question is of course the one that the management of the firm is most ready to answer. The task of answering these questions is part of the firm's internal marketing activities.

As employees, we have a responsibility not only to our employer but also to our colleagues. After all, we are all in the same boat – if one of us works poorly, it creates problems for the others.

So why are people paid different amounts of money? If we all depend on each other, shouldn't we all be paid the same? The managing director could hardly run the firm in splendid isolation – he or she needs the ground-floor workers! Yet the MD collects many times the salary of the lowliest clerk.

Or perhaps it's just the laws of supply and demand? Are clerks easier to find than top business brains? Or is there some other mechanism operating here?

public relations The practice of creating goodwill towards an organisation.

Because employee need goes beyond the monthly pay cheque, marketing has a role in managing the exchange. The marketing department within a firm is unlikely to be involved in the process, but nonetheless what happens is marketing. Since employees go home at the end of the day and discuss their employer with family and friends, it would appear to be sensible to ensure that they give a good account of the company. The members of the public that the employees encounter outside work are likely to believe employees rather than the propaganda of the marketing department, so such encounters are obviously of great importance. Word-of-mouth from employees is much more powerful than official communications from the company.

Public relations is the area of marketing concerned with developing a favourable image of the company. As far as internal markets are concerned, PR is mainly concerned with people whose work brings them into direct contact with people outside the company. These front-line staff include:

- Receptionists.
- Telephonists.
- Truck drivers.
- Warehouse staff.
- Serving staff in the company canteen.

This is apart from the marketing staff, such as salespeople, who are employed to contact customers. In a sense, everyone in the organisation has some input into the development of a favourable image for the firm.

Figure 3.3

Levels of contact with customers

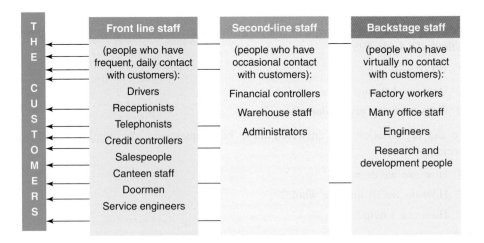

A further function of internal marketing is to overcome resistance to the plans of the marketing department. The days are gone when employers could simply tell staff what to do and expect to be obeyed to the letter: people need to know why they are being expected to carry out certain tasks, and in any case are more likely to contribute emotional labour if they are in favour of what is being proposed. Resistance to marketing plans may come from a number of directions, including people who are senior to the marketers proposing the plans: some examples are shown below.

- Production engineers may resist having to retool to produce new products. Customisation and product differentiation often disrupts production schedules.
- Finance directors sometimes feel that pricing according to what the market will bear is an unreliable method. Also, they tend to see spending on advertising as a cost rather than an investment.
- Lawyers are sometimes wary of apologising to customers when things go wrong, since this can be construed as an admission of liability.
- Boards of directors often cut the marketing budget when sales are poor, on the grounds that everyone's budget is being cut. This may be counterproductive: reducing the firm's voice in the market is likely to lead to a further reduction in sales.
- Salespeople can be resistant if they feel that the new plan will disrupt their chances of earning commission.

Kanter (1988) and Piercy (2001) identified 10 forms of resistance:

1 Criticism of the details of the plan.
2 Slow action in implementing the plan.
3 Slow response to requests.
4 Becoming unavailable.
5 Suggestions that resources would be better directed elsewhere.
6 Suggestions that proposals are too ambitious.
7 Setting up petty obstructions and annoyances to wear the proposer down.
8 Attempts to delay the decision, hoping the proposer will lose interest.
9 Attacks on the credibility of the proposer with rumour and innuendo.
10 Deflation of any excitement surrounding the plan by pointing out the risks.

From the viewpoint of almost everyone in the firm, producing a single product and generally operating on a 'one size fits all' basis is very much easier than trying to anticipate customers' needs, so resistance to change is extremely likely to happen. However, any marketing strategy will involve change, since the marketing approach must change to suit shifts in customer needs and expectations. **Internal marketing** is important in driving change within the organisation (Piercy and Morgan 1991).

internal marketing The practice of creating goodwill among employees.

The elements of the marketing mix still apply in internal markets. The product is the marketing plan and the actions necessary to make the plan successful. Price is what the internal customers will have to give up for the plan to be effective, and this will vary according to the internal customer – some will lose out badly because they have to make substantial adjustments, while others will have less difficulty or may even gain as a result of implementing the plan.

Communication (promotion) will obviously be a key area, not least because the internal customers may have a poor understanding of what marketing actually is. It may be necessary to explain the plan in terms which make sense to the audience, for example using phrases such as 'improving complaint response times'. Communication may come about through meetings, newsletters, email or any of a large number of ways, but it should (as far as possible) be a two-way process so that concerns can be addressed before

Figure 3.4

Marketing internal changes

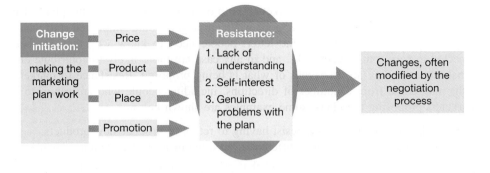

the plan is actually implemented. Sometimes companies use third parties (consultants) to deliver the message. This has the advantage of appearing impartial – the consultants have no interest in office politics, and are therefore seen to be doing their best for the organisation as a whole rather than (possibly) being seen as self-interested.

Distribution (or place) is about where the exchange takes place. In internal marketing, this could be a meeting room at the firm's offices, it could be a virtual meeting place such as a chatroom, or it could be an away-day (a meeting held at a neutral venue such as a hotel). Away-days are commonly used when a major change in policy is due to happen, because it allows staff to meet and discuss issues at a location which does not have the 'political' overtones of meetings at the office. It also signals the company's commitment to the plan, and allows people to interact socially at lunch and coffee breaks, helping to break down barriers between people at different levels in the organisation.

The internal market can be segmented, just like any other market. The obvious way of doing this is to divide the internal 'customers' into those who support the plan, those who might be persuaded to support it or who are neutral, and those who are likely to oppose the plan (often because they will be losers as a result of it) (Jobber 2004). Each of these groups needs to be approached in a different way, and has different sets of needs and concerns. These approaches are outlined in Table 3.2.

The techniques for rallying support for the marketing plan are similar to those used in any other area of marketing. Broadly, they fall into three categories: persuasion, negotiation and politics.

Persuasion is about changing attitudes. Attitude change always begins with finding out what the individual's current attitude is, so it is essential to understand the viewpoint of the opponent of the plan. It may well be that their concerns are justified: for example, the finance department may need to make major readjustments to their systems to incorporate a new credit system for customers. If so, the positive aspects of the change need to be emphasised: marketers can explain how, in the long run, the new system will mean more business from better-off customers who will represent less of a credit risk. Alternatively, some way might be found of minimising the disruption – in any case, the marketers should have spoken to the finance department before suggesting the change in the credit system.

The tactics of persuasion are as follows (Jobber 2004):

- *Articulate a shared vision*. The expected outcome of the plan is a corporate vision which needs to be disseminated to the internal market. In particular, the people who have the greatest influence over events need to be brought on board and to share the vision. If people do not understand the wider picture, they are liable to think that the plan is just another set of incomprehensible and futile changes (Piercy 1990). Almost all change involves a degree of risk and inconvenience for the participants. If they cannot see what the purpose is, they are unlikely to be prepared to take the risk.

Table 3.2   Internal marketing mix programme

Mix element	Supporters	Neutrals	Opposers
Product: the marketing plan, the attitude changes needed, the actions we want people to take.	Supporters will, by definition, be happy with the plan. No adaptation of the product will therefore be necessary.	Marketers should find out what the neutrals would need to have added to the plan in order to become supporters.	If the basis of the opposition is a feature of the plan that can be changed without upsetting the overall strategy, it may be possible to make the adjustments and thus remove the opposition.
Communications.	Marketers need to reinforce the existing positive attitudes and also recruit the help of supporters in persuading neutrals and opposers to come on board.	Communications should emphasise the benefits of the plan, and also indicate the support being obtained from others in the organisation. Negotiation to win commitment is also part of the communications package.	Marketers need to anticipate the arguments that opposers will use and prepare responses. Opposers can sometimes be bypassed, especially if senior management are in favour of the plan. If senior management are not in favour of the plan, of course, nothing will save it.
Distribution: meetings, presentations, away-days, informal conversations.	Supporters can be useful at meetings because they will apply pressure to the other groups. It may not always be possible to separate the groups for meetings, but often supporters will be concentrated in one or two departments.	Neutrals may or may not be involved in the process. Clearly some groups are unaffected by the marketing plan and will therefore not need to come to meetings (though they should be kept informed).	Opponents of the plan are more likely to be swayed at an away-day, particularly if the plan is being presented by a consultant. In any event, meetings between opponents and senior supporters are likely to be effective.

- *Communicate and train.* Many individuals will need to reorientate themselves and change their behaviour. This may mean developing new skills, and will almost certainly mean developing new habits and working practices, so training is essential. Changes require many meetings, presentations and written materials so that people become very clear about what is intended, what will be the outcome and what their own role in the process is.

- *Eliminate misunderstandings about what the plan is.* Sometimes people will have a garbled view of the reality of the plan, and such misconceptions will need to be dispelled. In some cases these misconceptions will have developed as a result of office rumour.

- *Sell the benefits of the plan.* Identifying the needs of the internal market is only the first stage: showing each individual or group what the benefits to them are of adopting the plan is the key to a successful adoption.

- *Gain acceptance by association.* Linking the plan to a widely-accepted organisational doctrine such as customer service or quality management will help its acceptance. The plan can also be associated with a powerful individual such as the managing director.

- *Leave room for local control over details.* This helps to generate a sense of ownership and avoids resentment. People who have the task of implementing the plan can do so with more conviction if they have had at least some say in what is being done.

Figure 3.5

Changing internal attitudes and actions

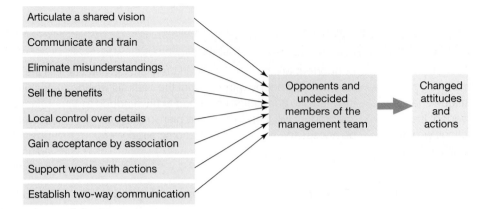

Articulate a shared vision

Communicate and train

Eliminate misunderstandings

Sell the benefits

Local control over details

Gain acceptance by association

Support words with actions

Establish two-way communication

Opponents and undecided members of the management team → Changed attitudes and actions

- *Support words with action.* There is no point in creating a plan and then failing to provide the necessary back-up for it, both in terms of management support for those who have to implement the plan and in terms of resources for its implementation. Unfortunately, managers often contradict their words by carrying out inappropriate actions – saying that the customer comes first is all very well, but if a manager then punishes a staff member for being over-generous in compensating a dissatisfied customer, the good work is undone.

- *Establish two-way communication.* People who are responsible for implementing the plan need to be able to communicate with senior management. Top-down management, in which staff are expected to obey orders and no more, is not the best way to run a company in the 21st century. Also, people lower down the hierarchy are often much nearer to customers and hence to the problem.

Negotiation is concerned with trading one concession for another. Since each party to the negotiation must be prepared to give up something in order to gain something else, it is advisable to decide in advance what concessions one is prepared to give, what concessions one is not prepared to give, and what one wants in return. Dividing these into 'must haves' and 'would likes' is a useful exercise.

Concession analysis is the process of evaluating the concessions one is prepared to give or wishes to gain. Each concession should be considered from the viewpoint of both the giver and the receiver: it may be possible to identify concessions which cost the giver very little, but which mean a lot to the receiver. For example, call centre operators may greatly resent having to man the telephones for longer hours in order to provide better customer service. At first they may demand large overtime payments for doing this, but an astute marketer may be able to offer a flexitime system which would overcome the problem at very little cost. Proposal analysis is the process of trying to predict the proposals (and demands) that the other party is likely to make. This will help to ensure that a response is ready, rather than waiting for the proposal to be put forward and thus being caught by surprise.

A useful negotiating ploy is to start by asking for much more than one is really prepared to accept. This has two advantages: first, the people on the other side might accept the proposal. Second, this approach leaves room for manoeuvre. The essence of negotiation is to exchange concessions, not to give them away.

Politics is about balancing pressures from different groups. Political expertise lies in recognising which groups are powerful and which are not, as well as recognising which groups are right in their view and which are wrong. There are five sources of power, as shown in Table 3.3 (French and Raven 1959).

Table 3.3 Sources of power

Source of power	Explanation
Reward power	This derives from the ability to provide rewards to members of the organisation. In some cases the plan itself provides rewards, but in others the implementer of the plan will need to build in extra rewards. For example, salespeople are sometimes wary of new products because there is a risk attached to selling them to existing customers – suppose the customer does not like the product? In these circumstances a sales manager might offer an extra cash incentive or a prize to the salespeople who sell the most of the new product.
Expert power	This is based on the belief that someone has special expertise. Major changes are more likely to be accepted if the proposer has a track record of success, and (as mentioned earlier) outside consultants are often seen to have expert power, and hence greater credibility.
Referent power	This derives from the charisma of the proposer. If people respect the proposer of the changes, they are more likely to go along with them, which is why charismatic leaders such as Richard Branson have been able to carry out radical business plans.
Legitimate power	Some power derives from the individual's role and position within the organisation. An instruction from a senior manager might be obeyed simply because he or she is the boss.
Coercive power	This is the opposite of reward power. It derives from the ability of the proposer to punish non-compliance. Punishment can range from loss of status, through sidelining for promotion, to actual dismissal. In practice, such bullying tactics are not only counterproductive in most cases, but may also be against the law. At best, use of coercive power may result in people going along with the plan, but it is unlikely to lead to permanent commitment.

Overt power plays are visible, transparent actions which determine the outcomes. Covert power plays are more subtle, and involve agenda setting and restriction of decision-making to specific individuals or departments. By defining what the input is or should be from different individuals, the covert operator can ensure the outcome of the process, but (in the same way as the use of coercive power) this may ensure compliance but does ensure commitment (Wilson 1993).

Getting the politics right can be challenging. Tactics for doing so are as follows:

- *Build coalitions*. Having identified the power sources which control the resources needed for implementation (money, expertise, opinion leadership etc.) the proposer of the plan can build alliances between them and with them. Stakeholders in the plan are those who will be directly affected by it, whether as winners or as losers: winners are obviously going to be in favour of the plan (provided they are aware that they will be winners, of course) but losers will need careful treatment (Kennedy, Benson and MacMillan 1984).

- *Display support*. Once the coalitions are in place, these powerful allies should be asked for some public demonstration of support. Powerful allies should be invited to meetings so that stakeholders can see that the plan has support in high places.

- *Invite the opposition in*. Opponents of the plan have good reasons for their opposition. It may be that they are able to see flaws in the plan which are not apparent to the proposers, or it may be that they will lose out as a result of the plan. Frank discussions with opponents can only lead to good outcomes – the more people who are in favour of the plan, or at least neutral about it, the greater its chances of success.

- *Warn the opposition*. In some cases, it may be possible to let the opposition know what the negative consequences of opposing the plan might be. This is a dangerous

referent power Potential for control derived from a position of authority.

legitimate power Potential for control derived from a legal or contractual position.

coercive power Potential for control derived from the ability to punish the other party.

tactic, because such a warning is likely to be perceived as a threat, which may make the opposition even more determined that the plan will not be implemented.

- *Use of language.* There are tactful ways of phrasing suggestions. To senior people, it is usually wise to talk in terms of 'I suggest this course of action' rather than 'This is the action we must take.' Senior managers are unlikely to be receptive to the idea of being taken for granted. On the other hand, with more junior colleagues, a stated assumption that the plan is going ahead anyway ('This is going to have to come sooner or later, the boss is all in favour') is likely to sway the uncommitted. Other useful ways of expressing political statements include suggesting that the opposition are 'set in their ways' or 'outdated'. The opposition would naturally use phrases such as 'half-baked' or 'ill-considered' when talking about the plan.

- *Decision control.* Office politics is often characterised by agenda setting, i.e. controlling what is and what is not discussed in meetings. Setting up committees and working parties which are composed of known allies, timing meetings for periods when opponents cannot be there because they are away on leave or on business trips, and limiting the scope of decisions which can be made by specific groups (usually by setting carefully-worded terms of reference) are some of the more dubious tactics used.

Political use can also be made of timing. Giving people enough time to adjust to the idea of change, and also allowing enough time for changes to be implemented, will improve the chances of the plan succeeding. As a way of overcoming opposition, the implementers of the plan can leave opponents insufficient time to formulate their alternative plans. This means that the proposer's plan must be acted on as there is no alternative.

As a last resort, the proponents of the plan can wait until opponents have left the company or new allies have joined. This could, of course, take a long time.

Internal Communications Media

House journal

house journal A medium for disseminating information within an organisation.

House journals are printed information books or sheets which are made available to employees. Journals may be of any of the following types (taking a broad definition):

- *Magazines*: Containing feature articles and illustrations, these magazines are relatively expensive to produce but have a professional, credible feel about them.

- *Newspapers*: These can be produced to resemble a tabloid newspaper, which makes them more accessible to some groups of employees. Content consists of news articles about the firm, with some feature articles.

- *Newsletter*: Common in small firms, a newsletter would probably be A4 or foolscap size, and will contain brief items, usually without illustration. Newsletters are cheap and easy to produce, especially in small numbers.

wall newspaper A poster giving information to employees.

- **Wall newspaper**: These look like posters and are fixed to walls. They are useful for brief communications about events or changes in company policies.

When planning a house journal, marketers need to consider the issues shown in Figure 3.6.

- *Readership.* Different groups of staff may have different needs, so it may be necessary to produce different journals for each. Research workers are likely to have different needs from truck drivers, for instance.

- *Quantity.* The greater the number of copies, the lower the production cost per copy. If the number of employees is large, a better-quality journal can be produced. If the

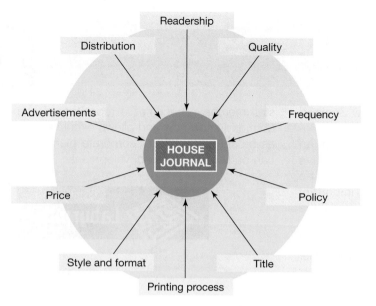

Figure 3.6

Issues in designing a house journal

numbers are small, the firm may need to produce newsletters or wall newspapers instead.

- *Frequency*. Frequent publication means that the journal is more likely to become part of the daily routine of staff. Some large firms even publish such journals daily.

- *Policy*. The journal should be more than simply a propaganda device for senior management: it should fit in with an overall PR programme and should have a clear editorial policy to ensure the quality of content.

- *Title*. The title should be characteristic of the organisation. Changing the title is difficult once it has become established, just as with any other brand name.

- *Printing process*. To an extent the printing process will affect the content, since some illustrations cannot be reproduced by simple, cheap printing processes. Cost will also affect the choice of process, as will the desire for a good-quality, credible journal.

- *Style and format*. Credibility is linked to the degree to which the journal resembles a commercial magazine. Style and format are part of the communication in the same way that packaging is part of a product.

- *Price*. Obviously the vast majority of house journals are free to staff, but it is feasible to make a charge if the journal is sufficiently interesting. There is no reason why a cover price should not be put on the journal in any case, even if it is free: this conveys to the staff that the journal is valuable, and thus is more likely to be read.

- *Advertisements*. Carrying advertising may be a useful way to reduce costs. If the circulation is sufficiently large, outside organisations might be prepared to place advertising – this is particularly true if the firm is large and in a single location, since local shops, restaurants and entertainment venues might well wish to promote their products. Employees may well want to advertise items for sale or forthcoming social events, and this also increases the readability of the journal.

- *Distribution*. Journals can be delivered by hand, by post to the employee's home address, or at distribution points within the firm (for example mail pigeonholes). The decision rests on the frequency of the journal, the location of employees and the type of journal involved.

E-Marketing in Practice
Labyrinth Solutions Ltd

Labyrinth Solutions Ltd of Auckland, New Zealand is a software company which specialises in producing intranets for companies. Labyrinth say that an intranet helps to ensure that a company's collective knowledge stays with the company and can be shared. Most companies have all their important information locked up in employees' heads – and if the employee leaves, the knowledge goes too.

Labyrinth say that an intranet allows free exchange of ideas, provides a forum for staff to ask for help from other staff members, becomes a repository of corporate wisdom and know-how and allows circulation of such items as brochure designs or corporate plans so that all staff can participate in their development.

House journals are often edited independently of senior management in order to ensure that the focus is on the employees' need for information rather than on the management's need to control or manipulate.

Websites

website A page on the Internet designed for and dedicated to an organisation or individual.

intranet A computer-mediated system for internal communications within an organisation.

Most firms' **websites**, where they exist, are mainly geared towards external marketing. In some cases, firms operate internal websites (**intranets**) aimed at employees. These sites are not accessible by outsiders, and they fulfil the same function as the house journal. The main advantage is that (once the site is set up) the costs are greatly reduced compared with producing a house journal: the disadvantage is that employees are unlikely to access the site except during working hours, and in some cases may not be able to access the site at all because the nature of their work does not involve using a computer.

Intranets are most useful in organisations in which virtually all employees are provided with computers, and in which there is no problem about allowing employees to scan the website during working hours. Website design is a specialist area, but some rules have been developed: sites need to be simple to access and use, graphics should be kept simple to minimise download time and articles should fit onto one screen as far as possible.

Internal briefings and open meetings

Some organisations give staff the opportunity to have access to senior management at open meetings or briefings. These briefings have the advantage of allowing senior management to gain direct access to grass-roots views from the workforce, as well as allowing the workforce the chance to question senior managers about company policies.

The overall effect is to increase openness within the firm and break down barriers. Employees (in general) work better if they understand why things are being done the way they are being done: this also enables them to use their initiative better if the system breaks down for any reason.

Communication with and from senior management is extremely important because of the way people process information. In the absence of solid information, the human brain has the facility to formulate hypotheses which will be used as a model for the universe until accurate information can be gained. In corporate terms, this means that lack of information about forthcoming changes will result in guesswork by staff, a flood of rumours, and even staff actions based on the rumours and hypotheses. At this point managerial attempts to 'scotch the rumours' are likely to be met with further suspicion.

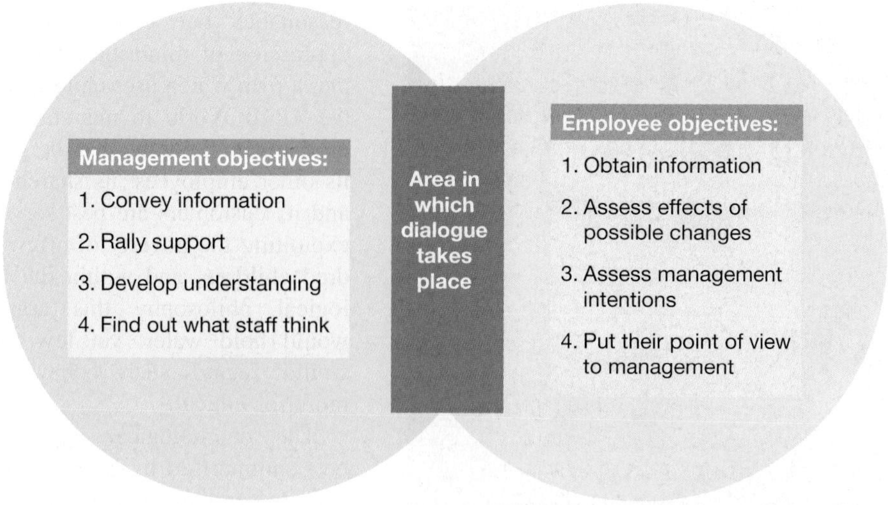

Figure 3.7

Dialogue between management and employees

Meetings can be categorised as follows:

- *Largely ritualistic.* The meeting is being held simply because it always has been, or it is expected that a meeting will be held. Nothing of any value will actually be decided at the meeting, since all the decisions have already been made.
- *Marginally informative.* The meeting is being held in order to pass on information. For example, a factory manager might call a meeting to tell the shopfloor workers that a major contract has been lost, and therefore there will be redundancies.
- *Nominally consultative.* Here the meeting is called to elicit suggestions from staff. In the example above, managers might ask if any of the workers have any ideas for mitigating the worst effect of the loss of the contract – but the final decision will still be made by senior management.
- *Democratically participative.* In this case the meeting is held with a genuine aim of involving staff in the decision-making. Often employees are unrealistic in their expectations of such meetings, however: some decisions are likely to be beyond their expertise. Equally, employers often exclude employees from decisions which they could cope with perfectly well.

Social Responsibility and Ethics

Social responsibility is about ensuring that the company acts within the accepted morals of the society in which it operates, as well as within the moral code of the employees and managers. The view that companies should exercise a responsible approach and consider their relationships with society at large is part of the societal marketing philosophy (see Chapter 1) but is also an important part of maintaining good public relations.

Ethics are the principles that define right and wrong. Ethical thinking divides into the teleological (the belief that acts should be defined as ethical or otherwise according to the outcome of the acts) and the deontological (that acts can be defined as ethical or unethical regardless of outcome). The teleological approach implies that the end can justify the means, in other words that an act which has a good outcome for most people can be justified, even when the act itself is damaging to some people. Teleology is concerned with the greatest good of the greatest number, which apparently seems

ethics A set of rules for good behaviour.

teleology The belief that acts can be judged by their outcomes.

deontology The belief that actions can be judged independently of outcome.

WE DON'T THINK GREED, DISHONESTY OR EXPLOITATION MAKE YOUR SKIN ANY SMOOTHER.

reasonable but can lead to the oppression of minorities. For example, a firm which uses child labour in the Third World to manufacture its products might argue that the good of its other employees, its shareholders and its customers are best served by exploiting the poverty of a few hundred children, and within the teleological philosophy this argument would hold water, yet few people would regard such behaviour as moral or ethical.

The deontological approach is best summarised by Kant's Categorical Imperative, which states that each act should be based on reasons that everyone could act on, and that actions must be based on reasons that the decision-maker would accept for others to use. The problem with deontology is that it involves considerable practical difficulties. For example, it implies that a company whose directors are able to gain a competitive advantage by misleading a competitor should also accept that their financial manager should be able to gain a personal advantage by misleading the company's auditors.

In most cases marketers do not become enmeshed in the philosophical arguments about ethics, but rely instead on the moral rules which are part of the corporate culture. Most business people have separate sets of ethics for their behaviour in work and at home (Fraedrich 1988) and corporations develop their own cultures and schemes of ethics. Where these accord broadly with the personal ethical values of the employees there will be less tension in the workplace – most employees would prefer to work for firms they consider to be ethical.

Many firms adopt codes of ethics. These lay down the rules by which the company operates, and these may be enshrined in a mission statement or corporate guidelines, intended to guide employees and to flag up the company's core values to outsiders. Carrying out good deeds does not guarantee customer acceptance, however: sometimes consumers become suspicious of companies, especially if there is a poor fit between the company's image and the cause it promotes (Becker-Olsen and Cudmore 2004). In some cases, a socially-responsible initiative carried out in one country backfires when the firm tries to act in the same way in another country, as happened when McDonald's tried to establish a Ronald McDonald House in Norway. Although these houses are established to benefit sick children, the action met with resistance from politicians, academics and the general public, to the extent that McDonald's abandoned the exercise (Bronn 2006).

In Figure 3.8, the firm's ethical environment is broken down into five basic components. Terpstra and David (1991) describe the corporate structure as being the lines of command, the formal administrative structures such as the organisation chart, and the assignment of authority, responsibility and information flow. The ways in which the structure is created and adapted are also highly relevant here: for example, Richer Sounds is a firm which finds new employees through word of mouth from existing employees. If a vacancy arises, it will be filled by someone who is a friend or relative of an existing employee. Within the firm, this is seen as a highly commendable and very effective way of ensuring that everyone works well together within a pleasant social environment. However, if this practice were to be adopted in a local authority or a Government office,

Figure 3.8
The ethical environment
Adapted from Terpstra and David 1991

it would be regarded as highly unethical. Government jobs are supposed to be open to all applicants, and giving jobs to relatives would go against the Government's Equal Opportunities rules.

The societal environment includes social relationships as well as the broader responsibilities towards society at large. Within the societal environment the firm would need to consider its near neighbours to ensure that its activities did not impact adversely on them (for example creating noise pollution near an office complex), the ecology, and its employment practices.

Industry considerations would include industry-wide codes of practice, fair competition, fair dealing with supply-chain members such as suppliers and customers and so forth. In some industries there are trade associations which lay down these rules, whereas in others the systems of behaviour develop as industry norms.

Corporate culture has been described as 'the way we do things round here'. The corporate culture often develops over time, but can be directed by a charismatic founder or head of the company. Entrepreneurs such as Richard Branson or Alan Sugar have stamped their personalities on their organisations: in an earlier era, the Quaker Rowntree family set up the firm around Quaker religious principles, which still colour the corporate culture to this day.

The physical environment is largely concerned with ecological issues, but also includes issues such as the exploitation of limited resources. For example, the world diamond trade is controlled by a very few companies, since diamonds are only found in any quantities in South Africa and Russia. These companies maintain the price of diamonds on the market by controlling the supply, in much the same way as the major oil-producing nations fix the price of oil. On the other hand, opals (which virtually all come from Australia) are free-mined: in other words, no restrictions are allowed on their mining and supply. Maintaining the value of diamonds means that there is stability of supply, and the end customers know that they have bought something of lasting value: the price of opals, on the other hand, fluctuates wildly according to whether the miners happen to have had a lucky strike. This means that opal mining is actually a high-risk business, unlike diamond mining, which is stable.

Three basic views of corporate ethical stances have been identified (Goodpaster and Matthews 1992). These are as follows:

1 The invisible hand.
2 The hand of Government.
3 The hand of management.

The invisible hand philosophy is that the sole responsibility of businesses is to make profits for their shareholders, within the law. This philosophy, often expressed by economists such as Milton Freidman, says that the marketplace will punish firms which do not conform or do not behave in acceptable ways, and that the greatest good of the greatest number (teleological approach) will result from the exercise of intelligent self-interest on the part of all. The invisible hand philosophy came to the fore during the 1980s, under the Thatcher Government in the UK and the Reagan administration in the United States.

The hand of Government philosophy, expressed by such people as economist John Galbraith, describes a system in which firms pursue economic objectives within a system of control developed by Government. This approach has become more prominent in the early 21st century, with Governments exercising more controls over corporations. It is the prevailing philosophy in Sweden, where Government not only regulates business activities, but frequently has large shareholdings in major Swedish companies.

Both of the foregoing philosophies have some common ground: each one assumes that morality and ethics have to be imposed on businesses from the outside, either by market forces or by Government intervention. The third approach described by Goodpaster and Matthew is the one by which corporations set their own morality, in a formalised structure which lays down the ethical stance of the company. In other words, executives (and indeed other employees) are not expected to work out their own ethical stances, but are shown the way by management. The hand of management approach therefore states that ethical and moral rules are generated from within the firm.

In practice, managements need to strike a balance between the three approaches. Quite clearly Government regulation plays a part in every business decision, but so does the imperative to make money for the shareholders. For marketers, the customer's interests come high up the list of priorities, so marketers are well aware that the market will punish unethical behaviour.

For marketers, there are specific customer-based issues which will impinge on ethical principles. Some examples are shown in Table 3.4.

Firms often establish ethical statements to guide employees. Figure 3.9 shows the Johnson and Johnson Credo.

Ecological environment

One of the key issues in social responsibility in recent years has been concern for the environment. Consumers consider the origins, content and manufacturing processes of the products they buy much more than they did in previous years, and therefore producers are concerned to be seen as being environmentally friendly. While adherence to the principles of environmentalism might be patchy and at times contradictory, there is little doubt that marketers need to take account of the feelings of consumers on this issue.

There are several sources of pressure for environmentalism. These are as follows:

1 *Customers.* The majority of customers in developed countries use some environmental criteria in making purchase decisions. These range from concern about the energy efficiency of appliances through to requiring assurances about the manufacturing processes involved in producing goods.

2 *Green pressure groups.* Pressure groups are organisations which conduct campaigns to influence policy and public opinion. In the environmentalist area, such groups carry out three main activities: first, they aim to provide information about environmental issues and bring these to the attention of the public and the policy-making bodies. Second, some groups (notably Greenpeace) take direct action against organisations which they perceive as being environmentally damaging. Such action ranges from peaceful protests through to driving steel spikes into trees to damage chainsaws, or hindering the progress of a vessel at sea by sailing across its course. Third, environmentalist groups offer consultation and consultancy about the environmental impact of proposed developments. Using these services can be a useful way for firms to avoid the negative consequences of (perhaps innocently) implementing a new development which impacts the environment negatively.

Table 3.4 Examples of ethical problems for marketers

Problem	Explanation
Products	These should be honestly made and described. Commercial pressures may encourage firms to use cheaper materials or to use inappropriate additives, but customers should be informed of these changes.
Promotion	Advertising is often accused of being misleading, and firms should obviously try to avoid this. Within the UK the advertising industry is policed by the Advertising Standards Authority, which is an example of an industry-based regulatory authority. The ASA is independent of Government, and polices the industry using the criteria 'legal, decent, honest and truthful'. In practice the ASA operates by responding to complaints from the public: it does not usually intervene unless the marketplace responds unfavourably to an advert. While a certain amount of advertising 'puff' is acceptable, it is clearly not acceptable to tell outright lies or even to use misleading phrases.
Pricing	Price fixing and predatory pricing (pricing below the cost of production in order to bankrupt competitors) are the two main areas where pricing practices fall foul of ethical standards. Price fixing, whereby the main firms in the industry agree to maintain prices at an artificially high level, is illegal in most countries when it happens through a formal agreement. However, it often happens through tacit agreements, whereby firms are extremely careful not to provoke a price war by undercutting their competitors. Another example of unethical pricing is situations where the full price is not disclosed – for example when prices are quoted without including VAT or other sales tax. Under EU law, all restaurants must display a menu with VAT-inclusive prices outside the premises so that customers can see what they are committing themselves to before they sit down. Even so, small print sometimes includes service charges which are not made apparent when the food is ordered. Similarly, some opticians fail to mention that the prices displayed are for the frames only – lenses cost extra.
Distribution	Abuse of power in managing distribution channels and failure to pay for goods within the specified credit terms of the supplier are both regarded as unethical, but frequently occur anyway. For example, several retailers operate no-quibble sale-or-return contracts which require suppliers to take back damaged goods even when there is no fault in the manufacture. This has been seen as unethical by some small manufacturers who have little bargaining power and few outlets for their products.

3 *Employees*. Increasingly, employees are acting to improve the environmental credentials of the firms they work for. In some cases (for example research and development staff and production engineers) they are able to act directly. In other cases employees have lobbied management or have even become 'whistleblowers' and taken their concerns to the news media.

4 *Legislation*. Politicians respond to the views of their constituents, and therefore will enact legislation concerning the environment. In some countries environmentalist political parties are powerful parliamentary groups in their own right (notably in the Netherlands and Germany). Pressure for legislation and regulation can also come from the industries themselves. This is because firms who wish to be environmentally friendly recognise that there are costs attached, and they do not want to be placed in an uncompetitive position against firms that ignore environmental issues. Legislation helps to ensure a level playing field.

5 *Media*. Most news media will report issues of environmental concern. Major oil spills and forest fires have always made the headlines, but in recent years stories about species extinction, wetlands draining and development and other somewhat more obscure and less dramatic issues have also been reported widely. This means that firms can easily find themselves the subject of unwanted media attention.

Figure 3.9

Johnson and Johnson Credo
Reprinted with permission from Johnson &
Johnson

Our Credo

We believe that our first responsibility is to the doctors, nurses and patients, to mothers and fathers and to all others who use our products and services. In meeting their needs everything we do must be of high quality. We must constantly strive to reduce our costs in order to maintain reasonable prices. Customers' orders must be serviced promptly and accurately. Our suppliers and distributors must have an opportunity to make a fair profit.

We are responsible to our employees, the men and women who work with us throughout the world. Everyone must be considered as an individual. We must respect their dignity and recognise their merit. They must have a sense of security in their jobs. Compensation must be fair and adequate, and working conditions clean, orderly and safe. We must be mindful of ways to help our employees fulfil their family responsibilities. Employees must feel free to make suggestions and complaints. There must be equal opportunity for employment, development and advancement for those qualified. We must provide competent management and their actions must be just and ethical.

We are responsible for the communities in which we live and work and to the world community as well. We must be good citizens – support good works and charities and bear our fair share of taxes. We must encourage civic improvements and better health and education. We must maintain in good order the property we are privileged to use, protecting the environment and natural resources.

Our final responsibility is to our stockholders. Business must make a sound profit. We must experiment with new ideas. Research must be carried on, innovative programs developed and mistakes paid for. New equipment must be purchased, new facilities provided and new products launched. Reserves must be created to provide for adverse times. When we operate according to these principles, the stockholders should realise a fair return.

green activist One who is proactive in espousing an environmentally friendly lifestyle.

green thinker One who believes in being environmentally friendly.

green customer One whose purchases are influenced by environmental concerns.

6 *Ethical investment*. Some banks and unit trust funds now offer ethical investment packages, allowing their customers to specify that they only want their money to be invested in projects with impeccable environmental and ethical credentials. Environmentally active investors are thus able to influence the funding of 'green' projects, making it marginally easier for firms to raise the necessary finance for environmentally-friendly projects.

Green customers can be segmented according to their degree of involvement in environmentalism. Firstly, '**green activists**' are those who are members of, or supporters of, environmental pressure groups. These people are the most environmentally active, and are the most likely to make purchasing decisions on the basis of environmental issues. The second group are the '**green thinkers**'. These customers seek out environmentally-friendly products and try to live in an environmentally-friendly way. Again, this group will base their purchasing decisions on the environmental credentials of the firm and its products. The third group are the '**green customers**'. These people have changed their behaviour in some way to be more environmentally friendly, for example by recycling, but have not made a radical change in their lifestyles. Some decisions will be based on environmental concerns, but these consumers are as likely to override their environmental concerns when other considerations (such as price) intervene. Extroversion (the degree to which people want to be seen to be doing good), agreeableness (the degree to which people want to get on with other people) and conscientiousness (the degree to which someone wants to 'do the right thing') are the key variables in environmentally friendly consumption (Fraj and Martinez 2006).

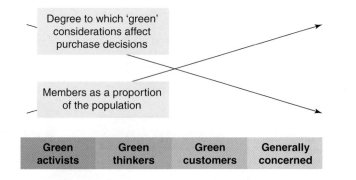

Figure 3.10

Degrees of environmental involvement

The final group is the '**generally concerned**' group. Currently, this group is thought to be the largest segment of the market. These people claim to concerned about the environment, but have made few if any concessions to it in terms of their purchasing behaviour. In general, this group will not act in an environmentally friendly manner unless they are forced to by legislation, or it becomes cheaper to do so. For example, when unleaded petrol was first introduced sales were extremely low, and motor manufacturers were unwilling to adapt cars to run on unleaded when availability throughout the country was so low. Equally, oil companies were unwilling to invest in increased distribution when relatively few cars could run on the new fuel. The UK Government, in common with many other governments worldwide, broke the impasse by giving a substantial tax break on the fuel, making it an average 5p a litre cheaper. This kick-started the move to unleaded, and now virtually all petrol-driven cars in the UK use it.

There is of course a group of people who are alienated by the environmental movement. These people see environmentalism as a passing fad, are pessimistic about the solutions, and are unlikely to be swayed by environmentalist claims on products. In general, this group are less educated, tend to be young families or elderly people, and also tend to lean to the left politically (Ogilvy and Mather 1992).

The response of marketers to environmental issues has occurred on several levels. At the lowest level, marketers have implied that their products have environmental credentials without actually making any changes to the products themselves. The use of words like 'recyclable' on packaging may be truthful in a strict sense, but this places the responsibility on the consumer to send the packaging for recycling, which is unlikely to happen since most consumers fall within the 'generally concerned' group. The problem with operating at this superficial level is that many consumers have become aware of this approach and suspicious of it. In general, people resent being manipulated, and the use of misleading wording is likely to be counterproductive.

At the next level, marketers have made real changes to the product, its packaging or its manufacture in order to accommodate environmentalist principles. These changes can range from using recycled paper to package the product through to a fundamental redesign of the product.

At the highest level the firm will examine all its activities throughout the supply chain, from raw materials to finished product, and will conduct an environmental impact study. Currently, relatively few firms do this, but some (notably Body Shop) have managed to make a virtue of this approach and have become extremely successful by positioning themselves as ethical marketers. This approach will only work if consumers are prepared to support it, since there are likely to be substantial cost implications.

Some issues have been prominent in the environmentalist movement. Figure 3.11 shows some of these.

generally concerned One who believes that the environment is important, but does little to change his or her behaviour accordingly.

Figure 3.11

Issues in environmentalism

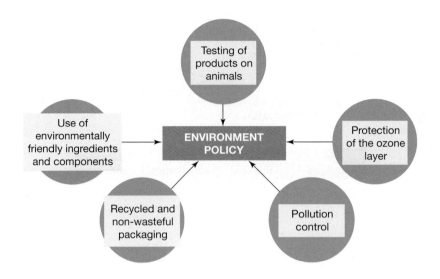

Use of Environmentally Friendly Components and Ingredients

In general, environmentalists encourage manufacturers to use ingredients and components which are environmentally friendly. This means that the sources of the ingredients should be sustainable, that they should be recycled, recyclable or bio-degradable and that the manufacturing processes involved should not in themselves be polluting or otherwise damaging.

Sustainable sourcing means, for example, that wood and paper should come from managed forests, not from virgin forest. Many magazine and newspaper publishers tell their readers that two trees are planted for each tree cut to make newsprint, and furniture manufacturers typically label wooden furniture to explain that the wood comes from sustainable forests.

Cosmetics companies also emphasise the use of naturally occurring products such as aloe vera and vegetable oils rather than animal products.

Talking Point

Saying that wood comes from managed forests is all very well, but is this really environmentally friendly? Should we be planting millions of acres of forest simply to make yet another magazine, when people are starving? Or should we using irreplaceable oil to make unleaded petrol? Or even biodegradable plastics?

Or maybe there is more to life than just feeding ourselves. Maybe it's important for us to have cosmetics, and cheap transportation, and news about our world, and entertainment. But is it environmentally friendly?

In recent years, the European Union has encouraged projects which reduce the EU's dependence on oil for fuel. This is largely because most EU countries do not have their own oil reserves: apart from Britain's North Sea holdings, there are few sources within the EU. One of the results of this has been the development of biofuel, which is diesel fuel produced from oilseed. While this fuel burns more cleanly than mineral oil, it requires a large acreage of land for its growth, and experiments have resulted in large areas of land becoming bright yellow as the oilseeds flower. Producing one ton of diesel fuel requires 0.77 hectares of land (International Energy Agency 1996). This is enough land to feed a family for a year, but one ton of diesel fuel is not enough to run a large lorry for a week.

The EU's target is for biofuel to account for 5 per cent of total fuel consumption by 2010 (Commission of the European Communities 2002). In 2008, the UK Government's chief scientist warned that producing biofuel on a large scale would adversely affect world food supplies, creating more famines.

Recycled, recyclable and non-wasteful packaging

Marketers have come in for much criticism about the quantity and type of packaging used for products. Packaging is intended to keep the contents safe from the external environment and vice versa, but marketers also use packaging as a promotional tool, making products stand out on retailers' shelves. Because modern packaging often uses different types of material (plastics, paper and metal might all be used in a single package) recycling can be problematical. One-way bottles (bottles which are not returned to the bottling company for refilling) were introduced in the late 1960s and have contributed greatly to the quantity of packaging which finds its way into landfill sites rather than being recycled. The reason for using one-way bottles is that it is cheaper and less time-consuming to buy a new bottle than it is to collect, wash and refill existing bottles. Interestingly, in the 1950s almost all bottles were returned because customers paid a substantial deposit on the bottle, refunded by the retailer when the bottle was returned.

Almost all packaging has the potential for recycling, either by using recycled materials in the packaging or by recycling the packaging after use. This would reduce the need for importing raw materials and would reduce the need for landfill sites for dumping rubbish.

Recycling of packaging is likely to become of even greater importance in the future as raw materials become rarer. The cost of using landfill sites is likely to rise as suitable sites are filled, and at the same time recycling technology can be expected to improve. In the meantime, marketers are faced with the problem of continuing to make products interesting and appealing without creating an excessive amount of wasteful packaging. The degree to which people can be persuaded to recycle when they dispose of their possessions depends largely on their personalities – 'packrats' (people who tend to hang on to their possessions) attach more meaning to their possessions than do 'purgers' (people who dispose of goods regularly). Packrats think that purgers are wasteful, and see themselves as thrifty, whereas purgers see packrats as being messy and disorganised (Coulter and Ligas 2003).

Protecting the ozone layer

The ozone layer is a protective layer of ozone gas which encircles the Earth and protects it from excessive radiation from the sun. Chlorofluorocarbons (CFCs) are a group of gases formerly used in aerosols and the manufacture of insulating materials. CFCs have the effect of combining with ozone and thus destroying it. World agreement was reached in Montreal in 1990 to phase out production of CFCs by 2000, but this target was not achieved: additionally, foam insulation which has CFC trapped in it is still in existence throughout the world in products which were made before the ban came into effect. It is likely to be many years before the situation is rectified and CFCs are finally removed from the environment.

The lesson to be learned is that companies need to be prepared for the possibility that a product which appears innocuous may have a hidden danger. Marketers need to be prepared for this possibility, since changes to products and their promotion may become necessary at any time.

Marketing in Practice
Recycling

Governmental attitudes to recycling vary greatly, even within the European Union. Germany, for example, has the Verpackvo, a law which allows consumers to return packaging to retailers, who are in turn required by law to return the packaging to the manufacturers. Manufacturers and suppliers assume responsibility for dealing with this packaging, which in practice means recycling. People are encouraged to return packaging to recycling bins: visitors to Germany are often surprised to see four separate slots on street rubbish bins to accommodate plastics, paper, metal, and miscellaneous rubbish. Recycling bags are supplied by an organisation set up by 400 major companies, and consumers are encouraged to separate out their rubbish for recycling.

Austria and Sweden also have comprehensive recycling systems. In Austria, potentially hazardous refuse such as batteries, old refrigerators and old computers must by law be returned to retailers for recycling or treatment. Householders typically sort their waste into separate components for recycling or disposal. In Sweden industry has established a special company to handle recycling, and in Finland 35 per cent of household waste is recovered. The rate for industry is much higher at over 60%. Finns also recycle bottles: 98 per cent of bottles in Finland are returned for refilling, rather than being smashed for re-melting or (worse) sent to landfills (http://virtual.finland.fi).

In the United States, each citizen produces 730 kilos of household refuse per annum, compared with just over 500 kilos per annum in Europe. America now has an official America Recycles Day, but recycling policy is left to each state to legislate. Some states, notably Oregon, have very strict environmental protection laws, and retailers are required to charge a small deposit on soft drink cans. Because each state has its own laws, however, the deposits vary from one state to another, and therefore it is theoretically possible for someone to pay a 5c deposit in one state, cross the state line, and have 10c or even 15c returned. The USA has an Environmental Protection Agency, which has the power to enforce environmental legislation, but the somewhat chaotic nature of the law in each state means that relatively little of each citizen's 730 kilos of refuse actually is recycled.

Much of the thrust towards recycling comes from the cost of using landfill. In the UK, landfill costs are relatively low at $30–35 a ton, compared with the USA at $50 a ton and Austria at $140 a ton (Kanari, Pineau and Shallari 2003). This may in part account for the UK's poor record on recycling.

Recycling is not a free option. Energy, time and effort are expended in returning materials and rendering them fit for re-use. Public acceptance of recycled (as opposed to all-new) products is still somewhat patchy. Often the materials sent for recycling need to be re-sorted, since people are not always as careful as they might be about separating the refuse correctly. An example is metal bottle-caps, which often find their way into glass-only recycling bins.

Testing of products on animals

Testing products on animals has been seen as a way of minimising the risk to humans. This has been particularly the case with products such as shampoos and cosmetics which come into prolonged contact with the skin or which may even be swallowed. Animal rights activists have protested at what they see as the unnecessary deaths of animals in these experiments, especially the notorious LD50 test in which a group of animals is fed the product until half of them are dead.

In 1998 the European Coalition to End Animal Experiments drew up an International Standard on 'Not tested on animals'. This international standard has been accepted by the world's animal protection pressure groups. For marketers, the standard presented an opportunity to establish the firm's animal-friendly credentials by enabling them to use the claim that their products are not tested on animals. This approach has been remarkably successful for some firms, especially in the absence of legislation: proposed European legislation banning all animal experiments has been postponed indefinitely.

Obviously nobody wants fluffy little bunnies to have shampoo put in their eyes. But isn't this better than having a damaging shampoo getting into a child's eyes? If we aren't going to test on animals, what *are* we going to test on?

Or should we maybe accept that we have enough shampoos and cosmetics, and call a halt to the 'arms race' of new products coming onto the market every day? Would it be realistic to try to prevent new product development in the cosmetics industry? Could our top models and actors manage without new cosmetics?

Maybe the fluffy bunnies are not safe just yet...

Pollution control

Preventing the escape of dangerous by-products into the environment has become a major concern in recent years. In many cases, firms have adopted **end-of-pipe solutions**: in other words, they have not made substantial changes in their production processes, but have instead tried to ensure that pollutants do not escape into the environment. Much of this effort has come about due to Government legislation rather than through a desire to protect the environment.

end-of-pipe solution Cleaning up pollution after it has been created rather than re-engineering the process so that pollution is not produced.

A better approach, in the longer term, is likely to be a change in the process so that the polluting by-products are not produced in the first place. However, in most Western countries manufacturing industry is in decline, and much manufacturing is carried out in Third World countries where pollution is lower on the political agenda than is poverty or job creation. This is, in itself, an ethical question for Western companies to address: on the one hand, moving production (and thus pollution) abroad solves the problem neatly. On the other hand, knowingly damaging the health of people in other countries would appear to be morally reprehensible.

Even service businesses create some pollution. Fast-food outlets create localised problems due to the amount of packaging they generate, but also create problems due to the amount of uneaten food which is discarded, creating a huge increase in the rat population of many cities. Cooking smells might also be considered a pollutant by many, and the smoke from frying is often greasy and unpleasant. Some fast-food chains employ people to collect discarded wrappers, etc. from the immediate radius of the outlet, but this is an end-of-pipe solution. Other firms use biodegradable packaging, but again this introduces nutrients into the environment, resulting in problems from bacteria and rats.

From a marketing viewpoint, having a reputation for creating pollution is not good public relations: pollution damages brand values as well as the environment.

Services Marketing

Much marketing theory has been developed around the marketing of physical products, but in fact the majority of day-to-day marketing is concerned with services. Marketing academics are divided on the issue of whether services marketing is actually a separate set of problems, or whether the principles of marketing remain the same whether dealing with a service or a physical product.

In fact, all physical products contain an element of service, and all services contain an element of physical product. In other words, products are on a continuum, with services at one end and physical products at the other. For example, a life insurance policy is very much a service, with virtually no physical existence apart from the glossy policy document. A bag of builder's sand, on the other hand, has a physical presence but almost no service aspects apart from delivery. Most products fall somewhere between the two, which leads many marketers to say that the differences between the two are negligible.

At the extreme end of the spectrum, service products have the following characteristics:

intangibility The inability to touch a service.

1 **Intangibility.** The product cannot be touched, which means that it is difficult to evaluate in advance of purchase. It also has no second-hand value, so in a sense cannot be owned. For example, a haircut cannot be tried out before purchase, nor can it be sold to a friend, unlike a guitar or a car.

inseparability In services, production and consumption occur at the same time.

2 **Inseparability** of production and consumption. In most cases, the production of a service and its consumption happen at the same time. A concert happens as it is being heard, and although the effects may last for some time afterwards in the memories of the audience, the main benefits are consumed at the time.

variability In services, there will be a difference between one service and the next, even from the same supplier.

3 **Variability.** Because services are produced on an individual basis, they are often variable in nature. In some respects this is a benefit for the customer: being able to ask the chef to cook one's steak rare rather than medium is useful, but on the other hand the chef might be having a bad day and may overcook the vegetables. Things go wrong with services because they are difficult to standardise.

perishability Services cannot be stockpiled.

4 **Perishability.** Services cannot be stockpiled for later use. An airline seat is only available for a specific flight on a specific day: once the aircraft takes off, the seat cannot be sold.

There are thought to be five dimensions of service quality in Internet marketing (Jayawardene 2004):

1 *Access.* The degree to which the website is easily found and navigated.
2 *Website interface.* The 'user-friendliness' of the website.
3 *Trust.* The degree to which the visitor feels that the website is safe to use.
4 *Attention.* The degree to which the website is engaging.
5 *Credibility.* The level of belief the user has in the website's integrity.

Services marketing therefore creates specific problems from the viewpoint of consumer behaviour. Consumers are expected to buy something which they cannot touch or feel, and which cannot be 'test-driven' beforehand. There is more on this in the chapter on consumer behaviour (Chapter 4), and also more on the development and management of service products in the chapters on products (Chapter 12 and 13).

For marketing academics, the issue is whether a service is equivalent to a physical product or not. Services provide benefits to customers, benefits for which they are prepared to pay: if a product is a bundle of benefits, then a service is also a bundle of benefits and we can use a broadly similar approach to marketing it. On the other hand, the issues of consumer trust, segmentation of the market, standardising production and so forth are very different for services and must be addressed in some way.

Branding

brand The focus of marketing activities.

The main vehicle by which marketers focus their activities is the **brand**. For marketing practitioners, the brand is the main area of responsibility – it is the one part of the business that is unquestionably their territory, and acts as the measure of the marketer's success. A brand which has a large market share, or which occupies a prestigious position in the market, demonstrates the marketer's skill in the profession. Some products are unbranded – building materials such as bricks and sand, for example. These products have virtually no input from marketing, whereas all the activities needed to establish a brand are contributed by marketers.

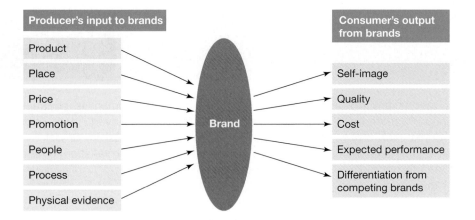

Figure 3.12
Brands as a contact point

Adding value to the product by branding involves a great deal more than merely giving the product a catchy name. Branding is the culmination of a range of activities across the whole marketing mix, leading to a brand image which conveys a whole set of messages to the consumer (and, more importantly, to the consumer's friends and family) about quality, price, expected performance, and status. For example, the Porsche brand name conveys an image of engineering excellence, reliability, sporty styling, high speed and high prices, and of wealth and success on the part of the owner. People do not buy Porsches simply as a means of transport; for that purpose a basic Ford is perfectly adequate.

Because branding involves all the elements of the marketing mix it cannot be regarded simply as a tactical tool designed to differentiate the product on the supermarket shelves. Instead, it must be regarded as the focus for the marketing effort, as a way of directing the thought processes of the management towards producing consumer satisfaction. The brand acts as a common point of contact between the producer and the consumer, as shown in Figure 3.12.

In Figure 3.12 the consumer benefits from the brand in terms of knowing what the quality will be, knowing what the expected performance will be, gaining some self-image values (for example, a prestigious product conveys prestige to the consumer by association – conversely, a low-price product might enhance a consumer's sense of frugality and ability to find good value for money).

In many cases the core product has very little to differentiate it from other products, and the brand is really the only differentiating feature. Despite the apparently artificial nature of differentiation by branding, the benefits to the consumer are very real; experiments show that branded analgesics work better than generic analgesics at relieving pain, even though the chemical formula is identical. This is because of the psychosomatic power of the brand. Someone driving a prestige

Branding enables people to judge the quality of a product without necessarily trying it first.

Marketing in Practice
The Pepsi Challenge

Every year, in towns and seaside resorts around Britain, Pepsi Cola set up a roadshow. Passers-by are asked to try two different cola drinks and say which they prefer. One of the drinks is Pepsi, the other is (of course) arch-rival Coca-Cola. Often to people's surprise, the majority of people prefer the Pepsi.

However, when the same experiment is conducted with the brand names clearly displayed, most people prefer the Coke. Coke outsells Pepsi in almost every market in the world – and the only explanation for this is the power of the brand!

car gains very real benefits in terms of the respect and envy of others, even if the performance of the car is no better than that of its cheaper rival.

Brands begin to exert influence early on in people's lives: an analysis of 422 letters to Santa Claus showed that most children are brand-orientated and are able to use sophisticated request strategies to get what they want (O'Cass and Clarke 2002). Also, children from poorer homes in the UK are acutely aware of the need to wear the right trainers, not only to appear 'cool' but also to avoid being bullied (Elliott and Leonard 2003). This effect was so strong that children actually said they preferred to talk to someone wearing branded trainers.

Brands can be looked at in a number of different ways. Table 3.5 shows eight different strategic functions of brands.

Branding clearly has advantages for the manufacturer and the retailer, since it helps to differentiate the product from the competitor's product. Economies of scale and scope are attributed to branding, and a brand with high sales will generate production economies (Demsetz 1973). A successful brand also creates a **barrier to entry**, so that competitors find it harder to enter the market (Demsetz 1982) Brands also allow firms to compete other than on price (Mercer 1993), which clearly has advantages since the firm does not have to cut its profit margins in order to compete.

Furthermore, brands which are held in high esteem tend to be more consistent in their sales, riding over the ups and downs of the market place (Png and Reitman 1995). Not all brands are priced at a premium; many brands are competitively priced in order to take advantage of consistent sales.

Branding has advantages for the consumer; it is easy to recognise the product, and easy to identify with it. Messages about the formulation and benefits are clearly conveyed, and in most cases the use of a particular brand says something about the consumer (for example, wearing designer clothes) (Bagwell and Bernheim 1996). Because most purchases only involve limited problem-solving behaviour, branding helps to reduce the decision-making time and also the effort of evaluating competing products. Consumers who either don't want to spend time on an extended information search, or who don't have the expertise to do so, can use the brand as an implicit guarantee of quality (Png and Reitman 1995).

Information storage and retrieval in humans is carried out by a process of '**chunking**' or collecting information in substantial quantities and storing it under a single 'file name' (Buschke 1976). In effect, the brand name provides an informational chunk; the individual is able to summon up a huge amount of information from memory using the brand name as the trigger.

From a strategic viewpoint, the brand image provides a focus for the creative energies of the marketing team. Koestler suggests that creativity involves the bringing-together of hitherto unrelated yet familiar objects to generate a creative insight (Koestler 1964). The difficulty for marketers is that product and brand development is often a team process, and as such the team needs to keep a firm picture of what the product is intended to

barrier to entry A factor which prevents a firm from entering a specific market.

chunking The mental process whereby information is stored alongside connected information.

convey – the 'personality' of the product – if they are to maintain consistency in the creative activities. One way of doing this is to use a **metaphor** for the product. For example, the Honda Accord developers used the metaphor 'Rugby player in a dinner suit' to achieve product coherence across the team, even though the entire creative team consisted of hundreds of people, from automotive stylists through to ad designers (Clark and Fujimoto 1990).

Brand planning is important, but time-consuming; often the job is given to brand managers, many of whom are young and inexperienced. Developing the brand is a process of integrating a number of strands of business activity, so a clear idea of the brand image is essential, as is a long-term view. To see branding as merely being about design or advertising or naming is inadequate and short-sighted; successful brands are those which

metaphor A sign which relates to an object.

Table 3.5 Strategic functions of brands

Function	Explanation
Brand as a sign of ownership	Brands were at one time a way of showing who had instigated the marketing activities for the brand. This was an attempt to protect the formulation of the product in cases where intellectual property protection is insufficient, and also to ensure that customers knew whether they were buying a manufacturer's brand or a retailer's brand.
Brand as a differentiating device	A strong brand undoubtedly does differentiate the product from similar products, but having a strong brand name is not enough. The product itself also needs to be different in some way; the brand image is the communicating device that conveys the difference to the consumer.
Brand as a functional device	Branding can be used to communicate functional capability. In other words, the brand conveys an image of its quality and expected performance to the consumer.
Brand as a symbolic device	The symbolism of some brands enables the consumer to say something about themselves. This is particularly apparent in the 'designer' clothes industry – a very ordinary T-shirt acquires added value because the name of the designer is printed on the front. If the consumers believe that the brand's value lies in its communication ability, they will spend considerable time and effort in choosing the brand that conveys the appropriate image.
Brand as a risk reducer	Every purchase involves a degree of risk; the product might not perform as expected, and if it fails to do so then the vendor might not be prepared to make restitution. Buying a strongly branded product offers the consumer a degree of reassurance about both the product and the producer. Astute marketers find out what types of risk are of most concern to the customers or consumers and develop a brand presentation which addresses those risks.
Brand as a shorthand device	Brands are used as a way of 'tagging' information about a product in the consumers' memories. This is particularly relevant when the brand is extended to other product categories, since the consumer's view of the parent brand is transferred to the new brand. For example, Virgin have successfully extended the brand image from records to retailing to airlines to financial services, all offering the same innovative approach and serving similar market segments.
Brand as a legal device	Brands give a certain amount of legal protection to the producer, since pack design and name can be protected where (often) the formulation of the product cannot. Strong branding offers some protection for the firm's intellectual property.
Brand as a strategic device	The assets constituting the brand can be identified and managed so that the brand maintains and builds on the added value which it represents.

act as a lens through which the consumer sees the corporation and the product. Constant evaluation of the image seen through the lens is essential if the brand is to retain its status.

When a new product has been developed, the producer will usually give it a brand name. A brand name is a term, symbol or design which distinguishes one seller's product from its competitors. The strategic considerations for brand naming are as follows;

1 *Marketing objectives*. The brand name should fit the overall marketing objectives of the firm; for example, a firm intending to enter the youth market will need to develop brand names which appeal to a young audience.

2 **Brand audit**. An estimate of the internal and external forces such as critical success factor (also known as the unique selling proposition),

3 *Brand objectives*. As with the marketing objectives, the overall intentions about the brand need to be specified.

4 *Brand strategy alternatives*. The other ways of achieving the brand's objectives, and the other factors involved in its success, have a bearing on the choice of brand name.

brand audit The process of determining whether a specific brand is being marketed effectively.

registration A system for protecting brand names.

Brand names can be protected in most countries by **registration**, but there is some protection for brands in that it is illegal to try to 'pass off ' a product as being a branded one when it isn't. For example, using a very similar brand name to a famous brand, or even using similar package design, could be regarded as passing off. This is a civil offence, not a criminal one, so it is up to the offended brand owner to take legal action.

Ries (1995) suggests that brand names should have the following characteristics;

1 They should shock, i.e. catch the customer's attention.

2 They should be alliterative; this helps them to be memorable.

3 They should connect to the product's positioning in the consumer's perceptual map.

4 They should link to a visual image; again, this helps the memorability.

5 They should communicate something about the product, or be capable of being used to communicate about the product.

6 They should encourage the development of a nickname (for example, 'Bud' for Budweiser Beer).

7 They should be telephone and directory-friendly.

Brands and Semiotics

semiotics The study of meaning.

Semiotics is the study of meaning, and is concerned with the symbolism conveyed by objects and words. Semiotics refers to systems of signs; the most obvious system is words, but other systems exist. For example, a film would use the sign systems of the spoken word, the gestures of the actors, the music of the soundtrack, and the conventions of movie direction and production to generate an overall meaning. The overall meaning is generated as a result of an interaction between the sign system and the observer or reader: the viewer interprets the information in the light of existing knowledge and attitudes, later including it in an overall perceptual map of reality (see Chapter 4 for more on consumer behaviour).

Brands are important symbols, often using more than one sign system to create meaning; the brand name, the logo, the colour and the design of the packaging all contribute.

In terms of semiotics brands have four levels:

1 A *utilitarian* *sign*. This is about the practical aspects of the product, and includes meanings of reliability, effectiveness, fitness for the purpose and so forth.

2 A *commercial sign*. This about the exchange values of the product, perhaps conveying meanings about value for money or cost-effectiveness.

3 A *socio-cultural* *sign*. This is about the social effects of buying (or not buying) the product, with meanings about membership of aspirational groups or about the fitness of the product for filling social roles.

4 A *sign about the mythical values of the product*. Myths are heroic stories about the product, many of which have little basis in fact; for example the Harley Davidson motorcycle brand has a strong mythical value due (in part) to its starring role in the film *Easy Rider*. The same is true of James Bond's Aston Martin and several brands of beer.

utilitarian Appertaining to the practical aspects of ownership.

socio-cultural Appertaining to the social effects of buying or not buying a product.

myths Heroic stories about a product.

Myths provide a conceptual framework through which the contradictions of life can be resolved, and brands can build on this. For example, modern industrial life is, presumably, the antithesis of frontier adventure. Yet the Harley Davidson, a product of twentieth-century industry, was used to represent the (probably mythical) freedom and adventure of the American West. Most powerful brands have at least some mythical connotations – in the UK, the Hovis bread brand has mythical connotations centred around corner bakery shops at the turn of the century; in Malaysia and Singapore Tiger Balm carries mythical connotations about ancient Chinese apothecaries; in Australia Vegemite carries mythical connotations about Australian family life which its main competitor, Promite, has never tapped into.

The association of different values with the brand name can be extremely useful when researching the acceptability of a brand's image. The importance that consumers place on these values can be researched using focus groups, with a subsequent analysis of the key signs contained within the brand, and consumers can be segmented according to their responsiveness to the particular signs contained within the brand and their relevance to the consumer's own internal values.

Research carried out by Gordon and Valentin (1996) into retail buying behaviour showed that different retail outlets convey different meanings to consumers in terms of a continuum from planned, routine shopping through to impulse buying. Each store type met the needs differently and conveyed different meanings in terms of appropriateness of behaviour. Convenience stores conveyed an image of disorder and feelings of guilt and confusion (perhaps associated with having forgotten to buy some items in the course of the regular weekly shop). Supermarkets represented planned shopping and conveyed an image of efficient domestic management and functionality. Petrol stations carried a dual meaning of planned purchase (for petrol) and impulse buying (in the shop). Business travellers seeking a break from work and pleasure travellers seeking to enhance the 'holiday' feeling both indulged in impulsive behaviour motivated by the need for a treat. Finally, off-licences legitimated the purchase of alcohol, allowing shoppers to buy drinks without the uneasy feeling that other shoppers might disapprove. Off-licences also provided an environment in which people felt able to experiment with new purchases.

convenience stores Stores which are located in residential areas and which stock frequently purchased items.

These signs are relevant not only for the retailers themselves in terms of their own branding, but also for branded-goods manufacturers who need to decide which outlets are most appropriate for their brands and where in the store the brand should be located. For example, snack foods and chocolate are successfully sold in petrol stations, where the travellers are often looking for a treat to break up a boring journey.

Summary

This chapter has been about the domains in which marketers work. Not all marketing is about physical products: some marketers deal with services, and even the marketing of ideas. Not all marketing is about money: many marketers deal with campaigns to persuade people to modify their behaviour, or even to volunteer for charitable work. In order to fulfil their roles, marketers are usually most concerned about the brand, and its place in the public consciousness.

The key points from this chapter are as follows:

- All donors to charity gain something from their donation, but different people gain in different ways.

- Change can come through rational appeal, or through emotional appeals: emotional appeals can emphasise the positive aspects of change, or can warn of the negative aspects of not changing.

- Work provides more than monetary benefits.

- All staff have a role in public relations.

- Marketers often face resistance to their plans.

- Concessions should be considered from the side of the giver and the receiver.

- In negotiation, one should consider the needs of one's opponents.

- Information is better than rumours.

- Ethical issues are best resolved at corporate level, but corporate ethics should match closely with the ethical stances of employees.

- The brand is the lens through which the company focuses its marketing efforts.

Chapter review questions

1　What are the main benefits a charitable donor might look for?

2　What is the difference between deontology and teleology?

3　Why might a company seek to establish a mission statement?

4　Why should a boss be prepared to negotiate with employees?

5　When would a rational advertising campaign be used rather than an emotional campaign?

6　Why are internal markets important?

7　How does branding help in focusing marketing effort?

8　What are the advantages of branding from the viewpoint of the consumers?

9　Why should responsibility for environmental issues rest with producers rather than consumers?

10　How does non-profit marketing differ from profit-based marketing?

Preview case revisited
Retired Greyhound Trust

The Retired Greyhound Trust's fundraising problem is chronic: no charity can ever have enough money, and the Trust is no exception. The Trust asks people to help in many ways:

- By adopting a greyhound as a pet. Obviously not everyone can do this – but those who do will be given every possible assistance. The dogs are carefully checked for health issues, and the new owners are given help and advice on how to look after their new pet.

- By spending money in the RGT Catalogue. Purchases can be made online, and include all kinds of greyhound-related products – everything from greyhound Christmas cards to children's books with a greyhound as the hero.

- By contributing a cash donation. For a flat donation of £100, donors can become a Lifetime Friend of the Trust, and will be given a badge, a sticker and a £20 voucher to spend in the Trust's catalogue.

- By becoming a Greyhound Guardian. Guardians contribute a regular minimum of £5 a month, in exchange for which they obtain the same benefits as the Lifetime Friends.

- By sponsoring a greyhound. Some dogs are not adopted, and may never be: perhaps the dog has been injured, or has a behavioural problem, or is just not pretty enough – whatever the reason, long stayers in the Trust's kennels can be sponsored. The sponsor gets a badge and sticker, a history of the sponsored dog and a Valentine's card every year from the dog.

Of course, once the Trust has the name and address of a regular contributor, it is able to contact the individual periodically to ask for more funds. Probably anyone who would like to get a Valentine's card from a dog would not object to this, but some people might.

The whole thrust of the Trust's approach to fundraising is that the charity has, like many others, moved beyond simply rattling a collecting tin in front of people on the street. The Trust management realises that people do not simply give to charities – they like to have some evidence of their own generosity, and like to have the gift recognised. Badges, stickers and vouchers do not cost a great deal, but they do show donors that their contribution is appreciated – an important factor in modern charity fundraising. However altruistic we may believe ourselves to be, there is still an exchange process going on.

www.retiredgreyhounds.co.uk

Charity No. 269668

I ♥ greyhounds
Retired greyhounds make great pets.

The Retired Greyhound Trust has placed over 40,000 greyhounds in loving homes, but we always need more people to adopt our dogs. The greyhounds for whom the RGT care for, deserve a good retirement after racing. They ask very little in return: regular walks and meals and the odd cuddle.

If you can offer an ex-racing greyhound a place in your home, or would like to find more about the work of the Trust, please log on to our website or call us on **0844 826 8424.**

Retired Greyhound Trust, 149A Central Road, Worcester Park, Surrey KT4 8DT
Email: greyhounds@retiredgreyhounds.co.uk
Web: www.retiredgreyhounds.co.uk

retired greyhound trust

Courtesy of the Retired Greyhound Trust

Case study
Morris Minor Owners' Club

Before he designed the iconic Mini (recently relaunched as the Mini Cooper), Sir Alec Issigonis designed another motoring legend – the Morris Minor. Looking rather like an upturned jelly mould, the Morris Minor was produced from 1948 to 1971. The perfect car for the austere 1950s, the Morris Minor was cheap to buy and run, simple to repair and easy to drive.

The car was manufactured in several versions. Early versions had an 800cc engine, which left the car somewhat underpowered (although it would do 40 miles to the gallon). Later, a 948cc engine was fitted, which improved the performance and gave a top speed of almost 70 miles per hour. A final version had a 1.1 litre engine, driving the car to a breathtaking 77 mph. Estate versions and van versions were also produced.

The cars were extremely reliable by the standards of the time – it was commonly said that there was nothing on the car to go wrong, due to its extremely simple design. Over the course of its life, 1.6 million Morris Minors were made, many for export to Commonwealth countries: even up until the 1980s they were the vehicle of choice for taxi drivers in Sri Lanka, and hundreds of thousands of the cars are still running. Which is, of course, where the Morris Minor Owners' Club comes into the picture.

The club was founded in 1976 for the purpose of encouraging the preservation of this classic vehicle. The club helps members in many ways – obvious issues such as sourcing spare parts (particularly rare spares from early models of the car), technical advice on maintaining the car, and obtaining insurance for the cars at a special rate are one thing. Less obviously, the club forms a powerful lobby to campaign on behalf of owners. Threats to classic vehicles are surprisingly common – legislation to force all vehicles over 10 years old off the road, legislation to tax all vehicles whether they are driven on the road or not, and even the threat to remove all leaded petrol from sale affect Morris Minor owners. Although the legislation is intended for the best of environmental reasons, it does affect older, less environmentally friendly cars and is no respecter of classic car status. To this end the club is affiliated to the Federation of Historic Vehicle Clubs, which acts together as a lobby.

The club has its own magazine, *Minor Matters*, which appears bi-monthly. The magazine is funded largely through advertising, and features articles written by Morris Minor enthusiasts as well as useful listings and technical information. The club also organises rallies, trips to the Continent, a members' website, swap meets, local branches which organise local events or just a social scene and so forth. Membership costs around £25 a year, depending on category of membership – most members would probably save the membership fee within a few months simply by using the technical advice service alone.

With 14 500 members worldwide, the Morris Minor Owners' Club represents a substantial force. Car enthusiasts are rarely drawn from the poorer sections of society – many members are well-heeled and influential, although of course this does not apply to all Morris Minor owners. Associating oneself with the Morris Minor brand is largely about nostalgia – like the VW Beetle the car is loveable, and members feel genuinely attached to their cars.

Presumably there will come a time when the last Morris Minor falls apart – after all, the cars were never intended to last forever. Meanwhile, the Morris Minor Owners' Club is doing its best to postpone the evil day.

Questions

1 What effect is the Morris Minor brand having on members?

2 How might companies affiliate themselves with the Morris Minor Owners' Club in order to tap into the potential market?

3 What funding problems might the club have?

4 Why does a club like this need to lobby Government?

5 How might the Morris Minor Owners' Club stand up against the environmentalist lobby?

Hanne Melbye-Hansen /istockphoto

References

Bagwell, L.S. and Bernheim, B.D. (1996): Veblen effects in a theory of conspicuous consumption. *The American Economic Review* **86**, 349–73.

Becker-Olsen, K, and Cudmore, B.A. (2004): When good deeds dilute your equity. *Advances in Consumer Research* **31**(1), 86–7.

Benady, D. (1997): Ofgas must dispel advertising hot air. *Marketing Week*, 4th December, pp. 19–20.

Bronn, P.S. (2006): Building corporate brands through community involvement: is it exportable? The case of the Ronald McDonald House in Norway. *Journal of Marketing Communications* **12**(4), 309–20.

Buschke, H. (1976): Learning is organized by chunking. *Journal of Verbal Learning and Verbal Behaviour* **15**, 313–24.

Clark, K. and Fujimoto, T. (1990): The power of product integrity. *Business Review* Nov/Dec, 107–18.

Commission of the European Communities (2002): *Communication from the Commission to the European Parliament concerning the Common Position of the Council on the Adoption of a Directive of the European Parliament and the Council on the Promotion of Biofuels for Transport.* (Brussels: Commission of the European Communities).

Coulter, R.A., and Ligas, M. (2003): To retain or relinquish: exploring the disposition practices of packrats and purgers. *Advances in Consumer Research* **30**(1), 38.

D'Apris, R. (1987): Quoted in Arnott, M: Effective employee communication in Hart, Norman (ed.): *Effective Corporate Relations* (London: McGraw-Hill).

Demsetz, H. (1973): Industry structure, market rivalry and public policy. *Journal of Law and Economics* **16**(1), April, 1–9.

Demsetz, H. (1982): Barriers to entry. *American Economic Review* **72**, 47–57.

Elliott, R. and Leonard, C. (2003): Peer pressure and poverty: exploring fashion brands and consumption symbolism among children of the 'British poor'. *Journal of Consumer Behaviour* **3**(4), 347–59.

Fock, H. K.Y., Woo, K.-S, and Hui, M.K. (2005): The impact of a prestigious partner on affinity card marketing. *European Journal of Marketing* **39**(1/2), 33–53.

Fraedrich J. (1988): Philosophy type interaction in the ethical decision making process of retailers. PhD dissertation (Texas: A&M University).

Fraj, E. and Martinez, E. (2006): Influence of personality on ecological consumer behaviour. *Journal of Consumer Behaviour* **5**(3), 167–81.

French, J.R. P. and Raven, B. (1959): The bases of social power. In Cartwright, D. (ed.) *Studies in Social Power* (Ann Arbor, MI: University of Michigan Press).

Goodpaster, K.E. and Matthews, J.B. Jr. (1982): Can a corporation have a conscience? *Harvard Business Review* **60**(1), 132–41.

Gordon, W. and Valentin, V. (1996): Buying the brand at point of choice. *Journal of Brand Management* **4**(1), 35–44.

International Energy Agency 1996: Automotive Fuels Survey 1: raw materials conversion. (Breda: Innash).

Jayawardene, C. (2004): Management of service quality in Internet banking: the development of an instrument. *Journal of Marketing* **20**(1),185–207.

Jobber, D. (2004): *Principles and Practice of Marketing*, 4th edn. (Maidenhead: McGraw Hill).

Kanari, N., Pineau, J-L. and Shallari, S. (2003): End-of life vehicle recycling in the European Union. *Journal of Metals*, August.

Kanter, R.M. (1988): *The Change Masters* (London: Allan and Unwin).

Kennedy, G., Benson, J. and MacMillan, J. (1984): *Managing Negotiations* (London: Business Books).

Koestler, A. (1964): *The Act of Creation* (London: Pan Books).

Kotler, P. (1982): *Marketing for Non-profit Organizations* (Englewood Cliffs, NJ: Prentice Hall).

Kottasz R. (2004): How should charitable organizations motivate young professionals to give philanthropically? *International Journal of Nonprofit and Voluntary Sector Marketing* **9**(1) 9–28.

Lichtenstein, D.R., Drumright, M.E and Braig, B.M. (2004): The effects of corporate social responsibility on customer donations to corporate-supported non-profits. *Journal of Marketing* **68**(4), 16–32.

Marchand, J. and Filiatrault, P. (2002): AIDS prevention advertising: different message strategies from different communication objectives. *International Journal of Nonprofit and Voluntary Sector Marketing* **7**(3), 271–87.

Maslow, A. (1954): *Motivation and Personality* (New York: Harper and Row).

Mercer, D. (1992): *Marketing Management* (Oxford: Blackwell).

Mortimore, R. (2003): Why politics needs marketing. *International Journal of Nonprofit and Voluntary Sector Marketing* **8**(2), 107–21.

Napoli, J. (2006): The impact of non-profit brand orientation on organizational performance. *Journal of Marketing Management* **22**(7/8), 673–94.

O'Cass, A. and Clarke, P. (2002): Dear Santa, do you have my brand? A study of brand requests, awareness and request styles at Christmas time. *Journal of Consumer Behaviour* **2**(1), 37–53.

Ogilvy, D. (1983): *Ogilvy on Advertising* (London: Pan).

Parker, A.M., Fischoff, B. and de Bruine, W. (2006): Who thinks they know more – but actually knows less? Adolescent confidence in their HIV/AIDS and general knowledge. *Advances in Consumer Research* **33**(1), 12–13.

Pegram, G., Booth, N. and McBurney, C. (2003): Full stop: an extraordinary appeal for an extraordinary aspiration – putting leadership theory into practice.? *International Journal of Nonprofit and Voluntary Sector Marketing* **8**(3), 207–12.

Piercy, N. (1990): Making marketing strategies happen in the real world. *Marketing Business*, February 20–1.

Piercy, N. (2001): *Marketing-led strategic change* (Oxford: Butterworth-Heinemann).

Piercy, N. and Morgan, N. (1991): Internal marketing: the missing half of the marketing programme. *Long Range Planning* **24**(2), 89–93.

Png, J.P. and Reitman, D. (1995): Why are some products branded and others not? *Journal of Law and Economics* **38**, 207–24.

Ries, A. (1995): What's in a name? *Sales and Marketing Management*, **Oct.** 36–7.

Rohrs, F.R. (1986): Social background, personality and attitudinal factors influencing the decision to volunteer and level of involvement among adult 4-H leaders. *Journal of Voluntary Action Research* **15**(1), 87–99.

Rose, J. (2003): Government advertising and the creation of national myths. *International Journal of Nonprofit and Voluntary Sector Marketing* **8**(2), 153–55.

Sego, T. (2002): Consumers' ethical judgement of issue advertising. *Advances in Consumer Research* **29**(1), 80–5.

Smith, D.H. and Macaulay, J. (1981): *Participants in Social and Political Activities* (San Francisco: Jossey-Bass).

Smith, K.H., and Stutts, M.A. (2003): Effects of short-term cosmetic vs. long-term health appeals in anti-smoking advertisements on the smoking behaviour of adolescents. *Journal of Consumer Behaviour* **3**(2), 157–77.

Terpstra, V. and David, K. (1991): *The Cultural Environment of International Business* (Cincinnati OH: South-Western Publishing Company).

Valor, C. (2007): The influence of information about labour abuses on consumer choice of clothes: a grounded theory approach. *Journal of Marketing Management* **23**(7/8), 675–95.

Wenham, K., Stephens, D. and Hardy, R. (2003): The marketing effectiveness of UK environmental charity websites compared to best practice. *International Journal of Non-profit and Voluntary Sector Marketing* **8**(3), 213–23.

West, D.C. and Sargeant, A. (2004): Taking risks with advertising: the not-for-profit sector. *Journal of Marketing Management* **20**(9/10), 1027–45.

Wilson, G. (1993): *Making Change Happen* (London: Pitman).

Wymer, W.W. (2003): Differentiating literacy volunteers: a segmentation analysis for target marketing. *International Journal of Non-profit and Voluntary Sector Marketing* **8**(3), 267–85.

Yavas, U. and Reicken, G. (1985): Can volunteers be targeted? *Journal of the Academy of Marketing Science* **3**(2), 218–28.

Further reading

Sargeant, A. (2004): *Marketing Management for Non-profit Organizations* (Oxford: Oxford University Press). This is a well-written and comprehensive text from one of the leading academics in the field. It covers all aspects of non-profit marketing from fundraising through to Governmental advertising and social marketing.

Drake, S.M., Gulman, M.J. and Roberts, S.M. (2005): *Light Their Fire: Using Internal Marketing to Ignite Employee Performance and Wow Your Customers* (Dearborn, MI: Dearborn Trade Publishing). This is an inspirational, very American, practitioner-orientated book. It explains how internal marketing can be used to motivate employees and create customer value. The book is full of examples and cases, including cases where things went badly wrong.

Part two
Markets and People

This section takes the theoretical underpinnings of marketing further. The section aims to show how marketing relates to the people it serves: the consumers, the firm, the employees and other stakeholders. Markets are the aggregate of consumers, suppliers and competitors: this section is concerned with techniques for dealing with all these elements, and especially with the people who make up these groups.

Chapter 4 covers consumer behaviour. Consumers are at the centre of everything marketers do, so the importance of understanding their behaviour cannot be overstated. We are all consumers, of course. This chapter includes the theoretical underpinning derived from behavioural sciences, and connects this to actual real-world purchasing behaviour.

Chapter 5 is concerned with organisational buying. There are differences between the ways people behave when they are buying for themselves or their families, and the ways they behave when buying on behalf of the firms they work for: this chapter shows how these differences manifest themselves in a business-to-business environment.

Choosing which customers to do business with is important when trying to allocate corporate resources. Chapter 6 looks at segmenting (dividing the market into groups of people with similar needs) and targeting (deciding which groups to approach). The chapter also covers positioning, which is about putting the brand into the correct place in the consumer's mind relative to competing brands.

Chapter 7 is concerned with information gathering. Good information about the market is a prerequisite for any decision-making: marketing research is the term for all the methods used for collecting and analysing data in order to generate knowledge.

For many people, marketing is all about communications. Of course, advertising and so forth are the most visible parts of marketing: Chapter 8 outlines the basic communications theories which underpin marketing communications, and also introduces some of the techniques which marketers use.

Chapter 9 looks at foreign markets. International marketing and globalisation have become hot topics in recent years – as has opposition to globalisation. This chapter looks at some of the theory and debate which surround international marketing, and also examines the practical aspects of entering overseas markets.

Chapter 4
Consumer behaviour

Learning objectives After reading this chapter, you should be able to:

1 Describe the decision-making process.

2 Explain the role of emotion in the decision-making process.

3 Explain the role of information processing in decision-making.

4 Describe the trade-offs in information collection and processing.

5 Understand the role of goals in motivating purchasing behaviour.

6 Develop ways of handling complaints.

7 Understand learning processes.

8 Explain the role of social groups in influencing behaviour.

9 Explain how perception operates.

10 Explain the role of self-concept in consumer motivation.

Introduction

Consumer behaviour consists of all the activities people undertake when obtaining, consuming and disposing of products and services (Blackwell, Miniard and Engel 2001). Studying consumer behaviour involves looking at what influences people to behave in particular ways when obtaining products, using them and disposing of them.

Understanding the way people think when they go about their purchasing behaviour is a key factor in successful marketing. The motivations, decision-making processes and post-purchase behaviour of consumers are useful when seeking to persuade people to choose one product rather than another, and to encourage people to recommend products to their friends.

In terms of studying marketing as an academic discipline, consumers are at the heart of any consideration of business policy. Understanding consumer behaviour is central to communications planning, to strategy planning and to segmentation and targeting. Reading this chapter will introduce you to the key issues and ways of thinking that inform everything marketers do.

Most retailers claim to reduce prices, and most of us only half-believe them. There has been a virtual price war raging for some time now throughout the Western world, but there are some stores that really do sell cheap goods. These are the cheap shops – the discount stores that carry a limited range of products, at unbelievably low prices. Service is often poor, quality is often low, but the appeal of a bargain encourages people to buy and buy again.

In Paris, the Tati store sells low-price goods, often imported from the Far East, at its huge department store in Montmartre. Montmartre is traditionally a poor area in the north of central Paris, between Sacre Coeur and Pigalle: nowadays, the area houses poor immigrants, and has a large number of cheap shops, but Tati is without doubt the king of them all. Tati has a branch in Boulogne sur Mer which specialises in wedding dresses and accessories – a somewhat remarkable concept for a cheap shop.

In the Netherlands, HEMA occupies a more upmarket position, with 280 shops and 10 000 employees, HEMA is a success story based on piling it high and selling it cheap. The initials stand for Hollandse Eenheidsprijzen Maatschappij Amsterdam (Standard Price Company of Amsterdam) because it used to operate on the basis of pricing everything at either 25c or 50c. After the Second World War this approach proved untenable, but the company still relies on selling basic housewares, mainly under its own brand name, at dramatically reduced prices. As a way of improving efficiency, HEMA recently installed a wireless-enabled system for reordering stock so that staff would not have to leave the shop floor. Recent bargains include 6 beer glasses for €1.95, an electric kettle for €11 and Jip en Janneke apple juice for €1.25 (Jip en Janneke is HEMA's children's brand).

In the grocery field, German companies dominate. Aldi and Lidl both operate stores throughout Europe: each category of product is stocked in few brands, so that there is little choice. Equally, there is very little overhead – the stores only have one or two brand of beans, for example, rather than carrying a broad range of brands for customers to choose from. This simplifies purchasing and reduces costs, since less shelf space is needed and consequently a smaller store is feasible. Fairly large discounts are possible on the few hundred products stocked – in each case, the stores make no guarantee to have a particular item in stock, since they tend to buy only when the price is right.

In Spain, prior to the adoption of the Euro, every village and suburb had its 'Todo a Cien' shop in which everything (or nearly everything) was sold for 100 pesetas. One hundred pesetas is only around 65c in Euros, which made everything very cheap indeed. Todo a Cien (usually written as Todo 100) was not a chain, however. Each store was entirely independent, but was served by the same group of importers and buyers. Nowadays, some stores advertise themselves as 'Todo a €1' or simply put '100' over the door: others trade under names such as 'Eugenio el Barato' (Eugene the Cheap).

In the UK there are many cheap shops. In South Wales, the Hypervalue stores became famous, being replaced eventually by Buyology. Nationally, Poundstretcher have stores throughout the UK. Poundstretcher operate a suppliers' open day, where potential suppliers can pitch to the buyers – the company looks for bankrupt stock, clearance sale goods, overruns, end-of-season clearances, cancelled orders and so forth. In fact, Poundstretcher will buy almost anything if the discount is big enough, and suppliers are more than happy to dump a job lot of goods in exchange for quick cash.

But what is the appeal? Someone going into a cheap shop may or may not find what he or she is looking for, the quality is likely to be extremely low (products may not last out the first usage) and in any case supermarket chains often have better-quality goods for less money.

The Decision-making Process

psychology The study of thought processes.

sociology The study of behaviour in groups.

economics The study of supply and demand.

anthropology The study of culture.

The study of consumers draws from other scientific disciplines: **psychology**, **sociology**, **economics** and **anthropology** among them.

Many different models have been developed for illustrating the consumer decision-making process. An early model was that of John Dewey (1910). Dewey's model is as follows:

1 A difficulty is felt.

2 The difficulty is located and defined.

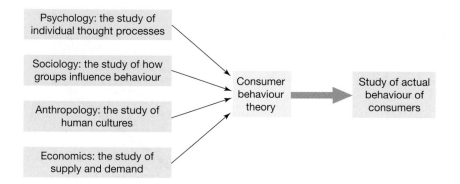

Figure 4.1

Contributions to studying
consumers

3 Possible solutions are suggested.

4 Consequences are considered.

5 A solution is accepted.

This model is, of course, somewhat simplistic. In most cases, people do not go through such an elaborate and considered process. Many purchases are made without apparent conscious thought – people often buy as a result of unexplained impulses, or simply fall in love with a product for no apparent reason. Later, Engel, Kollat and Blackwell developed the EKB model of consumer behaviour, which later became the CDP (Consumer Decision Process) model, and which follows seven stages (Blackwell *et al.* 2001).

These are:

1 *Need recognition.* The individual recognises that something is missing from his or her life.

2 *Search for information.* This information search may be internal (remembering facts about products, or recalling experiences with them) or external (reading about possible products, visiting shops, etc.)

3 *Pre-purchase evaluation of alternatives.* The individual considers which of the possible alternatives might be best for fulfilling the need.

4 *Purchase.* The act of making the final selection and paying for it.

5 *Consumption.* Using the product for the purpose of fulfilling the need.

6 *Post-consumption evaluation.* Considering whether the product actually satisfied the need or not, and whether there were any problems arising from its purchase and consumption.

7 *Divestment.* Disposing of the product, or its packaging, or any residue left from consuming the product.

The similarity between Dewey's model and the CDP model is obvious, and similar criticisms apply, but both models offer a basic outline of how people make consumption decisions. People do not buy unless they feel they have a need (see Chapter 1 for a definition of what constitutes a need). A need is felt when there is a divergence between the person's actual state and their desired state. The degree of difference between the two states is what determines the level of motivation the person feels to do something about the problem, and this will in turn depend on a number of external factors.

For example, a driver who is late for an appointment may feel thirsty, but not thirsty enough to stop at a motorway services and thus make himself even later. The thirst would have to become unbearable or the appointment would have to be unimportant for the driver to deviate from the purpose of the trip.

There are two possible reasons for a divergence between the **desired state** and the **actual state**: either the actual state has changed, or the desired state has changed. In

desired state The situation the individual wishes to be in.

actual state The situation the individual is currently experiencing.

Figure 4.2

The decision-making process

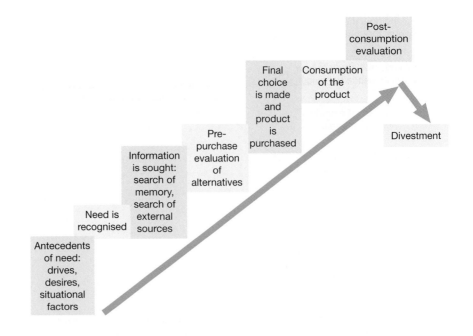

practice it is rare for the actual and desired states to be the same, but most people will tolerate a small discrepancy: if the actual and desired states were the same, the person would be perfectly happy and have everything he or she could want, which is unlikely in an imperfect world.

Causes of the shift in the actual state could be either of the following (Onkvisit and Shaw 1994):

assortment depletion Using up resources or wearing out products.

1 **Assortment depletion**. Consumption, spoilage, wear and tear or loss of a possession from the person's assortment of goods will cause a shift in the actual state.

2 *Income change*. An upward change in the individual's income will allow more purchases to be made: likewise, a downward shift in income will cause a reduction in the amount or quality of goods which can be purchased. The same applies to a windfall such as a lottery win or inheritance, or a sudden unexpected expense such as a lawsuit or accident.

Marketers have little control over the actual state of consumers. Causes of shifts in the desired state, on the other hand, often result from marketing activities. New information will often change a person's expectations because he or she becomes aware that there may be a better solution to his or her consumption problems than that currently being used. Marketers are often able to supply this new information through an advertisement or a news story about the product, or even through encouraging word-of-mouth. Much of what marketing is about is changing consumers' desired states by showing them products which will solve their needs better than the products they are currently using.

In some cases a shift in the actual state also leads to a shift in the desired state. For example, someone who receives a pay rise may develop new aspirations – having been perfectly happy driving a small basic car, the individual suddenly develops the desire to own a luxury car, for example. Previously the luxury car was not even under consideration because it would be totally out of reach, but the possibility of being able to buy it leads to the desire to own it, through a re-evaluation of the individual's desires (see Figure 4.3).

A lottery win would cause a shift in the person's actual state.

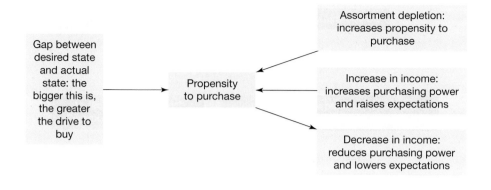

Figure 4.3

Influences on the propensity to purchase

Talking Point

Marketers are often accused of creating needs where no need previously existed. This they hotly deny – needs were there before marketing, after all!

And yet marketers do raise aspirations – nobody knew they needed a BMW until it was invented, nobody needed the electric toothbrush, nobody needed a computer in their living-room, let alone in their washing-machine.

On the other hand, nobody needed houses until they were invented – caves were perfectly adequate. Nor did we need fire, spears or bread. So at what point do we say that we have progressed far enough in making our lives more comfortable and convenient?

The **psychology of complication** states that people seek to complicate their lives: the **psychology of simplification** states that people seek to simplify their lives. In fact, at different times in our lives we may seek a more complex, interesting and stimulating life (psychology of complication), while at other times we find life too difficult and look for ways of simplifying our existences (psychology of simplification). Product purchases play a role in both systems (Hoyer and Ridgway 1984).

psychology of complication The desire to make one's life more complex and therefore more interesting.

psychology of simplification The desire to make one's life simpler and therefore less demanding.

Pre-purchase Activities

Having recognised the need, people undertake a series of pre-purchase activities. The information search may be internal or external: for most routine purchases, people need only remember which brand they usually buy, and even for less-frequent purchases people often already know a lot about the product category and even the brands involved.

In other cases, for example with high-value or infrequent purchases, consumers often need to carry out an **external search**. This means obtaining information from sources such as newspapers, brochures, TV programmes, friends, salespeople, helplines and of course the Internet. This information, combined with what is already known, completes the information search.

Sometimes an individual will set out with a belief that he or she already knows enough to be able to make the purchase, but is then confronted with new information at the point of purchase (see Figure 4.4). For example, the last time an individual might have bought a stereo system could have been 10 years ago: such a person would not necessarily be aware of the advances in technology that have occurred in the last

external search Looking for information in places other than memory.

Figure 4.4

Information search

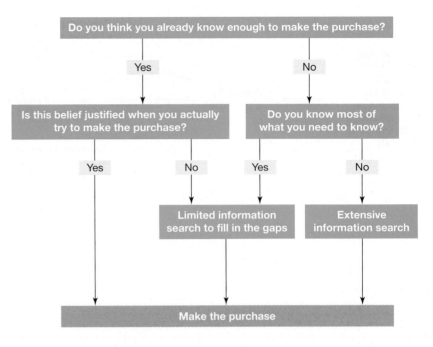

assortment adjustment Changing the proportions of products owned in order to increase satisfaction.

impulse purchases Purchases made without apparent conscious thought.

10 years and may be confronted by a huge array of new systems. This would cause the individual to reassess his or her level of knowledge and return to the information search stage of the process.

Information search efforts are not usually very extensive, even when major purchases are being considered. This is because of the amount of time and effort that needs to be expended when carrying out an extensive search. In fact, there is evidence to show that information overload will reduce the consumers' propensity to buy (Keller and Staelin 1987). Confusion can easily be created: research shows that consumer confusion has three dimensions, based on similarity with other information, information overload, and ambiguity of information (Walsh, Hennig-Thurau and Mitchell 2007). Such confusion obviously makes decision-making much harder, and also creates a degree of unease for consumers. People certainly go to considerable effort to avoid marketing communications, flipping past the advertisements in magazines and switching channels to avoid TV advertising. There is more on this in Chapter 8.

Assortment adjustment is the act of entering the market to replenish or exchange the assortment of goods the consumer owns. People recognise that their assortment of products is not what it should be in order to meet their needs (i.e. solve their day-to-day problems). Assortment adjustment can be programmed or unprogrammed: programmed assortment adjustment is about the habitual daily purchases which do not require much thought. Unprogrammed assortment adjustment needs much more thought, and refers to buying products which are new to the consumer. Non-programmed assortment adjustment falls into three categories, as follows (Onkvisit and Shaw 1994):

1 **Impulse purchases.** These are not based on any plan, and happen because the consumer is confronted with a stimulus, usually by happening to see something appealing. In fact, impulse purchases are not necessarily as impulsive as might be supposed, and impulse buying has been further divided into four categories (Stern 1962). Pure impulse is based largely on the novelty of the product, reminder impulse relates to products which have been left off the shopping list, suggestion impulse relates to products which fulfil a previously unfelt need, and planned impulse occurs when the individual has gone out to buy one type of product or one brand but is prepared to be swayed by special offers or new ideas.

2 **Limited problem-solving** takes place when the individual is already familiar with the product class and merely wants to update his or her available information. Limited decision-making is probably the commonest form of unprogrammed assortment adjustment, because most people are familiar with the product categories they buy, even if they are unfamiliar with new brands or new models of the products.

3 **Extended problem-solving** takes place when the product category is new to the consumer. For example, someone who has never owned a computer would need to gather a great deal of information and see a lot of machines before making a decision.

limited problem-solving Routine purchasing behaviour.

extended problem-solving Non-routine purchasing behaviour.

Factors affecting the search for information

The information search will be affected by a number of factors connected with the individual's situation. Assortment adjustment can take the form of either **replenishment** or **extension**. Replenishing the assortment (i.e. replacing worn-out or used items) requires the least information, since the consumer already knows what works and what does not. Extending the assortment requires much more information, since it implies learning about products which the consumer does not currently own.

The perceived value of the information is important in deciding whether it is worthwhile to collect it. For example, an information search on the Internet may be a very useful exercise provided it does not lead to paid-for sites. Some people would be prepared to pay for information about a potential purchase, whereas others would not. The relevance of the information is also a factor. If it has been a long time since the last purchase of the product category, new information might be highly relevant. Provided the consumer was happy with the last purchase, the internal information will be regarded as relevant, so there will be no need to seek out new information. In other words, if it ain't broke, don't fix it.

The perceived risk of the transaction refers to the possibility of unforeseen consequences (Bauer 1960). The risks fall into four categories:

1 **Physical risk.** Buying the wrong product might cause injury.
2 **Financial risk.** The product might prove to be a waste of money.
3 **Functional risk.** The risk that the product will not do the job for which it is intended.
4 **Psychosocial risk.** The purchase might prove to be embarrassing. This is especially true of items such as clothing.

All of these risks reduce as knowledge increases, so if the perceived risk is high the information search is likely to be more extensive.

The **perceived cost of the search** is the degree to which the consumer has to commit resources to the search. These resources are not necessarily only financial: for example, an individual might ask a friend for help, and thus incur a social obligation to repay the favour at a later date. In some cases, the cost of making a full search might exceed

replenishment Replacing products which have been worn out or used up.

extension Increasing the number of products owned.

physical risk The danger of physical harm as the result of a purchase.

financial risk The danger of losing money as the result of a purchase.

functional risk The risk that a product or service will not provide the expected benefits.

psychosocial risk The danger of looking foolish as a result of a purchase.

perceived cost of search The degree to which an individual believes that an information search will be too arduous or expensive.

		Value of the information	
		High	**Low**
Cost of obtaining the information	**High**	People are prepared to pay, albeit reluctantly	Extremely unlikely that people will pay for information
	Low	People will obtain the information readily	People may not even try to obtain the information

Figure 4.5

Trade-offs between cost and value of information

E-Marketing in Practice
Tesco

When Tesco introduced its loyalty card in 1995, the company little knew what a huge set of marketing problems – and a huge set of marketing solutions – the card would create. The card users win Clubcard points every time they use the card, so they present the card every time they shop at Tesco: Tesco has a fairly complete record of each customer's purchasing behaviour, because the checkouts store the information and pass it to the central computer.

At first, Tesco saw this as an opportunity to draw customers' attention to products which they were not, at present, buying. Customers were mailed special offers geared individually and based on products which they were not currently buying. This meant that someone who always buys basic ingredients for cooking would be sent offers for ready meals, customers who apparently never buy bread would be sent vouchers for money-off bread purchases, and so forth. Unfortunately, these vouchers were rarely redeemed – presumably an enthusiastic amateur chef would be unlikely to buy ready meals, and

someone allergic to bread would hardly be swayed by a money-off voucher.

Nowadays Tesco sends vouchers which offer products which are close to, but not exactly, what the consumer usually buys. This 'If you like that, you will probably like this' approach has paid off in a big way: Tesco's loyalty card is one of a very few such cards which really does inspire loyalty. This is because the company has ensured that it is customer-centred, not centred on what the store wants to sell. In 2004, Tesco announced record profits – perhaps not a coincidence.

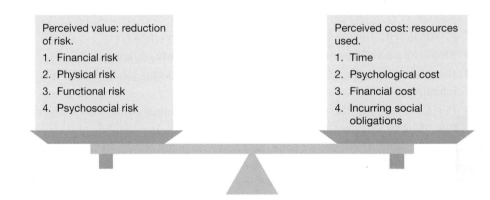

Figure 4.6

Risk management balance

Perceived value: reduction of risk.	Perceived cost: resources used.
1. Financial risk	1. Time
2. Physical risk	2. Psychological cost
3. Functional risk	3. Financial cost
4. Psychosocial risk	4. Incurring social obligations

the perceived risk of making a wrong purchase – for low-value items this is almost always the case. For example, buying the wrong type of shirt might result in a financial and social loss, but the financial loss is small and the social loss can be minimised by not wearing the shirt. Few people would expend a great deal of effort on an information search in these circumstances.

The perceived cost breaks down into time costs, money costs and psychological costs. Highly-paid people might have a greater appreciation of the value of time, and might be prepared to spend money in order to save time. Poorer customers may be more prepared to shop around in order to save money (Urbany 1986).

Money costs are the out-of-pocket expenses of searching. Comparing the prices of olive oil between supermarkets is relatively cheap, but few consumers would cross the Channel to see if the oil is cheaper in France or Spain.

The psychological cost of the information search includes frustration, the stress of finding the information or shopping around, talking to salespeople, and generally giving a lot of emotional energy to the search. Sometimes, of course, the search itself becomes pleasurable – many consumers enjoy shopping as an entertainment. This can be a more important motivator than an actual need to buy something (Bloch, Sherrell and Ridgway 1986).

Situational factors also affect the extent of the information search. In an emergency, for example a burst water pipe, few people would spend much time telephoning around several plumbers and comparing quotations for doing the work. Other situational variables might include product scarcity and lack of available credit.

Products can be classified as **shopping products** and **non-shopping products**. Shopping products are those which require a new solution every time they are purchased. Typically these products are higher-value items or rarely-purchased items. They require the greatest information search. Non-shopping goods are those for which the consumer already has full information: they are typically the products which are bought regularly and for which the consumer has an established brand preference (Bucklin 1963).

Since each consumer is an individual, individual characteristics play a part in the information search. Some people enjoy shopping around, others are bored by it: more importantly, most people like shopping for some categories of goods and not for others.

situational factors Elements of the immediate surroundings which affect decision-making.

shopping products Products which require extensive information search and decision-making.

non-shopping products Products which require little information search or decision-making.

Goals

Establishing a **goal** is the outcome of being motivated to do something about a problem. The basic outcome that the individual seeks to achieve is called an end goal, but it may be preceded by several sub-goals which lead to the end goal. For example, a simple goal hierarchy for buying a second-hand car might look like this:

goal An objective.

1 Find out which car would best suit the individual's needs.
2 Find out which is the cheapest way of financing the purchase.
3 Find out who has the right type of car at the right price.
4 Go and buy the car.

In order to act on this basic plan of action, the person will have to establish a series of subsidiary goals, with matching activities. This 'route map' to buying the car might look like this:

1 Buy a used-car guide.
2 Decide which models look as if they might meet the need.
3 Decide what prices are within an acceptable range.
4 Telephone banks and loan companies for loan quotes.
5 Buy the local paper.
6 Call up anybody who seems to have the right kind of car, call round and buy the right one.

An inexperienced car buyer may need to establish a more elaborate and lengthy plan, such as this:

1 Decide to buy a car.
2 Ask around among family and friends to find out which car might suit the purpose. An experienced car-owner among this group might point out needs which the actual consumer had not thought of – lack of experience sometimes translates into a lack of knowledge about one's own needs.
3 Go to used-car showrooms to examine the alternatives.
4 Find a helpful salesperson who appears honest and trustworthy.
5 Explain the needs to the salesperson.

Figure 4.7
Goal hierarchies

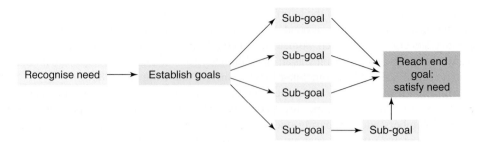

6 Listen to the salesperson's advice, perhaps with a knowledgeable friend on hand to assess the value and honesty of the advice.

7 Make the purchase decision, based on the closeness of fit between the salesperson's description of the car and the needs that have been identified.

8 Buy the car.

Experienced people tend to use shorter lists of sub-goals because they are able to cut out some of the stages. In the case of inexperienced buyers, the risk involved is greater, so they will go to some trouble to reduce the risk to a minimum. The degree of risk perceived by the consumer depends on two factors. Firstly, the seriousness of the possible damage caused by buying the wrong product, and secondly the likelihood that the negative consequences will occur. For example, a failed climbing rope would (possibly) kill the person using it, but the possibility of failure is fairly remote.

For experienced buyers, the decision process will be much faster. For example, when older drivers buy new cars they consider fewer brands and dealers, and are more likely to choose long-established brands with which they are familiar (Lambert-Pandraud, Laurent and LaPersonne 2005).

Making the choice

Choosing the right climbing equipment might be a matter of life and death.

Having recognised the need and collected the information, the customer is in a position to make the final choice of product. Making a final choice can be hard work – sometimes people end up making a bad choice simply because they get tired of trying to work out the best course of action (Baumeister 2004). People often begin by establishing a consideration set, which is the group of products any of which would provide an acceptable solution. The consideration set is usually small – only two or three choices – because too much choice leads to an inability to decide, or choice paralysis (Shankar, Cherrier and Canniford 2006). From a marketer's viewpoint, it is important to ensure that the company's product is in the consideration set, and this is actually the purpose of most advertising.

heuristic A decision-making rule.

consideration set The group of products which might be capable of meeting a need.

cut-off A filtering device which involves deciding the outer limits of acceptability for a given product's chatracteristics.

signal A feature of the product or its surrounding attributes which convey meaning about the product.

The consideration set is established from the information obtained in the information search. People will often use decision rules (**heuristics**) when establishing the **consideration set** – for example, someone may have a rule that they never buy Eastern European cars. This would mean that Skoda, Polski Fiat, Yugo and Lada would have no chance of being included in the consideration set. Another type of heuristic is a **cut-off**, by which the individual sets the limits of the decision. A cut-off may be based on price, i.e. no product above (or below) a particular price will be included, but equally a cut-off could be based on time (someone may not be prepared to consider any holiday that involves a flight of more than two hours) or product characteristics (no audio system will be considered that does not provide 7-channel home theatre sound).

Judging product quality is often a result of **signals**. A signal is a surrogate for knowing what the characteristics of the product actually are. For example, the retailer's reputation would be a signal for the quality of the products on offer. Price is often used as a signal:

people assume that the higher-priced products must be higher quality, even when there is no objective evidence to support this. Of course, if the consumer is able to inspect the product in detail, or has other evidence of the quality of the product, signals are less important.

Heuristics can be categorised as **compensatory** or **non-compensatory**. Compensatory heuristics can be offset against each other, whereas non-compensatory heuristics cannot. For example, someone may be prepared to accept a longer flight when going on holiday, because all the other characteristics of the holiday are exactly what is wanted. On the other hand, someone who becomes airsick if the flight is longer than two hours might be entirely unprepared to compromise on this aspect of the decision.

Some people adopt a **lexicographic** approach. This involves creating a hierarchy of attributes, and comparing products first against the most important attribute, then against the next one and so forth. Decisions might also be made by elimination of aspects, whereby the product is examined against other brands according to its attributes, but then each attribute is measured against cut-offs.

The **conjunctive** rule is the last of the non-compensatory rules. Here each brand is compared in turn against all the cut-offs. Only those brands which survive this process will be compared with each other.

Compensatory decision rules allow for trade-offs between attributes. This means that disadvantages in one area can be compensated for by advantages in another. The simple additive rule means that the individual makes a simple total of the product's positive attributes and compares this with a similar tally for other products. The weighted additive approach gives greater weight to some aspects than to others, and the phased decision strategy involves using rules in a sequence. This means that the individual might use non-compensatory heuristics such as cut-offs to reduce the number of options, then use a weighted additive rule to make the final choice between the remaining products.

Two more special categories of decision rule exist. First, people may use a constructive decision rule. This means that the rule must be established from scratch whenever a new situation is encountered. If the rule works, the consumer will store it in memory for use in the future when a similar situation arises. Second, affect referral is the process whereby consumers use a standard attitude (often based on emotional reasons) to make a decision. For example, someone may have a dislike of Japanese products, based on a negative experience with a Japanese person. This type of rule is usually non-compensatory.

compensatory Of a heuristic, one which allows negative features to be offset against positive features.

non-compensatory Of a heuristic, one which does not allow a positive feature to offset a negative feature.

lexicographic A hierarchy of heuristics.

conjunctive Heuristics which are considered together.

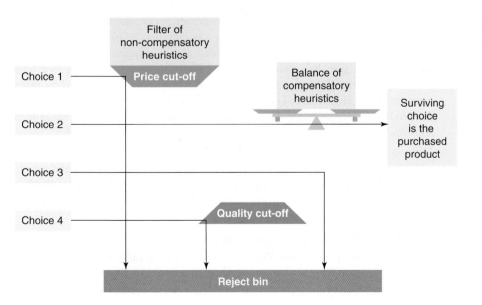

Figure 4.8

Decision rules

In fact, the bulk of consumer decision-making is not made in such a calculated manner. People decide their purchases at least as much on emotion as on logic, and rationalise the decision afterwards. Recent thinking is that complex decisions are made as a series of waves of thought and action, in other words a multi-phase, non-linear process occurs (Lye *et al.* 2005).

Consumption of the Product

Consumption of products appears at first sight to be an obvious area of consumer behaviour. However, from a marketing viewpoint, there are several issues around consumption which merit closer attention. For example:

1 *When is the product consumed*? In some cases this is known in advance – concert tickets, restaurant bookings and visits to the hairdresser or dentist are all pre-booked. In other cases the time of consumption is implied, as with breakfast cereals, summer holidays and take-away meals (which are consumed soon after purchase). In some cases marketers can increase sales by focusing on consumption rather than on purchase – for example encouraging people to eat breakfast cereal as a snack, or to take holidays at non-traditional times.

2 *Where is the product consumed*? Products might be consumed in public, in private or while doing something else. Consider the beer market. Some beer is consumed in bars and pubs, often on draught: some beer is consumed at home, indoors. Some beer is consumed outdoors, on picnics or when participating in an activity such as fishing or cricket. Each type of consumption has different implications for marketers – in particular, what type of container the beer is packed in and what the implications are for branding. Beer consumed in the home while watching TV may be a supermarket own brand, but the same individual might order a specific prestige brand in a pub, where friends can see what is being ordered. Beer carried on a picnic is easier to carry if it is in a can or a plastic bottle rather than in a heavy, breakable glass bottle.

3 *How is the product consumed*? Products have frequently been reinvented dramatically by purchasers (for example, using coffee filters to stop compost from leaking out of a plant-pot, or using coffee to transport earthworms on fishing trips) (Wansink 2004). Apart from these uses, which are clearly far removed from those the producer had envisaged, consumers may have other consumption habits. For example, it is useful to know whether people use rice as a side dish or as an ingredient in dishes such as paella. In a paella, people often use unbranded rice (except in Spain, where the rice is regarded as a key ingredient in the success of the dish). As a side dish, people are more likely to have a favourite rice brand, believing that the flavour is more important when it is not disguised by other ingredients. In either case, knowing that someone has found a new way to use the product is useful, since the producer can disseminate this knowledge to other consumers.

4 *How much is consumed*? Identifying which type of person is a heavy consumer, which type is a moderate consumer, which type is a light consumer, and which type is a non-consumer can be extremely useful. Producers have to decide whether they can identify potential heavy users in the population of non-users, but may find it equally useful to try to convert light users into heavy users.

Figure 4.9 shows how these consumption behaviours relate.

During the act of consumption, the individual makes a judgement about the experience. This is a post-purchase evaluation, leading to a decision about whether the product

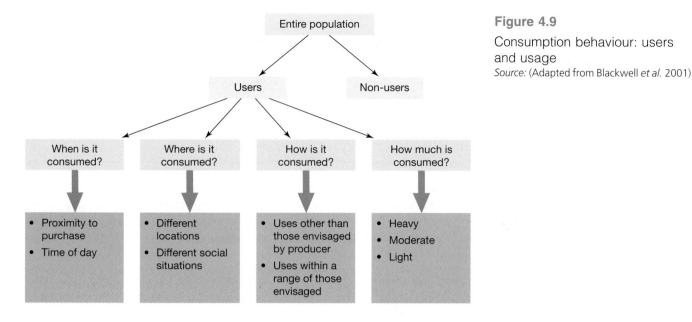

Figure 4.9

Consumption behaviour: users and usage
Source: (Adapted from Blackwell *et al.* 2001)

was satisfying or not – in other words, whether the product fulfilled the consumer's expectations. A critical part of this evaluation is the feelings experienced during consumption: these can vary from fear through excitement, pleasure, relief, boredom and anger to guilt and regret. These feelings should be appropriate to the product, or further purchase is unlikely. If the experience is largely emotional, the outcome will be evaluated by feelings: unsurprisingly, if the experience is largely practical, mental calculation is more important in evaluation (Hsee and Rottenstreich 2002).

For example, compare the feelings illustrated in Table 4.1. In each case the feeling is the same, but the situation is different – and would result in a different propensity to repurchase.

Pre-purchase expectations fall into three categories:

- *Equitable performance*. This is the performance one could reasonably expect, given the cost and effort involved in obtaining the product (Woodruff, Cadotte and Jenkins 1983).

- *Ideal performance*. What the customer hoped the product would do (Holbrook 1984).

- *Expected performance*. What the customer expects the product will actually do (Leichty and Churchill 1979).

Added to this is the concept of hope: hope is positive but uncertain, and has an effect on both involvement with the product and expectations about its performance (MacInnis and DeMello 2005).

After purchase, there are four possible post-purchase emotional states (Santos and Boote 2003): delight, satisfaction (positive indifference), acceptance (negative indifference) and dissatisfaction. Each will generate different levels of complaining or complimenting behaviour.

Satisfaction or dissatisfaction with the product arises because consumers try to establish a **perceptual map** of what their lives will be like with the product included. For example, someone contemplating buying a holiday home in France may well imagine sitting on the patio drinking a glass of wine, perhaps enjoying a meal at a local restaurant, even chatting to the locals over a *vin ordinaire* at a local bar. The reality is often very

perceptual map The individual's view of competing products.

Table 4.1 Feelings versus situations

Feeling	Situation One	Situation Two
Fear	White-knuckle ride at a theme park. In this situation, fear is fun because it provides the consumer with the confidence which comes from overcoming it, and also adds some excitement to his or her life.	Steering failure while driving one's new car on a motorway. In this case, the fear is genuinely life-threatening. It is not part of the expected benefits of the product.
Boredom	An afternoon spent game fishing when no fish were caught. Someone who books a game-fishing trip expects the thrill of the chase, the battle between angler and fish, and some impressive photographs to take home. Without the fish, all that results is a long ride on a boat.	An afternoon spent at a meditation centre. Here, boredom is the desired outcome, a chance to clear the brain and recharge the batteries. If the afternoon were exciting, it would not serve its purpose.
Anger	A football match during which the referee makes aseries of unfavourable decisions. Part of the pleasure of football matches is being able to shout at the referee – anger over something which is unlikely to affect one's lifestyle is part of the fun, releasing tension which may have built up as a result of not being allowed to shout at (say) the boss.	A hairdressing salon when the hairstyle has gone seriously wrong. In this circumstance, anger arises because there is probably not much that can be done to put matters right. In this case, anger is not part of the expectation.
Pain	At the dentist's, patients expect to feel some pain. Pain is seen as an acceptable part of the process, because there is a long-term benefit.	Almost any other location or consumption experience. People do not bargain for being hurt by the products and services they buy.

different – the locals might be unfriendly, the local restaurant atrocious and the weather rarely good enough for sitting outside. The level of dissonance will depend on the following factors:

1 The degree of divergence between the expected outcome and the actual outcome.
2 The importance of the discrepancy to the individual.
3 The degree to which the discrepancy can be corrected.
4 The cost of the purchase, in both time and money.

In some cases the results of the consumption experience are so positive that the consumer becomes 'hooked' on consumption. This may take the form of excessive consumption of a specific product (e.g. alcohol, chocolate, fatty foods etc.) or it may take a more general form, with the individual becoming a 'shopaholic' (O'Guinn and Faber 1989). **Compulsive consumption** has been defined as those practices that, though undertaken to bolster self-esteem, are inappropriate, excessive and disruptive to the lives of those who are involved (Faber, O'Guinn and Krych 1987). There is also evidence that compulsive behaviour in one area (for example buying lottery tickets and scratchcards) is linked to other addictive behaviours (such as smoking) (Balabanis 2002).

In general, **post-purchase evaluation** will be positive if the consumer's expectations were met or exceeded, and negative if these expectations were not met. Positive post-purchase evaluations will encourage repeat buying and positive word-of-mouth recommendations

compulsive consumption An obsessive need to buy and use products.

post-purchase evaluation The process of deciding whether the outcome of a purchase has been appropriate or not.

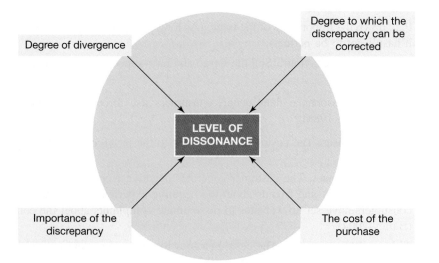

Figure 4.10

Factors in dissonance

to other potential consumers. Note that the objective experience is only partly relevant – what matters is whether or not the customer's expectations were met. This means that over-hyping a product may result in short-term sales as a result of the consumer's pre-purchase expectations being high, but will damage sales in the long run as consumers are dissatisfied, and tell others about their experience.

Apparently people sometimes enjoy complicating their lives, and sometimes enjoy simplifying them. Sometimes they like to be frightened, sometimes they like to be reassured. Sometimes they will tolerate pain as part of the process, more often they will regard pain as being the last thing they bargained for.

Everybody is different, and indeed everybody's mood shifts at different times: so how can marketers have any control whatsoever over post-purchase dissonance? One person leaves the white-knuckle ride excited and eager to go again – another person leaves the same ride threatening to sue the theme park.

Maybe it's about managing expectations. Provided the customers have a clear idea of what they are getting, they surely don't have any cause for complaint. Yet at the same time, marketers need to promote the products – encourage people to believe that product will meet their needs! So maybe it's also about managing the aftermath – having a good complaints procedure in place.

In practice, not every dissatisfied customer will complain. Some people will feel that it is not worth the trouble (especially if the problem is a minor one), some people will blame other factors and so forth. Some research has shown that only one-third of dissatisfied customers will complain (Day *et al.* 1981).

There are four general approaches that people take to reducing post-purchase dissonance:

1 Ignore the dissonant information and look for positive information about the product. (For example, the stereo system may not sound as good as one expected, but it looks really good).

2 Distort the dissonant information. (It sounds a lot better than the one you had before).

3 Play down the importance of the issue. (As long as it plays so you can hear the beat, it hasn't got to be perfect).

4 Change one's behaviour. (Sell the stereo and buy something else, listen to the radio instead).

If post-purchase dissonance does occur, consumers use three general approaches to complaining (Singh 1988):

voice responses Complaints made directly to the supplier.

private responses Complaints made to friends or family about a product or company.

third-party responses Complaints made via lawyers or consumer rights advocates.

1 **Voice responses.** The customer comes back to the provider to complain or seek redress.

2 **Private responses.** The customer generates negative word-of-mouth by talking to family and friends about the negative experience. In some cases, consumers have set up websites to disseminate complaints about the company (Bailey 2004).

3 **Third-party responses.** The customer goes to a lawyer or consumer champion to take up the case on their behalf.

Obviously the firm and the customer may well not agree on the legitimacy of the complaint: managers sometimes feel that the consumer wants something for nothing, or may even feel that there is an implied personal criticism in the complaint (Cobb, Walgren and Hollowed 1987). As the level of complaints increases, the willingness of managers to listen decreases (Smart and Martin 1991), presumably because they grow tired of hearing the same old problems. However, the way the complaint is handled affects satisfaction and dissatisfaction, and some research shows that loyalty will actually increase if the complaint is handled to the customer's satisfaction – in other words, customers whose complaints are handled well become more loyal than those who did not have a complaint in the first place (Coca-Cola Company 1981).

Third-party responses almost always occur after the consumer has been dissatisfied with the outcome of a voice response. Any lawyer will confirm whether the consumer has already complained directly to the company, since a court case is unlikely to succeed if the company has not had the opportunity to put matters right. The likelihood of a complaint being made depends on the following factors (Day 1984):

1 The significance of the consumption event in terms of product importance, cost, social visibility and time required in consumption. Consumers are unlikely to bother to complain if the product was cheap, unimportant and unlikely to last long anyway.

2 The consumer's knowledge and experience in terms of the number of previous purchases, level of product knowledge, perception of ability as a consumer and previous complaining experience. Consumers who have complained in the past are more likely to do so in the future: consumers with substantial knowledge of the product category are more likely to complain if things go wrong.

3 The difficulty of seeking redress. Customers are unlikely to complain if the product was purchased a long way away, or if complaining would take too much time and trouble.

4 The probability that a complaint will lead to a positive outcome (Halstead and Droge 1991). Complaints are more likely if the customer believes that the company is reputable or has a guarantee. Also, customers are less likely to complain if the problem is perceived as being incapable of being put right or compensated for.

The growth of the so-called compensation culture has led to a marked increase in third-party complaints. Partly this is due to the removal of restrictions on no-win-no-fee litigation, and partly due to increased expectations on the part of consumers.

Marketing in Practice
Granite Rock

Granite Rock supplies gravel for the building industry. They have an interesting and possibly unique approach to customer complaints – the invite customers *not* to pay the invoice.

On the back of each invoice is a statement to the effect that, if the customer is not satisfied with Granite Rock's performance (e.g. a delivery of gravel was late and held up construction), the client should deduct something from the invoice and only pay Granite Rock what they think the company has earned.

In practice, few customers feel the need to do this – and Granite Rock's trusting attitude means that many minor transgressions are simply forgiven. The end result is an increase in trust and an increase in business. What is more, Granite Rock's customers are prepared to pay (on average) 6 per cent more for their gravel than they would have to pay competing firms. The additional security of dealing with an honest company, prepared to admit its mistakes, is something worth paying extra for, even in an industry where the low bid typically gets the business.

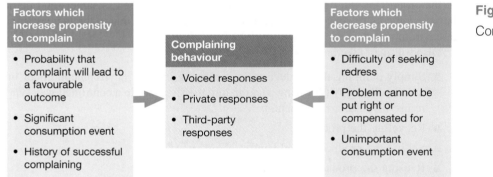

Figure 4.11

Complaining behaviour

From the viewpoint of the supplier, voice complaints are by far the least damaging. A voice complaint can be dealt with privately, and the supplier can retain a degree of control: also, a complaint well-handled results in a more loyal customer. Suppliers should, at least in theory, encourage people to voice their complaints.

In some cases, consumers **boycott** the company and its products and encourage others to do the same. Four factors predict boycott behaviour (Klein, Smith and John 2004):

boycott To avoid buying a company's products.

1 The desire to make a difference, in other words, to teach the company a lesson.

2 Scope for self-enhancement: the desire to make oneself feel important and powerful against the company.

3 Counter-arguments which inhibit boycotting: friends saying that it will make no difference to the company, that boycotting the product only means doing without it, and so forth.

4 Cost to the boycotter of constrained consumption: managing without the product may be harder on the boycotter than it is on the company.

Marketing in Practice
Trade-In

During the 1930s the new-car market was stagnant. Cars were then extremely expensive (even a cheap car would be several times the average year's salary for most people) and the vast majority of people had no cars. General Motors decided to stimulate the market by accepting used cars as part-payment for new cars. The second-hand cars could then be sold to people who could not afford a new car.

The idea quickly took root, and is now a feature of all car dealing. Second-hand cars are traded in for other second-hand cars, and even today few people would buy a brand-new car without offering their old car in part payment. General Motors' innovation has meant that, in the UK, there are slightly more than 22 million cars, which is more than one per household on average.

Disposal

Getting rid of the product after it has been consumed (or at least getting rid of what is left of the product) is the final stage in the consumption process. Consumers and marketers have become more concerned about disposal in recent years due to the increased interest in environmental issues.

Disposal may take any of the following forms:

- Simply dumping the product or its packaging into the environment, either in an uncontrolled way (throwing packing into the street) or in a controlled way (via local refuse disposal arrangements).
- Recycling the product.
- Selling the product second hand.
- Reusing the product in a novel way.

Marketers have an input into each of these possibilities, and in many cases can earn extra money for the company by providing facilities for consumers to dispose of unwanted or worn-out products.

People often sell their unwanted goods rather than dump them – a form of recycling?

For example, many fast-food companies now provide litter patrols near their premises to collect discarded packaging and food. Some computer peripherals firms provide freepost addresses for customers to return used ink cartridges for recycling, and even the so-called 'disposable' cameras are actually 70 per cent recycled each time they are returned for film processing.

Selling the product second hand has led to the growth of websites (eBay and Freecycle), specialist newspapers and magazines (Free-ads and Exchange and Mart), and even some amateur marketing such as cards in shop windows. In some industries, marketers have instituted trade-in arrangements.

Reusing products or packaging has become popular in some circles in recent years: many people keep the containers that takeaway foods come in and use them for the freezer: some companies encourage this behaviour by providing packaging which lends itself to reuse. For example, French mustard manufacturers typically package their product in jars which can be used as wine glasses afterwards. More novel uses for discarded products include use as garden ornaments or containers and even as part of artworks.

Influences on the Buying Decision

In 21st century Western society, people are faced with a vast range of possible ways of meeting their consumption needs. The variety of goods on offer and the unprecedented wealth of industrial society allow people to make extremely wide choices when satisfying their needs and the needs of their families. The basic necessities of life have long ago been taken care of – people are catering to higher-level needs.

For a supplier to make its voice heard amidst the almost overwhelming clamour of competitors, an understanding of what would sway customers one way or the other is clearly important. Individuals buy not only because they have a specific practical need for a product at a given moment: they also buy because they have social, psychological and cultural needs, needs which go beyond the merely physical needs for food, shelter and warmth.

Psychological influences include **perception**, **attitudes** and **motivation**. Sociological influences are about group behaviour: the respect of one's friends and colleagues and the influence of families. Cultural influences refer to religion, language and the shared beliefs and customs of the culture the individual is part of.

perception The process of building up a mental map of the world.

attitude A learned tendency to respond in a consistent manner to a specific stimulus or object.

motivation The force that moves an individual towards a specific set of solutions.

Drive, Motivation and Hedonism

Drive is the force that makes a person respond to a need. It is caused by the drift from the desired state to the actual state – the starting-point for recognising a need. If the drive state is at a high level, the individual becomes motivated to do something to correct the situation.

Allowing a gap to develop between the desired and actual states can be stimulating and enjoyable. Working up an appetite before a meal makes the meal more enjoyable, and achieving a goal may simply lead to developing a new goal. People often enjoy planning something more than they enjoy the actual experience (Raghunathan and Mukherji 2003).

Most people have a level at which this type of stimulation is enjoyable, stimulating and not yet unpleasant. This is called the **optimum stimulation level**, or OSL. If external stimulation goes above the OSL, the individual will seek to meet the need: if stimulation is below the OSL, the person will seek to increase the stimulation and bring it back up to the OSL.

The OSL varies from one individual to another, but research shows that people with high OSLs like novelty and risk-taking, whereas those with low OSLs prefer the tried and tested (Raju 1980). In general, people with high OSLs tend to be younger.

Motivation derives from drive. A drive only has quantity, whereas a motivation is directed towards a specific group of solutions. Much marketing effort is aimed at developing drives, but even more is aimed at developing motivations towards a specific product or group of products. Motives can be classified as shown in Table 4.2.

The current view of motivation is that there is a balance between the rational and emotional elements of motivation. There can be little doubt that emotion plays a large part in buying decisions, partly through the formation of attitudes. Also, needs can be classified into utilitarian needs, which are about the objective, functional aspects of life, and **hedonic needs**, which are about the pleasurable or aesthetic aspects of the products (Holbrook and Hirschmann 1982). It is common for both types of need to be considered in the same purchase decision: car purchase is a good example, since the practical aspects of owning a car are moderated by the pleasurable aspects of driving a car which is smart, comfortable, fast and so forth. People sometimes move towards hedonic needs as a result of shocking events: for example, after a near-death experience, people who normally look after their bodies tend to diet and exercise more, whereas people who

drive The force generated in an individual as a result of a felt need.

optimum stimulation level The level at which the gap between the desired state and the actual state has not yet become unpleasant.

hedonic needs Needs which relate to the pleasurable aspects of ownership.

Table 4.2 Classification of motives

Primary motives	The reason that leads to the purchase of a product class. The consumer may feel a need to buy a new car to replace a worn-out one.
Secondary motives	The reasons behind buying a specific brand. The consumer may have reasons for buying a Mercedes rather than a BMW.
Rational motives	These are based on reasoning, or a logical assessment of the situation. The consumer may have decided that the new car should be able to carry three children and their paraphernalia, and should fit the garage.
Emotional motives	These motives have to do with the consumer's feelings about the brand. This may include considerations such as what the neighbours might think of the car, what the car looks like, and how it feels to drive it.
Conscious motives	Motives of which the customer is aware.
Dormant motives	Motives operating below the conscious level. The car buyer may not be consciously aware that a sudden urge to buy a sports car is actually about approaching middle age, not about a need for transport.

Figure 4.12

Balance between rational and emotional needs

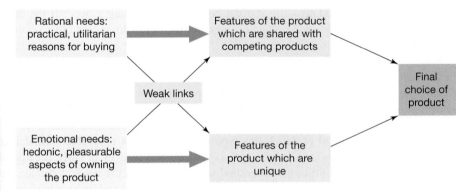

the break sensation...only 165 Calories

Courtesy of The Advertising Archives

Chocolate is marketed on hedonism.

have low body esteem tend to relax their diets and eat things they enjoy (Shiv, Ferraro and Bettman 2004).

Hedonic aspects of the product are often the main distinguishing feature between it and its competition. For example, car manufacturers design car doors so that they close with a satisfying 'thunk': this serves no useful purpose, but it does give the impression that the car is a solid machine. Heinz use turquoise for the label on their baked beans cans because it contrasts well with the colour of the beans, emphasising the orange colour of the sauce: the foil seals on jars of coffee are pleasurable to pop, and computer software uses amusing cartoon images for its Help sections. In some cases these hedonic aspects have been a by-product of packaging decisions, but in many cases the hedonic aspects of the product have been added at the design stage.

Advertising often uses hedonic imagery to promote products. Chocolate, beer, cars and even laundry products are promoted by emphasising fun, luxury, comfort or excitement – all of which are hedonic aspects of the products concerned.

Involvement

Involvement is the perceived importance or personal relevance of an object or event. In consumer terms, it is the degree to which the individual feels attached to the product or product category. For example, a professional musician may have a strong attachment to a particular brand of guitar string, whereas an amateur may not be so concerned since his or her livelihood does not depend on making choices of that nature.

Involvement is an important concept in marketing, since it relates strongly to repeat purchases. Involvement has both **affective** and **cognitive** elements, and is a part of attitude theory. High involvement comes about if the consumer feels that the product attributes are strongly linked to end goals or values; lower levels of involvement occur if the attributes of the product only link to function, and low levels occur if the attributes are irrelevant to the consequences. High involvement purchases are the ones that figure most in the purchaser's lifestyle.

Table 4.3 compares the different levels of involvement and how these impact on the decision-making process. High-involvement customers are difficult to persuade – they are unlikely to be moved by advertising, or even by persuasive sales pitches (Keisler, Collins and Miller 1969).

Levels of involvement are influenced both by **personal sources** and **situational sources**. Personal sources (also called intrinsic self-relevance) are the means-end knowledge stored in the individual's memory, and are influenced both by the individual's personality and by the product characteristics. If the individual thinks that the characteristics of the product relate strongly to life goals, or reflect strongly on the individual as a person, the intrinsic self-relevance will be high.

Situational sources of involvement relate to the immediate social or physical surroundings of the consumer. Social circumstances refer to the potential embarrassment factor of being seen wearing the wrong clothes or driving the wrong car. Physical factors relate to the use of the product in the 'real world'. For example, referring back to the climbing rope mentioned earlier, a climber might revise her view of the importance of reliability if the rope should break halfway up a rock face.

Sometimes marketers are able to emphasise the environmental sources of involvement in order to increase the consumer's involvement in the product. Clothes retailers can advise on appropriate dress for special occasions, and outdoors shops often offer advice on the necessity of buying the right equipment for outdoor pursuits such as camping or mountaineering.

Consumers frequently develop close relationships with brands, partly because the brand reflects their self-image. Cigarette smokers often become fiercely loyal to their

involvement Emotional attachment to a product or brand.

affective Relating to emotional factors.

cognitive Relating to rational factors.

personal sources The means–end knowledge stored in an individual's memory.

situational sources Sources of involvement derived from immediate social or cultural factors.

Table 4.3 Comparison of involvement levels

High involvement	Medium involvement	Low involvement
Attributes strongly linked to end goals	Attributes only link to function	Attributes irrelevant to consequences
Important to get it right first time	Need to have reasonably reliable results	Results perceived to be the same whichever product chosen
Consumer has in-depth knowledge and strong opinions	Consumer has knowledge of the product group, no strong feelings	No strong feelings, knowledge of product group irrelevant
Discrepant information ignored or discounted	Discrepant information considered carefully	Discrepant information ignored

E-Marketing in Practice
Manchester United

In the modern world communities have become fragmented. People live a long way away from their families, and a sense of belonging is often hard to come by. Football fans have a ready-made substitute for the tribe – they align themselves with their team.

The world's most successful football team is Manchester United, not so much because of the team's successes on the pitch, but because of its comprehensive approach to marketing. Manchester United sell everything from clothing to telephone cards with the team's brand on them – and fans lap it up. Manchester United Fan Clubs exist even in countries such as the United States where soccer is a minority sport – and fans who have never seen the team play happily pay out hundreds of pounds to buy Manchester United merchandise.

This level of involvement is fostered by online fan newsletters, by mailings to fans, by special events and prizes, and by (of course) the team's success on the pitch. There was a time when football fans' girlfriends were puzzled by their partners' apparent ability to commit to a football team for life but be unable to commit to a relationship – but nowadays so many of the fans are women that this no longer applies. Football fandom fulfils a need for belonging which is basic to all people, and Manchester United have been at the forefront of fulfilling that need.

© Ilian Studio/Alamy

Table 4.4 Categories of consumer according to involvement

Brand loyalists	Strong affective links to a favourite brand. Usually they tend to link the product category to the provision of personally-relevant consequences. These are people who go for the 'best brand' for their needs, but also feel that the product category itself is an important part of their lives.
Routine brand buyers	Low personal sources of involvement, but have a favourite brand. These consumers are more interested in the types of consequences associated with regular brand purchases (it is easier to buy the same one each week, and it is at least reliable). They are not necessarily looking for the 'best brand': a satisfactory one will do.
Information seekers	Have positive means–end information about the product category, but no one brand stands out as superior. These consumers use a lot of information to help them find a suitable brand from within the product category.
Brand switchers	Low brand loyalty, low personal involvement. These people do not see that the brand used has any important consequences, even if the product category is interesting. Usually they do not have a strong relationship with the product category either. This means that they are easily affected by environmental factors such as sales promotions.

(Source: J. Paul Peter and Jerry C. Olson, Understanding Consumer Behavior. Burr Ridge, IL: Irwin, 1994).

brands, although research shows that most smokers are unable to distinguish their own brand of cigarette in a blind taste test. Car drivers develop close relationships with their cars, often talking to the car and even giving it a name. People can be categorised according to their involvement level (see Table 4.4) but of course this categorisation only applies to particular product categories – someone may be extremely loyal to a specific brand of gin, but not care what brand of tonic goes in it. Equally, someone may be intensely loyal to a brand of tomato ketchup and have no loyalty at all to a car manufacturer: price is not relevant to involvement. Research shows that pre-teen children often link snack foods to lifestyle values, and become highly involved with their favourite brands (Dibley and Baker 2001).

Involvement is a function of loyalty, and therefore is of interest to marketers who seek to increase repeat purchases. There is strong evidence to indicate that it is approximately five times cheaper to retain an existing customer than it is to win a new one, and considerable effort on the part of many companies has gone into establishing systems for winning back customers who have defected to the opposition.

loyalty The tendency to repeat purchase of a brand.

Learning and Perception

Learning is not only about classroom-type learning. Most behaviour is learned as a result of external experiences; most of what people know (and almost certainly many of the things they are most proud of knowing) they learned outside school. People learn things partly through a formalised structure of teaching and partly through an unconscious process of learning by experience.

Learning is highly relevant to marketing, since consumers are affected by the things they learn, and much consumer behaviour is based on the learning process. Persuading consumers to remember the information they see in advertisements is a major problem for marketers: people are often able to remember the advertisement, but not the brand being advertised, for example.

Learning is defined as the behavioural changes that occur over time relative to an external stimulus condition (Onkvisit and Shaw 1994). According to this definition, activities are changed or originated through a reaction to an encountered situation. We can therefore say that someone has learned something if, as a result, their behaviour changes in some way.

The main conditions that arise from this definition are as follows;

1 There must be a change in behaviour (response tendencies).

2 This must result from external stimulus.

Learning has not taken place under the following circumstances:

1 **Species response tendencies.** These are instincts or reflexes; for example, the response of ducking when a stone is thrown at you does not rely on your having learned that stones are hard and hurt the skin. Learning has not taken place under those circumstances.

2 **Maturation.** Behavioural changes often occur in adolescence due to hormonal changes (for example), but again this is not a behavioural change as a result of learning.

3 Temporary states of the organism. Whilst behaviour can be, and often is, affected by tiredness, hunger, drunkenness etc. these factors do not constitute part of a larger learning process (even though learning may result from those states; the drunk may well learn to drink less in future).

species response tendencies Automatic behaviour as a result of instinct rather than learning.

maturation The development of the organism over time.

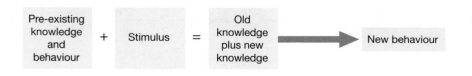

Figure 4.13

Development of learning

classical conditioning The instilling of automatic responses in an individual by repetition of stimulus and reward.

operant conditioning The instilling of automatic responses via the active participation of the individual.

unconditioned stimulus A stimulus which would normally produce a known reaction in an individual: this stimulus is offered as part of the conditioning process.

unconditioned response The existing automatic response of the individual to an unconditioned stimulus.

conditioned stimulus A stimulus offered at the same time as an unconditioned stimulus, with the intention of creating an artificial association between it and the unconditioned response.

Academic study of learning has two main schools of thought: first, the stimulus-response approach, which further subdivides into **classical** and **operant conditioning**, and second, cognitive theories, where the conscious thought of the individual enters into the equation.

Classical learning theory

The classical theory of learning was developed by, among others, the Russian researcher Pavlov (1927). Pavlov's famous experiments with dogs demonstrated that automatic responses (reflexes) could be learned. What Pavlov did was present a dog with an **unconditioned stimulus** (in this case, meat powder) knowing that this would lead to an **unconditioned response** (salivation). At the same time Pavlov would ring a bell (the **conditioned stimulus**). After a while the dog would associate the ringing of the bell with the meat, and would salivate whenever it heard the bell, without actually seeing any meat. This mechanism is shown in Figure 4.14.

Classical conditioning occurs in humans as well. Many smokers associate having a cup of coffee with having a cigarette, and find it difficult to give up smoking without also giving up coffee. Repetitive advertising jingles or strap lines become associated with the brands concerned: for example, the four-note tune associated with the Intel computer chip is recognised worldwide.

For this to work it is usually necessary to repeat the stimulus a number of times in order for the conditioned response to become established. The number of times the process needs to be repeated will depend on the strength of the stimulus and the receptiveness (motivation) of the individual. Research has shown that, although conditioning has been reported for a single conditioning event (Gorn 1982), perhaps as many as 30 pairings may be required before conditioning is maximised. (Kroeber-Riel 1984)

Behaviours influenced by classical conditioning are thought to be involuntary. If the doorbell rings, it is automatic for most people to look up, without consciously thinking about whether somebody is at the door. Most people are familiar with the start of recognition that sometimes occurs if a similar doorbell is rung during a TV drama. Classical conditioning also operates on the emotions: playing Christmas music will elicit memories of childhood Christmases, and advertising which portrays events of the recent past will generate feelings of nostalgia.

Figure 4.14

Classical learning theory

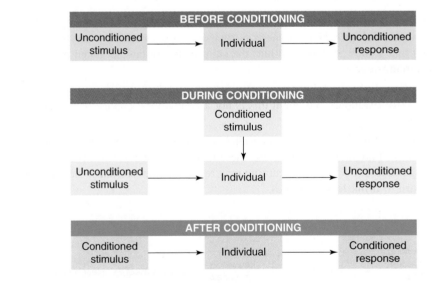

Another factor in the effectiveness of classical conditioning is the order in which the conditioned stimulus and the unconditioned stimulus are presented. In forward conditioning the conditioned stimulus (CS) comes before the unconditioned stimulus (US). In the case of conditioning via an advertising jingle, forward conditioning would mean that the product would be shown before the music is played.

In backward conditioning the US (unconditioned stimulus) comes before the CS (conditioned stimulus). Here the music would be played before the product is shown. Simultaneous conditioning requires both to be presented at the same time.

It appears that forward conditioning and simultaneous conditioning work best in advertising (McSweeney and Bierley 1984). This means that it is usually better to present the product before playing the popular tune, or play both together; the responses from this approach are usually stronger and longer-lasting.

Extinction occurs when the conditioned stimulus no longer evokes the conditioned response. This occurs in the ways shown in Table 4.5.

Generalisation happens when a stimulus that is close to the existing one evokes the same response. Pavlov found that a sound similar to the bell he used could also stimulate salivation, and it is often the case that a similar brand name can evoke a purchase response. A very common tactic in marketing is to produce similar packaging to that of one's competitor in order to take advantage of the generalisation effect. For an example of this, observe the similarity in the packaging between Tesco's Premium coffee and Nescafe Gold Blend (there is more on this in Chapter 12).

Discrimination is the process by which we learn to distinguish between stimuli, and only respond to the appropriate one. Consumers quite quickly learn to distinguish between brands, even when the design of the packaging is similar. Advertisers will often encourage discrimination by pairing a positive US with their own product, but not with the competitor's product. Classical conditioning is responsible for many repetitive advertising campaigns, and for many catchphrases which are now in common use.

forward conditioning The conditioned stimulus comes before the unconditioned stimulus.

backward conditioning The unconditioned stimulus comes before the conditioned stimulus.

simultaneous conditioning The conditioned stimulus and the unconditioned stimulus are offered at the same time.

extinction The gradual weakening of conditioning over time.

generalisation The tendency for the individual to react in several ways to the conditioned stimulus.

discrimination The ability to distinguish between similar stimuli.

Table 4.5 Extinction of conditioning

Reason for Extinction	Example	Explanation	Techniques to avoid extinction
The conditioned stimulus is encountered without the unconditioned stimulus.	The product is shown without the background music.	Seeing the product without the music tends to reduce the association of the music with the product; other stimuli will replace the music.	Ensure that all the advertising uses the same music, or imagery associated with the music.
The unconditioned stimulus is encountered without the conditioned stimulus.	The background music is heard without the product being present.	In this case, other stimuli may be evoked by the music; it will become associated with something other than the product.	Either ensure that the music is not played anywhere other than when the product is being shown, or ensure that the product is available when the music is played. For example, ensure that the club has an ample supply of the drink you are advertising.

Classical conditioning assumes that the individual plays no active role in the learning process. Pavlov's dogs did not have to do anything in order to be 'conditioned', because the process was carried out on their involuntary reflex of salivation. Although classical conditioning does operate in human beings, people are not usually passive in the process; the individual person (and most higher animals, in fact) is able to take part in the process and cooperate with it or avoid it. This process of active role-playing is called operant conditioning.

reinforcement Increasing the strength of learning by rewarding appropriate behaviour.

Skinner discovered operant conditioning by experimenting with rats.

Operant conditioning

Here the learner will conduct trial-and-error behaviour to obtain a reward (or avoid a punishment). Burris F. Skinner (1953) developed the concept in order to explain higher-level learning than that identified by Pavlov. The difference between Pavlov's approach and the operant conditioning approach is that the learner has choice in the outcome; the modern view of classical conditioning is that it also involves a cognitive dimension. In other words, Skinner is describing a type of learning that requires the learner to do something rather than be a passive recipient of a stimulus; the modern view is that even Pavlov's dog would have thought 'Here comes dinner' when the bell rang.

The basis of operant conditioning is the concept of **reinforcement**. If a consumer buys a product and is pleased with the outcome of using it, then he or she is likely to buy the product again. This means that the activity has had a positive reinforcement, and the consumer has become 'conditioned' to buy the product next time. The greater the positive reinforcement, the greater the likelihood of repeat purchase.

If the reward works, the consumer will try to think of a way to make it even better. 'If a little will help, a lot will cure'. This can lead to over-indulgence in food or alcohol, or indeed almost any other pleasurable activity. Typically this will happen if the consumer's need cannot be totally met by the product, but will be helped; a person with a serious psychological problem may well find that alcohol helps, but doesn't cure. An increasing intake of alcohol will never result in a complete meeting of the person's psychological needs because eventually sobriety will begin to set in again.

Airline loyalty schemes are aimed at reinforcing frequent flyers, whose loyalty is desirable since they are likely to be the most profitable customers. The airlines offer free flights to their most regular customers, and for many business travellers these free flights offer an attractive reason for choosing the same airline every time.

Talking Point

Operant conditioning appears to suggest that we are all simply acting on the basis of what is pleasurable or gratifying. But isn't this a rather depressing view of human beings? Don't people ever do things just to help others, even when it might be damaging to their own self-interest?

Or perhaps the warm glow we get from helping others is also part of operant conditioning? Maybe we hope that self-sacrifice will be our ticket to happiness – and that the reward of generosity is knowing that we have achieved the moral high ground.

On the other hand, maybe we should be admiring of people for whom altruistic behaviour is gratifying. After all, there are enough people around who appear to find antisocial behaviour gratifying, so why not accept that there is something in altruism after all?

Figure 4.15 shows three forms of operant conditioning. In the first example, positive reinforcement, the individual receives a stimulus and acts upon it. This action works, and the individual gets a good result; this leads to the behaviour being repeated if the same antecedent stimulus is presented at a later date. For example, in India many historic attractions have ladies-only ticket queues. The chivalrous Indian men form a very long

Courtesy of the BF Skinner Foundation

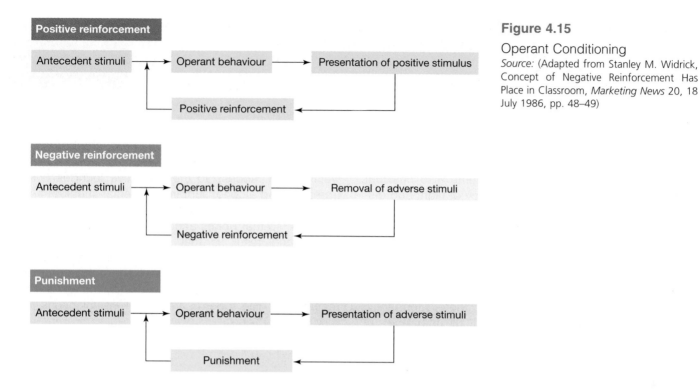

Figure 4.15

Operant Conditioning
Source: (Adapted from Stanley M. Widrick, Concept of Negative Reinforcement Has Place in Classroom, *Marketing News* 20, 18 July 1986, pp. 48–49)

queue to buy their tickets, while the Western tourists send their wives to buy the tickets at the ladies-only queue. This behaviour is rewarded by a shorter wait, so tourists quickly learn that this is the best way to buy tickets and repeat the process at every other opportunity.

The second example in the diagram shows a negative stimulus; this time the operant behaviour relieves the problem, and again the individual has learned how to avoid bad consequences when faced with a difficulty.

The third example shows how punishment fits into the learning process. If the operant behaviour leads to a bad result, for example the other people queuing become angry at the queue-jumping tactic, the individual won't try that tactic again. The problem with punishment as a motivator is that it may lead to the individual not visiting the attractions in future.

Operant conditioning does not necessarily require a product purchase; marketers will frequently give away free samples in the hope that a positive experience from using the product will encourage consumers to purchase in future. Likewise, car dealers always offer a test drive.

Operant conditioning is helpful in explaining how people become conditioned, or form habits of purchase; however, it still does not explain how learning operates when people become active in seeking out information. To understand this aspect of learning, it is necessary to look at the cognitive learning process.

Cognitive learning

Not all learning is just an automatic response to a stimulus. People analyse purchasing situations taking into account previous experiences, and make evaluative judgements. Learning is part of this, both in terms of informing the process as a result of earlier experiences, and also in terms of the consumer's approach to learning more about the product category or brand.

Marketing in Practice
KLM Flying Dutchman

KLM's frequent-flyer programme, Flying Dutchman, offers more than just free flights. Frequent flyers collect points which build towards various awards – free flights, free hotel rooms, upgrades, car hire discounts and so forth. But the scheme also has four different levels, based on frequency of flight and distance flown. At Blue Plus level, the frequent flyer can accumulate points towards rewards. Provided the individual travels frequently enough, he or she can be moved up to Silver Elite level, at which level the frequent flyer becomes entitled to use the executive lounges at airports, has priority check-in, an extra baggage allowance and so forth. More importantly, the rate of earning miles rises as the level of membership rises, so that points accumulate faster the higher up the scheme one rises. By the time the frequent flyer is at Platinum level, he or she has 20kg of extra baggage allowance, maximum priority for waiting lists, access to the executive lounges (with free food and alcohol supplied), special check-in and ticket-purchase priorities and 125 per cent bonuses on miles, so that points accumulate even faster.

The end result is that KLM frequent flyers are encouraged to stay with the scheme and try to increase the number and frequency of their flights – the system is as easy to get into as a pair of handcuffs, and as hard to retreat from. The rewards are almost instantaneous for KLM frequent flyers.

Figure 4.16

Cognitive learning

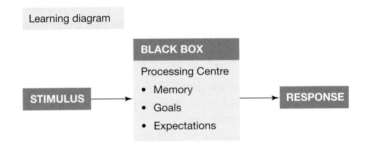

When considering cognitive learning, the emphasis is not on what is learned (as in stimulus-response theories) but on how it is learned. Classical learning and operant conditioning theories suppose that learning is automatic; cognitive learning theories assume that there is a conscious process going on.

The classical and operant theories assume that what goes on inside the consumer's head is a 'black box', in that we know that a given stimulus will prompt a particular response, but for most practical purposes we have no real way of knowing what is happening inside the black box. Within the cognitive learning paradigm, however, we are concerned with what happens inside the box, and we try to infer what is going on by analysing behaviour and responses from the individual. Figure 4.16 illustrates this.

The black box contains the cognitive processes; the stimulus is considered in the light of the individual's memory of what has happened in the past when presented with similar stimuli, his or her assessment of the desirable outcome, and an assessment of the likely outcome of any action. Following this processing the individual produces a response.

Cognitive learning expertise has five aspects:

- Cognitive effort
- Cognitive structure
- Analysis
- Elaboration
- Memory.

Cognitive effort is the degree of effort the consumer is prepared to put into thinking about the product offering. This will depend on such aspects as the complexity of the product, the consumer's involvement with it and the motivation for learning.

Cognitive structure is about the way the consumer thinks and the way the information is fitted into the existing knowledge. The analysis of information is concerned first with selecting the correct, relevant information from the environment, and second with interpreting the information correctly in order to obtain a clear action plan.

Elaboration is the structuring of the information within the brain, and adding to it from memory in order to form a coherent whole.

Memory is the mechanism by which learned information is stored. In fact, nothing is ever truly forgotten; information will eventually become irrecoverable by the conscious mind (forgotten), but the brain still retains the information and can be stimulated to recall it, either by hypnosis or by association of ideas.

Cognitive learning processes are important to marketers since they are helpful in predicting consumer responses to advertising. Hoch and Ha (1986) say that consumers view advertisements as tentative hypotheses about product performance that can be tested through product experience. Early learning about a product will affect future learning: this is called the **law of primacy**. For this reason first impressions count for a great deal.

Advertising will tend to be ignored if there is unambiguous objective evidence to hand. If the evidence is ambiguous or unobtainable at first hand (as is often the case) advertising appears to have an effect on consumer perceptions.

Learning from experience is a four-stage process, as Table 4.6 shows.

In most cases people prefer to learn by experience, especially for major product purchases; few people would buy a car without having a test drive first, and still fewer would buy one by mail order unless they were people with previous direct experience of the car. It is for this reason that mail-order companies have a no-quibble money-back guarantee; if this were not the case, few people would be prepared to buy by post rather than visit a high-street shop where they can see and feel the goods.

There are also three moderating factors in the cognitive learning process;

1 **Familiarity** with the domain. This is the degree to which the consumer has pre-existing knowledge of the product category.

2 Motivation to learn. If the purchase is an important one, or the possible effects of making a mistake would be serious, the consumer is likely to be highly motivated to obtain as much information as possible.

3 **Ambiguity** of the information environment. If the information is hard to get, contradictory or incomprehensible this will hinder the learning process. Sometimes consumers give up on the process if this is the case.

cognitive effort The degree of effort the consumer is prepared to put into thinking about the product offering.

cognitive structure The way information is fitted into the existing knowledge.

elaboration The structuring of the information within the brain, and adding to it from memory in order to form a coherent whole.

memory The mechanism by which learned information is stored.

law of primacy The law which states that early learning about an object will colour future experiences of the object, and future interpretations of that experience.

Visiting a motor show is a good way to learn about cars.

familiarity The degree to which an object is known.

ambiguity The degree to which stimuli can be interpreted in different ways.

Table 4.6 Learning from experience

Stage	Explanation	Example	Marketing response
Hypothesising	Developing a rough estimate of what's available.	Getting information from a friend, reading advertising material or brochures.	Have clearly written brochures and advertising, without too much jargon.
Exposure	Obtaining direct experience of the product.	Visiting a shop to try the product and ask questions about it.	Ensure that the product is on display, and allow plenty of opportunity for hands-on testing.
Encoding	Making sense of the information.	Translating the information, understanding what the product is and does in terms which fit in with previous experience.	Have sales people who can explain things in lay terms, and who do not frighten the customer off by using too much technical language.
Integration	Fitting the new information into the existing knowledge bank.	Thinking about the new information gained about the product, and discarding previous misconceptions.	Ensure that customers feel able to come back for further explanations if they still have problems. Make sure that customers understand everything before leaving the shop.

Figure 4.17 illustrates these moderating factors in terms of classifying readiness to learn from experience.

Cognitive theories recognise that consumers influence the outcome in an active manner, so the learning process is not always easy for an outsider (i.e. a marketing person) to manage. This may be part of the reason why new products fail so frequently: weak motivation to learn about new products leads to difficulty for marketers in starting the learning process.

Cognitive learning has five elements, as follows;

1 *Drive*. Drive is the stimulus that impels action. The impulse to learn can be driven by a fear of making an expensive mistake, or by a desire to maximise the benefits of the purchase.

cue An external trigger which encourages learning.

2 Cue. This is some external trigger which encourages learning. It is weaker than a drive, is external and is specific. For example, a public service such as the Health and Safety Council might exhort employers to send for a leaflet on safety in the workplace. Sometimes firms will use advertisement retrieval cues to trigger responses.

response The reaction the consumer makes to the interaction between a drive and a cue.

3 Response. This is the reaction the consumer makes to the interaction between a drive and a cue.

4 *Reinforcement*. Purchase response should be rewarded with a positive experience of the product. The object of reinforcement is to ensure that consumers associate the product with specific benefits.

How motivated are consumers to learn?	What do consumers already know?	How much can experience teach?	
		Little (high ambiguity)	**A lot (low ambiguity)**
HIGHLY MOTIVATED	**Unfamiliar**	Learning is most susceptible to management.	Learning is spontaneous, rapid and difficult to manage.
	Familiar	Formation of superstitious beliefs is possible. Existing beliefs inhibit suggestibility.	
WEAKLY MOTIVATED	**Unfamiliar**	Learning is slow to start and difficult to sustain, but is susceptible to management.	Learning is difficult to initiate and once started difficult to manage.
	Familiar	Complacency inhibits initiation of learning, so experience is unresponsive to management.	

Source: Hoch and Deighton (1989): Managing what consumers learn from experience. *Journal of Marketing* **53** (April), 1–20.

Figure 4.17

Moderating factors in cognitive learning

5 **Retention**. This is the stability of the learned material over time, or in other words, how well it is remembered. (The opposite of retention is extinction).

retention The stability of learned material over time.

Learned responses are never truly unlearned. The brain remembers (stores) everything, but rather like a computer with a faulty disk drive, it may not always be able to recall (retrieve) everything. Also, the human memory is huge; the *Encyclopaedia Britannica* contains 12 500 million characters, but the brain has a 125 000 000 million character storage capacity. This is enough storage to hold 10 000 *Encyclopaedia Britannicas*, which makes the human brain easily the world's most powerful computer (*Business Week* 1990).

Perception

Human beings have considerably more than five senses. Apart from the basic five (touch, taste, smell, sight, hearing) there are senses of direction, sense of balance, a clear knowledge of which way is down and so forth. Each sense is feeding information to the brain constantly, and the amount of information being collected would seriously overload the system if one took it all in. The brain therefore selects from the environment around the individual and cuts out the extraneous noise.

In effect, the brain makes automatic decisions as to what is relevant and what is not. Even though there may be many things happening around the individual, the person is unaware of most of them; in fact, experiments have shown that some information is filtered out by the optic nerve even before it gets to the brain. People quickly learn to ignore extraneous noises. For example, as a visitor to someone else's home you may be sharply aware of a loudly-ticking clock, whereas your host may be entirely used to it and unaware of it except when making a conscious effort to check that the clock is still

subjectivity Relating to the individual.

categorisation Filing information alongside similar information in the memory.

selectivity Selecting from external stimuli.

running. Therefore the information entering the brain does not provide a complete view of the world.

When the individual constructs a world view, he or she then assembles the remaining information to map what is happening in the outside world. Any gaps (and there will, of course, be plenty of these) will be filled in with imagination and experience. The cognitive map is therefore not a 'photograph': it is a construct of the imagination. This mapping will be affected by the following factors;

1   **Subjectivity.** This is the existing world view within the individual, and is unique to that individual.

2   **Categorisation.** This is the 'pigeonholing' of information, and the prejudging of events and products. This can happen through a process known as chunking, whereby the individual organises information into chunks of related items (Miller 1956). For example, a picture seen while a particular piece of music is playing might be chunked as one item in the memory, so that sight of the picture evokes the music and vice versa.

3   **Selectivity** is the degree to which the brain is selecting from the environment. It is a function of how much is going on around the individual, and also of how selective (concentrated) the individual is on the current task. Selectivity is also subjective: some people are a great deal more selective than others. Sometimes people select information simply because they assume it will be useful – this appears to be true of novel names for paint colours (Miller and Khan 2003).

4   **Expectations** lead individuals to interpret later information in a specific way. For example, look at this series of numbers and letters;

A 13 C D E F G H I
10 11 12 13 14 15 16

In fact, the number 13 appears in both series, but in the first series it would be interpreted as a B because that is what the brain is being led to expect. (The B in Matura MT Script looks like this; **B**)

5   **Past experience** leads us to interpret later experience in the light of what we already know. This is called the Law of Primacy by psychologists. Sometimes sights, smells or sounds from our past will trigger off inappropriate responses; the smell of baking bread may recall a village bakery from 20 years ago, but in fact the smell could have been artificially generated by an aerosol spray near the supermarket bread counter.

An example of cognitive mapping as applied to perception of product quality might run as follows. First, the consumer uses the input selector to select clues and assign values to them. For quality, the cues are typically price, brand name, and retailer name. There are strong positive relationships between price and quality in most consumers' perceptions, and brand name and quality; although the retailer name is less significant, it still carries some weight. For example, many consumers would feel confident that Harrod's would sell higher-quality items than the local corner shop, but might be less able to distinguish between Sainsbury's and Tesco.

subjective Appertaining to the individual.

The information is **subjective** in that the consumer will base decisions on the selected information. Each of us selects differently from the environment, and each of us has differing views. For example, illiterate people have different cognitive approaches as well as different heuristics: they tend to be swayed more by pictorial evidence, and prefer concrete reasoning (Viswathanan *et al.* 2005). Likewise, people tend to assess information as being stronger when it is framed within a short timescale – saying that almost 1000 people a day die of smoking is more powerful than saying that 440 000 people a year die of it (Chandran and Menon 2003).

Information about quality will be pigeonholed, or categorised; the individual may put Jaguars in the same category as BMW, or perhaps put Sony in the same slot as Hitachi.

Selectivity will depend on how much is going on in the environment, on the individual's interest and motivation regarding the subject area and on the degree of concentration the individual has on the task in hand. People with a highly-developed ability to concentrate select less from the environment, because they are able to 'shut out' the world much more. In a cluttered environment, the use of colour will reduce search times because it cuts through the selection process better (Jansson, Marlow and Bristow 2004).

Expectations of quality play a huge part: if the individual is expecting a high-quality item, he or she will select evidence which supports that view and tend to ignore evidence that does not. Past experience will also play a part in quality judgement. If the consumer has had bad experiences of Japanese products, this might lead to a general perception that Japanese products are of poor quality.

Weber's Law states that the size of the least detectable change depends on the size of the stimulus. This means that a very intense stimulus will require a bigger change if the change is to be perceived by the consumer. For example, twenty pence off the price of a morning newspaper is a substantial discount, and would attract attention in advertising, whereas twenty pence off the price of a BMW would go unnoticed. Clearly at this level of intensity (a price of a few pence compared with a price of thousands of pounds) Weber's Law may not work very precisely (Britt and Nelson 1976), but in the middle range of prices the law appears to work well. Incidentally, reducing the price from £10 to £9.99p is very noticeable even though the actual reduction is only 0.01 per cent of the initial price. The important element here is that the reduction be noticeable. There is more on pricing in Chapter 14.

Weber's Law also applies to product differentiation. The law can be applied to determine how much better the product has to be for the difference to be noticeable (Britt 1975), or conversely to determine how similar the product needs to be to be indistinguishable from the leading brand.

It should be noted here that perception and reality are not different things. There is a popular view that perception somehow differs from reality; in fact, reality only exists in the heads of individuals. If there is an objective reality, it is not accessible to us as human beings; we only have what our senses tell us, and for each of us reality is different because each of us selects and synthesises in a different way.

From a marketing viewpoint, the fact that perception is so nebulous and individual a thing is probably helpful in the long run. Peoples' views of products and services rely heavily on perceived attributes, some of which have no objective reality; the difficulty for marketers lies in knowing what will be the general perception of the members of the market segments with whom they are attempting to do business.

Peer and Reference Groups and the Family

A group is two or more persons who share a set of norms and whose relationship makes their behaviour interdependent. A **reference group** is 'A person or group of people that significantly influences an individual's behaviour' (Beardon and Etzel 1982). The reference groups provide standards or norms by which consumers judge their attitudes and behaviour.

reference group A group from which one takes behavioural cues.

Originally groups formed for the purpose of cooperating on survival activities. Because human beings could cooperate in such activities as hunting, food-gathering and defence from predators, they were able to increase the chances of survival for the species as a whole. Interestingly, this still appears to hold true: social researchers have reported that socially-isolated people have mortality rates between 50 per cent and 300 per cent higher than people who are strongly integrated into groups (Koretz 1990).

Most people prefer to fit in with the group (to a greater or lesser extent). This is either through politeness or through a desire not to be left out of things. Particularly with groups

of friends, people will 'go along with the crowd' on a great many issues, and will tend to adopt the group norms regarding behaviour and attitudes (Asch 1951).

Reference groups fall into many possible groupings; the following list is not intended to be exhaustive.

primary group The group of people who are closest to the individual.

- **Primary groups** are composed of those people we see most often; friends, family, close colleagues. A primary group is small enough to permit face-to-face interaction on a regular basis, and there is cohesiveness and mutual participation, which results in similar beliefs and behaviour within the group.

secondary group A group to which one belongs, but to which one does not relate on a regular basis.

- **Secondary groups** are composed of people we see occasionally, and with whom we have some shared interest. For example, a trade association or a sports club would constitute a secondary group. These groups are correspondingly less influential in shaping attitudes and controlling behaviour, but can exert influence on behaviour within the purview of the subject of mutual interest.

aspirational groups Groups the individual would like to be a member of.

- **Aspirational groups** are the groups which the individual wants to join. These groups can be very powerful in influencing behaviour, because the individual will often adopt the behaviour of the aspirational group in the hopes of being accepted as a member.

dissociative group A group to which one would not wish to belong.

- **Dissociative groups** on the other hand are those groups with which the individual does not want to be associated. This can have a negative effect on behaviour; the individual avoids certain products or behaviours rather than be mistaken for somebody from the dissociative group. Like aspirational groups, the definition of a group as dissociative is purely subjective.

formal group A group with a known, recorded membership list.

- **Formal groups** have a known list of members, very often recorded somewhere. An example might be a professional association or a club. Usually the rules and structure of the group are laid down in writing; there are rules for membership, and members' behaviour is constrained while they remain part of the group. However, the constraints usually only apply to fairly limited areas of behaviour.

informal group A group which does not have a fixed membership list or known rules.

- **Informal groups** are less structured and are typically based on friendship. An example would be an individual's circle of friends, which only exists for mutual moral support, company and sharing experiences. Although there can be even greater pressure to conform than would be the case with a formal group, there is nothing in writing.

automatic group/category group A group to which one belongs by virtue of birth.

- **Automatic groups** are those groups to which one belongs by virtue of age, gender, culture or education. These are sometimes also called **category groups**. Although at first sight it may seem that these groups would not exert much influence on the members' behaviour, because these are groups which have not been joined voluntarily, it would appear that people are influenced by group pressure to conform. For example, when buying clothes older people are sometimes reluctant to look like 'mutton dressed as lamb'. Sometimes people prefer to buy and wear second-hand clothes, either for nostalgic reasons or to show how thrifty they are (Roux and Korcha 2006), and shoes have been shown to carry many symbolic aspects (Belk 2003). Also, religion influences shopping behaviour even for apparently 'neutral' products such as television sets (Essoo and Dibb 2004).

The above categories of group are not mutually exclusive. A dissociative group could also be an informal one; a formal group can be a secondary group (and often is) and so forth. For example, one may not wish to become friends with a group of drunken hooligans (who see themselves as an informal group of friends having a good time). Likewise the golf club could be a place of refuge to which one retreats to have a quiet drink with like-minded people as well as a place where golf is played.

Marketing in Practice
Tribalism

Some recent thinking has likened groups to tribes. Neo-tribalism applies to primary groups and, to an extent, to secondary groups, but the emphasis on consumption is in the linking powers of the product rather than its utility as a product. For example, the France Telecom pager, Tatoo, has been marketed in a tribal way by using in-line roller skaters as an example tribe. Roller skaters are used in the firm's promotion, with events being organised for them and advertising built around them, even though (of course) the company's target market is much wider. The approach has been highly successful, but attempts by other firms to cash in on the idea have not always worked. Caisse D'Epargne, a French bank, tried launching a savings account called Tribu, but it was a complete failure because the account had no specific linking features. (Cova and Cova 2001).

Table 4.7 Group Influence

Type of	Definition	Explanation	Example
Normative Compliance	The pressure exerted on an individual to conform and comply.	Works best when social acceptance is a strong motive, strong pressures exist from the group, and the product or service is conspicuous in its use.	Street gangs require their members to wear specific jackets or other uniform. The members want to be accepted, the pressure to wear the jacket is great, and the jacket itself is a conspicuous badge of membership.
Value-Expressive Influence	The pressure that comes from the need for psychological association with a group.	The desired outcome is respect from others; this pressure comes from the need for esteem, rather than from the need to belong.	The businessman in his pinstripe suit, the hippy in his colourful shirt, sweatband and jeans are both seeking respect from others by expressing a set of values in the way they dress.
Informational Influence	The influence arising from a need to seek information from the reference group about the product category being considered.	People often need to get expert advice and opinion about their product choices. This can often be provided by the appropriate reference group.	Many professional organisations and trade bodies offer their members free advice about useful products for their businesses. Clearly a recommendation for, say, computer software for a hairdressing business would be well received if it came from the Hairdressers Federation.

(Source: After Engel, Blackwell and Miniard 1995)

Reference groups affect consumer choice in three ways, as shown in Table 4.7.

Of the above three influences, **normative compliance** is probably the most powerful. The source of normative compliance lies in operant conditioning: the individual finds that conforming behaviour results in group approval and esteem, whereas non-conforming behaviour results in group disapproval. Eventually the 'good' behaviour becomes automatic and natural, and it would be difficult to imagine any other way of doing things.

normative compliance The pressure to conform to group norms of behaviour.

8

Talking Point

The principles of good moral behaviour are not absolutes – they are the result (in most cases) of normative compliance with a reference group.

If moral behaviour is simply the result of normative compliance, where does that leave the world's major religions? Each one lays down a moral code, often on the basis of a set of laws for reasonable behaviour towards other people.

Or is it possible that the framers of such laws operate by considering what is reasonable group behaviour? Are they, in fact, setting out normative compliance parameters? Perhaps more to the point – if normative compliance is so powerful, why do we need such guidelines at all?

Of course, the pressure to conform will only work on someone who has a strong motivation to be accepted. If the pressure is coming from an aspirational group, this is likely to be the case; if, on the other hand, the pressure is coming from a dissociative group, the reverse will be the case and the individual will not feel under any pressure to conform. For example, most law-abiding citizens would comply with instructions from the police, and would usually go out of their way to help the police. Criminals, on the other hand, might avoid helping the police even in circumstances where their own crimes were not at issue.

The conspicuousness of the product or service is also crucial to the operation of normative compliance. For example, if all an individual's friends vote Labour the person might be under some pressure to do likewise, but since the ballot is secret nobody will know if he or she votes Conservative instead, so there is little pressure for normative compliance. Likewise, if one's friends all drink Stella Artois lager one may feel under pressure to do the same, but might be happy with supermarket own-brand when having a beer in the back garden at home.

Normative compliance is in decline in the Western world due to the shifting social paradigm towards a more **inner-directed** society (McNulty 1985). The reduction in face-to-face interaction may be leading to this move away from normative compliance; increasingly people communicate by impersonal means such as telephone, email and fax. Whether this is a cause of the paradigm shift or one of its effects is difficult to decide at present, but research by the Future Foundation indicates that people with a greater sense of independence, less concerned about material wealth and more concerned about experiences, and more idealistic (dubbed high-I people) are much more prolific users of the new communications technologies (Howard and Mason 2001).

inner-directed Motivated by forces originating within the individual.

The reference group will not exert influence over every buying decision. Even in circumstances in which group influence does come into play, the consumer will be influenced by other variables such as product characteristics, standards of judgement and conflicting influences from other groups. Table 4.8 shows some of the determinants of reference group influence.

The effectiveness of the role model in modelling behaviour will depend on the personal characteristics of the role model. Attractive models will be imitated more than unattractive ones, successful-looking models are given more credence than unsuccessful-looking ones, and a model who is perceived as being similar to the observer is also more likely to be emulated (Baker and Churchill 1977). There is also some evidence to show that observers are more likely to identify with role models who have some difficulty in completing the modelled task (Manz and Sims 1981).

Recent research seems to indicate that poor people are more influenced by informal reference groups, whereas wealthier people are more influenced by formal groups. The research was conducted with expectant mothers who were choosing maternity services, which is of course a high-involvement decision in virtually all cases. This may have had some effect on the findings (Tinson and Ensor 2001).

Table 4.8 Determinants of reference group influence

Determinant	Definition	Explanation	Example
Judgement standards	The criteria used by the individual to evaluate the need to conform.	Judgement standards are **objective** when the group norms are obvious and when the group approach is clearly the sensible course of action. The standards are **subjective** when it is not clear which is the most sensible course of action.	Decisions of the Government are often portrayed as being unanimous. This is to protect the illusion that the ruling party is united, since discord is often seen as a sign of weakness.
Product characteristics	The features of the product that are salient to the group influence.	The two main characteristics necessary for group influence to work are that the product should be **visible**, and that it should stand out (**non-universal ownership**).	Designer T-shirts have the designer's name written prominently across the front. This is often the only distinguishing feature of the product.
Member characteristics	The traits of the group member which make him or her more or less susceptible to group pressures.	People vary considerably in the degree to which they are influenced by the pressures from the group. Some people remain fairly independent, while others conform habitually. Personality, status and security all seem to play major roles in determining whether an individual will conform or not.	It transpires that university students are much more likely to conform with group norms than housewives (Park and Lessig 1977). This is possibly because the university students are young, poor and often away from home, so have a greater need to belong.
Group characteristics	The features of the group that influence individuals to conform.	The power of the group to influence the individual varies according to size, cohesiveness and leadership. Once the group is bigger than three members, the power to influence levels off. This is probably because the group has difficulty reaching a consensus. Likewise, the stronger the leadership, the greater the influence, and the greater the cohesiveness the stronger the influence, because the group reaches a clear decision.	Most smokers take up the habit as a result of peer group pressure when they are aged around twelve or thirteen. If a child's friends are strongly anti-smoking, the influence from advertisers and even family background is likely to be much less.
Role model	An individual whose influence is similar to that of a group.	A role model is a hero, a star, or just somebody the individual respects and admires, and wishes to imitate.	Imitating film stars has a long history. When Clark Gable removed his shirt in the 1930s to reveal that he was not wearing a vest, sales of vests plummeted. More recently, rap artist Nelly's style of sticking two adhesive plasters on his face has been copied throughout the UK by fans.

The Family

objective Not subject to bias from the individual.

subjective Appertaining to the individual.

visible Able to be seen by others.

non-universal ownership Not owned by people who are not members of the group.

Of all the reference groups, the family is probably the most powerful in influencing consumer decision-making. The reasons for this are as follows;

1 In the case of children, the parental influence is the earliest, and therefore colours the child's perception of everything that follows.

2 In the case of parents, the desire to do the best they can for their children influences their decision-making when making purchases for the family. Clear examples are the purchase of breakfast cereals such as Ready Brek, and disposable nappies, where the appeal is almost invariably to do with the comfort and well-being of the baby.

3 In the case of siblings, the influence comes either as role model (where the sibling is older) or as carer/adviser (where the sibling is younger).

Within the UK a family is usually defined in narrow terms – the parents and their offspring. However, in most families there will also be influences from uncles, aunts, grandparents and cousins. While these influences are often less strong in UK households than they might be in some other countries where the extended family is more common, the influences still exist to a greater or lesser extent. One of the changes currently occurring throughout Western Europe is the increase in the number of single-person households (European Commission 2005); there is, of course, a difference between a household and a family. A further change, coming about through the tremendous increase in the divorce rate, is the growing number of single-parent families.

There is also a problem here with terminology. Traditionally, studies of the family have referred to the male partner as the husband and the female partner as the wife. The increasing number of families in which the parents are not married has rendered this approach obsolete; even the definition of what constitutes a family is in doubt, because of the many different forms of relationships which have emerged. The traditional family group of a mother, a father and their children now accounts for less than 10 per cent of households in the UK, for example.

From a marketing viewpoint, the level of demand for many products is dictated more by the number of households than by the number of families. The relevance of families to marketing is therefore much more about consumer behaviour than about consumer demand levels.

In terms of its function as a reference group, the family is distinguished by the following characteristics:

1 *Face-to-face contact.* Family members see each other every day or thereabouts, and interact as advisers, information providers and sometimes deciders. Other reference groups rarely have this level of contact.

2 *Shared consumption.* Durables such as fridges, freezers, televisions and furniture are shared, and food is collectively purchased and cooked (although there is a strong trend away from families eating together). Purchase of these items is often collective: children even participate in decision-making on such major purchases as cars and houses. Other reference groups may share some consumption (for example, a model railway club may hire a workshop and share tools) but families share consumption of most domestic items. In some cases, products are handed down from one generation to another, reinforcing family values and traditions (Curasi 2006; Hartman and Kiecker 2004).

3 *Subordination of individual needs.* Because consumption is shared, some family members will find that the solution chosen is not one that fully meets their needs. Although this happens in other reference groups, the effect is more pronounced in families.

4 *Purchasing agent.* Because of the shared consumption, most families will have one member who does most, or all, of the shopping. Traditionally, this has been

the mother of the family, but increasingly the purchasing agent is the older children of the family – even pre-teens are sometimes taking over this role. The reason for this is the increase in the number of working mothers – women who work outside the home – which has left less time for shopping. This has major implications for marketers, since pre-teens and young teens generally watch more TV than adults and are therefore more open to marketing communications.

The above characteristics can also serve as a definition of a family. Whatever the composition of its members, the above list constitutes a convenient way of identifying what constitutes a family and what does not.

Family decision-making is not as straightforward as marketers have supposed in the past. There has been an assumption that the purchasing agent (e.g. the mother) is the one who makes the decisions, and while this is often the case, this approach ignores the ways in which the purchase decisions are arrived at.

Role specialisation is critical in family decision-making because of the sheer number of different products that must be bought each year in order to keep the family supplied. What this means in practice is that, for example, the family member responsible for doing the cooking is also likely to take the main responsibility for shopping for food. The family member who does the most driving is likely to make the main decision about the car and its accessories, servicing, fuelling and so forth; the family gardener buys the gardening products, and so on.

Product category affects role specialisation and decision-making systems. When an expensive purchase is being considered, it is likely that most of the family will be involved in some way, if only because major purchases affect the family budgeting for other items. At the other end of the scale, day-to-day shopping for toilet rolls and cans of beans entails very little collective decision-making. Where the product has a shared usage (a holiday or a car) the collective decision-making component is likely to increase greatly. Conversely, where the product is used predominantly by one family member, that member will dominate the decision-making even when the purchase is a major one (the family chef will make most of the decision about the new cooker, for example).

The family may well adopt different roles according to the decision-making stage. At the problem-recognition stage of, for example, the need for new shoes for the children, the children themselves may be the main contributors. The mother may then decide what type of shoes should be bought, and the father may be the one who takes the children to buy the shoes. It is reasonable to suppose that the main user of the product might be important in the initial stages, with perhaps joint decision-making at the final purchase.

Other determinants might include such factors as whether both parents are earning. In such families, decision-making is more likely to be joint because each has a financial stake in the outcome. Some studies seem to indicate that family decision-making is more likely to be husband-dominated when the husband is the sole earner, whereas couples who are both earning make decisions jointly (Filiatrault and Ritchie 1980). Males also tend to dominate highly-technical durable products (e.g. home computers).

Conflict resolution tends to have an increased importance in family decision-making as opposed to individual purchase behaviour. The reason for this is that, obviously, more people are involved, each with their own needs and their own internal conflicts to resolve. The conflict resolution system is as laid out in Table 4.9.

Influence of children on buying decisions

First-born children generate more economic impact than subsequent babies. Around 40 per cent of babies are first-born; they are photographed more, they get all new clothes

Table 4.9 Conflict resolution in families

Resolution method	Explanation
Persuasion through information exchange	When a conflict occurs, each family member seeks to persuade the others of his or her point of view. This leads to discussion, and ultimately some form of compromise.
Role expectation	If persuasion fails, a family member may be designated to make the decision. This is usually somebody who has the greatest expertise in the area of conflict being discussed. This method appears to be going out of fashion as greater democracy in family decision-making is appearing.
Establishment of norms	Families will often adopt rules for decision-making. Sometimes this will involve taking turns over making decisions (perhaps over which restaurant the family will go to this week, or where they will go on holiday).
Power exertion	This is also known as browbeating. One family member will try to exert power to force the other members to comply; this may be a husband who refuses to sign the cheque unless he gets his own way, or a wife who refuses to cook the dinner until the family agree, or a child who throws a tantrum. The person with the most power is called the **least dependent person** because he or she is not as dependent on the other family members. Using the examples above, if the wife has her own income she will not need to ask the husband to sign the cheque; if the other family members can cook they can get their own dinner; if the family can ignore the yelling toddler long enough, eventually the child will give up.

(Adapted from Onkvisit and Shaw 1994.)

least dependent person The individual with the most power in a group.

(no hand-me-downs) and get more attention all round. First-born and only children have a higher achievement rate than their siblings, and since the birth-rate is falling there are more of them proportionally. More and more couples are choosing to have only one child, and families larger than two children are becoming a rarity. Childlessness is also more common now than it was 30 years ago.

Children also have a role in applying pressure to their parents to make particular purchasing decisions. The level of 'pester power' generated can be overwhelming, and parents will frequently give in the child's demands (Ekstrom, Tansuhaj and Foxman 1987). Children often develop sophisticated negotiating techniques in order to get their own way, highlighting the benefits of purchase and forming coalitions with siblings or parents (Thomson, Laing and McKee 2007).

Although the number of children is steadily declining, their importance as consumers is not. Apart from the direct purchases of things that children need, they influence decision-making to a marked extent. Children's development as consumers goes through five stages:

1 Observing
2 Making requests
3 Making selections
4 Making assisted purchases
5 Making independent purchases.

Research (*Marketing News* 1983) has shown that pre-teens and young teens have a greater influence on family shopping choices than do the parents themselves for these reasons:

1 Often they do the shopping anyway, because both parents are working and the children have the available time to go to the shops.

2 They watch more TV, so are more influenced and more knowledgeable about products.

3 They tend to be more attuned to consumer issues, and have the time to shop around for (for example) free-range eggs.

In some cases children even have the role of teaching their parents about new products (Ekstrom 2007). For example, many parents ask their children to help with such new products as mobile telephones and DVD players.

Children have to learn to be effective consumers, and this training comes mainly (but not only) from the parents. Parents who are too strict with their children, or who insist on making all the decisions (even when they are being essentially indulgent) will create dependant adults who are unable to make their own consumption decisions (Rose, Dalakis, Kropp and Kamineni 2002). Families also develop consistent purchasing behaviours through the generations – children often buy the same brands they remember from their childhoods, for example (Epp and Arnould 2006).

Self-Concept

Self-concept is the individual's feelings about himself or herself. Beliefs about ourselves are often the main drivers in what we buy: we buy things which enhance our image of ourselves both in our own eyes and in the eyes of others.

Each of us projects a **role** which is either accepted or rejected by other people. In effect, we are each playing a part: Erving Goffman (1969) originally conceived this as the **dramaturgical analogy**, that life is theatre and that each of us uses props, costume, script and make-up to play our roles. We even have a backstage area, where our most intimate friends and family see us. If our role is accepted by others, we are rewarded with applause: if it is rejected, we are made to feel awkward by those around us.

Self-image has four components:

1 **Real self**. This is the objective self that others observe.

2 **Self-image**. This is the subjective self, as we see ourselves.

3 **Ideal self**. The person we wish we were.

4 **Looking-glass self**. The way we think other people see us.

Recently, the concept of 'worst self' has been added. This is the negative aspect of self, and is usually the self which people seek to reduce within themselves (Banister and Hogg 2003). Each of these components has purchasing implications. The real self drives conspicuous consumption of cars, fashion, hairdressing and all the outward manifestations of self. Self-image drives purchases of goods which fit the values and lifestyle of the individual, both conspicuously and inconspicuously. Ideal self drives self-improvement purchases such as education, cosmetic surgery, musical instruments and self-help books. Looking-glass self is a reflection of real self, so similar drives will result.

Self-concept has been shown to drive people's behaviour on holiday. Some people clearly behave very differently on holiday than they do when at home, almost becoming new people: this reflects in the type of holiday purchased and the types of activities undertaken (Todd 2001).

Self-concept is, like attitude, learned and purposeful. It is also stable over time, within limits, and is unique to the individual.

self-concept One's view of oneself.

role The position one has in the group.

dramaturgical analogy The view that life is essentially theatrical in nature.

real self The objective self that others observe.

self-image The subjective self: the person we think we are.

ideal self The person we wish we were.

looking-glass self The way we think other people see us.

worst self The negative aspects of one's personality: the aspects we wish to overcome in ourselves.

Summary

If consumers are at the centre of everything that marketers do, consumer behaviour should be the starting point in developing any marketing strategy. Consumer behaviour is not especially different from any other type of human behaviour: most behaviour is aimed at making life more convenient and comfortable. For human beings, this includes ensuring that we fit in with the people around us and do not attract ridicule or abuse from them. Human behaviour is complex, and involves many exchanges at many different levels. It is those exchanges which marketers seek to influence and facilitate.

The key points from this chapter are as follows:

- People are not entirely rational when making purchasing decisions – emotional issues are also involved.
- The less the individual knows about the product, the longer the problem-solving behaviour will take.
- The cost of obtaining information will be weighed against the value of the information.
- Goals operate in hierarchies: establishing an end goal will lead to establishing a set of sub-goals.
- Complaints should be encouraged, because a voiced complaint is easier to deal with and less damaging than either private complaints or third-party complaints.
- Operant conditioning involves action on the part of the person being conditioned.
- Families have the greatest influence on behaviour, but other groups are also important.
- Perception is both analytic and synthetic, but generates the only reality the individual has.
- Self-concept is one of the most important non-rational drivers for consumer behaviour.

Chapter review questions

1 What is the reason for developing a hierarchy of goals?

2 How does drive relate to motivation?

3 Under what circumstances would you expect someone to undertake an extensive external search?

4 Why do people become involved with specific brands?

5 What is the role of self-concept in buying fashion wear?

6 What are the factors which relate to the length of an information search?

7 What is the difference between perception and reality?

8 Why are families an important influence on decision-making?

9 Why is perception described as being both analytic and synthetic?

10 How might a service firm (such as a restaurant) minimise the perception of risk?

Preview case revisited
Cheap Shops

So what is the appeal for the customers? Perhaps it's the thrill of finding a real bargain. Perhaps it's the feeling of being a canny shopper. Perhaps it's simply a way of spending some time browsing (satisfying that hunter-gatherer instinct) without it costing too much.

People enjoy the shopping experience for itself. Practical shopping, for example buying in the week's groceries, is usually regarded as a chore rather than an enjoyable experience (even for foodies, going round the supermarket buying bread and eggs is hardly thrilling). Cheap shops provide the pleasure of browsing, for very

little outlay – and sometimes there will be something useful to be found. In many cases, the cheap plaster ornaments, badly-made clocks and flimsy kitchen utensils provide sources of humour, but in other cases the products on offer do actually work and are cheaper than would be paid elsewhere.

In some cases, products are available which are not on sale anywhere else: this is often the case with failed products, those which did not sell in sufficient numbers to interest a mainstream store.

Whatever the appeal, the stores keep bringing in the cash and sending out the tat!

Case Study
Comparison Websites

One of the arguments often put forward in the defence of marketing is that it increases consumer choice. Undoubtedly this is true – there are many more possibilities out there for consumers, and in fact there are so many different ways of meeting basic needs that people often become seriously confused by the choices which are available.

Traditional marketing communications methods (advertising, sales pitches and so forth) worked well until the advent of the Internet. Unfortunately, the Internet is able to provide so much information that people suffer from information overload – there is simply too much information out there! Even though the Internet has caused the problem, the Internet has also come up with the solution – comparison websites.

A comparison website searches the Internet for a solution based on customer need. Rather like a good salesperson, the website asks the individual to enter as much detail as possible about his or her needs and circumstances, then circulates the information to as many providers as are in the company's lists. Obviously not all providers are listed – comparison websites earn their keep from commissions paid by the ultimate service providers, and some companies are not prepared to pay the commission. Usually enough providers are listed for the consumers to make a reasonable choice, though, and it certainly does save time in terms of searching.

Or does it? A motorist looking for cheap car insurance may well find a good price comparison, but would then have to check that the policy covers him or her for driving in other countries, or allows him or her to drive occasionally for business purposes or even whether the policy covers legal expenses. Comparison sites appear to work best for intangible products which are fairly homogenous. Someone wishing to buy a sofa or a house will not be well-served by a comparison site: someone looking for house insurance or a new laptop probably will. Some of the big players in the market (such as confused.com) even play on the paradox that there are so many sites, all making the same claims, that it is difficult for consumers to choose between them.

Of course, people have to make the final decisions themselves. People are also responsible for the information they feed into the website – sometimes the questions can become tedious, and after filling several pages of forms on screen even the most avid bargain-hunter might become frustrated. As the confused.com website says, though, this is still better than filling in the same information over and over again on dozens of different companies' websites.

Since the information search takes up such a large amount of time, comparison websites certainly serve a purpose for consumers. However, comparison websites do have to make themselves known to consumers. Paradoxically, this usually means using traditional marketing communications media such as TV and radio.

As information clutter increases, and as consumers become more proactive in seeking information rather than simply being vessels for receiving advertising messages, comparison websites are likely to increase in importance. As vehicles for increasing consumer empowerment they have much to contribute – even if this means that companies are more likely to end up competing on price rather than on product benefits.

Questions

1 How do comparison websites affect the information search process?

2 What are the drawbacks of using a comparison website, from a consumer's viewpoint?

3 How might companies avoid competing on price?

4 What would drive someone to use a comparison website?

5 How can comparison websites meet consumer needs better?

References

Asch, S.E. (1951): Effects of group pressure on the modification and distortion of judgements. In H. Guetzkow (ed.) *Groups, Leadership and Men* (Pittsburgh, PA; Carnegie Press).

Bailey, A.A. (2004): Thiscompanysucks.com: the use of the Internet in negative consumer to consumer articulations. *Journal of Marketing Communications* **10**(3), 169–82.

Baker, M.J. and Churchill, G.A. Jr. (1977): The impact of physically attractive models on advertising evaluations. *Journal of Marketing Research* **14**(4), 538–55.

Balabanis, G. (2002): The relationship between lottery ticket and scratchcard buying behaviour, personality, and other compulsive behaviours. *Journal of Consumer Behaviour* **2**(1), 7–22.

Banister, E.N. and Hogg, M.K. (2003): Possible selves? Identifying dimensions for exploring dialectic between positive and negative selves in consumer behaviour. *Advances in Consumer Research* **30**(1).

Bauer, R.A. (1960): Consumer behaviour as risk taking. In R.S. Hancock (ed.) *Dynamic Marketing for a Changing World* (Chicago, IL: American Marketing Association).

Baumeister, R.F. (2004): Self-regulation, conscious choice, and consumer decisions. *Advances in Consumer Research* **31**(1).

Beardon, W.O. and Etzel, M.J. (1982): Reference group influence on product and brand purchase decisions. *Journal of Consumer Research* **9** (September), 184.

Belk, R. (2003): Shoes and self. *Advances in Consumer Research* **30**(1).

Blackwell, R.D., Miniard, P.W. and Engel, J.F. (2001): *Consumer Behaviour*, 9th edn (Mason, OH: South Western).

Bloch, P.H., Sherrell, D.L. and Ridgway, N.M. (1986): Consumer search: an extended framework. *Journal of Consumer Research* **13** (June), 119–26.

Britt, S.H. (1975): How Weber's Law can be applied to marketing. *Business Horizons* **13**(1), 21–30.

Britt, S.H. and Nelson, V.M. (1976): The marketing importance of the 'Just Noticeable Difference'. *Business Horizons* **14** (August), 38–40.

Bucklin, L (1963): Retail strategy and the classification of consumer goods. *Journal of Marketing* **27** (January), 50–4.

Business Week, 28th July 1990.

Chandran, S. and Menon, G. (2003): When am I at risk? Now, or now? The effects of temporal framing on perceptions of health risk. *Advances in Consumer Research* **30**(1).

Cobb, K.J., Walgren, G.C. and Hollowed, M. (1987): Differences in organisational responses to consumer letters of satisfaction and dissatisfaction. In M. Wallendorf and P. Anderson (eds) *Advances in Consumer Research*, vol. **14** (Provo, UT: Association for Consumer Research) pp. 227–31.

Coca-Cola Company, The (1981): *Measuring the Grapevine: Consumer Response and Word-of-Mouth.*

Cova, B. and Cova, V. (2001): Tribal aspects of postmodern consumption research: the case of French in-line roller skates. *Journal of Consumer Behaviour* **1**(1), 67–76.

Curasi, C.F. (2006): Maybe it is your father's Oldsmobile: the construction and reservation of family identity through the transfer of possessions. *Advances in Consumer Research* **33**(1), 83.

Day, R.L., Brabicke, K., Schaetzle, T. and Staubach, F. (1981): The hidden agenda of consumer complaining. *Journal of Retailing* **57** (Fall), 86–106.

Day, R (1984): Modelling choices among alternative responses to dissatisfaction. In T. Kinnear (ed.) *Advances in Consumer Research*, vol. **11** (Provo, UT: Association for Consumer Research), pp. 496–9.

Dewey, J. (1910): *How We Think* (Boston, MA: DC Heath and Co.).

Dibley, A. and Baker, S. (2001): Uncovering the links between brand choice and personal values among young British and Spanish girls. *Journal of Consumer Behaviour* **1**(1), 77–93.

Ekstrom, K.M. (2007): Parental consumer learning or 'keeping up with the children'. *Journal of Consumer Behaviour* **6**(4), 203–17.

Ekstrom, K.M., Tansuhaj, P.S. and Foxman, E. (1987): Children's influence in family decisions and consumer socialisation; a reciprocal view. In M. Wallendorf and P. Anderson (eds) *Advances in Consumer Research*, vol. **14** (Provo, UT: Association for Consumer Research), pp. 283–7.

Epp, A.M. and Arnould, E.J. (2006): Enacting the family legacy: how family themes influence consumption behaviour. *Advances in Consumer Research* **33**(1).

Essoo, N. and Dibb, S. (2004): Religious influences on shopping behaviour: an exploratory study. *Journal of Marketing Management* **20**(7/8), 683–712.

European Commission (2005): *Community Statistics on Income and Living Conditions* (Luxembourg: Statistical Office of the European Union.

Faber, R.J., O'Guinn, T.C. and Krych, R. (1987): Compulsive consumption. In M. Wallendorf and P. Anderson (eds), *Advances in Consumer Research*, vol. **14** (Provo, UT: Association for Consumer Research) pp. 132–5.

Filiatrault, P. and Ritchie, J.R.B. (1980): Joint purchasing decisions: a comparison of influence structure in family and couple decision-making units. *Journal of Consumer Research* **7** (September), 131–40.

Goffman, E. (1969): *The Presentation of Self in Everyday Life* (Harmondsworth: Penguin).

Gorn, G.G. (1982): The effects of music in advertising on choice behaviour: a classical conditioning approach. *Journal of Marketing* **46** (Winter), 94–101.

Halstead, D. and Droge, C. (1991): Consumer attitudes towards complaining and the prediction of multiple complaint response. In R. Holman and M. Solomon (eds), *Advances in Consumer Research*, vol. **18** (Provo, UT: Association for Consumer Research), pp. 210–16.

Hartman, C.L. and Kiecker, P. (2004): Jewellery – passing along the continuum of sacred and profane meanings. *Advances in Consumer Research* **31**(1).

Hoch, S.J. and Ha, Y-W. (1986): Consumer learning; advertising and the ambiguity of product experience. *Journal of Consumer Research* **13** (September), 221–33.

Holbrook, M.B. (1984): Situation-specific ideal points and usage of multiple dissimilar brands. In J.N. Sheth (ed.) *Research in Marketing*, vol. **7** (Greenwich, CT: JAI Press), pp. 93–131.

Holbrook, M.P. and Hirschmann, E.C. (1982): The experiential aspects of consumption: consumer fantasies, feelings and fun. *Journal of Consumer Research* **9** (September), 132–40.

Howard, M. and Mason, J. (2001): 21st century consumer society. *Journal of Consumer Behaviour* **1**(1), 94–101.

Hoyer, W.D. and Ridgway, N.M. (1984): Variety seeking as an explanation for exploratory purchase behaviour: a theoretical model. In T.C. Kinnear (ed.) *Advances in Consumer Research*, vol. **11** (Provo, UT: Association for Consumer Research), 114–19.

Hsee, C.K., and Rottenstreigh, Y. (2002): Panda, mugger and music: on the affective psychology of value. *Advances in Consumer Research* **29**(1).

Jansson, C., Marlow, N. and Bristow, M. (2004): The influence of colour on visual search times in cluttered environments. *Journal of Marketing Communications* **10**(3), 183–93.

Keisler, C.A., Collins, B.E. and Miller, N. (1969): *Attitude Change: a Critical Analysis of Theoretical Approaches* (New York: John Wiley).

Keller, K.L. and Staelin, R. (1987): Effects of quality and quantity of information on decision effectiveness. *Journal of Consumer Research* **14** (September), 200–13.

Klein, J.G., Smith, C.N. and John, A. (2004): Why we boycott: consumer motivations for boycott participation. *Journal of Marketing* **68**(3), 92–109.

Koretz, G. (1990): Living alone can be hazardous to your health. *Business Week* **3148**, 20.

Kroeber-Riel, W. (1984): Emotional product differentiation by classical conditioning. In T.C. Kinnear (ed.) *Advances in Consumer Research*, vol. **11** (Provo, UT: Association for Consumer Research), pp. 538–42.

Lambert-Pandraud, R., Laurent, G. and LaPersonne, E. (2005): Repeat purchase of new automobiles by older consumers: empirical evidence and interpretations. *Journal of Marketing* **69**(2), 97–113.

Leichty, M. and Churchill, G.A. Jr. (1979): Conceptual insights into consumer satisfaction and services. In N. Beckwith *et al.* (eds) *Educators Conference Proceedings* (Chicago, IL: American Marketing Association).

Lye, A., Shao, W., Rundle-Thiele, S. and Fausnaugh, C. (2005): Decision waves: consumer decisions in today's complex world. *European Journal of Marketing* **39**(1/2), 216–30.

MacInnis, D.J. and DeMello, G.E. (2005): The concept of hope and its relevance to product evaluation and choice. *Journal of Marketing* **69**(1), 1–13.

Manz, C.C. and Sims, H.R. (1981): Vicarious learning; the influence of modelling on organisational behaviour. *Academy of Management Review* **6**(1), 105–13.

Marketing News (1983): Teenage daughters of working mothers have a big role in purchase, brand selection decisions. *Marketing News* **18** (February).

McNulty, W.K. (1985): UK social change through a wide-angle lens. *Futures* August 1985.

McSweeney, F.K. and Bierley, C. (1984): Recent developments in classical conditioning. *Journal of Consumer Research* **11**(2), 619–31.

Miller, G.A. (1956): The magical number seven, plus or minus two; some limits on our capacity for processing information. *Psychological Review* (March).

Miller, E.G. and Khan, B.E. (2003): Shades of meaning: the effect of novel colour names on consumer preferences. *Advances in Consumer Research* **30**.

O'Guinn, T.C. and Faber, R.J. (1989): Compulsive buying: a phenomenological explanation. *Journal of Consumer Research* **16**(September), 151–5.

Onkvisit, S. and Shaw, J.J. (1994): *Consumer Behaviour, Strategy and Analysis* (New York: Macmillan).

Park, C.W. and Lessig, V.P. (1997): Students and housewives: susceptibility to reference group influence. *Journal of Consumer Research* **4**(September), 102–110.

Pavlov, I.P. (1927): *Conditioned Reflexes* (London: Oxford University Press).

Raghunathan, R. and Mukherji, A. (2003): Is hope to enjoy more enjoyed than hope enjoyed? *Advances in Consumer Research* **30**(1).

Raju, P.S. (1980) Optimum stimulation level its relationship to personality, demographics and exploratory behaviour. *Journal of Consumer Research* **7**(December), 272–82.

Rose, G.M., Dalakis, V., Kropp, F. and Kamineni, R. (2002): Raising young consumers: consumer socialisation and parental style across cultures. *Advances in Consumer Research* **29**(1).

Roux, D. and Korcha, M. (2006): Am I what I wear? An exploratory study of symbolic meanings associated with second-hand clothing. *Advances in Consumer Research* **33**(1).

Santos, J. and Boote, J. (2003): A theoretical exploration and model of consumer expectations, post-purchase affective states and affective behaviour. *Journal of Consumer Behaviour* **3**(2), 142–56.

Shankar, A., Cherrier, H. and Canniford, R. (2006): Consumer empowerment: a Foucauldian interpretation. *European Journal of Marketing* **40**(9/10), 1013–30.

Shiv, B., Ferraro, F.R. and Bettman, J.R. (2004): Let us eat and drink, for tomorrow we shall die: mortality salience and hedonic choice. *Advances in Consumer Research* **31**(1).

Singh, J. (1988): Consumer complaint intentions and behaviour: definitions and taxonomical issues. *Journal of Marketing* **52**(January), 93–107.

Skinner, B.F. (1953): *Science and Human Behaviour* (New York: Macmillan).

Smart, D.T. and Martin, C.L. (1991): Manufacturer responsiveness to consumer correspondence: an empirical investigation of consumer perceptions. *Journal of Consumer Affairs*, **26**(Summer), 104–28.

Stern, H. (1962): The significance of impulse buying today. *Journal of Marketing* **26**(April), 59–60.

Thomson, E.S., Laing, A.W. and McKee, L. (2007): Family purchase decision making: exploring child influence behaviour. *Journal of Consumer Behaviour* **6**(4), 182–202.

Tinson, J. and Ensor, J. (2001): Formal and informal referent groups: an exploration of novices and experts in maternity services. *Journal of Consumer Behaviour* **1**(2), 174–83.

Todd, S. (2001): Self-concept: a tourism application. *Journal of Consumer Behaviour* **1**(2), 184–96.

Urbany, J.E. (1986): An experimental examination of the economics of information. *Journal of Consumer Research* **13**(September), 257–71.

Viswanathan, M., Rosa, J.A. and Harris, J.E. (2005): Decision making and coping of functionally illiterate consumers and some implications for marketing management. *Journal of Marketing* **69**(1), 15–31.

Walsh, G., Hennig-Thurau, T. and Mitchell, V.-W. (2007): Consumer confusion proneness: scale development, validation, and application. *Journal of Marketing Management* **23**(7/8), 697–721.

Wansink, B. (2003): How resourceful consumers identify new uses for old products. *Journal of Family and Consumer Science* **95**(4), 109–13.

Woodruff, R.B., Cadotte, E.R. and Jenkins, R.J. (1983): Modelling consumer satisfaction using experience-based norms. *Journal of Marketing Research* **20**(August), 296–304.

Further reading

The very large number of books on consumer behaviour make it difficult to make specific recommendations: many of the texts are American, and should be treated with a degree of caution, since American consumption behaviour is not necessarily the same as that of other countries in the world. Having said that, much of the quoted research in consumer behaviour is American.

Here is a selection of texts.

Blythe, J. (2008): *Consumer Behaviour* (London: Thomson Learning). This text gives a more detailed account of consumer behaviour than is possible here.

Engel, J.F., Blackwell, R.T. and Miniard, P.W. (2000): *Consumer Behaviour* (Mason, OH: South Western). This text was written by the same writers who developed one of the most widely-quoted models of consumer behaviour. The text is comprehensive, well-argued and also readable and interesting.

Bagozzi, R.P., Gurhan-Canli, Z. and Priester, J.R. (2002): *The Social Psychology of Consumer Behaviour* (Milton Keynes: Open University Press). This is an erudite and academically advanced text, for those who are interested in the deeper issues underlying consumer behaviour.

Chapter 5
Organisational buying behaviour

Learning objectives After reading this chapter, you should be able to:

1. Explain the pressures which influence industrial buyers.

2. Explain the role of the decision-making unit.

3. Describe the main factors which influence industrial buyers.

4. Explain the role of customers in driving the reseller market.

5. Describe approaches to Government markets.

6. Explain how to approach institutional markets.

7. Show how industrial markets can be divided.

8. Describe the different types of buying situation, and the factors which are involved for making buying decisions within those situations.

9. Understand the role of team selling in industrial markets.

Introduction

Organisational buying is often supposed to be more rational and less emotional than consumer purchasing behaviour. However, it would be wrong to assume that organisational buying is always entirely rational: those responsible for making buying decisions within organisations are still human beings, and do not leave their emotions at the door when they come to work, so it seems unrealistic to suppose that they do not have some emotional or irrational input in their decision-making.

Businesses, Government departments, charities and other organisational purchasers actually represent the bulk of marketing activities, yet much of the attention in marketing is focused on business-to-consumer markets rather than on business-to-business markets. The reasons for this are obscure, but may have much to do with the fact that we are all consumers and can therefore relate more easily to consumer marketing issues.

This chapter looks at the ways organisational buyers make decisions, and also at some of the influences buyers are subject to.

The Decision-Making Unit

There are very few cases where an industrial purchasing decision is made by only one person. Even in a small business it is likely that several people would expect to have some influence or input into the purchase decision. Because of this, the decision-making process often becomes formalised, with specific areas of interest being expressed by members of the **decision-making unit** (DMU), and with roles and responsibilities being shared. This

decision-making unit A group of people who, between them, decide on purchases.

Preview case
Westinghouse Brakes

Railways have been around for two hundred years or more, beginning with the horse-drawn railways used in Cornish tin mines. Substantially a British invention, railways spread throughout the world throughout the 19th and 20th centuries, offering cheap and efficient long-distance transportation of people and goods.

Railways still form an important part of any country's transportation infrastructure. No longer a British monopoly, railway technology is global, and there are many hundreds of companies in the business of supplying railway companies with rolling stock, control systems, rails, marketing advice, ticketing systems and indeed anything that might make the railways run more efficiently, safely and profitably.

For example, in the 19th century an American by the name of George Westinghouse invented a braking system which used compressed air as the actuator for the brake pads. This meant that a long vehicle (such as a train) could have brakes in each of the carriages, thus reducing the risk of derailment in an emergency. Previous systems, in which the brakes were either applied in the locomotive

only or in a car at the rear of the train, put excessive strain either on the buffers or on the couplings as the full weight of the train forced itself onto the braked part of the train. Westinghouse had to overcome a number of technical problems, not least of which was the system for applying all the brakes at once along the length of the train – this was overcome by having separate compressed air reservoirs, each with an electric compressor, in each carriage.

Marketing the new product was not as easy as one might imagine. Westinghouse had to persuade railway companies to retrofit the air brakes to existing trains, or fit them as original equipment at the manufacturing yards. The system needed to be the same for all the different railway companies, since freight rolling stock was frequently switched from one company's network to another as it crossed the United States. For passengers, this was less crucial, since companies typically only ran their own passenger trains, with passengers physically getting off one train network and onto another in order to travel longer distances.

Getting the system adopted as standard was the challenge facing George Westinghouse.

---

group is also called the Buying Centre, and it cannot be identified on any company organisation chart: it varies in make-up from one buying situation to another. Individuals may participate for a brief time only or be part of the group from conception to conclusion.

The decision-making unit is thought to contain the following categories of member (Webster and Wind 1972):

initiator The person who first recognises a problem.

● **Initiators.** These are the individuals who first recognise the problem.

gatekeeper The person who controls the flow of information.

● **Gatekeepers.** These individuals control the flow of knowledge, either by being proactive in collecting information or by filtering it. They could be junior staff who are told to visit a trade fair and collect brochures, or a personal assistant who sees his or her role as being to prevent salespeople from 'wasting' the decision-maker's time.

buyer The person who negotiates the purchase.

● **Buyers.** The individuals given the task of sourcing suppliers and negotiating the final deal. Often these are purchasing agents who complete the administrative tasks necessary for buying. These people often work to a specific brief, and may have very little autonomy, even though they may be the only contact a supplier's salespeople have at the purchasing organisation.

decider The person who has the power to agree a purchase.

● **Deciders.** These are the people who make the final decisions, and may be senior managers or specialists. They may never meet any representatives of the supplying companies. Deciders generally rely heavily on advice from other members of the DMU.

user The person who uses the product.

● **Users.** These are the people who will be using the products which are supplied: they may be engineers or technicians, or even the cleaning staff who use cleaning products. Their opinions may well be sought by the deciders, and in many cases the users are also the initiators.

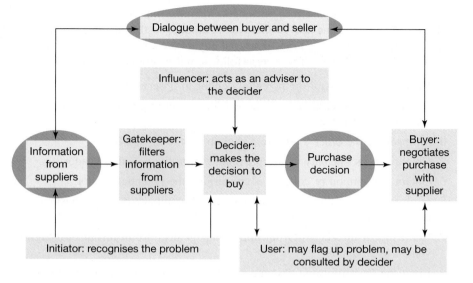

Figure 5.1

Relationships in the DMU

● **Influencers.** These people 'have the ear of' the deciders. They are trusted advisers, but from the supplying company's viewpoint they are extremely difficult to identify. Influencers may be employed by the purchasing firm (for example, engineers, information systems managers or research managers) or they may be consultants (for example, architects, acoustics and safety consultants). An influencer might even be the decider's golf partner, old college friend or teenage son.

influencer The person who has the ability to sway the judgement of a decider.

influencers Staff who can affect the way customers are treated, even though they have no direct access to them.

These categories are not, of course, mutually exclusive. A user might also be an influencer, or a gatekeeper might also be an initiator. The categories were originally developed to explain purchasing within families – which may be an example of the apparent similarities between business-to-business marketing and consumer marketing.

In fact, the members of the decision-making unit are affected both by rational and emotional motivations. Salespeople are well aware that buyers are affected by their liking or dislike for the suppliers' representatives, and buyers will often be working to their own agendas: for example, a buyer might be seeking a promotion, or might feel threatened in terms of job security, or may be conducting a vendetta with a colleague. Any of these influences might affect the buyers' behaviour, but all of them would be difficult or impossible for a supplier's salesperson to identify correctly and act upon.

In general, members of a decision-making unit tend to be more risk-averse than do consumers. This is because the Buying Centre (DMU) members have more to lose in the event of a wrong decision: for a consumer, the main risk is financial, and even that is limited since most retailers will replace or refund goods purchased in error. For the industrial purchaser, however, a serious purchasing mistake can result in major negative consequences for the business as well as loss of face at work, in shattered promotion dreams, or even in dismissal in serious cases. The professional persona of the industrial buyer is liable to be compromised by purchasing errors, which in turn means that the buyer will feel a loss of self-esteem.

Determining the relative power of each member of the Buying Centre (DMU) for each purchasing situation is a difficult task. Ronchetto, Hutt and Reingen (1989) identify these characteristics of individuals who may be most influential in a DMU:

● Important in the corporate and departmental hierarchy.

● Close to the organisational boundary.

● Central to the workflow.

● Active in cross-departmental communications.

● Directly linked to senior management.

It should be obvious that purchasing managers are most important in repetitive purchases, while the CEO will become heavily involved in unique, costly and risky buying decisions.

As a result of this increased risk, industrial buyers use a variety of risk-reducing tactics (Hawes and Barnhouse 1987). These are as follows, and are presented in order of importance:

1 Visit the operations of the potential vendor to observe its viability.

2 Question present customers of the vendor concerning their experience with the vendor's performance.

3 Multisource the order to ensure a backup source of supply.

4 Obtain contract penalty clause provisions from the potential vendor.

5 Obtain the opinion of colleagues concerning the potential vendor.

6 In choosing a vendor, favour firms that your company has done business with in the past.

7 Confirm that members of your upper management are in favour of using the vendor as a supplier.

8 Limit the search for and ultimate choice of a potential vendor only to well-known vendors.

9 Obtain the opinion of a majority of your co-workers that the chosen vendor is satisfactory.

Buyers are affected by individual, personal factors as well as environmental and organisational factors. Personally they exhibit many of the same influences on the buying decision that consumers have: the desire to play a role, for example, may cause a buyer to be difficult to negotiate with as he or she tries to drive a hard bargain. The desire for respect and liking may cause a buyer to want to give the order to a salesperson who is exceptionally pleasant or helpful, and to deny the order to a salesperson who is regarded as being unpleasant or pushy. Business buyers are likely to be affected by some or all of the following environmental influences (Loudon and Della Bitta 1993):

1 *Physical influences.* The location of the purchasing firm relative to its suppliers may be decisive, since many firms prefer to source supplies locally. This is especially true in the global marketplace, where a purchasing company may wish to support local suppliers, or may prefer to deal with people from the same cultural background. In many cases, buyers seem almost afraid to source from outside their own national boundaries, even when rational considerations of cost and quality would make the foreign supplier the better bet.

Figure 5.2

Environmental influences on buyer behaviour

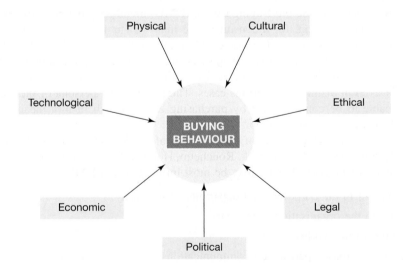

2 *Technological*. The level of technological development available among local suppliers will affect what the buyer can obtain. The technology of the buyer and the seller must also be compatible: in global markets this often presents a problem, since international technical standards remain very different for most products. Despite efforts within the European Union to harmonise technical standards, Europe still does not have standardised electrical fittings, plumbing fittings or even computer keyboards. Many European firms find it easier to trade with former colonies thousands of miles away then deal with countries within the EU, simply because the technical standards of the former colonies are identical with their own.

3 *Economic influences*. The macro-economic environment is concerned with the level of demand in the economy, and with the current taxation regime within the buyer's country. These conditions affect buyers' ability to buy goods as well as their need to buy in raw materials: if demand for their products is low, the demand for raw materials to manufacture them will also be low. On a more subtle level, the macro-economic climate affects the buyer's confidence in the same way as it affects consumer confidence. For example, a widespread belief that the national economy is about to go into a recession will almost certainly make buyers reluctant to commit to major investments in stock, equipment and machinery. In a global context, the fact that countries enter and leave recessions at different times will affect the timing of marketing efforts on the part of vendors. At the micro-economic level, a firm experiencing a boom in business will have greater ability to pay for goods and a greater level of confidence.

4 *Political influences*. Governments frequently pass laws affecting the way businesses operate, and this is nowhere more true than in international trade. Trade sanctions, trade barriers, specifically non-tariff barriers, preferred-nation status and so forth all affect the ways in which buyers are permitted or encouraged to buy. In some cases, Governments specifically help certain domestic businesses as part of an economic growth package. The political stability of countries is also a factor that vendors need to take account of.

5 *Legal influences*. Laws often lay down specific technical standards, which affects buyer decisions. Buyers may be compelled to incorporate safety features into products, or may be subject to legal restrictions in terms of raw materials. Often, vendors can obtain competitive advantage by anticipating changes in the law.

6 *Ethical influences*. In general, buyers are expected to act at all times for the benefit of the organisation, not for personal gain. This means that, in most cultures, the buyers are expected not to accept bribes, for example. However, in some cultures bribery is the normal way of doing business, which leaves the vendor with a major ethical problem – refusing to give a bribe is likely to lose the business, but giving a bribe is probably unethical or illegal in the company's home country, especially now that the OECD Anti-Bribery Convention has been widely adopted. As a general rule, buyers are likely to be highly suspicious of doing business with a salesperson whom they perceive as acting unethically – after all, if the salesperson is prepared to cheat on his or her employer, he or she cannot be trusted not to cheat on the buyer.

7 *Cultural influences*. Culture establishes the values, attitudes, customary behaviour, language, religion and art of a given group of people. When dealing internationally, cultural influences come to the forefront: in the UK it might be customary to offer a visitor a cup of tea or coffee, whereas in China it might be customary to offer food. Dim Sum originated as a way for Chinese businessmen to offer their visitors a symbolic meal, as a way of establishing rapport. Beyond the national culture is the corporate culture, sometimes defined as 'the way we do things round here'. Corporate culture encompasses the strategic vision of the organisation, its

Marketing in Practice
Bribery

Bribery is the act of giving someone a gift of money, goods or even services in order to change their behaviour in respect of their job. The problem is, the definition is subject to interpretation – for example, a tip is considered to be bribery in some cultures, whereas in other cultures giving an official a gift for speeding through some paperwork, or paying a police officer not to issue a traffic ticket, is regarded as normal practice and perfectly acceptable.

For the global marketer, the issue of bribes is a complex one. What is unacceptable in the company's home country may be entirely unacceptable abroad, and vice versa. For example, the United States has legislation (the Foreign Corrupt Practices Act) preventing American companies from bribing foreign companies – yet the practice is still widespread and prosecutions are few, simply because it is recognised that no business would result if bribes were not offered to the appropriate officials.

Even when cultures are close, bribery still happens. In 2006, Pierre Levi (the CEO and chairman of Faurecia, a French auto parts supplier) resigned over allegations that the company had bribed BMW buyers to specify Faurecia parts. In 2005, Sony BMG (one of the Big Four record companies that between them control 80 per cent of the record industry) admitted bribing radio DJs to plug Sony

records. Other bribery scandals crop up with monotonous regularity – everything from bribing tax officials to reduce the valuations they place on real estate to offering the Saudi Royal Family a bribe to agree to buying military aircraft.

Bribery can result in extremely dangerous situations. Zheng Xiayou, the head of China's drug regulatory body, accepted a total of $800 000 in bribes, which resulted in faulty or fake drugs being sold in China, and in one case toxic chemicals being added to toothpaste and cough medicine exported to Latin America, causing the deaths of over 100 people. The scandal almost derailed China's fledgling drug manufacturing and exporting business, but (far worse) the marketing of faulty drugs probably caused the deaths or at least the illnesses of millions of people. The scandal proved far more dangerous for Zheng, however – he was sentenced to death.

Ultimately, the morality of bribery is not in question, even in countries where it is rife. Bribery is immoral and in most cases illegal. It is damaging to business, to the countries where it happens, and to the people who give and accept the bribes. Yet it still goes on, because immediate gain often outweighs long-term disadvantages – especially when the stakes are as high as they are in the pharmaceutical industry.

ethical stance and its attitudes towards suppliers, among other things. In addition, many businesspeople act in accordance with their professional culture as well (Terpstra and David 1991). Each of these will affect the way business is done.

Organisational factors derive from the corporate culture, as well as from the strategic decisions made by senior management within the firm. Organisational policies, procedures, structure, systems of rewards, authority, status and communication systems will all affect the ways buyers relate to salespeople. Figure 5.3 shows the main categories of organisational influences on the buyers' behaviour.

Talking Point

The expansion of the European Union in 2004 was hailed (rightly) as an historic event, reuniting Europe peacefully for the first time in its long and bloody history. For business, the expansion was expected to bring great rewards in terms of bigger markets and greater choice of suppliers.

Yet many firms still preferred to deal with countries thousands of miles away, where the technical standards are the same as their own. So why not create closer links with these countries? Why did Britain, for example, join the EU and reject its former empire just at the time when transportation costs had fallen dramatically? Surely the wider range of climate, availability of raw materials and greater diversity of the Commonwealth made it a better bet?

Or perhaps the Commonwealth countries (for the most part) are so poor that they have no choice but to sell to us anyway – and we need to ally ourselves with the rich rather than with the poor!

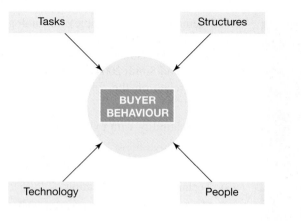

Figure 5.3

Organizational influences on buyer behaviour

Buying tasks differ greatly between firms, but may also differ significantly within firms. For example, the buying task for a supermarket clearly differs from that for a manufacturing company, since the supermarket intends to sell on the vast majority of its purchases unchanged, whereas the manufacturer is largely concerned with sourcing components and raw materials. Within this generalised structure the supermarket has other variations in the buying task: the buyers' approach to buying canned goods will be totally different to the approach used to buy fresh produce such as vegetables or fresh fish. Equally, the manufacturer will have a different approach when buying basic raw materials vs buying components, and a different approach again when buying lubricating oil or business services or new factory premises. The purchasing tasks will affect the buyer's thinking and negotiating approach, usually so seriously that firms will have separate buyers for each type of buying task.

The structure of the organisation falls into two categories: the formal structure is what shows on the organisation chart, and the informal structure which is actually what dictates staff behaviour in most cases. The informal structure is the network of social obligations, friendships and internal liaisons which influence day-to-day behaviour. The formal organisation structure determines such issues as the degree of centralisation in purchasing decision-making, the degree to which buying decisions follow a formal procedure (i.e. how constrained by the rules the buyers are) and the degree of specialisation in buying for different purposes or different departments in the organisation.

The informal structure dictates such issues as rivalry between buyers, 'brownie points' (recognition by management for jobs done well), cooperation between buyers in maintaining each other's status in the eyes of the boss, and so forth. The maze of informal relationships can be extremely complex, especially for a salesperson observing it from the outside, but often forms a key element in the success or failure of key-account selling. In the global context, the informal structure is subject to many cultural influences – the Oriental concern with gaining or losing face, for example, can be a crucial factor in doing business. The informal structure is also important in determining who will be the influencers in the decision-making unit; some colleagues' opinions may be regarded as more trustworthy than others, for example.

The technology within the organisation may act to control or circumvent much of the buyers' role. For example, computer-controlled stock purchasing, particularly in a just-in-time purchasing environment, will prevent buyers from being able to negotiate deals and in many cases removes the buyer from the process altogether. Models for inventory control and price forecasting are also widely used by buyers, so that in many cases the negotiating process is virtually automated with little room for manoeuvre on the part of the buyer. In these circumstances the selling organisation needs to go beyond the buyer to the other members of the DMU in order to work around the rules. More technology-minded companies are likely to use electronic communications systems more

Courtesy of The Advertising Archive

Virgin is inextricably linked to Richard Branson's personality.

(email being only one example): technology-mediated communications have a positive, direct effect on future intentions to buy, but of course this is mediated by factors of trust and commitment (McDonald and Smith 2004). E-commerce in business-to-business marketing relies on the following factors (Claycomb, Iyer and Germain 2005):

1 Compatibility with existing systems.

2 Cooperative norms with customers.

3 Lateral integration within the firm.

4 Technocratic specialisation.

5 Decentralisation of information technology.

The characteristics of the people involved in the organisation will, in part, determine the organisation culture, but will in any event control the interpretation of the rules under which the purchasing department operates. At senior management level, the character of the organisation is likely to be a function of the senior management, and in many cases the organisation's founder will have set his or her personality firmly on the organisation's culture. Virgin is clearly an offshoot of Richard Branson's personality, as Bodyshop is an offshoot of the late Anita Roddick's.

Talking Point

We frequently hear about the global village, about the convergence of cultures and about a new world order in which we accept and understand each other's cultures. So why is it necessary to consider cultural issues when we are marketing products and services? Surely the goods speak for themselves – does crude oil have a cultural value, or does a stamp mill have a cultural connotation?

Shouldn't buyers be prepared to accept and understand cultural differences? Otherwise how are we to do business? Or perhaps the buyers arrogantly believe that the sellers should adapt their approach to meet the buyers' culture – thus possibly missing out on getting the best deals for their organisations.

If we get clashes between corporate cultures within the same country, how much worse will the clashes be in globalised markets?

Classifying Business Customers

A business customer is one who is buying on behalf of an organisation rather than buying for personal or family consumption. For the purposes of discussion, we usually talk about organisations as the purchasers of goods, but of course this is not the case: business customers, in practice, are human beings who buy on behalf of organisations.

Organisations might be classified according to the types of buying and end-use they have for the products. Table 5.1 shows the commonly accepted classifications.

Business and commercial organisations

Business and commercial organisations can be segmented as original-equipment manufacturers (OEMs), users and aftermarket customers. OEMs buy foundation, entering and facilitating goods. Foundation goods are used to make other products: this includes machine tools and buildings. Entering goods are things that become part of other products, for example raw materials and components. Facilitating goods and services do not directly enter the product or production process but are necessary for the firm's business:

Table 5.1 Classification of buying organisations

Type of organisation	Description
Business and commercial organisations	These organisations buy goods which are used to make other goods and those that are consumed in the course of running the organisation's business. These organisations buy foundation goods and services used to make other products, facilitating goods and services which help an organisation achieve its objectives, and entering goods and services which become part of another product.
Reseller organisations	Resellers buy goods in order to sell them on to other organisations or to final consumers. Typically, resellers will be wholesalers or retailers, but they may also be agents for services, for example travel agents or webmasters who act as facilitators for other firms.
Governmental organisations	Governments buy everything from paperclips to aircraft carriers through their various departments. Because national and local government departments operate under specific rules, a different approach to that for businesses is usually required.
Institutional organisations	Institutional organisations include charities, educational establishments, hospitals and other organisations that do not fit into the business, reseller or Government categories. These organisations may buy any of the products, but they are used to achieve institutional goals, usually to provide services.

examples are accounting services, market research services, office cleaning, stationery and so forth. For example, computer manufacturers may buy machine tools to make computer cases and also buy silicon chips from specialist producers: the chips are incorporated into the final product, but the same type of chip might be incorporated in computers from several different OEMs. The Intel Pentium chip is an example.

For OEM buyers, the key issue will be the quality of the products or services. Such buyers are usually operating to fairly exact specifications laid down by their own production engineers and designers: it is unlikely that the supplying firm will be able to do very much to have the specification changed. This means that introducing a new product to an OEM will be a lengthy process, since the supplying company will need to establish a long-term relationship with the customer in order to become involved at the design stage for the new products.

User customers buy products which are used up within the organisation, either as components in their own equipment or to make the equipment perform properly, for example lubricating oils or cleaning products. These products are not resold, but may be bought in considerable quantities. Obviously some of these are service products – accountancy or legal services, cleaning services, maintenance or building services are all contained within the firm and not resold.

Aftermarket customers are those involved in the maintaining, repairing and overhauling (**MRO**) of products after they have been sold. For example, in the elevator business, independent contractors not affiliated with the original manufacturer perform most MRO. These contractors buy the components, supplies and services they need wherever they can find them.

The classification split between **OEM**, users and aftermarket customers is only relevant to the supplier. OEMs can also be user customers for some suppliers. For example, a plastic moulding company may sell components to an OEM and plastic tools to a user, as well as plastic replacement parts to an aftermarket organisation: in some cases these may even be the same organisation. Buying motivations for each type of purchase are clearly very different.

In Figure 5.4, the same suppliers sometimes provide goods or services for several firms in the supply chain. In some cases there will be considerable crossover between firms.

reseller organisation A firm which buys goods in order to sell them on to other firms or consumers.

mro Maintenance, repair and overhauling company.

oem Original equipment manufacturer.

Marketing in Practice
Ocean Rainwear

Ocean Rainwear is a Danish company, founded in 1958 to supply protective clothing to Danish fishermen. Until then, trawlermen and the like had worn heavy, uncomfortable oilskins which hampered movement and often funnelled water inside themselves, making the fishermen wetter than ever.

Ocean Rainwear supplies heavy duty polyurethane clothing with knitted polyester linings. The clothing is lighter and warmer than oilskins, and is much more effective in keeping the wearer dry: although it is more expensive than traditional clothing, its effectiveness means that the company is the market leader. Ocean Rainwear claim that they can manufacture clothing for any other industry – if your work involves getting wet, they can supply the protection.

In recent years, as the fishing industry has become more restricted by the European Union, Ocean Rainwear has branched out into supplying leisure clothing for outdoor pursuits such as hiking, fishing and hunting. It is in the industrial sector that their attention to quality and comfort has made them the leader, however.

Figure 5.4

Types of purchase

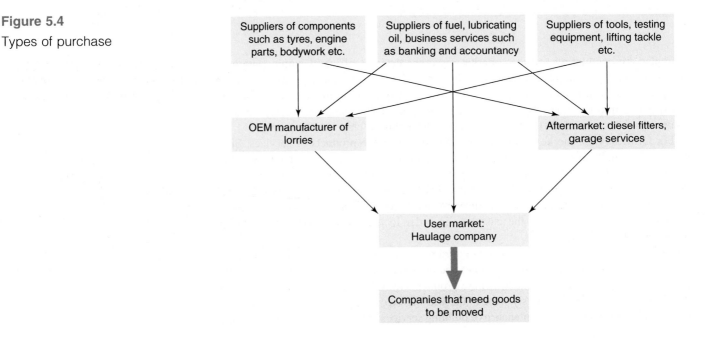

Reseller organisations

The majority of manufactured goods are sold through reseller organisations such as retailers and wholesalers. Intermediaries provide useful services such as bulk breaking, assortment of goods, and accumulation of associated product types: due to increased efficiencies resulting from these services, intermediaries tend to reduce overall prices for the final consumer. Cutting out the middleman usually reduces efficiency and tends to increase prices as a result; although there is a popular view that disintermediation reduces prices by cutting out the intermediaries' mark-ups.

E-Marketing in Practice
Bowers & Wilkins Group

Bowers & Wilkins Group is a company well-known to hi-fi enthusiasts. The company produces state-of-the-art loudspeakers which are sold worldwide: technical excellence is maintained by its research and development facility in the south of England.

The challenge for B&W is maintaining close relationships with manufacturers, retailers and the hi-fi media in the 70 countries in which it operates. The company is relatively small, and operates in a specialist area where maintaining contact by the traditional method of sending sales representatives to customers regularly is difficult or impossible.

B&W have therefore developed a sophisticated extranet which enables customers and others to log onto a special website. Each customer has a password, so the system can offer each one a personalised greeting and can also record the interactions for marketing research purposes. Distributors have access to all areas of the extranet, but retailers have less access and the media have their own section on the site. This helps to maintain confidentiality and protect corporate secrets. The extranet is multilingual, so that each customer, no matter what their native language, is able to access information much more easily than would be the case by using (for example) the telephone.

The result of using the extranet is increased service levels for all parties and enhanced communication with all relevant stakeholders. The extranet offers added value for distributors and retailers because the services provided are relevant to them and they have access to all relevant information instantly. B&W benefit because they have much more accurate and timely information about their distributors and retailers, and also have a more loyal group of customers.

Reseller organisations are driven almost entirely by their customers. This means that they will only buy products which they perceive to have a ready market: there is therefore a premium on employing buyers who have a clear understanding of marketing. Unlike the OEM buyers, there is little need for resellers to understand the technical aspects of the products they buy – they merely need to feel confident that the ultimate consumers will want the products.

Reseller organisations carry out the following basic functions:

1 Negotiate with suppliers.
2 Promotional activities such as advertising, sales promotion, providing a salesforce etc.
3 Warehousing, storage and product handling.
4 Transportation of local and (occasionally) long-distance shipments.
5 Inventory control.

6 Credit checking and credit control.

7 Pricing and collection of price information, particularly about competitors.

8 Collection of market information about consumers and competitors.

For manufacturers, this places a premium on establishing close long-term relationships with resellers. Shared information, as part of an integrated channel management strategy, becomes crucial to forward planning.

Government organisations

Government and quasi-government organisations are major buyers of almost everything. In some markets, the Government is heavily involved in industry. For instance, all insurance in India is a Government monopoly, and the oil industry in Mexico is controlled by PEMEX, a quasi-government entity. Governments are thought to be the largest category of market in the world, if all levels of Government are included in the equation (see Figure 5.5). The structure of Government varies from one country to another: for example, in Spain there is the national Government based in Madrid, the regional Governments (e.g. the Junta de Andalucía), the provincial Governments (e.g. Provincia de Granada) and the local town halls (e.g. Ayuntamiento de Ugijar). Sometimes these local town halls group together to form an alliance which carries out mutually beneficial activities such as tourism marketing or funding a local swimming pool, but frequently they act independently of one another within the frameworks of their own jurisdictions.

Because of the strict rules under which most Government organisations operate, special measures are often needed to negotiate deals. In particular, Government organisations are characterised by the tendering system, in which firms are asked to bid for contracts which are then usually offered to the lowest bidder. From a supplier's viewpoint, this can be seriously counterproductive, since the lowest price is likely to be also the least profitable price, so selling firms will often try to circumvent the process by ensuring that they become involved before the tender is finalised. In this way it is often possible to ensure that the tender is drawn up in a way that favours the proactive firm over its competitors, thus ensuring that competitors either do not bid at all or bid at too high a price.

In some cases, Governments need to purchase items which are not available to the general public or to other businesses. Military hardware is an obvious example: clearly ordinary businesses are not allowed to buy tanks or fighter planes. On a more subtle level, goods such as handguns are not permitted for private organisations in the UK, but can be sold to the Army or the police force. Some types of computer software are only appropriate for use by the tax authorities, and academic research is, in general, paid for entirely by the Government in the UK. From a marketing viewpoint, these specialist markets

Figure 5.5

Tiers of Government and their typical purchases

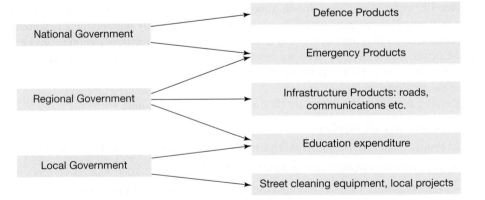

Marketing in Practice
The European Union

The European Union is intended to provide a 'level playing field' for companies within its borders. This has extended to tendering for Government (and even local government) buying. In the past, orders for such items as desks, computers, office supplies and so forth were commonly given to local companies within the Government's own country. This was seen as a way of supporting local firms, reducing imports, and securing jobs. Under EU rules, though, this type of selective purchasing is anti-competitive and is now banned.

Currently, any Government organisation within the EU must offer all contracts for tender throughout the EU, if the contract is above a specific value (currently around £100 000 for services and supplies and £4m for works). Contracts are advertised in the *Journal of the European Communities*, and also online at http://ted.publications. eu.int/. Local business organisations such as chambers of commerce also monitor tenders and pass them on to interested parties.

The end result of this process is that end users (the taxpayers, in the last analysis) get better value for money, and the most efficient companies have wider opportunities to expand their businesses.

---

present an interesting challenge, since in some cases the products need to be tailored to a specific Government or a specific Government department. This may mean that there is considerable scope for negotiation, but since the contract might still have to go out to tender, the company may find that it has merely wasted time unless it can demonstrate that no other company can carry out the work.

In some circumstances, Governments may issue a 'cost-plus' contract, in which the organisation is given a specific task to carry out and bills according to the cost of the contract plus an agreed profit margin. In the early days of space research this type of contract was common, since it was impossible to predict what the costs might be when dealing with an unknown set of circumstances. More recently these contracts have fallen into disrepute, since they reward inefficiency and waste.

Only Governments are able to buy heavy armaments.

Institutional organisations

Institutions include charities, universities, hospital trusts and non-profit organisations of all types, schools and so forth. In some cases these are Government-owned but independent for purposes of purchasing and supply (for example, secondary schools), in other cases they are totally independent (for example registered charities). The traditional view of these organisations is that they are chronically underfunded and therefore do not represent a particularly munificent market, but in practice the organisations actually have a very substantial aggregate spending power.

Because budgets are almost always very tight, the marketing organisation may need to be creative in helping the institution to raise the money to buy. For example, a firm which produces drilling equipment may find that it has a substantial market at Oxfam, since Oxfam drills wells in many arid regions of the Third World. Oxfam relies on public generosity to raise the money to buy the equipment, so the manufacturer may find it necessary to part-fund or even manage a fundraising campaign in order to make the sale.

Suppliers are often asked to contribute to charities, in cash or in products. This may not always be possible, since the supplier's only market might be the charities, but in some cases firms may find it worthwhile to supply free products to charities in order to

Figure 5.6

Factors in institutional marketing

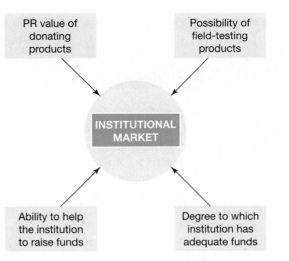

Talking Point

gain PR value, or sometimes in order to open the door to lucrative deals with other organisations. For example, a Third World charity might be prepared to field-test equipment which could then be sold to a Government department in the same country.

We are often told that marketing is about managing the exchange process, yet Government departments and many institutions seem to lay down the ground rules from the start. Marketers have to play by the buyer's rules to be in the game at all – so how can they possibly be managing the process? Pushed from one set of constraints to the next, it would seem that the average marketer is just a pawn in the buyer's hands!

Yet maybe that is how it should be, if customers are at the centre of everything we do. Not to mention that the management process itself could be construed as a clearing-house for pressures rather than as a directive force – in a sense, no manager is actually in control, so why should marketers be any different?

Buyers' Techniques

straight rebuy A repeat purchase with no modifications.

Buyers use a wide variety of techniques according to the buying situation they are faced with. The buying situations are generally divided into three types:

1 **Straight rebuy.** This is a situation in which the buyer is buying the same product in very much the same quantities from the same supplier. For example, an engineering company might buy the same quantity of components from its suppliers each month. In these circumstances the buyer needs no new information, and does not need to engage in much negotiation either. Prudent buyers may occasionally look at other possible sources of components in order to ensure that no new technology is available or that other suppliers are not able to supply the same components more cheaply, but in general the order placement is automatic. In many cases the buyer establishes an electronic data interchange (EDI) link with a supplier or establishes automatic buying procedures through the Internet so that orders are handled without any human interface. If the product is of minor importance, or represents a low commitment in terms of finance or risk, the buyer will not undertake any information search and will probably simply order the goods. This is called causal purchasing, because it results automatically from a cause such as low stock level. For example, a buyer for large engineering firm probably spends

very little time deciding on brands of paper for the photocopier. On the other hand, buying copper cable might be a routine purchase, but the buyer might monitor the market for alternatives occasionally. Such buying is called routine low-priority buying because it has a lower priority than would be the case if an entirely new situation were being faced. The company is unlikely to get into serious trouble if it pays 10 per cent more than it should for cable, for example.

2 **Modified rebuy**. In this situation, the buyer re-evaluates the habitual buying patterns of the firm with a view to changing them in some way. The quantities ordered, or the specification of the components, may be changed. Even the supplier may be changed. Sometimes these changes come about as a result of environmental scanning, in which the buyer has become aware of a better alternative than the one currently employed, or sometimes the changes come about because of marketing activities by the current suppliers' competitors. Internal forces (increases or decreases in demand for components) might trigger a renegotiation with suppliers or a search for new suppliers. In any event, the buyer is faced with a limited problem-solving scenario in which he or she will need to carry out some negotiation with existing or new suppliers, and will probably need to seek out new information as well. In a modified rebuy situation a buyer may well require potential suppliers to bid against each other for the business: the drawback of this approach, however, is that it often results in damaging the relationship with existing suppliers that may have been built up over many years.

modified rebuy A repeat purchase where some changes have been made.

3 **New task**. This type of buying situation comes about when the task is perceived as being entirely new. Past experience is therefore no guide, and present suppliers may not be able to help either. Thus the buyer is faced with a complex decision process. Judgemental new task situations are those in which the buyer must deal with technical complexities of the product, complex evaluation of alternatives and negotiating with new suppliers. Strategic new task situations are those in which the final decision is of strategic importance to the firm – for example, an insurance

new task A purchase which has no precedent.

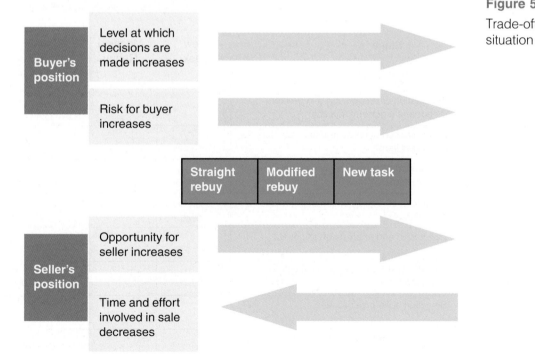

Figure 5.7

Trade-offs in type of buying situation

company in the market for new record-keeping software will be investing (potentially) hundreds of thousands of pounds in retraining staff, and in transferring existing records, not to mention the risks of buying software that is unable to cope with the tasks it is required to carry out. In these circumstances, long-range planning at Director level drives the buying process, and the relationship with the suppliers is likely to be both long-term and close.

From the viewpoint of the business marketer, the main chance of winning new customers will come in the new task situation. The risks for buyers involved in switching suppliers are often too great unless there is a very real and clear advantage in doing so: such an advantage is likely to be difficult to prove in practice. In the new task situation, potential suppliers may well find themselves screened out early in the process, and will then find it almost impossible to be reconsidered later.

The Buygrid Framework

Organisational buying can be seen as a series of decisions, each of which leads to a further problem about which a decision must be made (Cardozo 1983). From the viewpoint of the business marketer, it is possible to diagnose problems by examining the sequence of decisions – provided, of course, the decision sequence is known to the marketer. Marketers can identify the stage at which the firm is currently making decisions and can tailor the approach accordingly.

The industrial buying process can be mapped against a grid, as shown in Figure 5.8. The most complex buying situations occur in the upper-left portion of the framework and involve the largest number of decision makers and buying influences. This is because new

Figure 5.8

The Buygrid framework

(Source: From the Marketing Science Institute Series, 'Industrial Buying and Creative Marketing', by Patrick J. Robinson, Charles W. Faris and Yoram Wind. Copyright 1967 by Allyn and Bacon, Inc. Boston)

Stage	Buying Situations		
	New Task	Modified Rebuy	Straight Rebuy
Anticipation or recognition of a problem (need) and a general solution			
Determination of characteristics and quantity of needed item			
Description of characteristics and quantity of needed item			
Search for and qualification of potential sources			
Acquisition and analysis of proposals			
Evaluation of proposals and selection of supplier(s)			
Selection of an order routine			
Performance feedback and evaluation			

tasks require the greatest amount of effort in seeking information and formulating appropriate solutions, but also will require the greatest involvement of individuals at all levels of the organisation, each of whom will have his or her own agenda.

The Buygrid framework has been widely criticised, however. Like most models, it tends to oversimplify the case. As in consumer decision-making, the sequence may not be as clear-cut as the model implies, and events may take place in a different order in certain circumstances. For example, a supplier might approach a firm with a solution for a problem it didn't know it had, thus cutting out several stages of the process: the firm may well recognise the need and the problem, but will probably not need to acquire proposals and select a supplier, since the supplier is already on board with a solution. Second, suppliers go to great lengths to differentiate themselves from competitors as effectively as they can, so that the buyer may not have any other potential suppliers of the exact product on offer. Third, the model assumes a rational approach to purchasing which is often simply not there. Finally, the boundaries between new task, modified rebuy and straight rebuy are by no means clear-cut.

Because buyers are influenced by both rational and emotional considerations, the potential supplier needs to be aware of the buying motives of each member of the decision-making unit. What is more, each member of the DMU will apply different criteria for judging which suppliers should be included and which excluded (Kelly and Coaker 1976): the finance director might emphasise low prices, whereas the chief designer might be concerned with product quality and the production engineer with reliable delivery. The buyer might be concerned with the relationship with the supplier's sales people. In many cases, brand equity is less important than issues of price and delivery (Bendixen, Bukasa and Abratt 2004).

In the case of key-account management, this problem of dealing with different members of the DMU is often overcome by taking a team approach to the sale. While the **key-account manager** handles the initial contact and the management of the process, other specialists are brought in to deal with financial aspects, technical aspects and so forth. In this way each member of the DMU is speaking to someone with whom he or she has a common language and a common understanding of the conceptual environment within which each speciality operates. In some cases the number of people working on the account can become large: when IBM were dealing with Lloyd's Bank (one of the Big Four UK banks) they had over 100 people working on the account, and set up a special branch office in the Canary Wharf area to be near Lloyd's head office.

key-account manager Someone charged with the task of managing the relationship with a strategically important customer.

There are three types of business network (Moller and Svahn 2004):

1 *Stable.* These are networks which are perhaps still growing, but they are following a predictable course.

2 *Established.* These networks are fixed and relatively unchanging: the rules are known by the members.

3 *Emerging.* These networks are still growing and changing.

The internal culture of the firm (and the external culture, in an international context) affects the nature of each of these network types.

Managing the network means identifying the key network, developing a strategy for managing the individuals who operate within the network, and developing methods at the operational level for managing those actors (Ojasalo 2004). The responsibility for managing the actors is often divided between the members of the selling team.

Value Analysis

Value analysis is a way of determining where value is being added, or lost, throughout the production process. Value-in-use is defined as a product's economic value to the user relative to a specific alternative in a particular application (Kijewski and Yoon 1990).

value analysis A method of evaluating components, raw materials and even manufacturing processes in order to determine ways of cutting costs or improving finished products.

Table 5.2 Long-life bulb vs tungsten-filament bulb

1. *Annual cost of existing product:*	
250 replacement light bulbs × 45p =	£112.50
Cost of electricity: @ 6.7p per kilowatt × 60 watts × 150 bulbs =	£603.00
Cost of replacing bulbs assuming 10 minutes per bulb @ £10 per hour =	£416.00
TOTAL COST PER ANNUM:	**£1131.50**
2. *Cost of using long-life bulbs:*	
50 replacement bulbs per annum × £5 =	£250.00
Cost of electricity @ 6.7p per kilowatt × 11 watts × 150 bulbs =	£110.55
Cost of replacing bulbs assuming 10 minutes per bulb @ £10 per hour =	£83.20
TOTAL COST PER ANNUM:	**£443.75**

Value-in-use is the price that would equate to the overall costs and benefits of using one product rather than using another.

For example, consider long-life lightbulbs. These bulbs are usually between five and ten times as expensive as ordinary tungsten-filament bulbs to buy, but last five times as long and use only 20 per cent of the electricity. For a domestic consumer, this represents a considerable saving, more than enough to cover the initial outlay for the bulbs, but for a business customer the saving is even greater, since the cost of paying someone to replace the bulbs is significant. Assuming the life of a tungsten-filament bulb as being 1000 hours on average, compared with 5000 hours for a long-life bulb, the calculation would run as shown in Table 5.2.

Using this calculation, the company can make an immediate saving of just under £400 a year by switching to long-life bulbs. In fact, the capital cost of changing all the bulbs in the building would be recovered in the first year, although in practice the firm would probably only replace the tungsten-filament bulbs as they fail in use: in this way the labour cost of replacing the bulbs would be no higher than normal.

Because some buyers do use this type of calculation to assess alternative solutions to existing problems, the astute marketer will be prepared with the full arguments in favour of the new solution, including all the relevant factors, which make the product more attractive. On the other side of the coin, astute purchasers will involve potential suppliers in the discussions and in the value analysis process (Dowst and Raia 1990).

Evaluating Supplier Capability

Purchasers also need to assess the capability of potential suppliers to continue to supply successfully. This is a combination of assessing financial stability, technical expertise, reliability, quality assurance processes and production capacity. In simple terms, the purchasing company is trying to ensure that the potential supplier will be in a position to keep the promises it makes. Business customers that track the performance of suppliers gain competitive advantage because they are better able to manage the supply chain. (Bharadwaj 2004).

Table 5.3 illustrates some of the ways in which buyers can assess potential suppliers.

Table 5.3 Assessing suppliers

Attribute	Assessment method
Technical capability	Visit the supplier to examine production equipment, inspect quality control procedures and meet the engineering staff.
Managerial capability	Discuss systems for controlling processes, meet the managerial staff and become involved in planning and scheduling supplies.
Financial stability	Check the accounts filed at Companies House or other public record office, run a credit check, examine annual reports if any.
Capacity to deliver	Ascertain the status of other customers of the supplier – would any of these take priority? Assess the production capacity of the supplier, warehouse stocks of the product, reputation in the industry.

Whilst these methods are better than nothing, in most cases they rely on judgement on the part of the purchaser, who may not in fact have the necessary expertise to understand what the supplier's capability really is.

Talking Point

The methods of assessment shown in the table all rely on some kind of judgement on the part of the buyer. Even the financial figures filed at the company record office require interpretation – and may even have been 'massaged' to make the company look more financially viable than it actually is.

So why bother with what is, after all, a somewhat time-consuming exercise? Presumably a rogue supplier would have little difficulty in pulling the wool over the eyes of a buyer who probably lacks the engineering training to understand what is in front of him or her. On the other hand, an honest supplier would probably provide the 'warts and all' picture that might well lose the contract. Maybe buyers would be better advised to go for the supplier that looks the worst – at least we know they are being honest with us!

Evaluating Supplier Performance

Even after the contract is awarded, the purchasing company is likely to need to review the supplier's performance periodically. In some cases, suppliers have been known to relax once the contract is awarded, and of course the circumstances of the buying organisation are likely to change considerably in the course of what will be a lengthy relationship.

The basic evaluation methods are as outlined in Table 5.4.

Table 5.4 Evaluation approaches

Approach	Explanation
Categorical plan*	Each department having contact with the supplier is asked to provide a regular rating of suppliers against a list of salient performance factors. This method is extremely subjective, but is easy to administer.
Weighted-point plan*	Performance factors are graded according to their importance to the organisation: for example, delivery reliability might be more important for some organisations than for others. The supplier's total rating can be calculated and the supplier's offering can be adjusted if necessary to meet the purchasing organisation's needs.
Cost-ratio plan*	Here the buying organisation evaluates quality, delivery and service in terms of what each one costs. Good performance is assigned a negative score, i.e. the costs of purchase are reduced by good performance; poor performance is assigned a positive score, meaning that the costs are deemed to be greater when dealing with a poor performer.

*See glossary.

All of these methods involve some degree of subjectivity, in other words each method requires buyers to make judgements about the supplier. The fact that the outcomes are expressed in numbers gives each method a spurious credibility: those involved in evaluation exercises of this nature should be aware that the evaluation exercise itself should be evaluated periodically, and the criteria used by the various individuals involved need to be checked.

Talking Point

Much of the emphasis in the preceding sections has been on the purchaser's evaluation of suppliers. But what about the other way round? Customers are not always plaster saints – some are late payers, some impose unreasonable restrictions, some reject supplies for the flimsiest of reasons and some are just plain unpleasant to deal with.

So should suppliers have their own systems for assessing purchasers? Should we just grovel at the feet of any organisation willing to buy our goods – or should we stand up and be counted? After all, without supplies no company can survive – so presumably we are equally important to one another.

Maybe this is really the purpose of segmenting our markets – and what is really meant by segmentation.

In fact, suppliers tend to adapt more often than do purchasers when there is an ongoing relationship (Brennan, Turnbull and Wilson 2003). This is due to the relative power each has (buyers being more powerful in most circumstances), and managerial preferences. Suppliers that are market-orientated tend to develop a greater customer intimacy, which also may drive suppliers to change (Tuominen, Rajala and Moller 2004). Buyers who are themselves market-orientated tend to become more loyal to their suppliers (Jose Sanzo *et al.* 2003).

Summary

Buyers have a large number of influences on their decision-making. At the very least, buyers have their own personal agendas within the companies they work for: in the broader context, a wide range of political, environmental and technological issues will affect their decision-making. The end result is likely to be a combination of experience, careful calculation and gut feeling.

The key points from this chapter are as follows:

- Buyers are subject to many pressures other than the simple commercial ones: emotions, organisational influence, politics and internal structures are also important factors.

- The decision-making unit (DMU) or Buying Centre is the group of people that will make the buying decision. Roles and composition of DMUs vary widely.

- Business and commercial organisations are likely to be swayed most by past experience with a vendor, product characteristics and quality.

- Resellers are driven by their customers.

- Government markets are large, and almost always use a tendering system.

- Institutional markets may need special techniques to help them afford to buy the products.

- Markets can be divided into those buyers who buy products designed to make other products or who will incorporate the purchase into their own products (original equipment manufacturers), those who consume the product in the course of running their businesses (user markets) or those who serve the aftermarket.

- A purchase may be a straight rebuy a modified rebuy or a new task. These are given in order of increasing complexity, and do not have discrete boundaries.

- A team approach to buying usually dictates a team approach to selling.

Chapter review questions

1 How would you expect a Government department to go about buying a new computer system?

2 How might internal politics affect a buyer's behaviour?

3 What factors might be prominent in the buying decision for cleaning materials?

4 What factors might a supplier take into account when evaluating a purchasing company?

5 How might the directors of a company go about setting standards for evaluating suppliers? What objective criteria are available?

6 What are the main problems with evaluating supplier performance?

7 How should a seller approach a Government department?

8 What are the main differences between marketing to commercial organisations and marketing to charities?

9 How might a seller find out who the influencers are in the DMU?

10 How might a seller act to reduce the risk for the buyer?

Preview case revisited
Westinghouse Brakes

Westinghouse needed to convince railways throughout the United States to adopt his braking system – but how could he do it all in one go?

The answer lay in finding the most influential system and persuading them. Westinghouse identified the Burlington railroad in Chicago as a key account – Burlington had already opened up the prairies with its extensive rail network, but more importantly Chicago was the main hub for freight shipments from the East Coast to the West. If Burlington adopted the Westinghouse system, other rail systems would be forced to follow suit if they were not to have to unload freight cars and reload them onto other cars.

After a series of demonstrations, Westinghouse persuaded Burlington to adopt the system – in effect this forced other railways to do the same. Westinghouse's success was not built on the superiority of his product, in fact: many engineers still believe that vacuum brakes are better than air brakes, since they respond faster. The success of the Westinghouse brake lay in being adopted as the industry standard, in the same way as Microsoft has ensured that Windows is the industry standard. Such opportunities are rare: a later attempt by Westinghouse to establish their signalling system as the standard failed dramatically, probably because signals do not need to be standardised beyond the basic red-for-stop, green-for-go system.

To think of George Westinghouse as a sort of 19th century Bill Gates may seem far-fetched, but both entrepreneurs succeeded in the same way – by identifying the key customer and establishing their products as the industry standard.

Case study
Way Industry

When Communism collapsed in Eastern Europe in the late 1980s, considerable disruption followed in its wake. Virtually all enterprise had been State owned and controlled since the Second World War, and the military and economic power of the Soviet Union had kept tight control over the states of Eastern Europe.

In the aftermath, industrial policies became chaotic: suddenly companies which had hitherto been protected from competition were suddenly exposed to competitive practices from the West, In some cases, competition was ruthless – in East Germany, for example, West German mining companies bought out East German mines and promptly closed them down as a way of removing potential competitors, even though this put thousands of miners out of work and dealt the East German economy a death blow.

At the same time, new countries formed almost overnight. Yugoslavia split into several states which promptly went to war with each other, the Soviet Union broke up into dozens of tiny states and Czechoslovakia split to form Slovakia and the Czech Republic.

Eventually, of course, the chaotic conditions settled down and companies began to rise again. Eastern European manufacturers began the long climb back, but this time they had the advantage of knowing what they were up against: the fast learners survived, the managers who kept harking back to the Communist era disappeared. One such example of survival is Way Industry of Slovakia.

Courtesy of Way Industry

In 1999, Way Industry purchased the whole of the assets of Hontianske strojarne j-s at a bankruptcy settlement. The new company immediately embarked on a programme of new product development, beginning with the Locust 752 digger and the TALET 30 aircraft handling vehicle. Both were well-engineered, well-designed and versatile – the TALET 30 can be used to tow aircraft weighing up to 50 tons from their parking bays, but it can also be fitted with a snowplough, a grass cutter or sweeper so that it can act as a general-purpose vehicle for small airfields whether they have grass or tarmac runways. It is about the size of a saloon car and has a pickup-type load area at the back.

One of the company's most successful products has been the Bozena 4 mine-clearing robot. This is a tracked vehicle, remotely controlled, with a set of flails attached. The flails hammer the ground ahead of the vehicle, triggering any mines (this idea can be traced back to the Second World War, when manned tanks were used in this way). The machine is protected from the explosions caused by a steel shield, rather like a bulldozer share, at the front. The operator remains safely ensconced in an air-conditioned, armoured control room up to 2 kilometres away. The robot uses Deutz engines and Bosch-Rexroth hydraulic systems, so that spare parts are easily obtainable anywhere in the world: an essential consideration for a machine which is liable to be deployed in any of the world's trouble spots at any time. Since 2004, the company has been making the even bigger Bozena 5, which can clear even the most powerful anti-tank mines without difficulty.

Courtesy of Way Industry

The company is heavily involved in the clean-up operations in Iraq following the two wars there. Way Industry will provide training for operators, guaranteed supply of spare parts for up to 10 years after purchase, and technical support on-site if necessary. The company still reveals its Eastern European roots, however – the bulk of its dealers are based in Eastern Europe, with only a handful in Western Europe and none at all in the Americas.

Way Industry has become well established because of the continuing need for equipment to tidy up after wars. Wars continue to be fought worldwide – Way Industry supplies the United Nations and peacekeeping forces everywhere with the tools to carry out the job.

Questions

1 How might Way Industry seek to establish itself in Western Europe?

2 How might the company reduce its dependence on wars?

3 What is the role of agents and distributors in the success of a firm like Way Industry?

4 What business environment issues will affect Way Industry?

5 What type of buyer decision-making process would you expect Way Industry to need to deal with?

References

Bendixen, M., Bukasa, K.A. and Abratt, R.A. (2004): Brand equity in the business to business market. *Industrial Marketing Management* **33**(5), 371–80.

Bharadwaj, N. (2004): Investigating the decision criteria used in electronic components procurement. *Industrial Marketing Management* **33**(4), 317–23.

Brennan, R.D., Turnbull, P.W. and Wilson, D.T. (2003): Dyadic adaptation in business-to-business markets. *European Journal of Marketing* **37**(11), 1636–65.

Cardozo, R.N. (1983): Modelling organisational buying as a sequence of decisions. *Industrial Marketing Management* **12** (February), 75.

Claycomb, C., Iyer, K. and Germain, R. (2005): Predicting the level of B2B e-commerce in industrial organisations. *Industrial Marketing Management* **34**(3), 221–34.

Dowst, S. and Raia, E. (1990): Teaming up for the 90s. *Purchasing* **108** (February), 54–9.

Hawes, J.M. and Barnhouse, S.H. (1987): How purchasing agents handle personal risk. *Industrial Marketing Management* **16** (November), 287–93.

Jose Sanzo, M., Leticia Santos, M. Vasquez, R. and Alvarez, L.I. (2003): The role of market orientation in business dyadic relationships: testing an integrator model. *Journal of Marketing Management* **19**(1/2), 73–107.

Kelly, P. and Coaker, J.W. (1976): Can we generalise about choice criteria for industrial purchasing decisions? In K.L. Bernhardt (ed.) *Marketing 1776–1976 and Beyond* (Chicago, IL: American Marketing Association) pp. 330–3.

Kijewski, V. and Yoon, E. (1990): Market-based pricing: beyond price-performance curves. *Industrial Marketing Management* **19** (February), 11–19.

Loudon, D. and Della Bitta, A. (1993): *Consumer Behaviour: Concepts and Applications* (New York: McGraw Hill Education).

McDonald, J.B. and Smith, K. (2004): The effects of technology-mediated communication on industrial buyer behaviour. *Industrial Marketing Management* **33**(2), 107–16.

Moller, K. and Svahn, S. (2004): Crossing East–West boundaries: knowledge sharing in intercultural business networks. *Industrial Marketing Management* **33**(3), 219–28.

Ojasalo, J. (2004): Key network management. *Industrial Marketing Management* **33**(3), 195–205.

Ronchetto, J.R., Jr., Hutt, M.D. and Reingen, P.H. (1989): Embedded influence patterns in organisational buying systems. *Journal of Marketing* **53**(4), 51–62.

Terpstra, V. and David, K. (1991): *The Cultural Environment of International Business* (Cincinnati, OH: South-Western Publishing Company.)

Tuominen, M., Rajala, A. and Moller, K. (2004): Market-driving versus market-driven: divergent roles of orientation in business relationships. *Industrial Marketing Management* **33**(3), 207–17.

Webster, F.E. and Wind, Y. (1972): *Organisational Buying Behaviour* (Englewood Cliffs, NJ: Prentice Hall).

Further reading

There are many books on business-to-business marketing, including: Fill, C. and Fill, K. (2004): *Business to Business Marketing: Relationships, Systems and Communications* (Harlow: FT Prentice Hall). This is a comprehensive, readable textbook written from a marketing management perspective.

Blythe, J. and Zimmerman, A. (2005): *Business to Business Marketing Management* (London: Thomson Learning). This book takes a global perspective on B2B marketing.

Whitehead, M. and Barrat, C. (2004): *Buying for Business: Insights into Purchasing and Supply* (Chichester: John Wiley & Sons). This is a view from the other side. Written as a guide for practitioners, the book takes the buyer's viewpoint.

Chapter 6
Segmentation, targeting and positioning

| Part one
Concepts and Contexts | 1 Managing the exchange process
2 The marketing environment
3 Marketing domains |

| Part two
Markets and People | 4 Consumer behaviour
5 Organisational buying behaviour
6 Segmentation, targeting and positioning
7 Marketing information and research
8 Communications theories
9 International marketing |

| Part three
Strategy | 10 Creating competitive advantage
11 Building customer relationships |

| Part four
Marketing in Practice | 12 Product portfolio
13 New product development
14 Pricing
15 Advertising
16 Public relations and sponsorship
17 Selling and key account management
18 Exhibitions and sales promotions
19 Direct and online marketing
20 Managing channels
21 Intermediaries
22 People, processes and physical evidence |

Learning objectives After reading this chapter, you should be able to:

1. Understand the basic concept behind segmentation.

2. Explain the role of marketing research in segmenting markets.

3. Describe some of the commonest methods of segmenting markets.

4. Explain the role of targeting.

5. Explain the potential strategic issues in targeting.

6. Explain what positioning implies for customers.

7. Understand the key features of successful positioning.

Introduction

Segmentation is about separating the overall market into groups of customers with similar needs. Targeting is about developing variations on the basic product to meet the needs of these different groups. Segmentation can be defined as the grouping of individuals or organisations with similar needs, those needs being capable of being met by a single product offering.

Targeting also implies deciding which groups of customers are the best ones to aim for. A basic tenet of business (and of life in general) is that it is impossible to please everybody. This means that marketers need to consider which segments they cannot please and which they can, and then decide which of these segments will also be profitable.

There are very few products which please everybody – in fact, it is difficult to think of any. Even products such as Coca-Cola, which has penetrated soft drink markets in almost every country on the planet and is the world's most recognised brand, only has a minority share of the world's soft drinks market. Marketers therefore seek to position their products appropriately relative to competitors: positioning is, of course, in the minds of consumers.

The relationship between segmentation, targeting and positioning is shown in Figure 6.1.

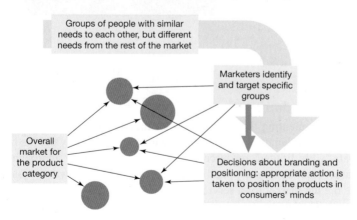

Figure 6.1

Segmentation, targeting and positioning

Preview case
Leger Holidays

Battlefields exert a considerable fascination for many people. For some, a visit to battlefield is a way of visualising a dramatic piece of history: others might be visiting the place where a relative of friend was killed. Still others visit the scenes of their youth – perhaps laying the ghosts of bad memories of the war.

Whatever the reason for travelling, finding a specific battlefield perhaps years after the war ended is not always easy. Time moves on, and large tracts of land are farmed, built on, quarried or otherwise altered beyond recognition. Most people have no real way of recognising the place, and still less ability to organise getting there, since the battlefields are usually in a foreign country and often in rural areas. There is therefore plenty of scope for a specialist package holiday firm – and that's where Leger Holidays steps in.

Leger was founded in 1983 as a standard holiday tour operator, not specifically as a specialist battlefield tour company. The company still offers other types of holiday (such as packages to Disneyland Paris or trips to Bruges) but Leger's main claim to fame is its battlefield tours. Over a third of all online bookings for Leger are for battlefield tours, and in February 2007 the company established a special section of its website devoted to battlefields. The web page includes a forum on which people can discuss their experiences, ask for help in identifying a particular part of a battlefield, and share news of veterans or relatives. Over 30 tours are available from this website, mainly in Europe, but with one tour going to the Falklands.

Tours are typically based around the two World Wars: visits to the battlefields of the Somme, Passchendaele and Gallipoli represent some of the World War I battles, while the Normandy beaches, the Dambuster raids and Colditz Castle represent some World War II iconic locations. Most trips are conducted by coach from the UK, although the Gallipoli trip and obviously the Falklands trip

are conducted by air. Each trip is guided by an expert, and includes lectures on the historical background to each battle – why it was fought, what its outcome was on the rest of the war and what its impact was on those who fought it. Guides are extremely well-qualified: Paul Reed, who has responsibility for World War I tours, is a historian who has written five books on World War I and who lived in the Somme region for 11 years. Other guides have a military background, or an in-depth knowledge of the history of the period.

The problem for Leger lies in meeting the needs of fairly disparate groups: young people visiting the scenes where their parents or grandparents fought, veterans (some of whom are likely to be elderly or disabled), widows and other relatives, and students of history, whether formal students on courses or amateur historians. Promoting to these different groups represents something of a challenge in itself, as each group has a different perception of war and its aftermath.

Segmentation

The purpose of segmenting the market is to ensure, as far as possible, that resources are directed at those individuals or organisations which are likely to yield the best returns. All firms operate with limited resources: taking a 'scattergun' approach to marketing activities rather than aiming at specific groups will inevitably waste those resources.

In Figure 6.2 the market for a service is broken down into groups with different ideas of what they want. The largest group is the one looking for a low-price, no-frills service – but

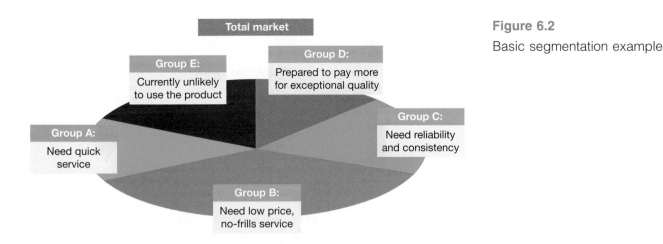

Figure 6.2

Basic segmentation example

of course low prices often go hand-in-hand with low profits. The group of people who are prepared to pay for exceptional quality is small, but probably more profitable as individuals. The company has to decide where its own strengths lie in terms of meeting customer expectations, and then decide whether it is able to meet the needs of its chosen target group better than the competition can.

The concept is, of course, much more straightforward than the practice. Deciding the basis on which the market should be segmented is only part of the problem – for example, one might assume that only young people visit nightclubs, and therefore target accordingly. However, it is actually the case that nightclubs cater for single people – most of whom are young, admittedly – but by targeting young people the nightclub might miss out on the growing number of divorced people in their thirties, forties and even fifties who might be customers. Since these people often have a great deal more money than their younger counterparts, the nightclub could miss out on a lucrative area of business.

Targeting might involve developing appropriate variations on the product (or new products), considering approaches to promoting the product to the different segments, and positioning the product against competitors in the same market.

Ultimately, the firm will want to use its segmentation policy to develop differential market strategies. Each segment will require a different approach, since each segment has different needs and characteristics and will therefore be interested in different aspects of the product offering. If the segmentation differs from that of the competition, the firm will be able to offer a product more closely tailored to the needs of the segment and will therefore obtain a competitive advantage.

Segmentation operates at four levels, as follows:

1 *Mass marketing*. The idea behind mass marketing is to produce something which almost everyone would want, then produce it in vast quantities at low prices and promote it heavily to gain market share. This approach is all but impossible to carry out in the modern world, because the markets are so diverse and consumer expectations have risen. Production has also become more efficient, so that the cost difference between the mass-produced, mass-marketed item and the more tailored product is smaller than it once was. Wealthy consumers, which includes almost everybody in the Western world, can easily afford the very tiny extra cost of a more customised product.

2 *Segmented markets*. Here the company seeks to identify substantial groups of individuals with similar needs, and aims to satisfy those needs. Competition will tend to be reduced by targeting a segment, and the company is able to direct resources more effectively.

3 *Niche marketing*. Niche marketers focus on small sub-groups within the larger segments and produce very carefully targeted products. The advantage of doing this

Even older people need to find new partners sometimes.

niche marketing Serving a small segment.

Figure 6.3

Segmentation trade-offs

is that the company is able to reach a group which is too small for larger firms to approach, and therefore will not experience much competitive pressure: the firm will also be able to operate with much less capital, since promotion will not need to be as powerful as it would if the company were competing against major firms for share of voice. Niche marketers usually get to understand their customers so well that they are able to charge a premium price for their products, and the approach is so successful that large companies sometimes also target niches within their overall market segment.

4 *Micromarketing*. This is the practice of tailoring products and marketing programmes to suit specific individuals and circumstances. For example, Dell Computers will produce a computer to the purchaser's specifications, within certain limits. Ultimately, micromarketing takes us full circle, to the days when craftsmen made everything to the customers' specifications – tailor-made clothing and furniture was, at one time, the norm. Micromarketing enables us to use modern production techniques to achieve similar outcomes. Mass customisation is the ability to prepare individual, custom-made products through a mass-production process. For example, Vision Express opticians manufacture lenses on-site, so that a customer can have an eye test, choose the frames for his or her new spectacles, and walk out with the finished product within an hour. In many cases people are not prepared to pay the increased cost of such good service, however (Bardacki and Whitelock 2004).

As the product becomes more customised, one would expect that customers would be prepared to pay more for it, so there is a trade-off between the extra cost of providing a more tailored product and the extra price that customers are prepared to pay. If the premium is small and the costs are large, the customisation is unlikely to be worthwhile. This calculation can be a difficult one for marketers to make.

Each level of segmentation has its own advantages and disadvantages (see Figure 6.3), but in general consumers expect a much higher standard of service than previously, and given the globalisation of world markets, consumers have a great deal more choice and variety than they have had before. People (understandably) want to be treated as individuals, and the marketer who ignores this does so at his or her peril.

Segmenting the Market

The starting point for successful segmentation is good market research. Understanding the needs of customers, and the characteristics of those customers the firm wants to reach, is basic to deciding how to meet those needs. Segmentation occurs in three stages, as follows:

1 An understanding of the needs of the various customers in the total market needs to be developed. This happens through market research, and sometimes through

internal knowledge within the firm (for example reports from sales people). There is more on market research in Chapter 7.

2 Customers are grouped according to their needs and characteristics. This can be a complex operation, since it is sometimes difficult to be clear about what the salient characteristics of the customers are (see the nightclub example above). There are a great many ways to segment the same market, and companies which are able to view markets from a fresh perspective are often able to find new ways of grouping customers. These new groupings may mean new advantages to customers, and competitive advantage to the firm.

3 Groupings are selected for targeting. Segmentation implies rejecting groups which are unprofitable, or which otherwise do not fit with the firm's strategic plans. For example, a firm may identify a lucrative market but be unwilling to compete directly with a major firm which already serves that market. Wiser counsels may dictate that the firm target a different group which would not pose a threat to the industry leaders.

Grouping people into segments can be carried out in a large number of ways, but the generally accepted view is that segmentation of consumer markets can be based on behavioural factors, on psychographic factors, or on profile factors.

Talking Point

There seems to be a view that people can be pigeonholed: that our reactions to marketing stimuli can be predicted, programmed, manipulated and filed away. Yet we all think of ourselves as individuals – making independent, even quirky, decisions without caring what other people think of us.

So which view is right? After all, it's easy to find examples of people acting like sheep, following the crowd: and it's easy to find people who follow the same routines day in and day out. Most people eat the same thing for breakfast every day, wear the same style of clothing, choose the same type of food in restaurants. On the other hand, people enjoy having a change now and then, doing the unexpected, and acting on impulse. If that's the case, how can we possibly expect to segment a market?

In practice, these different approaches are not mutually exclusive, and marketers often use more than one segmentation variable in order to focus on a very specific part of the market.

Behavioural segmentation

Basing segmentation on consumers' behaviour can be straightforward, but may also lack subtlety. For example, a manufacturer of fishing rods may not feel a need to know much about potential consumers in terms of their ages, incomes or attitudes: the fact that they go fishing is sufficient. Within that, the manufacturer might want to know what type of fish the angler is after, or on what occasions he or she goes fishing, but all of these questions operate within the behavioural segmentation area.

The main behavioural bases for segmentation are as follows (see Figure 6.4):

1 *Benefits sought*. Different people look for different things, even in the same product category. For example, some people buy a car because they need transport from one place to another, for themselves and their luggage. Others may be seeking the prestige which comes from driving an up-market car, and still others might be looking for hedonic aspects of the product (the fun of driving from one place to another). Sampson (1992) called these people respectively, functionality seekers, image seekers and pleasure seekers.

Figure 6.4
Behavioural segmentation

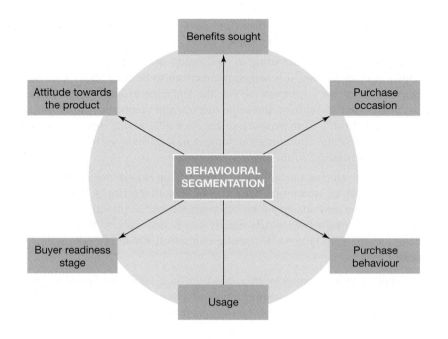

2 *Purchase occasion.* Some people might buy the product as a regular purchase, others might only buy as an occasional treat. For example, 40 years ago chicken was regarded as something of a luxury in the UK, and would only occasionally be eaten as a Sunday dinner – the staple of British Sunday dinners was beef. However, some people ate chicken frequently, either because they were wealthy enough to do so or because they considered the extra cost to be worthwhile. The same argument applies to lamb in the 21st century – it is one of the most expensive of meats, but to its aficionados it is worth every penny. Another type of purchase occasion relates to gift giving. The greater part of sales of aftershave is made to women: aftershave lotion is typically given as a gift, and relatively little is bought by men for their own use. Purchase occasion might also relate to situational factors: buying a new car battery might be a result of an awareness that the old battery is gradually becoming less efficient, or it may be the result of a sudden failure of the battery far from home. Purchase occasion may result in the same consumer buying different versions of the same product at different times. For example, someone might stay in a four-star hotel when travelling for business purposes, but stay in a crumbling old bed-and-breakfast when on holiday, because such places have more character. Equally, going out for a meal when one is too tired to cook results in a very different choice of restaurant from that chosen for a wedding anniversary or a first date.

3 *Purchase behaviour.* This could relate to time of purchase, place of purchase, quantities bought on each occasion, degree of willingness to buy innovative products and so forth. For example, books may be bought in a bookshop, in a newsagent's, in a charity shop, in a street market or over the Internet. Each type of purchase behaviour may be typical of the consumers concerned, but may not relate to other characteristics – the fact that someone enjoys bargain-hunting in a charity shop or second-hand book stall does not necessarily mean that he or she is poorer than someone who buys books on the Internet, for instance. Brand loyalty is also an element in purchase behaviour: if there is a group of consumers who regularly switch from one brand to another according to the price, this has implications for

the marketing approach. On the other hand, if there is a group of consumers who remain loyal to the product no matter what happens, the thrust of the marketing effort will lie in identifying and recruiting these people.

4 *Usage.* Consumers may be heavy users of the product category, medium users, light users, ex-users or non-users. Non-users are not, of course, consumers of the product, but may represent an opportunity if the supplying company can find out why they are non-users. Equally, light users and medium users can be encouraged to use more of the product – although this is almost certainly the easier option, many firms still concentrate on finding new users for their products from among the non-user category. For many firms, the obvious tactic is to target heavy users and try to steal these customers away from competing firms. This tactic is dangerous if all the firms in the market are targeting heavy users, however, because competitive pressure might prove too intense. In those circumstances, a firm might be better to target light or medium users. A neglected area of marketing is customer win-back, in which ex-users are brought back into the fold. An ex-user, after all, already knows all about the product and the company, and may have defected to the competition for a reason which can easily be corrected.

5 *Buyer readiness stage.* Some people are closer to buying the product than are others. People may be unaware of the product, others may be aware but not yet interested, others are aware and interested but do not yet need the product, others have an interest and a need but no money, and finally there are those who are actually in the market for the product. Being aware of these stages is important for firms selling major items such as houses or cars. Someone who recently moved house is unlikely to be in the market for another house, but after (say) seven or eight years a move is a likely option. Likewise, a couple who have recently started a family may well be interested in moving to a larger house, or to a house with a garden. Contacting people (for example by mail) when they are at the wrong stage of readiness is irritating and therefore counterproductive, whereas a contact at the right stage is helpful and useful.

6 *Attitude towards the product.* In some cases, the non-user's attitude towards the product is so hostile there is really very little point in trying to change it. For example, in political marketing it is well-known that the committed Labour (Socialist, Democrat) or Conservative (Christian Democrat, Republican) supporter is unlikely to change. Political campaigners know that there is little point in spending time either on committed supporters or on sworn enemies: better by far to concentrate on the 'floating voters' who might be swayed by argument. Also, some Party supporters may want a greater involvement than merely voting – some want to help with the election campaign, or contribute money to support the campaign, or become Party members.

Geographic segmentation

The area where people live can have a marked effect on their purchasing behaviour. An obvious example is the effect of climate – people in cold countries need to spend more on warm clothing, home insulation and heating products than do people in warm countries. The reverse is true for air conditioning, sun lotion, solar heating and barbecues. Less obvious examples are the effects of culture and the effects of location on shopping habits.

Culture is frequently geographically linked. Language tends to be a strong influence in linking people together, and language tends to be specific to particular localities. For example, research has

People living in cold climates need special products.

© Oleg Seleznev | Dreamstime.com

acorn A geographical segmentation method: A Classification Of Residential Neighbourhoods.

shown that Europe can be divided into five regions for the purpose of selling cars: the north (Scandinavia), the north-west (UK, Ireland, Belgium and Holland), the centre (Germany, Switzerland and Eastern Europe), the west (France and the French-speaking areas of Belgium and Switzerland) and the south (the Mediterranean countries). Each region tends to have its own attitudes to car purchase and ownership: the centre, for example, is more concerned about pollution than the other regions are, while the south region is more concerned about value for money. Cultural issues can be a basis for segmentation on their own – for example, African Americans sometimes wear African-style clothing to identify themselves with Africa, even though most of them are unlikely ever to visit Africa (deBerry-Spence and Izberk-Bilgin 2006).

Geographic segmentation can be taken to a micro level as well. One of the best-known examples of localised geographic segmentation is **ACORN**, a system for classifying consumers according to their postcodes. ACORN stands for A Classification of Residential Neighbourhoods, and it seeks to categorise households according to the type of housing which predominates within their postcode area. ACORN classifications are used by retailers to determine which products are the best to stock, by home-improvement companies to know which areas are likely to be most in need of the product, and by direct mail companies to know which areas are likely to be most receptive of mailings. Insurance companies are also able to tell which type of housing is most likely to result in claims.

The ACORN classifications are as shown in Table 6.1. The basic assumption underpinning ACORN is that the area one lives in has a strong influence on one's purchasing behaviour, partly because it relates to income level, partly because it relates to a local culture (the assumption being that similar types of people live in the same area) and partly because the type of housing one lives in has an effect on household purchases such as furniture and home improvements.

Marketing in Practice
Dutch Cheese

Holland is a small, very crowded country where the farms are wedged in between cities: land is at a premium and the cost of living is relatively high. Farming therefore needs to be high-value, producing value-added food products rather than commodity products such as wheat or rice. For centuries, the low-lying meadows of Holland have produced top-quality dairy products, and especially they have been famous for cheese production. Dutch cheese production is extremely well-integrated, with two main farmers' co-operatives and a few major cheese factories controlling the industry. About half of all the milk produced in Holland goes into cheese production, and the industry is so successful it even has to import dairy products to provide the raw materials for the cheeses.

The Dutch have been vigorous and indeed highly successful in exporting their Edam and Gouda cheeses,

recognised worldwide, but of course these cheeses are not exclusive to Holland any more – anyone can copy them. Also, of course, not everybody likes them – different countries have different ideas about what constitutes good cheese. The Dutch have therefore introduced new cheese products aimed at other markets. For example, much of the feta cheese sold in Greece now comes from Holland, parmesan is exported to Italy and quark is exported to Germany.

To some people, it comes as a surprise to visit a tiny village store in the mountains of Greece, buy some typically Greek feta cheese for a picnic lunch, and find 'Produce of the Netherlands' printed on it, but this type of segmentation of the market has enabled Dutch cheese producers to become one of the country's leading exporting industries.

Table 6.1 ACORN classifications

Category	Group		Type
A: Thriving	Wealthy achievers, suburban areas	1	Wealthy suburbs, large detached houses
		2	Villages with wealthy commuters
		3	Mature, affluent home-owning areas
		4	Affluent suburbs, older families
		5	Mature, well-off suburbs
	Affluent greys, rural communities	6	Agricultural villages, home-based workers
		7	Holiday retreats, older people, home-based workers
	Prosperous pensioners, retirement areas	8	Home-owning areas, well-off older residents
		9	Private flats, elderly people
B: Expanding	Affluent executives, family areas	10	Affluent working families with mortgages
		11	Affluent working couples with mortgages, new homes
		12	Transient workforces, living at their place of work
	Well-off workers, family areas	13	Home-owning family areas
		14	Home-owning family areas, older children
		15	Families with mortgages, younger children
C: Rising	Affluent urbanites, town and city areas	16	Well-off town and city areas
		17	Flats and mortgages, singles and young working couples
		18	Furnished flats and bedsits, younger single people
	Prosperous professionals, metropolitan areas	19	Apartments, young professional singles and couples
		20	Gentrified multi-ethnic areas
	Better-off executives, inner-city areas	21	Prosperous enclaves, highly qualified executives
		22	Academic centres, students and young professionals
		23	Affluent city centre areas, tenements and flats
		24	Partially gentrified multi-ethnic areas
		25	Converted flats and bedsits, single people
D: Setting	Comfortable middle agers, mature home-owning areas	26	Mature established home-owning areas
		27	Rural areas, mixed occupations
		28	Established home-owning areas
		29	Home-owning areas, council tenants, retired people

Table 6.1 ACORN classifications (continued)

Category	Group		Type
	Skilled workers, home-owning areas	30	Established home-owning areas, skilled workers
		31	Home-owners in older properties, younger workers
		32	Home-owning areas with skilled workers
	New home-owners, mature communities	33	Council areas, some new home-owners
		34	Mature home-owning areas, skilled workers
		35	Low rise estates, older workers, new home-owners
	White-collar workers, better-off multi-ethnic areas	36	Home-owning multi-ethnic areas, young families
		37	Multi-occupied town centres, mixed occupations
		38	Multi-ethnic areas, white-collar workers
F: Striving	Older people, less prosperous areas	39	Home-owners, small council flats, single pensioners
		40	Council areas, older people, health problems
	Council estate residents, better-off homes	41	Better-off council areas, new home-owners
		42	Council areas, young families, some new home-owners
		43	Council areas, young families, many lone parents
		44	Multi-occupied terraces, multi-ethnic areas
		45	Low-rise council housing, less well-off families
		46	Council areas, residents with health problems
	Council estate residents, high unemployment	47	Estates with high unemployment
		48	Council flats, elderly people, health problems
		49	Council flats, very high unemployment, singles
	Council estate residents, greatest hardship	50	Council areas, high unemployment, lone parents
		51	Council flats, greatest hardship, many lone parents
	People in multi-ethnic, low-income areas	52	Multi-ethnic, large families, overcrowding
		53	Multi-ethnic, severe unemployment, lone parents
		54	Multi-ethnic, high unemployment, overcrowding
	Unclassified	55	

Talking Point

Most of us live in cities. Even the relatively few people who live in rural areas (at least in Western Europe and the United States) live what is essentially an urban life – even farmers shop in supermarkets rather than grow their own food. Part of the advantage of living in a city is the variety of experience that cities provide – the entertainment facilities, the restaurants, the variety of people we can mix with and so forth. The whole point of living in a city is that we are *not* like our neighbours – so how does ACORN work?

Even more to the point, what about community workers who have to live in run-down areas as part of their jobs? What about University lecturers who act as wardens in student accommodation halls? What about caretakers who live in office blocks?

Perhaps ACORN provides a general overview of who is likely to live in a given area, but there may be plenty of exceptions!

Lifestyle choices are often geographically based. For example, American and Australian washing machines are almost always top-loading, whereas UK washing machines are typically front-loading. Because houses are bigger in Australia and the US, people have spare space for the easier-to-load top-loaders, whereas in the UK (and most of the rest of Europe) front-loaders are more convenient because they fit under a kitchen worktop. In hot countries people tend to live outside more, so there is less emphasis on furniture and home décor.

Demographic segmentation

Demographics is concerned with factors such as age, gender, sexual orientation, family size, family lifecycle stage, income, occupation, education, religion, ethnicity and nationality. Demographic factors are probably more widely used than any other factors for segmentation purposes, probably because the data is relatively easy to collect. Needs, wants and usage rates also correlate closely with demographic variables: for example, the wealthier an individual is, the more likely he or she is to consume almost any product one cares to mention. On the other hand, some demographic information can be misleading – age is particularly prone to this, but other demographic information can also be misinterpreted. For example, a product may appear to appeal to better-educated people, but in fact the appeal is to people with higher incomes. Since better-educated people tend to have higher incomes, the two factors can easily be confused.

Age segmentation

Some consumer needs and wants change with age. As people grow older, they will become more concerned with pensions and investments, for example. Physical changes such as greying hair, weight increase and increasing numbers of wrinkles also offer marketing opportunities, and in old age mobility is also likely to lessen. Age is not an adequate segmentation variable in itself, however, since the relationship between age and behaviour is far from linear (Simcock, Sudbury and Wright 2006). Age segmentation is sometimes carried out somewhat crudely, for example by categorising everyone over 65 as one group. This implies that a 65-year-old man has something in common with his 87-year-old mother, which is of course extremely unlikely.

At the other end of the scale, age segmentation is widely used in the children's toy market, and of course babies' and children's clothing is almost always designated by age rather than size. However, age is not the whole answer – apart from the obvious divergence in clothing as children leave the baby stage, their interests in toys is also

Figure 6.5

Demographic segmentation

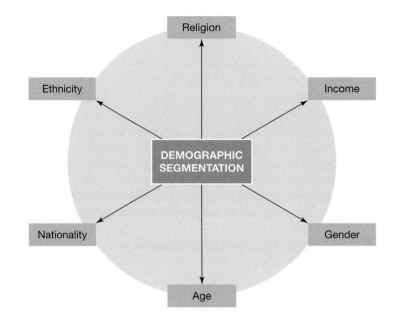

gender-specific to a large extent. As children develop interests of their own, and become more individual in their needs, other factors become more important than age. For example, Disneyland Paris know that around 20 per cent of children would not want to visit the theme park under any circumstances, even though the majority of children would love a visit.

A more subtle effect of segmentation by age is that different age groups have had different life experiences. People in their 80s remember living through the Second World War, people in their 70s were teenagers during the 1950s, people in their 50s remember Vietnam War protests, people in their 40s spent their early working lives in Thatcherite Britain, people in their 30s grew up with the telecommunications revolution and people in their 20s are faced with a longer working life than previous generations. These life experiences are particularly useful when tailoring communications because (for example) music from the specific era can be used to trigger memories. Some products also rely on nostalgia – DVDs, compilation albums of music from specific decades or 'best of' musicians who were popular at the time, and even DVDs or videos of newsreel events, are all aimed at specific age groups.

Gender

Segmentation by gender is not as clear-cut as it once was. Gender roles have shifted dramatically in the last thirty years, with men taking on more household tasks and women working outside the home and developing careers. For example, the highly successful advertising campaign for Flash cleaning products features a man doing the cleaning: the ads use the **strap line** 'Flash does the hard work so you don't have to', and implies that the man is cleverly gaining favour with his wife by cleaning the bathroom. Research by Mintel shows that 28 per cent of men take major responsibility for cooking, 20 per cent take responsibility for all the laundry and 40 per cent of men aged 55+ do at least half the grocery shopping. Men still take the bulk of the responsibility for gardening and DIY tasks, although women are encroaching on these traditional male preserves.

It seems likely that these trends will continue. While there are many older households in which the traditional gender division of household tasks continues, most younger couples have a more equal division of labour, and certainly younger women usually expect to have careers rather than 'pin money' jobs, which means that household tasks

strap line The slogan at the end of an advertisement.

need to be shared equally. The statistics may also be skewed by the number of women who remain at home to care for small children and therefore carry out more household tasks.

Astute marketers have taken note of these changes. Power tool manufacturers now offer smaller, lighter power tools with women in mind: the Black and Decker Mouse sander is an example. Instructions for assembling flat-pack furniture no longer assume that the reader will have studied woodwork in school, and men are shown cooking, cleaning and shopping in TV advertising.

Having said that, there are still products which are gender-specific, simply because of physical differences between men and women. Added to these are products which tend to be aimed at one gender because social mores still dictate some gender roles. For example, facial make-up for men is still somewhat rare in Western societies, and relatively few women take up boxing. The old gender roles may be eroding, but there will probably always be some products which meet the needs of one gender better than they do the other.

Sheila's Wheels specialises in car insurance for women.

OK, so gender roles have changed. Why do we care? Is it still an issue whether we show a man doing the hoovering, or a woman fixing the car? Haven't we moved beyond this need to make a conscious effort about gender stereotyping?

Or have we even gone too far the other way? Some advertising is derogatory to men, showing women rescuing men from their own folly, or implying that men are incapable of carrying out simple household tasks. Should such advertising be subject to the same protests that eventually removed advertising which demeaned women? A simple test for whether an advertisement is sexist: reverse the genders and see what happens.

Maybe it's men's turn to be demeaned in this way. But to be fair, the current generation of men are not responsible for past gender stereotyping, and anyway two wrongs don't make a right!

Within the gender debate there is also the question of sexual orientation. Homosexual people (gays) have specific characteristics from a marketing viewpoint: in general, gay people tend to be wealthier and have fewer outgoings, since they are less likely to have dependent children. In the UK, gays' disposable income is called the Pink Pound, valued at around £6bn a year, in the US it is the Dorothy Dollar and it is estimated to be worth around $350bn a year (BBC News 1998). This has meant that gays have been targeted as a group by financial institutions and by information services, clubs and even holiday companies such as Pink Pound Travel. Gays are estimated to represent about 4 per cent of the population, although this figure is doubtful because of a reluctance to 'come out' or identify oneself as gay due to the prejudice and stigma which still attaches to homosexuality in some quarters. Research carried out in Scotland for the Glasgow-based Beyond Barriers organisation indicated that two-thirds of gay people had been verbally abused or threatened.

Male homosexuals earn on average 23 per cent more than the average, have twice as many credit cards as the general population, and spend more than the average on entertainment (BBC 1998).

Income

Segmenting by income is widely practiced, although it is not as simple as might first appear. For example, an individual may have a high income coupled with high outgoings,

Pink Pound Travel is a brand name of Dovehouse Travel and is targeted at gay people. The organisation was founded as a result of the prejudice some gays have experienced when travelling – homosexuality is not always tolerated in some countries, and gay couples frequently find themselves subjected to verbal and even physical abuse.

The company organises holidays to many destinations worldwide: the Caribbean, the Mediterranean, city breaks and ski holidays. The company works closely with the Caribbean Tourist Authority and the Canadian Counsellors programme as well as with many other tourist organisations to ensure that customers can enjoy a hassle-free holiday.

The holidays are not cheap, but peace of mind on holiday is worth paying for.

or vice-versa. Income segmentation is often used for goods such as cars, luggage, holidays and fashion goods.

There is an assumption that rich people spend more money, and this is not unreasonable: the difficulty lies in deciding what a rich person would regard as being a desirable item. Income actually says very little about an individual's tastes and interests, and even less about what such people regard as value for money. Rich people are often very careful with their money – not surprisingly, since this is how many of them became rich in the first place.

Some firms have managed to grow successful on marketing to the poorer end of the market. Retailers such as Aldi and Lidl target less affluent market segments, offering basic products at knock-down prices in basic surroundings. By having a lean organisation, narrow product ranges, cheap store locations and a no-frills approach to store design, these companies have minimised their costs and can offer heavily-discounted products. During 2008, as the recession began to take effect and food prices rose, these stores reported substantial increases in business from middle-class consumers looking for ways to economise.

Religion, ethnicity and nationality

At first sight, these factors would have little bearing on consumption behaviour. In truth, their influence is limited and often affects only a small part of the consumer's purchasing behaviour, but each of the three factors has some effect.

For example, religion will have an effect on the purchase of religious artefacts and, in some cases, affects diet. Jewish people and Muslims avoid pork, Buddhists avoid meat in general, Jains and Parsees are strictly vegetarian, and many Catholics still eat fish on a Friday, although this is no longer a requirement of the faith.

ethnicity Cultural background.

Ethnicity is a combination of culture and race. The cultural element of ethnicity has clear effects on people's eating habits, clothing and even entertainment. The physical differences which go with racial characteristics may have some effect on purchasing: darker-skinned women use different cosmetics, and the characteristics of hair differ between black, Asian and white people, which means that slightly different formulations of hair care product are needed. In recent years some ethnic segmentation has become blurred because marketing activities have caused culture swapping: people have adopted products aimed at other cultures (food and clothing being good examples) and therefore ethnic segmentation for these products is no longer realistic (Jamal 2003).

Nationality is a legal state rather than an ethnic state, so has relatively little effect on purchase, but in global markets it is common to segment by nationality. This is because different legal restrictions apply within different countries. There exists a limited number of products which apply only to people of a particular nationality – flags, patriotic symbols and legal services for example.

Psychographic segmentation

People can be divided into groups according to lifestyle or personality characteristics. Lifestyles are both created by products and dictate which products will be bought: someone who owns a penthouse has a different lifestyle from someone who owns a farm, but those dwellings are products as well as lifestyle determinants.

Lifestyle segmentation has the major advantage that it relates directly to purchasing behaviour. It has been said that marketing delivers a lifestyle, so looking at consumers in terms of their chosen way of life seems logical on the face of it. One well-known lifestyle segmentation method is the VALS structure, shown in Figure 6.6.

The VALS structure postulates nine different lifestyle positions. At the poorer end of the scale, people are need-driven: they are concerned with survival, security and belonging. In the zone of the double hierarchy, wealthier people can be divided into the **outer-directed** (those whose main motivation derives from the respect or admiration of others) and the inner-directed (those whose main motivation derives from an inner drive).

outer directed Taking one's cue from the behaviour of others.

Finally, the theory postulates that people at the top of the hierarchy (the wealthiest or most secure people) have an integrated set of values and a balanced lifestyle.

At the bottom of the hierarchy, **survivors** are those people who can barely make ends meet. They are struggling to maintain any kind of lifestyle, and live in poverty. Slightly further up are the **sustainers**, who might typically be in a difficult position financially but can still maintain a reasonable level of existence above the subsistence point. **Belongers** are those whose basic needs have been met, and who seek to belong to society. They have not been totally excluded by reason of their circumstances: they would typically join clubs, do voluntary work and seek to fit in with other people. The need to belong can be a very powerful motivator – members of a football fan club often resist buying anything outside the group (Richardson and Turley 2006).

survivors Those people who struggle to maintain any kind of lifestyle.

sustainers People living close to the subsistence level.

belongers People who seek to join groups in society.

Inner-directed people divide into the I-am-me group, who seek to live their own lives regardless of what others think, the experiential group, who seek new experiences, and

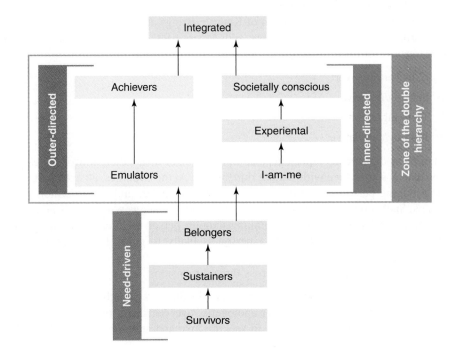

Figure 6.6
Values and lifestyles (VALs)

societally conscious Cause-oriented people who become involved in charitable work.

achievers People who seek respect by buying appropriate products.

the societally conscious group, who seek to do good in the world. Because these groups are less concerned about what others think of them, they are unlikely to buy goods simply because of the brand. The I-am-me group tend not to be heavy consumers, but are often creative. The experiential group are customers for travel, concerts, interesting foods, restaurants, cinema and theatre. The societally conscious group are cause-orientated people who enjoy getting involved in charity work or political parties (Donnelly 1970).

Among the outer-directed people, the emulators seek to copy other people, taking their cue from their neighbours. They are susceptible to suggestion from marketers, since they are keen to find out what is currently in fashion. Achievers, on the other hand, seek respect from other people and are therefore prime buyers of status symbol products such as designer clothing, branded goods and visible purchases such as cars (Zinkhan and Shermohamad 1986). People with an integrated set of values like to be respected, but do not let this drive their lives: they are often wealthy and care about other people, but have their own set of drivers.

Another possible segmentation method, still in its infancy, is the concept of interpretive communities. These are subcultures sharing a way of interpreting messages (and of course brands) (Kates 2002). Interpretive communities can only be identified by the way they process information, so they are difficult to identify except by running an advertisement and seeing who responds to it. For example, it is known that some people prefer to interpret messages visually, some prefer kinaesthetic (tactile) interpretations, while others process information aurally. Each group will respond to advertising differently (Skinner and Stephens 2003).

Personality characteristics

Segmenting by personality has a certain appeal about it, because personality changes only slowly over a long period of time. The difficulty lies in identifying a group of people with similar personality traits and targeting them successfully. For example, an insurance company might wish to target people with the personality traits of being security minded, being afraid of burglary, and of owning enough valuable objects to make the policy a large one. Such individuals would probably be careful to lock their houses, would have secure door and window locks and probably a burglar alarm, would be highly motivated to buy a policy and would be prepared to pay a lot for it. Unfortunately there is no easy way to target such a group: there is no single advertising medium directed at these people.

Psychologists have developed many ways of grouping people according to personality types. The mother and daughter team of Kathryn Briggs and Isabel Myers developed the Myers-Briggs Type Indicator (Briggs and Myers 1992) which has four personality dimensions, as follows:

- Extrovert/introvert
- Sensing/intuitive
- Thinking/feeling
- Judging/perceptive.

Each of these dimensions represents a continuum rather than a dichotomy, and each of us can be placed somewhere within those dimensions. At the extremes, an extrovert-sensing-feeling-judging person is warm-hearted, talkative, popular, and likes harmonious relationships. Such a person is likely to enjoy meals out, evenings with friends and romantic encounters. An introvert-intuitive-thinking-judging person is likely to be quiet, intelligent, cerebral and reclusive. Such a person is likely to enjoy the Internet, computer games, reading and learning.

Horney (1945) defined people across three dimensions:

compliant Someone who moves towards people, has goodness, sympathy, love, unselfishness and humility.

- **Compliant.** Moves towards people, has goodness, sympathy, love, unselfishness and humility. Tends to be over-apologetic, over-sensitive, over-grateful, over-generous and over-considerate in seeking love and attention.

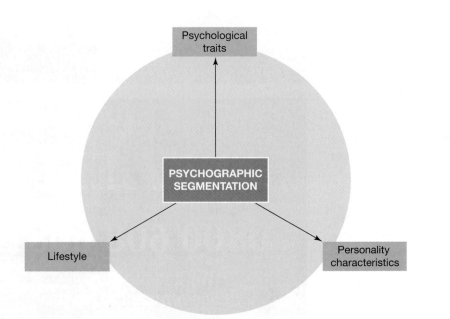

Figure 6.7

Psychographic segmentation

- **Aggressive**. Usually moves against people. Controls fear and emotions in a quest for success, prestige and admiration. Needs power, exploits others.

- **Detached**. Moves away from people. Conformity is repugnant to the detached person. Distrustful of others, these people are self-sufficient and independent, and value intelligence and reasoning.

There is some empirical evidence to show that these categorisations have some effect on people's buying behaviour. For example, it has been shown that compliant people use more mouthwash and toilet soap, and prefer branded products: aggressive people use more cologne and aftershave. Detached people show low interest in branding (Cohen 1967).

The main way of targeting by personality characteristics is to use similar types of individual in the advertising, so that the product is modelled (see Chapter 4). Thus a product aimed at extrovert people would show extroverts using the product.

Although personality traits can be linked to consumer behaviour, the problem lies in the sheer number of traits which have been identified. It has been estimated that there are some 18000 personality traits (Allport and Odbert 1936), and since each of these is interdependent, study of a few traits in isolation is unlikely to yield any concrete results (*Marketing News* 1985).

A relatively recent concept is that of the 'savvy' consumer. These are people who have in-depth understanding of consumption possibilities. They have the following characteristics (McDonald and Uncles 2007):

1 They are competent in technology, especially communications technology.

2 They are competent in interpersonal networking.

3 They are good at online networking.

4 They are marketing-literate; in other words, they understand how marketers are trying to influence them.

5 They are empowered by their own self-efficacy.

6 They are empowered by the expectations of firms, because they understand how to manipulate marketers.

aggressive Someone who usually moves against people, and controls fear and emotions in a quest for success, prestige and admiration.

detached Someone who moves away from people, and is self-sufficient and independent.

Marketing in Practice
Frizzell Insurance

Courtesy of The Advertising Archives

Motor insurance is a dangerous business to be in. Car accidents can be expensive, with personal injury claims, and competition is fierce. Many insurers operate on extremely narrow margins as a result, yet the industry is worth millions a year.

Frizzell Insurance has cornered a nice little niche within the market. For many years, the company has targeted public employees – civil servants, teachers, university lecturers and the like – people who do not drive much and who tend to like a quiet life. These are ideal people for a car insurer, because they do not have accidents and they tend to be loyal in a market known for shopping around. They are also easy to target: Frizzell recruited customers mainly by using leaflet drops and mailshots to the place of work.

The problem for the company is that there is only a limited number of such people, and (due to Government cutbacks) the numbers were declining. Frizzell therefore needed to find some other way of attracting similar types of people, and decided to go the mass-advertising route, using television as a medium. The company is too small to be able to handle large numbers of telephone calls, however, so the advertising needed to attract only those people whom the company was targeting.

Each advert was designed to show a couple who had been with Frizzell for many years. The couples were shown as they are now, and as they were then, with music from the period when they first insured with Frizzell. The adverts were tested with both the target audience and what Frizzell thought of as the 'undesirables' – people in the categories they did not want to attract. Potential customers thought the adverts were charming and engaging, whereas the 'undesirables' thought them boring, banal and condescending. The result was that target customers, who identified with the people in the advert, telephoned to buy insurance, whereas the 'undesirables' were repelled by the advert. Frizzell experienced its biggest-ever annual growth of business, outstripping arch-rival Direct Line and breaking into a new area of loyal customers.

Savvy consumers pose a special challenge to marketers because they know how to manipulate situations to their own advantage. This is particularly a problem in personal selling, for example in a retail store.

Segmenting Business Markets

Segmentation methods and criteria differ between consumer markets and business-to-business markets, for the following reasons:

1 Consumer markets are characterised by customers who are either the end user of the product or are very close to the end user. Business markets are characterised by buyers who do not themselves use the product.

2 The number of potential customers in business markets is almost always smaller, so a greater degree of customisation is likely to be necessary.

3 Psychographic and demographic variables are almost entirely inappropriate.

Business marketers should be careful about applying consumer segmentation techniques directly to business markets. Unrefined use of consumer segmentation techniques can lead a business marketer in the wrong direction.

Many firms define a market segment by product type or product size. This overly simplistic approach can have dire consequences, because it is product-focused rather than customer-focused. In the US computer hard disk drive (HDD) industry, suppliers identified customers for 14-inch drives as mainframe computer manufacturers, users of 8-inch drives as minicomputer makers, customers for 5.25-inch drives as personal computer manufacturers and for 2.5-inch drives as portable and laptop suppliers. Many firms focused on one or few segments and were unable to move into new segments as technology converged. A number of leading US HDD firms such as Memorex, Control Data and DEC were eventually forced to leave the HDD business. The leading Japanese firms continue to be the major suppliers, as they have been for the past 20 years (Chesbrough 2003).

Another common error business marketers make in segmenting is simply accepting the definition of an entire industry as one segment. For instance, a manufacturer of train control equipment might say 'we sell to electrified railways' and classify the Santiago Subway or London Underground in the same category as a surface electrified railway in India. The most obvious differences (such as the product being used underground as opposed to being used in full exposure to the elements) would thus be ignored. Some managers err on the other side of the spectrum, thinking about their segments in too narrow a fashion. They may think only about a particular industry dominated by a few major firms and not about new segments which could use their product that are entirely unrelated to the primary target segment.

Talking Point

If a whole industry is not a segment, then what is? If we define our segment as smaller than the whole industry, how do we decide who we are *not* going to sell to? And isn't that a little stupid anyway? If another firm in the same industry wanted to buy our products, are we going to throw them out on their ears? Or if a firm from another industry wants to buy, what do we say? Do we tell them their money isn't good enough for us? Obviously not – so what are we saying?

Is segmentation about who spends their money with us – or is it about how we spend our money?

Segmentation variables

Business marketing segmentation variables can be divided into two main categories.

In the first category, called **identifiers** by Day (1990), firms attempt to pre-establish segments a priori, that is before any data is collected. These are the more traditional segmentation variables because the data is easier to obtain through observation of the buying situation or from secondary sources. Some researchers call these macro variables. As can be seen from Table 6.2, they include demographic, operations, product required and purchasing situation variables related to current or potential customer market segments. Day (1990) also identified response profile characteristics 'unique to the product or service . . . based on attributes and behaviour toward the product category or specific brands and vendors in that category'. These include specific vendor attributes such as overall value offered, product quality, vendor reputation, on-time delivery and so on. In addition, customer variables such as the make-up of the decision-making unit (or buying centre), the importance of the purchase to the subject segment, and the innovativeness of the firms in this potential segment are examined. Another important aspect of the response profile technique is to review applications to determine how products are used. Finally, personal characteristics may be included to define a particular segment. These include variables related to individuals in the buying centre such as risk tolerance, loyalty, age, education and experience.

identifiers The major variables in segmentation which can be listed without carrying out extensive research.

Table 6.2 Segmentation variables

Identifier (a priori)	Response profile (a posteriori)

● **Demographic**
  – Industry classification
  – Firm type – OEM, end user, aftermarket (MRO)
  – Company size
  – Geographic location
  – Financial info/credit rating
 	
● **Operations**
  – Technologies used
  – Level of use – heavy, light, non-user
  – Centralised/decentralised purchasing
 	
● **Product Required**
  – Custom ↔ Standard
 	
● **Purchasing Situation**
  – Buying situation – new task, modified rebuy, straight rebuy
  – Current attitude toward our firm
  – Relationships
	● **Vendor Product Attributes**
	  – Overall value
	  – Product quality
	  – Vendor reputation
	  – Innovativeness
	  – On-time delivery
	  – Lowest cost
	
	● **Customer Variables**
	  – DMU (buying centre) make-up
	  – Purchase importance
	  – Attitude toward product
	  – Corporate cultural characteristics (innovativeness)
	
	● **Application**
	  – End use
	  – Importance of value in use
	
	● **DMU/Buying Centre Personal Characteristics**
	  – Risk tolerance
	  – Loyalty to current vendor
	  – Age
	  – Experience
	  – Education

Adapted from: Kotler (2003), Day (1990), Rao and Wang (1995), Malhotra (1989), Cardozo (1980).

These variables are often referred to as a posteriori, or after the fact variables, in which a 'clustering approach' is used to gather like customers together based on their particular needs. Some researchers call these micro-variables.

Looking at the usefulness of the two basic segmentation approaches as measured against the tests for a good segment, Malhotra (1989) claims the identifier approach is better than the response profile approach in terms of measurability and accessibility, since it is easy to find and reach the segments which already have established data classifications. He feels this method is particularly good for institutional markets where the number of establishments is small and the number of variables is large. On the other hand, Malhotra believes that using the response profile or clustering approach will produce more responsiveness from a particular segment, since the marketing mix will be closely tailored to the specific needs of the segment identified.

Generally speaking, business marketers have used identifiers in segmenting their customers. The major reason for this is simplicity. With the Internet, it is easy to get the kinds of information needed to segment markets using the identifier approach.

The use of the response profile approach is a subject of much discussion in the literature. While there is general agreement that the customer's view of vendor attributes, how the decision-making unit is constituted, or the risk tolerance of key members of the DMU is invaluable segmentation information, there is little agreement about how widespread this approach is.

Dibb and Simkin (2001) point out that although much has been written about segmentation, there is limited guidance for managers attempting to implement a true market segmentation process. They identified three major categories of barriers to segmentation: infrastructure, process and implementation. These can be further sub-divided into culture, structure and resources.

Infrastructure barriers include the support (or lack of support) from senior management, lack of intra-functional communications, entrenched organisational structures and the lack of financial and human resources. Process issues include the lack of practical advice on how to actually implement segmentation, the unwillingness to share ideas and data, the lack of a fit with corporate strategy and the misuse of the process because there is poor understanding of it. Implementation barriers include the difficulty of changing present segmentation in the firm. Since industries are often organised around product categories or distribution channels, it is extremely difficult to develop segments which are not congruent with those existing divisions. These barriers also include poor identification of responsibility and poor communications and lack of senior management involvement. In the end, the test is aligning budgets and assignments with the segmentation solutions. If this isn't accomplished, the entire process is a waste of time. A summary of the key segmentation barriers and recommended treatments is shown in Table 6.3.

Dibb and Simkin (2001) recommend treatments or solutions to the problems identified. As can be seen from Table 6.3, prior to the process it is important to find important data and identify the people and the skills required to get the segmentation process done. Senior management must strongly support the process, develop the proper communications channels, establish adequate budgets and set up training for people who will be assigned to do the process but may not have the necessary education or skills.

During the process, it is important to identify the segmentation steps, get the education gaps filled, then collect the data through internal and external sources (here a firm may employ a number of secondary and primary data techniques). It is also important to establish regular meetings for communications or progress and for senior management to be sure that the segmentation is going to fit into the overall corporate strategy.

Finally, to facilitate implementation the authors recommend identifying the specific audiences to whom the findings will be communicated and then to do that; to make changes to plans and programs congruent with the new segmentation solutions; to identify changes that are required in the culture and the structure of the firm; then to specify responsibilities, budgets and timing to make the segmentation work; finally to set up a monitoring process to see whether the segmentation process is being implemented and whether this implementation is effective.

The most widely accepted approach to segmentation is that proposed by Bonoma and Shapiro (1984). They describe the nested approach, starting with very general, easily available information and moving to the most specific variables which, incidentally, are the most difficult to obtain information about. See Figure 6.8.

The first and most obvious step is to group companies by industry classification. In the United States, the most common industry classification has been the Standard Industrial Classification (SIC), which was replaced in 1997 by the North American Industrial Classification System (NAICS). The NAICS was created to rationalise data among the three NAFTA countries – United States, Canada and Mexico. Other classification systems include the SITC System established by the United Nations in 1950. The US also participates in the Harmonised Commodity Description System, known simply as the Harmonised System, which has been used to classify goods in international trade since 1 January 1989. This system is in common use in more than 50 countries.

Industry classifications give a firm a start on a grouping of customers and prospective customers into potential segments.

Many firms simply divide their customers into heavy, medium and light users, the so-called A-B-C division. This may be useful for assigning salespeople to particular accounts, but is a poor substitute for the full segmentation process. Using firm demographics also includes dividing customers into types – OEM, user, and aftermarket (MRO) – and also to group them by company size, geographic location and by specific financial factors such as creditworthiness.

Table 6.3 Diagnosing and treating key segmentation barriers

Problems	Infrastructure	Process	Implementation
Culture	• Inflexible, resists new ideas • Not customer focused • Doesn't understand segmentation rationale	• Not committed to sharing data/ideas • Lack of 'buy in' • No fit with corporate strategy planning	• Product focus • Insufficient belief in the process • Unwillingness to change current segmentation
Structure	• Lack of intra-functional communications • Low senior management interest or involvement • Entrenched organisational structures	• Misuse of segmentation process	• Poor demarcation of responsibility • Ineffective communications of segmentation solution • Poor senior management involvement
Resources	• Too few or untrained people • Insufficient budgets	• Inadequate data available • Insufficient budgets • Too few or untrained people	• Lack of alignment of budgeting with segmentation • Insufficient time allowed
Solutions	**Prior to process:** • Find available data • Identify people/skills • Get senior management support • Develop communications • Establish adequate budgets • Train people – basic segmentation skills	**During process:** • Specify segmentation steps • Fill gaps in education/skills • Collect data – internal and external • Establish regular communications meetings • Review for fit with corporate strategy	**Facilitate Implementation:** • Identify and communicate findings • Make changes to plans and programmes • Identify changes required to culture and structure • Specify budgets, responsibilities and timing to roll out solutions • Develop method for monitoring roll out

Source: Based on Dibb and Simkin (2001).

Classifying customers according to OEM, end user or aftermarket (maintenance, repair and operations) gives important clues to their commonalities. An OEM or original equipment manufacturer buys components, systems, equipment and materials. In the case of components, these enter the OEM's final product, while materials are consumed in the manufacturing of their products. Systems and equipment are used to make the products. OEMs often purchase many different items to develop a particular product and frequently brand the product with their own name. Users obviously put the product to use. For instance, John Deere tractors are used by farmers, while Deere itself is an OEM (Hlavacek and Ames 1986). The after market, also called MRO, includes firms who offer add-on products, repair services or replacement parts. Often, a producer may sell his product or services to all three of these firm types, but each is a separate and different segment since requirements will probably be quite different (There is more on this in Chapter 5).

A second step involves more understanding of customer operations. In this step, the marketer would determine what technologies potential customers are employing, whether

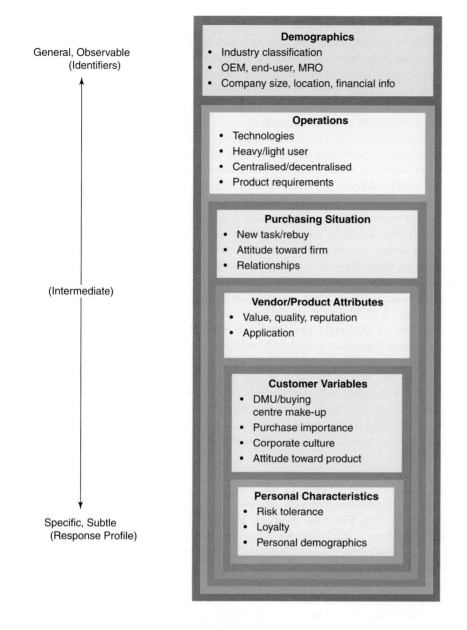

General, Observable
(Identifiers)

(Intermediate)

Specific, Subtle
(Response Profile)

Demographics
- Industry classification
- OEM, end-user, MRO
- Company size, location, financial info

Operations
- Technologies
- Heavy/light user
- Centralised/decentralised
- Product requirements

Purchasing Situation
- New task/rebuy
- Attitude toward firm
- Relationships

Vendor/Product Attributes
- Value, quality, reputation
- Application

Customer Variables
- DMU/buying centre make-up
- Purchase importance
- Corporate culture
- Attitude toward product

Personal Characteristics
- Risk tolerance
- Loyalty
- Personal demographics

Figure 6.8

The nested approach to segmentation
Source: (Adapted from Bonoma and Shapiro 1984)

Table 6.4 Classification of customers

Type of customer	Description
OEM	Original Equipment Manufacturer. These customers buy manufacturing equipment, raw materials and components to make into finished products. Examples would be car manufacturers or consumer durables manufacturers.
End user*	These customers consume the product entirely in the course of running the business. For example, a company will use cleaning materials, energy, copier paper, office furniture and so forth without incorporating any of these items into the finished products which it sells.
Aftermarket* (MRO)	Maintenance, repair and operations companies provide services to companies and consumers. For example, a computer repair company will use spare parts, tools and transport to repair or replace defective parts.

*See glossary.

they are heavy or light users of the product to be offered, whether they purchase in a centralised or decentralised way, and specifically what product requirements customers have, ranging from standard to custom products.

A third step is to look at the purchasing situation – whether for this firm the purchase is a new task, a straight rebuy or a modified rebuy, whether the potential customer has positive attitudes toward the firm and what relationships have been established by the marketing firm with potential customers.

The fourth step is to determine what commonalities there are among potential customers related to particular attributes by an offering firm. For instance, one customer group may be quite price-sensitive, where another emphasises delivery and still a third product quality defined in some specific manner. As an example, a firm supplying chemicals to an ink-maker might find that colour consistency was of primary importance and far outweighed price or delivery as a purchasing attribute. Another aspect of the vendor attribute would be the application in which the product may be used.

A more refined and more difficult set of variables to gain are identified in Figure 6.8 as customer variables. First and most important would be the make-up of the buying centre or DMU. Included here would be the importance of the purchase to the firm, the corporate culture, including the attitude toward innovation, and finally the attitude toward the product area. A final and most difficult set of characteristics which may be used for segmentation are personal characteristics of individuals in the DMU. These include age, experience and education, loyalty to current vendor and risk tolerance. A common saying used in many firms is 'no one ever got fired for buying IBM'. Individuals with low-risk tolerance would tend to choose a vendor like IBM, since the chances of negative consequences for an individual when choosing the pre-eminent supplier in any market are far lower than if that individual had chosen an unknown supplier. In nearly every industrial market, firms tend to stay with vendors who have satisfied them. Therefore the attitude toward the firm (as well as loyalty and tolerance for risk) will be important segmentation characteristics.

Robertson and Barich (1992) proposed a simple approach to segmentation based only on the purchase decision process. In this case, the authors claim that identifying potential customers as **first-time prospects**, **novices** and **sophisticates** yields all the segmentation information needed. First-time prospects are firms who see a need for the product, have started to evaluate possible suppliers, but have not yet purchased. Novices are customers who have purchased the product for the first time within the last 90 days, while sophisticates have purchased the product before and are ready to rebuy or have recently repurchased.

First-time prospects are seeking honest sales people who know and understand their business, a vendor who has been in business for some time, and they usually negotiate for a trial period. Novices are looking for technical support, training and knowledgeable sales reps. Sophisticates are seeking compatibility with existing systems, customised products, a successful record from the vendor, speed in sorting out problems and post-sales support. The main advantage of this simplified approach is the ability to implement it with the sales force, which is often the major hurdle for effective segmentation implementation.

Segmenting by customer benefits is recommended as the most effective approach; Rao and Wang (1995) found that identifiers do not correlate very well with profile or benefit sought variables. While these authors endorsed the nested approach to segmentation, they emphasised the importance of understanding specific customer benefits for the most effective segmentation.

Need to re-segment

Since business market segments change quickly, it is important to re-segment frequently. Some have suggested re-segmenting at the beginning of a new stage of the product lifecycle, but this is too difficult to determine. Nevertheless, changes in competition, technological advances, economic downturns or upswings and consolidation of an industry make re-segmentation very important. Once a firm begins to look at its existing

---

first-time prospects Potential customers with whom the company has never done business before.

novices Customers who have purchased the product for the first time within the last 90 days.

sophisticates Customers who have purchased the product before and are ready to rebuy or have recently repurchased.

segmentation on a regular basis, it may find it necessary to establish new segments for the most effective use of its marketing efforts. Managements should avoid being 'married' to the current segmentation and hold open the possibility of re-segmenting. It is a management task to question the assumptions which underlie the current segmentation on a regular basis.

Global segmentation

Segmentation strategy is not limited to any one country. Sophisticated business marketing firms look across countries for commonalities of market segments. For instance, ICI Nobel Explosives offers mining explosives across various countries to similar customer types, coordinating its activities in each country by segment and offering product and sales activities accordingly (Gillespie, Jeannet and Hennessey 2004). The same segmentation procedure described in Figure 6.8 can to be used across various countries, except that the data is much more difficult to get and developing common measures is often a real obstacle. Despite this, Schuster and Bodkin (1987) found that more than 40 per cent of firms they surveyed gathered segmentation information for the following macro-variables: geographic location, company size, usage, buying strategy, end market and decision-making stage. More than 40 per cent of firms gathered data for the following micro-variables: product attributes, purchase importance, attitudes and personal characteristics.

In business markets, it is not unusual to find commonalities among customers throughout the world. Electric utilities require the same products whether they are located in Kuala Lumpur or Caracas. A firm selling switchgear to electric utilities must look to a worldwide customer base in order to get the economies of scale necessary to be a global competitor. According to Yip (2003), customers can be segmented according to their purchasing patterns. **Global customers** are quite willing to purchase products outside their domestic markets and tend to have global control of purchasing from headquarters. Another important variable for segmenting these customers is the way in which the products are used. Yip defines **national global customers** as customers who use suppliers from around the world but employ the products in one country. **Multinational global customers** also buy from suppliers in many countries, but they use the products in many countries as well. Management should look for commonalities among customers using the segmentation process described in the earlier part of the chapter rather than accept that minor differences make serving one segment across countries too difficult to achieve. There are many benefits to serving multinational customer segments, not only including economies of scale, but also moving rapidly to world-class product and service offerings, making further expansion even easier.

A study of the purchasing decision process in a region of the United States, Sweden, France and five Southeast Asian countries found some differences in the decision-making process and the structure of the buying centre (Mattson and Salehi-Sangari 1993). This study also found differences in the most important purchase decision variables used by the decision-making unit for the same products. In short, this study serves as a caution that care must be taken in segmenting markets across countries. However, the benefits of international segmentation are worth the effort required.

Courier firms need to serve a global market.

global customers Firms which are willing to purchase products outside their domestic markets and tend to have global control of purchasing from headquarters.

national global customers Customers who source products globally, but only use them within their national borders.

multinational global customers Customers who source products globally, and also use the products globally.

Targeting

Targeting is a process of choosing a segment or segments, deciding on a tactical approach to marketing the products to that segment, and developing the tactics into practical actions.

Figure 6.9

Segment selection process
Source: (Adapted from Freytag and Clarke 2001)

FUTURE ATTRACTIVENESS

- Size and growth
- Profitability
- Relative risk
- Competition
- Government/environmental considerations
- Customer demands/technology
- Present relationships
- Development of new relationships

RESOURCE DEMANDS

- Technology
- Relationships
- Human resources – purchasing, sales, service, production
- Image
- Capital investment
- Product development

FIRM STRATEGY

- Corporate direction
- Management commitments
- Organisational requirements

For a segment to be viable, it must have the following characteristics:

- *It must be definable or measurable.* There must be some way of identifying the members of the segment and knowing how many of them there are.
- *It must be accessible.* This means it must be possible to communicate with the segment as a group, and get the products to them as a group.
- *It must be substantial,* i.e. big enough to be worth targeting.
- *It must be congruent.* The members must have closely similar needs.
- *It must be stable.* The segment should not change substantially over time, either in its needs or in its membership.

The three key criteria are accessibility, substance and measurability, but it is important to look at the causes underlying the segmentation.

Freytag and Clarke (2001) offer a segment selection process illustrated in Figure 6.9.

This process requires that a firm compare potential segments it may serve, estimating future attractiveness, resource demands and fit with firm strategy. First, the firm should decide whether this particular segment will be growing at a suitable rate and is large enough and profitable enough to serve. In addition, the firm should assess the competition and the risk, understand any governmental or environmental concerns, what demands customers may have and how serving this particular segment may affect present and future relationships with current and future customers. Second, the firm must look at demands on its resources in technology, relationships, human resources in each of the functional areas, image, capital investment and product development required. Finally, the firm should examine whether this new segment is congruent with its present or future strategy related to the overall corporate direction, management's commitment and organisational requirements required to implement the strategy.

Bonoma and Shapiro (1984) recommend choosing segments using two major criteria: Customer Conversion Analysis and Segment Profitability Analysis. The first simply means the attempt by a manager to determine how many potential prospects in a particular segment can be converted to customers and how large that served segment will be. This is based upon the number of prospects in a market (the density) which can be reached for a particular marketing expenditure.

Segment Profitability Analysis is an attempt to determine the contribution margin per pound invested to serve that segment. Bonoma and Shapiro recommend combining these approaches to determine which segments a firm ought to serve. To decide on which market segments to target, a firm would decide whether a segment is attractive, whether the firm has the resources to serve that segment and whether serving that segment fits with the company's overall objectives.

A firm may choose to apply undifferentiated marketing, which means focusing on commonalities among all segments, but in essence attempting to serve the entire market with only one marketing mix. This is found most often in the earliest stages of a product lifecycle when undifferentiated product will be accepted by customers because there is no other choice. Think for a moment of the early days of the personal computer market industry. Early personal computers were very heavy, very slow and had limited software capabilities. Yet many firms purchased large numbers of these personal computers because the productivity increases of their employees outweighed the difficulties of finding specific computers which satisfied their corporate needs. Undifferentiated marketing usually only lasts as long as competition is limited.

When a firm decides to use differentiated marketing, it designs specific marketing mixes to serve each segment. Obviously, differentiated marketing costs more than undifferentiated marketing and can only be justified when the results outweigh the cost. In order to differentiate its marketing, the firm changes the balance of the marketing mix elements (see Chapter 1) in order to vary its offering.

It is important to remember that not all marketing mix elements have to be changed to serve each segment. In many cases the same product, price and promotion may serve two different segments where the only variation required is distribution or service.

For firms with very limited resources the only choice may be concentrated marketing. In this case a firm concentrates on one or very few segments. The idea is to build a dominant position in that segment. For example, a firm manufacturing highly sensitive, low-light-level television cameras focuses its efforts on industrial applications of unauthorised entry or pilferage. Here again, the marketing mix must be carefully set to serve the specific segment(s) chosen. This is perhaps the most risky targeting strategy, since the possibility exists that the segment may experience economic difficulties or choose to use a substitute product. Firms using the concentration strategy must be vigilant about the possibilities of new segments.

Positioning

Positioning essentially means developing a theme which will provide a 'meaningful distinction for customers' (Day 1990). The concept of positioning was strongly advanced by Ries and Trout (2001). They state that many products already have a distinctive position in the mind of the customer. These positions are difficult to dislodge. For instance, IBM would be thought of as the world's largest and most competent computer company.

There are eight generic factors which are used in positioning products, as follows (Blankson and Kalafatis 2004):

1 Top of the range
2 Service
3 Value for money
4 Reliability
5 Attractiveness
6 Country of origin
7 Brand name
8 Selectivity.

These elements in a positioning strategy are not mutually exclusive, but obviously a firm cannot emphasise all of the factors because such a claim would lack credibility. For example, claiming to offer the best service, best country of origin and best value for money might sound unlikely (depending on one's definition of value for money).

Ries and Trout say that competitors have three possible strategies they may follow. First, the firm may choose to strengthen its current leadership position by reinforcing the original concepts that lead to the first position in the mind of the customer. Second, to establish a new position – 'cherchez les creneaux' – looking for new openings in a market. Third, to attempt to de-position or re-position the competition. Ries and Trout claim that customers establish a ladder for each product category in their minds. On these ladders, buyers establish possible suppliers as first, second or third level. This can offer an opportunity for positioning. Their most famous example of this comes from the car hire business and the car hire company, Avis. When Avis entered the market, Hertz held an unassailable position as the premier car rental firm. Avis was one of many other competitors, but Avis chose to position themselves as 'Number 2' which at that time was an unoccupied position. This immediately catapulted Avis to a position as an important competitor despite the reality that it was no larger than any of the other competitors fighting for a piece of the market with the pre-eminent Hertz. Avis established itself as the first alternative to Hertz in the minds of customers. This is also known as establishing the 'against' position – Avis placing themselves against Hertz.

Research shows that when people compare brands, the position of the product within the overall brand (for example, the best or worst model within the Ford range of cars) is more important than differences between competing brands (the difference between Ford and Renault). This implies that people tend to look at the overall, umbrella brand before they decide on products within the brand (LeClerc, Hsee and Nunnes 2002).

Treacy and Wiersema (1993) offer three value disciplines – operational excellence, customer intimacy or product leadership. They recommend that a firm should try to become a 'champion' in one of these areas while simply meeting industry standards in the other two.

Often, positioning is based upon a series of perceptual maps. An example is shown in Figure 6.10. This example shows two important variables, the horizontal axis for initial price and the vertical axis for technical assistance. It is obvious that the lower right-hand corner of this matrix is probably a poor position to be in. In this quadrant, a firm would be offering a high initial price with only adequate technical assistance.

Let us assume that three firms are in the market. Firm A is a low-priced firm offering little technical assistance. Firm B is a higher-priced firm with very good technical assistance. The management of Firm C may see an opportunity to stake out a position as a somewhat lower price offering than B with somewhat better technical assistance than A. (It might be noted here that a firm which could occupy the upper-left quadrant offering

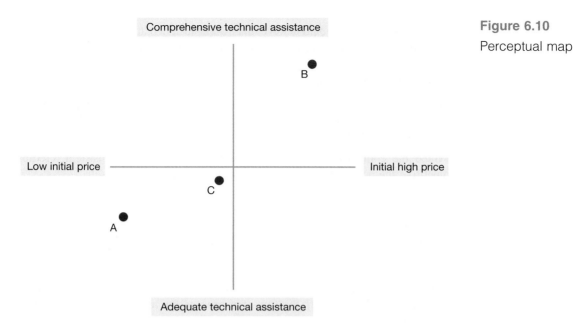

Figure 6.10

Perceptual map

low initial price and very good comprehensive technical assistance might win many more customers than either A, B, or C. However, for the purposes of this example, we assume that it is not possible in the industry to offer this combination.)

A critical point is that customers must place value on the variables being examined. In our example, if the customers had no particular need for technical assistance, this perceptual map would be virtually useless. However, if Firm C's market research shows that technical assistance and initial price are critical variables in the decision-making process, this map is quite useful in helping develop a position which can be clearly communicated to potential customers. In political markets there are five technical features of the political campaign: national policy, local policy, leaders, values and candidates. In fact, though, voters are most often swayed by service features – the degree to which their MP is supportive in the community and so forth (Baines *et al.* 2003).

A special consideration for international positioning is the country of origin effect. Buyers have already established perceptions of country capabilities, i.e. 'German engineering' develops positive associations. For example, an American office furniture firm decided to make products for the European Union countries in a new, state-of-the-art factory in Kells, Ireland. The products were equal in quality in every way to those produced in the US factory, yet Continental buyers often rejected the Irish-made product for competitive brands made in their home countries. Country of origin effect seems to be reduced as buyers become more informed, but it is important for a manager to know what perceptions already exist so that they can be addressed. Country of origin has less effect in consumer markets: a Canadian study showed that 93 per cent of consumers did not know the country of origin of the product they had just bought, and of the 6.5 per cent who did know, only 2 per cent thought that the knowledge might have played a part in their decision (Liefeld 2004).

Positioning a brand relies on four factors (the four Cs of positioning):

1 *Clarity*. It must be obvious to the consumers (or customers) what the brand is and where it sits relative to other brands.

2 *Credibility*. The position must be logical and believable – an obviously cheap and basic product cannot position itself as a premium brand. The reverse is also

true – few people would believe that a well-designed and well-made product can be sold for a low price: most people would suspect a catch!

3 *Consistency*. Whatever position is adopted, the marketers must maintain a consistent brand message.

4 *Competitiveness*. Successful positioning should mean that the company is not trying to occupy a position already taken by a competitor – it is far better to find a position which is currently not subject to competition.

Provided the company has a brand message which is clear, consistent, credible and competitive the positioning will be successful and the brand will sell.

Re-Positioning

If a current position has been rendered useless by competitor pressure or customer indifference, or because the results of the firm are less than expected, new positioning is necessary. Day (1990) offers the four-step process for reassessing a positioning theme shown in Table 6.5.

The main test in this approach is to be sure that alternatives are meaningful to customers and feasible and superior to what competition offers or may offer.

Designing the programmes to implement the chosen position can be a complex task requiring co-operation from all functional areas in the firm and sometimes requiring product and service modifications as well. Once a position is chosen, a firm must clearly communicate this position in a consistent way. The best positioning is simple to communicate: 'the fastest, the oldest or the most technically competent' are easy messages to communicate through advertising, public relations and especially through the sales force. It is especially important that a simple position be established when a firm is to communicate in many languages and across many cultures. Reducing the position to its irreducible simplest form will make it easy for the sales force to communicate what the company stands for, and this is a critical ingredient in global success. Choosing the right position is the culmination of all the market segmentation and targeting work which has been discussed in this chapter.

Table 6.5 Developing a new positioning theme

1 Identify alternative positioning themes.

2 Screen each alternative according to whether it is:
- Meaningful to customers;
- Feasible given the firm's competencies and customer perceptions of the firm;
- Superior/unique compared to competition; difficult for them to match;
- Congruent with company objectives.

3 Choose the position that best satisfies the criteria and generates the most enthusiasm and commitment within the organization.

4 Design the programs needed to implement the position. Compare costs of these programs with likely benefits.

Adapted from: Day (1990).

Summary

Choosing the right customers, for the right reasons, and presenting the product in the right way is how competitive advantage is achieved, no matter what the industry. Segmenting markets is key to allocating marketing resources effectively. Understanding which customer characteristics are most relevant in predicting their propensity to buy the firm's products is a matter of executive judgement, based on clear market research.

Targeting is the process of choosing which segments of the market will be most helpful to the company in achieving its strategic objectives. No company can please everybody, but more importantly no company should try to do so: choosing which customers are too expensive, too troublesome or too unprofitable to service is as important as choosing which are the most attractive customers.

Positioning the brand in the consumers' minds is the final stage in establishing a presence in the market. Correct positioning ensures that customers are not disappointed when they buy the product, and also ensures that the target customers will prefer the product over rival firms' products, ensuring long-term success for the company.

The key points from this chapter are as follows:

- Segmentation is about dividing the overall market into groups of people with similar needs.
- The starting point of segmentation is good market research.
- There are many ways of segmenting markets: the methods can easily be misidentified.
- Targeting implies choosing who *not* to do business with.
- The chosen target is not necessarily the most profitable: there could be strategic reasons for marketing to a particular segment.
- Positioning means providing a meaningful distinction for customers.
- Customers must place value on the variables on offer if positioning is to succeed.
- Positioning relies on clarity, credibility, consistency and competitiveness.

Preview case revisited
Leger Holidays

Leger is strongly committed to the Internet as a marketing medium. In January of 2008, Leger appointed Strange Corporation to handle its online marketing, including its affiliate strategy. Strange are expecting to build greater brand strength through a greater integration of Leger's online activities. Because the company deals largely with educated, better-off people who are Internet-savvy, promoting online is an obvious choice: coupled to this is the general trend in the travel business to run everything online.

As a specialist company, Leger's advertising is generally low key: the company does some TV advertising at off-peak times, and it sponsors some shows on the History Channel. Using the strapline 'Walk in the footsteps of heroes', Leger sponsors documentaries about battles and military equipment, thus getting directly to the target audience (people interested in history) in a way that mainstream free-to-air TV finds difficult to deliver economically.

The company runs its tours by coach, but it has pick-up points throughout the UK, so that those who are elderly or disabled do not need to make their way to (for example) a major airport to start their trip. This does help younger or fitter people as well, of course. The coaches themselves are modern, spacious and well-designed – they have on-board toilet facilities, extra legroom and extremely comfortable seats.

The key factor in the success of the company is, of course, its staff. The drivers, couriers, and especially the guides have extensive training in dealing with the different customer groups. Guides have in-depth knowledge of the battlefields themselves as well as the historical aspects of the battles, so that they are able to point out the places where specific actions took place and guide relatives or veterans to the appropriate locations.

Online reviews of Leger holidays by satisfied customers mainly rate the company extremely highly. Of course, you can't please everybody – some reviews are negative – but it is easy to see why Leger has been voted best tour operator to France in the British Travel Trades Awards 2006.

Case study
Heinz Salad Cream

Salad cream is a uniquely British product. Made from eggs, vinegar, oil, water, mustard and sugar, it is a somewhat more lively (tangy) salad dressing than mayonnaise, closer to the French vinaigrette in taste. It has been in use since the 18th century in England, and has been 'exported' as a concept by British ex-pats to former Empire countries, and (more recently) to the United States. HJ Heinz is the major manufacturer of salad cream in the UK, but several other versions exist, including store brands.

During the 1990s sales of salad cream dropped fairly dramatically. Mayonnaise, often regarded as more sophisticated than salad cream, began to replace it in the British consciousness, and the increasing fashion for cooking at home caused many people to make their own salad dressings rather than buy them in a bottle. People had warm memories of salad cream from their childhoods, but were too embarrassed to buy it – market research showed that, in the main, only people over the age of 45 bought it. Heinz threatened to withdraw the product altogether, but a public outcry caused them to back down and ask advertising agency Leo Burnett to develop a campaign for re-positioning the product. Leo Burnett had recently pitched for carrying out a tomato ketchup campaign: the salad cream brief was a bonus. Re-positioning is never easy. Existing customers can be alienated, while the intended new target market may not accept the product at all – so there is a very real risk of failure.

In 1998, salad cream was relaunched using the theme, 'Any food tastes supreme with Heinz salad cream'. Leo Burnett went for a retro appeal, and used a multimedia approach, advertising on TV, radio, posters, press and new media (websites). Their research had flagged up that younger people enjoyed mixing old and new, and salad cream was a 'blast from the past' which reminded them of their childhoods. Heinz commissioned well-known chefs to create recipes using salad cream: TV chef Gary Rhodes, an advocate of traditional British food, is on record as saying that salad cream is a 'classic'. The intention was to re-position salad cream as a more general product, not just something to pour over lettuce and tomatoes. Heinz have also emphasised that salad cream is lower in fat than mayonnaise, a factor which speaks to the 'healthy eating' consumer.

Overall, the advertising campaign was extremely successful – Heinz were new to radio, but research showed that 91 per cent of radio listeners had top-of-mind awareness of Heinz Salad Cream, compared with 79 per cent of non-listeners. The web campaign was equally successful – Heinz

hired top chef Dan Green to star in films showing him making various dishes using salad cream, with the theme 'It's not just for salads.' The promotional campaign aimed to make the product 'cool' again, and in that endeavour it has succeeded remarkably well. The product became re-established in the minds (and the shopping baskets) of consumers, now that they were no longer afraid to admit to buying it.

ATW Photography/photolibrary

As an example of how a product in the decline phase of the product lifecycle can be relaunched and regenerated to become successful again, Heinz Salad Cream takes some beating. As an example of how a product can be re-positioned (from being just for salads to being a more general condiment and ingredient), the campaign shows what can be done with an effective communications campaign.

Questions

1 Why is re-positioning from an older market to a younger market likely to be difficult?

2 Why is a younger segment often regarded as more attractive than an older segment?

3 How did Heinz avoid the problem of alienating older customers?

4 What were the main effects of the threat from Heinz to withdraw salad cream altogether?

5 How is Heinz salad cream positioned relative to its competitors?

References

Allport, G.W. and Odbert, H.S. (1936): Trait Names: A psycholexial study. *Psychological Monograph* **47**(211). (Princeton NJ: American Psychological Association).

Baines, P.R., Worcester, R.M., Jarrett, D. and Mortimore, R. (2003): Market segmentation and product differentiation in political campaigns: a technical feature perspective. *Journal of Marketing Management* **19**(112), 225–49.

Bardacki, A. and Whitelock, J. (2004): How ready are customers for mass customisation? An exploratory investigation. *European Journal of Marketing* **38**(11/12), 1396–416.

BBC (1998): BBC News Friday 1 July.

Blankson, C. and Kalafatis, S.P. (2004): The development and validation of a scale measuring consumer/customer derived generic typology of positioning strategies. *Journal of Marketing Management* **20**(1), 5–43.

Bonoma, T.V. and Shapiro, B.P. (1983): *Segmenting the Industrial Market* (Lexington, MA: D.C. Health Co).

Bonoma, T.V. and Shapiro, B.P. (1984): Evaluating market segmentation approaches. *Industrial Marketing Management* **13**(4), 257–68.

Briggs, K. and Myers, I. (1992): The Myers-Briggs Type Indicator. *San Jose Mercury News* 23 September.

Chesbrough, H.W. (2003): Environmental influences upon firm entry into new sub-markets: evidence from the worldwide hard disk drive industry conditionally. *Research Policy* **32**(4), 659–78.

Cohen, J.B. (1967): An interpersonal orientation to the study of consumer behaviour. *Journal of Marketing Research* **4** (August), 270–8.

Day, G.S. (1990): *Market-Driven Strategy: Process for Creating Value* (New York: The Free Press).

deBerry-Spence, B. and Izberk-Bilgin, E. (2006): Wearing identity: the symbolic uses of native African clothing by African Americans. *Advances in Consumer Research* **33**(1), 193.

Dibb, S. and Simkin, L. (2001): Market segmentation: diagnosing and treating the barriers. *Industrial MarketingManagement* **30**(8), 609–25.

Donnelly, J.H. (1970): Social character and acceptance of new products. *Journal of Marketing Research* **7** (February), 111–13.

Freytag, P.V. and Clarke, A.H. (2001): Business to business market segmentation. *Industrial Marketing Management* **30**(6), 473–86.

Gillespie, K., Jeannet, J.-P. and Hennessey, H.D. (2004): *Global Marketing: An Interactive Approach.* (Boston: Houghton Mifflin Company.)

Hlavacek, J.D. and Ames, B.C. (1986): Segmenting industrial and high-tech markets. *Journal of Business Strategy* **7**(2), 39–50.

Horney, K. (1945): *Our Inner Conflict* (New York: W.W. Norton).

Jamal, A. (2003): Marketing in a multicultural world: the interplay of marketing, ethnicity and consumption. *European Journal of Marketing* **37**(11), 599–620.

Kates, S. (2002): Doing brand and subculture ethnographies: developing the interpretive community concept in consumer research. *Advances in Consumer Research* **29**(1), 43.

LeClerc, F., Hsee, C.K. and Nunnes, J.C. (2002): Best of the worst or worst of the best? *Advances in Consumer Research* **29**(1).

Liefeld, J.P. (2004): Consumer knowledge and use of country-of-origin information at the point of purchase. *Journal of Consumer Behaviour* **4**(2), 85–96.

MacDonald, E.K. and Uncles, M.D. (2007): Consumer savvy: conceptualisation and measurement. *Journal of Marketing Management* **23**(5–6), 497–517.

Malhotra, N.K. (1989): Segmenting hospitals for improved management strategy. *Journal of Health Care Marketing* **9**(3), 45–52.

Marketing News (1985): 13 September, p. 56.

Mattson, M.R. and Salehi-Sangari, E. (1993): Decision making in purchases of equipment and materials: a four-country comparison. *International Journal of Physical Distribution and Logistics Management* **23**(8), 16–30.

Rao, C.R. and Wang, Z. (1995): Evaluating alternative segmentation strategies in standard industrial markets, *European Journal of Marketing* **29**(2), 58–75.

Richardson, B. and Turley, D. (2006): Support your local team: resistance subculture and the desire for distinction. *Advances in Consumer Research* **33**(1), 175–80.

Ries, A. and Trout, J. (2001): *Positioning: The Battle For Your Mind.* (New York: McGraw-Hill.)

Robertson, T.S. and Barich, H. (1992): A successful approach to segmenting industrial markets. *Planning Review* (November–December), 4–48.

Sampson, P. (1992): People are people the world over: the case for psychological market segmentation. *Marketing and Research Today* (November), 236–44.

Schuster, C.P. and Bodkin, C.D. (1987): Market segmentation practices of exporting companies, *Industrial Marketing Management* **16**(2), 95–102.

Simcock, P., Sudbury, L. and Wright, G. (2006): Age, perceived risk and satisfaction in consumer decision-making: a review and extension. *Journal of Marketing Management* **22**(3/4), 355–77.

Skinner, H. and Stephens, P. (2003): Speaking the same language: the relevance of neuro-linguistic programming to effective marketing communications. *Journal of Marketing Communications* **9**, 177–192.

Treacy, M. and Wiersema, F. (1993): Customer intimacy and other value disciplines. *Harvard Business Review* **71**(1), 88–93.

Yip, G.S. (2003) *Total Global Strategy II.* (Upper Saddle River, NJ: Prentice Hall.)

Zinkhan, G.M. and Shermohamad, A. (1986): Is other-directedness on the increase? An empirical test of Reisman's theory of social character. *Journal of Consumer Research* **13** (June), 127–30.

Further reading

Books purely on the subject of segmentation and targeting are not all that common: all introductory marketing texts cover the principles. Having said that, there are some segmentation texts available: here is a selection.

McDonald, H.B. and Dunbar, I. (2004): *Market Segmentation: How to Do It, How to Profit from It* (Oxford: Butterworth Heinemann). This is a textbook with a strong practitioner bias. Although it is aimed at marketing professionals, it is academically rigorous and also fairly readable.

Wedel, M. and Kamakura, W.A. (1999): *Market Segmentation: Conceptual and Methodological Foundations* (Norwell, MD: Kluwer Academic Publishers). This is a much more academic text, replete with theory.

Chapter 7
Marketing information and research

Learning objectives After reading this chapter, you should be able to:

1 Explain the role of marketing research in decision-making.

2 Describe the different subdivisions of marketing research.

3 Explain the benefits of secondary research and primary research.

4 Describe what is meant by qualitative and quantitative research, and explain the benefits of each.

5 Explain the differences between planning and execution.

6 Describe the most common techniques of marketing research.

7 Explain some of the ethical issues raised in carrying out marketing research.

Introduction

As with any other business function, marketing relies heavily on information. Some of this information already exists, buried within corporate records, and some of it needs to be collected from outside sources. These outside sources might be organisations which routinely collect market information and publish reports, or it may be necessary to collect data directly from consumers. Marketers need to decide which information-generating method is most appropriate, and which will be most cost-effective in generating the right information at the right price.

There is a degree of confusion in academic circles about what constitutes market research and what constitutes marketing research. A possible way of distinguishing between the two terms is to consider market research to be concerned with finding out about markets (customers, competitors, suppliers, market conditions in general), whereas marketing research takes the broader approach of researching anything which might be of use to a marketer. This debate overlaps into the debate about the boundaries of marketing. The American Marketing Association defines marketing research as follows:

The function that links the customer, consumer and public to the marketer through information – information used to identify and define marketing opportunities and problems: generate, refine, and evaluate marketing actions: monitor marketing performance: and improve understanding of marketing as a process. Marketing research specifies the information required to address these issues: designs the method for collecting information: manages and implements the data-collection process: analyses the results: and communicates the findings and their implications.

(AMA 1987)

Marketing research therefore looks beyond the immediate market and includes monitoring systems for marketing plans, identification of opportunities and threats, identification of what information is needed, and takes account of past experience and future expectations as well as looking at the present situation.

Preview case
LabOUR

Following Margaret Thatcher was not an easy task – even with the John Major administration in-between, the Labour Party had a difficult task ahead to win the 1997 UK General Election.

In order to stand a chance, the party had to bring in some radical new policies – and under Tony Blair they got them.

Tony Blair introduced New Labour to the world. Advocating a 'Third Way' of running the country, somewhere between the far-right policies of Margaret Thatcher and the middle-left policies of Jim Callaghan, Tony Blair managed to win the election in a landslide, and in fact held office for the next 10 years.

New Labour became famous for its use of focus groups. Focus groups were the trend in market research rather than surveys: surveys had consistently failed to predict the outcomes of previous general elections, while focus groups were equally consistent in giving a clear idea of what the electorate wanted. Focus groups showed New Labour how to get elected: introduce policies which were far further to the right than traditional Labour had generated in order to win over the centre ground, and don't worry too much about staunch Labour supporters because they will vote Labour whatever the policies are, simply because they have no choice.

Focus groups continued to be used by the party to gauge public opinion, but rumblings of discontent among traditional Labour Party supporters began to be heard. New Labour looked nothing like the Labour Party they had supported and worked for, and even though Labour has a history of being a 'broad church' that includes every viewpoint from the centrist Liberals through to Marxists, there was a distinct feeling that the party had moved too far from its roots.

One result of this discontent was the founding of LabOUR, a group of disgruntled Labour supporters, most of whom were party members, who wanted to reclaim the party they felt had got away from them. The aims of LabOUR are to:

1 Reintroduce democracy into the party
2 Expand and strengthen its members
3 Unite Government and party around its members.

Same old Tories. Same old lies.

BE WARNED: THE TORIES ARE SPENDING MILLIONS LYING ABOUT LABOUR, TO HIDE THE TRUTH ABOUT THEMSELVES.

Labour supporters have paid for this advertisement. If you want to help Labour beat the Tory Lie Machine call 0900 300 900.

Labour

Courtesy of The Advertising Archives

All business decisions involve an element of risk: the purpose of marketing research is to minimise the risk. In order to do this, of course, the new organisation would have to gather irrefutable evidence that the Parliamentary Labour Party was heading the wrong way, and leaving its members behind.

marketing research Information gathering for the purpose of improving the organisation's effectiveness in the market.

Types of Marketing Research

Marketing research divides into broad groupings. There are six main groupings (Proctor 2000), with some subgroupings (see Figure 7.1). These groupings are not mutually exclusive: aspects of each area of marketing might well be researched within the same study.

Figure 7.1

Components of marketing research

Customer research

customer research Investigations into the behaviour of purchasers of the product.

Confusingly, this is also sometimes referred to as market research. Customer research is concerned with the motivations and behaviour of customers, their geographical or demographic spread, their number and spending power and their creditworthiness.

Customer research provides information on market and market segment size, trends in the market, brand shares, customer characteristics and motivation, and competitor brand shares. It also provides information on the positioning of brands in the customers' minds.

Advertising research

advertising research Investigations into the effectiveness and potential effectiveness of marketing communications.

Advertising research is about measuring the success (or otherwise) of advertising campaigns or other promotional exercises. It provides marketers with information on the most appropriate media to use, the most effective type of campaign to use and the most effective design for the advertising. Because advertising research also looks at the motivations and perceptions of customers, it overlaps to an extent with customer research: understanding the impact of advertising on customers is of obvious benefit, especially when one considers the cost of running a major campaign.

Product research

product research Investigations intended to generate knowledge which can be used to inform new product development.

Product research is used to test new product ideas on potential customers. Often this type of research is carried out at the concept stage, even before a prototype is available: this avoids the company investing in an expensive research and development programme for products which have no market. Product research can also provide an assessment of the strengths and weaknesses of a firm's products against those of its competitors.

Once a prototype is available, the product can be test-marketed with a group of potential users to find out whether any final flaws exist which can be ironed out before the product is launched. Even at this late stage research is useful, because it often points up problems (or strengths) which are not apparent at the concept stage.

Product research also looks at the packaging of a product. This includes the appeal to the end consumer, the effectiveness of the packaging in protecting the product from the environment and vice versa, and the acceptability of the packaging to distributors, wholesalers, retailers and so forth.

Distribution research

Finding the most effective distribution channels is by no means an obvious exercise. Research can help to identify which distributors will be of most assistance, which have the appropriate facilities for the product and which are best connected to the end users.

Distribution research also considers physical distribution – the best location for warehouses, the best type of delivery systems and so forth.

Sales research

The effectiveness of the sales force can be the key factor in making or breaking a company. Sales research helps to assess the effectiveness of individual salespeople, of different sales techniques and of different management techniques. It helps to ensure that sales territories are of approximately the same value in terms of sales potential, and can also help ensure that the right salespeople are working in the right territories.

Sales research can also be used for establishing the right type of remuneration mix and the right type of training programme for salespeople. It therefore has a role in internal marketing.

Focus groups are often more reliable than surveys.

Marketing environment

Environment research looks at the political, economic, social and technological factors which affect marketing decision-making. Trends in the population, possible effects of proposed legislation and the likely effects of new technology are all within the remit of environmental research.

Knowing which factors are relevant and how they may impact on the firm and its marketing activities are of obvious importance.

Applied Marketing Research

The first stage of applied marketing research is often preliminary research intended to identify the dimensions of a problem. Understanding which factors go to make up the problem is only part of what companies need to know – they also need to know which other problems exist which may not have been identified as yet. Preliminary research is often known as exploratory research, because it sets out to examine unknown territory in terms of the information available to the firm.

Conclusive research is carried out in order to support (or refute) the theories generated by the preliminary research. Conclusive research is intended to generate conclusions – this may or may not always be possible. Conclusive research may use data which has already been collected, or may use field research in which new data is collected, or it may require a combination of both.

distribution research Investigations into the effectiveness of different outlets for products.

physical distribution The movement of products from producer to retailer and ultimately to the consumer.

sales research Investigations into aspects of the personal selling function, including the performances of individual salespeople.

environment research Investigations into the external factors which impinge on the organisation's activities.

preliminary research Investigations intended to outline the dimensions of a problem.

exploratory research Investigations intended to identify problems.

conclusive research Investigations intended to provide answers to problems.

field research Investigations carried out in the marketplace.

Figure 7.2

Applied marketing research

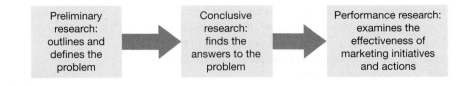

Performance research examines the effectiveness of marketing initiatives and actions, and therefore (in effect) provides information about whether the previous market research has been correctly carried out and interpreted. If the performance research shows that the company is not achieving its objectives, it is possible to make corrections and to re-examine the nature of the original problem – this may, in turn, lead to a revision of the previous preliminary and conclusive research.

Talking Point

If we don't know what the problem is, how do we know we have a problem at all? Is preliminary research really necessary? Surely what we don't know about can't hurt us, so why go looking for trouble?

Or is it better to identify potential threats before they become unmanageable? What we don't know may not hurt us – until the problem becomes so huge we can't miss it!

marketing information system
Mechanisms for providing a constant flow of information about markets.

internal continuous data Information supplied by systems within the organisation on a constant basis.

internal ad hoc data Information supplied by systems within the organisation for a specific purpose.

environmental scanning Continuous monitoring of external factors which might impinge on the organisation's activities.

marketing research Information gathering for the purpose of improving the organisation's effectiveness in the market.

Marketing Information Systems

A **marketing information system** provides a continuously updated stream of information on which decisions can be based. It has been defined as:

A system in which marketing information is formally gathered, stored, analysed and distributed to managers in accord with their informational needs on a regular planned basis.

(Jobber and Rainbow 1977)

Marketing information systems are built around the needs of managers, and should be designed to supply up-to-date information in a timely manner. A marketing information system consists of four elements: **internal continuous data**, **internal ad hoc data**, **environmental scanning** and **marketing research**.

Internal continuous data may consist of sales records, customer records, profitability calculations, customer feedback (positive and negative) and other management records

Figure 7.3

Marketing information system

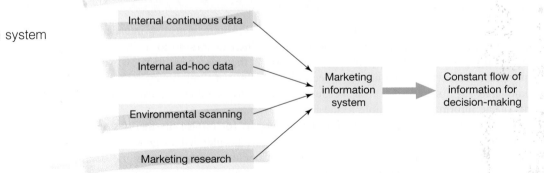

such as individual performance records for employees (e.g. salespeople). In many cases this information is already being collected by individuals within the firm, but is not being brought together in an appropriate form for the purposes of marketing management. In other cases, the information is not being collected at all – many firms, for example, calculate the profitability of each product in the range, but for a marketing manager it might be a great deal more useful to calculate the profitability of each market segment.

Internal ad hoc data is collected on an occasional basis for a specific purpose. For example, marketers might want to monitor the sales of a specific product following the introduction of a 'budget' version, with a view to seeing whether the cheaper product cannibalises sales of the original product. The marketing information system should already be capturing sales of the original product, so there should be little difficulty in providing the necessary information.

Environmental scanning has already been described in Chapter 2. Suffice it to say that monitoring the news media for potential threats and opportunities is part of the marketing information system.

Marketing research forms the final element of the marketing information system, and is used when specific answers to a specific problem need to be found. In this sense, marketing research fills in the gaps in the marketing information system.

Collecting such data is only the first stage, however: for raw data to become information it must be analysed and interpreted. Sophisticated marketing information systems are able to do at least some of the analysis automatically, although interpretation is likely to remain beyond the capability of computers for some time yet.

A good marketing information system will provide regular reports, or even real-time information on screen, to enable marketers to know what is happening in the marketplace. This allows managers to adjust tactics, formulate new policies and keep ahead of competitors. The evidence is that the ability to measure marketing performance has a significant positive effect on the firm's performance, profitability, stock returns and (not surprisingly) the status of marketing within the firm (O'Sullivan and Abela 2007).

Data Types

Data can be collected in many ways, but it falls into four main types, as shown in Table 7.1.

Qualitative data can also be secondary or primary data, and likewise quantitative data can be primary or secondary. Figure 7.4 shows some examples in each category.

Research data can come from custom-designed studies, tailored to meet the specific needs of the firm, from syndicated studies which are carried out on behalf of a group of

Table 7.1 Data typology

Primary data	Data which is collected from an original source, for example by running a questionnaire survey or by interviewing respondents.
Secondary data	Data which is secondhand. This is data which has been collected by someone else (for example, a commercial market research company) and which already existed before the problem was identified.
Quantitative data	Data which can be expressed numerically, for example in terms of percentages. This type of research is good for finding out what people do in terms of purchasing behaviour, but is not good for finding out why they do it.
Qualitative data	Data which cannot be expressed in numbers, for example interviews. This type of research is effective for finding out why people behave in the ways they do, but is not so good for finding out what people in general do.

Figure 7.4

Categories of data

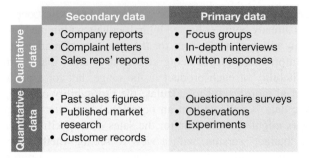

	Secondary data	Primary data
Qualitative data	• Company reports • Complaint letters • Sales reps' reports	• Focus groups • In-depth interviews • Written responses
Quantitative data	• Past sales figures • Published market research • Customer records	• Questionnaire surveys • Observations • Experiments

© iStockphoto.com

Traditional surveys are gradually disappearing.

firms (often competitors), or from standardised studies which are carried out by commercial research firms such as Mintel and sold to anyone who may find them useful.

Applied market research has undergone considerable change in recent years. Even 10 years ago, commercial applied research usually consisted of questionnaire research, in which researchers would go out with clipboards and stop people in the street to ask them questions. This approach has largely been abandoned in the 21st century – qualitative research (focus groups, depth interviews and so forth) have proved to be more reliable and to provide better insights into people's intentions and behaviour. The results are obtained much more quickly, and it is also cheaper since it requires a lot less people than questionnaire studies.

Planning for Research

The first stage in any planning process is to determine what the problem actually is. Defining the problem enables the planners to focus their efforts more precisely and therefore avoid being drawn into researching areas which might be interesting but which have little immediate relevance.

A goal-orientated approach to problem definition was suggested by Rickards (1974). This is shown in Table 7.2.

Table 7.2 Problem definition

Stage	*Example*
Stage One: Write down a description of the problem.	Problem: Our product line is becoming outdated and we need to create something new.
Stage Two: What do we need to accomplish?	We need to find out what people would like to see in a new product.
Stage Three: What are the obstacles?	Potential customers may not know what they would like in a new product. Competitors also have vigorous new-product programmes.
Stage Four: What constraints must we accept to solve the problem?	We have limited funds, we do not know which groups of people might be interested in our product.
Stage Five: Redefine the problem, taking into account the previous answers.	We do not understand our customers' needs adequately, and we do not know what other potential customers may exist.

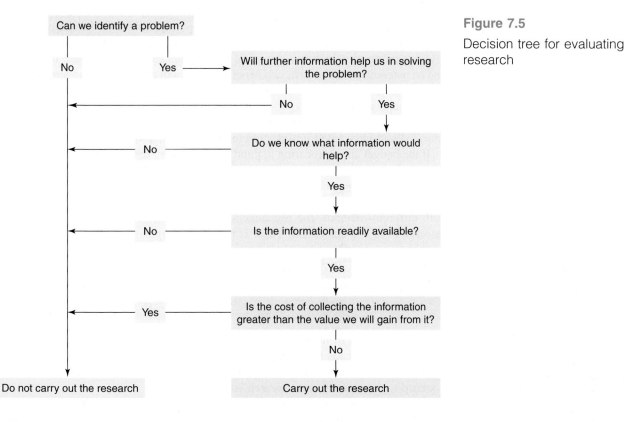

Figure 7.5

Decision tree for evaluating research

Having recognised the problem, managers need to consider whether carrying out research is a sensible option anyway. Sometimes the cost of the research exceeds any possible benefits which may accrue, so the managers need to decide whether the potential pay-off justifies the outlay. For example, a small restaurant may decide to offer a new main course. The cost of conducting a survey to find out whether the meal would prove popular would be far in excess of simply adding it as a 'special' for a few weeks to see the response of the diners.

The decision whether or not to carry out research can be based on a simple **decision tree**, as shown in Figure 7.5. The problem with this approach is that it gives a spurious credibility to the decision. In fact the decision tree is itself based on a set of judgements, but the impression given is that the outcome is objective. Management cannot know in advance how much the research is going to be worth: many research projects have proved to be worthless because the research question was wrong, or the research itself was poorly executed. Even worse, some projects have proved to be counterproductive because they have taken the company in an entirely wrong direction.

A further problem which arises is that those responsible for a new idea are often reluctant to carry out the research because they have such faith in the idea that they are unwilling to accept the possibility that it will not work.

Having decided that research is necessary and worthwhile, a detailed plan needs to be drawn up. A useful starting point is to hold discussions with the people who will be using the results of the research. Obviously there is a risk of producing a research exercise which tries to achieve too many objectives, but this is better than producing a research exercise which does not achieve the necessary objectives.

The **research plan** is the outline of the design, execution and monitoring of a study. The plan is not set in concrete – it can be changed, but the intention is that it provides a clear set of guidelines for those who will actually carry out the research and those who

decision tree A diagrammatic representation of the route a manager must take to reach a decision.

research plan An outline of the steps which must be taken in gathering information systematically.

will benefit from the findings. The plan contains a statement of the company's problem and the proposed means of collecting information to help solve it. The plan leads on to the research proposal, which is a statement of the plan, including the need for the research, and an assessment of the costs and benefits which will attach to it. The proposal is usually used to obtain approval of the plan from the various decision-makers involved in the problem and its solution.

The research plan and proposal will state exactly how the data is to be collected, analysed and interpreted in order to create the information the firm needs.

If the budget allows (bearing in mind that marketing research is an expensive exercise) it is good practice to use more than one research method to examine the problem. This is called triangulation: the purpose of the exercise is to reduce the risk that one or other method will provide a false result. By looking at the problem from different angles and with different methods, the researchers should be able to pick up on any errors in the research design or execution. There is more on triangulation later in the chapter.

Obtaining Information: Secondary Sources

secondary research Research which has already been carried out (often by someone else for another purpose), and which is available to the researcher for the current project.

primary research Research which is carried out from scratch for a specific project.

Secondary sources of information are those which already exist. In many cases, the information the firm needs has already been collected by someone else, often for some other purpose. Provided this information can be bought, or is published somewhere, the firm may not need to carry out its own research at all.

The main advantage of secondary research is, of course, cost. Secondary research is almost always cheaper than primary research, even when it has to be paid for. When it is already published in readily available form in libraries or on the Internet the advantage is clear.

The drawback with secondary research is that it often does not fit exactly to the firm's problem. Sometimes managers need to be creative in combining and interpreting information from secondary sources in order to create useable information.

Secondary sources include newspapers, journals, websites, published research, books, academic journals, Government reports, commercial research, European Union reports and research conducted by trade associations.

Another source of secondary data is internally generated information. Sales records often yield detailed data about customer behaviour: how often customers buy, how much they buy in any one order, where the customers are geographically, even what their delivery preferences are. Many firms have separate records of their customers' behaviour, held in different departments: for example, the sales manager may have records of which customers are difficult to sell to, which are likely to be increasing their orders in the near future and which are likely to be going bankrupt. The invoicing department will know which customers are bad payers and which are habitual complainers, the shipping department will know where the customers are and so forth. Combining this information could give a very clear picture of which customers are the most rewarding and which should be downgraded or dropped altogether.

Obtaining Information: Primary Sources

Primary research is carried out with the aim of generating original data. This means data that has not been collected before and which serves to fill a gap in the firm's knowledge. Primary research should only be carried out after secondary sources have been exhausted. This helps to minimise the cost by avoiding a reinvention of existing data. In marketing research, primary data can be collected in many ways: postal surveys, street

Marketing in Practice
Mintel

Mintel (Marketing Intelligence) reports are commercial marketing research reports produced for many industries. Mintel regularly generate industry reports based on panel surveys run by BMRB, a British marketing research consultancy. Reports cover virtually every conceivable area of consumer activity, and some business-to-business markets.

Although the reports are not specific to individual companies, they provide very broad and detailed information about the markets they cover. As a starting-point for research into any given market they are difficult to beat – and they often provide all the information a manager needs to be able to formulate a policy.

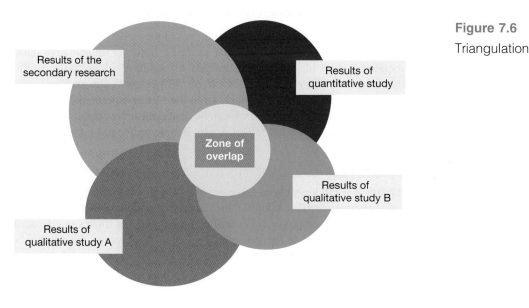

Figure 7.6
Triangulation

questionnaires, interviews, *focus groups* and so forth. Some of these generate quantitative data, some generate qualitative data. Some studies will use more than one method in order to triangulate on the problem or to examine different aspects of the same problem.

Triangulation means using different methods to focus on the same problem in order to confirm the accuracy of the answers. For example, a firm might run a questionnaire survey to find out how many people shop in a particular shopping mall, then send an observer to the mall in order to count the number of people passing through. This type of study allows the researchers to confirm that the questionnaire has been properly carried out, which may have a bearing on the reliability of any other questions contained in it.

Using different methods to attack different parts of the problem is also common. For example, a researcher might run a focus group to find out what the dimensions of the problem are, then use the results to design and run a questionnaire survey to find out how common the focus group's opinions are among the general population. Equally the reverse might happen – the researchers might run a questionnaire survey which tells them how people behave, then run a focus group to find out why.

focus group Respondents brought together to discuss a research question in a controlled and structured manner under the guidance of a researcher.

triangulation Using more than one research method to answer the same question in order to reduce the chances of errors.

Quantitative data is data which can be expressed numerically. Quantitative data can be collected by any of the following methods:

1 *Questionnaires*. These are quick to administer and analyse, but difficult to design.

2 *Interview surveys*. Similar to questionnaires, these surveys are carried out by interviewers. This ensures that respondents understand the questions, and also helps to ensure that they answer all questions appropriately.

3 *Observation*. Observing what people do and counting the numbers who behave in specific ways is a non-intrusive form of research. For example, a researcher might observe how many people enter a retail store, at what times of day, and to which shelves they go first. This could be extremely useful in managing the store, in terms of setting the right staffing numbers or laying out the store efficiently.

4 **Test marketing**. Putting a product onto the market in a limited geographical area, or with a few customers, enables the firm to gauge responses.

5 **Panels**. Many commercial marketing research companies recruit panels of respondents who participate regularly in marketing research studies in exchange for payment. Panels might be recruited from a wide range of individuals, who report on their buying behaviour across a wide range of products.

test marketing Offering a product to a small group of consumers in order to judge the likely response from a large group of consumers.

panel A permanently established group of research respondents.

Other sources of quantitative data exist, and techniques exist to extract numerical results from qualitative data. In the vast majority of cases, however, quantitative data collection means collecting a set of standardised answers to standardised questions. In this way, the researcher is able to make statements such as, '43 per cent of respondents said that they would buy the product if it were available from their local supermarket, but only 8 per cent would buy by mail order.' Provided we can be confident in this result, this is a useful piece of information: what it does not tell us is why people prefer to buy from the supermarket.

Sampling

In most cases it is not possible to ask everybody their opinions. Occasionally the number of potential respondents (for example, the number of people who might be expected to be in the market for a given product) is small enough that all of them can be questioned: this is called a census survey. In the vast majority of cases, however, the number of potential respondents is so large that only a small number of them can be included.

Figure 7.7
Sampling

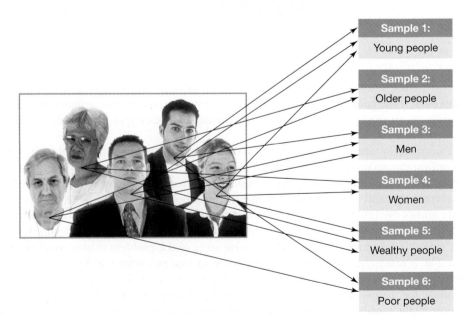

Table 7.3 Types of probability sample

Type of sample	Description	Advantages and disadvantages
Simple random sample	All members of the population have an equal chance of being included	Will provide a good cross-section of individuals, but in practice it is extremely difficult to achieve true randomness. Often an apparently random approach is biased because we do not have a complete list of every member of the population. The major difficulty is that some people refuse to participate in research, and are therefore left out of the study – which means the sample is no longer random.
Random walk sampling	Respondents are chosen on the basis of a 'random walk' around the area. Interviewers are given a route chosen at random and told to question (for example) every tenth household.	This method is simple to administer, but is not truly random.
Stratified random sample	The population is divided into mutually exclusive groups (for example by income or age) and interviewers are instructed to take a random sample from within each group.	This ensures that each group is represented in the final sample, for example to ensure that minority groups are adequately represented, but again is not truly random and is subject to errors in deciding what the stratifications should be.
Cluster sample	Clusters are chosen using a range of measures – geographical, income, age (for example). Individuals within the clusters are chosen at random.	Useful in cases where the population being studied is very large. Again, this method is not truly random, but does produce a representative sample.
Systematic sampling	Sampling units are chosen from the sampling frame at a uniform rate. For example, a business directory might be used, and every tenth firm sampled from it. In order to maintain randomness, the start point should be chosen at random, so if choosing every tenth respondent the start point should be a number between one and nine.	Again, this method works well for large populations. Care needs to be taken to ensure that the list of respondents being used is not affected by number – if companies are grouped in tens in some way, the sample will be seriously biased, for example.

Sampling from among all the potential respondents is therefore essential, but it is fraught with risk. How can we tell that the people being asked their opinions are the same in most essential aspects as the people who have not been asked? Such problems are susceptible to statistical analysis. At its most basic level, we can be fairly sure that if we ask one person's opinion the answers are unlikely to be representative of the population as a whole, since people differ widely in their opinions: on the other hand, if we ask everybody we know then the opinions will be absolutely accurate. It follows, therefore, that the larger the number of people whose opinions are included, the more reliable the results will be. In practice, reliable results can be obtained from relatively small samples, depending on the scale of the effect being measured: if the difference between two groups is large, the sample can be smaller, whereas if we are looking for subtle differences the sample size will need to be much larger.

Sampling types are shown in Tables 7.3 and 7.4. Table 7.3 shows probability samples, in which the inclusion of exclusion of respondents is largely a matter of chance, and therefore does not suffer from the bias of the interviewer.

Marketing in Practice
Sports Council for Wales

When the Sports Council for Wales wanted to investigate sports participation in the principality, it set up a simple survey. Interviewers stood outside the sports centres and stopped people at random, asking them how often they participated in sport, which sports they enjoyed most, and so forth. The Sports Council were amazed to find that a huge proportion of the respondents stated that they were frequent, enthusiastic participators in all kinds of sport. In fact, the reported results showed that participation in sport exceeded the capacity of the facilities available, if the results were projected across the population of Wales.

When the Sports Council called in a professional marketing research agency to explain the problem, the answer was obvious. By conducting the survey outside the sports centres the interviewers had picked up a large number of people who were either on their way in or on their way out of the sports centre. The sample was so biased the survey was effectively useless, and had to be conducted again from scratch.

Table 7.4 Non-probability sampling

Sample type	Description	Advantages and disadvantages
Quota sampling*	The researcher starts with the knowledge of how the population is divided, and instructs the interviewers to obtain data from a set number of representatives from each group.	The sample will be representative, provided the researcher really does know the structure of the population. Unfortunately it is easy to make errors and miss out important factors.
Convenience sampling*	A convenience sample has no sample design. The researcher simply interviews anyone who is available.	This method wins quick results, and often gives as good an outcome as a complex sampling method. Convenience samples often happen by accident when the researcher is actually trying to obtain a random sample, but has a high number of people who refuse to participate.
Judgement sampling*	The researcher selects a group of people who are believed (for whatever reason) to have opinions representative of the population at large.	Judgement samples obviously rely on good judgement on the part of the researcher. If he or she is wrong about the representativeness of the group chosen, the results will be seriously biased: on the other hand, judgement samples often give excellent results simply because they do include the people whose opinions count.

*See glossary.

delphi A system of research under which opinions are sought iteratively from experts.

Non-probability sampling seeks to avoid the potential pitfalls of probability sampling by deliberately choosing the sample. There are three forms of non-probability sampling, as shown in Table 7.4.

A derivative of judgement sampling is the **Delphi** technique. Delphi uses a small sample of experts to give their opinions. Initially, each expert is asked to give an opinion on a given topic, then the opinions are consolidated into a report which is circulated to the participants for further comment. The comments are then also consolidated and circulated, until either a consensus is reached or the experts agree to differ. Delphi is a widely-used method for obtaining useable opinions from a small group of people – it does not work well for larger groups, because the range of opinions becomes too unwieldy.

Sampling **bias** accounts for much of the inaccuracy in market research. Researchers often think they have taken a representative sample when in fact they have not, and often researchers are fooled into thinking that a large sample is a substitute for a representative sample. Statistical tools exist to help decide whether the sample was big enough, but there are no tools which can check on a researcher's judgement, good or otherwise.

Errors in sampling also occur because of non-response. Often people refuse to participate, which means that the researcher is forced to assume that people who do not participate are the same in all important respects as those who do participate. This is a considerable leap of faith – people who participate may have more time to spare, may be more likely to want to please the interviewer, or may simply be more interested in the subject matter of the research.

bias Errors in research results caused by failures in the research design or sampling method.

Talking Point

There seem to be so many sources of bias in sampling, we might wonder whether any research is reliable. What we cheerfully think is a random sample turns out to be non-random, and we might only find this out when we come to analyse the results after spending thousands of pounds paying people to stand on street corners questioning passers-by.

This is not to mention the non-response problem and the false-response problem. Opinion polls taken at the time of general elections have proved to be unreliable simply because people lie to the researchers about which way they intend to vote.

So should we just stop invading people's privacy in this way? After all, a nosy question deserves a short answer. On the other hand, understanding the market better means that we can plan products better, which should lead to a better life for everybody. Perhaps responding to marketing research should be made compulsory!

Questionnaire design

Questionnaires might be intended for self-completion, i.e. without the researcher being present, or for completion as part of a survey in which the researcher asks the questions and fills in the answers. Self-completion questionnaires are used if the respondents are geographically separated, or if the researcher is concerned that respondents might be influenced by the presence of the researcher and give inaccurate answers. They are also often used if the survey is to be conducted using a very large sample of respondents: an interviewer survey involving several thousand people would be too time-consuming to undertake.

The major drawbacks of self-completion questionnaires are that there is little or no control over the respondent (who can lie much more easily when completing a questionnaire than when answering questions from another person), there is no control over who actually fills in the questionnaire (a secretary might fill in the form rather than the executive it is aimed at), and the response rate tends to be very low, of the order of a few per cent in many cases. This means that the researcher may be in the position of assuming that the non-respondents are the same as the respondents, at least as far as any relevant characteristics are concerned. This is not always the case – for example, consider the lower literacy levels currently prevailing in most countries. Many people rarely read or write anything, and therefore are unlikely to complete the questionnaire: the fact that they are only semi-literate may well be a relevant factor in the research.

Figure 7.8

Factors indicating appropriateness of questionnaire delivery methods

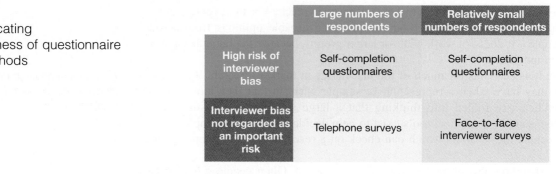

	Large numbers of respondents	Relatively small numbers of respondents
High risk of interviewer bias	Self-completion questionnaires	Self-completion questionnaires
Interviewer bias not regarded as an important risk	Telephone surveys	Face-to-face interviewer surveys

Researchers often use the total design method outlined by Dillman (1978). This has the following stages:

1 Identify aspects of the survey process affecting quantity or quality and design them for the best response.

2 Develop an administrative survey plan to accomplish the survey in complete detail.

3 Reward the respondents: this can take the form of positive regard, written appreciation, using a consultative approach, supporting his or her values, offering a tangible reward or even just providing an interesting questionnaire.

4 Reduce the costs to the respondent. This means making the task appear brief, reduce the effort required, eliminate embarrassing questions, eliminate subordination and eliminate any monetary costs.

5 Establish trust with the respondent. Provide a token of appreciation in advance, identify with a known and reputable organisation and build on other exchange relationships.

Following a total design approach will greatly increase response rate, though of course care must be taken not to compromise the research merely in order to win a large number of respondents.

Self-completion surveys are often used by restaurants and hotels to obtain feedback from customers. Most people are reluctant to complain in hotels and restaurants unless there is something seriously wrong or the problem is one which can easily be put right. Self-completion questionnaires left on the tables or in the rooms can allow people to comment in a non-threatening way, and can also direct people's attention to the areas which the firm is trying to improve. The drawback to this type of survey is that the respondents are self-selecting – only those who have a complaint or who are highly delighted are likely to take the time to fill in the questionnaire, so a quantitative analysis of the responses is likely to be of little use. Incidentally, some marketers regard anything less than a 'highly satisfied' score on these cards as a criticism which should be dealt with as if it were a complaint.

Surveys where the researcher is present have the advantage that the researcher can probe for answers if the respondent is unclear, and can also explain any ambiguities in the questions. They have the drawback that the researcher's body language or manner of speech might encourage the respondent in a particular direction, thus biasing the results of the survey, and they are much more labour-intensive than postal surveys and therefore much more expensive.

Telephone surveys occupy a half-way point between street surveys and self-completion questionnaires. Telephoning individuals and asking a series of questions has the advantage of being quick and relatively cheap, while ensuring that the right person is contacted and any ambiguous questions can be explained. The main drawback is that many people find it intrusive and will not respond, or respond with false answers in order to sabotage the research. A further problem is that many people now do not have landline telephones at all, relying on cell phones, for which there is no easily accessible national directory. These people are effectively excluded from any telephone survey, which may bias the results. This is not a problem when dealing with most business surveys, but may be in cases where (for example) salespeople form the target group of respondents.

Designing questionnaires is by no means easy. The first stage is to ensure that the problem to be tackled is clearly defined: it is all too easy to ask questions which are not relevant, and either over-extend the questionnaire so that respondents will not complete it, or create problems when it comes to analysing the results. On the other hand, leaving out questions which are relevant may result in incomplete and misleading results.

The questionnaire needs to be structured in three main parts: the introduction, the body of the questionnaire, and the demographic or basic data about the respondent. The introduction explains what the questionnaire is about, how the information will be used and what the researcher's policy is on confidentiality (usually a reassurance that the results will not be disclosed to a third party). This introduction should be brief and to the point: it should also seek to persuade the respondent to complete the questionnaire.

The body of the questionnaire should address the issues that the researcher is interested in. These are the basic questions for which the research was designed. The final part of the questionnaire should be about the respondents themselves: in the case of consumer surveys, these may be demographic questions (age, gender, income level and so forth) or in an industrial survey they may be questions about the firm, its turnover, the business it is in, number of employees and so forth. These questions are intended to allow the researcher to analyse the data according to respondent type. Such questions are usually put at the end of the questionnaire because they are generally considered to be sensitive: the received wisdom is that people are more likely to complete these questions when they have already invested some time in answering the earlier questions.

The questions themselves need to have the following characteristics:

1 They should address the problem itself.

2 They should not be leading questions; in other words, they should not favour one answer over another nor give any clue as to what the researcher wants to hear.

3 They should be broad enough to accommodate a range of opinions, but narrow enough to be easy to analyse.

4 Each question should be discrete, i.e. it should not require more than one answer.

The entire questionnaire should, of course, be written in simple and unambiguous language. Jargon, slang and unusual idioms should be avoided, and any terminology which might be offensive or incomprehensible to possible respondents should not be used.

The following checklist is a useful way of ensuring that the questions are appropriate.

1 *Is the question necessary*? If the question does not address the research problem, it should be removed.

2 *Will the respondents understand the question*? Questions may address areas which are not within the respondent's experience, or may be phrased in such a way that respondents cannot grasp the underlying concept.

3 *Does the respondent have the necessary information to answer the question*? For example, asking the chief buyer of a firm what the firm's annual expenditure is on salaries may not produce any answer. The respondent's memory may not be good enough ('How many chocolate bars did you buy last year?' is unlikely to be answered accurately), or the respondent may not have the necessary language skills to be able to formulate an answer.

4 *Is the respondent willing to answer the question*? Some questions are embarrassing or may seem intrusive: for example, people typically overstate their incomes on questionnaires rather than lose face by stating their true incomes. Respondents might be persuaded by a statement to the effect that an honest answer is essential to the accuracy of the research, but in many cases these questions can be removed or substituted without affecting the research adversely.

closed questions Enquiries to which there will only be a small range of possible answers, usually only yes or no.

open questions Enquiries to which there might be a wide range of possible answers.

dichotomous question An enquiry which can only be answered 'yes' or 'no'.

Negative questions ('Don't you think that . . .') are confusing and are likely to lead to biased answers. Hypothetical questions can also lead to hypothetical answers, although there are circumstances in which they can help overcome embarrassment.

Questionnaires usually use closed questions, where the answer is already reduced to only a few choices. This is because it is difficult to analyse open questions. For example, if a respondent is asked 'On average, how often do you shop in the city centre?' the question might have any number of answers. If the question is followed by a list such as 'Every day, once a week, once a month, once a year, less often' the responses will be categorised in a way which allows for easy analysis. A dichotomous question is one in which the answer can only be yes or no, which is of course the easiest type to analyse.

A problem in designing any research instrument is that respondents do not always reply accurately. For example, there is evidence that the fact that people are being surveyed affects their intentions to buy: the correlation between latent intention and subsequent purchase behaviour is 58 per cent greater among surveyed consumers than it is among non-surveyed consumers (Chandon, Morwitz and Reinartz 2005).

projective technique A research method which invites respondents to say what they think another person might answer to a specific question or problem.

Projective techniques

Overcoming embarrassment in questionnaires can be difficult. For example, asking people about their sexual orientation, personal hygiene purchases, attitudes towards their employer or racial attitudes is likely to lead to inaccurate responses. Projective techniques can help to overcome this problem by asking people to respond as if they were someone else. At least in theory, the individuals respond with their own attitude, since they are unlikely to have a very clear knowledge of what other people's attitudes are.

Talking Point

If people are embarrassed or made to feel uncomfortable when answering questions, why are we asking the questions at all? It's not a very nice way to make a living, and in any case a snoopy question deserves a lying answer! If people are uncomfortable with the questions, they are likely to give false answers – which doesn't help anybody.

On the other hand, maybe that's what a projective technique is all about. Making people feel more comfortable about helping with the research – which is ultimately going to benefit them anyway, if it means that we can met their needs better.

For example, someone might be asked what they think their work colleagues think about the boss, or what the average person thinks about people from another ethnic group. These questions might be asked in a fairly direct manner, or respondents might be asked to complete a sentence or say what a cartoon character might be saying. Projective techniques are useful, but often result in data which is difficult to analyse. As a way of reaching hidden attitudes they are often the only option, however.

In Figure 7.9 the character on the left is expressing an opinion which may not be one which everyone would be prepared to admit to in public (more controversial topics might include racism, sexual preferences or drug-taking). The respondent is invited to write in the response they would expect the other character to make to this statement. Responses might differ according to whether the respondent is told that the other character is male or female, and one might expect some differences in the answers given by men as opposed to women. There would also be differences if respondents were asked what the second character might be thinking, rather than what the character is saying.

Analysing questionnaires

Data, in itself, does not provide answers. It must first be analysed. The questionnaire should be designed so that the answers can easily be entered into a computer and totalled, but totalling does not equal analysis either.

Figure 7.9

Thematic apperception test

Table 7.5 Measures of statistical significance

Measure	Explanation
Student's t-test	Invented by a mathematician whose pen-name was The Student, this test measures the probability that an observed difference between two groups is the result of chance. It returns a percentage called a confidence interval: if this is (say) 95 per cent, the test says that the researcher can be 95 per cent confident that the difference is real, and not the result of a sampling error.
Mann–Whitney U Test	This compares two groups where the data is ordinal, i.e. is expressed as rankings.
Wilcoxon or Signed Rank Test	This is used where two matching samples are being compared using ordinal data.
Kruskal–Wallis test	Compares more than two independent samples using ordinal data.
Chi-square test	Used in checking whether cross-tabulated data is statistically significant, in other words if data which is distinguished by more than one variable shows differences which are unlikely to have occurred by chance.

For example, a survey of 6000 adults might show that 34 per cent of them regularly shop in out-of-town stores. This is vaguely interesting, but is not as useful as breaking down the sample according to demographic data. This might tell us that 74 per cent of people aged between 50 and 60 shop in out-of-town stores, and since this group is likely to be composed of the wealthiest members of society we now have something more important to go on. If we could also say that people with household incomes in excess of £50 000 a year shop in out-of-town stores, we have something very useful. This type of cross-tabulation is basic to analysis.

Researchers also need to be confident that the analysis is meaningful, and that the differences between different groups of respondents are real and not just the result of a chance combination. There are several ways of checking this using statistical tools which calculate the size of the difference between the groups, the overall sample size, and the size of the group concerned. In general, the larger the sample size, the more accurate the findings are likely to be. Table 7.5 shows the commonest methods of establishing statistical significance.

Having analysed the questionnaire, the researcher needs to consider interpreting the results. Interpretation means explaining what the results mean – it includes explaining why the results might have come about, what they say about respondents, and examining all the possible implications for the management of the firm. Interpretation is largely a matter of judgement, and different researchers might interpret the same data in different ways. For example, a finding that young people tend to live in small houses or apartments is probably a reflection of their incomes rather than a preference for small houses. It may also indicate their childless state, or even a low number of possessions and therefore a lower requirement for space. Questionnaires are not generally good for finding out definitive answers to this type of question, so researchers need to consider carefully what the answers actually mean. An alternative is to use qualitative research to back up the findings.

Questionnaire-based research has been criticised in other ways. Filling in questionnaires is a specific type of behaviour which has rules of its own: in order to understand consumers' responses to questionnaires, we may need to understand their behaviour towards the questionnaire itself (Grunert 2003). Also, Wefeld (2003) has criticised questionnaire surveys for the following reasons:

1 There is insufficient emphasis on external validity.
2 There is an implicit belief in the rationality of consumers which is not borne out in the real world.
3 Samples are often not representative due to high refusal rates.
4 Distortion and bias creep in because respondents will often give an answer rather than appear ignorant.

Talking Point

If questionnaires are so poor as a research instrument, why use them at all? After all, they are difficult to design, time-consuming to administer, and you need a degree in mathematics to interpret the results.

On the other hand, they do give a broad view of the opinions and behaviour of a lot of people at once. It would take years to run in-depth interviews with the thousands of people some questionnaire surveys deal with – and by that time the data would be no use anyway!

Observation and Experiment

One of the drawbacks of questionnaire research is that it relies on self-reports, i.e. people are being asked to report on their own behaviour and attitudes. This may not give accurate results for the following reasons:

1 People often cannot remember what their behaviour has been. For example, someone who is asked how many times they have bought a specific brand of biscuits this year is unlikely to remember accurately: and even a frequent-flying businessman may not remember how many flights he has taken in any given year.
2 People may be reluctant to admit to their behaviour. A heavy drinker who is asked about his or her alcohol intake is very likely to understate the amount, due to embarrassment or fear of being criticised.
3 If asked about their future behaviour, people may honestly provide an answer that they believe in but subsequent events prevent them from carrying out the proposed action. Future purchase intentions are notoriously inaccurate: an individual may intend to buy (for example) a new washing machine but in the event not have the money to do so.

Observing people's actual behaviour as it happens overcomes these problems. Three conditions exist for successful observation. First, the things to be researched must be observable. Attitudes, motives, emotions and so forth cannot be researched by observing behaviour. Second, the event must occur frequently or be predictable. Observing house purchases is unlikely to be very rewarding, although observing people's behaviour when they view properties might be feasible by accompanying the estate agent to viewings. Third, the event must be completed over a short period of time.

Marketing in Practice
Loyalty Cards

Many stores use information from their loyalty cards to observe customers' actual buying behaviour. The information is collected at the checkouts, and the stores are able to calculate how much people spend, what they spend it on, how often they spend and so forth. Coupled with the address data which the stores have in order to send out rewards, the retailer is able to develop a very clear profile of the customers and their behaviour – all through observation.

There is an ethical aspect to this approach, however. Many people feel that such observation is an invasion of privacy – even though we might expect our local butcher or greengrocer to remember what we like and don't like, many of us feel that keeping such information on a computer is a different matter entirely.

Presumably, if the information is only used in a general way (for example to estimate demand for a new product within an area by analysing purchases of similar products from the store in that area) there would be no problem. When the information is used to target individuals, the situation is entirely different.

There are of course exceptions. Longitudinal studies (studies carried out over a long period of time) have been carried out by observation – for example, Piaget's famous experiments and observation of child development – but in most cases lengthy observations are difficult or impossible to carry out.

longitudinal study Research which is carried out over a lengthy time period.

Observation needs to be carried out as far as possible without the knowledge of the people being observed. This can raise ethical problems regarding privacy – for example, there would be no ethical problem in counting how many people enter a shopping mall, but there may be a problem in following people around to see where (and if) they shop, and there would certainly be an ethical problem attached to observing known individuals (e.g. people selected as part of a sampling process) without their knowledge. On the other hand, people typically act differently if they know they are being observed, which will affect the results.

When setting up an observation, the observers need to be briefed carefully. In the case of an unstructured observation, the observers need to note everything and draw conclusions: unstructured observations work in much the same way as unstructured interviews or focus groups, in which the researcher does not know what might come of the research exercise. In the case of a structured observation, the observer is told what to look for, and

structured observation A marketing research technique which involves directly watching consumer behaviour.

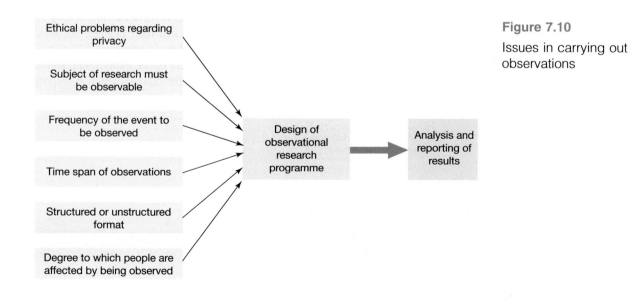

Figure 7.10

Issues in carrying out observations

Marketing in Practice
Fisher-Price

Fisher-Price is a subsidiary of Mattel, the world's largest toy manufacturer. At the company's headquarters in Chicago there is a free crèche for preschool children, and (of course) the toys are all made by Fisher-Price. What the toddlers neither know nor care about is that they are being observed by researchers all the time – how they play with the toys, which ones are the favourites, which ones become boring after a few minutes, which ones are worth fighting over, and so forth. This observational research is invaluable to the company in developing new toys.

is given a checklist. Structured observations are most often used for hypothesis testing, i.e. in situations in which the researcher has a clear idea what to look for.

Unstructured observations are often video-recorded to allow for more careful analysis of (for example) body language, but structured observations can often be carried out using a tick sheet.

mystery shoppers A marketing research technique whereby the researcher pretends to be a customer.

A common type of observation used in retail environments is to use 'mystery shoppers'. These are observers who pretend to be ordinary customers and who take note of such issues as staff courtesy, store layouts and cleanliness, store traffic and so forth. In some cases the retailer sends the mystery shopper to the company's own stores in order to check that management and staff are doing their jobs effectively, but more often the mystery shoppers are sent to competitors' shops in order to pick up useful ideas from the competition.

Experiments

In order to meet all three of the conditions for observation outlined at the bottom of p. 228 (observability, frequency and short-term completion), researchers may conduct an **experiment**. This enables the observation to happen under controlled conditions. In general, the subjects of experiments are well aware that they are part of a research study, but it is possible to conduct experiments without the subject being aware of the exact nature of the experiment. In recent years this type of experiment has sometimes been seen as unethical, however – there is a view that subjects should be willing, informed participants. For example, a retailer might want to find out whether customers are dishonest or not, and arrange for cashiers to give each customer slightly too much change. Observers could then see which customers return the excess change and which do not. There would certainly be an ethical problem with this type of research, because it involves setting a trap for the customers. Some customers might simply not have checked their change, but would be listed on the research as being dishonest – clearly an unfair description.

experiment A research technique in which a controlled situation is used to determine consumer response to a given stimulus.

dependent variable The stimulus which is applied to generate a response.

independent variable The response resulting from a dependent variable.

Experiments should have three components: the subject of the experiment, sometimes called the **dependent variable** or the test unit: second, the change which is imposed on

Figure 7.11

Components of experiments

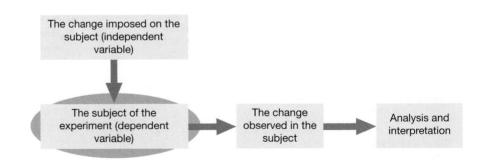

The change imposed on the subject (independent variable)

The subject of the experiment (dependent variable)

The change observed in the subject

Analysis and interpretation

the subject, also called the **independent variable**; third, the results which relate to the change introduced by the independent variable, also called the outcome or observation.

In an experiment the researcher manipulates selected independent variables and measures the effect of these manipulations on the dependent variables (Proctor 2000). This means that the researcher will observe what happens under one set of circumstances, then change one of the circumstances and see what the effect is on the outcomes. For example, a researcher wanting to test which of two instruction manuals is the clearer for the assembly of a piece of furniture might give a copy of each to two separate individuals and observe how quickly each can assemble the furniture. Carrying out this experiment with a number of people would give a clear idea of which wording is the most effective and where the problems might arise.

Experiments (and indeed all research) should have both internal and external validity. **Internally valid** experiments are those in which the independent variable is solely accountable for the changes observed in the dependent variable – in other words, the change the researcher introduced accounts for the change in the subject of the experiment. This is by no means certain: sometimes other factors creep in (or are already present) and the results become invalid. For example, in the experiment described above the experimenter might believe that it is the wording of the instructions which generates the difference between the two groups, whereas in fact the different wordings have caused the printer to rearrange the diagrams into a more easily understood format in one instruction leaflet. Thus it would be the change in the diagrams, not in the wording, which accounts for the differences.

External validity refers to the generalisability of the results, in other words whether the experiment's outcomes will work out under real-world conditions. Sometimes experiments are carried out under such carefully controlled conditions (in an attempt to ensure internal validity) that the results do not apply in the real world, when other factors are present. The problem for the researcher is that internal validity is best ensured by conducting the experiment under laboratory conditions, whereas external validity is best assured by conducting the experiment under field conditions. In some cases the research is conducted under both conditions in an attempt to ensure both internal and external validity.

Instructions for self-assembly furniture can be confusing if not researched properly.

Outside factors which may affect the validity of the experiment include the following:

1 *Repeated testing.* If the experiment is conducted with the same group of participants over and over again, the participants become used to the research method, and learn too much about the research topic to be able to react in the same way as someone would who was new to the research.

2 *Interviewer bias.* Sometimes the personality of the researchers will affect the outcomes because the research participants respond differently to different people.

3 *Maturation.* If research is being conducted over a period of time, the participants mature or change. These changes may easily be mistaken for effects of the research.

4 *History.* Current events outside the laboratory can affect the way participants behave. For example, research on responsiveness to advertising for cars would be affected by a large increase in the cost of fuel, or by a new tax on large cars.

5 **Mortality.** Over a period of time, participants drop out of the research, sometimes through actually dying, but more often through boredom, change of circumstances or simply becoming too busy to participate.

6 *Selection errors.* Like other sampling errors, selection of the wrong participants will affect the research outcomes adversely.

7 **Regression effects.** If the subjects for the experiment are chosen on the basis of a test (for example, a personality test), those at the extremes will often tend (over time) to move towards the middle. This is in part due to maturation and history effects.

internal validity A condition in which a research exercise provides evidence which supports what the exercise was intended to discover.

external validity A condition in which a research exercise would generate the same results if it were repeated elsewhere.

mortality The tendency for respondents to disappear over time.

regression effect The tendency for extremes to move towards the middle in longitudinal studies.

These factors tend to cause errors, but can often be overcome (controlled) by using an appropriate experimental design.

Experimental designs

The experimental design defines the way in which the experimental subjects will be treated, and the ways of measuring the outcomes of the experiment. The two broad categories of experimental design are basic (or informal) designs, which only measure the impact of the independent variable, and statistical (formal) designs, which also seek to measure the effect of other factors on the dependent variable.

Experimental designs come in many forms, but these are some of the main ones.

1 *After-only design.* Here the stimulus is applied, and the subjects' behaviour afterwards is measured. This design does not examine the subjects' behaviour beforehand, so it is difficult to know whether the change of behaviour came about as a result of the stimulus, or whether it would have happened anyway. In some cases this may not matter – for example, a marketer might place money-off coupons in different newspapers and measure which newspaper returns the most coupon redemptions.

2 *Before-after without control.* Here the researcher measures the subjects' behaviour, applies the stimulus, then re-measures the behaviour to see whether there has been a change. For example, sales for a given period might be recorded, then a sales promotion put in place and sales after the period measured. Clearly the problem with this design is that part of the change might have come from some other factor unconnected with the promotion. Other factors might have increased (or reduced) sales, so that the researcher ends up either overstating or understating the effect of the promotion.

3 *Before-after with control.* In this design, the researcher applies the stimulus to one group and not to another, so that most outside factors can be compensated for. For example, a company might record sales from two comparable parts of the country, apply the sales promotion in only one part, and see whether the change in the area where the promotion was offered is greater than the change in the area where the promotion was not offered.

4 *After-only with control.* In some cases, testing before applying the stimulus is difficult. For example, if an advertising agency wants to test the effectiveness of an advertisement for chocolate bars, the fact of questioning people about their chocolate-eating behaviour will sensitise them to the advertisement and their responses will not be spontaneous. With an after-only experimental design, the advertisement could be shown to one group (preferably buried among a group of advertisements for other products), then both groups can be questioned about their chocolate-buying intentions. Any differences should be due to the advertisement, provided the groups are well matched.

5 *Ex-post-facto design.* Here the groups are selected after the stimulus has been applied. For example, a market researcher might conduct a street survey in which people are asked whether they have seen a particular advertisement. Those who have seen the advert become the experimental group, while those who have not become the control group. Differences between the groups should be due to the advertisement. In practice, this type of study is difficult to carry out well, because people are often unable to remember what they have and have not seen – most advertising operates below the conscious level.

6 *Four-group six-study design.* This design was pioneered by Solomon during the Second World War as a way of testing the effects of training films on soldiers. The problem was that questioning soldiers prior to showing them the films made them pay more attention to the films: also, if they knew they were to be questioned

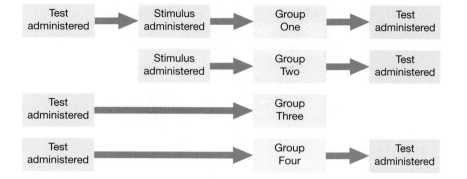

Figure 7.12

Four-group six-study design

afterwards, they paid more attention. Anecdotal evidence suggested that most of them, left to their own devices, slept through the films. Solomon's design involved selecting four similar groups of soldiers. One group was tested before the film and not afterwards, one group was tested afterwards, one group was tested both before and after, and one group was tested twice without being shown the film. In this way, it was possible to check what the effects were of being tested before the movie, being tested after the movie, and of being tested more than once. This allowed Solomon to calculate the effect of the movie, with the effects of the experiment 'tuned out'.

7 *Time series* design. This design assumes that the researcher will have access to the same group of people for a long period of time and that the testing itself will not affect the outcome. For example, a market research company might recruit a panel, perhaps of several thousand people, who record their purchases (or their TV viewing, or their leisure time activities, as appropriate) over a long period. Stimuli such as sales promotions, advertising, special offers and so forth may be offered during this period, and the effects measured on the group as a whole. Because of the long timescales involved, and the participatory nature of the exercise, effects arising from history, maturation and regression tend to be minimised.

time series Analysis which shows how the situation has progressed over a period, carried out in order to predict likely future trends.

Statistical designs

These designs use statistical techniques to assess the outcomes of the experiment. Statistical tools can be used to analyse the variance between the experimental groups and determine which of the changes come from the intended stimulus and which from extraneous factors.

A randomised design means that the stimulus is applied to participants (subjects) on a completely random basis. This should spread the effects of any other influences so as to ensure that any changes are the results of the stimulus, not of accidental influences.

Randomised block design is used when the researcher suspects that another major influence might affect the results. For example, leading up to Christmas 2003, exceptionally mild weather in the UK affected people's Christmas expenditure: it took longer for people to get into the Christmas spirit, and as a result some retailers panicked and slashed their prices (and profits) in order to clear Christmas stocks quickly. Unseasonable weather can be a major influence on behaviour and outcomes. For example, cutting prices might increase sales, but so might any one of a large number of factors. To allow for unseasonable weather, the researcher might run random tests across blocks of time – one in the spring, one in the summer, one in the winter and so forth. Differences between the blocks might relate to the seasonal weather.

Figure 7.13
Latin square design

Influence Two \ Influence One			
	Variable One	Variable Two	Variable Three
	Variable Two	Variable Three	Variable One
	Variable Three	Variable One	Variable Two

Latin square design allows researchers to isolate two major external influences. Each influence is laid out on one or other axis of a square and the variables entered in the boxes. The main problem with the Latin square is that it is expensive and complex to analyse. In circumstances where the cost is not a major consideration, and where the situation faced by the researcher is also complex, it can be well worth conducting a Latin square design.

Factorial design is used when the researcher suspects that some of the factors may also act on each other. A factorial design is likely to be of the same general type as a Latin square or randomised block study, but it uses more complex variance analysis to analyse the results.

The main problem with experiments in general is that they are undertaken under artificial conditions, with many of the possible influences deliberately left out in order to ensure validity. This means that the applicability of the results in the real world is limited – often the results are not generalisable to reality. One type of experiment which avoids these problems is test-marketing, in which the product is offered within a limited geographical area for a period of time to see how acceptable it is to the potential customers.

Test-marketing certainly gives a clear idea of the product's acceptability under real conditions, but it has the drawback of alerting competitors to the existence of the product. Also, test-marketing does not save the company the cost of developing the product and the marketing campaign – both of which are major elements in the cost of launching a new product. Thus test-marketing has limited benefits in most cases. An exception might be in retailing, where a store chain could order a small amount of a product and sell it through one or two of its stores, rolling it out nationally at a later date if it is successful.

Analysing and Interpreting Quantitative Data

Analysis is concerned with arranging the information in such a way that it acquires meaning. Interpretation is concerned with extracting useable recommendations from the data.

Analysis goes beyond simply listing the data. For example, a questionnaire survey may indicate that 20 per cent of the respondents regularly buy the product, 35 per cent occasionally buy it and the remainder never buy it. The same questionnaire may show that 52 per cent of the respondents are men, 48 per cent are women, 10 per cent are aged between 20 and 30, 23 per cent aged between 31 and 40, 45 per cent aged between 41 and 50, 18 per cent aged between 51 and 60 and remainder are over 60. Although this information is accurate and interesting, it does not mean much unless the researcher analyses it to show how many women aged 20–30 regularly buy the product, or how many people over 60 are occasional users. Also, it would appear that the sample is somewhat biased, since the age proportions do not correspond to those in the census. This means that the results of the analysis are likely to be inaccurate when taken as a whole, i.e. if conclusions are drawn based on (say) gender.

The first step in analysis is to edit the data. This means removing any anomalous or inaccurate data. Obviously it does not mean removing data which does not agree with the researcher's preconceptions: it does mean removing (for example) questionnaires where the respondent has obviously just ticked all the left-hand boxes in order to get the task out of the way (or, worse, sabotage the research). The intention is to eliminate errors, which come either from mistakes made by the interviewer or from mistakes or untrue statements from the respondents.

In some cases, computers can be used to detect inconsistencies. For example, if a respondent has indicated that he or she never uses a product, but then goes on to discuss the product in some detail, there is clearly an error somewhere. If the questionnaire is being completed online, the computer can pick up this error as it is being made and advise the respondent accordingly.

The next stage in analysis is to enter the data into a suitable software package. This allows responses to be grouped according to the answers given. Typically, questionnaires should have a coding frame in one of the margins. Answers can be numbered in the coding frame so that they become easier to enter into the computer for analysis. Figure 7.14 shows how this works in practice. In the figure, the researcher has converted the answers into numbers, which are entered in the final column. This makes entering the data into a computer much easier, and less prone to mistakes (this is particularly true if the researcher has to enter several hundred responses into a computer, or if a number of people will be working on data entry).

The next stage is to create tables of data. It is not sufficient merely to total the answers to each question: the researcher will be looking for groups of respondents who tend to answer in the same way, so cross-tabulations will be necessary. For example, in the case of the questionnaire used in Figure 7.14, respondents who are strongly against four-wheel-drive vehicles might be expected to answer the other questions differently from the way those in favour of four-wheel-drive vehicles would answer. For a motor manufacturer, a breakdown of attitudes of each group to the other factors in the questionnaire

Please read the statements below, then place a tick in the column which most closely matches your attitude to the statement. Tick Column One if you agree strongly with the statement, Column Two if you agree, and so forth with Column Five indicating that you disagree strongly with the statement.	1	2	3	4	5	Office use only
People who drive four-wheel-drive vehicles are selfish.	✓					
People should consider others when they choose a new car.	✓					
Cars are an essential part of modern life.		✓				
Cars are a luxury.				✓		
Cars are responsible for much of the high standard of living we enjoy.		✓				
Cars should be restricted in use because they damage the environment.			✓			
We should be seeking alternatives to car use.		✓				
People will never give up their cars.		✓				

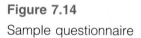

Figure 7.14

Sample questionnaire

Table 7.6 Statistical tools

Statistical tool	Purpose
Analysis of variance	Measures the degree to which the results vary from each other.
Correlation analysis	Measures the degree to which one variable is affected by another.
Rank order correlation	Measures the degree to which different aspects of the data end up being put into the same order by respondents.
Regression analysis	Establishes the relationship between different factors in the data.
Multivariate analysis	Establishes the relationships between a large number of variables, stating which of the variables accounts for the greatest amount of the observed variation in the outcomes.
Cluster analysis	Identifies similar entities from among a group of characteristics shared by the entities.
Factor analysis	Reduces the data and summarises it into a group of factors which account for the observed variance to a greater or lesser extent.
Conjoint analysis	Analyses the degree to which a change in one variable affects changes in another variable.
Multidimensional scaling (MDS)	Aimed at producing a visual set of relationships between different attributes based on a set of scales.

would be a great deal more useful than simply knowing how many people like four-wheel-drives and how many do not.

Finally, the data needs to be interpreted in order to extract meaningful information. Interpreting data is an area which requires considerable judgement, plus a degree of objectivity. For example, an American newspaper reported that there were more African-Americans in jail than there were in college. In itself, this statistic is perfectly true: however, the same is true of Anglo-Saxon Americans. When the comparison is made between black prisoners of college age and black students, it turns out that there are half a million black students compared with 200 000 black prisoners of the same age – still a shocking statistic, but with rather different implications from the one reported earlier.

Statistical analysis

A detailed account of all the techniques of statistical analysis which are available is beyond the scope of this chapter. Having said that, statistical tools are used to extract meaning from raw data, and to indicate the reliability of the data. Table 7.6 shows some of the statistical tools in current use.

These techniques (and many others) are available on computer software packages such as SPSS, Excel and Minitab.

Qualitative Research

Although much marketing research is carried out through surveys, the drawbacks of survey research are such that many researchers are using qualitative techniques instead of, or as well as, quantitative methods.

Qualitative research cannot usually be expressed in numerical terms. Typically, qualitative research results in expressions of opinion, and is usually therefore verbal. Qualitative techniques include the following:

1 *Open-ended interviews*. Respondents are asked an open-ended question (for example, 'What do you think of Cornish pasties?') and are then encouraged to talk freely about the topic. The responses could range from a discussion of the flavour and nutritional value of Cornish pasties to a discussion of the history of Cornish tin-mining. The problem for the researcher lies in deciding whether this is a digression or whether it is leading up to a relevant point – if the respondent is about to say something like 'The crusts had to be tough enough to survive being dropped down a mineshaft, so I never eat them' that would be relevant. A discussion of mine closures and consequent redundancies among miners probably would not.

2 *Group discussions or focus groups*. A group of people who have an interest in the subject or who are typical of the expected target market are brought together and invited to discuss a particular topic. The advantage of a focus group is that members will often trigger ideas in each other, and thus develop a wider-ranging set of responses.

3 *Analysis of written documents*. Respondents may be asked to write down their opinions on the topic under discussion. This has the advantage that they do not need to make statements directly to other people about subjects which may be embarrassing or otherwise hard to discuss. Other written documents (for example, letters of complaint) might be analysed as part of the secondary research carried out ahead of the primary research.

Qualitative data is useful for exploratory research. If the researcher has little or no idea which are the topics of importance within the research problem, a focus group or a series of depth interviews will reveal what questions to ask. The topics which the respondents discuss most often will be the ones of importance, and questionnaire questions can be suitably framed to find out the extent to which the views of the group apply to the general population. In other words, qualitative research defines the dimensions of the problem, and quantitative research finds out the size of those dimensions. As shown in Figure 7.15, either method can help with answering research questions, but quantitative research cannot answer 'why' questions very easily and qualitative research cannot answer 'how many' or 'how often' questions very easily.

Alternatively, qualitative research can be used after quantitative research as an aid to explaining the outcomes. A focus group might be briefed by telling them that, '74 per cent of people aged between 50 and 60 shop in out-of-town stores. Why do you think that might be?' If the focus group is drawn from that age group, they are very likely to be able to give some ideas as to why this behaviour occurs. In any event, they are more likely to be able to provide an answer than a 35-year-old researcher.

Focus groups are not without their problems, however. Firstly, much focus group research is carried out with people who do not, in fact form a group (Rook 2003). The

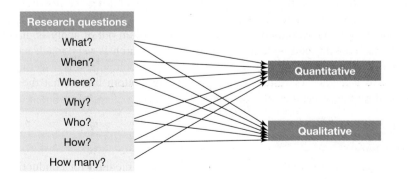

Figure 7.15

Qualitative vs quantitative research

Marketing in Practice
Biasing Respondents

The story goes that a radio station commissioned some focus group research to find out what people liked and disliked about the station. The researchers duly recruited a focus group, and decided that the group should be kept in the dark about who was paying for the research, in order to avoid biasing the results. They therefore planned to ask the group about radio stations in general, and three local FM stations in particular.

Unfortunately, on the day of the focus group interview, two executives from the station turned up in reception, and in front of the waiting focus group members, announced 'Hi. We're from the XYZ Radio station, we're here to observe the focus groups'. Not only had they given away the name of the commissioning company, but the group members now knew who they were. The researchers had no choice but to pay off the focus group respondents and cancel the research – an expensive error for the radio station!

groups are usually recruited as individuals, and may have met for the first time on the day of the discussion. Secondly, researchers often try to cover too much ground in a short period of time: perhaps because the research has been commissioned by an ambitious client, researchers may ask up to 40 direct questions of the group within an hour, which gives little time for discussion or reflection. Thirdly, people often lie in focus groups: they may give socially-acceptable answers in a group situation (especially when in the presence of a group of strangers), they may seek to please the researcher, there may be insufficient time to build trust, or they may give superficial replies about topics they have never considered and have little interest in (Zaltman 2003). Systems do exist to tell whether someone is lying in a focus group (Grapentine 2004) but such systems are of little help against someone who is an accomplished liar.

Analysing qualitative data can be complex. It is possible to extract numerical results from it, but in general it would be meaningless to make statements such as '25 per cent of respondents expressed doubt about the company's efficiency' since the sample sizes are usually too small for such a statement to have any significance.

How a researcher analyses the data will depend on the framework within which he or she is operating. A typical approach is to look for key words or phrases in transcripts of people's statements: for example, the word 'quality' might be regarded as a key word. Frequency counts of the word might give an indication of how important quality issues are to the respondents.

Searching for key phrases might be more problematic, since respondents may express the same concept in different ways. Selecting key themes from an initial read-through of the data might generate a large number of themes which can then be reduced to a smaller number of related themes: a second read through the data would allow the researcher to assign each phrase in the transcripts to one or other of the themes and thus develop an overview of the areas which concern respondents. This allows the researcher to understand the dimensions of the problem.

Although computer programs can help take the tedium out of analysis, it is important to recognise that the interpretation of qualitative research is very much an intellectual task, and therefore falls to the researcher. Using a computer may seem to be more objective as a method of research analysis, but the bottom line is that the computer is controlled by the researcher, not the other way round.

Internet research

In recent years the Internet has become a widely used medium for conducting research. Qualitative research has been carried out using chat rooms to conduct virtual focus

The key themes in the following transcript have been highlighted. This is an interview with a buyer for a major supermarket chain.

'**Actually, people often think that the sales people and the buyers are enemies. We're not. We're more like, sort of, helping each other.** We have to buy product, that's our job, I have to have product lines my customers want to buy. **Reps come in here to sell their stuff, and OK** they want to sell what they have to sell, **but if it's any good and we can use it, sure I'll buy it.** What I don't like is if they get pushy, **because if my customers won't buy it then I don't want it. I'm really acting as a sort of agent for the consumers, they're the ones paying my salary,** if I don't please them then that's me on my bike. On the other hand, if a rep can show me something we can sell, that is good, I'm grateful, I'll take his arm off I mean, we'll have to agree terms and so on, **but why not? It's my job. Just like selling is his job.** Sometimes they want to push it on merchandising – you know, shelf space, displays. OK the more we sell the better, but I have other lines to fit in, I have to make them understand that, once they understand that then we can talk.'

The key themes are:

1　Job/professional issues (In red)
2　Controlling the process (In yellow)
3　Roles (In blue)

Obviously these categories are arbitrary, and depend on the researcher's judgement: equally, it is sometimes difficult to see which category a statement should go in. However, themes do emerge from this type of analysis.

Figure 7.16

Analysing qualitative data

groups, and questionnaires have been emailed to existing customers. Automated survey websites such as surveymonkey.com have appeared, making it easy to carry out mass surveys online, and even to analyse the data automatically. Some websites include self-completion surveys, often offering prizes for completing the questionnaire.

The advantage of carrying out research on the Internet is that it is extremely cheap in comparison with other methods, and it frequently results in a very high number of responses. This can, however, give a spurious credibility to the results. The percentage of respondents on the Internet is approximately 4 per cent, which is low: the large number of respondents is due to the extremely large number of people who see the questionnaire (Grandcolas, Rettie and Marusenko 2003). The people who respond are extremely unlikely to be identical to the 96 per cent who did not respond, although whether the differences are material to the research will depend on what is being researched. Grandcolas *et al.* (2003) surmised that non-respondents may have ignored the survey because of several possible reasons: they may be poor typists, or perhaps less web-literate than respondents, or they may have less time, or may be using a dial-up connection for which they pay by the minute.

Sampling errors are considered to be the major cause of problems with Internet surveys (Ray 2003), since (according to some sources) around 30 per cent of UK households do not have Internet access. It is dangerous to assume that those who do not have Internet access are the same as those who do – they are likely to have lower incomes, be older and be less well-educated. A further sampling problem arises if respondents are rewarded: some people are suspicious of rewards, especially if being asked for personal information, while more materialistic people are prepared to volunteer information (Ward, Bridges and Chitty 2005).

Chat rooms also have a self-selecting sample base, which can lead to bias. A virtual focus group can be conducted with a group selected by the researcher, simply by using emails in which the comments go to all members. This method is advantageous because all the comments are recorded and the transcript is, in effect, already made.

In designing Internet-based surveys, researchers need to be aware of some of the general issues surrounding website design. For example, screen colour affects people's willingness to wait for material to download (Gorn *et al.* 2004), so the wrong colour might lead to a higher refusal rate as potential respondents log off rather than wait (relaxing colours give the impression that the wait is longer than it actually is).

There is little doubt that using the Internet will revolutionise marketing research. Three main areas have been identified as being particularly susceptible to change: sampling, marketing stimulus presentation and reporting (Wyner 2003). Sampling becomes easier in some ways because of the huge number of potential respondents: it is possible to find quite large numbers of obscure types of individual if necessary. Stimuli can be presented visually, aurally or in writing online: although this is not as good as, for example, giving someone a prototype of a new product to handle, it is certainly the next best thing. Finally, analysis and reporting of results can be largely automated. It is no longer necessary to enter data manually, which is a great saving in labour costs and time.

For Internet research to be successful, the software needs the following attributes (Deal 2003):

1 Direct and simple facilities for developing appropriate, flexible and attractive questionnaires.
2 Relatively easy fielding of questionnaires, including considerations of security and integrity control.
3 Ability to perform basic analysis.

There is some evidence that the widespread practice of paying people to participate in Internet-based surveys has created a group of professional respondents (Gillin and Sheppard 2003). There are obvious implications for this in terms of honesty of response and the quality of the sample.

Creating the report

The final stage of a research project is to create and present a report. The report should outline the background to the research (the research problem), the way in which the research was conducted and the rationale for doing so, the outcomes in terms of responses, the results (suitably analysed) and the interpretation of the results. The report should conclude with an outline of some recommendations for management, both in terms of an action plan resulting from the research and in terms of recommendations for any further research. The report should (in an ideal world) contain a statement regarding the limitations of the study.

In practice, many marketing research projects result in a less than fully frank report. Commercial marketing research companies may not be prepared to admit to their failings, and (worse) some researchers only provide the company with good news, suppressing any findings which may be unpopular. Managers who commission research should therefore examine the research method used as carefully as is feasible, and not simply rely on the bottom line.

A typical report is structured as follows:

1 *Executive summary.* This is at the beginning of the report, and allows executives to grasp the findings and recommendations quickly. It includes the basics of the research method (for example, how many respondents participated, and of what type), the main findings and the resulting recommendations.
2 *Introduction.* This includes the background to the research, the people involved and any acknowledgements.
3 *Research methods and methodology.* This includes the thinking behind the choice of method as well as a description of what was done and how it was done. The type of study, the purpose of the study, a description of the respondents and reasons for their inclusion, the sample design, data collection method and an example of the questionnaire (or other data-collection device).

4 *Analysis and findings.* The analytical approach adopted, tables and figures showing the results, and explanatory text.

5 *Recommendations* arising from the research results.

6 *Limitations* of the research.

7 *Appendices* containing any technical details or in-depth material regarding the data collection or analysis.

Ethics in Marketing Research

By its nature, marketing research seeks to elicit people's private thoughts and behaviour, and therefore depends heavily on establishing an atmosphere of trust and honesty between the researcher and the respondent. Unfortunately, abuse of this trust does occur, either deliberately or accidentally: Table 7.7 shows some of the possible ethical issues raised in marketing research.

As with any other ethical issue in business, managers need to consider the long-term effects of their actions. Apart from the obvious unease which most people feel when being dishonest, there is the practical aspect of the potential effect on the company's reputation. Having a reputation for underhand dealing is not good for business.

Table 7.7 Ethical Issues in marketing research

Ethical issue	Explanation
Intrusions on privacy	Most market researchers will need to know some private information about the respondents. Income, marital status and job status are commonly asked for, but sometimes researchers need to ask intimate questions about lifestyle and attitudes. Under no circumstances should this information be divulged to anyone: no information which could be used to identify respondents should ever be disclosed under any circumstances.
Misuse of research findings	If the findings are to be used in a promotional campaign, there is an obvious temptation to bias the results in order to support the advertiser's claims. This is a problem even when an agency is used to conduct the research: the agency often realises that a failure to produce the 'right' answer will jeopardise future business relations.
Competitive information gathering	Although competitors are naturally reticent in providing information about their plans, some methods of finding out what they have in mind are clearly unethical. Industrial espionage (where, for example, an employee of the company takes a job at a competing company in order to find out what their plans are) is not illegal in the UK, but is considered to be unethical. Bribing competitors' employees to pass on sensitive information is illegal, and is certainly unethical.
Sugging (selling under the guise of marketing research)	This practice is still fairly common, and is practised by sales-orientated companies. The company representative may begin by pretending to be conducting a survey, but quickly moves into a selling mode once he or she has found out about the respondent's personal circumstances. Sugging is very damaging to genuine marketing research because it makes people less likely to trust researchers in future. Unfortunately, it is difficult to prevent – despite the fact that it rarely works effectively since people are unlikely to buy from an organisation which has already demonstrated its dishonesty.

Summary

Marketing research supplies the information managers need to make decisions. Knowledge is power: without a continuous, timely and accurate flow of information about the external (and internal) environment marketing managers would be working entirely in the dark.

For marketers, all research is ultimately directed at meeting consumer needs better. Research will tell them what consumers want and need, what is already being supplied by competitors and what the consumers think of what they are being offered. Ultimately, the purpose of marketing research is to minimise risk in making business decisions. Using research to answer specific problems, marketing information systems to provide continuous updates and by triangulating on problems, managers can ensure the best possible basis on which to plan ahead.

Key points from this chapter are as follows:

- Marketing research supplies the information on which decisions are made.

- Marketing research can be divided into customer research advertising research, product research, distribution research, sales research and marketing environment research.

- Secondary research is cheaper than primary research but less well-tailored to the company's needs.

- Qualitative research is good for finding out people's deeper motivations, but does not have the statistical rigour of qualitative research.

- Research planning is based on what we need to know and how we are able to find it out. Execution is based on objectivity and avoidance of bias.

- Although questionnaire surveys are very common, focus groups, in-depth interviews, observation and experiments also have their place in marketing research.

- Secondary research is second-hand research – someone else collected it, usually for another purpose, but it can be recycled for the current purpose.

- Primary research is new, original research which is intended to be exactly tailored to find out information relevant to the company carrying it out.

- Research must be conducted honestly, and with respect for the individuals who have volunteered their time and trust to respond.

Chapter review questions

1 What is the difference between secondary and primary research?

2 What is the difference between preliminary research and conclusive research?

3 Which would be more suitable for preliminary research: qualitative or quantitative research?

4 How would a manager decide whether a piece of research is worth carrying out?

5 What are the main sources of inaccuracy in research?

6 What are the main drawbacks of questionnaires?

7 What ethical problems arise when conducting experiments?

8 How does triangulation improve the reliability of research?

9 What are the advantages of secondary research over primary research?

10 How can marketing information systems help in decision-making?

Preview case revisited
LabOUR

Gathering the evidence that Party members were unhappy really meant carrying out some kind of research exercise. Deciding to fight fire with fire, LabOUR began by commissioning focus groups composed of Labour Party members and recently-lapsed members.

LabOUR appointed Professor Stuart Weir, head of the Democratic Audit, to run the research for them. Between October and December 2005, LabOUR conducted focus groups in London, Birmingham, Cardiff, Glasgow and Manchester, recruiting members and former members for the focus groups. In February 2006, the members of LabOUR conducted informal sessions with members at the Blackpool Conference of the Labour Party, collecting anecdotal evidence: then in March 2006, they obtained funding to run a YouGov poll of members and former members.

Professor Weir and Professor Helen Margetts supervised the questionnaire design, and the poll was run during June 2006. The poll recruited 670 current Party members in an online survey, almost half of whom had been members for more than 10 years. The results went a long way to vindicating LabOUR's stance, producing the following statistics:

1 52 per cent believe that the war in Iraq was one of Labour's biggest mistakes.

2 49 per cent believed that being subservient to George Bush was a big mistake.

3 51 per cent thought that local party members had little influence on party policies.

The 704 lapsed members of the party that the survey picked up produced the following statistics:

1 65 per cent thought that Iraq was a mistake.

2 63 per cent thought that being subservient to President Bush was a mistake.

3 44 per cent thought that local party members had a great deal of influence on policy.

Obviously there were a great many more facts and figures that came from the survey: clearly LabOUR could go through and pick out the figures that suit their argument to some extent, and no doubt some of the responses may have been disappointing – but the fact remains that the survey was carried out fairly, and the findings are probably representative of the feelings of Labour Party members and ex-members in general.

Whether the research will bear any practical results is, of course, all a matter of politics.

Case study
Counter Intelligence Retail

Counter Intelligence Retail is a consultancy specialising in advising retailers about their store layout, merchandising and selling. The company goes beyond merely offering advice, however: Counter Intelligence Retail will go 'hands on' and help in implementing any policies they recommend.

The company has had particular success in the travel retail sector. Many airports make more money out of the retail shops than they do from the aircraft (Heathrow is a typical example) so getting the retailing right is of paramount importance. The stores have a captive audience who usually have little else to do but shop once they have checked in for their flights, but equally only have a finite period of time in which to browse and buy. Making the shopping process

more efficient for airline passengers is something that Counter Intelligence Retail can help with. If people can find what they are looking for quickly and easily, or can be directed to products of interest quickly, they are much more likely to buy. Good store layout and signage can only be achieved once the retailer knows exactly how people shop – and this is where Counter Intelligence Retail can help.

One area in which the company excels is in collecting data about how people shop. Some of this is collected via hidden cameras in-store, observing how people move around the store, which displays interest them and which do not, how they interact with the merchandise and so forth. Some of the data is collected via interviews, talking to people as they leave the store. Some of the data is collected in extremely innovative ways. For example, company founder Gary Stasiulevicuis is a frequent guest speaker at retail events: in April 2008 he spoke at the ACI Airport Business and Trinity Forum in Shanghai, where he explained the company's latest innovation – tiny digital cameras mounted on spectacles, worn by real shoppers. The special cameras record exactly what the shopper is looking at, how long they look at the object, and of course whether they choose to buy as a result.

Shoppers are frequently interviewed when leaving a store, in an attempt to find out why they made a particular purchase. Counter Intelligence Retail does this as well, but say that such interviews alone are not sufficient, because people find it difficult to analyse their own motivations. Often the decision to buy is made apparently on impulse, even though there may have been weeks or months of previous thought leading up to the final decision: it is not easy either to rationalise a decision afterwards, or to analyse one's own decision-making processes. A combination of observing through the customer's own eyes, observing through a hidden camera and post-event interviewing provides the triangulation necessary to fill in the gaps in the picture.

Counter Intelligence Retail say that they are 'Making it easier for retailers to sell more by making it easier for

shoppers to buy more'. This seems to sum up the whole philosophy of marketing in one sentence.

Questions

1 What ethical problems might arise from using hidden cameras?

2 What specific problems face retailers at airports, as opposed to other locations?

3 Why are post-purchase interviews likely to be unreliable?

4 What problems might there be in analysing the observation data?

5 How might retailers use observation to change store layout?

References

AMA (1987): New market research definition approved. *Marketing News* **2** January, p. 21.

Chandon, P., Morwitz, V.G. and Reinartz, W.J. (2005): Do intentions really predict behaviour? Self-generated validity effects in survey research. *Journal of Marketing* **69**(2), 1–13.

Deal, K. (2003): Do-it-yourself internet surveys. *Marketing Research* **15**(2), 40–2.

Dillman, D. (1978): *Mail and Telephone Surveys: The Total Design Method* (New York: Wiley).

Gillin, D.L. and Sheppard, J. (2003): The fallacy of getting paid for your opinions. *Marketing Research* **15**(3), 8.

Gorn, G.J., Chattopadhyay, A., Sengupta, J. and Tripathi, S. (2004): Waiting for the web: how screen colour affects time perception. *Journal of Marketing Research* **41**(2), 215–25.

Grandcolas, U., Rettie, R. and Marusenko, K. (2003): Web survey bias: sample or mode effect? *Journal of Marketing Management* **19**(5/6), 541–61.

Grapentine, T. (2004): Fuzzy math. *Marketing Research* **16**(1), 4.

Grapentine, T. (2004): To tell the truth. *Marketing Research* **16**(1), 4.

Grunert, K.D. (2003): Can we understand consumers by asking them? *Marketing Research* **15**(2), 46–8.

Jobber, D. and Rainbow, C. (1977): A study of the development and implementation of marketing information systems in British industry. *Journal of the Marketing Research Society* **19**(3), 104–11.

O'Sullivan, D. and Abela, A.V. (2007): Marketing performance measurement ability and firm performance. *Journal of Marketing* **71**(2), 79–93.

Proctor, T. (2000): *Essentials of Marketing Research* (Harlow: FT Prentice Hall).

Ray, N.M. (2003): Cyber surveys come of age. *Marketing Research* **15**(1), 32–7.

Rickards, T. (1974): *Problem Solving through Creative Analysis* (Aldershot: Gower).

Rook, D.W. (2003): Out of focus groups. *Marketing Research* **15**(2), 10–15.

Ward, S., Bridges, K. and Chitty, W. (2005): Do incentives matter? An examination of on-line privacy concerns and willingness to provide personal and financial information. *Journal of Marketing Communications* **11**(1), 21–40.

Wefeld, J.R. (2003): Consumer research in the land of Oz. *Marketing Research* **15**(1), 10–15.

Wyner, G.A. (2003): Reinventing research design. *Marketing Research* **14**(4), 6.

Zaltman, G. (2003): How Customers Think: Insights into the Mind of the Market (Harvard University Press).

Further reading

Proctor, T. (2000): *Essentials of Marketing Research* (Harlow: FT Prentice Hall). This book gives a good overview of current marketing research practice.

Dillman, D.A. (1999): *Mail and Internet Surveys: The Tailored Design Method* (Chichester: Wiley). Dillman was the inventor of total design, and he has applied the same thinking to Internet surveys. This is a book aimed mainly at practitioners, but is an extremely useful reference work for anyone engaged in marketing research.

Carson, D., Gilmore, A., Gronhaug, K. and Perry, C. (2001): *Qualitative Market Research* (London: Sage). This text provides a very comprehensive and erudite guide to qualitative research.

Chapter 8
Communications theories

Learning objectives After reading this chapter, you should be able to:

1   Explain how people interact with marketing communications.

2   Understand the interactive nature of communication.

3   Explain the role of redundancy in communication.

4   Describe the role of culture in communication.

5   Explain the sources of miscommunication.

6   Describe the taxonomy of marketing communication.

7   Explain the role of personal factors in communication.

8   Explain the difference between, and the role of, push and pull strategies.

9   Explain the role of negotiation in budget-setting.

10 Explain how competition affects communication strategies.

11 Describe the problems of integrating marketing communications.

Introduction

Marketing communications are the most visible part of marketing. Everyone is familiar with advertising, mailings, press releases, messages on T-shirts, spam emails and so forth. It is common to say that people are bombarded with advertising – but in fact this is not really true.

Human beings like to communicate. Conversation is still the most popular form of entertainment for the majority of us: we communicate with each other via telephone, newsprint, billboard, email, television, radio, text message and probably by jungle drum and sign language if nothing else is available. As a species, we love to exchange information, to argue, to persuade and to influence others. Communication about products and services is part of that mass of communication, and marketers are simply joining in with everyone else in the process. For marketers, communication about products and services is not just an entertainment, it is also a profession and a livelihood. Although communication is a major part of marketing, it is not the whole story: just as there is more to being a human being than just communication, there is more to being a marketer than just advertising.

This chapter examines the theoretical context of marketing communications. Beginning with theories of communication, the chapter continues into the structure and current thinking about the management of marketing communications.

Preview case
Citroën C4

For some time, Citroën had been suffering from a somewhat staid image: its 2CV model, originally developed immediately after the Second World War as a general-purpose utility vehicle for French farmers, was probably its best-known product. Although the 2CV's canvas roof made it the cheapest convertible on the market, and its large ground clearance meant it could be driven over a ploughed field with a box of eggs on the back seat, these were hardly features that endeared it to the kind of upmarket, educated people Citroën hoped to attract. The 2CV was certainly a reliable car – people said of it that it had so few refinements there was nothing on it to go wrong, and it was built to be maintained by amateurs. The low-tech image was one which Citroën wanted to shake off with its new generation of products, but shifting people's perceptions would be no easy task.

In 2005, Citroën asked advertising agency Euro RSCG London to come up with an innovative TV advertisement for their C4 car. The car was to be promoted as being 'alive with technology', not an easy concept to put across in a 30-second commercial. The result of their thinking was the astonishing 'Transformer' series of advertisements, in which the car transforms into a robot and dances (or, in later versions, ice-skates) before transforming back into a car. Marty Kudelka, Justin Timberlake's choreographer, was hired to create the dance sequence: he performed the dance covered from head to foot in motion sensors which

recorded his every move, then the 'robot' version was produced by Spy Films of Toronto using computer generated imaging (CGI). The actual visual effects were created by the Embassy visual effects company in Vancouver (which may explain why much of the background is recognisable by Vancouverites).

Of course, the key question was whether the advertising would succeed, considering that it said absolutely nothing whatsoever about the car, its features, or the company that made it.

Courtesy of The Advertising Archives

Attitude Formation and Change

A great deal of marketing communication (possibly even the majority of it) is aimed at either changing people's attitudes or encouraging specific attitudes to form among a target audience. The theory of attitude formation and change is therefore crucial to effective marketing communication.

Attitude is defined as a learned predisposition to respond to an object or class of objects in a consistently favourable or unfavourable way (Allport 1935). Attitudes represent what we like and dislike, so attitude determines to a large extent what people will and will not buy. Dismantling the definition, we find that:

1 *Attitude is learned, it is not instinctive.* We develop attitudes largely through experience, but partly through the experience of others, communicated through conversation or writing.

2 *Attitude is a tendency to respond, it is not the response itself.* Attitude does not always lead to action – someone might hate the boss, but not actually do anything about it.

3 *Attitude is consistent over time.* People tend to keep their attitudes intact unless some major new experience or information changes them.

4 *Attitudes can be favourable or unfavourable.* Since attitudes have a strength, an attitude is a vector: it has both strength and intensity.

5 *There is an implied relationship between the person and the attitudinal object.* The object of the attitude could be a product, a person or an idea: the word 'object' is used here in the sense of 'objective'.

Attitudes cannot be observed: they can be inferred from behaviour, or might be determined by market research, but often attitudes are hidden from the observer (and may even be unclear to the holder of the attitude).

Attitude has three dimensions: cognition, conation and affect. Cognition is what is known about the attitudinal object, in other words the facts about it. Affect is the emotional component of attitude, and is composed of what is felt about the object. Conation is the person's intended behaviour, resulting from holding the attitude.

Conation is only intended behaviour – it is not the behaviour itself. Someone may, for example, intend to change bank accounts on hearing that the bank has acted unethically in some way, but may find (on mature reflection) that switching to another bank is too much trouble. The attitude itself has not been affected by this, merely the outcome.

The components of attitude interact with each other in complex ways. Provided the three elements are in balance, the attitude is stable and is unlikely to change. Purchase intention is strongly linked to attitude, and some studies indicate that attitude to product is affected by attitude to the advertisements for it (Homer and Yoon 1992).

The traditional (and possibly intuitive) view of attitude is that attitudes are formed in a sequence, i.e. that knowledge (cognition) comes first, then emotional elements develop (affect) followed by behaviour (conation). In fact it has been shown that attitudes form in no particular order: someone can fall in love with, or take an instant dislike to, an attitudinal object without knowing anything substantial about it. In this way, affect can precede cognition (Zajonc and Markus 1985). Equally, someone might act on impulse to buy something which looks interesting, then learn about it and form an attitude later.

cognition The rational component of attitude.

conation Intended behaviour.

affect The emotional component of attitude.

Talking Point

Attitude seems to be a complex area. We don't know how a person's attitude formed, we don't know what it might lead to, and it's difficult to change anyway. So why not just ignore it, and go on how people actually behave? After all, people are not always rational anyway – they buy products they didn't really want, and form attitudes later!

Or should we perhaps be finding groups with positive attitudes towards our products and going to them? Why bother trying to change attitudes at all? In short, which is better – leave attitudes alone and just sell to people who like our products anyway, or go out and find people to whom we would like to sell and try to change their attitudes?

Attitude contains components of belief and opinion, but it is neither. Attitude differs from belief in that belief is neutral, and does not include connotations of good or bad. Belief is only concerned with the possession (or otherwise) of an attribute, and is usually

belief An understanding that an object possesses a particular attribute.

Figure 8.1
Stable attitude

Cognition

Affect   Conation

based on a judgement of the available evidence. Attitude contains an emotional element, and evaluates whether the existence or otherwise of an attribute will result in satisfaction or dissatisfaction. Believing that a luxury hotel has a reputation for comfort, for example, may be entirely irrelevant to a backpacker, and therefore not form part of his or her attitude to the hotel. Attitude differs from opinion in that opinion is an overt, vocalised expression of an attitude. Attitude is not always expressed, and may be expressed non-verbally, but opinion is always expressed.

Attitude formation

Attitude formation is by no means straightforward. As has already been seen, attitudes can form as a result of finding out facts about an object, as a result of forming an emotional attachment to an object, or as a result of acting towards an object. Each of these can lead to 'filling in' the other elements of attitude and thus forming a complete and stable attitude.

Because the cognitive system can only hold a relatively limited amount of information, people often use only a few beliefs to inform the cognitive element of attitude. These beliefs are called salient beliefs, and are usually the ones which the individuals believes to be most important. Salient beliefs could, of course, merely be the beliefs that were most recently presented (Fishbein and Ajzen 1975).

salient belief An understanding that an object possesses a relevant attribute.

The degree to which people form cognitions about attitudinal objects depends on their capacity to process information and also on the degree of attention they are prepared to give to the process. Ability to process information depends partly on intelligence and partly on existing knowledge of the product type. For example, someone who is a real computer buff will have a greater ability to process information about new software than someone who is a novice with computers, even though each person might be of equal intelligence.

The overall attitude is the result of formulating many attributes of the object. The multi-attribute model (Fishbein 1963) attempts to explain how the consumer's salient beliefs help to form the final attitude. The model proposes that the attitude towards the product is based on the summed set of beliefs about the product's attributes, weighted by the evaluation of those attributes. These attributes could include factors which are not directly part of the product, for example celebrity endorsement, slogans, relationships with charities, charisma of the company's founder and so forth. The multi-attribute model has remained one of the key concepts in attitude, but has been criticised because of its reliance on cognition as the starting point of attitude.

Forming a belief set about the object may result in a qualified attitude: for example, a restaurant may score highly on its food and service, but low on its atmosphere, which would make it a good place for a quick meal when one does not feel like cooking, but a bad place when one has a romantic dinner for two planned.

Attitudes clearly affect behaviour. Fishbein's theory of reasoned action says that individuals consciously evaluate the consequences of different behaviours and choose the one that will lead to the most favourable consequences. Beliefs about the intended behaviour and the likely outcome is what colours attitude, according to Fishbein: the theory assumes that consumers perform a logical evaluation procedure for making decisions about behaviour, based on attitude towards the behaviour, which derives from attitudes towards the brand.

Fishbein's model seeks to combine the internal influences on attitude with external influences. All of us are influenced by what other people think (there is more on this later in the chapter), so our attitudes towards other people and their expectations of us will affect what we do in the same way as our attitudes towards the behaviour itself will affect our behaviour. The model seeks to combine these factors into one unified explanation of behaviour.

Of course, the model assumes that people are rational, which is often not the case: emotions affect attitude, and also affect behaviour, so that people often act in ways which would not be predicted by their stated attitudes.

Attitudes can also be formed primarily through the affective route, or even through behaviour: they are not always formed as a result of conscious thought. People are not always rational: they form attitudes and opinions based on gut feeling, sometimes in the

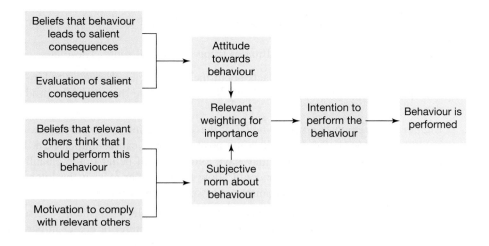

Figure 8.2

The theory of reasoned action

Source: Martin Fishbein, 'An Overview of the Attitude Construct'. In G.B. Hafer (ed.) *A Look Back, A Look Ahead*. Chicago, IL: American Marketing Association 1980

face of strong objective evidence to the contrary. A theory has been developed which states that there are two routes to attitude formation: the **central route**, which operates through cognition, and the **peripheral route**, which operates through affect (Petty and Cacioppo 1986). The elaboration likelihood model (Petty, Cacioppo and Schumann 1983) proposes that, in any situation, the person's level of involvement and ability to process information will be the key factors in determining which route predominates. If involvement is high and processing ability is also high, the central route will predominate. If on the other hand involvement is low and processing ability is low, the peripheral route is likely to predominate. In this case, the person will be influenced by cues which are incidental to the object in question (Chaiken 1980).

More recent studies have shown that peripheral processing may also influence consumers' beliefs as well as their feelings (Miniard, Bhatla and Rose 1990). This implies that peripheral processing supplements, rather than replaces, central processing.

central route Cognitive approach to changing behaviour.

peripheral route Affective approach to changing behaviour.

Changing attitudes

Attitude change is one of the key objectives of marketing communication. If an attitude is stable, it is extremely difficult to change – each element of the attitude supports every other element. The starting point of any attitude change is therefore to destabilise the attitude.

Attitudes can be destabilised by attacking any of the components. Changing the way a person feels about a product is likely to be as effective as changing some of their beliefs about the product, and marketers even try to change people's behaviour (for example by offering free samples or test drives) in order to destabilise the attitude. Very strongly held

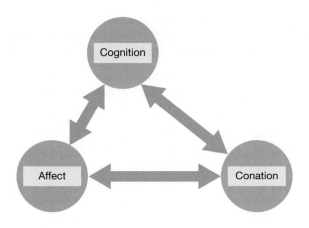

Figure 8.3

Unstable attitude

attitudes are unlikely to be changed greatly, but weakly held attitudes can certainly be shifted.

There are four ways of changing attitudes using the central route. These are:

1 *Add a new salient belief.* New facts about the product can change attitudes – for example, if a report from the Health and Safety Executive shows that the product is dangerous.

2 *Change the strength of a salient belief.* If the salient belief is a negative one, it can be discounted or played down: if it is a positive one, it can be emphasised. For example, a restaurant customer may have a low level of belief in the cleanliness of the kitchen, so the proprietor could allow the customer to visit the kitchen, or could fit a window so that customers could see into the kitchen.

3 *Change the evaluation of an existing belief.* For example, the reliability of a car may seem unimportant against the cost, but the manufacturer or dealer might point out that reliable cars cost a lot less to run because they need less servicing and fewer new components.

4 *Make an existing belief more salient.* Customers might believe (for example) that the waiters in a restaurant are friendly, but not regard this as particularly important until a friend points out that friendly staff make the evening more pleasant.

Inconsistency between the three components of attitude come about when a new stimulus is presented. When presented with a new stimulus, people have three ways of dealing with it, as shown in Table 8.1.

The three elements of attitude are so closely linked that a change in one element will almost always lead to a change in the others (Rosenberg 1960). Teasing out the individual factors in the attitude can be a time-consuming and conceptually difficult process: this is because so many factors go to make up an attitude, and in some cases the attitude will be affected by halo effect (sometimes also known as horns effect). Halo effect is the tendency to believe that, if one aspect of the product is good, then all other aspects are also good. Horns effect is the opposite side of the coin – if one aspect is bad, all aspects are bad.

Attitude measurement

Measuring attitude is clearly of considerable interest to marketers, since the strength and direction of the attitude have a strong effect on tendency to buy. Because attitude is so complex, it is often difficult to measure with any degree of accuracy, especially as some attitudes remain hidden – people are reluctant to reveal their true attitudes in some cases because of a fear of social stigma.

Table 8.1 Stimulus defence mechanisms

Defence mechanism	Explanation
Stimulus rejection	The individual simply ignores the stimulus, discounting the new information. By rejecting the new information, the individual is able to maintain the status quo and leave the attitude unchanged.
Attitude splitting	Here the individual only accepts the part of the new information that does not create an inconsistency. For example, someone might accept the truth of the new information, but regard it as a special case which does not apply to the actual situation.
Accommodate the new attitude	The individual accepts the stimulus as fact and changes his or her attitude accordingly.

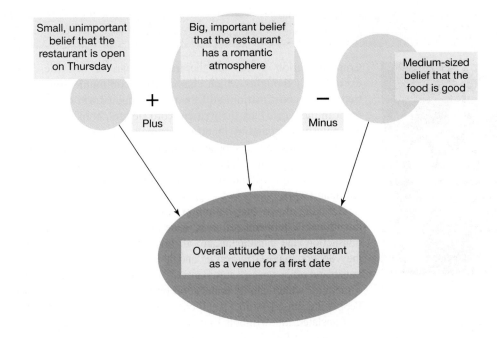

Figure 8.4

Beliefs in the formation of attitude

The Fishbein model mentioned earlier offers a formula for measuring attitude. By adding up the various beliefs and assigning scores to them, the model aims to generate a calculation of the strength of the attitude. The problem for the practical marketer lies in measuring the strengths of the beliefs (there is more on this in Chapter 7). For Fishbein, the focus is on the consumer rather than on the product, basing the analysis on belief and evaluation. Belief is the probability that the object possesses a particular attribute, and evaluation is the degree to which the attribute attracts or repels.

An alternative model was proposed by Rosenberg (1960). Rosenberg says that an individual's attitude towards an object represents the degree and direction of the attitudinal effect aroused by the object. Put more simply, attitude is composed of a quantity of feeling and a direction, and has two main components. These are perceived instrumentality, which is the subjective capacity of the object to attain the value in question, and value importance, which is the amount of satisfaction the person derives from the attainment of a particular value. In simple terms, the strength of the attitude can be measured by determining the degree to which the person believes that the product will perform, and the importance to the consumer that it should do so.

Theoretically, perceived instrumentality and value importance are independent, so when measured separately they are poor predictors, but taken together they have proven to be good measures of attitude.

instrumentality The subjective capacity of the object to attain the value in question.

The two models can be combined to give three aspects of attitude in terms of measurement:

1 Perceived instrumentality

2 Evaluative aspect

3 Value importance.

Examples of these aspects are as follows:

1 I believe the Lexus is the most comfortable car in its class.

2 I like comfort.

3 Comfort is important to me.

Note that the last two aspects are not identical. It is possible to like something without it being very important to you.

Communication

People like to communicate – often about products.

Communication is one of the most human of activities. The exchange of thoughts which characterises communication is carried out by conversation (still the most popular form of entertainment in the world), by the written word (letters, books, magazines and newspapers) and by pictures (cartoons, television and film).

Communication has been defined as a transactional process between two or more parties whereby meaning is exchanged through the intentional use of symbols (Engel, Warshaw and Kinnear 1994).

Breaking down this definition, we see that communication is intentional (a deliberate effort is made to convey information), it is a transaction (the participants are all involved in the process, even if they do not make a response) and it is symbolic (words, pictures, music and other sensory stimulants are used to translate thoughts into something which can be understood by the other person or people). People are not telepathic, so all communications require concepts to be translated into symbols to convey the required meaning.

This means that the individual or firm issuing the communication must first reduce the concepts to a set of symbols which can be passed on to the recipient of the message; the recipient must decode the symbols to get the original message. In fact, the parties must share a common field of experience which includes a common view of what the symbols involved actually mean.

A well-known and widely used model of communication was developed by Schramm (1948) and revised in 1971. This model is shown in Figure 8.5. The Schramm model views communication as a process which takes place between a sender and a receiver: there will be also a message, and a medium through which the message can be transmitted. The receiver may have a method of sending feedback on the message, to confirm that the message has been correctly received and understood, but noise and interference will affect both the ability of the message to get through and the content of the message.

The sender's field of experience and the receiver's field of experience must overlap, at least to the extent of having a common language, but in fact the overlap is likely to be much more complex and subtle in most marketing communications. Advertisements typically use references from TV shows, proverbs and common sayings: they often make puns or use half-statements which the audience is able to complete because they are aware of the cultural referents involved. This is why foreign advertising often seems unintentionally humorous or even incomprehensible.

Noise is the surrounding distraction present during the communications process, for example someone walking into the room during a commercial break. Interference is a

Figure 8.5

Schramm model of the communication process

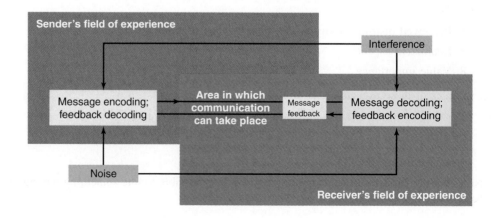

deliberate attempt to distract the audience's attention with intelligent communications. For example, a car driver may be distracted away from a radio advertisement by another car cutting in (noise) or by seeing an interesting billboard (interference). For most marketing purposes the difference is academic.

The Schramm model is useful, but it suffers from a number of weaknesses. First, it is essentially a one-step model of communication. This is rather over-simplified; Katz and Lazarsfield (1955) postulated a two-step model in which the messages are filtered through opinion leaders, for example magazine journalists, which alters both the content of the message and its impact on the receiver. Many marketing messages are filtered in this way, because the messages need to appear in a medium which might itself become part of the message. For example, an advertisement placed in a tabloid newspaper undoubtedly has a very different impact from that of the same advertisement placed in a glossy magazine. The image of the medium affects the credibility of the message.

Second, in most cases the message reaches the receiver via several routes. Sending the same message by more than one route is called **redundancy**, and is a good way of ensuring that the message gets through. Figure 8.6 shows this diagrammatically.

redundancy In communications, sending a message by more than one route to ensure correct delivery.

In the diagram, the sender sends almost identical messages via different routes. The effect of noise and interference is to distort the message, and the opinion leader will moderate the message, but by using three different routes the meaning of the message is more likely to get through. At first sight, this would be a good reason to integrate marketing communications, but in practice the message will tend to shift according to the route being used, which makes integration difficult. Because of the selective nature of perception (see Chapter 4), a radio advertisement is likely to have a different impact from that of a TV advertisement, and (even more so) from that of a press advertisement. Current thinking is that different media cannot deliver the identical message, so integrating communications is therefore more about delivering different parts of the same message.

Talking Point

If people are interested in the subject matter of the message, presumably they will pay attention to it. If they are not interested, presumably they will not act upon the message even if they are forced to hear it. So why do we need to worry about noise, interference, and so forth? Why not just put out messages and assume that people will take in the ones they are interested in and ignore the ones that are irrelevant?

Or is this a naïve view? Maybe people don't know whether they will be interested or not until after they have heard the message – so maybe we have to hammer it at them to get a result. Then again, is this really the way to treat our potential customers?

A further criticism of the Schramm model is that it tends to assume that the receiver is passive in the process. Human beings are not radio transmitters and receivers: they think about what they send and receive, adding the message to what is already known. The Schramm model does not address issues of persuasion, or even of outright lying. Furthermore, the model assumes that the receiver is either listening or is not listening, whereas in practice people may be listening only part of the time. In other words, selective attention will

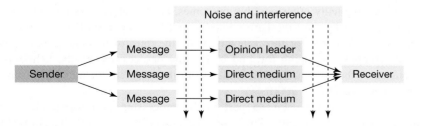

Figure 8.6

Redundancy in communication

Figure 8.7

Message plus person equals action

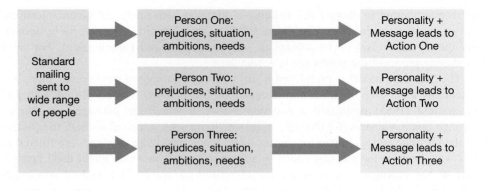

distort the message. Frequently communications are conducted as a dialogue of the deaf, in which each person wishes to make his or her point without actually listening to the other person's statements, or at best only picking up part of what is being said (Varey 2000). Despite these shortcomings, the Schramm model is not only widely taught, but is widely accepted as the expected model. People tend to imagine that what they say will be taken at face value, when of course this is unlikely to be the case. Consequently, people exaggerate, omit negative facts, and overstate the case in order to persuade other people to their point of view. This is particularly true in the organisational context, where much communication is 'political', i.e. aimed at creating an impression in the mind of the receiver.

In Figure 8.7, a standard message sent to a group of people will produce a different response from each person, because the message is added to the existing prejudices, needs, situation and ambitions of the specific individual. The actions which arise from the message will be different for each person.

For example, consider what happens when a householder receives an offer of a free holiday in exchange for attending a presentation on timeshare apartments. The householder might respond in any of the following ways:

1 Throw the mailing away, perhaps without reading it. The householder's view of reality is that timeshare salespeople are unethical, and that timeshare is at best poor value for money and at worst fraudulent.

2 Respond to the mailing by agreeing to go to the presentation, having no intention of buying a timeshare but simply attending in order to win the free holiday. The householder's view is that the timeshare company is stupid, and is 'fair game' for being exploited.

3 Respond to the mailing by agreeing to go to the presentation, with an open mind about whether or not to buy the timeshare. The householder's view here might be that timeshare is a popular way of buying holidays, so perhaps there are benefits attached to it: either way, the householder will win the holiday, so it is a 'win–win' proposition.

4 Examine the exact wording of the address on the envelope to find out which mailing list was used. Reality for the householder is that the timeshare company is not smart enough to outwit its target customers.

There are undoubtedly other possible outcomes, but the above example shows how the message sent out by the timeshare company creates a number of possibilities, most of which are not desirable for the company. Only the third of the above four outcomes is what the company is hoping for, and is the only one covered by the Schramm model. Acceptance of the communication comes from the recipient's choice, not from the initiator's intentions (Varey 2000).

Furthermore, emotion plays a part in the processing of information. Memory is stimulated by advertisements which produce powerful emotions (Baird, Wahlers and

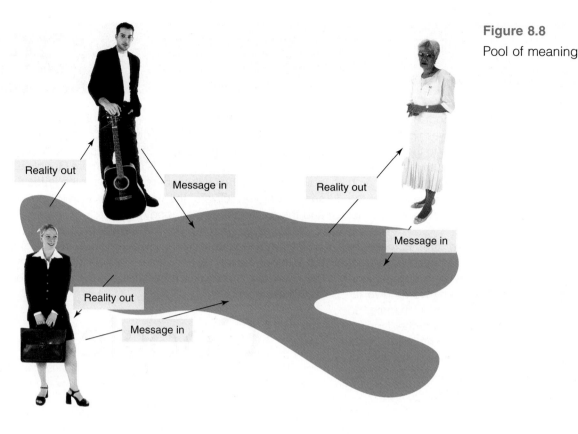

Figure 8.8
Pool of meaning

Cooper 2007), in some cases to the extent that bland messages are not processed at all. The effect appears to be stronger in women than in men, for reasons which are not clear.

Recently, an alternative view of the communication process has emerged. Communications theorists such as Deetz (1992) and Mantovani (1996) see communication as a cooperative process in which meaning is developed between individuals. Their joint perception of the world is developed through a co-construction of meaning, in which dialogue acts as the mediating device. In this model, communication is not something which is done to recipients: it is something which is shared with recipients. Research shows that people prefer interactive communications (Vlasic and Kesic 2007), probably because one-way communications are boring, and also somewhat patronising compared with a dialogue of equals.

An analogy for this is shown in Figure 8.8. Reality is represented as a pool of shared meaning into which people have an input. Each person adds something to the pool, and each person takes something out of the pool: what is put in is not necessarily the same as what is taken out, because each individual only takes what he or she wants from the pool. Also, what is put in is mixed with everything else in the same pool, so that the input is transformed.

If this alternative view of communication is accepted, it has far-reaching implications for marketers. In particular, the approach to marketing communications on the Internet is likely to be affected dramatically, since the Internet is above all an interactive medium.

The Hierarchy of Communication Effects

Communications are unlikely to create all their impact at once. Successive exposures to a communication will, if all goes well, move the recipient up a 'ladder' as shown in Figure 8.9. At the bottom of the ladder are people who are completely unaware of the product in question; at the top of the ladder are those who actually purchase the product.

E-Marketing in Practice
Search Engines

A different hierarchy of effects model operates in e-marketing, or at least that's what we might be led to believe. Marketing on the Internet seems to follow rules of its own, and communications is no exception. Apparently 85 per cent of visitors to websites are taken there by search engines such as Google or Lycos, which means that the websites need to be attractive to search engines, not necessarily to visitors.

Search engines such as Google are increasingly gearing up to search for strings rather than keywords, because relatively few people now type in a single key-word when making a search. Single key words give far too many results for the average person to handle, so instead of typing in, say, 'mortgage' the searcher types in 'mortgage rates'. Even this gives too many results, so a searcher might type in 'lowest mortgage rates UK' or 'lowest mortgage rates first time buyers UK' to limit the search to the areas he or she is interested in.

From the viewpoint of the people running Google, teaching the machine to recognise strings is good business. The better the searches, the less time people spend online tying up resources and the more Google are able to charge their subscribers. The better the leads the search engine delivers, the happier the subscribers are and the more money everybody makes.

Once again the key to the whole process lies in understanding what the customers do when they search the Internet. Which is, of course, a marketing problem – unfortunately, the research into this area is still far from complete.

Figure 8.9

The hierarchy of communications effects

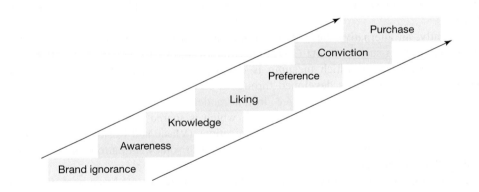

A problem with this model is that it implies the process is invariably linear. This is not necessarily the case; an individual can become aware of a product and form an instant liking for it, without having detailed knowledge of it. Equally, people often buy products on impulse and form an opinion about them afterwards.

Having said that, the hierarchy of effects model is helpful in planning communications campaigns, since different communications methods and styles can be used according to the consumer's level on the hierarchy. For example, when a new product is introduced (or a product is introduced into a new market) few of the target audience will know anything about it. Establishing the brand name in people's consciousnesses is therefore a realistic first move in the communications process. Later on in the campaign, more detail about the product can be introduced, and finally some more persuasive arguments might be used to encourage people to buy.

Table 8.2 Categorising signs

Type of sign	Definition	Example
Icon	A sign that looks like the object, or represents it visually in a way that most people would relate to.	A drawing of a tractor would represent the countryside and farming to most people.
Index	A sign that relates to the object by a causal connection.	A sweaty manual worker going into a bar would symbolise beer to most people: we are all familiar with the idea of becoming thirsty after working hard.
Symbol	An artificial sign which has been created for the purpose of providing meaning.	Most people would recognise the intertwined arrows used to denote recyclable or recycled materials. This conveys an image of 'greenness' to the products it appears on.

Signs and Meaning

A sign is 'anything that stands for something (its object) to somebody (its interpreter) in some respect (its context)' (Pierce 1986). Signs fall into three categories, as shown in Table 8.2.

The most obvious symbols are, of course, words. Words only have meanings as they are interpreted by people – and over long periods of time, even words change their meanings. For example, 'great' originally only meant 'large' but is commonly used to denote 'good'. 'Cool' referred only to temperature 50 years ago – it moved through meaning 'well-presented' or 'capable' to a current meaning signifying agreement with a proposed plan of action. The same words can also have different meanings in different languages: in Portuguese, 'mais' means more, whereas in French the word means 'but': in Spanish 'mas' means more, but in Portuguese it means 'but'. Considering that these three languages are closely related, one can imagine the wide range of meanings a word might have in all the languages of the world.

Meanings of words can be denotative, i.e. having the same meaning for everybody, or connotative, i.e. having a meaning which is unique to the individual. Although everybody knows what 'ship' is (denotative) some individuals become seasick and might associate 'ship' with the discomfort experienced when at sea (connotative).

Because connotative meanings vary among individuals, marketers need to develop empathy with their target audiences. This is easiest when the marketer and the audience are as similar as possible in terms of background and outlook. Semiotics, syntactics and semantics are fields of study which enable us to ensure that the correct meanings are attributed to symbols.

denotative Having a unique meaning for an individual.

connotative Having the same meaning for everybody.

Semiotics

Semiotics is the study of sign systems. It is really more of a theoretical approach than an academic discipline (O'Sullivan et al. 1983): spoken language is used as the main example of a sign system, but semiotics is not limited to language. Semiotics assumes that meaning can only be derived socially, so it agrees with the alternative view of communications described earlier. Communication is seen as an interaction between the reader and the text: texts are created by reworking signs, codes and symbols within the particular sign system in order to generate myths (stories which are not founded on evidence), connotations and meanings. The social process involved in communication is assumed to generate pleasure as well as cognitive, rational outcomes.

For example, a film (or indeed a TV advert) uses the sign systems of the spoken word, the actions of the actors, the music of the soundtrack and the conventions of direction and production to generate its meaning. People seeing the film filter the information and add it to their pre-existing attitudes, knowledge and prejudices in order to create a meaning. In this sense all communication is interactive to the extent that the observer edits and mutates the meanings offered. This is why people often have heated discussions about the meaning of film, the motivations of the characters and (of course) whether or not they enjoyed it.

Semiotics is an attempt to show how meaning is produced within a social context, implying that meaning is not produced by an individual but is subject to power plays, struggle and interpretation, much like any other social interaction.

Syntactics

Syntactics is about the structure of communications. Symbols and signs change their meanings according to the syntax, or contexts, in which they appear. For example, a road safety poster showing a 10-year-old boy holding his mother's hand to cross the road has a different meaning from that of the same 10-year-old holding his seven-year-old sister's hand. The boy means something different in each poster; in the first instance he is the protected person, in the second he is the protector, but there are greater connotations of vulnerability in the second example, which might make this poster more effective in alerting drivers to the dangers of children crossing the road.

In this picture the boy conveys a sense of vulnerability while helping his sister to cross safely.

Equally, the same word can have different meanings in different sentences, or the whole advertisement can acquire a different meaning when seen in different locations.

Semantics

Semantics is often thought to be about the study of meaning, but in fact it is concerned with the way words relate to the external reality to which they refer.

Communication is carried out in many other ways than the verbal or written word. Only 30 per cent of communication is conveyed by words; people communicate by pictures, non-verbal sounds, smell, touch, numbers, artefacts, time and kinetics. Most of these media are used by marketers – for example, women's magazines sometimes have scratch-and-sniff cards which contain new fragrances. Charities often send out free pens to prospective donors so that they can more easily fill in direct debit contribution forms: the gift of a pen also places the recipient under a small social obligation to make a contribution.

Table 8.3 shows some of the ways in which these silent communications methods are used by marketers.

In Figure 8.10 semantics overlaps into reality because it is about the relationship between words and reality. The words become the reality in the minds of the listeners. Semiotics feeds into syntactics, and thus the message is formulated: derived from reality, and moderated by the meanings and structures imposed by the composer of the message, the message becomes something new which is part reality, part messenger and part receiver.

Silent languages and culture

This gesture means 'OK' throughout the Americas – except in Brazil!

The main problem with silent languages is that they are not culturally universal. Most body language does not transfer well to other cultures, even when the cultures are otherwise close. Well-known examples are the two-finger sign which is highly insulting to British people but which can denote merely 'two' in the rest of Europe; the thumb and index finger circle which denotes 'OK' to Americans but which is a rude gesture in

Table 8.3 Silent communications

Medium	Example
Numbers	Heinz 57 Varieties is an example. There must have been a time when HJ Heinz produced exactly 57 varieties of canned food, but the range is very much larger than that now, and was very much smaller when the brand was established. The number implies a wide range of products.
Space	An image of people standing close together implies that they are good friends; likewise an image of wide open spaces implies freedom. Car advertising often uses this imagery.
Artefacts	Images of what people own imply their social status. Some artefacts (aircraft, cars, ships) might imply travel.
Time	An image of a clock's hands moving on might imply stress and pressure, or it might imply ageing.
Kinetics	People who are walking (or running) imply a fit and active lifestyle; those who are gesticulating with their hands imply intellectual discussion, or argument.

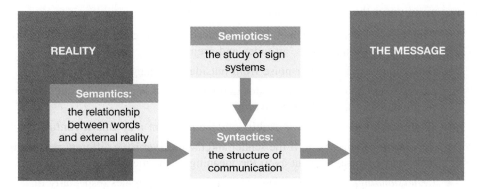

Figure 8.10

Semiotics, semantics and syntactics: structuring communication

Brazil; showing the soles of the feet to Thais is again insulting. Other examples are more subtle. Japanese people tend to show their emotions less in public than do Americans, Indians tend to regard shabby or torn clothes as denoting poverty, whereas North Europeans often associate this with independence and freedom, and numbers which are considered lucky in some cultures are neutral in others (Costa and Pavia 1992). Hong Kong and Shanghai Banking Corporation (HSBC) have made good use of these differences in their advertising, explaining that the bank has exceptional local knowledge and understands these cultural differences.

World communications are very well-established, and people are not all that stupid. Surely if the message we are conveying is 'Please buy this product' which is what most marketing communications are about, most people would get the idea. Buying and selling is straightforward enough, isn't it?

So why worry about culture? If people know that they are looking at a German company's adverts, or a Japanese company's ads, they *know* that these people are foreigners, and will make allowances. In fact, mistakes in language and so on are often charming rather than offensive.

Could it be that we are being over-sensitive?

The problem arises because of **ethnocentrism**, which is the practice of assuming that others think and believe as we do. Ethnocentrism is one of the few features of human behaviour that belongs to all cultures; the tendency is for people to believe that their own culture is the 'right' one and everybody else's is at best a poor copy (Shimp and Sharma

ethnocentrism The belief that one's own culture is superior to others.

1987). This easily leads to misunderstandings and outright rejection of the communication, and is remarkably common. Very few marketing communications can be applied worldwide, with the exception of one or two which apply to global markets (for example the global youth market, which responds to adverts for jeans and music CDs in a fairly consistent manner) (Steen 1995).

National cultural differences can sometimes be identified: the main researcher quoted in this context is Hofstede (1984) who researched 6000 respondents in many countries in order to find national differences in culture. This research is, however, now seriously out of date: world communications and extensive migrations have eroded national differences to the extent that generalisations cannot be easily made.

Symbols differ from one culture to another. British marketers might use a lion to symbolise patriotism, whereas French marketers would use a cockerel and Americans would use a bald eagle. Advertisements transfer cultural meanings into products (McCracken 1986).

Miscommunication

Failure to communicate can arise from several different causes. In essence, these can be categorised under the following headings:

- *Implication*. Recipients sometimes read meanings into communications, due to their previous experiences, attitudes and prejudices.
- *Distortion*. Interference or noise from outside can change the message.
- *Disruption*. The circumstances surrounding the message, or deliberate acts by the recipient, can change the message.
- *Confusion*. If the message is ambiguous the recipient may find it confusing.
- *Agreement/disagreement*. If the sender and the receiver have different perspectives, there may be disagreement as to the meaning of the message.
- *Understanding/misunderstanding*. Sometimes cultural issues (especially of language) or differences in perception mean that the message is simply misunderstood.
- *Personal transformation*. If the recipient is not prepared to change, the message may have little or no effect.

Figure 8.11

Causes of communication failure

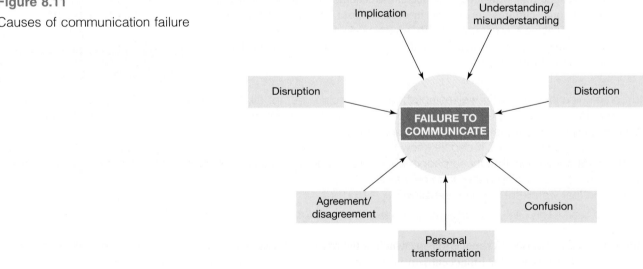

Each of these sources of miscommunication is present in marketing communications, as they are in interpersonal communications; the marketing implications of each are outlined in the following sections.

Implication

The implications of a communication are the meanings that are placed on it by the recipient. Miscommunication often arises between individuals because the communication raises unpleasant implications, and therefore the message is not stated clearly enough; for example, an employer telling staff that there might be redundancies might only intend to raise the possibility, but some staff will take it that their jobs are about to end, while others might take it that their own jobs are safe and others are under threat. Equally, marketing communications can fail because of implications. The implications of a message are peculiar to the individual: a mass communication will have different implications for each person who receives it, but marketers have to deal with people in the mass most of the time and therefore need to guess what the implications might be for most of the customers, not for a few individuals.

The main elements of implication are shown in Table 8.4.

Table 8.4 Elements of implication

Element	Explanation
Assumption	If the message is unclear, the receiver tends to 'fill in the gaps' by making assumptions about the message. These assumptions are subject to positive or negative slanting, may or may not be open to inspection and revision in future, and may turn out to be true or false when the recipient tries to act on them.
Inference	The recipient may add extra ideas to the message as received, adding information from memory. This can happen even when the message itself is clear and no misunderstanding is involved.
Expectation	Expectations about the communication may affect the meaning even before the message is delivered. People often respond to what they expected to hear, rather than what was actually said.
Reflection	Consideration of past communications affects the recipient's behaviour towards future communications. This is similar to expectation and inference.
Attribution	In the case of interactive communications, there will be a jointly produced outcome, but each party will attribute the outcome differently. For example, a salesperson may attribute a failed sale to the sales resistance of the customer, whereas the customer may attribute the failure to the salesperson's irritating manner.
Metacommunication	Metacommunication is about how things are said rather than what is being said. In marketing communications, metacommunication is manifested in two ways: the style of the communication (for example, different styles of press release) and the type of communication (television advertising as opposed to mailings).
The search for common ground	If there is no overlap between the sender's and recipient's fields of experience, the communication will fail. In most cases, both parties are likely to seek the common ground in which communication takes place, the sender because of the need for the message to get through, the recipient because of curiosity about the message content.

Table 8.5 Elements of distortion

Element	Explanation
Interference	To understand the message, the recipient must be able to concentrate on it to some extent. Other incoming messages may be inadvertently included in the interpretation of the main message, or may distract the recipient so that pieces of the main message are missed. The concept of interference relates mainly to the Schramm model described earlier: the 'pool' model of communication includes extra communications of this nature as part of the content of the pool.
Bias	Bias does not imply a malicious or negative mindset; it can simply mean that the recipient is likely to interpret the message in a particular way. Ideological, ethnocentric or egocentric biases all contribute to distortion of messages because all messages are added (in whole or in part) to the information in the individual's memory.
Miscalculation	Miscalculation occurs when the information presented is wrongly interpreted through a mistake in cognition. Sometimes this comes about through simple stupidity or mistakes; sometimes it comes about through a desire for an alternative truth to prevail. In marketing communication terms, a customer might misinterpret the terms of a special offer because he or she is unable to meet the true conditions and is hoping that other, simpler, conditions would be acceptable.
Pseudo-communication	Some communications are intended to cover up a true state of affairs in order to preserve appearances. Without actually lying about the true state of affairs, the communication is nonetheless a distortion of the truth. This is very much in accordance with Deetz' theories on political communication: for Deetz, the majority of communications within organisations fall into this category (Deetz 1992).

Distortion

Internal distractions and external interference often lead to distortions in the meaning of the message. For example, an individual may believe that German products are well-engineered, and from this be biased towards all German products. The messages conveyed by adverts for German goods will be distorted by this internal distraction. Table 8.5 shows the main elements of distortion.

Disruption

Disruption of communications can be caused by outside interruptions (not necessarily interference) or by internal misgivings on the part of the recipient. A typical example would be the breakdown of communication which happens when a prospective customer suddenly develops a dislike of a salesperson and calls the presentation to a halt. Disruption is only possible when the communications are two-way, as in personal selling or Internet transactions. Internet transactions are frequently curtailed by potential customers because the site is too slow to respond, or because the navigation around the site is too difficult, or (most commonly) because the customer is only seeking information and is not yet ready to buy.

The elements of disruption are shown in Table 8.6.

Confusion

Confusion arises from distortion, mistakes, disruption and conflict. Conflicting information about a product (for example, from a salesperson on the one hand and from a

Table 8.6 Elements of disruption

Element	Explanation
Unmanageable circumstance	The feeling that the situation is outside one's control can lead to disruption. For example, a complex mail-order form may never be completed because the customer feels unable to control the situation.
Relational instability	The consistency of people's behaviour derives from the type of situations they find themselves in. In an unfamiliar or awkward situation (for example, a young man meeting his girlfriend's parents for the first time) the recipient may not be able to respond to the messages being offered.
Conversational irregularities	Conversation normally involves statements, assessment of the meaning of the statements and responses. If statements meet with inappropriate or undesired responses the communication breaks down and is disrupted. For example, if a customer writes to complain about the company and in return receives a sales pitch for another product, the dialogue breaks down.
Lack of reciprocity	Life is a matter of give and take, and if (for example) a salesperson is clearly not prepared to give ground or allow the customer a chance to make a point, the dialogue will break down.
Mutual misconstruction	This applies to personal encounters where the participants are unable to translate their interpretations of self and other into a coherent vocabulary. The root of the problem is an inability to understand why someone else's viewpoint appears sensible to them; this can cause problems in negotiations.
Threat of dissolution	The knowledge that the relationship might end is one that can affect both parties. This is particularly relevant in business-to-business markets, where a disruption of supply can be as important to a customer as the disruption of income would be to the marketer. Without any stated threat by either party, the nature of the communications between them will be affected by the knowledge of their relationship (see Chapter 9 for more on relationship marketing).

friend on the other) creates confusion in the mind of the recipient. Avoidance of confusion is one of the main driving forces behind the integration of marketing communications: if everyone tells the same story, the possibilities for conflict and confusion are reduced dramatically.

The elements of confusion are shown in Table 8.7.

Agreement/disagreement

Disagreement occurs when the recipient understands but does not accept the message. The message might be discounted because of a bias against the source, or because of the style of the message, or because the recipient has a different frame of reference from the sender.

Table 8.8 shows the elements of agreement and disagreement.

Understanding/misunderstanding

There is always a risk of misunderstanding; part of the problem is that it is often impossible for the recipient of a message to know that there is a misunderstanding, at least until it is time to act on the information. Minimising misunderstanding is clearly of importance to marketers, since misunderstandings are a common cause for complaints against firms.

Table 8.7 Elements of confusion

Element	Explanation
Conflict	Disputes between the parties will almost always create confused communications, especially in negotiating situations. Tension tends to result in overstatement of positions, and attempts to resolve the conflict can also distract attention from the main issues. In many marketing situations the existence of serious conflict will disrupt the communication rather than merely confuse it, however.
Ambiguity	If the communication can be interpreted in two different ways it is ambiguous. This commonly happens in advertising, where the message is often so brief and so loaded with cultural connotations that it is easily misinterpreted.
Equivocation	If two messages are received which conflict with each other there is equivocation. Integrating marketing communications will reduce this problem, but it will always be present to some extent.
Vagueness	There will always be some uncertainty in communications, but some communications are so vaguely constructed that the meaning is lost. As the level of uncertainty increases, the frames of reference need to be expanded and the individual becomes confused.
Paradox	A paradox is a logical impossibility which creates confusion. For example, a sales promotion with an expiry date which has already passed (perhaps due to a printing error) creates confusion.
Contradiction	Similar to equivocation and paradox, contradiction is the appearance of irreconcilable differences in the communications received. Again this can be overcome to some extent by integrating marketing communications.

Table 8.8 Elements of agreement/disagreement

Element	Explanation
Relational ties	If the relationship between the parties is not a close one, disagreement is more likely. This is part of the reason for the increasing emphasis on relationship marketing.
Commonality of perspectives	If there is a foundation of consensus between the parties there will be a common perspective applied to discussions. This greatly increases the likelihood of agreement between parties.
Compatibility of values	If the personal value systems of the participants are close, there is less scope for disagreement. Marketers (especially salespeople) often go to considerable trouble to establish a rapport with customers.
Similarity of interests	If both parties stand to gain from the encounter, the interaction is likely to lead to agreement. Common experience and common goals both lead to closer agreement on other issues.
Depth of involvement	The importance of the issues under discussion will influence the degree to which the parties become involved. As involvement increases, so do the possibilities for both agreement and disagreement. A greater depth of involvement is more likely to lead to agreement in the long run, though, because the parties are less likely to withdraw from the discussions prematurely.
Quality of interaction	The quality of interaction is affected by the levels of agreement or disagreement. Disagreement will make the interaction unpleasant, and therefore more likely to terminate early.
Equality of influence	The party with the greatest power in the relationship will be able to enforce agreement from the other party. If the relationship is one of equals, then genuine agreement is more likely and a more lasting relationship becomes possible.

Table 8.9 Elements of understanding

Element	Explanation
Recognition of intent	It may not be possible to be sure of the other party's intentions, but having a clear recognition of them will help in understanding.
Multiple perspective taking	The more opportunity the recipient has to examine the information from different angles, the less likely it is that a misunderstanding will occur.
Warrants and reasons	When an observation leads to a conclusion, the explanatory mechanism is called a warrant. It is the reasoning process the individual goes through to arrive at an understanding. Reasons are the elements that serve as the basis for the warrant to operate on.
Tests of comprehension	The true measure of understanding is the degree to which the knowledge is effective when used to predict outcomes in the real world. Sometimes comprehension can be tested without making a commitment; for example, a consumer may call a helpline to check that the terms of a special offer are as they appear to be.
Code switching	The ability to understand is greatly improved if the participants are able to switch from one style of communication to another. Integration of marketing communications helps this process because it allows the dialogue to continue in a different way. Code switching is an element in redundancy; sending the message via different routes and using different codes will usually improve comprehension.
Synchrony and alignment of communicative styles	Synchronisation means that both parties follow through the dialogue at the same pace; alignment means that they follow through each stage together without being sidetracked. Understanding is improved if both parties can remain synchronised and aligned throughout the exchange.
Working through problematic concerns	More commonly found in personal selling situations, a preparedness to work through problems together is more likely to lead to mutual understanding. For this to happen both parties must perceive a mutually beneficial end goal.
Mutual struggle to minimise miscommunication	If both participants are prepared to make an effort to understand each other's viewpoint, accurate communication is more likely to result.

Sometimes basic disagreements lead to misunderstandings, sometimes it is the other way round. It is certainly easier to determine whether people agree with each other than whether they really understand each other, especially since people will sometimes act as if they understand each other in order to reach an agreement more quickly. Understanding is a construction of the mind; there are degrees of understanding, and the process of interpretation is (potentially) inexhaustible. The elements of understanding are shown in Table 8.9.

Personal transformation

The willingness of the recipient to be open-minded about the communication, and to be prepared to change, is of paramount importance. If the recipient of the message has already decided that the communication is not going to make any difference, then (in effect) he or she will not be listening to the message. Elements of personal transformation are shown in Table 8.10.

Perhaps the best way of minimising miscommunication is to ensure that the participants are motivated to seek understanding. Motivating the recipients to want to

Table 8.10 Elements of personal transformation

Element	Explanation
Receptivity to change	An individual who is not open-minded is unlikely to be receptive to communications; confusion is likely to result.
Supportive communication	Communications which support a customer through a change of attitude are usually helpful; this is why salespeople will often leave information about the products with a customer.

Talking Point

understand and learn from the communications is as important as (for example) motivating salespeople to go out and tell the story, or motivating creative people in advertising agencies to come up with a clever campaign.

It seems that there is so much that can go wrong with communications it's amazing we can speak to each other at all. Is it really worth bothering with all this stuff? Why not just drop the whole idea, put the goods in the shops where people can get at them and wait to see what happens?

After all, some companies operate very well without advertising at all – British Home Stores in the UK is one example. Maybe marketing communications are as likely to go wrong as to go right!

Elements of the Communications Mix

Marketers have many tactics at their disposal, and the best marketers use them in appropriate ways to maximise the impact of their communications activities. A very basic taxonomy of promotional tools is the four-way division into advertising, public relations, sales promotion and personal selling. This taxonomy is really too simplistic: each of the elements subdivides further, and there are several elements which don't readily fit into these categories. For example, T-shirt slogans are clearly communications, but they are not advertising, nor are they really public relations, yet T-shirts with brand logos on, or even adaptations of brand logos, are a common sight and can be considered as marketing communications.

Table 8.11 lists some of the elements of the mix. This list is unlikely to be exhaustive, and there is also the problem of boundary-spanning: some elements of the mix go beyond communication and into the realms of distribution (telemarketing and home shopping channels for example) or even into new product development (as with the websites which allow students to sell successful essays to other students).

Each of these elements is dealt with in more detail elsewhere in the book, in the Marketing in Practice section.

The range of possible tools at the marketer's disposal is obviously large; creating a good mix of communications methods is akin to following a recipe. The ingredients have to be added in the right amounts at the right time, and treated in the right way, if the recipe is to work. Also, one ingredient cannot substitute for another; personal selling cannot, on its own, replace advertising, nor can public relations exercises

Slogans on clothing create a powerful communication.

© Jeremy Sutton-Hibbert/Alamy

Table 8.11 Elements of the communications mix

Element	Explanation
Advertising	A paid insertion of a message in a medium.
Ambient advertising	Any message that forms part of the environment – for example messages placed on items such as bus tickets, stamp franking, till receipts, petrol pump nozzles and so forth.
Press advertising	Any paid message that appears in a newspaper, magazine or directory.
TV advertising	Commercial messages shown in the breaks during and between TV programmes.
Radio advertising	Sound-only advertisements broadcast on radio.
Outdoor advertising	Billboards, bus shelters, fly posters etc.
Transport advertising	Posters in stations and inside buses and trains.
Outside transport advertising	Posters on buses and taxis, and in some countries the sides of trains. British Airways have even carried other companies' logos on the tailplanes of aircraft.
Press releases	News stories about the firm or its products.
Public relations	The planned and sustained effort to establish and maintain goodwill and mutual understanding between an organisation and its **publics*** (Institute of Public Relations 1984).
Sponsorship	Funding of arts events, sporting events etc., in exchange for publicity and prestige.
Sales promotions	Activities designed to give a temporary boost to sales, such as money-off coupons, free samples, two-for-the-price-of-one promotions etc.
Personal selling	Face-to-face communications between buyers and sellers designed to ascertain and meet customers' needs on a one-to-one basis.
Database marketing	Profiling customers onto a database and sending out personalised mailings or other communications to them.
Telemarketing	Inbound (helpline, telephone ordering) or outbound (telecanvassing, teleselling) telephone calls. There are legal restrictions on outbound telemarketing.
Presence website	A website which acts as an advertisement, offering no interaction or ordering capability. Such websites only contain a telephone number or email link; they are increasingly rare as firms become more Internet-literate.
Interactive website	A website which offers the capability to order goods or to engage in a dialogue with the firm.
Spamming	Sending out mass email messages, usually (but not always) to a consenting mailing list (i.e. people who have asked for the mailings in some way, or who are voluntary members of a mailing list). In some countries there are legal restrictions on spamming, and sometimes irate Internet users retaliate in ways the spamming companies do not like.
Short-message texting	Messages sent out to the mobile telephones of consenting members of a mailing list. These range from sports results services to travel offers to telephone banking.
Direct-response TV advertising	Using TV adverts linked to inbound telephone operations to sell goods.
Exhibitions and trade fairs	Companies take stands at trade fairs to display new products, meet consumers and customers, and raise the company profile with interested parties.
Corporate identity	The overall image that the company projects; the company's 'personality'.
Branding	The mechanism by which marketing communications are coordinated.

*See glossary.

Figure 8.12

A taxonomy of marketing communications

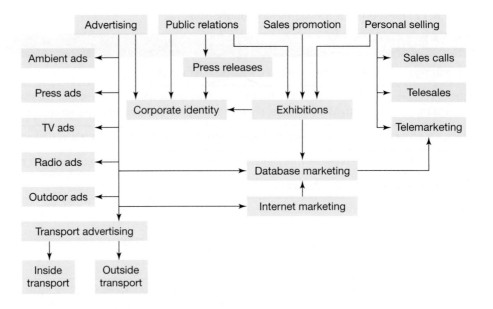

replace sales promotions. Figure 8.12 shows how the above elements of the mix relate to each other.

The interconnections between the various elements shown in Figure 8.12 are not the only ones; each marketing communication affects every other in some way or another.

Structuring the Communication Mix

Structuring the communications mix will differ from one firm to another, and indeed from one promotion to another within the same firm. Developing effective marketing communications follows a six-stage process, as follows;

1 *Identify the target audience.* In other words, decide who the message should get to.
2 *Determine the response sought.* What would the marketer like the audience to do after they get the message?
3 *Choose the message.* Write the copy, or produce an appropriate image.
4 *Choose the channel.* Decide which newspaper, TV station, radio station or other medium is most appealing to the audience.
5 *Select the source's attributes.* Decide what it is about the product or company that needs to be communicated.
6 *Collect feedback.* For example carry out market research to find out how successful the message was.

Communication is often expensive; full-page advertisements in Sunday colour supplements can cost upwards of £11 000 per insertion, and a 30-second TV ad at peak time can cost £30 000 per station. It is therefore worthwhile spending time and effort in ensuring that the message can be understood by the target audience and is reaching the right people. Figure 8.12 shows how the communication mix operates.

In Figure 8.13, messages from the company about its products and itself are transmitted via the elements of the promotional mix to the consumers, employees, pressure groups and other publics. Each of these groups receives the messages from more than one transmitter, so the elements of the mix also feed into each other, thus reducing conflict. The choice of method will depend upon the message, the receiver and the desired effect.

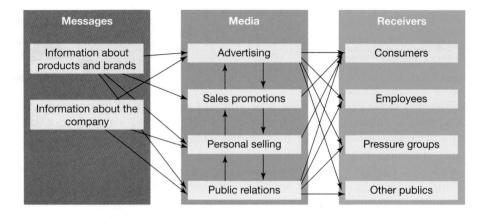

Figure 8.13
The promotional mix

The problem with this view of the promotional mix is that it is very much tied to the Schramm model of communication, which assumes that recipients are passive. For example, a recipient may feel perfectly comfortable with seeing a TV advertisement for the firm's products, less comfortable about receiving a mailing, and extremely uncomfortable about being telephoned at home. This will vary between different people – some people resent having their favourite programme interrupted by advertising, and prefer to have a mailing from a company they deal with frequently.

Mechanisms of Personal Influence

Overall, word-of-mouth influence is much stronger than advertising or other marketer-produced communications. For marketers, then, the problem lies in knowing how to use word-of-mouth to its best advantage. Table 8.12 offers some comparisons and strategies.

It is not usually possible to rely entirely on word-of-mouth, but marketers should take steps to stimulate it as a promotional tool. Advertising should be interesting and involving, perhaps even controversial so that debate ensues. It is not true to say that any word-of-mouth will be good for a company, but it is certainly true to say that controversy and debate will increase brand awareness. It does not always enhance brand image, however.

People often talk about things they have bought.

Table 8.12 Using word-of-mouth

Strong Influence	*Weak Influence*	*Tactical suggestions*
Seeker initiates conversation with source.	Source initiates conversation with seeker.	Advertising could emphasise the idea of 'Ask the person who owns one'. Network marketers could emphasise a more advisory role for their salespeople rather than a strongly proactive approach.
Negative information.	Positive information.	Because marketers are uniformly positive about the product, the seeker is more alert to any negatives. The essential thing for marketers to do is to ensure that any complaints are dealt with immediately and thoroughly.
Verbal communication is stronger for thinking and evaluation.	Visual communication is stronger for awareness and stimulation of interest.	Where appropriate, marketers could encourage satisfied customers to show their friends the product; this tactic is often used for home improvement sales, where customers are paid a small reward or commission for introducing friends to the product. This is also the basis for party-plan selling, e.g. Tupperware and Ann Summers.

E-Marketing in Practice
Viral Marketing

Website design has moved through a number of phases. During the late 1990s most websites were merely 'presence' sites, giving a brief outline of the company and its products and directing the interested potential customer to a telephone number or snail-mail address. As the decade progressed, more and more sites became interactive, allowing customers to navigate around the site, place orders online and email the company as appropriate for further information.

By the early 21st century, sites had gone a step further, and were offering the capability of involving visitors' friends. 'Email this site to a friend' buttons became commonplace, and eventually firms began to add value to the site by including games and puzzles, and even jokes, to encourage the site visitors to enrol their friends onto the site. This approach helped to overcome the major problem of internet marketing – making your voice heard through the clutter of almost 4 billion websites worldwide.

A recent development (and for many an unethical one) is the linking of marketing messages to self-replicating viruses. The virus operates by sending itself to everyone in the victim's address book, displaying the marketing message in the form of an email. It then copies itself into all the other recipient's address books and sends itself out again. Soon it has sent the message to everyone on the planet (often several times). Although in most cases recipients simply ignore the message and delete it, even a tiny response rate will represent a very large amount of business for the initiating firm.

Formulating a Strategy

As in any other issue in marketing, the first step in formulating a strategy is to find out what the target customers are looking for. In communications terms this means finding out which magazines they read, which TV stations they watch, what their leisure activities are, whether they are interested in football or opera or horse racing and so forth. Marketing research has the main role here; consumers not only consume products, they also consume communications media. Knowing which media the target customers consume enables the astute marketer to target communications accurately, and avoids wasting the budget on trying to communicate with people who have no need for the product.

Strategy must be integrated across the whole range of marketing activities; it must be formulated in the light of good analysis of the environment; and it must include a feedback system so that the strategy can be adapted in the light of environmental changes. Strategy is influenced by organisational objectives and resources, competitor activities, the structure of the market itself and the firm's willingness to make changes and take risks.

push strategy Promoting to channel intermediaries in order to 'push' products through the distribution channel.

pull strategy Promoting to end users in order to 'pull' products through the distribution channel.

Push vs Pull Strategies

Two basic strategic alternatives exist for marketing communications. **Push strategy** involves promoting heavily to wholesalers, retailers and agents on the assumption that they will, in turn, promote heavily to the end consumers. In this way the products are pushed through the distribution channel. **Pull strategy** involves promoting heavily to end users and consumers to create a demand that will pull the products through the distribution channel. Push strategies place the emphasis on personal selling and sales promotion, whereas pull strategies tend to place the emphasis on mass advertising. The two strategies are not mutually exclusive, but rather represent opposite ends of a spectrum; most campaigns contain elements of both.

Table 8.13 shows the functions which need to be carried out when planning the communications campaign.

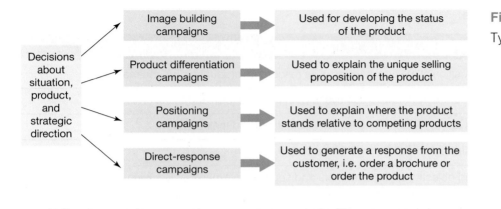

Figure 8.15

Types of campaign

Planning the Campaign

Whether this stage comes before or after the budget-setting will depend on whether the marketer is adopting an objective-and-task policy or not. In most cases, though, planning the campaign in detail will come after the budget is known and agreed; few companies give the marketing department a blank cheque for promotional spending. Campaigns can be carried out to achieve many objectives; a new product launch is often an objective, but in most cases the products will be in the maturity phase of the product lifecycle.

Image building campaigns are designed to convey a particular status for the product, and to emphasise ways in which it will complement the user's lifestyle. For example, Audi use the slogan 'Vorsprung durch Teknik' which means 'Progress through technology' as a way of showing that their cars are at the cutting edge of technology.

Product differentiation campaigns aim to show how the product is better than others by emphasising its differences. In most cases this will take the form of the **unique selling proposition** or USP for short. The USP is the one feature of the product that most stands out, and is usually a feature which conveys unique benefits to the consumer. Mature products often only differ very slightly from each other in terms of performance, so a USP can sometimes only be identified in terms of packaging, distribution or a prestigious brand. The USP will only be effective if it means something to consumers – otherwise the effect on the buying decision will be negligible.

Positioning strategies are concerned with the way consumers perceive the product compared with their perceptions of the competition (see Chapter 4 and Chapter 6).

Direct response campaigns seek an immediate response from the consumer in terms of purchase, or request for a brochure or a visit to the shop. For example, a retailer might run a newspaper campaign which includes a money-off coupon. The aim of the campaign is to encourage consumers to visit the shop to redeem the coupon, and the retailer can easily judge the effectiveness of the campaign by the number of coupons redeemed.

image building A type of campaign which is conducted for the purpose of conveying a specific perception of a product in the minds of customers.

product differentiation A type of campaign which emphasises the differences between a product and competing products.

unique selling proposition (USP) The factors which distinguish a product from its competitors.

direct response A type of advertising campaign which contains a method for the consumer to contact the supplier immediately and directly.

Tactical Considerations

Most of the tactics of marketing involve creativity on the part of practitioners, so it is virtually impossible to lay down any hard and fast rules about approaching different marketing problems. There is also a large number of alternative approaches available. However, the following might prove to be useful guidelines:

- Marketers should always try to do something that the competition hasn't thought of yet.
- It is important to consult everybody who is involved in the day-to-day application of the plans. Front-line people such as salespeople, receptionists, telesales operators and so forth are particularly important in this respect.

Table 8.15 SOSTT+4Ms

Element	Description
Situation	Current position of the firm in terms of its resources, product range and markets.
Objectives	What the company hopes to achieve in both the long term and the short term.
Strategy	Decisions about the correctness of the objectives and their overall fit.
Tactics	How the strategic objectives will be achieved.
Targets	Formalised objectives, target markets and segments of markets. Decisions about the appropriateness of these markets in the light of the firm's strategic objectives.
Manpower	Both genders, of course! Decisions about human resources; having the right people to do the job.
Money	Correct budgeting and allocation of financial resources where they will do the most to achieve the overall objectives.
Minutes	Timescales, deadlines and overall planning to ensure that everything happens at the right time.
Measurement	Monitoring and evaluation of activities to ensure that they remain on course and work as they should.

● Most marketing activities do not produce instant results, but results should be monitored anyway.

● The messages given to the consumers, the middlemen, the suppliers and all the other publics should be consistent.

● Competitors are likely to make some kind of response, so marketers should try to anticipate what the response might be when formulating plans.

The situation, objectives, strategy, tactics and targets plus manpower, money, minutes and measurement (SOSTT+4Ms) structure for planning gives a useful checklist for ensuring that the elements of strategy and tactics are brought together effectively. Table 8.15 shows how the structure works.

Cost-effectiveness will always be an issue in promotional campaigns, and it is for this reason that there has been a growth in direct marketing worldwide (see Chapter 9). The accurate targeting of market segments made possible by computer technology has enabled marketers to refine the approach, and hence increase the response rate. Marketers now talk in terms of response rates from promotions, not in terms of contact numbers.

Cutting through advertising clutter is a perennial problem. Most people skip past marketing communications, so marketers need to be creative in finding ways of making the communication eye-catching. Irritating or annoying slogans are often remembered better than others, and using variations on slogans also helps to make them more attention-getting (Rosengren and Dahlen 2006). Whether this approach makes people more likely to buy as a result is debatable, however.

Putting it All Together

To make the best use of the promotional effort it is worth spending time planning how the communications will fit together. The mix will need to be adapted according to what the product is and how the company wants to promote it, as well as according to the characteristics of the customers.

The elements marketers need to consider are:

- Size of budget
- Size of individual order value
- Number of potential buyers
- Geodemographical spread of potential buyers
- Category of product (convenience, unsought, shopping etc.)
- What the firm is trying to achieve.

It is impossible to achieve everything all at once, so marketers often plan the campaign as an integrated package. For example, Table 8.16 shows a product launch strategy designed to maximise penetration of a new food product.

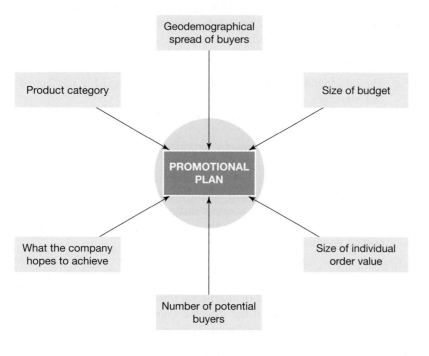

Figure 8.16

Factors in promotional planning

teaser campaign An advertising campaign in two stages: the first stage involves a message which in itself is meaningless, but which is explained by later advertisements in the second stage.

Table 8.16 Example of a promotional calendar

Month	Activity
May	Press release to the trade press, retailers.
June	Sales campaign to persuade retailers to stock the product. The aim is to get 50 per cent of retailers stocking the product, so the salesforce tell them a big advertising spend is forthcoming. Begin a **teaser campaign** (see Chapter 15)
July/August	Denouement of teaser campaign. Promotion staff appear in major retail outlets offering free samples. Press releases to cookery writers, possibly reports on daytime TV if product is newsworthy enough.
September/October	Once 50 per cent retailer penetration has occurred, start the TV campaign. Brief the advertising agency to obtain maximum brand awareness.
January/February	Begin a new campaign to inform consumers about the brand. Possibly use money-off sales promotion, linked promotions, etc. Review progress so far using market research. Possibly issue some press releases, if the product is innovative enough, to the business/cookery press.

Carrying out this kind of planning needs the cooperation of all the members of the marketing team. It is no use having the PR people doing one thing and the salesforce doing something else that negates their efforts. If the campaign is to be effective it is important that all the team members are involved in the discussions so that unrealistic demands are not made of them.

Integration of Marketing Communications

Integration of marketing communications has become a 'hot topic' among marketing academics and practitioners alike, and this is being extended to include all corporate communications (Nowak and Phelps 1994). The need for integration is shown in the following factors (Borremans 1998):

1 *Changes in the consumer market*
   - The information overload caused by the ever-increasing number of commercial messages.
   - Advertising in the mass media is increasingly irritating.
   - Media fragmentation.
   - Increasing numbers of 'me-too' products, where differences between brands are minor.
   - Complexity and change in fast-moving consumer goods markets, with increased distances between suppliers and consumers making it harder for suppliers to establish a consistent image.
   - Increasing media attention on the social and ethical behaviour of companies, putting goodwill at a premium.

2 *Changes in the supplier market*
   - Multiple acquisitions and changes in structure in and around corporations.
   - Interest of management in short-term results.
   - Increased recognition of the strategic importance of communication.
   - Increased interest in good internal communications with employees.

Integration aims to reduce ambiguity and increase the impact of messages emanating from the firm, and also should reduce costs by reducing duplication of effort. There are, however, barriers to integration (Petrison and Wang 1996); the following factors tend to mean that integration would actually detract from the effectiveness of communications:

- Database marketing allows customers to be targeted with individually-tailored communications.
- In niche marketing and micro-marketing, suppliers can communicate with very small and specific audiences, using different messages for each group.
- Specific methods and working practices used for different communication tools will affect the message each transmits.
- Corporate diversification means that different branches of the company need to send different messages.
- Different international (and even national) cultures mean that a single message comprehensible to all is difficult to achieve without producing 'lowest common denominator' messages, which have a low impact.
- Existing structures within organisations mean that different departments may not be able or willing to 'sing the same song'. For example, salespeople have to deal with customers as individuals: they may not agree with the advertising department's ideas on what customers should be told.

Table 8.17 Levels of integration

Level of integration	Explanation
Awareness stage	Those responsible for communications realise that a fragmented approach is not the optimum one.
Planning integration	The coordination of activities. There are two broad approaches: functional integration, which coordinates separate tools to create a single message where appropriate, and instrumental integration, which combines tools in such a way that they reinforce one another (Bruhn 1995).
Integration of content	Ensuring that there are no contradictions in the basic brand or corporate messages. At a higher level, integrating the themes of communication to make the basic messages the same.
Formal integration	Using the same logo, corporate colours, graphic approach and house style for all communications.
Integration between planning periods	Basic content remains the same from one campaign to the next. Either basic content remains the same, or the same executional approach is used in different projects.
Intra-organisational integration	Integration of the activities of everyone involved in communication functions (which could mean everybody who works in the organisation).
Inter-organisational integration	Integration of all the outside agencies involved in the firm's communications activities.
Geographical integration	Integration of campaigns in different countries. This is strongest in large multinationals which operate globally, e.g. the Coca-Cola Corporation (Hartley and Pickton 1997).
Integration of publics	All communications targeted to one segment of the market are integrated (horizontal integration) or all communications targeted to different segments are attuned (vertical integration).

● Personal resistance to change, managers' fear of losing responsibilities and budgets. This is particularly true of firms which have adopted the brand manager system of management.

In practice promotional mix elements often operate independently (Duncan and Caywood 1996) with specialist agencies for PR, advertising, exhibitions, corporate identity, branding etc. all working in isolation. Because each department or agency has its own budgets and concerns, integration may not happen simply because each wants to fight for its own part of the campaign, even when they understand that the needs of the campaign dictate that another department should have precedence.

There are nine types or levels of integration, as shown in Table 8.17: note that these do not necessarily constitute a process, or represent stages of development, and indeed there may be considerable overlap between the types.

Part of the reason for separating the functions is historical. Traditionally, marketing communications were divided into above the line communications and below the line communications. Above the line means advertising; below the line means everything else. This division came about because of the way advertising agencies paid commission by the media they place adverts in (usually the rate is 15 per cent of the billing), and/or by fees paid by the client. Traditionally, any paid-for advertising attracted commission (hence above the line) and any other activities such as PR or sales promotion were paid for by fees (hence below the line). As time has gone by these distinctions have become

above the line Advertising for which the advertising agency obtains a commission from the media.

below the line Promotional tools for which the advertising agency charges the client.

Figure 8.17

Ladder of integration

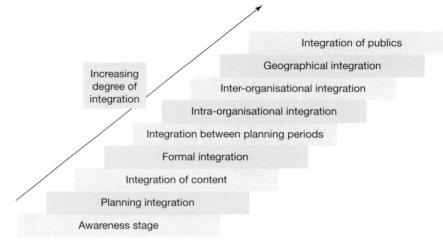

Increasing degree of integration

Integration of publics

Geographical integration

Inter-organisational integration

Intra-organisational integration

Integration between planning periods

Formal integration

Integration of content

Planning integration

Awareness stage

advertorials Advertisements which are written in the style of editorials (not to be confused with press releases).

more blurred, especially with the advent of **advertorials** (advertisements which look like editorial) which are usually written by journalists, and with ambient advertising and other new media which do not attract commission.

Overall, the advantages of integrating communications almost certainly overcome the drawbacks, since the cost savings and the reduction of ambiguity are clearly important objectives for most marketers. There is, however, the danger of losing the capacity to tailor messages for individuals (as happens in personal selling) or for niches in the market, and there are certainly some major creative problems attached to integrating communications on a global scale.

International Marketing Communications

Single communications strategies rarely work for firms in the global arena. In fact, the few exceptions are so notable that they are used as examples time and again – Marlboro cigarettes, Coca-Cola, Levi jeans – and nearly all are American. It is possible that the overwhelming influence of Hollywood in exporting American culture worldwide means that people in most countries are able to understand American cultural references (the Marlboro cowboy, for example) in a way that would not work for, say, the Brazilian gaucho or the Japanese samurai. Even within these examples, there are differences between campaigns in different countries: for example, UK legislation on tobacco advertising means that the Marlboro cowboy cannot be shown in the advertisements.

There is some common ground between countries, and there are identifiable international markets; the market for women's magazines has expanded in Europe as a result of deregulation, and magazines such as *Hello!* (originally *Hola!* in its native Spain) have managed to cross over successfully. This means that some print advertising within those magazines should also be able to make the transition.

Courtesy of The Advertising Archives

行 政 院 衛 生 署 警 告：吸 菸 有 害 健 康

Come to Marlboro Country.
自由不羈・豪邁作風

The Marlboro cowboy is instantly recognisable, even in Chinese.

Table 8.18 Basic international strategies

Strategy	Explanation
Same product, same communication	Can be used where the need for the product and its use are the same as in its home market.
Same product, different communication	Can be used where the need for the product differs in some way, but the basic method of use is the same, or when the cultural references differ. For example, soy sauce is considered an exotic product in western Europe, but is a regular purchase item in Oriental countries.
Different products, same communication	Sometimes the product formula has to change to meet local conditions, but the communication can remain the same. For example, the formulation of chocolate is different for hot countries due to the low melting-point of cocoa butter, but this need not affect the advertising.
Different product, different communications	Applies to markets with different needs and different product use, for example greetings cards or electrical appliances.

The main reason for standardising communications is cost. It is clearly much cheaper to produce one advert and repeat it across borders (perhaps changing the language as necessary) than it is to produce separate adverts for each country. However, the savings are most apparent in producing TV adverts, where the costs of production can easily approach the costs of airtime. This is not the case with press advertising, so pressure to internationalise is less apparent.

There are four basic strategies for international communications, as shown in Table 8.18 (Keegan 1984).

Most successful international campaigns are run on TV, which enables the advertiser to minimise or even omit words altogether. Standardising press communications is more difficult due to language differences. Some difficulties in this connection are subtle – some languages such as Arabic and Hebrew read from right to left, which can significantly alter the meaning of before-and-after pictures.

The following tips for translating advertising copy have been identified (Majaro 1982):

Global firms need to translate communications into many languages.

1 Avoid idioms, jargon or buzz words.

2 Leave space to expand foreign language text (Latin languages take 20 per cent more space than English and Arabic may need up to 50 per cent more space).

3 Check local legal requirements and codes of conduct.

4 Ensure that the translators speak the everyday language of the country in question. The Spanish spoken in Spain and Latin America differ, as does UK English and American English, or French French and Belgian French. (For obvious reasons, people who are not native speakers of the language should never be used.)

5 Brief the translators thoroughly so that they get a feel for the product, its benefits, the customer and competition. Do not just hand over the copy and expect it to be translated.

6 Check the translation with customers and distributors in the local market. This also gives local users the opportunity of being involved and raising any criticisms of the promotional materials before they are published for use.

7 Re-translate the materials back into English as a 'safety check'. They may not come back exactly as the original version, but there should be a reasonable commonality.

Figure 8.18

Cultural and product trade-offs in international markets

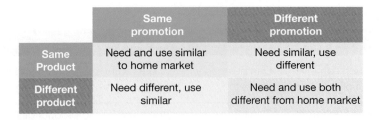

	Same promotion	Different promotion
Same Product	Need and use similar to home market	Need similar, use different
Different product	Need different, use similar	Need and use both different from home market

There are many (probably apocryphal) stories about translations of brand names and slogans that have gone horribly wrong: Pepsi's 'Come Alive with Pepsi' translating as 'Come Back from the Grave with Pepsi', or the Vauxhall Nova translating as 'Doesn't Go' in Spanish; any regular traveller will be aware of humorous (or obscene) brand names on foreign products.

Provided a universally recognisable icon is available, and it is possible to produce meaningful hooks in each language, it should be possible to produce good internationalised press advertising. Certainly factual information (e.g. 'Open Sundays') should translate fairly easily, so sought communications are presumably more likely to transfer easily.

A major headache for marketers is establishing meaningful websites. Since a website might be accessed from anywhere in the world, cultural differences need to be minimised – but at the same time, the site needs to have impact if it is to stand out from all the competing sites. Since some of these sites will be from the native country of the person accessing the site, they will inevitably be more appealing (or at least more comprehensible) than foreign websites. Even when the language is the same, cultural referents may differ in ways which make the site hard to understand. Additionally, websites may be accessed accidentally by foreigners, so website designers need to be aware of this. Often, websites contain contact telephone numbers which are devoid of the international dialling code, so that it becomes difficult or impossible for the observer to know which country the website originates in, and which offers are available. For example, someone in Cardiff, Wales may be looking for new curtains and may pick up a retailer in Cardiff New South Wales, Cardiff by the Sea in California or Cardiff, Canada. Although these retailers might offer free delivery, each would need to make clear how far they are prepared to go to meet this promise.

Researching the Effectiveness of Communications

Having developed and implemented the strategic and tactical plans, the next stage is to gather feedback as to the effectiveness of the communication. Much of the emphasis on effectiveness tests centres around advertising, since it is a high-profile activity and often a very expensive one. Four elements appear to be important in the effectiveness of advertising; awareness, liking, interest and enjoyment. There is a high correlation between brand loyalty and brand awareness (Stapel 1990); likeability appears to be the single best predictor of sales effectiveness, since likeability scales predict 97 per cent of sales successes (Biel 1990); interest clearly relates to likeability (Stapel 1991) and enjoyment appears to be a good indicator in advertising pre-tests (Brown 1991).

For many years effectiveness was measured in terms of sales results, the premise being that the purpose of advertising is to generate sales. The problem with this view is that sales can result from many other activities (personal selling, increased efforts by distributors, increased prosperity and so forth) so that it is difficult to assess the importance of advertising in the outcomes. A more recent view has been that the role of advertising is to communicate – to change awareness and attitudes (Colley 1961). This view crystallised as the DAGMAR model (Defining Advertising Goals, Measuring Advertising Results) (Colley 1961). DAGMAR implies that concrete and measurable communication

Marketing in Practice
HSBC

The Hong Kong and Shanghai Bank (HSBC) is one of the world's leading banks, with branches throughout the world. It uses a single global website as a portal through which customers can approach their local, national banks, and prides itself on its cultural sensitivity.

Each country in which HSBC operates has its own website and its own promotional campaigns, tailored to local needs: the bank even tailors its products to local needs (for example, in Saudi Arabia the bank offers Islamic banking, which conforms to the laws laid down in the Koran). Offering a Visa card which conforms to Shariah principles is clearly some achievement. In some cases the products offered in some markets would contravene the law in other markets – the special bank accounts for women offered in some Muslim countries, the 100 per cent car loans offered in the UK, some of the investment packages offered in Australia, to name but a few. HSBC calls itself the world's local bank, and it is in the realm of marketing communications that it makes this most obvious impact.

The bank allows its executives in each country to plan their own marketing campaigns, but under the umbrella of 'the world's local bank'. In the UK, the bank uses images from throughout the world which demonstrate cultural differences – the grasshopper, which is a pest in the USA but a delicacy in China, the various methods people use for curing headaches, the different items which denote good luck around the world. The bank's TV advertising follows the theme, showing the meanings of different gestures in different parts of the world.

Some of the communications are aimed at investors, some at personal banking customers, some at business customers: what the bank has as its strength is the ability to target so many different groups and persuade them all that they are dealing with the world's local bank.

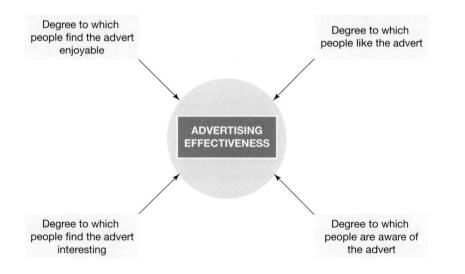

Figure 8.19

Factors in advertising effectiveness

objectives should be set for advertising, rather than sales turnover goals. Thus the outcomes that are measured are usually things like awareness, brand recognition, recall of content and so forth.

DAGMAR has been criticised on the grounds that it tends to lead planners to find out what can be measured easily, then set that as a goal (Broadbent 1989). The simple objectives which can be measured do not tell the whole story of major brand success;

Table 8.19 Evaluating advertising effectiveness

Technique	Description and explanation
Pre-tests	These are evaluations of the advertising before it is released. Pre-tests are commonly carried out using focus groups; research shows that this is the commonest method used by advertisers (Eagle, Hyde and Kitchen 1998).
Coupon returns, or enquiries	The advertiser counts up the number of enquiries received during each phase of an advertising campaign. This allows the marketing management to judge which media are working best, provided the coupons have an identifying code on them. This method assumes that it is the advertising which is generating the sales, which may or may not be the case.
Post-campaign tests (post-tests)	The particular testing method used will depend largely on the objectives of the campaign. Communications objectives (product awareness, attitude change, brand awareness) might be determined through surveys; sales objectives might be measured according to changes in sales which can be attributed to the campaign. This is difficult to do because of other factors (changes in economic conditions, for example) which might distort the findings.
Recognition tests and recall tests	In recognition tests, consumers are shown the advertisement and asked if they recognise it. They are then asked how much of it they actually recall. In an unaided recall test the consumer is asked which adverts he or she remembers seeing recently; in an aided recall test the consumer is shown a group of ads (without being told which is the one the researcher is interested in) and is asked which ones he or she has seen recently.

advertising does other things which are hard to measure, such as encouraging brand loyalty or increasing word-of-mouth communication between consumers themselves.

Advertising effectiveness can be assessed by market research, by returned coupons, and (sometimes) by increased sales. The last method is somewhat risky, however, since there may be many other factors which could have increased the sales of the product. Table 8.19 shows some common techniques for evaluating advertising effectiveness.

Any testing must be valid (must measure what it says it measures) and reliable (free of random error). A reliable test would provide consistent results every time it is used, and a valid test would enable the marketer to predict outcomes reasonably accurately. In order to ensure that this is the case, a set of principles called PACT (Positioning Advertising Copy Testing) have been established (*Marketing News* 1982). A good advertising testing system should:

1. Provide measurements that are relevant to the objectives of the advertising.
2. Require agreement about how the results will be used in advance of each specific test.
3. Provide multiple measurements, because single measurements, are generally inadequate to assess the advert's performance.
4. Be based on a model of human response to communication – the reception of a stimulus, the comprehension of the stimulus and the response to the stimulus.
5. Allow for consideration of whether the advertising stimulus should be exposed more than once.
6. Recognise that the more finished a piece of copy is, the more soundly it can be evaluated. It should also require as a minimum that alternative executions be tested to the same degree of finish.
7. Provide controls to avoid the biasing effects of the exposure content.
8. Take into account basic considerations of sample definition.
9. Demonstrate reliability and validity empirically.

Advertisements can be tested on two dimensions: those related to the advertisement itself, and those related to its contents. Since these two issues are sometimes difficult for the consumer to separate there is no real certainty as to which is actually being tested.

Pre-testing and post-testing

Pre-testing the advertisement to assess whether it is likely to be effective has a mixed history. There has been considerable debate as to whether it is really possible to predict whether an advert will work or not, and there is of course no certainty about this even when sophisticated copy-testing methods are used. Testing almost certainly reduces the risk of producing an ineffective advert, and it is better to find this out before expensive space is booked in the media, and possibly before an inappropriate message is sent out.

Post-testing is concerned with researching the effectiveness of the advert after it has appeared. Finding out whether the advertising has been effective in achieving the objectives laid down is much easier if clear objectives were set in the first place, of course, and if the advertising agency was given a clear brief.

Laboratory techniques

Testing can be carried out in the field, or in the laboratory; most pre-tests are carried out in laboratory conditions. Table 8.20 shows some of the available techniques.

Laboratory measures at first appear scientific and therefore objective, but this is often not the case. While the researcher might be able to maintain objectivity, it is unlikely that the subject (respondent) will and the knowledge of the artificiality of the situation is

qualitative data Information which cannot be expressed numerically.

Table 8.20 Laboratory techniques for testing advertising effectiveness

Technique	Explanation
Consumer juries	Groups of consumers are asked to judge whether they think the advertisement will work. This has the advantage that consumers (presumably) know what affects them most. The drawback is that they will sometimes 'play expert', trying to guess how other people would react to the advertisement rather than giving their own reactions.
Focus groups	A moderator conducts a loosely structured interview with six to twelve respondents simultaneously. The respondents tend to trigger comments from each other, so that a range of ideas is elicited. This data is qualitative; it is not usually possible or desirable to express it numerically, but it does raise issues effectively.
Portfolio tests	Respondents are shown test adverts (those the researcher wants to test) and control adverts (adverts whose effectiveness is already known) and asked to score them. The researcher can then compare the scores of the test adverts with the control adverts and see whether the test adverts will be as effective. This method may also mean that respondents try to 'play the expert'.
Readability tests	The copy is analysed for readability without consumer interviewing. The foremost method is the Fleisch formula (Flesch 1974). Readability is assessed by determining the average number of syllables per hundred words, the length of sentences, the human interest content and the familiarity of words. Results can be compared with predetermined norms for the target audience.
Physiological measures	Eye cameras can be used to record the route an individual's eye takes when seeing an advert. This can be unreliable; lingering on one part of the advert might denote interest, or it might denote incomprehension. Galvanic skin response and pupil dilation response measure different aspects of interest; pupils dilate and the electrical resistance of the skin decreases when an object of interest appears.

likely to cloud the respondent's judgement. Furthermore, the results of (for example) a galvanic skin response or pupil dilation response still need to be interpreted. Interest or excitement at seeing an advertisement does not necessarily stem from the communication itself, and almost certainly does not translate into the achievement of the communications objectives.

Summary

Communication is a very common human activity – some might even argue that it is a defining activity of human beings. Marketers are no exception, but marketers communicate about products and services on a professional basis. Communication is about establishing a common understanding of how the world works, and consumers are not passive in this process. Marketers therefore need to consider the personalities of their target audience, and the ways in which the messages will be interpreted – these interpretations may differ greatly from the message the marketers thought they were sending.

The key points from this chapter are as follows:

- People are not radios: they consider and interpret marketing messages in the light of their previous experience.
- Communications are rarely one-way.
- Redundancy in communication helps ensure clarity of the message.
- Meaning is derived from the message plus the personality of the person receiving it.
- Signs are not culturally universal.
- Miscommunication is common due to misunderstanding, implication, distraction, confusion and distortion.
- Marketing communication is a great deal more than just advertising, public relations, personal selling and sales promotion.
- Push strategies emphasise promotion to the distribution chain: pull strategies emphasise promotion to consumers. Most campaigns contain elements of both push and pull.
- Budgeting is more about negotiation than about the needs of the campaign.
- Marketers should aim to do things that their competitors are not doing.
- Integration of marketing communications is difficult because different departments and agencies each have different ideas.
- Integration is also difficult because each medium will inevitably colour the message.

Chapter review questions

1 How might you go about changing an attitude?

2 What is the difference between the central and peripheral routes to attitude change?

3 How might you overcome stimulus rejection?

4 What are the main criticisms of the Schramm model of communication?

5 What is meant by semantics?

6 How might ethnocentrism affect a communications campaign?

7 What are the main ways of stimulating word-of-mouth communication?

8 What is the difference between a push strategy and a pull strategy?

9 What are the advantages and disadvantages of integrating marketing communications?

10 How might symbols lead to miscommunication?

Preview case revisited
Citroën C4

The advertisements were an immediate success. To the generation brought up on Transformer toys, the theme evoked echoes of childhood fun and playfulness. The science fiction theme of the Transformers toys and TV series transferred easily to the idea that technology could be exciting as well as practical, and even for those not of the Transformers generation the innovativeness of the advertisements was eye-catching enough that they remained memorable.

Evidence of the impact of the advertising was quick to reveal itself. Chevrolet produced a spoof advertisement, in which the car continues to dance even when the owner wants to go home (meanwhile, the Chevvy driver just gets into his car and leaves). Three men in China built a full-size replica of the robot version of the car, using a Citroën, for a cost of $8000. Sui Lulu, Zhang Yiming and Li Wei, all from Nanjing, were all Transformers fans when they were younger: although the finished Transformer doesn't actually transform, it is a remarkable piece of artwork.

Elsewhere, the adverts became the subject of thousands or even millions of comments on weblogs. This in itself was a major boost for Citroën's campaign, since such 'word of mouse' carries the message even further. Comments included:

The Citroën commercials suggest the car is hip and rad and from the f***ing future. The Chevy suggests that the Citroën is hip and rad and from the f***ing future, and additionally suggests that the Chevy Aveo is a soulless chunk of plastic and steel designed for people whose lives consist of waiting to die.

Hey there . . . wow this has been the best advertisement 'i' ve' seen this year, i might be a lilo late on that but this is the first time I' ve seen this.

i think this is the best advert ever on tv! it rocks!! it really makes me want the car because it is so cool!

please put it back on our screens! i love it! thanx luv ema xxxxxxx I LOVE IT!'

From the viewpoint of Citroën, an advertisement that generated large amounts of word-of-mouth (and word of mouse) had to be a good thing. Further versions were produced in which the car ice-skates, and very soon the 'hi-tech' approach of the advertisement was being imitated by other manufacturers.

Certainly the advertising campaign met its objectives. The car was clearly regarded as a technologically-advanced, modern vehicle, even by those who were unimpressed by its looks or performance. Translating this into sales was another matter – although the adverts were well received, the car failed to make the Top Ten most popular cars in Europe, a position it might reasonably have attained, bearing in mind that the Renault Clio (a car in a similar target market) regularly appears in the league tables. Of course, there is no knowing what sales might have been like without the advertisement – or indeed what would have happened had the agency followed a less exciting approach.

Finance subject to status from Citroën Financial Services. A guarantee may be required. Terms and conditions apply. Metallic paint extra. Model shown C4 2.0i 16V Exclusive £16,095.

Courtesy of The Advertising Archives

Case study
Smart Cart

In recent years South Africa has experienced an economic boom. The country has always been the economic and industrial powerhouse of Africa, but since the ending of apartheid and the relative peace that has descended on the country as a result, business has boomed. South African goods and services are available throughout Southern Africa: for example, retailers such as Edgars Stores, founded in Johannesburg in 1929, now have branches throughout Southern Africa, and Celcom (the South African mobile telephone service provider) recently bought out Uganda's Nile Com mobile telephone provider.

The boom in South Africa's fortunes has meant a rapid rise of a black middle-class as well as increased wealth for everyone. As in any other industrialised economy, consumer power has come to the forefront – the range of goods available in South Africa, and the demand for them, has skyrocketed.

With the consumer boom has come an increase in the amount of marketing activity. Supermarkets have not been slow in adopting modern point-of-sale techniques, and this is where Smart Cart have been able to make their greatest contribution. Smart Cart is a Johannesburg-based marketing company, founded in 2004, specialising in ambient advertising within stores. The company places advertising on shopping trolleys and carts, and currently has the rights to over 200 000 supermarket trolleys, baskets and carts throughout Southern Africa. The company has a really international approach – it does business in South Africa, Zambia, Zimbabwe, Botswana and Namibia. Even the company's website is hosted in Zambia.

The company's latest innovation is the Smart Basket, a supermarket basket with an extending handle and two small wheels. This makes negotiating the supermarket aisles easier than would be the case with a full-size trolley, but the really subtle advantage of the Smart Basket is that it takes the weight off the shopper's arms. Someone who only intended to buy a few items (and therefore chose a basket rather than a trolley) is not prevented from buying more simply because the basket is getting too heavy to carry. Research by international consultants AC Nielsen showed that Smart Basket increases the time people spend in the store, and also increases the quantities purchased when compared with traditional shopping baskets.

Courtesy of Smart Cart

Placing advertisements on and in the trolleys and baskets is extremely powerful. A large supermarket may have 30 000 brands on the shelves, all vying for the shopper's attention: cutting through this clutter presents a problem for brand managers. On average, shoppers look into their trolleys or baskets every 8 to 10 seconds while in the store, either because they are placing goods in the trolleys or because they are checking their purchases. Each time the customer looks into the trolley, he or she sees the advertisement for whatever product is being promoted, so the 'opportunities to view' even in a minimum half-hour shopping trip would be around 180 or 200. Obviously such advertising is of prime importance from the viewpoint of the manufacturer, since it reaches directly to the consumer when he or she is engaged in the main activity of interest (shopping) and is in the right environment (the store). In addition, people see the advertisements on the trolleys elsewhere in the shopping environment – in the car park, in the street outside, even in other stores if the store is part of a shopping complex.

Smart Cart has contracts with Shoprite, South Africa's biggest retail group, which includes Dis-Chem, Checkers

Courtesy of Smart Cart

and Checkers Hyper. Sixty-five per cent of South Africans regularly shop in a Shoprite store, so the reach of the advertising is impressive. Furthermore, Smart Cart are able to segment the market fairly accurately by knowing the profile of the customers in specific stores and targeting accordingly. As a result, the company has a large number of major companies listed as clients – among them Nando's, Coca-Cola, Parmalat (the South African dairy products company), Unilever, Visa and MasterCard.

Ambient advertising is often associated with the weird and wacky – livery on motor vehicles, street sculptures and so forth. Yet the relatively simple idea of placing advertising on shopping baskets has created a South African success story for Smart Cart.

Questions

1 What are the main advantages for a firm advertising with Smart Cart?

2 Which advertisers are most likely to benefit from advertising on Smart Cart?

3 How might the advertising link to other promotional tools to create an integrated campaign?

4 What might be the limiting factors in Smart Cart's success?

5 What are the possible drawbacks of advertising on Smart Cart?

References

Allport, G.W. (1935): Attitudes. In C.A. Murchison (ed.) *A Handbook of Social Psychology* (Worcester, MA: Clark University Press).

Baird, T.R., Wahlers, R.G. and Cooper, C.K. (2007): Non-recognition of print advertising: emotional arousal and gender effects. *Journal of Marketing Communication* **13**(1), 39–57.

Biel, A. (1990): Love the advertisement, buy the product? *ADMAP* October.

Borremans T. (1998): Integrated (marketing) communications in practice; survey among communication, public relations and advertising agencies in Belgium. *Proceedings of the 3rd Annual Conference of the Global Institute for Corporate and Marketing Communications* (Glasgow: Strathclyde University).

Broadbent, S. (1989): *The Advertising Budget* (Institute of Practitioners in Advertising and NTC Publications Ltd).

Brown, G. (1991): Modelling advertising awareness. *ADMAP* April.

Bruhn, M. (1995): *Intergrierte Unternehmenskommunikation: Ansatzpunkte für eine strategische und operative Umsetzung intergrierter Kommunikationsarbeit.* (Stuttgart: Schaffer-Poeschel).

Chaiken, S. (1980): Heuristic versus systematic information processing and use of source versus message cues in persuasion. *Journal of Personality and Social Psychology* **39**, 752–66.

Colley, R.H. (1961): *Defining Advertising Goals* (New York: Association of National Advertisers).

Costa, J.A. and Pavia, T.M. (1992): What it all adds up to: culture and alpha numeric brand names. In J.F. Sherry Jr. and B. Sternthal (eds) *Advances in Consumer Research*, vol. 19 (Provo, UT: Association for Consumer Research 1992) p. 40.

Deetz, S.A. (1992): *Democracy in an Age of Corporate Colonization: Developments in Communication and the Politics of Everyday Life* (Albany, NY: State University of New York Press).

Duncan, T. and Caywood, C. (1996): The concept, process and evolution of integrated marketing communication. In E. Thorson and J. Moore, *Integrated Communication. Synergy of Persuasive Voices* (Mahwah, NJ: Lawrence Erlbaum).

Eagle, L., Hyde, K. and Kitchen, P. (1998): *Advertising effectiveness measurement: a review of industry research practices.* Proceedings of the Third Annual Conference of the Global Institute for Corporate and Marketing Communications (Glasgow: Strathclyde University).

Engel, J.F., Warshaw, M.R. and Kinnear, T.C. (1994): *Promotional Strategy* (Chicago, IL: Irwin).

Fishbein, M. (1963): An investigation of the relationships between beliefs about an object and the attitude towards that object. *Human Relations* **16** (August), 233–40.

Fishbein, M. and Ajzen, I. (1975): *Belief, Attitude, Intention and Behaviour: An Introduction to Theory and Research.* (Reading, MA: Addison-Wesley).

Hartley, B. and Pickton, D. (1997): *Integrated marketing communication – a new language for a new era.* Proceedings of the Second International Conference on Marketing and Corporate Communication, Antwerp.

Hofstede, G. (1984): Cultures Consequences: International Differences in Work-related Values (Beverley Hills, CA: Sage).

Homer, P.M. and Yoon, S.-G. (1992): Message framing and the interrelationships among ad-based feelings, affect and cognition. *Journal of Advertising* **21** (March), 19–33.

Institute of Public Relations (1984): *Public Relations Practice: Its Roles and Parameters* (London: The Institute of Public Relations).

Katz, E. and Lazarsfield, R (1955): *Personal Influence: The Part Played by People in the Flow of Mass Communications* (New York: New York Free Press).

Keegan, W. (1984): *Multinational Marketing Management*, 3rd edn (Englewood Cliffs, NJ: Prentice Hall International).

Majaro, S. (1982): *International Marketing* (London: Allen and Unwin).

Mantovani, G (1996): *New Communication Environments: From Everyday to Virtual* (London: Taylor and Francis).

McCracken, G. (1986): Culture and consumption: a theoretical account of the structure and movement of the cultural meaning of consumer goods. *Journal of Consumer Research* **13** (June), 71–81.

Marketing News (1982): 21Ad agencies endorse copy testing principles. 19 February.

Miniard, P.W., Bhatla, S. and Rose, R.L. (1990): On the formation and relationship of ad and brand attitudes: an experimental and causal analysis. *Journal of Marketing Research* **27** (August), 290–303.

Nowak, G. and Phelps, J. (1994): Conceptualising the integrated marketing communications phenomenon. *Journal of Current Issues and Research in Advertising* **16**(1), 49–66.

O'Sullivan, T., Hartley, J., Saunders, D. and Fiske, J. (1983): *Key Concepts in Communication* (London: Methuen).

Peirce C.S., quoted in Mick, D.G. (1986): Consumer research and semiotics: exploring the morphology of signs, symbols and significance. *Journal of Consumer Research* **13** (September), 196–213.

Petrison, L.A. and Wang, P. (1996): Integrated marketing communication: an organisational perspective. In E. Thorson and J. Moore, *Integrated Communication. Synergy of Persuasive Voices* (Mahwah: Lawrence Erlbaum), pp. 167–84.

Petty, R.E. and Cacioppo, J.T. (1986): Central and peripheral routes to persuasion: application to advertising. In L. Percy and A. Woodside (eds) *Advertising and Consumer Psychology* (Lexington, MA: Lexington Books).

Petty, R.E., Cacioppo, J. and Schumamn, D. (1983): Central and peripheral routes to advertising effectiveness. *Journal of Consumer Research* **10** (September), 135–46.

Rosenberg, M.J. (1960): An analysis of affective-cognitive consistency. In M.J. Rosenberg *et al.* (eds) *Attitude Organisation and Change* (New Haven, CT: Yale University Press).

Rosengren, S. and Dahlen, M. (2006): Brand-slogan matching in a cluttered environment. *Journal of Marketing Communications* **12**(4), 263–9.

Schramm, W.A. (1948): *Mass Communication* (Urbana, IL: University of Illinois Press).

Shimp, T. and Sharma, S. (1987): Consumer ethnocentrism: construction and validation of CETSCALE. *Journal of Marketing Research* August, 280–9.

Stapel, J. (1990): Monitoring advertising performance. *ADMAP* July/August.

Stapel, J. (1991): Like the advertisement but does it interest me? *ADMAP* April.

Steen, J. (1995): Now they're using suicide to sell jeans. *Sunday Express* 26 March.

Varey, R. (2000): A critical review of conceptions of communication evident in contemporary business and management literature. *Journal of Communication Management* **4**, 328–40.

Vlasic, Goran and Kesic, Tanja (2007): Analysis of customers' attitudes towards interactivity and relationship personalisation as contemporary developments in interactive marketing communication. *Journal of Marketing Communications* **13** (2—June), 109–129.

Zajonc, R.B. and Markus, H. (1985): Must all affect be mediated by cognition? *Journal of Consumer Research* **12** (December), 363–4.

Further reading

There are many books on marketing communications: the following only represents a small sample.

Smith, P.R. and Taylor, J. (2004): *Marketing Communications: An Integrated Approach* (London: Kogan Page). This is very much a practitioner's text, putting theory second to practice. On the other hand, it is extremely comprehensive.

Fill, C. (2001): *Marketing Communications: Contexts, Strategies and Applications* (Harlow: FT Prentice Hall). This is a classic student textbook on communications.

Pelsmacker, P. de, Geuens, M. and Bergh, J. van den (2004): *Marketing Communications: A European Perspective* (Harlow: FT Prentice Hall). This book provides a much deeper theoretical background than the others, but does not ignore practice.

Chapter 9
International marketing

Learning objectives After reading this chapter, you should be able to:

1. Explain different theoretical approaches to internationalisation.

2. Describe the factors involved in choosing and entering markets.

3. Explain how to calculate the profit potential of a national market.

4. Understand some of the difficulties involved in international marketing research.

5. Explain the relationship between product and promotion strategies in international markets.

6. Explain the main difficulties in setting up overseas branches.

Introduction

It has become almost impossible to escape from the effects of globalisation. Even companies which do not themselves sell their goods and services outside their national borders have found that they are competing with firms entering from overseas. Additionally, firms are finding that their home markets are changing as a result of foreign travel, mass migrations and other factors.

The Internet has also opened up global markets for even the smallest of firms – and has equally opened up global markets to consumers, so that competition truly crosses borders. The biggest change that the Internet has brought to business is that any company, no matter how small, can establish a presence on the global stage.

An understanding of the international nature of business is therefore at least as essential for marketers as it is for anyone else in business.

Globalisation of Trade

International trade goes back a long way. In about 4000 BC a stone axe factory was established in the Langdale Pikes, in the English Lake District. This factory was so successful that axes from it have been found as far away as the South of France – evidence that international trade occurred even before there were true nation states.

The thrust towards globalisation comes from the following factors (see Figure 9.1):

● *Comparative advantage*. Some countries are better placed to produce certain products than are others. Minerals such as oil and aluminium are obvious examples, but some countries develop expertise in service fields. For example, Holland has expertise in building dams and in handling large bodies of water, developed through the construction of its famous dykes.

● *Economies of scale*. For some goods the costs of development are so high that they can only be realistically amortised over very large production runs. For example, electronic products such as cellular telephones represent a huge cost in terms of

Preview case
Euro RSCG

Advertising has to be one of the hardest professions to be in in a globalising world. Taking account of the many different cultures, different nationalities, and different languages worldwide adds to the existing problem of balancing client need against customer receptiveness. From a management perspective, just keeping some kind of control over the many creative people needed in the business brings problems of its own.

Euro RSCG was formed in 1991 by the merger of eurocom (France's largest advertising agency) with RSCG (France's top creative agency). It is the world's biggest global advertising agency, employing 10 000 people in 75 countries. Although the company headquarters is now in New York (on Hudson Street rather than Madison Avenue), offices elsewhere in the world operate in a fairly autonomous manner – necessarily, since the whole point of having offices worldwide is to provide local knowledge about what will and will not work.

Advertising is a creative profession, of course, and Euro RSCG are proud of their creative credentials: they were the first agency to advertise on the Eiffel Tower, the first (and only) to put a statue on the empty fourth plinth of Nelson's Column in Trafalgar Square, London, the first to buy media space on the Internet (despite having no client who needed it at that time), the first to retain a reformed burglar to advise a client on security matters, and the first to change outdoor advertising on a twice-a-day basis. The company's slogan is 'the home of contagious ideas' and it certainly lives up to that ideal. Its Creative Business Ideas branding says that it seeks to produce ideas that revolutionise companies and the way they do business – no small ambition.

The company handles advertising for 10 of the top 100 largest global advertisers: Ford, Reckitt Bensicker, Danone, PSA Peugeot Citroën, Citigroup, Bayer, Schering-Plough Corp., LG Group, Carrefour and Sanofi-Aventis. Euro RSCG also handles many other accounts, not all of which are themselves global – although many of them aspire to be.

The problem for Euro RSCG is to be able to think global, but act local – and to create campaigns which resonate throughout the world.

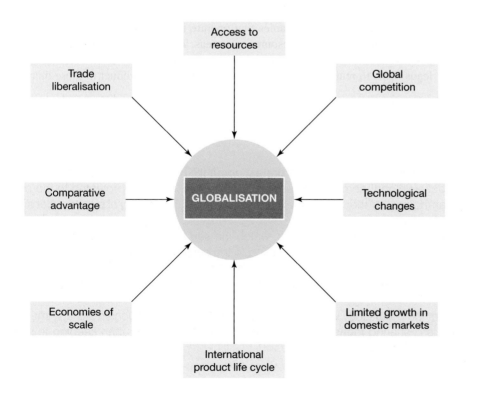

Figure 9.1

Forces for globalisation

research and development – only sales in the millions can justify the outlay, so a world market is essential. Also, modern automated production lines mean that manufacturing capacity has increased by orders of magnitude – few modern consumer-goods factories can function efficiently if only serving a domestic market.

- *Trade liberalisation.* The realisation that free trade creates wealth is not a new one – it was British Government policy for most of the 19th century. In recent years the idea has received a new boost with the creation of trading blocs such as the European Union, and the reduction of barriers to trade worldwide as a result of the World Trade Organisation agreements.

- *International product lifecycle.* As a product reaches the decline phase in one country, it can be introduced into a new country in order to prolong its life. In fact products cross borders even without the originating company trying to arrange this to happen – because of rapid world communications, ideas become disseminated and production of similar products in other countries will happen anyway.

- *Limited growth in domestic markets.* Most companies aim to grow, but clearly there will come a point at which the home market is saturated. Many firms become international because they cannot grow any more in their home markets.

- *Technological changes.* Improvements in air transport and telecommunications have made it much easier for firms to trade in other countries. Satellite TV has enabled firms to advertise internationally much more easily than they could before, and cheap airfreight has enabled firms to export small quantities of product relatively easily.

- *Global competition.* As foreign companies make inroads into a company's home markets, the company concerned might naturally decide that opportunities exist in the overseas markets. For example, an office furniture supply company in the UK, faced with competition from Italy, might reasonably conclude that opportunities would exist in the Italian market.

- *Access to resources.* Companies that operate internationally not only sell goods overseas, they also access resources overseas. The ease with which manufacture can be relocated to low-wage countries, or components sourced from overseas suppliers, leads firms to realise that they can easily sell finished product in those markets.

Talking Point

As globalisation increases, new market segments appear, and marketers seek to meet their needs.

If globalisation is such a great idea, why is it that so many people protest about it? The anti-globalisation movement has tried to disrupt trade talks, has attacked global companies such as McDonald's, and has protested to the point of rioting in all parts of the globe. Paradoxically, the anti-globalisation movement is itself global. So what's the problem?

Anti-globalists say that having everybody use the same products, watch the same TV shows, and wear the same clothes is destroying the world's cultural diversity and reducing everything to the same grey goo. Also, they argue that globalised companies are too powerful – they are more powerful than national governments, in fact, and can literally ignore democratically elected representatives. Eventually, the argument runs, we will all be controlled by big business – if we aren't already.

On the other hand, if people didn't want the goods they wouldn't buy them. We know that McDonald's is an American corporation – that's part of the fun. And isn't sharing ideas a positive thing for the world, rather than keeping to some dogmatic principle that our own culture is better than anyone else's?

International Business Perspectives

The philosophy behind the company's internationalisation effort is an important starting point for understanding the possible strategic and tactical approaches which might be taken to internationalisation. One classification of business perspectives is the EPRG classification (Muhlbacher, Dahringer and Leihs 1999). This classification is as shown in Table 9.1.

There are two main schools of thought on the internationalisation of the firm. The first is the Uppsala, or stages of development, approach, in which it is believed that firms go through a series of stages in becoming international and (eventually) global firms (see Figure 9.2). The stages are as follows:

1 *Exporting*. This implies the smallest level of commitment to the foreign market. The firm produces goods in its own country, and sells them in one or more foreign markets. The sales are made to a foreign importer, who then handles all the marketing in the foreign country. In some cases the exporting firm has acquired the business without actually seeking out an importer – the firm may have been approached at an exhibition stand, for example, or one of its own customers (a wholesaler or retailer) might have opened up a branch in the overseas market.

ethnocentrism The belief that one's own culture is superior to others.

polycentrism Viewing corporate activities as emanating from centres in a number of countries.

geocentrism Viewing corporate activities in a global manner.

Table 9.1 Classification of international perspectives

Ethnocentric perspective	An **ethnocentric** manager sees the domestic market as the most important, and the overseas markets as inferior. Often such managers do not perceive foreign imports as representing a serious threat at all.
Polycentric perspective	**Polycentric** managers look at each overseas market as if it were a separate domestic market. Each country is seen as a separate entity, and the firm seeks to be seen as a 'local' firm within that country. Each market has its own manufacturing and marketing facilities, and there is only limited overlap.
Regional perspective	Regional orientation means grouping countries together, usually on a geographical basis, and providing for the specific needs of consumers within those countries. National boundaries are respected, but do not have the same importance as cultural differences.
Geocentric perspective	The truly global – **geocentric** – marketer thinks of the world as a single market, with opportunities for procurement, production and sales in whichever market segments are the most appropriate. Global marketers look for global segments (for example the global youth market), and for global opportunities to rationalise communications, production and product development.

Figure 9.2

Stages of development approach

Control over foreign marketing activities increases

Global marketing

Overseas manufacture

Overseas distribution

Establish a sales office abroad

Exporting

Commitment and cost increases

The advantage of exporting is that it is cheap and relatively simple – the drawback is that the firm loses all control over the marketing of the product once it enters the foreign market.

2 *Establish a sales office in the foreign market.* Once export sales are becoming established, the exporting firm might consider it worthwhile to take an interest in the marketing of its goods in the overseas market. This involves increased financial commitment, but also offers greater control and tends to engender confidence among overseas buyers.

3 *Overseas distribution.* This would involve establishing a warehouse and distribution network in the overseas market. This gives even more control, and also shortens the lines of supply so that foreign buyers' needs can be met more quickly.

4 *Overseas manufacture.* The company sets up subsidiary factories in the countries in which it does business, to shorten lines of supply and to adapt the product to local market conditions.

5 *Global marketing.* At this stage the firm sources raw materials and components from the most cost-effective countries, and markets its products to the most appropriate market segments. Company ownership may be spread across stock markets in several countries, and the company may well employ far more foreigners than nationals of its country of origin.

eclectic All-encompassing, taking account of all factors.

An alternative view of the internationalisation process has been proposed by Dunning (1993). Dunning's **Eclectic** Theory says that firms enter foreign markets by whatever means are most appropriate to the firm. The decision will be based on the firm's specific advantage over its competitors, both at home and overseas, and the entry method decided upon without necessarily going through any intermediate stages. For example, a firm with a strength in franchising will enter overseas markets on a franchise basis rather than begin by exporting. The eclectic paradigm also has implications for manufacture, since a firm will produce in whichever country is most appropriate or convenient.

Some recent research indicates that there may be only small differences between firms which are 'born global' and those which take a traditional approach (Chetty and Campbell-Hunt 2004).

Globalisation occurs when managers concentrate on groups of customers with similar needs, regardless of country of residence. From a marketing viewpoint, this is obviously a customer-orientated approach, since country of residence actually says very little about a consumer's needs. The need for mobile telephones is the same whether the customer lives in Sweden or Zambia: only local systems and prices will change. Some cultural elements will, of course, need to be adapted: language, and use of the product might be factors which would change as the product moves into different markets.

Assessing Market Attractiveness

Mobile telephones are a global product.

Different markets have different levels of attractiveness. In some cases the overseas market may be less lucrative than the domestic market, but expansion may no longer be possible at home.

Assessing the attractiveness of the overseas market is not simply an issue of potential sales or potential profitability: it is also an issue of deciding the company's strategic direction. A firm might therefore enter one market in order to establish a position from which it can enter a more lucrative market. For example, when Honda entered the UK motorcycle market it began by selling small, low-powered motorcycles. This enabled the firm to become established, and eventually market large, high-powered bikes which are much more profitable.

Marketing in Practice
Tjaereborg

In the 1980s, Danish holiday tour operator Tjaereborg decided to enter the UK market. From across the North Sea, the UK looked attractive: with 10 times the population of Denmark, and an even higher propensity to travel than Denmark, the UK looked very promising indeed. Tjaereborg's chief competitive advantage in its home market is that it deals direct with the public rather than going through travel agents: the agents' commission could be saved and passed on to the customers, giving Tjaereborg a distinct price advantage.

Unfortunately the scheme did not work out. Tjaereborg did not take into account the entrenched British practice of buying holidays through high street travel agents.

Tjaereborg also did not consider the amount of money that would have to be spent on advertising in order to re-educate the UK public into the idea of booking direct. Finally, Tjaereborg were unable to offer the sheer variety of holidays that the much larger UK-based companies could offer. If the company had been able to exploit their 'Danishness' in some way they might have found a niche market, but this proved impossible. Had the Internet existed at the time, Tjaereborg would have been ideally placed to benefit, but the world wide web was in its infancy. The company had no realistic competitive position to obtain or maintain, and now no longer operates in the UK.

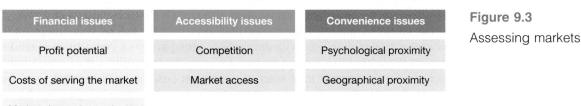

Financial issues	Accessibility issues	Convenience issues
Profit potential	Competition	Psychological proximity
Costs of serving the market	Market access	Geographical proximity
Market size and growth rate		

Figure 9.3

Assessing markets

Target markets might be chosen for any of the following reasons:

1 Geographical proximity
2 Psychological proximity
3 Market size and growth rate
4 Costs of serving the market
5 Profit potential
6 Market access
7 Competition.

Geographical proximity refers to the closeness of the market in physical terms. For example, trade within the European Union is based on the physical proximity of the markets – moving goods from Dortmund to Maastricht is easier in practice than moving goods from Dortmund to Munich, since Dortmund and Maastricht are much closer together. The German–Dutch border presents no real barrier to the movement of goods. However, there may be a psychological barrier, based partly on language and partly on history.

Psychological proximity refers to the cultural similarities which exist between some countries. For example, many UK firms regard the United States as an attractive market, simply because the US and UK are similar culturally. This can overcome the obvious advantages of trading with, say, France or Holland, which are much closer and which have virtually no border restrictions with the UK. Psychological proximity is often based on language – the UK feels closer to Australia, Canada, the United States, New Zealand

geographical proximity The closeness of the market in physical terms.

psychological proximity The degree to which countries are culturally close to each other.

Talking Point

and even India because these countries share a language. Likewise, Spanish companies often feel closer to Latin America than they do to Germany, and Portuguese companies feel closer to Brazil, Mozambique and Angola than they do to Italy or Greece.

Most English speakers get fairly lazy about learning foreign languages – after all, everybody speaks English nowadays, so why bother? This means, of course, that the English-speaking countries tend to trade with each other rather than with their nearest neighbours.

But if the neighbours speak English as well, because it is the world business language, where does that leave the argument? Why is it that British firms think first of trading with the United States, and second of trading with fellow EU members? Why do Americans only trade 10 per cent of their gross national product, and rarely venture out to other countries at all? If trade is always good, why are we so reluctant to do it?

Maybe it's more than language. Maybe we are just afraid of the unknown – and American films and TV make the United States seem very familiar!

Market size and growth rate can be important factors. A large market is likely to be more attractive than a small market, since there will be more niches available for the foreign company. Markets with high growth rates tend to offer less competitive pressure than stable or shrinking markets since all the companies in the market can grow without having to compete for market share with the other firms in the market. There is evidence that growth is a more important consideration than size (Whitelock and Jobber 1994).

The level and quality of the competition already in the market is an important factor, because a market with a heavily-entrenched, strong group of competitors is unlikely to respond favourably to a foreign entrant. Defining the competition is of course important here – a foreign entrant may enter at a different position in the market from the one occupied in the domestic market. Also, foreign goods sometimes gain (or lose) from country-of-origin effects, whereby some of the country's image attaches itself to the brand. For example, Germany has a reputation for good engineering, so German products are often assumed to be well-engineered. This is, of course, a ridiculous assumption to make, since there must be many German manufacturers who employ poor engineers, but nonetheless the view is widely held. Likewise, China has a long way to go to overcome its image of producing shoddy goods – yet many high-quality products carry the 'Made in China' label.

Sometimes the country of origin causes 'symbolic' consumption: people buy the product simply because of its country of origin (see Figure 9.4). This has been especially noticeable in transition economies (former Communist countries of Eastern Europe) where the consumption of Western products is symbolic of a desire for a Western lifestyle, and is even seen when individuals have no real knowledge of the products

Figure 9.4

Country of origin effects

| Actual features and benefits of the product | + | **Reputation issues** Reputation of brand Reputation of country of origin Reputation of company | = | Acceptability of product in foreign market |

themselves (Clark, Micken and Hart 2002). A particularly interesting example is the tortilla in Mexico. This is a culturally significant product, symbolising what it is to be Mexican, yet there is a strong belief that American-made tortillas are better than Mexican-made ones, simply because Mexicans tend to believe that anything American is better than anything Mexican (Gabel and Boller 2003).

The cost of serving the market can vary greatly between countries. For example, physical distribution costs can be extremely high in a country such as Australia, where distances are large between settlements: equally, in some countries (such as Japan) the distribution chains are long, with a large number of wholesalers and other middlemen involved in the process. Transportation costs in some developing countries vary with the seasons, as roads become flooded in the wet season or impassable deserts in the dry season. Advertising costs can vary dramatically – TV advertising in the United States is in general much cheaper than in the UK, for example. Some countries may lack a marketing infrastructure which would allow for cheap entry – for example, Germany has a well-developed system of manufacturers' agents, who are able to sell imported goods on a commission-only basis. This allows even the smallest firms to enter the German market (provided they can interest a good agent). Countries such as Zambia have no comparable system, so foreign companies need to set up their own sales organisation to do business there. Since salaries are generally low, this may not present the same problems it would in (say) Denmark, but the costs would undoubtedly be too high for a small firm.

Australian road trains cover vast distances.

Talking Point

Country of origin is commonly used as an advertising theme. Audi uses the strapline 'Vorsprung durch Teknik' in its world advertising, despite the fact that most non-German speakers would have no idea what this means (it means 'advance through technology' if you're curious).

So why put out an incomprehensible advertisement? Doesn't this fly in the face of everything we know about communication? Or is it that we are communicating the German-ness of Audi cars, in the hope that the German reputation for engineering will rub off on the Audi?

Does country of origin actually mean anything? On the one hand, one might expect that good engineers breed more good engineers, through training and education and by good example: on the other hand, why should a factory on one side of the Alps turn out better products than one a few miles away on the other side of the border?

Profit potential of the market is a function of the number of potential customers and the profit margin the product might command. In some cases the number of potential customers is so large that the market is worth approaching even though profit margins are small – an example is India. In other cases the margins are large but the number of customers is small, as in Denmark. Powerful buying groups, low per capita income, and strong competition are all factors which tend to reduce profit margins. High incomes, inefficient competition and good positioning within the market all help to raise profit margins (as of course is true in domestic markets).

Market access can be limited by the local industry structure, by Government restrictions on imports, or by local competition rules. For example, in Japan there is no legal problem with importing goods, but the monolithic structure of industry, with

Pure Audi. Vorsprung durch Technik.

Figure 9.5

Assessing profit potential

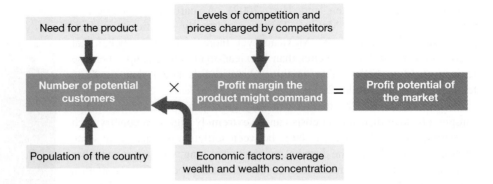

the giant *sogo sosha* general trading companies controlling every-thing, means that there are few openings for foreign companies. On the other hand, the Caricom countries in the Caribbean have high external tariffs on many goods in order to protect their fledgling manufacturing industries from cheap foreign imports.

Some firms use market attractiveness indexes to compare dif-ferent potential markets. Managers decide which are the factors which make a market attractive from the firm's viewpoint, and apply weightings to the factors, then assess each potential market against those factors. The stages of developing such an index are shown in Table 9.2.

As a result of the exercise, target countries can be classified as probables, possibles and 'no-hopers'. The last are discarded. Further information on the 'possibles' might be collected, and some of these might be promoted to 'probables', but the remainder will be discarded also.

The main problems with international marketing research also apply to market screening. These include:

- The high cost of gathering information, both in terms of money and in terms of time.

- The vast number of potentially relevant factors, and the difficulty of deciding which ones are truly relevant.

- The extent and frequency of changes in foreign market conditions. Often changes which are widely expected by local people (because they can read the clues well) are not apparent to foreigners, so that competitors in the foreign market are almost always better informed than foreign firms.

- The fact that the initial screening process relies on information which is published in the exporting firm's home country. Data for some countries is unreliable, and for most countries will be seriously out of date: the basis on which statistics have been collected will differ, with different factors being included for each country, so that 'educated guesses' will often need to be applied. For example, population age categories might vary: 'young' people might be defined as being aged under 15, from 13 to 18, from 10 to 20 and so forth. This makes comparisons extremely difficult.

A mitigating factor has been the Internet, and in particular sites such as the American CIA website which contains standardised information on each country. Unfortunately the data available is relatively limited, and is not likely to be very relevant to specific industries.

Table 9.2 Stages of developing a market attractiveness index

Stage	Explanation
Establish the criteria to be used for selecting countries	Criteria might include a significant proportion of the population wealthy enough to afford the product, a safe country to do business in, a country where the market should be easy to enter, or any of a dozen possible criteria.
Relate the selected criteria to appropriate variables	Wealth of the citizens might be linked to gross domestic product of the country, but might also be related to wealth concentration – there are more millionaires in India than there are in the UK, simply because the wealth is more concentrated. Relating criteria to variables which can be measured (or gleaned from published research) will involve assessing market potential, entry and operating costs and the competitive environment.
Determine the relative importance of each variable	This may involve obtaining advice from local contacts in the target market, considering which variables are most important for reaching corporate objectives, and considering the entry barriers to various national markets. Weightings are applied accordingly.
Evaluate each country and establish a rank order	Calculating the scores for each target market against the set of variables offered is straightforward, provided the weightings have been correctly evaluated and applied.
Conduct in-depth studies on highest-ranking countries	Having calculated the relative scores of the countries based on published records, managers can assess which countries appear to be the most promising and can act accordingly by carrying out further, first-hand, investigations.

Far and away the biggest problem with market screening techniques is that they require a great deal of arbitrary judgement on the part of managers. Selection of factors, and the weighting of factors, is purely speculative: the fact that the final outcome is presented numerically makes it appear to be a credible, scientific approach, but since the data going in is based on judgements by managers, the results are also simply based on managerial judgements. Having said that, market screening techniques can be a useful tool for clarifying management thinking and ensuring that all factors are taken into account, particularly if several people are involved in the process of deciding on the factors and their weightings.

A growing factor in globalisation is the existence of transnational market segments. These are groups of consumers with similar needs who inhabit different countries. This may occur because of migration (for example the substantial Malaysian and Chinese communities in Australia and British Columbia), because of similarities of age (as in the world youth market) or because of similarities in lifestyle (the international executive market). There is some debate about whether these segments exist in a real sense: some commentators say that they only exist because the members have no choice (Kjelgaard and Askegaard 2004).

Detailed information on global market segments is, of course, difficult to collect, because each country operates as a separate entity for the collection of statistics. From a conceptual viewpoint, the truly marketing-orientated company which wishes to go international should be looking for global segments rather than dividing up its customers according to country of residence. Country of residence is becoming less and less relevant as time goes by – mass migrations and foreign travel are having profound effects on the tastes and needs of consumers throughout the world, with ethnic segmentation growing steadily less easy to apply (Jamal 2003). Furthermore, people's desire for novelty is also driving the adoption of products from different cultures, so that items which are rooted in one ethnic context often sell well in other countries (Grier, Brumbaugh and Thornton 2006).

Figure 9.6

Global segmentation

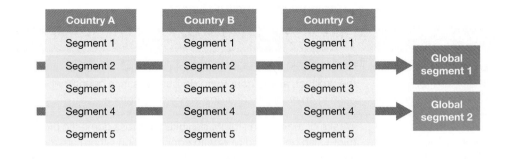

Strategy is about developing competitive capabilities and finding a competitive position within the marketplace. In international markets, the competitive capabilities that the firm has in one country may not be the same as those it has in another country: equally, the competitive position a firm adopts in one country may be different from that held in another. For example, Stella Artois beer is regarded as a standard, generic brand in its native Belgium, but in the UK it is marketed as a premium brand. Interestingly, the television advertisements for the beer are made predominantly in French, presumably as a way of increasing the apparent sophistication of the beer, but the brewery is in fact in Leuven, a predominantly Flemish-speaking city.

Firms wishing to enter a given overseas market will need to consider the same environmental issues as they would consider periodically within their home markets, but a key issue in global marketing is the degree to which the company is prepared to standardise its products and marketing approach (see Figure 9.7). There are five basic strategic stances available, as shown in Table 9.3.

Firms might decide on a globalisation strategy by which the company's products, attitudes, brands and promotion are standardised throughout the world, with global segments being identified, or conversely might decide on a customisation strategy whereby the company adapts its thinking (and marketing) to each new market. The companies which are most likely to seek a globalisation policy are those whose products are not culturally specific, and whose promotions can be readily understood throughout the world.

Research shows that relatively few companies standardise their advertising (Harris 1996). Of the 38 multinational companies surveyed, 26 said that they used standard

Global Strategy

Poor homme

Figure 9.7

Product/promotion strategy

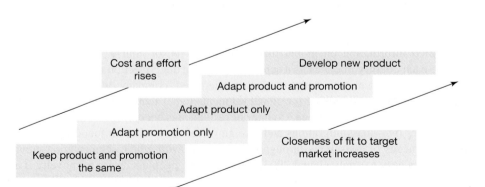

Table 9.3 International marketing strategies

Strategy	Explanation
Keep product and promotion the same	This strategy minimises entry costs, but relatively few firms have achieved success this way. Coca-Cola uses this approach, selling the same core product worldwide and using broadly the same promotional campaigns. This is possible for US companies because Hollywood has made the world aware of American icons and cultural norms, so that the promotions are comprehensible worldwide.
Adapt promotion only	The product remains the same, but the promotion is adapted to local cultural norms. Provided the product is acceptable in the local market, this approach works well and is commonly used.
Adapt product only	Some detergent manufacturers use this approach. The product itself is reformulated to take account of local water supply, local washing habits, and local washing machine designs. The promotion can remain broadly the same, because the brand values remain the same.
Adapt both product and promotion	Sometimes the product and the promotion need to be adapted. This was the case with the Procter and Gamble brand, Cheer, which had to be adapted for the Japanese market to allow for the extra fabric softeners the Japanese use. The promotion emphasised that the product works well in cold water, since most Japanese wash their clothes in cold water.
Invent new products	If existing products cannot meet the conditions in the target market, a new product must be invented. For example, the clockwork radio was invented for use in countries where mains power supply is not universal, and batteries are expensive or hard to obtain.

advertisements, but only four of these were completely standardised. The others varied from limited standardisation (perhaps only the corporate logo remaining the same) through limited standardisation of key elements, through to standard execution with some minor adaptations. Table 9.4 shows the factors which contribute to standardisation of the marketing programme (Cavusgil and Kirpalani 1993).

Political and legal environmental factors are important because they are likely to be different from those obtaining in the home market. For example, because alcohol is illegal in Saudi Arabia, hotels need to be designed and equipped differently. Also, the pricing structure of the hotels needs to different, since there will be no bar receipts, but there will be increased sales of coffee and soft drinks.

Technical and social norms differ according to culture and infrastructure. For example, in Zambia credit card transactions are routinely conducted using machines which take a carbon-copy impression of the card. This technology was largely superseded in the UK several years ago by the use of chip and PIN numbers, but because of the poorer telecommunications infrastructure in Zambia the system continues to be used. Technological norms sometimes persist due to cultural differences – for example, in Spain washing machines are often kept in outside areas because that is where the clothes are pegged out, so plastic covers are widely available to protect the machines from occasional rainfall. Having the washing machine in the kitchen is somewhat unusual, whereas in the UK that would be the logical place to keep a washing machine, since it makes the plumbing task a great deal easier.

Geographical similarity between countries contributes to standardisation for many products. For example, car manufacturers sometimes provide gearboxes with different gear ratios according to whether the car is to be sold in mountainous areas or flat country: also, cars intended for hot climates might typically be supplied with air conditioning, but not heaters (this is common practice in Brazil).

Table 9.4 Factors in
standardisation

Macro environmental factors	Similarity of legal requirements
	Political sensitivity
	Technical and social norms
	Geographical similarity
Product	Nature of the product
	Product uniqueness
	Cultural specificity
Market	Stage of the life cycle
	Degree of urbanisation
	Structure of distribution system
	Degree of technical orientation
	Price sensitivity
Internal environment	International experience
	Attitude of corporate management
	Goals of internationalisation
	Costs of research and development

Figure 9.8

Elements of culture

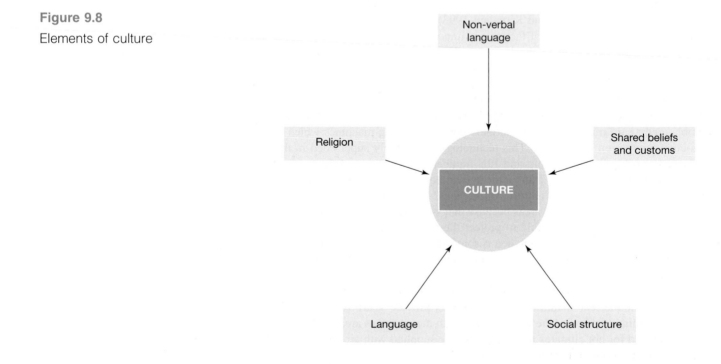

Culture

Culture is obviously a major consideration when crossing national boundaries: managers typically underestimate the possible impact of cultural differences, causing a 'shock' effect (Pedersen and Pedersen 2004). Culture is easier to recognise than define, but a nation's culture represents a collective frame of reference through which a wide range of issues and problems are interpreted. It determines how symbols, sounds, pictures and behaviour are perceived and interpreted by individuals and affects socialisation, friendship patterns, social institutions, aesthetics and language (Deyliner 1990, Ferraro 2001, Usunier 1993). Culture consists of the following main elements:

- *Religion.* Even if the bulk of the population is non-practising, the prevailing religion permeates the culture: this is the case with Christianity in Britain and with Islam in Turkey.

- *Language.* The language shapes the nation's thought, because some concepts are difficult (or impossible) to express in some languages, while others are easily expressed. For example, the Greek word for 'foreigner' (*xenos*) is also the word for 'guest'. When Greeks needed a word for 'foreigner' which did not imply guest status, they had to adapt a word from English – 'touristikos'.

- *Social structure.* This may range from the rigid caste structure of India through to the so-called 'classless society' of Australia. Social structure also includes gender roles and family patterns: the Indian practice of giving and lending family gold to a new bride purifies her, and also binds her to the new family (Fernandez and Veer 2004).

- *Shared beliefs and ethics.* Beliefs about what is and is not acceptable behaviour are largely cultural. Most (but not all) of these beliefs derive from religious principles.

- *Non-verbal language.* This includes gestures and body language: while some gestures are universal (for example smiling) most are not. Even nodding the head changes its meaning across national boundaries: in most of Europe an up-and-down nod means agreement, but in Greece a toss of the head accompanied by a click of the tongue means 'no'. Even smiling varies: Japanese people smile less in public than they do in private, whereas Americans smile more in public than they do in private.

Culture helps individuals to define concepts. A concept is a conscious linking together of images, objects, stimuli or events. Individuals receive huge numbers of messages, so the brain needs a system for classifying them into groups, which can then be dealt with efficiently. For instance, apples, oranges and bananas are all separate and unique items, but the brain can categorise them into a single concept of 'fruit'. Conceptualisations help the individual to manage data, identify relations among events and objects, and to discover similarities and differences that enable comparison of items of information. This is vitally important for the design of advertising images because culturally based conceptualisations can determine how a message is interpreted, and also how the message recipient responds to its contents. A particular example is the gender of brands. In languages where all nouns are either masculine or feminine (e.g. Spanish) a brand name can acquire gender (Coca-Cola is feminine, for example). This can affect consumer perception of the brand quite dramatically (Yorkston and deMello 2004).

National media that carry advertisements are themselves influenced by a country's culture. This can manifest itself in the following aspects of the national culture:

- The spoken and written language used. Even within a single country, these can vary according to social class or region.

Marketing in Practice
Watch Your Language!

The story goes that a major washing powder manufacturer produced a series of billboard advertisements for the Middle Eastern market in which a pile of dirty washing was shown on the left of the advert, followed by a packet of detergent in the middle and a pile of clean washing on the right. Unfortunately, the company had forgotten that Arabic reads from right to left – so the advert apparently showed that the detergent made clean clothes dirty, rather than the other way round.

Then there is the story that the slogan 'Come alive with Pepsi' translates as 'Come back from the grave with Pepsi'. Or that 'Avoid embarrassment – use Parker Pens' translated as 'Avoid pregnancy – use Parker Pens'.

Such cultural errors are common – but many of the stories are probably untrue. They still make good stories, and good cautionary tales for would-be international marketers.

- Whether a country has a tabloid press. The existence of a cheap, downmarket newspaper has an effect on who the message is aimed at, and also the content of the message.
- The editorial content of magazines, newspapers and broadcast media.
- Attitudes adopted by the media towards national issues (manifest in non-coverage of 'taboo' subjects, adoption of ideological lines etc.

Culture affects what people buy (taboos, local tastes, historical traditions etc.), when they buy (e.g. the spending boom around Christmas in most Christian countries), who does the purchasing (men or women) and the overall pattern of consumer buying behaviour. Culture can also affect consumer behaviour in relation to:

- Which consumer needs are felt more intensively.
- Which family members take which purchasing decisions.
- Attitudes towards foreign-supplied products.
- The number of people who will purchase an item during the introductory phase of its lifecycle.
- The segmentation of national markets.

On a wider level, cultural influences are evident in some aspects of a country's demographic make up. For example, household size is culturally determined. In Western Europe it is common for young single people to set up homes independently of their parents, whereas in many other cultures young people (especially women) only leave their parents' homes when they marry. Also, in Northern European countries the family is usually defined as the parents and their children, whereas in many countries unmarried aunts, uncles, cousins and so forth would live in the same house as the nuclear family. Kinship patterns, social mobility and social stratification are all culturally based, and all have an effect on purchasing behaviour as well as on responses to marketing communications.

At the same time, it is important to realise that culture only represents one aspect of the environment within which the firm operates. Political considerations and/or economic laws of supply and demand often outweigh cultural effects (Bangeman 1992), and some research indicates that in business-to-business markets cultural effects are far less important than language barriers, political barriers, geographic distance, technological differences and many other factors (Pressey and Selassie 2002).

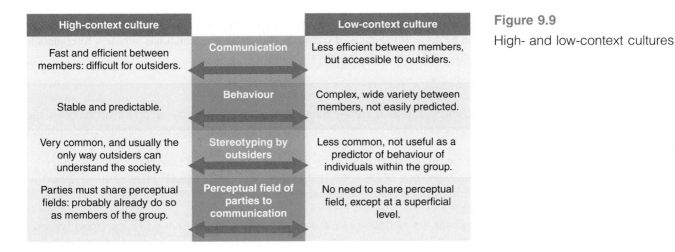

Figure 9.9
High- and low-context cultures

Models of culture

Three main approaches to the analysis of culture have been developed:

1 *Taxonomies of culture*. Dividing cultures into different levels and/or into high-context or low-context cultures.
2 *Lifestyle analysis*.
3 *Identification of cultural universals*. These are the aspects of culture found in all societies. Examples of cultural universals include bodily adornment, courtship, household hygiene, sexual taboos, gift giving and status differentiation (Murdock 1945).

A **high-context culture** is one in which the norms and values are deeply embedded within its members and not expressed in any explicit manner (Hofstede 1980). People sharing the same high-context culture do not feel any need to explain their thoughts and behaviour to each other, so they can rely heavily on non-verbal communication. Characteristics of high-context culture are as follows:

high-context culture A culture which is homogenous and has rigid rules.

- Communication within the high-context group is fast and efficient, but can break down in relation to outsiders who may not be able to understand what the group believes or is talking about.
- Behaviour within a high-context group is stable and predictable.
- The nature of a particular high-context group is likely to be understood by outsiders only by stereotyping the group as a whole.
- For effective communication to occur, all parties need to share the same perceptual field.

High-context cultures are orthodox, conservative and totalitarian: there is little room for personal expression within high-context groups, but on the plus side everyone has a clear understanding of what their role is and what they can expect from others within the group.

Low-context cultures, on the other hand, are characterised by the following features:

low-context culture A culture which is heterogenous and has tolerant rules.

- They are individualistic rather than collectivistic.
- Members communicate using clearly coded messages.
- Members' values, attitudes, perceptions and patterns of behaviour are diverse and liable to change quickly.

The United States and most of Western Europe have low-context cultures. Because of mass migrations and world travel, citizens of these countries have been exposed to many

cultural differences and tend not to assume that their own culture is the only way things can be done. Inhabitants of countries such as Japan, which has very few foreigners living there, tend to have high-context cultures.

The whole point of globalisation is that it makes us all more like each other: at the same time, world travel has given us a taste for the exotic. So why should we pander to local cultures? Having something very foreign on offer might be exciting for them!

After all, American firms have done extremely well by being as American as possible. Likewise, Dutch people enjoy Indonesian food, Americans have literally millions of Mexican restaurants, the most popular restaurants in Britain are Indian or Bangladeshi, and even in France, Chinese restaurants are springing up throughout the country. After all, nothing is as culturally specific as food!

On the other hand, the Mexican food served in Idaho or Wisconsin is far removed from the Mexican food served in Yucatan or Ciudad Mexico: the Indonesian food served in Haarlem is not the same as the Indonesian food served in Jakarta, nor is the Indian food served in Brixton the same as that served in Bombay (except for Leopold's restaurant and bar on Colaba Causeway, which is aimed at British tourists). So perhaps it isn't so much that we like foreign food, but more that we like the idea of eating foreign food!

Language and non-language influences

There are around 3000 languages and 10 000 dialects in the modern world. Many countries have several languages, often with a single 'lingua franca' spoken by everybody and a number of local languages. Many former colonies of European countries (for example India and most West African countries) use English or French as the official language of Government, and tribal or regional languages as the languages of ordinary day-to-day life.

An interesting development in recent years has been the adoption of English as the official corporate language of some multinationals, even when the country of origin of the company is not English-speaking. For example, Philips in the Netherlands conducts intra-firm communication in English, so company executives are expected to speak English as a matter of course. English has become the world business language in any case.

Many aspects of a community's culture are reflected in the language it uses. A detailed knowledge of a language reveals much about the relevant culture. Equally, ignorance of the subtleties of a language creates opportunities for absurdities in translation, mistaken messages and ambiguity. For example, linguistic communities have extensive vocabularies to describe activities and surroundings which are important to them (weather and agriculture in some societies, industry and commerce in others). Concepts of time, whether people approach issues analytically or intuitively, degrees of fatalism or of being organised and methodical, are all reflected in language.

Non-linguistic communication occurs through body language and gesture, but also through people's use of space. For example, standing close to someone is regarded as polite behaviour in the Middle East, but not in the USA, where it is regarded as a violation of personal space. Handholding and other forms of physical contact have different meanings in different cultures – in much of Africa it is normal to see friends walking in the street holding hands, but not lovers: the reverse would apply in most of Europe. These factors have very clear implications for advertising, and even for product adaptation.

The product itself will not need to be adapted if it is not culturally specific. Obviously a manufacturer of Buddhist prayer-wheels is unlikely to find a large market in a Moslem country, but there are more subtle examples: for instance, French people tend to spend more of their time outdoors than do British people, and therefore expect to find a wide range of high-quality garden furniture in their hypermarkets. French people are more

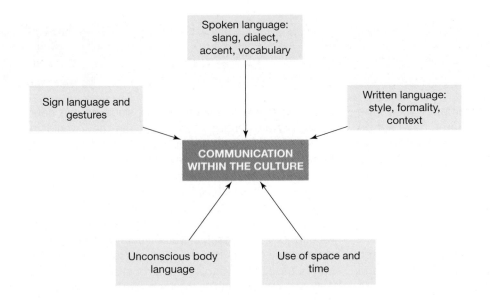

Figure 9.10

Language in context

prepared to spend large sums on products used outside the home. On the other hand, personal stereos and mobile telephones are not especially culturally specific, apart from the need to translate instructions into the language of the target country.

If the product is unique, it can remain standardised for all countries. If it has close competitors this is less likely to be possible: in order to offer something different to consumers in the target country, the product may need to be adapted substantially.

If a product is in the same stage of its lifecycle in two countries (for example, if it is growing rapidly in sales) the firm might be tempted to use a standardised promotional campaign. This could be a mistake if the product's growth is technology-driven in one market (for example it represents a major improvement over other products in the same market) and culturally driven in the other market (for example it has become the fashionable product to own).

The structure of the market itself contributes to the possibilities for standardisation. A highly urbanised country such as Holland or Singapore has very different characteristics from an essentially rural country like India, where more than half the population lives in villages or small towns. In the urbanised environment, a campaign can reach a large number of people relatively easily: rural countries require different techniques in order to reach enough people to make the campaign worthwhile.

The structure of the distribution system affects the degree to which products can be made available in specific markets. This applies both to the physical distribution of goods and to the structure of the retail and wholesale markets. For example, Spain has a large number of small grocery shops located in villages. The villages themselves often have extremely narrow streets, so physical delivery has to be made using small trucks which are able to negotiate winding alleyways. Order quantities are also much lower than is the case in countries like the UK, where food distribution is dominated by major supermarket chains such as Tesco and Sainsbury's. For manufacturers, this has implications in terms of packaging and shipping goods.

The degree to which the market is technologically orientated has a greater or lesser effect depending on the technology of the product. Markets such as the United States, which is heavily technology orientated, are more accepting of technologically advanced products. This is particularly apparent in fields such as computers, where the USA has overtaken the UK as the most computer-literate country in the world. For less technology-orientated markets computers need to be made simpler, and fewer accessories can be sold until the market becomes more used to the technology.

E-Marketing in Practice
Global E-tailing

Global marketing is apparently simple through the Internet, and many specialist stores have set up websites in the hopes of doing business worldwide. After all, if you have a website, people can access your products from anywhere in the world. Software firms have found this particularly useful: many of them operate their helplines, and even their sales, online, although few have succeeded in eliminating the salesforce (Moen, Endresen and Gavlen 2003).

In practice it is not that straightforward, as Amazon have found. Amazon began in the United States, and found that people from elsewhere in the world were accessing the site and ordering books – which was fine, except that the shipping costs often outweighed the savings made by online ordering. So Amazon established a presence in their major markets – there are separate websites for the UK, Germany, Japan, Canada, Austria and a separate site for Spanish books (although this site actually operates in English and runs from the United States). These physical presences in other markets have

been expensive to establish, and since people cannot easily browse through the books (as they would in a bricks-and-mortar bookshop) people tend only to buy books with which they are already familiar.

Many people visit the Amazon sites simply to research what is available, with no intention of buying. The sites are expensive to maintain, with constant updating being necessary, and the end result is that Amazon has yet to recoup its early losses. Twelve years of trading without making any money is hardly a success story – yet Amazon is easily the world's largest bookseller, so one can only assume that, in the long run, profits will follow.

Amazon are not alone in finding that cultural differences get in the way of e-tailing. Websites are usually firmly rooted in the country of origin, and even when companies develop country-specific websites they do not adapt them much (Singh, Kumar and Baack 2005). For services it is easier to adapt the site, so firms are more able to do this, but most still retain the main features of their home sites (Okazaki 2005).

Figure 9.11

Adapt or standardise?

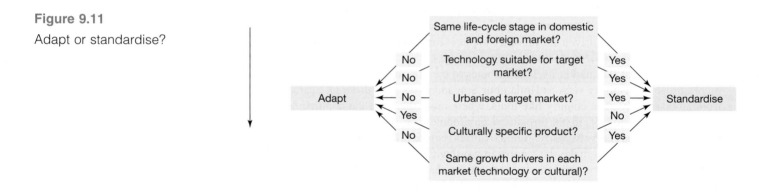

The internal environment of the company includes such factors as degree of international experience, attitude of management and goals of internationalisation. The international experience of the management needs to go beyond simply having travelled extensively. Managers need to have direct experience of doing business in the target countries. Inexperienced managers are more likely to believe that they can standardise the product, the promotion or both. The company's reasons for internationalising in the first place may affect standardisation: companies which are internationalising simply to dump excess production will not adapt the product, and may well not adapt their promotion either. Finally, some companies face high research and development costs – drug

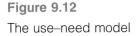

	USE CONDITION	
BUYER NEED	**Same**	**Different**
Same	Same product, same promotion Cost = 1	Adapt product, same promotion Cost = 3
Different	Same product, adapt promotion Cost = 2	Adapt product, adapt promotion Cost = 4

Unique promotion

Cost = ?

Figure 9.12

The use–need model

companies are unlikely to adapt products for overseas markets simply because of the cost of reformulating, testing and obtaining Government approval for new drugs.

Making the decision as to whether to standardise or not requires an evaluation of the overall situation in the market. One technique for doing this is the use–need model (Keegan 1989). This model evaluates the market need that is met by a given product against the way the product is used. Five combinations of use and need determine the degree of product and communication standardisation that is desirable, including consideration of their relative costs (see Figure 9.12).

If a product is to be used differently in each market, but fulfils the same basic need, adapting the product and standardising the communication would be an appropriate decision. On the other hand, if the use is the same but the need is different, a different communications programme should be put in place, although the product might be standardised. For example, mobile telephones in the UK are often used as a social tool, keeping friends in touch with each other. In some other countries the mobile telephone is seen as being essentially a business tool, with little use in a social context.

After a corporate policy has been developed and the products and markets have been identified, the managers need to decide which countries are to be targeted. This will require the same type of environmental audit as was described in Chapter 2: an assessment of the micro- and macro-environments within the target countries. The basic strategic decision to be made is whether the company can find a competitive position within the target markets, in other words whether the firm can marshal the capability to compete effectively against firms which are already established in the market.

Having established that there is a competitive position which can be filled, the company can examine the tactics and marketing mix decisions which need to be implemented.

Market Entry Tactics

Exporting is the practice of manufacturing a product in one country and selling it in another. Exporting is generally favoured by Governments, because it is helpful for the balance of payments: Governments need foreign currency coming into the country in order to fund essential imports such as raw materials and essential components, otherwise they need to raise interest rates in order to attract deposits of foreign currency into UK banks. The mechanisms for this are somewhat complex and outside the scope of this book, but suffice it to say that Governments in most countries offer a great deal of help to exporters.

Figure 9.13

Export routes

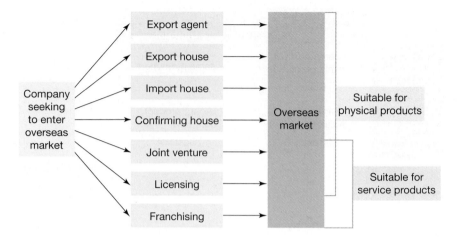

The problem with exporting is that the company loses control over the marketing of its goods. This can lead to problems later on as the company's reputation may be badly affected by inappropriate (or even unethical) marketing practices. The main advantage of exporting is that it is relatively simple once the company has found an importer in the target country. This is because the importer knows the local market, understands local consumers, understands the legal position on doing business in the country, and is unlikely to make the kind of mistakes a foreign company might make when starting out in a new country. There are several different ways in which export deals can be set up, as follows:

export agent A person or company that takes responsibility for organising the export of goods without taking title to the goods.

- **Export agents** bring together buyers and sellers, and are paid on commission: they do not actually buy the goods themselves. There is a wide variety of types of agent, and the use of agents is governed by different law in each target country: some care needs to be exercised when using an agent. For example, in France agents are protected by employment law and cannot be arbitrarily dismissed, whereas in the UK an agent is regarded as self-employed and is subject only to the terms of any contract agreed between the agent and the manufacturer. In some countries agents are salaried, particularly in cases where they are dealing with major capital goods such as machine tools or agricultural machinery.

export house An organisation which buys goods for sale abroad.

- **Export houses** buy goods for export to foreign countries. These are companies with contacts abroad, and with knowledge of the foreign markets in which they do business. In some cases export houses buy on the instructions of a foreign customer – for example, they may have been contacted by a foreign firm looking for a components supplier. In other cases they simply buy on their own account and find buyers in the foreign country.

import house An organisation which buys goods in from abroad.

- **Import houses** seek products in other countries and buy them for resale in their own countries. Sometimes importers will visit exhibitions and trade fairs in other countries looking for products to import (see Chapter 18). In some cases, overseas retailers maintain buying offices in other countries (for example Sears of the United States maintains a buying office in London).

confirming house An organisation which handles the mechanics of exporting and importing on behalf of manufacturers or buyers.

- **Confirming houses** arrange the details of credit and shipping on behalf of importers and exporters. The confirming house can arrange for the exporter to be paid, and will collect payment from the importer: one of the major barriers to exporting is the problem of credit. Many firms are reluctant to trust a foreign firm about whom they know nothing, and to risk the problems of having to sue in a foreign court for their money. Confirming houses remove this problem.

● *Joint ventures or export clubs.* Sometimes it is possible to agree to share the risks with other firms in a similar or complementary business. A joint venture might involve getting together with a foreign firm – perhaps with reciprocal agreements to market each others' products – or with a same-nationality firm which is already established in the foreign market. Sometimes these deals involve piggy-backing, which is the practice of selling a complementary product to the same customers through the same sales force. For example, an office-equipment supplier might join with an interior design firm to offer a complete service in fitting out new offices.

● Licensing agreements. A manufacturer of goods which do not travel well (for example glass or some food products) might allow a foreign producer to use the firm's patents in exchange for a royalty fee. For example, Pilkington Glass now earns more money from licensing the float-glass technique abroad than they do from actually making glass. Licensing relies on the firm having good patents or other protection for its intellectual property.

● Franchising is similar to licensing, but is used for service industries. The franchisor allows the franchisee to use its branding and business systems in exchange for royalties. McDonald's, Holiday Inn, and Dyno-Rod are all examples of successful franchises.

licensing An agreement to use a firm's intellectual property in exchange for a royalty.

franchising An agreement to use a firm's business methods and intellectual property in return for a fee and a royalty.

Rather than exporting, a firm might decide to set up a branch or a subsidiary in the target country. The difference between the two is that a branch is a direct extension of the parent firm into the foreign territory, whereas a subsidiary is legally a separate business. For example, Disneyland Paris is a separate company from the Disney Corporation, even though it is part-owned by Disney and pays the bulk of its profits to Disney in the form of royalties and license fees.

Branches are easy to set up (and easy to remove) but complex tax situations can arise because some countries, for example Spain and the United States, relate the amount of tax payable by the branch to the worldwide profits of the parent company. Normally branches are concerned with the transport and storage of goods, marketing, providing after-sales service and liaising with local banks about credit for customers. Local assembly or manufacture would normally be carried out elsewhere.

Since branches are considered as part of the parent company, the profits and losses of the branch are treated as part of those of the parent company and are shown in the latter's accounts. Subsidiaries prepare separate accounts, even when the parent company owns a large part (or even all) of the subsidiary's shares. A comparison of branches and subsidiaries is shown in Table 9.5.

The biggest advantage of setting up a subsidiary is that it acquires a local character and demonstrates to competitors and customers that the firm has a real commitment to the market. This can be especially important in a business-to-business context, where the company needs to be credible in the eyes of its customers.

Figure 9.14 compares the situation between a German branch and a French subsidiary. The German branch is actually part of the parent company, and is under direct control, whereas the French subsidiary is a separate entity with its own shareholders, banking arrangement and marketing.

In some major equipment contracts such as the construction of power stations or dockyards a firm is unlikely to want

During the 1970s Fiat sold its obsolete technology to Eastern European countries.

Table 9.5 Branches vs subsidiaries

Branches	Subsidiaries
Parent liable for all debts.	Subsidiary is liable for its own debts.
Does not require its own capital or directors.	Can raise capital in its own name.
Special tax rules apply, depending on the country concerned.	Taxed as if it were a separate local business.
No company formation or winding-up procedures involved.	Usually incorporated as a limited company.
Accounts are incorporated into those of the parent company.	Maintains its own accounts independent of the parent company.
Losses can be offset against the parent's profits.	Accounts must be independently audited.
Branch employees can be (but need not be) regarded as employees of the parent corporation.	Employees are only employed by the subsidiary, with the rights and obligations of local employment law.
Assets can be transferred between the parent and the branch without incurring tax liabilities.	Shares in the company can be sold to outsiders.
Often there are low rates of tax on repatriation of profits.	Carries a local identity.
Branch profits may be taxed in the parent company's country even if they have not been repatriated.	Internal reorganisations can occur without having to report this to the foreign authorities.

Figure 9.14

Branches and subsidiaries

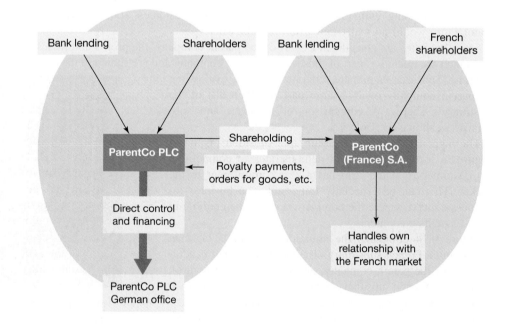

(or need) to establish a permanent base in a foreign country. In some cases these contracts are handled by agreeing a **turnkey contract**, in which the supplying firm builds the facility and operates it for a fixed period of time, eventually handing it over to local control. For example, during the 1970s the Fiat car company set up factories all over Eastern Europe as turnkey projects, selling off obsolete stamp mills and designs to Communist countries. This proved lucrative for Fiat, and allowed the client countries to develop their own car industries, which eventually became export industries for them.

Talking Point

Setting up factories for somebody seems like a fast way to create some extra competition. Why would a company help a low-wage economy establish itself with a modern manufacturing facility? Surely this is the road to ruin!

Or maybe the idea is *not* to establish a modern facility, but merely to provide some obsolete technology which will never succeed against the parent company's facilities. If so, isn't this a little bit unethical? Deliberately charging the foreign company a huge sum of money, and then setting them up to fail?

Perhaps the truth lies somewhere in between. Technology which is obsolete in one market may be just the latest thing in another – yet still not be able to compete outside its own area. In which case everyone is happy – at least for a while!

Turnkey contracts enable the client country to have a new system installed to a predetermined specification, acquiring new technologies quickly and relatively painlessly, and with a lower risk of failure. However, the contractor might be slow in handing over the facility to local workers, so that the client firm becomes totally dependent on the supplier.

Overseas manufacturing may be an option if there are high transportation costs, high external **tariff barriers**, import quotas or national rules on 'local content' (the percentage of the product which must be produced in the target country) which make exporting difficult. In a global context, overseas manufacture is likely to be based on costs of production: if it is cheaper to produce goods in a particular country, then that is where they will be produced regardless of end market. Two main options are available: the firm can set up its own factory in the target country, either as a branch or as a subsidiary, or it can contract the manufacture to a local firm. The latter option is more likely to generate economies of scale, but has the drawback that the company can lose control of its designs and technology. Often these are the only distinguishing features the firm has to bring to the new country, so their loss could be disastrous.

Another drawback to overseas manufacturing is the lack of economies of scale. Transportation costs are, in general, relatively low and tariff barriers are falling throughout the world, so the loss of economies of scale which come from large, automated production runs cannot be compensated for by lower transport costs and avoidance of tariffs. Many countries have come to realise that establishing high tariff barriers is usually counterproductive in the long run – Brazil's long-standing tariff against computer imports simply resulted in the country being left behind in the technological revolution.

'Screwdriver' establishments can sometimes overcome these problems. A 'screwdriver' factory is one which assembles components which have been manufactured overseas. Such an operation allows the company to label the product as manufactured in the destination country: it is difficult for national governments to define the point at which they are dealing with a foreign-made product. Japanese companies operating in Britain were accused of using screwdriver establishments to get round the European Union tariff barriers on imports of Japanese cars: content of such products must now be 65 per cent European to qualify as 'Made in the EU'. So contentious are these issues that the EU has set up a Committee on Origin to assess where the major part of the added value has come from.

Setting up and running a foreign presence is likely at some stage to involve sending staff from the home country to work in the foreign country for a substantial period of

turnkey contract An agreement whereby one firm establishes an entire business in a foreign country and subsequently hands over the business to another firm, in exchange for a fee and occasionally royalties.

tariff barriers Customs duties which make a product less competitive in an overseas market.

Figure 9.15
Screwdriver establishments

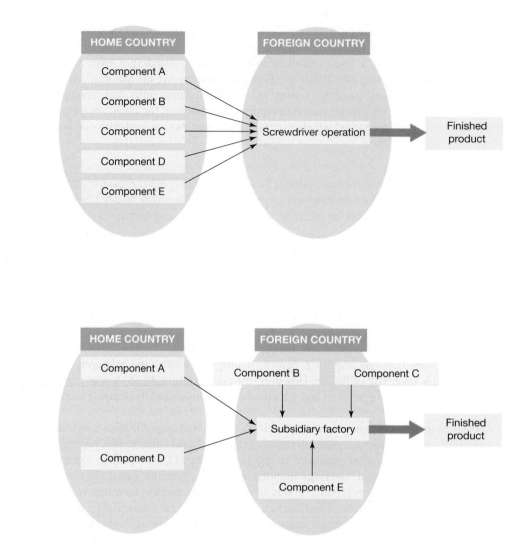

Figure 9.16
Overseas manufacturing
subsidiary

time. The number of expatriate staff has been in decline for some time now, however, at least in part because of the high cost of sending people to another country. An expatriate member of staff is likely to cost four times as much to employ as an equivalent member of staff in the home country (Boyacigiller 1991) and has limited effectiveness due to problems of language and culture. Failure of expatriates to settle effectively in the foreign country is common, due to the following factors:

- Children not making progress at school, either because they are studying in a foreign language, because they are in a special school for expatriates or because they have been left at home at boarding school.
- Concerns for family safety.
- Spouse not adjusting to the local physical and cultural environment (McEnery and Desharnais 1990). Many executives possessing qualifications suitable for expatriate assignments will have professionally-qualified spouses whose own career aspirations might make it difficult for them to move to a foreign country. In some cases the employing company needs to find a job for the expatriate's spouse as well as for the expatriate.

A further problem with employing expatriates in senior roles is that this blocks promotion prospects for local staff, who will then move to other companies, taking their new knowledge with them.

Getting employees to work well together in an international context involves two behavioural competencies (Vallaster and DeChernatony 2005). These are a clear brand vision, and facilitating both verbal and non-verbal social interactions.

Payment for Goods

An issue which is related to market entry decisions is that of payment for the goods. In most cases payment can be made in a mutually agreed currency: the astute marketer will accept payment in the currency of the customer's country, because this presents the minimum difficulty for the customer. Sometimes, however, the economy of the target country is such that the local currency is not acceptable. If the target country has a high inflation rate, for example, the currency can devalue quite dramatically between delivery of the goods and receipt of payment, so the exporting company may reasonably ask to be paid in a hard currency such as pounds, euros or US dollars.

In other cases, the country's Government may not have sufficient foreign exchange to allow importers to have access to hard currencies. In such cases the exporting firm may need to be creative. **Countertrading** is one way of overcoming the problem. In a countertrade deal no money changes hands. The exporter accepts payments in goods instead, then sells the goods for hard currency in another market.

countertrading Bartering of goods in international markets.

The system has many advantages for firms which are prepared to deal with the extra transaction costs. The value of the goods traded is often very much higher than their cash value, so that both parties gain: also, sale of the goods sometimes opens up contacts in third markets. Finally, many firms shy away from countertrade dealings, so there will be less competition in the markets concerned.

Countertrade can be used by exporters to offer favourable prices to potential customers in countries where there is fierce local competition. It may well be the case

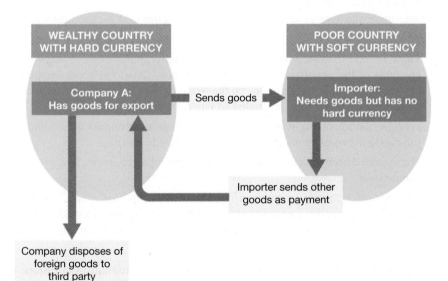

Figure 9.17

Countertrade in action

Marketing in Practice
McDonnell Douglas

During the 1990s many countries in Asia underwent major financial crises. The long period of rapid expansion that the 'Tiger' economies of the East had undergone suddenly turned to a collapse, leaving many countries short of the money to pay for goods they had already ordered.

McDonnell Douglas were required to accept a counterpurchase agreement when they sold eight F/A-18 fighter aircraft to the Thai government in 1995. Four-fifths of the contract was paid in hard currency, but McDonnell-Douglas found themselves the lucky owners of $12m worth of Thai rubber, ceramics, canned fruit, furniture and frozen chicken. The company disposed of most of the goods through a large Japanese trading company, and were allowed to sell the remainder in Thailand.

At the time, Thailand's balance of payments deficit was running at 8.1 per cent of gross domestic product – so there was little choice but to pay in frozen chicken. Equally, McDonnell Douglas was not well-placed to withstand the cancellation of such a large order – so the deal was a good compromise for both parties. Having said that, the real winner was the Japanese trading company that brokered the deal – they walked away with a pure profit, with no capital outlay whatsoever!

---

that a customer in a country where there are no foreign exchange problems would still prefer to countertrade, perhaps because of having access to a supply of a local export item.

Because countertrade typically involves dealing in goods which are unfamiliar to the exporter, intermediaries are crucial to the process. In some cases the intermediaries are able to offer complex deals involving several countertrade transactions. A variation of countertrade is **buyback**, which occurs when a firm supplies plant and equipment in exchange for a share of the future output of the equipment. For example, mining equipment might be supplied in exchange for payment in ore, to be supplied over a number of years. The exporter can sell the ore contract for immediate cash on the futures market, and thus recoup the investment immediately.

buyback An agreement on the part of a supplier to accept payment in finished products.

Counterpurchase deals are sometimes required by Governments of the target countries. In a **counterpurchase** deal, the company is paid in the currency of the target country, but must agree to spend the money on goods for export.

counterpurchase An agreement on the part of a supplier to accept payment in kind, or to spend the proceeds of the sale in the country in which the sale is made.

Countertrade and similar arrangements have been criticised for the following reasons, however:

● There is little evidence that countertrade actually improves the foreign exchange positions of the countries in which it is common. Often the goods supplied would have sold for much higher prices on the world market, which would have brought in more hard currency than is needed to pay for the imports.

● Foreign customers might be more interested in gaining unpaid distributors for their substandard export items than in buying the goods on offer.

● The system distorts the normal supply-and-demand mechanism, so it is damaging to competition.

● Disputes often arise over the quality of the goods supplied. There is considerable difficulty in agreeing a precise specification for the goods, and the exporter could be landed with shoddy goods that are difficult to sell. Slow-moving goods might impose a warehousing cost.

Countertrade has tended to decrease since the collapse of Communism in Europe and the increase in world trade, which has meant that most countries do not wish to find themselves outside the mainstream.

Summary

International marketing presents specific problems to marketers, but in fact the problems are no different from those faced by any company in a start-up mode. Managers need to understand that, in approaching a foreign market, they are in many ways starting with a clean slate – the environment, customers and competitors will probably all be different from the home situation. For most practical marketers this will be in itself a new situation, since they are unlikely to have been in at the start of the parent company, and will therefore have inherited most of the established customs and practice of the organisation. Also, most firms do not plan their growth – they simply solve problems as they arise, and eventually develop a way of functioning and an internal culture. International marketing enables marketers to plan from the outset – an opportunity not to be missed.

The key points from this chapter are as follows:

- Firms may go through a series of stages in developing their international marketing programme, or they may simply move straight to the most effective means of doing business in the foreign country.
- Markets might be selected for financial reasons, ease of access, convenience or a combination of all three.
- Profit potential is a function of the number of people who have a need for the product, their spending power and the level of competitive pressure.
- Cross-border comparisons in market research are likely to be badly flawed, especially in secondary research.
- Marketers can adapt the product, adapt the promotion, adapt both, or invent an entirely new product. It is rare that a product and its promotion can cross a border intact.
- Branches are easy to set up and easy to dismantle, but create problems in running efficiently because they do not demonstrate commitment to the market.

Chapter review questions

1 How does international marketing differ from domestic marketing?

2 What market entry methods are available?

3 How can overseas markets be assessed?

4 What are the cultural problems of marketing abroad?

5 What is globalisation?

6 How are marketing communications affected by crossing borders?

7 What is the difference between the Uppsala model and the stages of development model?

8 How is profit potential calculated?

9 What are the potential problems in sending expatriate managers to run foreign branches?

10 What are the advantages and disadvantages of countertrade?

Preview case revisited
Euro RSCG Revisited

Euro RSCG's work has won many awards from the advertising industry and from media owners, but the bottom line is, well, the bottom line! The company's adverts for Airbus Industrie, promoting the A380 Airbus, are one example. The A380 is the most expensive item ever advertised, at $230 million per aircraft. It is also the largest passenger aircraft ever built, and can therefore only be economical in a global market. Euro RSCG produced a series of advertisements comparing the Airbus to the seven wonders of the world, using straplines such as, 'Did the Pyramids have bedrooms?' 'Did the Statue of Zeus have a gym?' Enthusing potential passengers about the aircraft meant that airlines had to become interested – with the result that the A380 achieved the 50 initial orders needed to launch the project within five months of the campaign launch. A competing aircraft, the Boeing 747X Stretch, has yet to receive a single order.

Not all campaigns seek to encourage new customers. When Peugeot launched its first luxury sedan for many years, the 607, it aroused too much interest: too many people fancied having a test drive, despite having no interest (or indeed not enough money) to buy the car. Euro RSCG put together a campaign which combined direct mail, interactive and event marketing to identify and target the exact customers who would want the car, thus limiting the number of 'tyre kickers' who were just looking for a luxurious drive round for an hour or so.

Not all Euro RSCG's clients are global. When Belgian-based UCB Pharma developed a revolutionary new drug for treating epilepsy they had no global base at all. Euro RSCG knew that the global drugs market is dominated by very large companies with very deep pockets – and launching a drug which would comply with regulations, language and medical practice in so many countries was in itself a challenge. The agency used the slogan 'Simplifying Seizure Control' and concentrated its campaign on the decision-makers in the medical profession – the epileptologists and neurologists who would be prescribing the drug. Total sales for the first eight months topped $26 million, one of the fastest ever uptakes for a new drug.

Euro RSCG has certainly been a success story in its own right. Going global in advertising is not easy, and yet it is essential: If companies do not move outside their own countries to compete globally, they may be sure that foreign companies will enter their markets to compete with them. Euro RSCG makes sure that it, and its clients, are prepared.

Case study
International Herald Tribune

In 1887 the proprietor of the *New York Herald,* James Gordon Bennett, decided to create a European version of the paper. Based in Paris, the newspaper was intended to provide Americans abroad with all the news from home, but as time went by the newspaper developed a life of its own. In fact, when the New York paper closed its doors in 1966, the International edition continued independently, under the ownership of John Hay Whitney, who was then US Ambassador to Great Britain.

The *International Herald Tribune* has always been at the sharp end of communications. It was the first newspaper to be distributed by air (in 1928), was the first paper to be edited and typeset entirely on computer (1978) and the first to be transmitted electronically by satellite (in 1980).

As of 2008, the paper is printed at 33 sites around the world, has around 350 employees and a vast number of correspondents and contributors, and is edited in both Paris and Hong Kong.

The *IHT*'s circulation of around 250 000 is not large in newspaper terms: some newspapers number their readers in the millions. Even allowing for the fact that more than one person reads each issue, total readership only just scrapes over the half a million mark (compare this with the UK's tabloid, the *Sun,* which claims a circulation of over 4 million). What marks the *IHT* readership out, however, is that they are predominantly wealthy and influential.

IHT is widely available on long-haul flights, for example. Anyone who can afford the fare from the UK to Singapore is either fairly well-heeled or has a job in which the company is paying the fare. Either way, this is someone who is likely to be one of the world's movers and shakers. Also, the content of the paper is serious – this is not a paper the average gap-year student backpacker will seek out, although (again) those who do are likely to become movers and shakers in their turn. The paper speaks to the international executive or business person, providing a balanced view of world news plus some entertaining articles for the educated and sophisticated. Perhaps surprisingly, despite the newspaper's American origins, only 2 per cent of its readers live in the United States. This may be because Americans are no longer the world's great travellers, Europeans have long taken over this role, and indeed 60 per cent of the newspaper's readership is European, with 35 per cent coming from Asia.

Reaching this audience is by no means cheap, of course. A full-page ad in *IHT* can cost as much as $85 000, which means a cost-per-thousand readers of $1.70. (For comparison, the *Sun* charges around £60 000 for a full page, but has twelve times the circulation). The ability to deliver a wealthy and influential audience is a key plank in the *IHT* platform.

To back this up with figures, the *IHT* readership profile is as follows:

- Average age 50.
- 91 per cent are educated to degree level or above.
- 53 per cent live outside their country of citizenship.
- 98 per cent are in senior management jobs.
- Average household income is US$ 286 743.
- 72 per cent took at least three international flights in the last 12 months.

The overall picture is of a sophisticated, educated, wealthy group of global citizens – people who feel at home anywhere in the world. *IHT* has to have something for everybody within its pages if it is to live up to its title of 'The World's Daily Newspaper'. There is too much happening in the world to include everything, but what *IHT* does extremely well is provide the common denominator – the stories and articles which appeal to just such an international audience.

Questions

1 What policies would you expect *IHT* to have regarding segmentation?

2 How might *IHT* increase its circulation?

3 Why is *IHT* happy to appeal to an older audience?

4 What threats might there be to *IHT*'s position in the global marketplace?

5 Why would an advertiser be prepared to pay such high rates to advertise in *IHT*?

References

Bangeman, M. (1992): *Meeting the Global Challenge* (London: Kogan Page).

Boyacigiller, N. (1991): The role of expatriates in the management of interdependence, complexity and risk in multinational corporations. *Journal of International Business Studies* **21**(3), 357–81.

Cavusgil, S.T. and Kirpalani, V.H. (1993): Introducing products into export markets: success factors. *Journal of Business Research* **27**(1), 1–15.

Chetty, C. and Campbell-Hunt, C. (2004): A strategic approach to internationalisation: a traditional vs. a 'born global' approach. *Journal of International Marketing* **12**(1), 57–81.

Clark, I., III, Micken, K.S., and Hart, H.S. (2002): Symbols for sale – at least for now. Symbolic consumption in transituion economies. *Advances in Consumer Research* **29**(1).

Deyliner, N. (1990): The effects of religious factors on durable goods purchase decisions. *Journal of Consumer Marketing* **7**(3), 27–38.

Dunning, J.H. (1993): *The Globalisation of Business* (London: Routledge).

Fernandez, K.V. and Veer, E. (2004): The gold that binds: the ritualistic use of jewellery in an Indian wedding. *Advances in Consumer Research* **31**(1), 53.

Ferraro, G.P. (2001): *The Cultural Dimensions of International Business* (Harlow: Prentice Hall).

Gabel, T.G. and Boller, G.W. (2003): A preliminary look into the globalization of the tortilla in Mexico. *Advances in Consumer Research* **30**(1).

Grier, S.A., Brumbaugh, A.M. and Thornton, C.G. (2006): Crossover dreams: consumer responses to ethnic-oriented products. *Journal of Marketing* **70**(2), 35–51.

Harris, G. (1996): International advertising: developmental and implementational issues. *Journal of Marketing Management* **12**(6), 551–60.

Hofstede, G. (1980): *Culture's Consequences: International Differences in Work-related Values* (Beverly Hills, CA: Sage).

Jamal, A. (2003): Marketing in a multicultural world: the interplay of marketing, ethnicity and consumption. *European Journal of Marketing* **37**(11), 1599–620.

Keegan, W.J. (1989): *Multinational Marketing Management* (New York: Prentice Hall).

Kjelgaard, D. and Askegaard, S. (2004): Consuming modernities: the global youth segment as a site of consumption. *Advances in Consumer Research* **31**(1).

McEnery, J. and Desharnais, G. (1990): Culture shock. *Training and Development Journal* **44**(4), 43–7.

Moen, O., Endresen, I. and Gavlen, M. (2003): Executive insights into the use of the Internet in international marketing: a case study of small computer firms. *Journal of International Marketing* **11**(4), 129–49.

Muhlbacher, H., Dahringer, L. and Leihs, H. (1999): *International Marketing: A Global Perspective* (London: Thomson).

Murdock, G.P. (1945): The common denominator of cultures. In R. Linton (ed.) *The Science of Man* (New York: Columbia University Press).

Okazaki, S. (2005): Searching the Web for global brands: how American brands standardise their websites in Europe. *European Journal of Marketing* **39**(1/2), 87–109.

Pedersen, T. and Pedersen, B. (2004): Learning about foreign markets: are entrant firms exposed to a 'shock effect'? *Journal of International Marketing* **12**(1), 103–23.

Pressey, A.D. and Selassie, H.G. (2002): Are cultural differences overrated? Examining the influence of national culture on international buyer–seller relationships. *Journal of Consumer-Behaviour* **2**(4), 354–68.

Singh, N., Kumar, V. and Baack, D. (2005): Adaptation of cultural content: evidence from B2C e-commerce firms. *European Journal of Marketing* **39**(1/2), 71–86.

Usunier, J.C. (1993): *International Marketing: A Cultural Approach* (Harlow: Prentice Hall).

Vallaster, C. and DeChernatony, L. (2005): Internationalisation of service brands: the role of leadership during the international brand-building process. *Journal of Marketing Management* **21**(112), 181–203.

Whitelock, J. and Jobber, D. (1994): The impact of competitor environment on initial market entry in a new, non-domestic market. *Proceedings of the Marketing Education Group Conference*, Coleraine, July, pp. 1008–17.

Yorkston, E. and deMello, G. (2004): Sex sells? The effects of gender marking on consumers' evaluations of branded products across languages. *Advances in Consumer Research* **31**(1).

Further reading

There are many books on international business, most of them using the term 'global' rather than 'international'. Here is a selection.

Hennessey, H.D. and Jeannet, J.-P. (2003): *Global Account Management: Creating Value* (Oxford: John Wiley). This is a very comprehensive guide to global marketing, providing a well-structured, in-depth textbook on the topic.

For a more practitioner-orientated account of global marketing, Speare, N., Wilson, K. and Reese, S.J. (2001): *Successful Global Account Management* (London: Kogan Page) is a book which, although it intends to concentrate mainly on the personal selling and account management part of global marketing, actually gives a good deal of practical ideas on managing in a global market.

W.J. Keegan and B Schlegelmilch (2000): *Global Marketing Management: A European Perspective* (Harlow: FT Prentice Hall). This is a Europeanised version of Keegan's American text. As is often the case with European versions, the text has very high production values and is readable, with a great many useful features to help the learning process.

Part three
Strategy

This section is concerned with formulating appropriate strategies. The purpose of strategic planning is to put the firm in the best position possible to exploit the opportunities presented by the marketplace, while avoiding the threats presented by competitors and changes in the business environment.

Chapter 10 looks at creating competitive advantage through strategic planning. The chapter looks at strategy theory in general and marketing strategy in particular. It includes a discussion of the relationship between corporate strategy and marketing strategy, and at selecting the appropriate market stance and competitive moves. It also considers the issues surrounding problem-solving in complex environments and outlines some current thinking on the role of marketing in creating shareholder value.

Chapter 11 is concerned with establishing worthwhile relationships with customers. It looks at the value chain and value networks, customer retention and winback strategies, relationship marketing, the relationship between quality, service and value, and the relationship between all these issues and achieving strategic objectives.

The aim of this section is to lay the groundwork for the final and largest section of the book, which is about the practical issues of marketing. Although Part Three is the smallest section of the book, it contains the foundations for the more visible activities of marketing and places marketing in context within the firm.

Chapter 10
Creating competitive advantage

Learning objectives After reading this chapter, you should be able to:

1 Explain the strategic planning process.

2 Describe the relationship between marketing strategy and corporate strategy.

3 Explain how strategic plans are created.

4 Understand when to use formal planning and when not to.

5 Explain how strategic plans change when put into practice.

6 Explain the difference between aims and objectives.

7 Describe ways of dealing with complex problems.

8 Describe the three basic winning strategies.

9 Describe the implementation strategies for the three basic strategic positions.

10 Understand the role of innovation in strategic decision-making.

11 Understand the role of collaboration with competitors.

12 Explain the role of shareholder value in strategic planning.

Introduction

Strategy is not necessarily easy to define, and in particular the distinction between marketing strategy and corporate strategy is difficult to draw. This is especially true for organisations which consider themselves to be marketing-orientated, since one would reasonably expect that the marketing strategy would actually be the corporate strategy.

Because of the rapidly-changing nature of business life, strategy cannot be reduced to a simple set of rules, so managers need to consider the possibilities of creating new approaches. For marketers, the idea of differentiation is well understood, so the idea of adopting a different strategy from that of the organisation's competitors is straightforward and even obvious.

In most cases, marketing strategy is concerned with creating competitive advantage – in other words, improving the organisation's chances of surviving and prospering in the face of outside competition. All organisations compete for resources, customers, support from other organisations, employees and any of many possible factors which will enable the organisation to achieve its strategic objectives.

Preview case
Chardonnay

Contrary to what most people believe, Chardonnay is not the name of a wine – it is the name of a particular grape. The grape is similar to the Pinot grape (used to make Pinot Grigio, among others) and is the basic ingredient of many wines, including Chablis, Meursault and even champagne.

What has given the impression that it is a wine rather than a grape? The marketing activities of New World growers, for the most part. The European system of controlling wine production created a problem for wine producers in Australia, New Zealand, Chile, Argentina and California. Under the French 'Appellation D'Origine Contrôlée' regulations, a wine can only be called by the name of the region is comes from, and the annual production from that region is controlled – in other words, after a certain amount of wine from the region has been labelled as 'appellation contrôlée' any further production can only be sold as table wine, without the benefit of the 'appellation' branding. Similar systems exist in Germany ('Qualitatswein' designation) Spain, ('Denominacion de Origen' controls) and Italy ('Denominazione de Origine'). This left New World producers with nowhere to put their wines: under trade description laws, sparkling wine cannot be billed as champagne unless it actually comes from Champagne, in France. Calling the wines 'champagne style' only made the wines sound cheap and nasty – although many of them are substantially better than their European equivalents.

Developing a competitive advantage in a market which is several hundred years old is far from easy – especially when faced with international and national regulations which are designed to protect home producers from foreign competition. And yet the product itself – the wine – was of world-class standard.

© Sherri Camp | Dreamstime.com

Defining Strategy

Perhaps surprisingly, there is some disagreement among academics and practitioners about what strategy actually is. There are almost as many definitions as there are academics: here are some examples.

Strategies are means to ends, and these ends concern the purpose and objectives of the organisation. They are the things that businesses do, the paths they follow, and the decisions they take, in order to reach certain points and levels of success.

(Thompson 1997)

The positioning and relating of the firm/organisation to its environment in a way which will assure its continued success and make it secure from surprises.

(Ansoff 1984)

Strategy is making trade-offs in competing. The essence of strategy is choosing what not to do. Without trade-offs, there would be no need for choice and thus no need for strategy.

(Porter 1998)

An alternative approach is to define what strategy is and is not by listing its features. This is commonly done by describing what are tactics and what is strategy. Steiner and Miner (1977) drew up a list of the differences between strategy and tactics, as follows:

1 *Importance*. Strategic decisions are significantly more important than tactical ones.

2 *Level at which conducted*. Strategic decisions are usually made by top management.

3 *Time horizon*. Strategies are long-term: tactics are short-term.

4 *Regularity*. The formulation of strategy is continuous and irregular: tactics are periodic and fixed time, for example annual budget/plan.

5 *Nature of problem*. Strategic problems are usually unstructured and unique and so involve considerable risk and uncertainty. Tactical problems are more structured and repetitive and the risks easier to assess.

6 *Information needed*. Strategies require large amounts of external information, much of which relates to the future and is subjective. Tactical decisions depend much more on internally generated accounting or market research information.

7 *Detail*. Strategic decisions are broad, tactical decisions are detailed.

8 *Ease of evaluation*. Strategic decisions are much more difficult to judge.

In fact, all of the above features require further judgement to evaluate them. For example, how does one define importance? How does one define long-term or short-term? A year would be a long period in the fashion industry, but extremely short in the electricity generating industry.

Much of the conflict in the literature is actually the result of differing angles on the problem rather than fundamental conceptual difficulties. Strategic decisions are formulated at differing levels of the organisation, and certainly almost all decisions, at whatever level, may have strategic implications. Thus it may be argued that theoreticians offer differing theories because they are examining different parts of a complex structure.

The Nature of Strategy

Strategy has three dimensions: process, content and context (Pettigrew and Whipp 1991). Process is about the ways in which strategy comes about: content is about what is, or should be, the corporate strategy, and context is about the environment in which the strategy is to be implemented.

Strategy process is often assumed to be a linear progression through analysis of the situation the organisation is currently in, through formulation of a strategic plan, to implementation of the plan. In the analysis stage, the threats and opportunities inherent in the environment are examined. In the formulation stage, the strategic options are considered, and finally the strategy is implemented through a series of tactical decisions and activities. There is an underlying assumption that the whole process is rational – that managers act by reasoning through the situation and the possibilities, and then come to a logical conclusion.

Of course, this is often not the case at all. Managers act emotionally, decisions are made on an ad-hoc basis as crises arise and must be dealt with, and in any case good strategic thinking is creative and therefore not linear. The process is often messy: planners return to previous decisions and revise them in the light of experience, and may even go back to the analysis stage of the process as environmental changes appear. This is, of course, a sensible approach: carrying on blindly with an inappropriate strategy, ignoring

all changes around the organisation, will certainly lead to disaster. Strategy formation is therefore an iterative process, with the strategy growing incrementally in response to each new situation or each new idea from management.

If strategy has to be continually revised in the light of experience, what is the point of planning at all? Would it not be better simply to meet each problem as it arises and hope for the best?

Or perhaps we need a plan so that we have something to deviate from? General Eisenhower said that plans are nothing, but planning is everything – which maybe works fine in a war, but is it appropriate for business?

Strategy content will differ widely between organisations, and in fact each strategy should be unique, since it would be impossible to obtain competitive advantage were this not so. Strategy happens at three fundamental levels: the functional level, which is about strategic decisions made within the functional departments of the organisation, the business level or strategic business unit level, and the corporate level, which seeks to integrate the strategies from all levels of the organisation. In some cases there may be an even higher level where organisations group together to achieve a common overall goal. Trade organisations are examples of this, since they seek to improve the status of entire industries.

For many organisations, marketing is a function, and therefore the management would consider that marketing strategy belongs at the functional level. For more customer-orientated organisations, marketing strategy is the whole of the corporate strategy, so that marketing occupies the business level or the corporate level. At the industry level the strategy will almost certainly be a marketing strategy, even if only involving a public relations strategy.

In Figure 10.1, each level of the strategy feeds into each level above or below it in the hierarchy. Each level is influenced by environmental factors, and each level feeds into the overall corporate objectives (directly or indirectly). The interactivity of strategy is the main factor which makes formal planning difficult.

Figure 10.1

Levels of strategy

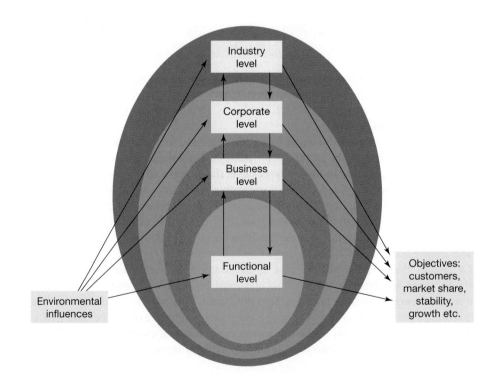

There are six dimensions of strategy (Hax 1990).

1 Strategy as a coherent, unifying and integrative pattern of decision.

2 Strategy as a means of establishing an organisation's purpose in terms of its long-term objectives.

3 Strategy as a definition of the firm's competitive domain.

4 Strategy as a response to external opportunities and threats, and internal strengths and weaknesses.

5 Strategy as a logical system for differentiating management tasks at corporate, business and functional levels.

6 Strategy as a definition of the economic and non-economic contribution the firm intends to make to its stakeholders.

Ultimately, strategy is what binds the organisation together and gives it direction.

Marketing Strategy and Corporate Strategy

If marketing strategy is regarded as residing at the functional level, marketers will only be concerned with manipulating the 7Ps (Booms and Bitner 1981). In this scenario, corporate strategy will stand above marketing strategy and will inform (or even dictate) the marketing strategy. If the firm is truly customer-orientated, the marketing strategy will in fact be the corporate strategy, since the company's whole approach is dictated by the marketplace, particularly customer needs (Webster 1992; McKinsey 1993). Some writers state that the market-orientated organisation is concerned not only with the interface between the firm and its customers, but with the relationships within the organisation (i.e. with employees) and with the relationships between the organisation and other organisations (Piercy and Cravens 1999).

In this model, every functional department of the organisation will be concerned with relationships rather than financial outcomes, presumably on the assumption that getting the relationships right will result in successful financial outcomes and enhanced long-term survival prospects. This might mean that the firm judges its success by the long-term loyalty of its customers rather than by the quarterly profit-and-loss statement, or it may mean that the personnel department recruits people who are already customer-orientated rather than people whose paper qualifications are outstanding. It will almost certainly mean that the production department will take its lead from the market researchers rather than from the scientific researchers.

Since the fundamental basis of the marketing concept is that organisations exist to satisfy the needs of the people and organisations on whom they depend for their survival, the marketing-orientated organisation will try to ensure that customers, shareholders, employees, suppliers and Government departments are all dealt with fairly. Managing the resulting conflicts of interest becomes a key factor in a successful strategy: need-satisfying objectives will take precedence over other objectives, since they are instrumental in achieving the most basic objective of all, which is the survival of the organisation.

Marketing management comprises the following elements:

1 Identifying needs among those on whom the organisation depends.

2 Developing methods of meeting those needs – providing products or services which do so.

3 Promoting those products to customers in order to demonstrate how their needs will be met.

Table 10.1 Levels and focus of organisational analysis in marketing

Strategic level	Unit of analysis	Examples of major issues	Examples of new organisational forms
Functional	Marketing sub-systems	Organising and coordinating sub-functions of marketing such as advertising, marketing research, sales operations.	Channel management. Logistics/services specialists.
Business	Marketing department	The department of marketing and internal structure of the marketing department. The integration of marketing sub-functions. Relationships with other functions.	Sector/segment management. Trade marketing. Investment specialists. Venture/new product departments.
Corporate	Divisional marketing responsibilities and group-wide marketing issues	Centralisation/decentralisation of marketing decision-making and relationship between central and peripheral marketing units.	Marketing exchange and coalition companies. Network organisations.
Enterprise	Strategic alliances and networks	External relationships and boundary-spanning with strategic marketing partners. Marketing 'make or buy' choices.	Partnerships. Alliances.

4 Handling the exchange processes which result.

5 Monitoring the overall process to ensure that changes in customer needs or competitive activity have not made the solutions inappropriate.

Piercy and Cravens (1999) offer a model which illustrates the level and focus of organisational analysis in marketing (Table 10.1).

One of the complexities inherent in this model is that there is a trade-off between forming competitive alliances and competing to meet customer needs. Marketing academics have consistently emphasised the need to generate competitive advantage by meeting customer needs better than the competition, but the Piercy and Cravens model seems to suggest that forming coalitions and partnerships at the corporate and enterprise levels will improve the prospects for survival. This has a certain logic to it: companies which do not compete with each other cannot lose out to each other. Presumably, though, organisations which collaborate rather than compete do not put the customer first, and therefore do not subscribe to the marketing concept.

Much depends on the breadth of definition of competition. A narrow definition (e.g. 'we are in the restaurant business') might mean entering into competition with other restaurants. A broad definition ('we are in the leisure industry') might mean forming strategic alliances with other restaurateurs to compete against the cinema industry or the sports-centre industry.

Modern leisure centres offer restaurants and bars as well as cinemas.

© Alex Segre/Alamy

Strategic Planning

Strategic planning is intended to generate a 'road map' for achieving the organisation's objectives. In most cases, this means obtaining some kind of competitive advantage: it may or may not be linked to profitability, since non-profit organisations also have strategies and also compete. The ultimate objectives may be linked to growth in market share, growth in shareholder value, achieving stability in an unstable market, developing a particular reputation in the industry, or any one of a large number of possible outcomes.

Figure 10.2 shows the traditional view of planning as cyclical in nature. The cycle continues indefinitely as the evaluation of the outcomes of previous plans and activities are used to inform the new strategic plans. The process may not always be as tidy as this, of course, particularly when firms are operating in conditions of continuous change.

Given the current emphasis on rapid change in most industries, planning may seem like a futile exercise. Plans are likely to be upset by technological changes, by competitor activity or by changes in legislation almost without any warning. On the other hand, if there is no road map, the organisation will lose its way very rapidly, and of course without having a clear idea of where the organisation wants to be, managers have no way of knowing whether their individual actions are helping or hindering.

There is no single rule for creating strategic plans. All managers carry out some planning, simply because they must ensure that resources are available in the right place, at the right time, and in the right quantities to ensure that objectives are reached. Equally, almost all managers are in the position of needing to manage change, since organisations must respond to changes in the environment. Managers therefore seek out opportunities to exploit and threats to avoid, playing to the strengths of the organisation and minimising the effects of its weaknesses.

In general, there are three approaches to planning: first, the fully-planned approach in which the organisation's future activities are detailed down to the finest level. At the opposite extreme, the adaptive model suggests that organisations change the strategy rapidly in the face of environmental changes, and by implication do not plan in detail or very far ahead. The third alternative approach is the incremental approach, in which an overall plan is in place but changes are made as circumstances change.

In the case of the fully-planned approach, planning may be formal, with many of the decisions already made or with established decision-making rules in place, or it may be

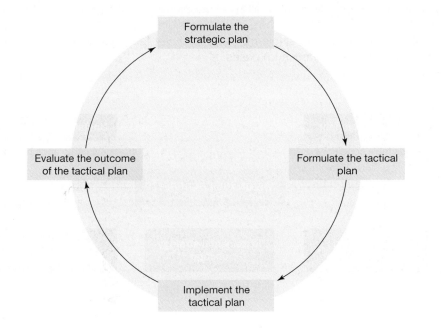

Figure 10.2

The cyclical nature of planning

informal and therefore carried out on an ad-hoc basis. Formal strategic planning works best in conditions of stability, where change is slow and where environmental conditions can be predicted fairly accurately. For example, the petroleum industry is fairly stable: the rules are laid down by the Organisation of Petroleum Exporting Countries, and by the seven largest oil companies. The number of producers is limited, and the oil companies control the process from extraction right through to delivery at the petrol pump. Demand is unlikely to vary very quickly, major competition is unlikely to enter the market unexpectedly, governments are unlikely to make major changes in legislation, and the companies themselves are powerful enough to control most of the potential changes which do exist. Oil companies are therefore able to plan years or even decades ahead with a fair degree of confidence.

On the other hand, the entertainment industry is extremely volatile. Consumer tastes are fickle, new competitors enter the market, fashions shift whether for nightclubs or for entertainers. Chaos theory (Stacey 1993) implies that intentional strategies are too inflexible for dealing with an inherently chaotic world, and therefore reliance on a tightly structured plan will lead to stagnation. Planning systems are useful in such circumstances, but are usually kept fairly loose and contain a lot of 'what-if' scenarios. This is more typical of adaptive strategic change.

Some organisations will be characterised by adaptive strategic change, in which managers throughout the organisation are empowered and encouraged to seek out new opportunities. The result of this is an increase in innovation at the business level, so that strategy develops from the bottom up: the rationale is that managers who are nearer to the customers (and other stakeholders) can respond much more quickly to changes in stakeholder needs. Adaptation to change will occur much more quickly in such organisations.

Many companies operating in an unstable environment rely on visionary leadership. The visionary leader (for example Sir Richard Branson of Virgin) has a clear idea of where the organisation is going and what the organisation stands for, and is able to communicate this to the employees of the organisation. Such leaders have a clear grasp of the products, services and activities which will be acceptable to the organisation's customers, suppliers, shareholders and other stakeholders.

Talking Point

Visionaries are often self-made, rising from poverty to huge wealth in a matter of a few years. Obviously visionary leadership works – so why don't all firms operate that way? After all, somebody sometime founded the firm, and presumably had dreams and the energy to turn them into reality!

Is it because there is a shortage of visionaries? Probably not – we all know people who have burning ambitions. Is it because visionaries can be hard to work with? Maybe. Or maybe we are losing sight of all the hundreds of people who start their businesses enthusiastically, energetically and single-mindedly, and yet fail anyway. Maybe visionary leadership only works in one in a thousand (or one in ten thousand) cases.

Figure 10.3

Planning and change

Incremental strategic change represents a half-way position between the fully-planned system and adaptive change models. The strategic leadership provides the overall direction, but strategies can and do emerge from within the decentralised system of the organisation. Managers meet regularly, both formally and informally, to discuss progress and to monitor environmental changes. They will plan new courses of action, and test them in small stages. The system works best in **organismic organisations** in which managers communicate freely and operate on a team basis: hierarchical organisations are less effective for implementing change. There is also an implication that the organisation must be tolerant of mistakes, which is of course not always the case: Mintzberg (1989) also states that managers must have access to a large amount of appropriate information, and must also be empowered to make the necessary changes in the organisation.

A major fire at the company's plant will also destroy the strategic plan.

The systems described above are not necessarily mutually exclusive: different divisions within the same organisation may be using different approaches. The management style of the people involved will also affect strategic planning: junior managers may well decide to ignore or pervert the overall strategic plan which has been handed down from the Board, perhaps on the grounds that what looks realistic in the boardroom is unworkable in the field. A rapid change in circumstances (for example, a major accident at a corporate factory) may result in the implementation of a predetermined crisis strategy, whereas another sudden crisis (entry of a foreign competitor into the market) may result in the scrapping of a detailed plan. Whatever happens, it is useful to remember that strategic planning does not happen in isolation: no battle plan ever survives first contact with the enemy, and no strategic plan is ever set in concrete. Planning is not a linear process, in other words.

organismic organisations Organisations which do not have a fixed structure: they adapt according to the task facing the organisation.

The Written Document

Sooner or later the strategy must be committed to paper. There are three categories of written statement, as follows:

1 *A vision statement.* This describes what the organisation is to become in the long term. The vision statement focuses on the values to which it is committed, and often sets appropriate standards of conduct for employees. The vision statement almost always contains marketing-led elements, such as a commitment to customer care or a pledge to become the market leader.

2 *The mission statement.* This contains the reasons for the organisation's existence, and states what the organisation seeks to achieve. Ackoff (1986) suggested that a mission statement should have five characteristics: it should contain a formulation of objectives that enable progress towards them to be measured, it should differentiate the company from its competitors, it should define the business that the company is in, it should be relevant to all stakeholders and it should be exciting and inspiring.

3 *The objectives statement.* This should lay down the immediate, long-term and medium-term objectives of the organisation. Usually these objectives will be linked to specific timescales. Obviously an objective must be measurable, or there will be

no way of telling whether it has been achieved. Also, if a given outcome cannot be measured, it is really an aim rather than an objective and should therefore belong in a mission statement or vision statement.

Each type of statement has its place in outlining and communicating the corporate strategy. The vision statement provides the basis for developing the organisational culture, the mission statement provides a checklist of what the organisation is for, and the objectives statement provides a set of criteria against which performance can be directly measured. Of the three documents, the objectives statement is the most likely to be changed over time, as old objectives are achieved and new objectives become necessary. As the environment creates new opportunities and threats, new objectives will be outlined, but the overall vision remains the same and the reasons for the organisation's existence remain constant.

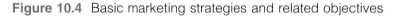

Setting Objectives

According to MacKay (1972) there are only three basic marketing objectives: to enlarge the market, to increase share of the existing market or to improve profitability within the existing market share. This somewhat simplistic view can be expanded by taking account of generic strategies for achieving those objectives. In setting objectives, one should move from the general to the particular, from the broad to the narrow and from the long-term to the short-term (McDonald 1984). This means that the objectives become more focused and therefore more attainable.

Figure 10.4 shows how MacKay's basic objectives fit with the generic strategies that flow from them.

Figure 10.4 Basic marketing strategies and related objectives

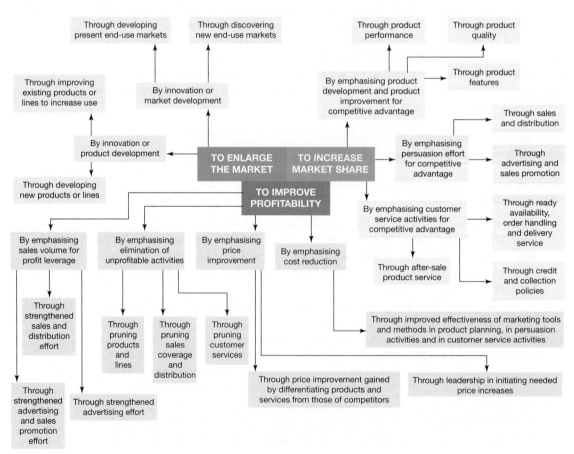

Some of the terminology used in the figure might cause disquiet among some marketers. For example, some of the objectives appear sales-orientated, and the idea of advertising being a strong persuasive force might seem a little odd in some quarters. The basic principle upon which the diagram is based still holds true: the core objectives need to be broken down into intermediate objectives, which in turn need to be broken down into initial objectives.

Complexity and Objective Setting

One of the problems of objective setting is that every problem impinges on every other problem. For example, Mason and Mitroff (1981) use the example of world problems to illustrate this principle. Figure 10.5 shows a matrix of world problems: try placing a tick in each box where you think the problems impinge on each other, in other words where the solution to one problem is related to the solution to the other problem.

When you have done this you will have few, if any, blanks. The exercise works equally well if the columns and rows are headed with business problems.

There are three main characteristics of complexity:

1 Any policy-making situation comprises many problems and issues.

2 These problems and issues tend to be highly interrelated, so that the solution to one problem creates other problems in its wake.

3 Few if any problems can be isolated effectively for special treatment.

Some problems are so complex that any solution creates many more problems. These problems are called 'wicked' problems because they tend to multiply (Rittel 1972), and the have the following characteristics:

1 *Inability to formulate the problem.* For example, planning an advertising campaign to run on TV this autumn is a tame problem, because the problem can be broken down into commissioning the production, setting the budget, booking the air time and so forth. Planning a product portfolio for 20 years' time is a wicked problem because there is no way of knowing what the competition will be doing, what the demographic profile of the consumers will be or what new technology might appear in the meantime.

2 *Relationship between the problem and the solution.* Tame problems can be formulated separately from the possible solutions. Wicked problems cannot be separated from the solution because the solution changes the nature of the problem.

3 *Lack of testability.* Solutions to tame problems will quickly reveal themselves to be effective or not. Solutions to wicked problems create too many other problems for a clear judgement to be made.

Figure 10.5 World problem matrix

	Peace	Energy	Starvation	Civil rights	Population	Balance of payments
Peace						
Energy						
Starvation						
Civil rights						
Population						
Balance of payments						

4 *Lack of finality.* Tame problems have solutions. Wicked problems create more problems so the solution will not end the process.

5 *Lack of tractability.* There may be several possible solutions for a tame problem, but these can be listed. For a wicked problem there is no exhaustive list available.

6 *Explanatory characteristics.* Tame problems can be stated as a gap between the desired state and the actual state. Wicked problems provide many possible explanations for the same discrepancy.

7 *Level of analysis.* Tame problems have an identifiable, natural form: there is no argument about the level of the problem. Wicked problems are symptoms of another problem, and therefore have no identifiable root cause: managers therefore cannot be certain that they are attacking the root cause rather than the symptoms of another problem.

8 *Reproducibility.* Tame problems can be abstracted and modelled: wicked problems are too complex for this.

9 *Replicability.* Tame problems have often cropped up before in some form, either in the same organisation or in another organisation. Wicked problems are essentially unique, so experience is of little help.

10 *Responsibility.* Would-be solvers of wicked problems are often blamed for creating more problems, but are unlikely to be praised because wicked problems are never solved in an absolute sense.

From the viewpoint of objective-setting, the existence of wicked problems means that objectives cannot be set in isolation. The implications of this are:

1 There must be a broad participation from all those affected by the decisions which are to be made.

2 Policy-making must be based on a wide spectrum of information gathered from many sources.

Wicked problem solving might be expected to use the following criteria (Mason and Mitroff 1981):

1 *Participative.* Since both the knowledge of the problem and the resources to solve it are scattered among many individuals, the problem-solving process must include a large number of people.

2 *Adversarial.* The best judgement of the assumptions in a wicked problem will be obtained as a result of scepticism and doubt, which implies a fair degree of debate and conflict among the individuals charged with solving the problem.

3 *Integrative.* A unified set of assumptions and a coherent plan of action will be needed to guide the problem-solving process.

4 *Managerial mind supporting.* Decision support systems are likely to be inadequate for solving wicked problems. Achieving insight into the nature of the complexity of the problem requires systems that support the policymakers' thinking process.

Market Strategies

Market-scope strategies deal with coverage of the market. There are three main alternative strategies, as shown in Table 10.2.

Market scope can change as the market changes or as the firm grows, so (like any other marketing strategy) the firm will need to reconsider the market scope as circumstances dictate. For example, an airline may start out by specialising in charter holidays but decide later on (as the firm acquires more resources and more routes) to develop

Table 10.2 Market scope strategies

Strategy alternative	Explanation and examples
Single-market strategy	The firm devotes all its efforts to one market segment. This is also known as niche marketing. In some cases the niche marketer seeks out a market which is too small or specialised for large firms to bother with (typically the route taken by small firms or those with limited resources), but in other cases there may be specialised capabilities which the firm can supply. For example, large washing-powder manufacturers specialise because of the prohibitive cost of the plant and equipment needed to manufacture washing powders.
Multi-market strategy	Here the firm seeks to serve several segments. For example, a glass bottle manufacturer may serve the food industry, the brewing industry, the soft drinks industry and even the gift and novelty industry. Each has different requirements, and each will need to be approached with a different tactical package.
Total-market strategy	Companies following a total-market strategy seek to serve every segment of their chosen markets. Motor manufacturers such as Ford seek to supply vehicles for every purpose, from compact cars through to heavy lorries.

scheduled routes as well. Equally, a company pursuing a multi-market strategy might fall on hard times and decide to concentrate on its core business.

Market-geography strategy takes geographic segmentation into the strategy area by concentrating the firm's resources in a key geographical area. In some cases this is an approach typical of very small businesses: local take-away food outlets operate within extremely small geographical areas, for example. On the other hand, some very substantial businesses also operate a market-geography strategy. The London Underground carries three million passengers daily over 235 miles of railway track and operates 257 stations. The Underground uses capital assets valued in the billions, but only operates within a relatively small geographical area, no larger than that covered by some taxi companies.

Regional-market strategy means that the firm operates within distinct geographical boundaries which go beyond the local area. For example, a brewery might have strong local ties but sell its beer nationally. The advantage of regional-market strategy is that it is easier to handle cultural characteristics of a region than to handle the different cultures which might be found across the country as a whole. The advertising campaigns of the SA Brain brewery, for example, might well be incomprehensible outside the company's native Wales.

National-market strategy is commonly adopted as the firm exhausts the possibilities within its own region. National-market strategy is relatively straightforward in small countries, but can prove difficult in large, diverse countries such as the United States or Brazil. Cultural differences between regions within one country can be substantial: residents of Munich have more in common with their Austrian neighbours in Salzburg than they do with their fellow Germans in Kiel or Rostock, for example. The main advantage of a national strategy is economies of scale in production, but there may also be some benefits in terms of spreading risk across the whole economy rather than relying on a regional economy which might be affected by (say) the closure of a major employer.

Another way of categorising market strategies is to consider the timing of market entry. Market-entry strategies fall into three categories: first-in strategy, early-entry strategy and laggard-entry strategy.

The London Underground operates within a relatively small area.

Marketing in Practice
Dover Loyalty Card

Dover is a seaport and former holiday resort in the south-east of England. Its main source of employment and income these days is its very large ferry port – Dover is the largest car ferry port in the UK, taking advantage of the narrow crossing between France and England at that point. Its other claim to fame is its chalk cliffs, which became symbolic of British independence and sovereignty during the Second World War.

From the viewpoint of local businesses, though, the ferry port is not really an advantage. Most traffic (and there is a lot of it) simply passes straight along the seafront to the port in a more or less continuous stream: with ferries leaving as regularly as every half-hour at peak times, Dover is not so much a port as a bridge. With the passing traffic just passing, Dover relies heavily on its local residents to keep businesses alive – and with other major towns such as Folkestone and Canterbury nearby, and with London only a short train ride away, locals have plenty of choice of shopping. To add insult to injury, some even use the ferries to do their shopping in the giant French hypermarkets just across the channel. The very existence of the port has created a local transport infrastructure which makes it easy for people to shop elsewhere – so if the town was not to die altogether, something needed to be done.

Local estate agent Paul Brown's stepped into the breach by creating the Dover Loyalty Card. The cards are free to local residents and can be collected from any participating business: the cards entitle users to discounts or special offers. Participating businesses pay a small amount to be in the scheme, in exchange for which they get a free listing in the local newspaper (which

sponsors the scheme) and access to the scheme's mailing list.

The scheme is sponsored by a wide variety of local organisations. Dover Council, the *Dover Express* newspaper, the Dover Guest House Owners' Association, NatWest Bank, and the Port of Dover all either contribute money or support the Loyalty Card in some other way (the newspaper provides a free listing, for example). Currently, 47 businesses are members of the scheme – everything from the local florist to a Buddy Holly impersonator – and Dover residents have signed up in their thousands for cards.

Clearly this is not a way of making a fast buck for Paul Brown's. Even if every business in Dover participated, the fees collected would hardly cover the running costs. Obviously, what is good for Dover is bound to be good for the local estate agent – but the Dover Loyalty Card is not about that, it is about helping one's local community.

First-in strategy means being the first to enter a given market. It has the major advantage of creating a lead which others then have to follow, but it carries the greatest risk in terms of possible failure in the market. This risk is high, since the market will be virtually unknown in the early stages. On the other hand, the first-to-market advantage means that a first-in strategist can cream off a large market share before competitors enter, and can maintain high profitability by price skimming in the early stages of the market's development. In general, first-in strategy is a high risk, high return approach.

Early-entry strategy means entering just after the first-in company. In most cases, the early-entry strategists have been developing products for the market, but were beaten by the other firm. In some cases the early-entry strategist deliberately holds back to allow another firm to test the market and make the early mistakes. Early-entry strategy works best for firms with a marketing advantage and the ability to learn from others – such firms also need sufficient resources to be able to take on the first-in strategist.

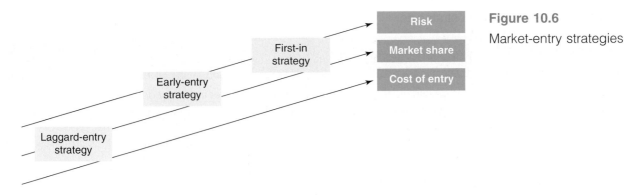

Figure 10.6
Market-entry strategies

Laggard-entry strategy means entering the market towards the end of the growth phase of the product life cycle, or when the market is mature. Imitators entering the market have the opportunity to learn from the market leaders' mistakes without the heavy research expenditure the first-in and early-entry strategists have incurred. Research shows that the chances of failure are very much reduced for laggards (Calentone and Cooper 1981). A laggard may enter the market with a new idea which enables the firm to make substantial inroads into the market – Amazon.com has made a considerable dent in the book market, for example, although this market was extremely well established.

Profitability will depend on the problems the first-in company encounters. For example, Philips of Holland introduced videodiscs in the 1980s, shortly after the introduction of video recorders. The project flopped completely, because the market was not yet ready. However, in the early 21st century the DVD system was introduced, using Philips' original technology, and became a runaway success. This demonstrates that the first-in companies must stay ahead of the competition throughout, or risk simply paving the way for competitors.

A further way of categorising strategies is to look at the level of commitment the firm has to the market. Firms might have strong, average or light commitment, as shown in Table 10.3.

Market-dilution strategies are ways of removing the firm from markets which are no longer profitable, or of divesting itself of unprofitable customers. There are four basic strategies in this category: demarketing, pruning, key-market strategy and harvesting.

- Demarketing is the process of discouraging certain groups of customers in order to reduce the costs of servicing unprofitable segments. Firms may decide to give preferential treatment to 'key' customers, they may ration supplies, or they may even recommend a competitor's product if the customer is really not worth keeping. Demarketing is directed at maintaining the goodwill of key customers at a time when demands cannot be met, for example during a crisis of supply.

- Pruning of marginal markets means pulling out of some segments altogether. Typically, firms will divest themselves of their low-commitment markets in order to concentrate on the core business, particular if business is going through a downturn at the time. Firms may also prune in order to divert resources into new projects which might pay better.

- Key-market strategy is the corollary of pruning strategy, in that the firm makes a conscious effort to concentrate on key markets at the expense of marginal markets. A key-market strategy requires strong focus, a reputation for quality and a strong position within the market.

- Harvesting strategy is one in which the company deliberately cuts investment in a given market (or for a given brand) and allows the sales to slide downwards, grabbing the profit from it without further investment in the market. This is a common strategy when a product is reaching the end of its lifecycle, and is also common if the market is

Table 10.3 Market-commitment strategies

Level of commitment	Explanation and examples
Strong-commitment strategy	These firms devote much greater resources to the market than they do to other segments. In some cases (particularly niche marketers) the firm commits all its resources to one market. Most managers are aware that the bulk of the firm's sales come from a relatively small group of customers, so the strong-commitment strategy means devoting most or all of the firm's resources to those customers.
Average-commitment strategy	This is typical of firms which lack the resources to commit fully to a given market, perhaps because the firm's resources are already committed elsewhere. Such firms may make mistakes in the average-commitment market because they are able to make up losses elsewhere, so in some respects the average-commitment firm is able to take more risks than the strong-commitment firm. The downside is that the average-commitment firm is likely to meet with strong opposition from high-commitment firms, as has been the case in the UK with the Direct Line insurance company. Direct Line is fully committed to telephone-based selling: other insurance companies which have tried to establish their own telesales operations have been unable to dent Direct Line's market. This is because telephone selling is the firm's entire *raison d'être*: for other firms it is merely a sideline.
Light-commitment strategy	This strategy is typical of firms with resources to spare from other activities. These firms may become market followers in a given market simply to shut out the competition, or to 'test the water'. Sometimes the firm's managers have a belief that the firm 'ought' to be in a given market.

disappearing. Harvesting is not always possible due to the existence of exit barriers. The company may have an investment in heavy equipment for which there is no resale market, there may be customer goodwill issues, or there may even be a reluctance on the part of management to let go of a brand which has historical significance.

Competitive Positions

Porter (1985) suggests four basic competitive strategies, of which three are winning strategies and one is a losing strategy:

1 *Overall cost leadership.* A company which is able to minimise its costs can obtain a competitive advantage over other companies either by reducing its prices or by increasing its profitability. Minimising costs may be an exercise in developing efficient systems, or it may mean moving production to Third World countries.

2 *Differentiation.* Companies which are able to show their customers that their products are significantly different from competing products are able to charge premium prices (provided, of course, that the customers believe that the differences make the product better). Differentiation comes from two sources: first, real differences in the features and benefits which the brand has to offer, and second, strong promotional activities to make the differences apparent (and important) to potential buyers. Both these sources of differentiation cost money to implement, so the firm needs to be confident that the premium which customers are prepared to pay for the differentiated product more than covers the extra costs.

3 *Focus.* Here the company concentrates on a few market segments rather than trying to compete in the whole market. Often these will be exclusive markets: the market for luxury yachts falls into this category. In the industrial context, Novo Nordisk of

Denmark specialises in producing industrial enzymes, and has become highly profitable by being the best in its chosen specialism.

The losing strategy is to try to achieve more than one of the above, and thus fail to achieve any of them. Combining low costs with differentiation is impossible, because a differentiation strategy requires higher expenditure on R&D and promotion if it is to be effective. Combining low cost with focus is also unlikely to work, because low cost depends on achieving economies of scale in production, which in turn means achieving high sales volumes across a very broad market. Focus and differentiation combine fairly well, but there are cost implications. The essence of the problem is to pursue a clear strategy which customers can identify with, so that the firm has a clear competitive position in the minds of the customers. If customers are unable to decide whether a firm is cheap, is best at serving its market segment, or is offering the highest specifications, the firm's products will not stand out from the competition and are thus likely to be relegated to a lower status in the decision-making framework.

Talking Point

The theory seems to show that only one firm can be the cost leader in any given market. So how do low-cost airlines fit into this equation? Many of them fly to the same destinations (Malaga, Prague, Alicante etc.) and they often do so from regional airports which are sufficiently close to each other to be realistic alternatives for many passengers.

Is the theory wrong? If so, where is it wrong? How can all these companies apparently compete on price without causing each other any major problems?

Firms occasionally try to carry out more than one strategy at a time because of a lack of consensus among managers. This can happen at all levels in the organisation, and is likely to be a result of poor communication of the corporate mission statement, vision or corporate objectives statement. Consensus among managers improves performance at the strategic business unit (SBU) level, especially for differentiation strategies (Homburg *et. al.* 1999) but appears unnecessary if the firm is pursuing a low-cost strategy. This may be because a low-cost strategy is easy to understand and relate to, even if disagreements occur elsewhere.

An alternative to Porter's categorisation of strategies is that proposed by Treacy and Wiersema (1993). This identifies three strategies of value disciplines aimed at increasing customer value. These are:

1 *Operational excellence*. Here the company provides better value for customers by leading the industry in price and convenience. Similar to the cost-leadership approach, the firm tries to reduce costs and create an effective and efficient delivery system.

2 *Customer intimacy*. This strategy requires the company to get as close as possible to its customers, usually by precise segmentation. This strategy is likely to be based on developing close relationships with customers, which in turn usually means empowering the grass-roots staff to make decisions close to the customers, and also developing very detailed knowledge of customers' needs and wants. Such companies attract customers who are prepared to pay substantial premiums to get exactly what they want and to be loyal to companies who deliver.

3 *Product leadership*. Companies pursuing this strategy offer leading-edge, state-of-the-art products and services, aimed at making the competitors' products (and indeed their own) obsolete as quickly as possible. A company following this strategy must be prepared to accept large R&D expenditure as part of the cost, as well as staff innovation programmes and systems for getting new products to market as quickly as possible. Examples are 3M and Sony, both of which have vigorous new product development systems and substantial rewards for innovative staff.

E-Marketing in Practice
BMI Baby

BMI Baby is a low-cost airline, set up in 2002 by its parent company, British Midland. BMI Baby is another in a series of low-cost airlines: the concept started in the United States in the early 1970s with Southwest Airlines. Ryanair was the first low-cost airline in Europe, based in Dublin: in the UK, Easyjet was the first low-cost carrier, starting in 1995. It was followed by BA's GoFly in 1998, and by KLM's Buzz in 2000. Meanwhile, other low-cost carriers were coming in from the rest of Europe: Germany's Germanwings and Air Berlin, Basiq in the Netherlands and Italy's Volare among them.

Where the airlines score is only partly due to the low cost of the flights. They also score on the ease of booking – which is all done via websites. This cuts costs because the work of making the booking is transferred to the customer, which saves on staff costs, and the passenger even supplies the paper to print the ticket.

The received wisdom is that only one firm can be the lowest cost carrier – but these airlines avoid that problem by flying from different airports, to different destinations. All have made extensive use of e-marketing, because the flights themselves are so cheap that it is difficult to maintain profitability. BMI Baby, for example, offers travel insurance, hotel bookings, car hire, car parking at airports and even travellers' cheques (through American Express). All of these can be bought online, automatically, with little or no intervention from airline staff.

every seventh flight out of Heathrow is one of ours

book now at flybmi.com

those who know fly **bmi**

Courtesy of The Advertising Archives

Unlike Porter's categorisation, the Treacy and Wiersema categories are not mutually exclusive. It is perfectly feasible to pursue operational excellence and product leadership, for example.

In practice, managers may not consciously decide to categorise the strategy according to either of these models. In most cases, senior managers will decide what the organisation should and should not be doing and strategy will develop from there: the categories are the result of observing reality, and are not necessarily intended to be prescriptive.

Competitive Moves

Retaining a position in the market, or carving out a new one, requires firms to attack competitors or defend themselves from attack. The moves that are available to each firm will depend in its position in the marketplace relative to its competitors. Figure 10.7 illustrates the four basic market positions.

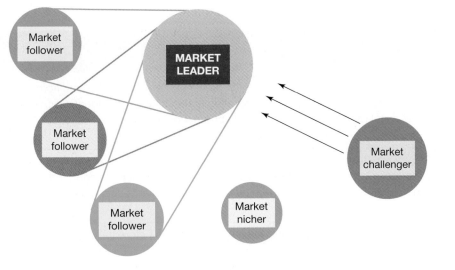

Figure 10.7
Basic market positions

In Figure 10.7 the size of the circles represents the relative market share of each firm. The market leader has by far the largest market share, and drags the market followers behind it. The niche marketer occupies a position which does not represent a threat to any of the other firms, while the market challenger seeks to steal market share from the market leader with the aim of becoming market leader in turn. Market challengers may have been market followers in the past, or may be entering from outside the market, for example a foreign company entering the market for the first time.

For market leaders, both market-orientated and relationship-orientated, strategies are important. For challengers, market-orientated strategies work best, and for followers and nichers relationship-orientated strategies work best (Tse *et al.* 2004).

market follower A company which follows the lead of the main company in the market.

Market leader strategies

Market leaders usually have the power to control the market to a large extent, but exercising this power too frequently might lead to the unwanted attentions of Government monopoly regulators. Market leaders therefore have two basic growth strategies: they can try to continue to win greater market share from their smaller rivals, or they can try to expand the total market.

Expanding the total market may well prove to be a viable option for a market leader, for two reasons. First, it may be easier to attract more customers into the market than it would be to try to steal customers from competitors, who are likely to defend their positions fiercely. Second, expanding the total market will not attract the attention of monopoly regulators, since the overall market share is likely to remain much the same. Expanding the total market will, of course, benefit the firm's competitors as well, but this is not an important consideration for a firm which already has the largest market share: in any case, the object of the exercise is to run a successful business, not merely to bankrupt one's competitors. Expanding the total market can be achieved by expanding the total number of users, by finding new uses for the product, or by encouraging greater usage among existing users.

Expanding market share is achieved at the expense of the weaker competitors. Monopoly regulators may investigate this activity, but for most firms this is not a serious threat, since regulators only come in when the market share is very substantial and where abuses can be proved. Basic routes to expanding market share are to win customers, to buy out competitors or to increase the loyalty of existing customers.

Table 10.4 Defence strategies

Defence strategy	Explanation
Position defence	A position defence involves building barriers which prevent or restrict competitors from entering the market. This may mean, for example, incorporating features into the product which require a large capital investment (and consequently a large production run) to make them economically viable.
Flanking defence	Market leaders can sometimes ignore parts of the market which offer an opening to competitors. For example, Japanese car manufacturers were extremely successful in entering the US small car market, which had been left almost untouched by the American giants such as General Motors and Ford.
Pre-emptive defence	Here the market leader begins by attacking the other companies before they can move against the leader. A threat of entry might be pre-empted by a large price cut, for example.
Counter-offensive defence	When attacked, the market leader launches an instant counter-attack. This can take the form of a promotion campaign, a price war or a new product development exercise to produce an improved version of the competitor's offering.
Mobile defence	The company is proactive in defending its current market position, by expanding into new markets ahead of the competition.
Contraction defence	If the company can no longer defend all its markets, it might decide to withdraw from some or all of those markets. In military terms, this is called a strategic withdrawal: however, the next phrase used by the Army is 'to previously prepared positions'. Sadly, some companies have managed the withdrawal part easily enough, but have not consolidated the positions which they can hold, and consequently have simply continued to retreat until there is nowhere left to go.

Market leaders can also improve productivity, squeezing more profit out of the same sales volume. This strategy is easy for market leaders because their relative size gives them a bargaining advantage with suppliers and distributors and also generates economies of scale.

More commonly, market leaders need to maintain their defences against attacks from market challengers. The basic defence strategies are shown in Table 10.4.

Market leaders need to be constantly vigilant: the most effective strategy for all the other companies in the market is likely to be to take market share from the leader. Once this process starts, it is all too easy for the market leader to continue to lose share until it ceases to be the market leader, or even goes bankrupt.

Market challenger strategies

Market challengers seek to increase their share of the market, usually by aggressive competitive tactics. Market challengers are in a different position from market leaders in that they have two choices of competitor to attack: they can attack the market leaders, which is risky but potentially has the highest rewards, or they can attack the smaller market followers, either by out-competing them or by taking them over. Attacking the market leader almost always means attacking a larger opponent which is well established in the market: the market leader almost certainly therefore has the resources and the experience to mount a vigorous defence. Smaller firms may not be so well-placed to defend themselves, but on the other hand defeating the market leader usually means becoming market leader in turn, which has obvious advantages.

Table 10.5 Market challenger strategies

Strategy	Explanation
Frontal attack	The challenger matches the competitor's marketing efforts across the board. It attacks the competitor's strengths, not its weaknesses, and in effect enters into a war of attrition. The company with the greater resources usually wins in these circumstances.
Flanking attack	Here the challenger concentrates on the competitor's weaknesses rather than its strengths. The challenger tries to find some portion of the competitor's business which is being poorly served or which it feels able to serve better, and attacks that. Sometimes the competitor will withdraw without much of a fight: a lot depends on the relative resources of the two firms.
Encirclement attack	This strategy involves attacking from several directions at once. This approach works best when the attacker has more resources than the defender.
Bypass attack	Here the challenger bypasses the market leader completely and targets new markets. This might involve entering new geographic markets, or using new technology to tap into new groups of customers. This has the advantage of not offering a direct threat to the competitor, thus minimising the risk of retaliation.
Guerrilla attack	The challenger makes occasional attacks on the larger competitor, using different tactics each time in order to demoralise and confuse the market leader. For example, a challenger might run a cut-price offer for one month only, followed the next month by a sales promotion, followed the next month by a promotional campaign. This constant switching of tactics does not allow the market leader time to organise a retaliatory strike, and instead forces the leader to become a follower, retaliating after the challenger has moved on to the next tactic.

Attacking the market leader means having a clear competitive advantage: a cost advantage, or the ability to provide better value for money by offering a better product. Attacking smaller competitors may only require an aggressive promotional campaign, a short price war or a takeover policy. The strategies open to a market challenger are shown in Table 10.5.

Guerrilla actions work best for small firms which are able to respond quickly and have the flexibility to move on as soon as their larger and perhaps more bureaucratic competitors try to retaliate.

Market follower strategies

Most firms operate with the view that competitors are 'the enemy' and will therefore try to attack them in order to seize market share. However, challenging the market leader or competing aggressively may not be the most effective strategy, since attack naturally leads to defence, followed by counter-attack. The primary task of any organisation is to survive, and an attack from a larger, better-resourced competitor may lead to the demise of the smaller firm.

Market followers typically allow the market leader to make most of the investment in developing new markets, then follow on to pick up any spare segments which might have been bypassed by the leader. The follower gains in terms of reduced costs and reduced risk, and although followers will never become market leaders, they are often as profitable as leaders (Haines, Chandran and Parkhe 1989). Market followers fall into three types, as shown in Table 10.6.

Since the vast majority of new products on the market fail, the market leader position is invariably risky. Successful products have to cover the costs of all the unsuccessful

Table 10.6 Market follower types

Category	Explanation
Cloner	These firms make almost exact copies of the leader's products, distribution, promotion and other marketing strategies. They can often do this at much lower cost, because they do not have the development costs or risks of the market leaders. Firms making exact copies of products are relatively rare, due to patenting and other intellectual property defences, but in some markets (particularly agricultural markets) cloning is perfectly feasible.
Imitator	Here the follower copies most of the leader's strategies, but retains some differentiation. This approach is more common than cloning, because it often avoids direct competition with the market leader, and can even help the leader to avoid charges of monopolistic behaviour. Typical imitator strategies would be supermarkets selling own brands which look like the market leader brands, or burger restaurants which imitate the McDonald's high-speed service system.
Adapter	Adapters go one step further than the market leader, producing improved versions of products or marketing programmes. Adapters can become industry leaders and are really only one step short of being challengers.

Talking Point

ones. Followers can be more confident that their products will succeed, because they are able to learn from the mistakes of the market leader and only copy products which are already successful. The same applies to promotional activities and distribution strategies: even though the bulk of the market is likely to go to the innovators, the costs of innovation are often large so that the profits often go to the followers.

If the safest way of running the business is to be a follower, why are so many firms so keen to be leaders? Why is it that firms spend millions on research and development when it would be so much easier simply to sit back and wait for the competitors to do all the hard work and take all the risks?

Or maybe there's more to it than this? After all, what happens if someone develops a product that completely destroys our market – and we have no way of copying it? What happens if another follower produces a better copy than ours? And presumably we need to bring in the occasional new product, or the competitors will cream off the best of the market first!

Market nicher strategies

market nicher A firm which is content with a small segment of the market.

Market nichers are firms which concentrate on small segments of the market, seeking to meet the needs of those customers as closely as possible. Nichers usually operate on a low-volume, high-margin basis, so this is often a suitable strategic position for medium-sized companies (Clifford and Cavanaugh 1985).

Competitors are often closed out of the niche because the niche strategist develops an intimate knowledge of customer needs which is difficult for a new entrant to acquire. Furthermore, the niche is often too small to support more than one company. Niche marketers run the risk of their chosen market declining or even disappearing altogether: the key to success in niche marketing is specialisation, but this can mean that the company lacks the flexibility to move on if the niche shrinks. Table 10.7 shows the ways in which niche marketers can specialise.

Table 10.7 Niche roles

Role	Explanation
End-use specialist	The firm specialises in meeting all the needs of one type of end user. For example, Radio Shack aims to supply all the needs of amateur electronics hobbyists.
Vertical-level specialist	The firm specialises in one level of the production–distribution cycle. For example, Pickford's specialise in moving heavy equipment and abnormal loads.
Customer-size specialist	Here the firm concentrates on marketing to firms of a particular size. Often smaller firms are neglected by the industry majors, allowing a foot in the door for nichers.
Specific-customer specialist	The firm specialises in supplying one or two very large firms. This is typical of small engineering firms: they offer specialist manufacturing expertise to larger firms who find it cheaper to outsource than to manufacture in-house. Weber carburettors are an example: the firm supplies high-quality carburettors to most car manufacturers for their high-performance cars.
Geographical specialist	Here the firm stays within a small geographical area. For example, Welsh-language book publishers do not operate outside Wales and Argentina, where the Welsh language is spoken.
Product or feature specialist	The firm specialises in producing a particular product or one with unique features. This type of specialisation is often based on a patented system or process.
Quality–price specialist	The firm operates within a niche at the top or bottom of the market. For example, the market for executive jet planes is dominated by Lear and Cessna.
Service specialist	The firm offers a service which is unavailable elsewhere. Only NASA offers a recovery and repair service for satellites, and only the Russian space agency offers space tourist flights (albeit at an extremely high price).

Collaborating with Competitors

Most strategy authors tend to think of business strategy in terms of warfare. The aim is to beat the competitors into submission in some way, to capture markets, to conduct campaigns, to attack competitors. Hamel, Doz and Prahalad (1989) move away from this approach and consider the possibilities for cooperating with competitors in order to ensure success for all. Strategic alliances generated through joint ventures, product licensing or cooperative research strengthen firms against competitors from outside the partnership by increasing market coverage, reducing costs, generating greater efficiency and raising the profile of both companies. Many Japanese firms have used this approach to enter European markets.

Hamel *et al.*'s (1989) research showed that collaboration between Japanese firms and Western firms often left the Western company worse off in the long run. This has been seen as the 'Trojan horse' effect, whereby the Japanese firm has entered into the collaboration only for the purpose of learning as much as possible from the Western firm before abandoning the partnership and setting up in competition. Hamel *et al.* (1989) contradict this to an extent, attributing the failure of Western firms to gain from the alliance to poor negotiating skills, poor fit between strategic goals and poor protection of sensitive information. On the other hand, more recent research from Hennart, Roehl and Zeitlow (1999) shows that, provided the partnership is well-managed, the benefits of collaboration outweigh the risks. Firms which benefit most from competitive collaboration tend to follow the principles outlined in Table 10.8.

end-use specialist A company specialising in customers who use the product in a specific way.

specific-customer specialist A company which specialises in dealing with a narrow range of customers.

Table 10.8 Principles for successful collaboration

Principle	Explanation
Collaboration is competition in a different form	Successful collaborators remember that their partner may well try to take over the whole market later on and become a major competitor. The collaboration may not last forever!
Harmony is not the most important measure of success	Occasional conflict may well lead to creative solutions for problems: like a marriage, if the partnership is a sincere commitment, arguments will happen now and then. Harmony usually only prevails where neither party really cares about the outcome, or indeed about the relationship.
Cooperation has limits	Strategic alliances often result in substantial transfers of information, perhaps well beyond that originally envisaged by senior management when they hammered out the deal. Successful collaborators will ensure that employees are well aware of what information can and cannot be passed on.
Learning from partners is paramount	Successful collaborators ensure that the new knowledge gained from the partner is diffused throughout their own organisation. This knowledge will remain even if the partnership dissolves.

Companies often enter into alliances in order to avoid making investments, either in developing new products or in entering new markets. Unfortunately this often allows the partner firm to control the situation to their own advantage. Mutual gain is certainly possible, but firms should conform to the following conditions:

- The partners' strategic goals converge while their competitive goals diverge. Each partner must allow the other to prosper in the shared venture, and should avoid competing directly.
- The size and power of both partners is modest compared with the industry leaders. This ensures that the mutual need to attack the market leader, or defend the partners against retaliation by the industry leader, keeps the partnership on track.
- The partners should be of similar size to each other. This helps to ensure that neither partner can develop a controlling interest in the venture.
- Each partner can learn from the other, but is able to restrict access to critically sensitive information.

Courtesy of Iveco

Collaboration offers a good way forward for many small companies, and indeed some larger ones. Highly-successful ventures include Iveco, the European alliance of truck manufacturers, and Transmanche Link, the consortium of civil engineering companies which built the Channel Tunnel.

Growth Strategies

As a general rule, most firms want to grow. Growth increases the firm's security in the market, it increases the power and influence of managers (not to mention their salaries) and it reduces costs. There are four generic routes to growth, as shown in Table 10.9 (Ansoff 1968).

Table 10.9 Growth strategies

Strategy	Explanation
Market penetration	This is the most common method of growing the business. The firm expands sales of its existing products in its existing markets, usually by taking business away from competitors.
Product development	Here the firm introduces new products within the existing market, either selling extra products to existing customers or offering a slightly different product to people who are not entirely satisfied with the existing products.
Market development	If a firm has saturated its existing markets, growth is still possible by introducing the existing products into new markets. This is a common reason for exporting.
Diversification	Taking new products into new markets appears to be a risky growth strategy, but firms sometimes do this because the new product has production synergies. A safer route would be to expand through acquisition, buying out a firm in the target market.

Growth in growing markets is likely to happen in any case, even without any formal strategic attempts to encourage it: the key to success here lies in measuring whether the company is growing faster than the market, slower than the market, or at the same pace as the market. Often firms which couch their growth objectives in financial terms fail to notice that they are growing more slowly than the market, and are thus (in effect) losing ground to competitors. Couching growth targets in terms of market share will avoid this pitfall, although obviously a reliable measure of the overall size of the market needs to be available.

During recessions most markets shrink, and a common response to this is for firms to retrench, put their expansion plans on hold, and wait for the economic climate to improve. In fact, for the astute firm a recession provides tremendous opportunities for growth, provided the company is prepared in advance. Growth in declining markets is likely to happen through acquisition of ailing competitors, and this is never easier than during a recession. Here is a list of strategies for riding a recession and coming out of it in better shape than when the recession started.

- *Cash is king*. During a recession, credit becomes tighter, so companies with cash reserves are able to force down prices from suppliers or buy out competitors much more easily.

- *Debtors default much more often*. Giving credit to customers is a bad idea during a recession: payment dates stretch out, and the debtor firm may well go bankrupt, leaving the debt unpaid. Debtors can be a useful source of expansion by takeover: some firms have achieved enviable vertical integration in this way.

- *Deals can be struck with liquidators*. If a competitor, supplier or distributor does go bankrupt, it is often possible to buy the firm from the liquidators for a fraction of its going-concern value. In fact, some firms even strike very lucrative deals with directors before the company goes under, in order to avoid the stigma of bankruptcy or even to save the directors from the scrutiny of regulators.

- *Markets shrink for suppliers as well*. A firm which has been a good customer in the past and shows signs of being a good payer is a valuable asset to a supplier, and one which is worth offering concessions to.

- *Good staff often become unexpectedly available*. As firms go bankrupt, some highly-skilled people enter the jobs market, often for salaries below what they might have commanded in their previous jobs.

- *Most financial managers insist on promotional budget cuts when times are hard*. This means that share of voice is easier to achieve, since competitors promote less, but it also means that advertising rates are likely to be cut as media struggle to sell space.

- *Raw material prices drop.* Many firms destock during recessions: towards the end of a recession, and indeed when dealing with liquidators, it is often possible to stock up with raw materials or components at very favourable prices.

Overall, recessions can be seen as an opportunity rather than a threat. The key to success in a recession is to ensure that the firm goes in with low financial gearing and preferably with a cash 'war chest' in order to snap up bargains. Recessions normally only last a few months, and are replaced within a year or two by boom conditions, during which it might be advisable to shed some assets while prices are high in order to have cash on hand for the next recession.

Value-based Marketing

Value-based marketing begins from the premise that the central task of management is to maximise shareholder value (Doyle 2000). This does not necessarily mean maximising profitability: shareholder value is more often related to capital growth, i.e. a rise in the value of the firm's shares, which is linked to many other factors than profit.

Maximising profit is often a short-term, tactical process involving cutting costs, reducing investment, downsizing, increasing sales at the expense of long-term customer loyalty and making short-term gains at the expense of long-term security. At the extreme, a profit focus can even lead to massaging the accounts to show a profit where there was not one before. Increased sophistication among shareholders has led to a realisation that long-term growth is likely to be more rewarding than immediate dividends: the spectacular collapse of firms such as Enron has led investors to avoid firms with spectacular short-term profits but little underlying substance. Therefore City analysts look more and more towards measures such as customer loyalty and brand awareness to judge whether stocks are likely to rise in value.

Unfortunately for investors, the marketplace is changing so rapidly that companies tend not to survive very long. The life expectancy of a company is now less than 20 years (De Geus 1997). Maintaining a profitable competitive advantage is likely to be even more elusive: as soon as it becomes apparent that a firm has found a profitable niche, competitors enter the market and profits are rapidly eroded until they reach the point where the company is unable to maintain an adequate return on its original capital investment (Black, Wright and Bachman 1998).

Obviously some companies are exceptions to this general trend. Large, well-established firms are able to retain shareholder value, using profits to increase the value of the firm rather than pay dividends. These blue-chip companies are regarded as safe investments because they maintain steady growth, although their dividend payouts are typically relatively low.

For marketers, the idea that the company should focus on maximising shareholder value rather than maximising consumer benefit may seem almost heretical. For the past 50 years, marketing academics have emphasised centrality of consumer needs in all strategic planning. Value-based marketing implies that customer satisfaction is not an end in itself: rather it is the route to maximising shareholder value.

In fact, because marketers have concentrated on customer satisfaction, while other (often more senior) managers have been concerned with the value of the shares, marketing has often been relegated to a function rather than a strategic driver. The result of this is that marketing thinking has not fulfilled its early promise, and will not do so until marketers accept that the customers and consumers are the means to an end.

Doyle (2000) has offered an alternative definition of marketing which encompasses this view.

Marketing is the management process that seeks to maximise returns to share-holders by developing and implementing strategies to build relationships of trust with high-value customers and to create a sustainable differential advantage.

This definition has the advantage of removing profitability from the equation and substituting shareholder value. It also includes a reference to the relationship marketing perspective: however, not all firms seek to build long-term relationships with customers, and in many cases it would be extremely unlikely that a long-term relationship would develop. Plastic surgeons, funeral directors and estate agents spring readily to mind. Also, many firms do extremely well dealing with a large number of low-value customers. From the viewpoint of value-based marketing, however, loyalty is important for building shareholder value, since a solid group of loyal customers is part of what ensures the long-term viability of a firm. Low-value customers are frequently not loyal.

The difference in orientation between aiming for an increase in shareholder value and aiming for an increase in customer satisfaction is a small one. It is really a difference in focus rather than a new philosophy altogether: a key focus for marketers is the twofold problem of how to increase the brand value and how to cash in on the increased value in the long term. Simply harvesting profits is not the way forward – reinvesting in further building of the brand, or in other ventures is realistic and will increase shareholder value.

Not all businesses have regular customers.

Does Strategy Matter?

Richard Whittington's 2001 text 'What is strategy – and does it matter?' questions the 'toolbox' approach of most strategy texts. Whittington examines four generic approaches to strategy, which are outlined in Table 10.10.

The generic perspectives on strategy can be mapped against processes and outcomes, as shown in Fig. 10.8.

Table 10.10 Generic approaches to strategy

Approach	Explanation
Classical	Relies on rational planning methods, using environmental analysis as the basis for decision-making and planning for the long term.
Evolutionary	Assumes that only the fittest will survive: correct strategies will result from adapting to the environment, and ad hoc solutions are used in response to environmental pressures. Evolutionary strategic thought is about accommodating to the law of the jungle: long-term planning is therefore not feasible.
Processualist	Strategy accommodates to the fallible processes of both organisations and markets. Strategy is therefore a bottom-up process, coming from the exigencies of the situations faced by the firm.
Systemic	The ends and means of strategy are linked to the cultures and powers of the local social systems in which it takes place. Companies therefore follow policies which are predicated by their local social constraints rather than by strict business considerations.

Figure 10.8

Generic perspectives on strategy

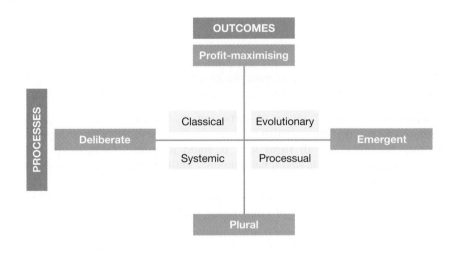

Each approach offers a different set of answers for what strategy is. Classicists say that strategy is rational and consists of a set of deliberate calculations aimed at achieving a market position and maintaining it in the face of opposition. It implies rationality, long-range focus, responses to environmental shifts in a calculated manner and so forth.

Evolutionists believe that the environment is too unpredictable for long-range planning to have any reasonable chance of success. For the evolutionists, it is the market not the managers that make the important choices, and firms are almost certainly unable to adapt quickly enough to make much difference to their survival chances (Hannan and Freeman 1988; Williamson 1991). Thus successful strategies only emerge as a result of ruthless natural selection, in which the firms with inappropriate strategies go broke and the ones who happen to have hit on a strategy which meets the needs of the market go on to succeed.

For processualists, the processes of organisations and markets are rarely perfect. This means that the market is not as implacable as the evolutionists believe, nor is the firm able to plan as thoroughly as the classicists would like. People are unable to be so precise and unvarying as to be able to carry through a detailed plan, particularly in the face of the difficulties and unforeseen circumstances which are bound to arise in an imperfect world. Therefore, firms develop strategy (or have it forced upon them) via a series of bodgings, ad-hoc decisions, compromises with reality and learning by mistakes rather than by long-range planning and rationality (Mintzberg 1994). For the processualist, failure to carry out the perfect marketing strategy is unlikely to prove fatal (although there may be some loss of ground).

Systemic theorists believe that people are capable of carrying out rational plans of action, and are also confident that it is possible to define strategies in the face of environmental forces. However, their view is that the objectives and practices of strategy are embedded in the social system to which they belong. This means, for example, that profit maximisation is not necessarily a strong factor in strategic planning. This argument carries considerable weight in a world in which the non-profit organisation and the 'fair trade' corporation are in the ascendant.

The systemic perspective also finds support in the fact that firms within different social systems have differing strategic perspectives. German and Japanese businesses were restructured after the Second World War to engender close cooperation between banks and enterprises, and to operate within a paternalistic state structure which encouraged worker participation and universal social security. The Anglo-American business structure, meanwhile, operated in an environment of hostile takeovers, impatient lenders, adversarial labour relations and (frequently) Governments committed to giving capitalism free rein.

Maybe the Germans and Japanese are right. Maybe cooperation between firms is the way forward, rather than destructive competition, which wastes resources.

On the other hand, we have monopoly regulators who take serious exception to companies which rig prices, cooperate in dividing up markets between them, and which agree to produce very similar products. So what's left to cooperate on? Staff training? Should we allow companies to work together more – or should we continue the pressure of the last 20 years, forcing more and more competition into the system?

In fact, all the generic philosophies of strategy have some facets which are evidenced in the real world. The business world is sufficiently complex to allow for a wide range of experiences and models. For example, some industries change very little over time: light-bulb manufacture has changed relatively little since the 19th century, and nor has house-building, even though the technology has shifted somewhat in the meantime. This means that it is reasonable to develop long-term strategies for these industries, to take account of fairly predictable economic or environmental shifts. In other industries, such as the restaurant trade, conditions can change rapidly and unpredictably, so an evolutionary paradigm prevails. Processualists find support for their arguments in those industries which are dominated by small firms, and in industries such as computer software where technological breakthroughs happen on an almost daily basis.

The differences between the generic strategies do matter, because they offer radically different recommendations for managers. For every manager, the strategy formulation process always begins with a decision as to which theoretical picture of the world best fits with his or her own experiences and attitudes. If the manager's view is that the world is orderly, with sufficient information and capacity to analyse, and sufficient availability of organisational control, then the classical paradigm would be most likely to be adopted. If, on the other hand, the manager believes that the environment is cut-throat and unpredictable, the evolutionist paradigm will prevail.

Some of the different contexts under which each strategic paradigm will succeed are shown in Figure 10.9. In the figure, profit maximising coupled with deliberation about strategy appears to operate best in mature, capital-intensive businesses with monopoly or oligopolistic power. These businesses live in a predictable world, where they can seek to

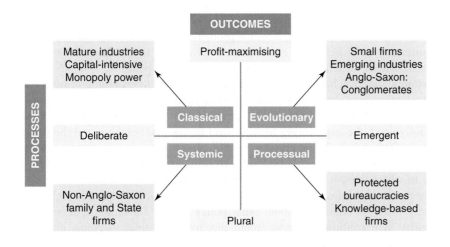

Figure 10.9

Contexts for strategy

make as much money as possible by thorough planning. Profit-maximising businesses which have emergent strategies are likely to be small firms, firms in new industries and conglomerates which follow the Anglo-Saxon model explained above. These firms live in a world of change, in which strategy has to emerge as events unfold. A situation in which firms have many outcomes other than profit, and in which the strategy cannot be planned in advance, suits protected bureaucracies such as Government organisations and knowledge-based firms such as consultancies or educational establishments. These organisations have to respond to changes, but are not necessarily seeking to make the maximum profit (or even any profit at all).

Finally, if firms are seeking many outcomes but operate in an environment which encourages deliberate strategic planning, they are likely to be non-Anglo Saxon firms (such as Japanese sogo sosha conglomerates), family-owned businesses or nationalised industries.

The consequences for government policy are also manifold. The four generic strategies have a profound effect on national policy: for classical strategists the national economic performance is rooted in individualism and rationalism. Evolutionary and processual managers would be sceptical of Government intervention, because the environment is viewed as being complex enough without 'artificial' interference from Government. The view would be that the Government might only act to spoil emergent successes. The systemic managers' view is that Government should make radical social and institutional change rather than tinker with the problem.

The classical viewpoint is that economic success comes through becoming cleverer and planning better: Baruch and Peiperl (1999) estimated that the UK economy needs approximately 75 000 MBA graduates per annum to replace managers who retire and to allow for some growth, compared with a total actual number of approximately 10 000 who graduate from business schools. Whittington (2001) claims that this under-investment in management education 'reinforces the characteristic shambolic and amateurish nature of British managerial elites.' Of course, other Master's programmes exist apart from MBAs: many more graduates have Master's degrees in accounting, in marketing, in human resources and so forth, but the picture still remains depressing for the classicists.

Processualists view the situation completely differently. Mintzberg (1996) believes that top-down, deliberate programmes of change are dangerous and probably unworkable anyway, and has expressed the view that conventional MBA programmes should be shut down altogether. Processualists believe in bottom-up strategy development, with policy growing as a result of historical and cultural accident.

Evolutionary managers go further. Since they believe that markets and entrepreneurship control the outcomes of business enterprises, they tend to value the visionary high-flyer above the rational, calculating MBA graduate. Many of the risk-taking, high-earning entrepreneurs who run fast-growing and fast-changing organisations are unburdened by too much education. Not having been told that there is a right and a wrong way of doing things, they invent their own rules as they go along, often with highly creative solutions as a result. Of course, it seems probable that most of these entrepreneurs either fail miserably or at best only ever scrape a living, but this is also true of most of the animal kingdom, which vindicates the evolutionist viewpoint.

Systemic theorists have yet another view of the route to economic growth. Since they believe that strategy develops from local social norms, they believe that the way forward is to establish clusters of firms in the same industry – examples include Silicon Valley and Hollywood, the engineering firms around Baden-Wurttemberg and the motor-racing cluster in Oxfordshire. These clusters exist because of the reluctance of key employees to move far from home when changing jobs, so firms setting up in the same industry tend to move to where there is a suitably skilled workforce already available.

The result of this disagreement about the basic shape of the business world is that there is really no clear consensus about what policy is best for national economic growth. Strategists will continue to argue about this for some time to come, and changes of Government will only exacerbate the problem as policies shift towards one view or another. Ultimately, the complexity of business life is such that it is unlikely that a definitive answer will ever arise: the truth is different according to one's circumstances and perspective.

Summary

Strategy and strategy planning are complex areas, mainly because it is difficult for firms to know where they are going and even harder to formulate a route for getting there. The conventional 'road map' analogy does not stand up well to close scrutiny: using a road map to go from one city to another works well because the cities are fixed geographically, the roads already exist and everything stays pretty much where it is while the planner moves from one place to another. This is not the case in the business world, where the goals shift, the road is frequently replaced or disappears and in most cases the planner actually has to build the road in any case. Business strategy has little in common with motorway driving: it is much more like white-water rafting, where rocks may suddenly appear, water is pouring into the boat, everybody on board is screaming at once and the paddle is less than adequate to steer the boat.

The key points from this chapter are as follows:

- Strategic planning is an iterative process, not a linear one.
- Marketing and corporate strategy will be the same if the company is customer-orientated.
- There is no single rule for creating strategic plans.
- Formal planning is only typical of firms in stable industries: firms operating in conditions of change are more likely to use adaptive strategic change.
- No battle plan survives first contact with the enemy.
- Aims are general: objectives are specific and measurable.
- Wicked problems have no absolute solutions.
- There are three basic winning strategies: overall cost leadership, differentiation and focus. They are mutually exclusive.
- Leaders defend, challengers attack, followers avoid conflict.
- Most new products fail, so safety lies in being a follower – and profitability may also be greater as a follower.
- Collaboration may be better than competition.
- Management's key objective may be increasing shareholder value rather than creating profits.

Chapter review questions

1 Under what circumstances would a company not bother with developing a strategic plan?

2 How might an evolutionary company go about planning an advertising campaign?

3 In terms of Porter's categories of strategic position, why would a combination strategy be a failing strategy?

4 Under what circumstances would collaboration with competitors be dangerous?

5 How might a processualist company approach solving a wicked problem?

6 If recessions offer such good opportunities for firms, why do governments worry so much about them?

7 What is the connection between increasing shareholder value and customer centrality?

8 How might a company quantify an aim such as 'provide the best service in the industry'?

9 If wicked problems have no definitive solution, why do firms try to solve them?

10 What is the difference between an evolutionist and a classicist?

Preview case revisited
Chardonnay

Quite clearly the New World wine producers could not use Old World names for their wines – the protection afforded by Government regulations were simply too strong. This led producers in Australia to bill their wines by the name of the grape: Chardonnay, Shiraz, Riesling and so forth. Breaking the near-monopoly of French vineyards in world markets was a challenge – but moving the wines from the shelves of cheap off-licences and onto the shelves of mainstream supermarkets involved a clear branding policy. Although each vineyard continued to use its own name, the practice grew up of adding the grape name – and this gradually spread throughout the New World. There was no overall plan, or collusion: the idea started off, and once the wineries could see the results they quickly jumped on the bandwagon.

The effect has been fairly dramatic. Chardonnay was one of the earliest wines to be marketed this way, and it was a shock to the wine industry – some traditionalists believed that it should not be allowed, but it was certainly a quick way of branding the wines. Australia in particular benefited from the move – so much so that imports of wines from Australia now outstrip imports from France, with the United States in third place. This is particularly striking because Australian and US wines have to overcome a European Union tariff barrier to enter the UK, whereas French wines do not – quite apart from considerations of transport half-way around the world rather than across 20 miles of English Channel. The UK imports the equivalent of 300 million bottles of wine a year from Australia, or 10 bottles for every adult in the country. This is still only one-sixth of what Brits drink in a year.

For French producers, the growth in New World wine has been a wake-up call. At first, French producers simply relied on their reputation as the best wine producers in the world: the New World wines, packaged imaginatively in airtight boxes or in carafes, did not seem like a threat. Then the sales started to shift to the New World and French producers had to react. Now many French producers make Chardonnay wines, and package them in boxes – it is, after all, a good way to get round the Appellation regulations, where previously the wines had to be sold for blending, a much less profitable way to go.

All in all, the Chardonnay revolution has been a good thing for the wine industry in general. It has made wine drinking more popular, as people are able to identify a dry, light wine no matter where in the world it has been produced: as their tastes develop, they may like a particular vintage or a particular vineyard's production, but meanwhile they can enjoy a reliable product. From the viewpoint of the producers, it has been a way to establish a competitive advantage by using a direct, no-nonsense (and quintessentially New World) approach to branding the wines. Converting the conservative French wine industry from market leaders to market followers has been an added bonus.

"It's going to be a great summer..."

Matt Gallo

Small things certainly make a difference. A few years back we wanted to find out how good our Lodi vineyards were at growing Chardonnay grapes.

Our Lodi vineyards sit right in the middle of the fruit basket of California. Great soils, balmy climate, and a weather pattern almost hand picked for grapes.

The result, our latest Chardonnay now displays even more ripe apple and citrus flavours, and is deliciously refreshing and crisp... Whatever the weather.

Ernest & Julio Gallo
WINE CELLARS
1999
CHARDONNAY
CALIFORNIA

🍇🍇 **Wines from the family of Ernest & Julio Gallo**

Case study
Standard Chartered Group

In 1969 two banks whose roots went back to the height of the British Empire merged to form the Standard Chartered Bank. The Standard Bank of British South Africa and the Chartered Bank of India, Australia and China had both been founded in the mid-19th century to offer banking services to the burgeoning trade of the Empire: the Kimberley diamond mines and (later) the gold strikes near Johannesburg were the foundation of the Standard Bank, while the trade in tea, indigo and cotton from India, silk from Japan, tobacco from Sumatra and hemp from Manila were the industries funded by the Chartered Bank.

By 1953, Standard Bank had 600 branches throughout most of Southern and Central Africa, and in 1965 it merged with the Bank of West Africa, thus gaining branches in Ghana, Cameroon, Gambia, Nigeria and Sierra Leone. Meanwhile, Chartered expanded into the Middle East as far as Cyprus.

The bank's geographical spread and its importance in many Third World countries mean that it needs to provide a wide range of services to meet the business needs of a culturally-diverse group of customers. The bank divides its activities into five areas:

1 *Personal banking*. With 1700 branches worldwide, the bank has 14 million customers. The bank is of course well-placed to offer international banking services to clients, and it offers the full range of services – mortgages, loans, credit cards, cheque accounts, savings accounts and so forth.

2 *SME banking*. Offering finance for small and medium enterprises is a crucial activity for any bank operating in the developing world, but it is also important in the more affluent markets of Hong Kong, Singapore and the Middle East.

3 *Wholesale banking*. This division deals with large deals, and with major cross-border financial packages. The wholesale division even offers a credit management service, collecting outstanding debts on behalf of its clients.

4 *Saadiq banking*. This division offers Shariah-compliant banking to Muslims. Standard Chartered has branches in 50 per cent of the Islamic world: under Shariah laws, Muslims are not allowed to accept or pay interest on loans, so banking has to follow very different rules from those which apply in non-Muslim countries. Standard Chartered is extremely well placed to offer these services.

5 *Private banking*. This service is aimed at high net worth individuals and corporations, and offers wealth management services. In other words, the Private Banking division exists to help wealthy people manage their money better, and it offers personalised, tailored solutions for these individuals and corporations. Again, Standard Chartered is well placed to offer global solutions for such clients.

On an absolute scale, Standard Chartered is not among the world's largest banks (HSBC has over 10 000 branches worldwide, for example). The bank has 73 000 employees, and claims to be 'passionate about our customers' success' which is no bad thing for a bank. The bank also aims to be a global bank with in-depth local knowledge of each of its markets, and in this it succeeds extremely well. Where Standard Chartered scores is in its strong presence in markets which other banks might find difficult – the unstable economies of Africa, the volatile Asian markets and the unusual banking situations in Islamic countries. The bank also scores highly on its ability to offer financial bridges between its customer countries: in many cases, the only secure way for firms to do business across these borders is by using Standard Chartered as the go-between. In Hong Kong, Standard Chartered is one of the three banks which issue Hong Kong dollars, providing the Special Administrative Region with its own currency independent of Chinese *renminbi* (or *yuan*).

Perhaps surprisingly, the bank has few customers in the UK, despite being headquartered in London. The bank's role in promoting trade into and out of the countries in which it does business is of paramount importance to individuals and businesses based in those countries. Promotion policy in such a diverse marketplace is far from simple, but Standard Chartered has managed to find a way which appeals to people worldwide. The bank sponsors marathons in many parts of the world, including Mumbai, Lahore, Dubai, Hong Kong, Nairobi and even Port Stanley in the Falkland Islands. This has culminated in what the bank has called The Greatest Race on Earth, in which teams of four people compete in marathons in four cities. One team member runs in each of the marathons, held in Singapore, Mumbai, Nairobi and Hong Kong, with an overall prize going to the best team. In 2008, the Kenyan teams swept the board – which fact did not go unnoticed in Africa.

Copyright © 2007 Standard Chartered Bank

Standard Chartered is a bank on a mission. Using a close understanding of its local markets, coupled with a global vision, the bank seeks to encourage trade and build up its customers' businesses. This can only be good for the bank in the long run.

Questions

1 What type of market scope strategy does Standard Chartered appear to be following?

2 What is Standard Chartered competitive position?

3 How might the Standard Chartered collaborate with other banks to strengthen its position worldwide?

4 What type of approach to strategy would work best for Standard Chartered?

5 Which of Treacy and Wiersema's competitive positions is Standard Chartered following?

References

Ackoff, R.L. (1986): *Management in Small Doses* (London: John Wiley).

Ansoff, H.I. (1968): *Corporate Strategy* (Harmondsworth: Penguin).

Ansoff, H.I. (1984): *Implementing Strategic Management* (Harlow: Prentice Hall).

Baruch, Y. and Pieperl, M. (1999): The impact of an MBA on graduate careers. *Human Resource Management Journal* **10**(2), 69–89.

Black, A., Wright, P. and Bachman, J.E. (1998): *In Search of Shareholder Value* (London: Pitman).

Booms, B.H. and Bitner, M.J. (1981): Marketing strategies and organisation structures for service firms. In J. Donnelly and W.R. George (eds.) *Marketing of Services* (Chicago, IL, American Marketing Association).

Calantone, R.J. and Cooper, R.G. (1981): New product scenarios: prospects for success. *American Journal of Marketing* **2**(45), 48–60.

Clifford, D.K. and Cavanaugh, R.E. (1985): *The Winning Performance: How America's High- and Mid-size Growth Companies Succeed* (New York: Bantam).

De Geus, A. (1997): *The Living Company* (Boston, MA: Harvard Business School Press).

Doyle, P. (2000): *Value-Based Marketing: Marketing Strategies for Corporate Growth and Shareholder Value* (London: Wiley).

Haines D.W., Chandran, R. and Parkhe, A. (1989): Winning by being first to market. … Or last? *Journal of Consumer Marketing* **6**(1), 63–9.

Hamel, G., Doz, Y. and Prahalad, C.K. (1989): Collaborate with your competitors – and win. *Harvard Business Review* January/February.

Hannan, M.T. and Freeman,.J. (1988): *Organisational Ecology* (Cambridge, MA: Harvard University Press).

Hax, A.C. (1990): Redefining the concept of strategy and the strategic formation process. *Planning Review* May/June, 34–40.

Hennart, J.F. Roehl, T. and Zeitlow, D.S. (1999): Trojan horse or workhorse? The evolution of US–Japanese joint ventures in the United States. *Strategic Management Journal* **20**(1), 15–29.

Homburg, C. and Krohmer, Workman, J.P. Jr (1999): Strategic concensus and performance: the role of strategy type and market related dynamism. *Strategic Management Journal* **20**(4), 339–57.

Mason, R. and Mitroff, I. (1981): *Challenging Strategic Planning Assumptions* (New York: Wiley).

McDonald, M.H.B. (1984): *Marketing Plans* (London: Heinemann).

McKay, E.S. (1972): *The Marketing Mystique* (New York: American Management Association).

McKinsey Quarterly, The (1993): *Marketing's Mid-Life Crisis*.

Mintzberg, H. (1996): Learning 1, Planning 0. *California Management Review* **38**(4), 92–4.

Mintzberg, H. (1989): *Mintzberg on Management* (New York: Free Press).

Mintzberg, H. (1994): *The Rise and Fall of Strategic Planning* (New York: Free Press).

Pettigrew, A. and Whipp, R. (1991): *Managing Change for Competitive Success* (Oxford: Basil Blackwell).

Piercy, N. and Cravens, D.W. (1999): Marketing organisation and management. In *Encyclopaedia of Marketing* (London: International Thomson Business Press), pp. 186–207.

Porter, M.E. (1985): *Competitive Advantage* (NewYork: Free Press).

Porter, M.E. (1996): What is strategy? *Harvard Business Review* (November/December), 61–78.

Porter, M.E. (1998): *Competitive Strategy: Techniques for Analyzing Industries and Competitors* (New York: Free Press).

Rittel, H. (1972): On the planning crisis: systems analysis of the first and second generations. *Bedriftsokonomen* **8**, 390–6.

Stacey, R.D. (1993): Strategy as order emerging from chaos. *Long Range Planning* **26**(1), 10–17.

Steiner, G. and Miner, J. (1977): *Management Policy and Strategy: Text, Readings and Cases* (New York: Macmillan).

Thompson, J.L. (1997): *Strategic Management: Awareness and Change* (London: Thomson).

Treacy, M. and Wiersema, F. (1993): Customer intimacy and other value disciplines. *Harvard Business Review* January/February, 84–93.

Tse, A.C.B., Sin, L.Y.M., Yau, O.H.M., Lee, J.S.Y. and Chow, R. (2004): A firm's role in the marketplace and the relative importance of market orientation and relationship marketing orientation. *European Journal of Marketing* **38**(9/10), 1158–72.

Webster, E. (1992): The changing role of marketing in the corporation. *Journal of Marketing* **56**(4), 1–18.

Whittington, R. (2001): *What is Strategy – And Does It Matter?* (London: Thomson).

Williamson, O.E. (1991): Strategising, economising and economic organisation. *Strategic Management Journal* **12**, 75–94.

Further reading

For general reading on management strategy, Thompson, J.L.'s (1997) *Strategic Management: Awareness and Change* (London: Thomson Business Press) provides a very good, comprehensive overview.

For greater depth on marketing strategy, *Marketing Strategy* (2003): by Blythe, J. (Maidenhead: McGraw Hill) is a concise and reader-friendly text. For even greater detail, Jain, S. (2000): *Marketing: Planning and Strategy* (Mason, OH: Southwestern) covers the subject admirably.

Chapter 11
Building customer relationships

Learning objectives After reading this chapter, you should be able to:

1. Explain how the value chain (and value network) concepts relate to supplying customer needs.

2. Understand the role of intermediaries in reducing costs.

3. Explain the core activities in the value chain.

4. Explain how the seller's activities affect the quality of the buyer–seller relationship.

5. Explain what is meant by quality.

6. Describe how service quality helps to differentiate suppliers.

7. Explain how to resolve customer complaints.

8. Describe the stages in customer defection.

9. Explain how to decide which customers should be encouraged to return.

Introduction

In the early days of marketing, the emphasis was on encouraging people to buy products and services from a specific producer. Advertising and other promotional activities were intended to bring in new customers, but once the customers had made their purchases companies tended to lose interest in them, assuming that they would remain loyal provided the products were satisfactory.

Recently this view has been challenged. Increased competition lures customers away: customers are, in any case, less loyal than they might have been in the days when there were few choices of product. A dwindling number of potential customers (as a result of falling populations) and a reduction in the effectiveness of advertising (as a result of an increase in clutter from excessive competition) means that there is a greater emphasis on retaining existing customers rather than attracting new ones. Various estimates have been put forward as to the relative costs of attracting new customers as opposed to retaining existing ones, but it is almost certainly cheaper to retain an existing customer than to recruit a new one.

The Value Chain

The first element in building customer relationships is the value the customer receives from the end product. In the past, marketers have tended to consider the product as being that which comes from a manufacturer, is passed through wholesalers and

Preview case
New Zealand Telecom

In common with many other national telephone systems worldwide, New Zealand Telecom has its roots in the Government-owned New Zealand Post Office. Originally, post offices were seen as the natural home for telephone operations – all long-distance communication came under their remit, including telegrams and even radio. However, the increasing complexity of telecommunications, plus the drive (during the 1980s) to make state-owned enterprises more efficient, led to the privatisation of telephone systems worldwide.

New Zealand Telecom was bought out by Bell Atlantic and Ameritech in 1990, and is now quoted on both the New Zealand and the New York stock exchanges. It is the largest company on the New Zealand exchange – perhaps not surprising, since New Zealand is a medium-size country with a small population, so it needs a large telephone infrastructure, but has few large businesses.

Like many other former nationalised industries, Telecom has had its share of teething troubles. In 2004 it won the Roger Award for the Worst Transnational Company Operating in New Zealand, and it has been criticised for

not developing a suitable broadband system for the country. It has competition – Telstra operates a competing landline system, and there are several mobile telephone providers in New Zealand, all competing against Telecom's mobile system. Telecom still has a monopoly on the New Zealand broadband network, but this is unlikely to last much longer. The company has also been in trouble over some of its advertising – one advertisement showed children saying, 'Only dumb kids read books, brainy kids have broadband'. This was widely condemned, not least by the New Zealand librarians' association.

In the days when the telecoms industry in New Zealand was a Government monopoly, there was no need for the company to worry about customer relationships. In the competitive climate of the 21st century, customers can easily go elsewhere – and in the interests of consumer choice and industry efficiency most telecom systems are being deregulated and competition is being encouraged. This has left New Zealand Telecom with a major problem and a steep learning curve.

---

retailers, and eventually lands with the end consumer. This view has been superseded to an extent by a holistic view, which examines the whole chain of events from raw material extraction through to the store shelf. This chain is called the value chain, because it is the means by which value is delivered to the end consumer in exchange for money.

value chain analysis Assessment of ways in which organisations add value to the products they handle.

Value chain analysis examines the ways in which organisations add value to the products as they pass along the chain. This involves analysis of the organisations themselves, and also the interactions between suppliers and distributors within the chain. Value chain analysis recognises that each organisation within the chain adds value to the product: this is an obvious proposition, since they would not be able to become part of the chain unless the other members thought that they had something to offer, yet people often talk of 'cutting out the middle man' as if these organisations were not adding value. Each increment of value added to the product needs to be greater than the cost of adding it, otherwise that particular member of the chain is not operating efficiently and will either be cut out of the chain or will be unable to show a profit and will disappear. Much of the efficiency gained by effective firms lies in their ability to manage the linkages between themselves and other organisations in an effective manner.

The implications of this are as follows:

1 Value creation requires cooperation from all the members of the chain. Whether this comes about through negotiated coordination of activities or through market forces does not matter greatly: the organisations rely on each other either way.

2 Those in the chain must consider the needs of other chain members if the process is to work to mutual advantage.

Figure 11.1

The value chain

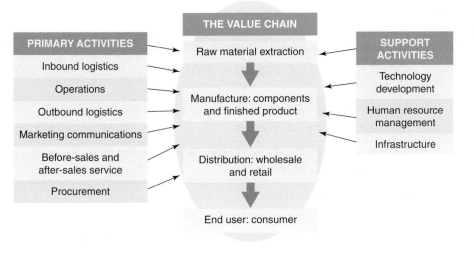

THE VALUE CHAIN

PRIMARY ACTIVITIES
- Inbound logistics
- Operations
- Outbound logistics
- Marketing communications
- Before-sales and after-sales service
- Procurement

Raw material extraction

Manufacture: components and finished product

Distribution: wholesale and retail

End user: consumer

SUPPORT ACTIVITIES
- Technology development
- Human resource management
- Infrastructure

3 Cost improvement and efficiency improvements will benefit everyone in the chain in the long run, but most especially will benefit the individual member because there is no need to renegotiate with other members in order to reap the benefits.

4 There is therefore a premium on managing the value chain within the firm itself.

5 There is a fundamental reliance on the contribution of people.

This management of the interfaces between organisations is also a manifestation of relationship marketing. Developing good working relationships with suppliers and customers means changing the organisation's working patterns to adapt to the needs of the other organisations, and also considering their profitability as well as the company's own profitability.

Within the value chain, there exist the categories of activity shown in Table 11.1 (Porter 1985). All of these activities must be carried out by some (or even all) of the members of the chain. Very few companies undertake all the activities in the value chain, from raw material extraction through to final retailing of the product: a notable exception is the major oil companies, which explore for oil, drill for it, refine it, package it and retail its products. Even these companies subcontract some of their activities – for example, oil well fires are typically handled by outside specialist companies.

In most cases, activities within the most efficient value chains are handled by specialist firms: for example, the food industry often works through a large number of intermediaries, each supplying specialist skills, which means that the value chain operates very efficiently. Hence a can of tuna, which has been handled by perhaps eight members of a value chain, can retail at 35p.

Many of the activities might be contracted-out to other members of the supply chain: for example, technological advances often come as a result of research grants to universities. Identifying the **core competences** needed for each member of the value chain (and for the chain as a whole) is a process which will vary from one industry to another, so that (for example) an accountancy firm which has a core competence in dealing with performing artists such as musicians and actors will not have the same level of expertise when dealing with small manufacturing businesses.

core competences The central, most important aspects of the company's abilities.

Oil companies carry out all the functions of the value chain, from exploration to retailing.

Table 11.1 Primary and support activities in the value chain

	Activity	Explanation and examples
Primary activities	Inbound logistics	Activities concerned with receiving, storing and distributing raw materials and components.
	Operations	Transforming inputs into outputs: raw materials into components, or components into finished products.
	Outbound logistics	Collection, storage and delivery to customers. This might be undertaken by a delivery or warehousing firm.
	Marketing communications	Functional aspects of marketing. Making customers aware of the product, and fine-tuning the offering.
	Before-sales and after-sales service	Activities which maintain or enhance product value. For example, repair services are often contracted-out.
	Procurement	Processes involved in obtaining the necessary resources for the primary activities. Raw material and equipment purchase, acquisition of office space etc.
Support activities	Technology development	Technological advances in product or process, or even in resource improvement, may be subcontracted.
	Human resource management	The activities involved in developing an effective workforce: hiring, training, motivating and rewarding.
	Infrastructure	Planning, financing, quality control, information management, communication and so forth.

The value chain is supported by four core activities:

1 **Procurement**. Acquiring the inputs used in the value chain is a key function: inputs must be of the right quality, the right quantity and at the right price, but they must also be delivered at the right time. Procurement is concerned with anything used in the course of providing marketing inputs, servicing inputs or materials used for outbound logistics.

2 *Human resource management*. This is the function of recruiting, training and rewarding staff members in the organisation.

3 *Technology development*. This includes know-how, research and development, product design and process improvement work.

4 *Infrastructure*. This includes working spaces (factories, offices, mines etc.), the organisational structure of the firm, the financial and operational control systems, and the feedback systems used by management.

procurement Obtaining goods to be used in production or running the organisation.

outbound logistics Controlling the flow of product from the organisation to its customers.

Each of the activities in the chain might lead to competitive advantage. In some firms, it is only the marketing that really distinguishes the product: in other value chains, the reliability of **outbound logistics** might be the deciding factor (especially if the customer operates a just-in-time purchasing system). However, one of the problems of value-chain analysis, from a marketer's viewpoint, is that marketing becomes relegated to a function within the system rather than the over-riding philosophy of the organisation. For a marketer, marketing should be the guiding philosophy in everything the firm does, from purchasing through to human resources and on into outbound logistics.

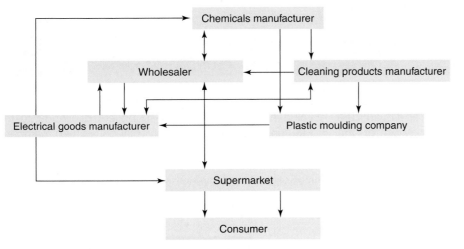

Figure 11.2
Value network

In some cases the value chain becomes a **value network**. Rather than a linear process in which raw materials progress through to consumers' homes in a straight line, with value being added at each stage, firms might contribute collectively to one stage, might be suppliers to one stage of the process and customers of another, and products might move back and forth between network members. This is illustrated in Figure 11.2. In this example, a chemicals manufacturer supplies raw materials to a cleaning products manufacturer, and also to a plastics moulding company. The plastics company supplies to a wholesaler, and to an electrical goods manufacturer. The cleaning products company supplies industrial cleaning products to the manufacturers in the network, and consumer products via the wholesaler, who also handles some of the products from the electrical goods manufacturer. The electrical goods manufacturer supplies products to the other companies and also supplies consumer products through the wholesaler and direct to the retailer.

Furthermore, each separate company in the chain has relationships with many other companies, in other words each firm is involved in several value chains at once. Adapting the firm's practices to each value chain becomes difficult or impossible – especially if members of one supply chain feel that they are being unfairly dealt with compared with members of another value chain. Obviously in such circumstances the management of the process relies heavily on developing close relationships within the network, on communicating effectively and openly between members and on developing a high degree of trust between the members of the chain.

For firms in global markets, many relationships in many different countries need to be considered. The value network may be different for each major customer: for example, Taylor Woodrow may form alliances with many companies in order to carry out a major construction project; intelligent managers know when to cooperate with competitors and when to compete. Marketing alliances of all kinds have been developed to serve customers. These may focus on product or service, promotion, logistics or joint pricing (Kotler 2003).

value network The group of organisations which collectively add value to raw materials.

Building Relationships

Building long-term relationships with customers has long been practiced in business-to-business marketing. This is because there are relatively few customers in business markets, so that the loss of even one customer can have serious consequences. For example, there are only nine major High Street banks in Britain: a company specialising

E-Marketing in Practice
Eurotunnel

Putting a tunnel under the English Channel to connect Britain with Continental Europe is an idea which has been around since 1802. Most of the opposition to the idea came from the military people – the English Channel has proved to be a successful defence for Britain for thousands of years. The growth of the European Union changed that, however – and the obvious fact that a bridge or tunnel is easily dynamited may have swayed the argument somewhat. In 1986 Margaret Thatcher (for Britain) and Francois Mitterand (for France) signed a treaty which authorised the tunnel to be built.

The tunnel was built by a consortium of British and French civil engineering contractors. For the British, Taylor Woodrow, Costain, Wimpey, Balfour Beatty and Tarmac: for the French, Bouygues, Dumez, Spie Batignolles, Société Auxiliaire D'Entreprises and Société Générale D'Entreprise. In normal times, these companies are competitors, but the sheer size of the project meant that one company alone could not handle the job. Each of the companies involved had, in typical builder fashion, other jobs on at the time. Wimpey was Britain's biggest house builder, Taylor Woodrow had a series of office-building contracts, Costain had road-building contracts and so forth. The companies were collaborators on the Tunnel, but competitors for the other jobs – yet managed to make the project work.

Eurotunnel was, and still is, the largest civil engineering project the world has ever seen. It could not have been completed without the establishment of a number of value networks – concrete suppliers delivering to the Eurotunnel as well as to individual consortium members, railway companies buying tunnel track as well as office buildings and so forth. The complexity of the total network involved almost every construction company, supplier and customer in both Britain and France, and affected firms throughout the world.

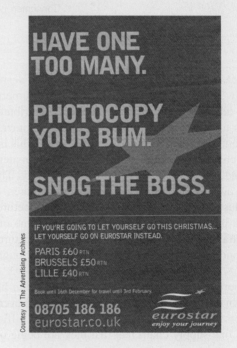

Courtesy of The Advertising Archives

relationship marketing The practice of concentrating on the lifetime value of customers rather than their value in the single transaction.

in computer software for cash point machines would be ill-advised to create a bad relationship with even one of them. Relationship marketing has met with rather less success in consumer markets, perhaps because consumers do not see any advantage in establishing a close relationship with the firms that supply the goods they use. There is, in fact, little research evidence to show that long-term customers are always more profitable than short-term ones, and also little evidence to show that satisfaction leads to loyalty (although it does lead to recommendations, which of course are likely to lead to acquisition of new customers) (East, Hammond and Gendall 2006). Other researchers claim that there is a relationship between customer loyalty and profitability (Helgesen 2006), so it seems likely that other factors (for example, industry and product types) affect the relationship.

The history of relationship marketing goes back to the Japanese *keiretsu* system, in which the companies in the value chain become extremely closely linked through a system of agreements, often for exclusive supply of components and raw materials. The *keiretsu* operate mainly on verbal agreements: Japanese businesses rarely worry too much about written contracts, since the Japanese legal system is not geared to enforcing such contracts. The result is a system which involves high degrees of trust and loyalty, and which apparently functions extremely efficiently.

The lesson was not lost on Western organisations. Companies such as Bose, Compaq and Motorola began to send their engineering personel to their suppliers in order to liaise on new product development and to consider ways of making the supply process more efficient, and they also stationed their salesforce in the retailers' offices to help in merchandising the products (Leenders and Blenkhorn 1988). Upstream and downstream involvement by the major companies in running the value chain made everything work more efficiently and therefore more profitably for all concerned. Another driver for relationship marketing may be that companies are often unskilled at managing customer acquisition: few companies have a coordinated system for acquiring new customers (Ang and Buttle 2006).

Talking Point

Are business relationships really that close? Do firms readily join together and fall in love with each other? Or are such relationships mere marriages of convenience?

After all, a firm has many people it has a much closer responsibility to – its customers, its employees, its neighbours, and not forgetting the poor old shareholders who put up the money in the first place! So is it right that the managers should try to create close relationships elsewhere? Aren't they being disloyal – some might even say unfaithful – in contracting relationships with other firms?

Or is it more the case that those close to the firm – customers, employees, etc. – are more like family, and they should encourage the firm to 'date' other firms?

A turning point in the thinking on relationship marketing came with the publication of research by consultants Bain & Co. in which they found that **cross-selling** to an existing customer costs one-sixth as much as selling to a new customer. What is more, they found that a 5 per cent increase in customer retention would increase the value of each customer by between 25 and 100 per cent (Reed 1999). Further research has supported this view of relationship marketing: firms which adopt relationship marketing have been shown to be more successful than firms which do not (Chaston *et al.* 2003), and the relationship between companies has been shown to be more important than either service quality (Roberts, Varki and Brodie 2003) or even price (Oederkerken-Schroeder *et al.* 2003). Even in consumer markets, loyalty is initially the result of perceived value, but later on affection for the company mediates the loyalty of customers (Johnson, Herrmann and Huber 2006).

cross-selling Selling new product lines to an existing customer.

How good the buyer–seller relationship remains is determined by how well the seller manages it (Weitz and Bradford 1999). Managing the relationship, in the business-to-business arena, is largely the responsibility of the sales force because it is the salespeople who regularly see the customers, but in a truly relationship-orientated company the whole firm should be involved in maintaining good relationships with customers. This means that the firm's engineers should be in contact with the other firm's engineers, the administrators should be seeking ways of making their interactions run more efficiently, the delivery drivers should be considerate of the customer's warehouse staff and so forth. Establishing such a broad range of contacts may not be simple, and it may not happen overnight, but such arrangements can only be beneficial for all parties: in business relationships, interactions range from the single exchange through to a full relationship portfolio of exchanges at every level (Holmlund 2004). The evidence is that empowering employees to manage problems between themselves will significantly increase customer satisfaction, loyalty and perceived quality (Evans and Laskin 1994; Dunleavy and Olivieri 2001).

Ultimately, good relationships depend on commitment and trust (Morgan and Hunt 1994). Trust moderates the effects of interdependence by enhancing the perception of the relational orientation of both manufacturer and supplier (Izquierdo and Cillan 2004). As the relationship deepens, the emphasis shifts from single transactions through to cooperation, and the nature of the problems being addressed by the partners also shifts (Wilson 1993). At the beginning of the relationship, the parties tend to be concerned with product-based problems: design, specifications, performance and so forth. As the

Table 11.2 KAM stages of development model

Stage of development	Objectives	Strategies
Pre-KAM: the relationship has not yet started: each partner is looking for the other.	Define and identify strategic account potential. Secure initial contact.	Identify key contacts and decision-making unit. Establish product need. Display willingness to address other areas of problem.
Early-KAM: The partners have made a start on doing business together.	Account penetration. Increase volume of business. Achieve preferred supplier status.	Build social network. Identify process-related problems and signal willingness to work together to provide cost-effective solutions.
Mid-KAM: The partnership is established and working well, the partners are looking for ways to make it even more effective.	Build partnership. Consolidate preferred supplier status. Establish key account in-house.	Focus on process-related issues. Manage the implementation of process-related solutions. Build inter-organisational teams. Establish joint systems. Begin to perform non-core management tasks.
Partnership-KAM. The partners are operating in a highly integrated way, dividing the work and the profits by mutual agreement.	Develop spirit of partnership. Build common culture. Lock in customer by being external resource base.	Integrate processes. Extend joint problem-solving. Focus on cost reduction and joint value-creating opportunities. Address key strategic issues of the client. Address facilitation issues.
Synergistic-KAM. At this point the companies are virtually indistinguishable. They operate almost entirely together.	Continuous improvement. Shared rewards. Quasi-integration.	Focus on joint value creation. Create semi-autonomous project teams. Develop strategic congruence.
Uncoupling-KAM. This can occur after any stage: the partners decide that the relationship is not working and they go their separate ways.	Disengagement.	Withdraw.

relationship deepens and the product problems are resolved, the parties tend to concentrate more on process issues – delivery times, relation to the value-creation processes of the customer. When the relationship is fully developed the parties become more concerned about facilitation, in other words the way in which business is carried out between them. At this point, the companies might be so close as to be almost indistinguishable to an outside observer.

In 1995 Millman and Wilson developed the KAM (key account management) stages of development model, which identified six stages of development in dyadic relationships. This model was later combined with the PPF model to shown how the problem-solving aspects link to the stages of development. This combined model is shown in Table 11.2.

The process of developing these relationships is a slow one – it would normally take several years to work through the process from initial contact to synergy, but the rewards make it worth the effort. The more efficiently the value chain (or value network) operates, the more likely it is that the partners in the chain will reach their strategic objectives. Developing the relationship is a worthwhile exercise for smaller, weaker firms: research shows that such firms can thrive in relationships with larger firms if they can develop high levels of trust (Narayandas and Rangan 2004).

Inevitably relationships will occasionally end. There are six basic types of ending for relationships (Michalski 2004):

1 *Forced*. This is a situation in which the relationship is dissolved by outside forces, for example Government monopoly regulators.

2 *Sudden*. One or other of the partners breaks off the relationship without warning.

3 *Creeping*. The partners gradually move their attention and business elsewhere.

4 *Optional*. An alternative set of relationships is offered.

5 *Involuntary*. One or other partner is compelled to withdraw.

6 *Planned*. The partners understand that there must be a separation, and they carry it out in the most equitable manner possible.

Suppliers are often reluctant to end relationships even if the relationship is unprofitable: this may be because the companies have little understanding of how to manage relationships (Helm, Rolfes and Gunther 2006).

Contracts provide the governing structure of relationships, especially in the early stages and the dissolution stages (Traynor and Traynor 2004), but it is the personal relationships between the individuals in the firms which decide the nature of the business relationship. For relationship marketers in business-to-business environments, products cease to be bundles of benefits as such, but become relational processes in which an overall value is created (Tuli, Kohli and Bharadwaj 2007).

Quality, Value and Service

Quality is the relationship between what customers expect and what they get. If a customer's expectations of a product are low, then he or she will not be disappointed: if, however, the customer has been led to expect a high-quality product and is in fact given a poor-quality one, he or she has the right to feel aggrieved. If the product exceeds expectations, the quality of the product will be perceived to be high.

Perception of quality is closely-related to the customer's views on what constitutes value for money. For example, a hotel room might cost anything between £50 a night and £500 a night – or more. The person staying in the £500 room clearly considers this to be value for money, as does the person staying in the £50 room: the difference lies in their relative perceptions of the value of money, and the level of comfort and service they expect for their money.

It follows from this that quality is not an absolute. Quality is in the eye of the beholder – or at least in the perception of the consumer, because each individual is starting with a different set of expectations. Service support is critical to relationship marketing, because it is during the pre-sale and after-sale support that customers are approached as individuals. It is at this time that customers' perceptions of quality will become apparent – and the front-line staff (salespeople, etc.) who deal directly with customers are able either to adjust the customers' expectations (pre-sale) or correct any problems with the product (after-sale).

In the past, quality was seen as the province of the production department, which led to the product concept mentioned in Chapter 1. Under a relationship marketing ethos, quality has become the integrating concept between production orientation and marketing orientation (Gummeson 1988). Marketing has the role of managing the customers' expectations – either by adjusting the expectations or by fine-tuning the product: concentration on the product alone is not enough.

For its guests, this luxury hotel in Dubai is worth what it costs.

Figure 11.3

Servqual model

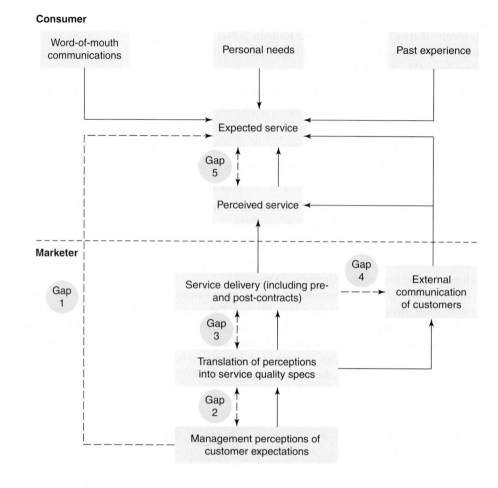

If we subscribe to this philosophy, then service quality can be defined as the ability of the organisation to meet or exceed customer expectations. The relationship marketer therefore needs to monitor the quality of the firm's output against two criteria: the customers' expectations and the firm's actual output. A well-known model for assessing service quality is Parasuraman, Zeithaml and Berry's (1985) Servqual model, shown in Figure 11.3.

The model shows various gaps which might develop and which need to be addressed. These are as follows:

- *Gap One*. The difference between actual customer expectations and management perceptions of customer expectations.
- *Gap Two*. The difference between management perceptions of customer expectations and service quality specifications.
- *Gap Three*. The difference between service quality specifications and the service actually delivered.
- *Gap Four*. The difference between service delivery and what is communicated about the service to customers.
- *Gap Five*. The difference between customer expectations and the perceptions of what is actually received. This gap is influenced by the other four.

In order to close the gaps, marketers may need to adopt a series of quality control procedures. Some of these may already be well-known to the production department, others are more specific to marketers.

E-Marketing in Practice
VSDA

The Vision Site Design Awards are given to the designers of excellent websites. VSDA is associated with the major design associations, and awards its prestigious design awards only to those websites which achieve brilliance in comparison with other websites.

Therein, of course, is the essence of this type of award. It is, in effect, a benchmarking award: the websites are not only compared with other sites in the same industry, they are compared with websites across the Internet. Thus a website for a bookseller might be compared with a website for an airline, for a Government department or for a university. For the e-marketer, the lesson is clear – customers will make similar comparisons across the range of websites they deal with on a daily basis.

Total quality management

The intention behind total quality management is to ensure that the firm and its associates does the right things at the right time in every stage of the value chain. The theory is that if every stage of the process is carried to the highest standards, or at least the appropriate standards, the outcome will be a product or service of the appropriate quality. The problem with this is that it does not take account of the customer's expectations, but instead relies on the firm's view of what constitutes a high-quality process. This means that the company will have difficulty in deciding at what level to pitch the quality assurance at each stage of the process.

The main contribution total quality management has is in the reduction of waste, and consequently a reduction in costs, because finished products will not need to be rejected due to component failures. The concept of zero-defect manufacture has led to dramatic cost savings in some industries, but apart from the cost savings has relatively little effect on marketing issues.

Benchmarking

Benchmarking is the process of comparing each element of the value chain, including company departments, with the most successful equivalent element in equivalent value chains. If each element in the value chain operates to a level equivalent to the best example from all other value chains, the result should be a value chain which is the best of the best. The value chains chosen are not necessarily those in the same business: for example, someone who is assessing the efficiency of the check-in procedures of an airline may well compare them with the queue-handling systems at his or her usual supermarket. Telephone call centres are compared with other call centres, not with other firms in the same industry.

In practice, benchmarking generates considerable difficulties. First, it is often very difficult to obtain truly accurate data on the functioning of other companies. Second, even when data is available, it may be difficult to decide which are the critical factors in the competitors' success. Third, at a conceptual level it would seem strange to allow the firm's quality control to be dictated by other companies. Fourth, if benchmarking is adopted by everybody, it will stifle innovation. Finally, the costs incurred in bringing all departments up to the best standards of all other companies are likely to be high, which will inevitably have an effect on prices.

Benchmarking is likely to lead companies back into the fallacious product orientation approach. Consumers do not necessarily want the highest quality at all times – they do want the highest quality they can get for the money they have available to spend, in other words best value for money.

> **benchmarking** Setting performance parameters by comparing performance with that of the best of the competing firms.

Figure 11.4

Benchmarking

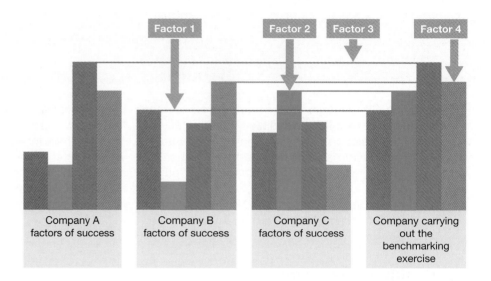

Service quality is often a major competitive differentiator for firms. For example, in the lubricating oil industry the specifications for the oil are laid down by engine manufacturers: the oil companies have to supply oil of a particular type, and this is the same across the industry with little opportunity to differentiate the physical product. Where the companies can differentiate themselves is in the service they offer: this may be concerned with delivery times, after-sales service, advice lines and so forth.

Christopher, Ballantyne and Payne (1991) have drawn up a five-stage approach to services benchmarking. This is as follows:

- *Stage 1.* Define the competitive arena, i.e. with whom are we compared by customers and with whom do we want to be compared?
- *Stage 2.* Identify the key components of customer service as seen by customers themselves.
- *Stage 3.* Establish the relative importance of those service components to customers.
- *Stage 4.* Identify the customer position on the key service components relative to the competition.
- *Stage 5.* Analyse the data to see if service performance matches customers' service needs.

Defining the competitive arena is not a simple matter, as we have seen in earlier chapters. Companies frequently define their competition in narrow terms, as simply being other companies which produce similar products rather than companies which offer consumers similar benefits. Firms need to consider which competitors the consumer compares them with – and these may well be firms in an entirely different industry. For example, Internet users might compare a retail website such as the bookseller Amazon with other retail websites in (say) the airline business. A telephone helpline for a computer software provider might be compared with the telephone helpline for a train company, and so forth.

The key components of customer service are often left to executive judgement without reference to the customers. For example, a computer owner might regard onsite maintenance calls as being far more useful and important than online support for software. A car owner whose car is in for its annual service might be more appreciative of a lift to the train station than of the car being ready by lunchtime. The problem for the service provider is that different people have different ideas of what is important – someone unfamiliar with computer software might set great store by a free helpline service, whereas someone who is very computer-literate but who lives a long way from a computer store might prefer on-site maintenance engineers to fix hardware faults.

Talking Point

There seems to be a growing view among companies that people want ever-better service and choice. This seems to have become the key to differentiating the product – but is it really the case?

Anyone who has visited the United States knows what restaurants are like there. The bewildering range of options for salad dressing, the many different options for how the food is to be cooked (low salt, low sugar, low fat, well-done, over easy, etc. etc.) and even the choice of bread rolls means that ordering a simple meal becomes a marathon task, not to mention the problem of remembering who ordered what. Compare this with the simplicity of ordering a meal in France, where the chef (as the acknowledged expert on food) *knows* what will taste good and what goes together well, and he makes sure you get it.

So do we really need all this service and choice all the time? Aren't there times when we just want to be told to sit down, shut up and eat the dinner? After all, which country has the better reputation for its food?

Once the key components are established, their relative importance needs to be assessed. This will vary from one person to the next, so it is helpful to segment the market: in the example given above, a computer retailer might deliberately aim for a 'beginners' market, or offer a beginners package, which would include a lot of online or telephone 'hand-holding'. An alternative package of after-sales service might be offered to the more computer-literate, perhaps offering free upgrades or more advanced software.

Identifying where we are in the customers' minds relative to the competition is a basic marketing function in any case. In the case of service provision, we should be doing this across a range of firms that offer similar types of after-sales and before-sales service, rather than simply firms which offer the same core product.

Having gone through the previous four stages, examining what we do in order to decide whether it fits with what the customers actually want us to do is relatively straightforward.

Managing the Relationship in Consumer Markets

Although relationship marketing appears to have flourished better in business-to-business markets, it has had some impact on consumer markets. The purpose of establishing a long-term relationship with the end consumers is to ensure that they come back, and keep coming back. This is in part a function of involvement (see Chapter 4). A loyal customer of a car manufacturer might easily spend £200 000 on cars over a lifetime, yet few manufacturers trouble to contact their end consumers regularly to check that the car is working well.

Companies need to recognise that people do not respond well to the idea of being managed – consumers will seek to control the relationship if they can. In some cases people have a fear of getting too close to a company or brand in case they are 'sold to': in other cases people might have a fear of loss, abandonment or rejection. People who are either low on both these dimensions, or high on both, report high satisfaction with brands: those who are high on one and low on the other report low satisfaction (Thompson and Johnson 2002).

In Figure 11.5, the cost of acquiring a new customer for each transaction is estimated at five times the cost of retaining an existing customer. Over the course of five transactions, the cost of finding new customers each time comes out to 10 per cent of the revenue obtained. Retaining the existing customer costs less than 4 per cent of the revenue. Over a longer period, the figures become even more favourable – for each

Figure 11.5

Relationship marketing in action

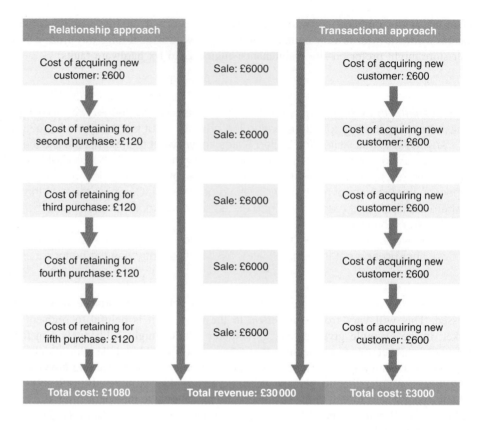

transaction, the existing customer costs only 2 per cent of the revenue obtained, whereas a new customer will still cost 10 per cent.

Part of the problem for marketers is that many consumers prefer not to establish relationships with the people who provide them with products and services. From a consumer's viewpoint, being telephoned or mailed regularly by everyone from whom they buy anything would be an imposition rather than a pleasure, and only in cases where the consumer feels heavily involved, or where there is some immediate material benefit, will they want to be troubled. Far too many companies use the 'courtesy call' approach when in fact they are only seeking to sell something else to the customer – only fairly sophisticated relationship marketers put the relationship first and the sales call second.

Having said that, there are some good examples of relationship management in consumer markets.

- *Supermarket loyalty cards*. These are used throughout the world to encourage shoppers to use the same supermarket for all their purchases. The evidence is that people frequently carry several loyalty cards for different supermarkets, thus somewhat reducing the usefulness of the system from the supermarket's viewpoint, but the cards do allow the supermarket to get a clearer picture of what each customer buys and enables the store to fine-tune its offering to ensure a closer fit with its customers. In theory, supermarkets should be able to predict the purchases of individual customers and thus be able to advise people better regarding special offers, new products and so forth, but in practice the Data Protection Act and the fact that people still shop in a wide variety of stores has made this somewhat difficult in practice. Loyalty cards no longer affect loyalty much, however, or change market structures, since most retailers offer loyalty cards and people simply use the appropriate card for the store they happen to be in at the time (Meyer-Waarden and Benavent 2006; Allaway *et al.* 2006).

Marketing in Practice
Brand Relationships

The brand is the focus for all marketing activities, so it is only natural that marketers should have had the idea of trying to encourage consumers to establish relationships with their brands. Some recent research has shown that the results of this are patchy and asked the question whether people actually do establish relationships with the products they buy. In other words, can people actually fall in love with a brand?

Brann Consulting's Relationship Marketing Survey of 1000 adults found that only 16 per cent thought that companies understood that they must give something back to consumers in order to maintain their trust. Forty-six per cent thought that companies think that they can manipulate people into buying more, and 48 per cent do not trust companies' marketing activities. Forty-four per cent thought that banks need to try harder to make customers feel valued, 28 per cent thought telephone companies should try harder and 36 per cent think that supermarkets should try harder.

The most important finding was in the field of relationships with brands. Respondents were asked whether they considered specific brands to be friends or casual acquaintances. Contrary to expectation, service brands such as banks, supermarkets and telephone companies were more likely to be considered casual acquaintances than were favourite tea and coffee brands, favourite beer or spirits, and even car brands and car dealerships, which were often considered to be friends. Interestingly, women were more likely to see their favourite brands as friends than were men: 58 per cent saw their favourite brand of coffee as a friend, for example.

On the plus side, people will admit to having relationships with favourite brands. On the minus side, the research seems to show that people are closer to their coffee than they are to their banks – which must make for depressing reading in financial services quarters.

- *Frequent flyer programmes.* Airlines (and others) operate loyalty schemes for passengers, some of which are extremely sophisticated. For example, KLM's Flying Blue programme has two parallel systems for earning points: one system provides the frequent flyer with free flights, upgrades and so forth, while the other system (which includes the number of flights taken within a given period as well as the distance flown) provides frequent flyers with extra baggage allowances, use of executive lounges at airports, rapid check-in etc.

- *'Friends' schemes for the Arts.* The Friends of Sadler's Wells Opera obtain 20 per cent discounts on tickets, get buy-one-get-one-free ticket deals, discounts on programmes and many other benefits. All these benefits are obtained in exchange for a £40 membership fee. Such schemes ensure loyalty at least until the initial fee has been recouped, and probably for some time afterwards.

In each of these cases the sponsoring company gains access to a list of names and addresses of people who have shown an interest in the firm, its products and its way of doing business. This is an essential stepping stone in developing direct marketing (see Chapter 19).

An important point to remember about relationship marketing is that many of the techniques used to generate loyalty are expensive and require considerable commitment: in the long run, the effort will pay off, but relationships are not built overnight and firms which try to cash in on the relationship too early are likely to do a great deal of damage to future business.

Loyalty and retention do not always come from satisfaction, however: switching barriers are also important (Patterson 2004). If it is difficult or expensive to switch from one supplier to another, people will apparently remain loyal – but of course, if it becomes easier to switch, or if the situation becomes intolerable, they may switch and will be difficult to win back. People who switch suppliers as a result of a recommendation from a friend or family member (referral switchers) are likely to become more loyal and have higher satisfaction ratings than switchers in general, and also are more likely to pass on the recommendation to others (Wangenheim and Bayon 2007). Switchers also tend to be more price-sensitive, whereas stayers are more sensitive to service quality (Leong and Qing 2006).

Loyalty sometimes comes about simply because the customer has little or no choice, or the switching costs are high: for example, even on the Internet (where the assumption has always been that there is very little to prevent people using different sites) research shows that people get bored with clicking through multiple sites to find bargains, and instead tend to stick to their usual supplier, where they know how to navigate the site and feel confident in what they are doing (Murray and Haubl 2002). People prefer not to spend a lot of time searching for information, another reason for staying with a familiar site (Zauberman 2002).

Customer Retention Strategies

Customer retention has become increasingly recognised as the key to long-term survival. In the past, most companies have operated on a 'leaky bucket' basis, seeking to refill the bucket with new customers while ignoring the ones leaking away through the bottom of the bucket. According to research by Gupta, Lehmann and Stuart (2004) a 1 per cent improvement in customer retention will lead to a 5 per cent improvement in the firm's value. A 1 per cent improvement in marginal cost or customer acquisition cost only makes 1 per cent increase in firm value respectively. In other words, according to Gupta *et al.* customer retention is five times as effective as cutting costs.

A study performed by the Cumberland Bank in the United States showed that the top 5 per cent of the customer base accounted for 40 per cent of total deposits, that a 5 per cent increase in retention of top customers added 4 per cent to the bank's profitability, and the minimum balance of the top 20 per cent of customers is $20 000. Reichheld

Figure 11.6

The leaky bucket

(1996) found that, in US corporations, 50 per cent of customers are lost over five years, 50 per cent of employees are lost in four years and 50 per cent of investors are lost in less than a year. Firms therefore need to recognise and reward loyal customers and ensure (as far as possible) that they remain as customers of the company's products.

Talking Point

Obviously it makes sense to retain customers if at all possible rather than have to go through the rigmarole of acquiring new ones. On the other hand, what are the implications?

Presumably a customer defected because he or she did not like what was on offer. In order to regain that lost customer, then, the firm has to offer something different and perhaps better. So what effect does that have on the thinking of the other customers? Presumably the best way to get some extras is to defect, then sit back and wait for the phone call! Is this the message we want our loyal customers to have?

Maybe we should think of a better way to regain lost customers!

Customers who remain with the firm are said to be loyal, but there are different types of loyalty. Table 11.3 shows the basic types of loyalty exhibited by customers.

Loyalty programmes which offer real economic benefits to customers affect both retention and customer share development positively (Verhoef 2003). The starting point for building trust is to keep promises, and the first set of promises any firm must keep is the promises surrounding the product and its performance. On the whole, customers

involvement Emotional attachment to a product or brand.

Table 11.3 Customer loyalty

Type of loyalty	Explanation
Price loyalty	Provided the organisation remains the price leader, these customers will remain loyal. If they do desert, it is more likely to be a result of a change of lifestyle (for example increased earnings) than a result of being lured away by a lower price elsewhere. Some businesses can make use of this fact: for example Tesco's supermarket own-brands cater for the wealthier customers (Tesco's Finest brand) and for the less wealthy (Tesco's Value brand).
Monopoly loyalty	The few firms who can exercise a monopoly have a captive customer base. However, as soon as an alternative becomes available they will defect.
Inertia loyalty	Most people are surrounded by different decisions which need to be made every day. This means that most of us remain loyal to most of the products we buy simply because it saves the trouble of finding a new product. Even though there might be major benefits attached to the new product, inertia prevents us from moving on. This is particularly true in banking: the vast majority of people stay with the same bank for most or all of their lives. Companies should beware of complacency, however – once defection starts, it will grow.
Emotional loyalty	Emotional loyalty is a function of **involvement** (see Chapter Four). Customers who are prepared to pay extra for the product, who are loyal to it whatever happens and who recommend the product to their friends are emotionally loyal.
Disloyalty	Dissatisfied customers will tell other customers of the same organisation about their experiences, and will often persuade the other customers to defect as well. This type of behaviour can be extremely damaging, because the experience of the disloyal customer is given great credence by other people.

understand that things do not always go perfectly, but a failure on the part of the firm to correct any faults in the product or the service means that the firm has broken its promises – a sure way to lose a customer. After a failure on the part of a supplying company, people adopt various coping strategies – re-evaluation of the brand's trustworthiness, apportioning blame or reinterpreting the brand into stereotypes. Sometimes the relationship actually strengthens if the problem is resolved, but the relationship may be renegotiated, or the customer may exit or avoid the brand in future. Forgiveness of the brand will involve a release of negative emotions (Chung and Beverland 2006). The possibility that the violation of trust might be repeated in future is more important in generating negative word of mouth and defection to the competition than is the magnitude of the violation (Wang and Huff 2007). In other words, people are more likely to forgive a major failure if they believe it is a one-off mistake rather than one of a series of even small failures.

The second area which any firm must get right is the interface with the customers. This is quite clearly the responsibility of the marketing people, but it is also the responsibility of everyone who comes into contact with customers in the course of the working day. Customer loyalty is positively related to technical service quality, functional service quality and customer education (Bell and Eisengrich 2007). The key to ensuring that customers are satisfied (better still, delighted) is to empower these front-line employees to make redress appropriately and on the spot. The relevance of the brand to the consumer is also relevant to defection – if the values expressed through the brand are salient, defection is less likely (Romaniuk and Sharp 2003). Customer satisfaction not only relates to greater return rates and word of mouth recommendations, it also makes advertising more effective and increases staff performance (dealing with satisfied customers is a great deal more pleasant than dealing with complaints) (Luo and Homburg 2007).

If a problem arises, there are three main elements in resolving the problem for the customer (Tax and Brown 1998). These are:

1 *Offer a fair outcome.* Refunds, replacements, credits, repairs and corrections of charges are typical forms of redress expected by customers. Most customers would also expect an apology as partial recompense for being treated unfairly or rudely, but Tax and Brown found that the majority of customers did not feel that their complaints had been met fairly. On the other hand, customers who felt that they had been treated fairly reported that they had received compensation for the inconvenience suffered as well as the basic exchange or repair. These customers also reported that they liked being offered a choice of compensation (for example a restaurant might offer a choice of vouchers against future meals, or a free liqueur with a customer's coffee).

2 *Offer a fair procedure.* Customers who thought that the procedure had been unfair had typically been frustrated by a prolonged procedure, often having to repeat their complaint to a number of different people, or being asked to deal with most of the problem themselves.

3 *Offer fair treatment.* Customers responded well to being treated honestly, politely and with concern. Making a genuine effort to resolve the problem was seen as a positive factor in remaining with the firm.

Perception of fairness depends on surrounding factors and social interactions: in other words, people will take account of mitigating circumstances, and are also affected by the way they are treated by staff (Carlson and Sally 2002).

Marketing in Practice
IKEA

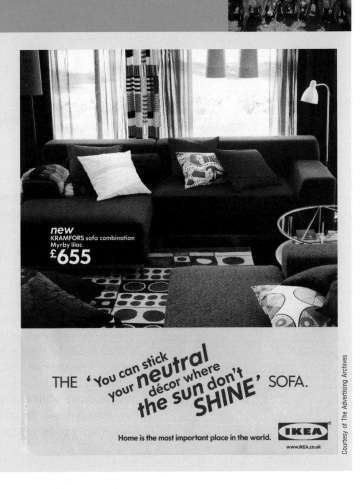

IKEA, the Swedish-based furniture retailer, runs huge warehouse-style retail outlets for its furniture and household goods. The furniture is mainly sold as flat-pack, self-assembly items, and the range of products is huge – perhaps 10 000 or more product lines under one roof.

IKEA's method of retailing furniture places heavy demands on shoppers. Making sure that they have picked up the three-drawer chest rather than the four-drawer is only one issue – customers need to navigate around the store and understand the system for buying the furniture. Inevitably, problems arise, but IKEA staff (called co-workers) are empowered to deal with problems instantly. They can give free meals at the in-store restaurant, free delivery, cash coupons, even instant discounts. Staff do not appear to abuse the system, and neither do customers. The result? IKEA turns over more than £6 billion worldwide in 160 stores, and is one of the fastest-growing retailers in the world.

Typically, people go through three distinct phases before finally terminating the relationship with a company which is giving unsatisfactory service (Griffin and Lowenstein 2001). These are:

1 **Value breakdown**. The service promise offered by the producer does not materialise. This may be a temporary failure, but much depends on how it is handled: for example, if a hotel has a breakdown in its hot water system, guests might be offered free drinks in the bar as a partial compensation while the system is repaired. If the failure is not addressed, the customer may simply accept the situation, and continue to buy, but with doubts.

value breakdown A situation in which the service offered by a producer does not materialise.

2 *The season of discontent*. After a series of value breakdown experiences, the customer will begin to look elsewhere, but may not actually defect yet. The warning signs for the firm are a reduced level of activity from this customer, and (in the case of business-to-business relationships) signs such as a reduced level of access to senior managers, a reduction in approvals for new proposals and negative feedback in the form of complaint letters or lowered performance ratings. Left unaddressed, the initial discontent will eventually lead the customer to defect to a competitor.

3 *Termination*. At this stage the customer either tells the firm that their relationship is over, or the customer simply takes his or her business elsewhere.

Figure 11.7

Segmenting the defectors

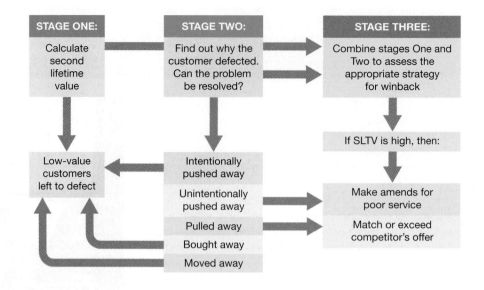

It seems that developing customer loyalty is not so much a matter of providing excellent service as it is of minimising service breakdowns. For example, people who are upgraded by an airline (perhaps due to overbooking of the economy class seats) become marginally more loyal, whereas customers who are downgraded or refused boarding because the aircraft is full become extremely dissatisfied and usually defect to a competing airline in future (Wangenheim and Bayon 2007).

In fact, if a customer does decide to go elsewhere, all is not lost. Studies show that the most lucrative source of new business prospects is customers who have defected: after all, they already know the company and its products, and provided the problems which drove them away can be resolved, there is no reason why they should not return.

Customer Winback

Customers do not always give companies a formal warning that they are about to defect. In many cases, they leave informally. For the manager, this can create a problem: do we in fact have a lost customer, or is this simply a seasonal downturn or a temporary loss of business?

The second decision point for the managers is to decide whether they actually want the customer back anyway. In some cases, the customer defects because they simply have no real need for the product, and have never bought in any substantial quantities. In these circumstances, there is little point in going to much effort to win back the customer, since the resulting business is not worthwhile.

Deciding on whether to win back the customer is a process of segmentation. The first stage in calculating this is to look at the customer's **second lifetime value** (Stauss and Friege 1999). Second lifetime value (SLTV) may differ from the same customer's first lifetime value for the following reasons:

1 The defected customer is familiar with the company and also with its competitors. Either of these factors might be positive or negative in terms of winback.

2 The company knows more about the defected customer than about any new customer – in particular the company should be able to work out what the customer does not like.

second lifetime value The value of a former customer who has been won back to the firm's products.

3 Recognition of the customer's needs expressed during the winback process might well lead to a sales performance better than that obtained first time round, because the customer appreciates the extra attention.

4 The length of the **sales cycle** will be shorter because the customer and the company know each other better.

sales cycle The series of activities undertaken by salespeople.

Calculating the actual SLTV for a given customer will depend greatly on the industry, and on what the individual customer's behaviour was previously. In business-to-business markets, firms may well be able to calculate the figures for individual customers, but in consumer markets the marketers will need to calculate on the basis of market segments instead.

Stauss and Friege (1999) identified five defector categories:

1 *Intentionally pushed away.* These are customers who are really not worth keeping: the costs of serving them outweigh the value the firm gains from them. The customer is sometimes wrong: sometimes people can be rude, unpleasant or expensive to do business with. Some companies even write to such customers and tell them to take their business elsewhere (Freiberg and Freiberg 1996). In other cases, companies might match the service level to the customer value, offering a low level of service to low-value customers. This may mean that those customers leave, but since they are low value this does not matter.

2 *Unintentionally pushed away.* These are customers whom we would like to continue serving, but who were pushed away by poor service or by mistakes on our part. Unhappiness with a product delivery, installation or service, improper handling of a complaint, disapproval of changes and feeling taken for granted are all reasons for customers feeling pushed away.

3 *Pulled away.* These are customers who were attracted by a competitors' better offer. This is not necessarily a cheaper offer – just one that offers better value.

4 *Bought away.* These customers are lured by low prices, and can easily be lured by an introductory pricing offer. Unfortunately, these customers can also be lured away again the next time someone comes up with an introductory offer, so they are probably not worth pursuing – especially as low prices usually mean low profits.

5 *Moved away.* Customers may move away geographically (a customer moves house or a business closes a regional office) or may move away in terms of needs (a customer gets married and has less need for mating-game products, or a business changes its production methods).

Finding out the reasons for the defection is the second stage in segmenting the defectors. Asking people within the selling company may give one side of the story, but ultimately the company must ask the customers themselves. When asking members of the company their side of the story, the following procedures might help:

1 Review the customer's history with the people who actually dealt with the customer.

2 Read through the customer's file.

3 Look for possible causes for defection in letters, salespeople's reports and so forth.

4 Look at the pattern of the customer's orders, and relate this to any changes in the company's business practices or in the customer's situation.

Customers who have defected should be interviewed to find out their reasons for leaving. Managers should bear in mind that customers may not always want to give the true reason, or may decide to embroider their reasons in the hope of gaining more concessions from the supplying company. It is important that the company does not try to re-sell the

Talking Point

customer when conducting an exit interview – the purpose of the exercise is to learn for the future, and this will not happen if the customer is suspicious that the interview is simply a sales pitch.

Presumably when people decide to defect, they do so because they do not like the company or its products. Imagine their delight when they are telephoned a few days later by someone trying to find out why they left.

Is it likely that the customer is going to tell the truth about why they left? Either they will not want to appear rude, or they will want to make a point, or they will want to 'get their own back' on the person telephoning. In any case, it is likely to be an embarrassing or painful experience for all concerned. So why put ourselves through it? Is it because we need to get some kind of feedback? Perhaps, at the least, we might get some idea of what annoys people about what we're doing – and in some cases maybe we can put the problem right for the defector!

The third stage in segmenting the defectors is to combine the SLTV with the reasons for defection. The most attractive segment will be the ones with the highest SLTV who are also in the unintentionally pushed away or pulled away categories. This is because bought-away customers are likely to be fickle, moved-away customers are unlikely to be persuaded to move back, and the intentionally pushed customers are undesirable anyway. These customers all left for reasons that would jeopardise any future relationship.

Obviously these rather long-drawn-out procedures are unlikely to be used in the case of a consumer who has decided to switch from one mobile telephone network to another, but in business-to-business markets the returns are potentially extremely high.

Customer retention and customer winback are both sides of the same coin: establishing and maintaining long-term relationships. Although relationship marketing has met with its main successes in business-to-business marketing, the future of consumer marketing is thought to lie with those firms that are able to retain customers and establish relationships with them. The most fertile ground for this approach is likely to be in services marketing environments, since the transactions always involve dealing with people. In some service industries (hairdressing, banking, restaurants, even hotels) people do establish relationships of trust which may last for many years.

Summary

Developing closer relationships with customers is a crucial part of business success. Given that the number of customers is shrinking in both consumer markets (due to falling birth rates in the developed world) and in business markets (due to increasing mergers and acquisitions), the importance of keeping the ones that remain is even greater than before.

Even when the relationship strategy fails, however, it is still possible to regain lost customers. Often these customers will be easier to win back than a new customer would be to gain: provided the company is careful in its approach, old customers can be persuaded to return to the fold.

The key points from this chapter are as follows:

- The value chain (and value network) concepts take a holistic view of supplying customer needs.

- Cutting out the middle man is likely to increase costs, not reduce them.

- There are four core activities in the value chain: procurement, human resource management, technical development and infrastructure.

- The quality of the buyer–seller relationship depends on how well the seller manages it.

- Quality is the relationship between expectation and reality.

- Service quality is often a major differentiator – sometimes it is the only differentiator.

- Solving customer complaints is a matter of offering a fair outcome, a fair procedure and fair treatment.

- There are three stages in customer defection: value breakdown, season of discontent and termination.

- Not all customers are valuable: not all should be encouraged to return.

Chapter review questions

1 What is the difference between the value chain and the value network?

2 Why do some firms concentrate on service quality?

3 How would you choose which customers were worth keeping or winning back if you were marketing manager for a bank?

4 Why is the onus on the seller to manage the buyer–seller relationship?

5 What are the key elements in building trust?

6 What types of problem would you expect firms to be dealing with in the mid-KAM stage?

7 What types of problem would you expect firms to be dealing with in the pre-KAM stage?

8 Why might someone regard a £50 000 car as value for money?

9 Why might there be a difference between customer expectations and management's perception of customer expectations?

10 Explain the leaky bucket theory.

Preview case revisited
New Zealand Telecom

Telecom needed to build up its connections with other telecommunications providers: the nature of telephone systems is that they need to connect with each other seamlessly, so competitors need to co-operate on many levels. In 2007, Telecom agreed number portability with its competitors, thus enabling customers to switch easily between providers – fine for companies which expect to gain customers, not so good for those expecting to lose them. Also in 2007, Telecom held talks with British Telecom in order to 'pick their brains' about BT's loss of the broadband monopoly in the UK. In January 2008, Telecom announced the formation of Chorus, its new infrastructure division: Chorus manages the installation and maintenance of the copper-based landlines for the whole of New Zealand, effectively providing a service which all telecoms companies in the country will use. The new division aims to create a level playing field for all telecoms companies, giving them equal access to the infrastructure rather than maintaining (and exploiting) the monopoly position previously enjoyed by Telecom. Although at first sight this may seem perverse, it does mean that Telecom remains 'in the driving seat' and avoids Government regulation, while at the same time creating the impression that remaining with Telecom as a customer is likely to be a safer option than going to a competitor, since the competitors do not even own the cables their systems use.

Unusually, New Zealand Telecom introduced a loyalty scheme. Initially this was called Talking Points, and its launch was accompanied by a questionnaire which asked people about their lifestyles and demographics: returning the questionnaire was itself rewarded by extra points towards the scheme's awards, which resulted in a 90 per cent response rate. Thus armed with detailed information about its customers, Telecom was able to tailor its services accordingly.

The loyalty scheme was eventually replaced by membership in Fly Buy, New Zealand's generic loyalty scheme which covers shopping in a great many stores. This may have diluted the effectiveness of the scheme from Telecom's viewpoint, but it does have advantages for customers – the points pile up faster. Telecom gives one Fly Buy point for every NZ$25 the customer spends on virtually any Telecom product, but there is a minimum NZ$50 a month spend needed in order to qualify. This means that only Telecom's more valuable customers are likely to benefit from the scheme, and it also means that there is an incentive for people to use more of Telecom's products, for example bundling their mobile, landline and broadband so as to maximise the gain from the scheme.

Telecom's slogan 'Connecting New Zealanders' may not be the snappiest in the world, but it does convey the company's basic ethos neatly. Telecom exists to connect people – obviously the firm needs to make money as well, but it is the connections that count.

Case study
Metflex

Metflex started out in 1930, in London's East End, as the Metropolitan Leather Company, manufacturing leather diaphragms for gas meters. In 1940, during the Blitz, its factory was bombed out, so the company relocated to Lancashire, taking 25 East End families with it to start new lives in the North, which at that time was away from the bombing.

In the 1950s and 1960s new plastic materials became available, and Metropolitan Leather became Metropolitan Flexible Products, or Metflex, and moved into making polymer diaphragms and precision plastic mouldings. The company was taken over by Thorn EMI in 1971, and around that time British Gas decided to use only synthetic diaphragms: leather diaphragms did not have the reliability of synthetics, nor were they as cheap. Metflex, having invested heavily in the new materials, were able to take full advantage of the switch and the company moved into high gear.

In 2002, Metflex won one of its biggest contracts to date. A major engineering company based close to Metflex headquarters was suddenly in need of a supplier when its rubber mouldings supplier ceased trading. They found Metflex on the Internet, and contacted them to find out whether they could fill the gap, despite having little experience of the tools and systems being used. Metflex rose to the challenge, which was to reinstate full production and supply within three months. Since the supplier was closing down, Metflex did not have access to the formulae for the specialist compounds they had been using, so the company chemists were forced to develop them from scratch.

The existing tools were delivered to Metflex from the former supplier – as is common in this industry, tools remain the property of the customer, not the moulding company – but Metflex were dismayed to find that over 100 tools, loaded on three lorries, arrived with no instructions for their use. The company's engineers had to work out which tools were which, and marry them to the company's existing equipment. In the meantime, the original three months' target was cut to only one month, since without these vital components the purchasing company could not produce its own products.

Metflex invested £80 000 in new plant and equipment specifically for the new customer. Metflex had many years experience in bonding metal to rubber, but up until now the company had generally handled components weighing less than 50 grams. Now they were expected to apply the same technology to components weighing 50 kilos – a thousand-fold increase in size. Metflex dedicated an entire unit to this one problem – with great success.

On a day-to-day basis, Metflex has a 'production cell' which only manufactures for this one client, with a 'cell leader' who liaises with the client on a regular basis to plan production schedules and ensure that blanks and tools are available on the dates the customer needs the products. Production is carried out exactly to order on a zero-stock basis, because there are over 500 components in all and the warehousing problem would be much greater than the relatively simply problem of resetting the equipment to produce a different component. Close liaison between customer and supplier are, of course, essential in this situation.

In 2003 the company again became independently-owned, and now has a turnover in excess of £6 million per annum. Although the company's main strength lies in manufacturing precision rubber diaphragms, Metflex also produce compression mouldings, injection mouldings, gaskets, seals and even loudspeaker surrounds, which are supplied to the hi-fi industry. There is more to a gas meter diaphragm than meets the eye – it must be of an exact thickness, it must flex evenly in every direction, it must of course be gas-tight, and it must be strong enough to last indefinitely. Most diaphragms are made of cloth-reinforced rubber, but Metflex have developed a fabric-free diaphragm which performs much better in use, being less variable in its flexibility.

Metflex has certainly come a long way from a bombed-out factory in London. It's a small company with a strong customer focus – something which is not always apparent in engineering firms.

Questions

1 What stage in key-account management is Metflex in with its new contract?

2 How might a cell leader initiate changes within Metflex to improve customer service?

3 What is the role of new investment in Metflex's customer care policy?

4 How might Metflex avoid losing its major new customer?

5 What are the main problems which might arise in using the make-to-order system?

References

Allaway, A.W., Goover, R.M., Berkowitz, D. and Davis, L. (2006): Deriving and exploring behaviour segments within a retail loyalty card programme. *European Journal of Marketing* **4**(11/12), 1317–39.

Ang, L. and Buttle, F. (2006): Managing for successful customer acquisition: an exploration. *Journal of Marketing Management* **22**(3/4), 295–317.

Bell, S. and Eisengrich, A.B. (2007): The paradox of customer education: customer expertise and loyalty in the financial services industry. *European Journal of Marketing* **41**(5/6), 466–86.

Carlson, K.A. and Sally, D. (2002): Thoughts that count: fairness and possibilities, intentions and reactions. *Advances in Consumer Research* **29**(1), 79–89.

Chaston, I., Badger, B., Mangles, T. and Sadler-Smith, E. (2003): Relationship marketing, knowledge management systems and e-commerce operations in small UK accounting practices. *Journal of Marketing Management* **19**, 109–29.

Christopher, M., Ballantyne, D. and Payne, A. (1991): *Relationship Marketing* (Oxford: Butterworth-Heinemann).

Chung, E. and Beverland, M. (2006): An exploration of consumer forgiveness following marketer transgressions. *Advances in Consumer Research* **33**(1), 98–9.

Dunleavy, J. and Olivieri, C. (2001): Relationship marketing: satisfaction, loyalty and perceived quality. *Journal of Selling and Major Account Management* **3**(3).

East, R., Hammond, K. and Gendall, P. (2006): Fact and fallacy in retention marketing. *Journal of Marketing Management* **22**(1), 5–23.

Evans, J. and Laskin, R. (1994): The relationship marketing process: a conceptualisation and application. *Industrial Marketing Management* **23**, 439–52.

Freiberg, K. and Freiberg, J. (1996): *Nuts: Southwest Airlines Crazy Recipe for Business and Personal Success* (Austin, TX: Bard Books).

Griffin, J. and Lowenstein, M. (2001): *Customer Winback* (San Francisco, CA: Jossey-Bass).

Gummeson, E. (1988): Service quality and product quality combined. *Review of Business* **9**(3).

Gupta, S., Lehmann, D.R. and Stuart, J.A. (2004): Valuing customers. *Journal of Marketing Research* **4**(1), 7–18.

Helgesen, O. (2006): Are loyal customers profitable? Customer satisfaction, customer (action) loyalty and customer profitability at the individual level. *Journal of Marketing Management* **22**(3/4), 245–66.

Helm, S., Rolfes, L. and Gunther, B. (2006): Suppliers' willingness to end unprofitable customer relationships. *European Journal of Marketing* **40**(3/4), 366–83.

Holmlund, M. (2004): Analysing business relationships and distinguishing different interaction levels. *Industrial Marketing Management* **33**(4), 279–87.

Izquierdo, C.C. and Cillan, J.G. (2004): The interaction of dependence and trust in long-term industrial relationships. *European Journal of Marketing* **38**(8), 974–84.

Johnson, M.D., Herrmann, A. and Huber, F. (2006): The evolution of loyalty intentions. *Journal of Marketing* **70**(2), 122–32.

Kotler, P. (2003): *Marketing Management* (Upper Saddle River, NJ: Prentice Hall).

Leenders, M.R. and Blenkhorn, D.L. (1988): *Reverse Marketing: The New Buyer–seller relationship* (New York: Free Press).

Leong, Y.P. and Qing W. (2006): Impact of relationship marketing tactics (RMTs) on switchers and stayers in a competitive service industry. *Journal of Marketing Management* **22**(1), 25–59.

Luo, X. and Homburg, C. (2007): Neglected outcomes of customer satisfaction. *Journal of Marketing* **71**(2), 133–49.

Meyer-Waarden, L. and Benavent, C. (2006): The impact of loyalty programmes on repeat purchase behaviour. *Journal of Marketing Management* **22**(1/2), 61–88.

Michalski, S. (2004): Types of customer relationship ending processes. *Journal of Marketing Management* **20**(9/10), 977–99.

Millman, T. and Wilson, K.J. (1995): From key account selling to key account management. *Journal of Marketing Science*, **1**.

Morgan, R.M. and Hunt, S.D. (1994): The commitment–trust theory of relationship marketing. *Journal of Marketing* **58** (July), 20–38.

Murray, K.B. and Haubl, G. (2002): The fiction of no friction: a user skills approach to cognitive lock-in. *Advances in Consumer Research* **29**(1).

Narayandas, D. and Rangan, V.K. (2004): Building and sustaining buyer–seller relationships in mature industrial markets. *Journal of Marketing* **68**(3), 63–77.

Oederkerken-Schroeder, O.H, Lemmink, J. and Semeijn, J. (2003): Consumers' trade-off between relationship, service, package and price: an empirical study in the car industry. *European Journal of Marketing* **37**(1), 219–42.

Parasuraman, A., Zeithaml, V.A. and Berry, L.L. (1985): A conceptual model of service quality and its implications for future research. *Journal of Marketing* **49** (Fall).

Patterson, P.G. (2004): A contingency model of behavioural intentions in a service context. *European Journal of Marketing* **8**(9/10), 1304–5.

Porter, M.E. (1985): *Competitive Advantage: Creating and Sustaining Superior Performance* (New York: Free Press).

Reed, D. (1999): Great expectations. *Marketing Week* 29 April, 57–8.

Reichheld, F. (1996): *The Loyalty Effect* (Boston, MA: Harvard Business School Press).

Roberts, K., Varki, S. and Brodie, R. (2003): Measuring the quality of relationships in consumer services: an empirical study. *European Journal of Marketing* **37**(1), 169–96.

Romaniuk, J. and Sharp, B. (2003): Brand salience and customer defection in subscription markets. *Journal of Marketing* **19**, 25–44.

Stauss, B. and Friege, C. (1999): Regaining service customers. *Journal of Service Research* May.

Tax, S. and Brown, S. (1998): Recovering and learning from service failures. *Sloan Management Review* **40**(1), 78.

Thompson, M. and Johnson, A.R. (2002): Investigating the role of attachment dimensions as predictors of satisfaction in consumer-brand relationships. *Advances in Consumer Research* **29**(1), 42.

Traynor, K. and Traynor, S. (2004): A Comparison of Marketing Approaches Used by High-tech Firms: 1985 versus 2001. *Industrial Marketing Management* **33**(5), 457–61.

Tuli, K.R., Kohli, A.K. and Bharadwaj, S.G. (2007): Rethinking customer solutions: from product bundles to relational processes. *Journal of Marketing* **71**(3), 1–17.

Verhoef, P.C. (2003): Understanding the effect of customer relationship management efforts on customer retention and customer share development. *Journal of Marketing* **67**(4), 30–45.

Wagenheim, F. and Bayon, T. (2003): Satisfaction, loyalty and word-of-mouth within the customer base of a utility provider: differences between stayers, switchers and referral switchers. *Journal of Consumer Behaviour* **3**(3), 211–20.

Wang, S. and Huff, L.C. (2007): Explaining buyers' response to sellers' violation of trust. *European Journal of Marketing* **41**(9/10), 1033–52.

Wangenheim, F. von and Bayon, T. (2007): Behavioural consequences of overbooking service capacity. *Journal of Marketing* **71**(4), 36–47.

Weitz, B.A. and Bradford, K.D. (1999): Personal selling and sales management: a relationship marketing perspective. *Journal of the Academy of Marketing Science* **27** (Spring), 241–54.

Wilson, K.J. (1993): A problem-centred approach to key-account management. Proceedings of the National Sales Management Conference, Atlanta, Georgia.

Zauberman, G. (2002): Lock-in over time: time references, prediction accuracy, and the information cost structure. *Advances in Consumer Research* **29**(1).

Further reading

Bank, J. (1992): *The Essence of Total Quality Management* (Hemel Hempstead: Prentice Hall). Although this book is now quite old, it offers a clearly-written and concise overview of Total Quality Management.

Egan, J. (2004): *Relationship Marketing: Exploring Relational Strategies in Marketing* (Hemel Hempstead: FT Prentice Hall). This text is up-to-date, readable, and shows how relationship marketing has a major role to play in strategy.

Plenert, G. (2001): *The eManager: Value Chain Management in an e-Commerce World* (London: Blackhall). Although e-commerce is a dynamic field, this text manages to give the reader a view which is sufficiently conceptual to be slow to age. Managing the value chain is often driven by IT, so this text is well worth reading for anyone who has an interest in managing suppliers and customers.

Part four
Marketing in Practice

The second half of the book is devoted to the practical aspects of day-to-day marketing. Having covered the theoretical groundwork in the first half, the book moves on to practicalities, describing the tools and techniques marketers use in their daily lives. This is linked throughout (and supported by) academic research in the field.

Chapter 12 is about managing the firm's range of products. Achieving a balanced portfolio of products is no small task: marketers need to consider the profitability of each market segment they approach, the effect each product has on sales of other products and the likely future sales of individual brands in the range. This chapter provides a set of approaches for making these decisions.

Chapter 13 looks at developing new products. Eventually, all products become obsolete, but in any case a firm which intends to expand needs to update its product range continually by adding new products to the portfolio. This chapter explains the process of new product development and the theoretical basis for adoption of innovation.

Chapter 14 is about pricing. Price can be used as a promotional device, as a communication tool, as a surrogate for judging quality and for many other things. This chapter outlines the various bases for pricing and the rationale behind pricing to meet consumer demand profitably.

Advertising is probably the most prominent of all marketing activities. Chapter 15 discusses various forms of advertising, and looks at media buying, budgeting, creative issues and choosing an agency. Planning for advertising and the use of new media are also covered.

Public relations and sponsorship are somewhat neglected in the academic literature, but have an important role to play in establishing both the credibility of the firm and the quality of its brands. Chapter 16 looks at practical aspects of PR and sponsorship, crisis management, choosing sponsorship targets and proactive public relations.

Chapter 17 is about selling and key account management. Personal selling is a very common first job in marketing, and for many it becomes a lifetime career: selling is marketing at the individual, personal level. Key account management is about handling customers who are of strategic importance to the firm, either because they represent a major part of the firm's turnover or because they represent a way into an attractive market. Managing key accounts is an extremely responsible job, because the future fate of the company may hang on how well the key account managers perform – but at the end of the day, it is still marketing.

Chapter 18 covers exhibitions and sales promotions. Exhibitions are a seriously under-researched and misunderstood area of marketing, yet they account for a significant proportion of expenditure. This chapter outlines ways of getting the best from exhibitions, and also looks at the emerging alternatives to exhibitions. The second part of the chapter looks at sales promotions: these are ways of gaining a short-term increase in business, and the chapter looks at sales pro-motion in the international context as well as the domestic context. Legal restrictions on sales promotions are also covered.

Chapter 19 covers the 'hot topic' of direct and online marketing. Direct mail, database marketing and Internet marketing are all covered. The future of electronic marketing is hard to predict, but some possible scenarios are discussed: there is little doubt that direct marketing will continue to grow in importance throughout the next decade or two, and this chapter provides a foundation for understanding the drivers for this growth.

Managing intermediaries effectively can make a very large difference to the bottom line for most firms. Chapter 20 looks at the practical aspects of controlling a distribution channel, whether from the viewpoint of a retailer, a wholesaler or a manufacturer. Logistics and physical distribution methods are also covered.

Chapter 21 takes a more detailed look at the day-to-day activities of retailers, wholesalers and agents. The chapter covers the nature of retailing and wholesaling, types of retailer, non-store retailing and retailer strategy.

Chapter 22 looks at the management of individuals involved in delivering marketing outcomes. Front-line staff are the people who deal with customers as part of their everyday jobs: they have specific responsibilities and pressures, and can be a crucial element in maintaining the corporate image. The chapter also looks at the process of delivering customer value, and at ways of improving the processes. Finally, the chapter covers physical evidence issues such as retail environment, decor and atmospherics, and such evidence as brochures and documentation.

Chapter 12
Product portfolio

Part one **Concepts and Contexts**	1 Managing the exchange process 2 The marketing environment 3 Marketing domains
Part two **Markets and People**	4 Consumer behaviour 5 Organisational buying behaviour 6 Segmentation, targeting and positioning 7 Marketing information and research 8 Communications theories 9 International marketing
Part three **Strategy**	10 Creating competitive advantage 11 Building customer relationships
Part four **Marketing in Practice**	12 Product portfolio 13 New product development 14 Pricing 15 Advertising 16 Public relations and sponsorship 17 Selling and key account management 18 Exhibitions and sales promotions 19 Direct and online marketing 20 Managing channels 21 Intermediaries 22 People, processes and physical evidence

Learning objectives After reading this chapter you should be able to:

1 Describe the stages a product goes through between launch and obsolescence.

2 Explain how to manage a portfolio of products.

3 Describe the role of executive judgement in managing the product portfolio, and show how theoretical models can help.

4 Explain the advantages and disadvantages of matrix models.

5 Describe the relationship between services and physical products.

6 Explain the transition from product orientation to service orientation in business markets.

7 Explain the role of packaging in marketing.

Introduction

Products, or bundles of benefits, are the main things that companies offer to their customers as their part of the exchange. A product provides benefits to its consumers, which is why they are prepared to part with their hard-earned cash to buy it: products might be anything which is put together by someone for the purposes of selling it. This includes services, of course – a haircut is as much a product as is a loaf of bread.

It is common to speak of 'the product', as if the company only offered one product, but in fact the vast majority of companies offer several, even many, products to their customers. Handling a portfolio of products is another aspect of the marketer's role.

In the nature of things, products become obsolete or unfashionable and competitors come up with new ideas: it would be an unwise company that hoped that its products would be saleable forever, so companies need to manage the portfolio of products in such a way as to ensure that it still meets the needs of the customers, dropping products which no longer meet customer needs effectively and introducing new ones which fit the market better.

This chapter looks at the management of the product portfolio, and explores some of the problems of managing products in the real world.

The Product Life Cycle

A key concept in product portfolio management is the product life cycle (see Figure 12.1). The basis of the PLC is that products move through a series of stages from their introduction to their final withdrawal from the market. Products tend to lose money when they are first introduced (because sales are low initially, and the costs of producing tend to be high because there are no economies of scale). Eventually, if all goes well,

Preview case
Sony

Sony is a giant Japanese electronics corporation, founded in 1946 by Akio Morita and Masaru Ibuka. Morita and Ibuka were ex-Japanese Navy electronics officers (which, at that time, meant radio engineers). The Japanese economy at the time was ruined: the partners earned a living repairing radios and manufacturing a limited number of voltmeters, but they hoped to expand more widely. Oddly, their first successful product was an automatic rice cooker which could sense when the rice was ready and switch off automatically.

In 1955 Sony manufactured its first transistor radio. At the time, transistors were a new breakthrough in electronics, so Sony was at the cutting edge – this was the first product to carry the Sony brand. The company went on to produce the first 'pocketable' transistor radio in the world, making radios truly portable for the first time.

In the ensuing years, as Sony became bigger and more successful, global expansion became a reality. Sony's commitment to being a global company is legendary – when the company wanted to enter the American market, Morita moved his entire family to the United States and told his wife she would have to become a typical American housewife – no small feat for a woman brought up in the traditional Japanese way, rarely leaving the house and never having learned to drive a car. When Morita decided that they needed a base in the European Union he sent his son to school in Wales so that he could gain insights into UK culture (Sony has two factories in Wales to this day).

The company's expenditure on research and development is intended to ensure that Sony stays at the forefront of technical innovation in consumer electronics. The company has tended to develop its own formats and systems rather than adopt those of other manufacturers: this policy culminated in the famous Betamax–VHS war of the 1980s, in which Sony's Betamax video recording system went head-to-head against JVC's rival VHS system. In the end, VHS gained the critical mass in the market despite being technically inferior to Betamax:

Sony were forced to adopt VHS, otherwise they would not have been able to remain in the video recorder market.

The Walkman portable stereo system is often held up as an example of an excellent new product. It was developed by Morita himself from a reporter's Dictaphone, and became hugely successful worldwide with many imitators. Therein lies the problem for Sony – consumer electronics is a volatile industry, with many companies competing or a vast global market. Sony needs to manage its product portfolio carefully if it is to remain ahead of the crowd.

EVERYBODY SHOULD OWN A COPY OF THIS.

NOBODY SHOULD OWN A COPY OF THIS.

SONY.

the product's sales improve and it begins to return a profit, but sooner or later the growth in sales will peak out, because the product reaches the limit of the number of people who want to buy it. As alternative products enter the market (perhaps because competitors seize an opportunity to bring out their own version, or perhaps because fashions and tastes change) the product will go into a decline and will eventually cease to have any market.

Figure 12.1

The product life cycle

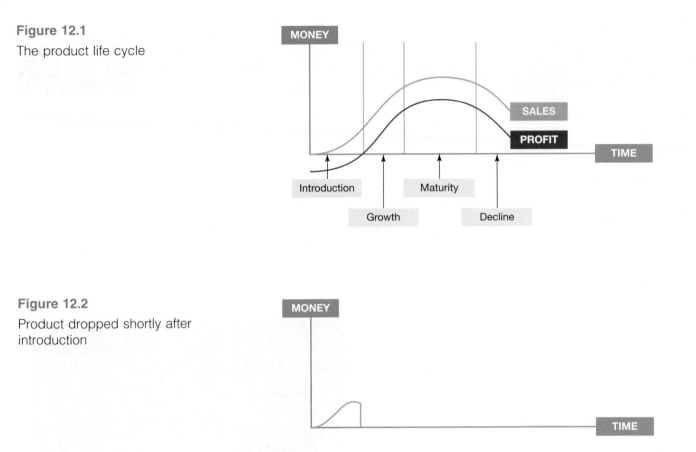

Figure 12.2

Product dropped shortly after introduction

In fact, the situation is often much more complex than this, so the basic product life cycle as shown in Figure 12.1 does not always describe what actually happens in practice.

The product life cycle is a useful concept for explaining what happens to products, but it suffers from a number of weaknesses. First, the model cannot predict with any accuracy what will happen, because there is no good way of knowing what the length of the maturity phase will be: for a fashion item, the maturity phase might only last a few months, whereas for a product such as pitta bread the maturity phase has already lasted several thousand years and shows no sign of changing.

Second, the model ignores the effects of marketing activities. If a product's sales are declining, marketers might decide to reposition the product in another market, might run a major promotional campaign, or might decide to drop the product altogether and concentrate resources on another product in the portfolio. These alternatives are shown in Figures 12.2 and 12.3.

Talking Point

It is not unusual for products to disappear almost as soon as they are launched: test marketing sometimes shows disappointing results, so the product is taken off the shelves. But the product life cycle tells us that products often lose money at first – and some products are 'sleepers' which do nothing for several years, then suddenly take off for no apparent reason.

There are also products which appear to be eminently sensible, and which do not find a market, possibly through a lack of professionalism on the part of the marketers. So should there be a marketer's life cycle instead? If the product doesn't perform, should we keep the product and fire the managers?

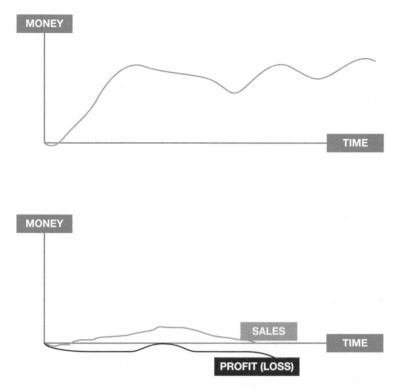

Figure 12.3

Effects of marketing activities on the product life cycle

Figure 12.4

Failed product

Third, the model does not account for those products which come back into fashion after a few years in the doldrums. Recent examples include the Mini Cooper, the Volkswagen Beetle and the yo-yo (which seems to undergo revivals every 10 to 15 years).

Fourth, the model does not take account of the fact that the vast majority of new products fail. This would give a life cycle such as that shown in Figure 12.4, where the product never moves into profit.

Finally, the PLC only looks at one product, whereas most marketing managers have to balance the demands of many different products and decide which of them is likely to yield the best return on investment (or perhaps which one will take the company nearest to achieving its strategic objectives).

Despite these weaknesses, the product life cycle is widely quoted and used in making decisions about marketing tactics. The type of decisions to be made might be as follows:

The hula-hoop undergoes periodic revivals.

- *Introduction phase.* The strategic objective will be to build the market as quickly as possible in order to shut out the competition. The product itself is likely to be a fairly basic model, since there has been no feedback from the market yet and therefore no opportunity to refine it or differentiate it. The focus of the firm's promotion effort will be on creating awareness and encouraging trial of the product: advertising is more effective in the introduction phase than it is later (Vakratsas and Ambler 1999). The price is likely to be high, since the firm needs to recoup development costs and (at least for the time being) does not have to compete, since competitors have yet to introduce their own versions of the product. Distribution of the product is likely to be patchy at this stage, since many distributors will not want to risk carrying an unknown product.

- *Growth.* The strategic thrust will still be on building the market as quickly as possible, but there will be a shift in promotional emphasis from creating awareness towards encouraging repeat purchases and brand preference. The product itself is likely to be available in several different versions by now, and the price will be lower as competitors enter the market: since their development costs will have been considerably lower (because they have an existing product to copy) they can still show a profit on a lower price. Distribution will be much wider in the growth phase as distributors become more confident of selling the product.

● *Maturity*. At this stage the strategy shifts to one of maintaining market share in the face of increased competition. The promotional thrust is concerned with maintaining brand loyalty and with maintaining awareness. The price will be at its lowest, and there will be several versions of the product available in order to meet the needs of several market segments. Competition will also be at its peak, especially as some competitors will be trying to increase market share by using aggressive marketing tactics. Distribution will be intensive.

● *Decline*. The strategy in the decline phase is likely to be one of harvesting, in which very little money is spent on promoting or developing the product further, and it is allowed to decline, with the company reaping profit from the remaining sales. The product will not be available in all its variants at this stage, since the company will be rationalising the range to reduce production costs. Promotional expenditure will be at a minimum, or cut out altogether, but the price will be rising in order to make as much as possible from the remaining sales. Distribution will shrink as some distributors find that they can no longer carry the product profitably. Eventually the product will be eliminated as it will no longer be viable. It should be noted that most decisions to eliminate products are made on the basis of intuition and judgement rather than any formal analysis (Greenley and Barus 1994), which is not surprising since there is always the option to try to revive the product's fortunes by investing in the brand.

For some companies, there are serious doubts as to whether it is worth investing in new products at all, and in fact there are companies which have produced essentially the same product for many years. These companies do not innovate at all, but as a result they run the risk of their product being superseded by a superior competitive product. Also, research shows that new products are more successful than sales promotions in producing the following results (Pawels *et al.* 2004):

1 Long-term financial performance and firm value.
2 Investor reaction (which grows over time).
3 Yielding top-line, bottom-line and stock market benefits.

This in itself means that new products are worth pursuing.

Managing Product Portfolios

The main lesson the PLC teaches us is that all products will, eventually, decline. This means that managers need to look at regular introduction of new products into the range (the portfolio) offered by the firm. At any moment in the company's existence it will have some products which have only just been introduced and are therefore losing money, some which are mature and are making at least some money, some which are doing extremely well, some which are weakening and dying, and so forth. Since any company only has limited resources at its disposal, marketing managers need to make decisions about which products need the most support and which ones can either manage with less support or need no support because they will shortly drop out anyway.

The decision is not necessarily a simple one: some products may be unprofitable in themselves, but may stimulate sales of other products. For example, a power-tool

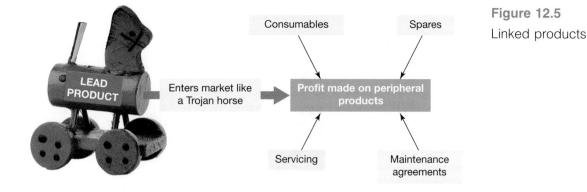

Figure 12.5
Linked products

manufacturer may make very little profit from sales of a power saw (due to competition from low-cost imports, or perhaps due to strong negotiating power of retailers) but may make much healthier profits from sales of replacement blades. Because many managers have specific, small ranges of product to look after, they will often lose sight of the big picture, so that the company's product portfolio is not a coherent, well-balanced mix but is rather an ill-matched assortment of products which do not have very much relationship to each other.

Portfolio planning is therefore a strategic issue, since it dictates the overall direction the company will go in. Portfolio planning is complex, but needs to be carried out if the firm is to direct its marketing resources in the most effective direction.

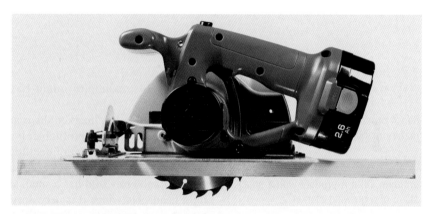

Power saw manufacturers make their profits from sales of replacement blades.

The Boston Consulting Group Matrix

It is possible to superimpose the PLC diagrams for each product onto the graph to give a composite view of what is happening to the firm's product portfolio. Apart from making the graph extremely complex, this will give a long-term overview, but the problems of prediction still remain; for many managers, a 'snapshot' of what is happening now is more useful. The Boston Consulting Group (BCG) developed a matrix for decision-making in these circumstances. The original BCG matrix is as shown in Figure 12.6.

Stars are products with rapid growth and a dominant share of the market. Often, the costs of fighting off the competition and maintaining growth mean that the product is actually absorbing more money than it is generating, but eventually it is hoped that it will be the market leader and the profits will begin to come back in. The problem lies in judging whether the market is going to continue to grow or whether it will go down as quickly as it went up. Even the most successful Star will eventually decline as it moves through the life cycle.

Cash Cows are the former Stars. They have a dominant share of the market, but are now in the maturity phase of the life cycle and consequently have low growth. A Cash Cow is generating cash and can be 'milked' of it to finance the Stars. These are the products that have steady year-in year-out sales and are generating much of the

stars Products with a large share of a growing market.

cash cow A product with a large share of a mature market.

Figure 12.6

Boston Consulting Group matrix
Source: (© The Boston Consulting Group)

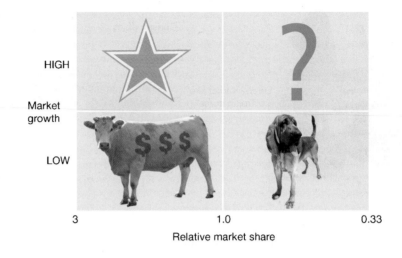

firm's profits; examples might be the Big Mac hamburger, Coca-Cola and the Ford Mondeo.

Dogs have a low market share and low growth prospects. The argument here is not whether the product is profitable; it almost always is. The argument is about whether the firm could use its production facilities to make something that would be more profitable, and this is also almost always the case.

The **Problem Child** has a small share of a growth market, and causes the marketer the most headaches, since it is necessary to work out a way of building market share so as to turn the product into a Star. This means finding out why the share is so low, and developing strategies to increase market share rapidly. The Problem Child (or question mark) could be backed with an even bigger promotion campaign, or it could possibly be adapted in some way to fit the market better. Market research plays a crucial role in making these decisions; finding out how to adapt a product is a difficult area of research, but the potential rewards are huge and adapting the product to meet people's needs better is almost always cheaper than increasing the advertising spend.

The policy decisions that arise from this view of the firm's product portfolio lie in the following areas:

- Which products should be dropped from the range entirely? This question not only hinges on how profitable the product itself is: sales of one product often indirectly generate sales of another more profitable product.
- Which products should be backed with promotion campaigns? Backing the wrong product can be extremely expensive: advertising campaigns have no second-hand value, so if it does not work the money is just lost.
- Which products could be adapted to fit the market better, and in what ways? This very much hinges on the market research findings and on customer feedback.
- Which new products could be introduced, and at what cost?

Like the product life cycle, the BCG matrix is a simple model that helps marketers to approach strategic product decisions; again like the PLC, it has a number of flaws. It is based on the following assumptions:

- *Market share can be gained by investment in marketing.* This is not always the case: some products will have lost their markets altogether (perhaps through environmental changes) and cannot be revived, no matter how much is invested.

dog A product with a small share of a mature market.

problem child A product with a small share of a growing market.

- *Market share gains will always generate cash surpluses.* Again, if market share is gained by drastic price cutting, cash may actually be lost.

- *Cash surpluses will be generated when the product is in the maturity stage of the life cycle.* Not necessarily so: mature products may well be operating on such small margins (due to competitive pressure) that the profit generated is low.

- *The best opportunity to build a dominant market position is during the growth phase.* In most cases this would be true, but this does not take account of competition. A competitor's product might be growing even faster.

Because of these limitations, the BCG matrix has been widely criticised (even though it has proved popular with planners for many years). Here are some of the criticisms leveled at the BCG matrix:

- Assuming that cash flow is determined by the product's position in the matrix is incorrect. Some Stars can show strong positive cashflows, and so can some Dogs, especially if there is little competition in the market.

- Focusing on market share and growth rates can be misleading because it ignores competitive advantage. Although market share might derive from competitive advantage, it is by no means certain, and a competitor might develop a new competency which could be missed by a manager who is concentrating on market growth rates. Competitive advantage might come from cost advantages, ownership of key assets and so forth.

- Market growth rate is not the same as market attractiveness. A small, stable market might be more attractive for a number of reasons than a rapidly-growing, volatile market which is attracting large numbers of competitors.

- Building market share is not always a good idea. Attempts to do so may provoke retaliation from a strong competitor, thus wiping out any gains made.

- Some products are interdependent (as in the example of the power saw mentioned earlier). More subtly, some distributors may want to be provided with a full range of products, or some customers might feel aggrieved if a favourite product were to be dropped from the range, and boycott other products.

- Some products have a very short life cycle, so instead of being groomed to become Cash Cows they should be heavily exploited while still in the Star stage. The matrix does not allow for this.

- The matrix does not consider potential competitive response. Whatever the firm does is likely to be met with retaliation of some sort.

- The matrix assumes that resources are limited, whereas in fact products which show a positive return can be funded from borrowed money or the capital markets relatively easily. Thus the kind of choice the matrix implies does not in fact always have to be made.

- The dividing lines between the boxes are vague and arbitrary. How is high growth defined? How is large market share defined? Indeed, how is market defined?

- The matrix is based on cash flow (revenue), whereas profitability might be a better criterion.

- The Problem Child remains a problem – the matrix offers no guidance.

- The matrix does not take account of the possibility of shrinking markets, which are of course a reality, especially during periodic recessions when most markets are shrinking.

In 1982 Barksdale and Harris proposed two additions to the BCG matrix, as shown in Figure 12.7. **War horses** have high market share, but the market has negative growth; the problem for management is to decide whether the product is in an irreversible decline, or

war horse A product with a large share of a shrinking market.

Figure 12.7

Expanded BCG matrix

		RELATIVE MARKET SHARE	
		High	Low
MARKET GROWTH	High	Star	Problem Child
	Low	Cash Cow	Dog
	Negative	War Horse	Dodo

dodo A product with a small share of a shrinking market.

whether it can be revived, perhaps by repositioning into another market. Dodos have a low share of a negative growth market, and are probably best discontinued.

The BCG matrix has proved a useful tool for analysing product portfolio decisions, but is really only a snapshot of the current position with the products it describes. Since most markets are to a greater or lesser extent dynamic, the matrix should be used with a certain degree of caution.

The size of the product portfolio and the complexity of the products within it can have further effects on the firm's management. For example, it has been shown that manufacturing a wide range of products with many options makes it difficult for the firm to use just-in-time purchasing techniques and complicates the firm's supply activities.

The General Electric Market Attractiveness-Competitive Position Model

The GE Matrix, developed by management consultants McKinsey, is wider-ranging than the BCG matrix. It is really a tool for deciding strategic direction, because it compares market attractiveness and competitive strength and can therefore be used to consider all aspects of the company's activities, not just its products. However, it can be used for product portfolio management, since the company is able to look at the competitive strengths of each product in the portfolio, measured against competing products in the same market.

The criteria for judging competitive strength are as follows:

- Market size
- Market growth rate
- Strength of competition
- Profit potential
- Social, political and legal factors.

The criteria for judging competitive strength are:

- Market share
- Potential to develop a differential advantage
- Opportunities to develop a cost advantage
- Reputation
- Distribution capabilities.

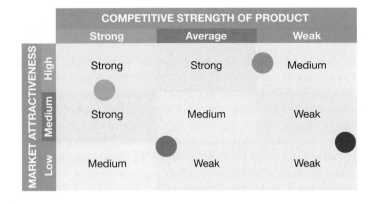

Figure 12.8

GE matrix

Management should be able to decide which criteria are most important for the specific products under consideration. This makes the GE matrix more flexible than the BCG matrix, since it can be tailored to specific circumstances. Managers should then agree on a weighting system for each criterion to reflect its importance in the product's potential success.

Managers then score each market attractiveness factor and each competitive strength factor on a scale of one to ten: each score is then multiplied by the weighting to obtain an overall score for both market attractiveness and competitive strength. These scores can be plotted on the matrix to give an overall picture of the firm's competitive position for each product.

In Figure 12.8, the yellow circle represents a strong product in a medium to highly-attractive market. The green circle represents a product which is in a highly-attractive market, but which is weak compared with competing products: this product is unlikely to succeed in this market, and managers should consider withdrawing it or repositioning it in another market. The blue circle represents a product in an unattractive segment, but with medium to strong capabilities. Managers have two choices here: either they can build up the market in some way, or they can seek a more attractive segment. Finally, the white circle represents a product with weak capabilities in an unattractive segment. There is a clear case here for pulling out and investing elsewhere.

Talking Point

Snapshots are all very well, but by the time the information has been collected and analysed, the world has moved on. Taking a photograph halfway through a race will not tell you who won – and by the time the picture is developed, the result is known anyway.

So what use are snapshots? Perhaps what we need is a video camera, giving us a constant view of the changes which are happening, with constantly updated projections of what is about to happen next.

The GE matrix is more detailed than the BCG matrix because more factors are taken into account, the weightings provide a finer discrimination between products, and it is more flexible so it can be tailored better to specific situations. The drawback is, of course, that it is more complex to use, and it requires considerable judgement on the part of managers, so there is a strong possibility of bias creeping in as managers try to secure more resources for their products, or simply try to champion their own products through the system.

Positives and Problems with Grid Analysis

Grid analyses such as GE and BCG matrices provide a useful tool for thinking about the problem. They clarify the issues, and in particular they stress that different products should be treated differently because they are at different stages in the life cycle, and they have different roles in the company's product strategy. For example, many companies act as if all products should return the same profit margin (this is especially the case in companies where **cost-plus pricing** is in evidence – there is more on this in Chapter 14). This is potentially damaging, because it would be unreasonable to expect a newly-launched product to show a profit immediately, and an attempt to do so might result in cutting the promotional budget associated with the product in order to increase the returns. Equally, a Cash Cow might be capable of returning a much larger profit margin than that set by a manager wedded to the idea of equal profits across all products.

As a consequence, there is an implication that products in different categories should be handled by different managers, and the reward systems for managers should also be different depending on which type of product they handle. For example, a manager in charge of new product launches might be targeted in terms of market share or sales growth rates, whereas a manager in charge of a product in the maturity phase of the life cycle should be rewarded on a profitability basis.

The main difficulty with matrices is that they provide a spurious credibility in decision-making. Managers still have to make arbitrary decisions about which segments, products or business strengths fit into which boxes. For example, it is easy to decide that a product has a competitive strength in one dimension, and be unaware that a competitor is about to launch a product which is even stronger in the same dimension. Equally, it is possible for a segment to be written off as unattractive until someone finds a product which fills a need for that segment.

A second problem with matrix planning is that it often leads firms to concentrate on growth, either through growing the firm's share of an existing market or through expanding into a growing market. While most firms do look for growth, an over-emphasis on entering growing markets can lead to the firm entering a market about which it knows very little, and abandoning or milking dry the stable, core products on which its success was founded. Going for high growth is a risky strategy, but is one which may well please the capital markets, and is thus often seen as a good way to go.

Matrix models should therefore be treated with a degree of caution: having said that, they do have the advantage of simplifying the problem and clarifying the issues, which is likely to help the planning process.

Service Products

For many marketers, the difference between service products and physical products is negligible, in marketing terms. The reason for this is that a service is also a bundle of benefits, and it is not hard to imagine circumstances where a service can provide the same benefits as a physical product. For example, someone who needs cheering up might eat a bar of chocolate (a physical product) or might watch a DVD of a favourite comedy show (a service product). A man wanting to impress his girlfriend might buy her a gift, or take her out to the theatre – the benefit to the customer is the same.

Categorising products as either service products or physical products is somewhat misleading. Almost all physical products contain an element of service, and almost all services contain physical elements. In effect, all products are on a continuum between the purely physical product (for example a bag of cement) to the purely service (life insurance). Even at these extremes there are no pure products: a bag of cement still has to be stocked by a builders' merchant, and an insurance policy still has a physical

cost-plus pricing Setting prices by calculating the outlay on producing the items, and adding on a profit margin.

The gift of a rose could be as effective as a dinner for two.

© Vgstudio | Dreamstime.com

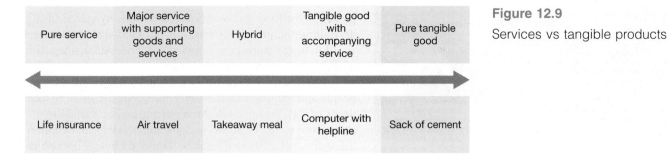

Pure service	Major service with supporting goods and services	Hybrid	Tangible good with accompanying service	Pure tangible good

Life insurance	Air travel	Takeaway meal	Computer with helpline	Sack of cement

Figure 12.9

Services vs tangible products

document to prove that it exists. It may therefore be more accurate to talk about service elements rather than service products. The factors distinguishing service elements are as follows:

- *They are intangible.* Service elements do not have any physical existence: the well-being one feels from spending time at the gym cannot be touched, sold, stored or given away to anyone else, but it is real nonetheless.
- *Production and consumption occur at the same time.* The airline passenger enjoys the flight at the same time as the aircraft flies: the theatregoer enjoys the play at the same time as the actors perform.
- *Services are perishable.* Once the aircraft takes off, any empty seats cannot be sold or stockpiled for later. If a restaurant is empty, the staff still have to be paid, and their time cannot be saved up for busy times.
- *Services cannot be tried in advance.* It is not possible to try out a haircut before the hairdresser starts cutting, nor can one eat a meal in a restaurant before ordering it.
- *Services are variable, even from the same supplier.* Sometimes the chef has a bad day, or the waiter is in a bad mood: on the other hand, sometimes a chef has an inspired day which transforms the food.

Each of these factors creates its own marketing problems. The intangibility of the product means that customers are, in effect, buying a promise: it is difficult for them to judge the product, and may even be difficult to judge it after it has been consumed (Zeithaml and Bitner 1996; Choi and Scarpa 1994). Intangibility therefore creates greater risk (there is more on this later).

Because consumption and production occur at the same time, the consumer is present for much of the production process, which means that there is much more contact between producer and consumer than would be the case with a physical product. This allows the service provider much greater opportunities to tailor the product to the customer.

The perishability of services has implications for pricing and promotion. The supplier must try to alter either the supply side or the demand side of the process in order to match production and consumption. Altering the supply side may mean employing part-time staff, working flexibly, and in general adding and subtracting people and equipment in order to meet a fluctuating demand. Evening out demand is often simpler – airlines offer cheap seats off-season, bars operate 'happy hours' for quiet parts of the day, restaurants offer 'early bird' meals early in the evening. Discount days for some groups of consumers (e.g. students and retired people) enable retailers to fill the store on quiet days, and so forth: there is more on this in Chapter 14.

Finally, the variability of services can be an asset or a liability. In some cases, variability is not good: restaurants rely on producing food of a consistent quality in order to maintain a reputation: this is difficult to do, since cooking is essentially a creative

process. Fast-food restaurants overcome this by standardising and de-skilling the process as much as possible, and employing low-skill low-wage workers to produce the food. Automating as much of the service as possible also helps.

An alternative approach is to employ educated, well-trained people and empower them to vary the service in order to meet the needs of the customers. In these circumstances, variability is seen as an asset to the business, because the service can be tailored to the individual customer's needs. Top-class hotels operate in this way, allowing desk staff to deal with customer complaints, solve customer problems, and make adjustments to the customer's experience of the hotel on an ad-hoc basis, without having to refer to senior managers. There is more on the empowerment of staff in Chapter 22.

Kotler (2003) suggested five categories of product, expressed as combinations of physical product and services:

1 *Pure tangible good.* This includes products such as paper, salt or computer disks which have almost no service attached to them.

2 *Tangible good with accompanying service.* This would include highly technical products which are dependent on installation, servicing, planning, training or maintenance.

3 *Hybrid.* This would be an equal offering of tangible and intangible benefits. In this case, the service portion of the product is as important as the tangible portion.

4 *Major service with supporting goods and services.* In this case, the important part of the product is the service element, but some physical goods and supporting services are required. Airline passengers, for example, are mainly buying transport services, but they also need some tangibles such as food and seating, and some support services (travel agents, etc.) are also needed.

5 *Pure service.* Here the product is almost entirely intangible, for example consultancy services or accounting services.

From the customer's viewpoint, buying a service is much more risky. Services are variable and cannot be tested, so the consumer has to take a great deal on trust: physical products can be returned if they prove to be faulty, but a bad haircut cannot be returned, and it may even prove problematical to avoid paying for it. Even a minor defect in a stereo system would justify returning it: an uncomfortable tram ride with a bad-tempered conductor will not result in a refund of the fare.

Because of this, consumers will need to spend more time on information-gathering, are likely to rely more heavily on word-of-mouth communications, and will want to know more about the qualifications and experience of the service provider. For example, someone looking for a hairdresser might want to know about the experience and qualifications of the stylist, whereas few people would care about the engineering qualifications of Sony's chief designer.

Most of the risk attached to buying a physical product is limited to the purchase price, unless of course the product is defective in a way which causes injury or property damage. Products with a high service element carry additional risks, however, as follows:

1 *Consequential loss.* These arise when a poorly-performed service causes loss to the customer. For example, a chartered accountant who fails to file a client's tax return on time might cause the client to be fined by the tax authorities, and perhaps be ordered to pay interest and surcharges. For this reason, service providers are usually careful to explain the risks beforehand, to put disclaimers into their contracts, and to carry professional liability insurance. Customers can take legal action if they have suffered consequential losses as a result of a poorly-executed service.

Marketing in Practice
Sixt Car Rentals

Sixt Car Rentals is far and away the largest car hire company in Germany, and is one of the largest in the world. The company has suffered dramatic setbacks in its time, which makes its current size and growth all the more remarkable.

Founded by Martin Sixt in 1912, in his home town of Munich, the company had scarcely got itself established when the cars were commandeered by the German Army for the First World War, which started in 1914. After the war, Sixt started up again, but in 1939 the cars were again confiscated for the Wehrmacht as the Second World War began. Martin Sixt died in 1945, heartbroken by the destruction of his offices and accommodation by Allied bombing.

In the 1950s the company started up again, using one car which Martin Sixt had hidden in a barn. The company grew largely through being innovative: it was the first taxi company in Germany to fit radios to the cars, using imported American equipment: it was the first car company in Germany to offer vehicle leasing, the first to have a website, and the first in the world to offer a self-service

system at airports. The company is also innovative in identifying and meeting customer needs – it offers a holiday rentals package in which the hire fee includes all the local waivers and guarantees, so that the customer simply turns up and drives the car away: any damage to the car is Sixt's problem. This takes away a major worry that many people have when driving in a foreign country – that there might be local regulations that either the driver or the car will not meet.

Sixt also has a low-cost subsidiary, Sixti, which offers a limited range of vehicles at extremely low rentals. Sixt claim that this is cheaper than owning a car – a claim which may well be true, given that most people use their cars fairly infrequently.

Sixt's growth outside Germany has been rapid. Now around half the size of Hertz, the largest car hire company in the world, Sixt is looking to spread its business model worldwide. Paying attention to the needs of its various market segments, and being prepared to innovate to meet the needs of a changing market, are the key factors which fuel Sixt's success.

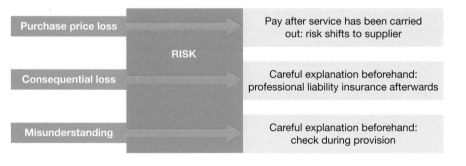

Figure 12.10

Risk in service purchases

2 *Purchase price risk.* This is the risk that the customer will lose the money paid for the service. In fact, this risk is lower for consumers in some service situations, because the service is only paid for after it has been consumed: in theory, a customer can refuse to pay for a meal which is not of the right quality. In practice, few people actually do this, but it is advisable for the supplier to check that everything is satisfactory during the service provision. This is why waiters will check that food is satisfactory while the diners are still eating, and why service stations call car owners if they find that extra work needs to be done. This type of check has two advantages for the supplier: first, it enables any problems to be corrected early, and second, it makes it much harder for the customer to claim that the service was faulty in order to avoid paying.

Marketing in Practice
Paying for Services

Payment for services is often culture-specific, in other words payments are made in different ways and at different stages of the service provision in different parts of the world. Nowhere is this more apparent than in bars.

In Spain, customers typically pay for their drinks when they leave the bar at the end of the evening. This creates complications for British tourists, who are used to paying for drinks as they get them, and who consequently sometimes walk out without paying. It also complicates matters when buying rounds of drinks – which is rare among Spaniards, who either pay for their own or treat their friends to an entire evening of drinking. Note that it is not common for Spaniards to spend an entire evening drinking – unlike the British, of course!

In Brazil it is common to pay for drinks before ordering them. Customers pay the cashier for what they want, and give the receipt to the barman who then pours the drinks. The barman never handles money: the cashier never handles drinks. In more expensive places customers pay when they leave – knowing which system is in operation is one of the puzzles for the foreigner.

Most countries have a system of tipping waiters and bar staff. In Spain, customers might leave a very small tip, just the odd few coins from their change. In the UK, nobody tips in pubs, but they do tip in restaurants (usually 10 per cent or so). In the United States, a 15 per cent tip is regarded as standard in bars and restaurants, and customers often leave 20 per cent or more if the service was good – which adds considerably to the cost of an evening out. Tipping is a minefield for the traveller – in the UK, customers tip hairdressers but not plumbers, in France customers tip waiters but not barmen, and tip staff when they sit at the tables but not when they sit at the bar.

3 *Misunderstanding.* Sometimes a customer does not understand the full implications of the service. For example, the client of a lawyer is unlikely to understand all the legal issues involved in the case (which is why he or she has hired a professional in the first place). The client may not understand the ramifications of (for example) conceding a point to the opposing lawyer.

Service purchasing therefore follows a somewhat different sequence from that of purchasing a physical good, as shown in Figure 12.11.

Because customers are buying a promise, they are much more likely to use indirect measures of quality when choosing a service. This means that they are likely to assume that the food will be better at a more expensive restaurant, that the hairdressing salon in the town centre will be better than the suburban one, and that the lawyer with the expensively-fitted offices will be more likely to win the case. These assumptions are, of course, irrational.

Figure 12.11

Service purchasing vs physical product purchasing

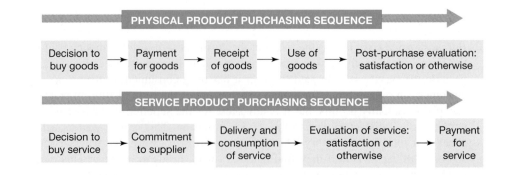

Involvement is also likely to be greater in service industries because of the additional risks involved. Customers tend to have favourite restaurants, hairdressers and family solicitors: even when problems become apparent, customers are reluctant to switch bank accounts, whereas they are prepared to switch brands of tuna in order to save a few pence. Note that the same customers who switch brands easily when buying physical products are likely to remain loyal to the same supermarket, which is after all a service provider.

In services markets there is more emphasis on Booms and Bitner's people, process and physical evidence (Booms and Bitner 1981). These have the following effects:

- *People*. Because most services are produced with the buyer present, there is usually direct contact between the producer and the consumer. Consumers need to relate to their hairdressers, lawyers and aircraft cabin crew, and the personalities of the providers affect the total experience. These front-line people who actually deliver the service have been called 'part-time marketers' (Gummeson 1991), and they often outnumber the full-time marketers in the marketing department.

- *Process*. Due to the customer's presence, the process becomes part of the total experience. There is a great deal of difference between a pizza served in an expensive restaurant and a pizza delivered by a local takeaway, but the difference is far more apparent in the process than it is in the physical product.

- *Physical evidence*. This usually refers to the tangibles which accompany a service product: the glossy brochure, the décor of the shop or offices, the appearance of the person after the hairdo is completed and so forth. Since virtually all products contain elements of both services and physical products, the tangible part of the product may constitute the major part of what the customer is paying for – a take-away meal is an example.

In many ways, marketing techniques for services are very similar to those for physical products, but it is important to remember that (from the consumer's viewpoint at least) the risks are greater, and therefore the decision process will be longer, and will rely on different criteria from those used for a physical product.

Industrial Product Strategy

Although there are many similarities between the marketing of consumer products and the marketing of industrial products, industrial (business-to-business) products differ from consumer products in a number of ways, as follows:

- First, consumer product strategies focus much more on brand identity and product appearance than do industrial products.

- Second, many industrial products are sold alongside related services such as installation, training, maintenance packages and so forth, so that industrial products need to be offered as a total package.

- Third, business buyers try to minimise the emotional content of the decisions they make, so they tend to be concerned with specific, tangible, measurable benefits of the products.

- Fourth, the marketing and design of a business-to-business product usually requires a full understanding of the customer's value-creating activities in order to understand how the product on offer can contribute to the customer's value chain (see Chapter 11).

Within the global context, firms will tend to produce a proliferation of different versions of the product, because each market will demand something different. In some industrial markets this will also happen, because each buyer is big enough to be able to negotiate changes to the product. For example, a supplier of components to car manufacturers (e.g. wiring harnesses) not only has to supply a slightly different version of the product to each manufacturer, but also has to supply different versions for each model of car.

In such circumstances, the company is producing customer-specified products, in which it is the customer that specifies exactly what is to be produced. The company is then in a position whereby its marketing activities revolve around demonstrating competency in being able to manufacture to the required specifications.

A recent trend in business-to-business markets has been the transition from product to service orientation. For firms based in the wealthy countries of Western Europe and the United States, manufacturing is often no longer viable: production of physical goods is handled better by firms in the developing world, where costs (especially labour costs) are much lower. Western firms therefore need to differentiate themselves by providing services (which have to be provided locally), leaving the production of the physical products to lower-cost providers who can then ship the products in.

Talking Point

Ultimately, every country in the world is likely to become industrialised, and presumably will then move towards a post-industrial society in which more companies will want to transit from production to services. How is it possible for everyone to become service providers? Can we all make a living opening doors for each other? Or should there still be some manufacturers around?

Or maybe the economies of scale in manufacturing are such that a very tiny number of highly automated factories will be able to produce all the manufactured goods we need. From a marketer's viewpoint this appears very risky – such a system would put too much power in the hands of a few members of the value chain. Perhaps the balance of power will shift away from retailers and back to manufacturers!

Greenberg (2000) suggests that, instead of firms being 'solutions providers' whereby they add a range of services to their traditional product ranges, they should become customer value providers. A customer value provider seeks to provide value further down the value chain, helping its clients to provide value to their customers. Majewski and Srinivas (2002) point out that managers often underestimate the true cost of shifting the company's orientation: they offer five business models for professional services, as shown in Table 12.1.

Figure 12.12

Transition from product to service orientation

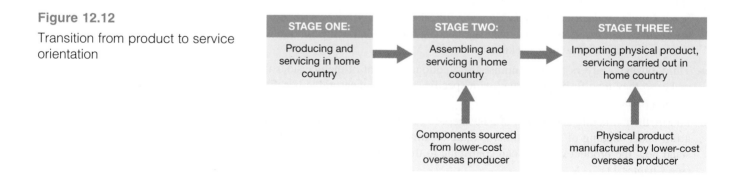

Table 12.1 Business models for professional services

	Product-centric	Professional services	Outsourcing	Information services	Financial services
Service value proposition	After-sales support Warranty services Maintenance offerings	Installation and support services Consulting services Other professional services	Lower fixed and/or variable costs Access to enhanced capabilities Increased flexibility Reduced head-count	Information-based for: maintenance, inventory management, supply chain, trading Remote monitoring and data aggregation	Financing for product purchases May include other value-added financial services Move assets from balance sheet to income statement
Operating model	Network or depot repair In-bound call centre Field service force Integrated sales force	Traditional leveraged engagement model Separate services organisation New channels to market	Head-count transfer of client Technology transfer or updating Scale economies Service-level tracking	Solutions selling skills Installed base of networked products Technology platforms and integration	Separate financial services organisation Financial operational processes (risk management, billing, etc.) Internal balance sheet

Packaging

Packaging is intended primarily to protect the product from the environment and vice-versa. For marketers, the packaging goes far beyond this, to the point where it conveys extra benefits to the customer, and thus becomes part of the product itself. Packaging carries out the following additional functions:

- Informs customers.
- Meets legal information requirements.
- In some cases aids use of the product (for example, ring pulls on cans of fish make it easier to open the can without spilling the contents or making the can opener smell of fish).

Packaging decisions might include such factors as tamper resistance (paper strips around caps to prevent bottles being opened in supermarkets), and customer usage (for example the development of beer packaging from bottles to cans, to ring pulls, to non-waste ring pulls, to draught beer systems). In recent years, environmental considerations have resulted in packaging which is either recyclable (or even recycled) or biodegradable. Customer acceptability is clearly a factor: packaging must be

hygienic and convenient for the customer, and it must look right as well. The ratio of the sides of the package affect people's perception of the product, but this depends also on the seriousness of the context – if the product is not important to the consumer, the shape of the packaging becomes less important as well (Raghubir and Greenleaf 2006).

Talking Point

Do people really care about the packaging of a product? Most of us just rip the packaging open as fast as possible to get our hands on the goodies – unless, of course, the product is packed in a shrink-wrap plastic shell!

Some packaging seems to have been designed for the maximum inconvenience of the customer. Unless you have a dog with strong teeth it's almost impossible to get into some packaging – so why do producers do this? Presumably it's to reduce pilfering – after all, if the customer can't get the packaging open without using bolt cutters, it's unlikely that the average shoplifter can sneak something out of its package in the store. So if the packaging is for the store's convenience, where does that leave customer centrality?

Some packaging has been designed in such a way that it can be protected by law: in the UK, this is covered by the 1994 Trade Marks Act, which enables producers to prevent competitors from selling their products in similar packaging. In some cases the packaging has been rendered expensive to copy, requiring special machine tools to produce complex shapes, or expensive printing processes. 'Me-too' packaging has become common among supermarket own-brand products, and there has been some debate about the ethics of this. In some countries these imitators contravene copyright or patent laws (Davies 1995).

Giant beer cans were fashionable in the 1970s.

Packaging can raise ethical issues: oversized packs can give the impression that the consumer is buying more than is in fact the case, for example. This is called slack packaging (Smith 1995). Manufacturers of products such as powder detergents and breakfast cereals usually print a statement to the effect that the contents of the box may settle in transit (which is of course true) in order to avoid claims of slack packaging. Misleading labelling is another area in which packaging can be deceptive – packaging is commonly labelled 'recyclable', which is true but not very helpful, since virtually everything is recyclable at a price. The implication is that the packaging is somehow more environmentally friendly than other packaging, which is unlikely to be the case. Foreign imports can be labelled as originating in the home country provided they have been packaged there, and there is a great deal of latitude in food labelling. Smoked bacon may well have had smoke flavour added, 'farm-fresh' eggs are likely to be from battery hens, and 'farmhouse' cheese may be from industrial cheese factories (Young 1999).

To counter these problems, the UK's Food Standards Agency has drawn up a list of commonly used words, and has made recommendations as to when the words can be used. They have also recommended that phrases such as 'natural goodness' and 'country style' should be avoided, since they have no definite meaning (Benady 2001).

Summary

The product is what the marketer is offering for exchange with the consumers, so getting it right is of considerable importance. Having the right products on offer at the right time is obviously important, but marketers also need to consider their resources and seek to ensure that the products they offer constitute the best use of limited resources. This means that they must manage the portfolio with regard to each product's performance, and also with regard to the overall mix of products.

Packaging performs a number of functions for both the producer and the consumer, but a key point is that the packaging actually forms part of the product, because it can offer definite benefits to the consumer (not to mention the retailers and wholesalers).

The key points from this chapter are as follows:

- The product life cycle, though severely flawed, offers a model for understanding the stages a product goes through.

- Products do not sell in isolation – they are often linked, and should be considered as a portfolio.

- The Boston Consulting Group Matrix offers a snapshot of the product's current position, but executive judgement still needs to be applied.

- Matrix analysis offers a spurious credibility, but does help to clarify the issues.

- Most products involve elements of both service and physical product.

- Many business-to-business companies are experiencing a transition from product orientation to service orientation.

- Packaging is part of the product: because it is the first contact many people have with the product, ethical issues might be raised.

Chapter review questions

1 What are the main drawbacks of the PLC?

2 What are the main drawbacks of the BCG matrix?

3 What strengths does the GE Matrix have over the BCG matrix?

4 How might a service company increase the consistency of its products?

5 How might service level increases help a company differentiate its products?

6 Why might a company drop a product shortly after its introduction?

7 Why might a company retain a product which actually loses money?

8 How might a chain restaurant company manipulate the physical evidence aspect of its activities to increase profits?

9 Why might a company move from a manufacturing to a services orientation?

10 How might packaging of take away foods help consumers to enjoy the product better?

Preview case revisited
Sony

For Sony to keep ahead of the game is not easy. The company has to keep producing new products, and of course has to market them effectively on a global scale: currently, Sony is pushing its Blu Ray high-definition DVD system. This had gone up against Toshiba's HD DVD system in a competition to decide which will be the world standard in DVD systems. Sony tied up deals with major film studios, effectively

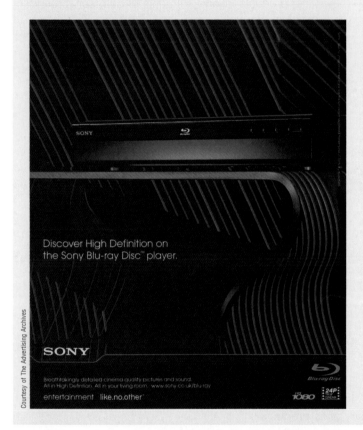

Discover High Definition on the Sony Blu-ray Disc™ player.

SONY

Breathtakingly detailed cinema quality pictures and sound.
All in High Definition. All in your living room. www.sony.co.uk/blu-ray
entertainment like.no.other™

Courtesy of The Advertising Archives

shutting Toshiba out of the prerecorded market: in February 2008 Toshiba admitted defeat and stopped supporting its own system.

Managing a portfolio of several thousand products and product variations creates major problems for Sony. Products become obsolete quickly, and therefore development costs need to be recovered fast if the company is to show a profit on its research and development commitment. Sony's designers have the philosophy of listening to customers' needs – in fact, Sony engineers are required to spend time working in Sony retail stores so that they have the opportunity to meet actual consumers face-to-face. This serves several purposes – first, it enables engineers to identify recurring problems with existing products. Second, it exposes them to the questions people have about products, which flags up areas of consumer concern which can be incorporated into new products. Third, and perhaps most importantly, it drives home to the engineers the fact that consumers are real people, not disembodied voices in a market research report.

Sony estimate that a new product has around three months to succeed or fail – after that period, it will be on its way out and its successor will need to be coming through the design pipeline. This rapid pace of change means that the only constant is the Sony brand, which has been attached to many subsidiary brands in order to maintain a presence in the various markets (Sony VAIO computers, Sony Ericsson mobile telephones, Sony Playstation video games and so forth).

In a rapidly changing world, only Sony's commitment to long-term research and development expenditure enables the company to keep ahead of the competition in generating consumer satisfaction.

Case study
Ovaltine

There are many nutritional drinks for children in the world, but for many people Ovaltine occupies a special place. First developed by a Swiss chemist, George Wander, in 1904, the drink sold in Switzerland under the brand name Ovomaltine (because it was made from eggs and malt) but when the product was exported to the UK in 1909 a typing error caused the name to be registered as Ovaltine.

The product was an instant success, and the UK factory began exports to the United States, but in 1915 a factory was built in Illinois for the manufacture of Ovaltine. In the 1930s and 1940s the American end of the company used the new medium of radio to promote the product – the company sponsored *Little Orphan Annie* and *Captain Midnight*, both popular children's shows. By saving up labels children could send in for special gifts – secret decoder rings, badges, and pins. Coded messages were sent out during the show, so children without a decoder ring would feel left out – a powerful persuasive tool. The connection between the product and children was one which the company fostered worldwide.

"Isn't it 'licious, Mummy!"

OVALTINE

for Radiant Health

Courtesy of The Advertising Archives

In the UK, commercial broadcasting did not exist until the 1950s (for television) and the 1960s (for radio). Government policy was that broadcasting was too powerful a communications medium to be left to commercial entities – or even political parties. The British Broadcasting Corporation was established as a State-owned but politically-independent broadcaster with a complete monopoly. It was funded by licence fees rather than by direct taxation, in order to maintain its independence from political parties and big business alike. However, during the 1930s the Duchy of Luxembourg established its own international broadcasting system, which could and did accept advertising, sponsorship and specially made programmes. The station used what was then the world's most powerful radio transmitter, easily powerful enough to reach the UK, and broadcast in English: programmes were recorded in the UK and sent out to Luxembourg. One such programme was The Ovaltineys.

The Ovaltineys were children who performed songs, set intriguing puzzles and played games on the air. The show was broadcast every Sunday from 5.30 in the evening until 6 pm, and was first aired in 1935. By 1939 the League of Ovaltineys, a children's club which was a spin-off from the show, had five million members: in the same way as American children sent off jars or labels to win special gifts, the UK's children collected labels to gain a membership badge and book, and the chance to enter competitions. Although the show went off the air during the Second World War, when Luxembourg was occupied by the Germans, the show resumed again in 1952: by then, post-war recovery had reached the point where rationing was ending and advertising could begin again. The show never regained its original popularity, however, perhaps because of the poor reception quality from Radio Luxembourg's new medium-wave transmitter. Many well-known British performers started their careers as Ovaltiney child stars, and many older people in the UK can still sing the cheery theme song from the show.

The Ovaltineys have occasionally been revived since, but largely as an exercise in nostalgia – modern children do not relate so readily to the format, which is seen as 'uncool', whereas adults who grew up with Ovaltine feel differently.

Ovaltine certainly has an international appeal – in Hong Kong it is served as a café drink in trendy cafes such as Maxim's Express or Café de Coral. In Brazil, the powder is often mixed with vanilla ice-cream.

Ovaltine is now part of the Twinings tea company. The malty flavour is as popular with adults as with children, and there is no doubt that Ovaltine will continue for another hundred years.

Questions

1 How might Ovaltine extend the brand?
2 How has the product life cycle been extended?
3 What are the main threats Ovaltine might face from competitors?
4 How might Ovaltine expand its market?
5 In terms of the BCG matrix, what is Ovaltine's likely position?

References

Barksdale, H.C. and Harris, C.E. (1982): Portfolio analysis and the PLC. *Long Range Planning* **15** (6), 74–83.

Benady, D. (2001): Will they eat their words? *Marketing Week* 2 August, 24–6.

Booms, B.H. and Bitner, M.J. (1981): Marketing strategies and organisation structures for service firms. In: J. Donnelly and W.R. George (eds) *Marketing of Services* (Chicago, IL: American Marketing Association).

Choi, C.J. and Scarpa, C. (1994): A note on small vs. large organisations. *Journal of Economic Behaviour and Organisation* **24** (July), 219–24.

Davies, I. (1995): Look-alikes: fair or unfair competition? *Journal of Brand Management* **2**(2), 104–20.

Greenberg, D. (2000): *Product Provider to Customer Value Provider: Escaping the Services Maze* (Somers, NY: IBM Institute for Business Value, IBM Global Services).

Greenley, G.E. and Barus, B.L. (1994): A comparative study of product launch and elimination decisions in UK and US companies. *European Journal of Marketing* **28**(2), 5–29.

Gummeson, E. (1991): Marketing orientation revisited: the crucial role of the part-time marketer. *European Journal of Marketing* **25**(2), 60–75.

Kotler, P. (2003): *Marketing Management* (Upper Saddle River, NJ: Pearson-Prentice Hall).

Majewski, B.M. and Srinavas, S. (2002): *The Services Challenge: Operationalising your Services Strategy* (Somers, NY: IBM Global Services).

Pawels, K., Silva-Risso, J., Srinavasan, S. and Hanssens, D.M. (2004): New products, sales promotions and firm value: the case of the automobile industry. *Journal of Marketing* **68**(4), 142–56.

Rhagubir, P. and Greenleaf, E.A. (2006): Ratios in proportion: what should the shape of the package be? *Journal of Marketing* **70**(2), 95–107.

Smith, N.C. (1995): Marketing strategies for the ethics era. *Sloan Management Review* **36**(4), 85–97.

Vakratsas, D. and Ambler, T. (1999): How advertising works: what do we really know? *Journal of Marketing* **63** (January), 26–43.

Young, R. (1999): First read the label, then add a pinch of salt. *The Times*, 30 November, 2–4.

Zeithaml, V.A. and Bitner, M.J. (1996): *Services Marketing* (Singapore: McGraw-Hill).

Further reading

There is a great deal written about new product development, but relatively little about product management. Here is one of the few books on the topic:

Gorchels, L. (2000): *The Product Manager's Handbook* (Mason, OH: Contemporary Books). This is a readable, practitioner-orientated American text. It uses interesting cases and examples to illustrate points, and concentrates strongly on the product manager's role.

Chapter 13
New product development

Learning objectives After reading this chapter, you should be able to:

1. Categorise products according to their degree of newness.

2. Assess the likely degree of success a particular product might have.

3. Explain the difficulties in establishing an innovative culture within the firm.

4. Outline ways of generating ideas for new products.

5. Explain the differences and similarities between project champions and project teams.

6. Describe the basic strategies for new product development.

7. Describe the factors in new product success.

8. Explain how innovations are diffused through the population.

9. Explain the role of newness in product acceptability.

10. Explain the factors which make up new product acceptability.

11. Describe the different characteristics of innovative consumers.

12. Show how marketers can affect the rate at which innovations are diffused.

Introduction

As we saw in Chapter 12, products pass through a life cycle and eventually cease to generate sales. For companies to remain in business, therefore, a constant stream of new products needs to be developed in order to replace those which have reached the end of their useful lives. Additionally, firms need to add new products to the range if they are to grow: new markets demand new products.

For marketers, there is likely to be a conflict arising from this. On the one hand, marketers need to look towards creating new products for their existing and potential customers, but on the other hand the products which customers might need may not be ones which can easily be produced by the company. For example, a company which produces guitars is unlikely to have the capacity or expertise to produce guitar strings, amplifiers or even plectrums. In most cases the production of such items would have to be undertaken by another firm.

Changing customer tastes, competitive pressures, technological advances and changing corporate strategy all contribute to the pressures to create new products. The rate of

Preview case
The Flying Car

The idea of owning a flying car has been around for a considerable time. In 1917, Glenn Curtiss (co-founder of Curtiss-Wright) unveiled an aluminium three-winged aircraft which could convert to a car and be driven on the road. It never managed to fly more than a short distance, however, and the project died for lack of financial backing. In 1937, the Arrowbile took to the skies: developed by Waldo Waterman, it was basically a car with a propeller attached to the back and detachable wings. The aircraft suffered from pitch instability because it had no tail as such, and earlier versions crashed fairly dramatically, but the finished version flew well: lack of financial backing (in the cash-strapped 'thirties) and the advent of the Second World War killed the project.

In the 1940s the Airphibian and the Convaircar both appeared, and flew: both were certified by the US Civil Aviation Authority, but the Airphibian did not attract funding and the Convaircar crashed on its third flight, ending the project. A military 'flying saucer' type vehicle was developed jointly by British and Canadian engineers, but the vehicle was never practical: the Aerocar was a fibreglass vehicle which obtained Federal Aviation Authority approval, and was scheduled to be manufactured by Ford in 1970, but was killed by the oil crisis in the early 1970s.

Part of the problem with a flying car is that it needs to be approved both by the civil aviation authorities and by the road traffic authorities. The requirements of each department often conflict – aircraft bodies are typically too flimsy to pass road traffic safety standards, and car bodies are too heavy to fly. A second problem is purely technical – aircraft wings are long (but can be folded, provide they can be braced sufficiently rigidly) but aircraft also typically have long tails to provide pitch stability. Although this problem can be overcome, the solutions usually require wing designs which become difficult to fold. A third problem is the need for a transmission system which can drive the road wheels and also a propeller, without creating too large a weight penalty – using the propeller to move the car on a road is simply too dangerous.

The real question is – what is the market for such a vehicle? For most people, the cost of flying is prohibitive, and in any case the necessary training in flying an aircraft is a major stumbling block.

Bob Giovioso

change differs between industries, but change is inevitable: firms which do not innovate will eventually disappear, along with their obsolete products. Firms which do innovate are likely to dominate global markets in future, provided they have the imagination to dominate fundamentally new markets (Hamel and Prahalad 1991).

Types of New Product

Various attempts have been made to define what is a new product. Products are not either new or old: there are degrees of newness, but in most cases the measurement of these degrees of newness is subjective.

One categorisation comes from Booz, Allen and Hamilton (1982). This is as follows:

1 *Product replacement*. This is essentially an improvement or redesign of an existing product. The new model of a car, the replacement of one formulation of shampoo for another, or the repositioning of an existing product into a new market are examples of product replacements. These account for around 45 per cent of new product launches.

2 *Additions to existing lines*. Brand extensions, complementary products such as coffee whitener, and products which make existing products easier to use or more effective come into this category. These are thought to account for about 25 per cent of new product launches. The fit between the parent brand and the extension product is crucial to the success of brand extensions (Volckner and Sattler 2006).

3 *New product lines*. Around 20 per cent of new product launches, these products are launched for the purpose of moving into new markets. Building on existing brand values, the products have only a small connection with the original product lines, and really constitute a new departure for the firm.

4 *New-to-the-world products*. These are products which create entirely new markets, and change the way people behave in a fundamental manner. Mobile telephones and the Internet are recent examples, but in the past radical inventions such as the car, the communications satellite and the aeroplane have achieved the same radical changes.

Figure 13.1

Categories of new product

Product replacement:
45 per cent of new product launches

Additions to existing lines:
25 per cent of new product launches

Total new product launches

New product lines:
20 per cent of new product launches

New-to-the-world products:
10 per cent of launches

Table 13.1 New product clusters

Clusters	Description
Cluster 1: The Better Mousetrap with No Synergy (36 per cent succeeded)	This is a product that, while being an improvement over existing offerings, does not fit in with the firm's existing product lines.
Cluster 2: The Innovative Mousetrap that Really Wasn't Better (No successes at all)	This might be a product that, while being technically excellent, has no real advantage for the consumer over existing products.
Cluster 3: The Close to Home Me-Too Product (56 per cent succeeded)	A copy of a competitor's offering. Not likely to be perceived as new by consumers.
Cluster 4: The Innovative High-Tech Product (64 per cent succeeded)	A truly new-to-the-world product.
Cluster 5: The Me-too Product with No Technical/ Production Synergy (14 per cent succeeded)	A copy of a competitor's product, but with no real connection with existing product lines.
Cluster 6: The Old But Simple Money-Saver (70 per cent succeeded)	Not a new product at all, except to the firm producing it.
Cluster 7: The Synergistic Product that was New to the Firm (67 per cent succeeded)	A product that fits the product line, but is new.
Cluster 8: The Innovative Superior Product with No Synergy (70 per cent succeeded)	A product that does not fit the existing product line, but is new.
Cluster 9: The Synergistic Close to Home Product (72 per cent succeeded)	A product line extension; perhaps a minor improvement over the firm's existing products.

The boundaries between these categories are by no means rigid, and sometimes the effects of a new product cannot be recognised until much later. A further drawback of these categories is that they tend to view the product from the producer's viewpoint: customers may not think that the new product line is really new at all.

An alternative, and more comprehensive, categorisation of products was developed by Calentone and Cooper (1981) (Table 13.1). These researchers also calculated the success rates for the new product clusters.

The evidence from Calentone and Cooper's study is that the less radical products are more likely to succeed than the radical, new-to-the-world products. Of course, the authors do not outline the extent to which a product succeeded – there is little doubt that a radical product such as the Sony Walkman made the company a great deal of money, more than compensating for the many other radical products launched by Sony which apparently sank without trace. On the other hand, products which have no synergy (either in production or in marketing) with the firm's existing products appeared to have no successes at all.

There is a problem with measuring the success (or otherwise) of a product, since success might be considered in terms of profit, of market share, of strategic outcomes, or of long-term sustainability. The most commonly used measures in consumer markets are as follows (Huang, Soutar and Brown 2004):

1 Customer acceptance

2 Customer satisfaction

3 Product performance

4 Customer perception of quality.

Talking Point

Innovation can be looked at from two viewpoints. Innovation on the part of a producer is the development of an idea which offers a new solution to an old problem, or a new solution to a new problem. Innovation on the part of a consumer is the degree to which new solutions are adopted.

It would appear from the Calentone and Cooper research that innovation is not a good idea after all. The most innovative products on the scale seem to be the ones most prone to failure, and the most successful ones seem to be the ones that are merely copies of competitors' products or minor alterations to existing products.

Or maybe we are only seeing part of the picture? Maybe the definition of success is at fault – after all, a new product might have strategic importance, taking the company into a new market. Or the new product might simply take a very, very long time to take off. Or maybe the new products which succeed succeed spectacularly, while the me-too products barely break even. Either way, companies continue to innovate!

A classification which is often quoted is that of Robertson (1967). Robertson classified products according to their effects on consumers' lives. The classification is as follows:

continuous innovation Incremental improvements in an existing product.

● **Continuous innovation.** An innovation which follows on incrementally from previous solutions, and offers only minor new benefits. It has been defined as the modification of the taste, appearance, performance or reliability of an existing product rather than the creation of a new one (Blackwell, Miniard and Engel 2001). Examples might include adding fluoride to toothpaste, 'lite' versions of beer brands or 'heavy-duty' batteries.

dynamically continuous innovation A product which is a substantial shift in technology but which does not change people's lives.

● **Dynamically continuous innovation.** This may involve the creation of a new product or the substantial modification of an existing product, but it does not lead to a change in people's shopping or usage patterns. DVD players do not significantly alter people's television viewing patterns in the same way that video recorders did: they simply replaced video recorders. Likewise, the electric toothbrush does not change the number of times people clean their teeth.

discontinuous innovation A new product which significantly changes consumers' lifestyles.

● **Discontinuous innovation.** This involves the creation of an entirely new product that significantly alters consumers' behaviours and lifestyles. Mobile telephones, video recorders, television and (in their day) cars and radio all changed the way people lived.

Firms wishing to be innovative need to establish a culture of innovation. Marketing orientation certainly tends to create an innovation culture, since products need to be developed to meet new customer needs, or to meet existing needs more effectively (Tajeddini, Trueman and Larsen 2006). New product development works best if the research and development (R&D) people get on well with the marketing people, in other words have a good working relationship (Rodriguez, Perez and Gutierrez 2007).

Figure 13.2

Degrees of innovation

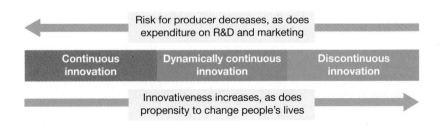

Marketing in Practice
James Dyson

When James Dyson was a twenty-three-year-old student at the Royal College of Art in London, he designed a novel boat, the Seatruck, which was able to carry cargo at high speeds. This won a Design Council award, and went on to earn $500 million in sales. Dyson later invented the ballbarrow, a wheelbarrow with a ball instead of a wheel (which made it less likely to sink in soft earth), a boat launcher using balls instead of wheels, and an amphibious vehicle for use on sand dunes and on the sea.

Eventually, though, Dyson invented the product which made him a household name – the Dyson vacuum cleaner. This cleaner was the first bagless cleaner: needing no bag, it is cheaper to own and use, and never loses suction. Dyson has promoted these benefits very ably, using advertisements showing people in the familiar position of having to dismantle the vacuum cleaner to find out what is clogging it up.

Dyson's success has been based on his ability to see the drawbacks with existing products, and engineer solutions. His most successful inventions (the ballbarrow, the seatruck and the vacuum cleaner) have been based on their practical advantages over existing products. The Wheelboat amphibian has been less successful – and Dyson has had many other inventions which failed to become a hit with the public. Perhaps this is because

they are technically interesting but lack a practical advantage over existing products.

Whatever the reason, Dyson continues to invent. He recently launched a washing machine which does not tangle clothes, and is working on improvements to his vacuum cleaners. The inventions are not revolutionary, but they are practical and they do improve the lives of millions of people – simply because they meet people's needs better than the competing products.

Courtesy of The Advertising Archives

Creating an innovative culture within the firm is not easy. Innovators run the risk of failure, and many firms are less than tolerant of failure. Some common methods of encouraging innovation are as follows:

1 Reward success, but tolerate failure.
2 Give a clear message that innovation is essential to the organisation.
3 Allow people time to develop their ideas.
4 Try to avoid the 'not invented here' syndrome in which ideas are discouraged simply because the manager did not think of the idea first.
5 Provide adequate resources for ideas to develop.
6 Be available to staff to discuss their ideas in a positive way.

The New Product Development (NPD) Process

Cooper and Kleinschmidt (1986) developed the following model for the new product development process:

- *New product strategy*. The firm needs to decide what its overall NPD process is expected to achieve in strategic terms: which markets should the firm be entering, which competitors should it be attacking and which should not be confronted, which customer needs is the firm best placed to serve, and so forth.

- *Idea generation.* Ideas might be generated by any member of staff, or might be generated by teams set up for the purpose. There is more on this later.

screening Selecting new product ideas for further development.

- **Screening.** Ideas need to be considered in terms of the firm's strategic intent and also in terms of feasibility. Feasibility includes production as well as marketing issues.

concept testing A market research exercise in which feedback is obtained on the basic idea for a new product.

- **Concept testing.** Having selected from the ideas, concept testing with customers and production people can take place. At this stage, no prototype is necessary: a mock-up and description of what the final product is intended to do will be sufficient.

- *Business analysis.* The products which survive concept testing will need to be considered in terms of their profitability, their effect on sales of other products, their strategic worth in terms of building the business and so forth.

- *Product development.* At this stage the research and development engineers take over. The final design of the product needs to reflect the results of the concept testing and needs to fit within the cost structures dictated by the business analysis.

- *Market testing.* The final product needs to be tested in the market. This could be carried out through focus group analysis of a prototype, or by test marketing (see Chapter 7). This is the final stage of the process before the company commits to mass production and mass marketing.

- *Commercialisation.* This is the point at which the company launches the final product onto the market and commits to major expenditure.

Products might be dropped at almost any point in the proceedings, but obviously the earlier the product is dropped the lower the cost implications. Products which do not meet the strategic intent of the company should really never even be considered at the idea-generation stage – people's thinking can be directed in other directions.

The model is useful in the sense that most products pass through most of the stages: however, some products will be rushed through some stages and will spend longer in others, and sometimes stages are omitted altogether.

Furthermore, in the real world many products are launched which are simply the brainchild of an influential person in the company. Such products are carried through by the determination (or power) of the **product champion**. One famous example is the Sony Walkman, which was invented by Akio Morita, the founder of Sony. As a former Navy electronics engineer, Morita built the first Walkman at home, in his spare time,

product champion An individual who has or is given the role of guiding a new product through the development process.

Figure 13.3
The NPD process

New product strategy
Idea generation
Screening
Concept testing
Business analysis
Product development
Market testing
Commercialisation

Initial large number of ideas whittled down to a few which are launched

Rejected ideas removed from the process

using a reporter's Dictaphone as the basis. Morita was able to force the product through into production over the protests of his marketing people, and of course it went on to be a worldwide success.

Talking Point

The Walkman is only one example among many radical inventions which appeared to fly in the face of conventional marketing wisdom. The Dyson vacuum cleaner, the clockwork radio, even the personal computer all started out as the ideas of engineers. They were products looking for a market – a concept which is anathema to marketers!

Yet these are products which have been phenomenally successful. So are the marketers wrong? Should we listen more to the engineers – who are, after all, consumers themselves and also know all about the art of the possible? Or perhaps the frame of the picture is too small to show the products which engineers loved, but the public hated – the products which clutter up the patent office and provide endless amusement for industrial historians!

Sources of Ideas

Ideas might come from any of the following sources:

- *Market feedback*. Sales people might bring back ideas from customers, or market research might generate some new concepts. Also, competitors might produce something new which can be adapted or copied: 'me-too' products are often highly successful, because the research and development has mainly been paid for by someone else.

- *Technological advance*. Often new technology becomes available through pure research: for example, the laser was originally an interesting laboratory phenomenon, but subsequently became a major force in telecommunications, being installed in everything from fibre-optic cables to DVD players.

- *Recycling of existing technology*. Applying existing technology to a new problem often generates new ideas. For example, when suspension bridge builders found that the support cables sometimes went into dangerous harmonic oscillations in high winds, they borrowed the technology of vibration dampers from electrical engineers, who had used the technology to prevent similar oscillations in overhead power lines.

- *Generation by employees and managers within the organisation*. To an extent, these ideas should be treated with a degree of suspicion, because they are often based on what the company is capable of doing rather than on what a suitable market segment would be prepared to buy. In terms of the Calentone and Cooper classifications, these products would be Synergistic Products New to the Firm, but could also be Innovative Mousetraps – i.e. technically-exciting products which actually do not offer the consumers anything new. These products showed no successes at all, because the market had no need for them.

- **Brainstorming**. Over 60 per cent of Dutch companies use brainstorming as a technique for generating new ideas (Nijssen and Lieshout 1995). Brainstorming involves getting a group of interested parties together and briefing them to generate new ideas, often around a strategic theme. Brainstorming teams are often interdisciplinary: marketers, designers, engineers and even delivery personnel might become involved on the team, so that ideas can be pre-screened for practicality. In general, brainstorming sessions can be extremely productive if the team approach them in a positive spirit.

brainstorming Generating new product ideas by group discussion.

Figure 13.4

Sources of ideas

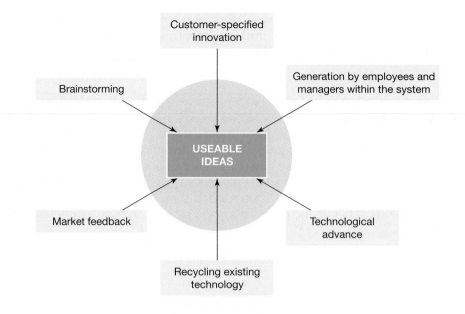

customer-specified innovation New product ideas which are generated by customers.

● **Customer-specified innovation**. In many business-to-business markets, innovation is forced by major customers. For example, if a motor manufacturer redesigns a vehicle, many (or all) of the components will need to be redesigned to a greater or lesser extent. In some cases, the component suppliers will need to expend substantial time and effort on research and development in order to meet the specification. In such circumstances, the engineers from the customer company are likely to become involved in the process, so a close relationship between supplier and customer is essential.

Organising for New Product Development

In too many firms innovation is stifled by the corporate culture or by the corporate structure. New ideas are easily discouraged – failure often brings criticism or even ridicule, so retaining the status quo is often seen as the low-risk option. Innovative firms therefore go to considerable effort to be proactive in encouraging innovation, and adopt many different structures for encouraging and developing new product ideas. **Project teams** are interdisciplinary groups composed of individuals from different departments.

project teams Groups of people with the responsibility for guiding products through the development process.

A project team might be formed from people from marketing, finance, engineering, even administration and shipping (depending on the product). They operate in a similar way to the brainstorming groups mentioned earlier, but the project team work together to carry the product right through the NPD process until it is launched. Such groups are also sometimes called venture teams.

The advantage of using a project team is that each member can carry the thoughts of the group back to their own departments and disseminate the ideas. The departments can then work on ways to implement their own part of the overall plan, so that the final launch of the product is carried out with the full knowledge and commitment of the whole firm. Project teams should meet regularly, although Internet technology means that meetings do not necessarily need to be physical: members can video conference from remote locations as necessary.

simultaneous engineering Carrying out development processes in parallel rather than sequentially in order to reduce time to market.

An extension of project teams is simultaneous engineering. In the past, designers would develop the product and then pass on the design to the production engineers, who

E-Marketing in Practice
Gadget Shop

Gadget Shop is a web-based mail order company which offers, well, gadgets. Some are truly useful, some are hilarious, some are virtually useless but look as if they ought to be useful.

The Paintball Magnum Duelling Kit is a home paint-balling set. The kit can be used for target practice against trees or walls, but it seems likely that it will be used by would-be jungle soldiers popping away at each other in the local woods. Then there is the Puchi-Puchi, an electronic device which duplicates the exact feel and sound of popping bubble wrap – the very thing for reducing stress in the office.

The Shake Torch is genuinely useful – it contains a powerful magnet and electric coil, so that 45 seconds of vigorous shaking generates enough electricity to power the torch for 45 minutes. There is a portable Jacuzzi – just add water – and even a rubber duck with a radio built in, to listen to in the Jacuzzi.

There are many more gadgets, of course: some will be bought as gifts, some as useful things to have around the house, and some for a good laugh. However, still others will be bought for no other reason than that they are novel – people's need for something unusual can be a powerful driver in this market.

Courtesy of The Gadget Shop

would organise the tooling and production line design in order to manufacture the finished product. Japanese companies moved over to a system of simultaneous engineering in which the designers and the production engineers work together throughout the process, thus cutting out one stage and speeding up the launch.

In some firms, product champions are appointed. A product champion has the role of taking the product through all its stages, and ensuring that colleagues contribute their part of the work at the appropriate time in the process. Product champions perform a useful

Figure 13.5

Project team structure

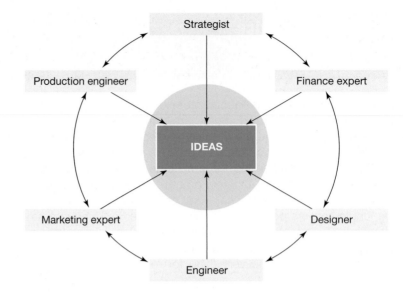

market challenger A company which seeks to grow at the expense of the market leader.

task in that they ensure the product actually comes into existence, rather than being sidelined by the routine tasks of making existing products. However, some researchers see product champions as a sign of a failed management: management, it can be argued, should be the ones who take responsibility for keeping the firm up to date (Johne and Snelson 1990).

There are six broad types of innovation strategy:

1 *Offensive.* Firms adopting an offensive strategy take pride in being the first to market. There are undoubtedly advantages in being the first with a new product: the firm can capture a substantial portion of the market before the competitors are off the starting blocks, and (provided the firm continues to innovate) can maintain the lead. This is the strategy adopted by Sony and 3M, both highly innovative firms.

2 *Defensive.* This strategy involves producing slightly improved copies of leaders' products. The defensive company only innovates in response to competitive challenges, either from leaders or from **market challengers**. Incremental innovations reduce risk for first movers in a market: early followers into a new market have some survival risks, but discontinuous innovation carries the greatest risks, so in fact there is only a disadvantage in being a first mover with a new product (Min, Kalwani and Robinson 2006). This means that a defensive strategy is probably the safest, even though rewards may not be high.

3 *Imitative.* Imitative companies simply produce copies of other firms' products, with few (if any) adaptations. These firms have the advantage of generating minimal R&D costs and of being sure that there is a market for the product. The main drawback is, of course, that the company which first developed the product has first-to-market advantages and will already have captured much of the market, which means that the imitative company needs to put in greater effort on promoting the product in order to poach customers, and probably has to sell at a lower price as well.

4 *Dependent.* The companies produce customer-specified innovations. For example, a component supplier to a major car manufacturer is not in a position to develop new products independently of the customer: the firm can only produce new components which are compatible with the car manufacturer's models.

5 *Traditional.* These firms are not really innovative at all: they resurrect old-fashioned designs or produce products which have been around for many years. In the UK, brands such as Hovis and Bovril have been manufactured in much the same way for over a hundred years: in Singapore, Tiger Balm is in this category, and in Australia Vegemite is a traditional product.

6 *Opportunist.* The opportunist company produces and markets inventions. The Dyson vacuum cleaner and the BayGen clockwork radio (invented by Trevor Bayliss) are examples of inventions which have succeeded. It should be pointed out that the vast majority of inventions actually fail to find a market, mainly because they tend to be technically-driven rather than market-driven.

Within the Traditional category, recent years have seen many 'new' products launched which are in fact reproductions of old designs. The Chrysler PSV, the Volkswagen Beetle and the Mini Cooper are all examples of 'retro' designs which have been revived (see Citroën C4 Preview case in Chapter 8, p. 248). There are also many household appliances such as fridges, toasters and the like which have been designed in Fifties styles. The desire for tradition extends to services as well – people prefer 'the real thing' when going to pubs, but often have trouble distinguishing them from 'replica' products (Lego *et al.* 2002). These products rely on the following factors for their success (Brown, Sherry and Kozinetts 2003):

Retro designs are popular again.

- *Allegory.* This is the mythology and story surrounding the original brand and its design. Allegorical impact is created when the original product has a well-known history: the original Beetle was so well-loved it even starred in a series of movies, for example, and the Mini starred in the original film of *The Italian Job*. Fifties-style toasters evoke memories of childhood, and myths grow up around products.

- *Aura.* This is the essence of the brand, the mystique surrounding it. The Chrysler PSV evokes imagery of 1940s America, and other retro products evoke similar auras.

- *Arcadia.* This is the idealised community in which such products might be used. Arcadia is based on nostalgia, but generally evokes a non-existent past: the 1950s is often seen as a golden age, for example, whereas in fact it was a decade filled with war, the fear of war and a general atmosphere of paranoia.

- *Antinomy.* This is brand paradox. New technology is viewed as unstoppable and overpowering, but at the same time is responsible for people's desire to return to a simpler, less high-tech past. People buy the retro products because they evoke the past, but at the same time expect the products to perform to modern standards: the original Mini Cooper was leaky, unreliable and uncomfortable both to drive and to ride in, but people liked the style. The new version is comfortable, reliable and efficient, but retains the style (albeit on a somewhat larger scale).

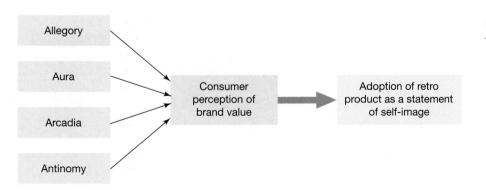

Figure 13.6

The four A's of retro design

Whether or not to go ahead with a new product is a decision which revolves around five dimensions (Carbonell-Foulquie, Munuera-Aleman and Rodrigeuz-Escudero 2004). These are as follows:

1 *Strategic fit*. This is the degree to which the new product fits in with the company's overall marketing and corporate strategy. The questions the company will ask are: Does this product take us nearer to where we want to be in the market? Does this product detract from our existing marketing plan? Does this product hurt our other products and cannibalise sales?

2 *Technical feasibility*. This is not just about whether the product can be made, or even whether it can be made economically: it is also about whether the product can be made economically within the product management portfolio (see Chapter 12).

3 *Customer acceptance*. Obviously no marketer should be launching a product which the customers do not like or would have difficulty accepting. Sadly, many products are launched every year which do not find a market – sometimes for no apparent reason.

4 *Market opportunity*. This is the level of competition the firm might have to face, and the current state of the external environment. The market opportunity takes account of all the elements which make up the market – the customers, the competitors, the macro- and micro-environment and so forth.

5 *Financial performance*. Firms do not necessarily aim to show a profit on every product they sell, but financial return is obviously important, and in the long run a product must be viable financially. If the product can never be profitable, the firm will have to make a decision as to whether there is any point in launching it at all.

Although all of the above factors are important, it is customer acceptance that decides the product's fate. If customers will not buy the product in sufficient numbers, all the other considerations are futile: if, on the other hand, customers have indicated that they will buy the product in large quantities, all the other problems can be overcome in time.

Retro products appear to be all the rage at present. Design styles from the 1950s and 1960s, revamped and updated models of traditional products, and even clothing fashions are being reissued to an eager public.

At the same time marketers are still using the word 'new' on almost everything from washing powder to cars. So which is the bigger selling point? New, or old? Modern/futuristic, or traditional/old-fashioned?

Figure 13.7

Factors in the launch decision

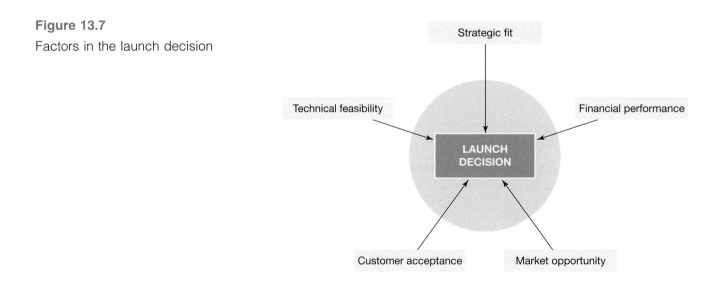

Diffusion of Innovation

New products are not immediately adopted by all consumers. Some consumers are driven to buy new products almost as soon as they become available, whereas others prefer to wait until the product has been around for a while before risking their hard-earned money on it. Innovations therefore take time to filter through the population: this process is called diffusion, and is partly determined by the nature of consumers and partly by the nature of the innovation itself.

Everett M. Rogers (1962) classified customers as follows:

- *Innovators.* Those who like to be first to own the latest products. These consumers predominate at the beginning of the product life cycle.
- *Early adopters.* Those who are open to new ideas, but like to wait a while after initial launch. These consumers predominate during the growth phase of the PLC.
- *Early majority.* Those who buy once the product is thoroughly tried and tested. These consumers predominate in the early part of the maturity phase of the PLC.
- *Late majority.* Those who are suspicious of new things, and wait until most other people already have one. These consumers predominate in the later part of the maturity phase of the PLC.
- *Laggards.* Those who only adopt new products when it becomes absolutely necessary to do so. These consumers predominate in the decline phase of the PLC.

The process of diffusion of innovation is carried out through reference-group influence (see Chapter 4). Groups and individuals obviously have a strong influence on people's attitudes and behaviour; the history of the theory is not so much one of advancing knowledge about the mechanisms involved, but is rather a history of the way society has changed in the period in which the theories were evolving.

Three main theories concerning the mechanisms for diffusion of innovation have been proposed: trickle-down theory, two-step flow theory and multistage interaction theory.

Trickle-down theory says that the wealthy classes obtain information about new products, and the poorer classes then imitate their 'betters' (Veblen 1899). This theory probably held true in the late 19th century, when class distinctions were much stronger than they are in the early 21st century, and also mass communication was not as widespread. Nowadays, the theory has been largely discredited in wealthy countries because new ideas are disseminated overnight by the mass media and copied by chain stores within days. There may be some vestiges of trickle-down theory, however: it is common for the designer dresses worn by film stars at movie premieres to be copied almost overnight by chain stores and sold to the general public within weeks or even days. The

Film premieres provide evidence to support trickle-down theory.

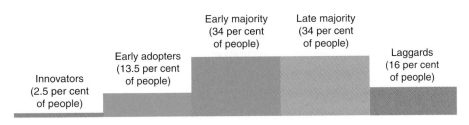

Figure 13.8

Adopter categories

homophilous influence The love of being like everyone else.

dress worn by Princess Diana at her wedding was available to the 'ordinary' bride within less than a week as chain-store tailors copied every detail of the dress from the TV coverage and reproduced it almost overnight. What is replacing trickle-down theory is **homophilous influence**, which refers to transmission between those of similar age, education, social class, etc. – in other words, those who already have a lot in common.

Two-step flow theory is similar, but this time it is 'influentials' rather than wealthy people who are the start of the adoption process (Lazarsfield, Bertelson and Gaudet 1948). This has considerable basis in truth, but may be less true now than it was in the 1940s when the theory was first developed; access to TV and other information media has proliferated and information about innovation is disseminated much faster. Certainly in the diffusion of innovative high-tech products there is strong evidence for the theory: however, there is a weakening of this mechanism due to the preponderance of mass media. In the 1940s most homes did not have TV and there was no commercial radio in the UK; the availability of commercial information was therefore more restricted to the wealthy. Also, the two-step flow assumes that the audience is passively waiting for the information to be presented, whereas in fact people actively seek out information about new things by asking friends and relatives and by looking for published information.

Influentials might include TV presenters (for example Trinny Woodall and Susannah Constantine influence women's thinking about what to wear through their many TV programmes, and Jeremy Clarkson presents programmes about new cars) or journalists (for example, there are several magazines devoted to new developments in IT).

The Multistage Interaction model (Engel, Blackwell and Miniard 1995) agrees that some people are more influential than others, but also recognises that the mass media affect both influential and seeker. The influential doesn't mediate the information flow, as the two-step model suggests, but rather acts as a mechanism for emphasising or facilitating the information flow. Within the model, there is a continuous dialogue between marketers, seekers and influentials with many stages of influence before the new idea is adopted or rejected.

Figure 13.9

Two-step flow theory

Figure 13.10

Multistage interaction model

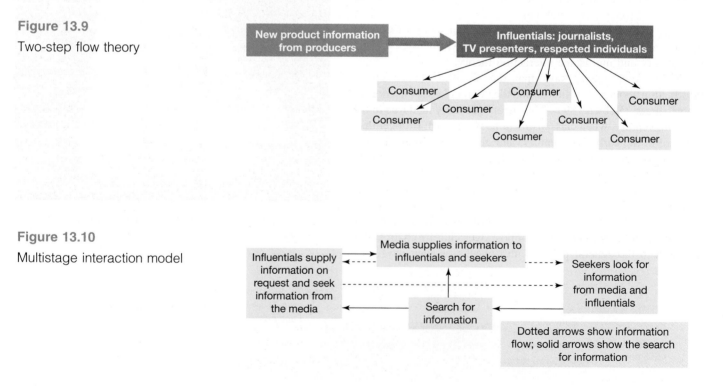

Table 13.2 Characteristics of influentials

Characteristic	Description of influential
Demographics	Wide differences according to product category. For fashions and film-going young women dominate. For self-medication, women with children are most influential. Generally, demography shows low correlation and is not a good predictor.
Social activity	Influencers and opinion leaders are usually gregarious.
General attitudes	Generally innovative and positive towards new products.
Personality and lifestyle	Low correlation of personality with opinion leadership. Lifestyle tends to be more fashion conscious, more socially active, more independent.
Product related	Influencers are more interested in the specific product area than are others. They are active searchers and information gatherers, especially from the mass media.

Source: Adapted from J.F. Engel, R.D. Blackwell and P.W. Miniard, *Consumer Behavior* (Fort Worth, TX: Dryden Press, 1995)

Clearly it is important for marketers to identify who the influential people are likely to be, and much research has been carried out into this area. Table 13.2 shows the main characteristics of influentials which have been identified so far, but this is probably not an exhaustive list, nor will it be generally applicable to all cases.

Influencers (and others) like to pass on their knowledge, and there are several reasons for doing this, as follows:

- *Involvement is a major force.* The influencer is actually interested in the subject area, and wants to share the excitement with others. A hi-fi enthusiast who buys a new Arcam stereo will want to tell friends and colleagues all about it on Monday morning. Telling other people acts as an outlet for the pleasure of owning the new product (Venkatraman 1990).

- *Self-enhancement is about airing one's superior knowledge.* Appearing to be a connoisseur, whether of fine wines or works of art or classic cars, is something many influencers strive for. Partly this relates to a need for the esteem of others, and partly it is a function of self-esteem.

- *Concern for others often precipitates influence.* The genuine desire to help a friend to reach a good decision often prompts the expert to say 'OK, I'll come with you when you go to the shop'. This factor works most strongly when there is a strong link between the individuals concerned, and when the influencer has been very satisfied with the product or service concerned (Bone 1992).

- **Message intrigue** is the factor concerned with comments about advertising messages. If an advertisement is particularly intriguing or humorous, people will discuss it; this enhances the message by repetition.

  message intrigue The increased interest developed by ambiguous communications.

- **Dissonance** reduction is about reducing doubts after making a major purchase (Gatignon and Robertson 1985). As word-of-mouth influence this can be good or bad; sometimes the influencer will try to reassure him or herself by telling everybody about the good points of the product; more often, though, the disappointed customer will use word-of-mouth to complain bitterly and explain how the wicked manufacturer has cheated him or her. This is sometimes a way of passing the responsibility over to the supplier rather than admitting that the influencer has made a bad decision or a bad choice.

  dissonance The emotional state created when expectations do not match with outcomes.

Consumers often need considerable persuasion to change from their old product to a new one. This is because there is always a cost of some sort. For example, somebody buying a new car will lose money on trading in the old car (a **switching cost**), or perhaps

E-Marketing in Practice
The Spidercatcher

Tony Allen, like most of us, prefers his house to be relatively free of creepy-crawlies. Also like many of us, he does not want to actually harm the animals – he just wants them to live elsewhere!

Hence the Spidercatcher. Tony invented this device as an alternative to standing on beds and chairs with a glass and a piece of cardboard, trying to evict spiders. The device has a long arm with a set of soft bristles on the end: the bristles can be dilated and then closed onto the spider, trapping it gently. The spider can then be removed to the outside world, where it can start a new life in the garden.

The problem for Tony is that this product is not exactly mainstream. Although it meets a long-felt need for many people, it does not fit neatly into a particular retail category – is it a garden tool, a DIY tool, a household cleaning tool or none of these? So Tony decided to market the product on the Internet. The results have been spectacular – the Spidercatcher has attracted a worldwide audience, and some impressive sales within a very short period of time.

Now the company has an Australian website as well as its UK site, and customers can pay in pounds sterling, Australian dollars, euros, or (through the firm's US distributors) in US dollars. Since the company accepts payments via credit card, and ships worldwide, there is really no reason why payment cannot be accepted from anywhere in the world, in any currency, at any time of the day or night.

The Spidercatcher seems to have become transformed into a moneycatcher for Tony Allen – and there are more ideas where it came from!

Figure 13.11

Motivation for influencers

- Involvement with the product category
- Self-enhancement: airing one's knowledge
- Concern for others
- Message intrigue: discussion of interesting communications
- Dissonance reduction: reducing doubts after a major purchase

→ **Motivation to discuss purchases with other people**

innovation cost The expenditure of money and effort resulting from adopting a new product.

somebody buying a new computer will also have to spend money on new software and spend time learning how to operate the new equipment (an **innovation cost**).

On the other hand there is strong evidence that newness as such is an important factor in the consumer's decision-making process (Haines 1966). This is why companies often use the word 'new' in advertising. In other words, people like new things, but there is a cost attached. Provided the new product offers real additional benefits over the old one (i.e. fits the consumer's needs better than the old product), the product will be adopted.

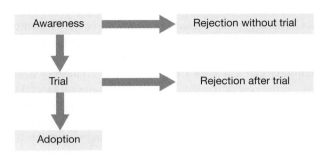

Figure 13.12
Adoption/rejection process

Consumers must first become aware of the new product, then become persuaded that there is a real advantage in switching from their existing solution. A useful model of this adoption process is as follows:

● *Awareness*. This will often come about as a result of promotional activities by the firm.

● *Trial*. For a low-price item (e.g. a packet of biscuits) this may mean that the consumer will actually buy the product before trying it; for a major purchase, such as a car, the consumer will usually need to have a test-drive. Increasingly, super-markets hold tasting sessions to allow customers to try new products.

● *Adoption*. This is the point at which the consumer decides to buy the product, or make it part of the weekly shopping list.

Obviously, not all products are successful. Many apparently promising new ideas sink without trace, others are popular for a while, then disappear. Successful products become culturally anchored, in other words become an integral part of people's lives in such a way that the person–product interface is a part of the individual's self-concept (Latour and Roberts 1991).

Everett M. Rogers (1962) identified the following perceived attributes of innovative products by which consumers apparently judge the product during the decision-making process:

● **Relative advantage**. The degree to which the innovation is perceived as better than the idea it supersedes. If the innovation does not offer something different from the solutions currently available, there is no reason to risk adopting it. Relative advantage is very much linked to cognition – it implies a rational calculation on the part of the prospective adopter of the product. Sometimes just the newness of the solution will create some sales, but these will tend to die out if the product really is not better (in terms of Calentone and Cooper, this would be designated as the Innovative Mousetrap That Really Wasn't Better).

relative advantage The degree to which a new product is better than the one it replaces.

● **Compatibility**. Consistency with existing values, past experiences and needs of potential adopters. If the product is compatible with existing knowledge and consumption practices, it is more likely to be adopted quickly: a new toothpaste does not involve any new learning or changed behaviour in brushing one's teeth, whereas a new diet requires changes in lifestyle.

compatibility The degree to which a product fits into the adopter's life.

● **Complexity**. Ideas that are easily understood are adopted more quickly. DVD players are actually a straightforward concept for someone who already owns a computer and a video recorder, but a digital camera presents the new owner with a great deal of learning if his or her previous camera used film. Software producers go to great effort to make their software user-friendly, with the least possible new learning necessary for users. Obviously someone who is using a computer for the first time is likely to find the software dazzlingly complex to use, compared with someone who has a few years' experience, so complexity is a subjective concept.

complexity The degree to which the product is difficult to understand.

trialability The degree to which the product can be tried out before adoption.

observability The degree to which the product can be seen by others.

- **Trialability**. The degree to which a product can be experimented with. Some products (notably service products) cannot be tested before purchase. Others can be tried out (for example cars can be test-driven). If the product is very innovative, lack of trialibility can kill sales from the outset. Trialibility is also a function of overall cost – if the cost of testing the product (whether financial or in terms of risk) is low, people will be more prepared to try it. For example, a new brand of biscuits is relatively cheap and easy to try out – if the biscuits are no good, the financial loss is only a few pence. On the other hand, trying out a new type of surfboard carries great risks in terms of finance and physical risk, so a surfer would be unlikely to buy such a board simply for the opportunity to try it out. Retailers and manufacturers need to address these issues when offering products.

- **Observability**. The degree to which the results of an innovation are visible to others. This has two main components: the degree to which the adopter is able to show friends and neighbours the advantages of the new product is likely to affect adoption, and also the degree to which prospective adopters can see the product being used by others will affect their decision to adopt (or not). Observability is largely an affective component of adoption: opinion leaders and influentials like to show off their new products, and (for the observer) there is an opportunity to see the product in action.

The five characteristics described above can be a guide as to the potential success of the product in the marketplace. Products which score highly on several characteristics are likely to succeed: those which score low, or which only score on one or two characteristics, are likely to fail. This is not, of course, an infallible guide, but in the long run successful products tend to conform to the characteristics outlined above.

Innovation is also a characteristic of consumers. Apart from the issue of adopting a new product as it stands, there is the concept of reinvention of existing products by the consumers. Sometimes users find new ways to use the product (not envisaged by the designers) and sometimes this leads to the creation of whole new markets. For example, in the 1930s it was discovered that baking soda is good for removing stale smells from refrigerators, a fact that was quickly seized on by baking soda manufacturers. Deodorising fridges is now a major part of the market for baking soda.

Figure 13.13

Characteristics of successful new products

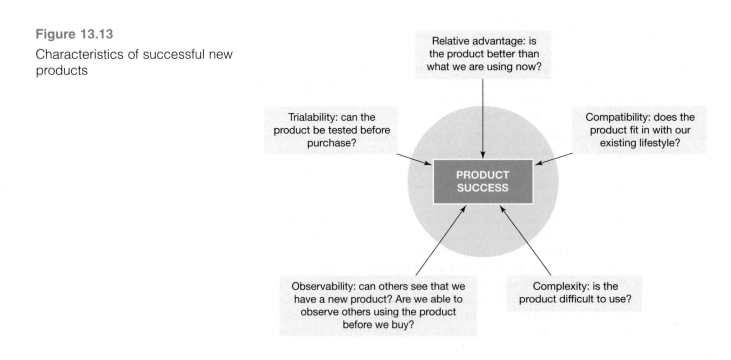

Influences on the Diffusion Process

The diffusion process is influenced by many factors. The first of these is innovation, both on the part of the producer and on the part of the consumer. The more innovative the consumer, the faster the product is adopted. Innovativeness is the degree to which an individual makes innovative decisions independently of the communicated experiences of others (Midgely 1977).

Innovativeness among consumers is somewhat difficult to assess, because innovativeness for one category of product does not necessarily equate to innovativeness for all categories. In other words, someone who is eager to buy the latest hi-fi equipment might have no interest at all in buying the latest digital camera. Innovativeness is linked to involvement (see Chapter 4), so people only become innovators for product groups they are involved with. Having said that, there is evidence that some people like gadgets and new technology generally – these are called **technophones. Technophobes**, on the other hand, exhibit reluctance to use new technology and are wary of it (Mitchell 1994). Innovation has both a cognitive element and an affective element: research using the Kirton Adaptive-Innovative Index (Kirton 1976) shows that there is a correlation between innovativeness and KAI scores (Foxall 1989). However, it transpires that involvement is a much more important factor (Foxall and Bhate 1993).

Second, communication is an influence. How consumers learn about new products, and the perceptions they form about them, affect the way they respond to the product offering. In some cases the communication is from producer to consumer, in other cases it is from consumer to consumer by word-of-mouth or by demonstration (see Observability above). There is some evidence that more rapid communications lead to more rapid diffusion (Olshavsky 1980). There is also evidence that people rely on different forms of communication according to their degree of innovativeness (Blythe 2002). Innovators tend to rely more on recommendations by friends and on hands-on experience with the equipment rather than on manufacturers' brochures or retailer's advice. Whether people are conspicuous consumers or not also seems to have some influence on communications: conspicuous consumers are more concerned with visual appearance, and less with technical brochures and descriptions (Blythe 2002).

Price does not appear to be significantly correlated with rate of diffusion, although it might reasonably be expected that more expensive products would diffuse more slowly because of higher financial risk.

technophone Someone who has an interest in new technology.

technophobe Someone who does not like new products.

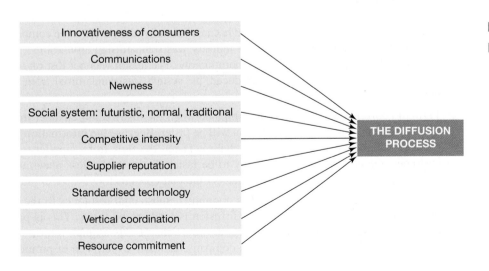

Figure 13.14

Influences on diffusion

One of the difficulties inherent in studying innovation is that there is no generally-recognised definition of newness. Because newness is an attribute accorded to a product by an observer, it is derived from two factors: the characteristics of the product and the characteristics of the observer. What is new to one person may not be new to another, and it may be possible for one person to accord a greater degree of newness to a given product than would another person. Equally, the same person may be able to observe two different products and ascribe different degrees of newness to each (Blythe 1999). A working definition for newness might be 'the degree to which a given product is outside the observer's experience'. Because newness is often used as a benefit in its own right in marketing communications, it would be useful to know what people mean by newness: unfortunately, because of the subjective nature of newness, this is unlikely to be possible.

Solar power has been slow to take off in Britain.

The social system to which individuals belong will affect the adoption of innovation. The rate of diffusion will be affected according to whether the society is futuristic, normal or traditionalist (Wills, Samli and Jacobs 1991). Some societies (such as the USA) tend to be futuristic, to welcome new inventions and ideas, whereas others (such as many European countries) are traditionalist and avoid new ideas. For example, in Andalucia (southern Spain) grants are available for the installation of solar power, yet the vast majority of people in Andalucia have not installed the systems yet, despite the obvious advantage of having free electricity as a result of innovating. On the other hand, many Northern European immigrants to the area have solar power.

Some of the factors which affect diffusion are under the control of marketers (Robertson and Gatignon 1986). These are as follows:

- *Competitive intensity*. Highly-competitive firms which adopt aggressive marketing strategies and often price competitively will speed up the process of adoption. Intense competition might lead to price wars: also, the more innovative a product is, the more likely a competitor is to retaliate with a similar product innovation (Kuester, Homburg and Robertson 1999).

- *Supplier reputation*. The better the reputation of the supplier, the faster the diffusion. This is because potential customers will perceive the source as being more credible, which reduces uncertainty and risk in the decision.

- *Standardised technology*. If there are several competing systems on offer, consumers are likely to be more cautious about adopting the product. For example, video recorders took a long time to be adopted because (initially) there were three competing systems. Once it became clear that the industry was standardising around the VHS system, adoption moved much more rapidly. The lesson was not lost on the industry – when DVDs were introduced, the system was standardised from the outset.

- *Vertical coordination*. If the relationships between the distribution channel members is close and interlocking, diffusion will be faster. Because the information flow between members of the distribution chain is faster, the flow from supplier to end customer (the consumer) is also likely to be faster. There is also less uncertainty between channel members and (ultimately) the end consumer.

- *Resource commitment*. If the firm has committed substantial resources to the product and to innovation generally, diffusion is likely to be faster. This is partly because the company will make efforts to ensure that it gets a quick return on its investment, and partly because the company has more experience of promoting innovation. Also, as the company's reputation for innovation grows, customers who are themselves innovative will be attracted to products from that company. Research indicates that more rapid adoption of innovations has shortened the product life cycle, which in turn forces managers to move faster in approving new projects (Olshavsky 1980, Rosenau 1988).

The speed at which innovation is adopted, and the success of innovation, appear also to be affected by the degree of marketing orientation of the firm. Some research suggests that market orientation facilitates technology-based innovation, but inhibits innovation aimed at emerging market segments (Zheng Zhou, Chi Kin and Tse 2005). Knowledge of the market, knowledge change, and sharing knowledge about the market all contribute to increased innovative effort (Marinova 2004), and (perhaps not surprisingly) firms which provide greater marketing support for radical new products are likely to gain higher rewards in the long run (Sorescu, Chandy and Prabhu 2003). Interestingly, acquiring another company also seems to stimulate innovation (at least in the pharmaceutical industry) (Prabhu, Chandy and Ellis 2005).

Summary

Innovation is the lifeblood of any company, and indeed this is so for most individuals as well: life would grow extremely tedious if nothing ever changed. The constant search for novelty on the part of consumers leads to a similar search on the part of companies. Organising for innovation is by no means straightforward: often there is resistance within the firm, and there are many influences on the new-product development process, as well as on the new-product diffusion process in the market.

Innovation can happen at many different levels, from the simple copying of a competitor's product through to the development of a radical new solution to a problem which people did not realise they had.

Key points from this chapter are as follows:

- Products can be replacements, additions, new lines or new-to-the-world.
- Less radical products are more likely to succeed than radical products, but may not succeed to the same extent.
- Creating an innovative culture within the firm is a useful but difficult step to take.
- Ideas can come from brainstorming, technological advance, recycling existing technology, market feedback, generation by employees or by customer specification.
- Project teams and project champions are both powerful in guiding new products through from idea to launch.
- There are six broad categories of NPD strategy: offensive, defensive, imitative, dependent, traditional and opportunistic.
- There are five necessary factors for a successful product launch: strategic fit, technical feasibility, customer acceptance, market opportunity and financial performance.
- Innovation diffuses gradually through the population: innovators for one product category are not necessarily innovators for another.
- Newness is a factor in product acceptability.
- The level of acceptability of a product depends on the following factors: relative advantage, complexity, compatibility, trialibility and observability.
- People have different communication styles according to their level of innovativeness.
- Some, though by no means all, of the factors which affect diffusion of innovation can be controlled by marketers.

Chapter review questions

1 What are the main problems in establishing an innovative corporate culture?

2 How might a firm identify innovators for its product category?

3 What is the role of a product champion?

4 What is the role of a project team?

5 How does the role of a project team differ from that of a brainstorming group?

6 What is the difference between an imitative strategy and a defensive strategy?

7 If newness is a factor in product acceptability, why does relative advantage matter?

8 What is the role of involvement in innovativeness?

9 How might a firm hasten the adoption of products?

10 What is the difference between a technophone and a technophobe?

Preview case revisited
The Flying Car

Despite the difficulties, efforts to build a flying car continue. A great deal of cash has been sunk into developing such a vehicle, even though it is doubtful whether it would ever find a mass market – however, even a small share of the world's light aircraft market would be a good thing to have, and of course the solutions to the technical problems might well find applications elsewhere.

Recent developments include Paul Moller's Skycar M400, which is designed to take off and land vertically. It uses eight engines to power ducted fans, which can be used to propel the car on the road, and is reputed to be able to achieve 350 miles per hour in the air. On the ground, it achieves 20 miles per gallon. Macro Industries' SkyRider X2R is a competing design which is intended to be available in five and seven-seat versions: in Israel, Urban Aeronautics are developing a car called the Cityhawk.

One of the most likely contenders for a true flying car may be Terrafugia's Transition. This is essentially a light aircraft adapted for the road: using a 100hp Rotax aero engine, the vehicle is intended to be driven to a nearby airfield, converted to aircraft mode, flown to its destination airfield, and driven from there to the driver's final destination. At a proposed price of $148 000 for the finished aircraft, the price is certainly not uncompetitive: the company is already taking orders, and is reputed to have more than 30 deposits for aircraft already paid up.

The Transition is clearly not intended for the school run or a grocery-shopping trip. It is intended as a hobby

Courtesy of MACRO Industries, Inc.

Transition is not). Many private pilots might be interested: having to drive to the airfield, get the aircraft out of the hangar, fuel it, carry out the pre-flight checks, and so forth could be avoided by simply driving the Transition out of the garage, filling up at a petrol station on the way, driving onto the runway and taking off (subject of course to permission from the control tower). Whether private motorists would be prepared to go to the trouble of obtaining a pilot's licence is, of course, another matter – but it would be a great way to beat the rush hour!

aircraft which will not need a hangar, and which can be driven home: it might be used for business trips or commuting for longer distances, but is unlikely to have the payload to be a realistic family vehicle. It is designed to fit within the FAA's Light Sports Aircraft category, which like the UK's Microlight category involves a great deal less regulation than heavier aircraft. Unfortunately, the Transition is too heavy to fit within European Microlight regulations, so would have to meet the full regulatory standards for Group A aircraft, which it is very unlikely to achieve.

The final problem with a flying car is, of course, licensing the pilot. Someone buying a Transition will need a full private pilot's licence: currently, the vehicle would be unlikely to be approved for road use in the UK or indeed anywhere else in Europe, and its projected performance does not match that of, say, a Cessna light aircraft. On the plus side, the cost of the vehicle will not be a problem for the market it is intended for – and there are savings to be made in terms of hangarage and maintenance. Insurance is another complex area, since there are no precedents for insurance companies to consider.

So who would buy a flying car? Anybody who has been stuck in a traffic jam will have wished at one time or another that the car could simply float up above the jam and carry on, but of course this would certainly violate any number of motoring laws, as well as civil aviation regulations, even if the car were capable of it (which the

Courtesy of Urban Aeronautics, Ltd.

Courtesy of Terrafugia

Case study
Yahoo!

Search engines are big business. When the Internet was first starting out, there were dozens – but gradually the market whittled down until there is now just a handful. The market leader is Google – so much so that the brand name has passed into the language and is now used as a verb. To Google something means to look it up on the Internet – so the brand has achieved the status of several previous brands such as Hoover.

Yahoo! was the brainchild of two PhD students, David Filo and Jerry Yang, who studied together at Stanford University. The system started out as a way of keeping their own files in order, and was originally housed on their student workstations at Stanford. As the system grew, and more of their friends began to use it, Yahoo! became too big for the Stanford computers and was transferred to Netscape's computers in California. This was in 1995: from then on, the company has grown and now has separate search engines for Japan, the UK, France, Canada, and Germany.

The brand name was not chosen through any careful planning system: Yang and Filo insist that it came about because they consider themselves to be yahoos (a name for wild people, derived from *Gulliver's Travels*). In fact, it's a brand that one might expect a couple of students to have come up with – but it is memorable, and it does convey a sense of joyfulness which much of the Internet lacks. Yahoo! continue with this theme on their website – the section on press releases says 'Follow our daring exploits', which of course is hardly the case when the most daring exploit being reported is a new deal with 3G. The exclamation mark had to be added because the name Yahoo was already in use for a brand of barbecue sauce.

Whereas Google is primarily a search engine with a few extras tacked on, Yahoo! has always aimed to provide much more – the company provides email, photo sharing, blogging, social networking, weather services and much more. Most of this expansion of services has come about through mergers and acquisitions, rather than developing software services itself, Yahoo! has operated by buying out other companies which already have working systems. This method avoids problems of glitches – by the time Yahoo! buys the companies, all the problems are out of the system.

This does not mean that Yahoo! has been entirely problem-free. The burst of the dotcom bubble in 2001 left a great many Internet-based companies in ruins – many went bankrupt altogether, but Yahoo! survived, albeit with a much-reduced share value. On 7 February 2000 the company was off-line for several hours as the result of an attack by hackers – luckily, the company recovered rapidly and its shares rose by 4.5 per cent the next day when it became clear that the problem was not an internal glitch.

In January 2008, Yahoo! was forced to announce job cuts as a result of failing to compete effectively against Google. Many of those made redundant were asked to apply for other jobs in the organisation, in areas which were expected to grow, but the fact remains that Yahoo! had to cut 1000 jobs out of a workforce of around 14 500.

Yahoo! aims to provide everything an Internet user needs apart from a computer (and they can even help there). Everything from search engines to email can be found, and users can find everything on the company's home page. Almost 90 per cent of Yahoo!'s income is derived from marketing services – charges to companies for directing people to their web pages, charges for display advertising on Yahoo! web pages and so forth. Yahoo! make around 2 to 3 cents on every search, which may not sound much but certainly mounts up when searches are numbered in the billions per day. Yahoo! is the second most visited website in the United States, and the most visited in the world (largely due to the wide range of services it offers).

The future is likely to hold more mergers and acquisitions for Yahoo! Talks have been held with Microsoft with a view to merging, although these seem to have derailed: meanwhile, there seems to be no reason to suppose that Yahoo! will stop seeking out companies to take over. Boardroom wrangles during 2008 did not seem to affect the company greatly – and the basic policy of offering everything an Internet user could want continues to be in place.

Questions

1 What long-term result might you expect from Yahoo!'s habit of adding extra features to the basic product?

2 How should Yahoo!'s management decide which products to add to the company portfolio?

3 What type of new product policy is Yahoo! apparently adopting?

4 What is the role of the company founders in new product development?

5 How might Yahoo compete with Google in terms of new product development?

References

Blackwell, R.D., Miniard, P.W. and Engel, J.F. (2001): *Consumer Behaviour*, 9th edn (Mason, OH: South Western).

Blythe, J. (1999): Innovativeness and newness in high-tech consumer durables. *Journal of Product and Brand Management* **8**(5), 415–29.

Blythe, J. (2002): Communications and imnovation: the case of hi-fi systems. *Corporate Communications: An International Journal* **7**(1), 9–16.

Bone, P.F. (1992): Determinants of word-of-mouth communications during product consumption. In J.F. Sherry and B. Strenthal (eds) *Advances in Consumer Research*, vol. **19** (Provo, UT: Association for Consumer Research) pp. 579–83.

Booz, Allen and Hamilton (1982): *New Products Management for the 1980s* (New York: Booz, Allen and Hamilton Inc.).

Brown, S., Sherry, J.F. and Kozinetts, R.V. (2003): Teaching old brands new tricks: retro branding and the revival of brand meaning. *Journal of Marketing* **67**(3), 19–33.

Calentone, R.J. and Cooper, R.G. (1981): New product scenarios; prospects for success. *American Journal of Marketing* **45** (Spring), 480.

Carbonell-Foulquie, P., Munuera-Aleman, J.L. and Rodriguez-Escudero, A.I. (2004): Criteria employed for go/no-go decisions when developing successful highly-innovative products. *Industrial Marketing Management* **33**(4), 307–16.

Cooper, R.G. and Kleinschmidt, E.J. (1986): An investigation into the new product process: steps, deficiencies and impact. *Journal of Product Innovation Management* **3**(2), 71–85.

Engel, J.F., Blackwell, R.D. and Miniard, P.W. (1995): *Consumer Behaviour*, 8th edn (Fort Worth, TX: Dryden Press).

Foxall, G.R. and Bhate, S. (1993): Cognitive style and personal involvement as explicators of innovative purchasing of 'healthy' brands. *European Journal of Marketing* **27**(2), 5–16.

Foxall, G.R. (1989): Marketing, innovation and customers. *Quarterly Review of Marketing* (Autumn), 14–22.

Gatignon, H. and Robertson, T.S. (1985): A propositional inventory for diffusion research. *Journal of Consumer Research* **11**(4), 859–67.

Haines, G.H. (1966): A study of why people purchase new products. *Proceedings of the American Marketing Association* (Chicago, IL: American Marketing Association), 685–97.

Hamel, G. and Prahalad, C.K. (1991): Corporate imagination and expeditionary marketing. *Harvard Business Review* (July–August), 81–92.

Huang, X., Soutar, G.N. and Brown, A. (2004): Measuring new product success: an empirical investigation of Australian SMEs. *Industrial Marketing Management* **33**(2), 101–23.

Johne, A. and Snelson, P. (1990): *Successful Product Development: Management Practices in American and British Firms* (Oxford: Basil Blackwell).

Kirton, M. (1976): Adaptors and innovators: a description and measure. *Journal of Applied Psychology* **61**(5), 622–9.

Kuester, S., Homburg, C. and Robertson, T.S. (1999): Retaliatory behaviour to new product entry. *Journal of Marketing* **63** (October), 90–106.

Latour, M.S. and Roberts, S.D. (1991): Cultural anchoring and product diffusion. *Journal of Consumer Marketing* **9** (Fall), 29–34.

Lazarsfield, P.F., Bertelson, B.R. and Gaudet, H. (1948): *The People's Choice* (New York: Columbia University Press).

Lego, C., Solomon, M.R., Turley, D., O'Neill, M. and Engels, B. (2002): Real or replica? Deciphering authenticity in Irish pubs. *Advances in Consumer Behaviour* **29**(1), 45.

Marinova, D. (2004): Actualising innovation effort: the impact of market knowledge diffusion in a dynamic system of competition. *Journal of Marketing* **68**(3), 1–19.

Midgely, D.F. (1977): *Innovation and New Product Marketing* (NewYork: Halstead Press, John Wiley and Sons Inc.).

Min, S., Kalwani, M.U. and Robinson, W.T. (2006): Market pioneer and early follower survival risks: a contingency analysis of really new vs. incrementally new products. *Journal of Marketing* **70**(1), 15–33.

Mitchell, S. (1994): Technophiles and technophobes. *American Demographics* **16** (February), 36.

Nijssen, E.J. and Lieshout, K.F.M. (1995): Awareness, use and effectiveness of models and methods for new product development. *European Journal of Marketing* **29**(10), 27–44.

Olshavsky, R.W. (1980): Time and the rate of adoption of innovations. *Journal of Consumer Research* **6**(4), 425–8.

Prabhu, J.C., Chandy, R.K. and Ellis, M.E. (2005): The impact of acquisitions on innovation: poison pill, placebo or tonic? *Journal of Marketing* **69**(1), 114–30.

Robertson, T.S. (1967): The process of innovation and the diffusion of innovation. *Journal of Marketing* **31**(1), 14–19.

Robertson, T.S. and Gatignon, H. (1986): Competitive effects on technology diffusion. *Journal of Marketing* **50** (July), 1–12.

Rodriguez, N.G., Perez, M.J.S. and Gutierrez, J.A.T. (2007): Interfunctional trust as a determining factor in new-product performance. *European Journal of Marketing* **41**(5/6), 678–702.

Rogers, E.M. (1962): *Diffusion of Innovations* (New York: Macmillan).

Rosenau, M.D. Jr. (1988): Speeding your new product to market. *Journal of Consumer Marketing* **5** (Spring), 23–35.

Sorescu, A.B., Chandy, R.K. and Prabhu, J.C. (2003): Sources and financial consequences of radical innovation: insights from pharmaceuticals. *Journal of Marketing* **67**(4), 82–102.

Tajeddini, K., Trueman, M. and Larsen, G. (2006): Examining the effect of marketing orientation on innovativeness. *Journal of Marketing Management* **22**(5/6), 529–51.

Veblen, T. (1899): *The Theory of the Leisure Class* (New York: Macmillan).

Venkatraman, M.P. (1990): Opinion leadership: enduring involvement and characteristics of opinion leaders: a moderating or mediating relationship. In M.E. Goldberg, G. Gorn, and R.W. Pollay (eds) *Advances in Consumer Research*, vol. **17** (Provo, UT: Association for Consumer Research) pp. 60–7.

Volckner, F. and Sattler, H. (2006): Drivers of brand extension success. *Journal of Marketing* **70**(2), 18–34.

Wills, J., Samli, A.C. and Jacobs, L. (1991): Developing global products and marketing strategies: a construct and research agenda. *Journal of the Academy of Marketing Science* **19**(1).

Zheng Zhou, K., Chi Kin, Y. and Tse, D.K. (2005): The effects of strategic orientations on technology and market-based breakthrough imnovations. *Journal of Marketing* **69**(2), 42–60.

Further reading

Johne, A. and Snelson, P. (1990): *Successful New Product Development* (London: Blackwell). This book is written by two of the foremost experts on innovation, and describes research carried out into new product successes in 40 British and American firms.

Markides, C. and Geroski, R (2004): *Fast Second: How Successful Companies Bypass Radical Innovation to Enter and Dominate New Markets* (Jossey Bass Wiley: New York). This book extols the virtues of being a follower rather than a leader in imnovation.

Chapter 14
Pricing

Learning objectives

After reading this chapter, you should be able to:

1. Explain the relationship price has with the other elements of the marketing mix.

2. Explain the importance of price in the marketing mix.

3. Show the important elements in the calculation of price.

4. Explain consumer perception of price.

5. Explain the relationship of price to the total cost to the consumer.

6. Understand which is the most customer-orientated pricing method.

7. Compare business-to-business pricing with business-to-consumer pricing.

8. Explain the role of competition laws on pricing.

Introduction

Pricing is often regarded as the least exciting element of the marketing mix. However, it is the only element that directly relates to income, and it is also an element which crosses over dramatically to the other elements. Promotional campaigns frequently carry messages about price, sales promotions are often based on price reductions and discounts, price conveys messages about the quality of the products, and it can even control the features and benefits of the products – after all, if customers are not prepared to pay the stated prices, the product needs to be built for a price customers will pay, which may mean cutting some corners on features and benefits.

Price also has a strategic element, since price is commonly how products become positioned against other products in the market: undercutting competitors on price is a common way of competing. Although several areas of marketing activity, including managing the supply chain, can lead indirectly to cutting costs, price is the only area where marketers can directly improve the profits of the firm. Even a small increase in the price can generate a very large increase in profits: for marketers, the problem often lies in finding ways to justify a price rise to consumers.

Price and the Bottom Line

As has been pointed out above, price is the only place where marketers can directly improve the bottom line. They do this by carefully pricing products for maximum profitability.

Figure 14.1 illustrates the mechanism by which this happens. At the original price of £10 the firm sells one million units for a total revenue of £10 million. The direct cost for

Preview case
Aldi

During 2008 UK food retailing underwent a subtle but far-reaching change. The rising cost of food, sparked by poor harvests and the conversion of agricultural land to biofuel production, caused people to rethink their shopping options, and many people moved away from shopping in the mainstream supermarkets such as Tesco, Sainsbury's and ASDA, and towards the discount food stores such as Aldi and Lidl. Previously these stores had been thought of as down-market shops for poor people – but increasingly the wealthier middle classes began to use them.

Aldi is of German origin: the name is short for Albrecht Discounts, and the company was originally founded by two brothers, Theo and Karl Albrecht. Aldi has been hugely successful in Germany – the vast majority of Germans shop in Aldi at least some of the time for some of their shopping (a survey conducted in 2002 by German market research company Forsa found that 95 per cent of blue-collar workers and 88 per cent of white-collar workers shop at Aldi).

Aldi operates on a low-cost basis. There are no frills or fancy displays in Aldi stores – goods are often simply stacked on the floor. Staffing is minimal, and the product range is also limited – almost everything is unbranded, and some products are sold at give-away prices. However, the quality is good, and some products are certainly in the 'luxury' class. In 2008, Aldi was the place to buy your jumbo king prawns, for example, as well as your champagne and German charcuterie: equally, it was the place to buy your baked beans (unbranded) and your cheap beer.

The Albrecht brothers were the sons of a coal miner from Essen in the Ruhr Valley. Their mother kept a small grocery shop as a way of supplementing the family income, and after Karl left the Wehrmacht at the end of the Second World War the brothers took over running the shop. They quickly expanded, by giving customers the maximum legal discount off the prices of the food. They cut costs ruthlessly by keeping the size of the store small, removing anything which did not sell quickly, not advertising at all and not selling fresh produce (thus eliminating a source of waste). By 1960, they owned 300 shops between them, but they split the business following a dispute over whether to sell cigarettes at the checkouts or not, and went their separate ways. The company now operates as two distinct halves (Aldi Sud and Aldi Nord), but this would not be apparent to the casual observer since the branding and the advertising are the same. The two companies even negotiate with suppliers on a joint basis.

Of course, the problem for Aldi is that all supermarkets claim to be the cheapest – making the claims stick is entirely another matter.

manufacturing the product (including all of the variable costs) at £6 per unit adds up to £6 million. Administrative costs are £3 million. In this case, as can be seen from our simple example, the profit to the firm is £1 million. Now let us assume that the marketing director decides to raise the price 5 per cent. Therefore, the product will now be sold at £10.50. If one million units are sold, the total revenue would be £10.5 million. The direct

Figure 14.1

Price and profitability

	ORIGINAL PRICE	NEW PRICE
		(increase price 5 per cent)
Sales Revenue (1 million units @ £10)	£10 000 000	£10 500 000
Direct Costs (Labour, materials, etc @ £6 per unit)	£6 000 000	£6 000 000
Administrative Costs (Overhead)	£3 000 000	£3 000 000
Profit	£1 000 000	£1 500 000

Figure 14.2

Stepped demand curve

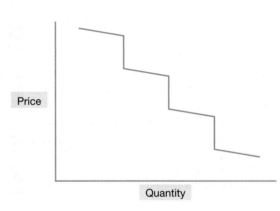

cost for making one million units remains £6 per unit for a total of £6 million and the administrative costs also remain the same at £3 million. This example shows how a 5 per cent increase in price results in a 50 per cent increase in profit from £1 million to £1.5 million.

Figure 14.1 shows how a small movement in price can result in very large benefits to the firm. However, this example has some obvious flaws. First, it assumes that the firm will still sell one million units even though the price is now higher. Basic economics teaches us that demand curves slope downward toward the right, as we saw in Chapter 1: that is to say, the higher the price, the lower the sales tend to be (depending on how elastic the demand curve is).

This demand curve certainly holds true for commodity products where all the offerings are exactly the same, such as sand or milk. However, in some consumer markets and in almost all business-to-business markets the demand curve actually looks more like the one shown in Figure 14.2.

This is a 'stepped' demand curve. The stepped demand curve implies that there are price ranges within which the demand will not change. If our marketing director is clever enough to determine that customers are not price sensitive to a difference between £10 and £10.50, he or she would realise the increased revenue from changing the price.

A second possible criticism of the example is that the increased price may require increases in expenses in order to justify the price rise. This may range from increased expenditure on advertising through to changing the product in some way to offer better value. Provided the extra costs are substantially less than the extra price which can be obtained, the changes should be made.

The Pricing Process

Figure 14.3 shows an overview of the pricing process. First, managers must set pricing objectives in line with the firm's corporate objectives. Second, the managers should develop the pricing strategy to be used in each market segment. In some cases, the prices charged for the same product will differ in different market segments: for example, the price charged to professional garages for spare parts for cars may differ from the prices charged to the general public. Likewise, prices often differ in international markets.

Managers should then try to determine what the demand will be at various pricing levels. This is by no means simple, because markets are dynamic: a prediction about demand in a given market may be completely overtaken by changes in consumer taste, by competitive activity, by a poorly-executed (or well-executed) promotional campaign or by any one of hundreds of possible eventualities. Having calculated an estimate of demand, he or she will estimate costs. This estimate will include manufacturing costs as well as marketing costs, and is intended to provide a profitability forecast.

The next stage is to review the competition. Competing offerings might offer better value for money, in which case the price will need to be adjusted: competitors may be planning a major promotional campaign, which might be countered by a price cut, or may be forced to raise their own prices, offering an opportunity to raise prices generally. Obviously, managers will not always know what their competitors are planning, and in most countries it is illegal for competitors to collude in fixing prices, since this always results in a worse deal for the consumers.

The final stage is to select a pricing method and policy, and determine the exact prices to be assigned to each individual product and product.

```
          Set pricing objective
                  ↓
        Develop pricing strategy
                  ↓
          Determine demand
                  ↓
            Estimate costs
                  ↓
  Review competitive offerings (and costs)
                  ↓
         Select pricing method
                  ↓
        Establish pricing policies
                  ↓
           Determine prices
```

Figure 14.3

The pricing process

Talking Point

Often, this somewhat complex approach to calculating the price will not happen, simply because the manager has inherited the pricing structure from a previous manager. This means that, in most cases, managers are not calculating prices from scratch, but are instead adjusting prices incrementally to meet changing market conditions.

There is a lot of data to support the idea that a firm with the largest market share also is the most successful in a particular industry. And what is the most effective way to gain the largest market share? Certainly to lower prices below competition. If this is true, wouldn't a smart marketing manager lower his prices below competitors' to get the biggest market share possible? What could possibly prevent him from taking this action?

Pricing Objectives

Generally speaking, pricing objectives can be divided into three major types as follows (McCarthy and Perrault 2002):

- *Profit-orientated.* Profit-orientated objectives include pricing to realise a target return on investment or to maximise profits. This is popularly supposed to be the commonest (or even the most intelligent) approach to pricing, but in fact firms frequently have other objectives.
- *Sales-orientated.* Sales-orientated objectives aim to increase sales either in currency or unit terms, or to penetrate markets and increase share. Firms will often aim for a sales-orientated approach when entering a new market, in order to maximise share and shut out competition: in the early stages of the product life cycle, this can be an effective strategy, with the ultimate aim of moving to a profit-orientated approach when the market matures.
- *Status quo-orientated.* Status quo-oriented pricing includes meeting competition or choosing to compete on a non-price basis. Many firms in well-established markets operate in this way in order to avoid triggering price wars, which would be to the detriment of all firms in the industry. Also, small firms will avoid direct attacks on market leaders, since it is too easy for the market leaders to retaliate.

In some cases, a firm does not have the luxury of pricing to maximise its profits: pricing is geared to survival in the face of an industry with very strong competition and overcapacity.

Some firms set an internal rate of return for particular product lines and set prices with this in mind, while other firms seek a particular margin on sales. The choice depends upon the nature of the industry. In a business where few sales are made per year, the target return on investment is most likely the best approach: in a high volume business, the margin on sales becomes more important. These accepted versions of pricing strategies do not include the most favourable approach, which is to establish pricing based on the value customers place on the product. This requires an in-depth knowledge of the customer's business and the ways in which the product is put to use by the customer.

Pricing Strategy

An overview of pricing strategy development is seen in Figure 14.4.

Considerations within the firm are (first) the corporate objectives that the firm has established. Pricing needs to fit within the overall corporate vision – is the firm aiming

E-Marketing in Practice
Crossing the Channel

The cross-channel ferry business is cut-throat at best. Several companies operate out of Dover, sailing to Calais, Boulogne and Dunkirk: they compete not only with each other, but also with the Eurotunnel undersea rail link, which operates trains direct from London to Paris and Brussels, and also a shuttle service which carries cars and trucks.

The Tunnel has never shown a profit (largely due to the huge cost of its construction – it is still the biggest civil engineering project ever undertaken) and teeters on the brink of bankruptcy. This would be a disaster for the ferry companies, because a new owner of the Tunnel would not have to service the debt or look after existing shareholders – bankruptcy means starting with a clean sheet, and the ferry companies' running costs are a great deal higher per passenger than what is, after all, a 25-mile stretch of railway line.

Ferries have therefore maintained an uneasy truce, keeping prices at the point where the Tunnel can still function: but then along came Speedferries to throw a spanner in the works. Speedferries operates a single fast catamaran between Dover and Boulogne, and uses airline-style online pricing. Book early and off-peak, and you can pick up a real bargain – book late and it will cost you. The impact has been severe: the other ferry companies have had no option but to follow suit, with the result that the cost of crossing the channel has fallen dramatically. Luckily, business has increased to compensate, and everyone is surviving so far – but an increase in capacity (perhaps by someone buying another vessel) could destabilise the market again. Travel has become extremely price-sensitive in recent years – and therefore the possibilities for competing on anything other than price are limited, especially when so many providers are offering the same core product.

p&ople want escape
not escape tunnels
our refreshing service will improve your view

POferries.com
08705 21 21 21
Or see your local travel agent

P&O Ferries

Courtesy of P&O Ferries

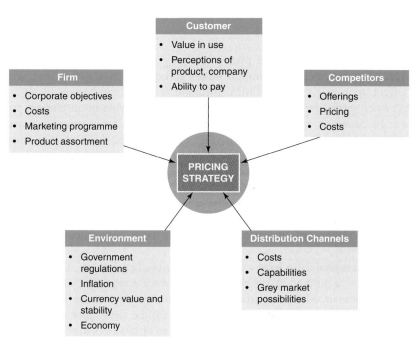

Figure 14.4

Pricing strategy development
Source: (Adapted from Hollensen 1998 and Cavusgil 1996)

to be at the cheap end or at the exclusive end of the market? Second, costs are critical. This not only means costs of the product but also the costs of marketing, including the market entry costs of foreign locations. An important factor in the cost of production is where the production facility is located – a location in a high-labour-cost region such as the United States, Western Europe or Japan will impact on the final cost of the product. On the other hand, the firm needs to take account of the shipping costs inherent in an overseas location.

Finally, the marketing programme in the firm is critical, since price must match up with the rest of the marketing. For instance, if a firm decides to offer a laptop computer which will withstand the rigours of a building site, it should charge accordingly. If the firm designs the product to be the most durable available, then advertises it as such and aims for the salesforce and distributors to place the product in the most difficult environments, it would hardly make sense to price the product below ordinary competing laptops.

Another consideration is the relationship of the price of the product to the pricing of other products in the line (and to other product lines). Often sales of one product are dependent on another – for instance, a firm may choose to price ink jet printers at low prices because they will make money on sales of ink cartridges over a significant period of time. Sometimes prices are set by customary practice: for example, the price of electric motors may be established by long tradition in the industry of pricing according to horsepower. Prices must be set to match these customer expectations even though they are not based on costs.

Talking Point

If price is a competitive tool and relates to the company's strategy, why would anyone want to follow a customary pricing approach? Shouldn't we be differentiating ourselves by offering something that the customer *isn't* expecting? Maybe something even better?

It's possible that too many companies just go along with what customers expect, instead of offering something new – after all, change is life!

Exclusive stores charge high prices in order to signal high quality.

The environment impacts the pricing strategy in many ways: Government regulations including price controls, import duties and quotas, as well as taxes, will have a major effect upon pricing possibilities. Inflation is another important factor in pricing strategy: often governments will impose strict price controls in an attempt to prevent inflation. In countries where governments do not allow rapid price increases, managers can avoid the restrictions by assigning the highest possible price to any product which is new or modified. The value of a currency in a particular market and the stability of that value will again impact whether a firm can feel comfortable with a particular price level or whether the firm needs to adjust the price frequently to meet changing market conditions. Finally, the relative growth or decline in a particular economy will have an obvious effect on pricing: declining economies are likely to exhibit greater downward pressure on prices as local competitors struggle to keep afloat.

Distribution channels also have an impact on the pricing strategy. The costs associated with the services performed by distributors will have a major effect upon the final price paid by the customer. Marketing managers need to be sure that the value added by the distributor exceeds the additional costs imposed by the distributor's profit margin. A further problem for marketing managers is that some distributors may see an opportunity for **grey market** re-export. This occurs when marketers offer the product at different

Marketing in Practice
Tesco and Levi's

I n July 2002 a landmark ruling was handed down by the UK High Court, preventing Tesco supermarket from selling cheap Levi jeans imported from Eastern Europe. This ruling marked the end of a four-year battle by Tesco to sell the jeans.

Levi's sell their jeans throughout the world, but the price at which they are sold varies greatly from one country to another, to match the value placed on the jeans in the various markets. A pair of Levi's which would cost around $30 in the United States might be sold for £35 in the UK and as little as £10 in Eastern Europe, where incomes are low and competition from local manufacturers is fierce. Levi price their jeans as a premium brand in all the markets they sell into, but because of widely-varying standards of living and consumer expectations, the actual price is very different in each market.

Levi's argue that they are entitled to retain their premium status in each market, and that Tesco were damaging their brand values by selling the jeans cheaply. Tesco argue that they are simply doing what every supermarket does – getting the best value for the consumers.

'For 130 years the Levi's name has been a promise of outstanding quality and value.' Joe Middleton of Levi's said. 'This decision allows us to carry on keeping that promise.'

'The EU must change this anti-consumer law, and change it quickly.' Phil Evans of the Consumer Association responded. 'Tesco may have lost their legal battle against Levi's – but the real loser is the consumer.'

The Mary Lynne Mini Skirt. levis-girls.com

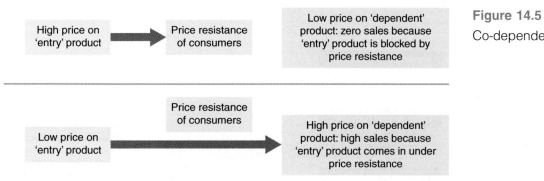

Figure 14.5
Co-dependent products

prices in different markets in order to meet local competition. Some distributors in the low-price market overbuy and sell the excess in the high-price market, beating the latter market's much higher prices and turning a neat profit. Dealing with these 'grey market' products is an ongoing problem for many international marketing managers.

grey market 1. Re-import of brands from markets where the prices are lower. 2. Older consumers.

Competitors have a major effect upon pricing strategy. First, one must examine their offerings in detail to understand the benefits and drawbacks of their approaches versus the firm's approach. Where products are sold in markets where bidding is not required to be made public and sales are infrequent, it may be difficult to obtain competitors' pricing. Nevertheless, an effort should be made. Finally, competitors' costs are a very important factor in pricing strategy, since a competitor with a high cost base will have difficulty in the event of a price war. Here again it may be difficult to obtain these costs, but the manager should attempt at the very least to estimate.

Talking Point

If we really have no idea what our competitors' costs are, or what their plans are, why are we even trying to guess? Why not just give our salespeople and distributors the power to negotiate price and make adjustments as they go along?

Or would this just lead to anarchy? Would it be better to sit down with our competitors and discuss things like civilised people? On the other hand, that would be collusion – which is illegal. So maybe we are doomed to continue with an inefficient system!

The most important factor in the pricing strategy is obviously the customer. Understanding how consumers use the product, and knowing what value they get from it, enables the marketing manager to establish true value-in-use prices. The perceptions customers have of the product and the manufacturer are also important: the ability to pay for the product is sometimes a problem, but astute marketers will find ways for potential customers to pay for the product on credit or through trade-in.

Determining Demand – Customer Perceptions of Price

As we have seen in Chapter 4, people perceive a total product including core benefits, product attributes and support services yielding a package of benefits they need. These benefits must be balanced against the various costs customers will incur. Usually, the most obvious cost is the net outlay of funds required from the customer to gain these benefits. This outlay includes not only the initial price, but the servicing and running costs over the useful life of the product. Customer perceptions of costs and benefits are shown in Figure 14.6.

Figure 14.6

Cost-benefit trade-offs

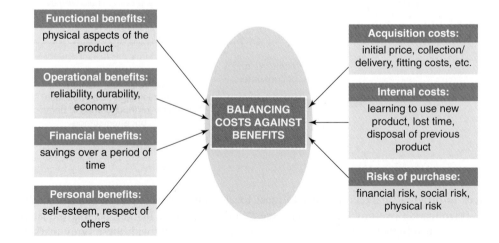

As can be seen in Figure 14.6, customer benefits fall into functional, operational, financial and personal categories. The functional are those that come to mind most readily, related to the physical aspects of the product – these often relate closely to the individual's cognition of the product. In the longer term, operational benefits such as reliability and durability, financial aspects such as savings made over the period of ownership, and personal benefits such as feelings of well-being and of ownership will assume greater importance.

Customer costs include acquisition costs such as the initial price plus delivery, fitting etc., internal costs, such as learning to use the product, lost time in buying it and getting it to work properly, and disposal: and finally, costs related to risk. Not all of these costs are financial, and not all of the price charged by the supplier is expressed financially, either. Suppliers might expect customers to accept a higher level of risk as part of the price of obtaining the product.

Consumers need to balance these factors carefully in order to arrive at a final evaluation of the product's worth. Provided the benefits exceed the costs, the consumer will be happy with the outcome: if the costs exceed the benefits, the consumer will not be happy with the outcome. In the long term, marketers should seek to ensure that benefits always outweigh costs, but either side of the equation can be adjusted: if the marketer can offer greater benefits without increasing the cost to the consumer, this is a valid way of achieving value for money. If benefits cannot be improved, then the only way to improve value for money is to reduce the costs – not necessarily the initial acquisition price, but (possibly) the other costs.

Research shows that a perception of loss of quality is more important to most people than a price loss – in other words, it's better to raise prices than to reduce quality (Hankuk and Agarwal 2003). The same researchers found that perceptions of loss are more important to consumers than comparable gains, which makes maintaining quality even more important.

Price Sensitivity

Establishing the needs of each segment is a precursor to developing appropriate pricing for each segment. In some cases, a product can be customised to meet the specific needs of a segment and priced at a premium because of the customisation. In setting prices for specific segments, the marketing director must estimate the price sensitivity of that particular market segment. Dolan (1995) listed factors that affect customer price sensitivity (see Table 14.1).

Table 14.1 Factors affecting customer price sensitivity

Economics
- Percentage of total expense
- Type of consumer
- Level of involvement

Search and usage
- Cost of information search
- Ease of comparing competitive alternatives
- Switching costs

Competition
- Differentiation
- Perception of price

The major categories are customer economics, search and usage and competition. Customers will be more sensitive if the percentage of the particular item is large in comparison to the total expense that the customer is incurring to achieve a particular end. Should the item be of extreme importance to the consumer, price sensitivity will tend to decline because reliability becomes paramount.

Reviewing the search and usage category, customers will be more price-sensitive if information search is easy and cheap, and competitive offerings are easily compared. In addition, the customer's price sensitivity is increased substantially where switching costs are low. Switching costs are all the costs associated with changing from one particular product or service to another. For example, a consumer might become persuaded that Apple Mac software is better than Microsoft, but would find it difficult to change because of the extra time needed to learn the new system. These costs may outweigh the benefits seen from a potential new system. Finally, price sensitivity is decreased where the manufacturer's offering is clearly differentiated from its competition and where price perception gives an aura of quality to a particular product.

Costs

For marketing managers, developing reliable costs to use in pricing decisions is often a frustrating process. Many products are made in the same factory and the allocation of costs by the finance department is often arbitrary. Products which are easy to manufacture and have low material costs often assume too much of the overhead of a facility, making the marketing manager's task in pricing to meet market conditions quite difficult. In this regard, marketing people are advised to study the costing process used at a particular facility in-depth so that they can convincingly present their case for proper costing of particular product lines.

Activity based costing (ABC) is a relatively new approach to establishing cost which allows hope for more accurately determining what costs should be assigned to particular product lines and customers. According to Narayanan and Sarkar (2002), under ABC, managers separately keep account of expenses required to produce individual units and batches, to design and maintain and produce and to keep the manufacturing facility running. ABC requires that costs be allocated not only to products but also to customers, so that a manager can determine the cost to serve a particular customer. In Narayanan and Sarkar's study, Insteel Corporation tracked the overhead needed to serve special customer needs including packing and loading, order processing and invoicing, post-sales service and the cost of offering credit. These costs were attributed to each customer and allocated to products based on the volume of each product purchased by a particular customer. Through the ABC approach, Insteel discovered that, at one factory studied, freight represented 16 per cent of the total people and physical resources cost. After the detailed analysis, management decided to increase the weight shipped per truck load, resulting in a 20 per cent reduction in freight expense. The visibility of the ABC system also allowed Insteel to change the product line and increase prices for less profitable products.

Talking Point

ABC certainly sounds like a wonderful way to increase efficiency – provided the forms are filled in properly! What happens when managers are too busy to work out the figures? What happens if the forms are too complicated?

In short, what happens when a manager is overworked, has a crisis to handle and simply shoves down any figures that come to mind? How can the system be made to cope?

Although the high risks associated with it have been well established, the idea of 'pricing down the learning curve' is one which has persisted for at least two decades. Learning curve (or experience curve) theory simply states that costs decline rapidly with each doubling of output of a particular product. Experience curve effects come from three major sources (Day and Montgomery 1983):

- *Learning*. Increased efficiency because of practice and skill or finding new and better ways to do things.
- *Technological improvements*. New production processes and product changes which improve yield.
- *Economies of scale*. Increased efficiency resulting from larger operations.

These improvements are especially relevant to investment and operating costs. Day and Montgomery found significant limitations of the strategic relevance for experience curve approaches, and they warn against an all-out dedication to this approach. While it may give some advantages in some markets, it also introduces rigidity that may make the firm slower and less flexible in its ability to respond to customer or competitive changes. The experience curve will only be strategically relevant when the three major effects identified above are important in the strategic environment of a particular firm. Ames and Hlavacek (1984) point out that slavishly following the experience curve approach has yielded disastrous results, especially for established or mature products where gains through experience diminish rapidly.

Competition

Understanding competitive offerings, including their prices, is critical. To begin with, a firm must be careful about setting its prices higher than the competition. This obviously depends upon the strategic position the firm finds itself in. Should the company be a leader in its market, it probably will price higher than competitors. In monopolistic competition situations, smaller firms would realise no benefit by attempting to price lower than the dominant competitor, since the large firm could easily match the smaller firm's prices or even retaliate by lowering prices further, putting a much larger financial strain on the smaller firm than it would realise itself. In high growth or hyper-competitive markets, some firms may attempt to disturb the status quo. An important tool in these markets is the race to the next price point, equivalent to the next step in the stepped demand curve (see Figure 14.2). While this is more common in consumer markets, there is a strong effect in business-to-business markets as well. Moore (1995) points out that when workstation prices were lowered to under £50 000 and then under £10 000 the result was 'huge boosts in sales volumes'. As the firm drops to the next price point, a new market segment will be in a position to buy the products, and competitors will need to follow suit. This is true even in the case where these smaller competitors have to sell below their costs.

Understanding your competitors' current position is an important factor affecting the price, but an equally important aspect of this decision is competitor reaction. Certainly, this aspect of pricing requires experience and knowledge. A correct assessment of competitors' potential reaction to increasing or decreasing price may determine whether the strategy chosen by the company is the correct one. Sophisticated companies are able to include in their data warehouse information about past competitive reactions to pricing moves. This knowledge can help the manager make more informed decisions about potential competitive actions.

Pricing Methods

Pricing methods are closely related to pricing objectives. The three basic methods are cost-based pricing, customer-based pricing and competition-based pricing (see Figure 14.7).

Cost-based pricing usually follows one of two methods: cost-plus pricing and mark-up pricing. Cost-plus pricing is often advocated by accountants and engineers because it is

Figure 14.7

Pricing methods

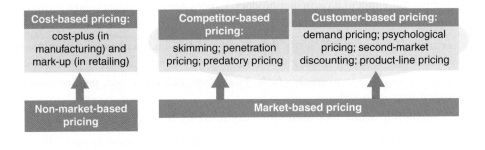

Table 14.2 Cost-plus pricing

Item	Cost per unit
Labour costs	£2.74
Raw materials	£4.80
Electricity	£0.08
Tooling costs (assuming production run of 50,000 units)	£2.71
Overheads (factory, office etc.)	£1.17
Total production cost per unit	£11.50
PLUS profit margin of 20%	£2.30
Total price, ex-factory	£13.80

simple to use and appears to guarantee that the firm will reach a predetermined profit level. Cost-plus pricing works by calculating the cost of producing the product, then adding on a fixed percentage profit to the total. An example of this type of calculation is shown in Table 14.2.

Although this pricing method appears logical and straightforward, it is actually fairly dangerous because it takes no account of the marketplace. If customers feel that the price is too high, they will not buy the product: on the other hand, if the price is much lower than customers would be prepared to pay, the company is losing out on potential profit.

Some government contracts are awarded on a cost-plus basis, but experience in the United States has shown that allowing cost-plus contracts to be granted will often result in the supplier inflating the costs to make an extra profit.

Mark-up pricing

shelf price The cost of a product when it is on the shelf, not including delivery costs etc.

Mark-up pricing is similar to cost-plus pricing, and is the method used by most retailers. Typically, a retailer will buy in stock and add on a fixed percentage to the bought-in price (a mark-up) in order to arrive at the **shelf price**. The level will vary from retailer to retailer, depending on the type of product; in some cases the mark-up will be 100 per cent

Table 14.3 Mark-up vs margin

Bought-in price	£4.00
Mark-up at 25 per cent of £4.00	£1.00
Price on the shelf	£5.00
Margin of 20 per cent of £5.00	£1.00
Bought-in price	£4.00

or more, in others it will be near zero (if the retailer feels that stocking the product will stimulate other sales). Usually there is a standard mark-up for each product category.

Profit margins can be expressed either in terms of a **mark-up** or of a **margin**. Mark-up is calculated on the price the retailer pays for the product; margin is calculated on the price the retailer sells for. This means that a 100 per cent mark-up equals a 50 per cent margin; a 25 per cent mark-up equals a 20 per cent margin (Table 14.3).

Retailers use this method because of the number of lines the shop may be carrying. For a hypermarket, this could be up to 20 000 separate lines, and it would clearly be impossible to carry out market research with the customers for every line. The buyers therefore use their training and knowledge of their customer base to determine which lines to stock, and (to some extent) rely on the manufacturers to carry out the formal market research and determine the recommended retail prices.

mark-up Gross profit calculated as a proportion of the price paid for an item.

margin Gross profit calculated as a proportion of the price a product is sold for.

Talking Point

Retailers nowadays usually hold the whip-hand in the distribution chain. They are closest to the consumers, they are the final customers in the chain and they have a wide range of possible suppliers. Manufacturers are in the unhappy position of having to meet the retailers' terms, or have no market.

So how might a manufacturer counteract this? Can a manufacturer be a price setter? Is there a case for manufacturers getting together to fight the power of the retailers – or would this simply mean that they would fall foul of the law on collusion? Retailers do not seem to have any difficulty in controlling the situation, whether by collusion or by consensus – so why have manufacturers allowed the initiative to be lost?

This method is identical to the cost-plus method except for two factors: first, the retailer is usually in close contact with the customers, and can therefore develop a good 'feel' for what customers will be prepared to pay, and second, retailers have ways of disposing of unsold stock. In some cases, this will mean discounting the stock back to cost and selling it in the January sales: in other cases, the retailer will have a sale-or-return agreement with the manufacturer, so that unsold stock can be returned for credit. This is becoming increasingly common with major retailers such as Toys Я Us which have sufficient 'clout' in the market to enforce such agreements. In a sense, therefore, the retailer is carrying out market research by test-marketing the product; if the customers do not accept the product at the price offered, the retailer can drop the price to a point that will represent value for money, or can return it to the manufacturer for credit.

Figure 14.8 shows the retailer's alternatives. Putting the goods into the annual sale, or selling them off at a discounted price, usually means that profit is small but it is still preferable to returning the goods to the manufacturer for credit, because that option means that the retailer makes no profit at all (and of course damages the relationship with the manufacturer).

E-Marketing in Practice
Last-Minute Holidays

There is nothing as perishable as an airline seat. Once the aircraft takes off, empty seats represent a dead loss to the airline or tour operator. The same is true of package holidays.

Tour operators are in a difficult position. In order to negotiate the lowest prices for flights and hotels, they need to block-book aircraft seats and hotel rooms months in advance, and then sell the holidays. Sometimes the holidays are slow to sell – in which case the tour operator needs to recoup whatever can be saved. For preference, tour operators would like to sell the whole package, even at a discount, because something is better than nothing – but if all else fails, the tour operator can sell off the flights at a discount and let the hotel rooms stay empty.

Before the Internet came along, holidaymakers could often pick up these 'last-minute bargains' from travel agents. Anyone who was able to be flexible about departure times and destinations could pick up really cheap deals, and the closer to the departure time, the cheaper the deal. Gradually, of course, people learned the system and would wait until the last minute before booking their holidays – which of course meant that fewer people booked in advance, which meant more holidays available at knockdown prices, to the detriment of the tour operators. The result was a waiting game on both sides – the tour operators would try to guess what the market was going to do, and the consumers were trying to guess at what point all the holidays would be sold and they would be going nowhere.

The Internet has changed all that. Now, holidays are offered online, and prices can go up as well as down – if more people try to book a trip, the price rises for the late bookers. For flights, the last-minute bargain is almost a thing of the past – tour operators and airlines have their computers programmed in such a way that increased interest in a particular destination causes the price to rise, so that in most cases it is much cheaper to book in advance. The last-minute bargain is not dead – in fact, Lastminute.com rely on these for their existence – but they are certainly harder to find than they once were.

Ready, steady, book.

No need to phone around, book a table for a top restaurant online.

do something
lastminute.com
gifts ∙ restaurants ∙ entertainment ∙ auctions ∙ travel

Courtesy of The Advertising Archives

Figure 14.8

Alternative price adjustment strategies

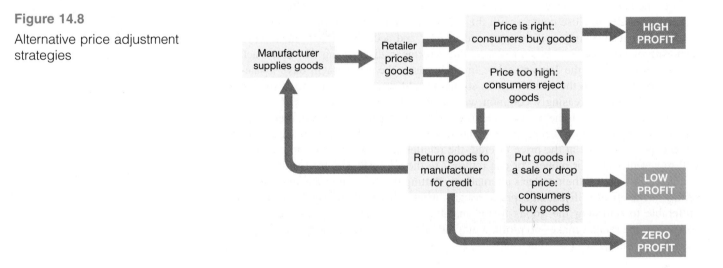

Customer-Based Pricing Methods

The various approaches to customer-based pricing do not necessarily mean offering products at the lowest possible price, but they do take account of customer needs and wants, and also of psychological factors in perception of price.

Customary pricing

Customary pricing is customer-orientated in that it provides the customer with the product for the same price at which it has always been offered. An example is the price of a call from a coin-operated telephone box. Telephone companies need only reduce the time allowed for the call as costs rise. For some countries (e.g. Australia) this is problematical, since local calls are allowed unlimited time, but for most European countries this is not the case.

The reason for using customary pricing is to avoid having to reset the call-boxes too often. Similar methods exist for taxis, some children's sweets and gas or electricity pre-payment meters. If this method were to be used for most products there would be a steady reduction in the firm's profits as the costs catch up with the selling price, so the method is not practical for every firm.

customary price The price a product has always been sold for.

Demand pricing

Demand pricing is the most market-orientated method of pricing. Here, the marketer begins by assessing what the demand will be for the product at different price levels. This is usually done by asking the customers what they might expect to pay for the product, and seeing how many choose each price level. This will lead to the development of the kind of chart shown in Table 14.4.

As the price rises, fewer customers are prepared to buy the product, as fewer will still see the product as good value for money. In the example given above, the fall-off is not linear, i.e. the number of units sold falls dramatically once the price goes above £5. This kind of calculation could be used to determine the stages of a skimming policy (see below), or it could be used to calculate the appropriate launch price of a product.

For demand pricing, the next stage is to calculate the costs of producing the product in the above quantities. Usually the cost of producing each item falls as more are made (i.e. if we make 50 000 units, each unit costs less than would be the case if we only make 1000 units). Given the costs of production it is possible to select the price that will lead to a maximisation of profits. This is because there is a trade-off between quantity produced and quantity sold: as the firm lowers the selling price, the amount sold increases but the income generated decreases.

The calculations can become complex, but the end result is that the product is sold at a price that customers will accept, and that will meet the company's profit targets.

demand pricing Calculating price according to what consumers are prepared to pay.

Table 14.4 Demand pricing

Price per unit	Number of customers who said they would buy at this price
£3 to £4	30 000
£4 to £5	25 000
£5 to £6	15 000
£6 to £7	5000

Table 14.5 Costings for demand pricing

Number of units	Unit cost (labour and materials)	Tooling-up and fixed costs	Net cost per unit
30 000	£1.20	£4000	£1.33
25 000	£1.32	£4000	£1.48
15 000	£1.54	£4000	£1.81
5000	£1.97	£4000	£2.77

Table 14.6 Profitability at different price bands

Number of units sold	Net profit per unit	Total profit for production run	Percentage profit per unit
30 000	£2.17	£65 100	62
25 000	£3.02	£75 500	67
15 000	£3.61	£54 150	66
5000	£3.73	£18 650	57

Table 14.5 shows an example of costings to match up with the above figures. The tooling-up cost is the amount it will cost the company to prepare for producing the item. This will be the same whether 1000 or 30 000 units are made.

Table 14.6 shows how much profit could be made at each price level. The price at which the product is sold will depend on the firm's overall objectives; these may not necessarily be to maximise profit on this one product, since the firm may have other products in the range or other long-term objectives that preclude maximising profits at present.

Based on these figures, the most profitable price will be £4.50. Other ways of calculating the price could easily lead to making a lower profit from this product. For instance, the price that would generate the highest profit per unit would be £6.50, but at this price they would only sell 5000 units and make £18 650. The price that would generate the highest sales would be £3.50, but this would (in effect) lose the firm almost £10 000 in terms of foregone profit.

A further useful concept is that of contribution. Contribution is calculated as the difference between the cost of manufacture and the price for which the product is sold – in other words it does not take account of overheads. Sometimes a product is worth producing because it makes a significant extra contribution to the firm's profits, without actually adding to the overheads. It is not difficult to imagine a situation in which a product carries a low profit margin and is therefore unable to support a share of the overheads. A calculation which included an overall share of the overheads might not give a fair picture, since the contribution would be additional to existing turnover.

Demand pricing works by knowing what the customers are prepared to pay and what they will see as value for money.

Product-line pricing

Product-line pricing means setting prices within linked product groups. Often sales of one product will be directly linked to the sales of another, so that it is possible to sell one item at a low price in order to make a greater profit on the other one. Gillette sells its Mach III system razors at a very low price, with the aim of making up the profit on sales of the blades. In the long run, this is a good strategy because it overcomes the initial resistance of consumers towards buying something untried, but allows the firm to show high profits for years to come (incidentally, this approach was first used by King C. Gillette, the inventor of the disposable safety razor blade).

Polaroid chose to sell its instant cameras very cheaply (almost for cost price) for the US market and to take their profit from selling the films for a much higher price. For Europe, the firm chose to sell both films and cameras for a medium level price and profit from sales of both. Eventually this led Kodak to enter the market with its own instant camera, but this was withdrawn from sale in the face of lawsuits from Polaroid for patent infringement.

product-line pricing In circumstances where sales of one product are dependent on sales of another, calculating both prices to take account of the price of each product.

Skimming

Skimming is the practice of starting out with a high price for a product, then reducing it progressively as sales level off. It relies on two main factors: first, that not all customers have the same perception of value for money, and second that the company has a technological lead over the opposition which can be maintained for long enough to satisfy the market.

Skimming is usually carried out by firms who have developed a technically advanced product. Initially the firm will charge a high price for the product, and at this point only those who are prepared to pay a premium price for it will buy. Profit may not be high, because the number of units sold will be low and therefore the cost of production per unit will be high. Once the most innovative customers have bought, and the competition is beginning to enter the market, the firm can drop the price and 'skim' the next layer of the market, at which point profits will begin to rise. Eventually the product will be sold at a price that allows the firm only a minimum profit, at which point only replacement sales or sales to late adopters will be made.

Figure 14.9 shows how skimming works. At each price level, the product shows a standard product life cycle curve: as the curve tops out and begins to fall back, the company lowers the price and the cycle starts again with a new group of consumers. The process continues until either the market is saturated or the company decides that it cannot make any further price reductions.

skimming Pricing products highly at first, but reducing the price steadily as the product moves through its life cycle.

Electronic products are frequently the subjects of skimming.

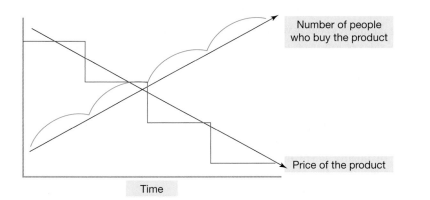

Figure 14.9

Skimming

The advantage of this method is that the cost of developing the product is returned fairly quickly, so that the product can later be sold near the marginal cost of production. This means that competitors have difficulty entering the market at all, since their own development costs will have to be recovered in some other way.

Skimming is commonly used in consumer electronics markets. This is because firms frequently establish a technological lead over the competitors, and can sometimes even protect their products by taking out patents, which take some time for competitors to overcome. An example of this was the Sony Walkman, which cost over £70 when it was first introduced in the early 1980s. Allowing for inflation, the price is now around one-tenth of what it was then. Recent research shows that customers are aware of skimming in the electronics markets, and are delaying purchases of new electronic devices until the prices drop. This may affect the way firms view skimming in the future.

Skimming requires careful judgement of what is happening in the marketplace, both in terms of observing customer behaviour and of observing competitive response. Market research is therefore basic to the success of a skimming policy, and very careful monitoring of sales to know when to cut the price again.

Psychological pricing

odd-even pricing Using '99c' or '95p' endings on prices.

Psychological pricing relies on emotional responses from the consumer. Higher prices are often used as an indicator of quality, so some firms will use prestige pricing. This applies in many service industries, because consumers are often buying a promise; a service that does not have a high enough quality cannot be exchanged afterwards. Consumer's expectations of high-priced restaurants and hairdressers are clearly higher in terms of the quality of service provision; cutting prices in those industries does not necessarily lead to an increase in business. **Odd-even pricing** is the practice of ending prices with an odd number, for example £3.99 or $5.95 rather than £4 or $6. It appears that consumers tend to categorise these prices as '£3 and a bit' or '$5 and change' and thus perceive the price as being lower. The effect may also be due to an association with discounted or sale prices; researchers report that '99' endings on prices increase sales by around 8 per cent (Schindler and Kirby 1997). However, there is some evidence to suggest that, in the case of first-time trial of products, rounding the price up to the nearest whole number can increase trials (Bray and Harris 2006).

Recent research has shown that odd-even pricing does not necessarily work in all cultures (Suri, Anderson and Kotlov 2004). In Poland, for example, the effects are negligible. Odd-even pricing also has effects on perceptions of discounts during sales. Rounding the price to (say) £5 from £4.99 leads people to overvalue the size of the discount, which increases the perception of value for money (Gueguen and Legoherel 2004). Thus the positive effect on sales of using a 99-ending can be negated by the effect when the product is on offer in a sale.

In China, there is evidence to suggest that prices ending in 8 are more effective than prices ending in 4, because 8 is a lucky number and 4 is unlucky (Simmons and Schindler 2003).

There are many other psychological effects in pricing – offering a high-priced product increases sales of lower-priced products (Krishna, Wagner and Yoon 2002), and bundling other services with the product (such as free shipping and handling) is a good purchase incentive (Roggeveen, Xia and Monroe 2006). The same researchers found that separating the price from the delivery charges led to more favourable memories of the transaction and fewer product returns, however.

One particularly interesting piece of research showed that the introduction of the euro in Germany (where it replaced the lower-value Deutschmark) resulted in higher perceptions of quality when the price was expressed in Deutschmarks than when it was expressed in euros. Presumably this is because the DM price was a higher number than the euro price (Molz and Gielnik 2006).

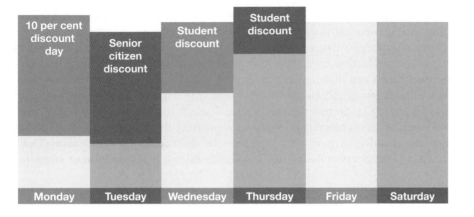

Figure 14.10
Second-market discounting

Second-market discounting

Second-market discounting is common in some service industries and in international markets. The brand is sold at one price in one market, and in a lower price in another: for example, museums offer discounts to students, some restaurants offer discounts to elderly people on week nights and so forth. Often these discounts are offered to even out the loading on the firm; week night discounts fill the restaurant on what would otherwise be a quiet night so making more efficient use of the premises and staff.

Figure 14.10 shows how second-market discounting works. At the bottom of each column is the amount of full-price business a retailer does on each day. Friday and Saturday are the busiest days, so on the other four days of the week the firm offers various discounts. On Monday the retailer offers 10 per cent off to all customers, which boosts business that day to a level higher than that of the weekend trade. Tuesday is senior citizen day, and Wednesday and Thursday are student discount days. These days are aimed at people who are able to shop mid-week.

Obviously these discounts may cannibalise sales on other days: a senior citizen might have been willing to shop on a Saturday and pay the full price (or might even have shopped on a Tuesday anyway, simply because the shop is quieter).

In international markets products might be discounted to meet local competition. For example, Honda motorcycles are up against strong local competition in India from Royal Enfield, so the price of their basic 100 cc motorcycle is around Rs 39 000 (about £600). A similar Honda motorcycle in the UK costs around £2000. The specifications of the motorcycles do differ somewhat – but it is difficult to see any difference that would account for a £1400 price differential.

second-market discounting Charging lower prices in some markets or some market segments than in others.

Competitor-based pricing

Competitor-based pricing recognises the influence of competition in the marketplace. Strategically, the marketer must decide how close the competition is in providing for the consumers' needs; if the products are close, then prices will need to be similar to those of the competition. A meet-the-competition strategy has the advantage of avoiding price wars and stimulating competition in other areas of marketing, thus maintaining profitability. An undercut-the-competition strategy is often the main plank in the firm's marketing strategy; it is particularly common among retailers, who have relatively little control over product features and benefits and often have little control over the promotion of the products they stock. Some multinational firms (particularly in electronics) have the capacity to undercut rivals, since they are able to manufacture in low-wage areas of the world, or are large enough to use widespread automation. There is a danger of starting

Many retailers offer price guarantees.

price wars when using an undercutting policy (see penetration pricing below). Undercutting (and consequent price wars) may be becoming more common.

Firms with large market shares often have enough control over their distribution systems and production capacity within their industries to become price leaders. Typically, such firms can make price adjustments without starting price wars, and can raise prices without losing substantial market share (see Chapter 2 for monopolistic competition) (Rich 1982). Sometimes these price leaders become sensitive to the price and profit needs of their competitors, in effect supporting them, because they do not wish to attract the attention of monopoly regulators by destroying the competition. Deliberate price fixing (managers colluding to set industry prices) is illegal in most countries.

Penetration pricing

penetration pricing Setting low prices in an attempt to capture a large market share.

Penetration pricing is used when the firm wants to capture a large part of the market quickly. It relies on the assumption that a lower price will be perceived as offering better value for money (which is, of course, often the case).

For penetration pricing to work, the company must have carried out thorough research to find out what the competitors are charging for the nearest similar product. The new product is then sold at a substantially lower price, even if this cuts profits below an acceptable level; the intention is to capture the market quickly before the competitors can react with even lower prices. The danger with this pricing method is that competitors may be able to sustain a price war for a long period and will eventually bankrupt the incoming firm. It is usually safer to compete on some other aspect of the offering, such as quality or delivery.

Predatory pricing

predatory pricing Pricing at extremely low levels (sometimes below the cost of production) with the intention of damaging competitors or forcing them to leave the market.

In some cases, prices are pitched below the cost of production. The purpose of this is to bankrupt the competition so that the new entrant can take over entirely; this practice is called **predatory pricing**, and (at least in international markets) is illegal. Predatory pricing was successfully used by Japanese car manufacturers when entering the European markets in the 1970s, and is commonly used by large firms who are entering new markets. For the strategy to be successful, it is necessary for the market to be dominated by firms that cannot sustain a long price war. It is worth doing if the company has no other competitive edge, but does have sufficient financial reserves to hold out for a long time. Naturally, this method is customer-orientated, since it can work only by providing the customers with very much better value for money than they have been used to. The company will eventually raise prices again in order to recoup the lost profits once the market presence has been established, however.

In Figure 14.11, the firm entering the market has a choice (basically) of three price levels. At the highest level, the firms are competing 'fairly': each is making a normal

Figure 14.11

Predatory pricing

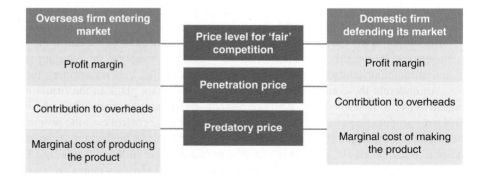

profit and covering the overhead. However, the foreign firm has a lower overall cost base – the manufacturing costs are lower, as are the overheads. At the second, lower, price level the foreign firm is still covering its overheads, but is now causing the domestic firm some difficulties because the domestic firm cannot cover its overheads if it meets the price. The lowest price is the predatory price – here the foreign firm relies on other markets to cover its overheads and profit margins, and sells into the new market at the marginal cost of production, which is actually below the price that the other firm can make for. At this level, it would be cheaper for the domestic firm to buy product from the foreign firm and resell it rather than manufacture itself. The domestic firm will lose money (and in fact will lose more money if sales increase), whereas the foreign firm can maintain this position indefinitely.

The ultimate in predatory pricing is **dumping**. This is the practice of selling goods at prices below the cost of manufacture, and was at one time commonly practiced by Communist countries desperate for hard currency. Dumping is illegal under international trade rules, but is difficult to prove, and by the time the victim countries have been able to prove their case and have the practice stopped, it is usually too late.

Competitor-based pricing is still customer-orientated to an extent, since it takes as its starting-point the prices that customers are currently prepared to pay.

dumping Disposing of products in a foreign market at prices below the cost of production.

Pricing in International Markets

International exporters use three basic methods (Cavusgil, 1996):

- *Rigid cost-plus pricing*: where the price is set simply by adding all the costs incurred for serving an international customer to the costs of manufacturing the product, plus a margin.

- *Flexible cost-plus pricing*: is similar to rigid cost-plus pricing but allows for some price variation, such as discounts for large orders or to meet local competition.

- *Dynamic incremental pricing*: assumes that fixed costs are incurred whether the firm sells outside its home market or not, so that the exporter seeks only to recover international variable costs.

Stottinger (2001) showed that most exporters use either the rigid cost-plus or flexible cost-plus approach, focusing on costs and competition rather than customer value in their pricing method.

More sophisticated firms analyse cost and demand and develop prices for a target return on investment. This method generally assumes demand at a certain level and does not sufficiently take into account the changes in demand resulting from changes in price or potential competitive moves.

Firms using sales-orientated objectives attempt to set prices which will grow their sales in units or currency or increase market share. These approaches have been discussed in some depth above. Those with status quo objectives generally set prices to meet competition. Finally, firms who attempt to use value-in-use pricing base their pricing decision upon extensive work with customers. While it would be naïve to say that they should ignore costs entirely, marketing managers who wish to be successful must price from the market in, knowing customer needs and willingness to pay as well as competitors' offerings, current and future possible pricing. Should market prices in a particular country fall below the costs to serve customers in that country, management must re-examine the entire marketing strategy for that particular market and take steps to lower costs or decide not to serve customers in that particular market at that particular time.

A special consideration for exporters is the escalation of price which can take place because of the additional costs of exporting, the import duties and value added taxes (VAT) applied in various markets.

Table 14.7 Escalation in export markets

Cost factors	Domestic	Export markets
Manufacturer's price at factory	5.00	5.00
+ Insurance, shipping (15 per cent) (CIF*)	—	0.75
Landed costs (CIF value)	—	5.75
+ Tariff (20 per cent of CIF value)	—	1.15
Importer/distributor's cost	—	6.90
+ Importer/distributor's margin (25 per cent of cost)	1.25	1.72
Subject to VAT (Full cost + margin)	—	8.62
+ VAT (18 per cent on cost + margin)	—	1.55
Retailer's cost	6.25	10.17
+ Retailer's margin (50 per cent on cost)	3.13	5.08
+ VAT (18 per cent on margin)	—	0.91
Consumer price (Retailer's cost + margin + VAT)	9.38	16.16
Percentage escalation over domestic price	—	72%

Adapted from: Becker (1980)

*CIF = cost, insurance and freight.

As can be seen from Table 14.7, a domestic product which is sold at the factory for £5 and is subject to the normal mark-ups by distributors and retailers might be sold to consumers for £9.38. This same product sent to an export market may be subject to the various costs escalations shown in Table 14.7, resulting in a consumer price 72 per cent higher than that of the domestic price. (This table makes the assumption that the domestic market has no VAT.) Even adding VAT for the domestic market, export pricing can often be much higher. Firms can take several actions to reduce this price escalation. As recommended by Czinkota and Ronkainen (2004), first the firm may attempt to eliminate some steps of distribution. In the example shown in Table 14.7, for simplicity, a number of wholesale steps were eliminated, but in some markets multiple steps of wholesaling are the norm, and are desirable for the good reason that they increase efficiency in those markets.

A second method to reduce a final price in exporting is to adapt the product using lower-cost components or ingredients and taking out costly additional features which can be made optional in particular markets. A third way to reduce escalation is to change tariff or tax classifications. This may require local lobbying of the taxing or importing authorities. A final method would be to assemble or produce overseas. Once foreign sourcing is established with lower cost components, all costs applied to the product will be reduced. Shipping components to the local market for assembly is often a good cost-cutting approach, because local tariffs may be much lower for components than for finished products: countries often prefer foreign firms to assemble locally, because it provides employment for local people.

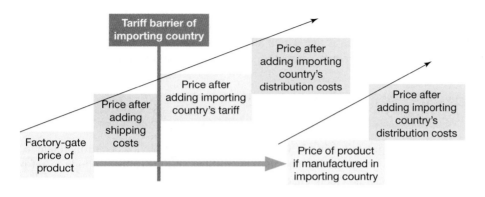

Figure 14.12

Effects of manufacturing in the target country

Pricing Policies in Business-to-Business Markets

In business markets, pricing has a somewhat different role because the purchasing process tends to be more rational, and is often much more price-sensitive. Pricing policies include deciding upon list price and discount levels, allowances, rebates and geographic differences (standardisation versus differentiation).

The question of list price varies by industry. In some industries, list prices are set in such a way that no customer ever pays that price. The list prices for a product line are set in order to provide various levels of discounts. Discounts can be given for volume purchases, whether cumulative or based on individual order, or based on time of order.

Allowances and rebates are simply price reductions given to dealers or distributors to help them promote a particular manufacturer's product. Some firms give advertising allowances to their distributors in order to encourage them to promote their particular product or even for identifying their facilities such as show rooms or service vehicles with a particular brand name. A firm may choose to offer a trade-in allowance for older products in order to replace them with newer versions. A rebate is a fee paid to a purchaser once the product is bought and installed.

A firm must decide on its geographic policies. First and foremost will be whether one standard price will be established in all markets, with the final local price determined by varying import duties, currency and local laws. Differentiated pricing allows local distributors or sales agents to set prices. In Stottinger's study of 45 industrial firms heavily involved in exporting, all but three made pricing decisions centrally and the largest firms were more likely to have centralised pricing decisions. Firms that used a company sales force internationally tended to standardise price, while those with independent distributors tended to allow differentiation.

Keegan and Green (2003) describe three global pricing policy alternatives:

- *Ethnocentric (extension)*, where a price per unit is the same no matter where in the world it is sold.

- *Polycentric (adaptation)*, which allows local managers or independent distributors to establish whatever price they feel is acceptable. In this case, prices are not coordinated between countries.

- *Geocentric*, where the firm does not use a single price worldwide or allow local managers or distributors to make independent pricing decisions. This is an intermediate approach which recognises that there are unique local market factors which impact the pricing decision and that price must be integrated with all elements of the marketing programme across the world. In this case, headquarters may decide to use a market-penetration approach for a particular market in order to gain short-term market share and a skimming approach elsewhere to reap profits used to offset low margins in markets where penetration is used.

Keegan points out that in global marketing, 'there is no such thing as a normal margin'. The geocentric approach is one which allows a true global competitive strategy in which a firm can take into account competitors and markets on a worldwide basis.

Legality of Pricing Policies

Many nations regulate pricing in various ways. The most obvious controls relate to anti-competitive actions. In the EU and the United States, firms cannot collude to set prices and this type of law is widely enacted (although intermittently enforced) in various other markets throughout the world. In the United States, a manufacturer must generally treat each class of customer equally. That is, the customer who buys a particular quantity of product should receive the same discount as another customer buying that same quantity. However, some exceptions to this rule are allowed. Manufacturers can use discriminatory pricing to meet a competitive threat in a particular market, or if it can be proved that their costs to serve one customer are lower than another.

In setting international prices, companies can sometimes be suspected of dumping. Dumping simply means that a product is sold at a level less than its cost of production. Anti-dumping penalties have increased in the United States, the EU, Canada and Australia and this will continue to be a key issue in international marketing. Managers must be careful that their pricing decisions can be defended against anti-dumping accusations.

Transfer Pricing

transfer pricing Internal pricing in a multinational company.

Transfer pricing can have an important effect on pricing decisions. Transfer prices are those set for goods or services which are bought by one division of a firm from another division. These are inside or intra-corporate prices. As might be expected, local tax authorities are quite interested in the transfer prices set inside corporations, since a firm can charge a high transfer price for components which it produces in a low-tax country, thus reducing the profits of its divisions in high-tax countries and effectively transferring the profits to a country where taxation is low.

Figure 14.13

Transfer pricing

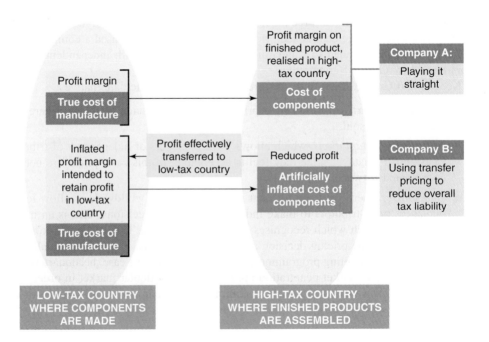

Transfer pricing can also have a significant effect upon the motivation of local partners. If for tax reasons prices are set in such a way as to reduce the profits of a local subsidiary or joint venture, managers of this entity may become demotivated. This 'softer' portion of the pricing decision between entities of a particular firm must also be taken into account.

Competitive Bidding

Business-to-business sales are often completed through competitive bids. This is especially true for Government institutions and non-profit organisations such as hospitals. Some non-governmental firms also use competitive bids. In some cases, a firm may require a bid to a particular specification and then reserve the right to negotiate further with the winning bidder. Firms use specification buying especially for large projects. These firms develop detailed specifications either based on the performance or description of a particular product, service or a combination of both. Firms supplying military products, large power stations or other major projects need to develop an expertise not only in the bidding process, but also in the specification process. 'Specmanship' means a firm's salesforce is expert at helping a customer develop specifications which will limit the bidders. The most successful salespeople can develop specifications with requirements that can be met only by their firm. When faced with a potential competitive bidding situation which will be based on specifications to be developed by a large customer, it is necessary to spend the required time to gain the most favourable specifications possible before bidding documents are released.

The development of a competitive bid should be viewed as equal in effort to developing a total business plan. It is not unusual for a firm to spend well over €100 000 to complete the analysis required to provide responsive bids to a particular customer. Before a firm decides to take on this major effort, a screening procedure should be completed.

Table 14.8 shows a procedure for evaluating bid opportunities. In this procedure, eight pre-bid factors should be examined. An analysis tool such as suggested in the table can be used to assign a weight to each factor and then rate the firm's capability for this

Table 14.8 Evaluating bid opportunities

Pre-bid factor	Weight (per cent)	Rating (1–10)	Value
Factory capacity	20	10	200
Competition	10	8	80
Follow-up opportunities	10	7	70
Quantity	10	7	70
Delivery	10	5	50
Profit	20	9	180
Experience	10	9	90
Bid capability	10	8	80
TOTAL	**100 per cent**	**N/A**	**820**

Adapted from: Paranka (1971)

particular bid. Multiplying the weights by the ratings gives a value for each factor, and adding all of the values together gives the firm some idea of whether they should pursue this particular bid. Of course if there are other opportunities these can be compared using this same tool.

The factors include (first) factory capacity. The firm must consider whether winning this bid will place an unusual strain on the factory where the product is made, or whether the factory is running at a relatively low level and has spare capacity. Competition must be considered as well, both in terms of the number of competitors and their possible bids. Past experience with competitors will serve as a guide here. A third and most important area is the possibility for follow-up opportunities. In some cases, a firm winning a bid will be placed on a preferred supplier list (such as with a government) and many additional orders may follow. In addition, a firm may receive orders for associated products. Here, the marketer must be careful because many sophisticated purchasers will indicate a large follow-up to a particular order with the goal of pushing the supplier to reduce the initial price.

Order size is another issue. Obviously, a very large order is more attractive than a smaller one, and large orders for a standard product with the same features are more attractive than an order for a mix of products. If the quantity can create economies of scale for a supplier, it will be more attractive than one which simply pushes a supplier past the point of diminishing returns.

In some cases, a large quantity of product is required to be delivered all at once, which may put an undue strain on the manufacturer's facilities. Marketers also need to consider the effect of accepting this order on customers, both from a delivery and factory capacity point of view. If a large order has the potential of reducing the manufacturer's capability to satisfy loyal customers in the future, it may not be as attractive. While this analysis must take place before final prices are determined, a general idea of the prices required to gain this order should be employed so that the firm can make an estimate of the possible profit to be realised. In some cases, a firm may decide that profit is not the overriding concern and that in order to fill the factory it will move ahead with a relatively unprofitable bid.

Another key factor is experience. Developing a winning bid for a particular project may take as much effort as an entire business plan for a new venture. If the firm has experience in developing bids of this particular kind, it should be looked upon more favourably. Finally, bid capability means the availability of people and financial resources to actually complete the work. There may be times when the firm simply does not have the capability to do the required work and therefore the project becomes less attractive.

Table 14.8 shows a hypothetical bid situation in which the firm has assigned weights to each of these factors and then rated the attractiveness of this bid along each one of the factors. The total value is then added, and as can be seen for this particular bid

Figure 14.14

Factors in bidding

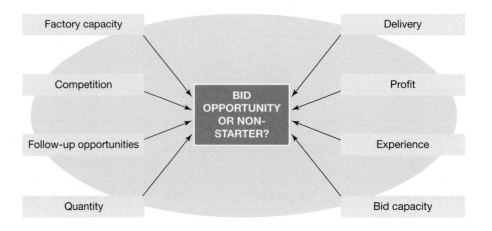

opportunity, the number is 820. It may be that the firm has set a minimum hurdle for proceeding with a bid. If we assume that hurdle might be 700 for this firm, it would proceed with the bidding process based on this score.

Once a firm has decided to move ahead it must develop a pricing strategy: the strategy for bids is the same as the general pricing strategy discussed earlier. In some cases, a firm may price simply for survival in order to get some business to keep the factory running. In most cases, the firm will decide whether it wishes to gain market share, increase profitability or use any of the other strategies described above.

Internationally, insisting on competitive bidding can be a problem in a high-context culture, where the project will probably be given to the firm the buyers feel is best positioned to do it based on the past establishment of trust. However, in a low-context culture a firm would develop specifications and push the supplier to meet the specifications as written (Hall 1976).

Credit

In business-to-business markets, credit is expected as a standard term of business. In some cases, firms will stretch the actual period of credit out – if the contract says 30 days' credit, they will pay in 90 days. This is especially prevalent when a large firm is dealing with a small supplier: in the UK, there is legislation which allows the small supplier to charge interest on late payments, but in practice few small firms are prepared to invoke this law since they are afraid of losing the customer. In consumer markets, the availability of credit can make a big difference to people's perception of price: people relate the hire purchase payments they make to the benefits gained from the product, for example, which means that their perception of value for money tends to fall as the product ages, but the payments remain the same (Auh and Shih 2006).

Interest-free credit can be affected by the way the time period is expressed. People tend to regard dates as abstract compared with a time period (LeBoeuf 2006), so stating 'Nothing to pay until 31 December' is less effective than saying 'Nothing to pay for six months'.

Summary

Price is not exciting, but getting it right is essential because it is the customer's half of the exchange. Although much of a marketer's attention focuses on the offer, the customer focuses on the total cost of purchasing the product – a consideration which includes the price the marketer is asking for the item. Price colours expectations as well – people tend to assume that the high-priced item is the high-quality item.

The key points from this chapter are as follows:

- Price affects all the elements of the marketing mix.
- Price is the only element of the mix which generates revenue.
- Price should relate to the market, not to the firm's costs of production.
- Consumer perception of price is functional, operational, financial and personal.
- Price is only one element in the total cost to the consumer.
- Demand pricing is the most customer-orientated method.
- Business-to-business markets tend to be more price-sensitive than consumer markets.
- Competition laws may affect pricing, whether prices are pitched excessively high (through collusion) or excessively low (in dumping).

Chapter review questions

1 List the factors in the pricing process.

2 What are the three major types of pricing objectives firms may use?

3 In developing a pricing strategy, what factors should a manager consider?

4 How does the customer perceive costs and benefits in weighing whether a price seems fair?

5 Explain the concept of switching cost.

6 When should the experience curve be used as a basis for pricing and when not?

7 What are the most common pricing methods used by international exporters? What are the drawbacks to these methods?

8 In developing pricing policies, what should an international firm consider?

9 How can transfer pricing affect the results realised by local partners?

10 When a firm enters a competitive bidding situation, how might they analyse the attractiveness of entering a particular bid?

Preview case revisited
Aldi

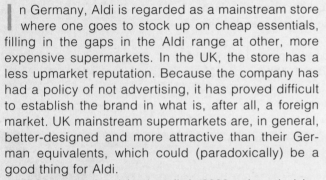

In Germany, Aldi is regarded as a mainstream store where one goes to stock up on cheap essentials, filling in the gaps in the Aldi range at other, more expensive supermarkets. In the UK, the store has a less upmarket reputation. Because the company has had a policy of not advertising, it has proved difficult to establish the brand in what is, after all, a foreign market. UK mainstream supermarkets are, in general, better-designed and more attractive than their German equivalents, which could (paradoxically) be a good thing for Aldi.

Aldi began advertising heavily in 2008, using television to convey the strapline 'Spend a little, live a lot' and promoting its upmarket products (such as the king prawns and the champagne) to communicate the message that the store is not only about cheap baked beans and cut-price corned beef.

Another departure from standard practice in Germany is that Aldi now accepts credit cards in the UK stores (German stores in general do not accept credit cards, and Germans rarely use them – unlike the British and French). Conveying the low-cost image is relatively easy in the UK, where the major supermarkets spend heavily on store design and frills in general – Aldi's stores are clearly run on a shoestring, with goods piled on the floor, no free carrier bags (as in Germany, UK Aldi customers pay for bags), and usually no more than one brand in each product category. The long queues at the checkouts are also a feature of Aldi – the company's minimalist approach to staffing ensures that no checkout operator is ever short of people to serve. The rapid checkout systems mean that people may not wait any longer in Aldi than they would in, say, Sainsbury's, however.

Overall, the low-cost low-price strategy has worked well for Aldi. Theo and Karl Albrecht (who both retired in 1993) are Germany's richest men, and the store chain is the world's 24th largest. Frau Albrecht, whose little grocery shop in Essen was the start of the whole business, has been quoted as saying, 'Je schlechter es den menschen geht, desto besser geht es uns' which loosely translates as 'The worse off people get, the better off we get'. Certainly the poor economic conditions in the UK during 2008 and 2009 were a bonus for Aldi – but whether this will be sustainable when the economy picks up again remains to be seen.

Case study
Auctionair

The Internet has opened up many opportunities for increasing consumer power, and nowhere has this been more apparent than in the proliferation of Internet auction sites. Sellers are able to post goods for sale on sites such as eBay or eBid, with or without a reserve price, and buyers are able to place their bids from (theoretically) anywhere in the world. The price rises as more people bid, until there is only one buyer left, who then buys the product at the final bid price. Buyers can pay by credit card through an escrow company (which holds the funds until the goods are delivered), or can make arrangements directly with the seller for payment.

Auctionair is a relative newcomer to this market, and has an unusual system: bids are sealed and unseen, just as they would be in a tendering situation. Potential buyers are invited to send their best offer, and the highest bid 'wins' the auction. The difference doesn't end there, however – bidders are not bound by their bid, and can withdraw afterwards, in which case the product is offered to the next highest bidder.

In some cases, products will have a 'secret price': above this price, every bidder will be supplied. Obviously this can only work when the company has multiple units of product to sell, but in some cases this will be the situation. The Auctionair system has the advantage that no-one can see the bids, which means that it is impossible for someone to 'snipe' a bid at the last minute. Unlike eBay, where sales are often snatched at the last minute by people who wait until they can see exactly what everyone else has bid, Auctionair buyers do not have to keep revisiting the site – they simply send in a bid for whatever they think the article is worth to them and wait to hear whether the vendor agrees.

Bidders pay a fee of £5 to take part in the bidding, but are not bound by the outcome: if a winning bidder decides to withdraw, his or her only cost is the entry fee. Auctionair make money from the entry fees, and also from profit on the sale items: over 40 per cent of their customers bid again, so the return rate of existing customers is satisfactorily high.

One of the most fascinating auction products offered by Auctionair is the low-bid auction, in which the lowest unmatched bid wins. Entry fee for this type of auction is anything up to £25, but the lowest bidder wins – provided no-one else has offered the same price. The lowest acceptable bid is £1, but if more than one person offers only £1 the product will be sold to someone else who has bid higher. For example, if two people bid £1, three people bid £2, one person bids £3, five people bid £4, two people bid £5 and three people bid £6, the person who bid £3 will be sold the product. Auctionair makes the bulk of its money on

the entry fees in this type of auction: the company sold a brand-new Mini Cooper for £5, and during 2007 they sold a total of 10 Mini Coopers, all for less than £110.

For low-price auctions the company sets the number of bids it will accept. Clearly this number of bids is calculated to ensure that the company still shows a profit on the product, and is balanced against the entry fee, which is in turn calculated against the likely amount the bidders would be prepared to pay for a chance to win the product. In effect, the low-bid auction is a lottery, but it avoids the UK's stringent gambling laws because the winner has to pay for the product, and there is an element of skill on the part of the winner in deciding how much to bid.

Again, unlike eBay and other auction sites, Auctionair sources all the products itself. People wanting to sell second-hand goods or unwanted gifts should go to eBay: Auctionair does not deal with vendors. What they do is contact suppliers and negotiate good deals for products, then auction them – presumably some unsold goods can be returned (or rather, not contracted for in the first place) – although the Auctionair site does include a 'Sale' section where unclaimed wins are sold off at low prices.

Auctionair offers a quirky, unusual auction system. The products tend to be high-value low-volume items such as luxury holidays or upmarket cars, but from the viewpoint of the manufacturers Auctionair offers an opportunity to move products on a website which doesn't suffer from the downmarket image of eBay. Suppliers are invited to put their products on the site: Auctionair ensure that only those suppliers with an appropriately reliable reputation are invited to supply goods and services.

Auctionair began as an experimental in-flight auction for British Airways (hence the company name), but became independent in 2003: in the intervening few years the response from the public has been very promising, with over half a million transactions conducted. In a crowded market, Auctionair certainly seems to have carved out a niche for itself.

Questions

1 Why would a manufacturer choose to use Auctionair?
2 What type of pricing method does Auctionair represent?
3 Why would someone be prepared to pay an entry fee to bid on Auctionair?
4 What is the rationale for the low-bid auctions?
5 Why does Auctionair only deal with invited companies?

References

Ames, B.C. and Hlavacek, J.D. (1984): *Managerial Marketing for Industrial Firms* (New York: Random House, Inc).

Auh, S. and Shih, C.-F. (2006): Balancing giving-up vs. taking-in: does the pattern of payments and benefits matter to customers in a financing decision context? *Advances in Consumer Research* **33**(1), 139–44.

Bray, J.P. and Harris, C. (2006): The effect of 9-ending prices on retail sales: a quantitative UK-based field study. *Journal of Marketing Management* **22**(5/6), 601–7.

Cavusgil, T.S. (1996): Pricing for Global Markets. *Columbia Journal of World Business* **31**(4), 66–78.

Czinkota, M. and Ronkainen, I.A. (2004): *International Marketing* (New York: Harcourt, Inc.).

Day, G.S. and Montgomery, D.B. (1983): Diagnosing the experience curve. *Journal of Marketing* **47** (Spring), 44–58.

Dolan, R.J. (1995): How do you know when the price is right. *Harvard Business Review* September/October, 174–83.

Gueguen, N. and Legoherel, P. (2004): Numerical encoding and odd-ending prices: the effect of a contrast in discount perception. *European Journal of Marketing* **38**(1), 194–208.

Hall, E.T. (1976): How cultures collide. *Psychology Today* **2**(1), 66–97.

Keegan, W.J. and Green, M.C. (2003): *Global Marketing* (Upper Saddle River, NJ: Prentice-Hall).

Hankuk, T.C. and Agarwal, P. (2003): When gains exceed losses: attribution trade-offs and prospect theory. *Advances in Consumer Research* **30**(1), 118–24.

Krishna, A., Wagner, M. and Yoon, C. (2002): Effects of extreme-priced products on consumer reservation prices. *Advances in Consumer Research* **29**(1).

LeBoeuf, R.A. (2006): Discount rates for time versus dates: the sensitivity of discounting to time-interval description. *Advances in Consumer Research* **33**(1), 138–9.

McCarthy, E.G. and Perrault, W.D. Jr. (2002): *Basic Marketing: A Global Managerial Approach* (New York: McGraw-Hill).

Moore, G.A. (1995): *Inside the Tornado* (New York: Harper Collins Publishing).

Molz, G. and Gielnik, M. (2006): Does the introduction of the Euro have an effect on subjective hypotheses about the price-quality relationship? *Journal of Consumer Behaviour* **5**(3), 204–10.

Narayanan, V.G. and Sarkar, R.G. (2002): The impact of activity-based costing on managerial decisions at Insteel Industries – a field study. *Journal of Economics and Management Strategy* **11**(2), 257–88.

Rich, S.A. (1982): Price leaders: large, strong, but cautious about conspiracy. *Marketing News* **25** June, 11.

Roggeveen, A.L., Xia, L. and Monroe, K.B. (2006): How attributions and the product's price impact the effectiveness of price partitioning. *Advances in Consumer Research* **33**(1), 181.

Schindler, R.M. and Kirby, P.N. (1997): Patterns of right-most digits used in advertised prices: implications for nine-ending effects. *Journal of Consumer Research* **24**(2), 192–201.

Simmons, C.L. and Schindler, R.M. (2003): Cultural superstitions and the price endings used in Chinese advertising. *Journal of International Marketing* **11**(2), 101–11.

Stottinger, B. (2001): Strategic export pricing: a long and winding road. *Journal of International Marketing* **9**(1), 40–63.

Suri, R., Anderson, R.E. and Kotlov, V. (2004): The use of 9-ending prices: contrasting the USA with Poland. *European Journal of Marketing* **38**(1), 56–72.

Further reading

Dolan, R.J. and Simon, H. (1997): *Power Pricing: How Managing Price Transforms the Bottom Line* (New York: Simon and Schuster). This book is aimed at practitioners, but has a wide range of genuine examples from major companies. The book is written in a lively and compelling way, and covers segmentation, promotional pricing, customary pricing, and indeed everything you need to know about pricing.

Marn, M.V., Roegner, E.V. and Zawada, C.C. (2004): *The Price Advantage* (New York: John Wiley and Sons Inc.). This is another practitioner book, written by three McKinsey consultants and based on experience with hundreds of companies. It provides a comprehensive and practical overview of pricing policies and methods, with some interesting case studies and examples.

Chapter 15
Advertising

Learning objectives After reading this chapter, you should be able to:

1. Explain the difference between the weak theory and the strong theory of advertising.

2. Understand the relationship between advertising, the marketing strategy and the corporate strategy.

3. Explain the relationship between advertising objectives and marketing objectives.

4. Explain the advantages and disadvantages of various media.

5. Explain how the theory of sought and unsought communication is applied in advertising.

6. Explain how people relate to television advertising.

7. Understand the role of music in advertising.

8. Explain the use of questions in advertising.

Introduction

To the lay person, advertising is often thought of as being the main activity of marketers. This is largely because it is far and away the most obvious of marketing activities: like the tip of an iceberg, it is the part of marketing which is most visible, although nine-tenths of marketing activities go on 'below the surface' and are not visible to the outside observer.

Advertising has been defined as a paid insertion of a message in a medium. This means that advertising is not messages on T-shirts, it is not messages contained in newspaper articles, and it is not messages passed on by word-of-mouth. It has a very specific and narrow meaning, in other words.

Advertising should be seen as part of an integrated communications strategy: there are things which advertising will do and things which it will not do. In general, it can create awareness, and move people closer to a purchase: it can help in positioning brands, and it can help in informing people about product attributes. It will not substitute for good product offerings, it will not persuade people to buy things they have little or no need for, and it will not cover up errors in other marketing areas.

How Advertising Works

How advertising works (and occasionally *whether* advertising works) has been a topic for debate in marketing academia for a number of years now. Part of the problem is that there is no way of telling whether something works unless one first defines what it is that one is trying to achieve. Since there are many possible objectives for an advertising campaign, ranging from increasing purchases through to reinforcing attitudes, there can be no single explanation for whether advertising works (Wright and Crimp 2000).

Preview case
L'Oreal

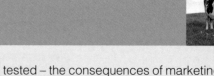

The beauty business is a surprisingly tough one. Charles Revson, the founder of Revlon, is famously quoted as saying, 'In the factory we make cosmetics, in the store we sell hope'. This idea that cosmetics are all about emotion and self-image is very much at the forefront of thinking in the cosmetics industry – and L'Oreal is no exception.

L'Oreal is the world's largest cosmetics company, with its headquarters in the Paris suburb of Clichy. The company started out in the hair-care business, having been founded by a young chemist who discovered a new method of dying hair which was less harsh and damaging than methods in use at the time. His daughter, Liliane Bettencourt, is reputed to be one of the world's richest women, even though she only holds a minority share in the business. The cosmetics business involves a great deal of chemistry – L'Oreal's research base employs over 3000 scientists. Since products must conform with strict health and safety norms, they are meticulously researched and tested – the consequences of marketing a dangerous skin or hair product could be disastrous for the company.

The problem for the company lies in creating effective advertising for their products. In general, L'Oreal's end consumers are unlikely to be very interested in the science of the products – their interest lies in what the product will do and in how their own self-image will be enhanced. L'Oreal's advertising agency, McCann Erickson, has been given the task of conveying the benefits of the product in a credible way without going too deeply into how the products work, at least in terms of not going too deeply into the science of the products.

McCann Erickson came up with the strapline 'Because I'm worth it!' This conveyed the impression that the products were high-quality, upmarket cosmetics, but also that the users of the cosmetics were valuable in themselves. This enhancement of self-image was clearly within the brief – but how could the company build on this and execute the advertising brief?

Two general theories about advertising have emerged from the debate. The strong theory suggests that advertising is a powerful force which can change attitudes and make a significant contribution to people's knowledge and understanding. The weak theory of advertising suggests that advertising can only 'nudge' people in the direction in which they are already moving; in other words, it reinforces rather than persuades (Ehrenberg 1992).

The main criticisms of the strong theory of advertising are first that there is little evidence to show that consumers develop a strong desire for the brand before trying it, and second, that the model only considers non-buyers who become buyers. In most

Figure 15.1

Strong and weak theories of advertising

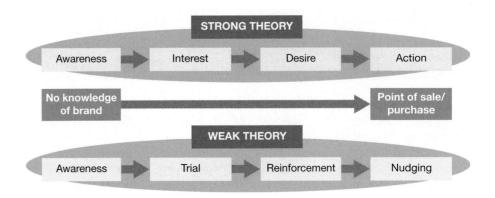

markets, advertising is intended to affect people who have already tried the product, either with a view to informing them about changes in the product, to remind them about the product or to encourage increased purchases of the product. The strong theory tends to be more prevalent in the United States, and it is of course possible that American experience is different from European experience: the weak theory tends to have more adherents in Europe. Research in FMCG (fast-moving consumer goods) markets shows that people are not usually loyal to one brand, and it is extremely difficult for a new brand to become established in the portfolio of brands which people buy. In these circumstances, most advertising is intended to improve brand loyalty and therefore defend the brand: this would tend to support the weak theory, because it implies that the main people to be affected by the advertising are existing customers for the brand.

Talking Point

If advertising is only a weak force, and doesn't persuade anybody, why is so much money spent on it by companies? Surely they wouldn't pay out billions of pounds, dollars, yen and euros every year just on the chance that it might work?

On the other hand, when was the last time you saw an advert and then went rushing out to buy a product? Have you *ever* been persuaded by an advertisement? Are advertisements like the bumble bee – in theory too aerodynamically unsound to fly, but in practice still able to?

Level of involvement has a role to play in determining the effects of advertising, and may also have a bearing on when the strong theory applies and when the weak theory predominates (Jones 1991). In the case of a high-involvement purchase, consumers are more likely to access sought communications (Blythe 2006, also see Chapter 8) and are likely to be more affected by advertising since they will be actively seeking out advertising messages. In the case of low-involvement purchases, consumers are less likely to seek out advertising and are therefore only likely to be moved slightly by the unsought communications around them.

One way in which advertising almost certainly does work is in reinforcing the value of companies' shares. Investors are affected by advertising as much as consumers (obviously, since they are all people), and research shows that advertising expenditures reduce the risk of stock falling in value (McAlister, Srinavasan and Kim 2007). This factor alone would justify a great deal of advertising expenditure, even without the potential effects on consumer attitudes and behaviour.

Developing an Advertising Strategy

The starting point for planning the advertising strategy is, of course, the marketing strategy. Knowing where the firm is planning to be in relation to its customers and the marketplace is an essential first step in deciding advertising's role in the process. It is

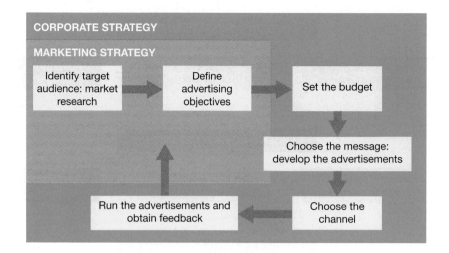

Figure 15.2

Stages in planning advertising

clearly not reasonable to take decisions about advertising without considering all the other elements of the marketing mix: advertising can be a crucial element in positioning the product, for example, but positioning also relies on pricing and product design.

Having developed a clear understanding of the overall marketing strategy, the advertising manager is in a position to identify the target audience. This is the group towards which the advertising is to be aimed, and usually corresponds to the market segment (although there are cases in which the advertising will be aimed towards people who influence the members of the market segment. For example, the market segment for textbooks is students, but promotional material is usually aimed at lecturers).

The next stage is to define the advertising objectives, or in other words decide how we would like the target audience to respond. The received wisdom is that advertising is intended to stimulate sales, but in fact this outcome cannot be guaranteed: advertising might be able to stimulate demand for a product category, but this does not necessarily translate into sales for the advertiser. It can just as easily translate into sales for competitors. A famous example of this was a series of advertisements for Cinzano vermouth, starring Leonard Rossiter and Joan Collins. Many viewers thought that the advertisements were actually for Cinzano's arch-rival Martini. Consequently, sales of Martini increased while sales of Cinzano remained little changed: as a result, the campaign was withdrawn. In general, managers should aim to set communications objectives rather than marketing objectives: raising awareness of the brand, repositioning the brand or correcting misconceptions about the brand are all reasonable objectives for advertising. Generating sales, increasing profits or improving customer loyalty may result from these communications outcomes, but cannot be guaranteed or measured realistically. There is more on measuring advertising effectiveness later.

The next stage in the process is to set the budget. Budget-setting has already been covered in Chapter 8: to recap, there are five basic approaches to budget-setting, as follows:

1 *Objective and task method*: the budget is set according to the tasks to be accomplished.

2 *Percentage of sales method*: the budget is set as a proportion of the company turnover.

3 *Comparative parity*: competitors' spending is matched in proportion to relative market share.

4 *Marginal approach*: spending continues up to the point where further spending will not generate extra sales.

Figure 15.3

Setting advertising budgets

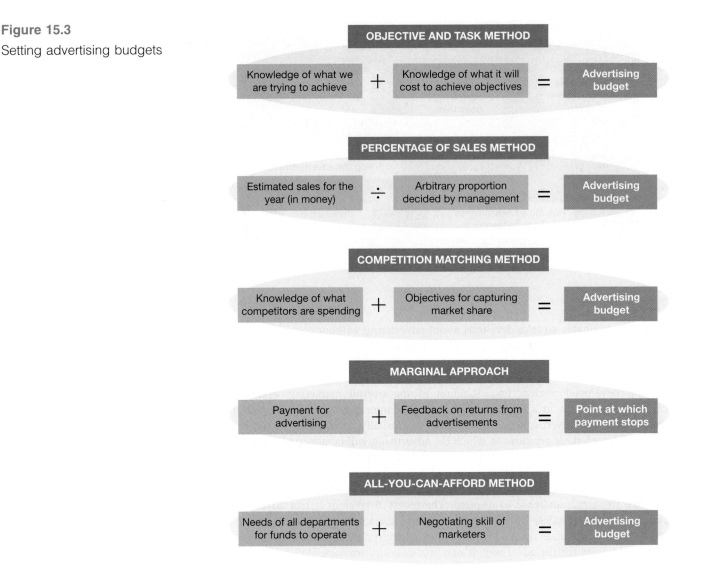

5 *All you can afford*: the budget is set through a process of negotiation with finance directors and colleagues from other departments.

These approaches are not necessarily mutually exclusive, and sometimes marketers will switch (or be forced to switch) from one to the other.

The budget has to reach a certain minimum level, because there is a great deal of advertising clutter around: no matter how creative the copywriters and artists are, a certain amount of money has to be spent in order to be heard at all.

Choosing the message is the next stage. Writing appropriate copy, or selecting an appropriate image, means selecting a communication platform which will appeal to the target audience as well as selecting a message which will result in the response the firm is hoping for. Producing an appropriate advertisement is a creative exercise, but cannot be carried out without regard for the characteristics of the target audience as well as the characteristics and needs of the firm and its brands. The starting point is to decide on the advertising platform: this is the basic selling proposition which is to be used in the advertising. For example, a car manufacturer may decide to sell on a platform of reliability (as Volkswagen does) or on a platform of style (as Ferrari does). The platform

Marketing in Practice
David Ogilvy

David Ogilvy, one of the world's most successful advertising practitioners, gave the following guidelines for press advertising:

1 The message appeal should be of benefit to the target audience.

2 The appeal should be specific: evidence to support it should be provided.

3 The message should be couched in the customer's language, not the language of the advertiser.

4 The advertisement should have a headline that might:

   a Promise a benefit.
   b Deliver news.
   c Offer a service.
   d Tell a significant story.
   e Identify a problem.
   f Quote a satisfied customer.

5 If body copy (additional copy following on from the headline) is to be used:

   a Long copy is acceptable if it is relevant to the needs of the target audience.
   b Long paragraphs and sentences should be avoided.
   c The copy should be broken up, using plenty of white space to avoid it looking heavy to read.

d If the advertiser is after enquiries, use a coupon and put the company address and telephone number at the end of the body copy. This is particularly important for industrial advertisements where more than one member of the decision-making unit (perhaps from different departments) may wish to send off for further details.

Ogilvy's advertising career was meteoric – despite the fact that he had been thrown out of Oxford University for 'indifference' and had tried various careers including tobacco farming, door-to-door selling and even a spell in British Intelligence. As a founder and senior partner in Ogilvy and Mather he became a multi-millionaire, with clients such as Rolls Royce and Nestlé to work for. With such famous statements as 'People do not buy from bad-mannered liars,' and 'The consumer's not a moron, she's your wife. Don't insult her intelligence,' he trained several generations of advertising executives and changed the shape of advertising.

Ogilvy and Mather became the world's largest advertising agency. When Ogilvy died in 1999, he left behind three excellent books on advertising and some of the biggest ideas in marketing – among them the concept of brand positioning and of using consumer research in advertising design.

should be something which is important to the target audience, and also should communicate competitive advantages. For example, research shows that some types of appeal work better than others for specific audiences: cosmetic appeals (statements about the effects on appearance and smell) work better in discouraging young men from smoking than do appeals about health risks. The reverse is true for young women (Smith and Stutts 2003).

The message itself is likely to be focused through the brand (see Chapter 3). The brand personality will be a key element in this: the personality is used to focus the brand attributes and allow for self-expression on the part of consumers.

Choosing the channel is an extension of developing the message, because the channel is itself part of the message. The newspaper, TV programme, radio station or billboard location each convey their own image, which reflects on the products. For example, the French station Canal 5 (which was once owned by Silvio Berlusconi, the Italian Prime Minister) faced falling audiences. The station owners decided to increase the audience numbers by showing soft-porn movies and sleazy game shows: audience figures improved dramatically, but advertising revenues fell because advertisers did not want to be associated with that type of programming. Canal 5 eventually went bankrupt, which is a considerable achievement for a TV station.

Figure 15.4
Focusing effect of the brand

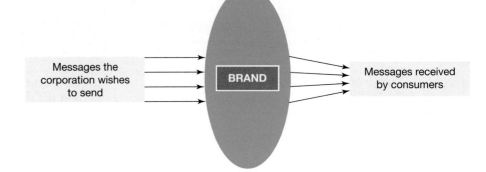

Looking at many advertisements, especially those for personal grooming, one might imagine that all advertisers ever think about is sex! Perfumes, after-shave lotions, hair gels, skin creams and even shampoo are all sold with a preponderance of semi-nudity and sexual innuendo. So what's the problem with booking these advertisements into shows with similar themes? Where do advertisers draw the line between what is shown in TV programmes and what they do themselves?

Looked at from the other direction, are regulators using double standards when they put prudish restrictions on advertising, while apparently 'anything goes' in the programming?

Finally, the advertisement should run and the company should collect feedback. Collecting feedback might involve carrying out formal market research, or it might involve checking coupon returns. Increases in sales are an unreliable method of judging advertising because too many other factors might come into play.

Types of Media

Advertising takes place through a number of media. More and more organisations are realising that advertising revenue can help to defray costs, so more and more media are being created. One of the criticisms levelled against advertising is that it adds to the cost of goods, because the advertising budget has to come from the prices consumers pay. However, advertising revenue subsidises public transport, virtually pays for our newspapers and commercial TV and radio, subsidises our theatres and cinemas and even contributes to our litter bins and bus shelters. The main media are as follows:

- *Print advertising*: newspapers, magazines, directories, freesheet newspapers.
- *Broadcast advertising*: radio, television, cable and even some pre-recorded DVD and video releases.
- *Outdoor advertising*: street furniture, billboards, posters.
- *Transport advertising*: adverts inside buses, trains, bus and train stations, and on the outsides of buses, taxis and (in some areas) trains.
- **Ambient advertising**: advertising on the risers of staircases, on the backs of bus tickets, on petrol-pump nozzles, in fact anywhere where the advertisement becomes part of the environment.

ambient advertising Advertising which becomes part of the environment.

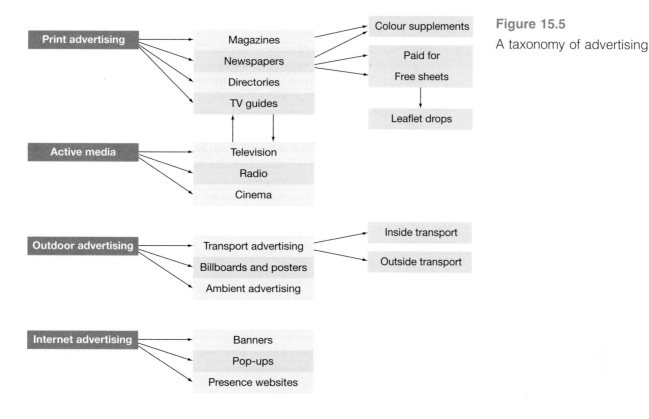

Figure 15.5

A taxonomy of advertising

- *Internet advertising*: banners, pop-ups, presence websites.
- *Cinema advertising*: both on the screen and inside the cinema.

Print advertising

Print advertising covers newspapers, magazines, technical press, directories and even leaflets handed out in the streets. It accounts for more than half of all advertising expenditure in the UK: several million advertisers use print media every day, and there are more than 12 000 publications in the UK alone. These figures do not necessarily relate to other countries, however: the World Association of Newspapers published a report in 2007 which showed that the Japanese are the world's biggest newspaper buyers, at 624 newspapers bought each day per thousand adults: (WAN 2007), whereas a BBC report stated that Italians buy only 104 copies per thousand adults per day (BBC 2006). Eighty per cent of Italians use only television for finding out the news, according to the BBC.

There is a huge range of newspapers and magazines, aimed at every type of consumer.

© David R. Frazier Photolibrary, Inc./Alamy

Print advertising has the following characteristics:

- *Permanence*. The print is permanent (unlike TV or radio) so the advertisement can be clipped and saved, or re-read. Newspapers tend to be thrown away soon after purchase, but magazines tend to be kept for long periods. In particular, magazines are often kept for months in doctors' waiting-rooms, hairdressing salons and even second-hand bookshops. Directories are often kept for years.

- *Variety of approaches*. This is particularly true of magazines. Magazines often target very tight segments of the market, so advertisers are able to reach very specific groups of people. In some cases, the market segment is actually defined by the medium: for example, *Cosmopolitan* readers are a very distinctive group which would be difficult to define except by saying that they are *Cosmopolitan* readers. Even newspapers attract specific types of reader, so that specific segments can be targeted easily.

- *Print media can be read on trains, in buses or on aeroplanes*. People rarely carry radios on public transport. In these circumstances the medium has the full attention of the reader.

- *Advertising success can often be assessed by checking coupon returns*. This is particularly true if the coupons are coded so that the individual periodical can be identified.

- *Statistics are usually available on sales, circulation and readership figures*. These are not necessarily the same thing – sometimes magazines are passed on to other readers, or placed in libraries and archives. This makes media planning easier. Also, many magazines collect data on the characteristics of their readers, and are able to tell potential advertisers what the demographic breakdown of the readers is and even what kind of purchases they make.

The advantages and disadvantages of print advertising are shown in Table 15.1.

Creative issues

Print advertising contains both sought and unsought communications (Blythe 2006). Sought communications are the classified advertisements, which are categorised according to product type or consumer need: these are the advertisements that people seek out. Unsought advertisements are the display advertisements, which are usually intended to be eye-catching. From a creative viewpoint, the approach to each advertisement type is very different.

Sought communications need to contain all the salient information needed by the reader to make a decision, including information about the firm's USP (unique selling proposition). This means that the advertisement can contain a relatively large amount of copy: the same is not true of unsought communications, i.e. display advertising.

When someone buys a newspaper, he or she has bought it for the news content, and is likely to flip past the display advertisements in the search for hard news. This means that the display advertisement will need to be eye-catching, and will need to get the main point across in a very few words, since the reader will almost certainly only retain a brief impression of the advertisement and will only remember the hook line (or strap line) at most. In terms of capturing the audience's attention, there are three key elements (Pieters and Wedel 2004), as follows:

1 *The brand*. If the brand is well-known already, it will tend to attract attention and direct it to the other two elements.

2 *The pictorial element*. Graphics are superior to everything else in capturing attention, regardless of the size of the picture.

3 *Text*. Text captures attention in a manner proportional to its size.

People are generally negative about the use of words such as 'probably', 'may' or 'could' in advertising (Berney-Reddish and Areni 2005). These words, known as 'hedges'

Table 15.1 Advantages and disadvantages of press advertising

Advantage	Explanation
Cheapness	Small advertisements can be placed very cheaply, and even a large campaign can be carried out relatively cheaply.
Adverts can be inserted quickly	TV stations normally need considerable notice before inserting advertisements. In Germany it can be over a year between booking a slot and the advert actually being aired; in the UK it would typically be approximately two months. Newspapers are able to accept advertising a day or two ahead of publication day.
Direct response is easy	Print advertising can carry coupons or order forms, unlike broadcast media. This makes mail-order purchase easier for consumers, and also provides instant feedback for the advertiser.
Targeting is easy	Because many magazines are aimed at specialist markets and hobbies, readers are likely to be interested in the advertising as well as in the editorial. Besides the ability to reach the exact audience who will be receptive to the product category, therefore, the advertiser is also reaching an involved audience who will read the advertising.
The press can always accept more advertising	Most European countries apply restrictions on the amount of advertising allowed on TV, and in any case airtime is limited because space must be left for programmes and there are only so many minutes in a day. The press need only add some extra pages to the publication.
Products are often grouped together	Classified sections in newspapers or specific trade sections in directories group products together. This means that consumers who are on an information search are likely to read all the advertisements, which means that advertisements can be smaller and cheaper without losing much impact.

Disadvantages	Explanation
Short life	This only really applies to newspapers. Apart from Sunday papers, which are often kept all week, most newspapers are thrown away within a few hours of purchase.
Poor print quality	Again, this applies to newspapers and to most directories. Magazines usually have high print quality, and can therefore carry high-resolution photographs and so forth.
Passive medium	The advertisements do not reach out to the reader in the way that a TV or radio advertisement would, and the medium is not interactive like the Internet.
Static medium	Because the advertisements are fixed, they are less eye-catching and engaging than moving advertisements would be.
Poorer literacy levels	In most of Western Europe and the USA, functional literacy levels are falling, and many people are not in the habit of reading. Many people watch TV news rather than read a newspaper, so circulation (and readership) levels have been falling for some time.

because they protect the advertiser from accusations of inaccuracy which might result from a definite statement, are often used in advertisements for products which may not work on everybody, for example slimming products. Other words, such as 'definitely', 'undoubtedly' and so forth (known as pledges) are also often viewed negatively because people simply do not believe them (Berney-Reddish and Areni 2005).

The creative aspects of the advertisement consists of two elements: the copy and the graphics. In many advertising agencies, the copywriter and the graphic artist work as a

Figure 15.6

Sought and unsought communications in print advertising

Figure 15.7

Creative briefs

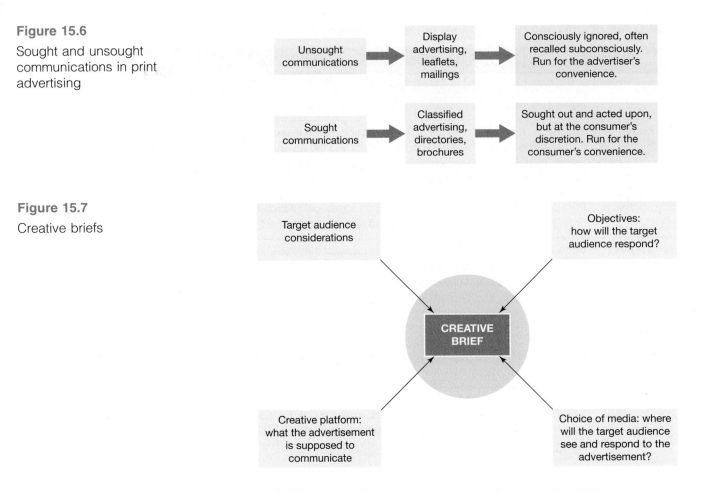

team, working on a creative brief given to them by the client. Creative briefs cover all the information the team needs, as follows:

- The target audience, its perceptions, motivations and buying criteria.
- What the advertisement is supposed to communicate, in other words the creative platform.
- Choice of media.
- The objectives of the advertisement, in other words the response expected from the target audience.

The creative brief is a contract between the client and the agency, so it merits careful reading before signing.

Copywriters are among the most creative writers in the world, because they need to get the message across in a very few words: some classic strap lines are as follows:

At 60 miles per hour, the loudest sound in this new Rolls-Royce comes from the electric clock. (Rolls-Royce cars: 1960s)

Heineken refreshes the parts other beers cannot reach. (Heineken beer: 1970s until now)

I can't believe I ate the whole thing! (Alka-Seltzer)

Freshly Squeezed Glaciers. (Canadian mineral water)

We're number two. We try harder. (Avis car hire)

All these slogans are clear, memorable and straight to the point, referring directly to the product's USP. However, in order to condense the message, copywriters often have to make cultural references: for example, a copywriter might use part of a well-known quotation, or may make a reference to a popular TV show in order to get the point across. These cultural referents may not cross borders very effectively, and indeed may not be understood even outside a specific region of the country.

Graphic artists have less of a problem in this area. Of course, what looks like a friendly smile to one person might look like a threatening grimace to another, and images of local places or buildings might not be recognisable elsewhere, but in general pictures are less of a problem than words.

If the client is a major one, the creative team will produce **roughs** or **scamps** for the client's approval. Sometimes these will be pre-tested with potential consumers (see Chapter 7). The agency will also produce a conceptual rationale which will explain how the advertisements are supposed to work and what the advantages of the approach are. Creatives in advertising see their managers and clients as being unprepared to take risks (El-Murad and Douglas 2003). This undoubtedly affects the relationships, but is understandable: creative people are likely to want to produce eye-catching, innovative advertising, whereas clients are likely to prefer something which will not cause offence to anyone.

roughs or **scamps** Draft advertising materials produced for a client's approval.

In the UK, advertisers will often seek the approval of regulatory bodies such as the Committee of Advertising Practice, which acts as a watchdog for the industry. The Advertising Standards Association is linked to the CAP and handles complaints from the public: it does not pre-approve advertising, but it does follow up on public complaints. If an advertisement causes offence, the ASA can ask for it to be withdrawn. Since the ASA has no statutory powers, advertisers can refuse to comply with the suggestion, but the ASA would then issue a media warning to its members, including newspaper and magazine publishers, which would effectively ban the advertisement from running. The vast majority of publications would not want to run advertisements which offend their hard-won readership.

Misleading advertisements can be forcibly withdrawn under the Control of Misleading Advertisements Regulations 1988, although this is rarely necessary since the ASA and CAP between them maintain effective control over offenders.

Active media: TV, radio and cinema

Radio, TV and cinema are powerful media because they are active – they actually do something. TV and radio are probably the most pervasive media in most countries – in Western Europe, TV ownership is almost 100 per cent, and many homes have several television sets. Radio ownership is at least as widespread. People watch TV while eating, doing housework, relaxing or even while entertaining friends. In some homes the set is rarely switched off. Significantly, the biggest-selling consumer magazines in most Western European countries and in the United States are the TV programme guides.

Because television advertising is an unsought communication (people rarely, if ever, switch on the TV in order to see a favourite advertisement) it works best for activating needs or providing information for the internal search. In most case advertisers are aiming to build the image of their product or firm, and to a large extent these aims can be met by television (McKechnie and Leather 1998). TV advertising has the advantages shown in Table 15.2 (Jefkins 1994). There are, of course, disadvantages of television as a medium. These are shown in Table 15.3.

Research at the London Business School shows that people do not necessarily watch the advertisements even if they are still in the room when the advertisement airs (Ritson 2003). The researchers identified a total of six behaviours which occur while the advertisement is on-screen: these are shown in Table 15.4.

Figure 15.8

Active media

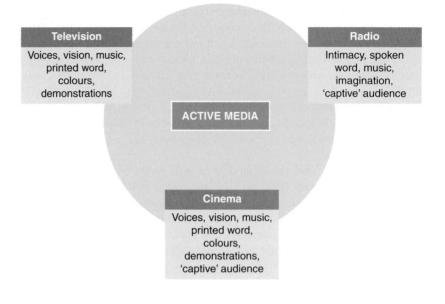

Table 15.2 Advantages of TV advertising

Advantage	Explanation
Realism	It is possible to show the product in use in a typical and realistic way. Because the audience can see how to use the product, and can see the kind of person who is using it, advertisers can position the brand appropriately. Often viewers are able to identify the social class of the person in the advertisement by their accent and clothing, which helps position the brand.
Receptive audiences	TV advertisements are often seen as entertainment: many are produced to high standards by world-class directors. Many advertisements tell a story, with surprising or amusing twists at the end.
Repetition	Advertisements can be repeated until sufficient of the audience have had an opportunity to see it. Agencies monitor this using published audience figures for each programme in which the advertisement appears.
Appeal to retailers	Most retailers have a strong belief in the power of television, and are more likely to give the product prominence on their shelves if they know a TV campaign is planned. Of course, the fact that the product has more shelf space might in itself increase sales, so there is no way of being sure that the advertisement actually increased consumers' propensity to buy.
Zoning and networking	In the UK and most other countries it is possible to localise advertising to the immediate TV region, or to 'go national' with advertisements which are broadcast throughout the network.
Links with other media	Further information, coupons and order forms can be printed in other media and the TV advertisement can direct people to look for them. Printing such items in TV guides is a useful ploy: this combines the strengths of both media.

Table 15.3 Disadvantages of television

Disadvantage	Explanation
Lack of selectivity	Television is a mass medium: it is hard to target specific audiences, even though some programmes appeal more to some people than to others. This means that advertisers are probably wasting the majority of their expenditure in talking to people who have no need for the product.
Impermanent medium	Once the advertisement has been aired, it has gone forever (barring repeat airings). It is difficult for viewers to take note of where products are available, or to note down telephone numbers and so forth.
Zapping and zipping	Remote controls allow audiences to 'zap' advertisements, either by muting the sound or by switching channels. If programmes have been recorded on a VCR or PVR, the viewers can 'zip' past the ads by using the 'cue' button. Zapping has been called 'The greatest threat to capitalism since Karl Marx' (Kneale 1988).
Clutter	In some countries TV advertising rates are so low that frequent and lengthy advertising spots are sold: the USA and Italy are examples of this. Viewers become bored with the sheer volume of advertising and frequently leave the room.
Audience fade-out	Audiences often leave the room while the advertisements are on, so although the ratings for the show might be high, the advertisements may not actually have been seen.
Cost	TV can be very expensive. Although it reaches a large audience, and therefore the cost-per-thousand-viewers might be low, the audience may not be composed of the right target group. The entry threshold is high: in the UK, which is admittedly one of the most expensive countries in the world for TV advertising, a nationally networked advertisement can easily cost £300 000 for one 30-second exposure.
Long lead times	Booking airtime can be a lengthy process, taking weeks or even months. Additionally, production times for a commercial are likely to be long.
Restrictions on content	Most broadcast regulatory authorities take a conservative view on what can be shown in TV advertising. Sexual imagery, swearing and some categories of product (tobacco and condoms being two examples) are absolutely banned (despite being common in programmes). Restrictions vary from one country to another – for example, in France it is illegal for retailers to advertise on TV, and in Germany toys cannot be advertised during children's TV programmes.
Dilution of audiences	As the number of available channels increases due to satellite and cable provision, plus DVD and VCR usage, the number of available viewers for any one programme has fallen. Also, high-quality programmes are spread across more channels, so that the average quality of programming has fallen. This has led to a reduction in time spent watching TV and an increase in other activities. This trend may be peaking out – there have been instances recently of cable TV channels going bankrupt, which indicates that there may be a limit to the number of channels audiences are prepared to support.

The first three activities in Table 15.4 are interesting in that the standard method of measuring advertising on TV, which is the people meter, would have shown that people were in the room and would therefore have assumed that they were watching the advertisement. In fact, in each of these three cases, presence in the room does not mean observation of the advertising.

Interestingly, there is research evidence that advertisements which are zapped are more likely to have a positive effect on brand purchase than those which are not (Zufryden, Pedrick and Sankaralingam 1993). This is presumably because the viewer has

zapping Using the TV remote control to avoid advertising messages.

zipping Using the fast-forward on a VCR to skip past TV advertising.

clutter Excessive advertising.

audience fade-out The tendency for TV viewers to leave the room or lose concentration when the commercial breaks occur.

Table 15.4 Behaviours in commercial breaks

Behaviour	Explanation
Social interaction	People often talk about their day discuss household problems or gossip while the commercial break runs.
Reading	Many people watch TV with a book or magazine at hand, to read during the breaks. Sometimes the reading will be a TV guide.
Tasking	The commercial break often affords an opportunity to load the dishwasher, clean the house, do the ironing, pay bills or make telephone calls.
Flicking	Jumping from one channel to another appears to be mainly a male activity. Flicking falls into two categories: almost random surfing across a number of other channels while waiting for the programme to restart, or alternatively going to a 'visit channel' such as a news channel for a specific length of time before returning to the programme.
Watching an advertisement	In many cases, advertisements are actually watched, and often commented on by the family members.
Advertising interaction	The final behaviour involves not only watching the advertisement, but commenting on it, singing along with the jingles, and even playing a game in which family members score 'points' by being the first to recognise the brand.

Figure 15.9

Activities in commercial breaks

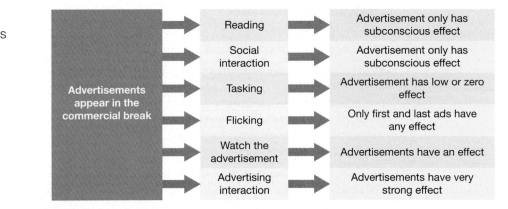

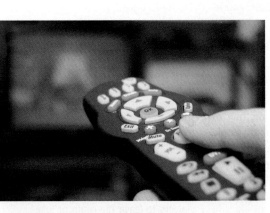

Zapping: a threat to capitalism?

to watch at least part of the advertisement and process the content before knowing that it is a candidate for zapping.

Fast-paced advertisements appear to have a positive effect on involuntary attention; in other words, they are more eye-catching, but have little effect on involuntary attention (they are no more likely to be watched actively) (Bolls, Muehling and Yoon 2003). Furthermore, fast-paced advertisements tend to focus people on the style of the advertisement, not on its content: people remember the advertisement but not the brand. Mood affects people's response to advertisements, so placing the advertisement in an appropriate programme may have a critical effect on its success or otherwise (Bakamitsios and Siomkos 2003).

There is a clear relationship between liking the advertisement and subsequent sales, but this is not always a positive relationship. Liking the advertisement seems to be related to whether the product is meaningful and relevant to the person at the time (Biel 1990), and there is evidence that advertisements relating to food and drink are more likely to be liked than are non-food advertisements (Biel and Bridgewater 1990). Liking is usually linked to a positive view of the product, which in turn is likely to lead to sales (Biel 1990; Stapel 1991). This situation is sometimes reversed when dealing with (for example) insurance products and the like, where the advertisement might contain shocking imagery as a 'cautionary tale' to show people what can go wrong if they do not have insurance. Messages which emphasise positive outcomes are more effective than those which emphasise negatives, however (Guangzhi and Pechmann 2006).

It may be difficult to deconstruct all the factors involved, since a truly unpleasant advertisement is likely to be ignored, so that the viewer is less likely to process the information cognitively. Such 'cautionary tale' advertisements are difficult to produce because the affective element is likely to repel the customer, whereas the cognitive element is likely to attract. Products can be placed on an approach-avoidance continuum, with products which are inherently attractive (food and beverages) at one end and products which are inherently unattractive and which are only bought out of dire necessity (pensions, life insurance) at the other (Wells 1980).

Talking Point

If people tend to 'switch off' from unpleasant advertisements, why produce them at all? Why show people scenes of crashed cars and devastated homes in order to frighten them into buying insurance? Maybe the school bully could frighten children into handing over their pocket money – but we're all grown-ups now!

Or maybe people have to be terrorised into buying insurance – otherwise they just keep putting it off until after they have been burgled or crashed the car! After all, in most countries it is a legal requirement to have car insurance – so doesn't this prove that people won't buy it unless they are threatened with jail?

Off-the-screen commercials (direct-response TV) appear to be a type of television advertising that breaks all the rules. These advertisements have high copy content, are extremely informative, and aim to obtain a direct response from viewers by getting them to call an order line and buy the product directly. In the United States, off-the-screen selling has gone a step further with the **infomercial**, a (typically) half-hour programme consisting of entertainment and news about a specific product. For example, an infomercial about a new type of fishing lure might show anglers using the device, show people catching fish, give tips about the most effective locations for using the lure and so forth. Infomercials are illegal on terrestrial TV in the UK, but they make up approximately 25 per cent of the programming on US cable stations (Steenhuysen 1994). Infomercials provide advertisers with enough time to inform and persuade people about the product's benefits: from the cable TV company's perspective, infomercials fill up air time which would otherwise have to be filled with paid-for programmes.

infomercial A feature-length programme about a product.

Radio advertising

Radio is the Cinderella of advertising, often ignored in favour of the higher profile of television. And yet, according to research conducted for Red Dragon Radio, commercial radio has a strong impact on people's lives. According to Red Dragon:

- Forty-four per cent of radio listeners wake up to a radio alarm.
- Twenty-seven per cent of people listen to radio in the bathroom, and forty-three per cent of the 15–24 age group do so.

Figure 15.10

FM vs AM radio

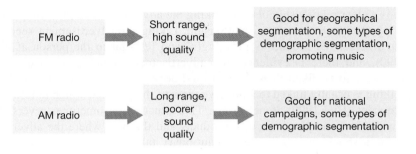

The pop of a champagne cork signifies a celebration to most Brits.

© Mikael Damkier |Dreamstime.com

- Seventy-two per cent of adult listeners listen to radio in the kitchen.
- Forty-four per cent of car drivers listen to the radio while driving.
- Forty-four per cent of employees listen to the radio in the workplace.
- Fifty-three per cent of adults aged 15–24 listen to their radios in the garden.

Most commercial radio is broadcast on the FM (frequency modulated) system, which gives short range but high sound quality. There are some commercial AM (amplitude modulated) stations which have a greater range but which give poorer sound quality. This means that the bulk of commercial radio is localised, and can therefore offer good geographical targeting. In the UK, independently-audited listener figures are compiled by the Radio Joint Advertising Research (RAJAR) organisation, which is jointly owned by the BBC and the independent radio stations.

The advantages of radio as an advertising medium are shown in Table 15.5. There are, of course, disadvantages to radio advertising. These are outlined in Table 15.6.

Radio advertising is often seen as a back-up medium for television, although in many countries it is a mainstream medium: for example, in much of Africa television coverage is sporadic and television ownership is low, whereas radio reaches everywhere.

Producing radio advertisements

Scripting radio advertisements is much like scripting TV advertisements, except that everything must be conveyed in the script. Sound effects become important as triggers for listeners' perception: the sound of waves on a beach and children playing signifies holidays, the sound of a champagne cork popping signifies a celebration and so forth. These triggers are culturally based: Muslims are unlikely to associate alcohol with celebrations, while many Australians have rarely visited the seaside. Radio requires imagination on the part of the listeners: in some cases this may actually be advantageous because it means that the advertisement is, in effect, more interactive (Ritson and Elliott 1995).

Music has a powerful role to play in radio advertising. It attracts listeners' attention and also helps position the brand by providing linking value – in other words, it helps the listener to make sense of the world (Cova 1997). It has been argued that pop music is most effective in adverts where the brand being promoted also provides linking value (Shankar 1998). For example, clothing provides linking value, so presumably music would work well in advertisements for clothes retailers.

Table 15.7 shows some ideas for writing slogans which will stick in the mind.

Questions are powerful in scriptwriting: a question tends to force the listener to think, in an attempt to find the answer. Questions can also contain assumptions which the listener does not query because he or she is distracted by the question itself. For example, asking listeners 'How can you remove those stale smells from clothing?' assumes that

Table 15.5 Advantages of radio

Advantage	Explanation
Radios are cheap and portable	Most people own a radio, and most households own several: they are often taken on outings or to work, so advertisements can be heard in most locations.
There is no need to be literate to enjoy radio	The spoken word is understood by everyone who is native to the country. In many Third World countries, literacy rates are so low that radio is the main means of communication, especially in remote areas.
Live medium	Like TV, radio is active, so it commands attention better than newspapers or billboards.
Does not require the listener's sole attention	Radio is often listened to while driving, working, doing housework or engaging in leisure pursuits.
Hard to zap advertisements	Unlike TV, radios are not usually fitted with remote controls, so listeners are unlikely to zap the advertisements. Frequently, changing station is also harder than is the case for TV, so surfing is less likely to happen.
Can be localised	Because much, if not most, radio is FM, advertising can be targeted to a small geographical area.
Can be targeted to different segments at different times of day	Workers listen for time-checks at around breakfast-time; drivers listen for traffic news on the way to and from work; housewives and factory workers listen during the day. The ability to target accurately has been called narrowcasting.
Cheapness and flexibility	Radio has much of the immediacy of TV, but at a fraction of the cost: in particular, production costs of radio advertisements are tiny compared with TV production costs.
Intimacy of the medium	People listen to the radio in a relaxed and often private location. Radio is more like a friend than an advertising medium – it is listened to in bed, in the bathroom, while driving or while at home.

Table 15.6 Disadvantages of radio

Disadvantage	Explanation
Audio medium only	This means that it is impossible to show the product, even as a static picture.
Relies heavily on audience imagination	Because audiences need to contribute a great deal to the joint development of knowledge, there is a greater emphasis on individual perception and consequently the advertiser has less control over outcomes. This makes it difficult to position the brand, because the listener has greater influence than the advertiser.
Transient, impermanent medium	Like television, radio is impermanent: listeners would need to be ready with a pen and paper to take down telephone numbers or addresses, and this is unlikely to happen given the circumstances under which most radio listening takes place.
Inattention of listeners	Radio is often used as a background noise to make tedious tasks more tolerable – the listener is rarely giving the radio his or her full attention.
Low number of listeners	The number of listeners to any given programme is normally low compared with the number of people within range of the station, which is itself a relatively low figure compared with television or even national press.
Difficult to measure	Much of the effect of radio advertising occurs below the conscious level: the lack of coupon responses or telephone calls as a result of radio advertising means that advertisers find it hard to measure the effects.

Figure 15.11
Creating radio advertisements

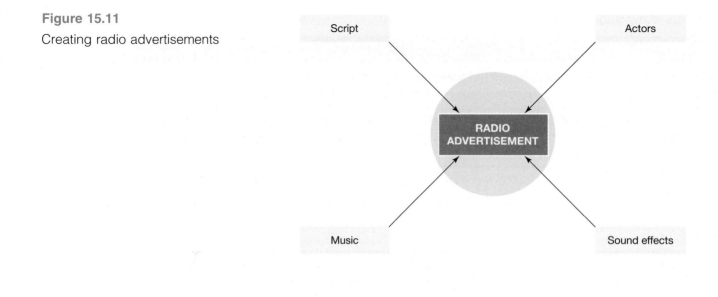

Table 15.7 Making slogans stick

Device	Explanation
Rhythm	Using a slogan with a natural beat aids memory. In the UK, Kwik-Fit car repairers used the phrase 'You can't get better than a Kwik-Fit Fitter', which has a natural rhythm: the phrase is almost instantly memorable.
Foregrounding	Bringing the slogan to the forefront of the mind can be achieved either by parallelism (an unexpected regularity, as in the Kwik-Fit slogan) or by an unexpected irregularity.
Alliteration	Using the same sound repeatedly creates a resonance. This does not necessarily mean using the same initial letter: the 'nb' in 'Canberra' sounds like an 'm', for example.
Assonance	The repetition of vowel sounds, as in 'Gillette – the best a man can get!' The assonance of 'Gillette' and 'get' make the slogan more memorable.
Rhyme	Some languages have more rhymes than others. Welsh, Spanish and Italian are particularly rich in rhymes: these languages also have a natural rhythm because the emphasis in the words tends to fall in the same place. German and Greek are less rhythmic, and have fewer rhymes.
Intonation	Stressing different syllables from those expected in ordinary speech can add to the deviation effect.
Puns	Homophones are words which sound similar but have different meanings, for example 'grate' and great'. Carefully used, these can have a high impact: foreign languages are a rich source of possibilities. Homophones work better in print than on radio, however.

Table 15.8 Main provisions of the Radio Authority Code of Practice

Provision	Explanation
Prohibition of some products entirely	Cigarettes, pornography and escort agencies are banned completely.
Endorsement by presenters	Station presenters may not recommend advertisers' goods, so advertisers cannot employ them to do voice-overs on their advertisements.
Advertisements must not offend against taste or decency	No racist, sexist or obscene language is allowed (even as a joke). Obviously standards of what is acceptable change over time: the Code of Practice applies the standards of the 'reasonable person', or relies on complaints from listeners.
Advertisements must not use 'knocking copy'	Advertisers are not allowed to make derogatory comments about rivals' products, even if they are true: they may not make comparisons between their own products and competitors.
Advertisements must not use sound effects which might endanger drivers	Sounds of police sirens, tyres squealing or sounds of crashes might distract drivers. This restriction only applies to radio – there is no problem with using such sound effects on television, since drivers cannot watch TV while driving.
Advertisements must not mislead the audience	Although a certain amount of 'puff' is expected, advertisements must not deliberately set out to deceive the listeners. This means that advertisements are expected to be reasonably truthful – and this especially applies to medicines, financial services and environmental (green) claims.

the listener's clothing smells stale, and the listener can easily accept this idea unquestioningly while still trying to think how to remove the smells.

Most questions asked in radio scripts are rhetorical: asking listeners 'Would you like to save money on car insurance?' does not really invite a 'No' answer. Listeners can easily assume that what follows (the advertisement for an insurance broker) will solve the problem for them.

In the UK, radio advertising is regulated by the Radio Authority Code of Practice, in addition to the advertising industry regulators mentioned earlier. The main provisions of the Code are shown in Table 15.8.

Because radio advertisements are quick to produce, and air time is usually readily available, they can be used for emergency advertising or for advertising that is timely: for example, in the event of a sudden snowstorm, advertisements for weather-related products can be aired.

Cinema advertising

For many years the cinema was the only visual advertising medium. Television meant that cinema audiences declined dramatically in the 1950s and 1960s, but in recent years the trend has reversed. A combination of 'blockbuster' movies which have attracted audiences and the emergence of comfortable well-equipped cinemas in entertainment complexes has led to a resurgence of cinema attendance as part of a night out.

From the advertiser's viewpoint, cinema has all the advantages of television plus one other: it is impossible to zip, zap or leave the room while the advertisements are on.

Consequently cinemas provide an unrivalled opportunity to speak to a captive audience. UK Film Council statistics show that cinema attendances have risen from 34 million per annum in 1988 to 167.3 million visits in 2003: no small audience for advertising. Another factor in rising cinema attendance is the relatively poorer quality of television programming.

Typical cinema audiences are young people in their teens and early twenties: 56 per cent of cinema-goers are aged 15 to 24, although they represent only 18 per cent of the UK population aged over seven (Cinema Advertising Association 1997). The audience is also strongly ABC1 in socio-economic profile. In some Third World countries (notably India) cinema attendance is widespread because of the relatively low level of television ownership.

The medium is extremely flexible – cheap packages are available for local firms, using stock film to which a voice-over is added, while at the same time major corporations can screen their TV commercials on the big screen. In most countries cinema advertising is less regulated than TV advertising: in the UK, advertisements have to be passed by the British Board of Film Censors, but the restrictions are much less stringent than those for television, since the cinema audience has already been pre-screened.

Cinema is probably under-used as a medium. It accounts for only 0.5 per cent of advertising expenditure in the UK (Advertising Association 1998) yet it offers a relatively cheap way of reaching a key target audience.

Billboard advertising

Outdoor displays are the oldest form of advertising: such displays have been in use for thousands of years. Outdoor signs have been found in the ruins of Pompeii and in medieval towns throughout Europe. Probably the most ubiquitous and obtrusive of outdoor advertising media is the billboard. Most vacant sites in cities have billboards on them, and they appear on the sides of buildings, beside major roads, beside railway lines and even mounted on trailers and towed through the streets.

Billboards have the following advantages:

teaser campaign An advertising campaign in two stages: the first stage involves a message which in itself is meaningless, but which is explained by later advertisements in the second stage.

● *Low cost*. A billboard poster is relatively cheap to design and print, and the site rentals are also low.

● *Can be targeted geographically*. If the company wishes to reach a specific geographical market segment, billboards in that area can be booked. One site can be booked to promote a local retail outlet, for example.

● *Can be used seasonally for short periods*. Posters can easily be changed, so that the products advertised can be adjusted according to the season or to other changing circumstances.

Billboards are exceptionally useful for **teaser campaigns**. A teaser campaign is one in which an apparently meaningless advertisement is run for a few weeks, then another advertisement is run which explains the original one. Teaser campaigns work by using message intrigue: the observer becomes intrigued as to what the advertisement actually means, and is thus sensitised to look out for the answer when it finally arrives. Billboard advertising is also widely used during political campaigns, because the posters can be changed quickly as different issues come to the fore.

Because of their public nature, billboards can often be used to generate controversy. This has been the case (famously)

By permission of Joshua Benton

Harveytiles used a billboard campaign which many Christians found offensive – but it created controversy and thus a greater impact.

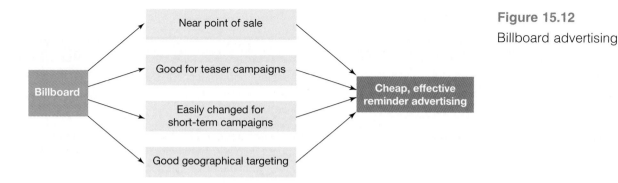

Figure 15.12
Billboard advertising

with Benetton, but in Zambia the Harveytiles company has used controversial bill-boards to advertise its roofing tiles. In many cases, the religious references in Harveytiles billboards have caused considerable offence to local Christian groups, and the company has attracted a great deal of criticism, but the posters remain and the result is that everyone has heard of Harveytiles in Southern Africa. However, in most countries billboards are among the least regulated of advertising media – in the UK, the only regulation is the Advertising Standards Authority, which of course only acts after complaints have been received (i.e. after the billboards have appeared).

Talking Point

We are often told that some advertising is offensive, or is offensive to some religious group or ethnic minority. Yet advertising has to cut through the clutter and be noticed – what better way than to be shocking? And anyway, in a pluralist society it is really very difficult to produce advertising which offends no-one: if we were really strict about this, there would be no advertising for alcoholic drinks, no advertising for cosmetics, no advertising for many movies, and no advertising even for tea or coffee, because all of these products are prohibited by one religious sect or another.

So why not go the whole hog, and produce *really* offensive advertisements? Why not have everyone reeling in horror at what is on the billboard? In short, why not produce advertisements that shock people all the time?

Advertising folklore has it that two-thirds of consumer decision-making takes place immediately before the purchase, at the point of sale (Brierley 1995). Billboards are often used as a last reminder before purchasing, which is why they are widely used to advertise frequently purchased items such as soft drinks and snacks. The disadvantages of billboard advertising are as shown in Table 15.9.

Billboards can be extremely effective as a support medium for other advertising. They can be used as reminders for advertising such as TV or radio, and can be used to direct people to websites: because billboards are a more or less permanent medium, a commuter (for example) can take note of a web address when returning home or going to work the next day (or next week).

Designing outdoor advertising

With the exception of inside transport advertising, outdoor advertising must use a minimum of copy and a maximum of imagery, because observers will only see it very briefly

Table 15.9 Disadvantages of billboards

Disadvantage	Explanation
Limited capacity	Since billboards are read literally in passing, copy must be extremely brief and to the point. Often billboards can only be used as a reminder, or to direct potential customers to another information source (e.g. a website).
Difficult to evaluate	Audience figures are extremely hard to measure, because they may be walking or driving past, or be on a bus. Traffic counts help somewhat, but there is no way of telling how many of the passers-by actually looked at the advertisement.
Difficult to target	Segmentation by ethnic group might be possible in cities where such ethnic groups live in the same area, but segmentation by (for example) age would be impossible. A billboard on a main road is likely to be passed by people from all backgrounds and income levels.
Vulnerability	Billboards are often vandalised or defaced.
Noise	Passing traffic, crowded pavements or the problems of driving in a city centre will often prevent people from paying attention to billboards. Sometimes this can work to the advertiser's advantage, though: an advertisement for car air-conditioning might work well on a hot, dusty day.
Environmental restrictions	In many countries there are strict restrictions on the design, location and number of billboards. This is a response to the proliferation of outdoor advertising in some areas, where it has become an environmental problem, inasmuch as it obscures views of the countryside.

Anyone seeing this poster would know what 'you' means!

in most cases. Icons, symbols and indices play a large part in this (see Chapter 8), but there is a strong tendency to use stereotypes because this is the quickest way to get the message across. Whereas in most writing authors try to avoid being gender-specific, copywriters have little choice, because gender-neutral words are less appealing (DeVoe 1956). 'He' or 'she' would be interpreted as someone known to the reader, and 'you' of course means the reader. The famous World War I recruiting poster showing General Kitchener apparently pointing at the reader and saying, 'Your country needs YOU' needed to be interpreted by the observer – clearly an 85-year-old woman would know that the poster does not mean her, but a man of military age would know that it meant him (Myers 1994). This poster was highly successful, and was later copied by the Americans, using Uncle Sam instead of Kitchener.

Language can also be used as a sign. Using French words in an English-speaking country can convey an image of chicness and sophistication which goes beyond the meaning of the slogan itself. Phrases such as 'Je ne sais quoi' or 'Savoir-faire' are in common use, at least in Britain, so most people would understand them. In Australia, Aboriginal words such as 'corroboree' would convey an Australian image: some Australian words (such as 'barbie') would convey an Australian image to British people, whereas the equivalent South African word for a barbecue (braai) would not be understood. Americans, on the other hand, would probably associate 'barbie' with Mattel's Barbie doll.

Use of accent (different pronunciation) or dialect (different words) can also convey impressions of wealth, of solid down-to-earth character, of traditional values, of youth, and of modern go-getting attitudes. Accent can be conveyed by different spellings for common words, and in some cases standard spelling for dialect words already exist. This foregrounds the information and makes the communication more noticeable as well as

E-Marketing in Practice
The London Underground

In the London Underground posters are erected on the tunnel walls opposite the platforms. In deep-level tunnels there is no opposite platform, and the tunnels are relatively small (unlike the cut-and-cover stations on the Paris Metro, for example). This means that there are no distractions, and the posters are near enough for passengers to read them while they wait for their trains.

Although the Tube runs trains very frequently, passengers often have time to read as much as 1000 words of copy. Advertisements in the deep-level Tube lines have therefore taken on a life of their own – they have story lines and intriguing beginnings and endings. The history of Jack Daniels whiskey, the story of Henry VIII, or the process of making cheeses have all appeared at one time or another. Copywriters can at last let themselves go, because Tube travellers (over 4 million of them every day) are more than happy to have something to look at other than their fellow-passengers!

more memorable. Advertisements using accent are common in the UK, perhaps because of the wide range of accents and dialects.

Transport Advertising

Transport advertising falls into two categories: inside transport and outside transport. Inside transport advertising is carried inside trains, buses, railway stations and bus stations. It provides travellers with something to look at, and is unusual in that it can use a great deal more copy than any other form of unsought communication.

Advertising on stations and inside trains is more tightly targeted than advertising in the street because it will be seen predominantly by commuters and tourists (at least in London, Paris, Athens or other major cities). As with billboards, zoning is possible to an extent, but specific campaigns can be aimed at a commuter audience. For example, the UK charity, the Samaritans, which has an emergency helpline for people who are depressed or suicidal, ran a highly-successful campaign aimed at commuters. Posters on bus stops and stations in the suburbs read, 'Can't face going to work? Call the Samaritans'. Posters in city-centre locations read, 'Can't face going home? Call the Samaritans'.

On public transport, people often try to avoid eye contact with their fellow passengers: this means that advertisements are likely to be read several times in each journey, especially when the trains are crowded and people are forced to stand, since reading a book or newspaper is much harder in these circumstances.

Advertising on the outsides of buses, taxis and trains has much the same advantages as billboard advertising, except that this time it is the medium that moves, while the audience may or may not be static. Advertisements low down on the backs of buses are at eye level for any motorists following the bus, so this is a good location for advertising anything to do with cars, from tyre fitting to insurance. In some cities it is possible to have whole buses painted with the company's design: this is called **livery**. Taxis often carry advertising, and a recent development in some UK cities is the bicycle rickshaw, which gives free rides to passengers but carries advertising. The advertising fees are enough to cover provision of the service.

livery Painting a public-transport vehicle in corporate colours or advertising.

Liveried vehicles are eye-catching.

© Helene Rogers/Alamy

Airborne media

Airships, blimps, banner-towing, hot-air balloons and even skywriting are all eye-catching methods of advertising outdoors. Airborne advertisements have the advantage of being visible over many miles, although the message is liable to be limited because of legibility from a long distance: in most cases only the brand name and perhaps a logo can be used.

Probably the best-known airship is Goodyear's. In itself, the airship conveys a message of unhurried freedom from care (Bounds 1994), but airships attract attention, so the brand name is seen by anyone the airship flies over. The Goodyear airship is often used as a camera platform at sporting events and major concerts. In these circumstances it gives triple value, because it is filmed as part of the coverage of the event, it is in constant sight of the audience at the event, and it is mentioned by the commentators every time the view switches to the camera on the airship. The cost of operating an airship is high – around £250 000 a month – but the impact is also high.

A cheaper alternative is the unmanned blimp. These inflatables cost around £20 000 and can be tethered above business premises. Unfortunately, they have become commonplace, and as a result have lost most of their impact: any advertising method which relies on novelty will lose its impact if it is overused.

Towing a banner behind a light aircraft or underneath a helicopter is another high-impact method of advertising. It tends to work best at locations where people are congregated in a long line (for example a beach) but the signs can be hard to read unless the aircraft flies too low for safety. As with any other outdoor advertising, the copy needs to be as brief as possible: confining it to the logo and a slogan is usually sufficient. Helicopters were widely used by the Conservative party during the UK's 2005 General Election.

In 1919, a former Royal Flying Corps major called Jack Savage bought a war-surplus fighter aircraft and fitted smoke canisters to it. He then sold his services to major companies as a skywriter: he would fly in patterns which spelled out messages. The messages were sometimes a mile or more long, written in smoke against the sky. Skywriting became popular because it is extremely eye-catching: Savage wrote 'Persil', 'Castrol' and 'Daily Mail' over the skies of London, and wrote 'Hello USA' on a visit to New York in 1922.

Skywriting has fallen out of fashion in recent years, and has been banned in several countries (including the UK) because of the risk of collisions between aircraft. The medium is not, of course, permanent: Savage's message to New York only lasted 10 minutes. On the other hand, the message can be read by a very large number of people – skywriting over cities such as London or New York would reach millions of people and would certainly be eye-catching.

Hot-air balloons have proved to be extraordinarily effective for corporate advertising. The balloons can be made in the shape of the product (provided the product is a suitable shape, of course) and the balloons are often seen at displays or competitive events which draw large crowds. The main drawback of hot-air balloons is that they are extremely affected by adverse weather conditions, so that their use is seasonal at best, and unreliable at worst.

Aerial message are very prominent.

At present, there is little or no academic research into flying media. The only regulation on flying media is that imposed by air traffic control regulations and Civil Aviation inspectors, whose concern is safety not advertising appropriateness – for example, aircraft are not allowed to fly within 500 feet of the ground or of any group of people, which

Marketing in Practice
Baconinflate

Baconinflate Ltd has been in the outdoor advertising business for 22 years. Based 60 miles from London, the company can offer anything that inflates – with your company logo on it.

Baconinflate offer blimps, temporary inflatable event stations, air-powered sculptures, inflatable Santa Clauses and Frankenstein's Monsters, inflatable polar bears, and even an Event Tower, which is a 30-foot-high inflatable with a TV camera on top, offering a panoramic view of the event. The company even offer a service for obtaining the necessary planning permissions from the Civil Aviation Authority and local government planning departments.

The company's own graphics department will transfer corporate logos onto any inflatable, matching the colours exactly. Baconinflate customers include blue chip companies such as Ford, BT, Renault, Sainsbury's and Royal Jordanian Airlines, but the company also offers its services to smaller companies such as car dealers, conservatory suppliers and retailers.

The problem for Baconinflate is that inflatables are becoming more and more commonplace, and thus are losing their impact: the company has to keep thinking up new ideas to make inflatables exciting.

naturally affects the legibility of the copy. The effectiveness of flying media is therefore highly debatable, although such an eye-catching medium is likely to be effective.

Ambient advertising

Traditional marketing communications techniques are becoming less effective as markets fragment, costs increase, audiences diminish and clutter worsens (Evans, O'Malley and Patterson 1996). Therefore, new routes for communicating with customers and consumers are being sought.

Ambient advertising is somewhat difficult to define, although plenty of examples of it are around: in general, it is advertising which becomes part of the environment, where the message becomes the medium. For example, for one campaign an underarm deodorant manufacturer arranged to replace the hanging straps in London Underground carriages with empty bottles of the deodorant. Strap-hanging commuters are acutely aware of underarm odours, and holding onto the bottles instead of the usual straps meant that they had already assumed the position one uses when applying the deodorant. Another development is the invention of a device which converts shop windows into loudspeakers so that window can 'talk' about the products on display (Grapentine 2003).

Ambient advertising offers the following advantages:

● It is often cheaper than sales promotions, and when used near the point of purchase gives a good incentive without the loss of profit associated with sales promotion discounts.

● Well-executed ambient campaigns enhance brand image and cut through clutter.

● Novel ambient campaigns often create press coverage: some ambient campaigns are designed with this in mind.

● They are very effective for activating needs.

Ambient advertisers need to consider the relationship between the medium being used, the advertised product or service and the proximity to the point of sale, as well as the basic objectives of the campaign. Ambient advertising works best when it is either close to the location of problem or close to the point of purchase. For example, Kellogg's Nutrigrain bar was promoted as a snack for commuters who had missed breakfast, so Kellogg's arranged for advertisements for the product to be printed on bus and train tickets. Many travellers were reported to have bought the bars as a result, buying them from station newsstands or kiosks near bus stops.

Placing the advertisement near the point of sale might involve, for example, using petrol nozzles to promote goods which are available from the petrol station shop. Equally, nozzle advertising was used by Volkswagen to publicise the fuel efficiency of the Volkswagen Golf TDI, thus using a medium which is close to the problem.

Advertisements printed on eggs cause an impact at breakfast time, adverts printed on the rising barriers at car parks are guaranteed to make an impact, and art installations in city centres often attract audiences. Ambient media can be classified according to campaign objectives and proximity to the point of sale, as shown in Table 15.10 (Shankar and Horton 1999).

Consumers tend to exhibit little pre-purchase decision-making for low-involvement purchases (Foxall and Goldsmith 1994), and some studies have shown that 70 per cent of all decisions to purchase specific brands are made inside the store (POPAI 1995). Trolley advertising makes around 19 per cent difference to the purchase of specific brands (Shankar 1999a), which demonstrates the power of ambient advertising to nudge consumers. Table 15.11 maps ambient advertising against Ehrenberg's ATRN model of advertising effects (the weak theory) (Ehrenberg 1997; Barnard and Ehrenberg 1997).

Ambient advertising is difficult to measure. First, the creativity of some campaigns is such that no advance predictions can be made. Second, research into the effects of ambient advertising has been relatively small as yet, so suitable test instruments have not

Table 15.10 Classification of ambient media

Objectives of the campaign	High proximity to the point of sale	Low proximity to the point of sale
Strategic: designed to create long-term effects	Toilet walls (e.g. anti drink-driving campaigns).	Stunt ambient media designed to gain publicity: sky banners, skywriting, art installations, painted aeroplanes, risers on staircases.
Tactical: designed to create immediate response	Petrol pump nozzles, toilet walls, in-store floor advertising, supermarket till rolls, credit card vouchers, stair risers, supermarket trolleys.	Ticket advertising, supermarket till rolls, credit card vouchers, betting slips.

Table 15.11 Mapping of ambient advertising against the ATRN model

Stage	Explanation	Role of ambient advertising
Awareness	Consciousness of a new brand is followed by interest.	Consciousness is developed by a high impact, innovative campaign, e.g. replacing straps with deodorant bottles.
Trial	Trial purchase of the brand may occur, perhaps with the consumer in a sceptical frame of mind.	Ambient advertising close to the point of sale may be enough to nudge the consumer towards one brand rather than another.
Reinforcement	Satisfactory use of the brand will encourage further purchase, or even establish a habitual propensity to buy the brand.	Ambient advertising only has a reminder role to play at this stage, and may be no more effective than other advertising.
Nudging	Propensity to buy may be enhanced or decreased by the nudging effect of advertising – either the firm's own or that of competitors.	Ambient advertising is thought to be better than other advertising for nudging consumers, since it has greater proximity both to the problem and to the point of purchase.

been devised. Third, there is no industry-wide evaluation system: there is no estimating system to find out how many people picked up a particular petrol nozzle and therefore saw the advertisement, for example (Shankar 1999b).

In the future it seems likely that ambient advertising will grow. Although greater creativity is involved in developing campaigns, the impact is high and the cost is relatively low, especially considering the potential spin-off in terms of news coverage. Ambient advertising fits well within an integrated marketing communications approach because it both supports, and is supported by, other communications tools.

Internet Advertising

Internet advertising is distinct from Internet marketing, which also includes online purchasing, online market research and many other interactive processes. Internet marketing is covered more fully in Chapter 19.

Advertising on the Internet is usually seen as complementing other media, and even now advertisers are still struggling to learn how to use the Internet as an effective element in the marketing mix (McLuhan 2000). There is some evidence that people who visit a firm's website are more likely to visit its premises, and that a good website improves brand image (Muller and Chandon 2004).

Internet advertising breaks down into the following elements:

- **Banners**. These are small advertisements placed on host websites. The host website is often a free site, in other words it offers something attractive (such as stock market information) at no cost to the Internet user, but the site is paid for by banner advertisers. A banner advertisement usually carries a hyperlink to take the surfer to the advertiser's website, where more information (and often an order form) will be available.

  banners Advertising messages on websites.

- **Pop-ups**. A pop-up is an advertisement which automatically appears on screen when the Internet user accesses a site. Pop-ups are widely regarded as a nuisance, and software is available to block them, but advertisers continue to use them because people do occasionally respond.

  pop-ups Advertising messages which appear on websites.

E-Marketing in Practice
thisismoney.com

Thisismoney.com is a website run by the *Daily Mail*, the *Mail on Sunday*, the *London Evening Standard* and *Metro*. These newspapers are all part of Associated News Group, and the website is operated by Associated New Media, a subsidiary of the group.

Thisismoney.com provides news and views about all financial issues, from the stock market through to pensions advice. The site costs relatively little to run, because the journalists would be producing the stories for their respective newspapers anyway: stories are simply reprinted on the website. There is no cover price, no need to register to use the site, and no cost to the visitor – so how is this paid for?

The site is paid for in the same way as newspapers are paid for – through advertising. Thisismoney.com's website carries banners, pop-ups and hyperlinks to other websites where financial services companies offer their products. The site is highly lucrative as an advertising site, because people go there to seek solutions for their financial problems – also, the people who access the site are likely to be the wealthier members of society, who are (first) able to invest in financial products and (second) are wealthy enough to own Internet access, or be in jobs where Internet access is part of the job.

This highly desirable audience is channelled to the site where they not only have potential problems flagged up by the journalists, but also have the advertisers offering potential solutions.

---

presence website A website which is not interactive, but directs customers to another medium.

spam Unwanted commercial emails.

- **Presence websites.** Although these are growing rarer, presence websites are sites which do not contain any interactive features. A presence website usually explains what the company does, and directs visitors to a telephone number, email address or 'snail mail' address to find out more. Such sites really do not take advantage of the possibilities of the Internet.

- Email advertising. This can take the form of **spam** (unsolicited emails about products or services) or can be opt-in newsletters. Spam, like pop-ups, is regarded as one of the less desirable features of the Internet, and in the past spammers have experienced retaliation from disgruntled recipients of spam. Retaliation has taken the form of flaming (sending insulting messages by email), mail-bombing (sending large files such as telephone directories, book manuscripts or picture files to the spammer) or complaints to the spammer's Internet Service Provider (ISP). Opt-in newsletters are commonly used by firms with whom the Internet user already has a relationship – for example, a low-cost airline might send out special offers to people who fly with them regularly.

In the UK, spam was made illegal in 2003, but this only applies to UK companies: since most spam originates in the United States, the anti-spam legislation has had little effect. It has been estimated that spam accounts for two-thirds of all emails (The Register 2004). Spam creates problems for companies because it clogs email systems and wastes the time of employees – very little of it is relevant, but it takes time to delete the files.

Talking Point

There seems to be a great deal of interest in the ethics of Internet advertising, especially spam and pop-ups. OK, these forms of advertising are a nuisance to many people – but are they really more of a nuisance than, say, mailings through the letterbox? Or billboards which obscure the view?

The bottom line, surely, is that advertisers would not use these methods if people did not respond – so somebody obviously likes the adverts! After all, they must occasionally have something to offer – so what's the problem?

A recent development in Internet advertising has been the use of viral spam programs. Virus writers have been hired by spammers to develop viruses which will propagate spam messages through the address books of infected computers. In late 2004 such a viral spam program was used to promote a database of American medical institutions. Infected computers spread the spam around the world, with some users receiving five to 10 copies of the advertisement per day. Clearly such tactics are unethical, and will almost certainly be banned: the difficulty is that the Internet is largely unregulated, messages can originate anywhere in the world, and therefore legislation would need to be ratified by virtually every nation on earth if unethical practices are to be stamped out entirely. It may be possible in the future for ISPs to be forced to develop ways of filtering spam from unregulated countries, but in the current state of the art this is extremely difficult, and many ISPs would regard such measures as being counterproductive, since the whole point of the Internet is that it offers worldwide access.

Consumer Responses to Advertising

People respond to advertising on both an emotional and a cognitive level. If advertisements are more emotionally-based, people tend to remember them better (Williams 2003), but of course this does not necessarily mean that they are more likely to buy as a result. When people pay conscious attention to advertising at all, which may not be often, they will seek to process the information in some way. The more the person already knows about the subject, the less likely he or she is to rely on the advertisement for information, and therefore the less likely he or she is to make a purchase (Wang 2006).

Sometimes people become activists, and complain about advertising on a regular basis: according to research conducted by Volkov, Harker and Harker (2006), people can be categorised according to their responses to advertising as follows:

1 *Advertising aficionados*. These people tend to believe that advertising is in general a good thing, providing valuable information, and that it paints a reasonably fair picture and is essential for decision-making.

2 *Consumer activists*. These people are regular complainers, who complain to suppliers or via the media in an attempt to improve the lot of the consumer. They are campaigners, on a crusade to make things better for everyone. People who counter-argue against an advertisement show increased strengths in their attitudes afterwards (Rucker and Petty 2004), probably because they persuade themselves more than they persuade others.

3 *Advertising moral guardians*. Moral guardians believe that advertising is creating a materialist society in which people's baser needs are encouraged and which erodes the values of a decent society.

4 *Advertising seekers*. These people watch a lot of advertisements on TV and become expert on their content – for them, the advertisements are a form of entertainment.

The implication of this research is that people always respond in some way to advertising: the responses are not always positive, and do not always result in a sale, but people do process the information and it does have an effect. Even when advertisements have apparently failed to persuade, they often reduce certainty levels (Tormala, Brinol and Petty 2004).

Summary

Advertising is the most visible of marketing activities, and yet often the most misunderstood, even by marketers themselves. Advertising is, at the end of the day, a communications medium, with all that that entails. It can only be judged for its effectiveness in communicating, not in terms of its effects on sales, yet discussions of advertising (and evaluation of it) often centre around real or imaginary increases in sales as a result of the campaigns undertaken.

Advertising is essentially a creative exercise – at the same time, marketers need to consider the effects of the advertising on the population at large, as well as on the target consumers and customers. The many media which are available, and the new media which are emerging on an almost daily basis, place a premium on maintaining that creative thrust.

The key points from this chapter are as follows:

- Opinion is divided as to whether advertising is a strong force or a weak force, but it quite clearly is not able to persuade people against their will.
- Advertising fits within the marketing strategy, but also relates to the corporate strategy.
- Advertising is about communications objectives, not sales objectives.
- Print advertising is cheap and durable, but is a passive medium.
- Display advertising should be concise: classified advertising should be detailed.
- Television is engaging and versatile, but advertising is often zipped or zapped.
- People do not necessarily watch television advertisements even when they are in the room.
- Radio offers good geographical targeting.
- Pop music is most effective in advertising when the brand also provides linking value.
- Questions are powerful in communications because they force people to think.
- Billboards are cheap, are good for geographical targeting and can be changed easily.
- Inside transport advertisements are often read in their entirety.
- Airships often gain extra coverage because they are newsworthy.
- Ambient advertising works best close to the point of purchase.

Chapter review questions

1 What is the difference between the strong theory of advertising and the weak theory?

2 Why might a company switch from the objective-and-task method of budgeting to the all-you-can-afford method?

3 What is the main drawback of the proportion-of-sales method of budgeting?

4 What type of advertising would you expect a small service business such as a plumber to use?

5 How might television advertisers increase the number of people who actually watch the advertisements?

6 What advantages does radio advertising have over billboards?

7 Why do advertisements often use questions?

8 What are the main differences between inside transport advertising and outside transport advertising?

9 Why does ambient advertising work best when it is close to the problem?

10 Why might a firm use pop-ups, despite the fact that many people now block them?

Preview case revisited
L'Oreal

The company has a long history of using celebrity actresses and models in its advertising. Jennifer Aniston, Cindy Crawford, Jane Fonda, Penelope Cruz, Beyonce Knowles, Diane Keaton, Jerry Hall and Jennifer Lopez are just a few of the big names who have appeared in L'Oreal advertising. Recently, the 'face of L'Oreal' has been Andie MacDowell, famous for her role in 'Four Weddings and a Funeral'. In each case, the celebrity is someone who is glamorous, but at the same time is someone the consumer can realistically relate to. For example, Jane Fonda appeared for L'Oreal at the age of 68, to demonstrate the quality of L'Oreal's anti-wrinkle skin care products.

Using Andie MacDowell as the 'face of Revitalift', McCann Erickson created advertisements showing how the skin care products made her look younger. MacDowell was portrayed as a confident, fulfilled woman: in a few of the early advertisements, male actors were included as the romantic interest, but later these were dropped as being unnecessary to the message.

The strapline was also altered after research showed that people thought it was too 'money-orientated' and made MacDowell sound self-centred. The current strapline is 'Because you're worth it', which includes the consumer and increases the self-image enhancing aspect of the products.

Some campaigns ran into trouble. One featuring Penelope Cruz, in which the company claimed that their mascara made eyelashes '60 per cent longer' had to be withdrawn after it was revealed that Cruz had worn false eyelashes for the 'after' shot. In May 2007, the Therapeutic Goods Administration in Australia ordered L'Oreal (among others) to withdraw advertising of their wrinkle creams, on the basis that the creams were not as effective as claimed in the advertising. Other claims have been upheld by the Advertising Standards Authority, and in the United States a class action suit was brought against L'Oreal in California, alleging that Garnier Fructis hair strengthening products did not, in fact, strengthen hair at all.

Such outcomes are ever likely in an industry which is built on the premise that every woman (and man) can be beautiful if only they use the right cosmetics. Disappointment is likely to set in – but the fact remains that L'Oreal remains hugely successful, with a reputation untarnished by such accusations.

Case study
Vegemite

To Australians, Vegemite is more than just a salty yeast spread for their toast – it is a national cultural icon. Similar to the British Marmite (and not dissimilar to its main Australian rival, Promite) Vegemite is made from brewer's yeast, a by-product of beer manufacture: it is rich in B vitamins, which makes it ideal for vegetarians since the alternative sources of B12 are mainly of animal origin. Not that vegetarianism is very big in Australia – most Australians just eat Vegemite because it tastes good on toast or crackers.

Following the First World War, exports of Marmite from Britain to Australia were seriously disrupted: to fill the gap, Australian food company Fred Walker and Co. commissioned food technologist Cyril P. Callister to develop a replacement. In 1923, Vegemite was first registered as a trademark. Meanwhile, in New Zealand, the Sanitarium company began manufacturing Marmite and shipping it to Australia. As a way of combating this competition, Fred Walker rebranded Vegemite as Parwill (from 1928 to 1935) in order to use the advertising slogan 'If Marmite, then Parwill!' Not surprisingly, this attempt at humour didn't work, so the company reverted to the original name.

Trying to usurp the market leader (Marmite) was far from simple. Up to the reversion to Vegemite as the brand name, Parwill had only sold in Queensland: Fred Walker's problem lay in getting Australians to try his product. In 1937, the company ran a national limerick contest, with substantial prizes (including Pontiac cars). To enter, people had to prove they had bought Vegemite: having bought it, they would naturally try it. The resulting publicity, and the huge number of product trials, established Vegemite firmly in the Australian market.

The product received another boost just before the Second World War, when it was officially endorsed by the British Medical Association for its nutritional value. During the war, Australian soldiers were issued with Vegemite rations, leading to shortages of the product back home – the company was quick to point out the reason for the shortages, and rationed civilians on a strict per-capita basis. This had the effect of making Vegemite seem even more attractive and valuable – for soldiers, it was a taste of home, for civilians it was the hard-to-find elixir of taste.

The post-war baby boom created a whole new market, with Vegemite featuring as the vitamin source for the new little Australians. In 1954 the company produced a radio show featuring 'The Happy Little Vegemites', a group of bright, lively children modelled on the Ovaltineys, who had been used to promote British bedtime drink, Ovaltine, in the 1930s and 1940s. The Happy Little Vegemites had their own song, and the advertising campaign continued until the late 1960s, transferring to television along the way. Even now, most adult Australians can sing the Happy Little Vegemites song, and the phrase has even passed into the language – calling someone a 'happy little vegemite' means that the person is cheerful. The campaign was revived in the 1980s, following nearly two decades of emphasising the nutritional value of Vegemite, and continues to this day in some form or another. Nostalgia is an important part of Vegemite's success – each generation remembers it as a childhood food, and indeed some advertising has used famous people such as sports stars and entertainers to say 'I'm still a Vegemite kid'.

The strength of feeling towards Vegemite has resulted in some remarkable outcomes. In 2006, Melbourne newspaper the *Herald Sun* mistakenly published a story which claimed that Vegemite had been banned in the United States and that Australians were being searched for it on entry. The story may have resulted from a traveller's anecdote, but it was given wide credence and many Australians emailed President Bush's office to protest. Anti-American comments appeared on blogs and in letters to newspapers, and the *Herald Sun* encouraged readers to protest about the ban – with great effect. Despite official denials by US Customs, the rumour still persists that Vegemite was banned – although it is actually available in some speciality stores in the United States.

Vegemite has made very little impact outside Australia, even though the brand is now owned by American giant Kraft. This is despite the fact that the brand name is well-known outside Australia, due to its appearance in popular culture: Vegemite has featured in pop songs, comedy routines (notable Barry Humphries' character, Sir Les Patterson) and even in *The Simpsons*. Possibly the company has not made much effort to market the product elsewhere in the world (unlike other Australian products such as Foster's Lager), possibly there is a country-of-origin effect, since Australia is not renowned for its cuisine, or maybe the product is such an Australian icon the company wants to keep it exclusively for Australians. Whatever the reasons, with 21 million jars of Vegemite a year being sold, Kraft have a highly successful brand on their hands.

© Colin Underhill/Alamy

Questions

1 How has Vegemite integrated its communications campaigns?

2 What are the key features in Vegemite advertising?

3 How could Vegemite use advertising to enter overseas markets?

4 What would be the best media for promoting Vegemite?

5 How might country of origin be used to good effect in overseas advertising?

References

Advertising Association (1998): *Advertising Association Yearbook* (Henley: Advertising Association).

Bakamitsos, G. and Siomkos, G.J. (2003): Context effects in marketing practice: the case of mood. *Journal of Consumer Behaviour* **3**(4), 304–14.

Barnard, N. and Ehrenberg, A. (1997): Advertising: strongly persuasive or nudging? *Journal of Advertising Research* **37**(1), 21–31.

BBC 2006: *The press in Italy:* http://news.bbc.co.uk/1/hi/world/europe/4373775.stm

Berney-Reddish, I.A. and Areni, C.S. (2005): Effects of probability markers on advertising claim acceptance. *Journal of Marketing Communications* **11**(1).

Biel, A.L. (1990): Love the ad. Buy the product? *ADMAP* September, 21–25.

Biel, A.L. and Bridgewater, C.A. (1990): Attributes of likeable television commercials. *Journal of Advertising Research* **30**(3), 38–44.

Blythe, J. (2006): *Essentials of Marketing Communications*, 2nd edn (Harlow: FT Prentice Hall).

Bolls, P.D., Muehling, D.D. and Yoon, K. (2003): The effects of television commercial pacing on viewers' attention and memory. *Journal of Marketing Communications* **9**(1), 17–28.

Bounds, W. (1994): Fuji's spirits soar as its blimp is winner of a World Cup contest. *The Wall Street Journal* 21 June.

Brierley, S. (1995): *The Advertising Handbook* (London: Routledge).

Cinema Advertising Association (1997): *UK Cinema Audience Profile* (London: Cinema Advertising Association).

Cova, B. (1997): Community and consumption: towards a definition of the linking value of products and services. *European Journal of Marketing* **31**(3/4), 297–316.

DeVoe, M. (1956): *Effective Advertising Copy* (New York: Macmillan).

Ehrenberg, A. (1997): How do consumers buy a new brand? *ADMAP* March.

Ehrenberg, A.S.C. (1992): Comments on how advertising works. *Marketing and Research Today* August, 167–9.

El-Murad, J. and West, D. C. (2003): Risk and creativity in advertising. *Journal of Marketing* **19**, 657–673.

Evans, M., O'Malley, L. and Patterson, M. (1996): Direct marketing communications in the UK: a study of growth, past present and future. *Journal of Marketing Communications* **2** (March), 51–65.

Foxall, G. and Goldsmith, R.E. (1994): *Consumer Psychology for Marketing* (London: Routledge).

Grapentine, T. (2003): Window shopping. *Marketing Research* **15**(4), 5.

Guangzhi, Z. and Pechmann, C. (2006): Regulatory focus, feature positive effect, and message framing. *Advances in Consumer Research* **33**(1).

Jefkins, F. (1994): *Advertising* (London: M&E Handbooks).

Jones, J.P. (1991): Over-promise and under-delivery. *Marketing and Research Today* (November), 195–203.

McAlister, L., Srinavasan, R. and Kim, M. (2007): Advertising, research and development, and systematic risk of the firm. *Journal of Marketing* **71**(1), 35–48.

McKechnie, S. and Leather, R. (1998): Likeability as a measure of advertising effectiveness: the case of financial services. *Journal of Marketing Communications* **4**(2), 63–85.

McLuhan, R. (2000): A lesson in on-line brand promotion. *Marketing* 23 March, 31–2.

Muller, B. and Chandon, J.-L. (2004): The impact of World Wide Web site visits on brand image in the motor vehicle and mobile telephone industries. *Journal of Marketing Communications* **10**(2), 153–65.

Myers, G (1994): *Words in ads* (London: Edward Arnold).

Pieters, R. and Wedel, M. (2004): Attention, capture and transfer in advertising: brand, pictorial and text size effects. *Journal of Marketing* **68**(2), 36–50.

POPAI (1995): Point of purchase consumer buying habits study. In T.A. Shimp (1997), *Advertising, Promotion and Supplemental Aspects of Integrated Marketing Communications*, 4th edn (Fort Worth, TX: Dryden Press).

Ritson, M. (2003): *Assessing the Value of Advertising* (London: London Business School).

Ritson, M. and Elliott, R. (1995): A model of advertising literacy: the praxology and co-creation of meaning. *Proceedings of the European Marketing Association Conference*. Paris: ESSEC.

Rucker, D.D. and Petty, R.E. (2004): When counter arguing fails: effects on attitude strength. *Advances in Consumer Research* **31**(1), 87.

Shankar, A. (1998): Adding value to the ads? On the increasing use of pop music in advertising. *Proceedings of the Academy of Marketing Conference*. Sheffield: Sheffield Business School.

Shankar, A. (1999a): Ambient media: advertising's new opportunity? *International Journal of Advertising* **18**.

Shankar, A. (1999b): Advertising's imbroglio. *Journal of Marketing Communications* **5**(1), 1–17.

Shankar, A. and Horton, B. (1999): Ambient media: advertising's new media opportunity. *International Journal of Advertising* **18**(3), 305–22.

Smith, K.H. and Stutts, M.A. (2003): Effects of short-term cosmetic versus long-term health fear appeals in anti-smoking advertisements on the smoking behaviour of adolescents. *Journal of Consumer Behaviour* **3**(2), 155–77.

Stapel, J. (1991): Like the advertisement, but does it interest me? *ADMAP* April.

Steenhuysen, J. (1994): Adland's new billion-dollar baby. *Advertising Age* **65**(15), pS-8-S-14, 2.

The Register (2004): htttp://www.theregister.co.uk.

Tormala, Z.L., Brinol, P. and Petty, R.E. (2004): Hidden effects of persuasion. *Advances in Consumer Research* **31**(1), 81.

Volkov, M., Harker, M. and Harker, D. (2006): People who complain about advertising: the aficionados, guardians, activists and seekers. *Journal of Marketing Management* **22**(3/4), 379–405.

WAN annual survey of world press trends (2007): World Newspaper Congress and 15th World Editors Forum, Göteborg, Sweden.

Wang, S.-L.A. (2006): The effects of audience knowledge on message processing of editorial content. *Journal of Marketing Communications* **12**(4), 281–96.

Wells, W.D. (1980): Liking and sales effectiveness: a hypothesis. *Topline* **2**(1).

Williams, P. (2003): The impact of emotional advertising appeals on consumer implicit and explicit memory: an accessibility/diagnosticity perspective. *Advances in Consumer Research* **30**(1), 88.

Wright, L.T. and Crimp, M. (2000): *The Marketing Research Process* (London: Prentice-Hall).

Zufryden, F.S., Pedrick, J.H. and Sankaralingam, A. (1993): Zapping and its impact on brand purchase behaviour. *Journal of Advertising Research* **33** (January–February), 58–66.

Further reading

Ogilvy, D. (1985): *Ogilvy on Advertising* (New York: Random House). Straightforward, practical analysis and suggestions about how to advertise, from the legendary David Ogilvy.

Ogilvy, D. (1988): *Confessions of an Advertising Man* (London: Southbank Publishing). This is Ogilvy's autobiography, a fascinating look at how David Ogilvy almost accidentally became one of the world's top advertising men.

Cook, G. (1992): *The Discourse of Advertising* (London: Routledge). This is an academic text about advertising as communication: the interplay between advertising and other texts around them, with the people who make and see them, and the interactions between advertising and society are contained in this text.

Chapter 16
Public relations and sponsorship

Learning objectives After reading this chapter, you should be able to:

1 Explain the difference between PR and spin-doctoring.

2 Explain how corporate reputation affects stock market valuations.

3 Demonstrate the internal role of public relations.

4 Describe how to organise a crisis team.

5 Explain the role of outside agencies in public relations.

6 Explain the relationship between sponsorship and advertising.

Introduction

corporate reputation The overall image of the organisation.

Public relations is about making the world feel good about the organisation and its products. This is partly about establishing a **corporate reputation**, and partly about establishing the firm's activities in a positive way in people's minds. Changing people's attitudes about the company can be a long-drawn-out process (see Chapter 4), but well-managed public relations lead to very real benefits to the firm. PR should not be confused with spin-doctoring: spin-doctoring is about covering up bad news and twisting the truth in a crisis. PR is about ensuring that the company does the right things at the right times, and ensures that its publics know what it is doing.

Sometimes PR is seen as being solely the responsibility of the public relations department, but in fact everyone in the firm has a role in public relations: many of the firm's employees have direct contact with people outside the organisation during their working day, but in any case everybody goes home and talks to friends and family about the company's activities.

Corporate reputation management goes a step beyond PR in that it involves a web of interactions between members of the corporation's publics (see p. 516), as well as simply dealing with outbound communication from the firm itself.

PR and External Communication

Public relations or PR is the management of corporate image through the management of relationships with the organisation's publics. Hayward (1998) offered an alternative definition, as follows.

Those efforts used by management to identify and close any gap between how the organisation is seen by its key publics and how it would like to be seen.

PR has more than just a role in defending the company from attack and publicising its successes. It has a key role in relationship marketing, since it is concerned with building a

Preview case
Friends of the Earth

The environment has become the hot issue of the early 21st century, yet relatively few people realise that environmental concerns have been expressed for over 200 years. In the 19th century, people were concerned about the rising population: Thomas Malthus published several essays on the topic, pointing out that population grows exponentially while food supply only grows arithmetically – in other words, population expands much faster than the food supply, and starvation would result. In the middle of the century the first sewage schemes were installed in London to improve the environment. In the 20th century, many books were published on environmental issues – in 1953, the sci-fi book *The Space Merchants* by Pohl and Kornbluth appeared, in which the villains were big business and the good guys were the conservationists. In 1962, Rachel Carson published *Silent Spring*, a best-selling book on the effects of DDT on wildlife.

So how is it that the environment is suddenly on the agenda, after 200 years of being largely ignored by an indifferent world? Much of the credit for raising the profile of the environment in the public consciousness can be given to pressure groups such as Friends of the Earth.

Friends of the Earth (conveniently abbreviated to FOE) is an environmental lobby group which started in the United States but which is now worldwide. FOE started out in 1969, campaigning for more recycling: the UK branch of FOE famously dumped 1500 bottles outside the Schweppes factory to emphasise the waste involved in using non-returnable bottles (these had recently been introduced in the UK, replacing bottles which were returned for reuse). FOE have been at the sharp end of campaigning ever since: they are probably the UK's leading pressure group on environmental issues.

Of course, it is one thing to dump bottles outside soft-drinks factories, and quite another to create the kind of cultural sea-change needed to make the general public stop buying drinks in disposable containers. Recycling, reducing carbon emissions and reducing waste are difficult areas to gain consumer acceptance – for many people, they imply a substantial reduction in standard of living, so getting people to act is difficult. There are three main elements in creating environmental change: getting businesses to change what they are doing, getting government to pass suitable legislation so that everyone is on a level playing field, and getting the general public to act appropriately. For FOE, this is a major public relations exercise.

© Paul Doyle/Alamy

Figure 16.1

Publicity, PR and press relations

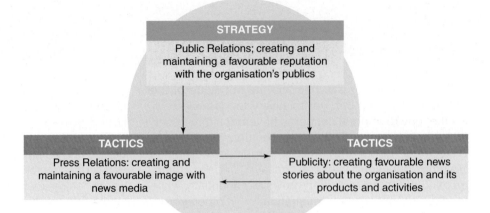

long-term image rather than gaining a quick sale. There is a strategic relationship between publicity, PR, and press relations; see Figure 16.1. PR occupies the overall strategic role in the relationship.

Many firms use PR solely for crisis management, seeing it either as a tool for complaint handling (usually by employing somebody with a nice smile and a friendly voice to handle complaints), or as a tactical tool, whereby the firm only formulates a plan for handling problems after things have gone wrong. This is a fire-fighting or reactive approach to public relations, and is generally regarded as being far less effective than a proactive approach which seeks to avoid problems arising.

PR managers have the task of coordinating all those activities which make up the public face of the organisation, and will have some or all of the following tasks to handle.

- Organising Press conferences
- Running staff training workshops
- Organising social events
- Handling incoming complaints or criticism
- Grooming senior management for TV or Press interviews
- Moulding the internal culture of the organisation

PR people talk about 'publics' rather than 'the public'. This is because they are dealing with a wide range of people, all with differing needs and preconceptions. The following publics might be part of the PR manager's remit.

1 Customers
2 Suppliers
3 Staff
4 Government and Government departments
5 Local government
6 Neighbours
7 Local residents
8 The general public
9 Pressure groups such as environmentalists or trade unions
10 Other industry members

In each case the approach will be different, and the expected outcomes will also be different. The basic routes by which PR operates are word-of-mouth, Press and TV news stories, and personal recommendation. The aim of good PR is to put the name of the firm and its products into people's minds in a positive way.

PR is not advertising, because it is not directly paid for. Advertising can be both informative and persuasive, but PR can only be used for conveying information or for placing the company before the public eye in a positive way. PR does not generate business directly, but achieves the company's long-term objectives by creating positive feelings. The ideal outcome is to give the world the impression that this is 'a good firm to do business with'. In some cases this will result in more sales, in other cases it might result in reduced costs (for example less absenteeism, less time wasted dealing with complaints and less money spent compensating disgruntled customers).

PR and marketing do not always fit together well: there is often a lack of fit between the information processing requirements of marketers and those of PR professionals (Cornelissen and Harris 2004).

Tools of Public Relations

PR people use a number of different ways of achieving their aims. The list in Table 16.1 is by no means comprehensive, but does cover the main tools available to PR managers.

Of these, the press release and sponsorship are probably the most important.

Table 16.1 Tools of PR

Tool	Description and examples
Press releases	A press release is a news story about the organisation, usually designed to put the firm in a good light but often intended just to keep the organisation in the public eye. For example, a community arts group might write to the local newspapers to tell them about a forthcoming performance or event. The newspaper might run this on its 'what's on' page, or might use it as a human-interest story about how community arts organisations benefit the community.
Sponsorship	Sponsorship of events, individuals or organisations is useful for creating favourable publicity. For example, many firms sponsor sporting events, putting the company name in the public eye.
Publicity stunts	Sometimes firms will stage an event specifically for the purpose of creating a news story, for example a publisher might arrange a book-signing session involving a famous author. Such events are often reported in local news media: if the author is famous enough the story might even make the national news. This is less common in business-to-business markets, since mass-media publicity is of less value.
Word-of-mouth	Generating favourable word-of-mouth is an important aim of PR. For example, a firm might book seats at a sporting event such as the Wimbledon Tennis Championships in order to invite good clients. The clients are almost certain to talk to colleagues and friends about their day out, and will certainly recall the name of the company that provided them with the seat.
Corporate advertising	Corporate advertising is aimed at improving the corporate image rather than selling products. Such advertising is very common in the trade press, but occasionally appears in the mass media. British Airways have successfully used television to promote the company's image, aiming specifically at business-class sales: this is a rare example of using mass-media advertising in a business-to-business market.
Lobbying	Lobbying is the process of making representations to members of Parliament, congressmen or other politicians. For example, the tobacco industry has lobbied against banning smoking in pubs in the UK, and won a temporary success in that smoking was only be banned in pubs which serve food until a total ban was introduced in 2007.

Table 16.2 Criteria for successful press releases

Criterion	Example
Stories must be newsworthy, i.e. of interest to the reader.	Articles about your new lower prices are not newsworthy; articles about opening a new factory creating 200 jobs are.
Stories must not be merely thinly disguised advertisements.	A story saying that your new processing equipment is a bargain at only £23 000 is not news. A story saying that you have concluded a partnership agreement with a machine tool manufacture in Poland probably is, at least in the trade press. A story that you are financing a new training initiative for underprivileged teenagers is probably news in the national press.
Stories must fit the editorial style of the magazine or paper to which they are being sent.	An article sent to *Cosmopolitan* about your new machine tools would not be published. An article about your new female marketing director probably would.

A press release is a favourable news story about the organisation, which originates from within the organisation itself. Newspapers and the trade Press earn their money mainly through paid advertising, but they attract readers by having stimulating articles about topics of interest to the readership. Editors need to fill space, and are quite happy to use a press release to do so if the story is newsworthy and interesting to the readership. In a business-to-business context, the trade Press relies heavily on press releases, since industry news would be difficult to collect in any other way, but even the popular Press relies on individuals and companies to alert them to news stories. This is the essence of the press release.

The advantages of using press releases are that they are much more credible than an advertisement, they are much more likely to be read, and the space within the publication is free. There are, of course, costs attached to producing press releases – someone has to be paid to write the story, and often some effort needs to be made to cultivate journalists so that they are alerted to the press release before it arrives. Table 16.2 shows the criteria under which the press stories must be produced if they are to be published.

Increasing scepticism and resistance to advertising has meant that there has been a substantial growth in the use of press releases and publicity in recent years. Press stories are much more credible, and although they do not usually generate business directly, they do have a positive long-term effect in building brand awareness and loyalty. It should be said that advertising alone also does not usually generate business immediately: as outlined in Chapter 15, communications tools can only be judged by communications outcomes, not by marketing outcomes.

Editors do not have to publish press releases exactly as they are received. They reserve the right to alter stories, add to them, comment on them or otherwise change them around to suit their own purposes. Editors will frequently cut stories in order to fill a specific space in the newspaper, so journalists are taught to write in an 'inverted pyramid' style, so that stories can be cut from the bottom. Figure 16.2 shows an example of this, using a story about a company's new initiative to help homeless people.

The story in Figure 16.2 could be cut at any point, starting from the bottom up, without losing the sense of a complete story. Each paragraph adds something else, but

Bellingham Industries offers new hope to the homeless

Bellingham Industries Ltd today announced a new work-for-housing initiative which will enable homeless people to get off the streets. The company is offering training and housing for homeless people, in an effort to break the cycle of deprivation which keeps people on the streets.

The scheme will work by giving homeless people on-the-job training and accommodation at Bellingham's own hostel, which is situated near the factory. Bellingham, which manufactures electrical appliances, will initially employ twelve people under the scheme, but hopes to expand the scheme in future.

James Whittle, Bellingham's personnel director, said, 'The tragedy of homelessness is that many of these people are unable to find work because they have no fixed address, and of course they cannot rent or buy a home because they have no jobs. We are delighted to be able to offer a way out of the cycle, at least for some homeless people.'

Once established in the hostel, the new employees will be able to seek work and housing elsewhere, though it is anticipated that most of them will be in the scheme for at least a year.

Headline: contains the main feature of the story

First paragraph contains the essence of the story. The story could be cut at this point, and it would still make sense and give the reader the gist of what has happened.

Second paragraph provides more detail of how the scheme works, but could still be cut at this point without any sense of loss.

Third paragraph gives the company's viewpoint, and further raises the corporate reputation. It also explains the rationale behind the scheme.

Final paragraph gives more detail, and the prognosis for the future of the scheme.

Figure 16.2

Example press release

does not have to be there for the story to make sense: the reader would not be left with a feeling of needing more if the story were cut after the second or third paragraph, or even after the first paragraph. Obviously the company would prefer it if the story appeared in its entirety, but this will not always happen: editors need to make the stories fit the page.

Editors will occasionally change a story, or incorporate the press release into a story about something else, and of course stories are often simply scrapped if something more newsworthy comes in. There is nothing substantial that company press officers can do about this. Cultivating a good relationship with the media is therefore an important part of the press officer's job.

Sometimes this will involve business entertaining, but more often the press officer will simply try to see to it that the job of the Press is made as easy as possible. This means supplying accurate and complete information, it means writing press releases so that they require a minimum of editing and rewriting, and it means making the appropriate corporate spokesperson available when required.

When business entertaining is appropriate, it will often come as part of a media event or press conference. This may be called to launch a new product, to announce some major corporate development such as a merger or takeover or (less often) when there has been a corporate crisis. This will involve inviting journalists from the appropriate media, providing refreshments, and providing corporate spokespeople to answer

Press conferences are useful for disseminating news about the company.

questions and make statements. This kind of event only has a limited success, however, unless the groundwork for it has been very thoroughly laid: journalists are often suspicious of media events, sometimes feeling that the organisers are trying to buy them off with a buffet and a glass of wine. This means they may not respond positively to the message the PR people are trying to convey, and may write a critical article rather than the positive one that was hoped for.

To minimise the chance of this happening, media events should follow these basic rules:

1 Avoid calling a media event or press conference unless you are announcing something that the Press will find interesting.

2 Check that there are no negative connotations in what you are announcing.

3 Ensure that you have some of the company's senior executives there to talk to the press, not just the PR people.

4 Only invite journalists with whom you feel you have a good working relationship.

5 Avoid being too lavish with the refreshments.

6 Ensure that your senior executives, in fact anybody who is going to speak to the press, has had some training in doing this. This is particularly important for TV.

7 Be prepared to answer all questions truthfully. Journalists are trained to spot lies and evasions.

8 Take account of the fact that newspapers (and indeed broadcast media) have deadlines to adhere to. Call the conference at a time that will allow reporters enough time to file their stories.

It is always better from the press viewpoint to speak to the most senior managers available rather than to the PR people. Having said that, the senior managers will need some training in handling the Press and answering questions, and also need to be fully briefed on anything the Press might want to ask. In the case of a press conference called as a result of a crisis this can be a problem: there is more on crisis management later in the chapter. Press officers should be prepared to handle queries from journalists promptly, honestly and enthusiastically, and arrange interviews with senior personnel if necessary.

Creating and Managing a Reputation

corporate reputation The overall image of the organisation.

Corporate reputation has been defined as the aggregate perceptions of outsiders about the salient characteristics of firms (Fombrun and Rindova 2000). In other words, an organisation's reputation is composed of the overall view that people have about the organisation. Reputation is important for two reasons: first, it has a direct effect on the bottom line, because organisations with good reputations are more likely to attract customers, and second a good reputation acts as a buffer should a crisis occur.

A favourable reputation is a resource that increases performance (Deephouse 1997). One of the main advantages of a favourable reputation is that it cannot be copied by other organisations, so it becomes a differentiator for the firm (Roberts and Dowling 1997).

Of course, reputation is more than simply good or bad. In some cases the organisation's reputation will be good in some respects and bad in others, or it may be that the organisation has a reputation for a particular type of behaviour that is perceived as good by some people and bad by others. For the manager, therefore, the problem is not so much one of creating a good reputation rather than a bad one: it is rather a problem of creating the right reputation so that the organisation's publics are clear about what to expect. Attempts to create the wrong reputation (good or bad) will result in frustrated expectations.

Talking Point

For most individuals, reputation is something which just happens. We acquire a reputation for telling funny stories, or being tight with money, or being good to talk over problems with, without actually trying all that hard or being self-conscious about it. In fact, the worst reputation someone can have is one of being manipulative and self-obsessed – in other words, trying to create a particular reputation is frowned upon by most people.

So why should companies be any different? Why would we be prepared to trust a firm which is apparently out to establish a reputation for being trustworthy? Surely the words 'Just trust me', are the surest way to make anyone suspicious!

Managing reputation is more than just an exercise in **spin-doctoring**. Spin-doctoring is a process of putting a good face on unacceptable facts, whereas managing reputation is a process of ensuring that the facts themselves are acceptable. It is about ensuring that everyone's experience of the organisation is in keeping with the reputation the organisation has or hopes to build. This means that everyone within the organisation has a role to play: each member of staff has the power to work well or badly, each shareholder has the power to affect the share price, each customer has the power to buy or not to buy. More importantly, each stakeholder has the power to make or break the organisation's reputation simply by saying or doing the right things, or the wrong things, when dealing with those outside the organisation.

Corporate communications officers have responsibility for **boundary scanning**. This means that they should be aware of what is happening at the boundaries between the organisation and its stakeholders, and need also to be aware of what can be done to improve interactions at the boundaries. This is similar to the role of marketers: marketers are responsible for what is done at the boundaries, communications officers are responsible for what is said.

The sources of knowledge which influence reputation are:

1 Direct experience of dealing with the organisation.

2 Hearsay evidence from friends, colleagues and acquaintances.

3 Third-party public sources such as newspaper articles, TV documentaries and published research.

4 Organisation-generated information such as brochures, annual reports and advertising.

The degree to which the corporate communications officer has influence over these sources is in inverse proportion to the influence on attitude. This is illustrated in Figure 16.3. A corporate communications officer has the role of seeking to influence communications about the company, whatever the source of those communications might be: this moves the role away from one of simply managing outgoing communications from the company, and towards one of seeking to create an atmosphere in which even

spin-doctoring Attempts to cover up bad news by slanting it in a way which puts the organisation in a favourable light.

boundary scanning The practice of monitoring the interfaces between the firm and its publics.

Ability of the corporate communications officer to control the information is greater lower down the scale	Direct experience ↑ Hearsay from friends Third-party sources Organisation-generated information	Influence on attitude is greater the higher up the scale

Figure 16.3

Hierarchy of information sources

Figure 16.4
Creating a reputation

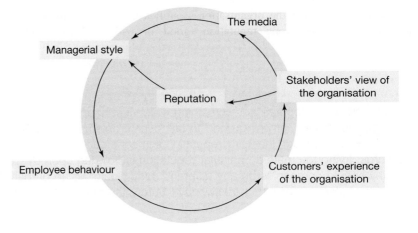

word-of-mouth between people unconnected with the firm still conveys the desired image.

Reputation affects decision-making on the part of all stakeholders, so the reputation of an organisation is both created and consumed by its members. In other words, someone who is a customer or an employee of the firm has that role in part because of the corporate reputation, and in turn adds to the reputation by telling others about the firm and its products. There is an element of positive feedback involved – a particular reputation will attract people who feel positive about the organisation and will repel those who feel negative about it. Once inside the organisation, people will act in ways which reflect the reputation. For example, a company with a reputation for treating its staff well will attract managers who like to work in that type of managerial paradigm: these are likely to be managers who, in turn, try to treat their staff well. Figure 16.4 shows how these elements relate.

One of the problems with reputation management is that different reputations may be attractive to different stakeholders. Stakeholders are people or groups of people who are affected directly or indirectly by a firm's activities and decisions (Post, Lawrence and Weber 2002). An employee may be attracted by an organisation's reputation for paying its staff generously, but this same attribute might repel a shareholder. Likewise, customers might be attracted to a firm with a reputation for keeping its prices, staff costs and profits at rock-bottom, but this would hardly attract either staff or shareholders. Ultimately it is not possible to please everybody, so managers need to identify who are the key players, and should seek to establish a good reputation with those people.

In practice, organisations acquire reputations rather than develop them. While it may be possible to re-establish a better reputation (or at least a more appropriate one) this is likely to be off-putting to some stakeholders, even if it is attractive to others. In practice managers are unlikely to create a reputation from scratch – they are much more likely to be tinkering with the organisation's existing reputation to make it more attractive to some people, or to make it more explicit to the stakeholders.

Maintaining a strong reputation pays direct dividends for the enterprise. Research shows that investors are prepared to pay higher prices for the shares of companies with good reputations, even when risks and returns are comparable with other firms in the same industry. Cordeiro and Sambharaya (1997) showed earnings forecasts made by financial analysts were heavily influenced by the non-financial component of the corporate reputation. Surveys of MBA students show that they are attracted to companies with good reputations, which means that companies which are larger and more visible are apparently better to work for. Part of this attraction is the reflected glory of working for a high-profile company, and part of it is about a perception that working for a major company is likely to be more secure and better rewarded.

Marketing in Practice
Best-Laid Plans

During the 1960s town planners in Spain had the idea of creating a quiet respectable resort for the wealthier middle-classes of Europe, foreseeing (correctly) that these people would have large disposable incomes and would be prepared to spend increasing amounts of their money on leisure, particularly as air travel became more widely available. The intended image of the resort was that of a peaceful town with an old quarter at its heart and upmarket, comfortable hotels around it.

The chosen area for the new resort was a small fishing village of 2000 people, located about half an hour from the nearest airport, in an area with little in the way of natural resources apart from fairly constant sunshine all the year round. In 1958, the village mayor decided to hold a song contest to establish the town's reputation, and to encourage the kind of respectable, middle-class arts lovers the town needed to feed its fledgling tourist trade and fill its hotels. The contest was a runaway success, mainly because the first contest spawned a major hit, over seventy versions of which were recorded worldwide.

The resultant publicity would have put the town on the map even if the contest had never run again.

Unfortunately, although the publicity put the town on the map and started the developments rolling, the image of a quiet resort for the wealthy never materialised. The result of the careful planning was Benidorm – now widely regarded as the epitome of rampant overdevelopment, and used as a byword for appalling resorts even by people who have never been there. The existing beach is excellent, but is now topped up with sand shipped in from the Sahara: acres of high-rise hotel and apartment development run for several miles along this seafront, and the original village is almost invisible. The original 2000 inhabitants have been supplanted by hotel workers, waiters, bar-owners and the like from all over Europe, and the resort is capable of coping with five million visitors a year. Maybe the original planners of Benidorm are not unhappy with the outcome – the town is nothing if not prosperous – but as a demonstration of the way things can turn out unexpectedly, Benidorm takes some beating!

The reputation of the organisation is important to all stakeholders, but there may be conflicts between the groups: this means that the board of directors often finds itself in the position of being a clearing house for pressures from different stakeholder groups. Even when stakeholders are in broad agreement as to where the company should be heading there will be differing opinions on how to get there.

For companies, there is a problem in meeting the differing needs of different market segments while still maintaining a consistent corporate reputation. For example, a major supermarket needs to meet the needs of many different income groups. This means that most major supermarket chains offer a budget range of products as well as the mainstream branded goods, but the quality of the budget range still needs to be of a reasonably good standard to avoid damaging the corporate reputation.

Image

Image is the affective component of attitude towards the organisation. It is the gut feeling or overall impression that the organisation's name and brands generate in the minds of the organisation's publics. The overall image created is not necessarily the one that managers intended.

image The overall impression a company or brand has in the eyes of its publics.

Corporate image is the image of the organisation, as opposed to the image of its products and services. Corporate image is composed of organisational history, financial stability, reputation as an employer, history of corporate citizenship and so forth. It is possible to have a good corporate image and a poor reputation for products and vice versa. For example, IBM has an exemplary corporate image, although its products are not

Figure 16.5

Types of image

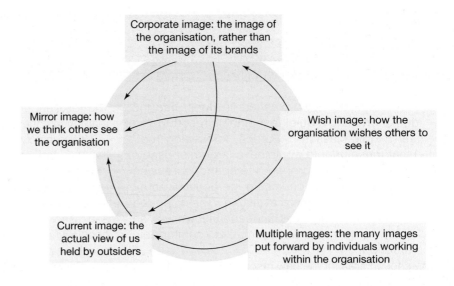

greatly different from those available elsewhere, whereas Rolls Royce has an outstanding image for its products despite a somewhat chequered corporate history involving several bankruptcies and relaunches.

A multiple image occurs when separate branches of the business or even individuals within the business create their own image within that of the overall corporation. An obvious example is that of sales representatives, who each have a personal image and reputation with customers which may or may not accord with the overall corporate image. Organisations such as IBM try to overcome this by using very strict selection criteria when employing salespeople: at one time, IBM salespeople wore a company uniform of blue blazers and grey trousers, but this was discontinued after a 'revolution' by French IBM salespeople, who simply refused to wear the uniform. Even now, IBMers tend to have a similar appearance, conforming to the strong corporate culture.

Talking Point

Creating a standard corporate image is obviously desirable. Yet for most purchasing firms, the only real contact they have with the supplier is through the sales representatives – who are all individuals.

We are told that the strength of the sales function is the ability to provide a personalised, individual service. But if we insist on hiring a group of clones, how are we to individualise what we do? And even if the salespeople are very similar, the simple fact of tailoring the company's service to each customer is bound to lead to variations in the image.

So is it really possible *ever* to generate a consistent corporate image? Or are we left with the unpalatable truth that we cannot force our employees into neat little moulds?

Corporate Image and Added Value

Corporate image is not a luxury. The image of a corporation translates into hard added value for shareholders. This is partly because of the effect that image has on the corporation's customers, but is also a function of the effects it has on staff, and is very much a result of the influence the image has on shareholders. High-profile companies are more attractive to shareholders, even if the firm's actual performance in terms of profits and dividends is no better than average. Since the central task of management is to maximise shareholder value, image must be central to management thinking and action.

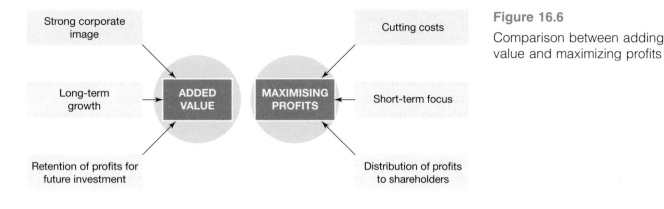

Courtesy of Eddie Stobart

Figure 16.6

Comparison between adding value and maximizing profits

Maximising shareholder value is not the same as maximising profits. Profit maximisation tends to be short-term, a matter of cutting costs, reducing investment, downsising, increasing sales volumes at the expense of long-term customer loyalty and so forth. Adding value to the shareholders' assets is about creating a secure, growing long-term investment. Since the dot.com bubble burst investors have become painfully aware that investments in firms with spectacular profits but little underlying solidity is a quick way to lose money. City analysts look more and more towards using measures such as customer loyalty, brand awareness and investment levels in judging the long-term prospects for firms.

The counter argument for this is that the shifting global marketplace has reduced survival prospects for companies. The life expectancy of a firm is now less than 20 years (De Geus 1997). Maintaining a profitable competitive advantage is also problematical. If a firm finds a profitable market niche, competitors respond rapidly and profits fall to the point where it is almost impossible to maintain an adequate return on the original capital investment (Black, Wright and Bachman 1998).

The value which accrues from image management has always been accounted for under the heading of 'goodwill' on the firm's balance sheet. The goodwill element of the firm's value is the difference between the value of the firm's tangible assets and its value on the stock market. For some firms, the value of goodwill is actually the bulk of the firm's overall value. For example, Coca-Cola's goodwill value is more than 80 per cent of the firm's total value. Much of this goodwill value comes from the Coca-Cola brand itself. This approach to valuing the firm's reputation and image is now regarded as being somewhat crude, and new measures are being developed to take account of brand value, customer loyalty values and so forth to move away from the reliance on financial measures when assessing firms' successes.

Eddie Stobart has one of the UK's strongest brands.

Talking Point

Boards of directors often use the stock market valuation of the company's shares as a barometer of the company's success. Yet this is rarely reflected in the corporation's mission statement. Most of these talk about caring for staff and customers.

Does this mean that the mission statement is not strictly true? Or does it mean that staff and customers are mere instruments in attaining the goal of share value? And if a higher share value is independent of profit, does that mean that the wool is being pulled over shareholders' eyes? In short, are most boards of directors behaving in some Machiavellian way in order to shore up their own positions? Or are they perhaps merely trying to balance the needs of a wide group of people?

Risk Management

No matter how carefully PR activities are planned and prepared for, crises will develop from time to time. Preparing for the unexpected is therefore a necessity. Some PR agencies specialise in crisis management, but a degree of advance preparation will certainly help if the worst should happen. Preparing for a crisis is similar to organising a fire drill. The fire may never happen, but it is as well to be prepared.

Crises may be very likely to happen, or extremely unlikely. For example, most manufacturing firms can expect to have a product-related problem sooner or later, and either need to recall products for safety reasons, or need to make adaptations to future versions of the product. On the other hand, some crises are extremely unlikely. Assassination or kidnapping of senior executives is not common in most parts of the world, nor are products rendered illegal without considerable warning beforehand.

Crises can also be defined as within the firm's control or outside the firm's control. Many firms have been beset by problems which were really not of their making: however, very few problems are entirely outside the firm's control. In most cases, events can at least be influenced, if not controlled. Sometimes, however, the cost of such influence is out of all proportion to the level of risk involved.

Establishing a crisis team

Ideally, the organisation should establish a permanent crisis management team of perhaps four or five individuals who are able to take decisions and act as spokespeople in the event of a crisis. Typical members might be the personnel manager, the safety officer, the factory manager, the PR officer and at least one member of the board of directors. Keeping the crisis team small means that communication between members is easy and fast.

The team should meet regularly to review potential risks and formulate strategies for dealing with crises. It may even be possible to rehearse responses in the case of the most likely crises. Importantly, the team should be trained in presentation techniques for dealing with the media, especially in the event of a TV interview.

Figure 16.7

Elements of good crisis management

Marketing in Practice
Bhopal

On December 2nd 1984 over 40 tons of lethal gas was released into the air from the Union Carbide chemical factory in Bhopal, India. The accident was caused by water entering a tank containing chemicals: the resulting reaction generated great heat and vented the poisonous gases into the atmosphere. As a result, thousands of people in the area were killed – estimates vary between 3800 and 8000 – and hundreds of thousands have suffered ill-health ever since.

Union Carbide was held accountable by the world's Press and the company was widely criticised by environmental groups. Union Carbide was seen as being slow to pay compensation, slow to make reparations at the plant and slow to implement a clean-up operation. Often, the American parent company was accused of not caring simply because the victims were Indian.

Union Carbide have pointed out that only 51 per cent of the plant was owned by the company, the rest being owned by the Indian Government (26 per cent) and private shareholders (23 per cent). The Bhopal plant was staffed and managed entirely by Indians. In 1989, an Indian court ordered Union Carbide to pay US$470m in damages in full and final settlement, and the company did so, but the trouble has not gone away: campaigners say that birth defects in the area are caused by chemicals from the plant. This is denied by Union Carbide, who say that soil contamination is caused by chemicals which were never used at the plant, and that close interbreeding (a feature of marriages in the Bhopal area) is what is causing the birth defects. The US company denies any liability whatsoever, and has the backing of the Second Circuit Court of Appeals in Manhattan, which ruled in 1987 that the case belongs solely in India and the US company has no liability. The Indian Government was held partly liable and has bought health insurance for the 100 000 people who are thought to have been affected.

The case has been further complicated: in 2001 Dow Chemical bought Union Carbide. Dow, understandably, does not feel any responsibility whatever for Bhopal and is refusing to consider any further claims. Meanwhile, campaigners have persuaded an Indian court to issue a warrant for the arrest of Union Carbide's former CEO, Warren Anderson, on charges of culpable homicide. Anderson is unlikely to be extradited from the United States, but probably should not visit India any time soon.

Meanwhile, the survivors of Bhopal wait. The case has dragged on for more than 25 years: the compensation worked out to only $500 for each victim, which may be a lot of money to someone who only earns $2 a day, but still won't cover the medical bills. Union Carbide (India) is now owned by an entirely different company, which (like Dow in the USA) feels no responsibility for the disaster. The campaigning continues, however, and presumably will until the last of the survivors has died.

The team should be able to contact each other immediately in the event of a crisis, and should also be provided with deputies in case of being away on business, on holiday, off work sick or otherwise unavailable. The essence of planning for crises is to have as many fall-back positions as possible. Having a Plan B is obvious, but it is wise to have a Plan C or even Plan D as well.

Dealing with the media in a crisis

One of the main PR problems inherent in crisis management is the fact that many crises are newsworthy. This means that reporters will be attracted to the company and its officers in the hope of getting comments or newsworthy statements which will help to sell newspapers.

Provided the groundwork has been laid in advance, the company should have a good relationship with the news media already. This will help in the event of a crisis. However, many managers still feel a degree of trepidation when facing the Press at a crisis news conference. The journalists are not there to help the company out of a

Figure 16.8

Crisis management

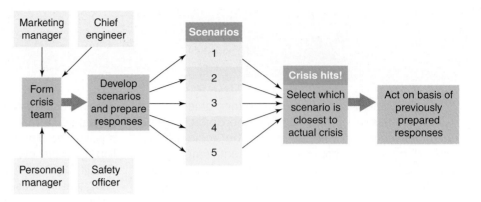

crisis, they are there to hunt down (or create) a story. Their objectives are probably not compatible with those of the company, but they are under an obligation to report the news reasonably accurately.

Preparation is important. As soon as the crisis breaks, the crisis team should be ready to organise a press conference, preferably on the company's own territory. The press conference should be held as soon as is reasonably possible, but it allows the spokespeople sufficient time to prepare themselves for the journalists and gives a reasonable excuse for not talking to reporters ahead of time. The crisis team should remember that they are in charge. It is their information, their crisis, and their story. They are not under an obligation to the news media, but they are under an obligation to the company's shareholders, customers, employees and other publics. The media may or may not be helpful in communicating with these publics in a crisis situation.

Another important consideration is to ensure that the situation is not made worse by careless statements. Insurance and legal liability may be affected by what is said, so this should be checked beforehand.

Crisis teams need to have a special set of talents, as well as the training needed to perform their ordinary jobs. Rapid communication and rapid response are essential when the crisis occurs. Good relationships with the news media will pay off in times of crisis.

Crisis management should not be left until the crisis happens. Everyone involved should be briefed beforehand on the crisis policy. This enables everyone to respond appropriately, without committing the company to inappropriate actions – in simple terms, being prepared for a crisis will help to prevent panic reactions and over-hasty responses which might come back to haunt the company later.

The Role of PR in the Organisation

Organisations, just like people, have needs. Some of these needs are common to all organisations, and have different levels of importance according to the circumstances of the organisation, or the particular stage in its development. A hierarchy of organisational needs was developed by Pearson (1980). Table 16.3 shows how PR can help in satisfying those needs.

Table 16.3 The hierarchy of organisational needs

Organisational need	Requirements	Typical PR activity
Output	Money, machines, manpower, materials.	Staff programmes to attract the right people.
Survival	Cash flow, profits, share performance, customers.	Publicity aimed at customers; events publicising the firm and its products.
Morale	Employee job satisfaction.	Staff newsletters, morale-boosting activities, etc.
Acceptability	Approval by the external stakeholders (shareholders, Government, customers, suppliers, society in general).	External PR, shareholder reports, lobbying of Government departments and MPs, events for suppliers and customers, favourable press releases.
Leadership	Having a respected position in the company's chosen field; this could be customer satisfaction, employee involvement, industry leadership in technology, or several of these.	Corporate image-building exercises, customer care activities, publicity about new products and technological advances, sponsorship of research in universities, sponsorship of the Arts.

Adapted from: Pearson (1980).

Pearson's hierarchy is useful as a concept but less useful as a practical guide because so many firms deviate from the order in which the needs are met.

Internal Communications Media

House journal

House journals are printed information books or sheets which are made available to employees. Journals may be of any of the following types:

- *Magazines*. Containing feature articles and illustrations, such magazines are relatively expensive to produce but have a professional, credible feel about them.
- *Newspapers*. These can be produced to resemble a tabloid newspaper, which makes them more accessible to some groups of employees. Content consists of news articles about the firm, with some feature articles.
- *Newsletter*. Common in small firms, a newsletter would probably be A4 or foolscap size, and will contain brief items, usually without illustration. Newsletters are cheap and easy to produce, especially in small numbers.
- *Wall newspaper*. These look like posters and are fixed to walls. They are useful for brief communications about events or changes in company policies.
- *Electronic newsletter*. Internal email systems offer great potential for disseminating newsletters. The medium is cheap to use, effective, and often increases the likelihood that the newsletter will be read. Furthermore, it is possible to tell who has opened the newsletter and who had deleted it without reading it – although, of course, opening it is not the same as reading it.

Figure 16.9

Issues in designing a house
journal

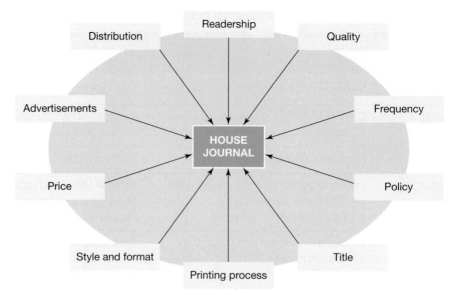

When planning a house journal, you need to consider the issues shown in Figure 16.9.

- *Readership*. Different groups of staff may have different needs, so it may be necessary to produce different journals for each. Research workers are likely to have different needs from truck drivers, for instance.

- *Quantity*. The greater the number of copies, the lower the production cost per copy. If the number of employees is large, a better-quality journal can be produced. If the numbers are small, the firm may need to produce newsletters or wall newspapers instead.

- *Frequency*. Frequent publication means that the journal is more likely to become part of the daily routine of staff. Some large firms even publish such journals daily.

- *Policy*. The journal should be more than simply a propaganda device for senior management. It should fit in with an overall PR programme, and should have a clear editorial policy to ensure the quality of content.

- *Title*. The title should be characteristic of the organisation. Changing the title is difficult once it has become established, just as with any other brand name.

- *Printing process*. To an extent the printing process will affect the content, since simple, cheap printing processes cannot reproduce some illustrations. Cost will also affect the choice of process, as will the desire for a good-quality, credible journal.

- *Style and format*. Credibility is linked to the degree to which the journal resembles a commercial magazine. Style and format are part of the communication in the same way that packaging is part of a product.

- *Price*. Obviously the vast majority of house journals are free to staff, but it is feasible to make a charge if the journal is sufficiently interesting. There is no reason why a cover price should not be put on the journal in any case, even if it is free. This conveys to the staff that the journal is valuable, and thus is more likely to be read.

- *Advertisements*. Carrying advertising may be a useful way to reduce costs. If the circulation is sufficiently large, outside organisations might be prepared to place advertising – this is particularly true if the firm is large and in a single location, since local shops, restaurants and entertainment venues might well wish to promote their products. Employees may well want to advertise items for sale or forthcoming social events, which also increases the readability of the journal.

- *Distribution*. Journals can be delivered by hand, by post to the employee's home address, or at distribution points within the firm (for example mail pigeonholes). The decision rests on the frequency of the journal, the location of employees and the type of journal involved. Distribution via email is probably the quickest and cheapest method.

House journals are often edited independently of senior management in order to ensure that the focus is on the employees' need for information rather than on the management's need to control or manipulate.

Websites

Most firms' websites, where they exist, are mainly geared towards external marketing. In some cases, firms operate internal websites aimed at employees. These sites are not accessible by outsiders, and they fulfil the same function as the house journal. The main advantage is that the costs are greatly reduced compared with producing a house journal. The disadvantage is that employees are unlikely to access the site except during working hours, and in some cases may not be able to access the site at all because the nature of their work does not involve using a computer.

Internal websites are most useful in organisations in which virtually all employees are provided with computers, and in which there is no problem about allowing employees to browse the website during working hours. Website design is a specialist area, but some rules have been developed. Sites need to be simple to access and use, graphics should be kept simple to minimise download time, and articles should fit onto one screen as far as possible.

Internal briefings and open meetings

Some organisations give staff the opportunity to have access to senior management at open meetings or briefings. These briefings have the advantage of allowing senior management to gain direct access to grass-roots views from the workforce, as well as allowing the workforce the chance to question senior managers about company policies.

The overall effect is to increase openness within the firm, and break down barriers. Employees (in general) work better if they understand why things are being done the way they are being done. This also enables them to use their initiative better if the system breaks down for any reason.

Sponsorship

Sponsorship has been defined as 'An investment, in cash or kind, in an activity in return for access to the exploitable commercial potential associated with this activity' (Meenaghan 1991). Sponsorship of the Arts or sporting events is an increasingly popular way of generating positive feelings about firms.

Sponsorship in the UK grew a hundredfold between 1970 and 1993, from £4m to £400m. It has continued to grow ever since, with estimates for 2009 ranging between £2000m and £3000m. However, a large part of this increase came from tobacco firms, due to global restrictions on tobacco advertising. Sponsorship of Formula One motor racing, horse racing, cricket and many arts events such as the Brecon Jazz Festival by tobacco companies allowed them to promote their products despite the Europe-wide ban

Table 16.4 Reasons for sponsorship

Objectives	Percentage agreement	Rank
Press coverage/exposure/opportunity	84.6	1
TV coverage/exposure/opportunity	78.5	2
Promote brand awareness	78.4	3
Promote corporate image	77.0	4
Radio coverage/exposure/opportunity	72.3	5
Increase sales	63.1	6
Enhance community relations	55.4	7
Entertain clients	43.1	8
Benefit employees	36.9	9
Match competition	30.8	10
Fad/fashion	26.2	11

on tobacco advertising on TV, but the UK Government (responding to a European Union directive) banned any new tobacco sponsorship deals in 2003, and is requiring organisations to phase out tobacco sponsorship over a period of time. Some events have disappeared altogether as a result of the ban on tobacco sponsorship, having been unable to find alternative sponsors, and the ban has certainly had a detrimental effect on the Arts, whatever its effect on the nation's smokers.

The value of sponsoring events is in little doubt: as a way of promoting a firm and its products, and in particular as a way of improving the corporate image, sponsorship has much to offer. Sponsorship has been shown to create a sustainable competitive advantage (Fahy, Farrelly and Quester 2004). Companies sponsor for a variety of different reasons, as shown in Table 16.4 (Zafer Erdogan and Kitchen 1998).

The basis of sponsorship is to take the customers' beliefs about the sponsored event and link them to the company doing the sponsoring. Thus a firm wishing to appear middle-class and respectable might sponsor a theatre production or an opera, whereas a company wishing to appear to be 'one of the lads' might sponsor a football team. As far as possible, sponsorship should relate to the company's existing image.

Sponsoring sports teams has a degree of risk attached to it, since the fortunes of the sponsor are linked to the fortunes of the team: if the team perform badly, the team's supporters are less likely to buy the sponsor's products (Lings and Owen 2007). Some firms have tried to get round this problem by sponsoring rival teams – in the hope that if one fails, the other will succeed. This tends to alienate committed supporters of both teams, however, because they feel betrayed by the sponsoring company (Davies, Veloutsou and Costa 2006).

Sponsorship will only work if it is linked to other marketing activities, in particular to advertising. Hefler (1994) estimated that two to three times the cost of sponsorship needs to be spent on advertising if the exercise is to be effective. The advertising should tell

Marketing in Practice
Lincoln Mercury

I n 1996 sales of the upmarket Lincoln-Mercury car were at an all-time low – and the company (a Ford subsidiary) had an even worse problem on its hands. Analysis of the ownership of Lincoln-Mercury cars revealed that the average age of owners was 57. This meant that the lifetime value of Lincoln owners was low – these drivers were heading rapidly towards old age and would not be driving much longer, and in particular would not be changing their cars very frequently. It seemed highly likely that many Lincoln drivers would never buy another car, especially since the cars themselves are built to last.

Jim Rogers, Lincoln's new marketing manager, realised that drastic action would have to be taken. He moved production to California and introduced a new

Courtesy of Lincoln © 2008 Ford Motor Company

2008 NAVIGATOR

LINCOLN
REACH HIGHER

model (the Lincoln Navigator) which stopped the rot temporarily, but Rogers knew that he had to attract the 35 to 49-year-olds who were currently buying BMW and Lexus cars. 'Changing the product was not enough' Rogers said. 'We needed to change what the brand stood for on an emotional basis. After all, nobody needs to pay $40–50,000 for a car.'

Rogers committed $90 million to the most integrated car publicity campaign ever undertaken. The campaign centred around another new model, the Lincoln LS, and was linked by the innovative Cirque du Soleil, a Montreal-based circus group. Lincoln arranged for three of the circus acts to conduct a mini-tour of eight major cities, ahead of the main tour of the circus (also sponsored by Lincoln). The mini-tour pulled in hundreds of potential buyers, identified by local Lincoln dealers in each city and invited specifically to the circus. These people in turn talked to friends and work colleagues about Cirque du Soleil, so that the main tour was a sell-out: of course, at each performance the Lincoln LS was available for circus goers to inspect, and even book test-drives.

The result of this sponsorship was that by August 1999 Lincoln had sold all the LS sedans they could make – 30 000 cars in all, representing $1.4 billion gross revenue. The company had been able to approach potential LS customers who would otherwise have been completely unavailable, a lucrative group of people who change their cars every two years or so. Cirque du Soleil also gained: apart from the sponsorship, the group now has a high profile in the United States as well as in its native Canada. Overall, the campaign was outstanding value all round for only $90 million.

customers why the firm has chosen this particular event to sponsor, so that the link between the firm's values and the sponsored event is clear. A bank which claims to be 'Proud to sponsor the Opera Festival' will not do as well as they would if they were to say 'We believe in helping you to enjoy the good things in life – that's why we sponsor the Opera Festival'. A recent development in sponsorship is to go beyond the mere exchange of money as the sole benefit to the sponsored organisation or event. If the sponsored organisation can gain something tangible in terms of extra business or extra publicity for their cause, then so much the better for both parties.

There is evidence that consumers feel gratitude towards the sponsors of their favourite events (Lacey *et al.* 2007), but there is no evidence regarding business buyers. Any feelings of gratitude may be an emotional linking between the sponsor and the event rather than a feeling of gratitude that the sponsor made the event possible. The difference between these emotions is merely academic in any case – if sponsorship leads to an improvement in the firm's standing with customers, that should be sufficient. There are

Figure 16.10

Considerations in sponsorship

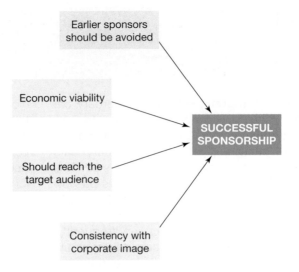

also spin-offs for the internal PR of the firm: most employees like to feel that they are working for a caring organisation, and sponsorship money often leads to free tickets or price reductions for staff of the sponsoring organisation.

The following criteria apply when considering sponsorship (Hefler 1994).

- The sponsorship must be economically viable; it should be cost-effective, in other words.
- The event or organisation being sponsored should be consistent with the brand image and overall marketing communications plans.
- It should offer a strong possibility of reaching the desired target audience.
- Care should be taken if the event has been sponsored before; the audience may confuse the sponsors, and you may be benefiting the earlier sponsor.

There is certainly a long-term effect from sponsorship – following the ending of a long-term relationship between a sponsor and an event, regular audiences of the event still demonstrate strong awareness of the sponsoring brand (Mason and Cochetel 2006).

In the business-to-business arena, one of the main benefits of sponsorship of sports events and arts events is the availability of tickets or reserved seating for sponsors. This enables the sponsoring firms to offer seats as a relationship-builder or deal-sweetener to possible customers.

Talking Point

Anyone watching a major sporting event such as the Wimbledon tennis tournament will have noticed many empty seats. Anyone wanting to obtain tickets for such events finds them hard to get. So why does this happen?

Corporate sponsorship is the culprit. Corporations are given many free seats which they are unable, or unwilling, to use on the days they are available, and therefore seats are empty while real sports fans are unable to obtain tickets. This naturally causes a degree of resentment among fans – and a feeling that 'Big Business' is acting against the interests of ordinary people.

So how do corporations gain by this? What does this achieve for enhancing the corporate reputation? Perhaps in the business-to-business environment there is no need to care about Joe Public, but isn't that attitude somewhat cynical?

Or perhaps there is an opportunity for someone. Could corporations make unwanted seats available to the public on a first-come-first-served basis?

Using Outside Agencies to Build Corporate Image

Outside public relations agencies are frequently used for developing corporate image. The reasons for doing this might be as follows:

1 The firm is too small to warrant having a specialist PR department.
2 External agencies have expertise which the company lacks.
3 The external agency can provide an unbiased view of the firm's needs.
4 External agencies often carry greater credibility than internal departments or managers.
5 Economies of scale may make the external agency cheaper to use.
6 One-off events or campaigns are more efficiently run by outsiders, without deflecting attention away from core activities.

The Public Relations Consultants' Association lists the following activities as services that a consultancy might offer:

- Establishing channels of communication with the client's public or publics.
- Management communications.
- Marketing and sales promotion related activity.
- Advice or services relating to political, Governmental or public affairs.
- Financial public relations, dealing with shareholders and investment tipsters.
- Personnel and industrial relations advice.
- Recruitment training and higher and technical education.

This list is not exhaustive. Since outside agencies often specialise, the firm might need to go to several different sources to access all the services listed above. Even firms with an in-house public relations department may prefer to subcontract some specialist or one-off activities. Some activities which might involve an outside agency might be as follows:

- *Exhibitions*. The infrequency of attendance at exhibitions (for many firms) means that in-house planning is likely to be disruptive and inefficient. Outside consultants might be setting up four or five exhibitions a week compared with the average firm's four or five a year, so they will quickly acquire strong expertise in exhibition management.
- *Sponsorship*. Outside consultants will have contacts and negotiating expertise which is unlikely to be available in-house. In particular, an outside firm will have up-to-date knowledge of what the 'going rate' is for sponsoring particular events and individuals.
- *Production of house journals*. Because of the economies of scale available in the printing and publishing industry, house journals can often be more cheaply produced by outsiders than by the firm itself.
- *Corporate or financial PR*. Corporate PR relies heavily on having a suitable network of contacts in the finance industry and the financial press. It is extremely unlikely that a firm's PR department would have a comprehensive list of such contacts, so the outside agency provides an instant network of useful contacts.
- *Government liaison*. Lobbying politicians is an extremely specialised area of public relations, requiring considerable insider knowledge and an understanding of current political issues. Professional lobbyists are far better able to carry out this work than a firm's public relations officer would be.
- *Organising one-off events*. Like exhibitions, one-off events are almost certainly better subcontracted to an outside agency.
- *Overseas PR*. Firms are extremely unlikely to have the specialist local knowledge needed when setting up public relations activities in a foreign country.

Figure 16.11

Example of task division between
in-house staff and agency staff

	THINGS THE FIRM NEEDS TO DO	
	Lobby parliament →	
	Sponsor an athlete →	
Things to do in-house	← Sponsor an arts event	Things to farm out to an agency
	← Write press releases	
	← Publish a staff newsletter	
	Train executives for TV →	

Figure 16.12

Choosing a PR consultancy
Source: (Harley W. Warner, APR, Fellow
Warner Communication Counselors Inc.
Reprinted with permission of Public Relations Review)

Competence and Reputation
- Years in business.
- Size – people and billings
- Full service or specialisms.
- Reach: local, national, international.
- Growth pattern and financial stability.
- Types of accounts.
- Experience with accounts similar to yours, or conversely conflicts of interest with competitors' accounts.
- Samples of work.
- Sample list of suppliers used.

Staff
- List and qualifications of staff – full time, project clients, freelance/consultants.
- Names of several former employees.
- Staff to be assigned to your account – qualifications and length of time with the firm.
- Percentage of their time to be devoted to your account – other accounts they will handle.
- Staff or personnel back-up available.
- Staff turnover in the past two years.

Clients
- Existing client list.
- Past clients.
- Average number of clients during the last five years – retainer clients, project clients.
- Oldest clients and length of service.
- Average length of client–firm relationship.
- Clients lost in the last year.

Results and measurement
- Does the firm understand your objectives and needs?
- How will progress be reported?
- How will results be measured?
- What will it cost – billing process, hourly rate, expenses billed, approval process?

Choosing an appropriate agency or consultancy begins with the agency's ability to carry out the specific tasks you need. Deciding which tasks the agency should do can be a process of elimination. Begin by deciding which tasks can be completed in-house, then whatever is left is the task of the agency. The checklist for choosing a PR consultancy shown in Figure 16.12 was developed by Warner Communication Counselors Inc.

Unless the outside agency has been called in as a result of a sudden crisis (which is possibly the worst way to handle both PR and consultants), the consultancy will be asked to present a proposal. This allows the consultancy time to research the client's situation, and its existing relationships with its publics. The proposal should contain comments on the following aspects of the problem:

- Analysis of the problems and opportunities facing the client company.
- Analysis of the potential harm or gain to the client.

- Analysis of the potential difficulties and opportunities presented by the case, and the various courses of action (or inaction) which would lead to those outcomes.
- The overall programme goals and the objectives for each of the target publics.
- Analysis of any immediate action needed.
- Long-range planning for achieving the objectives.
- Monitoring systems for checking the outcomes.
- Staffing and budgets required for the programme.

Client firms will often ask several agencies to present, with the aim of choosing the best among them. This approach can cause problems, for several reasons. First, the best agencies may not want to enter into a competitive tendering situation. Second, some agencies will send their best people to present, but will actually give the work to their more junior staff. Third, agencies in this position may not want to present their best ideas, feeling (rightly in some cases) that the prospective client will steal their ideas. Finally, it is known that some clients will invite presentations from agencies in order to keep their existing agency on its toes.

Such practices are ethically dubious and do no good for the client organisation's reputation. Since the whole purpose of the exercise is to improve the firm's reputation, annoying the PR agencies is clearly not an intelligent move. To counter the possibility of potential clients stealing their ideas, some of the leading agencies now charge a fee for bidding.

Relationships with external PR consultancies tend to last. Some major firms have used the same PR consultants for over 20 years. Changing consultants frequently is not a good idea. Consultants need time to build up knowledge of the firm and its personnel, and the firm needs time to develop a suitable atmosphere of trust. Consultancies need to be aware of sensitive information if they are not to be taken by surprise in a crisis, and the firm is unlikely to feel comfortable with this unless the relationship has been established for some time.

Developing a Brief

The purpose of the brief is to bridge the gap between what the firm needs and what the consultant is able to supply. Without a clear brief, the consultant has no blueprint to follow, and neither party has any way of knowing whether the exercise has been successful or not.

Developing a brief begins with the firm's objectives. Objective setting is a strategic decision area, so it is likely to be the province of senior management. Each objective needs to meet SMARTT criteria, as follows.

1 **S**pecific, in other words it must relate to a narrow range of outcomes.
2 **M**easurable. If it is not measurable, it is merely an aim.
3 **A**chievable. There is no point in setting objectives which cannot be achieved, or which are unlikely to be achieved.
4 **R**elevant to the firm's situation and resources.
5 **T**argeted accurately.
6 **T**imed: a deadline should be in place for its achievement.

The objectives will dictate the budget if the firm is using the objective-and-task method of budgeting. This method means deciding what tasks need to be undertaken to achieve the final outcome, and working out how much it will cost to achieve each task. Most organisations tend to operate on the all-we-can-afford budgeting method, which involves agreeing a figure with the finance director. The SMARTT formula implies that, in these circumstances, the budget will dictate the objectives, since the objectives must be achievable within the available resources.

Figure 16.13

Criteria for objective setting

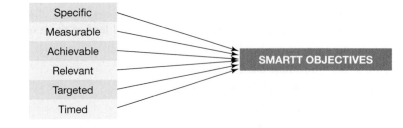

Setting the objectives is, of course, only the starting point. Objectives need to be translated into tactical methods for their achievement, and these tactics also need to be considered in the light of what the company is trying to achieve.

The brief will be fine-tuned in consultation with the PR agency itself. From the position of their specialist knowledge, the agency will be able to say whether the budget is adequate for what needs to be achieved, or (conversely) say whether the objectives can be achieved within the budget on offer. The agency can also advise on what the appropriate objectives should be, given the firm's current situation.

Measuring Outcomes

If the outcomes from the PR activities do not match up with the budgeted objectives, conflict between the client and the agency is likely to be the result. The most common reason for the relationship breaking down is conflict over the costs and hours billed compared with the outcomes achieved. From the agency's viewpoint, much of what happens is outside their direct control. Sponsored events might not attract sufficient audiences, press releases might be spiked as a result of major news stories breaking, and special events might be rained off. Many a carefully planned reputation-enhancing exercise has foundered when the celebrity athlete involved has been caught taking drugs, for example.

Measuring outcomes needs to be considered at the objective setting stage. A good PR agency will not offer any guarantees of outcomes, but it should be feasible to assign probabilities to the outcomes and to put systems in place for assessing whether the objectives were achieved. Table 16.5 shows some possible evaluation methods.

Evaluating activities is never an easy task. It is difficult to be objective, and some activities are too difficult or expensive for evaluation to be worthwhile, but without evaluation managers have no way of knowing what corrective action to take.

Table 16.5 Evaluating PR

Activity	Possible evaluation methods
Press campaign to raise awareness	Formal market research to determine public awareness of the brand/company.
Campaign to improve the public image	Formal market research. Focus groups for perceptual mapping of the firm against competitors. Measures of attitude change.
Exhibition or trade show	Records of contacts made, tracking of leads, formal research to determine improvements in image.
Sponsorship of a sporting event	Recall rates for the sponsorship activity.

Word-of-Mouth

Word-of-mouth is probably the most powerful PR tool available, but it is also the hardest to control. People often discuss products and services: most people like to pass on good advice about products they have bought (or avoided buying), and recent purchases are a common topic of conversation between friends.

The reasons for the effectiveness of word-of-mouth are as follows:

- It is interactive, because two or more parties discuss the product or the company. This forces both parties to think about the product or company and its features and benefits – which in turn helps to fix the brand in the individuals' memories. For marketers, the problem here lies with the fact that neither of the individuals concerned is under the control of the company.

- As a communication, word-of-mouth allows for confirmation of messages through feedback.

- A message from a friend or relative carries a great deal more credibility than a message from a corporation – after all, people know full well that the company is trying to sell its products.

People who switch brands as a result of a recommendation from a friend or family member are much more likely to stay loyal to the brand than are people who switch as a result of marketing activities (Wangenheim and Bayon 2003). People who switch brands are also much more likely to be big users of word-of-mouth, both in terms of relying on it when making decisions and in passing good advice along to others.

Positive word-of-mouth can be generated (or at least encouraged) by using press releases, but a more proactive way is to use 'bring a friend' schemes. This is often seen as a sales promotion device (see Chapter 18) but it also generates word-of-mouth if the scheme is handled well. It is usually better to offer a benefit to the 'friend' rather than to the existing customer – people often feel guilty at recommending something to a friend in exchange for a reward. Awards and certificates often form the basis for word-of-mouth: someone receiving a loyalty gift is likely to talk about it, particularly if it is conspicuous (for example a clock or a barometer). Promotional clothing can sometimes generate word-of-mouth: T shirts or fleeces with logos can provoke comment.

The richness of the message and the strength of its advocacy (i.e. the enthusiasm of the person talking about the brand) are the key factors in successful word-of-mouth (Mazzarol, Sweeney and Soutar 2007). In some cases word-of-mouth can be powerful even before the product has been tried out, provided the product is innovative enough: for example, when a blockbuster movie is about to be released, word-of-mouth is strongest before release, i.e. before anyone has seen the movie (Liu 2006).

Product Placement

Arranging to have a brand featured in a movie or TV show has a strong impact on people's impressions of the product. In some cases the product placement is subtle (for example, most American movies are likely to feature Coca-Cola at some point, even if only as a background advertisement or a shot of a Coca-Cola vending machine) or the placement can be more overt, as in the case of the Mini Coopers used in the remake of *The Italian Job*.

Because the products appear quite naturally, cinema audiences tend not to filter out the message: when the film's hero orders a Jim Beam on the rocks, the brand becomes associated with the hero without any overt effort. The same is true of James Bond's Aston Martin, which was replaced by a BMW in *Tomorrow Never Dies,* reputedly because Aston Martin could not afford the placement fee (Oakes 1997). From the viewpoint of a film

Courtesy of Aston Martin

Associating a product with James Bond is a powerful way to position the brand.

producer, product placement and merchandise spin-offs can easily cover the entire cost of making the movie – films such as *Toy Story* and *Godzilla* could have been complete flops at the box office and still made money simply on the placement and merchandise deals.

A major advantage of product placement from the marketer's viewpoint is the longevity of films. The film may be shown all over the world, then released on DVD, then be shown on TV perhaps for many years to come – some products might not be permitted in TV advertising (cigarettes are an obvious example) but can appear in films screened on TV. Likewise, some TV broadcasters such as the BBC are not allowed to carry advertising, but a product placed in a film will appear.

If products can be placed in soap operas, this also has a powerful effect, because soaps have a parasocial function for many people: in other words, they replace the real social life that such people lack (Russell and Stern 2006). This means that featured products have a greater importance, almost as great as they would have if they were used by friends.

The evidence is that people remember 'placed' products better than they do advertised products, but in some cases there can be a backlash because sometimes people feel that product placement is equivalent to manipulation. This in turn leads to mistrust of the brand (Bhatnagar and Aksoy 2004).

The most extreme example of placement is when the brand becomes an intrinsic part of the plot line. This is called branded entertainment, and was commonplace in the United States in the 1940s and 1950s. TV shows commonly plugged the sponsors' products, often in such a blatant way as to cause people to become confused about the actual story-line. To some extent branded entertainment still exists (although shows such as *The Kraft Theatre* no longer exist) in the form of films where a specific brand is the mainstay of the film. The popular *Herbie* films of the 1970s are an example, where the hero of the story is a Volkswagen car. More recently, *The Italian Job* features Mini Coopers as the stars. There may be moral and ethical issues attached to this extreme form of placement, however (Hudson and Hudson 2006).

Summary

Corporate reputation goes beyond merely putting spin on the corporation's activities. It is a co-ordinated effort to influence communications to and from stakeholders, and also between stakeholders, in order to improve the corporation's position in the minds of its publics. In this sense, corporate reputation has a strategic role, because it involves positioning the corporation in the public consciousness: this has real pay-offs in terms of share values, employee satisfaction and behaviour, and customer perceptions of the firm.

The key points from this chapter are as follows:

- Corporate reputations are not built through spin-doctoring.
- Corporate reputation has a stock market valuation.
- Public relations has an internal role.
- Crises will happen: having a crisis team in place is prudent.
- Outside agencies are often cheaper and more effective than carrying out PR tasks in-house.
- Between two and three times the cost of sponsorship should be devoted to other communications efforts in order to support the sponsorship expenditure.

Chapter review questions

1 Why might a firm prefer to handle its corporate reputation activities in-house?

2 What are the key issues in building a crisis team?

3 If corporate reputation has such a strong effect on the firm's stock market valuation, why bother with any other activities?

4 What are the main criteria for deciding to sponsor an event or organisation?

5 How might a company avoid PR disasters such as that resulting from the Bhopal tragedy?

6 What are the main advantages of publishing an in-house newsletter?

7 How should a firm handle internal PR when recruiting new staff?

8 How might a firm resolve conflicts between stakeholders?

9 Why might an individual's opinion about a firm change as a result of sponsorship?

10 Which components of attitude are likely to be most affected by PR activities?

Preview case revisited
Friends of the Earth

FOE realised fairly quickly that the voluntary, small-scale approach would take far too long to work, if it worked at all. Getting people to change wasteful habits takes time – recycling takes effort, turning down the heating means being less comfortable, insulating the house is an expense and an effort, and so forth. Equally, businesses have to show a profit – a firm which acts alone to become more environmentally friendly is likely to lose out against firms which don't bother. Governments are in the business of doing things which will please the electorate – legislation limiting people's activities would not be popular. In other words, there has to be a pay-off for anyone who becomes more eco-friendly.

FOE has a somewhat unusual approach to changing hearts and minds. First, they focus on the solutions, not the problem. This means that they emphasise different, less damaging ways of doing things rather than simply complaining to stakeholders about the issues. Second, everything is based on credible research: they back things up with the facts, drawn from credible scientific research conducted by independent bodies such as universities. Third, FOE tries to get a lot of people involved, whether as campaigners, as lobbyists or even simply as voters. Governments and businesses are always interested in what the public are doing, either because they want votes or because they want more business. Finally, FOE uses its network of interested parties and organisations – the group is active in 70 countries, and has 200 groups within the UK. Many members of these groups are in positions of influence – FOE membership is not solely confined to people in rope sandals.

FOE in the UK has had major successes in lobbying government, to the extent that the organisation is usually called in as a consultant on environmental issues. FOE's focus on finding alternatives pays off handsomely in this way – the organisation often has viable suggestions to offer to Government and industry when environmentally-damaging proposals are put forward.

Of course, it is not all plain sailing. FOE has enemies, and sometimes mistakes are made – the biofuels controversy is one, since many environmental pressure groups initially campaigned in favour of using biofuels, until it became clear that rainforests were being cut down to make way for biofuel farms and food crops were being diverted to manufacture biofuels.

FOE also issue a constant stream of press releases. These can be accessed through the FOE website, and they are categorised as being suitable for the Press, suitable for general readers, suitable for experts (such as scientists) and suitable for campaigners. There are no problems in accessing all four categories, but the classification does help in finding information of an appropriate type.

FOE also supplies spokespeople whenever there is anything concerning environmental issues in the news. These spokespeople are experienced and trained in appearing on TV or in talking to the Press: they are always well-briefed, and capable of talking at different levels of complexity according to the audience.

Despite being (in many ways) antibig business, FOE have adopted many of the methods of large companies. In fact, FOE is better than most large firms at handling public relations.

Case study
Brecon Jazz Festival

Every August the small Welsh market town of Brecon becomes packed to the rafters with jazz enthusiasts for the Brecon Jazz Festival. Every hotel room in the town is booked, every space in campsites and fields for miles around is taken and every day thousands of visitors arrive on day trips.

The Festival began in 1984, partly at the instigation of jazz singer George Melly, who was active in persuading world names in jazz to perform in this somewhat unlikely location. In the ensuing years, more and more top names appeared at the Festival – names such as John Dankworth, Cleo Laine, Van Morrison, Paula Gardiner, Lee Konitz, Courtney Pine, Sonny Rollins and of course George Melly, have all appeared at Brecon – but the Festival also includes lesser-known performers, giving newcomers a chance to showcase their music.

The Festival divides into three categories – the Concert Programme, which features major stars and for which tickets need to be booked in advance, the Stroller Programme, for which a pass can be bought (for 2008 the full weekend pass cost £48) entitling the holder to unlimited access to any of the venues around the town (and there are more than a dozen), and the Street Programme, which is free to anyone attending the Festival. The Street Programme features various groups or individual musicians, not all of whom are jazz musicians.

The festival has had a number of setbacks, some of which looked as if they might close it altogether. Resistance from a substantial group of local residents who object to their quiet town being overrun with thousands of boisterous visitors every year is only one problem: new regulations on public performance, coupled with policing problems, took the Street Programme off the agenda on more than one occasion. The organisers were forced to move the Street Programme to a single fixed venue when the police were unable to direct traffic around the town, but objections from residents (and the difficulties of mixing motorists with somewhat inebriated revellers) caused the policy to be reversed in time for the 2007 festival. George Melly died in 2007, depriving the Festival of one of its most prominent advocates.

One of the biggest setbacks was the European Union ban on tobacco sponsorship. Until then, Brecon Jazz Festival's biggest sponsor was British cigarette brand Lambert and Butler. The brand was shown throughout the Festival programme, and there was a Lambert and Butler stage on which many big names appeared, but the funding disappeared overnight, leaving the Festival bereft.

Other sponsors needed to be found quickly – and, if possible, sponsors who would be useful allies in other respects, such as dealing with local objections and handling policing issues. The first port of call was the government and local government agencies. The Welsh Assembly now gives Brecon Jazz Festival both practical and financial help, having given the Festival major event status in recognition of its contribution to promoting Wales and Welsh tourism. HSBC have become major sponsors, since Brecon Jazz Festival usually attracts a wealthier, older audience than (say) a rock festival – these people represent desirable potential customers. Powys County Council have been brought on board – they have an interest in anything that brings money into the county, and Brecon Jazz Festival certainly does that. Many local businesses find the Festival a major boost to their turnover and profile, with every hotel, café, restaurant and pub packed to the roof for the entire weekend. Welsh TV channel S4C also sponsor the Festival – as does *Buzz*, the events magazine.

Music charities and organisations also feature – the Royal Welsh College of Music and Drama, the Performing Rights Society's Foundation for New Music and of course the Welsh Arts Council all contribute in cash or in kind.

Of course, the Festival is not out of the woods yet. Sponsorship can be withdrawn at a moment's notice, volunteers can un-volunteer, regulations can change overnight, policing policy can be changed and governments can fail to be re-elected, but whatever happens the Brecon Jazz Festival will continue as an important flagship event for Wales, and indeed for the UK.

Questions

1 Why is it important to have the Welsh Assembly on board as sponsors?

2 What other sponsors might Brecon Jazz encourage?

3 How should Brecon Jazz Festival's organisers deal with protests from local people?

4 What is the pay-off for S4C in sponsoring the Festival?

5 Why would Powys Council sponsor the Festival, despite protests from local residents who are, after all, its electorate?

References

Bhatnagar, N. and Aksoy, L. (2004): Et tu, brutus? A case for consumer scepticism and backlash against product placements. *Advances in Consumer Research* **31**(1).

Black, A., Wright, P. and Bachman, J.E. (1998): *In Search of Shareholder Value* (London: Pitman).

Cordeiro, J.J. and Sambharaya, R. (1997): Do corporate reputations influence security analyst earnings forecasts? *Corporate Reputation Review* **1**(2), 94–8.

Cornelissen, J. and Harris, P. (2004): Interdependencies between marketing and public relations disciplines as correlates of communicative organisation. *Journal of Marketing* **20**(1), 237–65.

Davies, F., Veloutsou, C. and Costa, A. (2006): Investigating the influences of a joint sponsorship of rival teams on supporter attitudes and brand preferences. *Journal of Marketing Communications* **12**(1), 31–48.

De Geus, A. (1997): *The Living Company* (Boston, MA: Harvard Business Press).

Deephouse, D.L. (1997): The effect of financial and media reputations on performance. *Corporate Reputation Review* **1**(2), 68–71.

Fahy, J., Farrelly, F. and Quester, P. (2004): Competitive advantage through sponsorship: a conceptual model and research propositions. *European Journal of Marketing* **38**(8), 1013–30.

Fombrun, C.J. and Rindova, V. in M. Schultz, M.J. Hatch and M.H. Larsen (2000): *The Expressive Organisation* (Oxford University Press).

Hayward, R. 1998): *All About PR* (London McGraw-Hill).

Hefler, M. (1994): Making sure sponsorship meets all the parameters. *Brandweek* (May).

Hudson, S. and Hudson, D. (2006): Branded entertainment: a new advertising technique or product placement in disguise? *Journal of Marketing Management* **22**(5/6), 489–504.

Lacey, R., Sneath, J.Z., Finney, Z.R. and Close, A.G. (2007): The impact of repeat attendance on event sponsoring effects. *Journal of Marketing* **13**(4), 243–55.

Lings, I.N. and Owen, K.M. (2007): Buying a sponsor's brand: the role of effective commitment to the sponsored team. *Journal of Marketing Management* **23**(5/6), 483–96.

Liu, Y. (2006): Word of mouth for movies: its dynamics and impact on box office revenue. *Journal of Marketing* **70**(3), 74–9.

Mason, R.B. and Cochetel, F. (2006): Residual brand awareness following the termination of a long-term event sponsorship and the appointment of a new sponsor. *Journal of Marketing Communication* **12**(2), 125–44.

Mazzarol, T., Sweeney, G.C., and Soutar, G.N. (2007): Conceptualising word-of-mouth activities, triggers and conditions: an exploratory study. *European Journal of Marketing* **41**(11/12), 1475–94.

Meenaghan, J.A. (1991): The role of sponsorship in the marketing communications mix. *International Journal of Advertising* **10**(1), 35–47.

Oakes, P. (1997): Licensed to sell. *The Guardian*, 19th December.

Pearson, A.J. (1980): *Setting Corporate Objectives as a Basis for Action* (Johannesburg: National Development and Management Foundation of South Africa).

Post, J.E., Lawrence, A.T. and Weber, J. (2002): *Business and Society: Corporate Strategy, Public Policy, Ethics* (New York: McGraw-Hill).

Roberts, P.W. and Dowling, G.R. (1997): The value of a firm's corporate reputation: how reputation helps attain and sustain superior profitability. *Corporate Reputation Review* **1**(2), 72–6.

Russell, A. and Stern, B. (2006): Aspirational consumption in US soap operas: the process of parasocial attachment to television soap characters. *Advances in Consumer Research* **33**(1), 136.

Wangenheim, F. von and Bayon, T. (2007): Behavioral consequences of overbooking service capacity. *Journal of Marketing* **71**(4), 36–47.

Zafer Erdogan, B. and Kitchen, P.J. (1998): The interaction between advertising and sponsorship: uneasy alliance or strategic symbiosis? *Proceedings of the Third Annual Conference of the Global Institute for Corporate and Marketing Communications*. Strathclyde Business School.

Further reading

Penn, W. (2004): *Be Your Own PR Expert* (London: Thomson). This is a 'how-to' book with a direct style, written by an industry expert. Penn outlines the practical aspects of running one's own PR campaigns in a lively, engaging style. He also wrote *Market Yourself through the Media*, which explains how the news media operate and how to use the media to get your message across.

Regester, M. and Larkin, J. (2001): *Risk Issues and Crisis Management: A Casebook Of Best Practice* (London: Kogan Page). This book covers crisis management, using case studies from famous companies to illustrate the points made. It is intended for students rather than practitioners, but has something to offer everyone.

Chapter 17
Selling and key account management

Learning objectives After reading this chapter, you should be able to:

1. Explain the philosophy behind selling.

2. Explain the role of selling in communications.

3. Describe the relationship between salespeople and customers.

4. Explain the difference between objections and conditions.

5. Understand the importance of after-sales activities.

6. Describe the main differences between key account selling and small account selling.

7. Explain how management techniques differ between small-account selling and key-account selling.

8. Explain the role of commission in motivating salespeople.

9. Understand some of the key issues in recruiting, training and motivating salespeople.

Introduction

Personal selling may sometimes be regarded with some suspicion: it is often associated with high-pressure techniques, and with the needs of the seller rather than the needs of the buyer. In fact, this view of selling is false: in practice, successful salespeople succeed because they are able to find solutions to customers' problems. The practice of selling has little or nothing to do with the selling concept described in Chapter 1, because customers are not generally stupid enough to buy from someone who is pushy or who clearly does not have the customer's interests at heart. Personal selling is more about establishing personal relationships with customers.

Marketing is frequently about personal relationships, especially in the business-to-business area. Even though business people often aim to be totally rational in their buying behaviour, the personality of the people they see conveys an image about the personality of the supplying corporation: for the buyer, the sales representative *is* the company. Personal selling has a special place in business-to-business transactions. Because of the higher order values and smaller number of buyers, suppliers feel the need to offer a personal service, supplied by the salesforce.

Equally, in many areas of consumer marketing personal selling has a strong role. For major purchases such as cars, houses, home improvements and even timeshare apartments, the personality and professionalism of the salesperson is the deciding factor in purchase. For complex products such as consumer electronics, holidays and financial products such as insurance and pensions, the salesperson can provide importance guidance and help in tailoring the product to suit the individual's needs.

Preview case
Jewson

Jewson is one of the UK's largest chains of builder's merchants. It is part of the Saint-Gobain Building Distribution Group, which includes plumbers' merchants, tile merchants, timber merchants and so forth, but Jewson aims to provide a one-stop service for everything – in fact, its advertising strapline for many years was 'We've got the Jewson lot!' implying that they can supply everything a general builder might need. The company deals largely with the trade (professional builders) but will supply the householder and DIY enthusiast. Jewson prides itself on its wide range of stock and its friendly, professional staff: the company has over 500 stores throughout the UK, and maintains an extremely high standard of sales service throughout.

Although the company's management have always been satisfied with the professional way in which their salespeople handle customers, the firm decided to go for the British Standards Institution's ISO 9001 accolade.

ISO 9001 is a quality assurance standard developed for all businesses, not just selling organisations: it is an international standard which operates in many countries, and it is administered locally in each country throughout the world by national standards agencies (in the UK, this is the British Standards Institution). In order to obtain ISO 9001 status, firms have to demonstrate compliance with a wide range of quality procedures.

First, companies need to have a stated quality assurance policy, and employees must have clear objectives to work towards. All the key processes in the company need to be mapped out, and quality objectives need to be put in place: monitoring systems must be developed to ensure that the objectives are met.

Second, the company needs to determine customer requirements and develop systems for communicating product information, inquiries, contracts, orders, feedback and complaints.

Third, the company needs a system for regular monitoring through meetings and internal audits.

Fourth, the company needs documented procedures for dealing with actual and potential deviations from the standard procedures.

There are many more procedures enshrined in ISO 9001, and the above categories have a great deal more detail attached to them – compliance is a major undertaking for any firm, and cannot happen overnight.

© Everyday Images / Alamy

Talking Point

The Role of Personal Selling

Personal selling is probably the largest single budget item in most marketing departments. Salespeople earn high salaries and need expensive back-up: company cars, administration assistance, expensive brochures and sales materials and so forth. Allowing for travelling time, preparation time, and so forth salespeople spend only a fraction of their time actually making sales presentations. This therefore begs the question: why have we not been able to find a cheaper way to get business?

The reason is that salespeople provide a personal touch. A salesperson is able to meet a customer, discuss the customer's problems and develop a creative solution. The customer understands his or her present situation and needs, the salesperson understands the capabilities of the supplier and their products, and (usually) the two share knowledge about the context of the problem and the solution. This relationship is illustrated in Figure 17.1.

The key point in this is that selling is about establishing a dialogue: it is not about persuading people to buy things they don't really want, it is not about fast-talking a buyer into making a rash decision, and it is most definitely not about telling lies about the firm's products.

There is a great deal of talk nowadays about establishing relationships, generating dialogues, asking people's opinions, and even about choice. But is this really what customers want? Do people really want dialogue and choice – or would they be happier if they simply had a product which really worked and did the job for them?

Would it, in fact, be better if companies simply said 'Here it is – take it or leave it'. Or would that seem too direct altogether?

Salespeople can give advice to people in the market for a complex product.

For example, an amateur astronomer who intends to buy a new telescope would have knowledge of what types of astronomical body he or she is most interested in, and might have some knowledge of the telescopes on the market. An amateur astronomer would probably know the differences between reflecting and refracting telescopes, but might not have specific knowledge of the telescopes available from a particular supplier. The salesperson would be able to fill this gap, and would probably also be able to make recommendations about how to use the new telescope to make best use of its features.

Salespeople exist to carry out the following functions:

● Identify suitable possible customers.

● Identify problems those customers have or might have.

● Establish a dialogue with the potential customer.

Figure 17.1

The function of selling

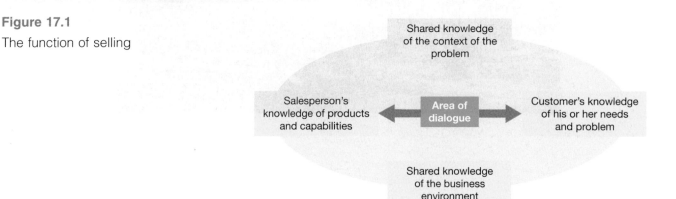

E-Marketing in Practice
Handbag.com

Handbag.com is a website owned by Boots PLC, the UK pharmacist, and Press Holdings Limited. It is, in effect, an online women's magazine: it has a target audience of career women in their mid-thirties, and has a 'readership' of almost a million readers per month.

Ford saw this group as a potentially key market for the Ford Focus. The Focus is a small car, light to drive and easy to manoeuvre, and Ford saw these features as having a particular appeal to women. Part of the problem for car manufacturers is that car purchase is often seen as predominantly a male activity – it can be difficult to encourage women to go to a car dealer and take a test-drive, not least because car salespeople are predominantly male, which many women find intimidating. Ford therefore ran a year-long campaign on Handbag.com to encourage women to visit the dealerships. The campaign involved sponsorship of Handbag.com's Business Plan Awards advertorials, advertisements, pop-ups, banners and (crucially) test-drive promotions with vouchers.

The campaign was aimed at directing women to the Focus website, and (of course) to the Ford dealerships. The response was excellent: apart from changing the perception of the Focus among the target audience (a primary objective of advertising), the campaign encouraged thousands of women to test-drive the cars.

Undoubtedly the women-only nature of the website helped to counteract the men-only image of car dealerships, but whatever the reasons, the salespeople at Ford had a lot more people to talk to as a result of the advertising support.

The personal selling process relies on having people to talk to: integrating the Handbag.com campaign into Ford's sales process provided the salespeople at the dealerships with a stream of prospective customers, most of whom would not have visited the dealerships without the campaign.

it goes with **everything**

the ford**focus** *Ford*

Courtesy of The Advertising Archives

- Refine the view of the problem to take account of the dialogue.
- Identify solutions which are within the supplying firm's capabilities.
- Explain the solution.
- Represent the customer's views to the supplying company.
- Ensure a smooth process of supply which meets the customer's needs.
- Solve any after-sales problems which may arise.

Marketers usually think of personal selling as part of the promotional mix, along with sales promotion, advertising and publicity. Personal selling is different from the other elements in that it always offers a two-way communication with the prospective customer, whereas each of the other elements is usually a one-way communication. This is partly what makes personal selling such a powerful instrument; the salesperson can clarify points, answer queries and concentrate on those issues which seem to be of greatest interest to the prospect. More importantly, the salesperson is able to conduct instant 'market research' with the prospect and determine which issues are of most relevance, often in an interactive way which allows the salesperson to highlight issues which the prospect was not aware of.

As with other forms of marketing communication, selling works best as part of an integrated campaign. Salespeople find it a great deal easier to call on prospects who have already heard something about the company through advertising, publicity or exhibition activities, and many salespeople regard it as the main duty of the marketing department to deliver warm leads (or even hot ones). Equally, marketers regard it as part of the salesperson's responsibility to 'sing the same song' by communicating the company's core message, in conjunction with the other communications methods.

Salespeople and marketers often have divergent views about the relationship between selling and marketing, and this is occasionally a source of conflict between them (Dewsnap and Jobber 1998).

A Marketer's View

Salespeople are able to find, inform and persuade customers in a way that has yet to be bettered by any other communications medium.

This view of personal selling emphasises heavily the provision of information and the element of persuasion. Personal selling is one of several possible options available to the marketer for communicating the company's messages to the customers; its major advantage over other communications is that the message can be tailored to fit the prospect's need for information. This is very much a marketer-oriented view; marketers appear to be working to the model shown in Figure 17.2.

Because of the supposed high cost of personal selling, and the knowledge that there are many other ways of communicating effectively with customers, marketers will sometimes look for ways to eliminate the salesforce.

At first sight the marketer's model of the role of personal selling appears to allow for the replacement of selling with other (often IT-based) techniques. Since personal selling is regarded as an expensive option, this viewpoint is wholly understandable. A mailing which contacts 5000 good prospects for a cost of £15 000 is a great deal cheaper than a sales rep who would contact around half that number of prospects in a year at a cost of £50 000; even allowing for the sales rep's much better success rate, the cost advantage is obvious. If the marketers are right in thinking of selling as a communication tool, it is obviously cost-effective to seek other ways of communicating.

Undoubtedly personal selling does have a strong communications element, involving as it does a two-way dialogue between salesperson and prospect, but there is a great deal more to personal selling than this. An examination of what salespeople actually do will make this clearer.

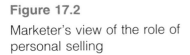

Figure 17.2

Marketer's view of the role of personal selling

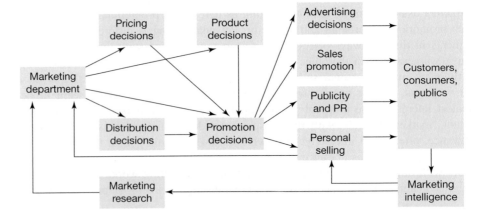

The Salesperson's Eye View

Research into sales practice shows a somewhat different picture from that conveyed by most marketing texts.

The emphasis in selling practice is not on telling prospects about the products, but on asking questions about the prospect's needs. The salesperson's role in the sales presentation is not about delivering a persuasive sales talk, but rather is about using appropriate questions. The questions not only help in finding out what the prospect actually needs, but also help to lead the discussion and the subsequent negotiations in a particular direction. DeCormier and Jobber (1993) found a total of 13 different types of question in use by salespeople; some of these were for information-gathering purposes, others serve to control and direct the discussion. Rackham (1991) categorised questions in four dimensions; situation, problem, implication and need-payoff. In each case the emphasis is on asking the prospect about his or her situation, with a view to finding a solution from among the salesperson's portfolio of products. The three key elements in this are first that the needs of the buyer are paramount, second that the salesperson is asking questions, not making statements, and third that communicating the marketing department's 'message' is not relevant to this core process.

Sales trainers and writers have emphasised the problem-solving aspects of selling for many years now (see Figure 17.3), and salespeople are usually told that the most successful presentations are those in which the customer does most of the talking (Lund 1979). Problem-solving is at the core of the activity rather than communication; if the customer is allowed to talk, he or she will (in effect) tell the salesperson how to sell the product.

Talking Point

Marketers have been talking for years about putting the customer at the centre of everything the firm does. Salespeople live with this philosophy every day – after all, they spend most of their time dealing with customers, relatively little of their time dealing with the company that pays their salaries.

So why the conflict? Why don't marketing professionals just back off and let the salespeople run things? In fact, why not go further – why not give the salespeople complete control over the company?

In the case of services, the marketer and the salesperson will also be concerned with the people, process and physical evidence (Booms and Bitner 1981). Salespeople have a role to play here as well; for example, it is common practice for salespeople to leave something with the customer once the sale is closed (a copy of the order, a brochure about the product, etc.) The salesperson is the main individual in the 'people' element, at least in most service industries, and also often has considerable input into the process. In fact, a comparison of the salesperson's activities and the marketer's activities shows considerable common ground, as Table 17.1 shows.

The main difference between selling and marketing is that selling is concerned with individuals and individual relationships, whereas marketing is concerned with market segments. Although direct marketing and database marketing seek to target very small segments (even a segment of one) by using information technology, salespeople already do this, face-to-face and in real time, without the benefit of the marketing department's range of resources.

The salesperson's model of the relationship between marketing and sales will look more like that shown in Figure 17.4. From the salesforce viewpoint, it is the salesforce

Figure 17.3

Problem-solving

Table 17.1 Comparison of marketers' and salespeople's activities

Marketer's activities	Salesperson's activities
Research into the needs of consumers.	Needs analysis based on situation and problem questions.
Gap analysis.	Analysis of needs to identify problems.
New product development, designed to meet the consumers' needs.	Selection from among the existing range of products to find closest fit for prospect's needs.
Pricing: selecting a price which meets the needs and expectations of both the customer and the firm.	Price negotiation: negotiating a price which meets the needs and expectations of both the customer and the firm.
Promotion: developing an appropriate promotion strategy which will equate to the consumers' psychological and behavioural characteristics.	Promotion: explaining the features and benefits of the product in terms of the customer's needs, psychology and behavioural characteristics.
Distribution decisions: ensuring that the product is in a convenient place for the consumer to buy it.	Distribution negotiations: ensuring that the product reaches the customer in the right quantities and at the right time.

Figure 17.4

Salesperson's model of the relationship between marketing and selling

who do the 'real' work of finding out the customer's needs and fulfilling them, with the marketing department providing the back-up services of advertising, public relations and sales promotion. Marketers provide information (gained by market research) to the salesforce, and also to the production department, but the salesforce exists to identify and solve customer's problems. They do this using the range of products supplied by the production department.

In the salesperson's model, the marketing department occupies a subservient role. Since the salesforce are in the 'front line', dealing directly with the customers, it is clear that every other department in the firm depends on them to bring in the business. They are, in fact, the only department which brings in money: everything else generates costs. Sales training programmes sometimes emphasise this; salespeople are told that the average salesperson supports five other jobs, they are told that 'nothing happens until somebody sells something', and they are encouraged to think of themselves as the most important people in the firm.

Many salespeople regard their relationship with their customers as being more important than their relationship with the firm that pays their salaries – further evidence that salespeople regard themselves as being the most important people in the firm.

Research shows that salespeople are often defensive of their good relationships with customers, even when this conflicts with instructions from the marketing department (Anderson and Robertson 1995). This may be due to the belief that it is easier for salespeople to find a new company to work for than it is to find new customers. Salespeople also know that establishing a social rapport with customers is important, and there is research evidence to show that they are right to believe this (Geiger and Turley 2005). Learning about customers in order to develop the relationship is often unconscious – it is simply a process of getting to know someone on a personal level in most cases, rather than a calculated effort (Turley and Geiger 2006). The same researchers found that extensive use of IT can actually make the process less effective, reducing the salesperson's relational competencies – clearly a dangerous outcome (Geiger and Turley 2007).

While there may be some justification for the salesperson's model, the model ignores the interrelated nature of the firm's activities. Salespeople would have nothing to sell were it not for the efforts of the production department, would have no pay-packet and no invoicing without the finance department, would have no deliveries without the shipping department, and so forth. Salespeople may have been given a false view of their own importance, but trainers may feel justified in doing this in order to counteract the often negative image and low status that selling has in the eyes of other departments.

silent seller The book of sales materials carried by sales representatives.

In this model, the salesforce collects information about the market from the marketing department's research, and information about the individual customer directly from the customer. Information about the product range, prices and discount structures, delivery lead times and methods, sales promotion and the use of advertising and PR materials (contained in the salesperson's 'silent seller') are all used in negotiation with the customer. This is done with the aim of obtaining an acceptable solution for both parties, regarding both information exchange and product and price exchange.

For many salespeople, the marketing department also has the role of 'softening-up' prospective customers by providing publicity and advertising; the salesperson feels more confident about making a call knowing that the prospect has already heard of the company and has had the opportunity to form some favourable impressions. In this model the marketing department performs a support function, providing a set of products for the customer to choose from, a price structure for the salesperson and the customer to negotiate around, a distribution system which can be tailored to suit the customer and promotional back-up in the form of advertising and publicity. Sales promotions might be useful as ways of closing sales (they are sometimes called deal-makers) but the basic problem-solving and decision-making is done by the salespeople when they are with the customer. There is research evidence to show that collaboration between sales and marketing, not surprisingly, improves business performance: however, the driver for this needs to come from senior management (Le Meunier-Fitzhugh and Piercy 2007).

Salespeople see brochures as being part of the support provided by marketers.

Talking Point

If customers are aware of their problems, why do we need salespeople at all? Why not simply provide all the information on a website, make it as interactive as possible and let people get on with it? After all, the social side of selling is hardly worth bothering with – buyers are paid to buy, not to sit chatting to sales reps!

Not to mention that too cosy a relationship between salespeople and customers might lead to all sorts of complications – favouritism and so forth. So isn't it far and away the best and cheapest option to get rid of the salesforce and use the money to buy a really good website?

On the other hand, most of us like to socialise in work. We are social animals, are we not? And if that's the case, why do we limit corporate contacts just to salespeople and buyers? Why not expand our range of contacts between the firms and get everybody to meet up?

In fact, it is this problem-solving and decision-making function that distinguishes the salesforce from other 'promotional tools'. The salesforce do not think of themselves as being primarily communicators: they think of themselves as being primarily decision-makers.

If the salespeople are correct in this view, then it would be impossible to replace them with a database (at least, given the current state of the art). Computers can hold and manipulate information very effectively, but they are unable to solve problems creatively or negotiate effectively, or indeed establish a long-term relationship on a human level. For these functions a human being is necessary.

A problem that arises from this perspective is that salespeople tend to identify very much with the customers. They will, and indeed should, be prepared to represent the customers' views back to the company, and even fight the customer's corner for them within the firm, because this leads to a more customer-orientated attitude within the company. On the other hand, the firm is entitled to expect a certain amount of loyalty from its employees, so the salesforce's over-identification with the customers is likely to lead to conflict between salespeople and their colleagues back at head office.

For these reasons salespeople find it is easier and more beneficial to begin by finding out the customer's needs, and then apply a solution to those needs based on the firm's product range. Although marketing writers commonly refer to 'the product', it is very rarely the case that a salesperson will only have one product to offer; in many cases, salespeople even have the capacity to vary products or tailor them to fit the customer's needs. For example, computer software houses selling to major customers are able to write customer-specific software for the client; services salespeople (for example selling training services) will almost always have to tailor the product.

Types of Salesperson

Donaldson (1998) offers the following classification of selling types:

1 *Consumer direct.* These salespeople deal with consumers: they are order-getters who rely on selling skills, prepared presentations (canned presentations) and conditioned response techniques to close sales. Timeshare salespeople are typical of this group.

2 *Industrial direct.* These salespeople are also order-getters, but operate on a much larger scale. Usually these salespeople deal with one-off or infrequent purchases such as aircraft sales to airlines, machine tools, greenfield civil engineering projects and so forth. The emphasis for these salespeople is on negotiation skills.

3 *Government institutional direct.* Similar to industrial direct, these salespeople specialise in dealing with institutional buying. Because institutions typically operate by putting purchase contracts out to tender, these salespeople need special techniques: on the other hand, many of these organisations issue publications which explain how to sell to them, sometimes specifying the rules of business and acceptable profit levels. Often the salesperson's main hurdle is to become accepted as an approved supplier.

4 *Consumer indirect.* These salespeople call on retailers. Selling is normally on a repeat basis to established customers, but the main thrust of the salesperson's effort goes into understanding the consumer market. This means that the salesperson needs to help the retailer sell more of the product, by using creative

merchandising, by advising on sales techniques, and (in the case of fast-moving consumer goods) negotiating with the retailer for extra shelf space for the products.

5 *Industrial indirect.* Most of the activity of these salespeople is in supporting distributors and agents. They need strong product knowledge, and will need to concentrate on defending existing business from incoming competition: this is because it is typically the case that product and price are similar between competitors. The service level the salesperson offers is therefore the main competitive tool.

6 *Missionary sales.* **Missionary** selling is most effective when the selling cycle is long but the information needs of potential specifiers are immediate, when other forms of communication cannot convey the whole picture, and when the buying process is complex.

missionary A salesperson who does not sell directly, but who has the task of 'spreading the word' about a product to people who influence purchase.

7 *Key account salespeople.* A **key account** is one which is of strategic importance, which represents a substantial proportion of the supplier's turnover, or which is likely to lead to a change in the way the firm does business. Key account salespeople need very strong negotiating skills, a high degree of confidence and the ability to relate to people at many different levels in the organisation (Cespedes 1996; Millman and Wilson 1995; Millman and Wilson 1996).

key account A customer or potential customer with strategic importance to the firm.

8 *Agents.* A manufacturer's agent represents many different suppliers, but does not take title to the goods. Agents typically call on the same regular group of customers, but offer a wide range of goods: the skills required are therefore the ability to understand a wide range of products, the administrative ability to keep track of the orders and to meet the differing order formats of client companies, and the ability to work efficiently, often on low margins. Good agents do not carry products which compete directly, although there are exceptions to this general rule.

9 *Merchandisers.* **Merchandisers** call on large and small retail outlets specifically for the purpose of maintaining in-store displays and point-of-sale materials. In some cases (for example Procter and Gamble) suppliers have their own employees stationed in supermarkets to improve the coordination of their supply operations. These salespeople are sometimes called customer account managers, which more accurately describes the breadth of their role.

merchandisers A type of sales person who has the responsibility of establishing and maintaining in-store displays

10 *Telesales.* Telephone selling can be either inbound or outbound. Inbound **telesales** involves responding to customer enquiries, often generated by advertising or exhibitions. Outbound telesales usually involves cold-calling prospects, or replacing a personal visit with a telephone call. The main advantage of telesales is that it is very much cheaper than personal calls: the main disadvantage is that it is considerably less effective on a call-for-call basis. Telesalespeople need good communication skills, including a clear speaking voice: on the plus side, the telesales operator usually has better access to customer information than a field salesperson would have, due to the availability of VDU screens.

Gaining shelf space is a key goal of indirect salespeople.

11 *System selling.* **System selling** involves teams of salespeople, each of whom brings a different skill to bear on the problem. Missionary salespeople, new-business salespeople and technical salespeople may all be involved in selling to the same account, see Figure 17.5.

12 *Franchise selling.* Franchising is much the same as licensing, but is much more extensive. The franchisor grants the franchisee the right to use its business system,

telesales Selling over the telephone.

system selling Marketing on a one-to-one basis by a team of salespeople.

E-Marketing in Practice
Mitsubishi-Tokyo Pharmaceuticals

The pharmaceuticals industry is highly competitive, complex and dominated by major firms – so it is hardly surprising that it presents unique problems for the salesforce. Pharmaceuticals fall into two categories: over-the-counter (OTC) medicines which can be bought from a pharmacist and prescription drugs (the so-called ethical medicines), which can only be obtained on prescription.

Because doctors do not buy drugs in any quantity (but do decide on which drugs to prescribe) the ethical medicines market is served by missionary salespeople. Because pharmacists do buy OTC medicines, this market is served by order-takers who call on the pharmacists.

Mitsubishi-Tokyo Pharmaceuticals was formed in October 2000 by the merger of Mitsubishi Chemicals and the pharmaceutical division of Tokyo Tanabe Seiyaku Co. Ltd. The new company supplies medicines to both OTC and ethical markets: as a result of the merger, it found itself with 530 sales representatives who had various levels of training, differing knowledge of the drugs and markets they were dealing with, and little knowledge of the product ranges of each others' companies. The new

company therefore needed to develop the salesforce rapidly, and in particular to provide them with high-quality, detailed information about the products and the market. Tokyo Tanabe's previous software, Zaurus, proved to be wholly inadequate to handle the task of dealing with the larger salesforce.

The solution was to introduce a new software system from Dendrite, a software company which specialises in systems for pharmaceutical salesforces. Dendrite developed a system called MUSE (medical, useful, sensible, expert) which allowed the salesforce to share information about products, physicians and hospitals. The system was later expanded to allow information sharing with office-based salespeople and marketers.

Allowing different categories of salespeople to share information has proved of immense value to Mitsubishi Tokyo Pharmaceuticals. Training time has been cut, and effectiveness has increased: working together more has improved the cohesiveness of the salesforce, and propelled Mitsubishi Tokyo to the leading position among Japanese pharmaceutical companies.

Figure 17.5

System selling

and provides extensive support services and promotional input. In exchange, the franchisee pays a substantial royalty and an up-front franchise fee, and agrees to conduct the business exactly according to the instructions from the franchisor. An example of this in the business-to-business field is Snap-On Tools, which supplies tools to the light engineering and motor trade.

There are, of course, many other ways of describing types of salesperson. Suggestions have included customer partner, buyer–seller team coordinator, customer service provider, buyer behaviour expert, information gatherer, market analyst, forecaster and technologist (Rosenbloom and Anderson 1984; Wilson 1993a). As personal selling develops in complexity, other classifications may well emerge.

The Selling Cycle

Figure 17.6 shows the selling cycle. The selling sequence is drawn as a circle to indicate that it is an ongoing process, although in practice each salesperson will divide up his or her day in such a way as to carry out several, or even all, of the separate processes at once.

Lead generation activities are sometimes also called prospecting, although in fact they differ considerably. Lead generation is concerned with finding people who are prepared to meet the salesperson and hear what he or she has to say. **Prospects** are potential buyers who have a need for the product and the means to pay for it. Lead generation is a process of establishing first contact: leads are generated via advertising, cold-calling (making visits or telephone calls without an appointment), by running exhibition stands, by sending out mail shots or by personal recommendation.

Prospecting is about establishing that the lead has a need for the product, and also has the means to pay for it. In some cases these issues cannot be clearly determined in advance of meeting the potential customer, but a good salesperson will try to investigate a prospect as thoroughly as possible before wasting time on making a sales call.

Preparing for the sale involves preparing both physically and mentally: wearing the right clothes, having the right presentation materials to hand, having the right mental attitude and having the appropriate knowledge of the prospect's circumstances. Physical appearance is especially important – looking the part is at least halfway to being the part, and there is even evidence that salespeople's appearance affects the way they are assessed by sales managers (Vilela *et al.* 2007). Preparing is likely to be complex in business-to-business sales, since in many cases the salesperson will be calling on several firms in one day, each with a separate set of data to remember and each with a separate set of needs.

Appointing means making appointments to see the appropriate decision-maker. In consumer sales, this probably means ensuring that both husband and wife are present: salespeople are often advised to ensure that all the decision-makers are present, but in a business-to-business context this is unlikely to be possible. Therefore the salesperson may well go through a process of using one appointment to generate the next until all the decision-makers have been seen.

The **sales presentation** is a process of conducting a directed conversation in which the prospect's need is established and agreed, the supplier's solution is explained and the sale is closed. Closing the sale may mean that the order is placed or it may not: the purpose of the presentation is to get a decision, which may or may not be in favour of purchase. There is a section on the sales presentation later in the chapter.

leads People who are prepared to hear what a salesperson has to say.

prospects People who have a need for a product and the means to pay for it.

sales presentation A structured interview in which a salesperson ascertains a customer's needs and offers a solution which will meet those needs.

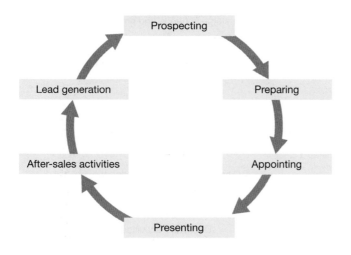

Figure 17.6
The selling cycle

After-sales activities include calling on the customer afterwards to ensure that the process went smoothly, to learn lessons for the future and perhaps to correct any shortcomings in the delivery or the product. Often salespeople are apparently afraid of carrying out follow-up calls, perhaps because of a fear that the customer will have a complaint: however, it is far better to find out from the customer that there is a problem than to be told that the customer has complained to the company. After-sales visits also offer opportunities for making further sales or asking for recommendations. Other after-sales activities include ensuring that the paperwork is correctly completed for the company's systems, ensuring that the products are delivered on time, representing the customer's views back to the company and providing other appropriate market information.

The Sales Presentation

Figure 17.7 shows the sequence of events which leads to an eventual sale.

Opening the sale

Particularly when first meeting a new customer, the salesperson needs to establish a personal rapport. This is established by showing a genuine interest in the customer and his or her problems: the traditional view of the salesperson as being a backslapping individual with a fund of good jokes is a long way from the truth.

icebreaker A statement or question used at the beginning of a sales presentation, with the intention of establishing a rapport with the buyer.

Typically salespeople begin with an 'icebreaker'. This is an opening remark or series of comments which tend to put the relationship on a human level; they are polite comments which anybody might use when meeting someone new. Comments about the weather or the state of the traffic help to put both parties at ease before getting down to business, but it is usual to proceed fairly quickly to the business at hand. Often the aim of the exercise is to create a perceived similarity between the salesperson and the prospect; if the prospect feels that they have something in common, this will increase the level of trust in what the salesperson has to say (Dion, Easterling and Miller 1995). Salespeople seek to establish relationships with their prospects, because this is a more certain way of

Figure 17.7

The sales visit

making sales (McKenna 1991); it is also a way of making the working day more pleasant.

The presentation

In the first instance, salespeople should be prepared to listen to what their customers have to say; selling is not about talking well, it is about listening to people's problems and finding solutions.

Second, salespeople need to be ultra-polite, and very aware of the customer's sensibilities. The overall impression should be that the salesperson is a 'friend in the business' – and in fact most salespeople will agree that it easier to find another company to work for than it is to find new customers. Good salespeople look after their customers.

Finally, telling lies to customers is counter-productive, since the lie will inevitably come to light once the customer takes delivery of the product. This leads to cancellation of contracts, return of the goods and even lawsuits – which the customer will almost certainly win. Unfortunately, the same is not true when the situation is reversed: it is a paradox of selling practice that the customer is free to tell any number of lies but the salesperson must tell the truth, despite popular belief to the contrary.

Although some customers regard salespeople with suspicion, the evidence is that salespeople actually seek to develop and maintain good relationships with their customers even when this conflicts with instructions from their marketing departments (Anderson and Robertson 1995). For the customer, the salesperson is a source of information, a source of help in problem-solving and is an advocate back to the supplying company. Good salespeople are also adept at helping their customers through the decision-making process; often this is the hardest part of making a sale.

Asking questions

The obvious way to find out the customer's needs is by asking questions. The traditional approach, which was developed by E.K. Strong in the 1920s, is to divide questions into two types: open questions and closed questions. An open question has a number of different possible answers, whereas a closed question can only be answered 'yes' or 'no' (Strong 1925). Here are some examples of open questions:

What sort of maintenance bills are you paying at the moment on your equipment?
Who is in charge of the budgets for maintenance?
Where should the shipment be delivered?

And some examples of closed questions:

Would you like me to show you how you can save on maintenance?
Shall I put you down for the 24-hour call-out service?
Should we deliver to the main warehouse?

Open questions are actually opening questions; they are the main tool the salesperson has for finding out about the customer's needs. Closed questions tend to be closing questions, used towards the end of the sales presentation to bring the customer to the decision point. Questions have a further important function, in that they enable the salesperson to keep control of the direction in which the presentation is going. Questions are powerful in directing people's thoughts; anybody with small children knows that the constant stream of questions is both distracting and wearing, because the child keeps triggering the adult's mind to think of a response. Questions demand attention in a way that statements do not.

The presentation itself is, in part, the transfer of knowledge from the salesperson to the prospect. Salespeople will, of course, have considerable knowledge about the products in the range, and probably of the industry in general.

Table 17.2 The NASA model

N	Needs. The salesperson asks the prospect about his or her needs: what problems does the prospect have?
A	Acceptance. Having ascertained the needs, the salesperson confirms with the prospect that these are in fact the needs, and obtains the prospect's acceptance of the problem.
S	Solution. The salesperson shows the prospect how the solution will meet his or her problem.
A	Acceptance again. This time the salesperson seeks the prospect's acceptance of the proposed solution.

Figure 17.8

Narrowing the problem

One method of structuring the presentation to the customer's needs is to adopt the NASA structure, shown in Table 17.2. If at any stage the salesperson is unable to get an acceptance, he or she should go back to the needs and review what the prospect's problem is. The NASA system places the emphasis on finding solutions to the prospect's need problem; researchers have demonstrated that this is the most effective way to achieve success in selling (Lund 1979).

During the solution part of the presentation, the salesperson explains about the particular product which seems to fit the prospect's needs. Because the presentation revolves around the specific customer, it is essential to refer back to those needs at each stage. People do not buy physical products, they buy what the product will do for them. The classic example is the hot water bottle: people do not buy a rubber bag with a stopper in it, they buy a warm bed.

Talking Point

If the sales presentation is a directed conversation, with the salesperson doing the directing, where is the consideration of the customer's needs? If the customer is being directed to say certain things, and answer certain questions in a particular way, and is (in short) being manipulated, how can we possibly then assert that his or her needs are being dealt with?

Or is it, perhaps, that the salesperson is somehow better qualified to lead the customer through the decision-making process? Do salespeople have some kind of special talent in problem-solving?

This means that a simple description of the product's features is entirely inadequate: the features must be converted to benefits if a sale is to result. Features are about what the product is; benefits are about what it will do for the customer.

Handling objections

Objections are queries or negative statements raised by the prospect in the course of the presentation. The prospect may, for example, say that a particular feature of the product is not wanted, or is an expensive frill. In most industries the same objections tend to crop up over and over again: common ones are 'We can't afford it', and 'I need to consult someone else about this'.

Although objections are often seen as being barriers to making the sale, good sales-people recognise them as requests for further information. Provided the objection is successfully answered, the negotiation can continue until a mutually acceptable solution is reached. Objections can be handled in the following way:

1 Repeat the objection back to the prospect, to confirm that both the salesperson and the prospect understand each other and the nature of the problem.

2 Isolate the objection; in other words, confirm that it is the only problem with the product.

3 Apologise for not having explained properly. This avoids making the prospect lose face or feel silly.

4 If the objection is false (i.e. has no basis in fact) explain how the product actually meets the problem; alternatively (if the objection is real), show how the benefits of the product outweigh the disadvantages.

5 Confirm with the prospect that the objection has been overcome.

Objections should be distinguished from conditions; a condition prevents the sale going ahead. The commonest ones are as shown in Table 17.3.

Often, conditions do not really exist, and are being used to cover up another objection which the prospect would prefer not to raise. Hidden objections need to be brought out into the open if the salesperson is to be able to answer them; this can sometimes be a difficult process, and relies heavily on the trust of the prospect. Salespeople can some-times use the direct approach of simply saying 'I get the feeling there's something else troubling you about the product – what's the problem?' Commonly the objection will be expressed as a desire to 'think about it'. In this case, the salesperson can say 'Yes, I

objections Questions raised by a prospect in the course of a sales presentation.

conditions Situations which make a sale impossible.

Table 17.3 Common conditions

Condition	What the salesperson should do
The prospect has no authority to make the decision.	Find out who does have the authority, and ask the prospect to make an appointment to see that person.
The firm has no money.	If this is true, the sale cannot go ahead. In most cases it is not true; buyers will often say that the budget has run out as a way of extracting extra concessions from the salesperson. Astute salespeople will find out who has the authority to increase the budget, or will arrange for payment to be deferred into the next financial year.
The firm has no need for the product.	Unless there is a need, no purchase will take place. This is a problem which the salesperson has caused by not properly identifying the needs in the first place.

Talking Point

understand that. But just to clarify things for me, what is it you particularly want to think about?' Often this will lead to a statement of the real objection.

If a customer is claiming that there is a condition in order to avoid raising an objection, shouldn't we respect that? Where does the salesperson get off, making people feel uncomfortable in order to get a sale?

Or is it simply that people are afraid of making a wrong decision, so they try to avoid making any decision at all? Are salespeople really more in the role of therapists, getting people to stand up and be counted when hard decisions have to be made?

Objections can also be classified as real and false. A real objection is a genuine problem with the product; a false objection arises from a misunderstanding, or refers to something that has not yet been covered in the presentation.

Objections can sometimes be used for a trial close: the salesperson says 'If we can overcome that problem for you, are we in business?' This can sometimes mean closing the sale early, but at the very least it brings out any other objections. As a general rule, it is advisable to deal with objections as they arise; leaving them all to the end of the presentation means that the prospect is sitting with negative feelings about the product for a long time. Objections must always be taken seriously; even if the salesperson feels that the problem is a small one, and the prospect is getting too concerned over a triviality, it may not seem that way to the prospect.

Closing the sale

closing techniques Those questions and behaviours which end the sales presentation and elicit a decision from the buyer.

Once all the objections have been answered, the sale can be closed. **Closing techniques** are ways of helping the prospect over the decision-making hurdle. Perhaps surprisingly, most people are reluctant to make decisions, even more so if they are professional buyers. This is perhaps because of the risks attached to making a mistake, but whatever the reason buyers often need some help in agreeing to the order. Salespeople use a number of closing techniques to achieve this: Table 17.4 has some examples.

There are, of course, many other closing techniques. Salespeople will typically use whichever one seems most appropriate to the situation.

Table 17.4 Examples of closing techniques

Technique	Explanation	Example
Alternative close	The prospect is offered two alternatives, each of which leads to the order.	'Would you like them in red, or in green?'
Order-book close	The salesperson writes down each feature in the order book as it is agreed during the presentation	'OK, you want the green ones, you want four gross, and your best delivery date is Thursdays. If you'll just autograph this for me, we'll get it moving for you.'
Immediate gain close	The prospect is shown that the sooner he or she agrees to the deal, the sooner he or she will get the benefits of the product	'Fine. So the sooner we get this paperwork sorted, the sooner you'll start making those savings, right?'

Salespeople should avoid asking prospects to 'sign' the order. This has negative connotations because it implies a final commitment – people talk of 'signing your life away' or 'signing your death warrant'. It is better to ask people to 'OK that for me' or 'Autograph this for me'.

Talking Point

We are told that selling is about solving problems. All well and good, but what happens when the customer says that the solution being offered isn't good enough? Does the salesperson give up? No. Apparently he or she then goes into objection-handling mode, then rapidly into closing mode using all sorts of psychological gymnastics to get the buyer signed up.

Is this behaviour peculiar to salespeople, though? How about when we are persuading a friend to come out for the evening or to go on a trip together? Even more so, when we are persuading our wife or husband (or girlfriend or boyfriend) to lose weight or give up smoking? We know it would be good for them to do this, and they know it too, but can they make a firm commitment?

Could it be that we are all salespeople at heart, just that some of us are not trained enough to do it well?

The astute reader will have recognised that the above sequence of events ties in closely with the NASA model described earlier. During the face-to-face part of the salesperson's job the prospect's needs always come first, followed by an acceptance of the needs, followed by the presentation of the solution to the need problem. Acceptance of the solution, or rejection of it, determines whether the sale goes ahead or not.

Post-presentation activities

It would clearly be rude simply to pack up the order forms and leave immediately after making the sale, so it is good practice to stay for a few moments and discuss other matters, or at the very least to recap on the sale and make sure the customer is happy with everything. In most cases the customer has (so far) only bought a promise to deliver, so it is also a good idea to leave behind some information about the product, a set of contact telephone numbers and copies of the documentation. This serves two purposes: first, it ensures that problems can be nipped in the bud because the customer can contact the firm at any time. Second, it gives the customer a sense of security and tends to reduce the incidence of cancellations. Buyer's remorse is the term for post-purchase regrets; some of these second thoughts come about because the buyer acquires new information or remembers something important which wasn't covered in the presentation, and some of them come from a feeling of mistrust which arises because the customer has nothing tangible to show for the commitment made at the close.

Sometimes salespeople are afraid that, by leaving information and contact telephone numbers, the customer will be encouraged to cancel. The reverse is the case. Customers who are able to telephone are (a) more confident that they don't need to and (b) able to do so if there is a problem, which means that the problem can be solved before the goods are delivered.

After-sales service

Sometimes salespeople are nervous about going back to customers they have sold to, for fear of cancellations or for fear of having to deal with complaints. The reason for this is that salespeople need to maintain a positive outlook about the company, the products and themselves, and dealing with customer complaints may mean that the salesperson becomes infected with negativity.

Figure 17.9

Benefits of revisiting customers

REVISIT THE CUSTOMER AFTER THE GOODS HAVE BEEN DELIVERED

Can resolve any problems with the goods or the delivery before the customer contacts the office

Can obtain positive feedback from the customer, generating 'feel-good factor' for the salesperson

Can generate repeat business from satisfied customers

In fact it is always worthwhile revisiting customers once the delivery of the product has been made. The reasons for this are as follows:

● If there is a problem, the visit offers the opportunity to rectify matters. Research shows that customers whose complaints are dealt with to their complete satisfaction become more loyal than those who didn't have a complaint in the first place (Coca-Cola Company 1981). Perhaps salespeople should actually encourage customers to complain, so that they can demonstrate how well they can handle complaints!

● If the customer is completely satisfied with the product (which is usually the case) this helps the salesperson feel even more positive about the firm and the products.

● Repeat sales often result, and a longer-term relationship can develop.

Salespeople usually find that only positive outcomes result from maintaining a good after-sales service.

Key Account Selling

A key account is one which possesses some or all of the following characteristics:

● It accounts for a significant proportion of the firm's overall sales. This means that the supplying firm is in a vulnerable position if the customer goes elsewhere. This in turn means that the supplier may be expected to negotiate significant changes in its methods, products, and business practices in order to fit in with the customer's business practices and needs.

● There is cooperation between distribution channel members rather than conflict. This places the emphasis strongly on good, effective channels of communication, with the salesperson in the front line.

● The supplier works interdependently with the customer to lower costs and increase efficiency. This again implies lengthy negotiations and frequent contact between the firms.

● Supply involves servicing aspects such as technical support, as well as delivery of physical products. Servicing aspects will often fall to the salesperson, and because of the intangible nature of services, good communication is at a premium.

Key account selling has the following features:

1 There will be many decision-makers involved, with very little likelihood of being able to meet all of them at one time.

2 It is frequently the case that the salesperson is not present when the final decision is made, and he or she may never meet the most senior decision-makers.

3 The problems which the salesperson is expected to address are complex and often insoluble in any permanent sense.

4 The consequences of the problem are often much more important than the immediate problem would suggest.

Traditional selling emphasises objection handling, overcoming the sales resistance of the buyer and closing the sale. This naturally tends to lead to a focus on the single transaction rather than on the whole picture of the relationship between the supplier and the buyer.

In itself, this may not matter for many purchases. A firm selling photocopiers, for example, has many competitors who are supplying broadly similar products. This means that a quick sale is essential, since otherwise the buyer will be getting several quotes from other firms and will probably make the final decision based on the price alone. In addition, repeat business will be unlikely to materialise, and will be a long time coming if it does, so the salesperson is not looking to establish a long-term relationship with the buyer, nor is the buyer particularly interested in establishing a long-term relationship with the salesperson. Both parties are mainly interested in solving the customer's immediate problems, then moving on to other business.

Selling to major accounts cannot follow the simplistic approach of finding out needs and closing which is used in traditional selling situations; it involves a much more drawn-out procedure. Buyers who are considering a major commitment to a supplier, either for a single large purchase or for a long-term stream of supplies, are unlikely to be impressed with a one-hour presentation followed by an alternative close. Also, the salesperson will need to sell the solution to his or her own firm, since major changes in products and practices are often needed.

In major account selling the emphasis shifts from objection handling towards objection prevention. The salesperson is concerned to ensure that objections do not arise, or at least if they do, that the answers are already in place. This means that the questions that need to be asked are a little more sophisticated than just the open-or-closed dichotomy. The system of classifying questions as open or closed is inadequate in a key account situation. Rackham (1995) identified four groupings of question types, as follows:

1 *Situation questions.* These questions are about finding out the current situation of the prospective customer, in terms of the customer's strategic direction, financial position, status of the problem and so forth.

2 *Problem questions.* These questions relate to the specific problem the buyer has at present. These questions help to develop mutual understanding of the problem and reveal the implied needs.

3 *Implication questions.* These explore the wider implications of the problem, and often reveal that the problem has much greater ramifications than were at first apparent. This makes the buyer feel the problem much more acutely.

4 *Need-payoff questions.* These questions enable the buyer to state explicit needs, which allows the seller to explain the benefits of the product.

This classification of questions has been registered as SPIN by Huthwaite Research Group Ltd. The process of working through these questions and covering all the implications of the proposed solution is time-consuming and will involve many people; this means that the one-call approach to selling which is typical of small sales will not apply to major accounts.

From a sales management viewpoint this has major implications. In small account sales, the one-call sale is the norm; typically, sales managers operate on the basis that the more calls the salespeople make, the more sales will result. On the face of it,

Major projects such as dams are typical key account situations.

Figure 17.10

Sales process in major accounts

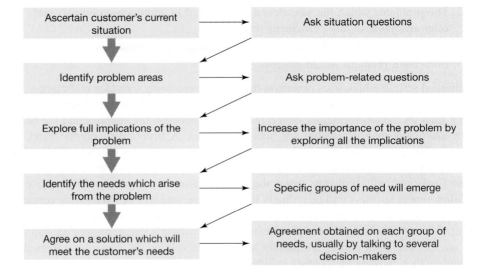

this is perfectly logical. If a salesperson has a closing rate of one in four (one sale for every four calls) then 20 calls will produce five sales, 40 calls will produce 10 sales, and 12 calls will only produce three sales. Therefore most sales managers apply pressure to their salesforces to make more calls.

In major account selling this approach would be disastrous. Encouraged (or compelled) to call on more customers, the salesperson will inevitably begin to call on only those customers who can be sold to quickly and easily, in other words the smaller accounts.

Sales productivity actually comes from two components: sales efficiency and sales effectiveness. Efficiency is about getting in front of the maximum number of prospects for the minimum cost; sales effectiveness is about maximising the sales potential once in front of the prospects. Both elements are important, but small account selling puts more emphasis on efficiency, whereas major account selling puts more emphasis on effectiveness.

In small account sales, managerial involvement is not usually hands-on. The managers who are most successful concentrate on managing sales team activities, but do little or no selling themselves and do not become involved directly with customers unless there is a major problem (Rackham 1995). In major account selling, though, the sales manager is almost certain to become directly involved with the customer at some stage, if only because such a large commitment on the part of the customer demands that he or she should speak to the senior management of the supplier firm. Sales managers should follow these principles when becoming involved in major sales:

● Only become involved when your presence makes a unique difference. The salesperson involved on the account is probably very deeply immersed in it, and will know a lot about the customer and the state of the negotiation; you cannot possibly know as much.

● Do not make sales calls on a customer unless your salesperson is with you. You could upset a delicate stage of the negotiation, or at the very least introduce new factors.

● Before any joint call, agree on specific and clear selling roles with your salesperson. Again, control needs to be strongly with the salesperson who is responsible for the account, so it is essential to trust that person's judgement.

● Be an active internal seller for your salespeople. The solution arrived at for the client is likely to involve internal changes for the supplier, some of which will not be popular with the other people in the firm. They will need to be convinced, and the sales manager is the best person to do this.

● Always have a withdrawal strategy that prevents any customer becoming too dependent on you personally. Customers may prefer to deal with 'the boss' rather than with the salesperson, but a sales manager cannot afford to spend all of his or her time out of the office selling to major accounts.

Problems arise for the sales manager in coaching major sales. In small sales, where the salesperson is perhaps making four or five calls a day, it is easily possible for the sales manager to accompany the salesperson for a day and observe what happens in calls. Corrections can be made to the salesperson's approach, and within a week or so the improvement in sales should become apparent. In major sales, the lead times between first contact with the client and the final agreement to the sale are likely to be very long indeed, often months and sometimes years; in those circumstances, coaching becomes difficult, to say the least. Improvements in methods may not show results for years, and therefore it may be difficult to motivate salespeople to make changes in their practices.

One of the biggest problems for the sales manager is that it is relatively easy to get people to work harder – extra incentives will usually motivate people to put in more hours, or otherwise increase sales efficiency. Increasing sales effectiveness, though, means getting people to 'work smarter', and since most people are working as 'smart' as they know how to already, extra incentives will probably not help.

The KAM/PPF Model

For the purposes of discussion, the Millman and Wilson definition of a key account will be used. For Millman and Wilson, a key account is a customer in a business-to-business market identified by a selling company as being of strategic importance (Millman and Wilson 1994). This definition avoids the problem of linking key account status to size, geographical location or volume of business. The implication is that an account can be small in volume terms, or can be a small company, but can represent a major breakthrough for the selling company, perhaps because the account opens the door to other, larger volumes of business. Key account management encapsulates all those activities intended to establish or maintain a relationship with a strategically important customer.

The Millman-Wilson (1995) relational development model is a tool for examining the initiation, growth and eventual demise of the relationship between firms. Linked to the Product, Process, Facilitation (PPF) model of relational interaction (Wilson 1993b), as shown in Table 17.5, it is possible to show that the types of problem being addressed

Table 17.5 The PPF model of problem characteristics

Problem category	Nature of problem
Product	Availability, performance, features, quality, design, technical support, order size, price, terms.
Process	Speed of response, manufacturing process issues, application of process knowledge, changes to product, project management issues, decision-making process knowledge, special attention in relation to deliveries, design, quotes, cost reduction.
Facilitation	Value creation, compatibility and integration of systems, alignment of objectives, integration of personnel, managing processes peripheral to customer core activity, strategic alignment.

and resolved by the partners in the relationship will vary according to the stage of the relationship.

The PPF model postulates that the nature of dyadic organisational relationships is directly related to the nature of the problems that the parties focus on resolving. In dyadic business relationships these problems are hierarchical, in that a more distant relationship between the parties will only generate problems related to products. The higher order problems of process and facilitation will only become apparent as the relationship becomes closer.

The Millman-Wilson relational development model describes the stages firms go through as the relationship achieves key account status (Millman and Wilson 1995). In the pre-KAM (key account management) stage, the firms do not have a relationship but are assessing whether there is potential for establishing key account status. In the early-KAM stage the supplying firm might develop preferred-supplier status. In the mid-KAM stage the partnership builds further, consolidating the preferred-supplier status. In the partnership-KAM stage the firms develop a spirit of partnership and build a common culture and the supplier locks in the customer, thus becoming the external resource base. In the synergistic-KAM stage the firms share rewards and become quasi-integrated. The final stage is the uncoupling-KAM stage in which the firms disengage.

The combined KAM/PPF model categorises the types of problem, and shows how these can be related to the stages that firms go through when establishing a key account relationship. Table 17.6 shows the PPF strategies mapped against the stages of the relational development model (Wilson 1999).

Table 17.6 KAM/PPF strategies

Development stage	Objectives	Strategies
Pre-KAM	Define and identify strategic account potential. Secure initial contact.	Identify key contacts and decision-making unit. Establish product need. Display willingness to address other areas of the problem. Advocate key-account status in-house.
Early-KAM	Account penetration. Increase volume of business. Achieve preferred supplier status.	Build social network. Identify process-related problems and signal willingness to work together to provide cost-effective solutions. Build trust through performance and open communications.
Mid-KAM	Build partnership. Consolidate preferred-supplier status. Establish key account in-house.	Focus on product-related issues. Manage the implementation of process-related solutions. Build inter-organisational teams. Establish joint systems. Begin to perform non-core management tasks.
Partnership-KAM	Develop spirit of partnership. Build common culture. Lock-in customer by being external resource base.	Integrate processes. Extend joint problem-solving. Focus on cost reduction and joint value-creating opportunities. Address key strategic issues of the client. Address facilitation issues.
Synergistic-KAM	Continuous improvement. Shared rewards. Quasi-integration.	Focus on joint value creation. Create semi-autonomous projects teams. Develop strategic congruence.
Uncoupling-KAM	Disengagement.	Withdraw.

The strategic issues raised at different stages of the relationship connect with the firm's communication strategies, and particularly with the stated strategies of firms at trade fairs. In the early stages, communication might be dominated by outbound messages from the selling company, but in the later stages a true dialogue is likely to be the prevailing paradigm.

Negotiation

'You don't get what you deserve in this life; you get what you negotiate.' Negotiation is about coming to a mutual agreement, where each party is prepared to give up something in order to obtain concessions from the other party. The emphasis on negotiation that is so apparent at present has come about largely because of the emphasis on establishing long-term relationships between customers and suppliers, and is particularly important in major account selling.

The basis on which negotiation rests is that both parties will benefit as a result of the trade. In everyday terms, a shopkeeper would prefer to have money than have the goods on the shelves, whereas the customers would prefer to have the goods than have the money. If this were not the case, trade would be impossible. The contract results at any point along a line drawn between the maximum amount of money the customers are prepared to pay and the minimum amount the retailer is prepared to accept. In a Middle Eastern bazaar, the price would be subject to negotiation by the parties, with the shopkeeper trying to get the highest price and the customer trying to pay the lowest. In Western shops there is only an indirect negotiation, with the customer going to the retailer who offers the best deal; this can scarcely be called negotiation at all.

Negotiating follows eight stages, as shown in Table 17.7. Negotiation takes practice and a considerable degree of empathy; good negotiators need to be able to judge other people's behaviour accurately and reliably, and do this in real time with the customer present. Having a negotiation orientation from the start will underpin behaviour throughout the presentation (Brooks and Rose 2004).

Negotiation is the norm in Asian street markets.

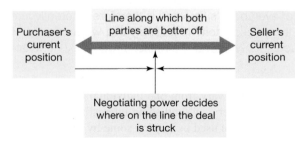

Figure 17.11

Benefit of negotiation

Table 17.7 Eight stages of negotiation

Stage	Explanation
Preparation	Good negotiators set targets: what is the maximum they might achieve, what is the minimum they are willing to accept and what is the most probable outcome. This may mean working out detailed costings. More importantly, the negotiator needs to work out what it is the other side are likely to want and be prepared to give – this avoids surprises in the discussions.
Discussion	Listening carefully to what the other party is saying usually gives a clue as to how to express a counter-offer, or even to what it is the person really wants from the negotiation.
Signals	Negotiators need to give clear signals when the discussion is going in the right direction. This encourages further movement and helps the negotiation to proceed.
Proposition	The proposition being offered needs to be fair and flexible. Nelson Rockefeller's business maxim was 'Always leave something for the next guy'. What he meant was that negotiators should always allow the other party to make something from the deal: in following this rule, Rockefeller ensured that everybody wanted to do business with him, because they knew they would always benefit from it.
Presentation	It is essential to communicate effectively so that the both parties are clear about exactly what is on offer and what each is going to gain.
Bargain	Bargaining is about getting something back for what one is prepared to offer. If the other party says, 'Can you cut the price another 5 per cent?' the salesperson should not just agree to do it. The salesperson needs to say 'OK, we'll cut it if you'll guarantee to order 20 per cent more goods'. In other words, salespeople should negotiate, not donate.
Close	At some point both parties will need to summarise their positions and come to an agreement. This should be done once both parties are happy with the deal they are getting, so the close need not be aggressive or manipulative.
Agreement	Any agreement made needs to be put in writing to ensure that there is no misunderstanding. Salespeople should also seek some kind of formal commitment from the other party, either in cash or as a contract.

Talking Point

Negotiation seems to be a fact of life in Middle Eastern bazaars and indeed in most developing countries, and in the past was a regular feature of life in every country. So why have we (largely) given up on it in industrial countries? Why don't we haggle in supermarkets, or agree a price with a taxi driver before we get in?

Is it because haggling simply takes up too much of everybody's time and is therefore inherently inefficient? Is it that people are not confident of their ability to outsmart the salesperson? Is it simply that we are so rich that we just pay whatever is asked, without considering the consequences? Whatever the reasons, we rarely negotiate!

Techniques of negotiation vary from one individual to the next, but the list shown in Table 17.8 gives a useful overview (and some interesting names) for some of the main ones. Some of these tactics are used by buyers, some by salespeople, some by both; some are acceptable bargaining ploys, some are somewhat dubious ethically and are intended to get the best deal in a one-off selling or buying situation.

Table 17.8 Negotiating tactics

Tactic	Description and explanation
Act Crazy	Moving around from one topic to another can sometimes disorientate the other party and cause their carefully prepared position to collapse. This is a tactic sometimes used by buyers in traditional selling situations, where they want to confuse the salesperson.
Big Pot	Here the salesperson quotes a high price initially, in order to have room to manoeuvre later. Equally, a buyer may imply that a very large order will be placed in order to negotiate a better deal.
Prestigious Ally	Mention of an existing customer who has influence over the prospect may sway the sale. For example, a computer salesperson selling to a car component manufacturer is more likely to get the sale if he or she is already selling to Ford.
The Well is Dry	The negotiator says that there is no further room for negotiation: the deal must either go ahead as it is, or not at all. This is a somewhat dangerous tactic, since the other party might well call a halt at that point; it is advisable to leave the door open, perhaps by appealing to senior management to allow a little more room for negotiation.
Limited Authority	This is similar to The Well is Dry. Here the negotiator says that the deal has gone as far as she or he is authorised to take it. This can have the effect of producing a little more from the other party, or it could lead to a demand to speak to someone who does have the authority to negotiate.
Whipsaw!	This needs two negotiators, one to play 'good cop' and the other to play 'bad cop'. The 'bad cop' tries to drive as hard a bargain as possible, then when that is rejected the 'good cop' (the other negotiator) speaks privately to the other party and says 'Maybe I can talk him round. Can you go just a little bit higher?'
Divide and Conquer	This is very commonly used in industrial selling due to the large number of people involved in the buying process. The salesperson approaches each one in turn, separately, and gets some kind of agreement to go ahead 'provided the others agree'. Finally there is no-one left to veto the deal.
Get Lost	Very common in the legal profession, the negotiator simply is unavailable for comment. This tactic is intended to unnerve the other party, who then may offer more than was intended in order to secure the deal.
Wet Noodle	The negotiator simply doesn't respond to anything. This tends to make the other party improve the offer in the hopes of provoking a reaction and kick-starting the negotiation.
Be Patient	Just being quiet and letting the other person keep talking will often lead them into persuading themselves.
Split the Difference	Probably the most common bargaining tactic of all, 'Let's split the difference'. The person who first suggests it probably has the most to gain; it is worth waiting it out to get an even better deal.
Play Devil's Advocate	The negotiator gives the other party some good reasons *not* to accept the deal. Often this will provoke the other party into justifying why the deal should go ahead – the tactic works by using reverse psychology.
Trial Balloon	'I suppose you'd go ahead if we were to offer…'. This type of statement allows the negotiator to judge whether the other party is open to an offer, without actually committing to making the offer.
Surprise!	The negotiator suddenly slips in some new information which puts everything else in a different light and restarts the negotiation on different lines. Sometimes this is done in order to unsettle the other party; more often it is done to restart a stalled negotiation.

Ultimately, the deal that is struck will depend on the relative strength of each party in terms of their firms' negotiating positions, and on the skills and charisma of the negotiators. The process is not a mechanical one; as pointed out at the beginning of this chapter, business is not done by companies, it is done by people. The chemistry between two individuals is at least as important as the final economics of the deal itself.

Managing the Salesforce

Possibly the most expensive marketing tool the company has, the salesforce, is in some ways the hardest to control. This is because it is composed of independently-minded people who each have their own ideas on how the job should be done and who are working away from the office and out of sight of the sales managers. Sales managers are responsible for recruitment, training, motivation, controlling and evaluating salesforce activities, and managing sales territories.

Recruitment is complicated by the fact that there is no generally applicable set of personality traits that go to make up the ideal salesperson. This is because the sales task varies greatly from one firm to another, and the sales manager will need to draw up a specific set of desirable traits for the task in hand. This will involve analysing the company's successful salespeople – and also the less successful ones – to find out what the differences are between them.

Some companies take the view that almost anybody can be trained to sell, and therefore the selection procedures are somewhat limited, or even non-existent: other companies are extremely selective and subject potential recruits to a rigorous selection procedure.

Sources of potential recruits are advertising, employment agencies, recommendations from existing sales staff, colleges and universities and internal appointments from other departments. Training can be long or short, depending on the product and the market. Table 17.9 illustrates the dimensions of the problem.

The role the salesperson is required to take on will also affect the length of training; missionary salespeople will take longer to train than order-takers and closers will take longer than telesales operators. Traditional salesforces are under pressure from direct channels and from key account sales approaches: the solution to this is to improve training so that people 'work smart', to manage interfaces between customer and salesperson better, and to integrate processes better (Piercy and Lane 2003).

Table 17.9 Factors relating to length of training of sales staff

Factors indicating long training	Factors indicating short training
Complex, technical products	Simple products
Industrial markets with professional buyers	Household, consumer markets
High order values (from the customer's viewpoint)	Low order values
High recruitment costs	Low recruitment costs
Inexperienced recruits – for example, recruited directly from university	Experienced recruits from the same industry

Typically, training falls into two sections: classroom training, in which the recruits are taught about the company and the products and may be given some grounding in sales techniques, and field training, which is an ongoing training programme carried out in front of real customers in the field. Field training is often the province of the sales managers, but classroom training can be carried out by other company personnel (in some cases, in larger firms, there will be specialists who do nothing else but train sales people). Sales team learning is impacted by the salesforce's perception of the organisation's willingness to change, however: if salespeople feel that the organisation will still expect them to continue with the same processes and procedures, they are unlikely to want to study new methods (Rangajaran *et al.* 2004).

People tend to learn best by performing the task, so most sales training programmes involve substantial field training, either by sending out rookies (trainees) with experienced salespeople, or by the 'in-at-the-deep-end' approach of sending rookies out on their own fairly early in their careers. The latter method is indicated if there are plenty of possible customers for the product; the view is that a few mistakes (lost sales) won't matter. In business-to-business selling, though, it is often the case that there are fewer possible customers and therefore the loss of even one or two could be serious. In these circumstances it would be better to give rookies a long period of working alongside more experienced salespeople.

Ultimately, of course, salespeople will lose more sales than they get. In most industries, fewer than half the presentations given result in a sale: a typical proportion would be one in three.

Payment for salespeople traditionally has a **commission** element, but it is perfectly feasible to use a straight salary method or a commission-only method. Although it is commonly supposed that a commission-only salesperson will be highly motivated to work hard, since otherwise he or she will not earn any money, this is not necessarily the case. Salespeople who are paid solely by commission will sometimes decide that they have earned enough for this month and will give themselves a holiday; the company has very little moral power to compel them to work, since there is no basic salary being paid. Conversely, a salesperson who is paid salary only may feel obligated to work in order to justify the salary.

commission Performance-related payments made to salespeople.

Herzberg (1975) says that the payment method must be seen to be fair if demotivation is to be avoided; the payment method is not in itself a good motivator. Salespeople are out on the road for most of their working lives and do not see what other salespeople are doing; whether they are competent at the job, whether they are getting some kind of unfair advantage, even whether they are working at all. In these circumstances a commission system does at least reassure the salesperson that extra effort brings extra rewards. There is evidence that salespeople also judge pay fairness on supervisory behaviour, trust and interactional fairness, i.e. negotiation and explanation (Ramaswamy and Singh 2003).

Table 17.10 shows the trade-offs between commission-only and salary-only; of course, most firms have a mixture of salary and commission.

Motivation, perhaps surprisingly, tends to come from sources other than payment. The classic view of motivation was proposed by Abraham Maslow (1954). Maslow's Hierarchy of Need theory postulates that people will fulfil the needs at the lower end of a pyramid (survival needs and security needs) before they move on to addressing needs at the upper end (such as belonging needs, esteem needs and self-actualisation needs). Thus, once a salesperson has assured his or her basic survival needs, these cease to be motivators; the individual will then be moving onto esteem needs or belonging needs. For this reason sales managers usually have a battery of motivational devices for salespeople to aim for.

For **rookies**, the award of a company tie might address the need to belong; for more senior salespeople, membership of a Millionaire's Club (salespeople who have sold more than a million pounds' worth of product) might address esteem needs. Many sales

rookie A new sales recruit.

Table 17.10 Trade-offs in salespeople's pay packages

Mainly salary	*Mainly commission*
Where order values are high	Where order values are low
Where the **sales cycle** is long	Where the sales cycle is short
Where staff turnover is low	Where staff turnover is high
Where sales staff are carefully selected against narrow criteria	Where selection criteria for staff are broad
For new staff, or staff who have to develop new territories	For situations where aggressive selling is indicated (e.g. selling unsought goods)
Where sales territories are seriously unequal in terms of sales potential	Where sales territories are substantially the same

sales cycle The series of activities undertaken by salespeople.

Figure 17.12

Motivation tools

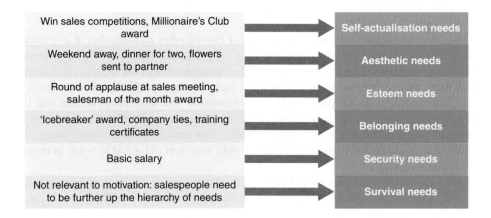

Win sales competitions, Millionaire's Club award	Self-actualisation needs
Weekend away, dinner for two, flowers sent to partner	Aesthetic needs
Round of applause at sales meeting, salesman of the month award	Esteem needs
'Icebreaker' award, company ties, training certificates	Belonging needs
Basic salary	Security needs
Not relevant to motivation: salespeople need to be further up the hierarchy of needs	Survival needs

managers offer prizes for salespeople's spouses or partners. This can be a powerful incentive, since salespeople often work unusual hours and thus have disrupted home lives; the spouse or partner is sometimes neglected in favour of the job, so a prize aimed at them can help assuage the salesperson's natural feelings of guilt.

Sales **territory** management involves ensuring that the salesforce have a reasonably equal chance of making sales. Clearly a garage tools salesperson in a major city will have an easier task than one in a rural area, simply because of the shorter distances between prospects; such a salesperson would spend more time in presentations and less time driving. On the other hand, the city salesperson would probably face more competition and might also have to spend more time caught in traffic during rush hour periods.

Territories can be divided geographically or by industry; IBM divide territories by industry, for example, so that salespeople get to know the problems and needs of the specific industry for which they have responsibility. IBM salespeople might be given responsibility for banks, insurance companies or local government departments. This sometimes means that salespeople have greater distances to travel in order to present IBM products, but are more able to make sensible recommendations and give useful advice.

territory The geographical area or group of potential customers allocated to a salesperson.

Geographical territories are more common, since they minimise travel time and maximise selling time.

It is virtually impossible to create exactly equal territories. Thus it is important to discuss decisions with salespeople in order to ensure that people feel they are being treated fairly. For example, some salespeople may be quite happy to accept a rural territory because they like to live and work in the country, even if it means earning less.

Summary

The salesforce is a major part of business-to-business budgets. In many cases, salespeople spend relatively little time actually selling, and a great deal of time filling in paperwork, travelling between appointments and so forth. This means that much sales management effort is directed towards ensuring that the salespeople spend as little time on administration as possible and are effective when they are in front of a customer.

The key points from this chapter are:

- Selling is about solving problems for customers, it is not about persuasion.

- Selling may not belong in the communications mix at all.

- Salespeople often identify with customers.

- Objections are requests for information: conditions are states of affairs which make the sale impossible.

- After-sales activities are essential, but are often neglected.

- Techniques used in small-scale accounts are counterproductive in key account selling.

- The same is true of management techniques.

- Commission is a way of ensuring fairness: it is probably not a strong motivator.

Chapter review questions

1 What are the main differences between key account selling and small account selling?

2 Which remuneration system would you expect to be more highly motivating: a commission-only system or a straight-salary system?

3 Why is ice-breaking important?

4 Why do salespeople tend to identify with customers more than with the firms they work for?

5 Why are after-sales activities often neglected?

6 What type of territory design would you expect to see in the pharmaceutical industry?

7 What is the difference between an objection and a condition?

8 Why is it counterproductive to pressure key account salespeople into increasing their activity levels?

9 Why is it effective to pressure small account salespeople into increasing their activity levels?

10 Why should salespeople try to develop negotiating skills?

Preview case revisited
Jewson

In 2004, Jewson began the process of redesigning the company's internal sales systems to conform with ISO 9001. The process took six months, during which time the company assessed their existing systems and generated a gap analysis. Areas for improvement were identified, but this process continues to this day – part of the ISO 9001 accreditation involves building in systems for continuous improvement. One key area which Tony Newman (then the Sales Director of Jewson) identified was customer enquiry and quotation turnaround – the quicker customer enquiries could be followed up with a quotation the better, and the new systems meant that Jewson could respond more quickly than competitors were able to when asked to quote for supplying materials.

Jewson also run regular surveys of their major customers in order to identify areas where further improvements in service can be made. Staff members were very supportive of the changes – they had always been concerned about ensuring customer satisfaction, but the ISO 9001 compliance meant that they had a framework in which to operate. Following the procedures meant that they could offer top-flight service every time: it also provided reassurance that, provided they followed the set procedures, any failures would be the fault of the system rather than being blamed on the staff member. Tony Newman is quoted as saying that the new standard did not fundamentally change the staff attitude to customers – it simply provided them with a set of procedures which soon became second nature to follow.

The result of the implementation of ISO 9001 was an overall increase in efficiency. The company found that it was having to issue fewer credit notes, because sales staff were making fewer errors. Business from public sector organisations increased, because for many such organisations compliance with ISO 9001 is a prerequisite for doing business. Customer complaints coming into the sales offices have been reduced to an absolute minimum – which is of course good for sales staff morale as well as for customer relations.

As Sales Director, Tony Newman has no hesitation in recommending ISO 9001 to other companies as a way of reducing customer problems, improving staff morale and increasing business. Less time spent on correcting errors and dealing with complaints means more time available for looking after customers – which is exactly what every sales office seeks to achieve.

Case study
Snap-On Tools

Few garages or light engineering firms would not have heard of Snap-On Tools. This tool supply franchise is ubiquitous, supplying high quality tools to engineers throughout the world.

Snap-On had its beginnings in the 1920s when two Americans, Joseph Johnson and William Seideman, formed a company which manufactured and sold socket sets which fitted onto interchangeable handles. The advantages of the new system were obvious – the average engineer's tool box became substantially lighter and less bulky as a result of the innovation, but of course the benefits of the new system had to be demonstrated. The fledgling company's first salesman, Stanton Palmer, took the tools directly to potential customers and demonstrated them at the customer's own place of business.

This approach proved too slow: Palmer could not possibly call on enough people, and the number of tools in the range was steadily increasing, so the company began to sell franchises to independent distributors. In the 1950s, Snap-On introduced walk-in vans which were fully stocked with Snap-On products, By this time the company had spread outside the United States and was becoming a world leader in tool supply. The company's reputation for high quality, coupled with the convenience of having the van call to the workplace, quickly turned Snap-On into a success story.

Many Snap-On franchisees are themselves from engineering backgrounds. This means that they can 'talk the talk' with fellow engineers and mechanics, and they are often already familiar with the tools. Some are from business backgrounds of course – having run everything from market stalls to restaurants before choosing to buy a Snap-On franchise.

The fact that the franchisees are their own bosses does not mean that Snap-On can ignore motivation issues, of course. While most franchisees are self-motivated to a very large extent, they all still need some extra goals and incentives from time to time. Snap-On run a series of sales contests and incentive schemes – for example, the top-selling franchisees are often given foreign holidays on which they can take their wives (or husbands, as the case may be). This is a well deserved 'thank you' not only to the franchisees, but also to their partners, who often have to put up with disrupted home lives as a result of the dedicated approach successful franchisees need to have in this demanding business. Other prizes have included motor racing experiences, a natural type of prize for a firm in the engineering business.

Franchisees are required to meet minimum service levels each week (this helps to protect the Snap-On brand) but they are then able to set their own schedules and relate to customers in their own way. This gives franchisees a great deal of flexibility – though if course if they are to succeed they do need to work as much as possible during the periods when their customers' businesses are operating.

Becoming a Snap-On franchisee is by no means a matter of simply handing over the franchise fee. The minimum personal investment is £11 000, with a total investment of £60 000 needed (some of which can be borrowed). The applicants will need a certain amount of engineering knowledge, but undergo extensive training in product knowledge and sales techniques before going out on the road. Training is a continuing affair, however – franchisees are assigned to a Field Group of approximately 10–12 franchisees. The group meets periodically for training sessions, and the Field Group manager goes out with franchisees to provide field training.

In 2007, Snap-On was awarded the British Franchisor of the Year award, in recognition of the company's professionalism and top-class training and support. For the 400 and more franchisees, Snap-On's approach to sales management has meant an opportunity to create a successful business – and earn some serious money.

Questions

1 Why would someone who has invested £60 000 in a business need motivation from a sales manager?

2 What other motivational tools might Snap-On use?

3 How can Snap-On improve its recruitment?

4 What are the advantages of requiring an up-front investment from franchisees?

5 What specific training problems might there be for Snap-On?

References

Anderson, E. and Robertson, T.S. (1995): Inducing multi-line salespeople to adopt house brands. *Journal of Marketing* **59**(2), 16–31.

Booms, B.H. and Bitner, M.J. (1981): Marketing strategies and organisation structures for service firms. In J. Donnelly and W.R. George (eds) *Marketing of Services* (American Marketing Association).

Brooks, B.L. and Rose, R.L. (2004): A contextual model of negotiation orientation. *Industrial Marketing Management* **33**(2), 125–33.

Cespedes, F.V. (1996): *Managing Marketing Linkages Texts, Cases and Readings* (Upper Saddle River, NJ: Prentice-Hall.).

Coca-Cola Company, The (1981): *Measuring the Grapevine: Consumer Response and Word of Mouth*.

DeCormier, R. and Jobber, D. (1993): The counsellor selling method; concepts, constructs, and effectiveness. *Journal of Personal Selling and Sales Management* **13**(4), 39–60.

Dewsnap, B. and Jobber, D. (1998): The sales and marketing interface: is it working? *Proceedings of the Academy of Marketing Conference*. Sheffield.

Dion, R, Easterling, D. and Miller, S.J. (1995): What is really necessary in buyer–seller relationships? *Industrial Marketing Management* **24**, 1–9.

Donaldson, W. (1998): *Sales Management Theory and Practice* (London: MacMillan).

Geiger, S. and Turley, D. (2005): Socialising behaviours in business-to-business selling: an exploratory study from the Republic of Ireland. *Industrial Marketing Management* **34**(3), 263–73.

Geiger, S. and Turley, D. (2006): The perceived impact of information technology on salespeople's relational competencies. *Journal of Marketing Management* **22**(7/8), 827–51.

Herzberg, F. (1975): *Work and the Nature of Man* (London: Crosby Lockwood).

Le Meunier-Fitzhugh, K. and Piercy, N.F. (2007): Exploring collaboration between sales and marketing. *European Journal of Marketing* **41**(7/8), 939–55.

Lund, P.R. (1979): *Compelling Selling* (London: Macmillan).

Maslow, A. (1954): *Motivation and Personality* (New York: Harper and Row).

McKenna, R. (1991): *Relationship Marketing* (London: Century Business).

Millman, T. and Wilson, K.J. (1995): Developing key account managers. *IMP Twelfth International Conference Proceedings*. Manchester Federal School of Business and Management, 1995.

Millman, A.F. and Wilson, K.J. (1996): Developing key account management competencies. *Journal of Marketing Practice* **2**(2), 7–22.

Piercy, N.F. and Lane, N. (2003): Transformation of the traditional salesforce: imperatives for intelligence, interface and integration. *Journal of Marketing Management* **19**, 563–82.

Rackham, N. (1991): *The Management of Major Sales* (Aldershot: Gower).

Rackham, N. (1995): *Spin Selling* (Aldershot: Gower).

Ramaswamy, S.N. and Singh, J. (2003): Antecedents and consequences of merit pay fairness for industrial salespeople. *Journal of Marketing* **67**(4), 46–66.

Rangajaran, D., Chonko, L.B., Jones, E. and Roberts, J.A. (2004): Organisational variables, salesforce perceptions of readiness for change, learning, and performance among boundary-spanning teams: a conceptual framework and propositions for research. *Industrial Marketing Management* **33**(4), 289–305.

Rosenbloom, B. and Anderson, R.E. (1984): The sales manager: tomorrow's super marketer. *Business Horizons* (**March–April**), 50–6.

Strong, E.K. (1925): *The Psychology of Selling* (New York: McGraw-Hill).

Turley, D. and Geiger, S. (2006): Exploring salesperson learning in the client relationship nexus. *European Journal of Marketing* **40**(5/6), 662–81.

Vilela, B.B., Gonzalez, J.A.V., Ferrin, P.F. and delRio Araujo, L. (2007): Impression management tactics and affective context: influence on sales performance appraisal. *European Journal of Marketing* **41**(5/6), 624–39.

Wilson, K.J. (1999): Developing key-account relationships: the integration of the Millman-Wilson relational development model with the problem-centred [PPF] model of buyer–seller interaction in business-to-business markets. *The Journal of Selling and Major Account Management* **1**(4).

Wilson, K.J. (1993a): A problem-centred approach to key account management. Proceedings of the National Sales Management Conference, Atlanta.

Wilson, K.J. (1993b) Managing the industrial sales force of the 1990s. *Journal of Marketing Management* **9**(2), 123–39.

Further reading

Blythe, J. (2005): *Sales and Key-account Management* (London: Thomson Learning). This is a current academic textbook on the sales process.

Rackham, N. (2000): *Spin Selling* (Aldershot: Gower). This is the classic book on key-account selling. Although it is intended for practitioners and managers, it is based on sound research and offers exceptionally good, clear advice for salespeople.

Chapter 18
Exhibitions and sales promotion

Learning objectives After reading this chapter, you should be able to:

1. Explain how exhibitors should evaluate their activities.

2. Plan suitable objectives for an exhibition.

3. Decide on staffing issues for manning exhibition stands.

4. Explain how to link sales promotions to exhibitions.

5. Describe the difference between push strategies and pull strategies.

6. Explain how to plan for an exhibition.

7. Select sales promotions to accomplish specific tasks.

8. Explain how sales promotions can be used by salespeople.

9. Explain how sales promotions can be used to create permanent rises in sales.

Introduction

Exhibitions and trade fairs are among the most widely used marketing tools, and yet at the same time they are the least well-researched. Even experienced exhibitors have very little idea of how, or even whether, exhibitions are effective.

Sales promotions allow free rein to the imagination of the manager. So many sales promotion activities are used by clever managers, yet this area has received only limited attention from academics. In business-to-business marketing, sales promotions are often played down, yet they still have a potentially important role to play.

Exhibitions and Trade Fairs as Communication

Exhibitions and trade fairs represent a substantial commitment on the part of marketers. Total expenditure on exhibitions and trade fairs in the UK is consistently higher than the spend on magazine advertising, and is also higher than the combined expenditure on outdoor, cinema and radio advertising. Yet few exhibitors assess the effectiveness of this activity in any realistic way, and there is continuing academic debate about whether exhibitions are actually effective in communicating with target markets. Attitudes are polarised

Preview case
Sixth China International Auto Supplies Sourcing Fair

China has come a long way in only 30 or so years: until the mid-1970s China was a closed country, with few (if any) imports or exports and little contact with the outside world. This state of affairs began to change after the death of Chairman Mao Tse-Tung (sometimes spelled Mao Zhedong), the Communist leader of China since the 1940s.

Opening up for trade really began to take off in the mid-1990s, but the country is on a steep learning curve and there are still many restrictions on trade both into and out of the country. Chinese industry began by competing on price – in a command economy, there need not be any connection between the costs of manufacture and the selling price, especially if the product is to be sold for much-needed hard currencies such as pounds, euros, US dollars or yen. At first, China's cheap, shoddy products flooded into Western markets, usually being sold in 'cheap shops'. Soon, though, Taiwanese and Hong Kong entrepreneurs took over, instituting quality control procedures which dramatically raised the standards of manufacture, and also bringing much-needed marketing skills to the mainland.

2008 saw China hosting the Olympic Games, symbolically bringing the country into the world family of nations. The same year brought the Sixth International Auto Supplies Sourcing Fair, held in Shanghai. The fair is one of the biggest exhibitions of its kind in China, with 500 exhibitors and around 50 000 visitors – and it has been growing dramatically year-on-year, to the point where it had to be moved from its first home (Shanghai Intex Expo) to the Shanghai New International Expo Centre, the largest exhibition centre in China.

The exhibition is organised by a consortium of local auto trade associations, including the China Auto Fitting Industry Federation and the Shanghai Auto Parts Circulating Trade Association. The State Administration for Industry and Commerce has overall administrative responsibility for the event – a clear reminder that the major part of Chinese industry is still State owned and controlled.

Shanghai is well-connected to the rest of the world, and even during the Mao era, when China was highly regimented (even to the point of the entire population being dressed in identical jackets) Shanghai maintained its cosmopolitan character – Shanghai natives dressed in fashionable clothes and had fewer restrictions than elsewhere in China. Pre-Communism, Shanghai welcomed foreigners, and many foreign-owned enterprises were based there. The problem for the exhibition organisers lies in establishing credibility both for the exhibition and for the exhibitors, many of which are Chinese-owned companies, given the poor reputation of Chinese goods in the past.

Another problem lies in language. China simply lacks sufficient good linguists: European languages are difficult for Mandarin speakers to learn, and (as is clear from even a casual investigation of Chinese websites) the English is variable to say the least – and the lack of sufficient native English speakers to check the spelling and grammar compounds the problem.

among exhibitors: some believe strongly that exhibitions are excellent promotional tools, whereas others believe exhibitions are marginal at best (Blythe and Rayner 1996).

One of the areas of dispute is the split between activities relating directly to making sales (generating leads, identifying prospects, even making sales pitches on the stand) and the non-sales benefits of exhibitions (public relations, enhancing corporate reputation, carrying out market research, etc.). Most exhibitors are concerned mainly with immediate sales (Shipley, Egan and Wong 1993; Kijewski, Yoon and Young 1992; Blythe 1997). Having said that, some exhibitors are more concerned with non-selling activities.

Exhibitions occupy a key role in business-to-business marketing, since they allow contact with buyers who otherwise might never meet due to geographical or time constraints. This is particularly the case with international trade fairs such as those held in Germany, where exhibitions occupy a more important role than in most other countries. Exhibitions such as these can bring together people who might otherwise not have known of each others' existence. Since contact at a fair takes place on neutral territory, both

Figure 18.1

Selling and non-selling activities at exhibitions

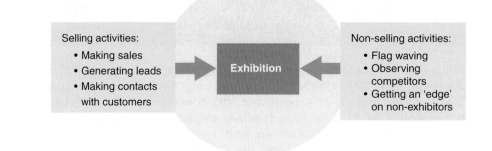

Talking Point

parties can feel more relaxed, so exhibitions offer an opportunity for the relationship between buying company and selling company to develop more fully, and perhaps develop in unexpected directions. Since many visitors are technical people or administrators rather than buyers, there are many opportunities for establishing contacts at all levels of the organisation.

It's interesting to note how people seem to separate marketing from selling. Of course, personal selling is a separate activity within marketing, but presumably the aim of *all* marketing is to increase the amount of business the firm does? Or at the very least, to persuade customers and others to behave in particular ways towards the firm and its products?

Let's not get too precious here – Alan Sugar once famously said, when asked what his corporate mission was, 'We want your money!' So how do we divide selling activities from non-selling activities? And does it matter?

As a public relations exercise, exhibitions have much to offer. Since buyers are only a tiny minority of visitors to exhibitions (less than 10 per cent at most) (Blythe 2000; Gramman 1994), selling objectives are probably not the most important activities to be undertaken. Yet, almost everybody who visits has some interest in the industry for which the exhibition is organised. This means that many of them will be influential in the buying decision, or at the very least might talk to people who are influential.

In terms of semiotics, trade fairs provide signs about the company and its products. For some firms, the sign is the main reason for exhibiting – being at the exhibition at all gives a signal that the company is at the forefront of the industry, or at least is not one of the laggards. In most cases, though, trade fairs are the vehicle by which signs are delivered. Sign systems of trade fairs are well-known – the stand, the suited personnel, the product samples, the free gifts, the product demonstrations and set-piece displays are typical of trade fairs. Each system has an accepted etiquette, so that visitors and exhibitors know what their role is when attending the show.

Syntactically, trade shows tend to be stylised. The meaning of a brochure offered at a trade show is not the same as the meaning of a brochure offered by a salesperson at a customer's office. Because trade shows have a cultural context of their own, the resulting meanings differ from those encountered outside the exhibition hall.

Research Into Exhibitions

Research into managers' perceptions of exhibitions confirms that most managers see them in terms of making sales. This is true of both US and UK shows: even when managers do not expect to take orders at the exhibition, they do see the exhibition as an opportunity to generate leads, qualify prospects and open sales. This is particularly apparent in the staffing of stands: managers predominantly staff them with salespeople, even though there is evidence to suggest that visitors do not like this (Tanner and Chonko 1995; Skerlos and Blythe 2000).

Shipley *et al.* (1993) identified 13 reasons for exhibiting, of which seven were directly related to selling while six represent non-selling activities. Research conducted by Blythe (1997) showed that the selling aims were ranked highest in importance by the majority of exhibitors (see Table 18.1).

Attempts to determine whether exhibitions are effective or not are also coloured by the assumption that they are primarily selling devices. Sharland and Balogh (1996) defined effectiveness as the number of sales leads generated, followed up and successfully closed, and efficiency as the comparison between the cost of trade show participation versus other sales and promotion activities. US research by the Trade Show Bureau in 1988 put the cost of a trade show lead at $132, compared with $251 per call in the field (Trade Show Bureau 1988). UK research showed the comparable figures to be £30 per useful contact at a trade show, compared to £150 for a field call (Exhibition Industry Federation 1994). Although a 'useful contact' may not be the same as a sales lead, the general conclusion of researchers is that trade shows and exhibitions generate leads more cheaply than other methods.

The problem lies in determining the strength of these 'leads'. A useful contact may not be a buyer at all – which is not a problem if the individual might act as a gatekeeper or influencer in reaching the decision-makers. Even a qualified lead from a buyer may not be strong, since such a buyer will almost certainly be visiting the firm's competitors, who will undoubtedly be at the same venue.

Some early research by Kerin and Cron (1987) showed that some exhibitors do pay attention to the possibilities of non-selling activities. Although the emphasis was still on selling, other aims were present (see Table 18.2). For this particular group of respondents, corporate image came out highest, although the next two highest-scoring aims were selling aims.

Table 18.1 Ranking of exhibition aims

Reason for exhibiting	*Ranking*
Meeting new customers	1
Launching new products	2
Taking sales orders	3
Interacting with existing customers	4
Promoting existing products	5
Enhancing the company image	6
General market research	7
Meet new distributors	8
Keeping up with the competition	9
Getting information about the competition	10
Interacting with existing distributors	11
Getting an edge on non-exhibitors	12
Enhancing the morale of the staff	13

Figure 18.2
Strength of leads

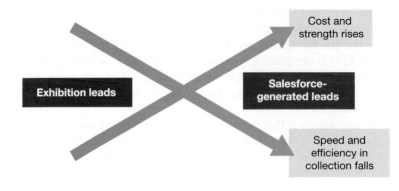

Table 18.2 Importance of trade show aims

Aim	Mean score (out of 10, with 10 as highest)
Enhancing corporate image	5.32
Introducing new products	5.14
Identifying new prospects	5.08
Getting competitive information	4.94
Servicing current customers	4.69
Enhancing corporate morale	3.75
Selling at the show	2.79
New product testing	2.17

Those who contend that exhibitions are not primarily useful as selling tools may well be right, since there is a discrepancy between the exhibitors' view of exhibitions and the visitors' view. If exhibitions are about communicating, it would seem reasonable to suppose that the visitors and the exhibitors should have compatible aims in attending: that is to say, their aims will not be the same, but they should be complementary. In the case of exhibitions, visitors are quite clearly seeking out at least some of the communication. Figure 18.3 shows the comparison between visitors' tactics and strategies and exhibitors' tactics and strategies.

Personal selling clearly happens on exhibition stands, although probably not to the extent that exhibitors believe it does.

Visitor Expectations

Research conducted among visitors to trade fairs shows that most of them are not directly involved in purchase decisions, and many of them have no role whatsoever in purchasing. (Skerlos and Blythe 2000; Gramman 1994; Bello and Lohtia 1993; Munuera and Ruiz 1999).

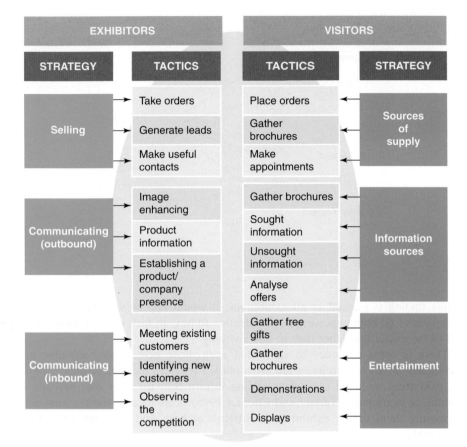

Figure 18.3

Exhibitors and visitors strategies and tactics

Various categorisations of visitors have been proposed, many of them based on job titles: Blythe (2002a) categorised visitors according to their aims in attending the exhibition, and came up with the following categories:

- *Tyre kickers*: have no purchasing intent or power, but pretend that they do.
- *Wheeler-dealers*: have power and intention to buy, but go round all suppliers as they want the best deal.
- *Technocrats*: engineers or technicians – mostly information seekers.
- *Foxes*: have their own agenda, for example spying on competitors or selling their own products to exhibitors.
- *Day trippers*: students, retired people or just people generally having a day out of the office.

This categorisation was validated by Schwartz and Blythe (2003) in a study of German trade fair visitors, and again by Price and Blythe (2004) in a UK study. In this study, the following proportions of visitors were found at two exhibitions studied:

- Tyre kickers   6%
- Wheeler-dealers   8%
- Technocrats   20%
- Foxes   59%
- Day trippers   7%

Exhibitions offer opportunities to make contacts – but buyers are in the minority.

© Ulrike Hammerich | Dreamstime.com

Figure 18.4

Exhibition visitors

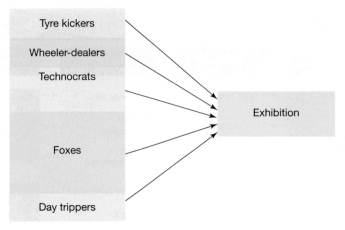

If this finding is general to all exhibitions, it would appear that the vast majority of visitors have no buying power and no intention to buy: in fact, most of them are there to sell to the exhibitors rather than to buy anything.

There is some evidence to show that even those people who are able to make recommendations or purchases are often not yet ready to make decisions – they attend the exhibition with the idea of collecting information for later use, perhaps several months or years later (Tanner and Chonko 1995). This means that tracking sales and attributing them to the exhibition is difficult at best, and in many cases is simply impossible.

If exhibitors are solely exhibiting in order to make sales, it would appear that they are likely to be disappointed: the number of visitors who can influence sales, or even directly make purchases, is small. However, exhibitors who set other objectives can certainly gain from exhibiting, and of course some good sales leads are generated at exhibitions, mainly from visitors who are in a position to influence purchase decisions at their companies.

Exhibitions and Key Account Management

Key account management is about creating long-term relationships with other firms (see Chapter 17). As we saw in that chapter, relationships go through stages, at each stage of which the focus is on a different type of problem.

In the context of key account management, exhibitions offer few opportunities to make immediate sales. What they do offer is an opportunity to initiate relationships by approaching influencers and users, for example technical people and administrators: these opportunities are much greater than the opportunity to meet buyers, simply because of the numerical preponderance of these people. Opportunities to deepen existing relationships by meeting key account firms' technical or administrative people are obviously present, and may represent the real strength of exhibitions. In some cases these people may not have been involved directly with the supplying company as the relationship is being established, but are able to become part of the process by meeting people on the exhibition stand.

Using the KAM/PPF model outlined in Chapter 17 (Wilson 1999), it is possible to map visitors' and exhibitors' reasons for attendance (Blythe 2002b). Table 18.3 shows this mapping.

Marketing in Practice
ExpoInter

Every year the city of Porto Alegre in Brazil is host to the ExpoInter agricultural show. The show is the biggest in South America, attracting visitors from Uruguay, Paraguay, Argentina, Chile and of course from all over Brazil. From the Amazon to the pampas, and from the Andes to the Atlantic, ranchers and agricultural suppliers flock to the show.

ExpoInter runs at the end of August, and typically receives 120 000 visitors a day on weekends – 800 000 visitors will come to the show while it is on. Obviously many of these visitors are there simply for a day out, and many are from the city of Porto Alegre.

The ranchers who come to the show to enter the competitions and displays bring their prize cattle: the gauchos (South American cowboys) who tend the cattle look forward to the show as a chance to meet old friends, to see the big city (many of them rarely sleep indoors, let alone visit a town) and to swap stories. The ranchers,

some from remote *fazendas* (ranches) in the border country or on the vast plains of Argentina, see the show as an opportunity to find out about the latest equipment, while their wives seize the chance to shop in Porto Alegre or enjoy a concert or the theatre.

For residents of Porto Alegre, the show brings visitors to the city: business booms, the shopping malls and markets are packed and special events occur throughout the city. The Rio Grande do Sul Tourist Office even promotes ExpoInter as a tourist attraction for foreigners.

Every agricultural supplier in Latin America aims to be represented at ExpoInter, but in fact most of the benefits from the show have nothing to do with agriculture. The show itself has become such an important event on the calendar of Porto Alegre (and indeed most of South America) as a celebration of gaucho culture that the sale of tractors or welding equipment almost pales into insignificance.

Table 18.3 Exhibitions and the KAM/PPF model

Development stage	Visitors' reasons for attendance	Exhibitors' reasons for attendance
Pre-KAM: defining and identifying strategic account potential.	See new companies, make business contacts, compare products and services.	Meet new customers, launch new products, meet new distributors, promote existing products.
Early-KAM: account penetration, seeking preferred-supplier status.	Obtain technical or product information.	Interact with existing customers, interact with existing distributors, enhance the company image, take sales orders.
Mid-KAM: building partnership, consolidate preferred-supplier status.	Discuss specific problems/talk with the experts.	Interact with existing customers, interact with existing distributors.
Partnership-KAM: develop spirit of partnership, build common culture, lock-in customer.	Discuss specific problems/talk with the experts.	Interact with existing customers and distributors (possibly by sharing exhibition space).
Synergistic-KAM: continuous improvement, shared rewards, quasi-integration.	No real role. At this stage the companies are very close together, and may even be sharing their promotional activities, including exhibiting at trade fairs.	No real role.
Uncoupling-KAM: disengagement.	To see new customers, products, developments and companies.	To meet new customers and distributors and to take sales orders.

Figure 18.5

Key accounts and exhibitions

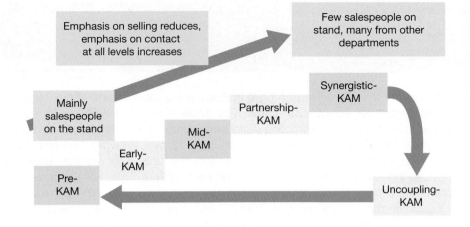

For key account managers, trade fairs offer three main opportunities:

1 First contact at the pre-KAM or even early-KAM stage.
2 Building partnerships and establishing a common culture at the mid-KAM and partnership-KAM stages.
3 Offering an opportunity for a shared voice at the synergistic-KAM stage.

The first contact is far more likely to be with a technical person or an administrator than with a buyer or decision-maker, which means that the key account manager needs to use these people as product champions in order to enter the prospective customer's firm. Given that these technical people are at the trade fair for the purpose of finding out what is new in the field, exhibitors might be well advised to put some of their own technical people on the stand in order to explore possible synergies. In the pre-KAM stage, when the parties are feeling each other out, it appears that exhibitors place a high importance on finding new customers and launching new products.

At the early-KAM stage, when the parties are aiming to increase the volume of business and build a social network, the exhibitor's aim of interacting with existing customers will be most appropriate. Where the prevailing strategy is concerned with building networks, the trade fair offers a neutral territory on which people who would not normally have the chance to meet are able to network with the exhibiting firm. For the exhibitor, the key strategy here is to ensure that the partner firm's technical, administrative and marketing people are specifically invited to the stand, possibly with the objective of meeting their opposite numbers. Interaction between these individuals is likely to encourage the identification of problems, the finding of creative solutions and a closer relationship between the organisations. However, research indicates that many technical people's needs are not being met – the opportunity to discuss specific problems, which is a common reason for visiting the exhibition, is unavailable because the exhibiting firms tend to concentrate mainly on selling activities.

In the mid-KAM stage, visitors may wish to discuss specific problems. Exhibitors will wish to interact with existing distributors and customers, the latter of which aims is rated fourth in importance by exhibitors.

At the partnership-KAM stage the two parties are probably too closely intertwined to need to meet in an exhibition hall, and may even be sharing stand space. Nevertheless, social activities built around the exhibition, such as dinners together, can help cement relationships.

At the synergistic-KAM stage, firms develop strategic congruence. At this point, trade fairs provide the opportunity to share a voice. This is, of course, true of other communications media, but trade fairs allow congruence across a broader spectrum of activities than most because of the interactive nature of the medium. For example, trade fairs can be used for concept testing of new products, allowing the partners to obtain quick feedback on the market viability of the product.

At the uncoupling-KAM stage, when the partnership is dissolving, the parties are likely to use the trade fair to seek new partners. Obviously there is likely to be considerable overlap between the separate stages and activities, but as the relationship deepens the role of trade fairs is likely to become less important.

Talking Point

Exhibitions are busy places at the best of times – at the worst of times, of course, they are empty. So exhibitors are hard-pressed to talk to so many people, and to find out who is from which company, and what their role is and so forth. The question arises, therefore – how many different departments are we going to have represented on the stand? How big is this stand expected to be?

With exhibition space being charged by the square yard, and exhibition stands themselves not exactly cheap, having a stand which will accommodate someone from every department is clearly going to be prohibitively expensive. Also, who is going to be minding the store if everyone's at the exhibition?

How can we set the priorities, when most firms might be expected to have at least five or six key accounts (possibly dozens, if the firm is large) and perhaps hundreds of small account customers? When do we get the chance to speak to new customers?

Using trade fairs effectively as a tool in key account management means understanding how trade fairs work and who the visitors are. As in any other area of marketing, the key issue is to meet the needs of those visitors effectively in order to facilitate exchange. Using the courtship analogy, the exhibition hall is the business equivalent of the dance hall. It is a place for chance encounters that may lead to romance, or it is a place to go to on a date. Whether chance or prearranged, the key account manager can only make the best of the event by setting objectives and being clear about achieving them.

An important issue here is to ensure that the right people are on the stand in order to discuss issues with the visitors. If the exhibitor intends to relate to technical people, it would seem sensible to ensure that some of the exhibitor's technical people are on the stand to answer questions. If the intention is to establish links with key accounts at other levels in the organisation, it may be sensible to arrange for senior managers to be on the stand, at least for part of the time: these people frequently have few opportunities to meet customers.

Why Exhibitions Fail

Exhibitions frequently do not work for firms. In most cases, this is because exhibitors have not thought through their strategies clearly enough, have not set objectives and have not evaluated their activities sufficiently rigorously (or at all, in many cases) (Blythe 2000). As in any other area of marketing, failure to meet the needs of the customer (in this case the visitor) will result in a failure to communicate effectively and hence a failure of the exhibition.

In other cases, exhibitions fail because the exhibitors have inappropriate objectives. Although orders are sometimes placed at exhibitions or shortly afterwards, going to an exhibition with the sole objective of making sales is almost certainly unrealistic in most cases, because so few buyers are present as a proportion of visitors. Even when buyers are present, they are likely to be in the information-gathering stage of the buying process and are unlikely to be in a position to place an order anyway.

As in other areas of business, much of the risk of failure can be reduced by planning ahead. Unfortunately, many exhibitors leave the planning of the exhibition to the last minute and do not prepare sufficiently in advance.

Figure 18.6

Why exhibitions fail

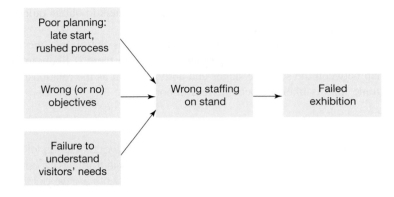

Planning for Exhibitions

Failure to plan an exhibition may be caused by the view that exhibitions are merely flag-waving exercises aimed at showing the corporate face and nothing more. In other cases, companies do not plan because they regard the exhibition as a one-off event, and so do not wish to impose extra burdens on the marketing team. In other cases, however, failure to plan is simply a result of lack of knowledge or lack of the will to take trouble over ensuring that the exhibition is successful.

Planning an exhibition properly can easily take up six months or more, if pre-preparation and post-exhibition activities are taken into account. The stages of planning an exhibition are as follows:

1 *Decide on the objectives.* This goes beyond merely deciding what the reasons are for exhibiting: the objectives need to be measurable (and systems need to be in place to do this), achievable (within the context of the firm's resources), and realistic (considering the visitor profile and competitive pressures at the exhibition).

2 *Select which exhibition to attend.* This relies on the range of choice, the visitor profiles (obtainable from the organisers, though the figures may have been massaged), the cost of exhibiting, the availability of suitable space in a good location, the timing of the exhibition relative to the firm's business cycle, the competitive level and the prestige value of the exhibition. It is good practice to attend the exhibition as a visitor before committing to exhibiting the following year.

3 *Plan the staffing of the stand.* Most managers tend to use the salesforce to staff the stand, but often this is inappropriate: much depends on what the objectives of exhibiting are. Using salespeople also has the disadvantage of taking them off the road at a time when enquiries are likely to be at their highest. Since visitors are likely to be in the information search stage of the buying process, it is probably too early to involve salespeople anyway.

4 *Plan the support promotions.* These may include direct mailshots to visitors, advertising campaigns in advance of the exhibition, press releases in the trade press, and salesforce activity before the exhibition (inviting existing customers to visit the stand) and afterwards (following up on enquiries), including a wide variety of social events.

5 *Decide on the layout of the stand and its contents.* Since visitors are usually information-gathering, the layout needs to be attractive and eye-catching, but should also convey solid information. It is often a good idea to have a private area so that customers can discuss business in private: this area can double as a rest area for stand personnel. Refreshments can be made available within this area: opinions are mixed as to whether alcoholic drink should be available.

6 *Arrange the follow-up activities after the exhibition.* A surprising number of exhibitors fail to do this, with the result that the salesforce is not able to follow up on leads generated, the company is not prepared to send information out to those who requested it and the PR momentum obtained from the exhibition is wasted (Blythe and Rayner 1996). The biggest problem with delaying follow-ups is that prospective customers will almost certainly have contacted the firm's competitors at the same exhibition, so a delay is likely to mean that the competitors will get the business.

7 *Plan the logistics of the exercise.* Ensure that sufficient promotional material has been produced, that the staff are transported to the exhibition, that the hotels are booked and are of a suitable standard, that stand personnel are briefed and prepared, that equipment, furnishing, samples and so forth all arrive at the right time and in the right condition.

The job is not finished when the exhibition closes – evaluation is essential.

Once the exhibition is over, evaluation needs to take place. Many firms do not evaluate their activities effectively (or at all), which seems perverse considering the amount of money and effort which is expended on exhibition attendance. The reasons for not evaluating might be as follows (Blythe 1997):

1 The firm lacks the resources to carry out the evaluation.

2 The activity is not important enough within the firm's overall marketing strategy to warrant evaluation.

3 The evaluation would be too difficult or expensive.

4 The firm is owner-managed and therefore the owner feels able to estimate the effectiveness of the exhibition without formal evaluation.

Managing the Exhibition Stand

Stand management is straightforward provided the planning has been carried out effectively and the necessary equipment and staff have arrived. Designing the layout of the stand is an important part of the process; most exhibitors tend to make the company name the most prominent feature of the stand, with brand names and product specifications lower on the list of priorities. This is a reasonable policy if the purpose of the stand is to raise the corporate profile, but in most circumstances the visitors' need for solid information will dictate the design and layout of the stand.

In many cases firms assume that the visitors will recognise the company's name and will know what products are available. This is something of a leap of faith; overseas

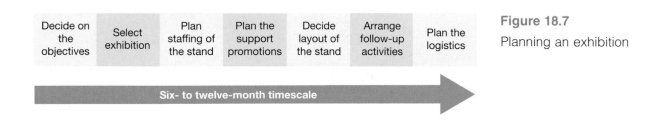

Decide on the objectives	Select exhibition	Plan staffing of the stand	Plan the support promotions	Decide layout of the stand	Arrange follow-up activities	Plan the logistics

Six- to twelve-month timescale

Figure 18.7

Planning an exhibition

visitors to exhibitions may not be familiar with the firm and its products, and even domestic visitors may be more familiar with brand names than with company names, since that is what is usually given the heaviest promotion.

Exhibitions are tiring for the visitors as well as for the exhibitors, so visitors usually only spend significant time at a few stands. This may be as few as 10 or 12, and this figure does not rise if the exhibition is larger, since most visitors only spend one day at an exhibition. This means that large exhibitions with many stands do not increase the number of visitors who will see the stand; statistically, large exhibitions actually reduce the chances of particular visitors seeing a particular stand, since there are more to choose from. The problem of clutter is probably greater at exhibitions than in any other environment, as exhibitors all compete for the visitors' limited attention. For this reason the stand must be designed with the visitors' as well as with the exhibitor's objectives in mind.

For example, if the exhibition objective is to raise corporate awareness, the company name needs to be prominent and a plentiful supply of brochures and leaflets needs to be available. Temporary promotion staff could be employed to hand out leaflets in other parts of the exhibition, so that exhibitors who do not plan to visit the stand might be encouraged to do so, or at least go away with some information about the firm. The stand might have some kind of stunt or gimmick to raise awareness: a product demonstration or some spectacular event will attract attention.

All this planning is fine and dandy if the exhibitors have only one or two objectives. Yet we have seen already that exhibitors might have many objectives, and a lot of aims which are not quantifiable as well.

How can firms reconcile the different objectives? How is it possible to plan around six objectives and five aims and to prepare for old customers, new customers, key customers, general visitors and the inevitable time-wasters? Maybe it isn't possible at all – so we might as well just do what is convenient!

On the other hand, if the aim is to make sales or generate leads, the stand should show the brand names prominently, with plenty of information on product benefits. The stand should be staffed with some technical people and some sales people, and brochures should only be given to visitors who are prepared to leave their names and addresses (some exhibitors will only mail out brochures rather than give them out on the stand). This ensures that follow-up calls can be carried out. Promotions and stunts should be used to collect names and addresses: for example, a free draw for a prize. Special 'exhibition-only' discounts or promotions can be used, and pre-publicity can reflect this in order to get buyers onto the stand. In these circumstances, casual non-buying visitors are less important and might even be actively discouraged – although (for the reasons outlined earlier in the chapter) this may

Figure 18.8

Motivating stand staff

be a short-sighted policy, since most exhibitions are probably not good selling venues, and the casual visitors may be the exhibitor's best future customers.

The following is a checklist for organising the stand itself:

- Ensure that displays are easily accessible and are informative.
- Check that stand members have a clear brief.
- Have clear objectives in place and, where possible, set targets for stand members.
- Have an area where prospects can be taken for a private conversation if necessary.
- Ensure an adequate supply of drinking water and other refreshments.
- Establish a rota for stand staff to ensure regular breaks.
- Have a record-keeping system for leads and useful contacts.
- Have a feedback system for visitors' comments.
- Set up some 'fun' activities for stand staff.

It is useful for stand staff to have the opportunity to tour the rest of the exhibition (this also gives them a break) and it is worthwhile to give them objectives for doing this, for example, making it the time for gathering information about competitors. Staff will need a break at least every hour; long periods of standing, smiling and relating to large numbers of people is both physically and psychologically exhausting. This requires careful planning to ensure that there are enough suitably qualified people left to man the stand during breaks.

The main problem concerning stand staff is maintaining their motivation over the period of the show. After a few hours on the stand the visitors seem to meld into a single mass, most of the enquiries seem like a waste of time and the smile begins to wear a little thin. For this reason it is a good idea to have some activities running which keep the stand personnel interested. For example, a competition for collecting business cards, with an appropriate small prize, can keep staff motivated. Demonstrations throughout the day can help to break the monotony for staff as well as visitors, particularly if the demonstrations are given by stand members in rotation. Again, a small prize could be offered for the best demonstration.

Exhibitions are often held away from the firm's home base, and therefore away from the staff's homes and families. Sometimes it might be appropriate to allow staff to bring their partners with them, but in most cases this is problematical, so every opportunity should be given for staff to telephone home, and it almost goes without saying that their accommodation and meals should be of a high standard – this compensates to a small extent for being away from home, but in any case it reflects better on the firm.

Overall, exhibitions need to be planned in fine detail, with everything leading towards the planned objectives. Choice of exhibition, pre-publicity and post-follow-ups, stand design, staffing and choice of what to exhibit should all be chosen with clear objectives in mind.

Good hotel accommodation is essential for staff manning exhibition stands.

Alternatives to Exhibitions

Because of the cost and commitment attached to exhibiting, not least the disruption to the exhibitors' normal routine, firms are beginning to look for alternative routes for meeting buyers and promoting their products. Since one of the major advantages of exhibitions is the 'neutral territory' aspect, allowing buyers and sellers to discuss matters in a more relaxed way, many exhibitors are moving towards private exhibitions or roadshows to exhibit their products.

Private Exhibitions

A private exhibition is one to which specific people are invited: it is organised by one firm, or sometimes by a group of firms, independently of an exhibition organiser. Private exhibitions are sometimes run at venues near to the public exhibition, and coinciding with the main event. Typically such events are held in hotels or small halls where the buyers are invited.

The main advantages are as follows:

- The atmosphere is usually more relaxed and less frenetic than in the main exhibition.
- No competitors are present to distract the visitors.
- The exhibitor has much more control over the environment than would be the case at the public exhibition, where the organisers may impose irksome regulations.
- Superior refreshment and reception facilities are available.
- If the event is held in a hotel the staff will have access to their rooms and can easily take breaks.
- Sometimes the overall cost is less.

The main drawback of the private event is that visitors will only come to it if they are given advance warning, and even then may decide only to visit the main exhibition. The invitations need to be sent out early enough for visitors to make allowance for the event, but not so early that they forget about it, and some incentive to make the necessary detour may also need to be in place. It is extremely unlikely that the list of desirable visitors will be complete – one of the main advantages of the public exhibition is that some of the visitors will be unknown to the exhibiting company, and a first contact can be made.

Private exhibitions work best in situations in which the company has a limited market, where the costs of the main exhibition are high and where a suitable venue is available close to the main site.

Roadshows

A roadshow is a travelling exhibition which takes the product to the buyer rather than the other way round. In some cases these are run in hotels, in other cases trailers or caravans are used. Roadshows are useful in cases where large numbers of buyers are concentrated in particular geographical areas, and where many of them would not make the journey to visit a national exhibition. In some countries (for example the United States) industries may be geographically concentrated (e.g. the film industry in California or the steel industry in Pennsylvania), making a roadshow more economical.

Like private exhibitions, roadshows allow the exhibitor to control the environment to a large extent. Roadshows can be run in conjunction with other firms, which reduces the cost and increases the interest level for the visitors; this can be particularly effective if the firms concerned are complementary rather than competing.

In common with private exhibitions, the roadshow's organiser is entirely responsible for all the publicity. In the case of a major public exhibition the exhibition organisers and even the firm's competitors will ensure that a certain minimum level of visitors will attend; in the case of a roadshow the exhibitor will need to produce considerable advance publicity and even send out specific invitations to individual buyers and prospects. This adds to the risk as well as the cost.

Sales Promotion

Sales promotions are intended to create a short-term increase in sales. They can take many forms, from short-term discounts through to extra quantities, free packs and free gifts. Sales promotions are typical of push strategies: this is one in which the goods are heavily promoted to distributors rather then to the end customer. The theory is that the distributor will, in turn, promote the product heavily, thus pushing the goods through the distribution chain. The converse of a push strategy is a pull strategy, in which the goods are promoted heavily to the final users in order to create demand which will pull the goods through the distribution chain. Push and pull strategy is explained in Chapter 8.

Expenditure on sales promotion has increased in recent years as producers find that push strategies can be more accurately targeted and are less prone to clutter (the effect of too much promotion vying for the customer's attention). One of the major benefits of sales promotion is that it deflects interest away from price as a competitive tool, particularly if the promotion is not of the 'extra discount' variety. Creating the campaign should be based on the 'who do I want to do what?' question (Cummins 1998). In other words, the objective of the campaign needs to be couched in precise terms – an aim 'to increase sales' is too vague, whereas an aim 'to encourage customers to recommend the product to their friends' is one which can be used as the basis for creative thinking.

Sales promotions can be used to encourage trial, to **trade up** (buy a more expensive version of the product), or to expand usage: when aimed at distributors, they can encourage distributors to increase stock levels (load up). This may only move sales from the future to the present: when the promotion is over, the distributor may de-stock and therefore reduce purchases for a period. This may not matter if the purpose of the promotion is to even out demand in order to schedule factory production better, or if the purpose is to lock out competitors from shelf space at the warehouse, but it is important to understand that sales promotions usually have a short-term effect.

trade up Buy the more expensive model.

In capital-goods markets such as cars, major household appliances and (in business-to-business markets) heavy machinery, reduced-interest or zero-interest deals can be powerful incentives, as can leasing deals. These incentives can overcome situations in which the customer has little or no money, or where (in business markets) the finance director has declared a moratorium on expenditure. The problem for the supplier can lie in working out the cost of such deals, so many firms involve an outside bank or finance company to handle the details. Finance companies judge the supplier against the following criteria:

1 The goods need to be durable, identifiable and movable (in case of repossession).

2 The goods should have a value greater than the outstanding debt at all times, which means there should be a well established second-hand market.

3 The supplier must itself be a reliable, well established business.

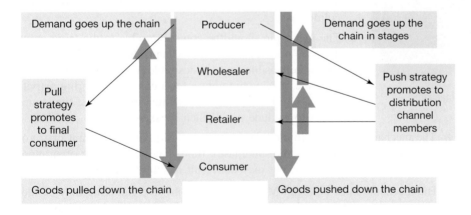

Figure 18.9

Push vs pull strategies

Marketing in Practice
Goldwell

Goldwell is a German hair cosmetics manufacturer, dealing exclusively with hairdressing salons. When the firm entered the UK market they found themselves facing an established market in which L'Oreal, Schwarzkopf, Wella, Clynol and Clairol had sewn up the bulk of the market between them. All of these companies were bigger than Goldwell, and consequently had much bigger marketing budgets – they also had nationwide distribution, both directly to salons and through cash-and-carry wholesalers.

Goldwell began by equipping their salespeople with vans, so that stock could be delivered immediately – no waiting for the order to be processed and delivered. Although some salespeople thought this approach seemed unorthodox at best, and unprofessional at worst,

it did give the company a slight edge over the others in the market. Where Goldwell really scored, though, was in its sales promotions. Salespeople were empowered to give away free samples of product – but if a salon placed an order, the free samples would be of a different product in the Goldwell range. Salon owners would use the products, and perhaps order them next time – thus obtaining free samples of yet another product. This approach meant that Goldwell gradually displaced other companies' products.

Sales promotion bought Goldwell a substantial share of the professional market in the UK, and coupled with its rapid delivery system made the company a major player within five years of entering the market.

Some suppliers are large enough to act as their own finance companies. This was notably the case for IBM, which from its foundation until the mid-1980s did not sell any of its equipment outright: everything was leased. This meant that IBM retained ownership of all its equipment throughout the world, which gave the company a substantial measure of control over its customers, though at the cost of cash flow problems in the early years.

mechanics In sales promotion, the activities the customer must undertake.

Many sales promotions involve the customer in doing something: filling in a form, scratching panels on a scratch card, collecting tokens towards a prize and so forth. These actions are called **mechanics**, and need to be carefully designed so as to maximise the effectiveness of the promotion. The following considerations apply to designing a mechanic:

Scratch cards provide a simple but engaging mechanic.

- The mechanic should not involve a task which is too complex, or might be seen as too much trouble. A task which is too complex will result in people giving up or not attempting the mechanic: on the other hand, those who do carry out a complex task are likely to be the most highly motivated and therefore may be highly desirable customers.

- Embarrassing or personally intrusive mechanics should be avoided. The feelings of the person carrying out the mechanic need to be considered, and particular note needs to be taken of cultural issues.

- The mechanic should be comprehensible to the target group. There is no reason why a mechanic should not be made incomprehensible to an undesirable market segment – for example, a sales promotion for a company offering activity holidays in France might be written in French if the company wants to exclude non-French speakers.

- The mechanic might be immediate (a scratch card giving an instant prize) or delayed (a discount of a future purchase). Immediate rewards are often more appealing to the consumer, but may not result in future purchases.

- The mechanic must be legal. Mechanics which involve gambling may be illegal in some countries, and even in the UK a mechanic involving a game of chance cannot be dependent on a purchase. In other words, the consumer can demand a scratch card without actually buying anything – though few people would do so.

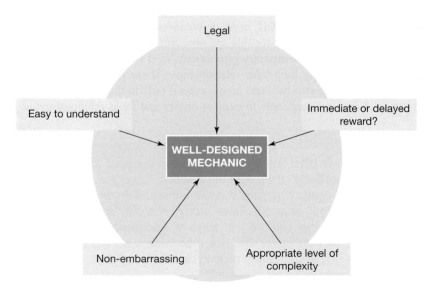

Figure 18.10
Issues in designing mechanics

Categories of Sales Promotion

Sales promotions fall into three categories: promotions aimed at the sales team, promotions aimed further down the value chain at middlemen and promotions aimed at the consumer.

Promotions aimed at the salesforce are part of the motivational programme, covered in Chapter 17. Prizes, cash rewards and extra benefits such as 'salesman of the month' status all come under this category, and can be considered as sales promotions since they are aimed at gaining a short-term increase in sales. Such promotions work well in single-transaction type selling, but can be seriously counterproductive in key account management, since salespeople are encouraged to go for quick results rather than build long-term relationships.

Sales promotions aimed at channel intermediaries form part of a push strategy. Early in the product life cycle, incentives to middlemen may be necessary to gain acceptance of new products by channel members. This can be an important consideration for the customer, since onward sales of the goods needs to be assured. Incentives to encourage distributors to carry the product will also help in shutting out later competition. For example, a manufacturer of an artificial sweetener may want to encourage food manu-facturers to incorporate the sweetener. In order to do this, a sales promotion encouraging retailers to stock products containing the sweetener would clearly help. Promotions aimed at customers might be used to shift the time of purchase, stimulate trial or encourage continued use of a product. These probably represent the mainstream of sales promotions.

Figure 18.11
Categories of sales promotion

Talking Point

Sales promotion is less widely used in business-to-business markets than it is in consumer markets. The reasons for this are obscure: it may be that business buyers are less likely to be swayed by temporary promotions, or it may be that a sales promotion is not conducive to building long-term relationships. There is, however, a role for sales promotion in the business-to-business arena, even if only in the form of 'deal sweeteners' which are available to salespeople to cement orders and build relationships.

Sales promotions to consumers often take the form of free gifts, and the same is true in business-to-business markets. Where, then, is the difference between this and a straight bribe? If we offer the business buyer (say) a 'training course' which just happens to take place in Tenerife or the Bahamas, why does this not constitute an arrestable offence?

In a sense, does it matter if we do this? Who loses out, after all? Sales promotions only shift sales – they don't necessarily increase sales over the year. Maybe gifts of this sort are just ways of smoothing the path of business, making things more flexible and providing all of us with an easier life. But if so, where do we stop? How do we distinguish between a reasonable business gift, or the simple courtesy of picking up the bill for lunch, and the seduction of a buyer into doing something which is not in his employer's best interests?

Sales Promotion Techniques

Sales promotions aimed at consumers come in many varieties, but some of the more common ones are as follows:

- *Free tastings*. New food products are often promoted in supermarkets by companies who offer free tastings to shoppers. This technique is expensive, because the demonstrators have to be paid to give away free product, but it is extremely effective in encouraging trial. The consumer often feels under a small obligation to buy the product, having accepted the 'gift' of a taste.

- *Money-off vouchers in press advertisements*. The main advantage of this type of promotion is that the marketers can check the effectiveness of one print medium over another, i.e. the managers can see which newspaper or magazine generates the highest number of coupon redemptions. The main drawback is that it tends to lead to short-term brand switching: when the offer ends, consumers are likely to revert to their usual brand.

- *Two-for-one*. Customers pay for the product, but are given an extra one free. This is equivalent to a generous price discount, so it will appeal to price-sensitive consumers, who will typically switch brands to take advantage of the offers without demonstrating any subsequent brand loyalty. Two-for-one offers are useful for disposing of excess stock (especially perishable stock) and for shutting out competitors, but they are of course expensive.

- **Piggy-backing** *or bundling*. This promotion works by providing a free sample of a product, attached to a complementary product. For example, Amazon (the online book retailer) frequently offer an extra book, on a complementary subject, to textbook purchasers.

- *Instant lottery or scratch cards*. This type of promotion is commonly used in petrol stations, with the intention of encouraging motorists to stop at the same petrol station. In many countries these promotions are illegal, because they involve gambling: in the UK the promoters cannot require customers to make a purchase, nor can the scratch cards be linked to purchases of a specific minimum amount. In other words, people can (in theory) demand a scratch card without buying anything, although in practice few people would have the courage to do this.

piggy-backing Attaching one product to another for the purposes of sales promotion.

- *Free gift with each purchase*. Free gifts are often enclosed with children's breakfast cereals, but other promotions have ranged from a free Frisbee with suntan lotion to a free sunroof with a new car. Free gifts can encourage brand switching: this can be particularly effective when selling to children, because children are less likely to switch back again: children are not price-sensitive, and will tend to keep to their favourite brand.

- *Loyalty cards*. These cards offer rewards to customers for shopping at the same retailer, or (in the case of airlines or ferry companies) using the same company for travel. Usually the rewards are given as discounts or vouchers against future purchases, but sometimes (notably in hypermarkets in France and Spain) in-store discounts are available for loyalty card holders, and sometimes points can be redeemed against goods which are only available to card holders. Likewise, some airlines allow frequent flyers to use the Business Class lounges, or to bring a partner on a business flight.

In general, sales promotions involve giving something away. The gift should (ideally) be something which is not too expensive for the promoter to supply, offers extra added value for the consumer and is relevant to the product being promoted. The offer should not look 'too good to be true' for two reasons – first, the company might find itself unable to fulfil the promotion, and second, consumers might suspect that there is a 'catch', which would certainly be counterproductive.

An interesting variation on the standard sales promotion (which benefits the purchaser only) is to offer something to a friend of the purchaser. This can be surprisingly powerful, especially if the product is regarded as a luxury or a treat – people often feel guilty about spending money on treating themselves, but if a friend will also benefit, this helps reduce the guilty feelings and makes the purchase more likely (Lee and Corfman 2004). For example, somebody who buys a week at a luxury hotel might be given a voucher for a friend to have a one-night stay during the week, or the purchaser of a new hairdo might be given a discount voucher to give to a friend. Promotions such as this also have the advantage of encouraging word-of-mouth.

Off-the-shelf promotions are provided by suppliers which specialise in sales promotions. For example, a common promotion is to offer free hotel accommodation to customers. The customers are usually required to take their evening meal and breakfast at the hotel, and pay for these, so the hotel is guaranteed some revenue. This makes the promotion relatively cheap for the promoter. Often the vouchers are only valid for off-peak periods, when the hotel rooms might be empty anyway: the hotelier would obviously rather have some income than none, and also the guests may like the hotel and return at a later date, paying the full price.

Off-the-shelf promotions do require a certain degree of trust on all sides, since the company offering the promotion has very little control over the quality of the service provided, or the terms on which other people are benefiting from the same offer. For example, a discount voucher for a meal at a posh restaurant will not seem like a bargain if it turns out that the restaurant offers the same discount to anyone who turns up on the same night. If run well, though, off-the-shelf promotions provide benefits to all parties – the promoter gains because customers want the discounts, the firm giving the discounts gains because of the extra business during an off-peak period, and the customer gains by obtaining a cheaper deal than would otherwise be the case.

Joint promotions are a way of reducing the costs of promotions by sharing them with another (related) firm. Entering into a joint promotion agreement with another company allows the firm to gain in several ways: the cost of the promotion is reduced, the scope of the promotion is increased because the other firm will contact its own customer base, and the customer's perception of value is often increased. Piggybacking (bundling) promotions operate this way, but joint promotions can be linked to a charity or cause, or can link to products or companies with which the promoter might have a marketing synergy. For

Marketing in Practice
Hoover

In August 1992, Hoover introduced a remarkable sales promotion: anyone spending more than £100 on Hoover products would be given two free flights, within Europe. This offer seemed too good to be true – and in fact it was!

TWO RETURN FLIGHT TICKETS. UNBELIEVABLE.

Courtesy of The Advertising Archives

At the time, the UK was in recession. Airlines had spare capacity, which they were prepared to allocate to Hoover at discount prices. At the same time, sales of domestic appliances were in the doldrums. The promotion sought to use the surplus aircraft seats as a way of stimulating demand for products, and the cost of the exercise was supposed to be covered (at least in part) by

sales of expensive extras such as hotel accommodation, travel insurance and so forth. Unfortunately these sales failed to reach expected levels – and at the same time, response to the promotion reached epic proportions. Hoover's travel agents were inundated with applications, far exceeding the fairly modest allocation of seats by the airlines. Hoover then compounded the problem by extending the offer to return flights to the USA, again hoping to use surplus seats on those routes.

Clearly the company was not in a position to honour the promotion. Demands from disgruntled Hoover customers grew, questions were asked in Parliament and consumer action began to take a practical turn.

One man (whose washing machine had broken down before he ever got the chance to fly) became a national hero overnight when he seized the Hoover engineer's van and held it to ransom until he got his flights. The engineer had made an unfortunate comment to the effect that, 'If you think you're going to get two free flights just for buying a washing machine, you must be an idiot,' which proved to be the final straw. 'I'm not as stupid as you are,' the customer replied. 'I'm not going to have to walk home.'

Eventually, 220 000 people were awarded their flights. Court cases continued for six years after the original promotion ended, and the parent company was forced to bail out Hoover UK to the tune of £48 million.

example, Kimberley Clark (manufacturers of Kleenex) ran a highly successful promotion during the summer months based on hay fever sufferers. Kleenex sells best during the winter, when people have colds or 'flu: hay fever sufferers who could supply three proofs of purchase of Kleenex were sent a free 'hay fever kit' containing an Optrex eye-mask, Merethol lozenges, a travel pack of Kleenex and a batch of money-off coupons for hay fever-related products.

Price promotions are an obvious form of sales promotion, but are risky because they inevitably reduce profit margins. Price promotions might involve immediate discounts (see Table 18.4) or delayed discounts. A delayed discount might be a voucher valid against future purchases, or a coupon from a newspaper advertisement. There are three drawbacks to coupon redemption schemes: first, it is difficult to estimate the redemption rate of coupons in advance, and therefore difficult to estimate the cost of the promotion. Second, coupons are sometimes cut from batches of newspapers and redeemed through a retailer who is an accomplice. Third, some retailers will accept coupons against any purchases, regardless of whether the customer is actually buying the product being promoted or not. Some retailers even honour vouchers from other retailers, as a way of sabotaging the rival firm's promotion.

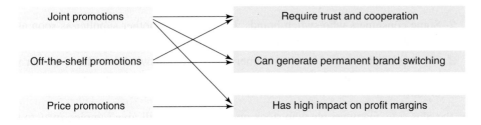

Figure 18.12

Strengths and weaknesses of sales promotions

Table 18.4 Immediate discounts

Type of discount	Example
Seasonal discount	January sales and summer sales are both ways of boosting business during times when consumer spending is often low. In recent years, however, many people in the UK have been deliberately delaying their purchases until the January sales, seriously affecting the pre-Christmas trade of many retailers.
Multibuys	Offering discounts for bulk purchase (two-for-one offers) is actually a price promotion. A study by London Business School found that 95 per cent of multibuys are bought by only 27 per cent of households, who then promptly switch to a competitor's product when the multibuy promotion ends.
Banded packs	Banded packs are similar to multibuys, but in this case, the goods are wrapped together in an outer package, thus forcing the customer to buy two or more.
Reduced shelf price	Grocery retailers frequently reduce the price of goods which are approaching their sell-by dates. Such promotions can reduce the propensity of consumers to pay the full price: near to closing time, groups of customers can often be seen hovering around the 'reduced items' shelves of supermarkets.
Extra-fill packs	Special extra-large packs are produced, labelled (for example) '25% Extra Free'. The main advantage of this type of promotion is that the cost of the extra product is relatively small: distribution, packaging and marketing costs far outweigh the cost of the product.

Whatever type of sales promotion is used, marketers should be careful not to overuse the technique. Sales promotions work because they offer something unusual: if the product always has a 'special' price reduction consumers will come to expect it, and will switch away from the product when the promotion ends. This in turn forces the company to reintroduce the promotion, so that (in effect) the company has simply cut its profit margins, often by a substantial amount.

Integrating Sales Promotions with other Communications Tools

Sales promotions are often thought to be relatively ineffective because the temporary increase in sales is followed by a fall in sales, as customers have stocked up on the product. If the purpose of the promotion is to even out seasonal sales, this may not matter, but the view is based on the following assumptions:

1 Loyal customers will stock up on the product (where this is possible) and will therefore not need to buy any more of the product for some time.

2 Some consumers who switch brands will switch to another supplier as soon as the promotion ends (Krishna, Currim and Shoemaker 1991).

3 There is a hard core of loyal consumers who will not switch brands, no matter what incentives are offered. These are likely to be the most valuable customers for the brand.

On the plus side, many people who stock up on the brand will give samples away to their friends (Wansink and Deshpande 1994). Second, some people will stay with the new brand – even habitual brand switchers will often stay with the brand until there is some reason to switch (competitors running a promotion, for example). Third, even hard-core loyal customers eventually switch brands, if only because their own brand ceases production.

Integrating sales promotion with other communications is intended to create what is called the ratchet effect. This is the process whereby sales are sharply increased as a result of a sales promotion, and sustained at the new level by the judicious use of other promotional tools. A clever or controversial sales promotion can create publicity: a sales promotion with a good mechanic can create a database, and a good retailer promotion can support the salesforce in winning orders from retailers.

As with any other form of integration of communications, clarity of objectives, consistency of message and consideration of the synergy between the different tools will always benefit the campaign.

Summary

Although exhibitions and trade fairs are often considered as a form of sales promotion, they do in fact have totally separate features and advantages. Exhibitions offer a wide range of communications possibilities between all levels of the organisations which exhibit and those visitors who attend. Like an old-fashioned marketplace, exhibitions allow all interested parties to meet if they so wish, but this opportunity is often squandered by an over-emphasis on making immediate sales.

Sales promotions offer a valuable tool for creating temporary increases in sales, but may or may not lead to long-term increases in business. Like any other marketing tool, sales promotions need to be placed in a context: they should operate within an overall framework of marketing communications.

The key points from this chapter are as follows:

- Buyers are very much in the minority at most, if not all, exhibitions.

- Most visitors are on an information search, not on a shopping trip.

- Most exhibitors are focused strongly on selling, whereas they should be focused on making useful contacts.

- The dissonance between exhibitors' aims and visitors' aims often results in disappointment for both parties.

- Exhibitors should establish objectives for their activities, but rarely do so.

- Sales promotions can be useful as deal sweeteners or facilitators.

- Sales promotions often only result in shifting sales forward, rather than increasing sales in the long term.

- Sales promotions can be used for the salesforce, for intermediaries, for customers or for the customers of customers.

- Promotions can backfire: although the best ones are highly innovative, so are the disastrous ones.

Chapter review questions

1 How might an exhibitor evaluate the aim of enhancing the company image?

2 What objectives might be appropriate for a first-time exhibitor?

3 What would be the most appropriate staffing approach for an exhibitor seeking to relate to existing customers?

4 What type of sales promotion would be most effective for a firm entering a new market?

5 How might salespeople use sales promotions to close deals? What might be the dangers of doing this?

6 How might a company use a sales promotion to generate a permanent rise in sales?

7 What are the pitfalls of using push-strategy sales promotions?

8 How might a sales promotion be linked to an exhibition?

9 Why do exhibitors often fail to evaluate their activities?

10 What should exhibitors be doing (say) six months ahead of time to prepare for an exhibition?

Preview case revisited
China International Auto Supplies Sourcing Fair

The exhibition organisers obviously lack some of the skills and knowledge that more experienced Western organisers would have acquired. For example, booths are allocated on a first-come-first-served basis, rather than on the basis of charging more for booths in better locations. Each three-metre by three-metre booth costs US$2500 for the three days of the show, and each has only standard fittings and equipment – there is no hire facility to allow exhibitors to obtain non-standard fittings or equipment. The visitor registration form is somewhat naïve – it asks visitors to state the purpose of the visit, but does not consider the possibility that visitors may not be buyers.

The organisers still show a somewhat China-centric attitude: their publicity refers mainly to Chinese car manufacture and growth prospects (China will have more than 80 million private cars on the road by 2010, for example), and perhaps this is not surprising since the exhibition attracts a mainly Chinese audience (perhaps 2 to 3 per cent of the visitors were from outside China). The organisers even regard Hong Kong as a foreign country.

In some other respects the organisers showed a great willingness to make life as easy as possible for overseas buyers – notably, they pre-booked 1000 hotel rooms to accommodate the foreign visitors. In part, this may have been because Chinese hotels are not all allowed to accommodate foreigners – they need a special licence to do so. Visitors who register as 'VIP' visitors are given free hotel accommodation, free meals, free entry to all seminars and free assistance with pre-booking meetings with potential suppliers.

The exhibition has, however, grown rapidly since its inception. Growth has been of the order of 50–60 per cent per annum, with 70 per cent of exhibitors at the 2007 event immediately booking for 2008. Opportunities to meet foreign buyers and suppliers are still few and far between in China – the International Auto Supplies Sourcing Fair provides just such an opportunity.

Case study
HSBC in the UAE

Hong Kong and Shanghai Banking Corporation (HSBC) is one of the world's largest and best-known banks, priding itself on being 'the world's local bank', a slogan which is intended to sum up the bank's ability to operate in many different cultures and business climates. HSBC certainly lives up to its global claims – and nowhere more so than in the United Arab Emirates, or UAE.

The UAE is a federation of Middle Eastern countries, with Dubai as its richest city-state. It is a wealthy part of the world – oil has accounted for much of its wealth, but Dubai has made an impressive name for itself as a trading and tourism centre. Dubai was wealthy even before oil was discovered there, due to its trading activities: in the 1960s a deliberate decision was made that Dubai should be the playground of the oil sheiks, and so it has proved to be. Dubai's shops are largely duty-free, taxation is low and hotels are luxurious.

HSBC has found itself at the heart of this consumer paradise. The bank offers credit cards, of course, but in the UAE they also offer a wide range of sales promotions – after all, every other bank would like to tap into this lucrative market. HSBC's promotions are intended to cover every possible need that a credit card holder might have, anywhere in the UAE.

For example, during August and September 2008 HSBC offered a joint promotion with Air Miles. Customers using both the HSBC credit card and the Air Miles card were entered in a draw to win one million air miles – enough for 10 return trips to Mumbai, five return trips to London, or three return trips to New York. Each week a new winner would be chosen, so there would be eight lucky winners over the course of the promotion, all names to be announced at the end of the promotion.

HSBC also teamed up with Radisson Dubai (part of the Radisson hotel group) to offer 30 per cent off room rates and food at Radisson restaurants in Dubai, provided the customer paid using the HSBC card. This promotion ran for the entire summer of 2008. Similar offers were in place at Oriental Stores: customers could obtain 15 per cent off the list price of top-of-the-range watches such as Tissot and Odeon. Restaurants at the Wafi City Mall offer a 20 per cent discount to HSBC card holders: these restaurants include Planet Hollywood, Seville's, Thai Chi and Ginseng.

Until 31 August 2008 any HSBC card holder buying an Apple computer was given six months' interest-free credit on the purchase, as was any purchaser of jewellery from Joyalukkas or Damas jewellery stores.

Between 1 June and 31 August, any HSBC Visa card holder who used their card abroad could win a four-night stay in a luxury castle hotel in Europe: this promotion was run in conjunction with the Visa organisation.

Of course, as a bank operating in an Islamic area of the world, HSBC has to offer banking services which comply with Shariah law, so the bank offers an Al Wafah card, which complies with strict Islamic banking laws. Naturally, the Al Wafah card is eligible for all the sales promotions, including free breakdown assistance for motorists.

Many of the promotions seem exceptionally generous – 20 or 30 per cent off a restaurant bill is rather a lot of discount. In the context of Middle Eastern bazaar culture, however, such discounts are not unusual. The overall effect of the promotions is, of course, that HSBC has a very substantial share of the credit card market in the UAE, as indeed it does worldwide. Truly the 'world's local bank'.

Questions

1 What types of sales promotion is HSBC using in the UAE?

2 Why does HSBC offer such large discounts for using the card?

3 How has HSBC used its understanding of the local culture to promote the card?

4 What are the potential disadvantages of the sales promotions HSBC are using?

5 Why the emphasis on travel-linked promotions?

References

Bello, D.C. and Lohtia, R. (1993): Improving trade show effectiveness by analyzing attendees. *Industrial Marketing Management* **22**(22), 311–18.

Blythe, J. (1997): Does size matter? Objectives and measures at UK trade exhibitions. *Journal of Marketing Communications* **3**(1), 22–4.

Blythe, J. (2000): Objectives and measures at UK trade exhibitions. *Journal of Marketing Management* **16**(1).

Blythe, J. (2002a): The huckster and the fox: a fable from the exhibition hall. *International Journal of Management and Decision-Making* **3**(3 & 4), 280–90.

Blythe, J. (2002b): Using trade fairs in key account management. *Industrial Marketing Management* **31**(7), 627–35.

Blythe, J. and Rayner, T. (1996): The evaluation of non-selling activities at British trade exhibitions – an exploratory study. *Marketing Intelligence and Planning* **14**(5), 20–4.

Cummins, J. (1998): *Sales Promotion: How to Create and Implement Campaigns That Really Work* (London: Kogan Page).

Exhibition Industry Federation (1994): *EIF Exhibition Effectiveness Survey* (London: Centre for Leisure and Tourism Studies).

Gramann, J. (1994): *Independent Market Research* (Birmingham: Centre Exhibitions with National Exhibition Centre).

Kerin, R.A. and Cron, W.L. (1987): Assessing trade show functions and performance: an exploratory study. *Journal of Marketing* **51** (July), 87–94.

Kijewski, V., Yoon, E. and Young, G. (1992): *Trade Shows: How Managers Pick their Winners* (Pennsylvania, PA: Institute for the Study of Business Markets, Penn State University).

Krishna, A., Currim, I.S. and Shoemaker, R.W. (1991): Consumer perceptions of promotional activity. *Journal of Marketing* **55** (April), 4–16.

Lee, S.N. and Corfman, K.P. (2004): A little something for me, and maybe for you too. Promotions that relieve guilt. *Advances in Consumer Research* **31**(1).

Munuera, J.L. and Ruiz, S. (1999): Trade fairs as services: a look at visitors objectives in Spain. *Journal of Business Research* **44**(1), 17–24.

Price, E. and Blythe, J. (2004): *Information Source Usage by Trade Show Attendees* (Academy of Marketing Conference, Cheltenham, July).

Sharland, A. and Balogh, R (1996): The value of non-selling activities at international trade shows. *Industrial Marketing Management* **25**(1), 59–66.

Shipley, D., Egan, C. and Wong, K.S. (1993): Dimensions of trade show exhibiting management. *Journal of Marketing Management* **9**(1), 55–63.

Skerlos, K. and Blythe, J. (2000): Ignoring the audience: exhibitors and visitors at a Greek trade fair. Proceedings of the Fifth International Conference on Corporate and Marketing Communication. Erasmus University, Rotterdam, 22 and 23 May (Rotterdam: Erasmus University).

Schwartz, A. and Blythe, J. (2003): Visitor typology and the trade fair servicescape. Proceedings of the Academy of Marketing Conference, Aston University (July) (Birmingham: Aston University).

Tanner, J.F. and Chonko, L.B. (1995): Trade show objectives, management and staffing practices. *Industrial Marketing Management* **4**(24), 257–64.

Trade Show Bureau (1988): *Attitudes and Opinions of Computer Executives Regarding Attendance at Information Technology Events*, Study no. 1080 (East Orleans, MA: Trade Show Bureau).

Wansink, B. and Deshpande, R. (1994): Out of sight, out of mind: pantry stockpiling and brand-use frequency. *Marketing Letters* **5**(1), 91–100.

Wilson, K.J. (1999): Developing key account relationships: the integration of the Millman-Wilson relational development model with the problem-centred [PPF] model of buyer-seller interaction in business-to-business markets. *The Journal of Selling and Major Account Management* **1**(4), 11–32.

Further reading

In both the sales promotion and the exhibition fields, relatively little has been written. Both areas are little-researched by academics, and although there have been a number of books published in the past, few up-to-date and accurate books exist on either topic.

Cummins, J. and Mullin, R. (2002): Sales Promotion: *How to Create, Implement and Integrate Campaigns that Really Work* (London: Kogan Page). This is an updated and much-expanded new edition of a sales promotion classic, aimed at practitioners. It has some very useful checklists, and provides a quick-reference text.

Friedman, S. and Kepler, K. (1992): *Exhibiting at Tradeshows: Tips for Success* (Boston, MA: Crisp Publications Inc.). This book is packed with tips and advice on exhibiting, but is now somewhat out-of-date and of course applies to the American market, so should be used with some caution.

Chapter 19
Direct and online marketing

Learning objectives After reading this chapter, you should be able to:

1. Describe the key elements on which direct marketing rests.

2. Show how successful direct marketing can be made interactive.

3. Explain the role of the database in direct marketing.

4. Identify sources of information which can be used to build a database.

5. Explain the difference between direct marketing and junk mail.

6. Understand the importance of customer retention.

7. Explain ways of making direct response advertising more effective.

8. Explain the importance of information in the success of the Internet.

9. Describe some of the barriers to Internet adoption.

Introduction

Direct marketing is marketing without intermediaries. Direct marketers go straight from producer to final consumer, without using wholesalers or retailers to mediate between them and the customers – and therefore without having to build in a profit margin for the distributors. Naturally, this means that the direct marketer has to fulfil all the functions normally associated with wholesalers and retailers, including delivery of the goods, after-sales service, promotion and so forth.

Because direct marketers deal with customers without going through intermediaries, they are normally much better placed to tailor the product offering than traditional marketers would be. They are also better placed to assess the effectiveness of their marketing activities, because the responses from customers are also direct.

The Direct Marketing Association defines direct marketing as follows:

Direct marketing is an interactive system of marketing which uses one or more advertising media to effect a measurable response and/or transaction at any location.

For the Direct Marketing Association, then, the key issue is the measurability of the activity.

An example of direct marketing is online marketing. Firms using the Internet to promote and sell products are, by definition, direct marketers. The growth in the use of the Internet for marketing purposes has been astronomical: buying goods online is becoming a significant proportion of total retail sales, and in some industries (notably the travel industry) online booking may eventually become the commonest way of buying travel.

Preview case
Arabella Miller

Arabella Miller is a retailer of children's clothing – but with several differences. First, the company adopts an ethical stance: the company donates 1 per cent of its turnover to global charities, and has a detailed ethical code which covers issues such as fair trade, good working conditions in factories supplying the company and of course environmental policies which encourage sustainable production. The company's founders began the business when they were unable to find organic clothing for their daughter, who suffered from eczema as a baby.

Clothing made from natural fibre is one thing, but Arabella Miller went one step further by insisting that everything should also be organic. All the clothing on sale is certified by the Soil Association as being entirely organic – which means that the cotton in an individual T-shirt can be traced back to the field it came from. Even the ink used for printing is certified organic and entirely natural.

The potential market is large, of course, with hundreds of thousands of babies born every year, and a growing interest in all things environmentally-friendly and ethical. In addition, many children have developed allergies to artificial fibres and even the inks used in printing on T-shirts and other clothing. The problem for Arabella Miller is that the market is geographically dispersed – and clearly, opening a retail shop in every major town in the country would be an expensive undertaking. Luckily, salvation is at hand in the form of the Internet.

Retailing online is an obvious option for the company. In general, the likely clientele for the products is going to be educated, computer-literate and probably comparatively well-off. Poorer members of society often cannot afford to be overly concerned about ethical issues – price is all that matters, and man-made fibres are almost always cheaper than organic material. However, the Internet has become an extremely crowded marketplace, and people often prefer to see and feel clothing for themselves – especially if it is for a baby's delicate skin.

Direct marketing is much more than a sub-section of the communication mix (Tapp 2004). Because direct marketing also encompasses fulfilment of orders, it in fact encompasses all marketing activities in some way, but does so on a direct basis.

The Basis of Direct Marketing

Direct marketing rests on four key issues (Holder 1998):

1 *Targeting.* Customers need to be identified and targeted accurately. For example, a direct mailing which is sent to people who have no need for the product is not only wasteful, it is also annoying for the recipients and therefore counter-productive in the long run.

2 *Interaction*. Getting a response from the customers is key to direct marketing's success. The responses may be in the form of a purchase, in the form of a request for information or in the form of supplying information: for the long-term management of databases, however, any responses from customers must be captured and recorded.

3 *Control*. Direct marketers have a great deal more control over events than do conventional marketers, simply because there are fewer organisations involved in providing value to the end consumer. It is also possible to pre-test almost every aspect of the direct provision.

4 *Continuity*. The aim in direct marketing is to use the information gathered to develop an ongoing, continuous relationship with the customer: each transaction should refine the firm's knowledge of the customer's needs and wants, and this knowledge should be reflected in future dealings.

Unwanted promotions are annoying for the recipient and wasteful for the sender.

Direct marketing is not a new activity: catalogues have been distributed almost since the invention of printing, and such institutions as mail-order catalogues and book clubs have been around for over 100 years. What has brought direct marketing to prominence in recent years is the dramatic fall in the cost of computers and the parallel increase in their power, and hence the possibilities for developing sophisticated databases.

There are three categories of direct marketing: stand alone, integrated and peripheral. Stand alone direct marketers have no other means of managing the relationship with the customer. The UK's First Direct bank operates in this way: it has no branches, so customers can only access the bank via the telephone or (more recently) the Internet. The bank sends out information by post or online, and customers have their salaries paid directly into their accounts. There are limitations for the bank, of course: they deal only with private banking, not business banking, and there are products which they either do not supply or cannot supply as economically as can a bank with branches, simply because banking regulations require hard copies of some documents and witnessed signatures for others.

Integrated direct marketing implies that the firm's direct marketing activities form part of an overall integrated communications strategy. This does not imply that direct marketing is subordinate to other marketing communications: it can equally mean that direct marketing activities are supported by other communications, or that all communications occupy an equal status. What the term does imply is that the firm's communications are seen as a total package, not as a series of separate activities.

Figure 19.1

Issues in direct marketing

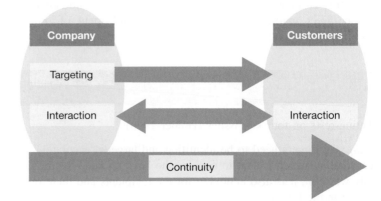

Marketing in Practice
Garden Organic

Garden Organic, formerly The Henry Doubleday Research Association, had its beginnings in the 19th century, when a Quaker named Henry Doubleday introduced Russian comfrey into Britain and spent his life promoting the use of this remarkable herb. Although Doubleday himself had no connection with Garden Organic, his single-minded dedication to promoting horticulture was the inspiration for one Lawrence Hills, who in 1954 took an interest in organic gardening. Like Doubleday, Hills spent his life advocating organic gardening and encouraging others to do likewise.

In 1954, organic gardening was firmly in the realm of 'crank' pursuits. Hardly anybody took the idea seriously, and there was no money available to research the possibilities, so Hills simply asked people to experiment in their own gardens and send the results in to him. By the early 1970s the environmental movement was just beginning and interest in organic gardening increased somewhat, but Hills and his friends were still regarded as being somewhat eccentric, to say the least. Hills worked for 10 years for no pay whatsoever: he funded the whole association by writing articles for the newspapers.

In 1986, Garden Organic opened a showplace garden near Coventry, where visitors could see the benefits of organic gardening. The finances were still very tight, however, but eventually, direct marketing came to the rescue. Garden Organic set up the Organic Gardening Catalogue, a complete ordering system for all things related to organic gardening.

The catalogue offers gardening tools, organic seeds (and a few non-organic seeds for plants for which organic seeds are not available), books on organic gardening, and indeed anything an organic gardener might need. The catalogue comes in hard copy and online formats.

The proceeds from the catalogue are used to fund the ongoing work of Garden Organic: as time goes by, the catalogue is not only the main source of income for the Association, it is also becoming the main way of recruiting members and spreading the word about organic gardening. For a very small, cash-poor organisation, running a mail-order catalogue has proved to be the perfect solution.

Peripheral direct marketing is used as an occasional tactical tool by firms which usually market their products via other means. Sometimes firms undertake some direct marketing as a result of competitive pressures, or to fill a temporary gap in the market (for example if a distributor goes out of business).

Direct marketing has undergone rapid growth in the past 30 years or so. The drivers for this are shown in Table 19.1.

Database Marketing

Database marketing has been defined as:

An interactive approach to marketing that uses individually addressable marketing media and channels (such as mail, telephone and the salesforce) to provide information to a target audience, stimulate demand, and stay close to customers by recording and storing an electronic database memory of customers, prospects, and all communication and transactional data. (Stone, Davies and Bond 1995).

Database marketing is characterised by its two-directional, interactive nature. The database is used to send out information, but is then improved and refined by collecting the information which is returned from the recipients of the first contact. This is true even

Table 19.1 Drivers for growth for direct marketing

Driver	Explanation
Changing demographics and lifestyles	More people living alone and a greater degree of difference between individuals due to fragmenting markets mean that consumers demand a more individualised approach. Dealing direct with suppliers often offers more flexibility than going through retailers.
Media fragmentation	The number of specialist magazines in the UK is now over 6000, compared with only a few hundred forty years ago. Increasing numbers of cable and satellite TV channels allow advertisers to 'narrowcast'*, targeting specific audiences with a special interest (for example, the History Channel would be a good place to promote books, magazines and courses on history).
Increasing salesforce costs	The cost of employing salespeople to call on customers is often prohibitive. For example, home-improvement companies employing a direct sales force would expect to pay 35–40 per cent of their turnover to sales people in salaries and commission: an interactive website costs a fraction of this amount.
Alternative distribution channels	The Internet, direct-response television, interactive terminals in banks, email, fax, and teletext were all unknown thirty years ago. The huge increase in direct mailings and telephone marketing has come about because of improvements in data management techniques.
Changing business focus	The focus in many businesses has shifted from customer acquisition to customer retention. The reason for this is the discovery that it is very much cheaper to retain an existing customer than it is to recruit a new one.
The list explosion	As databases have become more widespread, the names and addresses of individuals have been passed around from one list broker to the next. Lists have been combined and reanalysed and can be rented from list brokers or even bought outright in some cases. Lists have often been created for the specific purpose of renting them – perhaps by using an omnibus questionnaire with a prize attached to it. The creation and combination of lists is restricted by the Data Protection Act in the UK, and by similar legislation in many other countries.
Sophisticated analytical techniques	At one time, consumers were defined by somewhat inexact methods such as income group, gender or age. Modern analysis can define people by lifestyle, by tastes and preferences or by behaviour. More accurate targeting means less wastage in communication terms.

*See glossary.

Talking Point

if the targeted individual does not respond at all – non-response demonstrates that this individual is either not interested in the offer, or did not receive it in the first place (perhaps because he or she has moved away, or even died). Increased use of IT has also increased consumer empowerment – direct marketing has made it very easy for people to switch suppliers, either by going through the Internet or by responding to approaches by direct marketers (Pires, Stanton and Rita 2006).

Direct marketing seems to embody everything that people object to in business, and in marketing in particular. Direct marketers send out mailings, they telephone people at home just as they are sitting down to dinner, they collect personal information about people and use it to sell to them. All in all, direct marketers sound like a real bunch of rascals.

So why do they carry on doing it? Is it some malevolence, some personality disorder, that makes them be such a pain to the rest of us? Or is it something else?

Is it, perhaps, that people respond to the offers? Perhaps people are (don't say it) actually *pleased* when someone contacts them to tell them about something they will like. Perhaps people like to be told that their usual ferry operator has a special deal on trips, or their local fast-food delivery service is giving away free pizzas, or their car dealer has a 0 per cent finance deal on new cars.

It's all about the relevance of the offer, isn't it?

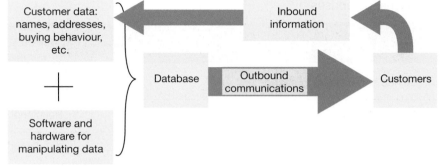

Figure 19.2

Database marketing

The key to all direct marketing, and in particular the key to Internet-based direct marketing, is the creation of a suitable database. A database consists of two elements: a collection of customer data and a software program designed to manipulate the data. Databases can be sequential, relational or object-orientated: a sequential database contains a number of fields against which the data can be sorted. For example, a bank might keep customer files which contain the customer's name, address, account number, occupation category and income level. The bank would be able to sort customers against each of these criteria and offer products which would be of most interest to the customer.

A relational database might be regarded as a set of tables which can be related to each other by the computer. The relationships do not have to be specified at the outset, so a relational database is much more flexible than a sequential database, but on the other hand tends to be slower to use and more expensive to set up. Table 19.2 shows the considerations that need to be taken into account when deciding whether to use a sequential database or a relational database.

Object-orientated databases are a relatively new phenomenon. They operate on the basis of **polymorphism**, bundling together both code and data to create an 'object'. This object is able to carry out much of the routine cross-checking and validation which needs to be done in order to insert a new customer into the database.

polymorphism Bundling data and code to create an object.

The data needed to populate the database might come from a large number of sources. Typical sources might be:

- *Company records.* Companies keep records of the sales made, delivery addresses and so forth (particularly in business-to-business marketing), but at a more subtle level the records can be analysed to show the type of product each customer buys and the frequency of purchase.

- *Responses to sales promotions.* A sales promotion not only tells the firm the name and address of a potential regular customer, it can also provide the firm with information about the customer's likes and dislikes, and (if the appropriate form is used) may even provide information about the customer's situation in terms of earnings, family size and so forth. The difficulty with collecting information in this way is that customers are likely to give misinformation if they perceive the questions as being intrusive.

- *Warranty and guarantee cards.* Returned warranty registrations provide information on the location of the end customers, and often give details about how the customer intends to use the product (this is especially true of computer users). Again, respondents might be less than truthful about how they intend to use the product, in case this affects the guarantee. Also, people frequently do not return warranty cards.

- *Enquiries from potential customers.* The fact that an enquirer does not buy the product is actually a useful piece of information. If marketers know why people

Table 19.2 Sequential vs relational databases

Marketing requirements	Sequential or Relational
Data requirements are clearly defined and unlikely to change	Sequential
Reporting requirements are likely to change	Relational
Market structure is complex and likely to change	Relational
Need to integrate with other systems	Relational
System is likely to be enhanced to include other applications in future	Relational
There is a need for quick development	Sequential
Initial cost is an important factor	Sequential
There is a requirement to add, modify or browse data online	Relational
There is a need for a user-friendly, flexible environment	Relational
The type of queries to be made are known, as are the type of reports required	Sequential
It is acceptable for selections and queries to be carried out by specialists	Sequential
There will often be long-batch processing runs	Relational
Queries need to be made on an ad hoc basis	Relational

do not buy the product, they are able to consider ways of adapting the product or producing a different version in order to capture a new market segment.

● *Exchange data with other organisations*. This type of exchange is severely regulated by the Data Protection Act in the UK and is restricted in many other countries by similar legislation. It is, however, permissible if customers have agreed to allow it. When companies exchange data, they are able to build up a fuller picture of the customer's needs and tastes, as well as obtaining details about new customers.

● *Salesforce records*. Salespeople frequently maintain detailed records of customers' details, such as customers' preferred ways of doing business, their personal details (names, number of children, etc.) and their attitude towards the company and competitors. This information is in addition to the basic information about what they buy, when and in what quantities. The problem for managers lies in finding ways to encourage the salesforce to give up this information.

● *Application forms*. Applications for credit cards, for membership of clubs or credit unions or for loyalty schemes can provide detailed personal information. The drawback is that people occasionally lie on the forms in order to gain the benefits they are looking for from the membership, and also a form which is seen as intrusive might be off-putting for the applicant.

● *Complaints*. Customers who complain will often provide useful information on what is wrong with the product or the company. If a particular complaint arises frequently, this is an obvious indication: however, it is also useful to take details of dissatisfied customers because a pattern may emerge – the type of customer, the circumstances of use of the product, the way the complaint was handled or the circumstances in which the product failed might all provide useful information. Equally, customers whose complaints are handled to their complete satisfaction often become more loyal than customers who did not have a complaint in the first place.

● *Responses to previous direct marketing activities.* Whether the response was positive or negative, the company can use the information to refine the existing database.

● *Organised events.* Exhibitions, trade fairs or conferences can provide a list of interested potential customers. In-store tastings and special evening events can also be useful, since presumably those present are already interested in the general product area.

● *Loyalty cards.* Supermarket loyalty cards and frequent-flyer programmes provide extremely detailed information about customers' buying behaviour. This information can be analysed to give a very accurate portrayal of each customer: at first, supermarkets used this information to offer customers products which they did not usually buy, but this approach turned out to be naïve since customers (for the most part) already knew about these products and did not want them. Subsequently, supermarkets realised that they would be more successful in notifying customers of special offers on products which they were known to buy, but perhaps only occasionally.

● *Surveys.* It is important to note that, for ethical reasons, it must be made clear to people that they are participating in a survey which will lead to them being contacted by firms. This is different from a market research survey in which consumer attitudes are being sought out: using data of this sort for purposes for which it was not given is at least unethical, and in some countries illegal. However, there is no problem with asking people whether they intend to switch their mortgage to another bank, or whether they intend to change their car in the next year, provided it is clear that this will result in offers being made to respondents.

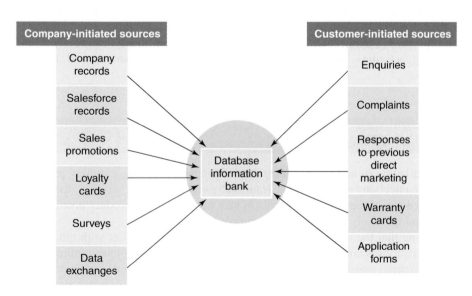

Figure 19.3

Sources of information

Table 19.3 Typical information stored on databases

Type of information	Explanation and examples
Customer and prospect information	Basic data about existing customers and future prospects would include contact details, personal characteristics (in consumer markets) or information on decision-makers and their buying criteria (for business-to-business markets).
Transaction information	Transaction information can be categorised under frequency (the number of times the customer buys), recency (the latest transaction carried out), amount (the quantity purchased) and category (the type of product being bought). More frequent customers are obviously valuable, but if the frequency rate is declining this may mean that the customer is buying elsewhere. Recency is useful because recent customers are more likely to recommend the product to others. Amount purchased is usually recorded in value terms: this is often regarded as the most important factor, but in fact the amount purchased needs to be measured against frequency of purchase and category. Category defines the type of product which is bought.
Promotional information	Databases should include information about the promotions which have been run, particularly when the promotion has been offered to different segments within the overall customer group. Knowing which customers respond best to particular types of promotion is invaluable information for the marketers.
Product information	Again, knowing which customers respond best to which type of product is invaluable for the marketers. Also, knowing which customers do not respond to a product may be helpful in developing new products.
Geodemographic information	Where possible, the database should contain information about people's incomes, family size, lifestyle and so forth. If the customer's postcode is available (which is almost certainly the case) a MOSAIC or ACORN analysis can be conducted to provide an approximation of the information, but detailed information can often be gleaned from the customers themselves.

The types of information stored on a database are shown in Table 19.3.

The database is the starting point for most direct marketing. Databases are used to identify customers for mailings or telephone campaigns, for improving customer relationship management, for managing distributors in the supply chain, for evaluating marketing activities, for identifying potential new target markets and for planning campaigns.

Managing Direct Marketing

Direct marketing should be fully integrated with other marketing activities, particularly in the communications area. Building from the overall marketing strategy, the direct marketing element of the campaign needs to take account of the product positioning in the market and the likely responses from competitors.

Ensuring that the messages from the campaign do not conflict with other marketing communications is not as simple as it might sound, because recipients of direct marketing communications consider the medium as well as the message. Indiscriminate mailings or telephone calls can lead potential customers to rank the communications along with junk mail and nuisance calls, so considerable care needs to be taken with both the style and the method of the communication. Low conversion rates (from initial contact to sale) in direct marketing are usually caused by consumer frustration at information which is inaccurate, poorly-presented, insufficient or of doubtful credibility (Grant, Clarke and Kyriazis 2007).

Talking Point

We are told that people consider the medium as well as the message, but is this really so? Are TV advertisements really different from mailings? After all, a mailing is simply another communication, which can be read at leisure (or not at all), whereas a TV advert always seems to interrupt the programme at the point where it's just getting interesting (which is, of course, deliberate on the part of the TV company).

Presumably, then, mailings would be seen as a benign and pleasant way to receive information from companies, while TV and radio advertising would be an unpleasant and intrusive way.

The target audience for the campaign should be tightly defined. Sending out mailings to people who have no interest in, or need for, the product is not only wasteful, it is also counterproductive. Poorly-targeted mailings are perceived as '**junk mail**' and are usually thrown away, often without being read: this makes future, better-targeted mailings less likely to be received positively. For this reason, direct marketers must understand their customers' needs as much as any other marketer does, but with the difference that direct marketers often have better information about customers than do other marketers. Segmentation can be carried out using the same categories as for other marketing activities; a useful segmentation system for direct marketers is shown in Table 19.4.

The database of existing customers can be used to identify potential customers from bought-in or rented databases. The risk here is that existing customers may not actually be the best customers: there may be a more lucrative group of people with whom we do not currently do business, perhaps because they are unaware of the firm and its products.

junk mail Poorly-targeted direct mailings.

©iStockphoto.com/Feng Yu

Table 19.4 Segmentation in direct marketing

Criterion	Explanation
Competitors' customers	Sometimes these can be identified from lists of people who have indicated that they do not buy our products (perhaps as a result of an omnibus survey – but note the ethical warning issued earlier).
Prospects	People who have not previously purchased the product, but who qualify as having a need for the product and the means to pay for it. In general, prospects would be potential purchasers with a similar profile to our existing customers.
Enquirers	People who have contacted the organisation (for example, at an exhibition or trade fair) but have yet to make a purchase.
Lapsed customers	People who used to buy our products, but no longer do. These people are frequently the most cost-effective to target, because they already know the product and the company and may have stopped buying for a reason which is easily addressed.
Referrals	People who have been recommended to the company by a friend or family member. Many companies run 'bring a friend' schemes to encourage referrals, often giving gifts to both the existing customer and to the new customer.
Existing customers	People who currently buy the products, and can be encouraged (first) to continue to do so and (second) to buy more of the product.

Marketing in Practice
Heist

Heist is an unusual organisation – it is a consultancy which deals entirely with marketing in higher education. Among the many marketing services provided by Heist, database cleaning is among the most important.

Because higher education institutions only send out mailings relatively infrequently, the databases are often inaccurate and should be cleaned before every use. Alumni move away, die or emigrate, and sending mailings to these addresses can be wasteful at best, acutely embarrassing at worst.

Heist check university databases against the following lists:

1 *The Post Office Address File*. This checks that the Post Office has not changed the address: half a million addresses or postcodes are changed each year in the UK.

2 *The Read Group Gone Away Suppression File*. This is a list of addresses where mail has been returned as 'gone away'. This happens when people move without leaving a forwarding address.

3 *The National Change of Address file*. This file (run by the Post Office) can help trace people who have moved house.

4 *The Bereavement Register*. Recently, the National Register of Births, Deaths and Marriages opened its files on deaths to the direct mail industry. This move was intended to reduce the number of mailings sent to the recently-bereaved.

After running the university database through these filters, it is usually fairly clean – but Heist can also help in developing and managing the database. Heist can advise on creating a database of prospective students, of alumni, and even of existing students – universities frequently forget that existing students represent a rich source of marketing information, and can also be encouraged to continue their education by studying for higher awards.

Probably the majority of people never consider that institutions such as universities have the need to manage a database – yet alumni represent an ideal opportunity to establish a lifetime relationship with an individual. Few commercial organisations can match that.

There have certainly been cases where companies have underpriced their products, thus giving a 'cheap' image to more upmarket customers.

Having identified the groups to be targeted, a list can be developed either from the company's own database or from a rented database. Buying names from a rented database carries some risks: the list may not be 'clean' – in other words, some of the people on the list might have moved house or died: other names on the list might be duplicated. This happens when an individual's address or name can be written in different ways. For example, an individual might be called Mr Alan James Fuller, Mr A.J. Fuller, Mr Alan J. Fuller, Al Fuller and so forth. Computers are notoriously bad at picking up such variations. Similar problems arise in business-to-business markets, where standard industry classification numbers may not accurately describe the business the company is in, and companies sometimes change their names, merge with other companies, move headquarters and so forth.

The next stage in the process is to set the campaign objectives. These can be expressed financially, of course, and in most companies this is likely to happen, but marketers might consider setting marketing objectives such as response rates to mailings, acquisition or retention of customers, or communications objectives such as increasing awareness or reputation.

Acquiring new customers is almost always more expensive than retaining existing ones, so marketers might well look towards reducing customer churn (the rate at which customers leave and are replaced). Retaining customers also has the advantage that loyal customers are often prepared to recommend friends to use the product, are less likely to switch to competing brands, and often buy new products from the same company

(Stone *et al.* 1995). This is why companies adopting a relationship marketing approach (which has been closely associated with direct marketing) calculate the lifetime value of a customer rather than the immediate transaction value – a loyal customer is worth a great deal more to the firm than is an occasional customer.

As we saw in Chapter 11, many firms concentrate too much on acquiring new customers at the expense of retaining existing ones: this has been called the 'leaky bucket' syndrome.

A retention objective often comes about as the result of a relationship marketing perspective. A 2 per cent increase in customer retention has the same effect as a 10 per cent reduction in overheads (Murphy 1997), because a loyal customer provides opportunities to persuade the customer to trade up to a more expensive version of the product, to sell the customer more products in the company's portfolio, and to sell customers a replacement product when the existing one is likely to be coming towards the end of its useful life.

Direct marketing can be used as a sales promotion tool, sending special offers to people who are known to respond to them. For example, ferry companies and low-cost airlines send special offers by email to frequent travellers: this is usually welcomed by the recipients, because they enjoy travel and welcome the opportunity to save money.

Tools of Direct Marketing

Direct mail

Direct mail is material sent via the postal service to the recipient's home or business premises. The purpose is to generate a response or a transaction: the mailing may contain information, may request information or may make a proposition for an exchange (offer something for sale, in other words). In some cases the mailing is intended to maintain a relationship with the customer: many banks send out information about new services, or changes to existing services, simply in order to make sure that customers do not suddenly have a nasty surprise when they try to carry out a transaction.

Direct mail is often equated with junk mail. There is, however a distinction: junk mail consists of indiscriminate, untargeted mailings, whereas direct mail is (or should be) carefully targeted. Although no company wants to waste money sending offers to people who will not respond, sometimes firms lack the sophistication to be able to target mail accurately. Also, firms often use outdated mailing lists, sending out mailings to people who have moved house or died, or whose circumstances have changed.

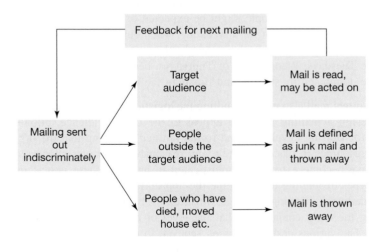

Figure 19.4

Targeting mailings

Apart from the waste, there is also the risk of damaging the brand by the use of poorly-targeted and indiscriminate mailings. Since people have a negative view of junk mail, there is a very real danger of transferring that negativity to the brand – people might feel less well-disposed towards a company which is perceived as harassing them.

Of course, there will always be a certain amount of room for error – direct mail companies cannot be completely up-to-date. For example, someone who was very interested in the possibility of moving his or her mortgage to a cheaper lender six months ago might have inherited some money and paid the mortgage off in the meantime, and thus has no interest in the offers coming through the door. Likewise, people move house on average every seven years, which means that some people move house much more frequently than this. Mailings sent to these addresses are, of course, wasted.

Within the UK, approximately 100 million pieces of mail are returned each year marked 'Return to Sender' or 'Gone Away'. This represents over £4 million in wasted postage and around £200 million in wasted mailings. This does not take account of the (perhaps larger) number of mailings which are simply thrown away. Much of this wastage could be reduced: agencies exist to clean mailing lists. One such agency, ReAD, claims to identify over 94 per cent of gone-aways and 80 per cent of deceased people, by comparing records with the Registrar of Births, Deaths and Marriages and by examining records at the Land Registry (Reed 1996). Cleaning the in-house database should be even easier: if a target customer has failed to respond to a certain number of mailings, he or she could be struck off the list or perhaps even contacted by telephone to check that they are still a potential customer for the product.

The major advantage of direct mail is that it is relatively cheap compared with other communications methods, especially considering that it is (or should be) accurately targeting the most likely prospective customers. Managers of direct mail should ask the following questions (Bird 2000):

1 *Who is the target market?* In other words, who are the people the mailing is intending to influence, persuade or inform?

2 *What response is required?* What is it that we would like these people to do? Are we expecting them to make a purchase, or merely to make an enquiry? Are we expecting them to keep the information for future use, or make use of it immediately?

3 *Why should they act on what we are sending them?* What reasons for action are we giving them? What's in it for them?

4 *Where is the target audience?* What addresses do we have for the target audience, and would it be better to contact them at work or at home? Where in the country do they live, and how does that affect their propensity to respond?

5 *When is the best time to reach them?* Should we aim for the mailing to arrive at the weekend, when people might be expected to have the time to read it and act on it, or should we aim for a weekday, when our offices are open and they will be able to respond? For business people, the best days to receive mailings are likely to be Tuesdays, Wednesdays or Thursdays, because Mondays and Fridays tend to be dominated by starting and finishing the week's work.

Managing direct mail also means handling the logistics of the exercise: allowing plenty of time to design a mailing that will appeal to the target audience, allowing sufficient resources for stuffing envelopes, and (often omitted) ensuring that the organisation has sufficient resources in place to handle any reasonable level of responses. Some organisations have become extremely sophisticated in handling these issues: many will test different types of mailing to determine the appropriate style. This is done by designing different mailings (changing headings, illustrations, type of copy, mechanics and so forth) and coding the reply coupons so that the level of response from each mailing can be measured. The various designs are then sent out to representative samples of the target group and the subsequent responses are checked against the codes.

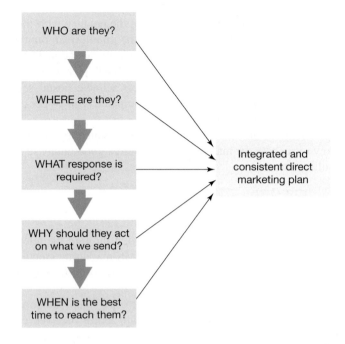

Figure 19.5
Planning direct marketing

Table 19.5 Direct mail in Europe

Country	Items of direct mail per head of population
Belgium	107
Netherlands	97
Finland	97
Austria	90
UK	79
Germany	78
Sweden	75
France	70
Denmark	45
Ireland	30
Italy	26
Spain	22

Direct mail is big business throughout Europe, and despite the problems of poor targeting and consequent low response rates (3 per cent is regarded as typical) the medium does work. Even a 3 per cent response rate is a vast improvement on the response rates to, for example, television advertising. Table 19.5 shows the annual figures for European direct mail.

There is, of course, a large discrepancy between the country with the highest amount of direct mail (Belgium) and the country with the smallest amount (Spain). This is probably a reflection on the different infrastructures of these countries: Belgium has a largely urban population and a well-developed and reliable postal service, whereas Spain has a largely rural population and a somewhat less reliable postal service. There is a slightly lower literacy rate for Spain (97 per cent compared with 98 per cent for Belgium), but this is unlikely to have had any real effect.

Overall, direct mail is an effective way of communicating directly with a target audience: the key to success for managers is to ensure a good database and consequently an accurate mailing list.

Telemarketing

telemarketing Selling or researching via the telephone.

Telemarketing is the name given to direct marketing through the telephone system. In general, it refers to communication via landline: SMS marketing (sending text messages to mobile telephones) is generally regarded as a separate form of marketing, because it is less interactive.

Telemarketing falls into two main categories: inbound telemarketing, in which a call centre receives calls from people responding to advertisements or other marketing communications, and outbound telemarketing, in which the call centre personnel initiate the calls.

Telemarketing is versatile and has the advantage of being immediately interactive – the prospect and the telemarketer can develop a conversation instantly. The main drawback is that customers often see it as intrusive (at least as far as outbound telemarketing is concerned) and the UK's Telephone Preference Service, which circulates lists of people who do not wish to be telephoned by telemarketers, has experienced a large increase in subscribers in recent years. Recent legislation in the United States introduced a Federal Trade Commission Do-Not-Call list, which allows consumers to register their names and telephone numbers on a list of people who do not want to receive unsolicited telephone calls. The Do-Not-Call list was overwhelmed by requests from consumers within the first few days of its existence: if companies continue to call people on the list the firms are liable for fines of up to $11 000 per violation. Similar legislation is currently going through the European Union system, and is likely to be in force in EU member states in the near future. The legislation in the United States covers calls from outside the US, provided the calls are being made on behalf of a US company, but the European legislation does not seem to cover this eventuality at the time of writing.

Telesales staff can call up customer details on computer screens.

In some ways these do-not-call lists might seem to be a problem for telemarketing companies, but in fact they simplify matters in the long run by eliminating people who would otherwise put the phone down, or (worse) be abusive to the telesales staff. From the viewpoint of a telemarketer, being able to talk to someone who is prepared to listen is a major advantage. Also, the legislation does not cover companies with whom the consumer already has a relationship. This has to be an exception, otherwise it would be impossible for a firm to telephone a customer (for example) to say that his or her order has arrived, or for a bank to call a customer to warn of an excess overdraft situation.

A major problem with do-not-call lists is that the people who do not register with them will receive more and more calls as the options for outbound telesales targets reduces. Since some people are unaware of the existence of do-not-call lists, the degree of annoyance experienced is likely to increase. In the long run, this is in no-one's interests:

essentially, firms need to be extremely careful about targeting the right customers, but in practice few firms are because many telesales companies are selling-oriented and therefore adopt a short-term attitude.

Talking Point

People often seem to regard companies as somehow being the enemy. Why should this be? If it were not for companies, we would have no clothes to wear, no food to eat, no houses to live in and no jobs to go to. Companies are actually just groups of people, all trying to provide something which we will like enough to give them our hard-earned cash – so shouldn't we be helping them as much as possible?

Or could we argue that, by saying we don't want any 'phone calls, we are actually helping by preventing those companies from wasting their time? On the other hand, might we not be missing out on offers which would really help us out?

Telemarketing is, in common with other 21st century communications media, technology-driven. Apart from the storage of large databases which can be made available to call-centre staff, computers can do much of the dialling. Rather than telesales operators pushing buttons to dial the numbers, predictive dialling systems are used to call up large numbers of people. The computer makes the outbound calls, only passing on the call to an operator when a person answers. This cuts out a lot of wasted time calling answering machines, fax machines and empty houses, although it does put a lot of extra pressure on the telesales staff, who often work under heavy pressure anyway. Automated systems can also arrange for automatic call-backs to customers at a later date, connecting to the same telesales operator and calling up the relevant information on the operator's screen.

Outbound telemarketing is useful for the following activities:

- *Direct selling*. Telemarketing is often used to service smaller accounts in the business-to-business environment, where the cost of sending a salesperson is not justified by the size of the business. Telesales cannot really replace a face-to-face call where the product is new or complex, because nothing really replaces the kind of detailed discussions which can take place between a salesperson and a buyer, but telesales is certainly capable of dealing with reordering situations, or with interim calls between sales visits.

- *Supporting the salesforce*. Telemarketers can contact buyers between salesperson visits, to inform buyers of the impending visit of a salesperson or to make and confirm appointments. Inbound telemarketers perform the same function, but the process is instigated by the customer in those circumstances.

- *Generating and screening leads*. Telemarketers can establish an initial contact with a prospective customer, and set up an initial visit from the salesperson. Outbound telemarketers can also check on leads which have come in as a result of exhibition attendance or magazine advertising, and can qualify the lead (i.e. ensure that the person has a need for the product and the means to pay for it).

- *Marketing database building and updating*. Checking that the details on the company database are still relevant and correct is a useful task for telemarketers. Also, if the database has come from a source such as an industry directory, a telemarketing call might need to be made to fill in gaps in the information supplied.

Inbound telemarketing does not suffer from the same restrictions and problems as outbound telemarketing. Inbound calls are those initiated by the customer, perhaps as a result of visiting a website or seeing an advertisement. Telephoning a call centre is a quick and flexible way for most people to do business, and provided the call centre staff are trained properly and have the time to deal with the call fully, the chances of doing business are strong.

Figure 19.6

Outbound telemarketing

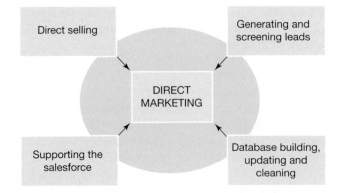

The main advantage of telemarketing is that it has many of the advantages of face-to-face selling but is orders of magnitude cheaper. It has the same flexibility and immediacy and much, of the same personal elements, but a telephone call is likely to cost around £5 at most, whereas a personal sales call is likely to cost £150 or more. Telemarketing can have any of the following roles in the selling process:

- *Primary role*. Here the telemarketing exercise is also the selling (telesales) exercise. The telemarketer is expecting to obtain an order as a result of the telephone call. Using telemarketing as the primary sales method will only work if the selling process is essentially routine (not a problem-solving role, but an explanation of features and benefits), the price of the product being sold is relatively low, the products are not technical and there is a widely spread customer base.

- *Supporting role*. Telemarketing helps (as explained earlier) in situations where some face-to-face contact is indicated, but telemarketers can carry out some routine aspects of the process such as making and confirming appointments or carrying out follow-up and after-sales calls.

- *Combination role*. In some cases, and for some products, telemarketing can take the primary role while still acting in a supporting role for other sales. For example, a field salesforce might have responsibility for selling major capital equipment to firms, using the telemarketing people to support them in this, but subsequently telemarketing people might handle sales of peripherals and consumables. In some cases, for example the computer industry, the sale of a new computer system to a company might be enhanced by offering rapid telephone ordering of printer cartridges, special paper, CD-RW disks and so forth.

- *No role*. Some selling situations, notably key account selling, allow no real role for telemarketing. Apart from a purely 'secretarial' role of confirming appointments, telemarketing is unlikely to work in a key account scenario.

The main disadvantages of telemarketing, which may preclude it from consideration, are as follows:

- It does not have the same power as a personal visit. Around 70 per cent of communication is non-verbal: facial expressions, body language, physical appearance and the ability to show samples or photographs of the product are much more powerful than any purely verbal presentation.

- It is easier for a customer to reject a telephone call: being rude to someone face-to-face is a great deal harder than simply putting the telephone down.

- Telephone selling is often regarded as an invasion of privacy, so a telemarketing call starts off on the wrong basis.

- Labour costs are higher than for direct mail (though the impact is likely to be higher).

- There is growing pressure on the industry in terms of Government regulation. This will inevitably lead to restriction, do-not-call lists and possibly even the outright banning of outbound telemarketing.

- The Internet represents a cheaper, more consumer-friendly and faster method of achieving similar results.

SMS marketing

SMS (short message service) systems, commonly known as texting, have become a new tool in the hands of direct marketers. SMS has the advantage of reaching a predominantly young audience, who might be expected to have a high lifetime value: although often their overall incomes are relatively low, the lack of mortgages and other major outgoings often means that young people have relatively high disposable incomes.

sms Short Message Service, or texting on cellular telephones.

The audience for SMS messages is likely to be interested in fast food, music, films, alcoholic drinks, magazines, books and mating-game products such as clothes, concerts and cosmetics: typically the SMS recipients opt-in to being contacted by the firms concerned, subscribing to newsletters about issues they might be interested in. Banks now use SMS to contact customers about their bank accounts, and some SMS systems exist to update people about stock exchange movements.

The main advantages of SMS marketing are as follows (Anon 2002):

- *Cost effectiveness.* The cost per message is between 15p and 25p, compared with 50p to £2 for a direct mailing.

- *Personalised messages.* The messages can easily be addressed to individuals or to subgroups within the database. This means that subscribers can opt to be informed about specific types of product.

- *Targeting.* SMS use among 15 to 25-year-olds is 86 per cent, and among 25 to 34-year-olds it is 87 per cent (Middleton 2002). This means that SMS can target a relatively young audience fairly easily (although it should be noted that SMS use is rapidly spreading amongst older age groups). Because of the opt-in nature of SMS, the audience selects and segments itself, however.

Texting has shown great potential for marketing to young people.

- *Interactive capability.* The recipient of the message can easily text a reply, often to make a purchase or (for example) book a concert ticket.

- *Customer relationships can be built.* Because the SMS system is interactive, dialogues can become established.

- *Time flexibility.* The messages can be sent at any time of day, and of course can be read by the recipients whenever it is convenient to do so.

- *Immediacy and measurability.* Because replies can, and usually are, made very shortly after the messages have been sent out, the response rates can be measured fairly easily.

- *Database building.* The information which is sent back from subscribers can be used to improve the detail and accuracy of the database.

There are, of course, limitations. The messages generally have to be fairly short, 160 characters or less (although messages can be split into two), and the messages are visually unexciting. Third-generation (3G) technology does permit good quality pictures to be sent, but these telephones are not yet universally distributed, and the extra cost of sending such large amounts of information may prove prohibitive. There is also the possibility of wear-off – as SMS marketing becomes more widespread, the initial novelty

Talking Point

is likely to wear off, and it will become regarded as just another nuisance call. Poor targeting is likely to contribute to this, and SMS marketing is as prone to this as any other direct medium (McCartney 2003).

SMS is the defining communication medium of the early 21st century. Texting is almost an obsession among some young people: it has even been credited with reducing smoking among young people, because their hands are too busy to light a cigarette. Receiving a text message is exciting – it could be from a hot date, from a friend in trouble or from... a marketing company.

So is there a moral dimension here? Should companies be tapping into something as personal, and indeed as culturally embedded, as texting? If not, why not? Radio, television, cinema, newspapers, magazines and indeed the Internet would not exist in their present forms if it were not for advertising, so why not subsidise SMS the same way?

The key elements for success in SMS marketing are shown in Table 19.6.

SMS marketing is governed by the Mobile Marketing Association in the UK. This organisation was set up with the aim of preventing SMS marketing from suffering from the same excesses which have brought Internet marketing (and particularly spamming) into a degree of disrepute. The MMA conducted research which indicated that 68 per cent of consumers would recommend the service to friends, and 43 per cent said they would respond to messages positively (Blythe 2003).

Direct response advertising

Direct response advertising differs from ordinary advertising as follows:

1 It seeks to elicit a direct response from the target audience.
2 It provides a communications channel for the responses (a coupon, telephone number, website etc.)
3 It has a strong call-to-action in the advertisement (for example, it will say 'Call this number now').

The purpose of direct response advertising is to use the mass media to reach a wider audience than would be possible with, for example, a mailing. Also, it can be used in

Table 19.6 Key elements for success in SMS marketing

Element	Explanation
Targeting	As with any other direct medium, targeting correctly is essential. Apart from wasted messages going to people who have no interest in the product, 'junk' messages only serve to annoy recipients.
Value added	The communication must be valuable to the recipient in its own right. This means that it should go beyond a mere advertising plug and provide real information or entertainment value. This is difficult in only 160 characters.
Interactive	The message should encourage recipients to respond, thus setting up a dialogue: this means that the company sending out the message will need people at the other end of the communication to text back to the subscribers.
Permission	Consumers must have a clear and easy way of opting out from receiving marketing communications to their mobiles (this is part of the New Electronic Communications Directive from the European Union).

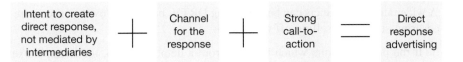

Figure 19.7

Direct response advertising

circumstances where direct mailing could not be used – typically, when there is no mailing list available. Direct response advertising can appear in print media, billboards or broadcast media (though direct response television is more common than direct response radio).

A typical print-based direct response advertisement will incorporate the telephone number or web address into the advertising itself, although many advertisements still only add on the telephone number at the end, almost as an afterthought. The number should be a free number, or at least a local-rate number: the fewer obstacles in the way of responding, the better.

Direct response television demands considerable creativity on the part of the marketer, and also requires fairly frequent repetition of the advertisements. Because there is no hard copy, the target audience need either to be able to remember the contact details (which is unlikely unless the telephone number or address is very easily memorable) or need enough time to write the details down. The advertisements vary in length worldwide: in the UK, the standard 30-second advertisement is usual, although sometimes the advertisements are 60 seconds or even 120 seconds during off-peak times. Shorter slots are rarely used because of the need to ensure that people have enough time to act on the call-to-action, enough time to write down telephone numbers and so forth.

In other countries, longer time slots may be available: in the United States, the infomercial (a half-hour programme about the product) is common on some cable stations, and in Spain it sometimes seems as if the entirety of TV advertising consists of direct response advertising.

Digital TV has made a substantial difference to the way people interact with direct response advertising. Because digital TV has a degree of interactivity built in, people are able to press the red button on their remote control handsets to find out more about products, and even to order a brochure or free sample. Eventually, digital TV will be even more interactive: there are currently three modes in which this could happen. First, the viewer has the single mode in which he or she can switch between the normal TV programming and the interactive mode. This is the system which allows viewers to access a purchase site after seeing the advertisement. Second, there is the simultaneous mode, in which the viewer can split the screen or use a picture-in-picture (PIP) window, either to continue watching the programme while interacting with the site through the PIP window, or using the PIP window to keep up with the show while using the main screen to choose products. This is particularly useful if one member of the family wants to follow up on the product but the others would prefer to watch the programme.

The third model is the pause mode, in which the programme is downloaded to a hard disk so that the viewer can pause the programme while interacting with the advertising, then return to the programme afterwards. This system allows viewers to customise their viewing, downloading programmes of interest and watching them later (much the same as using a VCR or DVD recorder, but faster and simpler).

Direct response television (DRTV) is undoubtedly going to grow in importance in the next few years: in the UK digital TV is expected to be the broadcasting standard by 2012, at which time the current analogue broadcasting will stop altogether, making most TV sets obsolete without a set-top digital converter. Although this date is not set in stone, and consumers are being consulted, there will come a point when the analogue signal will be switched off (as happened in 1985 with the old 405-line broadcasting standard in the UK) and any remaining TVs which have not been converted will be scrapped.

A wide range of products can be sold using DRTV, but the following criteria are useful in ensuring success in selling off the screen:

1 If the product is one which benefits from a demonstration, for example exercise equipment or clothing.

2 If the product has mass consumer appeal (since TV is a mass medium) or if it has appeal to a specific group of people who might be expected to watch a specialist cable channel (for example, history books might sell well to people who watch the History Channel).

3 The advertising itself must be engaging and interesting (see Chapter 15 on zipping and zapping).

4 The company needs an efficient inbound telemarketing operation to be able to respond to calls. This is especially important since the calls will tend to bunch up immediately after the advertisement is aired: the call centre might be overwhelmed for 10 or 15 minutes, then be idle until the advertisement airs again.

Catalogue marketing

Catalogues have proved to be an enduring form of direct marketing in several countries. Catalogues are distributed to consumers and agents, and orders are placed by mail: goods are then delivered either through the post or via parcel delivery services.

The USA had the first mail-order catalogues during the 19th century, serving remote farms and communities: the steadily-spreading rail network made catalogue shopping possible and the idea caught on in other countries. The drivers for catalogue shopping are as follows:

1 *Availability of credit.* In many cases, people from poorer backgrounds (especially people who are unemployed) have little or no access to credit. The local catalogue agent (a friend or neighbour) who is creditworthy takes on the credit risk, offering credit in turn to the end consumer. The agent earns commission, and is less exposed to the credit risk than the company would be, because he or she has a social link with the end consumer. This has been an important driver in the growth of the UK catalogue industry, although as credit has become more readily available to people at all levels of society, the availability of credit has become less important.

2 *Convenience.* In circumstances where people live a long way from shops (as was the case in the early days in the United States, and is still to an extent the case), or when shopping hours are restricted (as was the case in Germany), catalogue shopping presents an attractive alternative. Catalogues might also present a useful alternative for people who find it difficult to get to the shops, either because they have small children or because they are housebound through illness or disability.

3 *Range of goods.* Many catalogues have an extremely wide range of products, meaning that people can quickly find exactly what they need.

Figure 19.8

Advantages of catalogue marketing

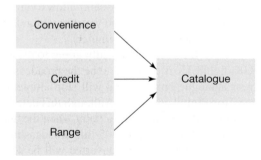

Many catalogues operate alongside retail operations: firms such as Next, essentially a store retailer, can run a catalogue operation alongside the store. Likewise, firms like Argos (which is essentially a catalogue retailer) runs stores in which the catalogue is the starting point for buying. Customers enter the store, find the goods in the catalogue, fill in a form and then collect the goods from a counter at the back of the store. The advantage of this system is that there is no need to wait for delivery (or pay for it), and customers can browse the catalogue at home before visiting the store (or perhaps asking a friend to collect the goods).

The UK, Germany and the United States are the three countries which make most use of catalogue buying. In each country the market accounts for approximately 4 per cent of retail sales, which represents a substantial amount of business, but hardly threatens traditional High Street retailers.

Direct response radio

Direct response radio advertising is less common than DRTV: the problem of delivering a response channel is much greater, because of the lack of visual clues or the permanency that comes from print media. Radio advertising therefore needs to be more creative in finding ways to make telephone numbers (or even websites) memorable. Sometimes this is done by using a memorable telephone number which fits the advertising platform, sometimes it is done by linking the telephone number to a catchy jingle. The key to this is repetition – interested customers are not likely to have a pen handy to write down the numbers, especially considering that many people only listen to commercial radio when they are driving.

The main advantage of direct radio is, of course, cost. Radio advertising is far cheaper than TV advertising, and reaches a wider audience than press advertising: it also has the advantage that the advertising is difficult to zip or zap (see Chapter 15). It is probable that direct radio advertising is currently an underused medium.

Internet Marketing

Much has been written about the Internet and its impact on marketing, particularly in the area of retailing: it is true to say that the Internet and e-commerce have changed the way firms do business in many areas. On the other hand, e-commerce still only represents a relatively small part of the world's business, and although the various aspects of the Internet which impinge on business have played a huge role in facilitating exchange, it will be some time yet before traditional High Street retailers need to become overly worried.

Talking Point

Because the Internet is virtually unregulated (because no Government has yet worked out a way of doing so – but watch this space) it has been a medium for disseminating both the best and the worst of human communications. Children who lost their parents in the 2004 tsunami in Asia were reunited through the Internet: charitable aims, enlightening messages, support for the lonely, help for the needy have all happened through the Internet. Like a bush telegraph for the global village, the Internet keeps us all in touch.

On the downside, the Internet has been the medium for disseminating the worst pornography available, for showing beheadings and torture, for publishing malicious falsehoods and Nazi propaganda, for showing the worst of humanity. In the past, advertisers have boycotted media such as soft-porn TV channels and malevolent magazines because they do not want their brand names to be associated with such communications. So what's happening with the Internet? Will we see advertisers deserting in droves, as a protest against the excesses of the medium? Or will we, instead, see advertisers jumping on the bandwagon, with the realisation that they are no longer bound by the fetters of Government regulation?

Figure 19.9

Electronic communications media

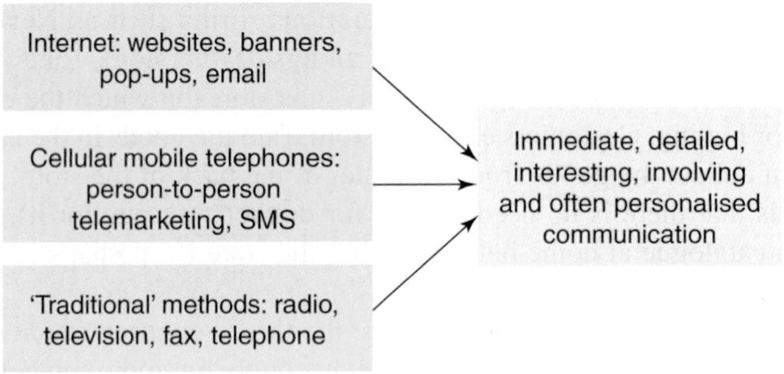

From its early beginnings as a communications medium for academic and military uses, the Internet has grown to the point where virtually all firms have a website, and in most cases the websites allow at least some interactivity. Websites fall into two main categories: presence websites, which merely give information about the company and usually include contact telephone and email addresses, and interactive websites, where customers can navigate around the site, obtain more information about the company and its products and even place orders. As firms become more sophisticated in their use of the Internet, presence sites are disappearing in favour of the more complex, more expensive interactive sites.

Part of the problem in writing about the Internet is that the technology is progressing extremely rapidly, as are the computer skills of the general public. Communications technology is converging rapidly, so that telephone, television, Internet, email, SMS, fax and even radio are combining to offer seamless, interactive exchange of information anywhere in the world. Ultimately, the new technologies will need to be considered as a whole rather than as separate entities, but at present they are still operating independently to a large extent.

To cover all the methods of doing business electronically, the term 'e-commerce' has been coined. E-commerce is generally applied to business conducted over the Internet, but strictly speaking it also refers to business conducted via other electronic means. E-marketing refers to the marketing elements of e-commerce, with a sub-category of online marketing which refers to Internet marketing activities.

In the business-to-business environment, many major firms have moved over to electronic data interchange (EDI) protocols to manage their relationships with both suppliers and customers. EDI involves setting up dedicated network connections with trading partners so that orders, invoices and even payments can be made electronically, without the use of paper invoices and orders and consequently with many fewer staff involved in the process.

The most prominent form of e-commerce is business-to-consumer marketing, however. It is here that some industries have been revolutionised: online travel booking is an obvious example, with low-cost airlines such as Ryanair and EasyJet conducting virtually all their bookings online. The advantages are many for the companies concerned: the work of making the booking is shifted to the customer, the company's pricing is shifted to the computer, and even the cost of printing a ticket is borne by the customer. On other websites it is possible to book hotel rooms, book bus and train tickets, arrange for transfers from airports and so forth.

One of the problems for companies is that the Internet has put considerable power in the hands of consumers. Customers can behave badly online, perhaps by setting up a shadow website which attacks the firm, and most companies are not prepared for handling this type of attack (Conway *et al.* 2007). Sometimes consumers develop innovative (or devious) ways to use company websites – for example, using the Internet to gain information about products, but then making the purchase from a bricks-and-mortar retailer. Consumers have been known to be even more devious – booking a number of

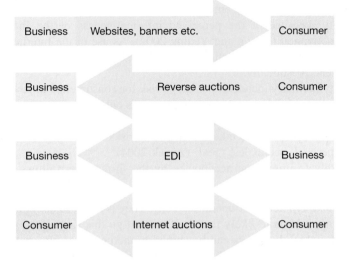

Figure 19.10

E-business relationships

hotel rooms online, cancelling at the last minute, then contacting the hotel to ask for a last-minute discount. The Internet is still working out the power relationships between consumers and suppliers – what is deviant and what is merely innovative is still being negotiated (Denegri-Knott 2006).

Consumer-to-business e-commerce also exists, on a relatively small scale: in this model, consumers group together to make offers to suppliers in a so-called 'reverse auction'. If the suppliers feel that the combined offer makes it worthwhile to meet the consumers' bid price, the deal goes ahead. This type of trading has had limited success, partly because of the effort of getting enough people together (even online) to make a realistic bid, and partly because of the uncertainty about whether the goods will eventually materialise. The majority of people are prepared to pay more for the convenience and certainty of buying from a conventional retail outlet.

Consumer-to-consumer e-commerce is represented by firms such as eBay, the Internet auction site, on which consumers can sell secondhand goods, unwanted concert tickets and so forth. eBay has proved to be hugely successful, with millions of people worldwide logging on to buy or sell items. Consumers also form virtual communities based around common interests, often including product categories or even specific brands as the focus of the group. There are four basic types of virtual community: brand communicators, who discuss specific products; communities of interest (hobby sites such as sailing enthusiasts); fantasy communities (based around playing games such as Dungeons and Dragons); and relationship communities (based on shared problems and experience) (Muniz and O'Guinn 2001).

Such communities replace some marketer-led sources of information such as salespeople or advertising, but only replace primary sources to a limited extent (Jepsen 2006). The satisfaction from such communities comes from interacting with other members rather than anything the organisers do, so establishing such a community on a corporate website may not be as powerful as some companies might hope (Langerak *et al.* 2004).

Adoption of Internet marketing

Two factors are key in the growth of Internet marketing: its acceptance by consumers and its acceptance by marketers. Acceptance by consumers depends on a degree of computer literacy, access to computers, a belief that the companies online are honest and reputable and reassurance about security of cash transactions online. In general, the people who are most likely to respond favourably to Internet marketing are those with high levels of social

escapism (people who enjoy the entertainment value of the Internet, in other words), high Internet ability (because of the perceived informativeness of the Internet) and high information motivation (Zheng and Yeqing 2002). As use of the Internet becomes more widespread, however, such distinctions are likely to be eroded – eventually everyone will be Internet users, presumably.

Intangibility normally increases perceived risk for consumers, but research shows that the main concerns people have about doing business online revolve around privacy issues and security, not about the products themselves (Eggert 2006). Interestingly, online investors are often prepared to take much greater risks than they would offline, because the online experience seems less 'real' (Zwick 2004).

Factors likely to impact on acceptance by the firm are as follows (Van Slyke and Belanger 2003):

1 *Operational efficiency*. If operational efficiency is likely to be improved by Internet marketing, it is more likely that the firm will go this route: for example, if the work of making bookings can be shifted to the customer, this will improve operational efficiency, which is a clear benefit for the firm.

2 *Channel conflict*. If other distribution channel members (e.g. retailers and whole-salers) feel threatened because the company is going direct to consumers via the Internet, this may inhibit adoption of the Internet as a medium for marketing.

3 *New markets and competition*. As new markets appear, they are likely to be Internet-driven: at the same time, if competitors are marketing on the Internet, there will be pressure for other firms to follow suit.

4 *Financial investment*. Setting up a website can be an expensive and time-consuming option (although equally, a small website can be set up relatively cheaply compared with many other marketing activities). Firms need to decide on the level of investment which is appropriate to what the firm seeks to achieve.

5 *Market changes*. Consumer tastes and behaviours change, and undoubtedly there has been a revolution in the way consumers shop, at least for some items. For example, the past 30 years has seen a tremendous growth in air travel, particularly connected to foreign holidays. E-commerce has enabled people to book more of these trips online.

The rate at which firms become fully Internet-competent also depends on a range of factors, as shown in Table 19.7.

Table 19.7 Factors in the rate of adoption of Internet marketing by firms

Factor	Explanation
Internal factors	These are the factors which arise from within the firm itself. This could include personnel, existing processes and procedures, current strategic aims and so forth.
Environmental factors	These result from influences outside the firm, over which the firm does not have direct control. Examples might be the degree to which competitors are using the Internet or the extent to which potential customers might be using the Internet.
Comparative advantage	This is the extent to which using the Internet offers real advantages over existing methods of trading. If the Internet offers no real advantage (which is entirely possible), then there is no point in using it. For example, a company selling home improvements would find it difficult to do business solely via the Internet (although a presence website might be used to drive business to the company's offices).

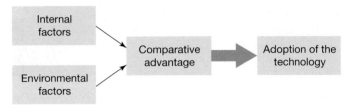

Figure 19.11

Adopting the Internet

Table 19.8 Ladder of e-business initiatives

Stage	Explanation
Information sharing	E-business is viewed as an activity within the existing business framework. There is little or no integration with other communications or marketing activities. Most of the effort comes from the 'grass roots' of the organisation, and most of the outcomes relate to increased efficiency.
Automation of business processes	At this stage, e-business affects the firm's processes. There is some integration with other systems and processes, with the e-business team taking the lead. Most of the outcomes relate to effectiveness.
Integration	At this stage e-business becomes integrated into the firm's processes. It operates at the enterprise level, integration is tight and e-business drives the business's marketing efforts. The outcomes relate mainly to revenue.
Reinvention of the industry and the markets	Here the use of e-business revolutionises the value network. There is real-time integration of the value chain from end to end, and the process is driven from the top of the company. The outcomes relate to transformation of processes and behaviours throughout the value chain.

It has been suggested that e-business initiatives are like a ladder (Sawhney and Zabin 2001): businesses progress incrementally from the bottom to the top of the ladder, beginning with using the Internet to share information. The next stage is the automation of business processes, followed by the integration of processes and relationships with business partners. The final stage is the transformation of industries and markets. This is expanded on in Table 19.8.

As the industry progresses up the ladder, the emphasis shifts from evolutionary initiatives to revolutionary initiatives: the focus becomes longer-term, external away from the 'bottom line' (the final profit figures) and towards the 'top line' (the company's strategic direction).

Companies which operate purely in cyberspace (i.e. companies which do not have a physical store chain) have had a somewhat patchy success rate. Some, such as Amazon.com, have survived and grown and have recently begun to show a profit (although Amazon have yet to recover the losses made in earlier years). Others have failed dismally, while yet others have been hugely successful (eBay among them). The current thinking is that firms which have a physical presence as well as a cyber presence are likely to be the most successful (Fletcher, Bell and McNaughton 2004).

E-Marketing in Practice
Boo.com

The power of e-business to change business practice is undoubted: what many strategists fail to see is that e-business also changes business strategy. This was part of the problem surrounding the dot.com crash of April 2000. At that time, there were many companies setting up with the intention of exploiting the possibilities of the Internet. Backed by private capital, each company thought that it had a sure-fire way of making millions from the Internet. In practice, many of the companies were badly run and did not follow the basics of prudent business practice – so sure were they that the Internet would solve all their problems by making the tactical and process aspects of the business work better, they lost sight of the overall strategic impact. For a while, dot.coms were the stock market favourites, but the collapse of boo.com triggered a wave of panic which wiped billions from stock markets throughout the world.

Boo.com was set up as an online fashion retailer, and was founded by Kajsa Leander (a Swedish fashion model) and Ernst Malmsten (a well-known poet). The website used state-of-the-art graphics packages to show the clothes, and the firm was lavish in publicising itself.

Funded with a £100m war chest from Wall Street banks, the company became famous for throwing lavish parties and for the rock star mentality of its founders, who would fly first-class around the world for high-level discussions where (strangely) no decisions were apparently made. Having been told by their backers that the firm was worth $1 billion, they hired 40 Ghurkha soldiers as bodyguards.

Unfortunately the firm had lost sight of even the simplest business principles. The financial director resigned after two months, horrified by the waste of money surrounding the company. The launch of the website was heralded by a lavish party for several thousand people, with top rock bands and caviar: the fact that the website was not actually ready until several months later had little impact on the company's thinking. The technology, when it finally did work, proved to be far too advanced for the computers of most potential customers – the wonderful graphics took so long to download that most people gave up in frustration and went to a normal retailer.

The carnival atmosphere at the group's London headquarters was legendary. Vans would turn up daily with supplies of cake, fruit juice and chocolate for the staff, many of whom had been recruited from other countries and did not speak English. Since staff were often unable to communicate with each other, the delays in the launch were exacerbated – the actual launch was six months late, after seven false starts.

In the end, Boo.com burned through the £100 million within eighteen months. For several months the Ghurkha bodyguards, loyal to the end, refused to let the liquidators into the company headquarters (despite not having been paid). In the end, when the liquidators did gain access, they were only able to sell Boo.com's technology for £170 000, and the brand name for a similar sum.

The founders of the firm, Leander and Malmsten, have since sold their story in book and film form, and have a lucrative income from lecturing to bankers and venture capitalists on the dangers of giving 20-somethings millions of pounds to play with without checking their business credentials first. On the downside, disgruntled former employees run a website dedicated to blackening Leander and Malmsten's characters, and creditors are still trying to salvage something from the wreckage – but with little chance of success.

Table 19.9 Problems of internationalisation and the Internet

Problem	Explanation and solution
Global from inception	The Internet is an inherently global medium, so firms have no opportunity to build expertise and a financial base in domestic markets before being forced into the global arena.
Rapid entry by 'me-toos'	Internet-based firms find their systems and software are easily copied by firms in other countries. Also, foreign firms are often able to register foreign versions of the URL almost as soon as the company starts trading: it is virtually impossible to register the URL in all countries simultaneously.
Difficulty of meeting cultural differences	The Internet crosses cultural boundaries as well as national boundaries. This means that websites might be seen to be offensive in some cultures, or at least might be irritatingly irrelevant. Designing a site that offends no-one is almost impossible.

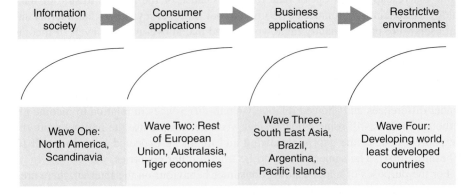

Figure 19.12

Global Internet adoption

Internationalisation and the Internet

Internet-based companies face serious problems in the international context. Some of the problems are outlined in Table 19.9.

The Internet has gone through four stages of international development (Commonwealth of Australia 1999). These are as follows:

- *Wave One:* The USA, Canada and the Nordic countries. These countries adopted the Internet from the start, in the 1980s, and are now the heaviest users of the technology.

- *Wave Two:* The rest of the European Union, Australia, New Zealand, Japan, Republic of Korea, Taiwan, Singapore, Hong Kong and Israel. This wave was characterised by high levels of private and public sector interest in developing broad information societies. There has been a high level of interest in consumer focus, and some of these countries (notably the UK and Germany) are virtually indistinguishable from first-wave countries in terms of Internet usage.

- *Wave Three:* Developing countries across South East Asia, China, Brazil, Argentina, South Africa, Egypt and small island states such as Tonga, Fiji, Barbados and French Polynesia. Characterised by high levels of interest in business applications of the Internet; in these countries, most people are too poor to be able to afford a private Internet connection.

- *Wave Four:* Least developed countries, or countries that deliberately avoid use of the Internet. These countries have unattractive investment environments, or attempt to ban the Internet for political, social or religious reasons. For example, in Myanmar all fax machines and modems not used for teaching or business have to be registered, and in Laos the government screens Internet content available to subscribers, censors any information exchanged and approves all connections to the Internet (Fletcher *et al.* 2004).

The effect of privacy and security protection on the perceived value of a website is stronger in countries where the rule of law is weak – in other words, if the residents of the country do not believe that the law is capable of protecting them, they will only use websites which promise high levels of security. People give more weight to cultural congruity between themselves and the website if they live in a country with a strong sense of national identity, and people from individualistic cultures (such as the United States and the UK) give greater weight to privacy and security issues (Steenkamp and Geyskens 2006).

Buyer Behaviour and the Internet

Buyer behaviour on the Internet has been the subject of considerable interest in recent years, but research goes out of date rapidly because of the rapid diffusion of the technology: for example, Monnier (1999) found that most surveys about the Internet showed that users were predominantly male, young, and had above-average levels of income and education. This profile has undoubtedly changed in the meantime, as access to the Internet has spread to other socio-economic groups: research conducted in 2003 by National Opinion Polls showed that Internet usage in the UK matched closely across the population spread in all age groups except the 55+ group, were virtually unaffected by gender differences and showed relatively small differences in relation to income groups. Although there is still some evidence that wealthier people use the Internet more than do the poorest people, the gap is narrowing and might be expected to narrow still further (Cheshire 2004). The same is likely to be true in other countries.

virtual products Anything which can be sold and delivered via the Internet.

For the purposes of understanding consumer behaviour on the Internet, there are three types of product: physical products, transaction-related products and **virtual products** (Craig, Douglas and Flaherty 2000). The characteristics of these in terms of behaviour are as follows:

- *Physical products*. The information search can be conducted online, but when it comes to actually making the purchase the customer either needs to go to a bricks-and-mortar store or the product needs to be delivered. Delivery may not always be easy or possible, depending on the product: for example, buying a motorbike online would almost certainly require the customer to collect the bike. Thus the final stage of the process depends on traditional marketing infrastructures. Additionally, people like to inspect physical products, which is not possible online (Dailey 2003).

- *Transaction-related products*. Products such as airline tickets and car hire can be researched and booked online, but the actual consumption of the product takes place offline. The marketing infrastructure therefore still needs to operate on traditional lines – the airport check-in desk and aircraft will operate in the same way whether the customer bought the ticket online or not.

- *Virtual products*. Music, computer software, news services, stock market advice and so forth have no physical existence and can therefore be bought and delivered entirely online. Virtual products can easily reach global segments, because there is no need to consider the marketing infrastructure in the countries concerned: for example, when Amazon first started in the United States, the company had difficulty fulfilling orders from the UK because of the costs of shipping books across the Atlantic. This difficulty does not exist for online music retailers. Virtual products can easily be adapted to market segments and even individual customers.

Information is, of course, the key contribution the Internet makes. External search costs are reduced by using the Internet, but because of the large number of websites and the need to interact both with the computer and with each website, cognitive search cost is

high. In other words, although the search can be conducted quickly and easily without leaving the house, there is considerable effort in operating a computer and in navigating round an unfamiliar site (Chiang, Dholakia and Westin 2004). This may be why people often limit their searches to one or two regularly-used sites: research shows that people only visit an average of 1.1 book sites, 1.2 CD sites and 1.8 travel sites before making a decision (Johnson *et al.* 2002).

For virtual products, information actually is the product, but for transaction-related products the extra information enhances the product. For example, many airlines allow online customers to choose their seat on the aircraft at the time of booking, and many hotels provide digital photographs of their rooms online. For physical products, the extra information improves decision-making and refines choice criteria. Although personal service is still important for assessing satisfaction with transaction-related products, self-service technology often helps to tie consumers into relationships with providers (Beatson, Coote and Rudd 2006).

For companies supplying physical products online there will always be a likelihood that people will carry out an information search online but then buy the products from a bricks-and-mortar retailer. The reason for this is that nothing substitutes for a hands-on experience of the product, and in many cases the product needs a much closer examination than can be carried out online. In order to overcome this problem, online retailers need to offer something extra, either in terms of convenience or (more commonly) in terms of price. Given that the costs of running a website are likely to be much lower than the costs of running a bricks-and-mortar store, prices should be lower: however, in many cases the extra cost of delivering the goods eats into the overhead savings, so that firms find that their profit margins are squeezed.

People look for sensory stimulation from an e-tailer exactly as they would from a bricks-and-mortar retailer, so the sites should be designed to be as interesting as possible (Parsons and Conroy 2006). One way of doing this is by using avatars (animated cartoon characters) which create a friendly impression, which in turn leads to increased pleasure and arousal (Wang, Wager and Wakefield 2007). Avatars also appear to lead to a greater purchase intention (Holzwarth, Janiszewski and Newmann 2006).

McKinsey (McKinsey Marketing Practice 2000) researched Internet users in order to identify segments of the market. The segments they identified were as follows:

- *Simplifiers*. These are experienced Internet users who seek convenience and low prices. They spend relatively little time online, but they account for half of all Internet purchases.
- *Surfers*. This is a small segment of people who enjoy novel approaches and enjoy the control they have over the transaction process.
- *Bargainers*. This group are price-driven and use the Internet to seek out the best deals.
- *Connectors*. These people are newcomers to the Internet who use it to connect to others via chat facilities, etc. Due to a lack of confidence in their own technical ability, they are looking for reassurance when using the Internet.
- *Routiners*. These users visit few sites but use the sites intensively. They have a specific routine, perhaps for booking travel or for online banking.
- *Sportsters*. This group spend only a small amount of time online, visiting sites which focus on sports and entertainment.

The segments are compared in Table 19.10.

Buyer behaviour itself differs on the Internet. Diffusion of innovation is likely to be faster, because the geographical proximity is less of an issue: especially in the case of virtual products, innovation adoption can (and does) proceed much faster than normal.

The evaluations a consumer has to make before buying are likely to be more complex, partly because there is simply more information available and partly because the cues are different. For example, evaluating a hotel in another country might prove difficult if the consumer does not understand the local star rating system.

Table 19.10 Online consumer segments

Segment	Percentage of Internet users	Hours active per month	Unique domains accessed per month	Pages accessed per month	Percentage buying
Simplifiers	29	7.1	62	1021	87
Surfers	8	30.2	224	4852	71
Bargainers	8	8.3	43	1295	64
Connectors	36	5.7	54	791	42
Routiners	15	8.2	32	624	50
Sportsters	4	7.1	47	1023	51
Total/Average	100	9.8	74	1398	61

Source: McKinsey Marketing Practice, *All Visitors Are Not Created Equal* (April 2000).

Country of origin effects are likely to be less important as cues because of increased exposure to a wider range of information from other countries. Finally, the role of opinion leaders is likely to diminish because of the proliferation of chat rooms, bulletin boards and 'customer review' boxes on websites.

Barriers to Use of the Internet

In the international context there are several barriers which will limit growth of the Internet, at least in the short term. First, there is the language barrier. The Internet is heavily biased in favour of English: of the 150 million websites functioning in 2000, 129 million were in English. This is despite the fact that English speakers only account for some 497 million people, about one-twelfth of the world's population (Craig *et al.* 2000). The world's most-spoken language, Mandarin, accounts for more than one-sixth of the world's population, but only 6.6 per cent of its websites. Partly this is because written Mandarin does not lend itself to websites because it consists of pictograms rather than alphabetically derived words.

Information can become misrepresented because people from different cultures read icons and signs in different ways (see Chapter 8). A symbol such as a horse or a fish might have totally different meanings, depending on the cultural context of the observer.

Information may be less credible on the Internet, or it may acquire a spurious credibility: for example, information posted on bulletin boards or in chat rooms would not have the same credibility as a statement from a trusted friend (word-of-mouse versus word-of-mouth). On the other hand, some completely false information is posted on the Internet, but because it is well-produced and well-written it is often accepted as true by the less discerning surfers.

From a company viewpoint, the level of clutter on the Internet represents a potential problem. Ensuring that one's own website is visited more than others is a function of the following factors (Wolk and Theysohn 2007):

● *The quality of the offering.* The actual products on offer are the main reason for visiting.
● *The level of interactivity.* The more interactive the site, the more people will enjoy visiting and the longer they will stay.

Security fears	Infrastructure problems
Local laws and customs	Language
Credibility	Cross-border differentials
Computer literacy	Misunderstanding
Misrepresentation of information	
Lack of consumer protection	

Figure 19.13

Barriers to Internet use: the brick wall

- *Accessibility and relevance.* If the site appears in the first 10 or so on a search engine, and is relevant, the visitor will stay longer. Accessibility may reduce the number of page views, however.
- *Credibility.* A site which appears honest and informative will be visited more often than one which appears devious or unhelpful.
- *Branding.* Better-known companies will have more hits.
- *Visibility.* The degree to which the site is known outside cyberspace will influence the number of hits.

The number of page views is influenced by credibility, interactivity, accessibility and relevance.

Other barriers include the technical capabilities of the consumers (which may be high in countries where most of the population is well-educated, but low in countries where education is at a lower level), and difficulties in maintaining cross-border differentials, especially in pricing. For example, second-market discounting (see Chapter 14) is extremely difficult: even if customers cannot actually buy the products at the lower price because the company refuses to ship to their country, they will still be able to see what people in other countries are paying, which leads to resentment. Equally, companies may not be able to do other than charge the same price across the board, which disadvantages poorer countries and may lead to losing market share to local competitors whose cost base is lower.

Internet sites also face local laws and customs: for example, comparative advertising (making comparisons between the company's products and its competitors) is illegal in Germany, advertising to children is illegal in Denmark and English-language advertising is illegal in France. Local customs may also inhibit Internet use: Germans have proved to be highly resistant to credit cards, which means that buying online becomes difficult or impossible. A study by TGI Global showed that less than a third of German adults have a credit card, and less than one-fifth of Italians have one (compared with 62 per cent of Britons and a massive 81 per cent of French adults). This disparity undoubtedly has an effect on people's ability to buy online.

Talking Point

There seem to be so many problems with using the Internet, it's a miracle it ever got off the ground in the first place! How is it that a medium with so many barriers, so many negatives, has become so important in people's lives?

Could it be that part of the success is the complexity of the medium? Could it be that people actually like it because of the technology? Any sufficiently advanced technology is indistinguishable from magic, as Arthur C. Clarke once wrote: so does the Internet bring some magic into our lives?

Security issues also concern web users, and have acted as an inhibitor in the past. More secure websites have certainly helped, as have guarantees from credit card companies that they will carry the losses resulting from fraudulent transactions, but many people are still fearful of losing money through fraud or simple error. Ordering the wrong goods, having one's credit card cloned, or simply being defrauded by a bogus website are all real problems (even though such events are rare).

Legal issues can also affect Internet adoption, both by consumers and by marketers. Consumer protection laws can often be circumvented by Internet-based firms, because the firm would be hard-pressed to obey every piece of consumer legislation in every country in the world. No national government has control over the Internet, so although a government might clamp down on companies within its own borders, it has little or no powers to prevent foreign companies from trading online. Personal information is often collected by online firms and compiled to provide a detailed picture of the consumer's lifestyle. The fact that some countries ban this type of activity will not prevent companies from other countries from doing it, and of course many companies would not see any ethical problem in doing so either.

Finally, logistics issues can affect Internet entry to a given market. If there is a poorly-developed infrastructure for delivering orders, or the topography of the country is such that deliveries are difficult (for example if the country is mountainous or homes are widely separated, as in outback Australia) there may well be problems with online ordering.

Summary

Direct marketing is likely to increase in importance as time goes by, because it offers the chance to customise the offering to consumers. At its best, direct marketing allows the producer and the consumer to interact in a way which improves the exchange process and tailors the product to the consumer's exact needs, while allowing the producer to win a loyal customer. At its worst, direct marketing annoys people by offering products for which they have no need, through a system of intrusive communications which can only be a waste of time and money for the producers.

Poor planning and execution of direct marketing exercises are commonplace, and will probably lead (eventually) to Government controls on mail and telephone marketing. In the meantime, provided the databases are well-maintained, companies and consumers can expect to continue to reap the benefits of an interactive dialogue.

The key points from this chapter are as follows:

- Successful direct marketing rests on four issues: targeting, interaction, control and continuity.

- Direct marketing is two-directional, therefore it is interactive.
- The foundation of all direct marketing is the quality of the database.
- There are many sources of information for building a database, but they divide broadly into company-based sources and customer-based sources.
- Poorly targeted direct marketing becomes classified as junk mail.
- Acquiring new customers is always more expensive than retaining existing ones.
- A 2 per cent improvement in customer retention equates to a 10 per cent reduction in overheads.
- Repetition is the key to success in direct radio advertising.
- Information is the most important product of the Internet.
- There are many barriers to Internet adoption, both by consumers and by companies.

Chapter review questions

1 What differences would you expect to see between a direct response newspaper advertisement and a traditional newspaper advertisement?

2 How might you begin to establish a database for marketing a flying school?

3 How would you minimise the risk of producing junk mail?

4 If you were running a pizza delivery service, what steps might you take to use direct marketing as a customer retention strategy?

5 If you were running a website aimed at Germans or Italians, how might you overcome the problem of lack of credit card penetration in those countries?

6 How would you attract simplifiers to a website?

7 What steps might you take to reduce some of the negative connotations of the Internet?

8 How might you use customer complaints to build a database?

9 What steps could you take to improve customer retention?

10 How could you use the database to win back customers who have defected to competitors?

Preview case revisited
Arabella Miller

The Internet is a wonderful medium for direct sales, but it does suffer from the problem that people cannot handle the goods – and when parents are buying clothes for their children, they do like to see what they are getting. Also, postage and packing adds considerably to the cost of the goods – especially when ordering a small quantity. So Arabella Miller introduced Party Plan selling, recruiting mothers from all over the UK to sell the clothing.

The agents are expected to organise party evenings at friends' homes. The host of the party can be paid a commission for her efforts, and Arabella Miller sells the products to the agent at a 40 per cent discount. This means that the agent is paid on the night of the party, since everything must be pre-paid before dispatch. Goods are sent out to the host's address, and distributed from there to the party guests.

Agents are paid a further 10 per cent on sales each month, so in theory they will be paid 50 per cent on sales. In practice, of course, agents will need to pay a cut to the hosts of the parties – but this can be negotiated. Agents can even recruit a team of people to sell at parties, and can then keep the 10 per cent bonus on all the sales made.

Agents are supplied with a full set of marketing materials (party invitations, carrier bags, a clothes rail, coat hangers, etc.) but these have to be paid for by the agents themselves. Agents also need to pay for their demonstration kits – they can opt for the baby-only kit, the kids-only kit or a full kit which contains everything.

Arabella Miller has a policy of never selling its mailing list or agents' names. Although this cuts off a potentially lucrative source of income, the company's stance would not permit it.

For a small company in a highly competitive business, Arabella Miller has got off to a flying start. Whether the party plan approach is as successful as the Internet sales remains to be seen – but the company has come a long way in only a few years.

Case study
Betterware

Betterware is a major catalogue direct marketing company based in the UK. Founded in 1928 in Romford, Essex, the company is now headquartered in Birmingham, in the West Midlands. Its rise to its current FTSE 500 status has not been entirely smooth – the company was in the hands of the receivers in 1983, and was bought out by the Cohen family (for only £253 000) and relocated to the Midlands. Revamping the company's manufacturing and marketing took some time – Betterware had been manufacturing all its own products, but the new owners subcontract manufacture to cheaper factories in the Far East and Latin America: however, the company still owns 70 per cent of its moulds and patterns, so most of the products are unique to Betterware.

Initially, the company sold houseware and cleaning products, but in the 80-plus years since its foundation the range has grown dramatically. Betterware now offers gifts, beauty products, personal care products, outdoor products, home office equipment such as shredders and computer accessories, and even pet care products. The total number of products is still relatively small, however: there are only around 400 products in the catalogue in total.

Betterware sells its products through two main routes: its website and its catalogue. The website is extremely easy to navigate, with products neatly arranged in categories and with more detailed descriptions of each product available at the click of a mouse. Goods are delivered within five working days, at a nominal charge or free (if the order is over £35 in value, it will be delivered to most mainland UK and European destinations free). Products can be returned within 28 days for a refund provided they are undamaged, unused and in the original packaging – this goes well beyond the statutory seven-day cooling-off period required under the UK's direct selling regulations.

Where the company scores most strongly, however, is in its catalogue sales. Betterware uses the traditional method of appointing self-employed agents to distribute the catalogues and collect orders from interested customers. The standard Betterware method is for the agent to drop off catalogues with potential customers within his or her local area, then call back later in the week to collect the catalogue and take any orders. There are three levels to the Betterware sales team: Distributors work part-time, delivering catalogues and collecting orders. They are often people who, for whatever reason, are unable to take on a full-time job: for example, mothers of young children might only be able to work during school hours or in the evenings when their husbands can mind the children for a few hours.

Seventy per cent of Betterware's distributors are women, which is probably a result of recruiting young mothers. The hours of work are completely flexible for Distributors, and they can work as much or as little as they are able, but obviously they only earn relatively small amounts and probably need to work a minimum of 15 to 20 hours a week to build up enough of a customer base to make the exercise worthwhile. Distributors are paid a commission of 20 per cent of sales, but a bonus scheme can raise these earnings to 27 per cent in some cases.

Level two is the Territory Sales Agent, or TSA. TSAs are expected to work full-time, and must have a car and a computer. TSAs are given an exclusive territory, and have the responsibility of distributing and collecting catalogues and orders (just like the Distributors) but additionally take on the administrative role of processing orders, organising returns, taking bulk delivery of goods from Betterware and distributing them to customers, and dealing with the banking of payments and all the associated paperwork. TSAs are paid on a commission-only basis, earning 30 per cent of the sales on their territory.

The next level up is the Coordinator. Coordinators have the responsibility of recruiting and motivating distributors, as well as handling their orders and taking delivery of goods from Betterware. Unlike TSAs, Coordinators operate through their distributor team, and are expected to spend a lot of time on motivating and training people. Coordinators earn 12.8 per cent of the sales on their territory, which can be a substantial sum for someone running a large Distributor group. Again, this is a full-time role, and one which demands considerable people- and organisational-skills: as with most other direct sales companies, Distributor turnover is high. The average time someone spends as a Distributor for Betterware is 10 weeks (up from four weeks only a few years ago), but of course the average is dragged down by the large number of people who only last a few days – successful Distributors often stay for years. The Coordinators have probably contributed more than any other factor to the improvement in retention rate, since Betterware's sales director is on record as saying that the motivational 'meetings' operated by firms such as Amway are a waste of time and money.

Many other catalogue companies have run into a motivation problem with their distributors because there is nothing to stop someone browsing the catalogue, then ordering online or by telephone. Betterware have overcome this by taking an unusual step: the company gives each Distributor a fixed territory and pays commission on sales from that territory no matter whether they come through the Distributor or via the Internet. This means that Distributors still get paid, even if they do not initiate the order – which in turn encourages them to promote the company at every opportunity, since clearly an Internet sale is a lot less hassle than a sale made face-to-face.

Distributors are not, in fact, expected to 'sell' anything. They are only expected to say one sentence to prospective customers – 'Good morning, madam. I'd like you to accept this catalogue with our compliments'. This somewhat taciturn approach means that anyone who can walk and talk can succeed as a Betterware Distributor, and there is no need for any expensive and time-consuming sales training.

Certainly the company has done extremely well since 1983 – although an exact valuation is difficult to come by, since the company is privately-owned: it is estimated to be worth well over £100 million. Not a bad return on £253 000.

Questions

1 Why bother with Distributors at all, when the website functions so well and Distributors are not allowed to deliver sales pitches?

2 The costs of paying commission and administering the delivery of relatively small quantities of goods is obviously fairly high – at least 50 per cent of the turnover. Why not simply distribute through traditional retailers and wholesalers?

3 What might Betterware do to improve Distributor retention rates even more?

4 Why might motivational meetings be a waste of time and money?

5 Why does Betterware pay commission on Internet sales?

References

Anon (2002): Can SMS ever replace traditional direct mail? *Marketing Week* 26 September, 37.

Beatson, A., Coote, L.V. and Rudd, J.M. (2006): Determining consumer satisfaction and commitment through self-service technology and personal service usage. *Journal of Marketing Management* **22**(7/8), 853–82.

Bird, D. (2000): *Commonsense Direct Marketing* (London: Kogan Page).

Blythe, J. (2003): RU receiving me? In D. Jobber and G. Lancaster, *Selling and Sales Management* (Harlow: Financial Times Pearson).

Cheshire, S. (2004): *Latest trends in the GB Online marketplace*. Interactive Advertising Bureau, http://www.iabuk.net/.

Chiang, K.-P., Dholakia, R.R. and Westin, S. (2004): Needle in the cyberstack: consumer search for information in the Web-based marketspace. *Advances in Consumer Research* **31**(1), 88.

Commonwealth of Australia (1999): *Creating a Clearway on the New Silk Road. International Business and Policy Trends in Internet Commerce* (Canberra: Commonwealth of Australia).

Conway, T., Ward, M., Lewis, G. and Bernhardt, A. (2007): Internet crisis potential: the importance of a strategic approach to marketing communications. *Journal of Marketing Communications* **13**(3), 213–28.

Craig, C.S., Douglas, S.P. and Flaherty, T.B. (2000): Information access and internationalisation – the internet and consumer behaviour in international markets. *Proceedings of the eCommerce and Global Business Forum*, 17–19 May, Santa Cruz, California. (Vera Cruz, CA: Accenture Institute for Strategic Change), pp. 31–7.

Dailey, L. (2003): Understanding consumers' need to personally inspect products prior to purchase. *Advances in Consumer Research* **30**(1).

Denegri-Knott, J. (2006): Consumers behaving badly: deviation or innovation? Power struggles on the Web. *Journal of Consumer Behaviour* **5**(1), 82–94.

Eggert, A. (2006): Intangibility and perceived risk in on-line environments. *Journal of Marketing Management* **22**(5/6), 553–72.

Fletcher, R., Bell, J. and McNaughton, R. (2004): *International E-Business Marketing* (London: Thomson Learning).

Grant, R., Clarke, R.J. and Kyriazis, E. (2007): A review of factors affecting online consumer search behaviour from an information value perspective. *Journal of Marketing Management* **23**(5/6), 519–53.

Holder, D. (1998): The absolute essentials of direct marketing. IDM Seminar, Bristol.

Holzwarth, M., Janiszewski, C. and Newmann, M.M. (2006): The influence of avatars on online consumer shopping behaviour. *Journal of Marketing* **70**(4), 19–36.

Jepsen, A.L. (2006): Information search in virtual communities: is it replacing use of off-line communication? *Journal of Marketing Communications* **12**(4), 247–61.

Johnson, E., Moe, W., Fader, P., Bellman, S. and Lohse, J. (2002): On the depths and dynamics of on-line search behaviour. *Advances in Consumer Research* **29**(1).

Langerak, F., Verhoef, P.C., Verlegh, P.W.J. and De Valck, K. (2004): Satisfaction and participation in virtual communities. *Advances in Consumer Research* **31**(1), 56–7.

McCarhley, N. (2003): Getting the message across. *Financial Times IT Review* 15 January.

McKinsey Marketing Practice (2000): All visitors are not created equal. www.mckinsey.com.

Middleton, T. (2002): Sending out the winning message. *Marketing Week* **25**(20), 43–5.

Monnier, P.D. (1999): *Cybermarketing: A Guide for Managers in Developing Countries* (Geneva: International Trade Centre).

Muniz, A. and O'Guinn, T. (2001): Brand community. *Journal of Consumer Research* **27**(4), 412–32.

Murphy, J. (1997): The art of satisfaction. *Financial Times* 23 April.

Parsons, A. and Conroy, D. (2006): Sensory stimuli and e-tailers. *Journal of Consumer Behaviour* **5**(1), 69–81.

Pires, G.D., Stanton, J. and Rita, P. (2006): The Internet, consumer empowerment, and marketing strategies. *European Journal of Marketing* **40**(9/10), 936–49.

Reed, D. (1996): Direct flight. *Marketing Week* 1 November, 45–7.

Sawhney, M. and Zabin, J. (2001): *The Seven Steps to Nirvana* (Maidenhead: McGraw-Hill).

Steenkamp, J.-B.E.M. and Geyskens, I. (2006): How country characteristics affect the perceived value of websites. *Journal of Marketing* **70**(3), 136–50.

Stone, M., Davies, D. and Bond, A. (1995): *Direct Hit: Direct Marketing with a Winning Edge* (London: Pitman).

Tapp, Alan (2004): *Principles of Direct and Database Marketing* (Harlow: FT Prentice Hall).

Van Slyke, C. and Belanger, F. (2003): *E-Business Technologies: Supporting the Net Enhanced Organisation* (Wiley: New York).

Wang, L.C., Wager, J.A. and Wakefield, K. (2007): Can a retail web site be social? *Journal of Marketing* **71**(3), 143–57.

Wolk, A. and Theysohn, S. (2007): Factors influencing website traffic in the paid content market. *Journal of Marketing Management* **23**(7/8), 769–96.

Zheng, Z. and Yeqing, B. (2002): Users' attitudes towards web advertising: effects of Internet motivation and Internet ability. *Advances in Consumer Behaviour* **29**(1).

Zwick, D. (2004): Online investing: derealization and the experience of risk. *Advances in Consumer Research* **31**(1), 58.

Further reading

Tapp, A. (2004): *Principles of Direct and Database Marketing* (Harlow: FT Prentice Hall) is a very readable and comprehensive text.

Chapter 20
Managing channels

Learning objectives After reading this chapter you should be able to:

1. Explain the value of 'middle men'.

2. Explain some of the problems of obtaining distribution.

3. Describe the issues in deciding on market coverage.

4. Explain the basis of business relationships.

5. Describe ways of controlling distribution channels.

6. Explain the difference between logistics and physical distribution.

7. Explain the issues surrounding the calculation of service levels.

8. Show how good supply chain management conveys competitive advantage.

9. Show how a logistics approach helps corporate growth.

10. Describe the drawbacks and advantages of just-in-time purchasing.

Introduction

The distribution of products is an essential part of the marketing mix, and getting the products into the right place at the right time and in the right quantities is the prerequisite for consumers to buy the products. Managing the channels of distribution by which products move from producer to consumer is a task which may fall to any or all of the members of the distribution chain: in some cases it is the manufacturers who call the tune, in other cases it is retailers or wholesalers.

Choosing the right distribution channel can also be a strategic issue: some distribution routes will provide competitive benefits, and of course different routes carry different risks. Choice of channel will depend in part on the segmentation of the market, as well as on the characteristics of the products and the state of the competition. Also, developing a new or unconventional channel of distribution can give the company a competitive edge which the product alone will not provide.

Functions of Intermediaries

Although people often talk about 'cutting out the middle man' as a way of reducing prices, this actually does not work out in practice. Intermediaries provide important services in smoothing the path between producers and consumers, almost invariably reducing costs by increasing efficiency. For example, a can of tuna goes through

Preview case
First Scotrail and Unipart

First Scotrail took over the franchise to run Scotland's rail network in 2004. At the time, the service had a reputation for unreliability, lateness, high fares and a general poor service. The First Group already had a highly successful long-distance coach service, and ran local bus services throughout Scotland and even parts of England: First is the UK's biggest bus operator, running one in five of all local bus services in the country, carrying 2.8 million passengers a day. The transition to providing rail services should have been a simple one, but in fact railway systems have particular problems which coach systems do not have, not least of which is the maintenance of the locomotives and the rolling stock.

Fortunately, under the UK system of railway management, maintenance of the permanent way (the actual tracks) is carried out by a different organisation, otherwise the problem would be almost insuperable. First Scotrail's aim, from the start, was to provide safe, reliable transport at a reasonable cost: the previous franchise owners had allowed things to slip, and many staff on Scotland's railway system had become demoralised. The travelling public also had little faith in rail travel – yet Scotland has a good rail infrastructure, and as a relatively large but underpopulated country (Scotland is almost the same size as England but has one-eighth of the population), the rail network provides a crucial transport system.

Clearly First needed to do something, and do it fast – so they called in logistics experts Unipart to help. Unipart was, in its early days, simply a distribution service for motor spares. Following the decline of the British car manufacturing industry, Unipart developed total logistics systems and consultancy systems for maintenance depots, and has grown to employ 9000 people

worldwide, with a turnover of £1.1 billion per annum. Unipart has a specialist railway division, with depots at Crewe, York and Doncaster (all centrally located in the north of England), established in the former British Railways maintenance depots at these important rail hubs.

Unipart Rail found that there was poor communication between management and staff at the maintenance depots in Scotland. Staff had little or no idea of the reasons for train failures, and shop floor workers were excluded from the decision-making process, so their experience and knowledge was effectively being wasted. Unipart needed to develop a new way of working – and quickly!

numerous intermediaries on its way from fisherman to pantry. The canners, the exporters, the importers, the food brokers, the wholesalers and the retailers all add a small margin of profit at each stage, ending up at the point of sale for a cost of less than 50p. It would clearly be inefficient for a wholesaler to deliver single cans to people's homes: still less would it be efficient for the fisherman to can his own fish and deliver to supermarkets. Intermediaries reconcile the needs of producers and consumers: producers need to manufacture a small range of products in large quantities, whereas consumers need to consume a wide range of products in small quantities.

Figure 20.1 shows how a wholesaler might rearrange shipments from producers into more convenient shipments for retailers. Intermediaries do this in two ways: first, by breaking bulk deliveries into single units, and second by assorting these units into a range of goods available off-the-shelf to consumers or even to the next intermediary. Using the

Figure 20.1

Bulk breaking and assortment

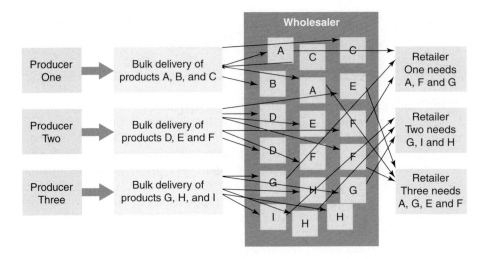

example of the tuna canneries, a delivery from the food importer of several tons of canned tuna might be broken down into separate cases of fish at the wholesaler: retailers are then able to buy a few cases of tuna, alongside cases of canned vegetables, cold meats and so forth, to retail one can at a time to consumers.

The net result is a reduced number of transactions across the system as a whole, with a consequent rise in efficiency. The increased efficiency will almost always more than compensate for the intermediaries' profit margins.

Apart from improving efficiency, intermediaries improve accessibility to the product from consumers. In many cases, the products are actually made hundreds or thousands of miles from where they are consumed, so intermediaries are able to close the location gap and supply the goods at a more convenient place. There is also a time gap: the manufacturer may produce the goods during daylight hours, Monday to Friday, but the consumer may wish to buy the goods outside working hours or at weekends. Retailers therefore stay open in the evenings and at weekends to meet this need.

Intermediaries provide ownership utility, in that the goods are available immediately from the intermediary's stocks. If goods were supplied direct from the factories, there would probably be a delay while goods are made (this is the case with many goods which are supplied directly from the producer to the consumer – as anyone who has ever bought double glazing knows).

Finally, intermediaries may provide specialist services such as after-sales, maintenance, installation or even training in the use of the products. These services are often best performed by the firms which are closest to the consumers, in other words the retailers. Retailers provide information utility, in that they can usually answer questions about the products immediately before and after sales.

Distribution channels may be of any length, ranging from direct channels from producer to consumer (common in the home-improvements industry), through to the seven or eight-member channels common in the food industry. The longer channels are often used by firms moving into foreign markets, and are often associated with lower-priced goods which are distributed in very large quantities.

The following factors influence the way distribution affects strategy:

1 Distribution adds value to the product by increasing utility (of place or of time).

2 The channel is the producer's main link to its ultimate consumers.

3 Choice of channel affects the rest of the marketing mix, so it affects overall strategy.

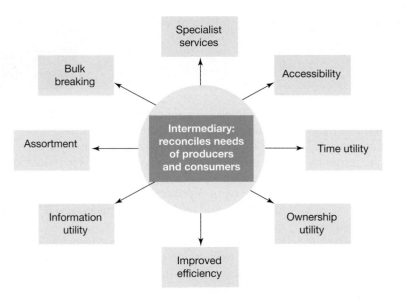

Figure 20.2
Functions of intermediaries

4 Building appropriate channels takes time and commitment (especially in a global context), so distribution decisions are difficult and expensive to change.

5 The distribution system itself often determines segmentation and targeting decisions. Conflicts may arise between the firm's strategic goals and those of the distributors, especially in global markets where timescales may differ.

6 Intermediaries in foreign countries may weaken the supplier's control over marketing decisions.

Intermediaries in Industrial Channels

For manufacturers in business-to-business markets, distribution can be the make-or-break factor for the firm. Because industrial markets are often widespread geographically, manufacturers would have great difficulty in serving the markets directly.

Intermediaries in global business-to-business markets serve customers in the following ways:

1 *Provide fast delivery*. Local distributors will hold buffer stocks, so that end users will not be held up by (for example) a shortage of spare parts.

2 *Provide a segment-based product assortment*. Distributors such as motor-spares factors carry a wide range of stock appropriate to a specific industrial sector.

3 *Provide local credit*. Distributors may be able to provide credit facilities in the country in which they operate, whereas the producer may be unable to do this due to being in a different country.

4 *Provide product information*. Distributors can explain about the products in the local language and with knowledge of local conditions.

5 *Assist in buying decisions*. Distributors can often give advice about several manufacturers' products, and can help in decision-making since they are likely to have knowledge of (for example) reliability and availability of spare parts.

Marketing in Practice
Tyron

Tyron Automotive Group Ltd. manufactures and markets safety systems for vehicle tyres. The main customers for the systems are police forces, security companies, the armed forces and the emergency services. The systems allow the vehicle to continue to be driven after a tyre blows out or is shot out by terrorists or enemy action.

Systems range from a simple steel band which allows the car to stay under control after a tyre blows, up to a 'run-flat' system which allows the vehicle to be driven for 50km or more on flat tyres. The latest product will cope with a blow-out at 150 mph, and is expected to be a big success with police forces.

In 1984, Tyron allowed its products to be manufactured under licence overseas, and although this gave the company a global presence, a problem arose when the licensing agreements ran out because Tyron had a major gap in its marketing. The company eventually recruited more than 1000 distributors in the UK, but its lack of foreign representation left it severely limited in its growth potential.

Eventually, Tyron contacted Trade Partners UK, a Government organisation set up to help small firms to export. TPUK provided training for Tyron's salesforce, and also arranged for Tyron's MD, Tony Glazebrook, to attend two trade fairs – Meplex in Dubai, and Intersec. Intersec was followed up by a trip to Australia and New Zealand, under the guidance of TPUK's export experts.

Tyron appointed several new distributors in the Middle East and won immediate orders worth over £110 000. The company went on to appoint distributors in France, Benelux, Australia, Trinidad and Tobago, Germany, the USA, Singapore, Sweden and Oman. These lead distributors are expected to appoint sub-distributors in their own countries.

Tyron tends to be a product-orientated company, but the marketing input provided by TPUK has proved invaluable. The company now exports 70 per cent of its output, and is hoping to persuade vehicle manufacturers to fit its products as original equipment.

6 *Anticipate needs.* Because the distributors know the local market, they are often able to guess what customers might need and advise manufacturers accordingly.

Because these advantages are apparent to the end customers, choosing the right distributor can mean the difference between success and failure for the manufacturer. However, distributors also serve manufacturers in the following ways:

1 *Buy and hold stocks.* Distributors are the customers of the manufacturers, because they actually buy the goods. This frees up working capital for the manufacturer.

2 *Combine manufacturers' outputs.* Customers almost always buy from several manufacturers. This means that they will be exposed to the firm's products whenever they buy from other manufacturers.

3 *Share credit risk.* Although the manufacturer will offer credit to the distributors, this is less risky than offering credit to the hundreds of customers the distributor deals with – at the same time, the distributor is better placed to assess the creditworthiness of the end customers.

4 *Share selling risk.* The distributors have a stake in selling the products, since they have themselves made a commitment by buying the products in the first place. Obviously there is an assumption that the products are saleable, but in the event that the sales do not materialise both parties share the loss.

5 *Forecast market needs.* Distributors are close to the market and are better placed to forecast what their customers will need.

6 *Provide market information.* Distributors are well-placed to feed back information about the market, about competitive activity and so forth.

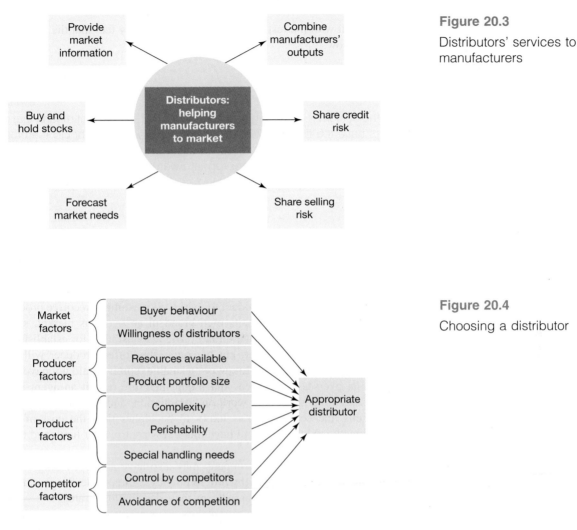

Figure 20.3

Distributors' services to manufacturers

Figure 20.4

Choosing a distributor

Channel Strategy

Channel strategy is about choosing the right distributors. This will involve selecting the most effective distributors, the appropriate level of distribution intensity and the degree of channel integration.

Selecting the most effective distributors depends on market factors, producer factors, product factors and competitive factors. Market factors include buyer behaviour, much of which is about the expectations buyers have of where the product might be found. At the most obvious level, people do not expect to buy books at the greengrocer's, and yet Boots (the UK pharmacist) has been successful in selling computer equipment and cooking utensils. In some cases, the distribution network will be suited to the profile of the target audience, who have come into the shop for something else but buy the product on impulse: in other cases it will have been chosen because the shop sells similar products and customers might reasonably expect to find the product category there.

Willingness of distributors to handle the product is also a market factor. Distributors may be unwilling to market the product for any number of reasons: they may feel that it would not sell in sufficient quantities to their customer base, it may be that the product

Talking Point

does not sit well with the rest of their range, or they may feel that the profitability of the product is too low.

In marketing we are supposed to begin with the customer. If we begin with the customer, surely that means that retailers should be choosing suppliers, since retailers have the best knowledge of the customers and should therefore know what people want? In which case, retailers should be at the sharp end of new product development, hiring engineers and manufacturers to design and make the products, booking out appropriate warehouse space and so forth.

In other words, if we are customer-centred, the present system is working backwards, isn't it? Perhaps we aren't as customer-centred as we like to pretend!

Producer factors include the resources the producer can bring to bear on the distribution problem. In some cases, producers do not have the resources to approach the market in the ideal manner, so they rely on the distributors to provide more of the necessary services to bring the product to market. For example, a coffee producer may not have enough money to establish its own brand in an overseas market, so it produces coffee for a supermarket as an 'own-brand'. The responsibility for establishing the brand then transfers to the supermarket, but of course the coffee producer will be paid proportionately less for the product. Likewise, a small exporter would not have the resources to establish an overseas salesforce, and might therefore recruit an agent in the foreign country: although the agent may work on commission, and therefore only be paid when he or she sells, the commission is likely to be higher than the cost of employing a salesforce directly and the firm will have much less control over how (and if) the product is marketed.

The product portfolio of the company may also have an effect. Single-product companies are unlikely to find it worthwhile to employ a direct salesforce: multiple-product companies need to consider the breadth of their distribution strategy.

Product factors might include complexity. If a product is complex, or needs to be tailored to individual customer requirements, direct distribution from producer to customer is more likely. This will allow the firm to discuss requirements and adjust the product: also, a high-priced product will usually mean that the customer prefers to talk directly with the supplying company. Perishable goods usually require short distribution channels and minimal handling (which is a major problem for supermarkets), and products which require special handling may require direct distribution simply because distributors do not want the problem of handling the products.

Distribution channels are sometimes controlled or at least heavily influenced by competitors. The means by which channel control can be exercised are described later in the chapter – but if a competitor has seized control first, there may be a serious problem in obtaining distribution. In some cases, excessive control of a channel might be construed as a restrictive practice, and a company which is shut out of a market might be able to take the distributor to court, but this is hardly a good way to start a business relationship. Producers would be better advised to seek a non-traditional outlet for their products. Influences on channel design are shown in Table 20.1 (Czinkota and Ronkainen 2004).

In many cases, firms might use different distribution routes for different customers. Some customers might be supplied direct, others might be supplied by agents, still others might be supplied via wholesalers and retailers. Many firms in business-to-business markets divide their customers into A, B and C-type customers. The As might represent the top 10 per cent of customers, large firms perhaps accounting for 50 per cent of the company's turnover. B-type customers might be medium-size companies accounting for 30 per cent of sales, with the remainder being small firms which only place small orders.

E-Marketing in Practice
Dell Computers

When the PC market took off in the 1980s, major suppliers such as IBM, Amstrad and Apple quickly tied up deals with High Street distributors. In the UK, outlets such as Dixon's, Curry's and Comet were rapidly signed up, in many cases with exclusive deals under which the manufacturers were not allowed to sell their products in other outlets.

This left the smaller independent PC manufacturers out in the cold. In 1984, Dell Inc. was founded by Michael Dell (who was then aged 19). The company decided to deal directly with the public from the outset. The Internet added hugely to the company's effectiveness – people were able to buy online, specifying exactly what they wanted in a computer and in effect building their own PC online.

The company's attitude has always been that dealing directly enables them to get closer to the customer, and Dell certainly goes to some considerable trouble to do this: customers have online or telephone technical support, and can even talk to the person who assembled their computer. Field support is provided if necessary, and the company runs training programmes for its business buyers.

Dell's products are not necessarily cheaper than its competitors' products, despite the retailers' markups, but what Dell does do extremely well is maintain a closeness with its customers that Toshiba, IBM, Apple and the like can only envy from afar.

A-type customers might be dealt with directly, B-type customers through wholesalers or local distributors and C-type customers through mail order or the Internet.

This approach certainly applies the appropriate level of resources to each group of customers, but at the same time it may result in losing control of some customers who might be of strategic importance – for example small firms who have strong growth potential. There is also a potential 'turf war' problem if a small firm becomes larger (perhaps because the distributor did a good job in helping the firm) and, in moving from a B classification to an A classification, is immediately 'stolen' by the manufacturer.

Distribution Intensity

Producers also need to consider the intensity of their market coverage. In some cases and for some products, the producer might be looking for as wide a coverage as possible – this would be the case for a mass-market product such as a chocolate bar or a coffee brand. Ideally, the producer would like the products to be available in as many

Table 20.1 Influences on channel design

Influence	Explanation
Competitors	In some cases, marketers will be looking for a different distribution route from that used by competitors: in other cases, they will need to follow a similar route because that is what customers expect. As a general rule, if the product can be differentiated from its competitors in a way which is not related to distribution, it should be distributed through the same channels as competitors in order to allow customers to compare the products. If there are no differentiating features between the product and its competitors, the distribution channel might be an effective way of competing.
Availability	In international markets, it is often the case that distribution can only be carried out through the one or two channels which are available: on the other hand, other channels may be available which are not common in the home country. Finally, competitors in the target country may already have tied up the existing distributors in exclusive contracts.
Culture	Culture affects the systems and negotiating tactics of distributors in foreign countries. Business culture varies considerably: for example, in Italy hypermarkets are rare, whereas in France they are commonplace. This is due to a cultural difference, in that Italians believe in supporting small local businesses, which are often destroyed by hypermarkets.
Company objectives and resources	Some distribution decisions link to overall corporate strategy. For example, a company might seek to become pre-eminent in direct distribution worldwide (e.g. Avon Cosmetics). Corporate resources also have an effect: it may be impossible to distribute through all possible outlets simply because the company does not have the resources to produce the amount of stock required, or provide the credit needed by the retailers. In other markets, distributors need a great deal of support from suppliers: this can range from providing printed materials such as brochures, to providing online technical support, through to full-scale training programmes.
Distribution strategy	The intensity of distribution (see next section), the competitive advantage being sought and the characteristics of the market will all affect distribution decisions.
Product characteristics	Some products, especially fragile or perishable products, demand very specific distribution techniques. For example, microlight aircraft are usually supplied in kit form from the factories for assembly at airfields. This means that local distributors need a high level of technical ability, either to assemble the aircraft or to advise would-be aviators who assemble their own planes.
Customers	Obviously, all distribution decisions have to be made in the light of what customers need and expect. If customers normally expect a product to be available from a particular type of outlet, there would have to be a compelling reason to distribute the product elsewhere. Such a compelling reason might be that the company sees a competitive advantage in not distributing the product on the same shelves as its competitors, of course.

outlets as possible, because sales are directly related to the number of outlets where the products are available. Since consumers probably have a wide range of products in the consideration set, another brand would almost certainly be an adequate substitute if the firm's brand is unavailable from the shop the consumer happens to be in at the time of purchase.

Selective distribution means that the producer uses a limited number of specialist outlets in a given area to stock the products. This type of distribution works best for shopping products such as hi-fi systems, bicycles, toys and so forth which need a

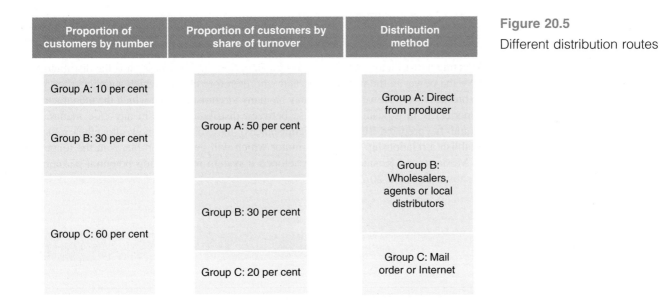

Proportion of customers by number	Proportion of customers by share of turnover	Distribution method
Group A: 10 per cent	Group A: 50 per cent	Group A: Direct from producer
Group B: 30 per cent	Group B: 30 per cent	Group B: Wholesalers, agents or local distributors
Group C: 60 per cent	Group C: 20 per cent	Group C: Mail order or Internet

Figure 20.5

Different distribution routes

specialist retailer who might be expected to offer expert advice. For this type of product, the manufacturer benefits by being able to concentrate on a few retailers, ensuring that they are trained in selling the product and (in particular) ensuring that the retailers understand the product's features and benefits so that they do not make promises which cannot be kept, and can provide suitable after-sales service. From the retailer's viewpoint, this arrangement also means that they can agree on an exclusive territory and thus reduce competition.

Exclusive distribution is an extreme form of selective distribution. Retailers or wholesalers are given the sole rights to sell the product within their area: in effect, this cuts out competition from other distributors as far as the individual product or brand is concerned. Exclusive agreements can work both ways: a retailer might seek the exclusive rights to a product, or the manufacturer might want to prevent the retailer from stocking competing brands. Some exclusive agreements can be against consumers' interests when they aim to reduce competition, however, so courts will occasionally overturn them if they are challenged by competitors or consumer groups.

'Exclusive' retail outlets create a higher–level perception of the brands they sell.

Talking Point

If consumers are kings, then presumably they are supposed to be given the greatest possible choice of goods to buy. If that's the case, why are exclusive agreements allowed at all? These agreements must *always* be in restraint of trade because they don't allow some people to have access to the goods!

Or is this a rather simplistic view of consumer needs? Most of us don't need to have Cartier jewellery displayed in Tesco, and those who can afford Cartier want to feel that it has come from an exclusive outlet. If some people feel that they do not want to mix with the riff-raff, why not indulge them? Isn't this one of the pleasures of being wealthy?

Selecting a Distributor

Selecting a distributor may not always be an option: in many cases it is the distributors who have the power in the relationship, and who therefore choose which suppliers they want to do business with. However, there may be many circumstances in which the manufacturer (or importer) is in a position to choose between distributors, and in any case manufacturers should be prepared (in some circumstances) to avoid a market altogether rather than establish a relationship with a distributor which will generate problems in the longer term.

Moriarty and Kosnik (1989) developed a system for profiling potential partners. This is shown in Table 20.2.

Table 20.2 Partner profile

Characteristics	Weight (1–10)	Rating (1–10)	Total
Past performance			
Profitability			
Sales growth			
Market share			
Cooperation with other partners			
Experience with market/product			
Financial strength			
Capabilities			
Facilities			
Marketing/sales			
Design/technological			
Size of firm			
Language			
After-sales			
Knowledge of local business customs			
Reputation/relationships			
With suppliers			
With customers			
With financial institutions			
With government(s)			
Goals and strategies			
Short-term			
Long-term			
Compatibility			
Product lines			
Markets			
Style/personalities			

The weight refers to the importance placed on the characteristic by the company, and the rating relates to the actual performance by the prospective partner in regard to that rating. By multiplying one figure by the other an overall rating can be produced, against which the various alternative partners can be judged.

The partner profile chart is similar to the marketing audit in that it provides a 'snapshot' of the current situation regarding the prospective partner. It suffers from the same weaknesses as the marketing audit: it has a substantial degree of subjectivity despite appearing to be objective, and the situation may change over time (in fact, it may change before the assessment exercise has been completed). The major problem lies in collecting the necessary data to fill in the boxes, however – not all of it is likely to be available, and in particular there will be major gaps in the information when dealing across national borders, simply because the company is not in touch with local business information.

In international markets, similar organisational cultures are more important than similar national cultures when looking for business partners (Pothokuchi *et al.* 2002). This means that companies should look for distributors with a similar business philosophy, of a similar size and with compatible business objectives.

Once a distributor has been agreed on, it is difficult to change the decision. The distributor, not unnaturally, will feel aggrieved at any changes, having perhaps committed resources to the supplying firm. Likewise any new distributor is likely to be suspicious if the previous relationship broke down. In most cases, the agreement will be regulated by a contract or at least written agreement of some sort which outlines each party's rights and responsibilities. The key contract areas are shown in Table 20.3 (Fitzpatrick and Zimmerman 1985).

The type of relationship refers to whether the distributor will take title to the products or not. This means deciding whether the distributor will buy the goods from the supplier, or simply find orders for the supplier who will then collect the money from the end customer. In an international distribution agreement, this is important, because the distributor will be in a much better position to assess the creditworthiness of local customers than will the supplier. The risk will therefore be a great deal less for the supplier, but of course the distributor will want to take a larger profit on the deal in exchange for carrying the risk. The second contract area describes the type of entity the supplier is dealing with – it is, in general, better to make distribution agreements with corporations rather than individuals, because some countries regard individual agents or distributors as employees of the supplying company, which may mean liability under employment protection legislation (this is substantially the case in France, for example).

Taxation will arise in the country where the distributor is established, but there may be regulations about customs duties and VAT which might affect the overseas supplier.

Table 20.3 Agent/distributor agreements

Key contract areas	Key contract areas (continued)
Types of relationship	Terms/conditions of sale
Corporation vs individuals	Facilities and personnel
Taxes	Inventory
Duration of agreement	Confidentiality
Termination of agreement	Proprietary information (trademarks, trade name, etc.)
Records and communication	Product sale or service agreement
Arbitration and governing law	Advertising and promotion
Payment and compensation	Other provisions

Figure 20.6
Distributor contracts

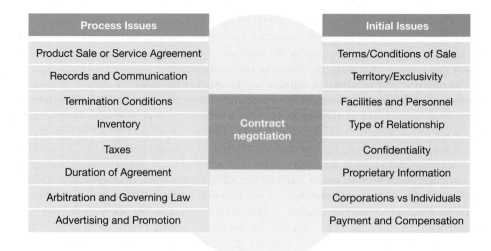

The distribution agreement should lay down who has the responsibility for dealing with these taxes.

The duration of the agreement should be limited, but should be sufficient to allow the distributor time to build a reputation. Too short an agreement will demotivate the distributor, which is not in anybody's interests: too long an agreement leaves the supplier at risk of being stuck with a distributor who is unable to deliver sales. Termination of the agreement will be governed by law in most countries: from the supplier's viewpoint, it would certainly be advisable to lay down standards of performance from the distributor, failure in which would lead to termination of the agreement. Again, in fairness to distributors the supplier should offer renewal agreements regularly, preferably well before the existing agreement runs out. Termination agreements should include clauses on how the termination is to be handled – what is to happen to unsold stocks, for example. Suppliers might well consider that it is worthwhile buying back any unsold stocks rather than have the distributor sell them off at a discount, potentially damaging the brand.

The product sale or service agreement identifies which products or services the distributor will be handling. This links with territory, because the supplier may prefer one distributor to handle some of its products in a given territory, while another distributor handles different products in the same territory. This may happen, for example, because the supplier produces a 'domestic' range and a 'professional' range of products. Each would be serving a different market, and therefore might require different distribution.

Arbitration and governing law refers to the ways in which disputes will be settled. Arbitration by a specified professional body is almost always cheaper and less damaging to the relationship than resorting to the law courts. In international agreements, it is usual to specify the country whose laws will be applied to any disputes between the parties. At one time it became common in Eastern European countries to specify that contracts would be decided under English law, even when both parties to the contract were from the same Eastern European country: the reason for this was that 50 years or more of Communism had left those countries with little or no effective commercial law.

The payment and compensation clause refers to the way commissions or profits will be divided between the parties. In many countries, anti-corruption laws mean that all transactions need to be traceable through clear accounting pathways.

confidentiality agreement A contract between two parties containing clauses to the effect that each will keep the other's secrets.

Confidentiality agreements exist to protect the intellectual property rights of the supplier, and to preserve corporate information from being leaked out to competitors. Confidentiality clauses should outlive the overall agreement: a disgruntled distributor should not be in the position of being able to pass on company secrets to competitors after the agreement has terminated. The same applies to the distributors' use of trademarks, trade name and copyright.

Records and communication need to be specified so that both parties can verify that business has been conducted fairly. Perhaps most importantly, the level and type of marketing activities to be undertaken by the distributor and the supplier need to be specified. Here a balance needs to be struck between the supplier's knowledge of the products, and a desire to maintain brand values, and the distributor's knowledge of the local market and desire to meet and overcome local competition.

Here is a checklist for selecting and motivating distributors:

1 Ask potential customers to recommend possible distributors.

2 Determine which distributor fits the company's overall strategy best. The goals of each should be compatible: an aggressive, high-growth strategy on the part of the supplier would not work well with a cautious, steady distributor.

3 Visit the distributor regularly. Apart from ensuring that the distributor is keeping to both the letter and the spirit of the agreement, visits enable the supplier to understand the market better and work more closely with the distributor in developing the market.

4 Visit overseas customers with the distributor. Although some distributors might regard this with suspicion in the early stages of the relationship, visits are usually appreciated by the overseas buyers, and in the long run they help to support the distributor. They also enable the supplier to understand the market better.

5 Provide training and support. If possible, distributor's staff should be given the opportunity to visit the supplier's factories or head office, perhaps for some formal training in the characteristics of the company's products. These exchanges will help both companies to understand each other's corporate culture.

Managing Distribution Channels

Channels can be led by any of the members. In some cases, manufacturers have the power (especially when the manufacturer is large and the products have few close substitutes). In other cases wholesalers or importers have the power, because they form the interface between manufacturer and retailer: in many cases, retailers hold the power, because they are closest to the end consumers.

In Figure 20.7, there is a continual tension between cooperation and conflict: power and leadership act as modifying influences, moving the balance between the two extremes.

Figure 20.7

Factors in channel management

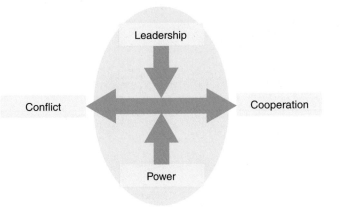

Channel cooperation is an essential part of the functioning of channels. Because each channel member relies on the other, members must cooperate if the goods are to flow freely along the channel. The problem is that conflict arises: although everyone agrees that cooperation is the best way forward for the overall success of the channel, each link in the channel has its own interests to consider, and short-term advantage might be gained at the expense of other members. Conflicts often centre around strategic non-compliance, perceptual disagreements and demarcation of decision-making responsibility (Moore, Birtwistle and Burt 2004). Power and conflict are equally important, but are exploited differently by managers (Gadde 2004).

Channel cooperation can be improved by using some or all of the following methods:

1 Channel members can agree on target markets, so that each member can direct effort towards meeting the common goal.

2 Define the tasks each member will contribute. This minimises duplication of effort, and also prevents the end consumer being given conflicting messages.

In some cases channels can become highly integrated: this has been termed co-marketing (Marx 1995). Co-marketing involves sharing market information, and agreeing on strategic issues. Co-marketing can work extremely well if a condition of trust has been

Table 20.4 Channel power

Economic sources of power	Non-economic sources of power	Other factors
Control of resources. The degree to which the channel member has the power to direct goods, services or money within the channel.	Reward power. This is the power to provide benefits to channel members, for example to grant credit.	Level of power. The economic or non-economic sources of power are only effective provided the members value them.
Size of company. The bigger the firm is compared with the other members, the more likely it is to be able to exercise economic power.	Expert power. This arises when the channel leader has a special expertise which the other members need.	Dependency of other channel members.
Referent power. This is the power which emerges when other members seek to copy the leader.		Willingness to lead. In some cases, only one firm is prepared to take the responsibility (and carry out the work) of coordinating and controlling the channel.
Legitimate power. This arises from a legal relationship. This could be contractual, or it could come about because one channel member has a substantial shareholding in another member firm.		
Coercive power. This exists when one channel member has the power to punish another channel member, for example by withholding stock.		

created between the channel members: however, there are some potential problems, as follows:

1 Channel members are likely to have relationships with other firms at the same time (because they are members of other channels). This can give rise to conflicts of interest.

2 Power in the channel is rarely equally divided, so one member is likely to dominate the others, with potentially damaging consequences.

3 Expectations are sometimes not fulfilled, leading to disappointment and mistrust.

Sources of channel power are shown in Table 20.4 (Bitner 1992).

A power imbalance is not necessarily a barrier to entering a relationship, nor is it a bar to success for the relationship (Hingley 2005), but it clearly has an effect on the ways companies behave towards each other. Managing the channel in practice can be carried out either by cooperation and negotiation, or by coercion, with the most powerful member laying down the rules and compelling the others to follow. Attempts to control distribution channels by the use of power may well be looked on with disfavour by law courts, however, as they imply a restriction of trade. Table 20.5 shows the main channel management techniques.

Sometimes the simplest way to control a distribution channel is to buy out the members. This leads to vertical integration of the channel, an extreme example of which is the major oil companies, which carry out all the distribution functions from extraction of crude oil through to sales at petrol pumps.

Table 20.5 Channel management techniques

Technique	Explanation	Legal position
Refusal to deal	One member refuses to do business with one or more other members. For example, a food wholesaler might refuse to supply private clubs on the grounds that this would be unfair on grocers and caterers.	In most countries suppliers do not have to sell their goods to anyone they do not wish to deal with. However, if the refusal to deal is based on a restriction of trade (for example, if a retailer is blacklisted for refusing to go along with a restrictive agreement) there may be grounds for a lawsuit.
Tying contracts	The supplier (sometimes a franchiser) demands that the channel member carries other products as well as the one the channel member wants to stock. If the supplier insists that the channel member carries the full range, this is called full-line forcing. For example, fast-food franchisees are usually required to buy all their supplies from the franchiser, and must carry the full range.	In the UK, most of these contracts would be illegal. They can be justified if, for example, only the supplier can provide goods of acceptable quality, or if the purchaser is free to carry competing products as well. Some agreements are accepted if the supplier is new to the market.
Restricted sales territories	Intermediaries are prevented from selling outside the area. Intermediaries usually prefer this arrangement, because it prevents other intermediaries from competing directly with them.	Courts have conflicting views about these arrangements. On the one hand, they do help weaker distributors, and can increase competition if other local dealers carry different brands: on the other hand, such agreements are a clear restraint of trade.

physical distribution The movement of products from producer to retailer and ultimately to the consumer.

logistics The coordination of the supply chain to achieve a seamless flow from raw materials through to the consumer.

Logistics and the Supply Chain

Physical distribution is concerned with the movement of goods via road, rail, sea and air. Physical distribution is therefore about organising transportation to move goods in a timely and secure way from producer to consumer, taking all factors into account including budget.

Logistics, on the other hand, takes a holistic view of the process. A logistics approach to physical distribution considers the entire process of delivering value to customers, starting with raw materials extraction. Logistics takes the whole transport problem and integrates it into a smooth system for moving goods from where they are produced to where they are needed.

For example, until the early 1970s goods being moved internationally would be loaded onto lorries at the factory, driven to a sea port, unloaded into a warehouse, reloaded onto a ship, taken to the overseas port and unloaded into another warehouse, then reloaded onto lorries for delivery to distribution warehouses and, ultimately, to retailers. Loading cargo onto the ship (and off again at the other end) required 18 men for each cargo hatch: eight on the quayside, eight on the ship and two winch operators. This did not include the ship's officers, who were needed to supervise the work.

During the 1970s the cargo container was developed. This allowed firms to fill the container at the factory, load the entire container onto a lorry (or train) for delivery to the ship, where it could be loaded onto the ship by (at some ports) one man in a specialised crane. The result of this has not only been a dramatic reduction in the number of dock workers needed, but also a dramatic reduction in the number of ships needed, since each ship only spends a few hours in port instead of the days formerly needed.

Logistics is central to supply chain management. Transport and warehousing links are the intermediate links in the supply chain, rather than the main concern as they are in physical distribution orientation. It is in these areas that the biggest cost reductions can be made, with consequent increase in profit or reduction in price to the consumer (in either case, competitive advantage improves).

In the past, cargo handling was very labour-intensive.

© The Print Collector/Alamy

Figure 20.8

Elements in logistics management

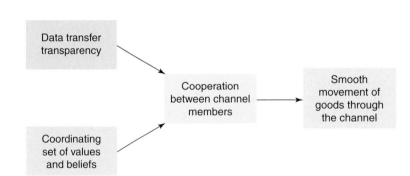

Coordinating the supply chain requires the following factors to be in place:

1 Data communication needs to be transparent, with all those involved being kept informed as to what is happening to the goods.

2 There must be a coordinating philosophy or set of rules to which all those involved should subscribe.

IT systems have enabled logistics coordinators to track consignments in real time wherever they are in the world. This enables effective use of resources: aircraft can always fly full, ships can be loaded swiftly and spend more time at sea, warehouses can be smaller because goods stay for shorter periods of time. For example, Chevron Oil introduced SAP logistics software in 1992 at a total cost of $160m. By 1997 the software had been responsible for reducing purchasing-related costs by 15 per cent. In addition, purchase transactions were facilitated electronically instead of using paper transactions, which greatly improved the reliability of the process and improved response times.

Another use of IT has been to minimise wasted journeys or part-full journeys. An example of how IT has been successful in this way is the Delego company of Sweden. Delego was started by two truck drivers who met by chance on a ferry from Denmark to Germany. Chatting to other drivers over a few beers, the two truckers realised that several of their erstwhile colleagues were travelling between the same two points, but with only half-full or even empty trucks. The two truckers planned a new system for organising part-loads, and eventually gave up their trucking jobs, borrowed some capital and started the Delego website. The system works through the Internet: when a transport company has an empty or part-empty truck on a given route, the company enters its details on the Delego website (or by telephone) and Delego tries to match up the truck with a cargo, providing an estimate of the financial return for the trucker.

Talking Point

Whenever firms talk about becoming more efficient they seem to regard job losses as inevitable. In fact, many go further – they actively try to get rid of staff. And yet business is about people. Without people nothing happens – and if people are not earning money, how are they going to buy the goods that the manufacturers produce?

Furthermore, if firms keep on firing their staff, the company is shrinking – yet isn't it part of the imperative for companies in a capitalist world that they should grow?

Or maybe it's about restructuring – shifting people from inefficient jobs into efficient ones, and from jobs which are basically 'make-work' into jobs which produce real value for everybody – company, customers and yes, even the workers! One thing's for sure – continual changes in working practices make for interesting times.

Logistics has become widely adopted by global firms. Shipping and trucking companies are therefore redefining themselves as logistics facilitators. This means that such companies take responsibility for the whole process, moving goods from the factory gates to the final destination by whatever means are available. This leads to even greater savings for the businesses involved, since the process operates much more smoothly.

Logistics managers are responsible for some or all of the following interfaces:

1 Collaboration with physical distribution. Selecting transportation methods such as road, rail, sea or air.

2 Optimisation of the material flow within the work centre.

3 Planning and organising the storage area layouts and the type of handling equipment involved.

4 Selection of suppliers for raw materials, price levels and specifications.

5 Selection of subcontractors to perform specific tasks.

6 Organising after-sales activities, including problem resolution with supplied products.

7 Verifying that sales forecasts accord with the real needs of the client.

8 Developing delivery schedules.

9 Developing packaging to meet the need for physical strength and security.

Not all elements of the logistical system are controllable by the logistics manager. Transport delays, changes in legislation requiring new documentation, the bankruptcy of distribution channel members, or even the weather can play havoc with the best-laid logistical systems. This means that even greater care should be taken with those elements which are controllable. Table 20.6 shows the elements which are controllable.

As with many other complex decisions, each element of the logistics system impacts on every other element. If the supplier fails to become reliable, the customer may have to bear the extra cost of holding large buffer stocks: additionally, if supplies fail, the customer may lose production or even customers. Clearly customers in many markets will

Table 20.6 Controllable elements in a logistics system

Element	Description
Customer service	Customer service is the product of all logistics activities. It relates to the effectiveness of the system in creating time and place utility. The level of customer service provided by the supplier has a direct impact on total cost, market share and profitability.
Order processing	This affects costs and customer service levels, because it is the starting point for all logistics activities. The speed and accuracy of order processing clearly affects customer service: this is particularly true in global markets, where errors or delays become multiplied by distance and by the time which it takes to make corrections.
Logistics communications	The way in which information is channelled within the distribution system affects the smooth running of the logistics. For example, a good progress-chasing system will allow deliveries to be tracked and therefore customer reassurance will be greater.
Transportation	The physical movement of the goods is often the most significant cost area in the logistics process. It involves the most complex decisions concerning carriers and routes, and is therefore often most prone to errors and delays.
Warehousing	Storage space serves as the buffer between production and consumption. Efficient warehousing reduces transportation costs by ensuring that (for example) containers are shipped full and transport systems are fully utilised.
Inventory control	This ensures that the correct mix of products is available for customers, and also ensures that stocks are kept at a reasonable level to avoid having too much capital tied up.
Packaging	The purpose of packaging is primarily to protect the contents from the environment and vice-versa. It also serves as a location for some shipping instructions, e.g. port of destination.
Materials handling	Picking stock to be included in an order is potentially a time-consuming and therefore expensive activity. Some warehouses have the capacity to automate the system, so that robots select the products and bring them to the point from which they will be shipped.
Production planning	Utilised in conjunction with logistics planning, production planning ensures that products are available in the right quantities and at the right times.
Plant and warehouse location	The location of the firm's facilities should be planned so as to minimise delivery times (and therefore minimise customer response times) as well as ensure that the costs of buying or renting space are minimised. This will often result in difficult decisions, since space near customers is likely to be more expensive than space in (for example) remote rural locations.

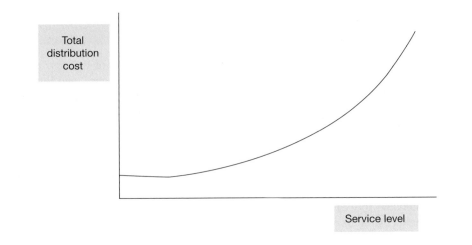

Figure 20.9

Logistics trade-offs

favour reliable suppliers, and will even pay premium prices for this, so a good logistics system is likely to have pay-offs on the bottom line in terms of improved profits and possibly improved competitor advantage.

In practice, two main variables must be traded off against each other (see Figure 20.9). The first is the total distribution cost, which would generally be regarded as something which should be kept to a minimum. The second variable is the level of logistical service given to customers. As service improves, costs will rise, and there is likely to be a diminishing return for extra expenditure: in other words, there is a point at which further expenditure is unlikely to make a material improvement in service levels.

Firms need to trade off these cost and service level considerations in such a way as to maximise the firm's ability to achieve its strategic objectives. The total-cost approach to logistics management attempts to balance these by assuming that all logistical decisions impact on all other logistical problems, so management needs to look at the efficiency of the system as a whole rather than only concerning itself with individual elements of the structure. The interactions between the elements are described as cost trade-offs, because an increase in one cost may be matched by a decrease in another. Reducing overall costs is the aim of this approach, but there are difficulties.

For example, the separate elements of the logistical system will almost certainly be controlled by different firms, each with its own cost structure and strategic aims. Thus an increase in cost for one element of the system will not be offset by a reduction in cost elsewhere, since the gainer and the loser are actually different firms. Even within a single firm, different departments will have their own budgetary constraints – managers may not be prepared to lose out so that someone else in the organisation can gain. Any attempt to organise the logistical system as a seamless whole must take account of these problems, which of course places a premium on supply chain integration.

In some cases, the business must maintain the highest possible service levels whatever the cost. For example, delivery of urgent medical supplies is not cost-sensitive, but it is highly service-sensitive. At the other extreme, delivery of paper for recycling is unlikely to be service-sensitive, but almost certainly will be cost-sensitive.

Determining the level of service is a complex problem because it is difficult to calculate the possible revenue gains from an improvement in customer service levels. This calculation needs to be made in the light of competitive pressures, customer preferences, industry norms and so forth. The cost element is much easier to calculate, and the net result needs to be a trade-off between the two elements. One study found that a 5 per cent reduction in customer service levels resulted in a 20 per cent decrease in sales (LaLonde *et al.* 1988).

Managing the Supply Chain

supply chain The organisations which add value to the product as it moves from raw materials to consumer.

Supply chain management has been described as the integration of business processes from end user through original suppliers to provide products, services, and information that add value for customers (Cooper, Lambert and Pugh 1997). The critical element in managing the supply chain is to ensure that value is added for customers: in order to do this, the supply chain needs to be coordinated and needs to become as seamless as possible.

For business-to-business marketers this has two implications. First, it implies that the marketer needs to work at establishing relationships with both suppliers and customers, and in most cases will need to be prepared to change the firms working practices in order to accommodate the needs of other firms in the supply chain. Second, it means that seeking new customers will mean fitting into an existing supply chain, where the rules and practices are already well established.

In order for relationships to work at optimum efficiency within the supply chain, the members need to share information about strategic plans, new product development, customer profiles and much else. For example, e-marketing firms need to integrate their internal and external supply chain activities as well as share strategic information if they are to succeed (Eng 2004). This information is commercially sensitive, so a great deal of trust is necessary. Goods flow down the supply chain, but information flows up it, enabling the various members of the chain to plan around the reality of existing market conditions. Effective supply chain management is a powerful tool for creating competitive advantage for the following reasons (Quinn 2000):

1 It reduces costs.
2 It improves asset utilisation.
3 It reduces order cycle time, thus speeding up delivery of customer satisfaction.

Effective supply chain management can also shut out competitors by denying them access to sources of components or raw materials. For example, when CD players were first marketed the only source of supply for the CD drives were three factories in Taiwan, all of which were under exclusive contract to Japanese electronics manufacturers. This effectively shut out European and US manufacturers until they could develop the manufacturing capacity themselves – a somewhat ironic position for the Europeans, since the technology was originally developed in the UK.

The goals of supply chain management are shown in Table 20.7. If the supply chain is properly managed, it should create tangible benefits for customers in terms of reduced waste, more flexible and reliable deliveries and improved costs. For the members of the supply chain, it should increase security of supply, make planning easier, reduce costs and reduce competitive pressures. There have been many studies which have demonstrated the advantages of integrating the supply chain: Ferguson (2000) demonstrated that best-practice SCM companies have a 45 per cent cost advantage over median supply chain competitors. On the other hand, supply chain glitches have been shown to cause an average 9 per cent drop in the value of the company's shares on the day the problem is announced, and up to 20 per cent decline in the six months following the announcement (Bowman 2001).

In global supply chain management, there are four strategic marketing challenges (Flint 2004). These are:

1 *Customer value learning.* Finding out what customers regard as valuable is complex in the global environment, because supplying firms need to consider differing decision-making processes, differing decision-maker values, different importance rankings of service versus physical attribute values and so forth. The value chain may span several different cultures, so that each link in the chain must be considered separately as well as how it fits into the whole.

Table 20.7 Goals of supply chain management

Waste reduction	By minimising duplication, harmonising operations and systems and by reducing inventories waste is reduced. For example, harmonising materials handling equipment reduces the need for loading and unloading components and also creates economies of scale in purchasing equipment and containers.
Time compression	Improved information flows about market conditions enable supply chain members to predict demand more accurately and thus make response times quicker. Also, preferred-customer status within the supply chain means that each member responds more quickly to the needs of other members than to the needs of non-members. Reducing response times improves cashflow for all members because deliveries happen faster, so invoices are paid sooner.
Flexible response	Ensuring flexibility in the supply chain means that all the members are able to adjust more quickly to changing market conditions. This can lead to major improvements in competitive advantage.
Unit cost reduction	Good supply chain management seeks to reduce unit costs, which will either allow the firms in the chain to make more money or will allow them to reduce the price to the end consumer, which again offers a competitive advantage. Cost is not necessarily the same as price: a customer operating a just-in-time manufacturing system may accept a slightly higher price for receiving small daily deliveries rather than paying a lower price for one large monthly delivery, because the savings in terms of holding stocks will outweigh the extra outlay.

2 *Understanding customer value change*. Customers often change what they value as changing circumstances dictate. Because changes happen at different times in different countries, customer value is a moving target.

3 *Delivering value in a world of uncertainty*. Because change is constant, and may even be accelerating, it is virtually impossible to integrate the strategies of firms which are often thousands of miles apart and being pulled in different directions by local changes in the business environment.

4 *The customer value process*. In order to meet the problems raised by the first three challenges, marketers may need to shift from a functional towards a process orientation. This may be difficult, in that shareholders believe that they have invested in a company rather than in a supply chain, which makes it difficult for the process to be seamless.

These challenges will differ in importance from one firm to another, and the solutions will be widely varying, but these are not challenges which a global firm can ignore. Success in integrating the supply chain provides an important competitive advantage, and given that globalisation also provides the best opportunities for minimising total costs, managing the global supply chain effectively is a powerful route to growth.

Establishing and Maintaining Relationships

Relationships exist not only between suppliers and purchasers, but also across several other categories of partner. Morgan and Hunt (1994) offered the following categorisation:

1 Supplier partnerships
- Goods suppliers
- Services suppliers

Figure 20.10

Supply chain management

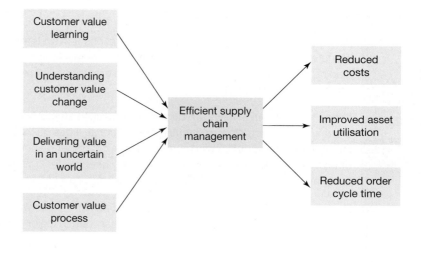

2 Lateral partnerships

- Competitors
- Non-profit organisations
- Government

3 Buyer partnerships

- Intermediate customers
- Ultimate customers

4 Internal partnerships

- Business units
- Employment
- Functional departments

From a marketer's viewpoint, the most important set of relationships here will be the buyer relationships, but this does not mean that the other relationships can safely be ignored. In terms of supply chain management, these relationships are important, as they ensure that the firm's place in the supply chain and its ability to contribute effectively are assured. For Morgan and Hunt (1994), relationship marketing refers to all marketing activities directed towards establishing, developing and maintaining successful relational exchanges. This led them to develop the commitment-trust theory, which states that those networks characterised by relationship commitment and trust engender cooperation, a reduced tendency to leave the network, the belief that conflict will be functional rather than damaging and reduced uncertainty.

All relationships (whether business or personal) are affected by the degree of trust which exists between the parties. Establishing a relationship of trust between businesses can be a complex affair, since many different individuals will need to be part of the process and consequently part of the outcome. There was more on this in Chapter 11.

Channel System Orientation

In order to overcome some of the problems inherent in having a logistical system made up of several companies, supply chain management seeks to synchronise channel activities through a series of negotiations which divide up the overall profits between members. At least in theory, this should make all members better off, since overall costs will fall and service levels will rise. In this scenario, relationships between the channel members must be seen as long-term, permanent, totally honest and highly cooperative if savings are to result.

Figure 20.11

Profit sharing

Companies with effective logistics systems grow 8 per cent faster than those without, realise a 7 per cent price premium and are 12 times as profitable as firms with inferior service levels (Novich 1992). Setting the service level may or may not be a function of profitability: much depends on the strategic aim of the company involved. This means that it may be possible to help a partner firm to achieve a strategic aim in exchange for a concession on profitability.

Key elements in welding the channel into a single system are as follows:

1 Develop information systems which provide realistic sales forecasts for channel members.

2 Standardise packaging and handling systems (for example by using palletisation or containerisation).

3 Provide services (e.g. warehousing or data handling services) which improve efficiency for everyone (usually provided by the channel leader).

4 'Pooling' of shipments to avoid the 'empty truck' problem.

Since the service level is often the only strategic advantage the channel has, there are obvious advantages in coming to an agreement and integrating the system. Unfortunately, such integration may take some years to achieve, since relationships of trust take time to establish. Supply chain management implies a greater degree of integration than does logistics management: SCM implies integration of all the business systems of the channel members, whereas logistics is only concerned with integrating the systems relating to the movement of goods.

Inventory Management

Inventory management is the buffer in the logistical system. Inventories are essential in business-to-business markets because production and demand never quite match. This means that there are times when the producers need to stockpile product, and times when the demand outstrips supply and stockpiled products are released onto the market. This ensures a smooth flow of goods to the final users.

Operating deficiencies in the system will sometimes result in delays in delivery, in which case stocks can be used: also, industrial buyers cannot predict demand accurately because they are themselves relying (ultimately) on consumer demand, which is volatile. As we saw in Chapter 5, demand in business-to-business markets is much more volatile than that in consumer markets because of stocking and destocking effects.

Table 20.8 Effects of JIT on marketing firms

Activity	Impact
Transportation	Because the number of shipments increases, the quantity ordered each time decreases. The shipments also need to meet the exact demands of the customer, and are non-negotiable, so the supplier must be flexible. In one study, 49% of companies using JIT said that the inability of suppliers to deliver to their specifications was a problem (Celley *et al.* 1986).
Field warehousing	Shipping over long distances may not be feasible because of the inherent unreliability of transportation, so smaller, more numerous warehouses will be needed. In addition, the use of third-party warehousing may be unsuitable because the customer will require absolute reliability: the supplier may not feel that a third party can be trusted sufficiently.
Field inventory control	Inventory levels of producers may need to be increased as customers will be totally unable to tolerate stock-outs under any circumstances. Because of the need for 100 per cent control of inventory, the producer may need to take over all the distribution functions.
Protective packaging	Packaging may be changed or even eliminated in some cases because the goods will be used immediately in production. This is a rare case where just-in-time might benefit the vendor.
Materials handling	There may be few changes here, but because quantities delivered are much smaller, it may not be feasible to use (for example) containerisation as a way of reducing handling.
Order processing	The simplest way of dealing with this is electronically. The situation will inevitably become more complex as more frequent deliveries, at clearly specified times, become necessary.

Talking Point

During the 1980s and 1990s there was an attempt by some firms to introduce just-in-time (JIT) purchasing, in which the purchasing firm does not hold stocks, but instead shifts the responsibility for maintaining inventories onto the suppliers. This does not accord with the systems approach to logistics, since it does not take account of the whole supply chain. Some have questioned the efficiency of JIT recently because of the tendency for it to contribute to traffic congestion as trucks make more frequent deliveries, and also its tendency to increase costs for suppliers. See Table 20.8 for a summary of the impact of just-in-time on the marketing firm.

Just-in-time inventory management means arranging for components to arrive almost exactly at the moment when they are needed at the customer's factory. This obviously results in savings for the customer – but what about the supplier? Suppliers need to deliver small amounts frequently rather than large amounts periodically – so they use smaller vehicles, and more of them, and often park just outside the customer's gates until the exact minute for delivery.

Fine for the customer, of course, but wouldn't the supplier pass those costs on? Somebody has to keep the inventory – and somebody has to pay for it. Ultimately it's the end customer. And what about the impact on the environment? All those extra vehicles clogging the streets and parking spaces cannot be a good thing!

Yet if *all* firms could arrange the logistics in a JIT manner, wouldn't the flow of goods from raw materials to finished products be a real process, instead of a lot of starts and stops? Maybe JIT has something to offer after all!

Estimates of future sales are the key element in controlling the logistics system. These estimates need to be far more accurate than the general ones used for planning sales promotions or other long-term marketing plans: the logistics and inventory forecast needs to be flexible enough to operate on a day-to-day basis if necessary. This requires some fairly sophisticated computer technology, which should be linked throughout the supply chain so as to enable firms further up the chain to predict demand. Falling inventory at the retailer means increased demand at the wholesaler, the manufacturer, the component supplier and the raw material supplier in that order, but delays in the system mean that increased demand at the retail level will perhaps take several months to filter through to the raw material level.

International Trade

Table 20.9 shows the commonest documents used in international trade.

This comprehensive list of paperwork may not be necessary for all shipments. There is considerable duplication, in other words. Having said that, trucks travelling through Europe may need to carry large amounts of paperwork to satisfy the formalities at each border once the truck has left the European Union. Standardising the documentation for trucks was a major issue within the EU in its attempts to maximise the free flow of goods throughout the Union, but of course the system is not perfect because member states are still permitted to ban imports from other member states if their Governments believe that

Table 20.9 Trade Documentation

Export document	Description
Ocean bill of lading	The contract between the shipper and the carrier. The bill of lading is a receipt given by the carrier (often issued by the ship's purser) which proves that the goods were loaded. It is often used as proof of ownership, so that it matches with the cargo unloaded and can be bought and sold.
Export declaration	This includes complete particulars of the product and its destination, and is used to control exports and compile statistical information about exports.
Letter of credit	This is a financial document issued by the importer's bank, guaranteeing the exporter's payment subject to certain conditions (often the presentation of the bill of lading to prove that the goods were shipped)
Commercial invoice	The bill for the goods from the seller to the buyer. Often used by customs officials to determine the true value of the goods.
Certificate of origin	This document assures the buyer that the goods have not already been shipped from a country with which, for example, a trade embargo applies. These certificates are often provided by a recognised chamber of commerce in the exporting country.
Insurance certificate	This assures the importer that insurance is in place to cover the loss of or damage to the goods in transit.
Transmittal letter	A list of the particulars of the shipment and a record of the documents being transmitted, together with instructions for disposition of documents.
Customs entry	This provides information about the goods, their origin, estimated value and destination. This is for the purpose of assessing customs duty.
Carrier's certificate and release order	A document to advise customs of the details of the shipment, its ownership, port of loading and so forth. This certificate proves the ownership of the goods for customs purposes.
Delivery order	The consignee, or his customs broker, issues this to the ocean carrier as authority to release the cargo to the inland carrier. It includes all the data necessary to ascertain that the cargo may be released.

E-Marketing in Practice
Little Old Wine-Drinker Me

Within the United States there are many wine-producing states – even New York and Michigan produce wine, though it is California that has the world markets. But 70 years after prohibition was repealed, some states are still battling it out for control of drinking.

In December 2004 a case went before the Supreme Court which challenged the rights of states to control sales of wine within their borders. New York and Michigan both had laws which allowed their own wine-makers to sell their products direct to customers, but which made it virtually impossible for out-of-state producers to do so. This has not mattered much in the past, but with the advent of direct ordering via the Internet the situation has become a hot issue. Essentially, both states were using the 21st Amendment to the Constitution as a way of shutting out competition. The 21st Amendment repealed prohibition, but gave each state the power to regulate importation of alcoholic drinks from other states, since some states (and counties within the states) wished to remain alcohol-free – in fact, some are still alcohol-free to this day.

The argument from the other side is that New York and Michigan were simply using the law to institute old-fashioned protectionism, preventing competing wines from entering their markets and thus protecting their own small wineries. New York requires out-of-state wineries to establish offices within New York State, but does not say whether they expect the winery to ship wines from those offices: the court case revolved around a conflict between two clauses of the Constitution, one of which regulates commerce and provides for free and uninhibited trade between the states, the other of which apparently allows states to ban products from other states.

New York and Michigan further argued that they had the right to levy taxation on alcohol and tobacco (among other things) and this would be difficult if they allowed direct shipment. The opposition argued that 29 other states did not appear to be having any difficulty with this.

In 2005, the law took an unusual course. The court found in favour of the state of Michigan and gave summary judgment, but the plaintiffs appealed and the Appeal Court overturned the decision of the lower court, saying that Michigan's behaviour was clearly discriminatory and also unconstitutional, because the ban was not covered by the 21st Amendment. This meant that Michigan now must allow out-of-state wineries to deliver within its borders. Oddly, though, the case against New York went the other way – at first the court found in favour of the out-of-state wineries, but on appeal New York was able to have the decision overturned, with the Appeal Court ruling that New York had acted entirely within the 21st Amendment.

the imports represent a threat to human or animal life. This was the justification for the French ban on British beef imports during the late 1990s, and is the justification for the British ban on the import of live shellfish from the rest of the European Union. In the United States virtually all border controls between the states have been abolished, but differences in state taxation mean that some products (for example cigarettes) are still worth smuggling internally, and California maintains restrictions on imports of plants and fruit for fear of importing an epidemic which would damage the state's lucrative fruit farming.

The most important document from the international marketer's viewpoint is the bill of lading, since this is proof of ownership. It is a document of possessory title, which means that only the holder of the bill of lading can collect the goods. There are exceptions to this general rule: if perishable goods arrive before the bill of lading has arrived (for example if the bill of lading has been posted but the goods were sent via airfreight) the shipper can release the goods to a third party on receipt of a letter of indemnity from the part collecting the consignment. Possession therefore passes when the bill of lading is transferred, but ownership only passes when the parties intend it to pass, as evidenced by the sales contract.

As receipts, bills of lading provide only prima facie evidence that a certain quantity was received on board, that packaging marks were in order and that the goods were apparently in good condition. Nevertheless it is up to the carrier to prove that the items stated were not put on board, or that they were loaded in good condition. Obviously a

ship's master is only required to attest that the goods appeared to be in good condition: with a few exceptions the ship's officers are not expected to carry out detailed internal inspections of cargoes to investigate their inner qualities.

Obviously world trade is important. We can each make what we are good at making, and we can profit from ideas from other countries. Also, of course, more trade usually means less war – it is not a good idea to shoot the grocer. So why not just remove all trade restrictions immediately? Certainly there would be a painful period of readjustment, but after that, wouldn't life be so much easier? After all, poor countries frequently complain that they don't have fair access to rich markets while wealthier countries complain that they are paying too much for goods.

Or is free trade just a rich country's response? Do we only consider this approach because we know we have the economic power to clobber any opposition? A 10 per cent drop in our standard of living during a period of readjustment would hardly be noticed – but in Mali or Ethiopia it would mean millions of deaths. So how *do* we control trade? Simply by more paperwork? Or by a controlled and calculated regime of duties and documents? And if so, who does the controlling and calculating?

Another problem in international transport is ensuring that everyone involved is clear about what is meant by specific terms. 'Incoterms' refers to a set of words and phrases which have been agreed upon internationally to describe specific types of shipping conditions, so that importers and exporters know exactly who is paying for what.

Transportation Methods

Selecting a transportation method for a global market can be complex. As a general rule, the faster the shipment, the higher the cost, but standby air freight (in which the shipment is sent on the next available aircraft with spare capacity) can be relatively cheap, and when the costs of having capital tied up in goods in transit is also taken into account, can actually be cheaper than surface transportation. Obviously for perishable or highly valuable goods such as computer chips, air freight is almost always cheaper, because there is less spoilage and the capital is tied up for a shorter period.

Five basic modes of transportation are used in business-to-business marketing. Goods are shipped by road, by rail, by air freight, by water, or in some cases by pipeline. Often combination systems are used, for example the ro-ro (roll on, roll off) ferries which transport lorries (or even just the trailers) across the English Channel, Irish Sea and North Sea routes.

Figure 20.12 shows the factors which a marketing manager will typically take into account when choosing a transportation method.

Shipping by road is fast and direct but can be labour-intensive.

In most cases, each of the factors will trade off against each of the others in some way. For example, sea transport (or indeed inland waterway transport) will be substantially cheaper than air freight, but will be much slower. Equally, the reliability of rail transport may compare unfavourably with road transport, but may protect the goods better.

In some circumstances accessibility is an issue. The city of Iquitos, in Peru, is only accessible by water or air – there are no rail or road links into the city. This obviously limits the choices somewhat. Less obviously, some towns in Australia which are accessible by rail may only see one freight train a week, and are much better served by road transport, since Australian buses tow trailers for limited amounts of freight and usually offer a daily service.

Figure 20.12

Trade-offs in transportation

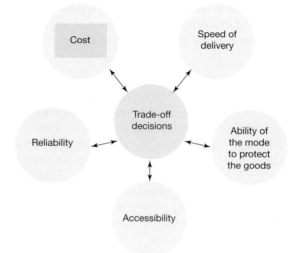

liner A ship or aircraft which operates on a regular route at fixed times.

tramp ship A ship which does not follow set routes, but which sails when it has a cargo for a particular port.

Costs obviously vary in different countries. Inland waterways are widely used in Continental Europe, but are not commercially viable within the UK. Railway systems are heavily subsidised in Switzerland and the United States for environmental reasons, but not in the UK, where the system has deteriorated dramatically in the last 15 years or so.

Sea freight includes scheduled services (**liners**) which operate according to a fairly strict schedule, visiting specific ports at specific dates, and tramp services which sail once they have a full cargo for a specific destination. Liner services charge fixed rates, **tramp ships** (which are frequently modern, fast vessels) have variable rates which are almost always cheaper than the scheduled rates. Sea freight charges are based on either volume or weight, with extra charges for extra services, for example tallying cargo on and off (tallying means that a ship's officer counts the units of cargo as they are loaded).

Shipping agents will carry out all the functions of booking space on the ship and arranging for the loading of the cargoes: they are paid commission by the ship owners. The details of the shipment are contained on a standard shipping note (SSN) which advises the shipping company on what is to happen to the goods on arrival at the foreign port.

Airfreight used to be an expensive option, but is now much cheaper due to increased efficiency of aircraft and the introduction of standby airfreight (this means that goods are sent on the next aircraft with spare space on board). Speedy delivery means less stockholding, more rapid settlement of invoices, less insurance and therefore faster turnover of working capital. International airlines' cargo rates are fixed through IATA (International Air Transport Association) but carriers such as DHL are free to fix their own prices, and of course it is feasible to charter a cargo aircraft for a particularly large shipment. For air transport, the air waybill is the equivalent of the bill of lading, but it does not prove title to the goods. One of the problems with air transport, however, is that aircraft do not carry the standardised containers used by road and sea transport, so cargo has to be re-packed, increasing handling costs.

Road transport is usually very flexible in that goods can be collected and delivered door-to-door, a factor which offsets the sometimes high costs per mile when compared with sea or even air. In combination with roll-on-roll-off ferries, truckers can operate throughout Europe, much of the United States seaboards, the Far East and North Africa, but for longer distances containers are more useful. Many countries restrict cabotage (the collection of cargoes en route) so that a vehicle may make a delivery in one country and be unable to pick up a return cargo. Road cabotage has been abolished within the European Union, but still exists in most of Africa and non-EU countries.

Rail transport varies greatly between countries, largely due to the differences in rail and road infrastructure. In some countries (e.g. Germany) rail transport is well-developed and competes well with road transport. In other countries (e.g. Thailand) the rail network is by no means national, but is effective and efficient over the routes it does cover. In yet other countries (e.g. the UK) the rail network is capable of carrying only a tiny fraction of the freight transport needs of the country, due to an aging and poorly-maintained infrastructure and an emphasis on passenger transportation, which pushes the system close to capacity on many routes. The main drawback of rail transport in a small country like the UK is that the goods need to be loaded onto a lorry, unloaded onto a train, then reloaded onto a lorry at the other end. Normally it is simpler and quicker to drive the lorry directly to the customer's premises. Within continental Europe, the United States and Australia distances are great enough to make transferring cargoes worthwhile, although in all three cases the long-distance truck (or road-train, in Australia) are much more widely used.

Summary

Intermediaries perform important functions, more than justifying their existence. Managing the supply chain is by no means simple, and it is not always the role of the manufacturer to do so – many supply chains are managed by wholesalers, retailers or other members, using negotiation, coercion or reward to make the system operate more smoothly. In an ideal world, the supply chain will take a logistics approach and will function as a single entity, but in practice this is difficult because each member of the chain is probably a member of several other chains as well, creating conflicts of interest.

Key points from this chapter are as follows:

- Cutting out the middle man raises costs.
- Distribution channels may already be controlled by competitors.
- Market coverage may be intensive, selective or exclusive: this depends largely on the product category, but also on the target market.
- Relationships need to be long-term and based on trust.
- Channels can be controlled by cooperation or by coercion.
- Logistics takes a holistic view of the supply chain.
- The level of service offered trades off against the overall cost.
- Good supply chain management can shut out competitors altogether.
- Companies with effective logistics systems grow 8 per cent faster than those without.
- Just-in-time purchasing can create more problems than it solves.

Chapter review questions

1. What is the difference between logistics and physical distribution?
2. Why do international agreements often specify the governing law of the contract?
3. Why would a firm prefer to limit the number of outlets its products are available from?
4. Refusal to deal is an example of which type of power?
5. How does culture affect choice of distributor in international markets?
6. What factors help in reconciling conflict and cooperation?
7. What are the key elements in developing a single channel system?
8. What factors might be relevant in determining which firm in the supply chain holds the power?
9. What factors might determine the level of service offered by the supply chain?
10. Why might companies with effective logistics systems experience greater growth than those without?

Preview case revisited
First Scotrail and Unipart

Unipart consultants began by talking to the shop floor workers in the depots at Haymarket (near Edinburgh) and other smaller depots in Scotland. Having discovered that these workers were rarely, if ever, consulted or kept informed about train failures, Unipart decided that ownership of the systems had to be devolved to the depots themselves.

Unipart has a policy of worker empowerment within its own organisation, and so it was easy for them to set about introducing similar methods within Scotrail. Over a 70-day period, Unipart established Performance Improvement Boards within a Communications Centre in each depot. The Boards were there to inform the shop floor workers of their own progress and the progress of First Scotrail as a whole: each Board has an appointed 'owner' charged with the responsibility of keeping it up-to-date. Each morning, meetings between the managers and the maintenance teams review the previous day's performance (as measured against the Headline Board), and review the coming day's workload. Once a week, the overall Performance Board is reviewed so that problems can be identified, shortfalls flagged up and achievements rewarded.

Once a month the processes within the Communication Centre are reviewed to identify possible changes and improvements. Using the Boards and the Communications Centres allows shop floor workers to track the progress of maintenance improvements – and, crucially, enables them to feel like part of the overall process rather than simply wage-slaves.

The results are startlingly good. Train failures from the Haymarket depot have been cut by 50 per cent, there has been a 40 per cent reduction in impact minutes (the penalty payments franchise owners have to make in the event of trains running late) and up to 60 per cent improvement in productivity in some areas of maintenance. The improved reliability of train services means that over 90 per cent of Scotrail trains arrive within 10 minutes of the advertised times: apart from the customer care issues, this represents a huge cash saving in terms of penalties.

It is unlikely that all trains will always run on time – there will always be incidents of vandalism, accidents caused by road transport (such as the time in 2007 when a truck ran into a rail bridge, causing extensive damage and delays), people trespassing onto the track and bad weather. These are beyond the control of First Scotrail, of course – but the company, with Unipart's help, has at least taken control of the factors within its control, to great effect.

Case study
Sri Lankan Tea

Sri Lanka is perhaps best known for its tourism nowadays, but it was (and is) a major producer of tea. Tea is the most popular beverage in the world after water, and Sri Lanka (formerly known as Ceylon) is one Commonwealth country that produces huge amounts of it. Tea is an important part of British culture as well – it is significant that 75 per cent of the world's tea comes from Commonwealth countries: in other words, Britain's former Empire. Commonwealth countries also account for more than half of the world's tea consumption, but substantial amounts of tea are consumed in Russia and Eastern Europe as well as elsewhere in the world.

Sri Lanka's tea exports account for 13 per cent of its merchandise exports: it is the world's second largest tea exporter (with a 19.2 per cent share of the world market),

despite being a relatively small island off the southern coast of India. The industry was established by British colonialists in the mid-19th century, and in common with other industries of the Empire the basic commodity was produced in Sri Lanka, while the value-adding processes of packaging, distribution and marketing took place in Britain. Tea produced in Sri Lanka was taken to London to be auctioned, blended and packaged. Even after Sri Lanka became independent in 1948, the basic system still continued and does so to this day – except that, after independence, the British planters moved their operations to Africa, taking their buyers and distributors with them. This left something of a gap in the Sri Lankan distribution system.

Much of the African tea is produced using the cut tear and curl (CTC) process, which is industrially efficient but which damages the tea and affects the flavour. Perhaps only a real connoisseur of tea would notice the difference, but the Sri Lankan 'orthodox' method creates much more fragrant tea, as less of the aromatics are destroyed in processing.

Because Sri Lankan producers have little or no control over the blending, packaging and distribution of their products, they have little control over the prices paid to them. Prices paid to growers have remained virtually static for nearly 30 years: if costs rise in the UK, the producers are pushed to reduce their prices, and if they cannot or will not do so the buyers simply remove the Sri Lankan component from the blend and replace it with African tea. Once the Sri Lankan component has been removed, it is extremely difficult to have it put back in again. Even in the 'orthodox' market Sri Lankan producers have to compete with newcomers from Vietnam and Indonesia who can offer very similar teas at lower prices.

Most of the tea is sold at the twice-weekly Colombo tea auction. Under Sri Lankan law 90 per cent of the country's tea must pass through this auction, leaving 10 per cent which can be sold privately. Many buyers would much prefer to have this arrangement, but cannot do so because of the 90 per cent rule: many Sri Lankan factories can only produce in relatively small quantities compared to their Kenyan counterparts, so larger buyers find it much easier to deal with Kenya. If major buyers boycotted the auction, the Sri Lankan Government would be forced to change the rules, but this would almost certainly disadvantage smaller buyers and might also damage the new markets Sri Lankan tea is beginning to penetrate. For example, by 2004 23 per cent of Sri Lankan tea was going to the Commonwealth of Independent States (the former Soviet Union). Some of these countries are relatively small and lack the buying power of the giant UK tea importers.

Tea changes hands many times before it reaches the final consumer, and since Sri Lanka does not carry out many of the functions of tea distribution itself, the flow of information from consumer to producer is extremely limited: in effect, the distributors have all the power in the relationship, and do not hesitate to use it. Since tea is a global product, producers need to know what producers in other countries are doing, but this information only reaches a nexus with the distributors – who of course do not pass it on. Many growers lack the business skills to correct the situation – they fail to plan far enough ahead, they measure their progress against what they did in previous years, and they tend to believe that they are powerless in the face of global economic forces.

In a situation in which the major tea blenders have control of the distribution network, the producers have little or no choice but to produce what they are told to produce at prices they are told to accept. Even with a differentiated product, the true situation is that the tea importers can choose between 15 or more countries when sourcing tea – it is easy simply to cut out one tea from the blend entirely, leaving the producer with no market. Unless Sri Lanka takes some drastic action, the future of a 150-year-old industry is in some doubt.

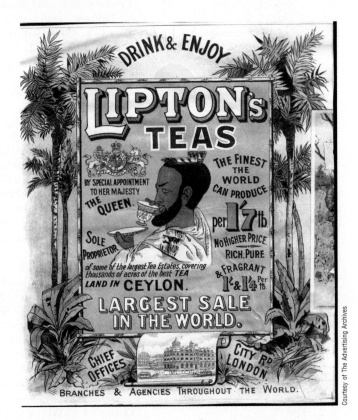

Courtesy of The Advertising Archives

Questions

1 What type of power are the tea importers using to control the market?

2 How might Sri Lankan producers control distribution in new markets?

3 What routes are open to the Sri Lankan Government to improve the situation?

4 What might producers do in order to improve their chances of being included in UK blends of tea?

5 How can a logistics approach be applied to the industry to the advantage of Sri Lankan producers?

References

Bitner, M.J. (1992): Servicescapes: the impact of physical surroundings on customers and employees. *Journal of Marketing* **56**(2), 57–71.

Bowman, R.J. (2001): Does Wall Street really care about the supply chain? *Global Logistics and Supply Chain Strategies* (April), 31–5.

Celley, A.F., Clee, W.H., Smith, A.W. and Vonderembese, M.A. (1986): Implementation of JIT in the United States. *Journal of Purchasing and Materials Management* **22** (Winter), 13.

Cooper, M.C., Lambert, D.M. and Pugh, J.D. (1997): Supply chain management: more than a new name for logistics. *International Journal of Logistics Management* **8**(1), 1.

Czinkota, M.R. and Ronkainen, I.A. (2004): *International Marketing*, 7th edn (Mason, OH: Thomson-Southwestern).

Eng, T.-Y. (2004): The role of e-marketplaces in supply chain management. *Industrial Marketing Management* **33**(2), 97–105.

Ferguson, B. (2000): Implementing supply-chain management. *Production and Inventory Management Journal* (Second Quarter), 64.

Fitzpatrick, P.B. and Zimmerman, A.S. (1985): *Essentials of Export Marketing* (New York: AMACOM).

Flint, D.J. (2004): Strategic marketing in global supply chains. Four challenges. *Industrial Marketing Management* **33**(1), 45–50.

Gadde, L.-E. (2004): Activity coordination and resource combining in distribution networks – implications for relationship involvement and the relationship atmosphere. *Journal of Marketing Management* **20**(1), 157–84.

Hingley, M.K. (2005): Power imbalance in UK agri-food supply chains: learning to live with the supermarkets? *Journal of Marketing Management* **21**(1/2), 63–88.

La Londe, B.J., Cooper, M.C. and Noordewier, T.G. (1988): *Customer Service: a management perspective* (Oak Brook, ILL; The Council of Logistics Management).

Marx, W. (1995): The co-marketing revolution. *Industry Week* 2 October, 77–9.

Moore, C.M., Birtwistle, G. and Burt, S. (2004): Channel power, conflict and conflict resolution in international fashion retailing. *European Journal of Marketing* **38**(7), 749–69.

Morgan, R.M. and Hunt, S.D. (1994): The commitment–trust theory of relationship marketing. *Journal of Marketing* **58** (July), 20–38.

Moriarty, R.T. and Kosnik, T.J.: High-tech marketing: concepts, continuity and change. *Sloane Management Review* (Summer).

Novich, N.S. (1992): How to sell customer service. *Transportation and Distribution* **33** (January), 46.

Pothokuchi, V., Damanpour, F., Choi, J., Chen, C.C. and Park, S.H. (2002): National and organisational cultural differences and international joint-venture performance. *Journal of International Business Studies* **33**(2), 243–65.

Quinn, F.J. (2000): A supply chain management overview. *Supply Chain Yearbook* (Mason, OH: McGrawHill), 15.

Further reading

Christopher, M. (2005): *Logistics and Supply Chain Management: Creating Value-added Networks* (Harlow: Financial Times Prentice Hall). This is the latest edition of a leading text on logistics. It is easy to read, and is also full of examples and cases.

Hugos, M. (2003): *Essentials of Supply Chain Management* (New York: John Wiley and Sons). This is a more practice-orientated book, written by an American author who has very wide experience of distribution.

Chapter 21
Intermediaries

Learning objectives After reading this chapter, you should be able to:

1. Explain the roles, responsibilities and rights of agents.

2. Describe the differences between intermediaries who buy goods and those who do not.

3. Be able to decide when licensing and franchising agreements would be better than wholesaler–retailer distribution.

4. Explain the relationships between wholesalers, retailers and consumers.

5. Be able to decide on the appropriateness of service levels in retailing.

6. Explain the key issues in deciding on the location of retail outlets.

Introduction

As we saw in Chapter 20, intermediaries perform vital functions in managing the delivery of goods and services from producer to consumer. In this chapter we will be looking at specific types of intermediary, the functions they perform and the particular issues each has in performing profitably within the marketing function.

Intermediaries exist in many forms, from corner shops to multinational export houses, and perform many different functions. Choosing an appropriate intermediary is not necessarily a simple matter, especially as intermediaries frequently have more power in the supply chain than do producers, and can therefore pick and choose between suppliers.

Categorising Intermediaries

Intermediaries can be categorised in several different ways: one way is to divide them into those which take title to the products (buy the products from the producer or from another intermediary) and those which do not (see Figure 21.1). Intermediaries which take title to the products can be considered as customers: they have specific needs which must be met by the producer, and will have similar decision-making procedures to those of any other business-to-business customer, with the exception that (in general) much more of the decision-making is devolved to the buyers rather than to other members of the decision-making unit.

Intermediaries which do not take title to the goods may require more support and management, because their commitment to the producer and the brand is less – in general, they are taking a much smaller risk, since they are not actually parting with any money to buy the goods themselves. These intermediaries are called agents, and they are subject to special rules of contract. An agent is usually appointed for a fixed period of time, under specific contractual arrangements, and has the role of obtaining orders for the product. Agency salespeople call on wholesalers and others, take orders and arrange delivery, usually on a commission-only basis.

Preview case
Gift House International

Gift House International is a wholesaler based in Sully, South Wales. Formed in 2002, the company has rapidly acquired a reputation for efficient distribution of novel products. The company has a 40 000 square foot warehouse and specialises in gifts and novelties. The company's product range includes 'geek T-shirts' with messages such as 'No I won't fix your computer' and 'Insufficient memory', boys' toys such as remote-controlled helicopters and a bottle opener that will open two bottles at once, gadgets such as emergency reading glasses and talking key clips, and novelty gift items such as football club mints (with the club crest on them) and slot machine drinks dispensers.

The company has an office in Hong Kong which can arrange bulk shipments FOB (free on board – i.e. the customer pays the shipping and insurance) but Gift House International can supply most products ex-warehouse.

Orders over £500 are dispatched free, and there is a sliding scale for shipping charges for other orders. In most cases Gift House International can arrange next-day delivery within the UK provided orders are received by 1.00 pm the day before, but customers are asked to allow 3 to 5 days in case orders are delayed by the carriers.

Many of Gift House International's customers are small retailers or even market traders. Ordering in sufficient quantities to be economic from the company's Hong Kong office would clearly be impossible, but many of them can easily order a selection of products to arrive at the £500 level required for free delivery.

Most of the products on offer are imported from China via the Hong Kong office: customers are based throughout the UK, with a growing customer base in the rest of Europe. The problem for Gift House International lies in making their presence known in what is a very competitive market.

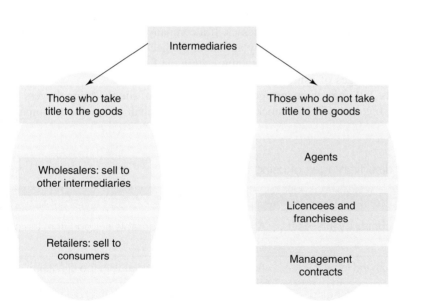

Figure 21.1

Categorising intermediaries

Intermediaries which take title to the product divide into wholesalers, who only deal with other intermediaries, and retailers, who deal with the end consumers.

Agents

Agents are commonly used in international marketing, but are also used within national borders, typically by small firms which cannot afford to run a national salesforce, or which have only a few products. Although agency law differs from one country to another, there are some factors which all agency agreements will have in common: these are as follows.

- An agent cannot take delivery of the principal's goods at an agreed price and resell them for a higher price without the principal's knowledge and permission. In other words, the agent cannot make secret deals behind the principal's back.
- Agents must maintain strict confidentiality regarding their principal's affairs and must pass on all relevant information.
- The principal is liable to third parties for wrongs committed by an agent 'in the course of his or her authority'. For example, if the agent fraudulently misrepresents the product, the principal is liable to the customer for any compensation. In effect, the agent is the principal as far as the customer is concerned: a company would not be allowed to disclaim liability if its agent had cheated a customer.

Within the European Union, agency law was harmonised in 1994 to include the following clauses to protect agents when their agreements are terminated.

- The agent will be entitled to full payment for any deal resulting from his or her work (even if it was concluded after the end of the agency).
- The agent will be entitled to a lump sum of up to one year's past average commission.
- The agent will be entitled to compensation (where appropriate) for damages to the agent's commercial reputation caused by an unfair termination of the agreement.

brokers Intermediaries who bring buyers and sellers together, but do not themselves handle goods.

factors Intermediaries who hold stocks of product, but do not take title to the goods.

In some countries outside the European Union, agents are regarded as essentially employees of the client organisation, whereas in other countries they are regarded as independent, self-contained businesses. If a company is considering employing an agent in a foreign country, it is certainly advisable to check the legal position of agents – it is unlikely to be the same as that obtaining within the EU. Table 21.1 shows the advantages and disadvantages of using agents.

Agents fall into three categories: brokers, who simply bring buyers and sellers together; factors, who hold stocks of the goods on behalf of the client company and who

Table 21.1 Advantages and disadvantages of using agents

Advantages	Disadvantages
Operations are subject to direct control by the client.	Agents require considerable support from the client company.
Agents are usually very familiar with the local market.	Agents may not be familiar with the client firm.
Agents have appropriate contacts for arranging after-sales service, etc.	Agents act independently, so may set up deals with firms with whom they have a special arrangement.
Financial risk is low – no sales, no costs.	Unless sales happen quickly and easily, the agent might decide to concentrate efforts on a different client firm.
Agents usually act for other firms as well, so may be able to create marketing synergies.	Because agents usually work for several firms, they may have conflicts of interest.
The lack of long-term commitment on the part of the client means that it is easy to withdraw from the arrangement.	The lack of long-term commitment may reduce the incentive to sell.

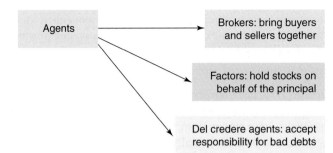

Figure 21.2

Categories of agent

may have discretion to negotiate prices, and **del credere agents** who also accept responsibility for bad debts. Del credere agents offer an extra level of security, particularly in overseas markets, for two reasons: first, they are better able to assess the creditworthiness of customers, and second, they are less likely to be tempted to sell to someone who is not creditworthy – an agent who has no responsibility for credit is likely to sell to anyone who is prepared to place an order.

In the main, agents are effectively salespeople who act for several firms at once. A manufacturer's agent usually specialises in particular categories of buyer: some call on food wholesalers, some on novelty-goods wholesalers and so forth. A manufacturer's agent might carry products from a dozen different manufacturers, increasing the efficiency of each call.

del credere agents Intermediaries who do not take title to the goods, but who do accept the credit risk from customers.

There seems to be a lot of trust involved in hiring an agent. After all, as principal the company is bound by any agreement the agent makes, and is responsible (ultimately) for anything the agent does or says. Added to that, agents seem to have all sorts of rights in law – so why bother with an agent at all?

Taking on an agent might seem to be the simplest route to internationalising: a local person, who has the contacts and the local knowledge, can just be plugged into the firm's existing systems. But isn't this just a short cut, and what's more one which will lead to problems later? Taking a short cut down a dark alleyway at dead of night might save some effort – but it's no use if you get mugged halfway through!

Licensing and franchising

In some cases firms will own intellectual property (brands, patents, registered trade marks or specialist knowledge) but lack the resources to exploit them effectively. For example, a firm may have a patented product with global potential, but lack the necessary financial or organisational resources to set up a global marketing operation before the patent expires or is rendered obsolete by technological advances elsewhere. In these circumstances, the firm might arrange a licensing agreement or a franchising agreement with other firms, either at home or abroad, under which the licensee is allowed to exploit the intellectual property in exchange for a fee or a royalty.

Licensing is appropriate in the following circumstances:

● Where it is not feasible to set up business in a particular foreign country (perhaps because of local laws preventing foreign businesses from entering the market) but where intellectual property such as patents are protected.

● Where the cost of shipping goods to the foreign market would be prohibitive.

● Where the target market is particularly patriotic, so that 'home-produced' products will sell better than imports. This is often the case in France and in Australia.

● The licensee will have to purchase materials or components from the licensor. This gives a substantial degree of control over the process, and also ensures that the licensor knows exactly how much of the product is being sold.

● The licensor is already overstretched in terms of the markets it is selling to.

The main categories of licence are shown in Table 21.2.

Licensing is often used in cases where the product is perishable or fragile: for example, Pilkington Glass make more money from licensing their intellectual property in the float-glass technique than they do from actually making glass. This is because it is extremely difficulty to ship glass over long distances.

The advantages and disadvantages of licensing agreements are shown in Table 21.3.

Licensing contracts are complex, and need to cover specific elements, as follows:

● Fees and royalties.

● Geographical area covered by the agreement.

● Permissible selling prices.

● Quality control arrangements.

● Frequency of payments.

● Confidentiality requirements.

● Procedures for settling disputes, and which country's law should apply to the agreement.

● Minimum production levels.

● Termination and renewal arrangements.

● Ownership of new inventions resulting from the licensor's work.

● Licensee's capacity to become involved with competing products.

Glass is difficult to ship, so is usually made under licence.

● Licensee's capacity to subcontract.

● Support services to be provided by the licensor (for example, training and technical support).

A variation in licensing is franchising. Franchising is commonly used when a company has the rights to a brand name or a business format: it is commonly used in services market where patents do not apply. A large number of well-known service businesses are

Table 21.2 Categories of license

Category	Explanation
Assignments	The licensor hands over all its intellectual property rights to the licensee in exchange for a royalty. The licensee can then use the information in any way.
Sole license	The licensor retains the rights to the patents, brands etc. but agrees not to extend licenses to anyone other than the licensee during the period of the agreement.
Exclusive license	The licensor agrees not to use the patents, trade marks etc. for its own business during the life of the agreement. This means that the licensee has the sole use of the intellectual property for a specified period, which is of course a favourable position for the licensee.
Know-how license	These cover confidential but not patented (and perhaps non-patentable) intellectual property. This may be a process, or a specific way of exploiting knowledge which is in the public domain.

Table 21.3 Advantages and disadvantages of licensing

Advantages	Disadvantages
No capital investment for the licensor	May be difficult to verify sales figures
Can be undertaken by small firms	Lower revenues to the licensor
Immediate access to local expertise	Licensee acquires know-how and may set up in competition once the agreement expires
No import tariff or transportation costs	Quality levels may not be maintained
Materials and components might be sold to the licensee	Complex contractual arrangements may be necessary
Licensor usually receives an initial lump sum payment, which helps defray development costs	Many possibilities for conflict and misunderstanding
Risk of failure shared with licensee	Licensee might not fully exploit the local market
Allows entry to markets which might otherwise be closed to foreign firms	Licensee's firm could become insolvent and cease production, causing damage to the brand in the foreign country
No export knowledge required	Licensee might be less competent either as a producer or as a marketer than at first appeared
Provides income to help offset future research and development expenditure	

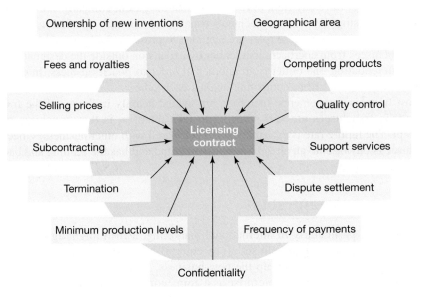

Figure 21.3

Elements in licensing contracts

franchises: McDonald's hamburgers, Holiday Inn hotels, Dyno-Rod drain-cleaning services and many others.

The franchisee is entitled to use the brand name, business systems, trade marks and indeed the entire business format within a given locality in exchange for paying a lump sum up-front followed by a regular royalty based on turnover. In most cases, the franchisee also has to buy its supplies from the franchisor: in effect, the franchisor retains complete control over the running of the business, and especially over the marketing of the brand, but the franchisee bears most of the risks of failure.

Marketing in Practice
Holiday Inns

Holiday Inns is an international chain of hotels, nine out of 10 of which are franchised and are therefore independently owned and operated. Holiday Inn began in 1952, and in almost 60 years has expanded to the point where the chain comprises over 2000 hotels worldwide, with 284 000 rooms. Because the hotels are franchised, the hoteliers who own them benefit from a centralised reservation system, and from a brand which prides itself on a friendly approach and what Holiday Inns call a 'can-do' service, by which they mean that whatever a guest needs, the hotel staff will do their best to provide.

The hotel chain has an internationally-consistent image, which reassures customers that they will get the same level of service whether they are in Singapore or Sacramento: this can be particularly important for business travellers, who have enough to think about without having to consider choosing a hotel and finding out which services are available and which are not in each case.

Franchising enabled Holiday Inns to create an international hotel network at a speed that would have been impossible if the parent company had tried to set up a new hotel in each location directly. Local franchisees were able to cut through red tape, and establish a presence in local markets, at a rate which could not be equalled by an incoming firm.

Marketing is centrally administered in order to keep the brand values consistent across all the countries the chain operates in. Since 1988, the chain has been part of the Intercontinental Hotels Group, but it still retains its franchise system: 139 hotels were being built at the time of writing, and more will be added as the century progresses.

Franchisees are independent self-employed businesses, not employees of the franchisor, and rarely have any right of redress against the parent company in the event of the business collapsing. Franchise agreements usually contain very detailed rules about how the business is to be run: these rules are intended to preserve the brand values and protect other franchisees from encroachment, either by expansion outside the designated territory or by differentiating one outlet from another in order to poach business. In effect, franchisees are prevented from competing against each other.

Most franchise agreements, therefore, are loaded heavily in favour of the franchisor. The reason franchisees are still prepared to take them on is that franchises rarely go bankrupt. The failure rate is extremely small compared with other businesses, because the franchisee is buying into an already-established brand and has the training and back-up of the parent company.

Management contracts

In some cases, particularly in international marketing, a firm might agree to provide a team of expert managers to help set up an enterprise in the foreign country. Typically the management team will set up the new business, train local personnel in running it and eventually hand over the enterprise as a going concern to the foreign company. This is called a turnkey contract, and is often used for such major enterprises as hydro-electric generating systems or heavy industrial complexes such as car factories. During the 1960s and 1970s, Fiat set up several car factories in Eastern Europe, passing on obsolete Fiat technology and designs (which were still far advanced of anything available in the East).

The advantage for the supplying firm is that there is very little risk attached, and the returns can be predicted very accurately. Problems include the potential for disagreement with the foreign company, and in some cases of course the supplying firm will be setting up a competitor in business. Disagreements might include arguments about best working practices and about training: it is easy for the supplying company to claim that the staff are untrainable and for the commissioning company to claim that the training programme is at fault, for example.

For the commissioning company, the main advantage is that they obtain a working installation far more quickly than would be the case if they had to begin building expertise from scratch: new technology can be acquired quickly, although the commissioning company is often reliant on the goodwill of the supplying company for providing the appropriate level of training. Also, the arrangement might end up more expensive than simply hiring appropriately qualified consultants to carry out the work.

Wholesalers

Wholesalers are organisations which take title to the goods but who sell only to other intermediaries. They carry out the following functions, which are of importance to manufacturers:

- Negotiating with suppliers (manufacturers, importers, other wholesalers, etc.)
- Carrying out some promotional activities within the trade. Some wholesalers have their own salesforces, and they also carry out some sales promotion, advertising and publicity.
- Warehousing, storage and product handling.
- Transporting of local and sometimes long-distance shipments.
- Controlling inventory: some even do this on behalf of the retailer, at the retailer's premises.
- Credit checking and credit control.
- Pricing and collection of pricing information, particularly about competitors.
- Acting as a channel of information up and down the supply chain.

These are all functions which the manufacturer would have to carry out on an individual basis if the wholesaler were not available to do them. The wholesalers also provide services to retailers, as follows:

- Information gathering and dissemination.
- One-stop shopping for a wide range of products from a wide range of manufacturers.
- Facilities for buying relatively small quantities.

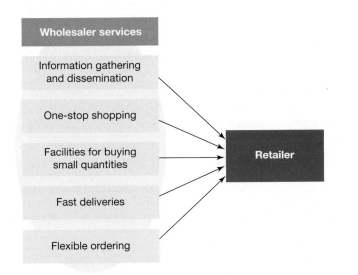

Figure 21.4

Wholesalers' services to retailers

● Fast deliveries, often on a cash-and-carry basis.

● Flexible ordering – amounts can be varied as consumer demand fluctuates.

For most retailers, it is clearly much more economical to use a wholesaler than to buy direct from the manufacturer. Only if a retailer is big enough to order economic quantities from a manufacturer (e.g. a major supermarket chain) will it be worthwhile to do so, and in most cases such large retailers operate their own warehouse and central bulk-breaking facilities in any case, in effect carrying out the wholesaler's job in-house.

There are many different types of wholesaler, as listed in Table 21.4.

Table 21.4 Types of wholesaler

Wholesaler	Description
Merchant wholesaler	These firms buy-in goods and sell directly to retailers, usually delivering the goods and having a salesforce calling on retailers in their geographical area.
Full-service merchant wholesaler	These provide a wide range of services for retailers, including shop design, sales promotion, advertising, coupon redemption, own-brand products, management support and so forth. For example, Spar is a grocery wholesaler which supplies small corner grocery shops throughout the UK and parts of the rest of Europe. Each shop is individually owned and managed, but carries the Spar logo and stocks Spar own-brand products (Happy Shopper brand).
General-merchandise wholesalers	These wholesalers carry a wide product mix, but have little depth. They deal mainly with small grocery shops and general stores, operating as a one-stop shop for this type of retailer. Cash-and-carry warehouses are a good example, where the retailer collects the stock and takes it away using his or her own transport.
Limited-line wholesalers	These outlets offer only a limited range of products, but stock them in depth. They are often found in industrial markets, selling specialist items such as building materials and equipment: they are often able to offer specialist advice and expertise in the field.
Speciality-line wholesalers	Speciality-line wholesalers carry a very narrow range, perhaps concentrating on only one type of product. They are typically found in industries where the products require special handling, or require specialist expertise in the buying or marketing of the product. For example, there are wholesalers who specialise only in coffee. In many cases, they sell only to other wholesalers.
Rack jobbers	These are wholesalers who maintain their own stands or displays in retail outlets. The wholesaler takes responsibility for stocking and maintaining the stand, the retailer collects the money from consumers and keeps a share of the proceeds. This saves the retailer's working capital, and in some cases removes the need for expertise in buying the stock: for example, rack jobbers might put a stand selling cosmetics in a clothing shop.
Limited-service wholesalers	These take title to the goods, but do not actually take delivery, store inventory or monitor demand. An example might be a coal wholesaler, who orders from an importer or from a coal mining company and arranges delivery direct to a coal merchant without actually storing the coal.
Cash-and-carry wholesaler	This is a category of general-merchandise wholesaler: the wholesaler acts like a giant supermarket where retailers come and choose goods, using their own transport to take the goods away.
Drop shipper (or desk jobber)	This is similar to a limited-service wholesaler. Drop shippers have a salesforce which obtains orders from retailers: the orders are passed directly to manufacturers, who then arrange delivery direct to the retailer.
Mail-order wholesalers	In some industries, orders can be taken and goods despatched through the post or via the Internet. Mail-order wholesalers produce catalogues to sell to retailers.

Retailers

Retailers deal with any sales that are for the customer's own use, or for the use of family and friends. In other words, any purchases that are not for business needs are the domain of the retailer.

Therefore, a retailer is not necessarily a High Street shop, or a market trader; mail order catalogues, TV phone-in lines, even door-to-door salesmen are all retailers. Tupper Corporation (which sells Tupperware using party plan) is as much a retailer as Aldi, Makro or Coles' even though the product is sold in the customer's own home.

Traditionally most retail outlets have been in city centres or suburban high streets. Partly this was for convenience, so that shoppers had a central area to visit for all their shopping requirements, and partly it was due to planning regulations which zoned most retail shops in traditional retail areas, away from industrial parks and housing estates.

Within the last 20 years out-of-town hypermarkets and shopping parks have been growing up. This is in response to the following factors:

Courtesy of Tupperware

- Greater car ownership means an increase in **outshopping** (shopping outside the area where the consumer lives).

- High city-centre rents and property taxes make out-of-town sites more attractive for retailers.

- Town planners have used retail parks as a way of regenerating decaying industrial sites on the edges of towns.

outshopping Shopping outside the area in which one lives.

Such out-of-town sites have not necessarily damaged all town-centre retailers, although there has been a shift in the composition of city-centre retail districts. For example, food retailers have largely gone from central sites in major cities, except for delicatessens and speciality food outlets. In the United Kingdom, the supermarket chain Tesco has recently begun to reverse this trend with the establishment of the Tesco Metro stores in city centres, closely followed by arch-rival Sainsbury's Central Stores. These stores carry a limited range of products, usually in smaller pack sizes, and aim at office workers shopping in their lunch hours or convenience shopping.

Here are some descriptions of different types of retail outlet:

- *Convenience stores*, or corner shops, offer a range of grocery and household items. These local shops often open until late at night. They are usually family-run, often belong to a trading group such as Spar, Circle K and 7-Eleven, and cater for last-minute and emergency purchases. In recent years, the Circle K and 7-Eleven franchises have expanded internationally from the United States and are making inroads into the late-night shopping market. Convenience stores have been under threat from supermarkets as later opening has become more common and the laws on Sunday trading in many countries have been relaxed.

- *Supermarkets* are large self-service shops, which rely on selling at low prices. Typically they are well-laid-out, bright, professionally-run shops carrying a wide range of goods.

- *Hypermarkets* are even bigger supermarkets, usually in an out-of-town or edge-of-town location. A typical hypermarket would carry perhaps 20 000 lines. The true hypermarket sells everything from food to TV sets.

- *Department stores* are located in city centres and sell everything; each department has its own buyers and functions as a separate profit centre. Examples are Harrods of London, El Corte Ingles in Spain and Clery's in Dublin. Within department

concessionaires Firms which rent space in department stores, paying a rental and usually a commission on sales.

stores, some functions are given over to **concessionaires**, who pay a rental per square foot plus a percentage of turnover to set up a store-within-a-store. Miss Selfridge, Brides and Principles all operate in this way within department stores. The trend is towards allowing more concessionaires, and around 70 per cent of Debenham's floor space is allocated this way.

- *Variety stores* offer a more limited range of goods, perhaps specialising in clothes (e.g. Primark) or in housewares and music (e.g. Woolworths).

- *Discounters* (sometimes called baby sharks) are grocery outlets offering a minimum range of goods at very low prices. Often the decor is basic, the displays almost non-existent, and the general ambience one of pile-it-high-and-sell-it-cheap. Kwik Save, Lidl and Aldi are examples of this approach; such stores typically carry only 700 lines or so.

- *Niche marketers* stock a very limited range of products, but in great depth. Examples are Sock Shop and Tie Rack. They frequently occupy tiny shops (even kiosks at railway stations) but offer every possible type of product within their very narrow spectrum. Niche marketers were the success story of the 1980s, but declined somewhat during the 1990s.

- *Discount sheds* are out-of-town DIY and hardware stores. They are usually businesses requiring large display areas, but with per-square-metre turnovers and profits that do not justify city-centre rents. Service levels are minimal, the stores are cheaply constructed and basic in terms of decor and ambience, and everything is geared towards minimising the overhead.

- *Catalogue showrooms* have minimal or non-existent displays, and are really an extension of the mail order catalogue. Customers buy in the same way as they would by mail order, by filling in a form, and the goods are brought out from a warehouse at the rear of the store. These outlets usually have sophisticated electronic inventory control.

Many niche marketers operate small outlets at major railway stations.

© Len Green | Dreamstime.com

Shopping Behaviour

People have many motives for shopping, going beyond a simple need to obtain goods and services. These can be divided into social motives and personal motives, each of which determine the choice of retailer, the time spent shopping and much of the effort which is expended.

Social motives include the following:

- *Social experience outside the home.* Talking to shop assistants, going shopping with a friend or friends, getting out of the house for a while.

- *Communication with others having a similar interest.* Whether shopping for clothes or computers, people enjoy taking a friend along, especially if the friend has a specific expertise which can be used.

- *Peer group attraction.* Going to specific shops means mingling with people from a similar social background. This is reassuring in terms of self-image.

- *Status and authority.* Being a customer is a pleasant experience – the shop assistants (if they are well-trained) are attentive and interested in the customers' needs, which means that customers enjoy the warm glow of being looked after.

- *Pleasure of bargaining*. In some situations in every country bargaining is acceptable, and in some countries it is normal practice almost everywhere. The bargaining process is enjoyable because it has the elements of power, of exercising skill and of getting a bargain.

Personal motives include the following:

- *Role playing*. Playing the part of the customer is a pleasant experience: some people even adopt a new persona when shopping, in order to enhance their own self-esteem.
- *Diversion*. Looking at new products is an entertainment in itself, and browsing around the shops can be a relaxing way of spending some time.
- *Self-gratification*. Meeting one's own needs by buying goods relieves the tensions set up by lacking something which is regarded as essential.
- *Learning about new trends*. Learning is, in itself, a pleasurable thing. Being the first to know about new products is important for some people's self-esteem.
- *Physical activity*. Often people have sedentary lives: going for a walk round the shops can relieve this. Often people experience this motivation when on holiday – relaxing on the beach or by the pool quickly becomes boring.
- *Sensory stimulation*. Simply exposing one's senses to new sensations is pleasurable, and shopping fulfils this role admirably.

Shoppers can be categorised according to their shopping behaviour, as shown in Table 21.5.

Table 21.5 Shopper profiles

Profile	Explanation
Yesteryears	Approximately 17 per cent of shoppers fit this profile. Yesteryears are insecure, conservative, somewhat anti-social and are risk avoiders. They are typically older females, and are looking for low prices, guarantees, convenient retailer location and speedy service. They are light consumers who like chain stores and discount stores.
Power purchasers	Representing about 15 per cent of shoppers, this group are self-indulgent variety seekers. They are risk-takers and big spenders, and tend to be young. They are looking for friendly salespeople, easy-to-find merchandise, high quality, fast service and are brand-conscious. They are very heavy consumers, and like department stores, chain stores and speciality shops.
Fashion foregoers	These are fashion laggards, and are unconcerned about image or style. They tend to be mundane and anti-social, and are typically single men living alone. They look for low prices, ease of finding merchandise, convenient location and a wide selection of products. They are light consumers who shop infrequently, and they like DIY outlets. They represent around 16 per cent of shoppers.
Social strivers	This group are style-conscious fashion experimenters who like shopping, are social people and are brand-aware. They are young, female, often somewhat downmarket and are heavy consumers. They like guarantees, friendly salespeople, a wide selection of goods and high quality. Typically they shop anywhere and everywhere (except DIY stores) and shop as often as possible. Because of this, they represent 20 per cent of shoppers.
Dutifuls	16 per cent of the country's shoppers, these people are sacrificial, practical risk avoiders. They are comparison shoppers (they like to shop around). Typically, they are downmarket mid-life households or down/middle market older households. They look for low prices, guarantees, ease of finding merchandise, convenient location, friendly salespeople and speed of service. They shop relatively infrequently, and are light consumers.
Progressive patrons	These are self-confident, artistic, variety-seeking, open-minded, risk-taking, innovative and imaginative people. They are often male, but may also be middle to upmarket mid-life families. They look for ease of finding merchandise, high quality, wide selection and specific brands. They are very heavy consumers, and like speciality stores, catalogue outlets, convenience stores and DIY outlets. They account for the remaining 16 per cent of shoppers.

Choice of retailer is determined by the proximity of the store (the closer, the better), the store design and physical facilities, the merchandise on offer, advertising and sales promotion activities, store personnel, customer service and the other clients. This last is an interesting example of a factor over which the store does not have direct control, but it clearly has an influence on the image of the store and the shopping experience. A store with an upmarket clientele and image will attract people who associate themselves with that image: a store with a downmarket image and a disreputable clientele will repel more upmarket clients. One of the problems inherent in self-service retailing is the problem of shop soiling. Goods may be handled by many people, and even if the goods are not damaged in any way (having been protected by the packaging) customers will often regard the products as having been contaminated by the touch of others. Anthropological studies of this relate the phenomenon to bad magic – the previous person to have touched the product is thought to have transferred some of the essence of themselves into the product. This can be a powerful influence, operating below the conscious level – few people would be aware of it, yet it is there all the time (Argo, Dahl and Morales 2006).

Non-Store Retailing

Non-store retailing includes door-to-door selling, vending machines, telemarketing (selling goods by telephone), mail order, in-home selling and catalogue retailing.

Door-to-door selling has suffered a decline in recent years, largely because of the changing role and working patterns of women. Forty years ago most married women would be at home during the day, so that door-to-door sales of everything from brushes to kitchen knives was a viable option for companies. Low overheads for the firm coupled with convenience for the housewife meant that door-to-door salesmen could count on a reasonable success rate, with few empty houses. By the 1990s, however, most women worked outside the home so houses were empty during the day, and calling in the evenings was perceived as intrusive by most householders – it would be difficult to imagine householders giving a warm welcome to a knife salesman turning up on doorsteps at nine o'clock at night, for example.

party plan A direct-marketing tool in which the salesperson holds private presentations for groups of friends in a private home.

A more acceptable from of in-home selling is the **party plan**. Pioneered by firms such as Tupperware, party plan selling involves a local agent for the firm, who recruits homeowners to run a 'party' for friends and work colleagues. The party will involve the usual food, drink and conversation, but will also be centred around a demonstration of the firm's products. The party organiser will be given a commission (often in the form of free product, but sometimes in cash) for his or her efforts in organising the party. Party plan retailing seems to be a predominantly female activity.

Mail order and teleshopping were covered in Chapter 19: they are, of course, forms of retailing because they involve direct sales to consumers.

E-commerce refers to retailing over the Internet. Currently, e-commerce is dominated by business-to-business marketing, but dot.com firms such as Amazon.com, Lastminute.com and Priceline.com are making inroads into consumer markets. The growth of such firms is limited mainly by the growth in Internet users; as more people go online, the potential market increases and is likely to do so for the foreseeable future. Traditional retailers have not been slow to respond to the perceived threat: in the United Kingdom, many supermarkets now offer an Internet service, with free delivery. There is more on this in Chapter 19.

Because consumer needs change rapidly, there are fashions in retailing (the rise and fall of niche marketing demonstrates this). Being responsive to consumer needs is, of course, important to all marketers, but retailers are at the 'sharp end' of this process and

Marketing in Practice
Party Time!

Many firms sell their products via party plan – everything from sex aids to kitchen utensils is sold in people's own homes. Perhaps one of the most successful areas, though, is cosmetics. Firms like Moor@Home, which sells products extracted from lowland moors (essentially, mudpacks and similar skin treatments), and Oriflame, the Swedish cosmetics company, are cashing in on the boom in party plan.

Party plan makes a good choice for selling cosmetics because it allows the customers to try products out in a private atmosphere but with friends presents to give feedback. Women particularly seem to find party plan attractive: virtually all party plan companies direct their activities at women, perhaps because women tend to see shopping as a social activity, whereas most men view shopping as a solitary activity usually connected with utilitarian needs.

Moor@Home is a small company, just starting out in party plan, but its sales of natural products for the skin are burgeoning. At the other end of the scale, Oriflame operate in 55 countries worldwide, with a salesforce of

1.5 million (most of whom are part-time). These companies offer women the chance to earn extra money without compromising their careers, family lives or social lives, and offer the customers the opportunity to try products in a non-threatening environment.

Party plan has also been successful in the sex aids and lingerie industry. Few women would want to be seen in public buying sex aids, but in a party atmosphere the situation is totally different. Parties such as those run by Ann Summers or Justdelites are hugely successful because (perhaps strangely) they remove the embarrassment factor surrounding the products. Women are able to rationalise their presence at the party by saying 'It's a bit of a laugh', and indeed the parties are conducted in a light-hearted way, with plenty of giggling and jokes.

From their roots in the Tupperware parties of the 1950s party plan events have come a long way. The need for some kind of social event to liven up a lonely day has disappeared, but the pleasure of meeting friends and sharing buying experiences has not.

need to be able to adapt quickly to changing trends. The following factors have been identified as being crucial to retail success:

- *Location.* Being where the consumer can easily find the shop: in other words, where the customers would expect such a shop to be. A shoe shop would typically be in a High Street or city-centre location, whereas a furniture warehouse would be typically out of town.

- *Buying the right goods in the right quantities.* Being able to supply what the consumer wants to buy.

- *Offering the right level of service.* If the service level is less than the customer expects, he or she will be dissatisfied and will shop elsewhere. If the service level is too high, the costs increase, and also the customer may become suspicious that the prices are higher than they need be. Discount stores are expected to have low service levels, and consumers respond to that by believing that the prices are therefore lower.

- *Store image.* If the shop and its goods are upmarket, so must be the image in the consumer's mind. As with any other aspect of the product, the benefits must be as expected, or post-purchase dissonance will follow.

- *Atmospherics.* The physical elements of the shop design that encourage purchase. Use of the right colours, lighting, piped music and even odours can greatly affect purchasing behaviour (Bitner 1992). For example, some supermarkets use artificially generated smells of fresh bread baking to improve sales of bakery goods. Aromas in retail shops can create a sense of place and familiarity, and it is even possible to create a 'corporate odour' (Davies, Kooijman and Ward 2003).

Figure 21.5

Factors in retail success

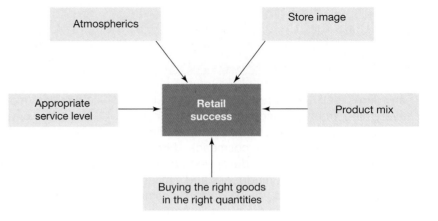

- *Product mix.* The retailer must decide which products will appeal to their customers. Sometimes this results in the shop moving away from its original product range into totally unrelated areas.

Recent trends in retail include the greater use of EPOS (electronic point-of-sale) equipment and laser scanners to speed checkout queues through (and, incidentally, to save staffing costs), and the increasing use of loyalty cards. These cards give the customer extra discounts based on the amount spent at the store over a given period. The initial intention is to encourage customers to buy at the same store all the time in order to obtain the discounts, and in this sense the cards are really just another sales promotion. This type of loyalty programme, involving economic benefits, does have a positive effect on customer retention. The schemes also tend to help in terms of increasing the retailer's share of the customers (Verhoef 2003).

There is a further possibility inherent in EPOS technology, however. It is now possible to keep a record of each customer's buying habits and to establish their purchasing pattern based on the EPOS records. Theoretically, this would mean that customers could be reminded at the checkout that they are running low on certain items, since the supermarket computer would know how frequently those items are usually bought. The phrase Domesday marketing has been coined by Professor Martin Evans to describe this; whether it could be seen as a useful service for consumers or as an unwarranted invasion of privacy remains as a topic for discussion (Evans 1994). EPOS systems in the UK were redesigned in 2004 to allow for the introduction of chip-and-pin credit cards. These have been used in France and Spain for many years to reduce credit card fraud and reduce time spent at the checkouts.

Talking Point

Most of what we do is recorded on computer somewhere – in fact, firms and Government departments know a great deal more about us than we like to think. If the police or the tax authorities really want to know about our expenditure and lifestyles, they can find out very quickly and easily – almost at the touch of a button, in fact.

So how does that make you feel? In George Orwell's book, *1984*, he described a society in which everyone was under surveillance all the time by the dictator, Big Brother. The TV show *Big Brother* has shown how people crack under the strain of being watched all the time – and yet we are quite happy to hand over our loyalty card at the supermarket and have all the details of our purchases recorded, including our credit card number, home address and even email address and telephone number. Big Brother knows what you bought – even those personal items that you wouldn't want your mother to know you buy! All in the name of providing a better service.

But does it matter? We live in a goldfish bowl anyway – privacy is dead! At least the supermarket only wants this information so they can tell us about good deals on stuff we might want to buy: it isn't the Secret Service after us for imaginary crimes against the State. So why not let everybody know everything and have done with it?

Forms of ownership in retail are also diverse. Although most retail outlets are still owner-managed and independent (around 62 per cent of UK retailers fall into this category), the sales volume for independents is well behind that of the majors. Independents account for less than 30 per cent of UK retail sales, and much of this is concentrated in the CTN (confectionery, tobacco, news) sector. This sector continues to survive because it offers more personal service and more flexible opening hours, although this advantage has been eroded markedly by major supermarket chains, who now offer very extended (even 24 hour) opening times.

A second category of ownership is the corporate chain. This has multiple outlets under common ownership, and is the usual form of ownership for major supermarkets, High Street clothing chains such as Next and pharmacies such as Boots. Many of these chains are long-established and have built their success on their skills in purchasing rather than on selling. Most of the major chains operate centralised purchasing so that they are able to gain maximum bulk discounts from suppliers, and have maximum control over the supply chain. Some, such as Marks & Spencer, commission small manufacturers to produce items exclusively for the chain. This maximises the control the retailer has over the supply chain.

Although some of these chains allow a degree of local flexibility in purchasing (for example, Tesco allows its Welsh, Scottish and Irish branches to stock a small range of locally-produced goods to capitalise on the patriotic feelings of its customers), their main strength comes from bulk purchasing. Many of them offer extensive ranges of own-brands (products which carry the retailer's name rather than the manufacturer's). These own-brands compete with manufacturer's brands, although a recent piece of research has indicated that they often help to increase sales of manufacturers' brands. At the same time, the evidence is that heavy own-brand users contribute less to store profits than other shoppers (Ailawadi and Harlam 2004). The key factors consumers use in judging the store's own brands are the perceived quality of the store brand versus the national brands, the individual's familiarity with the store brands, and confidence in the extrinsic (that is, external) attributes of the brand (Gonzales-Mieres, Diaz Martin and Trespalacios Gutierrez 2006).

The third type of ownership is the contractual system, whereby independent retailers band together, either as a cooperative between the retailers or as a system sponsored by a wholesaler (such as the Spar system discussed earlier). The advantage is that the group can still benefit to some extent from bulk buying, but this is mitigated somewhat by the costs of running the group and inherent inefficiencies in having a large number of independent managers, each of whom has his or her own ideas about running the business. The lack of a consistent brand image is a major problem for these chains: some of the stores are indistinguishable from mainstream supermarkets, while others show the lack of investment which is often the hallmark of small businesses.

Franchising has been discussed earlier in terms of service industries such as fast food and hotel services, but it also exists in retailing. Benetton is the prime example: most Benetton retailers are franchises, and thus many of the risks are passed on to the retailer. Benetton franchisees in Germany have raised objections to Benetton's infamous advertising campaigns, because they found that the campaigns were losing them business: from Benetton's viewpoint, this was simply part of a normal business risk, but the risk was being borne by the franchisees, since Benetton continued to show profits in other countries without any difficulty.

Service Levels

In common with other service industries, retailers need to set a service level which their customers will find acceptable. There is, of course, a trade-off in terms of cost – the higher the service level, the greater the cost. The service level varies considerably from retailer to retailer, but broadly comes down to the categories in Table 21.6.

Table 21.6 Service levels

Service level	Explanation
Full service	Full-service retailers pay close personal attention to the customer, offer a range of account and delivery services, and charge premium prices as a consequence. Such stores as Harrod's, Cartier and Tiffany's are in this category.
Limited service	These stores do not offer the full 'red carpet' service, but do offer extras such as credit facilities, technical advice or home delivery. The driver for deciding the service level is what the consumer must have: for example, a computer retailer must offer technical advice because few consumers would be sufficiently IT-literate to be aware of the latest technology.
Self-service	Typical of supermarkets, self-service offers the minimum service level possible in exchange for low prices. The customer performs most of the in-store functions, selecting goods and taking them to a checkout to pay. Having said that, many supermarkets offer a little more than the minimum (for example offering to wrap cut flowers, or offering a home delivery service for larger orders). Lidl is an example of a 'no-frills' self-service store, whereas Tesco offers small extras which make shopping easier.

Figure 21.6

Service levels and price

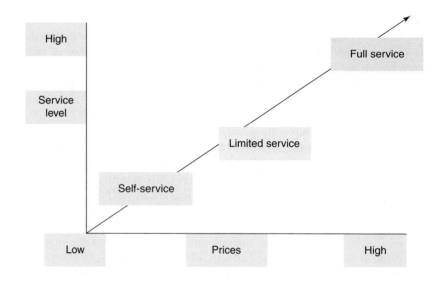

Merchandise Levels

There are two dimensions of range for retailers: breadth of range, which means the variety of different product lines stocked, and depth of range, which refers to the amount of choice within the product line. Department stores represent the greatest breadth of range, aiming to offer everything from clothing to food to electrical goods to hairdressing under one roof. The original aim of a department store was to ensure that customers would not need to go anywhere else to do their shopping – a revolutionary concept in the 19th century when the first such stores were opened.

Depth of range usually means that the retailer specialises in a particular type of product and stocks every conceivable variant on the product. Niche retailers such as Tie Rack and Knickerbox are examples of this.

Marketing in Practice
Tie Rack

In 1981, the first Tie Rack store opened its doors. The concept was simple: using extremely small outlets in railway stations and airports, within department stores and in shopping arcades, the company aimed to specialise only in neckwear. Tie Rack sold every type of tie and scarf, and nothing else.

Ties have the advantage of being small and highly priced. This meant that even a small shop could carry a very large range – much more than would be available in most general fashion outlets. Overheads, on the other hand, were extremely low. Locating the stores in railway stations and airports was a stroke of genius – per square foot, these locations are expensive, but there is a very high footfall of relatively well-off people who often have time to kill while waiting for their train or plane.

The success of the chain means that it now operates in 24 countries, through 330 outlets (most of which are tiny, in retail terms) and has amalgamated with Frangi SPA, the Italian fashion company.

Specialising has proved to be the way forward. In the 1960s and 1970s the trend was towards ever-larger stores selling everything – the 1970s saw the first hypermarkets, and department stores were in their heyday, so Tie Rack was swimming against the tide. On the other hand, Tie Rack's success certainly proved the adage that marketers should do something different from the crowd!

In recent years, shopping malls have largely replaced department stores. The advantage of the shopping mall is that it allows specialist retailers (who stock a deep range of products) while at the same time offering the main advantage of department stores, which is the breadth of range. Because many of the niche retailers are also chain stores, they can take advantage of bulk buying and so forth in a way that traditional department stores are unable to do. The result of this is that some department stores and department store chains are closing their doors. Most spectacular of these in recent times was the Allders department store chain, which went into administrative receivership in February 2005 with the loss of hundreds of jobs.

Shopping malls are the new department stores.

Strategic Decisions in Retailing

Location is a key decision in retailing, because the whole point of being a retailer is to place the goods at the most convenient point possible for the consumers to make their purchases. If the wrong location is chosen, the store will not generate enough trade to remain viable (Anderson 1993). In addition to lost business, relocation costs can represent a very substantial drain on capital, since the cost of fitting out a store can be extremely high.

The location decision hinges on two key factors: catchment area and the type of goods being sold. Catchment area refers to the radius around the store within which customers might reasonably be expected to travel, and an astute retailer will look towards investigating the profile of the customers within that area. A useful tool for doing this is a geodemographic rating tool such as ACORN or MOSAIC, which gives a fairly detailed description of the type of people living within the area. Catchment area analysis should also look at competition already in the area, and potential competitive responses. Stores do not necessarily avoid areas where there are many competitors, of course – it is equally valid to go to an area where there are already successful businesses, because splitting the

Table 21.7 Location-decision factors

Factor	Explanation
Population	This refers to the size of the population, the age profile, income, housing type, unemployment level, lifestyle and ethnic mix.
Accessibility	This refers to pedestrian flow (also called footfall), public transport, car access, parking, visibility, staff access and delivery access.
Competition	The existing activity of competitors, the saturation level of competition, the cash turnover, the age of the outlets, the trade areas, the design and facilities offered by competitors and the future potential for competitive activity all need to be taken into account.
Costs	The costs of acquiring a site, the development of the site, shop fitting, rent and local property taxes, maintenance of premises, security, staffing and delivery costs come under this heading.

market may still provide the store with enough business to be profitable, and the presence of competitors indicates that there is business to be done.

The second main factor in location decisions is type of goods. Some goods require a city-centre location, others do better in out-of-town locations. Fashion retailers tend to congregate in city centres, because fashion retailing tends to be a social event as much as a utilitarian, practical exercise. A day out in town is an appealing prospect for many consumers, because of the hedonic aspects of shopping. Convenience goods need to be readily available near to where the consumers live or work: shopping goods can be less conveniently situated because people are prepared to spend more time in travelling and searching.

Another factor is the cost of premises. For bulky goods such as consumer appliances (washing machines, fridges etc.) the high cost of city-centre premises mean that retailers have difficulty in displaying a wide enough range of goods. Most such products are infrequently bought, so people are prepared to travel outside the city centre: edge-of-town retail parks with their lower rents and easy car parking are the obvious site for such products. Another classification of location-decision factors was offered by McGoldrick in 2002. This is shown in Table 21.7.

Locations can be classified as follows:

- *City centre.* City centres are usually the focal point for office development and transport connections, so they offer a large footfall. At ground level, most city centres are dominated by retail outlets, but such sites are expensive in terms of rent and taxes, so they tend to be dominated by high-margin products such as fashion, jewellery and financial services. City centre locations are often called prime, or primary locations.
- *Suburban.* Suburban locations are predominantly in residential areas. Often called secondary shopping centres, these parades of shops may run for whole streets in suburban locations, or may be a small row of six or seven convenience stores.
- *Out of town.* Edge-of-town or out-of-town retail parks have sprung up in the last 30 years or so, often near to major trunk roads. They take advantage of low rents and (in some cases) subsidies from local government departments, especially when they occupy 'brownfield' sites formerly used for industry. During the 1990s the concept was expanded to include the idea of an out-of-town shopping and entertainment complex (for example the MacArthur Glen centres) which include cinemas, restaurants and even bowling alleys. These centres are often some distance from major cities (for example, the MacArthur Glen complex at Sarn Park is about half-way between Cardiff and Swansea, in a rural area just off the M4 motorway).

Figure 21.7
Location factors

The location-decision process follows three stages:

1 *Search for good locations*. The retailer needs to decide which regions, towns, or areas of the city to locate in. Areas can be defined by socioeconomic categories, and retailers can establish retail spend potential by using geodemographic profiling.

2 *Assessment of viability*. Forecasting turnover using multiple regression techniques may be a possibility for comparing different locations. Often, such techniques give a spurious credibility to the results, when in fact most of the information included in the calculation is subjective. For example, a firm may decide that being near to a competitor is a good thing because the management believe they have a better selling proposition: on the other hand, if the competitor's selling proposition is actually better in the eyes of consumers, the store would be better locating elsewhere.

3 *Assessment of micro factors*. Issues such as footfall, presence of other retailers who are not competitors but who might attract customers, nearness of car parks and ease of parking, and security levels might all be taken into account. The site itself (which may well be an existing building) needs to be assessed in terms of ease of access for deliveries, length and terms of the lease, planning permission issues and even local environmental factors. For example, one major food retailer fell foul of the health inspectors during 2004 because of a rat infestation of epidemic proportions. The store owners had failed to take account of their location next to a large river, which of course is a breeding ground (and major highway) for rats.

Having selected a location, the retailer needs to consider competitive factors and competitive positioning within the chosen marketplace.

Competitive Positioning for Retailers

A key aspect of positioning is the store image and atmosphere. The shop front, the interior décor, the lighting, the display units and the fixtures and fittings all contribute to the overall impression customers have of the store. The elements which go to make up the overall perception of the store are listed in Table 21.8.

Figure 21.8

Location-decision process

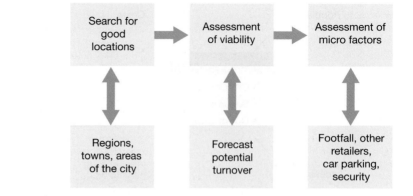

Table 21.8 Elements in store Image

Element	Explanation
Sight	Lighting and colour are the two chief elements in sight. Most supermarkets now use green around the vegetable section, because this gives an impression of coolness and freshness: yellow appears bright and sunny, but also induces anxiety, which may make shoppers hurry past that part of the store.
Scent	Many supermarkets have in-store bakeries which generate the smell of fresh bread, but those which do not have space for a bakery will sometimes use aerosol scents to generate the same aroma. Another ploy is to have a hot-chicken counter: these counters are not especially profitable in themselves, but they do generate smells which encourage shoppers to buy more food.
Sound	Many stores have background music playing, because research shows that music tends to make shoppers spend more time in the store (and consequently spend more money). Also, a silent atmosphere can seem unfriendly and unsettling for shoppers.
Other sensory experiences	Tactile factors such as the feeling of walking on carpet, the use of natural materials in display areas and the provision of comfortable seating (depending on the store) all affect the shopping experience. Some stores (e.g. bookshops, women's fashion shops) provide seating – the bookshops do so to allow customers to browse books more easily, women's fashion stores often provide seating for accompanying husbands and boyfriends.
Other shoppers	The degree of crowding in the store and the behaviour of other customers are important parts of the shopping experience, but are less controllable by the retailer. The store should not be overcrowded, but neither should it be empty: also, customers prefer to shop where they feel that similar people to themselves shop. Wealthier customers prefer not to shop at the same stores as poorer people, and vice-versa: young people prefer to buy their clothes at stores where other young people shop.

Layout and Display Strategies

Store layout and display affects customer perception of the store as well as their buying behaviour within the store. Store layouts conform to one of three main types, as shown in Table 21.9 (McGoldrick 2002).

Hypermarkets and other large stores might use a combination of these layouts, using a grid layout for FMCG (fast-moving consumer goods) lines and a free-flow layout for shopping goods or gift items.

Table 21.9 Store layouts

Layout	Description
Grid pattern	Aisles are arranged systematically so that customers walk in straight lines past the displayed merchandise. This layout is typical of supermarkets. This layout makes it easy for customers to find what they are looking for: supermarkets typically label each aisle so that shoppers can go straight to the goods they need.
Free flow	Displays are laid out in an irregular pattern, making a more interesting store layout for browsing. Free flow layouts encourage customers to wander around and browse the products on display: they are not conducive to quick decision-making.
Boutique layout	Boutique layout separates the store into smaller sections. This layout might be used in a fashion shop, where different types of clothing might be displayed in different sections – the impression is of a set of small stores within the larger store.

Products can be displayed in one of five basic formats (Rosenbloom 1981). These are:

1 *Open display*. The goods are displayed on racks or counters where customers can pick them up and examine them. This type of display maximises customer involvement with the product and encourages trial, but can clearly lead to deterioration of the products due to excessive handling (shop soiling).

2 *Theme display*. The retailer may decide to base a display around a theme – summer holidays, Mother's Day, Easter, gardening etc. These displays are intended to be eye-catching and to give customers a reminder of the various items they will need to enjoy the forthcoming event.

3 *Lifestyle display*. Here the display revolves around a particular lifestyle or life stage – a furniture shop might display the products in a room setting, for example.

4 *Coordinated display*. This is similar to theme displays and lifestyle displays – for example, a display might revolve around physical fitness, with mannequins dressed in sports clothes, accompanied by exercise equipment or sports equipment.

5 *Classification dominance display*. Here the retailer groups similar products together to give the impression that the store specialises in that category of product.

Retailing has gone through many changes in the last hundred years or so, but the end result is that retailers frequently have the strongest influence in the distribution channel because they are, by definition, closest to the consumers. As retailers have grown in size, they have been able to exert much greater influence on producers, telling them what to produce and when to produce it: retailers have even been able to specify the sizes, colours and quality of agricultural produce such as tomatoes and chickens.

Perhaps the biggest revolution in retailing will come from the Internet. As we saw in Chapter 19, more and more products are being bought online, and traditional bricks-and-mortar retail outlets need to take this into consideration. The most successful retailers online appear to be the 'clicks and mortar' outlets which combine a website with a physical High Street shop. This allows customers to check on the website whether the shop stocks the product category, but to visit the shop to see the actual product: likewise, consumers can see the product in the shop, go home to think about it, then order online. Having a physical presence improves the trust level between consumer and retailer, and reassures the customer that there will be a line of recourse if anything goes wrong with the purchase.

Summary

Wholesalers, agents, retailers and other inter-mediaries perform useful functions in ensuring that the right products reach the right customers at the right time and in the right condition. Their activities account for the major part of the cost of goods in most cases, but without them there would be great ineffi-ciencies and duplicated effort in the supply chain.

The result of their proximity to customers is improved fit between need and supply, and also an increase in power in the supply chain, with wholesalers and retailers gen-erally having more bargaining power than manufacturers. Although consumers have the ultimate power (simply by choosing to spend their money elsewhere) their spokes-person is the retailer, who gauges consumer need and translates this into purchases from wholesalers and manufacturers.

The key points from this chapter are as follows:

- Agents are, for all practical purposes, the principal. The principal is bound by any acts of, or agreements made by, its agents.
- Intermediaries do not necessarily buy the products they handle.
- Licensing is most appropriate if products are perish-able or fragile.
- Not all retailers have shops: a retailer is any firm which sells direct to consumers.
- Service levels have to be traded off against costs, and ultimately against prices.
- Location decisions are based on population, acces-sibility, competition and costs.

Chapter review questions

1 What is the difference between a licensee and a franchisee?

2 How might an Internet retailer set up a bricks-and-mortar store?

3 What factors might a retailer take into account when deciding on service levels?

4 Why might a wholesaler provide a support service for consumers?

5 How might a discount grocery store decide on where to locate new stores?

6 What type of store layout would you expect in an electronic goods retailer?

7 How might a retailer encourage lower income shoppers?

8 What advantages might there be for a wholesaler in becoming a full-service wholesaler?

9 What advantages are there for retailers in dealing with full-service wholesalers?

10 How would ACORN help a retailer make a location decision?

Preview case revisited
Gift House International

Gift House International has a website on which all products are displayed, but this alone is not sufficient for the company to promote its products. Advertising in the trade press is another way forward, but the company finds that one of its best ways of meeting new customers is to exhibit at the trade fairs, at the National Exhibition Centre in Birmingham.

The two main events for the gift and novelty trade are the Spring Fair and the Autumn Fair. The Spring Fair takes place in February each year, and is attended by 4000 exhibitors and tens of thousands of visitors. The Spring Fair is the time when some buyers are looking towards the Christmas trade (such are the lead times in wholesale) but it is the show at which people set up business deals for the entire year. The Autumn Fair is smaller but is equally important, and is held in September each year.

Gift House International attend both fairs each year, with a view to finding new retailers and making useful contacts with potential suppliers. Not all exhibitions work for the company though – although Gift House International exhibited at the Erotica 07 show in London during November 2007, the company had no plans to attend the 2008 exhibition.

Gift House International has a difficult market to deal with: it varies from small novelty shops in seaside resorts through to major retailers, and each type of customer requires a different approach. Some require large quantities of a single item shipped direct to their own warehousing facility, others require a mixture of a few products shipped to their own store. Gift House International has to remain flexible enough to cope with these different needs while maintaining a single brand image, and needs to carry out its task efficiently. Computerised stock control systems and a 'can-do' attitude among its small workforce are obviously a great help. The key factor in success, however, lies in buying the right products in the right quantities at the right price – a skill which can make or break any intermediary.

Case study
Argos

When Richard Tompkins was on holiday on the Greek island of Argos in the early 1970s he came up with a brilliant idea. Tompkins was the founder of Green Shield trading stamps in the UK: these were an early form of loyalty scheme, by which retailers gave out the special stamps to shoppers according to how much they spent. Shoppers stuck the stamps in a book, and could exchange the filled books for goods at special 'redemption centres' in High Street locations. The scheme was a huge success – at one time Green Shield Stamps was the largest outlet for bathroom scales in the UK – but Tompkins knew that the scheme wouldn't last forever. With the ending of resale price maintenance the way was open for discount stores, which would cut the foundations away from Green Shield. Tompkins' brilliant holiday idea was that he could allow people to buy goods from the redemption centres using cash instead of (or as well as) the books of stamps. He named his new company Argos, in memory of his holiday destination.

Argos is an unusual retailer. Rather than having goods on display, Argos has a catalogue from which people choose goods: the stores have a few items where they can be seen, but the main display medium is the catalogue itself.

Customers fill in a form listing what they want to buy, take it to a delivery counter, pay for the goods and wait for a warehouseman to bring the packages out to them. New catalogues are produced twice year, in spring and autumn, and are adapted for in-store use by being ring bound and laminated to stand up to the heavier use they take from hundreds of customers a day.

This way of handling products means that costs are dramatically reduced. Goods do not become shop-soiled, fewer staff are needed because displays do not have to be replenished and there is negligible shoplifting. The downside is the cost of printing the catalogue – but even this is offset by the fact that the catalogue is available to mail-order and even telephone shoppers who never visit the store at all.

Customers can also purchase online, and there are automated tills within each store where customers can enter the code numbers for each item and pay by credit card, thus cutting out the need for a cashier. Customers can ensure that goods are in stock by using the 'check and reserve' option, which checks that the goods are in stock and allows customers to reserve them using the website, the telephone or a text messaging service. Argos also offers a home delivery service, and indeed some large items can only be bought by home delivery.

Argos now has 700 stores throughout the UK and Ireland, and the store employs 34 000 people. In 2007, the company turned over £4.2 billion and served over 130 million customers, making it the UK's largest general goods retailer.

Courtesy of The Advertising Archives

Using the strapline 'Don't shop for it – Argos it' Argos advertises widely on TV and in the press. Advertising reaches its peak when the catalogues are due out, and potential customers are advised to obtain a catalogue as soon as possible before they all go – the intention is that people will keep a catalogue at home, thus reducing browsing time in-store. Everything is designed around convenience and cutting overheads, with the result that Argos has become the great success story of the last 40 years in UK retailing.

Questions

1 What is the trade-off between service level and costs for Argos?

2 How might Argos segment its market?

3 What is Argos's main competitive advantage?

4 Why would someone buy from a store which does not have the goods on display?

5 What are the main drawbacks of the Argos system from the viewpoint of a customer?

References

Ailawadi, K.L. and Harlam, B. (2004): An empirical analysis of the determinants of retail margins: the role of store brand share. *Journal of Marketing* **68**(1), 147–55.

Anderson, C.H. (1993): *Retailing* (St Paul, MN: West Publishing).

Argo, J.J., Dahl, D.W. and Morales, A.C. (2006): Consumer contamination: how consumers react to products touched by others. *Journal of Marketing* **70**(2), 81–94.

Bitner, M.J. (1992): Servicescapes: the impact of physical surroundings on customers and employees. *Journal of Marketing* **56**(2), 57–71.

Davies, B.J., Kooijman, D. and Ward, P. (2003): The sweet smell of success: olfaction in retailing. *Journal of Marketing Management* **19**(5/6), 611–27.

Evans, M. (1994): Domesday marketing. *Journal of Marketing Management* **10**(5), 409–31.

Gonzalez-Mieres, C., Diaz Martin, A.M. and Trespalacios Gutierrez, J.A. (2006): Antecedents of the difference in perceived risk between store brands and national brands. *European Journal of Marketing* **40**(1/2), 61–82.

McGoldrick, P. (2002): *Retail Marketing*, 2nd edn (Maidenhead: McGraw Hill).

Rosenbloom, B. (1981): *Retail Marketing* (New York: Random House).

Verhoef, P.C. (2003): Understanding the effect of customer relationship management efforts on customer retention and customer share development. *Journal of Marketing* **67**(4), 30–45.

Further reading

There are a great many practitioner-type books available on retailing, but relatively few on wholesaling.

Among the more 'academic' books on retailing, Cox, P. and Brittain, R. (2004): *Retailing – An Introduction* (Harlow: Prentice Hall) offer a very readable but academically rigorous text. One author is a very experienced retail practitioner, the other is a respected academic, so the balance is a good one and the subject is approached well from both perspectives.

Regarding wholesaling, there are very few books on the topic at all, and most of these are economic analyses of the availability of wholesalers in different industries. The few 'how-to' books on wholesaling which exist are seriously out of date, and most are out of print.

Chapter 22
People, process and physical evidence

Part one **Concepts and Contexts**	1 Managing the exchange process 2 The marketing environment 3 Marketing domains
Part two **Markets and People**	4 Consumer behaviour 5 Organisational buying behaviour 6 Segmentation, targeting and positioning 7 Marketing information and research 8 Communications theories 9 International marketing
Part three **Strategy**	10 Creating competitive advantage 11 Building customer relationships
Part four **Marketing in Practice**	12 Product portfolio 13 New product development 14 Pricing 15 Advertising 16 Public relations and sponsorship 17 Selling and key account management 18 Exhibitions and sales promotions 19 Direct and online marketing 20 Managing channels 21 Intermediaries 22 People, processes and physical evidence

Learning objectives After reading this chapter you should be able to:

1. Explain the role of service in increasing customer loyalty.

2. Explain how the purchase of services differs from that of physical products.

3. Describe how risk increases in service purchases.

4. Explain how failures occur in service provision, and outline ways of dealing with it.

5. Explain the role of staff empowerment in service industries.

6. Explain how processes create strategic capabilities.

7. Show how consumers can also be producers.

8. Categorise services against the dimensions of complexity and divergence.

9. Explain the role of physical evidence in improving future business.

Introduction

Although the original idea of including people, process and physical evidence in the marketing mix came about because of a need to account for services marketing, all marketers need to understand the role of these three extra Ps in making products more attractive to consumers.

Business is not conducted by companies: companies are a legal fiction, without any real existence except through their employees. Business is conducted by people, and the relationships between the individuals concerned are probably the most important factor in many business transactions. The process of purchase and supply of products is also important in terms of assessing value for money, providing convenience and (often) differentiating one product from another. Physical evidence is what we use to confirm our possession of the product – think how often people use the phrase 'Nothing to show for it!'

Ultimately these three elements can be all that differentiates one product from another.

Services Marketing

As we saw in Chapter 3, services are characterised by being intangible, perishable, variable and inseparable from their production. In fact, the distinction between physical products and services is becoming more blurred as time goes on, because marketers of physical products are using service attributes to augment their products, and service marketers are including more physical evidence in their offerings for the same reason.

Preview case
Thomas Cook

In 1841 a young cabinet maker called Thomas Cook set out from his home in Market Harborough to walk the few miles to Leicester in order to attend a temperance meeting. On the way he was struck by a great thought – believing as he did that drinking alcohol was the curse of the British working classes, he decided to arrange special rail excursions so that people could attend temperance meetings. His first excursion transported 500 people in open railway carriages the 12 miles between Leicester and Loughborough to attend a temperance rally: the trip cost a shilling per person. Cook made no money on these tours – he simply ran them in order to further the aims of temperance. It was 1845 before he decided to run a profit-making tour, when he organised a trip to Liverpool, producing a printed brochure explaining the route and the local sights.

The opening up of the railway network in the UK allowed Cook to expand his operations, and by the time of the Great Exhibition in 1851 he was in a position to transport 150 000 people from the Midlands to see the exhibition. The success of this venture encouraged him to expand internationally: in 1855 he set up his first overseas tour, to visit an exhibition in Paris. The cross-Channel ferry companies refused to deal with him, though, so he had to set up a route from Harwich to Antwerp: this gave him the idea of expanding the tour to include Brussels, Heidelberg, Baden-Baden, the Rhine, Strasbourg and Paris, returning via Le Havre. Cook accompanied his customers on this tour to show them the way, arrange hotels and guide them generally.

To make things easier for his customers Cook made two important innovations: first, he negotiated with hoteliers to provide discounted rooms in exchange for vouchers issued by Cook. Second, he provided people with 'circular notes' which could be exchanged for local currency in any of his destinations. These were the forerunner of the traveller's cheque.

As the nation's wealth increased, Thomas Cook found itself with an ever-increasing group of competitors and imitators, as well as an increasingly broad spectrum of clients – foreign holidays were no longer the sole province of the wealthy: even by the 1930s, middle-class Britons were perfectly able to travel to France or Germany on holiday. By the 1960s, package holidays by air were on offer at low enough prices that most people could at least consider taking a foreign holiday – and by the 1990s many people took two or three trip abroad every year. Extending the service to meet the needs of these broader audiences presented a challenge to Thomas Cook.

Clearly people, process and physical evidence rise in importance as products move closer to the 'service' end of the spectrum: most services involve direct input by human beings, so the personal interaction between provider and customer is crucial to the customer's experience. An unfriendly taxi-driver, an irritating hairdresser or a careless air hostess can damage the customer's experience of the service even when the practical aspects (the taxi journey, the hairstyle, or the flight) are all perfect.

Some service industries encourage strong customer loyalty. These are typically personal services such as hairdressing and beauty therapy, food and beverage services such

Figure 22.1

Services marketing

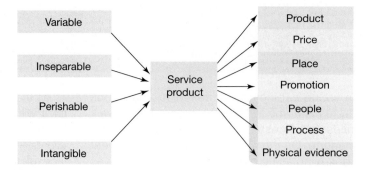

as pubs and restaurants, and some technical services such as car maintenance and computer technical support services. Banks often engender strong customer loyalty, in part because people find it difficult to switch banks: transferring standing orders and direct debits is time-consuming, and many people feel that a long-term relationship with a bank is more likely to lead to preferential treatment in case of unexpected overdraft or loan situations arising. Loyalty here is generated through the negative stimulus of high switching costs.

Talking Point

There is a lot of talk about loyalty, customer relationships and so forth. But do we really want this, as consumers? What's in it for us? Do we really *want* to have a relationship with the bank manager, or go on a nice holiday with our insurance company?

Wouldn't we rather they just served us in a friendly and efficient manner when we need them, and then just get back in the box and leave us alone until the next time? On the other hand, perhaps it's rather comforting to know that the bank is thinking about us when we're gone!

On the other hand, some services do not automatically engender customer loyalty. Taxis and buses are prime examples; although someone might use the same taxi firm when travelling from home, this is unlikely to be the case for someone arriving at an airport or train station. At these times, one simply takes the first available taxi. It would be extremely rare for someone to have a regular taxi driver, although most people use the same hairdresser on each visit. Other services such as airlines need to work hard to encourage loyalty, primarily through their use of frequent-flyer programmes: most airline passengers are simply looking for the lowest fare between their chosen departure point and destination – apart from business travellers, who often travel the same route anyway, loyalty is low.

Figure 22.2

Benefits of loyalty

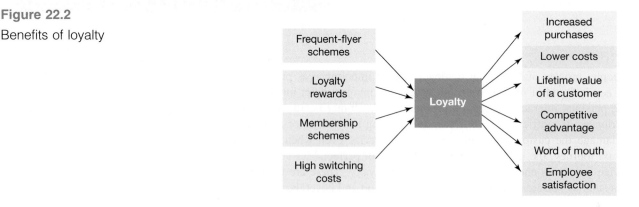

If loyalty can be generated, the benefits for the organisation are considerable. There are six main benefits, as follows:

1 *Increased purchases* (Reichheld and Sasser 1990). Customers tend to increase their purchases year-on-year with firms with whom they have a relationship. Of course, there must be a limit to this, but it is logical to assume that people are more likely to spend money with firms in whom they trust.

2 *Lower cost.* Attracting new customers is always more expensive than retaining existing ones.

3 *Lifetime value of a customer.* As we saw in Chapter 11, customer value should be measured in terms of how much the customer spends in a lifetime, rather than in a single transaction.

4 *Sustainable competitive advantage.* The intangible aspects of a service relationship are difficult to copy: a loyal group of customers are, by definition, difficult to lure away by competitors (Roberts, Varki and Brodie 2003).

5 *Word-of-mouth.* This is much more important in services marketing because of the intangibility of services. It is not possible, in most cases, to try out a service before purchase, so people rely heavily on the recommendations of friends. Firms with large numbers of loyal customers are more likely to benefit from this. If the service is a complex one, the consumers' choice is based primarily on direct experience, and then on recommendations from family and friends (Devlin 2007).

6 *Employee satisfaction.* Staff are more likely to stay with a firm which has a large group of loyal customers. Because staff in service industries are close to the customers, they are subject to direct customer feedback: praise is welcome, but regular complaints will demoralise staff and make them doubt whether they are working for a good company. Employees in the service sector are certainly attracted by the branding of the companies they choose to work for (Knox and Freeman 2006).

Lowering the rate of customer churn (plugging the holes in the leaky bucket – see Chapter 11) causes a substantial rise in overall profits (Reichheld and Sasser 1990).

Service purchasing follows a slightly different sequence from purchase of a physical good, as shown in Figure 22.3. Most of the risk attached to buying a physical product is limited to the purchase price (though no doubt there will be exceptions to this general rule). Services carry additional risks.

Consequential losses arise when a service goes wrong and causes a loss to the customer. For example, a poorly handled legal case could result in the loss of thousands of pounds, or even loss of liberty in a criminal case. Service providers usually are careful to explain the risks beforehand, use disclaimers in contracts and carry professional liability insurance. Consumers can sue for consequential losses.

Purchase price risk is the possible loss of the purchase price when the consumer buys a service that does not work. The usual consumer response is to refuse to pay for the service, so it is advisable for the supplier to check during the service process that everything is satisfactory. This is why waiters will check that the food is satisfactory during a meal out, and why service stations call customers when they find something serious is wrong with the car. Checking during the service provision not only makes it easier to correct problems early, it also makes it harder for customers to claim that the service went wrong in order to avoid paying.

Misunderstanding is common in service provision because of inability to try out services (trialibility). Particularly in professional services, the provider may feel that the customer would not understand the finer details of what is being done, and may therefore not bother to explain properly. This can easily result in post-purchase dissonance and refusal to pay.

Professional services like legal representation are difficult to understand and carry high risks.

©iStockphoto.com / John Steele

Marketing in Practice
Credit Card Tarts

American Express, in common with many other financial service providers, likes to hang on to its customers. The cost of acquiring customers is high: apart from the cost of advertising and handling incoming enquiries, financial services companies have to generate large amounts of paperwork in the form of application forms and statutory statements. They also have to run credit checks on all applicants, and since American Express cards have no upper credit limit, the credit checks need to be bullet-proof!

For most such companies, there is a fine line to be drawn between recruitment and retention. If the offer made for recruitment purposes is too generous, people will take out the cards with no intention of ever using them, just to gain on the special offer. This increases the defection rate when the offer expires. For example, American Express made a generous offer to KLM frequent-flyer members in early 2004. Anyone taking out an Amex card would be given 25 000 frequent-flyer miles on KLM, which is almost enough for a return flight within Europe. Thousands of KLM customers took up the offer, then cancelled the cards before the first year was up (thus avoiding the £105 membership fee charged by Amex). In effect, these people had obtained free flights just for the effort of filling out some forms and sending them to Amex.

Naturally, when these 'customers' cancelled their cards, they were passed to Amex's customer-retention people, who are empowered to make extra offers in an attempt to keep the customer. Some people were offered interest-free credit cards, others were offered extra concessions on the membership fee, but in all cases these people were treated as if they were customers, whereas in fact they had never, or hardly ever, used the cards at all.

Other companies have taken a more logical view of this type of behaviour. They look at the customer's actual usage of the product. There is no point in offering someone extra concessions if they have already proved that they are simply taking advantage of the situation.

Giving all and sundry zero-interest deals on credit cards is a way of recruiting new customers: continuing to offer the so-called 'card tarts' extra concessions is simply giving money away. In one case reported in the UK newspapers, one man saved £3000 a year on his mortgage simply by using interest-free credit card money in a savings account linked to a Tracker mortgage. He was able to keep switching the money from one card to another, cancelling cards as the offers expired, confident that credit card companies would continue to offer him new deals every time. The same companies would come back to be cheated over and over again – poor behaviour for a credit card company!

This is not to say that credit card providers cannot learn, of course. By 2008 the free deals were over. Although 0 per cent interest was still being offered on transfers, the companies began charging a 2 or 3 per cent transfer fee, which went some way towards discouraging the card tarts. Also, some companies (notably Egg) introduced a deliberate policy of cancelling the cards of people who were unprofitable customers – in Egg's case, this was a controversial move, since they cancelled the cards of many people who pay in full at the end of each month, thus demonstrating financial probity but also avoiding paying any interest. Some commentators saw this as simply getting rid of the most creditworthy customers – but of course people who run a permanently maxed-out card are the ones who pay for managing directors' company cars!

Figure 22.3

Service purchasing sequence compared with physical product purchasing sequence.

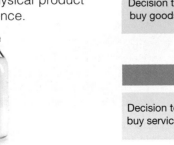

Purchase of a Physical Product

Decision to buy goods → Payment for goods → Receipt of goods → Use of goods → Post-purchase evaluation: satisfaction or otherwise

Purchase of a Service Product

Decision to buy service → Commitment to supplier → Delivery and consumption of service → Evaluation of service: satisfaction or otherwise → Pay for service

Because consumers are buying a promise, they are more likely to use indirect measures of quality such as price. Diners tend to assume that more expensive restaurants will provide better food and/or service, that expensive hairdressers will provide better hairdos and that expensive lawyers are more likely to win cases. Having made a purchasing decision, the consumer is more likely to become involved with the service provider. Consumers therefore tend to have favourite restaurants, hairdressers and family solicitors with whom the relationship might continue for a lifetime. Customers are reluctant to switch bank accounts, even when problems have become apparent; even though customers will readily change brands of canned tuna in order to save a few pence, they will still buy the tuna from the same supermarket as usual. This is because the customer knows where everything is kept in the supermarket, understands the store's policy on returned goods, knows which credit cards are acceptable and perhaps even knows some of the staff on the tills.

People

Company employees can be divided into four main groups (Judd 1987):

1 **Contactors**. These people have frequent and regular contact with customers. They are typically heavily involved with marketing activities: they are salespeople, telesales operators and customer service people. Because they are dealing with customers on a day-to-day basis, they need to be trained in customer relations and should be motivated to deal with customers. They should also be recruited on the basis of their ability to deal with people.

2 **Modifiers**. These people deal with customers regularly, but have no direct marketing role. They are receptionists, truck drivers, switchboard operators and (sometimes) warehouse personnel or progress chasers. They need a clear view of the organisation's marketing strategy and to be aware of their own role within it. Modifiers need good people skills, and training and monitoring of performance regarding their customer contacts.

3 **Influencers**. These people are involved with the traditional elements of the marketing mix, but have little or no contact with customers. Influencers need to be evaluated and rewarded according to customer-orientated performance standards.

4 **Isolateds**. Isolateds have no customer contact and very little to do with conventional marketing functions. Examples are accountants, personnel people and office cleaners. Although they need to be alerted to the idea that their efforts are important in supporting the other staff, they do not need any specific training for dealing with customers. In essence, their role is to create the right conditions under which the customer-focused staff can do their jobs.

Of course, everyone goes home at the end of the day and talks to family and friends about the firm, and as such everyone in the firm bears some responsibility for the corporate image and for marketing (see Chapter 16). Creating shared values and especially creating a feeling of corporate justice (that one is working for a fair-minded company) affects how employees deal with customers. This in turn affects

contactors Staff who have daily contact with customers.

modifiers Staff who have some contact with customers for specific purposes.

influencer The person who has the ability to sway the judgement of a decider.

isolateds Staff who have no relationship at all with customers.

Courtesy of J Sainsbury Plc

Expert staff are a key asset in many retail stores.

Figure 22.4

Employees and customers

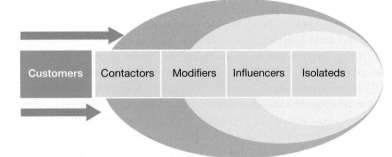

Talking Point

customers' perception of the organisation (Maxham and Netemeyer 2003). In some cases, employees are crucial in establishing the credibility of the brand – research into Irish theme pubs revealed that the employees and other patrons are at least as important as the 'Irish' decor in creating a feeling of authenticity (Munoz, Wood and Solomon 2006).

In practice, no matter how hard companies try to deliver the perfect service, the natural variability of employee performance will mean that there will always be some occasions on which the service falls below standard. This means that firms need to concentrate on recovering from service mistakes when they do occur (Rasmusson 1997). The first step in this is to empower front-line employees.

Companies expect more and more of their employees nowadays. Not so many years ago, people had nine to five jobs – they would sit at their desks, or on the production line, from nine in the morning until five in the afternoon, then get paid on Friday. Some people did exactly the same job for 50 years and ended up with a gold watch at the end of it – but not any more! Employers expect people to be able to multitask, to switch jobs with each other and to take on an ever-wider range of tasks.

Empowerment seems to be following along the same lines – employers expecting people to take on responsibility for customer satisfaction as well as carry out their normal jobs! On the other hand, maybe customer satisfaction is what all our jobs are about at the end of the day, and empowerment just recognises that fact!

empowerment Giving staff the ability to resolve customer problems without recourse to higher management.

Empowerment means giving employees the authority to sort out problems without having to refer to management. This approach to managing people makes the employees responsible for their own actions, and more importantly makes them responsible for controlling the service delivery. The purpose of the exercise is to ensure that problems are dealt with as soon as they happen, without the customer having to wait for a decision from management. Because many services are carried out on a one-to-one basis, managers would find it difficult or impossible to supervise every aspect of the process, so employees need to be empowered if the system is to operate smoothly: the efforts of a factory worker can be checked by examining the tangible output (a physical product), but because production and consumption of services take place at the same time, it is often not possible to check outputs, and therefore the onus must be on the staff member to act professionally and on the employer to provide the staff member with the authority to do so.

Research shows that customers who encounter failures in service provision expect the following five elements in complaint-handling (Gruber, Szmigin and Voss 2006):

1 Positive non-verbal signals from the employees who handle the complaint. This would include appropriate body language such as nodding to demonstrate understanding and being genuinely interested in solving the problem.

Marketing in Practice
IKEA's Co-Workers

IKEA is a gigantic operation. The stores cover several acres, and each store employs 60 or more staff (called co-workers). The stores carry thousands of different products, and the whole experience can be so confusing for people who are shopping there for the first time that IKEA provide pencils, paper, tape measures and maps so that people can find their way around the vast stores and can make notes on what they want to purchase.

Inevitably some people become confused, disorientated, frustrated and error-prone in such an environment. Sometimes they will pick up the three-drawer model when they meant to pick up the four-drawer one, or they will get lost and wander in circles. Staff at IKEA are extremely well trained: they are cross-trained in sales and stock operations, so that they can usually solve any customer problem, but more importantly they are trained to spot customers who are struggling or frustrated.

Co-workers are empowered to take a wide range of corrective actions. Apart from solving the immediate problem (being out of stock of an item, or helping the customer to find something) they can, when the situation requires it, offer customers a free meal in the IKEA on-site Swedish restaurant, free delivery of an item, cash coupons or even money off the purchase price of the product.

Over 200 million people visit IKEA stores in any one year – testimony to the effectiveness of the company's customer-care policies.

Table 22.1 Options for empowering staff

Option	Explanation
Encourage employees to contribute ideas	This needs to go beyond simply putting up a suggestion box. Some firms (notably Ford) pay substantial cash rewards to employees who think of money-saving ideas for the company.
Establish work teams	Work teams are allowed to share and manage their own work, which enables them to help each other and establish quality controls within the group. This is seen by most employees as less threatening than management controls.
Empower staff to change strategic parameters	This allows employees to take responsibility for the overall outcome, rather than simply having responsibility for their own actions.

2 Employees should have sufficient product and process knowledge to handle the complaint and resolve the problem.

3 Employees should have sufficient authority to deal with the problem.

4 Employees should be seen to try hard to solve the problem.

5 The customer should be taken seriously.

All of these elements are critical factors in staff empowerment. There are three basic objectives of staff empowerment, as follows:

1 To make the organisation more responsive to pressures from outside.

2 To remove layers of management in order to reduce costs. Less supervision means fewer supervisors: managers are left free to coach and support staff rather than direct them, which also reduces workload and stress for managers.

3 To create employee networks. This encourages collaboration, teamwork and horizontal communication, which in turn tends to improve employee motivation.

The basic empowerment options are as shown in Table 22.1.

Figure 22.5

Trade-offs in staff empowerment

	High customer contact	Low customer contact
Highly structured, rigid competitive environment with little change	Limited empowerment	No empowerment
Unstructured, rapidly changing competitive environment	High empowerment	Limited empowerment

For most staff, empowerment is a powerful motivator because it increases job satisfaction: if they are not empowered, staff can feel like small cogs in a very large machine, especially in modern global organisations. Being part of a smaller, empowered team brings the workplace down to a human scale. There are, of course, trade-offs in staff empowerment. These are illustrated in Figure 22.5.

Purely from the viewpoint of how the customers will be treated, the deciding factors in empowerment are the competitive environment and the relative importance of close linkages with the customers. If there is little customer contact, there is little need for staff empowerment, and none at all if the competitive environment is rigid and unchanging. On the other hand, if there is high customer contact, empowerment will need to be in place, and staff will be highly empowered if they have to deal with an unstructured, rapidly-changing environment.

Problems can arise from empowerment. Some people are risk-averse, and therefore reluctant to assume the responsibility which goes with empowerment: managers might overcome this by giving extra support to these staff and by putting in reward systems for correct decisions. There should not be a culture of blame: punishing staff for making wrong decisions is a sure way of ending up with staff who make no decisions at all, which is of course the worst outcome. Problems arise from the following areas:

1 When the empowerment is taken away as soon as the most important and interesting decisions have been made.

2 When the parameters are not clear, so that employees become afraid of making wrong decisions.

3 When communication is poor, both between managers and staff and within the staff teams.

When setting parameters, clear guidelines should be given: at the same time staff should not be overly burdened with fixed rules, because the whole point of empowerment is to enable staff members to act when something unexpected occurs. If all the possible circumstances could be outlined in advance, presumably they could be prevented from happening.

Murphy (2001) points out that empowerment does not always benefit employees. Many find it threatening, and others see it as a way for management to abdicate responsibility without paying the staff any extra for doing what they see as a management job. Staff who become alienated from the process (either because they feel they have been given extra responsibility without being given extra pay, or because the empowerment is too restricted to be of any use) may act in ways which are detrimental to the firm or to customer relations. For example, an employee might be over-generous to a favourite customer, or neglect a customer who is regarded as a nuisance.

Here is a checklist for successful empowerment of employees:

1 Employees need to be selected, trained and nurtured with empowerment in mind.

2 Employees should be given clear guidelines without being bound by rules which cannot, in any case, cover every eventuality.

3 Empowerment works best when combined with a team approach: the support of other members of the team offers invaluable reassurance.

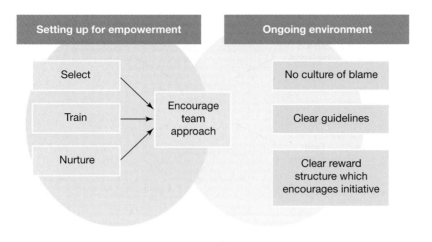

Figure 22.6
Successful empowerment

4 Rewards must reflect the contribution the employee makes.

5 There should not be a culture of blame. Failure should be seen as an opportunity to learn, not as a matter for punishment.

The concept of empowerment implies that power is being devolved from senior managers to junior staff: this may be unhelpful. It may be better to think of empowerment as being about encouraging staff to use their initiative: it does, in any case, require skilful management.

Team-building is itself a marketing task. Individual contributions to the team's efforts are almost always determined by the needs of the individual employee – the need for promotion, for personal development, for job satisfaction or for the esteem of the group (Cummings 1981). Successful teams need shared objectives, preferably agreed within the group rather than imposed from outside. Belbin (1981) suggests that teams should be able to perform the following tasks between them:

1 Create useful ideas.

2 Analyse problems effectively.

3 Get things done.

4 Communicate effectively.

5 Have leadership qualities.

6 Evaluate problems and options logically.

7 Handle technical aspects of the job.

8 Control their work.

9 Report back effectively either verbally or in writing.

Leaders should be able to shape and share a vision which gives point to the work of others (Handy 1989).

Process

A process is a series of actions taken in order to convert inputs to something of greater value (Finlay 2000). If the process does not create greater value, it is neither efficient nor effective: a dysfunctional process can actually reduce value. For example, a chef might take basic ingredients such as flour, eggs, apples and so forth and create a pie, adding to the value of the ingredients. A great chef can take the same ingredients and create a work of art: a bad chef might take the already-valuable ingredients and create an inedible mess.

Figure 22.7

Development processes

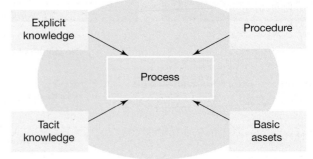

In marketing, every process combines the following basic resources:

1 *Basic assets*. These are the tangible and intangible assets of the business: they appear on the balance sheet, and include tangible assets such as plant and equipment, cash in hand, work in progress, buildings, and fixtures and fittings. Intangible assets include the reputation of the firm, the reputation of its brands, and a factor which accountants call 'goodwill', which acts as a catch-all for any other intangible assets.

2 *Explicit knowledge*. This is knowledge which can be written down or otherwise recorded. It includes patents, market research, customer databases and so forth.

3 *Tacit knowledge*. This is knowledge which is difficult or impossible to write down, because it resides mainly in the heads of employees. Skilled workers or professionals within the firm may have industry-specific skills which cannot easily be replaced. Consider a restaurant which intends to specialise in Tibetan food: finding a Tibetan chef might be a difficult task if the existing chef decides to leave. Equally, a skilled buyer or corporate lawyer would be equally difficult to replace.

4 *Procedure*. This is the mechanism by which the basic assets, explicit knowledge and tacit knowledge are brought together to create a process.

Procedure is often mistaken for process, but in fact the two differ: a good procedure which lacks the necessary staff skills will not produce an effective process, for example. Unfortunately, because procedure is easy for management to change, it is the element which changes most often. Changing the procedure means that staff have to readjust and reorder their knowledge, so there is inevitable disruption to the process and wasted time and effort.

When processes are linked together to deliver a set of benefits to customers, they become part of the firm's overall capability. A capability should be more than the sum of the individual processes, but this will not happen if the processes are not linked correctly or if they are mutually damaging in some way (Stalk, Evans and Shulman 1992).

Talking Point

Surely one of the problems companies have is controlling the processes? Employees cut corners, figure out new ways to do things, and try to make things easier for themselves and (sometimes) the customers as well. Not to mention that middle managers are actually expected to change things and adapt to changing circumstances.

If so, how can processes ever realistically be combined to create capabilities? Or are we actually saying that the ability to create and adapt is also part of a process, and consequently part of a capability the firm has?

In services markets, the consumers can sometimes be seen as a co-producer of the service. For example, live theatre clearly has serious drawbacks over television: it cannot hope to provide the same level of special effects and scenes, and the actors' performances may not always be perfect (whereas on TV an imperfect performance is simply re-shot). Additionally, going to the theatre involves booking seats, going out in the cold and finding one's way to the theatre, sitting in what are often uncomfortable seats, not being able to have a drink or a snack during the performance and not being able to press the pause button. The theatre does not allow one to change channels if the play is boring, it does not allow one to turn up the volume if the actors are speaking too quietly, and it does not allow one to watch the play wearing a dressing-gown. For these people pay for a ticket – what is the attraction? The main attraction is that there is an atmosphere in the theatre generated by the presence of an audience – the other consumers. A half-empty theatre seems bleak: a theatre full of people responding to the show helps to generate a response in the person watching the play.

Developing services processes

As with any other question in marketing, the starting point for developing a service process is the customers' needs. In some cases the needs can be presented as a hierarchy – for example, an aircraft manufacturer may not require new engines to be delivered urgently, but probably would need spare parts to be delivered quickly, as a grounded aircraft is an expensive item. The aero engine manufacturer would therefore see the supply of engines as being less important than the supply of spare parts, and would therefore seek to ensure that the stock of spares is kept up to an appropriate level even if this delayed the completion of new engines.

The atmosphere at a live concert is part of the product.

Service processes fall into three general categories:

1 *Before-sales service processes.* These might include helpful sales staff, readily available information, availability of samples and availability of supplies.

2 *During-sales processes.* These might include progress-chasing of orders, prompt and reliable delivery and helpful delivery staff.

3 *After-sales processes.* Courtesy calls, prompt attention to complaints, warranties and service agreements would all be after-sales services.

These processes all involve human interaction, so they all provide opportunities to improve customer loyalty. Unfortunately, they are also easy to copy, and not very difficult to exceed, so it may be difficult to maintain competitive advantage. Also, there is a trade-off between service level and cost: some firms (as we saw in Chapter 21) have been successful by cutting back dramatically on service and reducing prices accordingly. Retailers, low-cost airlines, and some restaurants offer minimal service, but have streamlined processes which reduce cost and deliver the core product efficiently. In some cases, the streamlined process might actually be preferable to the more staff-intensive process it replaces – many people find that booking flights on the Internet is a great deal easier than going through a travel agent.

Setting the right level of service can therefore be a source of competitive advantage. The emphasis here is on setting the right level – too high a level of service and the price will have to rise or the profits will have to fall. At too low a level, many customers will go elsewhere. Many firms still try to provide a high level of service for a low price – often at the expense of their employees – but this can only be done by shaving profits or otherwise acting in ways which reduce longer-term competitiveness. Note that segmentation still applies – some people are happy to pay for an enhanced service, while others prefer to buy the cheapest. Indeed, individuals often shift between the two levels, depending on the occasion – a couple going out for their 25th wedding anniversary dinner will not eat at the same restaurant they might go to for a quick lunch during the working week.

Processes can be considered as structural elements which can be used to deliver a strategic position. A process-orientated approach to strategy involves the following steps (Shostack 1987):

1 Break down the process into logical steps to make control easier.

2 Take the more variable processes into account: variability leads to different outcomes at different times, because of variations in the judgement of the people delivering the service, because of human error or because of customer choice. Naturally this problem is made worse by staff empowerment, especially if the boundaries are not clearly drawn.

3 Set tolerance standards which recognise that service processes do not always run smoothly, but rather function within a performance band. For example, it would be uneconomic (if not outright impossible) to ensure that no-one queues for longer than two minutes in a supermarket, but it should be possible to set a target such as 95 per cent of customers queuing for less than two minutes.

Service processes have aspects of both complexity and divergence. Complexity is about the number of stages the process has to go through and the number of separate processes involved: divergence is about the variability of the stages and the consequent variability of the outcomes.

To illustrate, an airline is an example of a complex service. Several hundred different tasks need to be undertaken and dozens of entirely separate service processes need to be coordinated for the passengers to reach their destinations. First, a travel agent needs to sell the ticket, which means ensuring that the passenger is on the right plane at the right time, leaving from the right airport and arriving at the right airport. Second, the aircraft needs to be correctly serviced and fuelled – services often carried out by separate companies. Food for the passengers needs to be provided by yet another service company, both airports (and any intermediate airports, if the journey is a long one) need to be prepared to handle the aircraft and its passengers, and several air traffic control agencies in different countries need to become involved. Alcoholic drinks, in-flight entertainment, in-flight magazines, and (on scheduled aircraft) in-flight packs of earplugs, headrests, eyeshades and so forth also need to be provided. Even at the airports several companies will be involved in the process – airport caterers, bookstores, travel goods shops, duty-free shops, baggage handlers, car parks, taxi firms and bus companies.

On the other hand, the service is not very divergent. Apart from the differences between flying economy, business-class or first-class the experience is much the same for all passengers. Caterers go to great efforts to ensure that all meals are standardised, flight attendants go to equal efforts to treat everyone with the same degree of formality and friendliness (and of course are in uniform), and obviously all the passengers depart from, and arrive at, the same airports. The entire process is so formulaic that frequent flyers find

Figure 22.8

Process-orientated approach to strategy

| Break down the process into logical steps | → | Take account of the more variable processes | → | Set appropriate tolerance standards |

	High divergence	Low divergence
High complexity	Unstable, unreliable, high-cost service	Stable, reliable, high-cost service
Low complexity	Variable, customised, simple to provide service	Simple, reliable, easily provided, cheap service

Figure 22.9

Complexity vs divergence

it difficult to remember which airline they are flying with, because each one treats its customers virtually identically.

By contrast, hairdressers exhibit almost exactly the opposite characteristics. In most hair salons the client will only be attended by one or two of the staff, in a process which does not involve any other companies apart from the salon's suppliers of hair products, electricity and so forth. The end result, however, varies considerably – if the salon is any good, each customer is dealt with as an individual and receives an individual hairstyle based on the client's physical features, age, lifestyle and so forth. On the other hand, things can go wrong more often in a hairdressing salon than on an aeroplane – there are perhaps too many variables in the equation, not least of which is the characteristics of the client's hair.

A hairdressing salon represents a process which is divergent but not complex. Most services fall somewhere between airlines and hairdressing, but the complexity and divergence of the service can often be adjusted to establish a competitive position. The possible effects of adjusting these factors are as follows:

- Reducing divergence will reduce costs, improve productivity and make distribution easier. A typical example would be a fast-food restaurant, which offers a limited menu of standardised food at low cost.

- Increased divergence allows greater customisation, greater flexibility, and (usually) premium pricing. High divergency is found among niche businesses and small, flexible businesses such as bespoke tailors.

- Reduced complexity usually means specialising in a basic, no-frills service offered by one firm, offering the core benefits of the product.

- Increased complexity increases customer choice by offering a wider range of products, but it also offers a wider range of separate features within the main product on offer. An example might be a computer retailer which offers free delivery, onsite maintenance and online technical support: each of these separate processes adds to the core service of selling the computer, and each is almost certainly offered by a company other than the retailer through a totally separate service process.

Low and high complexity may not always be apparent from the consumer's viewpoint, however. Divergence will always be apparent, because it is the degree to which the outcomes vary for each consumer.

Physical Evidence

The intangibility of most of the benefits of a service means that consumers do not have any evidence that the service ever took place. The evidence might be useful to show to other people (a certificate from a training course, a life insurance policy to show to a

Marketing in Practice
Vidal Sassoon

At the beginning of the 1960s Britain was a dynamic place. Recovered from the Second World War, prosperous and with a large younger generation of war babies (now in their teens and early twenties), the country was full of new ideas. One of the areas in which Britain was booming was in fashion – and hairdressing was no exception.

A young hairdresser called Vidal Sassoon was about to revolutionise thinking in the hair business. Before Sassoon, the client was queen: hairdressers did clients' hair exactly in the way they were told to, hardly even daring to offer advice. Hair was typically curled and bouffed to create almost hat-like effects. Sassoon changed all that. He began by taking an idea from the clothing industry – that the cut is everything. Sassoon developed an entirely new way of cutting hair, using fingers and scissors rather than combs, razors and scissors. Haircuts became precise, and hairstyles became geometrical – Sassoon did not use hair lacquer, he simply allowed the hair to fall naturally, perhaps blow-drying it to create movement without using hair rollers and permanent waves.

The second innovation on Sassoon's part was that he would not follow orders from the clients. At first sight, this flies in the face of customer centrality, but Sassoon's argument was that he was the expert in hairdressing, and therefore he was in the best position to decide what style would suit the customer and how the look would be achieved. He also offered only a small range of hairstyles – almost in the same way as clothes designers offer collections. The outcome of a visit to a Sassoon salon was, and still is, a fairly standardised 'look' which others can recognise as a Sassoon cut. By limiting divergence, Sassoon established a brand.

Sassoon quickly became *the* hairdresser for the Swinging Sixties, and indeed continues to set the pace for others even to this day. The Sixties Baby Boomers have now moved on into wheezy middle age, but a new generation of young hairstylists have picked up the Sassoon challenge, and Vidal Sassoon salons, hair care products, and (importantly) training schools for hairdressers are found throughout the world. Not bad for a poor young boy from the East End of London.

© Andrew Hamilton / Alamy

bank), or it might be simply something to act as a reminder of the pleasure the consumer obtained from the service (a souvenir of a holiday, a menu from a restaurant, a travel kit from an airline). Physical evidence might also be used as a way of assessing the quality of a product before committing to a purchase (the bank branch's décor, or the menu in the window of a restaurant).

Talking Point

It's commonly said that you can't judge a book by the cover – yet apparently we are expected to believe that we can judge a bank by its décor. Are we really as naïve as that? Do people seriously think that reading a restaurant menu gives any idea of the quality of the food?

There again, what else do we have to go on? We can hardly go into the restaurant and taste the food first! Maybe restaurants should try this as an experiment – let people have a small taste of the food before they commit to buying a meal. This is, after all, what happens in Spain, in many tapas bars.

Some people might think that banks would be better spending their money on reducing their charges or improving their service – but the evidence is that having a smart interior really does affect people's decisions about where to bank. So maybe we really *are* judging the book by the cover!

In some cases the physical element of the product itself is sufficient to act as physical evidence. A meal in a restaurant fulfils this: the food, the surroundings, the quality of the crockery and cutlery all convey evidence about the quality of the experience, even though the greater part of the bill will be absorbed by the chef's time in cooking the food and the waiter's time in delivering it (not to mention the washing up). In other cases, for example life insurance or other financial services, the physical evidence is likely to be much less or lacking altogether, in which case the firm may need to produce something which will provide evidence, for example a glossy brochure or policy document. For practical and legal purposes, most insurance documents could be printed on one or two sheets of paper, but for marketing purposes the document needs to be much more substantial.

There are four generic ways to add value through physical evidence:

1 Create physical evidence which increases loyalty.
2 Use physical evidence to enhance brand image.
3 Use physical evidence which has an intrinsic value of its own, e.g. a free gift.
4 Create physical evidence which leads to further sales.

Airlines use their frequent-flyer programmes to increase loyalty: the physical evidence of the flights taken is the regular newsletter which is sent out and the plastic card which the frequent flyer uses to gain access to the executive lounges at airports en route. Some airlines (KLM for example) also issue special plastic baggage tags which let the baggage handlers know that they are dealing with a very important suitcase: what effect this has on the baggage handlers is debatable, but the effect for the customer is a feeling of importance. At each level of membership of KLM's frequent-flyer programme the colour of the card changes, as do the benefits to which the holder is entitled. These physical elements of the service are intended to encourage the customer to fly more often with KLM: failure to fly a set number of

Figure 22.10

Adding value through physical evidence

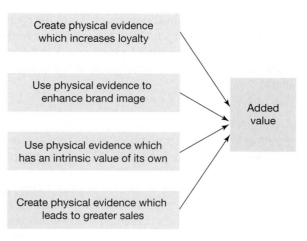

times a year with the airline will result in a downgrade to a lower level. An intangible benefit of membership for the customer is the occasional free flight – membership points can be exchanged for free flights at a set rate per distance travelled, or for upgrades into business class.

Brand image can be enhanced by using physical evidence which fits in with the brand's essential qualities. For example, an insurance company which wishes to convey a solid, respectable image will produce a glossy policy document full of high-flown legal phrases and reassuring photographs of solid corporate headquarters. A company aiming to convey a more down-to-earth, welcoming image might produce a policy couched in simple language, with photographs of smiling staff and policyholders. Physical evidence need not always be up-market: most low-cost airlines emphasise the cost-cutting aspects of their businesses by requiring passengers to print off their own tickets on their computers, or by having no tickets at all. This is about as basic as physical evidence can get, but it does emphasise the point that the airline does not waste passengers' money on anything which is not absolutely necessary.

Physical evidence which has an intrinsic value of its own would include free gifts: this is a common ploy in the financial services industry. Clocks, pen sets, DVD players, radio alarm clocks and so forth are often given out to people who take out insurance policies or pension plans. Clearly very few people would take out an insurance policy simply to win a carriage clock, but the existence of the clock on the policyholder's mantelpiece is good evidence of the existence of the policy.

Physical evidence which leads to further business might include reminder cards sent out by garages to let drivers know that their cars are due for a service. Dentists, opticians, hairdressers and some hospitals use reminders like this to tell people they need check-ups: the physical evidence of the previous visit serves to generate more business. Some business gifts fulfil a similar function: a desk calendar, notepad or pen given away at the conclusion of a sale may serve as a reminder when a future need arises.

Marketing services is far from straightforward: the intangibility of the service naturally affects people's perceptions, and (in the short term, at least) the risks attached are higher. People therefore use a number of surrogates – for example, people tend to trust firms which have been around for a long time (Desai, Kalra and Murthi 2008) or which contribute to the wider community and invest in good marketing communications (Gray 2006). In the long run, though, services do form the greater part of 21st century marketing, and are therefore of increasing importance to marketers.

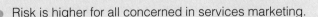

Summary

Although people, process and physical evidence are often associated with service industries, the fact is that every product involves some service element. Business is not conducted by companies: it is conducted between human beings, carrying out processes which improve the lives of other human beings. In some cases, they also need to provide some kind of proof that the service has been carried out – hence the physical evidence aspect.

The key points from this chapter are as follows:

- Service industries often command greater loyalty than do industries which deal with physical products. This is because of the higher risk to the consumer of buying services.
- Services purchasing follows a somewhat different route from purchasing physical products.
- Risk is higher for all concerned in services marketing.
- There will always be some failures in providing services.
- For empowerment to work there should be clear guidelines, a no-blame culture and clear rewards for success.
- Process combines basic assets, explicit knowledge, tacit knowledge and procedure.
- Consumers can be seen as co-producers of services in many cases.
- Services are characterised in two dimensions: complexity and diversity.
- Physical evidence can be used to increase loyalty, enhance brand image, increase value and increase future sales.

Chapter review questions

1 What mechanisms might a restaurant chain use to improve customer loyalty?

2 What are the main factors in risk for customers of service firms?

3 What are the main differences between services and physical products?

4 What are the key differences between contactors, modifiers, influencers and isolateds?

5 How might physical evidence be used to increase loyalty?

6 How might improved service provision help sales of physical products?

7 What are the advantages of empowering staff?

8 What differences in decision-making might consumers exhibit when purchasing services?

9 How might a firm minimise the effects of variability in service provision?

10 What factors combine to produce service process?

Preview case revisited
Thomas Cook

The travel industry has, of course, moved on greatly since the 19th century. Foreign travel is now commonplace, and the majority of British people holiday in other countries – few Brits are without a passport. Thomas Cook has also gone through a number of changes – nationalised in 1948 as part of the British Railways nationalisation, the company returned to private ownership in 1972 and was bought up by Westdeutsche Landesbank in 1992. The company decided to concentrate on long-haul package holidays in the 1980s, leaving the short-haul package holiday market altogether in 1988. The greater profitability of long-haul holidays was evident, as was the cut-throat nature of the price-conscious short-haul market. However, in 1996 Thomas Cook bought out Sunworld, a short-haul package company, and returned to the market.

The Internet has changed the market dramatically – more and more people book their holidays independently, and as people are becoming more used to foreign travel (and less afraid of it) the days of the package tour are numbered. Proposed legislation in the UK to provide similar protection to independent travellers as already exists for package holidaymakers may remove one of the main advantages of the package holiday – its security in the event of something going wrong, for example an airline going bankrupt.

As of 2008, Thomas Cook UK and Ireland is part of Thomas Cook PLC, a major company formed from the merger of Thomas Cook and MyTravel. This company owns some of the best-known travel brands in the UK: Club 18–30, Airtours, Cresta, CruiseThomasCook, Sunset, Sunworld Holidays and Tradewinds, to name but a few. The group employs a total of 30 000 staff, has 3000 offices, operates 97 aircraft and has a £9 billion annual turnover.

Thomas Cook, were he to return, might feel justly proud of the travel empire that has grown up from his first temperance excursions. On the other hand, it is a sad reflection that much of the business is devoted to Brits going abroad for sunshine and cheap alcohol – the man who ran trips to temperance meetings simply for the love of it and to help his fellow man might well be despondent at having his name attached to Club 18–30 holidays.

Case study
Capita

Government departments are always under pressure to reduce costs, and one of their main costs is, of course, staff. Public sector workers are expensive to employ – apart from their salaries, which are now often equal to or higher than those paid for equivalent work in the private sector, public employees have negotiated a wide range of fringe benefits. Pensions, generous sick pay schemes, maternity benefits and enhanced job security are all 'perks' of working for the Government. Originally intended to compensate for low salaries, these benefits have proved to be a major cost for national government and local authorities in the UK – with the result that outsourcing many services makes sense, since the company contracted to deliver the service takes on the problem of staffing and does not have the history of employee fringe benefits that the public sector has.

This situation became particularly interesting for the public sector during the 1980s, when the Thatcher Government sought to overturn the old systems of secure employment for public sector workers. Departments were encouraged to outsource as much as possible, and most departments were targeted to show a 'profit' and in fact some (such as Companies House, the record-keeping department for limited companies) were expected to become self-financing. Into this new climate for public services stepped Capita.

Capita was founded in 1984, as a subdivision of CIPFA (the Chartered Institute of Public Finance and Accountancy). At the time, it comprised two people, but rapid growth meant that, in 1987, it was bought out by its management (with the help of venture capital financing) and became a private company. The new company was obviously in the right place at the right time, because it grew from 33 people to over 2000 in the following 20 years, and is now a FTSE 100 company, one of the select few to be used to gauge the health of the UK economy.

Capita provides outsourcing services under eight headings: local government, central government, education, transport, health, life and pensions, insurance and other private sector organisations. Capita does not limit itself exclusively to the public sector – although circumstances have combined to make the public sector the company's biggest market. For example, Capita administers the BBC's licence fees, a contract the company won from the Post Office: London's congestion charging is run by Capita, as is the Criminal Records Bureau and the Education Maintenance Allowance for the Learning and Skills Council.

Of course, things do not always run smoothly. In 2002, the Government introduced mandatory criminal record checks for anyone working with children. Capita, as the company running the Criminal Records Bureau, was inundated with requests for checks from schools throughout the country. At the same time, Estelle Morris, the Secretary of State for Education, put in some last-minute changes in the legislation that threw the system into chaos. In some places the start of the academic year had to be postponed as teachers, some of whom had been working with children for years, were banned from teaching until their CRB checks were delivered.

Capita's client list is extensive – Birmingham City Council, Co-Operative Insurance, Zurich Insurance, Harrow Council, the Health and Safety Executive, Salford Council and many more. The company turns over more than £2 billion per annum, with pre-tax profits around £250 million. Capita offers permanent services (such as the BBC licence fee contract) or can handle one-off, time-limited situations (Capita administered the miners' personal injury liability claims for the Department of Trade and Industry). Around one-fifth of the company's business comes from local government,

13 per cent from education and 12 per cent from central government. Insurance services account for a further 10 per cent of the company's turnover, and the related life and pensions industry accounts for a further 11 per cent.

What Capita offers is economies of scale. The company has an army of administrators and another army of call-centre staff – it can easily switch people around from one contract to another, making better use of people's time and evening-out peaks and troughs in demand. The company's computer capacity is equally impressive, and can easily cope with the very large number of individual accounts which characterise insurance services, congestion charging and other large contracts. Probably most people in the UK feature somewhere in Capita's databases, and many will feature several times – an interesting thought when one considers privacy and confidentiality issues.

Whatever future changes might happen in Government, Capita is now so well-established in both the private and public sectors that the company is unlikely to suffer major financial setbacks or even competitive threats. The main problem Capita might fear is that a computer glitch damages its databases or renders it unable to deliver on its promises – this could result in a mass withdrawal on the part of its customers. On the other hand, there are few other places for the customers to go, once they have committed to Capita.

Questions

1 What is the role of process in Capita's service provision?

2 What problems might a local Government department face when using Capita to provide services on their behalf?

3 How might Capita have sought to resolve the service failure over the CRB checks on teachers?

4 How might economies of scale manifest themselves in provision of services?

5 What problems regarding their own staffing might Capita experience?

References

Belbin, R.M. (1981): *Management Teams: Why They Succeed or Fail* (London: Heinemann).

Cummings, T.G. (1981): Designing effective work groups. In P.C. Nystrom and W.H. Starbuck, *Handbook of Organisational Design* (Oxford University Press).

Desai, P.S., Kalra, A. and Murthi, B.P.S. (2008): When old is gold: the role of business longevity in risky situations. *Journal of Marketing* **22**(1), 95–107.

Devlin, J.F. (2007): Complex services and choice criteria: an example from the life assurance market. *Journal of Marketing Management* **23**(7/8), 631–50.

Finlay, P. (2000): *Strategic Management: An Introduction to Business and Corporate Strategy* (Harlow: Financial Times Prentice Hall).

Gray, B.J. (2006): Benchmarking services branding practices. *Journal of Marketing Management* **22**(7/8), 717–58.

Gruber, T., Szmigin, I. and Voss, R. (2006): The desired qualities of customer contact employees in complaint-handling encounters. *Journal of Marketing Management* **22**(5/6), 619–42.

Handy, C. (1989): *The Age of Unreason* (London: Hutchinson).

Judd, V.C. (1987): Differentiate with the fifth P. *Industrial Marketing Management* **16**, 241–7.

Knox, S. and Freeman, C. (2006): Measuring and managing employer brand image in the service industry. *Journal of Marketing Management* **18**(7/8), 695–716.

Maxham III, J.G. and Netemeyer, R.G. (2003): Firms reap what they sow: the effect of shared values and perceived organisational justice on customers' evaluation of complaint handling. *Journal of Marketing* **67**(1), 46–62.

Munoz, C.L., Wood, N.T. and Solomon, M.R. (2006): Real or blarney? A cross-cultural investigation of the perceived authenticity of Irish pubs. *Journal of Consumer Behaviour* **5**(3), 222–34.

Murphy, J.A. (2001): *The Lifebelt: The Definitive Guide to Managing Customer Retention* (Chichester: John Wiley).

Rasmusson, E. (1997): Winning back angry customers. *Sales and Marketing Management* (October), 131.

Reichheld, F.F. and Sasser, W.E. Jr. (1990): Zero defections, quality comes to services. *Harvard Business Review* (September–October), 105–11.

Roberts, K., Varki, S. and Brodie, R. (2003): Measuring the quality of relationships in consumer services: an empirical study. *European Journal of Marketing* **37**(1/2), 169–96.

Shostack, G.L. (1987): Service positioning through structural change. *Journal of Marketing* **51** (January), 34–43.

Stalk, G., Evans, P. and Shulman, L. (1992): Competing on capabilities. *Harvard Business Review* (March–April).

Further reading

Palmer, A. (2004): *Principles of Services Marketing* (Maidenhead: McGraw-Hill) is a well established, readable and comprehensive textbook. Now in its fourth edition, this book has become established as the leading text in the field.

Zeithaml, V. and Bitner, M.J. (2002): *Services Marketing* (Mason, OH: McGraw Hill) is an American text with a good pedigree. Zeithaml and Bitner almost invented services marketing between them, so the text is certainly definitive, but of course uses American examples and contexts which are not always familiar to non-Americans.

Glossary

Above the line advertising for which the advertising agency obtains a commission from the media.

Achievers People who seek respect by buying appropriate products.

ACORN A geographical segmentation method: A Classification Of Residential Neighbourhoods.

Actual state The situation the individual is currently experiencing.

Adapter A company which produces new products, superior to those produced by the market leader.

Advertising A paid message inserted in a medium.

Advertising research Investigations into the effectiveness and potential effectiveness of marketing communications.

Advertorials Advertisements which are written in the style of editorials (not to be confused with press releases).

Affect The emotional component of attitude.

Affective Relating to emotional factors.

Aftermarket See MRO.

Aggressive Someone who usually moves against people and controls fear and emotions in a quest for success, prestige and admiration.

Alliteration Using similar sounds in a slogan to aid memory.

Ambient advertising Advertising which becomes part of the environment.

Ambiguity The degree to which stimuli can be interpreted in different ways.

Anthropology The study of culture.

Aspirational groups Groups the individual would like to be a member of.

Associative group A group to which one would like to belong.

Assonance Repetition of vowels in a slogan to aid memory.

Assortment adjustment Changing the proportions of products owned in order to increase satisfaction.

Assortment depletion Using up resources or wearing out products.

Attitude A learned tendency to respond in a consistent manner to a specific stimulus or object.

Audience fade-out The tendency for TV viewers to leave the room or lose concentration when the commercial breaks occur.

Automatic group/category group A group to which one belongs by virtue of birth.

Backward conditioning The unconditioned stimulus comes before the conditioned stimulus.

Banners Advertising messages on websites.

Barrier to entry A factor which prevents a firm from entering a specific market.

Belief An understanding that an object possesses a particular attribute.

Belongers People who seek to join groups in society.

Below the line Promotional tools for which the advertising agency charges the client.

Benchmarking Setting performance parameters by comparing performance with that of the best of the competing firms.

Bias Errors in research results caused by failures in the research design or sampling method.

Boundary scanning The practice of monitoring the interfaces between the firm and its publics.

Boycott To avoid buying a company's products.

Brainstorming Generating new product ideas by group discussion.

Brand The focus of marketing activities.

Brand audit The process of determining whether a specific brand is being marketed effectively.

Brokers Intermediaries who bring buyers and sellers together but do not themselves handle goods.

Buyback An agreement on the part of a supplier to accept payment in finished products.

Buyer The person who negotiates the purchase.

Cash cow A product with a large share of a mature market.

Catalogue showrooms Retailers which have a bricks-and-mortar presence but which use a brochure to display the goods rather than display shelves.

Categorical plan An approach to valuing suppliers based on salient performance factors.

Categorisation Filing information alongside similar information in the memory.

Central route Cognitive approach to changing behaviour.

Chunking The mental process whereby information is stored alongside connected information.

Classical conditioning The instilling of automatic responses in an individual by repetition of stimulus and reward.

Cloner A company which produces copies of products sold by the market leader.

Closed questions Enquiries to which there will only be a small range of possible answers, usually only yes or no.

Closing techniques Those questions and behaviours which end the sales presentation and elicit a decision from the buyer.

Clutter Excessive advertising.

Coercive power Potential for control derived from the ability to punish the other party.

Cognition The rational component of attitude.

Cognitive Relating to rational factors.

Cognitive effort The degree of effort the consumer is prepared to put into thinking about the product offering

Cognitive structure The way information is fitted into the existing knowledge.

Commission Performance-related payments made to salespeople.

Comparative advantage The degree to which one country is better at producing certain goods than another.

Compatibility The degree to which a product fits into the adopter's life.

Compensatory Of a heuristic, one which allows negative features to be offset against positive features.

Competitor orientation The belief that corporate success comes from understanding competitors.

Complexity The degree to which the product is difficult to understand.

Compliant Someone who moves towards people, has goodness, sympathy, love, unselfishness and humility.

Compulsive consumption An obsessive need to buy and use products.

Conation Intended behaviour.

Concept testing A market research exercise in which feedback is obtained on the basic idea for a new product.

Concessionaires Firms which rent space in department stores, paying a rental and usually a commission on sales.

Conclusive research Investigations intended to provide answers to problems.

Conditioned response A response which results from exposure to a conditioned stimulus.

Conditioned stimulus A stimulus offered at the same time as an unconditioned stimulus, with the intention of creating an artificial association between it and the unconditioned response.

Conditions Situations which make a sale impossible.

Confidentiality agreement A contract between two parties containing clauses to the effect that each will keep the other's secrets.

Confirming houses An organisation which handles the mechanics of exporting and importing on behalf of manufacturers or buyers.

Conjunctive Heuristics which are considered together.

Connotative Having the same meaning for everybody.

Consideration set The group of products which might be capable of meeting a need.

Consumer One who obtains the benefits from a product.

Consumerism The set of organised activities intended to promote the needs of the consumer against those of the firm.

Contactors Staff who have daily contact with customers.

Continuous innovation Incremental improvements in an existing product.

Convenience sample Selecting respondents by availability, without regard to the characteristics of the respondents.

Convenience stores Stores which are located in residential areas and which stock frequently purchased items.

Core competences The central, most important aspects of the company's abilities.

Corporate reputation The overall image of the organisation.

Cost-plus pricing Setting prices by calculating the outlay on producing the items, and adding on a profit margin.

Cost-ratio plan A method of evaluating suppliers based on the costs of doing business with them.

Counterpurchase An agreement on the part of a supplier to accept payment in kind, or to spend the proceeds of the sale in the country in which the sale is made.

Countertrading Bartering of goods in international markets.

Cross-selling Selling new product lines to an existing customer.

Cue An external trigger which encourages learning.

Culture The set of shared beliefs and behaviours common to an identifiable group of people.

Customary price The price a product has always been sold for.

Customer One who decides on payment for a product.

Customer intimacy The degree to which a firm is close to its customers.

Customer orientation The belief that corporate success comes from understanding and meeting customer needs.

Customer research Investigations into the behaviour of purchasers of the product.

Customer size specialist A company which specialises in dealing with customers of a specific size.

Customer-specified innovation New product ideas which are generated by customers.

Cut-off A filtering device which involves deciding the outer limits of acceptability for a given product's chatracteristics.

Database marketing Using a list of customers or potential customers stored on a computer to drive the marketing effort.

Decider The person who has the power to agree a purchase.

Decision tree A diagrammatic representation of the route a manager must take to reach a decision.

Decision-making unit A group of people who, between them, decide on purchases.

Del credere agents Intermediaries who do not take title to the goods, but who do accept the credit risk from customers.

Delphi A system of research under which opinions are sought iteratively from experts.

Demand pricing Calculating price according to what consumers are prepared to pay.

Demographics The study of the structure of the population.

Denotative Having a unique meaning for an individual.

Deontology The belief that actions can be judged independently of outcome.

Dependent variable The stimulus which is applied to generate a response.

Desired state The situation the individual wishes to be in.

Detached Someone who moves away from people, is self-sufficient and independent.

Dichotomous question An inquiry which can only be answered 'yes' or 'no'.

Differentiation Factors which distinguish one product from another.

Direct-response advertising Messages inserted in a medium with the intention of generating a dialogue with potential consumers.

Direct response A type of advertising campaign which contains a method for the consumer to contact the supplier immediately and directly.

Discontinuous innovation A new product which significantly changes consumers' lifestyles.

Discount sheds Out-of-town stores offering a wide range of products at low prices.

Discounters Retailers that carry a limited range of stock at low prices.

Discrimination The ability to distinguish between similar stimuli.

Dissociative group A group to which one would not wish to belong.

Dissonance The emotional state created when expectations do not match with outcomes.

Distribution research Investigations into the effectiveness of different outlets for products.

Dodo A product with a small share of a shrinking market.

Dog A product with a small share of a mature market.

Dramaturgical analogy The view that life is essentially theatrical in nature.

Drive The force generated in an individual as a result of a felt need.

Dumping Disposing of products in a foreign market at prices below the cost of production.

Dynamically continuous innovation A product which is a substantial shift in technology but which does not change people's lives.

Eclectic All-encompassing, taking account of all factors.

Economic choice The inability to spend the same money twice.

Economics The study of supply and demand.

Economies of scale Cost savings resulting from large production runs.

Elaboration The structuring of the information within the brain, and adding to it from memory in order to form a coherent whole.

Elasticity of demand The degree to which people's propensity to buy a product is affected by price changes.

Empowerment Giving staff the ability to resolve customer problems without recourse to higher management.

End user The person or company who uses the product, without selling it on or converting it to something else.

End-of-pipe solution Cleaning up pollution after it has been created rather than re-engineering the process so that pollution is not produced.

End-use specialist A company specialising in customers who use the product in a specific way.

End-use specialist A firm which specialises in supplying all the needs of a specific group of customers.

Environment research Investigations into the external factors which impinge on the organisation's activities.

Environmental scanning Continuous monitoring of external factors which might impinge on the organisation's activities.

Ethics A set of rules for good behaviour.

Ethnicity Cultural background.

Ethnocentrism The belief that one's own culture is superior to others.

Experiment A research technique in which a controlled situation is used to determine consumer response to a given stimulus.

Exploratory research Investigations intended to identify problems.

Export agent A person or company that takes responsibility for organising the export of goods without taking title to the goods.

Export house An organisation which buys goods for sale abroad.

Extended problem-solving Non-routine purchasing behaviour.

Extension Increasing the number of products owned.

External environment Factors which operate outside the organisation.

External search Looking for information in places other than memory.

External validity A condition where a research exercise would generate the same results if it were repeated elsewhere.

Extinction The gradual weakening of conditioning over time.

Factors Intermediaries who hold stocks of product but do not take title to the goods.

Familiarity The degree to which an object is known.

Field research Investigations carried out in the marketplace.

Financial risk The danger of losing money as the result of a purchase.

First-time prospects Potential customers with whom the company has never done business before.

Focus group Respondents brought together to discuss a research question in a controlled and structured manner under the guidance of a researcher.

Focus strategy The practice of targeting a small segment of the market.

Foregrounding Bringing an advertising slogan to the forefront of customer's minds.

Formal group A group with a known, recorded membership list.

Formal structure The official relationships between members of an organisation.

Forward conditioning The conditioned stimulus comes before the unconditioned stimulus.

Franchising An agreement to use a firm's business methods and intellectual property in return for a fee and a royalty.

Frequency Number of times each consumer is exposed to the communication.

Functional risk The risk that a product or service will not provide the expected benefits.

Gatekeeper The person who controls the flow of information.

Generalisation The tendency for the individual to react in several ways to the conditioned stimulus.

Generally concerned One who believes that the environment is important, but does little to change his or her behaviour accordingly.

Geocentrism Viewing corporate activities in a global manner.

Geographical proximity The closeness of the market in physical terms.

Global customers Firms which are willing to purchase products outside their domestic markets and tend to have global control of purchasing from headquarters.

Globalisation The view of the world as a single market and single source of supply.

Goal An objective.

Green activist One who is proactive in espousing an environmentally friendly lifestyle.

Green customer One whose purchases are influenced by environmental concerns.

Green thinker One who believes in being environmentally friendly.

Grey market 1. Re-import of brands from markets where the prices are lower. 2. Older consumers.

Hedonic needs Needs which relate to the pleasurable aspects of ownership.

Heuristic A decision-making rule.

High-context culture A culture which is homogenous and has rigid rules.

Homophilous influence The love of being like everyone else.

House journal A medium for disseminating information within an organisation.

Icebreaker A statement or question used at the beginning of a sales presentation with the intention of establishing a rapport with the buyer.

Ideal self The person we wish we were.

Identifiers The major variables in segmentation which can be listed without carrying out extensive research.

Image The overall impression a company or brand has in the eyes of its publics.

Image building A type of campaign which is conducted for the purpose of conveying a specific perception of a product in the minds of customers.

Imitator A company which makes somewhat differentiated products which are similar to those produced by the market leader.

Import house An organisation which buys goods in from abroad.

Impulse purchases Purchases made without apparent conscious thought.

Independent variable The response resulting from a dependent variable.

Indifference curve A diagrammatic representation of the trade-offs people have between products.

Influencer The person who has the ability to sway the judgement of a decider.

Influencers Staff who can affect the way customers are treated, even though they have no direct access to them.

Infomercial A feature-length programme about a product.

Informal group A group which does not have a fixed membership list or known rules.

Informal structure The unofficial relationships between members of an organisation.

Infrastructure The physical resources available to the firm for logistical processes.

Initiator The person who first recognises a problem.

Inner directed Motivated by forces originating within the individual.

Innovation cost The expenditure of money and effort resulting from adopting a new product.

Inseparability In services, production and consumption occur at the same time.

Instrumentality The subjective capacity of the object to attain the value in question.

Intangibility The inability to touch a service.

Internal ad hoc data Information supplied by systems within the organisation for a specific purpose.

Internal continuous data Information supplied by systems within the organisation on a constant basis.

Internal environment Factors which operate within the organisation.

Internal marketing The practice of creating goodwill among employees.

Internal validity A condition where a research exercise provides evidence which supports what the exercise was intended to discover.

Intranet A computer-mediated system for internal communications within an organisation.

Involvement Emotional attachment to a product or brand.

Isolateds Staff who have no relationship with customers.

Judgement sample Selecting respondents according to criteria established by the researcher.

Junk mail Poorly-targeted direct mailings.

Key account A customer or potential customer with strategic importance to the firm.

Key-account manager Someone charged with the task of managing the relationship with a strategically important customer.

Law of primacy The law which states that early learning about an object will colour future experiences of the object and future interpretations of that experience.

Leads People who are prepared to hear what a salesperson has to say.

Least dependent person The individual with the most power in a group.

Legitimate power Potential for control derived from a legal or contractual position.

Lexicographic A hierarchy of heuristics.

Licensing An agreement to use a firm's intellectual property in exchange for a royalty.

Limited problem-solving Routine purchasing behaviour.

Liner A ship or aircraft which operates on a regular route at fixed times.

Livery Painting a public-transport vehicle in corporate colours or advertising.

Lobbying Making representations to politicians with the aim of changing legislation.

Logistics The coordination of the supply chain to achieve a seamless flow from raw materials through to the consumer.

Longitudinal study Research which is carried out over a lengthy time period.

Looking-glass self The way we think other people see us.

Low-context culture A culture which is heterogenous and has tolerant rules.

Loyalty The tendency to repeat purchase of a brand.

Macro environment Factors which affect all the firms in an industry.

Margin Gross profit calculated as a proportion of the price a product is sold for.

Market challenger A company which seeks to grow at the expense of the market leader.

Market follower A company which follows the lead of the main company in the market.

Market nicher A firm which is content with a small segment of the market.

Market research Investigations intended to improve knowledge about customers and competitors.

Market segment A group of people having similar needs.

Marketing information system Mechanisms for providing a constant flow of information about markets.

Marketing orientation The belief that corporate success comes from understanding the relationships in the market.

Marketing research Information gathering for the purpose of improving the organisation's effectiveness in the market.

Mark-up Gross profit calculated as a proportion of the price paid for an item.

Maturation The development of the organism over time.

Mechanics In sales promotion, the activities the customer must undertake.

Memory The mechanism by which learned information is stored.

Merchandisers A type of sales person who has the responsibility of establishing and maintaining in-store displays

Message intrigue The increased interest developed by ambiguous communications.

Metaphor A sign which relates to an object.

Micro environment Factors which only affect one firm.

Missionary A salesperson who does not sell directly, but who has the task of 'spreading the word' about a product to people who influence purchase.

Modified rebuy A repeat purchase where some changes have been made.

Modifiers Staff who have some contact with customers for specific purposes.

Monopolistic competition A situation in which one company exercises strong influence in the market, but other companies can still enter the market and compete effectively.

Monopoly A situation in which one company controls the market.

Mortality The tendency for respondents to disappear over time.

Motivation The force that moves an individual towards a specific set of solutions.

MRO Maintenance, repair and overhauling company.

Multibuys A sales promotion in which customers are offered extra packs of product when they buy one or more packs.

Multinational global customers Customers who source products globally, and also use the products globally.

Mystery shoppers A marketing research technique whereby the researcher pretends to be a customer.

Myths Heroic stories about a product.

Narrowcast Accurate targeting of audiences in broadcast media.

National global customers Customers who source products globally but only use them within their national borders.

Need A perceived lack of something.

New task A purchase which has no precedent.

Niche marketing Serving a small segment.

Non-compensatory Of a heuristic, one which does not allow a positive feature to offset a negative feature.

Non-shopping products Products which require little information search or decision-making.

Non-universal ownership Not owned by people who are not members of the group.

Normative compliance The pressure to conform to group norms of behaviour.

Novices Customers who have purchased the product for the first time within the last 90 days.

Objections Questions raised by a prospect in the course of a sales presentation.

Objective Not subject to bias from the individual.

Observability The degree to which the product can be seen by others.

Odd-even pricing Using '99c' or '95p' endings on prices.

OEM Original equipment manufacturer.

Oligopoly A situation in which a group of companies control the market between them.

Open questions Enquiries to which there might be a wide range of possible answers.

Operant conditioning The instilling of automatic responses via the active participation of the individual.

Optimum stimulation level The level at which the gap between the desired state and the actual state has not yet become unpleasant.

Organismic organisations Organisations which do not have a fixed structure: they adapt according to the task facing the organisation.

Outbound logistics Controlling the flow of product from the organisation to its customers.

Outer directed Taking one's cue from the behaviour of others.

Outshopping Shopping outside the area in which one lives.

Panel A permanently established group of research respondents.

Party plan A direct-marketing tool in which the salesperson holds private presentations for groups of friends in a private home.

Penetration pricing Setting low prices in an attempt to capture a large market share.

People The individuals involved in providing customer satisfaction.

Perceived cost of search The degree to which an individual believes that an information search will be too arduous or expensive.

Perception The process of building up a mental map of the world.

Perceptual map The individual's view of competing products.

Perfect competition A state of affairs where everyone in the market has perfect knowledge and no one buyer or seller can influence the market.

Peripheral route Affective approach to changing behaviour.

Perishability Services cannot be stockpiled.

Personal sources The means–end knowledge stored in an individual's memory.

Physical distribution The movement of products from producer to retailer and ultimately to the consumer.

Physical distribution Moving goods from the producer to the consumer along the value chain.

Physical evidence The tangible proof that a service has taken place.

Physical risk The danger of physical harm as the result of a purchase.

Piggy-backing Attaching one product to another for the purposes of sales promotion.

Place The location where the exchange takes place.

Polycentrism Viewing corporate activities as emanating from centres in a number of countries.

Polymorphism Bundling data and code to create an object

Pop-ups Advertising messages which appear on websites.

Positioning Placing the product in the appropriate location in the consumers' perceptual maps.

Post-purchase evaluation The process of deciding whether the outcome of a purchase has been appropriate or not.

Predatory pricing Pricing at extremely low levels (sometimes below the cost of production) with the intention of damaging competitors or forcing them to leave the market.

Preliminary research Investigations intended to outline the dimensions of a problem.

Presence website A website which is not interactive but directs customers to another medium.

Press releases News stories about the organisation.

Price The exchange that the customer makes in order to obtain a product.

Primary data Information collected first-hand for a specific purpose.

Primary group The group of people who are closest to the individual.

Primary research Research which is carried out from scratch for a specific project.

Private responses Complaints made to friends or family about a product or company.

Problem child A product with a small share of a growing market.

Process The set of activities which together produce customer satisfaction.

Procurement Obtaining goods to be used in production or running the organisation.

Product A bundle of benefits.

Product champion An individual who has or is given the role of guiding a new product through the development process.

Product differentiation A type of campaign which emphasises the differences between a a product and competing products.

Product life cycle The process of launch, growth, maturity and decline which products are thought to go through.

Product orientation The belief that corporate success comes from having the best product.

Product portfolio The range of goods offered by a firm.

Product research Investigations intended to generate knowledge which can be used to inform new product development.

Production orientation The belief that corporate success comes from efficient production.

Product-line pricing In circumstances where sales of one product are dependent on sales of another, calculating both prices to take account of the price of each product.

Project teams Groups of people with the responsibility for guiding products through the development process.

Projective technique A research method which invites respondents to say what they think another person might answer to a specific question or problem.

Promotion Marketing communications.

Prospects People who have a need for a product and the means to pay for it.

Psychological proximity The degree to which countries are culturally close to each other.

Psychology The study of thought processes.

Psychology of complication The desire to make one's life more complex and therefore more interesting.

Psychology of simplification The desire to make one's life simpler and therefore less demanding.

Psychosocial risk The danger of looking foolish as a result of a purchase.

Public relations The practice of creating goodwill towards an organisation.

Publics The groups of people with whom the organisation interacts.

Pull strategy Promoting to end users in order to 'pull' products through the distribution channel.

Push strategy Promoting to channel intermediaries in order to 'push' products through the distribution channel.

Qualitative data Information which cannot be expressed numerically.

Quantitative data Information which can be expressed numerically.

Quota sampling Selecting respondents according to a set of prearranged parameters.

Reach Number of potential consumers a communication reaches.

Real self The objective self that others observe.

Recession A situation in which gross national production falls for three consecutive months.

Redundancy In communications, sending a message by more than one route, to ensure a correct delivery.

Reference group A group from which one takes behavioural cues.

Referent power Potential for control derived from a position of authority.

Registration A system for protecting brand names.

Regression effect The tendency for extremes to move towards the middle in longitudinal studies.

Reinforcement Increasing the strength of learning by rewarding appropriate behaviour.

Relationship marketing The practice of concentrating on the lifetime value of customers rather than their value in the single transaction.

Relative advantage The degree to which a new product is better than the one it replaces.

Replenishment Replacing products which have been worn out or used up.

Research plan An outline of the steps which must be taken in gathering information systematically.

Reseller organisation A firm which buys goods in order to sell them on to other firms or consumers.

Response The reaction the consumer makes to the interaction between a drive and a cue.

Retention The stability of learned material over time.

Role The position one has in the group.

Rookie A new sales recruit.

Roughs Draft advertising materials produced for a client's approval.

Sales cycle The series of activities undertaken by salespeople.

Sales orientation The belief that corporate success comes from having proactive salespeople.

Sales presentation A structured interview in which a salesperson ascertains a customer's needs and offers a solution which will meet those needs.

Sales research Investigations into aspects of the personal selling function, including the performances of individual salespeople.

Salient belief An understanding that an object possesses a relevant attribute.

Sampling Selecting appropriate respondents for research.

Scamps See **Roughs**.

Screening Selecting new product ideas for further development.

Second lifetime value The value of a former customer who has been won back to the firm's products.

Secondary data Information collected secondhand: information which was originally collected for a different purpose from that for which the researcher now wants to use it.

Secondary group A group to which one belongs but which one does not relate to on a regular basis.

Second-market discounting Charging lower prices in some markets or some market segments than in others.

Secondary research Research which has already been carried out (often by someone else for another purpose), and which is available to the researcher for the current project.

Segmentation Dividing the market into groups of people with similar needs.

Selectivity Selecting from external stimuli.

Self-concept One's view of oneself.

Self-image The subjective self: the person we think we are.

Semiotics The study of meaning.

Shelf price The cost of a product when it is on the shelf, not including delivery costs etc.

Shopping products Products which require extensive information search and decision-making.

Signal A feature of the product or its surrounding attributes which convey meaning about the product.

Silent seller The book of sales materials carried by sales representatives.

Simultaneous conditioning The conditioned stimulus and the unconditioned stimulus are offered at the same time.

Simultaneous engineering Carrying out development processes in parallel rather than sequentially in order to reduce time to market.

Situational factors Elements of the immediate surroundings which affect decision-making.

Situational sources Sources of involvement derived from immediate social or cultural factors.

Skimming Pricing products highly at first, but reducing the price steadily as the product moves through its life cycle.

SMS Short Message Service, or texting on cellular telephones.

Societally conscious Cause-oriented people who become involved in charitable work.

Socio-cultural Appertaining to the social effects of buying or not buying a product.

Sociology The study of behaviour in groups.

Sophisticates Customers who have purchased the product before and are ready to rebuy or have recently repurchased.

Spam Unwanted commercial emails.

Species response tendencies Automatic behaviour as a result of instinct rather than learning.

Specific-customer specialist A company which specialises in dealing with a narrow range of customers.

Spin-doctoring Attempts to cover up bad news by slanting it in a way which puts the organisation in a favourable light.

Sponsorship Payment to a cause or event in exchange for publicity.

Stakeholders People who are impacted by corporate activities.

Stars Products with a large share of a growing market.

Straight rebuy A repeat purchase with no modifications.

Strap line The slogan at the end of an advertisement.

Structured observation A marketing research technique which involves directly watching consumer behaviour.

Subjective Appertaining to the individual.

Subjectivity Relating to the individual.

Sugging Selling under the guise of market research.

Supply chain The organisations which add value to the product as it moves from raw materials to consumer.

Survivors Those people who struggle to maintain any kind of lifestyle.

Sustainers People living close to the subsistence level.

Switching cost The expenditure of money and effort resulting from changing from one product to another.

System selling Marketing on a one-to-one basis by a team of salespeople.

Targeting Choosing which segments to service.

Tariff barriers Customs duties which make a product less competitive in an overseas market.

Teaser campaign An advertising campaign in two stages: the first stage involves a message which in itself is meaningless, but which is explained by later advertisements in the second stage.

Technophobe Someone who does not like new products.

Technophone Someone who has an interest in new technology.

Telemarketing Selling or researching via the telephone.

Teleology The belief that acts can be judged by their outcomes.

Telephone selling The practice of using telephone communications as a personal selling medium rather than face-to-face meetings.

Telesales Selling over the telephone.

Territory The geographical area or group of potential customers allocated to a salesperson.

Test marketing Offering a product to a small group of consumers in order to judge the likely response from a large group of consumers.

Third-party responses Complaints made via lawyers or consumer rights advocates.

Time series Analysis which shows how the situation has progressed over a period, carried out in order to predict likely future trends.

Trade association A group of companies in the same industry, set up to look after the collective interests of the group.

Trade up Buying the more expensive model.

Tramp ship A ship which does not follow set routes, but which sails when it has a cargo for a particular port.

Transfer pricing Internal pricing in a multinational company.

Trialability The degree to which the product can be tried out before adoption.

Triangulation Using more than one research method to answer the same question in order to reduce the chances of errors.

Turnkey contract An agreement whereby one firm establishes an entire business in a foreign country and subsequently hands over the business to another firm, in exchange for a fee and occasionally royalties.

Unconditioned response The existing automatic response of the individual to an unconditioned stimulus.

Unconditioned stimulus A stimulus which would normally produce a known reaction in an individual: this stimulus is offered as part of the conditioning process.

Unique selling proposition (USP) The factors which distinguish a product from its competitors.

User The person who uses the product.

Utilitarian Appertaining to the practical aspects of ownership.

Value The benefit a customer obtains from a product.

Value analysis A method of evaluating components, raw materials and even manufacturing processes in order to determine ways of cutting costs or improving finished products.

Value breakdown A situation in which the service offered by a producer does not materialise.

Value chain The firms involved in the process of turning raw materials into products.

Value chain analysis Assessment of ways in which organisations add value to the products they handle.

Value network The group of organisations which collectively add value to raw materials.

Value-based marketing Marketing whose end goal is raising the share value of the company.

Variability In services, the difference between one service and the next, even from the same supplier.

Vertical integration A situation in which one company controls or owns suppliers and customers throughout the supply chain.

Virtual products Anything which can be sold and delivered via the Internet.

Visible Able to be seen by others.

Voice responses Complaints made directly to the supplier.

Wall newspaper A poster giving information to employees.

Want A specific satisfier for a need.

War horse A product with a large share of a shrinking market.

Website A page on the Internet designed for and dedicated to an organisation or individual.

Weighted-point plan A method of evaluating suppliers based on factors which are of greatest importance to the company.

Wicked problem A problem whose solutions create more problems.

Worst self The negative aspects of one's personality: the aspects we wish to overcome in ourselves.

Zapping Using the TV remote control to avoid advertising messages.

Zipping Using the fast-forward on a VCR to skip past TV advertising.

Index